EARLY RESPONSES TO HUME

Volume 7

Edited and Introduced by
James Fieser
University of Tennessee at Martin

THOEMMES CONTINUUM

Early Responses to Hume

Edited and Introduced by **James Fieser**

University of Tennessee at Martin, USA

Volumes 1 and 2
Early Responses to Hume's Moral, Literary and Political Writings

Volumes 3 and 4
Early Responses to Hume's Metaphysical and Epistemological
Writings

Volumes 5 and 6
Early Responses to Hume's Writings on Religion

Volumes 7 and 8
Early Responses to Hume's *History of England*

Volumes 9 and 10
Early Responses to Hume's Life and Reputation
Bibliography of Early Responses to Hume, with Indexes

EARLY RESPONSES TO HUME'S
HISTORY OF ENGLAND

Second Edition, Revised

I

Edited and Introduced by

James Fieser

University of Tennessee at Martin

thoemmes

First published by Thoemmes Press, 2003

Thoemmes Continuum
11 Great George Street
Bristol BS1 5RR, England

http://www.thoemmes.com

Early Responses to Hume
Second edition, revised, 2005
10 vols : ISBN 1 84371 114 1

Early Responses to Hume's *History of England*
Second edition, revised, 2005
2 Volumes : ISBN 1 84371 119 2

© J. Fieser, 2002, 2005

British Library Cataloguing-in-Publication Data
A CIP record of this title is available from the British Library

Printed and bound in Great Britain
by Biddles Ltd, Kings Lynn, Norfolk

CONTENTS

EARLY RESPONSES TO HUME'S *HISTORY OF ENGLAND*

VOLUME 1

VOLUME 2

INTRODUCTION

Although David Hume (1711–1776) is now widely recognized as one of the great British philosophers, in his own day he had at least as much impact as a historian. His *History of England* appeared in four instalments between 1754 and 1762. It was quickly established as a classic, overshadowing most other multi-volume histories of Great Britain that followed during the 18th and 19th centuries. The work far outlasted the expected lifespan of histories of this sort. Even after Hume's death, the *History* was revised and adapted by others, and by the end of the 19th century it went through over 100 editions and reprintings. In spite of its great popularity, the early responses to Hume's *History* have been among the least explored areas of Hume scholarship.

Hume's Place among 18th-Century Histories of England.

The success of Hume's *History* owes partly to his exceptional writing skill and partly to the limitations of rival histories of England at the time. Although many histories prior to Hume adequately presented factual information, readers believed they lacked spirit, and were poor rivals to the productions of classical historians as well as modern histories by French and German writers. Francis Palgrave, in "Hume and his Influence upon History" (1844) discusses in detail the faults of Hume's precursors. Two figures deserve special mentioning here. The first was French writer Rapin de Thoyras (1661–1725), whose 17 volume *Histiore d' Angleterre* was translated into English and published several times in the years following his death. For a time his was the only complete account of English history. As a researcher, Rapin consulted only printed authorities, not manuscripts. Politically, he advocated republicanism and was highly critical of monarchy. Hume, from a more conservative spot on the political spectrum, wrote that Rapin's works – and those by similar anti-royalist writers – were "most despicable, both for style and matter, have been extolled, and propagated, and read; as if they had equalled the most celebrated remains of antiquity" (*History*, Chapter 71).

The second figure was Thomas Carte (1686–1754), a researcher in the true sense of the word, who accessed every manuscript archive he knew of relevant to English history. He published collections of some of these manuscripts and near the end of his life the fruits of his research appeared in his *General History of England* (1747–1755), the last volume of which was published posthumously. Unlike Rapin, Carte was strongly royalist, although he usually kept his political preferences hidden. Praised for his research, some critics nevertheless believed that he placed too much importance on manuscript content, at the expense of conventional printed authorities. Hume relied heavily on Carte's works, even to the point of fault.

Regardless of the merits and demerits of these earlier historians of England, Hume entered the picture at just the right time since other such histories were simply unavailable in bookshops:

> Formerly we had few histories of England. Before the publication of Mr. Hume's first volume, in 1755, we could seldom find above half a score in folio, and two or three of a smaller size, in the shops of our eminent booksellers; but since that time they have multiplied upon us in great abundance. Compilations of this kind have been repeated in a variety of different forms; and now every stall in London, from Piccadilly to Moorfields, is loaded with this species of literary lumber. [*Critical Review*, 1771, Vol. 31, p. 361]

Hume published his *History* in reverse chronological order, beginning with the Stuart monarchs (1754, 1757), moving to the House of Tudor (1759), and ending with the earlier periods (1762). The retrograde appearance of the volumes itself became a matter of discussion for several critics. Once finished, the volumes were republished as complete sets in the proper chronological order. Hume intended to continue his *History* past the period of the Restoration, but his plans were never fulfilled. He initially hesitated for fear that the "prejudices" against his former volumes had not yet subsided (Hume to Andrew Miller, January 14, 1765). James Boswell notes later that Hume abandoned his plans since "we have not yet had access to papers sufficient to let us know, with authenticity, the state of affairs; and it was disagreeable to write history which afterwards might be proved not to be true" (Boswell to William Temple, June 19, 1775).

Even as Hume's *History* was leaving the press, other histories of England began to appear, most notably by Tobias Smollett, Robert Henry, Catherine Macaulay, Oliver Goldsmith, and Charles Coote. Each of these had ample admirers, but they lacked one thing that Hume had, namely, a philosophical pedigree. To his 18th and 19th century critics, Hume was not just a historian, but a *philosophical* historian. For example, Smollet (1759) writes that Hume has "involved the reflections of a philosophical historian in the detail of his facts, in a manner which throws a light upon every subject, without sensibly interrupting the course of the narration." An anonymous author for the *Critical Review* (1762) offered a more detailed explanation of Hume's role as a philosophical historian:

> No writer hath more fortunately hit upon the method of rendering history instructive than our ingenious author, whose work may be regarded as a

table of the human passions, stripped of all disguise, laid naked to the eye, and dissected by the masterly hand of a curious artist. We see actions traced up to their first springs and actuating principles, in so natural a manner, that we cannot avoid giving our assent to Mr. Hume's conclusions, even when they disagree with those we should have formed from a perusal of the simple facts.

The emphasis here is Hume's ability to look into the minds of historical figures and uncover the motives behind their conduct. In the following decades, attitudes about historical scholarship changed, and, by the early 19th century, notions of the "philosophy of history" developed – a concept distinct from earlier notions of a "philosophical historian." In an 1825 essay, John Allen offered the following account of Hume as the quintessential philosopher of history:

The philosophic historian troubles himself little with the characters of individuals, or with the motives that influence their actions. His object is to trace the general causes in the state and condition of society that determine events, independent, and often in spite of the individuals who appear to conduct them. He neglects the fly, to study the wheel on which it revolves. The fault to which he is most prone, is indifference about individuals. He neither interests himself nor his readers in their fate or fortunes. Instead of a dramatic story, his work becomes a dry dissertation. Content with enlarging our views, and enlightening our understanding, he aspires not to warm our passions, or excite our feelings.

Allen recognizes that Hume in fact excelled at portraying individual characters and exciting the reader's feelings. His point, though, is that Hume's contribution as a philosopher of history was his ability to understand the larger causes of social events, independent of history's key players.

Royal Prerogative vs. Individual Liberty.
A political theme underlying the whole *History* is a conflict between Tory and Whig ideology. Hume felt that he was politically moderate, tending to see both the strengths and the weaknesses in opposing viewpoints:

With regard to politics and the character of princes and great men, I think I am very moderate. My views of things are more conformable to Whig principles; my representations of persons to Tory prejudices. Nothing can so much prove that men commonly regard more persons than things, as to find that I am commonly numbered among the Tories. [Hume to John Clephane, 1756]

Indeed, to some 18th century American respondents, Hume was even a politically liberal historian, insofar as he traced the history of political liberty. But to radical Whig British readers, who were wrestling with a different set of political issues, Hume was a conservative Tory. In the Britain of Hume's day, a major point of contention between the two parties concerned whether the English government was historically an absolute or limited monarchy. Tories believed that it was traditionally absolute, with governmental authority being grounded in royal prerogative. Whigs, on the other hand, believed that it was traditionally limited, with the foundation of government resting in the individual liberty of the people, as expressed in the parliamentary voice of the commons.

Hume took two distinct positions on the prerogative issue. From a theoretical and idealistic perspective, he favoured a mixed constitution, mediating between the authority of the monarch and that of the Parliament. Discussing this issue in his 1741 *Essays*, he holds that we should learn "the lesson of moderation in all our political controversies." However, from the perspective of how British history actually unfolded, he emphasized royal prerogative. And, as a "philosophical historian," he tried to show how human nature gave rise to the tendency towards royal prerogative. In his brief autobiography, "My Own Life," he says that he rejected the "senseless clamour" of Whig ideology, and believed "It is ridiculous to consider the English constitution before that period [of the Stuart Monarchs] as a regular plan of liberty." Gilbert Stuart (1778) best encapsulated Hume's historical stance on the prerogative issue: "his history, from its beginning to its conclusion, is chiefly to be regarded as a plausible defence of prerogative."

Early respondents to Hume's *History* saw an irony to his preference for prerogative over civil liberty. Hume's philosophical writings were among the most controversial pieces of literature of the time, and would have been impossible to publish if Britain was not a friend to liberty. Hume, though, was certainly no enemy to liberty; it is just that he believed liberty was best achieved through moderation rather than Whig radicalism. He writes, "If any other rule than established practice be followed, factions and dissentions must multiply without end" (*History*, Appendix 3). To Hume's way of thinking, the loudest voices favouring liberty were Calvinistic religious fanatics who accomplished little more than dissention. A strong, centralized and moderating force was the best way to avoid factious disruption from the start.

In any event, Hume's Whig critics believed that he intentionally constructed a Tory narrative. That narrative, in a nutshell, is this. As early as the Anglo Saxon period, the commons did not participate in the king's advisory council. The Witenagemot, for example, was only a council of nobles and bishops, which the king could listen to or ignore as he saw fit. Throughout the succeeding centuries, England's great kings were those who exercised absolute rule, and took advantage of prerogative courts such as the Star Chamber. Elizabeth – England's most beloved monarch – was in fact a tyrant, and her reign was much like that of a Turkish sultan. Charles I – a largely virtuous man – tried to follow in her footsteps as a strong monarch. After a few minor lapses in judgement, and a few too many concessions to Catholics, Protestant zealots rose up against him, and he was ultimately executed. To avoid over-characterizing royal prerogative, Hume occasionally condemns arbitrary actions of monarchs and praises efforts for preserving liberty. Nevertheless, Whig critics argued, Hume's emphasis was decisively in favour of prerogative.

Whig advocates were bothered by the *History*, not simply because of the Tory ideology that they perceived in it, but because Hume's brilliant writing style made the Tory narrative so psychologically compelling. In their view, Hume's attack on liberty was as dangerous as it was misguided. Consequently, the Whig assaults on Hume are quite passionate. Shortly after the publication of his first volume, Hume wrote to a friend, "I observe that some of the weekly papers have been busy with me. I am as great an atheist as Bolingbroke; as great a Jacobite as Carte; I cannot write English, &c." (Hume to Balcarres, December 17, 1754). From the first selection in this collection, dated 1754, to the final one in 1844, the Whig fury against him never died, and if anything only increased in vehemence.

Many of Hume's Whig critics singled out specific episodes of his Tory narrative. His account of the Anglo Saxon period was criticized by Owen Ruffhead (1763), John Whitaker (1773), Gilbert Stuart (1778), John Millar (1787), and Francis Palgrave (1826). His view of Elizabeth's tyrannical reign was countered by John Millar (1787), William Belsham (1789), and George Brodie (1822). The account of Charles I was criticized by Thomas Birch (1756), the *Monthly Repository* (1821), J.S. Mill (1824), and Francis Palgrave (1844). Two writers – Joseph Towers (1778) and William Smyth (1840) – looked at Hume's view of prerogative throughout several periods of English history. More general critiques of Hume's stance on the prerogative issue were offered by Richard Hurd (1765), John Pinkerton (1785), Francis Garden (1791), Francis Jeffrey (1824), and John Allen (1825).

In addition to such attacks on Hume's view of prerogative, many of his critics focused on specific portions of his *History* that were politically sensitive for other reasons. Hume writes that there are three events in British history "which may be regarded as touchstones of partymen":

An English Whig, who asserts the reality of the popish plot, an Irish Catholic, who denies the massacre in 1641, and a Scotch Jacobite, who maintains the innocence of queen Mary, must be considered as men beyond the reach of argument or reason, and must be left to their prejudices. [Chapter 39, Note]

Indeed, these were three issues that generated many critical responses to Hume's *History*.

Religious Fanaticism and Superstition.
The first of these three issues – the Popish Plot of 1678 – is discussed by Hume in Chapter 67. The specific "plot" was that Jesuits and other Roman Catholics were conspiring to kill Charles II and place his Catholic brother James on the throne. Although the whole plot was fabricated by Titus Oates, a former priest, a reign of terror gripped London and 35 people were executed. The larger issue surrounding the plot involved tensions between Protestants and Catholics, which predated that episode. Hume had strong views about the nature of both Protestantism and Catholicism, which he candidly expressed in the 1754 volume of his *History*. In one passage he argues that the first Protestant reformers were fanatical or "inflamed with the highest enthusiasm" in their opposition to Catholic domination. He was particularly critical of the unsettling effect that Protestant extremism had on society – such as intolerance towards Catholics and even civil war. The second passage labels Catholicism a superstition which "like all other species of superstition ... rouses the vain fears of unhappy mortals." Although critical of both Protestantism and Catholicism, to his Protestant readers the brunt of Hume's attack appeared to be directed towards Protestants. Roger Flexman (1754) and Daniel MacQueen (1756) directly criticized these two controversial passages.

Hume recognized that he struck a raw nerve, and wrote to a friend, "I am convinced that whatever I have said of religion [in the 1752 volume] should have received some more softenings" (Hume to John Clephane, 1756). In response to his critics, Hume included a note to the 1757 instalment of his *History*, which defends his comments on religion in the earlier volume. Hume contends here that he was simply pointing out the abuses of religion, and not arguing against the practice of religion per se. William Warburton criticized this note in his 1757 *Remarks* (included in *Early Responses to Hume's Writings on Religion*). Hume's footnote was actually an abridged version of a Preface he had drafted for the 1757 volumes, but never included. The complete draft of the unpublished Preface is reprinted in E.C. Mossner's *The Life of David Hume* (1954, pp. 306–308). The controversy surrounding the original two passages prompted Hume to delete them in the 1759 second edition of that volume. They appear in this collection as quoted by Flexman and MacQueen; they are also reprinted in the Foreword to the Liberty Classics edition of Hume's *History of England* (1983, pp. xiv-xvii). Hume eventually dropped the abridged footnote from later editions of the *History*; it appears in this collection as quoted by William Rose in his 1757 review. Even after the two original passages were removed, they were later criticized by Archibald Maclaine (1765), Joseph Towers (1778) and William Smyth (1840).

Hume continued discussing religion in successive volumes of the *History*, and in the 1757 instalment, under the House of Tudor, his assaults on the Protestant Reformation were as harsh as what appeared in the 1752 volume. Also in the Tudor volumes, he considers the advantages of a centralized, state-sponsored religion (Chapter 29). Without state regulation, he believes, competition between religious sects will produce sensationalism and fanaticism. Accordingly, Hume was sympathetic with the organized structure and rituals of Catholicism and the Church of England, and suspicious of Presbyterianism. Adam Smith (1776) rejected Hume's argument and maintained that religious practice would become more refined in a free market environment. This issue is also addressed by Francis Garden (1791). Other critics – most notably Francis Jeffrey (1824) and Francis Palgrave (1844) – speculated about Hume's grudge against religion in general and Calvinist Protestantism specifically.

Irish Rebellion of 1641.

The second touchstone of party men concerns the Irish Rebellion, which originated in the Irish province of Ulster on October 23, 1641. The stage for the rebellion was set by an increased conscription of Irish Catholics into the militia, and the active conspiring of traditional Irish Catholics, especially Rory O'More, to revolt and return Irish Catholicism to its previous splendour. Under the mistaken belief that Dublin had already been taken by Catholic rebels, the allied rebels of Ulster expelled local English Protestants from their homes and killed many of them. The rebellion was a surprise to everyone, including the chief conspirators. Explanations varied concerning the ultimate cause of the rebellion. Catherine Macaulay maintained in her *History of England* (1763–1783) that, even before the Reformation, there existed an initial strife in Ireland based on social policies, and not on religion. After the Reformation, she argues, denominational differences became the pretence for dispute. Hume's account of the Irish rebellion is given in the 1754 volume of his *History*. He begins arguing that the Irish were originally barbarians and became civilized only through English rule. According to Hume, when the revolt broke out, the native Irish barbarism re-emerged and was further supplemented by national and religious prejudice. Drawing heavily from John Temple's eyewitness account in *The Irish Rebellion* (1646), Hume graphically describes how Irish Catholic men, women and children tortured and killed their defenceless English neighbours. Hume notes that estimated death tolls were as high as 200,000, but suggests that 40,000 is more believable.

Roger Flexman's 1754 review applauds Hume's "exquisite and affecting description of the insurrection and massacre" although he believes that the death toll was much higher than Hume contends. In late 1754, Adam Smith sent Hume a letter criticizing Hume's account of the Irish massacre. Although Smith's letter has not surfaced, we have Hume's reply:

Your Objection to the Irish Massacre is just; but falls not on the Execution but the Subject. Had I been to describe the Massacre of Paris, I shoud not have fallen into that Fault; But in the Irish Massacre no single eminent Man fell, or by a remarkable Death. If the Elocution of that whole Chapter be blameable, it is because my Conception labord with too great an Idea of my

Subject, which is there the most important. But that misfortune is not unusual. [Hume to Adam Smith, January 9, 1755]

Smith appears to have criticized Hume for sensationalizing an unextraordinary group of events.

The first systematic attack on Hume's account of the rebellion was by Sylvester O'Halloran (1772), who argues that Hume greatly exaggerated the number of Irish who were excessively violent during the revolt. Three years later John Curry criticized Hume for taking far too seriously the "stupid legend" conveyed by John Temple. Hume also disputed the issue of the Irish Rebellion with Edmund Burke, which Robert Bisset discusses in his 1799 biography of Burke. According to Bisset, Burke was convinced that Hume had him in mind when citing the prejudice of the "Irish Catholic, who denies the massacre in 1641."

Mary Queen of Scots.
The third volatile political issue mentioned by Hume concerns Mary Queen of Scots, who was imprisoned and ultimately executed for the murder of her husband Henry Stewart, Lord Darnley. The case against her hinged on an alleged extramarital affair she had with James Hepburn, Earl of Bothwell, evidence of which was supplied by a collection of documents. These included eight letters and twelve sonnets to Bothwell, and two marriage-contracts – all of which supposedly were written prior to the death of Darnley. The letters and sonnets were reported to be written in Mary's own hand in the French language. The documents were brought to light by Mary's enemy, the Earl of Morton, who claimed that his servants seized them from Bothwell's servant. Mary denounced the letters as forgeries of Morton and others, but she and her supporters were denied access to the original French versions. The text of the original French manuscripts was printed in George Buchanan's *Detection* (1572), which also presented a detailed case for her guilt. The letters were also published in Latin and Scottish-dialect versions, supposedly translated from the original French. The original French manuscripts themselves became lost after Morton's execution in 1581.

The earliest published vindication of Mary was Scottish Bishop John Lesley's *Defence of the honour of Mary Queen of Scotland* (1571), which was subsequently suppressed by Queen Elizabeth. The question of Mary's guilt continued to be debated, but the controversy took on new life with the appearance of Walter Goodall's *Examination of the Letters said to be Written by Mary, Queen of Scots* (1754), which argues that the letters were forged. In the absence of the original letters, he noted that there were inconsistent statements about whether the letters were both written and signed by her. Specifically, in the act of council the letters are described as "written and subscribed with her own hand" and in the act of parliament, as "written wholly with her own hand." Goodall further pointed out problems in the chronology laid out by her accusers. Perhaps most importantly, he argued on linguistic grounds that the letters and sonnets were forged. Analysing the three language versions side by side, he contended that the French was translated from the Latin, and the Latin from an original Scottish-dialect version. There was, in fact, no original French manuscript. In their respective histories, Hume and Scottish historian William Robertson both argued for Mary's guilt and the authenticity of the letters. They both concede Goodall's chief point that the surviving French copies printed in Buchanan's *Detection* were ultimately derived from the Scottish. However, they insist that there was an original French version – which quickly disappeared – upon which all other versions are based. In a note to his narrative of Queen Mary in Chapter 39 of his *History* (first published in 1759), Hume offers fifteen arguments for the authenticity of the letters. Robertson made his case in his *History of Scotland* (1758–1759).

In his 1760 *Historical and Critical Enquiry*, William Tytler defends Goodall's position against Hume and Robertson. According to Tytler, there are simply no grounds to postulate the existence of an original French version. The letters, thus, must be rejected as frauds created by Mary's enemies, and, consequently, the case against Mary collapses. Hume was unhappy with Tytler's critique of him and, in the 1770 edition of his *History*, Hume inserted a footnote stating that Tytler's work contains "scandalous artifices" from beginning to end. Tytler responded to this in the 1772 edition of his *Enquiry*. The consensus at the time was that Tytler was victorious over both Hume and Robertson. Critics felt that Hume's harsh response to Tytler was an embarrassment, and, by not responding at all, Robertson conceded to Tytler by default – although a 1760 letter from Hume to Lord Elibank indicates that "it was Contempt, & not Inability" that kept Robertson from publicly responding to Tytler. Hume's views on the subject were critiqued further by Henri Griffet (1766), David Dalrymple (1784), and John Whitaker (1787).

Hume's Reputation and Historical Accuracy.
Most respondents praised the engaging style of Hume's narrative in the most glowing terms. For example, in 1763 James Boswell wrote in his private journal, "I employed the day in reading Hume's *History*, which enlarged my views, filled me with great ideas, and rendered me happy." Even one of Hume's harshest critics, Richard Hurd (1759), states that his *History* is "the most readable *general* account of the *English* affairs, that has yet been given to the public." Mixed with such praise, though, was usually a list of stylistic and factual errors that critics urged Hume to tend to. An anonymous article in *Gentleman's Magazine* (1772) criticized the historical accuracy of Hume's account of the Quakers. Hume's account of Richard third was attacked by Horace Walpole in two publications (1768, 1769). Invariably, Hume made a large number of the recommended changes in subsequent editions of his history – particularly those changes suggested by Roger Flexman (1754), William Smellie (1756, 1759), Owen Ruffhead (1759, 1762, 1763), William Tytler (1760), and Sylvester

O'Halloran (1772). The most dramatic list appears in Joseph Priestley's *Rudiments of English Grammar* (1768), which selects over a hundred passages from Hume's *History* as examples of bad writing style. Hume was angered by this, but made virtually all of the changes that Priestley suggested.

Even after his death it was routine for critics to point out stylistic and factual flaws in the *History*. The following anecdote printed in 1794 is indicative of this attitude:

> DAVID HUME knew so little of the Law and the Constitution of England, that he one day, in company with a celebrated Lawyer of the kingdom of Ireland, was praising the system of the old Crown Law of England, as a mild and liberal one. His friend reminded him of several instances of its severity and injustice, which have within these two last centuries been done away. "Alas!" cries David, "I knew nothing of them – I must own, then, that the old Crown Law was a very cruel and a very arbitrary system. [*European Magazine and London Review*, 1794, Vol. 25, p. 431.]

In the beginning of the nineteenth century, attacks on the veracity of the *History* took a different turn as more precise notions of historical methodology took shape. Inconsistencies in Hume's narrative of Charles I were exposed in an anonymous article in the *Monthly Repository* (1821). John Stuart Mill (1822) argued that Hume was immoral for putting his own ideological interests above the greater good of his mass readership. Francis Palgrave (1826) attacked Hume's uncritical reliance on secondary sources in his account of early periods of English history. In an 1831 article, Henry Hallam excerpts a passage from Hume's history, and places it alongside Carte's account of the same event; the strong parallels between the sentence structure of each showed that Hume relied too heavily on Carte. In 1844 Palgrave revisited the issue of Hume's authority as an historian. His essay – one of the most important in this collection – attempts to understand and entirely discredit Hume's historical methodology. To that end, he relates the following anecdote:

> The only glimpse we gain [of Hume's study method] is through a story told by a late venerable Scottish crony. Some one having hinted that David had neglected an authority he ought to have consulted, the old gentleman replied, – 'Why, mon, David read a vast deal before he set about a piece of his book; but his usual seat was the sofa, and he often wrote with his legs up; and it would have been unco fashious to have moved across the room when any little doubt occurred.' [Palgrave (1844)]

Around this time, Robert Chambers's popular *Cyclopædia of English Literature* (1844) appeared, which consists largely of an assault on Hume's accuracy as an historian.

In spite of these efforts to dethrone Hume, there remained a strong general feeling about Hume's authority, as we see in the following 1844 passage by Archibald Alison:

> In other departments of knowledge, a certain degree of information is felt to be requisite before a man can presume to write a book. He cannot produce a treatise on mathematics without knowing at least Euclid, nor a work on history without having read Hume, nor on political economy without having acquired a smattering of Adam Smith. [Archibald Alison, *Blackwood's Edinburgh Magazine*, November 1844, Vol. 56, 658]

Other histories came along to rival Hume's, but, because of its classic status as a work of literature, it held its place in the market long after its scholarship was superseded. Two nineteenth-century rivals are worth mentioning. One is *A History of England* (1819–1839) by Catholic priest John Lingard. A more objective historian than Hume, Lingard had a greater command of primary sources, and, by virtue of this, had the greater long-term impact in the discipline of history. However, he never achieved Hume's popularity, largely as a result of the prevailing anti-Catholic climate. Thomas Macaulay's *History of England* (1849–1861) was similar to Hume's in terms of strong narrative. He also had a political agenda for the times and was a founder of what is known as the Whig interpretation of history. But during his life his work could do no more than rival Hume's, and it was only posthumously that he came to dominate the market.

One indication of the lasting popularity of Hume's *History* is the many student abridgements that appeared throughout the nineteenth century. The most abundant of these in the United States was *The Student's Hume*, which saw over thirty editions, the last of which was in 1910. Such abridgements unfortunately downgraded Hume's *History* – eliminating the more extraneous philosophical discussions and controversial passages.

Editorial Conventions and Acknowledgments.
In preparing these selections, spelling and punctuation have not been modernized. Some original printers' conventions have been altered; for example, footnote references follow punctuation marks, rather than precede them. Unless noted otherwise, comments contained in square brackets are mine. The authorship of anonymous reviews in the *Monthly Review* is based on Benjamin Christie Nangle's *The Monthly Review First Series 1749–1789* (1934) and *The Monthly Review Second Series 1790–1815* (1955). Authorship of anonymous articles in nineteenth-century journals is based on *The Wellesley Index to Victorian Periodicals, 1824–1900* (1966–89), edited by Walter E. Houghton. I thank Mark Spencer and M.A. Stewart for input on this collection.

1
ROGER FLEXMAN,
THE MONTHLY REVIEW

[Roger Flexman], review of *The History of Great Britain. Vol. 1. Containing the Reigns of James I and Charles I*, in *The Monthly Review*, March 1754, Vol. 12, pp. 206–229.
Complete review.

When the first volume of Hume's *History* appeared in 1754, Great Britain's sole book review journal at the time – the *Monthly Review* – took notice of it. By that time Hume was no stranger to the journal; his *Enquiry Concerning the Principles of Morals* and *Political Discourses* were favourably reviewed by William Rose. The journal also reviewed dozens of books that discussed Hume, and reviewers routinely made additional evaluations of Hume in these. The *Monthly Review* was founded in 1749 by Ralph Griffiths (1720–1803), a regular reviewer for earlier journals. The articles in the *Monthly Review* appeared anonymously. However, each month Griffiths penned abbreviations of the names of the reviewers into his personal copy of the *Monthly* (his annotated copy now resides in the Bodleian Library, and a microfilm of it is available in the *English Literary Periodicals* microfilm series). Most of Griffiths's abbreviations have been identified and catalogued by Benjamin Christie Nangle in *The Monthly Review First Series: 1749–1789* (1934), and *The Monthly Review Second Series: 1790–1815* (1955). According to Nangle's catalogue, the reviewer of the article on Volume 1 of Hume's *History* was Roger Flexman (1708–1795), a dissenting clergyman and author of several historical works including *Critical, Historical, and Political Miscellanies* (1752). Flexman wrote approximately 50 review articles for the *Monthly* and ended his association with the journal in 1762, under strained circumstances. Less generous in his evaluation of Hume than was Rose, Flexman charges Hume with partiality and inconsistency, and he expresses regret that Hume even attempted a history of Great Britain. Common for review articles of the time, Flexman's review consists mostly of excerpts. The segments he selects, though, are among the most controversial in this volume of Hume's *History*, and Hume removed some of these paragraphs in later editions. These segments included here cover the Gunpowder Plot, Roman Catholic superstition, the Irish massacre, Scottish Protestant fanaticism, and Glamorgan's allegedly forged commission.

ART. XXX. *The History of* Great-Britain, *Vol.* I. *containing the reigns of* James I. *and* Charles I. *By* David Hume, *Esq*; Edinburgh *printed by* Hamilton, Balfour, *and* Neill. 4to. 14s. *in boards. Sold also by the Booksellers in* London.

It will be unnecessary for us to repeat here, what we have already more than once had occasion to say, with respect to the abilities of this very ingenious writer; abilities, that we shall always with pleasure see him employing on subjects to which they are adequate: among which we are sorry to say (convinced by the work now before us) this history of his own country is the last he ought to have attempted. The capacity of this gentleman, for an orderly, and even *elegant* narration of facts and events, (if *elegance* were necessary in an historian) and for a pleasing, animated delineation of characters, is freely acknowledged: but the more essential articles of IMPARTIALITY and CONSISTENCY, will ever be regarded as the most valuable and most indispensable qualifications.

If any peculiar indulgence may be claimed by an historian, who seems to have adopted a favourite system of religion or politics, it is only when such systems appear reconcilable to the real constitution of the government, and look with a benevolent aspect on the rights and liberties of the subject.

It is foreign to our design to offer any conjecture concerning the particular views of our author in compiling this history; in the perusal of which we have met with many strong indications of direct opposition to the genuine maxims of our civil polity, as well as indecent reflections on the protestant religion, as if it were rather the casual effect of enthusiasm and fanaticism, than the amiable offspring of free enquiry, and rational conviction.

After he hath sufficiently apprised us of his attachment to the justly exploded doctrine of hereditary Right, and lineal Succession, he offers some cursory remarks upon the reign and character of Queen *Elizabeth*; and mentions several incidents which are commonly taken notice of by the rest of our historians. He then proceeds to give his sentiments upon some religious subjects, with which he appears not to be thoroughly acquainted; and intersperses such reflections and censures with his account of the conference at *Hampton-Court*, as seem calculated, not so much to expose and deride the *Puritans*, as to fix deep marks of reproach upon the protestant religion itself.

'The first reformers,' says he, 'who made such furious and successful attacks on the *Romish* SUPERSTITION, and shook it to its lowest foundations, may safely be pronounced to have been *universally* inflamed with the highest ENTHUSIASM. These two species of religion, the superstitious and fanatical, stand in diametrical opposition to each other; and a large portion of the latter must necessarily fall to his share, who is so courageous as to control authority, and so assuming as to obtrude his own innovations upon the world. Hence that rage of dispute which every where seized the new religionists; this disdain of ecclesiastical subjection, that contempt of ceremonies, and of all the exterior pomp and splendor of worship.'

This obstinate and uncomplying species of religion, he represents as necessarily receiving some alteration, according to the different situation of civil affairs, and the different constitutions of government, it met with in its progress. In *Germany, Denmark,* and *Sweden*, he observes, the spirit of enthusiasm was somewhat tempered by a sense of order, so that episcopal jurisdiction, with a few decent ceremonies, was preserved in the new establishment; but that in *Switzerland, Geneva, France, Scotland,* and the *Low Countries*, fanaticism displayed itself in its full extend, and affected every circumstance of discipline and worship. He asserts, that

'they were the preachers of *Switzerland, France,* and the *Low Countries*, who carried the reformation into *England*; but as the government was there monarchical, and the magistrate took the lead in this grand revolution, though the speculative doctrines were borrowed from the more fanatical churches, yet were the discipline and worship naturally mitigated with a more humane spirit of religion.'

In the next chapter Mr. *Hume* gives a particular account of the *Roman* catholic superstition, its genius, and spirit. This he introduces with a narrative of the *gunpowder treason*, which he justly declares to be an event amongst the most memorable which history has conveyed to posterity; and contains at once

'a singular proof of the strength and weakness of the human mind; its widest departure from morals, and its most steady attachment to religious prejudices. – A fact as certain as it appears incredible.' We think it not improper to give our author's account of this affair, as one specimen, among others, of his manner.

The roman catholics had expected great favour and indulgence on the accession of *James*, both as he was descending from *Mary*, who had sacrificed her life to their cause, and as he had himself, in his early youth, shewed some partiality towards them; which nothing, they believed, but interest and necessity had since restrained. It is pretended, that he had even entered into positive engagements to tolerate their religion, as soon as he should mount the throne of *England*; whether their credulity had interpreted in this sense some obliging expressions of the king, or that he had employed such an artifice, in order to render them favorable to his title. Very soon, they discovered their mistake; and were at once surprised and enraged to find *James*, on all occasions, express his intention of executing strictly the laws enacted against them, and of persevering in all the rigorous measure of *Elizabeth. Catesby*, a gentleman of good parts, and of an ancient family, first thought of a most extraordinary method of revenge; and he opened his intention to *Piercy*, a descendant of the illustrious house of *Northumberland*. In one of their conversations, with regard to the distrest condition of the catholics, *Piercy* having broke into a sally of passion, and mentioned the assassinating the king, *Catesby* took the opportunity of revealing to him a nobler and more extensive plan of treason, which not only included a sure execution of vengeance, but afforded some hopes of restoring the catholic religion in *England*. In vain, said he, would you put an end to the king's life; he has children, who would succeed both to his crown, and to his maxims of government. In vain would you extinguish the whole royal family: the nobility, the gentry, the parliament are all infected with the same heresy, and could raise to the throne another prince, and another family, who, beside their hatred to our religion, would be animated with revenge for the tragical death of their predecessors. To serve any good purpose, we must destroy, at one blow, the king, the royal family, the lords, the commons; and bury all our enemies in one common ruin. Happily, they are all assembled on the first day of every session, and afford us the opportunity of glorious and useful vengeance. Great preparations will not be requisite. A few of us, combining, may run a mine below the hall in which they meet, and chusing the very moment when the king harangues both houses, consign over to destruction those determined foes to all piety and religion. Mean while, we ourselves standing aloof, safe and unsuspected, shall triumph in being the instruments of divine wrath, and shall behold with pleasure those sacrilegious walls, in which were passed the edicts for proscribing our church, and butchering her children, tost into a thousand fragments; while their impious inhabitants, mediating perhaps still new persecutions against us, pass from flames above to flames below, there for ever to endure the torments due to their offences.

Piercy was charmed with this project of *Catesby*; and they agreed to communicate the matter to a few more, and among the rest to *Thomas Winter*, whom they sent over to *Flanders*, in quest of *Fawkes*, an officer in the *Spanish* service, with whose zeal and courage they were all thoroughly acquainted. Whenever they inlisted a new conspirator, in order to bind him to secrecy, along with an oath, they always employed the sacrament, the most sacred rite of their religion. And it is remarkable, that no one of these pious devotees ever entertained the least compunction with regard to the cruel massacre which they projected, of whatever was great and eminent in the nation. Some of them only were startled by the reflection, that of necessity many catholics must be present; as spectators, as attendants on the king, as having seats in the house of peers: but *Tesmond*, a jesuit, and *Garnet*, superior of that order in *England*, removed these weak scruples, and shewed them, how the interests of religion required, that the innocent should here be sacrificed along with the guilty.

All this passed in the spring and summer of the year 1604; when the conspirators also hired a house, in *Piercy's* name, adjoining to that in which the parliament was to assemble. Towards the end of that year they began their operations. That they might be less interrupted, and give less suspicion to the neighbourhood, they carried in store of provisions along with them, and never desisted from their labour. Obstinate to their purpose, and confirmed by passion, by principle, and by mutual exhortation, they little valued life in comparison of a disappointment; and having provided arms, along with the instruments of their work, they resolved there to perish in case of a discovery. Objects of pity as well as of horror, barbarous and pious, traitorous and faithful, they fancied themselves favourites of heaven while enemies to mankind, and drowned all sense of crime in their pretensions to superior excellence and merit. Their perseverance advanced the work, and they soon pierced the wall, though three yards in thickness; but on approaching the other side, they were somewhat startled with hearing a noise, which they knew not how to account for. Upon inquiry, they found it came from the vault below the house of lords; that a magazine of coals had been kept there, and that, as the coals were selling off, the vault would be let to the highest bidder. The opportunity was immediately seized; the place hired by *Piercey*; thirty-six barrels of powder lodged in it, the whole covered up with faggots and billets; the doors of the cellar boldly flung open, and every body admitted, as if it contained nothing dangerous.

Confident of success, they now began to look forward, and to plan the remaining part of their project. The king, the queen, the prince of *Wales*,[1] were all expected to be present at the opening of the parliament. The duke, by reason of his tender age, would be absent; and it was resolved that *Piercey* should seize him, or assassinate him. The princess *Elizabeth*, a child likewise, was kept at Lord *Harrington's* house in *Warwickshire*; and Sir *Everad Digby, Rookwood, Grant,* being let into the conspiracy, engaged to assemble their friends, under pretext of a hunting match, and seizing that princess, immediately to proclaim her queen. So transported were they with rage against their adversaries, and charmed with the prospect of revenge, that they forgot all care of their own safety; and trusting to the general confusion which must result from so unexpected a blow, they foresaw not, that the fury of the

---

[1] Mr. *Hume* should have known, that at this time there was no Prince of *Wales*; Prince *Henry*, eldest son to King *James* I. was not created Prince of *Wales* until 4 *June* 1610. See *Review*, vol. VIII, page 223.

people, now unrestrained by any authority, must have turned against them, and would probably have satiated itself by an universal massacre of the catholics.

The day so long wished for, now approached, on which the parliament was appointed to assemble. The dreadful secret, though communicated to above twenty persons, had been religiously kept, during the space of near a year and a half. No remorse, no pity, no fear of punishment, no hope of reward, had, as yet, induced any one conspirator, either to abandon the enterprize, or make a discovery of it. The holy fury had extinguished in their breasts every other motive; and it was an indiscretion at last, proceeding chiefly from these very bigotted prejudices, and partialities, which save the nation.

Ten days before the meeting of the parliament, Lord *Monteagle*, a catholic, son to Lord *Morley*, received the following letter, which had been delivered to his servant by an unknown hand.

"My Lord, Out of the love I bear to some of your friends, I have a care of your preservation. Therefore I would advise you, as you tender your life, to devise some excuse to shift off your attendance at this parliament. For God and man have concurred to punish the wickedness of this time. And think not slightly of this advertisement; but retire yourself into your country, where you may expect the event in safety. For though there be no appearance of any stir, yet, I say, they will receive a terrible blow this parliament, and yet they shall not see who hurts them. This council is not to be contemned, because it may do you good, and can do you no harm: for the danger is past, as soon as you have burned the letter. And I hope God will give you the grace to make good use of it; to whose holy protection I commend you."

Monteagle knew not what to make of this letter; and tho' inclined to think it a foolish attempt to frighten and ridicule him, he judged it safest to carry it to Lord *Salisbury*, secretary of state. Though *Salisbury* too was inclined to give little attention to it, he thought proper to communicate it to the king, who came to town a few days after. To the king it appeared not so light a matter; and from the serious earnest style of the letter, he conjectured, that it implied something very dangerous and important. *A terrible blow* and yet *the authors concealed*, a danger so *sudden* and yet so *great*, these circumstances seemed all to denote some contrivance by gunpowder; and it was thought advisable to inspect all the vaults below the house of parliament. This care belonged to the Earl of *Suffolk*, lord-chamberlain; who purposely delayed the search till the day before the meeting of the parliament. He remarked those great piles of wood and faggots, which lay in the vault under the upper house; and he cast his eye upon *Fawkes*, who stood in a dark corner, and passed himself for *Piercy's* servant. That daring and determined courage which so much distinguished his conspirator, even among these heroes in villany, was fully painted in his countenance, and was not passed unnoticed by the lord-chamberlain. Such a quantity of fuel too, for the use of one who lived so little in town as

Piercy, appeared a little extraordinary: and upon comparing all circumstances, it was resolved, that a more thorough inspection should be made. About midnight Sir *Thomas Knevet*, a justice of peace, was sent with proper attendants; and before the door of the vault finding *Fawkes*, who had just finished all his preparations; he immediately siezed him, and turning over the faggots, discovered the powder. The matches, and every thing proper for setting fire to the train, were taken in *Fawkes's* pocket; who finding his guilt now apparent, and seeing no refuge but in boldness and dispair, expressed the utmost regret, that he had lost the opportunity of firing the powder at once, and of sweetening his own death by that of his enemies. Before the council he displayed the same intrepid firmness, mixt even with scorn and disdain; refusing to discover his accomplices, and shewing no concern but for the failure of the enterprize. This obstinacy lasted for two or three days; but being confined to the *Tower*, left him to reflect on his guilt and danger, and the rack being just shewn to him, his courage, fatigued with so long an effort, and unsupported by hope or society, at last succumbed, and he made a full discovery of all the conspirators.

Catesby, Piercy, and the other criminals, who were in *London*, though they had heard of the alarm taken at the letter sent to *Monteagle*; though they had heard of the lord-chamberlain's search, yet were resolved to persist to the utmost, and never abandoned their hopes of success.[2] But at last, hearing that *Fawkes* was arrested, they hurried away to *Warwickshire*; where Sir *Everard Digby*, making account that success had attended his confederates, was already in arms, in order to f seize the Princess *Elizabeth*. She had escaped into *Coventry*; and they were obliged to put themselves on their defence against the country, who were raised from all quarters, and armed by the sheriffs. The conspirators, with all their attendants, never exceeded the number of eighty persons; and being surrounded on every side, could no longer entertain hopes, either of escaping or prevailing. Having therefore confessed themselves, and received absolution, they boldly prepared for death, and resolved to sell their lives as dear as possible to the assailants. But even this miserable consolation was denied them. Some of their powder took fire, and disabled them for

---

[2] Some historians have imagined, that the king had secret intelligence of the conspiracy, and that the letter to *Monteagel* was wrote by his direction, in order to have the fame of penetration in discovering the plot. But the known facts refute this supposition. That letter being commonly talked of, might naturally have given an alarm to the conspirators, and made them contrive their escape. The visit of the lord-chamberlain ought to have had the same effect. In short, it appears, that no body was arrested or enquired after, for some days, till *Fawkes* discovered their names. We may infer, however, from a letter in *Winwood's* Memorials, vol. 2. that *Salisbury's* sagacity led the king in his conjectures, and that the minister, like an artful courtier, gave his master the praise of the whole discovery. – *This note is Mr. Hume's.*

defence. The people rushed in upon them. *Piercy* and *Catesby* were killed with one shot: *Digby, Rookwood, Winter,* and others, being taken prisoners, were tried, confessed their guilt, and died, as well as *Garnet,* by the hands of the executioner.

Neither had the desperate fortune of the conspirators urged them to this enterprize, nor had the former profligacy of their lives, prepared them for so great a crime. Before that audacious attempt, their conduct seems, in general, to be liable to no reproach. *Catesby's* character had entitled him to such regard, that *Rookwood* and *Digby* were seduced by their implicite trust in his judgment; and they declared, that from the motive alone of friendship to him, they were ready, on any occasion, to have sacrificed their lives. *Digby* himself was as highly esteemed and beloved as any man in *England*; and he had been particularly honoured with the good opinion of Queen *Elizabeth.* It was bigotted zeal alone, the most absurd of prejudices masqued with reason, the most criminal of passions covered with the appearance of duty, which seduced them into measures, that were fatal to themselves, and had so nearly proved fatal to their country.'

Our author having given the foregoing narration of this most *detestable* conspiracy, judges it proper to add a brief account of the *Roman* catholic superstition. He observes that 'history addresses itself to a more distant posterity than will ever be reached by any local or temporary theology; and the characters of sects may be studied, when their controversies shall be totally forgotten.' He proceeds –

'Before the reformation, all men of sense and virtue wished impatiently for some event, which might repress the exorbitant power of the clergy all over *Europe,* and put an end to the unbounded usurpations and pretensions of the *Roman* pontiff: but when the doctrine of *Luther* was promulgated, they were somewhat alarmed at the sharpness of the remedy; and it was easily foreseen, from the offensive zeal of the reformers, and defensive of the church, that all Christendom must be thrown into combustion. In the preceeding state of ignorance and tranquillity, into which mankind were lulled, the attachment to superstition, though with reserve, was not extreme; and, like the ancient pagan idolatry, the popular religion consisted more of exterior practices and observances, than of any principles, which either took possession of the heart, or influenced the conduct. It might have been hoped, that learning and knowledge, as of old in *Greece,* stealing in gradually, would have opened the eyes of men, and corrected such of the ecclesiastical abuses as were the grossest and most burthensome. It had been observed, that upon the revival of letters, very generous and enlarged sentiments of religion prevailed throughout *all Italy,* and that during the reign of *Leo,* the court of *Rome* itself, in imitation of their illustrious prince, had not been wanting in a just sense of freedom. But when the enraged and fanatical reformers took arms against the papal hierarchy, and threatened to rend from the church at once all her riches and authority; no wonder she was animated with equal zeal and ardor, in defence of such ancient and invaluable possessions. At the same time, that she employed the stake and the gibbet against her avowed enemies, she extended her jealousy even towards learning and philosophy, whom, in her supine security, she had formerly overlooked, as harmless and inoffensive. Hence, the severe check, which knowledge received in *Italy*: hence, its total extinction in *Spain*: and hence, the slow progress which it made in *France, Germany* and *England*. From the admiration of ancient literature, from the inquiry after new discoveries, the minds of the studious were every where turned to polemical science; and in all schools and academies the furious controversies of theology took place of the calm disquisitions of learning.

Meanwhile, the rage of dispute and the violence of opposition rivetted men more strongly in all their various delusions, and infected every intercourse of society with their malignant influence. The *Roman* pontiff, not armed with temporal force sufficient for his defence, was obliged to point anew all his spiritual artillery, and to propagate the doctrine of rebellion, and even of assassination, in order to subdue or terrify his enemies. Priests, jealous and provoked, timerous and uncontrouled, directed all the councils of that sect, and gave rise to such events as seem astonishing amid the mildness and humanity of modern manners. The massacre of *Paris*, that of *Ireland*, the murder of the two *Henrys of France,* the gunpowder conspiracy in *England*, are memorable, though temporary instances of the bigotry of that superstition. And the dreadful tribunal of the inquisition, that utmost instance of human depravity, is a durable monument to instruct us what a pitch iniquity and cruelty may rise to, when covered with the sacred mantle of religion.

Though the prospect of sharing the plunder of the church, had engaged some princes to embrace the reformation, it may be affirmed, that the *Romish* system remained still the favourite religion of sovereigns. The blind submission which is inculcated by all superstition, particularly by that of the catholics; the absolute resignation of all private judgment, reason, and inquiry; these are dispositions very advantageous to civil, as well as to ecclesiastical authority; and the liberty of the subject is more likely to suffer from such principles, than the prerogatives of the chief magistrate. The splendor too and pomp of worship, which that religion carefully supports, are agreeable to the taste of magnificence that prevails in courts, and form a species of devotion, which, while it flatters the pampered sense, gives little perplexity to the indolent understandings of the great. That delicious country where the *Roman* pontiff resides, was the source of all modern art and refinement, and diffused on its superstition an air of politeness which distinguishes it from the gross rusticity of the other sects. And though policy made it assume, in some of its monastic orders, that austere mien which is acceptable to the vulgar, all authority still resided in its prelates and spiritual princes, whose temper, more cultivated and humanized, inclined them to every decent pleasure and indulgence. Like all other species of superstition, it rouses the vain fears of unhappy mortals, but it knows also the secret of allaying these fears, and by exterior rites, ceremonies, and abasements, though some times at the expence of morals, it reconciles the penitent to his offended deity.'

To this representation of the genius, the spirit, and maxims of the popish superstition, it may not be improper to annex our author's exquisite and affecting description of the insurrection and massacre in *Ireland*, which commenced *October* 23, 1641.

There was such a propensity to a revolt, he tells us, discovered in all the *Irish*, that it was esteemed unnecessary, as it was dangerous, to entrust the secret to many hands. The appointed day drew nigh, and no discovery had been yet made to the government. The king, indeed, had been informed by his ambassadors, that something was in agitation among the *Irish* in foreign parts; but though he gave warning to the administration in *Ireland*, the intelligence was entirely neglected. Secret rumours likewise were heard of some approaching conspiracy; but no attention was paid to them. The Earl of *Liecester*, whom the king had appointed lieutenant, remained in *London*. The two justices, Sir *William Parsons* and Sir *John Borlace*, were men of small ability, and owed their advancement to nothing but their zeal for that party by whom every thing was now governed. Tranquil from their ignorance and inexperience, these men, according to our author's account, indulged themselves in the most profound repose, on the very brink of destruction.

'But they were awakened from their security, the very day before that appointed for the commencement of hostilities. The *Castle* of *Dublin*, by which the capital is commanded, contained arms for 10,000 men, along with thirty-five pieces of cannon, and a proportionable quantity of ammunition: yet was this important place guarded, and that too without any care, by no greater force than fifty men. *Maguire*, and *More*, were already in town with a numerous band of their retainers; others were expected that night; and next morning they were to enter upon what they esteemed the easiest of all enterprizes, the surprize of the *Castle*. *Oconolly*, an *Irishman*, but a protestant, betrayed the secret to *Parsons*. The justices and council, for safety, fled immediately into the *Castle*, and reinforced the guards. The alarm was conveyed to the city, and all the protestants prepared for defence. *More* escaped; *Maguire* was taken; and *Mahone*, one of the conspirators, being likewise seized, first discovered to the justices the project of a general insurrection, and redoubled the apprehensions which were already universally diffused throughout *Dublin*.

But though *Oconolly's* discovery saved the castle from a surprize, the confession extorted from *Mahone* came too late to prevent the intended insurrection. *Oneale*, and his confederates, had already taken arms in *Ulster*. The *Irish*, every where intermingled with the *English*, needed but a hint from their leaders and priests, to begin hostilities against a people whom they hated on account of their religion, and envied for their riches and prosperity. The houses, cattle, goods, of the unwary *English*, were first seized. Those who heard of the commotions in their neighbourhood, instead of deserting their habitations, and flocking together for mutual protection, remained at home, in hopes of defending their property; and fell thus separately into the hands of their enemies. After rapacity had fully exerted itself, cruelty, and the most barbarous that ever in any nation was known or heard of, began its operations. An universal massacre commenced of the *English*, now defenceless, and passively resigned to their inhuman foes. No age, no sex, no condition was spared. The wife weeping for her butchered husband, and embracing her helpless children, was pierced along with then, and perished by the same stroke. The old, the young, the vigorous, the infirm, underwent a like fate, and were confounded in one common ruin. In vain did flight save from the first assault: destruction was every where let loose, and met the hunted victims at every turn. In vain was recourse had to relations, to companions, to friends, all connexions were dissolved, and death was dealt by that inhuman hand from which protection was implored and expected. Without provocation, without opposition, the astonished *English*, living in profound peace and full security, were massacred by their nearest neighbours, with whom they had long upheld a continued intercourse of kindness and good offices.

But death was the lightest punishment inflicted by those more than barbarous savages: all the tortures which wanton cruelty could devise, all the lingering pains of body, the anguish of mind, the agonies of despair, could not satiate revenge excited without injury, and cruelty derived from no cause. To enter into particulars would shock the least delicate humanity. Such enormities, though attested by undoubted evidence, appear almost incredible. Depraved nature, even perverted religion, though encouraged by the utmost licence, reach not such a pitch of ferocity; unless the pity inherent in human breasts be lost, by that contagion of example which transports men beyond all the usual motives of conduct and behaviour.

The weaker sex themselves, naturally tender to their own sufferings, and compassionate to those of others, here emulated their most robust companions in the practice of every cruelty. Even children, taught by the example, and encouraged by the exhortation of their brutal parents, essayed their feeble blows on the dead carcasses, or defenceless children, of the *English*. The very avarice of the *Irish* was not a sufficient restraint to their cruelty: such was their frenzy, that their cattle which they had seized, and by rapine had made their own, yet because they bore the name of *English*, were wantonly slaughtered, or, covered with wounds, turned loose into the woods and desarts.

The stately buildings, or commodious habitations of the planters, as if upbraiding the sloth and ignorance of the natives, were consumed with fire, or laid level with the ground: and where the miserable owners, shut up in their houses, and preparing for defence, perished in the flames, along with their wives and children, a double triumph was afforded to these insulting butchers.

If any where a number assembled together, and assuming courage from despair, were resolved to sweeten death by a revenge on their barbarous assassins; they were disarmed by capitulations and promises of safety, confirmed by the most solemn oaths; but no sooner had they surrendered, than the rebels, with perfidy equal to their cruelty, made them share the fate of their unhappy countrymen.

Others, more ingenious still in their barbarity, tempted their prisoners, by the fond love of life, to embrue their hands in the blood of friends, brothers, parents; and having thus rendered themselves accomplices in guilt, gave them that death which they thought to shun by deserving it.

Amidst all these enormities, the sacred name of RELIGION resounded on every side; not to stop the hand of these inhuman savages, but to enforce their blows, and to steel their hearts against every movement of human or social sympathy; the *English*, as heretics, abhorred of God, and detestable to all holy men, were marked out by the priests for slaughter; and of all actions, to rid the world of these declared enemies to catholic faith and piety, was represented as the most meritorious. Nature, which, in that rude people was sufficiently inclined to atrocious deeds, was farther stimulated by precept, and national prejudices empoisoned by those aversions, more deadly and incurable, which arose from an enraged superstition. While death finished the sufferings of each victim, the bigotted assassins, with joy and exultation, still echoed in his expiring ears, that these agonies were but the commencement of torments infinite and eternal.

Such were the barbarities by which Sir *Phelim Oneale*, and the *Irish* in *Ulster*, signalized their rebellion: an event memorable in the annals of human kind, and worthy to be had in perpetual detestation and abhorrence. The generous nature of *More* was shocked at the recital of such enormous cruelties. He flew to *Oneale's* camp; but found that his authority, which was sufficient to excite the *Irish* to an insurrection, was too feeble to restrain their inhumanity. Soon after he abandoned a cause polluted with so many crimes, and retired into *Flanders*. Sir *Phelim*, recommended by the greatness of his family, and perhaps too by the unrestrained brutality of his nature, though without any courage or capacity, acquired the entire ascendant over the northern rebels. The *English* colonies were totally annihilated in the open country of *Ulster*: the *Scotch*, at first, met with more favourable treatment.

In order to engage them to a passive neutrality, the *Irish* pretended to distinguish betwixt the *British* nations; and claiming friendship and consanguinity with the *Scotch*, extended not over them the fury of their massacres. Many of them found an opportunity to fly the country; others retired into places of security, and prepared themselves for defence: and by this means the *Scotch* planters, most of them at least, escaped with their lives.

From *Ulster*, the flames of rebellion diffused themselves, in an instant, over the three other provinces of *Ireland*. In all places, death and slaughter were not uncommon; though the *Irish*, in these other provinces, pretended to act with more moderation, and humanity: but cruel and barbarous was their humanity! Not contented with expelling the *English* their houses, with despoiling them of their goodly manors, with wasting their cultivated fields; they stripped them of their very cloaths, and turned them out naked and defenceless, to all the severities of the season. The heavens themselves, as if conspiring against that unhappy people, were armed with cold and tempest, unusual to the climate, and executed what the merciless sword of the barbarians had left unfinished. The roads were covered with crowds of naked *English*, hastening towards *Dublin* and the other cities, which yet remained in the hands of the countrymen. The feeble age of children, the tender sex of women, soon succumbed under the multiplied rigors of cold and hunger. Here the weeping husband, bidding a final adieu to his expiring family, envied them that fate, which he himself expected so soon to share. There, the son, having long supported his aged parent, with reluctance obeyed his last commands, and abandoning him in this uttermost distress, reserved himself to the hopes of revenging that death, which all his efforts could not prevent nor delay. The astonishing greatness of the calamity, deprived the sufferers of any relief from the view of companions in affliction. With silent tears or lamentable cries, they hurried on through the hostile territories, and found every heart which was not immured in unrelenting barbarity, guarded by the more implacable furies of mistaken piety and religion.

The saving of *Dublin*, preserved in *Ireland* the relics of the *English* name. The gates of that city, though timorously opened, received the wretched supplicants, and displayed a view of human misery, beyond what any eye had ever before beheld. Compassion seized the amazed inhabitants, aggravated with the fear of like calamities, while they observed the numerous foes, without and within, which every where environed them, and reflected on the weak resources by which they were themselves supported. The more vigourous of the unhappy fugitives, to the number of three thousand, were inlisted into three regiments. The rest were distributed into the houses, and all care taken, by diet and warmth, to recruit their feeble and torpid limbs. Diseases of unknown name and species, deprived from those multiplied distresses, seized many of them and put a speedy period to their lives: others, having now leisure to reflect on their mighty loss of friends and fortune, cursed that being which they had saved. Abandoning themselves to despair, refusing all succour, they expired, without other consolation than that of receiving, among their countrymen, the honours of a grave, which, to their slaughtered companions, had been denied by the inhuman barbarians.'

Our author observes, that by some computations, those who perished by all these cruelties, are made to amount to a hundred and fifty or two hundred thousand: this calculation Mr. *Hume* imagines is too immoderate; and that, by the most *reasonable* account, they must have been near forty thousand. Upon this we beg leave to subjoin, that above one hundred and fifty four thousand protestants were massacred in *Ireland*, from the 23d of *October*, 1641, to the 1st of *March* following, according to the computation of the priests themselves who were present. See *Rushworth*, vol. v. p. 355, 734. But according to Sir *John Temple*, who wrote a particular account of this shocking scene of desolation, from the time the rebellion first broke out, unto the cessation *September* 15, 1643, there were above three hundred thousand *British* and [*Irish*] protestants cruelly murdered in cold blood, destroyed some other way, or expelled out of their habitations. See *Temple's; Irish* Rebellion, page 6, and *Cox*, p. 73.

Mr. *Hume* very industriously labours to clear King *Charles* from the imputation of having encouraged the *Irish* to take arms against his protestant subjects; his observations relating to this matter are before the public, to whose impartial judgment we leave them. But his assertions relating to the commission said to be given to *Edward* Lord *Herbert*, Earl of *Glamorgan*, seem to require a more particular notice.

'After the cessation with the *Irish* rebels,' he tells us, 'the king was desirous of concluding a final peace with them, and obtaining their assistance in *England*; and he gave authority to *Ormond*, lord-lieutenant, to promise them an abrogation of all the penal laws enacted against catholics, along with the suspension of *Poyning's* statute, with some particular bills which should be agreed on. Lord *Herbert*, created Earl of *Glamorgan*, (tho' his patent had not yet passed the seals) having occasion for his private affairs to go to *Ireland*, the king considered that this nobleman, being a catholic, and allied to the best *Irish* families, might be of service; and he accordingly desired him, to promote, by his good offices, the negotiation which was then on foot with the rebels. *Glamorgan*, bigotted for his religion, and passionate for the king's service, but guided in these pursuits by no manner of judgment or discretion, secretly, of himself, without any communication with *Ormand*, concluded a peace with the council of *Kilkenny*, and agreed, in the king's name, that the *Irish* should enjoy all the churches, which they had ever in possession of, since the commencement of their insurrection; on condition that they should assist the king with a body of ten thousand men. As soon as this transaction was divulged, *Ormand*, who was well assured that the king had never consented to a treaty, by which the catholic was, in a manner, made the established religion of *Ireland*, immediately threw *Glamorgan* into prison, and charged him with high-treason on account of his temerity. The king disowned the giving him any authority for this pacification; and sent to the parliament an account of the whole matter. The prejudices which prevailed against him, made his relation meet with no manner of credit with the parliament or their partizans: and to this day, his veracity in this point is, by some historians, very much called in question.'

Mr. *Hume* here subjoins an attempt to persuade his readers that *Glamorgan's* commission was either forged, or surreptitious, or limited by *secret* instructions, which he did not regard; but he thinks the supposition of its forgery is by far the most probable. He also refers to Mr. *Carte's* Life of the Duke of *Ormond*, as furnishing sufficient evidence on this occasion. He asserts, that the Earl of *Glamorgan* was a man of so little probity, or so great levity, that his forgeries, in other instances, are palpable and avowed: that in order to render himself considerable among the *Irish*, he shewed them a paper, pretended to be signed by the king; wherein *Charles* promises his daughter to *Glamorgan's* eldest son, and gives him the right of coinage, &c. That the paper in which the king promised to give his daughter to *Glamorgan's* son, was not forged, seems evident from a remarkable commission which Mr. *Collins* has published in his account of the family of the Duke of *Beaufort*.[3] See Peerage of *England*, Vol. I. page 75, edit. 1735. In this commission the abovesaid earl was invested with the office of generalissimo of three armies, *English*, *Irish*, and foreign, and admiral of a fleet at sea, &c. It is also added,

"And for persons of generosity, for whom titles of honour are most desirable, we have entrusted you with several patents under our great seal of *England*, from a marquis to a baronet, which we give you full power and authority to date, and dispose of, without knowing our further pleasure. So great is our trust and confidence in you, as that, whatsoever you do contract for or promise, we will make good the same accordingly, from the date of this our commission forwards, which, for their better satisfaction, we give you leave to give them, or any of them, copies thereof, attested under your hand and seal of arms. And for your own encouragement, and in token of our gratitude, we give and allow forward such fees, titles, preheminences, and privileges, as do and may belong unto your place and command above mentioned, with promise of our dear daughter ELIZABETH, to your son PLANTAGENET, in marriage, with three hundred thousand pounds in dower

---

[3] Lineally descended from the Earl of *Glamorgan*.

or portion, most part whereof we acknowledge sent, and disburst by your father and you in our service; with the title of Duke of *Somerset* to you, and your heirs male for ever. And from hence forward to give the garter to your arms, and at your pleasure to put on the George and blue ribbon: and for your greater honour, and in testimony of our reality, we have WITHOUT OWN HAND, affixed our great seal of *England* unto these our commission and letters, making them patents. Witness our self at *Oxford*, the first day of *April*, in the twentieth year of our reign, and the year of our Lord one thousand six hundred and forty-four."[4]

We refer the curious, for further satisfaction on this subject, to a valuable tract, intitled, *An Inquiry into the Share which King* Charles *had in the Transactions of the Earl of* Glamorgan, etc. printed 1747.[5] But to return to our author.

It may not be disagreeable to our readers to make some extracts from Mr. *Hume's* work, relating to the principal characters drawn in this history; wherein, we apprehend, he has given various proofs both of his judgment, and command of expression.

Having intimated the King *James*, by his journey into *Scotland*, 1617, proposed to enlarge episcopal authority, to establish some few ceremonies in public worship, and to fix a superiority of the civil above the ecclesiastical jurisdiction, he proceeds to sketch out a view of the religion which then prevailed in that kingdom. 'The fire of devotion,' says he,

'excited by novelty, and inflamed by opposition, had so possessed the minds of the *Scotch* reformers, that all rites and ornaments, and even order of worship, were disdainfully rejected, as useless burthens; retarding the imagination in its rapturous extasies, and stinting the operations of that divine spirit, by which they supposed themselves to be animated. A mode of worship was established, the most naked and most simple imaginable; one that borrowed nothing from the senses, but reposed itself entirely on the contemplation of the divine essence which discovers itself to the understanding only. This species of devotion, so *suitable to the supreme Being*, but so little suitable to human frailty, was observed to occasion the most enormous ravages in the breast, and to subvert every rational principle of conduct and behaviour. The mind, straining for these extraordinary raptures, reaching them by short glances, succumbing again under its own weakness, rejecting all exterior aid of pomp and ceremony, was so occupied in this inward life, that it fled from every intercourse of society, and from every sweet or

---

[4]   This commission is also inserted, at large, by the authors of the Parliamentary History of *England*, in their fourteenth volume, just published.

[5]   [Selections from a later edition of this work are contained in this volume.]

chearful amusement, which could soften or humanize the character. – In order to mellow these humors, *James* endeavoured to infuse a small tincture of superstition into the national worship, and to introduce such rites and ceremonies as might, in some degree, occupy the mind, and please the senses, without departing too far from that simplicity, by which the reformation was distinguished. The finer arts too, though still rude in these northern kingdoms, were employed to adorn the churches; and the king's chapel, in which an organ was erected, and some pictures and statues displayed, was proposed as a model to the rest of the nation. But music was grating to the prejudiced ears of the *Scotch* clergy; sculpture and painting appeared instruments of idolatry; the surplice was a rag of popery; and each motion or gesture prescribed by the liturgy, was a step towards that spiritual Babylon, so much the object of their horror and aversion. Every thing was deemed impious but their own mystical comments on the scriptures, which they idolized, and whose eastern prophetic style they employed in every common occurrence of life.

It will be sufficient to give an account of one or two of the ceremonies, which the king was so intent to establish. Such institutions, for a time, are esteemed, either too divine to have proceeded from any other Being than the supreme creator of the universe, or too diabolical to have been derived from other than an infernal demon. But no sooner is the mode of the controversy past, than they are universally discovered to be so frivolous, as scarce to be mentioned with dignity, or even decency, amidst the ordinary course of human transactions. On these occasions, history is sometimes constrained to depart a little from her native and accustomed gravity.

As episcopal ordination was still wanting to the *Scotch* bishops, who derived their character merely from votes of parliaments and assemblies, *James* had called up three of them to *England*, [1610.] By canonical ceremonies, and by imposition of hands, they received from the *English* bishops that unknown, and therefore the more revered virtue, which through innumerable prelates had been supposed to be transmitted, without interruption, from the first disciples and apostles. And these three bishops were esteemed sufficient to preserve alive that virtue, to transport it into *Scotland*, and to transfer it by their touch to their brethren and successors in that kingdom.

Great controversies arose, even after every other dispute seemed to be adjusted, betwixt the king and the ministers, about the manner of receiving the sacrament: the king still insisted, that the communicants should rest on their knees; and he regarded that posture as the most respectful, because the most uneasy: the ministers strenuously maintained the privilege of reposing on their seats, during the performance of that sacred rite; and would by no means submit to the posture prescribed to them.

– Every prudent man agreed in condemning the measures of the king, who, by an ill-timed zeal for insignificant ceremonies, had betrayed, though in an opposite manner, equal narrowness of mind, with the persons whom he treated with such contempt. It was judged, that had not these dangerous humours been irritated by opposition, had they been allowed peaceably to evaporate, they might at last have subsided, within the limits of law and civil authority. And as all fanatical religions naturally circumscribe to very narrow bounds, the numbers and riches of the ecclesiastics; no sooner is their first fire spent, than they lose all credit over the people, and leave them under the natural and benevolent influence of their legal and moral obligations.'

We have been agreeably entertained with the characters our author hath attempted of some celebrated personages, who make no inconsiderable figure in this history. *Henry*, Prince of *Wales*, he remarks, has been justly mentioned by historians with peculiar applause; and observes, that his merit, in every respect, seems to have been very extraordinary.

'He had not reached his eighteenth year, and he possessed already more dignity in his behaviour, and commanded more respect, than his father with all his age, learning, and experience. Neither his high fortune, nor his youth, had seduced him into any irregular pleasures; business and ambition seem to have been his sole passion. His inclinations, as well as exercises, were entirely martial. – He had conceived great affection and esteem for the brave Sir *Walter Raleigh*. It was his saying, "Sure no king but my father would keep such a bird in a cage." He seems, indeed, to have nourished too violent a contempt for the king, on account of his pedantry and pusillanimity; and by that means, struck in with the restless and martial spirit of the *English* nation. Had he lived, he had probably promoted the glory, perhaps not the felicity, of his people. The unhappy prepossession, which men commonly entertain in favour of ambition, courage, enterprize, and other warlike virtues, engages generous natures, who always love fame, into such pursuits as destroy their own peace, and that of the rest of mankind.'

Lord *Bacon's* character, in our author's view of him, seems to be pretty justly delineated; 'a man,' says he,

'universally admired for the greatness of his genius, and beloved for the courteousness and humanity of his behaviour. He was the great ornament of his age and nation; and nought was wanting to render him the ornament of human nature itself, but that strength of mind which might check his intemperate desire of preferment that could add nothing to his dignity, and restraining his profuse inclination to expence that could be requisite neither for his honor nor entertainment. His want of œconomy, and his indulgence to servants had involved him in necessities; and, in order to supply his prodigality, he had been tempted to take bribes, and that in a very open manner, from suitors in chancery.'

The Duke of *Buckingham*, who was in such high esteem, both with *James I.* and *Charles I*. Mr. *Hume* represents as governing the court and nation with an uncontroled sway; but altogether unfit for the high station to which he was raised.

'Some accomplishments of a courtier he was possessed of: of every talent of a minister he was utterly devoid. Headlong in his passions, and incapable equally of prudence and of dissimulation: sincere from violence, rather than from candour; expensive from profusion more than from generosity: a warm friend, a furious enemy; but without any choice or discernment in either: with these qualities he had early and quickly mounted to the highest rank; and partook at once of the insolence which attends a fortune newly acquired, and the impetuosity which belongs to persons born in high stations, and unacquainted with opposition.'

In his portrait of King *James I.* this delineator's artful disposition of his lights and shades deserves particular notice. 'No prince,' says he,

'so little enterprising, and so inoffensive, was ever so much exposed to the opposite extremes of calumny and flattery, of satire and panegyric. And the factions, which began in his time, being still continued, have made his character be as much disputed to this day, as is commonly that of princes who are our contemporaries. Many virtues, however, it must be owned, he was possessed of; but no one of them pure or free from the contagion of the neighbouring vices. His generosity bordered on profusion, his learning on pedantry, his pacific disposition on pusillanimity, his wisdom on cunning, his friendship on light fancy and boyish fondness. While he imagined that he was only maintaining his own authority, he may be justly suspected in some of his actions, and still more of his pretensions, to have encroached on the liberties of his people: while he endeavoured, by an exact neutrality, to acquire the good will of all his neighbours, he was able to preserve fully the esteem and regard of none. His capacity was considerable; but fitter to discourse on general maxims, than to conduct any intricate business: his intentions were just; but more adapted to the conduct of private life, than to the government of kingdoms. Aukward in his person, and ungainly in his manners; he was ill qualified to command respect; partial and undiscerning in his affections, he was little fitted to acquire general love. Of a feeble temper more than of a frail judgment. Exposed to our ridicule from his vanity, but exempt from our hatred by his freedom from pride and arrogance. And upon the whole, it may be pronounced of his character, that all his qualities were sullied with weakness, and embellished by humanity. Political courage he certainly was devoid of; and from thence chiefly is derived the strong prejudice which prevails against his personal bravery: an inference, however, which must be owned, from general experience, to be extremely fallacious.'

If any reader should suspect, that in drawing the several limbs and features of the preceding portraiture, a greater regard hath been shewn to the spirit and elegance of the colouring and drapery, than to the true resemblance of the original, we refer to the fifth and sixth volumes of the *Parliamentary History*, and Mr. *Harris's Historical and Critical Account, etc.* of James I wherein a variety of evidence will appear against Mr. *Hume's* representation: and indeed the facts which he himself has related, concerning this monarch, cannot easily be reconciled with the character he hath drawn for him.

In the account Mr. *Hume* gives of Archbishop *Laud*, he tells us, this prelate

'was virtuous, if severity of manners alone, and abstinence from pleasure, could deserve that name. He was learned, if ecclesiastical knowledge could intitle him to that praise. He was disinterested; but with unceasing industry he studied to exalt the priestly and prelatical character, which was his own. His zeal was unrelenting in the cause of religion; that is, in imposing, by the most rigourous measure, his own tenets and pious ceremonies on the obstinate puritans, who had profanely dared to oppose him. In prosecution of his holy purposes, he overlooked every human consideration; or, in other words, the heat and indiscretion of his temper made him neglect all views of prudence, and all rules of good manners. He was, in this respect, happy, that ALL his enemies were also declared enemies to loyalty and true piety; and that every exercise of his revenge, by that means, became a merit and a virtue. This was the man who acquired so great an ascendant over *Charles*, and led him, by the superstition of his temper, into a conduct which proved so fatal to himself, and to his kingdoms.'

The panegyric our historian has wrought up, to embellish the character of *Charles I.* which he allows to be a *mixed* one, is not only repugnant to historical truth, but even refuted and exposed by Mr. *Hume's* own view of this prince's arbitrary administration; however, we shall only observe, that if the account which his son and successor, *Charles II.* gave of his father's conduct, in the affair of the *Irish* rebellion and massacre, may be depended upon, the virtue and piety of this unhappy king, will appear in a very disadvantageous light; the second *Charles* acknowleges, that

"besides letters and orders, under his majesty's own hand, there was sufficient evidence and testimony of several messages and directions, sent from our royal father, and our royal mother, with the privity and direction of the king our father, by which it appears, that WHATEVER CORRESPONDENCE or ACTINGS the said marquis [of *Antrim*] had with the confederate *Irish* catholics, were DIRECTED AND ALLOWED by the said letters and instructions: and that the KING himself was well pleased with what the marquis did, after he had done it, and approved of the same."

See *An Essay towards obtaining a true Idea of the Character and Reign of* Charles I. *page* 126, 8*vo*. 1748.

We shall close our account of this work with a reflection or two upon it. – And *first*, If it is considered only as a work of *genius*, or, as consisting of *general remarks* and *observations* on the history of the period to which he confines himself, it has, undoubtedly, on several accounts, a very considerable share of merit. The author's reflections, in many instances, are striking and manly, his manner masterly, and, when prejudice does not warp and bias his judgment, his characters are strongly and clearly marked. – *Again*, If we take our notions of the two reigns this author assumes to write the history of, from what he says of them, we shall certainly form a very inadequate and unjust idea of those times. Many facts are concealed, or partially exhibited, that are necessary to be rightly viewed, in order to throw a true light upon them; and instead of a full and faithful representation of facts, the reader is often presented with half-views and side-glances of them. – *Once more*, We cannot but observe, how singular Mr. *Hume* is in his notions of religion. He seems to be of opinion, that there are but two species of it in all nature, *superstition* and *fanaticism*; and under one or other of these, he gives us to understand, the whole of the christian profession is, and ever was, included. His treatment, indeed, of every denomination of christians, to speak the most favourably, is far from being such as becomes a gentleman, and may, we apprehend, prejudice his reputation *even as an historian*, in the opinion of many intelligent and considerate readers.

2
GÖTTINGISCHE ANZEIGEN

Review of *The History of Great Britain*, Vol. 1, in *Göttingische Anzeigen von gelehrten Sachen*, December 8, 1755, Nr. 147, pp. 1350–1354. Complete review.

*G*öttingische Anzeigen was one of the world's longest serial publications, covering over 200 years, from 1739–1940. The journal went through several name changes, and was devoted to the review of scholarly books.[1] By the time the first volume of Hume's *History* appeared, *Göttingische Anzeigen* had already reviewed most of Hume's previous publications. The anonymous reviewer of the article here is impressed with Hume's writing style and his ability to grasp the context of past times and guide readers through historical obscurities. The reviewer, though, notes disagreement with Hume, particularly "in religious matters where he expresses his opinion at the expense of the truth." Below is the first published English translation of the complete review, by Nels Jeff Rogers. Bracketed comments in the notes below are those of the translator.

Edinburgh.

Last year Mr. David Hume's *The History of Great Britain*, volume one, was published by Hamilton, Balfour and Neil. The 473 page volume in large quarto contains the histories of King James the First and Charles the First. The name of the author is well enough known and indicates in advance that this volume distinguishes itself from the common fare. We read the volume with much pleasure, not necessarily because of the unknown information – we didn't compare the volume–; but rather more so because of the pragmatic writing style of which this volume is exemplary. It is well known that Mr. Hume is well acquainted with the world and is wont to serious observation of

---

[1] *Göttingische Zeitungen von gelehrten Sachen* (1739–1752); *Göttingische Anzeigen von gelehrten Sachen, unter der Aufsicht der Königl. Gesellschaft der Wissenschaften* (1753–1801); *Göttingische gelehrte Anzeigen, unter der Aufsicht der Gesellschaft der Wissenschaften* (1802–1940).

customs. In this volume we find the quite rare talent of using this knowledge for the purpose of enlightenment and promoting the usefulness of history. It is a well known rule that the historian, if he wants to uncover the historical motivations of the period in question, must put himself in the times about which he writes and that he must judge the action of people not according to principles popular today, but rather, according to those principles which predominated in those days about which he writes. This rule is least observed by those historians who work on the history of recent times, probably due to the prejudice that, as they believe, in such a short period of time no noticeable changes in the political mind-set can be discerned. Other historians err by not giving the reader any guidance in order that they themselves might see the differences between past and present constitutions and the rules of the state that derive from them. To his advantage Mr. Hume has generally avoided these errors and from his book one becomes well acquainted with what Great Britain looked like at the time of King James and King Charles. In Queen Elizabeth's time the court ruled almost monarchically and the favour of the nation toward this Princess and her external affability allowed her to do everything she wanted. The rights of parliament were generally reduced. Church issues belonged solely before her majesty who dealt with the Popes and Puritans in an extremely strict manner.

King James ascended to the throne with the most sublime thoughts of his own power – thoughts which could not co-exist with the freedom of the people as he lacked the artistry to win their love and the favour of the regional courts. For this reason he could not easily bring the Parliament to his purpose. Moreover, his weaknesses, which were known to the people and the regional courts, gave the parliament the opportunity to consider renewing and reasserting its old rights. Parliament involved itself in both state and church issues and as the King was often dependent upon their approval, so it was that they had to give him the means by which to arrive at his purpose. Under this government there were certainly noteworthy occurrences. King James, however, did not know how to put these to the service of his advantage. His pedantic desire to become famous as a writer; his exaggerated love for those in his favour, who themselves accomplished very little for him; and his peaceable manner led him to make irresponsible political errors. Yet what made him so hated by the people was that for reasons of simple vanity he entered into negotiations with the Spanish Crown to provide the then Prince of Wales a royal bride and in turn made the Prince in question into a knight errant. It also prevented the King from providing his son-in-law, the misfortunate Christian Fredric of the Palatinate, with the help the people demanded for reasons of religious enthusiasm. Despite this the King in the end wed the Prince of Wales with a French Princess. In relation to this marriage Mr. Hume makes a note that we cannot skip over here. It is true that in the marriage agreement it was promised that the education of children would be left to the catholic mother for thirteen years. That this agreement was made only in order to deceive the Roman Court, and was in no way intended to be adhered to, can be seen in the success with which King Charles the First raised his children in the Protestant religion from the earliest years of childhood.

We have here inadvertently arrived at the last main section of the history of King James the First, which was the section that best pleased us because it gives news of the civil government, ecclesiastical government, manners, finances, navy, commerce, manufacture, colonies and learning and the arts in England during the time under discussion. Of this we will share a few samples. To begin with it is shown that at the time King James came to the throne the power of the King was almost unlimited and that even among writers who were otherwise good patriots a type of passive obedience was adopted and defended. In the church an exaggerated religious enthusiasm that burned heretics and persecuted nonconformist still dominated. The freedom of the press, of which the English are today so proud, was virtually unknown and King James, who contrary to all assumptions was a loyal supporter of the of the episcopal church, directed the libraries of both the Archbishop of Canterbury and York, the library of London and of both vice-chancellors of the universities. The manners of the English were moderate and they kept to the middle of the road better than they do today; while at the same time there reigned more harmony and the elite had more respect for common men. The nobleman loved life in the country and it was an error in governing by King James that he no longer gathered these men at his court, which must be excused because of the inordinate expenditures associated in so doing.

In 1617 the income of the King was 450,000 Pounds Sterling. Expenditures however exceeded this sum by 36,000 Pounds. The price of grain from which afterwards all other necessities were dependent was not less, but rather more, than it is now. So is also the price of wool and other processed goods less today now than it was then. Both land and sea power were weak. Trade in contrast had grown more than one then thought, though it was still in its infancy. There were counted no more than 10,000 mariners on trade-ships, which is barely a sixth of today's number. The export of raw wool, before it was banned, enriched only the Dutch yearly in the amount of 700,000 Pounds. Linen manufacture was still completely unknown. At the same time King James introduced the planting of Mulberry trees and the manufacture of silk. Trade in the East Indies was expanded, though also impeded and interrupted by the Dutch. Yet it was the American Colonies that were the most important part of the gains made in English trade. Agriculture was very underdeveloped as one began under this government to encourage the people to make improvements in this area. Still one had to buy bread from foreigners. We will skip over the critical examination of the state of the sciences and note only that Mr. Hume in his evaluation of the King holds the middle-ground between those who praise him in exaggerated fashion for his erudition and writings and those who demean him.

Since we have already said so much of the history of King James, we only see it as necessary to point out that the second book is composed in the same style and that the sources and means of conveyance uncover the disagreements between King Charles and his people which eventually cost the former his head. One cannot better convey Mr. Hume's view of these events than in the terms with which he himself describes the King on page 468. For that reason we want to cite a short passage of this description. He writes: "The virtues of King Charles in general surpass his vices, or more properly speaking, his imperfections: For scarce any of his faults rose to that pitch as to merit the appellation of vices. He deserves the epithet of a good, rather than of a great man; and was more fitted to rule as an absolute monarch than at a time when the genius of the people ran violently toward liberty. Some historians do him an injustice when they cast doubt upon his honesty and his faithfulness to his promises."[2] That there are moral and political remarks mixed in with the historical reports is to be assumed of Mr. Hume, even if we do not agree with all of them, least of all in religious matters where he expresses his opinion at the expense of the truth.

---

[2] [This is not a direct quote but a summary of the contents as appears in pages 542–543 in David Hume, *The History of England. Vol. V.* (Indianapolis, IN: Liberty Classics, 1983). – N.J.R.]

3
THOMAS BIRCH

Thomas Birch, *An inquiry into the share, which King Charles I. had in the transactions of the Earl of Glamorgan, ... for bringing over a body of Irish rebels to assist that King, in the years 1645 and 1646. ... The second edition; to which is added an appendix, containing several letters of the King to the Earl of Glamorgan, ...* London: printed for A. Millar, 1756, viii, 376 p.
Selections from Appendix; from 1756 edition.

Thomas Birch (1705–1766) was born in the Clerkenwell borough of London, and raised a Quaker. In 1731 he was ordained priest in the Church of England, from which time he was appointed to several London rectories. Birch was a voluminous writer in the areas of history and literature. Ideologically he was strongly Whiggish. In 1747 he published his *Inquiry*, which discusses the relation between Charles I and Edward Somerset (1601–1667), Earl of Glamorgan. In 1644 and 1645 Charles hoped to receive military assistance from Ireland in his conflict with English Parliamentarians. He assigned the task of mediation with the Irish to James Butler (Earl, later Duke of Ormonde, lieutenant general of the English Army). However, Glamorgan – a Catholic – was involved in more clandestine mediation efforts; claiming to act on the authority of Charles, he signed a controversial treaty with Irish Roman Catholics. The treaty was publicly exposed, and, under pressure from Irish Protestants, Charles renounced Glamorgan's efforts, and Glamorgan himself was imprisoned for treason. Questions arose about the extent to which Glamorgan acted in concert with Ormonde and Charles. Birch – siding with the Parliamentarians – argued that Glamorgan acted with the full authority of the king. In the 1754 volume of his *History*, Hume sided with the Royalists and argued that Glamorgan concluded the controversial treaty on his own, without communication with Ormonde. In fact, following historian Thomas Carte, Hume argued that Glamorgan was a known forger and probably counterfeited his royal commission to mediate in Ireland during the rebellion. In 1756 a second edition of Birch's *Inquiry* appeared, which, according to Birch's Preface, is "exactly reprinted from the former published in May 1747, with the addition of an Appendix written in January 1755." In this Appendix he attacks Hume for not consulting the first edition of Birch's *Inquiry* and instead relying on Carte's groundless assessment that Glamorgan forged his commission.

Hume had some communication with Birch at this time. The 1756 edition of Birch's *Inquiry* was published by Andrew Millar – who was also Hume's bookseller and friend. Perhaps alerted to Birch's forthcoming publication, Hume wrote Millar the previous year concerning Birch and the issue of Charles I's arbitrary rule:

> Pray tell Dr Birch, if you have Occasion to see him, that his Story of the Warrant for Lord Loudon's Execution, tho' at first I thought it highly improbable, appears to me at present a great deal more likely. ... I own it is the strongest Instance of any which History affords of K. Charles's arbitrary Principles. [Hume to Andrew Millar, April 12, 1755]

Hume also had indirect communication with Birch through another mutual friend (see Hume to John Clephane, April 20, 1756). Shortly after, Hume requested that Millar arrange a meeting with Birch:

> You would oblige me much, if you woud prepare the way for an Acquaintaince between Dr Birch & me, when I shall be in London. I have a great Esteem for his Character; have heard that he is very communicative; and is very willing, and even desirous, to give Information to any Body that applies to him. Such an Acquaintance woud be very useful and agreeable to me. [Hume to Andrew Millar, April 6, 1758]

Two years later Hume solicited help from Birch in acquiring some hard-to-find historical works (Hume to Andrew Millar, March 22, 1760). In 1763 a dinner meeting with Birch and other notable writers finally took place when Hume stopped through London on his way to Paris (Mossner, *Life of David Hume*, p. 438).

Personal communication aside, Hume responded more officially to Birch's attack. In the 1759 second edition of his *History*, Hume abandoned Carte's theory that Glamorgan forged his commission from Charles. Nevertheless, Hume retained his Royalist version of the Glamorgan episode, and included a lengthy note to Chapter 58, which offers six arguments against Birch's position. The following year, Hume wrote John Douglas concerning Birch's account of the Glamorgan issue. Hume states that "Dr Birch has totally mistaken the Point in Question" and that Birch's "Style suits well enough those puritanical Times, when Popery was the Height of all Reproaches" (Hume to John Douglas, October 27, 1760). At the time, Douglas was editing a collection of letters of Henry Hyde, second Earl of Clarendon, which ultimately appeared in 1763. Hume heard through Millar that one of the letters "clears up the Question of Glamorgan's Transactions." Hume requested access to the letter, but Douglas, not permitted to give him the original, responded with only a summary of the document (Douglas's correspondence to Hume is included in Burton's *Letters of Eminent Persons*, 1849, pp. 16–19).

Birch's *Inquiry* is favourably mentioned by Francis Jeffrey in his 1824 review of Brodie's *History*, contained later in this collection. The following is from the 1756 and final edition of Birch's *Inquiry*.

AN
APPENDIX
TO THE
Inquiry into the share, which King Charles I. *had in the transactions of the Earl of* Glamorgan, *afterwards Marquis of* Worcester, *for bringing over a body of* Irish *rebels to assist that King, in the years* 1645 *and* 1646. In which *Appendix* are now published several letters of the King to the Earl of Glamorgan, from the originals in the Harleian library of manuscripts.

At the close of the *Inquiry* I declared, that *if any new evidence could be produced to shew, that King* Charles I. *neither authorised, nor was privy to, nor connived at the proceedings of the Earl of* Glamorgan *with the* Irish *rebels, I should with the utmost readiness submit to the force of truth, which ought to be the chief aim of every writer.* It is now above seven years and an half since the publication of that book, which has hitherto received not the least answer to any part of it; though Mr. *Carte*, whose character as an historian was brought into question by it, frequently assured his friends, that he would give a thorough confutation of it. An advertisement indeed, imputed to him, appeared in the *Gazetteer* of *Wednesday February* 6, 1754, and in the *London Evening Post* of *Saturday* the 23d of that month, in the following terms:

"*Shortly will be published,*
The CASE of the ROYAL MARTYR considered with candour; wherein, amongst other libels upon his Majesty, a treatise, intitled, *An Inquiry into the share, which King* Charles I. *had in the transactions of the Earl of* Glamorgan, *&c.* is examined; and the chief positions and insinuations of that author shewn to be weak, groundless, and utterly inconsistent with the character of a critic or a scholar"

What *candour* might have been expected from that writer, may be judged of, both from his other performances, and from his giving the name of *libel* to a discourse drawn up with the utmost moderation of style, as well as fidelity in the representation of facts. And how little additional evidence would have been produced by him upon this subject, is evident from his pretending only *to shew,* that my chief *positions* and *insinuations,* as he is pleased to describe a detail of facts supported by the best authorities, and a few clear observations deduced from them, are *weak, groundless, and utterly inconsistent with the character of a critic or a scholar;* as if the question was not a point of history, but of mere criticism or literature. But the book thus advertised was never published, either before or since Mr. *Carte*'s death on the 2d of *April*, 1754, near two months after the first advertisement; nor can I find, upon the strictest examination, that any such piece was in the press, or even prepared for it.

Mr. *Guthrie*, whose third volume of his history was published in 1751, takes no manner of notice of the *Inquiry*, which had then seen the public light four years; but in a very imperfect account, which he gives of the affair of the Earl of *Glamorgan*, contained in less than a quarter of a page, first stiles his lordship's authority from the King a *pretended* one; and then affirms, that "*in the whole of the negotiations there were such intricacies and inconsistencies*, as ought to have rendered it very doubtful, whether *Glamorgan* had such a power as he pretended from *Charles*, who loudly disclaimed it."

Mr. *Hume*, the latest of our historians, preserves the same silence concerning the *Inquiry*; and in the first volume of his *General History of Great-Britain*, p. 412. where he remarks, that King *Charles* I.'s *veracity*, in disowning his having given any authority to the Earl of *Glamorgan*, *is to this day by some historians very much called in question*, he declares for the supposition of the forgery of his lordship's commission. But in support of this notion this ingenious writer contents himself with a repetition of Mr. *Carte*'s assertions and reasonings, which had been examined and confuted in a book, which from the subject of it, and the course of Mr. *Hume*'s historical researches, could scarce have escaped his knowledge.

Nor has the *Inquiry* only passed hitherto unimpeached in its credit in the smallest article, but it has likewise received new confirmation from evidence of the strongest kind, by the discovery of several original letters of king *Charles* I. himself to the Earl of *Glamorgan*, in the Harleian library of manuscripts, purchased in 1753 by the Parliament, and intended to be part of the British Museum. These letters are proper to be laid before the public, in justice to it, and to myself; and shall therefore be inserted, with some other additional facts and remarks, in this *Appendix*, with reference to the respective pages of the *Inquiry*, to which they relate.

...

4
DANIEL MACQUEEN

[Daniel MacQueen], *Letters on Mr. Hume's History of Great Britain*. Edinburgh: printed by Sands, Donaldson, Murray, and Cochran. For A. Kincaid and A. Donaldson, 1756, [4], 328 p.[1]
Complete; from 1756 edition.

Daniel MacQueen (d. 1777) was minister of the Old Kirk in Edinburgh and author of *Observations on Daniel's Prophecy of the Seventy Weeks* (1748). His *Letters on Mr. Hume's History of Great Britain* appeared anonymously two years after Hume's first volume of the *History* was published, and is principally an attack on Hume's portrayal of the Protestant Reformation. The nine Letters of MacQueen's polemic are directed towards an imaginary friend. In Letter 1 MacQueen presents Hume's two infamous passages about Catholic superstition and Protestant enthusiasm – passages which Hume removed from later editions of the *History*. MacQueen agrees that Catholicism is indeed superstitious, but questions Hume's claim that superstition and enthusiasm are diametrically opposed. In Letter 2 he turns to Hume's accusation that the Protestant reformers were excessively fanatical. According to MacQueen, the reformers were anything but fanatical insofar as they rejected all religious authority except that of the Bible. Letter 3 highlights inconsistencies with Hume's various criteria of enthusiasm, and MacQueen discusses the true non-fanatical character of the early reformers. And even if at times the reformers did act zealously, this, he believes, is excusable in view of the fiery political environment of the time.

Letter 4 addresses Hume's suggestion that the Reformation was not really necessary, and that a more leisurely internal reform of Catholicism would have been effective. MacQueen counters that Papal obstinacy prevented any internal reform, and Luther's own experiences regarding Papal indulgences confirm this. In Letter 5 MacQueen considers Hume's view that the reformation was premature, and the reformers should have waited for a sweeping

---

[1] Title Page: LETTERS | ON | Mr HUME's HISTORY | OF *GREAT BRITAIN.* | EDINBURGH: | Printed by SANDS, DONALDSON, MURRAY and COCHRAN. | For A. KINCAID and A. DONALDSON. | MDCCLVI.

internal event that would have suppressed the power of the clergy across Europe. In response, MacQueen argues that the Catholic hierarchy had been inherently resistant to major changes, and it was unrealistic for the reformers to patiently wait for this to happen. Letter 6 examines Hume's claim that the revived interest in ancient Greek thought at this time would open people's eyes and correct ecclesiastical abuses. MacQueen disagrees on the grounds that ancient Greek philosophy in its own day did not expel superstition from Greek religion.

In Letter 7 he looks at Hume's treatment of the various Protestant denominations. Contrary to Hume's assessment that Elizabeth exercised "good taste and sound judgment" in her authority over the Church of England, MacQueen believes that many of her actions were severely oppressive. Letter 8 discusses Hume's views of civil liberty, particularly during the reign of Charles I. In many passages of the *History*, Hume appears to be a strong advocate for liberty and harshly condemns Charles's infringements on freedom – specifically the ship-money tax. However, Hume then quite inconsistently claims that these infringements were minor and in fact had a positive impact on the country's economy. MacQueen asks, "Can you imagine yourself to be reading the same author?" He contests Hume's claim that the civil war owed more to disputes over religion than to disputes over liberty. The ninth and concluding Letter criticizes Hume's "loose and irreligious sneers" that prevail throughout the *History*. MacQueen notes that even ancient pagan philosophers such as Marcus Aurelius advocated piety and worship. He concludes extolling the virtues of true piety.

MacQueen's *Letters* was favourably reviewed in both the *Monthly Review* and the *Critical Review*. Writing for the *Monthly Review*, William Rose criticizes Hume's lack of partiality and recommends MacQueen's *Letters* for those who share Hume's views on religion:

Whoever peruses Mr. Hume's History with attention and impartiality, how much soever he may be pleased with his animated and entertaining manner of writing, and with the many marks of a lively genius, that are interspersed throughout his work, will not be of opinion, we apprehend, that the author's merit consists in giving an impartial representation of facts, or exhibiting characters in just and proper colours: nor will what he has advanced in regard to Religion, the Genius of the Protestant Faith, and the Characters of the first Reformers, be accounted, we presume, any recommendation of his History. If there are any, however, as perhaps there may be some, who agree with Mr. Hume in their sentiments upon these subjects, the Letters now before us may very properly be recommended to their attentive perusal. They are penned in a genteel, spirited, and candid manner; the author writes like a Gentleman, and a Scholar; and appears to be animated with a hearty concern for the interests of truth and virtue. It will not, we hope, be disagreeable to our readers, to present them with a pretty full account of what is contained in them. [*Monthly Review*, April 1756, Vol. 14, pp. 309–322]

Tobias Smollett opens his discussion in the *Critical Review* noting the "private criticism" surrounding Hume's *History*:

> Mr *Hume*'s history of *Great Britain*, which ever since its publication hath been the subject of much private criticism, is here submitted to public censure by a few very just though severe animadversions on some particular parts of it. The ingenious author of these letters seems principally to have confined his remarks to a defence of the Reformation, which Mr. *Hume* had thought fit to attack in two or three passages quoted by our letter-writer, wherein *there is* (he observes) *a peculiar and extravagant train of thought which those will not be surprised at who are acquainted with some other writings of this extraordinary author.*

Smollett concludes praising MacQueen's efforts:

> The work upon the whole we would venture to recommend to our readers as capable of affording him some pleasure in the perusal, as it seems to be written by a man of piety and virtue, and a zealous friend to the Protestant religion. We could wish to see the rest of Mr. *Hume*'s performances as impartially canvassed and as fairly refuted as those parts which have fallen under the inspection of the author of these letters. [*Critical Review*, 1756, Vol. 1, pp. 248–253]

In his 1775 review of John Whitaker's *History of Manchester*, Gilbert Stuart – writing for the *Edinburgh Magazine and Review* – harshly criticizes Macqueen (for quotations, see the selection on Whitaker's *History*, contained later in this collection). MacQueen's *Letters* is favourably mentioned in Joseph Towers's *Observations on Mr. Hume's History of England* (1778), which also appears later in this collection.

Hume did not think highly of McQueen, as reflected in one of his letters to Stuart (for the context of this letter see the entry on Gilbert Stuart later in these volumes). The following is from the 1756 and only edition of McQueen's *Letters*. The text below is complete, with the exclusion of several Greek quotations in footnotes from classical philosophers. McQueen provides English translations of these passages in the body of the text, and I have retained his bibliographical references to these passages in the footnotes. Bracketed comments in the text are McQueen's; bracketed comments in the footnotes are mine.

L E T T E R S

O N

Mr H U M E's H I S T O R Y

O F

G R E A T   B R I T A I N.

E D I N B U R G H :

Printed by Sands, Donaldson, Murray, and Cochran.

For A. Kincaid and A. Donaldson.

M D C C L V I.

LETTERS
ON
MR HUME's HISTORY

LETTER I.

As the conversation of friends is at all times agreeable, so when these friends are men of virtue and learning, mutual improvement will be added to social delight. The last of these is perhaps best promoted by a general uniformity of sentiment; but the first, by such diversity of opinion as is accompanied with candid and calm debate, and prompts them to an accurate investigation of truth. New ideas will be thus suggested; prejudices removed; the subject opened; and what is of most weight, and may be certainly known, will be distinguished from what is doubtful, and of less importance. But as the attention of the mind is not to be fixed too long on intricate subjects, such conversation is happily diversified with various reflections on this or the other writer, whose sentiments and composition are particularly considered. Men pronounce upon these according to their different abilities and taste: neither is it easy for them to throw off that bias, which is derived from their own preconceived opinions, and from their favourable or unfavourable thoughts of the main design which the author appears to have had in his view.

You will remember, I had lately an opportunity to see all this fully exemplified in that company of your friends, to which you introduced me; where, after an hour or two had been spent in other matters, the merits of a certain history began to be canvassed. The gentleman who spoke first, gave it as his judgment, that VOLTAIRE'S manner of writing was the most instructive and agreeable; that a minute detail of particular incidents was of little significancy in history; and as it perplexed the mind, and overloaded the memory to no purpose, so it was impossible for one to keep up the spirit of a narrative, who should write in this taste: he therefore approved of distinct and comprehensive views of things, interspersed with lively description, with pertinent reflections, and an exact delineation of characters. This he thought was peculiarly proper, where the subject of the history was well known; and he was of the mind, upon the whole, that the composition of Mr Hume's history was elegant, the diction generally clear and correct, and the narrative succinct and animated.

Your other friend, whose turn it was, talked of this author's declining the trouble of inserting any new materials, with which he might have been supplied from many valuable collections published within these few years: he represented the consequence of being thoroughly acquainted with the history of our own country, and mentioned impartiality and a scrupulous regard to truth, as essential to the character of a good historian: these, he said, would determine him to give a fair representation of facts, and would equally restrain from ill-grounded flattery, and unjust reproach. Having given his opinion of Mr Hume's history in this light, which was not a little unfavourable, he proceeded to distinguish betwixt history, and memoir writing; and to speak of his style, with which in the main he was pleased; adding withal, that, so far as he could perceive, the chief merit of the history must be rested there. At any rate, he hoped, that, corrupted as is the age wherein we live, there would be but a few who would esteem this history on account of the author's indecent excursions on the subject of religion, the genius of the Protestant faith, and the characters of the first reformers. He concluded with a warmth of expression, that seemed to flow from an honest and pious heart, affectionately concerned for the important interests of religion.

It gave me pleasure to observe, that his animadversions on this last point were approved; the justness of which, I took occasion to say, might be apparent to all, who would attentively peruse but a few passages of the history; on which I at that time offered several remarks, together with some reflections on the political sentiments of the historian. These you afterwards asked me to put in order: you obtained my promise; and I now sit down to discharge the obligation. The two passages to which I chiefly referred, are to be found in the 8th and 26th pages. In the first of these we read what follows.

"The first reformers, who made such furious and successful attacks on the Romish superstition, and shook it to its lowest foundations, may safely be pronounced to have been universally inflamed with the highest enthusiasm. These two species of religion, the superstitious and fanatical, stand in diametrical opposition to each other; and a large portion of the latter must necessarily fall to his share, who is so courageous as to controul authority, and so assuming as to obtrude his own innovations upon the world. Hence that rage of dispute, which every where seized the new religionists; that disdain of ecclesiastical subjection; that contempt of ceremonies, and of all the exterior pomp and splendor of worship. And hence too that inflexible intrepidity with which they braved dangers, torments, and even death itself; while they preached the doctrine of peace, and carried the tumults of war through every part of Christendom. However obstinate and uncomplying this species of religion, it necessarily received some alteration, according to the different situation on civil affairs, and the different species of government which it met with in its progress. In the electorates of Germany, in Denmark, and in Sweden, where the monarch was early converted, and, by putting himself at the head of the reformers, acquired authority amongst them; as the spirit of enthusiasm was somewhat tempered by a sense of order, Episcopal jurisdiction, along with a few decent ceremonies, was preserved in the new establishment. In Switzerland and Geneva, which were popular governments; in France, Scotland, and the Low Countries, where the people reformed themselves in opposition to the prince; the genius of fanaticism displayed itself in its full extent, and affected every circumstance of discipline and worship," &c.

The other passage relating to the same subject, is in the 25th and 26th pages; in which this author delivers his sentiments with great formality.

"Here it may not be improper," says he, "in a few words, to give some account of the Roman-Catholic religion, its genius and spirit. History addresses itself to a more distant posterity than will ever be reached by any local or temporary theology; and the characters of sects may be studied, when their controversies shall be totally forgotten. Before the reformation, all men of sense and virtue wished impatiently for some event, which might repress the exorbitant power of the clergy all over Europe, and put an end to the unbounded usurpations and pretensions of the Roman Pontiff: but when the doctrine of Luther was promulgated, they were somewhat alarmed at the sharpness of the remedy; and it was easily foreseen, from the offensive zeal of the reformers, and the defensive of the church, that all Christendom must be thrown into combustion. In the preceding state of ignorance and tranquillity into which mankind were lulled, the attachment to superstition, though without reserve, was not extreme; and, like the ancient Pagan idolatry, the popular religion consisted more of exterior practices and observances, than of any principles, which either took possession of the heart, or influenced the conduct. It might have been hoped, that learning and knowledge, as of old in Greece, stealing in gradually, would have opened the eyes of men, and corrected such of the ecclesiastical abuses, as were the grossest and most burthensome. It had been observed, that, upon the revival of letters, very generous and enlarged sentiments of religion prevailed throughout all Italy; and that, during the reign of Leo, the court of Rome itself, in imitation of their illustrious prince, had not been wanting in a just sense of freedom. But when the enraged and fanatical reformers took arms against the papal hierarchy, and threatened to rend from the church at once all her riches and authority; no wonder she was animated with equal zeal and ardour, in defence of such ancient and invaluable possessions. At the same time that she employed the stake and gibbet against her avowed enemies, she extended her jealousy even towards learning and philosophy, whom, in her supine security, she had formerly overlooked as harmless and inoffensive. Hence the severe check which knowledge received in Italy; hence its total extinction in Spain; and hence the slow progress which it made in France, Germany, and England. From the admiration of ancient literature, from the inquiry after new discoveries, the minds of the studious were every where turned to polemical science; and, in all schools and academies, the furious controversies of theology took place of the calm disquisitions of learning. Mean while the rage of dispute and the violence of opposition riveted men more strongly in all their various delusions, and infected every intercourse of society with their malignant influence. The Roman Pontiff, not armed with temporal force sufficient for his defence, was obliged to point anew all his spiritual artillery, and to propagate the doctrine of rebellion, and even of assassination, in order to subdue or terrify his enemies. Priests jealous and provoked, timorous and uncontrouled, directed all the councils of that sect, and gave rise to such events as seem astonishing amid the mildness and humanity of modern manners. The massacre of Paris, that of Ireland, the murder of the two Henrys of France, the gunpowder-conspiracy in England, are memorable, though temporary instances of the bigotry of that superstition. And the dreadful tribunal of the inquisition, that utmost instance of human depravity, is a durable monument to instruct us, what a pitch iniquity and cruelty may rise to, when covered with the sacred mantle of religion."

These, my friend, are the two passages on which, at your desire, I am to bestow some remarks. If there is found in them a peculiar and extravagant train of thought, it needs be no great surprise to those who are acquainted with some other writings of this extraordinary author. He seems willing to inform us, that his sentiments and expressions have been fully weighed, as this laboured description of the genius of Popery, and the spirit of the reformation, is, in effect, addressed to a *distant posterity. Distant* indeed they must be, whom no knowledge of the capital articles of distinction betwixt the Popish and Protestant churches shall be able to reach; and who are to be wholly indebted for their instruction to those short sketches, which are presented in this or the like history, that is intended to outlive the wreck of ages. A more full delineation perhaps might be expected from those writers of eminent merit, who are animated by such pleasing prospects; as they may well conclude, that if this *distant posterity*, of which we speak, shall have any resemblance of their forefathers, in the features of the mind, their curiosity and thirst of knowledge will be but slightly gratified by these general descriptions and succinct memoirs. But are they at least just and unexceptionable, so far as they go? or, if there are mistakes, are they but of a trivial nature, not at all affecting the main subject, and so inconsiderable as not to deserve a particular regard? Hardly will any one pronounce so, I think, even at first reading.

Waving, at present, some general reflections on this subject, I would proceed to observe, that the distinction which he establishes betwixt the genius of the Roman-Catholic, and that of the Protestant religion, is a leading idea, which runs through all his speculations; or rather, it is the idea upon which they are all founded. Superstition, we are told, is the characteristic of the former, and fanaticism or enthusiasm of the latter. In his account also, "these two species of religion, the superstitious and fanatical, stand in diametrical opposition to each other."

The forms and degrees of superstition may be infinitely varied. Among the Heathens their δεισιδαιμονια included in it a sacred dread of invisible powers, in consequence of their wretched sentiments concerning the objects of their false worship; by which sentiments they were led into all that medley of insignificant, absurd, and very oft barbarous rites, which made up so great a part of their established religion. In general, mean and unworthy notions of God, and of that service which is acceptable to him, seem to be the source of all superstition. Hence its irrational fears and perplexities of mind, which may be further strengthened by disease and melancholy; hence its various devices in order to conciliate the favour of an offended Deity; and hence too its extreme regard to certain rites of worship, to prescribed austerities, or to whatever services are deemed conducive to this great purpose of divine forgiveness and acceptance.

That this character of superstition is, by our author, very justly affixed to the Roman-Catholic religion, I shall readily admit; and would only further remind you of the nature of that superstition, and of its diffusive influence through the whole Popish system. It is indeed to be plainly discerned in the general plan of their religious worship, which is so highly solicitous about the external garb of devotion, and has so much incumbered the service of the sanctuary; particularly in some of its most solemn acts. Hence an air of empty pageantry is spread over them, while the attention is withdrawn from the ideas and sentiments of a rational and manly piety. But this is not all: it is further affirmed by Protestants, that this superstition of theirs wears an idolatrous form; and that this is discovered in the worship of God by images, in the worship of the host in the sacrament, of the virgin Mary, of saints and angels; and in the adoring and burning incense before their images. It is added, you know, that as all this bears a near resemblance to Pagan idolatry and superstition, so the plea which the doctors of that church would urge in their own defence is exactly similar to those distinctions, and that method of reasoning, by which the ancient idolatry was defended by some of its zealous votaries.

Is not the same resemblance to be further traced in most of their public rites? Do but reflect, for instance, on all the apparatus of sacred vestments, – on their solemn processions, and carrying about with them the images of their saints, – on the annual festivals set apart for their honour, – on the absurd design, and the glaring pomp of their canonization; do but think of the exorcisms, lustrations, consecrations of water, oil, bells, lights, and the rest, which are so well known in that church; and must not the ancient fabric of Gentile superstition be immediately presented to your mind, and the perfect similitude strike at the first view?

The general tenets of superstition too will ever have a baleful influence on life and morals. False notions of religion contract and pervert the understanding; a wrong bias is fixed upon the mind; what is of no real worth is too often substituted in the room of what is intrinsically good; a sense of moral obligations is weakened; and a mighty stress is laid on the forms of religion, and on certain external acts of obedience, as in themselves of great importance, nay, perhaps, as highly meritorious in the sight of God. And may not this spirit be discovered in too many doctrines of the Popish church? Must it not evidently appear to every one, who takes a comprehensive view of their established tenets concerning the effect of the mere outward participation of the sacraments, – concerning injoined penances, or voluntary austerities, – private masses, – indulgences, – auricular confession, and the consequent absolution; – concerning distinction of meats, – frequent repetition of prayers, which most of them do not understand, – pilgrimages to this or the other celebrated shrine or image of some eminent saint? Are not their doctrines on these, and the like subjects of the most unhappy influence on vital religion and Christian morals; on purity of heart and manners? Do they not tend to excite a sacred regard to what is either quite foreign to religion, or of no great value in it; to what is only a corruption of it, and is perhaps inconsistent with its clearest and most salutary precepts? And are they not apt to mislead the submissive and credulous devotee, and to encourage that delusive trust in many of little or no consequence, which numbers of mankind are so ready to entertain?

This now is *the full sway* of superstition. Thus does its genius exert itself in the Popish plan: and by these means has true Christianity been disfigured, its genuine tendency misunderstood or neglected, its amiable doctrines debased, its pure precepts perverted, and its worship *in spirit and in truth* most shamefully obscured. When we speak of the superstition of the Roman church, let this complete view of it be present to our thoughts. Then, indeed, shall we have other sentiments concerning it, than if we had only the idea of a multiplicity of outward rites, and of any pomp and pageantry of worship whatsoever.

It is admitted, then, that superstition is the distinguishing characteristic of that church; and it is affirmed withal, that it is a superstition of the worst kind. Neither shall it be contested by me, that they are its truest sons, who receive all its dictates in humble reverence, and comply with its injunctions in the spirit of bigotry and awful submission.

But is it also to be granted, that "these two species of religion, the superstitious and fanatical, stand in diametrical opposition to each other?" Our author is positive on this head: but as he is no great dogmatist in most things, perhaps it might have been as well not to have shewn himself so peremptory *here*.

The essence of enthusiasm or fanaticism seems to lie in the strong delusion of an over-heated imagination, which prompts to wild excess in what respects the principles and practice of religion. The weak mind, so deluded, flatters itself with the conceit of extraordinary illumination, and of its having an immediate intercourse with heaven. – Pride, ignorance, and blind zeal, are mingled in the character. If these meet with a morose temper, we have the idea of a sullen and obstinate fanatic; if with a quite different disposition, we have that of a lively and bold enthusiast. This irregular principle must, of course, afford but an unsteady direction; and be also naturally productive of extravagant effects, as in all its operations it disclaims an alliance with reason, and disdains a subjection to her conclusions. Accordingly, we have heard of the high conceits of some, who talk of an internal light, as the guide of their conduct, very different from the light of reason and the word of God: – we have heard of the dark and unintelligible jargon of some of the mystic tribe, and of the more elevated pretensions of others to extraordinary visions, rapturous ecstasies, and prophetic dreams. And what is the reverse of this spirit, and of these wild excursions? What other than sober and just sentiments of things; than the habit of a pious and well-regulated mind, properly influenced by the wise and worthy principles of true religion? In *these* my friend, there is a native truth, an excellence and dignity, however they may be debased by superstition on the one hand, or disgraced by fanaticism on the other. Unhappy they (if there are any such) who would blend them all together in one promiscuous ruin. The wise and good must abhor the impious design. Even a sober Heathen has recommended to us,[2] "so to fly from superstition, as not to fall into the opposite extreme of Atheism, while we overlook true piety, that is seated between them." The sense is plain and strong, and the caution of no small importance in every age.

But our author states a diametrical opposition betwixt superstition and fanaticism; for what purpose, he best knows; but with what reason, let us now inquire. These two species of religion (to use his style) are evidently distinct the one from the other: but they do not appear to me to be "diametrically opposite." I can perceive no absurdity in supposing, that one may embrace the tenets, and practise the rites of superstition, who notwithstanding may be possessed of no inconsiderable portion of the fanatical spirit. Nay, I can easily imagine a plan of religion, which, in some of its doctrines and institutions, may be extremely favourable to superstition; in others again, to fanaticism. What is still more, I do not see why this latter may not prompt one, in many instances, to a compliance with the dictates of the former: so that instead of enmity and diametrical opposition, they may very often afford mutual assistance to each other. All this I can easily suppose; and account it no difficult matter to explain. But, instead of entering into abstract reasoning, give me leave to confirm what I have now said by a palpable proof, with which we are furnished by the present subject. For is it not true in fact, that this same superstitious Roman-Catholic church is not a little celebrated for its fanaticism? – that in various ways it has given encouragement and support to this principle, and its operations? – and that some of its most superstitious bigots have been justly ranked in the number of the most illustrious fanatics?

For ascertaining this last point, we are provided with very ample materials in the *Aurea Legenda*, as it is called, and in the voluminous records of the *Acta*

---

[2]   [Greek quotation removed.] Plutarch.

Sanctorum, published with all the proper marks of authority. But, without prejudice to the cause, one may safely confine himself to the lives of some of their most distinguished saints, and in particular of those who founded their religious orders. As you are not unacquainted with this biography, I appeal to you, and in like manner to every one who has looked into those books, whether there are not, in the lives and characters of these saints of theirs, perfect examples and exhibitions of the fanatical spirit, in all its forms of extravagance, from the most childish and silliest reveries of a disordered fancy, to its elevated conceits of inspiration, – of peculiar intercourse with heaven, saints, and angels, – and of ecstatic visions, and prophetic illumination. To give particular instances under each of these heads, were to go about to confirm what no body will contest. And yet some of these very persons, as St Francis, Dominic, and Ignatius, are known to have been the most determined bigots, the most zealous devotees to the superstition of the Roman church in all its branches, and to have exerted all their power in its support. These were the men who promoted the measures of violence and cruelty against all, who, in their times, presumed to differ in their sentiments and practice from established doctrines and rites. One of them is infamously distinguished by his scheme for erecting the court of inquisition, and by having its dreadful power committed to him and his associates: (and with their successors it remains to this day). Another is the founder of an order, whose disciples have done infinite mischief to human society; and whose barbarous and sanguinary zeal is as well known, as are their schemes of dissolute morals, and their shocking maxims of wicked policy.

But fools and fanatics, you will say, may start up every where. Doubtless they may; and if their fanaticism is disapproved and checked by that church of whose profession they are, surely no reproach ought to be derived to it, on their account. Thus all reasonable men will judge. But what if peculiar marks of respect are bestowed upon them by the church of which they are members? – if credit is given to their pretended revelations, a sanctity supposed to belong to their character, and the utmost deference be shewn to their opinions and dictates? – if their examples are, by the public authority of the church, recommended to imitation, and their names transmitted with honour to posterity? By all this, one would think a pretty full sanction were given to their delusions, and to the spirit with which they were animated.

Let us next consider the principles and institutions of the monastic life, which has been so favoured by the church of Rome, in every age. What high encomiums of that state, and of the manner of devotion that is practised in it? Has not the idea of spiritual perfection been annexed to it, and the title of *religious*, in an appropriated sense, conferred on those who embrace it, as though they only merited the appellation? With what various colouring has it been set off, that it might suit different views and tempers, and that the number of votaries to the monastic state might be enlarged? Yet what more proper to cherish a gloomy turn than such an absolute retreat from the world? from all its business, enjoyments, and social intercourse? A total renunciation of these is professed; perhaps it is honestly intended: but nature may soon reclaim against the force that is put upon her, and dejection of spirit become the consequence of a choice that cannot be remedied. The rules that are prescribed to them, the books in which they are conversant, the restraints under which they are laid, abstinence, penances, and other austerities, do still more strengthen the melancholy habit, and must have great influence in producing a disordered state of imagination. The peculiar practices of their devotion, and the general patterns of it that are set before them, in the lives of this and the other eminent saint of their respective orders, are obviously of the same tendency. If their minds receive the tincture, which all these are apt to convey, the fanatical spirit will be strongly imbibed. How much more, if they are well acquainted with the reveries and visions of St Francis and St Dominic, of St Bridget and St Theresa; and if those wonderful tales are believed and affectionately entertained? When such a breach is made on the ideas of rational religion, what a flood of visionary extravagance may rush in upon the human mind? thus may it be hurried along by every delusion, and retain at length but little force to resist any fanatical impressions whatsoever: the effects of which may be perhaps mistaken for the evidences of a seraphic devotion, and considered as marks of the extraordinary favour of heaven. As visions, dreams, and prophecies have been long familiar to their imaginations, they may now, in their turn, lay claim to these; and with as good reason also, (to do them justice), as ever those friends of theirs had, who have gone before them in the same pretensions.

Such is the nature of the monastic state, which is so zealously supported by the church of Rome; and which yet in its institution, in its rules, and in the manner of life and devotion that is peculiar to it, hath been always so favourable to fanaticism, and is indeed so naturally productive of it. But has this *species of religion* banished from the walls of monasteries and nunneries, that other which is affirmed to be *diametrically opposite* to it? Let me rather ask, where else shall we find persons so warmly attached to all the superstitions of that church? *There* are its most submissive votaries, whom it approves and applauds: thence an air of sanctity is, in the eyes of the vulgar, spread over that religion: and thence too is derived the confirmation of some favourite and gainful doctrines. From cloysters and cells have issued the dreadful tales concerning souls in purgatory, and their importunate requests to their friends on earth for deliverance. For this purpose, and for the atonement of their own sins also, have the superstitious and opulent been prompted to the erection and endowment of religious houses, as a work of eminent merit; while those equally superstitious and less wealthy are directed to the treasures of the church, to the merits of saints, to indulgences and private masses. Thus are the vitals of religion deeply wounded by the combined influence of these two principles, of which we speak: thus fanaticism is rendered subservient to the interests of superstition, and, on many occasions, is made use of to bear up the unwieldy fabric. All the world knows, that popular superstitions have been thus upheld, and that they are so to this day. Nay, some of their learned doctors are ready to appeal to the visions of their saints, to voices from heaven, and I know not what; not to mention the tales of cures performed by means of relics. In this manner, and by these subsidiary proofs, do they endeavour to support the adoration of the host, – that most profound doctrine from which it is derived, – the whole system of the worship of saints and images, and the peculiar excellence of such worship at some noted shrine. These and the like are the subjects into which this sort of proof has been admitted: and thus are superstition and fanaticism combined and complicated in the Popish model. – Shall I mention one instance more, that seems to merit our particular notice? But a little ago I hinted at their giving marks of distinguished respect to several persons, in whom the latter of these principles or *species of religion* was signally displayed: but all this is nothing, in comparison of their setting them up as objects of worship, of religious trust and veneration. How amazing! that those who call themselves Christians, should thus transform a spiritual and rational service into so perfect a resemblance of the Heathen plan; and that multitudes should co-operate in promoting the delusion? The forms of canonization do indeed exhibit a most extraordinary scene. – In the steps that are preparatory to it, they shew themselves well affected towards all that is told or recorded concerning the visions and miracles of the saint; for these are the two main pillars on which the fabric of canonization has ever rested. There is some sort of evidence offered of the truth of those wonderful things: proper application is made to the court of Rome, and to its principal ministers: their consent is obtained: public prayers and processions are appointed: the day is fixed: and at length the decree of canonization is pronounced by the Pope himself, in the most solemn manner, according to the authority, which, as he avers, he has received from God.[3] What folly, or rather what impiety is here? – But it is most to our present purpose to observe, that if one reads the account of the preparatory process, and of the lives of those canonized saints, he will soon perceive, that what relates to visions and revelations, is no inconsiderable part of the subject, and is one of the principal causes that is assigned for this

---

[3] There is now before me a copy of one of those bulls. It is that of the late Pope Clement XI. The words are, "Ad honorem, &*c.* beatos Pium Quintum Pontificem, Andream Avellinum, Felicem a Cantalice confessors, et Catharinam de Bononia virginem, sanctos et sanctam esse decernimus, definimus, atque ordinamus, ac sanctorum catalogo *nostra divinitus tradita auctoritate* adscribimus: statuentes ac jubentes illorum sacratissiman memoriam ab ecclesia universali quolibet, anno die eorum, natali, nempe, &*c.* sancta ac pia devotione recoil ac adorari debere," – The following prayer too was pronounced by him on this occasion. "Magnificantes, Domine, clementiam tuam, suppliciter exoramus, ut illorum, quos hodie *nostra divina auctoritate* sanctificavimus, præsidio, nos salves semper ac munias per Christum Dominum nostrum." – Such is the style of the prayer and decree.

canonization. Thus has the spirit of fanaticism been cherished; thus has it been dignified, and consecrated in that church; and in so many different ways have superstition and fanaticism become subservient to each other.

May I be allowed therefore, upon the whole, to reject our author's favourite maxim on this head; and to suppose, that what has been now remarked is sufficient to discredit it? The reason of the thing and the plainest facts are against it. After all this, it is surely unnecessary to subjoin the sentiments of some ancient and modern writers: but there is one authority of such distinction that I cannot well omit it; an authority that must needs be of the greatest weight with MR HUME, and with all his admirers: – in one word, it is *his own*. You may judge of it by what I am now to transcribe from the 27th page of his history, in which he gives us a short description of the superstition of the Roman system. "The blind submission," says he,

"which is inculcated by all superstition, particularly by that of the Catholics; the absolute resignation of all private judgment, reason, and inquiry; these are dispositions very advantageous to civil as well as to ecclesiastical authority. – The splendor too and pomp of worship, which that religion carefully supports, are agreeable to the taste of magnificence that prevails in courts; and form a species of devotion, which, while it flatters the pampered senses, gives little perplexity to the indolent understandings of the great. That delicious country where the Roman Pontiff resides, was the source of all modern art and refinement, and diffused on its superstition an air of politeness, which distinguishes it from the gross rusticity of the other sects. And though policy made it assume, in some of its monastic orders, that austere mien which is acceptable to the vulgar; all authority still resided in its prelates and spiritual princes, whose temper, more cultivated and humanized, inclined them to every decent pleasure and indulgence. Like all other species of superstition, it rouses the vain fears of unhappy mortals; but it knows also the secret of allaying these fears, and by exterior rites, ceremonies, and abasements, though sometimes at the expence of morals, it reconciles the penitent to his offended Deity."

Elsewhere he speaks of a "superstitious regard to days, postures, meats, and vestments."

In this portraiture of Popish superstition, it would seem, he intends to mark its striking features. They are, blind submission to civil and ecclesiastical authority; the absolute resignation of all private judgment, reason, and inquiry; splendor and pomp of worship, which gives little perplexity to an indolent understanding; – its rousing vain fears in deluded mortals, and its allaying these by exterior rites and abasements, though sometimes at the expence of morals; to which he adds a superstitious regard to days, postures, meats, and vestments.

Now, a plan of religion that is directly opposite to this, will be one, I presume, that prescribes no such blind submission to ecclesiastical dictates; that admits and asserts the right of private judgment in all matters of religion; that doth not affect an empty splendor, and glittering pomp of worship; nor injoin a superstitious regard to meats, days, and vestments; that doth not intend, and is not calculated to rouse vain fears in the breasts of men; and knows nothing of the method of allaying them by exterior rites, or any unworthy means whatever, at the expence of morals. I would ask, then, if this plan, and the temper adapted to it, is to be called fanatical? If not, our author's favourite maxim falls to the ground. – But if it is so affirmed, I would not chuse further to contest this matter; and would only beg leave to put the assertion into other words, – Light is darkness; and Wisdom is folly.

I am, &c.

LETTER II.

It is admitted to be the mark of a good genius, to reduce a complicated subject to a few plain principles, or to exhibit a just representation of it, in some one striking point of view. But many, we know, are apt to fail in such attempts, if they have not measured their own strength, if their minds are warped by strong prejudice, if they are extremely fond of new or uncommon sentiments, and adventure to interpose their decisions in matters which they have not deliberately and dispassionately considered. Where-ever this is the case to any considerable degree, the cause of truth will proportionably suffer, the subject itself be misunderstood, or perhaps grossly misrepresented; as the principles, the reasoning, the conclusions concerning it, will take the tincture of those sources from which they flow.

We have seen how this author has failed in his general and fundamental proposition; and it falls next in our way to consider what he has connected with it. This now is nothing less than a charge of fanaticism against the Protestant profession, and of the highest degree of it against the first reformers. Fanaticism is made the characteristic of that religion, and of those worthy personages who promoted and defended it. –

"The Protestant fanaticism, more rapid in its progress – The Catholic superstition, as usual, had ranged itself on the side of monarchy; the Protestant enthusiasm on that of liberty – The spirit of enthusiasm – The genius of fanaticism – The enraged and fanatical reformers – The more fanatical churches – The first reformers, who made such furious and successful attacks on the Romish superstition, and shook it to its lowest foundations, may safely be pronounced to have been universally inflamed with the highest enthusiasm. These two species of religion, the superstitious and fanatical, stand in diametrical opposition to each other; and a large portion of the latter must necessarily fall to his share, who is so courageous as to control authority, and so assuming as to obtrude his own innovations upon the world."[4]

Such is his uniform tenor of expression on this subject: As to which I may be allowed to observe, that although this intemperate and abusive style had met with no check from any regards to religion itself, yet a sense of decorum might have been of some avail to restrain it; – even but a slight consideration of what is due to the public, to the established religion of one's country, and to that numerous and respectable body of men, respectable in *every view*, who heretofore embraced the Protestant profession of Christianity, and who now adhere to that communion. But since this polite writer has so far broke through these restraints, let us now attend to the manner in which the bold accusation is supported. *Quid dignum tanto?* How is this high and peremptory charge maintained? By repeated and strong assertions; by a supposed opposition of the fanatical to the superstitious species of religion; and by ascribing several things concerning the reformation to the influence of the former principle, which he seems to think cannot be well accounted for in any other way. This is the sum of the evidence: the last part of which shall be fully considered in the course of these letters: the other points may be more easily discussed. As a proportional strength of proof had need to accompany a continued peremptory form of expression, so this might well be expected in the writings of those authors, who shew themselves to be generally well affected to the sceptical species of philosophy. That such persons should give way to hasty and presumptuous conclusions, is surely quite out of character, and not a little inconsistent with their profession of perfect freedom from prejudice, and with their pretension to the spirit of calm and candid inquiry. But to take things as we find them:

The argument that is drawn from the opposition of fanaticism and super-stition, has been already in part considered; and what remains may be finished in a few words. It was proved, as I apprehend, in the former letter, that these *two species of religion* are far from being *diametrically opposite:* and therefore the application which he would make of this maxim to the reproach of the Protestant cause, must fall of course. The principle itself, and the deduction from it, must equally and at once be rejected. – It was also observed before, that, in his particular description of Romish superstition, he has unwarily furnished us with a strong argument against his main position, and in favour of the plan and spirit of Protestantism. But I would not chuse to rest the defence here, in using his own authority against himself. The subject is of the

[4] P. 60. 75. 8. 26. 7.

greatest consequence, and merits the utmost attention of those who bear a due regard to our Christian and Protestant profession.

The charge, you see, is laid against the Protestant religion, against the first reformers, and against all the Protestant churches; some of which, however, are treated with a less degree of reproach and insult. Now, if this charge were well founded, we might, no doubt, expect to meet with strong discoveries of fanaticism in the general tendency of the reformation; in the leading principles, by which it was conducted, and upon which it was supported; in the religious scheme which it introduced; in the characters and conduct of those who were most distinguished by their zeal for its interests; and in the writings and tenets of its avowed friends, in every age. These, as I conceive, are the chief topics, from which the proof, if proof were to be had, should be deduced: and according to the same plan may one proceed in the refutation of the charge that is now before us.

It is not my intention, to enter into a long detail of particulars relative to the gross corruptions and spiritual tyranny of Popery. To oppose these, you know, was the general purpose of the reformation; to give a check to this tyranny; to remove those corruptions; and to restore the knowledge of true Christianity, and its sacred doctrines, as they were delivered by our Lord himself, and by his apostles. Are these, my friend, matters of light concern to one who has the spirit of a Christian, and who wishes well to the greatest and best interests of mankind? Had the question been only concerning a few speculative points, and some other things of little consequence, there might have been reason to talk of folly and fanaticism: but if the reverse of this is the truth, the grand scope, at least, was wise, good, and honourable.

Was it not, for instance, a question of importance, Whether religious worship was to be offered to the Creator, to God *alone?* or whether creature-worship was not likewise to be admitted, though in opposition to the pure dictates of reason, and the express prohibition of the divine law? Was it not of consequence to determine, whether Christians were to present their spiritual sacrifices of prayer and thanksgiving, through the one Mediator betwixt God and man? or whether they were to be directed also to the merits and intercession of the Virgin Mary, and of this or the other real or imaginary saint? Was not a matter of the greatest moment included in the question respecting the adoration of the host in the sacrament? which idolatrous practice, by the way, is grounded on a doctrine repugnant to common sense and feeling, and had been introduced and propagated in the darkest and most barbarous ages. Does not all the world know to what an amazing excess the worship of saints and images was carried, with all its appendages? to the derogation of the worship due to the true and living God, through Jesus Christ our Lord; and almost to the extinction of those sentiments and dispositions which animate a pure and rational devotion. Nay, may we not here appeal to the present state of things in Popish countries, particularly in those which are most firmly attached to that communion? The distinctions and apologies that are offered on this subject, are, in truth, of no great weight: at most, they do but reach the men of learning; to the vulgar they are unknown. Even their public forms[5] are not very favourable to these distinctions, how much soever their doctors may attempt to disguise and conceal the truth.

Further, were they not justly charged with perverting the doctrines of Christianity, in many important instances; with giving a false and unworthy representation of its spirit and precepts, and weakening the force of religious and moral obligations? while, instead of the amiable views of divine mercy to guilty creatures in Christ Jesus; instead of the repentance and faith of the gospel, and that sanctity of heart and life which it prescribes and promotes, the minds of men were much turned aside to quite different objects, and to a fallacious trust in the merits of saints, in priestly absolution, penances, pilgrimages, the observation of fasts and festivals, in the repetition of a few *Pater nosters* and very many *Ave Marias*, in the veneration of saints and relics, and I know not what other outward observances of a like nature and of equal insignificancy. By these means is the mind unhappily deluded, and Christianity debased; whilst an airy phantom assumes the form, and claims the regard that is due to true religion. At best, salutary truths are mingled with noxious errors; and things that are in their own nature insignificant, perhaps irrational and absurd,

---

[5] The following prayers are a specimen of their style. "Maria mater gratiæ, mater misericordiæ, tu nos ab hoste protege, et hora mortis suscipe. – Sub tuum præsidium confugimus, sancta Dei genitrix: nostras deprecationes ne despicias in necessitatibus, sed a periculis cunctis libera nos semper, virgo gloriosa et benedicta." *Offic. B. V.*

Accipe quod offerimus, redona quod rogamus, excusa quod timemus; quia tu es spes unica peccatorum. Per te speramus veniam delictorum, et in te beautissima nostrorum est expectatio præmiorum. Sancta Maria, succurre miseris." *Brev. Rom.*

Deus qui per gloriosissimam Filii tui matrem – præsta, quæsumus, ut quam pie veneramur tanti operis institutricem, ejus pariter meritis et intercessione a peccatis omnibus et captivate dæmonis liberemur." – *Missa de B. V. de mer.*

Deus qui B. Nicolaum Pontificem innumeris decorasti miraculis, tribue, quæsumus, ut ejus meritis et precibus a gehennæ incendiis liberemur, per Dominum." *Brev. Rom.*

As to the consecration of an image.

"Omnipotens, sempeterne Deus, clementissima cujus dispositione cuncta creantur ex nihilo, hanc imaginem, in honorem piissimæ genitricis Filii tui Domini nostri Jesu Christi venerabiliter adaptatam, benedicere et sanctificare digneris; et præsta, misericordissime Pater, – ut quicunque eandem misericordæ reginam et gratiosissimam dominam nostram coram hac effigie suppliciter honorare studuerint, et de instantibus periculis eruantur, et in conspectu divinæ majestatis tuæ de commissis et omissis veniam impetrent, per eundem Dominum." – *Pontif. Rom.* And with respect to other images, – "Præsta ut quicunque coram illa ipsum gloriosissimum apostolum tuum vel martyrem – supplicater honorare studuerint, illius precibus ac obtentu a te gratiam in præsenti, et æternam gloriam obtineat in futurum, per Dominum." – *Pontif. Rom.*

Sanctificetur istud lignum, in nominee Patris, et Filii, et Spiritus Sancti: et benedictio illus ligni in quo sancta membra Salvatoris suspensa sunt, sit in isto lingo, ut orantes inclinantesque se propter Deum, ante istam crucem, inveniant corporis et animæ sanitatem." *Pontif. Rom.*

This is a specimen of the language of their public liturgies.

are blended with what is in itself essentially good. Every thing of this sort must needs lose its virtue, in consequence of the unnatural mixture.

And were not men industriously detained in a state of ignorance? had it not been long so? was not the reading of sacred scripture denied to the laity; while they were taught to receive all that the church propounded and injoined, without hesitation, without inquiry? It is but of a piece with the other parts of the absurd plan, that the public service of the church should be in an unknown tongue; *unknown* indeed to almost all those who joined in that service, and to a great number of those too, who heretofore did, and who, at this day, do preside in it. Need I speak of their doctrines concerning the sacraments, concerning traditions, purgatory, indulgences, the propitiatory sacrifice of the mass, &c.? And was not the whole corrupt system imposed in the most arbitrary manner? Supported by ecclesiastical authority, and by the supposed infallibility of popes, or of councils, it is further guarded by awful sanctions and sanguinary laws.

How amazing to think of the progress and strength of that spiritual monarchy, which had been erected in the Christian church? of its unbounded dominion, its numberless oppressions and diffusive devastation? how the foundations of it were laid in the most extraordinary manner, and the super-structure reared, by a thousand devices, in successive ages? The scheme of power, of wealth and worldly grandeur, is uniformly prosecuted. Nothing is rejected that may tend to its advancement. Corruptions of Christian doctrine, superstitious fears, lying wonders, a mixture of humility and pride, of craft and violence in the Roman pontiffs, together with the most refined arts of human policy – all are employed, and made subservient to the great purpose that is in view. How piteous the condition of the Christian world under this despotic rule? The different princes and states of Europe had, in their turns, very often felt its deplorable effects: and although, before the æra of the reformation, they had many a time complained of the oppressive exercise of this power, yet they still continued in subjection to it. But the principles of the reformation had much influence in scattering the mists of ignorance and superstition. How beneficial its tendency in every respect? while it contributes to the interests of religion, and the good of mankind; to the deliverance of Christians from a state of slavish submission to an usurped authority, at the same time that it aims at restoring Christianity itself to its original purity and native honours.

Was there not here a cause, a great and noble cause, worthy of the interpo-sition of the wise and good? and were not they who thought it so, and who had reason to conclude, that they might be of service in it, obliged to support it, and to exert themselves in its behalf? – It were easy to prosecute this subject, and to urge the points now mentioned with a convincing evidence; at least, with an evidence, that would be held such by all, who have not thoroughly imbibed the spirit, and who are not friends to the mystery and vassalage of Popery.

But let it suffice to have said thus much concerning it: and let us suppose, that the general purpose of the reformation is admitted, as well it may, to have been unquestionably good and excellent: the next inquiry will be, with relation to the main principles on which it was founded, and according to which it was conducted. How are we to think of these? were they irrational? were they wild and irregular? Then indeed would they have been known to be of the enthusiastic kind. But did the first reformers ever speak of any new revelation of the divine will, that had been made to them from heaven? did they lay claim to prophetic inspiration? and, in consequence of such claim, did they mean to impose any doctrines of religion on the credit of their own testimony, and the weight of their own authority? Were these their pretensions? and was this the manner of their address?

In answer to these questions, I appeal to their history, to their writings yet extant, and even to what their enemies have said concerning them. Was it not their avowed principle, That the faith of Christians was to rest on the word of God, and on this alone? and therefore, that any doctrine or practice whatever not so grounded, ought not to be received with religious regard; and if it was condemned by the holy writ, that it ought to be rejected, even though long prescription, and the sanction of ecclesiastical authority, could be pleaded in its behalf; neither of which can stamp a value on error and folly, nor change the internal nature, though they may indeed the outward attire of truth and falsehood. Thus did they proceed in rejecting Popish errors, and in propounding and confirming the opposite truths. They objected; they argued; they drew their conclusions from reason and scripture; they called upon their adversaries to try their doctrines by this test; and they exhorted Christians to judge for themselves, to search the scriptures, and to be on their guard, against the influence of specious forms, of crafty arts, and timorous superstition. They had themselves shaken off the prejudices that were so apt to intangle them in the search of truth; they led the way to others in the noble path, and incited them to follow their example, and to assert their religious liberties, to which they had a native, an unalienable right, as men and Christians.

To the charge of novelty that was brought against their doctrine, they made answer, That it must appear *new* to those alone, who were unacquainted with the true doctrine of the gospel, as contained in sacred writ.

"Novam quod appellant doctrinam nostram," says one of the first reformers, in his elegant apology addressed to a great monarch, "Deo sunt vehementer injurii, cujus sacrum verbum novitatis insimulari non merebatur. Illis quidem novam esse minime dubito, quibus et Christus novus est, et evangelium novum: sed qui illam Pauli concionem veterem esse noverunt, Jesum Christum mortuum propter peccata nostra, resurrexisse propter justificationem nostram, nihil apud nos deprehendent novum. Quod diu incognita sepultaque latuit, humanæ impietatis crimen est: nunc cum Dei benignitate nobis redditur, saltem postliminii jure suam antiquitatem recipere debebat."

But as the plea of antiquity was strenuously urged, and the fame of the ancient doctors of the Christian church was loudly sounded by those who defended the Popish system; to the writings of the primitive fathers also did the reformers make their appeal, (though with a regard in no sort equal to that which they yielded to holy scripture), and to the doctrines and practices of the purest, that is, of the three first ages of Christianity. They did not decline even this inferior tribunal; well knowing that the Roman-Catholic cause could not be defended before it. Nay, they undertook to prove, that many of those corruptions of which they complained, had not been heard of in the church, during the space of six or seven hundred years. Some others might be traced backwards to the fifth, or perhaps the fourth century; but what they were at that time, was as much to be distinguished from what they were become in the fourteenth and fifteenth centuries, as is the small stream of a river near its source, from its deep and overflowing waters when it is poured into the ocean.

To the most ancient general councils they professed regard, though they denied infallibility. Neither could they perceive any sort of reason for granting it to the papal chair, which had so long, and so arrogantly claimed it. In short, as they were not wanting in a proper respect to antiquity, so they adhered to the word of God, as a perfect rule of Christian faith and practice, according to which all religious doctrines were to be tried, and by whose authority they were to be finally determined. They translated the scriptures into different languages, they earnestly recommended the study of them, and they generously asserted the right of private judgment, in the most important of all concerns, *Religion*.

Is this now, my friend, the manner of fanaticism or enthusiasm? Was it ever known to be directed by such principles as these? Or rather, does it not fly the test of reason, and fail in the reverence that is due to holy writ? whilst in their stead it appeals to internal light and perception, to strong impressions or impulses on the mind, in a word, to something extraordinary and supernatural. Is this the spirit of Protestantism? Are these its principles and pretensions? Was this the spirit of the first reformers? and this the plan upon which they acted? – How absurd, will you say, to think of it in this manner? Give me leave to add, how absurd therefore is it to affix the general character of enthusiasts and fanatics to those, who, upon the slightest attention, must be fully and at once acquitted as to the essential part of this charge? and how much more absurd to speak of this *irrational* principle, as the spirit of that profession of religion, which is so *rationally* grounded, and which, according to its original constitution, ought ever to maintain a friendly regard to the freedom of inquiry and the rights of conscience, these capital articles in the Protestant scheme?

The matter, as I apprehend, will not bear a dispute; and therefore I shall go on to observe, that, after having said so much of the general design of the reformation, and its leading principles, it is not surely necessary to enter upon the particular consideration of the doctrines of Protestantism, as they stand distinguished from the Roman system. In the former, the manifold corruptions of religion that had been introduced into the latter are rejected, in order to the restoring the knowledge of the genuine truths of Christianity. I have nothing to do at present with the differences of opinion, in relation to points of less import, that arose among the first reformers; and shall only say, that it is pity they should have suffered those differences to be inflamed by an honest, but mistaken zeal, which might have been at first in a great measure composed by the prudence, learning, and temper of a Bucer and Melancthon. The union of Christian affection, notwithstanding these, might well have been maintained; and in this manner, the interests of the reformation would have been further promoted and strengthened. But it is to the purpose of our present argument to take notice, that in vain are the marks of fanaticism sought after, in the peculiar distinguishing tenets of the Protestant faith. No vestiges of it are to be discovered *there*; unless perhaps by those persons who may be so extremely sagacious, as to discern them in every thing that is opposite to approved super-stition and established error. They indeed may fancy that they perceive them, where no one besides could possibly expect to find them.

But if not in the doctrines of the Protestant persuasion, perhaps they are to be met with in the scheme of religious worship introduced by the reformation. – Let us remark the most essential points on this subject. Public service had been long performed in an unknown tongue: the reformers rejected the practice; and the plainest dictates of reason condemn it. – A number of rites had entered into divine worship, and a variety of ornaments had been affected: the first reformers were generally of opinion, that a great part of these ought to be removed, as superstitious, and by no means conducive to the interests of true piety; or rather, as plainly obstructive of the worship of the heart and understanding. And in this matter of retrenching rites and ornaments, some of them went further than the rest. – But with respect to the worship of saints and images, and all its ceremonies and decorations, there was no sort of difference in opinion amongst them. This kind of religion, if it merits the name, had been long recommended to the world; and long had it almost entirely absorbed the devotion of the vulgar: but as it was irrational in its own nature, and directly contrary to the divine law, it was unanimously and strongly condemned by all who joined in the refor-mation. And in consequence of this rejection of it, there was a new face of things every where, in the worship of the Protestant churches.

What now remained after the removal of those various corruptions, which had gone on from bad to worse, for a course of ages? What other than the pure and simple plan of Christian worship? the worship of the true God, through Jesus Christ our Lord, and outward acts of worship offered up in a becoming manner, and animated by internal piety; without which all external services, however costly and decorated, are but as the sounding brass and tinkling cymbal. These are the sentiments which the first reformers warmly inculcated on Christians; and which ought ever to be in their eye, in all their devotions, whether they confine themselves to some stated forms, whether they add to these, or whether they express their pious thoughts and desires in other words, and with a peculiar respect to the language of holy writ. And an acquaintance with the scriptures, it may be observed by the way, is to be assiduously cultivated in an especial manner, by all those who are not injoined the reading of established forms of prayer in their sacred ministrations; that they may be the better qualified for the right discharge of an important part of their duty, as the public ministers of religion. But whether we may approve of the one or the other scheme; of that which would confine public worship to the regular use of stated forms, or of that other, which would go no further than a general directory, and a recommendation of useful patterns of devotion, above all, of those in sacred scripture; this, I say, is not the question at present. The question is concerning Protestants in general, and their sentiments with regard to religious worship, in opposition to the depraved scheme of the Roman church. As to essential articles, there was an uniformity of judgment amongst the first reformers; how much soever they might differ in their opinions about some things of less consequence. And were not the doctrines in which they perfectly agreed, most important, and most excellent? were they not grounded on the nature of Christian worship, and on the plainest truths of the word of God? – They were apparently so grounded; and, I trust, will still remain firm and unshaken, notwithstanding the unwearied and combined efforts of superstition and irreligion.

Before concluding this letter, I shall just remind you of what has been already hinted at before, namely, that the genius of any particular profession of religion, will, in one degree or other, discover itself in the writings of its avowed friends, who have all along maintained its principles and interests. It is impossible that it should be otherwise: and I add, how paradoxical would it be for any one to affirm, that the works of a Chilingworth and a Tillotson are marked with the character of enthusiasm? If the scheme of the Protestant religion, which they so zealously defended, had been liable to this imputation, the enthusiastic spirit or principle must not only have left its perceptible traces, but have impressed a manifest signature on their writings: a signature this, however, that hitherto hath not been visible, and, I suppose, will never hereafter become so, in the writings of these great men, or in the works of those authors, who, since the æra of the reformation, have been engaged in its defence.

I have done, Sir, with what I proposed to remark on this subject, in relation to the genius or spirit of the Protestant religion. We have considered it as it is exhibited in the general tendency of the reformation; in the great principles on which it was established; in the peculiar distinguishing doctrines of the Protestant faith; in its plan of religious worship; and something too has been now said relative to the writings of its avowed and zealous friends. Upon the whole, then, the falsity, the folly of the charge of enthusiasm or fanaticism is, I think, abundantly evident. The true genius of the Protestant religion is as much to be distinguished from that wretched principle and spirit, as knowledge from ignorance, truth from error, wisdom from wild extravagance, and as what is great, and good, and worthy, is to be distinguished from what is mean, hurtful, and contemptible. Dark colours indeed may be thrown over the fairest objects, or they may be presented to our view in a false light, and be likewise blended with objects of deformity; by which means their native grace and luster may be sullied or impaired: but an attentive eye will soon perceive the deviation from truth and nature, which proceeds either from gross mistake, or from unworthy artifice. Thus also it is with respect to the objects of the understanding, and to the intellectual eye, which beholds and judges concerning them. And whosoever, my friend, has a right sense of God and religion, must be solicitous to know the truth; and to guard against those deceptions, which may be of dangerous consequence to his truest and best interests. But they who have no such sense, may roam at large, and talk of those truths and objects with light indifference, which others, taught by the purest reason, and by heavenly wisdom, are disposed to consider with reverend regard. May these benign and salutary dictates be ever rightly attended to by us. Their importance, their excellence is best known to those who feel their amiable influence on their hearts and manners.

I am, &c.

LETTER III.

It is true indeed, as you well affirm, that not one article of the Protestant faith can be affected by what concerns the temper and conduct of the first reformers: and I fully assent to what you add, that, notwithstanding this, they who bear a sincere regard to the Protestant religion, must be sensibly affected when they see their characters traduced and vilified. Besides, there is something due to injured worth, and to violated truth; and the friends of truth and virtue will never be insensible to the obligation. It appears also to be not a little ungenerous, to exaggerate every failing, and to heighten every harsh feature; as it is neither just nor candid to disguise or disfigure what is good and amiable. On some occasions this author well knows how to give the most favourable representation of things, and to admit every sort of apology even for gross defects, and the most culpable actions. Neither is this excess of mildness confined to the maleadministration of princes: it reaches now and then to the conduct of bigots, in particular to those devoted to the Roman superstition, and in some measure even to their acts of violence in its support.

But the first reformers are treated in a manner entirely different; nay, in a manner, I am sorry to say, that is by no means agreeable to the dictates of truth and candor. We have seen how they are characterized as enthusiasts in the highest degree; as fanatics, and as fanatics of the worst kind, furious and enraged: and to this disgraceful principle of enthusiasm or fanaticism their whole conduct is ascribed. "Hence that rage of dispute which every where seized the new religionists; that disdain of ecclesiastical subjection; that contempt of ceremonies, and of all the exterior pomp and splendor of worship. And hence too, that inflexible intrepidity, with which they braved dangers, torments, and even death itself; while they preached the doctrine of peace, and carried the tumults of war through every part of Christendom." The very first deduction in this paragraph does not appear to be rightly formed; since a fanatic, I suppose, is rather inclined to peremptory dictating, than to an eagerness of reasoning and dispute. But be this as it will, whatever is included in this same *rage of dispute*, seems to belong in an equal degree, according to our author's own account, to the character that he has stated in opposition to fanaticism: for of the superstitious Roman Catholics he says, "No wonder the church was animated with equal zeal and ardor, in defence of their ancient and invaluable possessions." and he adds a little below, "Mean while the rage of dispute, and the violence of opposition, riveted men more strongly in all their various delusions."

"A disdain of ecclesiastical subjection" is the next mark of fanaticism. That the first reformers would not yield obedience to the rulers of the Popish church, is confessed; and that they withdrew from their subjection, or, if this author pleases, that they disdained it. And does not he himself disdain such subjection? – I dare say, that he reckons it mean and sordid: and yet that he never once suspected himself liable to the charge of fanaticism on that account. – A slavish subjection to the dictates of men in matters of religion, is, in truth, wholly inconsistent with the spirit of Protestantism: but is it not equally so with the principles of the clearest reason, and with the natural rights of mankind? How ridiculous the proposition, – To refuse such blind and implicit submission, is a characteristical mark of fanaticism? – I leave it with you to determine, whether this proposition is not here in effect affirmed by this author.

Ill must it fare with the reformers, if they are to be judged by such a rule; and very hard it is, if they could not declare against the service in an unknown tongue, and against the multiplicity of rites and decorations which had been introduced into public worship, without being chargeable with pure fanaticism.

Intrepidity of spirit is the concluding article of proof in the above paragraph; concerning which every one knows, that as it is grounded in the natural constitution, so it may be strengthened in different persons, by various principles and motives that are suited to affect them. A sense of duty, a sense of honour, a sense of religion, each of these will, in its turn, confirm it. Where the cause is good, intrepidity of spirit in its defence is an honourable distinction. But boldness and intrepidity may be likewise exerted in a quite opposite cause, and in prosecution of the worst of purposes. In the concerns of religion it may be exerted by the inflamed bigot, and the wild enthusiast, as well as by the wise and worthy friends of truth. Here then is another supposed mark of enthusiasm, which is in itself wholly ambiguous, and from which therefore no conclusion can be drawn. What relates to the happy, and *perfectly new* antithesis, betwixt the "doctrine of peace," and "the tumults of war," will fall afterwards more properly in our way.

Such is the evidence contained in that important paragraph; and evidence much too slender to support the weighty charge that is brought against the first reformers. But not to rest in these general strictures, let us proceed a little further in this subject, and take a short view of their character and conduct.

Even their enemies found themselves obliged to admit, that they were men of good endowments, and of uncommon erudition. Some of them were justly reckoned amongst the first geniuses and scholars of the age in which they lived. They set themselves against the reigning barbarity of scholastic learning, and contributed largely to the introduction and advancement of ancient literature. In their writings they soon discovered a strength of genius, a skill in the learned languages, an acquaintance with the holy scriptures, and a knowledge of Heathen and Christian antiquity, greatly above the rate of those who were accounted eminent doctors in the Roman church: and in some of their compositions, about which most care was employed, a purity and elegance of style were to be discerned, together with a manly and perspicuous manner of reasoning, little known to those times.

In their natural tempers there was obviously a great disparity. In Luther and Zuinglius, for instance, we may perceive a more active and intrepid spirit than belonged to their worthy friends Oecolompadius and Bucer, to Calvin, Peter Martyr, and the mild Melancthon. Some of them were of a severe, others of a lively turn. As to their moral character, it is not enough to say that it was irreproachable: their lives were holy and exemplary: they felt the influence of religion; and they acted according to its dictates. Being powerfully animated by the faith and hope of Christians, they studied to live up to their sacred obligations, and to approve themselves to God.

Again, let it be remembered, that visions, revelations, and the pretension of immediate inspiration, are the highest degree of enthusiasm, the very summit of fanatical phrenzy. Say, my friend, were such things ever heard of amongst the first reformers? Their works are open to our inspection: is there any thing of this kind to be found in them? Did they not strenuously oppose and refute the wild and destructive principles of the enthusiastic sect which arose in Germany, and which was indeed the disgrace of the Protestant name? And yet they must be charged with enthusiasm, even in its *highest degree*. It was observed in the preceding letter, that fanaticism flies the test of reason, and fails in the regard due to holy writ; whilst it appeals from them to internal light and perception, to strong impressions or impulses on the mind, to something extraordinary and supernatural: add to this what has been now hinted at concerning its *highest degree*; and let the matter be rested here. Has this author any where shewn, or will he undertake to shew, that the first reformers so pretended, and so appealed? If not, why is this character, to the exclusion indeed of every other, affixed to those persons, to whom, in its distinctive and essential part, it is no wise applicable? And if not applicable in its essential part, how absurd to speak of it in its *highest degree?*

But, you will say, was there nothing intemperate in their zeal, nothing irregular in the manner of their prosecuting the great ends they had in view? Who ever affirmed that there was not? they were men; consequently neither infallible nor impeccable. But then, my friend, intemperate zeal is not enthusiasm. They are no less distinct than effect and cause. Neither does the effect here follow necessarily from the cause; for we have many a time heard of *harmless* enthusiasts: nor is it an effect of this cause alone, as it may be at least equally derived from credulous and blind bigotry. Nay, I will venture to affirm, that furious and desolating zeal hath been found in alliance with the superstitious principle more frequently than with the enthusiastic one; and that its ravages, when thus allied, have been more deplorable and dreadful.

Let us now therefore dismiss these two conjuring terms, *Enthusiasm* and *Fanaticism*, which are so familiar to this historian, and with the help of which he has thought himself able to perform such mighty feats. Suffer me, however, to remark a few things further as to the charge of intemperate zeal that is brought against these truly eminent men.

I have already acknowledged, that in this respect they are not blameless. The particular conduct of one amongst them, whose natural temper was the most apt to hurry him into this extreme, shall be considered by itself in a following letter. In general, it must be confessed with regret by the friends of religion, that an indiscreet and excessive zeal has been too often employed to advance its interests. It is pity, sure, that ever it should be so; as this sort of zeal has a tendency to hurt and to disgrace any cause into which it enters. But when one gives evidence of an integrity of heart and purpose, favourable constructions are to be admitted, and the censure of what is amiss ought to be more mild; especially if the subject about which this zeal is exercised is of considerable, still more, if it is of the last importance. Indeed, when the question relates to something of the greatest moment, whether in religious or civil concerns, it is not easy for the wisest and the best of men to keep within the exact bounds of what is right and fit; and even an open generous honesty of heart may betray one, in the warmth of opposition, into such actions, and such expressions about persons and things, as he will not, and cannot approve in his cooler moments. In all cases of this kind, we are allowed to disapprove, but without rigour; we may condemn, but with reluctance, and with all favourable abatements. Moderation and candour will dictate an apology for human frailty.

If ever such apology is to be admitted, surely it ought to be admitted in the matter now before us. Grant that the public conduct of the reformers in various instances was not unexceptionable; and that their zeal was not always rightly directed, nor restrained within due bounds. But let the austerity of censure be softened by an attention to the peculiar circumstances in which they were placed, to the importance of the end in view, and to their steady honesty in its pursuit; – by an attention to the number and power of their enemies, to the deplorable state of religion in the Roman church, to the mighty opposition they had to encounter, and to all that refined policy, that insidious craft and determined violence, which were by turns exerted against them. Amidst all their difficulties they held on their course, trusting in God, and commending themselves to his protection; animated by a good conscience, and by the principles, the prospects and aids of the gospel. For let sceptics and infidels sneer as they will, we can without hesitation affirm, that the divine blessing rested on them, and on their labours; and that the almighty arm, which upholds the upright and the oppressed, sustained and strengthened them.

It is well known, that the objections which they raised at first against certain doctrines, that had not then received the full sanction of ecclesiastical authority, were unanswerably strong. The whole business indeed of indulgences, in itself, and as it was then transacted, was plainly liable to such objections. These were published, and calmly submitted to the judgment of the learned. At the same time, they who had it in their power to redress what was complained of, were properly supplicated for that effect. Instead of a favourable hearing, menaces are poured out; and the grossest errors are obstinately defended. However, those who had so well begun, persist, like honest and good men, in shaking off their prejudices, and in cultivating the study of the scripture, of Christian antiquity, and the writings of the most approved doctors in the church. What light they derived from these was imparted to the world; till at last the errors of Popery were pretty fully detected; its departure, in most important instances, from the genuine doctrines and spirit of our holy religion, was evidently demonstrated; and the weak, the irrational grounds of its spiritual dominion were laid open; – of that dominion, which was so absurdly claimed, and had been so widely extended, and so boldly exercised. If we have a right sense, my friend, of the piteous state of the Christian church, amid all this degeneracy and oppression, we must admit, that the cause in which the reformers were engaged, was of the highest moment, in every respect. But the alarm was soon taken by ignorant bigots, and by those whose interest it was that things should remain as they were. They began to be more afraid, when they understood that the doctrines of liberty and truth were listened to with pleasure and approbation. Various councils are held; different measures are proposed for giving a check to the progress of these doctrines, and for enticing or intimidating those who taught them. By and by anathematizing bulls are published, imperial edicts are solicited, and the power of spiritual tyranny is put forth with strong effort against all who dared to contest established tenets, and to urge the necessity of a reformation. And were they to renounce, to abjure the truth, that they might escape the danger? to make shipwreck of faith and of a good conscience, and to profess a solemn falsehood in the sight of God and man? or else, were they to sit down tamely and passively, till they should be dragged to prisons, to tortures, and a cruel death? How shocking to nature the latter choice? and is not the former impious to an high degree? Well therefore might they request the protection of their natural princes, against those cruel designs which were meditated, and in part executed, by their powerful enemies. The truth was to be vindicated; the corrupted state of the Roman church to be fully represented; the attention of the stupidly inconsiderate to be roused; the writings of their adversaries to be refuted; the prejudices of ignorance and folly to be withstood; and the violence of their enemies to be opposed; of enemies who were ever forward to spread all manner of falsehoods against them, to pronounce them guilty of heresy and blasphemy, and to expose them to the hatred and rage of bigotry blind and inflamed.

Now, as the great importance of the cause might well allow of an ardour of spirit, and did indeed require it; is it any wonder, if, in such difficult and dangerous circumstances, the weakness and perturbation of human passions mingled sometimes with their religious zeal? They did sometimes mingle with it, especially in one of them, who was naturally of a warm temper, who was obliged to pass through a turbulent scene, and against whom the resentment and malice of the enemies of the reformation were chiefly pointed. But surely a candid judge will be ready to make all reasonable allowances in so peculiar a case. Nay, I do not know, whether they may not be entirely acquitted with relation to some things which have been imputed to an overheated zeal.

For example, my friend, I am free to own, that heretofore, in reading some passages of their writings, concerning the prevailing impiety, and flagitious manners of the court of Rome, I was apt to suspect a height of colouring in the descriptions, till I found that similar accounts were given by men of great character in their own communion.[6] Even Pope Adrian himself had so much honesty, as fairly and publicly to acknowledge, that, "for some time past, many

---

[6] "Fieri potest," says Erasmus, in one of his letters, "ut in Germania sint qui non temperant a blasphemiis in Deum, sed in hos horrendis suppliciis animadvertitur. At ego Romæ his auribus audivi quosdam abominandis blasphemiis debacchantes in Christum, et in illius apostolos, idque multis mecum audientibus, et quidem impune. Ibidem multos novi, qui commemorabant se dicta horrenda audisse, a quibusdam sacerdotibus aulæ pontificiæ ministries, idque in ipsa missa, tam clare ut ea vox ad multorum aures pervenerit." *Bayle's dict. art. Calvin.*

"Memini eum aliquando," says the writer of Castellan's life, "cum pontificum Romanorum supinas libidines, avaritiam, et rapacitatem, religionis contemptum, superbiamque cardinalium, luxum, et ignaviam, nundinationesque, cauponationes, et flagita reliqua aulicorum Romanensium describeret, et cætera quæ tunc vidiffet commemoraret, ita animo concitari et indignatione commoveri consuevisse, ut ei non modo in facie color, sed et toto corpore gestus motusque immutarentur; ut etiam mihi frequenter diceret, sibi esse persuasissimum, ne pontifices quidem Romanos religionis et sacrorum antistites, tot suis suorumque flagitiis sceleribusque contaminatos, vere et ex animo Christum colere; quæ autem in religione facerent, retinendæ dominationis causa, veluti larva ad fallendum apposite, egregie simulare." *Ib. art. Castellan.*

Scimus in hac sancta sede, aliquot jam annis, multa abominanda fuisse; – et omnia denique in perversum mutata. Nec mirum, si ægritudo a capite in membra, a summis pontificibus in aliod inferiores prælatos, descenderit." – *Instrutio Adriani pro D. Francisco Chiregato* – *in fasciculo rerum expet. et fugiend.*

abominable things had prevailed in the Roman court; that the disease had been derived from the head to the members; and that all was changed to the worse." A politic Cardinal, it is true, thinks but meanly of his prudence on account of this open confession: (*Troppo aperto*, as I remember, are Pallavicini's words). But we may be well assured, that the disorders of that court were extreme, and the marks of the distemper flagrant, when such confession was made of its malignity by the Roman Pontiff. However, after this declaration, his days were but few, and his successors never again addressed the public in this manner.

Let it be further remarked on the whole of this subject, that the apology which is now offered in their behalf, may likewise be reasonably urged in the case of those who are liable to the same charge, for their conduct in advancing the interests of the reformation, in those countries where the princes adhered to the Roman-Catholic religion. In some of them the reformation at last prevailed; in others it was checked and borne down by ecclesiastical tyranny, unworthily abetted by the civil power. It is observed by a celebrated historian, in speaking of the reformation in Scotland, "that in the methods by which it was advanced, there was too great a mixture of the heat and forwardness that is natural to the genius of that country." Be it so, if you will: but let it not be forgot, that ere things came to a crisis in the year 1558, and during the space of thirty years preceding, many of those who espoused the Protestant principles, had felt the weight of persecution in one or other of its various forms. Besides imprisonment, banishment, and different species of rigorous treatment, there had been but too many instances of inhuman violence and blood cruelty. Every one knows by whom these measures were carried on, and how little the civil power interposed, in order to control this tyranny of the Popish clergy. The case of *extreme necessity* at last took place; and a great many of the nobility and barons associated themselves for mutual defence, in their profession of the Protestant religion. In a short time after, the parliament approved of the confession of faith that was presented to them; and Popery was proscribed.

It is, no doubt, perfectly easy for us, at this distance, to sit down in great tranquillity, and sagely to pronounce, that this or the other measure was too precipitate; and that the zeal of certain persons, at such a time, and of the multitude, at such another, was quite irregular. But if we look backwards, and impartially consider the general state of things at that period, and the different circumstances affecting it, our censure must needs be more modest; and we shall probably find ourselves inclined to admit an apology for that which cannot obtain our approbation. In the midst of a storm at sea, it is not surely to be expected, that things should be managed so calmly and prudently as in moderate weather and an easy voyage.

Upon the whole; as the blessings of the reformation are truly inestimable, so we cannot help admiring those worthy men who were so unwearied in the prosecution of its noble purposes. Their merit was distinguished; their integrity approved; their qualities were eminent, and their lives exemplary; their task was arduous; their labours incessant, and their success, through the divine blessing, proportionable; they were honoured to be the instruments of diffusive and lasting good to the Christian church: and therefore their names, on all these accounts, and notwithstanding their failings, ought to be transmitted with respect and honour among Protestants from age to age. They have been thus transmitted, and they will be so; at least by all who deserve to wear that name, by all who have a due regard to the united interests of truth, liberty, and religion.

I am, &c.

LETTER IV.

After the interruption I met with from some necessary avocations, I now go on to consider what is contained in the second passage concerning the refor- mation, which I transcribed in my first letter.

"Before the reformation, all men of sense and virtue wished impatiently for some event, which might repress the exorbitant power of the clergy all over Europe, and put an end to the unbounded usurpations and pretensions of the Roman Pontiff. But when the doctrine of Luther was promulgated, they were somewhat alarmed at the sharpness of the remedy," *&c.* – "It had been observed, that, upon the revival of letters, very generous and enlarged senti- ments of religion prevailed throughout all Italy; and that, during the reign of Leo, the court of Rome itself, in imitation of their illustrious prince, had not been wanting in a just sense of freedom. But when," *&c.*

The general meaning of the whole passage seems to be this, That men of sense and virtue longed for a reformation of those ecclesiastical abuses which were extremely grievous; that they waited for some event, which might be happily improved to this purpose; that the attachment of the multitude to the Romish superstition was not very strong; that the revival of learning, in all probability, would have been of influence, by itself, to have corrected what was most complained of; that in fact Pope Leo and the court of Rome were not wanting in a just sense of freedom; and therefore it would appear, that it was by no means necessary for the first reformers to stir in that matter, and far less to be so deeply engaged in it. Very probably too, had they proceeded more leisurely, much might have been granted, and some things extremely disagreeable would never have happened.

This, my friend, is the general train of sentiment which is set before us in the above passage, and is now to come under our review. Nothing can be more certain, than that long before the age of Luther, many wise and good men had expressed their sense of the degenerate state of the Christian church, of the corruptions which prevailed, and the oppressive tyranny that was exercised in it. In the fourteenth and fifteenth centuries, to go no further back, their complaints were loud and frequent. They who considered things in a religious light, were much affected with the depravations of Christian doctrine and worship, with the prevalence of superstition in its noxious and extensive influence, and with the gross ignorance and corruption of manners which were spread through all the orders of ecclesiastics. But they who considered things in a political light, were chiefly attentive to what regarded the external government of the church, and the exercise of that unlimited power to which the Roman see laid claim. Against this the princes of Europe had, from time to time, remonstrated, and some attempts had been made to restrain it; which however, for the most part, proved to be but weak and ineffectual.

In these two centuries, we know that, both in England and Germany, there were some eminent doctors, who declared against many things that bore the marks of a state of religion exceedingly vitiated; and whose writings are to be considered as a sort of dawn of the morning, breaking out after a long and dismal night of Gothic darkness. This dawn was joyfully beheld by many; and its progress was gradual towards the age of the reformation, in which the more perfect light of religious knowledge began again to shine on the Christian world. The books of Wickliff, and of his followers, had been dispersed through England, and afterwards they found their way into foreign parts. The doctrines contained in them were highly relished by not a few, both at home and abroad; to the indignation of all who chose to retain their primitive ignorance and submission; and of those too whose interest it was to defend the cause of superstition and slavery, to support every ancient error, all tenets of whatsoever kind, which had been heretofore embraced by the church; and to guard against dangerous innovations, and the dreaded incroachments of reason and free inquiry.

Let us now attend to our author's account of this matter. What is it that "all men of sense and virtue wished for impatiently before the reformation? – For some event, which might repress the exorbitant power of the clergy all over Europe, and put an end to the unbounded usurpations and pretensions of the Roman Pontiff." And was this all that they wished to see redressed? Were the views of the wise and good wholly confined to the restraint of the power of the clergy, and of the Pontiff's usurpations? Was this the whole of what was intended by the first reformers? and if "such of the ecclesiastical abuses as were the grossest and most burdensome had been corrected," would this have sufficed? By no means; it was not, it would not have been so.

The reformation, no doubt, was favoured by many on account of its influence on the political interests of the several states: but there was another, and a most important view of it. The very name of *reformation of religion* points to this different, and higher view. To remove its deplorable corruptions, to restore the knowledge of Christian truth, to disclose the falsehood and fatal tendency of those tenets and practices of superstition which had so baleful an aspect on worship, life, and morals, to the end that the Christian church Might assume a better and a purer form; this, I say, was a good and noble aim, and this was the aim of the reformers.

Just reason too had the world to complain of the numberless oppressions under which they groaned, in consequence of the bold and shameful exercise of that usurped power, to which they had been so long subjected. If the reformation prevailed, it would naturally put an end to these. But this was not the main, far less the sole intention of Luther, and of those who first moved in it; and is rather to be considered as a consequence of their original design. Their general aim, then, is by this historian presented in a false light. It was in truth more the business of the princes of Europe than of private doctors, to fall upon measures for the restraint of exorbitant power, and for the redress of enormous abuses. What may be our author's opinion, with regard to the other purposes of the reformation, is not the question; or whether he thinks these were worthy of the attention of men of sense and virtue. He writes as an historian; and therefore it was incumbent on him to give a full representation of facts, at least of important ones, whatever were his own sentiments about them. But to go on with his narrative:

"In the preceding state of ignorance and tranquillity, into which mankind were lulled, the attachment to superstition, though without reserve, was not extreme." And therefore it might have been concluded, that it would be no difficult matter to disengage them; the rather that learning and knowledge began to be introduced. This, I think, is the consequence that is meant to be insinuated. But it is opposed by history and experience; by the history of the reformation, and by the state of the Roman-Catholic religion at this day. As the great progress of learning in Europe, during the two last centuries, has not produced any considerable change to the better in many nations, which still retain their warm affection to ancient superstition; so is not this a demonstration, in fact, that our author's reasoning is fallacious? The truth is, the knowledge of arts and sciences may flourish, where the knowledge of true religion makes but slow advances; especially, if means of every kind are used to interrupt its progress. That this was the case here, we certainly know; and the consequences are in our time manifest in Popish countries, where ignorance and bigotry are cordially allied in the breasts of multitudes, and where too many causes concur to maintain their empire.

Neither can I assent to the proposition itself, that, "in the preceding state of ignorance, the attachment to superstition, though without reserve, was not extreme." It would seem, that attachment may well be called "extreme," which is accompanied with a full and implicit resignation of the understanding and will to the doctrines and dictates of superstition. Can it be said, that the attachment to the church and its superstitions was not "extreme," when, in the history of some preceding centuries, we read so often of the furious efforts of the multitude in their defence, and of that outrageous bigotry of theirs, which even monarchs dreaded, and whose terrors added so mighty an efficacy to ecclesiastical menaces, and papal thunders? Was not the attachment "extreme," which so frequently prevailed over the respect and allegiance that subjects owed to their natural princes, and which armed them against those princes, of whose conduct towards themselves they had not the least reason to complain? May not this epithet "extreme" be well affixed to that sort of attachment and zeal, which prompted them to put in execution the violent edicts of the Roman Pontiffs against all who dared to oppose them? The raging zeal of persecution, and of the croisades, is but too conspicuous in the history of several ages. I do not mean here the wild expeditions into the east, which were first known by the name of croisades; but those others that were afterwards distinguished by the same appellation, and were published against the cities, states, or princes, who became, from time to time, obnoxious to the Roman see. All this, I think, will go far towards confirming the negative of the above proposition.

"It might have been hoped," adds he, that learning and knowledge – would have opened the eyes of men, and corrected such of the ecclesiastical abuses as were the grossest and most burdensome. It had been observed," &c. He seems to affirm, that learning and knowledge would probably have had a happy influence on the Pope himself, and have induced him, and the great prelates of his court, to redress those grievances which were most oppressive. And was it only requisite in order to this, that they should know they had little reason and right on their side? Had they, good men, been hitherto acting wrong merely thro' ignorance and mistake? And was it to be hoped, that so soon as they were apprised of what was just and right, things would be reduced to a regular order enough? and that, as they were unbiased by ambition, pride, and interest, they would be ready to comply with the directions of equity and sound reason? – According to this scheme, I cannot possibly assign any reason why they should have been so enraged at those who honestly endeavoured to set all these matters before them in the clearest light, and to hold up to them the glass of reason, as well as that of holy scripture and primitive antiquity, in which they might view the very deformed nature of those corruptions which had so long prevailed in the Christian church.

But perhaps the above conjecture may be propped by the following paragraph. "It has been observed, that, upon the revival of letters, very generous and enlarged sentiments of religion prevailed throughout all Italy; and that, during the reign of Leo, the court of Rome itself, in imitation of their illustrious prince, had not been wanting in a just sense of freedom." As he is here speaking of ecclesiastical abuses and usurpations, he may be thought to insinuate, that the court of Rome, and the Pope himself, had given evidence of their being inclined to quit some of their unjust pretensions, and to despoil themselves of a part of their usurped authority. Upon what occasion they did so, I own myself entirely ignorant. What I know is, that nothing of this sort is to be met with in the proceedings of the Lateran council, that was assembled during his pontificate. On the contrary, he was not only solicitous to retain, but he strove to enlarge the Papal power, and to get rid of some restraints which had been laid on it by the council of Basil, about seventy years before. Neither was his attempt without success; as, in that council of his, the famous constitution of Boniface VIII. which affirms, that the authority of the Pope ought to be held uncontroulable, and indisputable, was approved and renewed.[7] Any one indeed who reads the history of that council, will soon observe, that this Pontiff was but little inclined to the reformation even of those abuses which had been of a long time the subject of complaint. What has the appearance of reformation in the acts of this Lateran council, relates, for the most part, to matters of small consequence; and where any thing of considerable importance is touched, the redress is plainly delusory, by means of the reserving clauses annexed to some wholesome canons. Accordingly, several of their own writers exclaim against the scene of formal mockery, and against the obstinate opposition to all proposals for a reformation, that was apparent in the rulers of their church; and they conclude with lamenting its incurable state.[8] So that the learning of this "illustrious Pontiff," and his supposed "just sense of freedom," were of no great influence in all this matter.

Let us now consider this same "just sense of freedom" in another light; and as it is blended with what this author calls "very generous and enlarged sentiments of religion." The meaning of these last words, according to his sense of things, may be perhaps easily ascertained. "That philosophical sect, who have of late received the appellation of *freethinkers*,"[9] was not first heard of in our age. The Pope of whom we speak, and some of his chief counsellors, were heretofore shrewdly suspected of a warm attachment to it: in a word, it was said that they had no great regard to some of the essential principles of religion and the Christian faith; and the charge, it would appear, is not without foundation. Certain it is, that *infidelity* began at that time to spread through Italy. This was the extreme into which many were thrown, who considered the

---

[7] Sess. II.

[8] "Hæc illa est eximia," says Richer, "et tantopere a Christianis nationibus, ducentis abhinc annis, exoptata reformatio: vel, ut verius dicamus, abusuum curiæ Romanæ incrustatio atque involutio." And again, in speaking of the court of Rome, "Cum igitur morbi, injuriæ atque corruptelæ illinc unde medicina juraque salutaria debebant promanare, scaturiunt; quotusquisque et de ecclesiæ in melius instauratione, et de publica salute, spem omnem non merito abjiciat?" *Richerii hist. concil. generlib.* 4. – "Vale, Christiane lector," says another Roman doctor, "et ecclesiasticæ disciplinæ ad deteriora prolabanti quotidie, quoniam aliud nihil fere restat, communibus mecum suspiriis ingemisce."

[9] P. 6.

Christian doctrine as it was exhibited in the tenets of that church; to some of which they could not possibly yield their assent. Thus, without entering into a detail, without distinguishing betwixt the genuine doctrines of Christianity, and the infusions of folly and superstition, they were but too ready to form their conclusions on the side of infidelity. These received an additional force from their knowledge of the licentious manners of the ecclesiastics, from their attention to the frame of worship that was established, to the variety of gainful tenets that were strongly inculcated, and of shameful impostures that were publicly authorised; and, in a word, to those pretensions and maxims of the Roman see, by which what was called the government of the church had been converted into a mere secular empire, whose concerns were managed according to the usual methods of conducting the schemes of interest and ambition. When they thought of all this, and did not make proper distinctions on the subject, they were still further confirmed in their prejudices, and conclusions, against the Christian religion itself. Pity indeed that it should have been so disfigured; and that a hideous phantom, should have been presented to view instead of an angelic form! But no great compliment, however, is due to their discernment, who did not perceive the fallacy and gross imposture; or to their love of truth, who were not anxious to discover its delusive representation.

Others there were of a different turn, of a better spirit, and of just discernment, who soon favoured the doctrines of the reformation, and in a little time after embraced them with pleasure; although, on this account, several of them were obliged to abandon their native country, that they might escape the violence of those very persons who are said to have had "a just sense of freedom."

This same illustrious Pontiff, with all his "just sense of freedom," exerted himself in the manner of the most determined bigot, in many instances; particularly so with regard to the first reformers in Germany. What though he may be supposed to have been a sceptic, an infidel, an Atheist, if you will; it doth by no means follow, that he would allow others to espouse what opinions they pleased, to judge for themselves, to declare their sentiments, and to act according to the dictates of conscience, in the business of religion. The reason is plain; because the consequences might have been fatal to those interests which were supreme in his affection. Some of the most irreligious and profligate of his predecessors had shewn themselves, upon occasions, to be the most violent persecutors of all those who refused their assent and submission to authorised doctrines and rites. Whether bigot or infidel, is of little importance here: the outward conduct will be the same. All history attests it; the reason of the thing persuades it; and the uniform behaviour of the Popes Leo and Adrian towards the first reformers, (without going any further), is fully sufficient to confirm it. In their outrageous treatment of them, the honest bigot and the illustrious sceptic most cordially agree; however widely they might differ in their own private sentiments about religion. There is then no sort of connection, so far as

I can perceive, betwixt the Deistical principles of Pope Leo and his courtiers, and their bearing the least good-will to the reformation of the church. Had there been any such connection, a change would have commenced long before, as this was not the first Pontiff who was suspected of these principles. Some others had been accused of them, in the most public manner, and in the face of general councils. To say truth, it is somewhat ludicrous in our author, to talk of any hope of reformation, or even of indulgence to it, from that quarter: and in fact, this same "just sense of freedom," which is by him ascribed to the Pope and his friends, did not hinder them from entering into all measures of severity and persecution, against those who honestly and openly professed their opinion and belief.

As to what he calls "generous and enlarged sentiments of religion," I am bold to affirm, that very different epithets are due to the principles of scepticism and infidelity, which would despoil us of all noble sentiments and aims, which would deprive us of all rational grounds of inward tranquillity, would extinguish our hopes with respect to a better and a happier world, and would present to us a dejecting and debasing view of nature, of mankind, and of God. – But what is in itself absurd and sordid, may be dignified, or may be meant to be dignified, by quite opposite titles: and some of those who do so, may perhaps dream of their making great progress in the paths of learning and true knowledge; while, in reality, they are bewildered in a maze of dark notions, and are apt to stumble at every obstacle that lies in their way.

See then, my friend, how we are to conclude, upon the whole, concerning that train of sentiments and hints which is furnished out by this historian. They are intended, you see, to persuade, that it was not at all necessary for the first reformers to bestir themselves as they did; since it might have been hoped, that, upon the revival of learning, a reformation would have followed of course; especially as the attachment of the multitude to those superstitions, to which they had been long accustomed, was not extreme: nay, it was to be hoped, that a wished-for reformation would have been favoured and promoted even by the court of Rome itself; and the rather, that the Pope and his chief friends, in consequence of their sceptical or libertine principles, would probably have very little regarded what opinions were prevalent; and would not only have allowed men to think and profess as they pleased, but would have also corrected what had been most complained of, and put a final period to the oppressive exercise of spiritual dominion.

Here, I think, one might safely dropt the subject: but, that you may have a more full view of it, it may not be improper to enter into some further particulars, and to remind you of a few passages relative to the first steps of the reformation; by an attention to which, it will be easily discerned what was the spirit of the court of Rome, and to whom the epithets "furious and "enraged" do most justly appertain. We have seen to whom this historian would appropriate them: but that they may be more properly ascribed to very different persons, we shall soon, if I mistake not, find reason to conclude.

Luther, it is well known, first set himself against the notorious abuse of indulgences. These the Pope had caused to be published every where, that he might remedy the disorder of his finances, which had been much exhausted; and might likewise have it in his power to bestow large sums on his friends, by assigning them the revenues that were to be derived from those indulgences in this or the other province. F. Paul (whose account of things I have not chiefly in my eye) has remarked, that Pope Urban, towards the end of the eleventh century, first granted plenary indulgences to all who would join in the intended expedition to the holy land. The example, adds he, was followed by several of his successors; who refined upon this new invention, and extended their indulgences to those who should furnish men or money for that service; and in the course of time to those also who should, in like manner, assist in the croisades against those Christians who fell under the displeasure of the Roman Pontiffs. He goes on to inform us, that the world had frequently seen these sums, or at least a great part of them, applied to purposes very different from that, under the pretext of which they had been amassed. As to Leo's indulgences, they were given to all without exception who would purchase them; and were intended for the good, as he said, not only of the living, but likewise of the dead; as their influence was supposed to reach the state of souls in purgatory, in order to their instant deliverance. In the distribution of the revenue that was to be raised from the sale of his indulgences, he made a gift of what should be levied in Saxony and the northern parts of Germany, to his sister, who was married to a natural son of Pope Innocent VIII.

They who published the indulgences behaved themselves in the most scandalous manner; so that wise and sober men were quite shocked at the shameful tenets which they maintained, and at the nature and circumstances of this infamous brokage. In speaking of this subject, a famous Italian author says, that "the Bishop Arembaud, who received his commission from the Pope's sister, was a minister worthy of such a commission, and that he executed it with great extortion and avarice; that many of those persons who were employed under him, gamed away these indulgences in taverns; and since it was known through all Germany, that the money arising from them was not to be remitted to the Pope's treasury, from whence part of it might have been afterwards issued for some good use, but that the whole of it was destined to satisfy the avarice of a lady; therefore an indignation of spirit, and an abhorrence of this exaction, and of its ministers, had been raised in the breasts of men; and that the character and authority of the Pope himself suffered greatly on this occasion."[10] Although Guicciardini, the author I now point at, was not

---

[10] "– Haveva concitato in molti luoghi indegnatione, & scandalo assai, & specialmente nella Germania; dove a molti de' ministri erano veduta vendere per poco prezzo, o giocarsi su le taverne la faculta del liberare l'anime de' morti dal purgatorio. Et acrebbe che il pontefice, il quale per facilita della natura sua, essercitava in molte cose

a friend to the reformation, yet he is not unwilling to allow, that Luther had but too good reason to oppose these indulgences, and to question the authority upon which they were founded.

He did oppose them, and spoke against the dangerous doctrines and licentious behaviour of those who distributed them. He laid the case before the Bishop of Brandenburg and the Archbishop of Mentz, to whom he directed very submissive letters, though without effect. Afterwards having carefully considered the subject, he published his sentiments about indulgences, purgatory, penance, and other points intermixed with them. This small tract was writ in the scholastic way: and his opinions were formed into a great many theses or conclusions, to the examination of which the learned were invited. He sent it to the vicar-general of his order, about Midsummer 1518, and prefixed to it a submissive dedication to the Pope; in which he acquaints him, that the preachers of indulgences had openly taught the most impious and heretical doctrines; that they had imposed an oath upon confessors, binding them to inculcate these; and that they were guilty of insatiable avarice, reckoning themselves secure under the protection of his great name, which many had taken occasion on their account to reproach. He adds, that he was much affected with all this scene; and that as he was destitute of authority, he had addressed himself to some of the great prelates of the church concerning it; that their treatment of him was different; and that the terror of his Holiness's name, and the threatenings of church-censures, had much influence upon them: at length, as he goes on, when he could do nothing else, he resolved at least gently to oppose these corrupt teachers, by calling in question their tenets, and proposing a disputation upon them. To this end he had wrote and printed a short treatise; which he might well do, who was, by his apostolic authority, a professor of theology, agreeably to the usual manner in all universities, where subjects of superior importance to any he had touched were every day canvassed. It was composed in the form that is familiar to the schools, but not at all adapted to the understandings of the vulgar. Now that he had declared

con poca maesta l' ufficio ponteficale, dono a Maddalena sua sorella lo emolumento, et l'esattione delle indulgenze di molte parti di Germania; la quale havendo fatto deputare commessario il Vescovo Aremboddo, ministro degno di questa commessione, che l'essercitava con grande avaritia et estorsione, e sapendosi per tutta la Germania che i danari, che se ne cavavano non andavano al pontefice, o alla camera apostolica, donde non sarebbe forse stato possibile che qualche parte sene fusse spesa in usibuoni, ma era destinato a satisfare all'avaritia d'una donna; haveva fatto detestabile non solo l'esattione, et i ministri di quella, ma il nome ancora, e l'autorita di chi tanto inconsultamente le concedeva. La-qual occasione havendo prefa Lutero, et havendo comminciato a disprezzare queste concessioni, et a tassarre in queste l'autorita del pontefice, multiplicandogli in causa favorevole a gli orecchi de' popoli, numero grande di auditori; commincio ogni di piu scopertamente a negare l'autorita del pontifice. Da questi principii forse honesti, o almeno per la guista occasione, che gli era data, in qualche parte scusabili, &c." *L' hist. d'Italia di Guicciardini, lib.* 13.

his sentiments, he asks what he should do. He was conscious to himself of his own defects in point of genius and learning: he had been unwilling to appear in public: he was sensible, that he had incurred the hatred of many: he wished to mitigate it, and to guard against its effects; and therefore would he commend himself to his protection: he refers the whole matter to his Holiness; and concludes with expressing his submission to his judgment and authority in very humble terms. This is the substance of that famous dedication.[11]

Mean while they who were most concerned in the shameful traffic, were further alarmed and enraged at Luther's conduct. Obloquy, harsh names, and high threatenings were poured out against him: and some of his adversaries, particularly Prierias and Eckius, wrote answers to his book, which were penned with the utmost acrimony of style. As any thing that had the shew of argument in those compositions, was grounded upon the supposed infallibility of the Roman Pontiffs, Luther entered into an examination of this matter, and declared his assent to the judgment of the council of Constance, which affirms, that the authority of a general council is superior to that of the Pope. By and by he was summoned to Rome; and at the same time Leo sent a brief to the

---

[11] Cœpit apud nos, diebus proximis, prædicari jubilæus ille indulgentiarum apostoli-carum, profecitque adeo ut præcones illius, sub tui nominis terrore omnia sibi licere putantes, impiissima hæreticaque palam auderent docere, in gravissimum scandalum et ludibrium ecclesiasticæ potestatis, ac si decretales de abusionibus quæstorum nihil ad eos pertinerent. Nec contenti quod liberrimis verbis hæc sua venena diffunderent, insuper libellos ediderunt, et ita statuerunt ut confessors juramento adigerent, quo hæc ipsa fidelissime instantissimeque populo inculcarent. Vera dico – extant libelli, nec possunt negare. – Unum erat quo scandala sedabant, sciz. terror nominis tui; (insuper) iguis comminatio, et hæretici nominis opprobrium. – Verum nihilominus crebrescebant fabulæ per tabernas de avaritia sacerdotum, detractioneque clavium summique pontificis, ut testis est vox totius hujus terræ. Ego sane (ut fateor) pro zelo Christi, sicuti mi videbar, aut, si ita placet, pro juvenili calore, urebar; nec tamen meum esse videbam in iis quicquam statuere aut facere; proinde monui privatim aliquot magnates eccle-siarum. Hic ab aliis acceptabar, aliis ridiculum, aliis aliud videbar: prævalebat enim nominis tui terror, et censurarum intentatio. Tandem cum nihil possem aliud, visum est saltem leniuscule illis reluctari, id est, eorum dogmata in dubium et disputationem vocare. Itaque schedulam disputatoriam edidi, invitans tantum doctiores, siqui vellent, mecum disputare. – Ecce hoc est incendium, quo totum mundum queruntur confla-grare; forte quod indignantur me unum autoritate tua apostolica magistrum theologiæ, jus habere in publica schola disputandi, pro more omnium universitatum et totius ecclesiæ, non modo de indulgentiis, verum etiam de potestate, remissione, indul-gentiis divines, incomparabiliter majoribus rebus. – Nunc quid faciam? revocare non possum; et miram mihi invidiam ex ea invulgatione video conflari. Invitus venio in publicum, – præsertim ego indoctus, vacuus eruditione, &c. – Sed cogit necessitas; – itaque quo et ipsos adversaries mitigem, et desideria multorum expleam, emitto ecce meas nugas declaratorias mearum disputationum; emitto autem, quo tutior sim, sub tui nominis præsidio, et tuæ protectionis umbra, Beatiff. Pater. – Quare, Beat. Pater, prostratum me pedibus tuæ Beatitudinis offero, cum omnibus quæ sum et habeo. Vivifica, occide, voca, revoca, approba, reproba, ut placuerit," &c.

Elector of Saxony, exhorting him not to afford his protection to a man who deserved it so little. He wrote also to Cardinal Cajetan, his legate at the diet of Ausburg, that he might use means to get him sent prisoner to Rome. The Pope was afterwards prevailed with to refer the judgment of the cause to this legate. Having received a safe conduct from the Emperor, Luther appeared before the Cardinal; who first represented to him the danger he was in, if he persisted in his way; and then attempted to allure him by the fair prospect of wealth and honours, of which he gave him liberal promises in the Pope's name, if he would retract his sentiments. But he soon found, that this was not the proper method of dealing with one who had neither a timorous nor a sordid spirit, and whose steady regard to virtue and religion kept him at a distance from a compliance with any thing that might violate his conscience, upon any consideration whatsoever. The haughty Cardinal was much provoked at his firmness, and at the honest freedom of his discourse, so that he broke out into passionate expressions and menaces. Luther patiently bore with this harsh usage; nay, when he was on his journey homeward, he wrote him a submissive letter, in order to soften his displeasure.

But new adversaries were stirred up against him, and against the doctrines he taught; which still continued to gain ground, notwithstanding all this opposition. At length, the Pope, afraid of some incroachment upon his authority, sent a *bull* into Germany; in which he asserted his own plenary power, and the validity of his indulgences in their largest extent, as reaching both to the living and to the dead; which plenitude of power belonged to him, as he was successor of St Peter. He further declared, that this was the doctrine of the Roman church, and that it ought to be received by all Christians. Copies of this bull were dispersed through Germany by his legate, who injoined the bishops to denounce severe punishment against those who did not believe agreeably to what was contained in it.

After this plain condemnation of his doctrine, Luther and his friends might well look for the worst of treatment. And in the apprehension of this, was he basely to give up with the truth, and tamely to bow down under this despotic power? Thus did his enemies fondly hope; but he still adhered to the honest and generous purpose he had formed. He implored the protection of his prince; and it was granted. The university of Wittemberg openly befriended his cause, and multitudes every where embraced his principles. Being thus encouraged, and commending himself to the divine care, he ventured to protest against the judgment of the Pope exhibited in his bull, and to appeal from it to the decision of a general council, to which he maintained the preference ought, on all accounts, to be given. Such appeal was not indeed an unheard-of thing; or rather it was a regular and legal measure, supported by the authority of two famous councils in the fifteenth century. Father Paul acquaints us, that this protestation and appeal was soon spread over Germany; and that, generally speaking, it was thought just and reasonable.

In the following year, 1519, Luther proceeded to the examination of several important articles of religious faith and practice, and shewed the corruptions of the church of Rome in these points. At the same time Zuinglius, a doctor of theology, was at the head of the opposition to indulgences in Switzerland. He had, in like manner, been led from one subject to another; and declaring against many established opinions and rites, he appealed to scripture and primitive antiquity. But the enemies of the reformation were extremely unwilling to carry up their researches so high; and would rather have had every thing tried by the decretals of Popes, the practice of a few preceding ages, the sentiments of some of the later fathers, and by the venerable authority of the schoolmen. These were the foundations upon which they settled the vindication of the Popish plan; while the supposed guilt of heresy, and their real danger who embraced the reformation, were represented in the strongest light.

At this time too the Pope was solicited to a more strenuous exertion of his authority; and he consented to refer the cognisance of this whole affair to a select congregation of prelates, divines, and canonists. By their advice, a bull was drawn up (*anno* 1520), in which the Pope talks in the style of a bigot; condemns a great many articles of Luther's doctrine as heretical, false, scandalous, and contrary to catholic truths; denounces high penalties against all who should teach or espouse them; gives orders to all into whose hands they may come, to burn Luther's books; and he is pleased to add, that since Luther had, for a year past, continued to disregard the censures of the church, had refused to appear at Rome, though he made him the offer of a safe conduct, and had even dared to appeal from his judgment to the decision of a future council, in direct contradiction to the peremptory prohibitions of the Popes Pius II. and Julius II. he might therefore now proceed to his condemnation, without any further delay. Nevertheless, he once more exhorts him, and all his adherents, to renounce their errors, within the space of sixty days, and to burn the books in which they are contained; otherwise he determines and declares, that they are to be held and treated as notorious and obstinate heretics. He prohibits all intercourse with them, lays all places to which they may go under an interdict, and commands them to be seized, where-ever they are to be found, in order to their being brought prisoners to Rome. In the conclusion, he directs this bull to be published every where, and excommunicates all those who should obstruct the reading and publication of it.

Such was the tenor of the bull, and this the behaviour of Leo and his court, notwithstanding their "generous and enlarged sentiments of religion," and notwithstanding their "just sense of freedom." Thus did they fully comply with the advice which Father Paul tells us, the inquisitor Friar Hogstrat, in the true spirit of his office, had given at first to the Pope, concerning the proper method of refuting the doctrines of Luther, which he thought was to be done by means of fire and faggot. No wonder then, that this worthy man, so assaulted, found himself animated to write in his own defence, in the defence of sacred truth, and of all its friends. Accordingly, as soon as he was apprised of the contents of the papal bull, he renewed his appeal to the future council, complained of his being condemned without having been heard in his own defence, took notice of the unwillingness which the Pope shewed to subject his doctrines to the trial of scripture, and the decision of a general council; and then he intreats the Emperor, and all princes and magistrates, to admit of his appeal, in maintenance of the authority of those councils, without regarding the illegal and unrighteous decree of the Pope against him.

Towards the beginning of the next year, the diet of the empire was assembled at Worms; and Luther had a summons to attend it, together with a safe conduct from the Emperor Charles V. that he might there give an account of the doctrines which he taught. He obeyed the summons, and appeared before that grand assembly. Being asked, If he was the author of those books which bore his name, whose titles were then read to him? and, Whether he adhered to the tenets which were to be found there, or would retract any of them? he made answer to the first question, That he acknowledged these books to be of his composure; and with regard to the second, as it was a point of great importance, he asked a little time to deliberate on the return he should make. He was allowed till next day; when the questions being repeated, in the introduction of his answer, he made an apology for his not having addressed himself the day before to that august assembly in the most proper terms, and for his having failed in not giving every one the titles of honour which appertained to him. As to his writings, he said they were of three sorts; the first of which concerned the doctrines of faith and piety; the second impugned the tenets and practices of the court of Rome; and the third consisted of replies to his adversaries. In relation to the doctrines, he said, That as he was fully persuaded of their truth, he would neither act as a Christian, nor even as an honest man, if he renounced them, or professed to renounce them. He appealed to themselves, whether there was not too good reason for his writings of the second sort, since all Christian states, particularly those of Germany, had been pillaged with impunity, and groaned under a heavy yoke; adding withal, that a retraction of his sentiments on this head, might tend to the strengthening of that tyranny which had been so long exercised. As to the third class, he acknowledged, that he had wrote some of those pieces with too much heat and passion; and told them further, that as he could not lay claim to an exemption from faults, so he would not defend them; but that he adhered to his general doctrines as Christian truths, and was ready to explain the grounds of his persuasion to every one that asked him; declaring at the same time, that if any person should convince him of error by the holy scripture, he would himself throw his books into the flames. He concluded with a plain and honest address to the Emperor and princes, concerning the importance of religious truth, and the great guilt and danger of despising or rejecting it. – A little after, the Emperor put the question to him, and required him to declare at once, whether he was resolved to defend his writings? His answer was, That he could not retract what he had wrote or taught, till his adversaries, either by reason or scripture, should prove it to be erroneous. He was next called to a private meeting of some ecclesiastical and secular princes; where it was proposed and urged, that he should refer himself to the judgment of a council which was soon to be assembled. To this proposal he consented, upon two conditions; one of which was, that the judgment should be formed on the testimony of holy writ. But the Emperor was resolved on severe measures, without violating, however, the safe conduct that he had given; to which violation there were not wanting some who endeavoured to incite him, and who talked of the decree of the council of Constance, about a hundred years before, which determined, that faith was not to be kept with heretics. The Elector Palatine vigorously opposed the infamous counsel; and the Emperor himself refused to comply, saying very honourably, as Mr Lenfant informs us, "that he did not chuse to blush with his predecessor Sigismund;" meaning the prince who had allowed his safe conduct to John Huss to be basely violated, and who could not restrain himself from blushing in a public meeting of the council, when he was reminded of it by that much-injured, eminent man.

Soon after Luther's departure from Worms, the Emperor issued a rigorous edict against him, and against all who were of the same sentiments; in which, among other things, he declares, that agreeably to the Pope's sentence, and in execution of it, Luther is to be considered as a notorious heretic; and he commands him to be treated as such, by the princes and states of the empire; who were charged, under the usual penalties, to imprison him after a certain term of days, and every where to punish all who adhered to him with the confiscation of their goods. The whole strain of the edict is to a high degree severe; and there are some virulent expressions in it, which inflamed bigotry alone could dictate. But as Luther, and the university of Wittemberg, had the protection of their natural prince; and as the friends of the reformation soon became a respectable body in Germany, neither the Pope's menacing bull, nor the Emperor's violent edict produced their intended effect. In course of time, Charles was obliged to abate much of his severity towards them; especially when he stood in need, as was frequently the case, of the assistance of Protestant princes, in the prosecution of his various political schemes. Concord was at length, in some measure, established; and the free exercise of both religions was allowed of in the empire. But not to go further in this detail; wherein I have purposely followed the account of a Roman Catholic, rather than that of any Protestant historian; and indeed the integrity and candour of the celebrated Father Paul may well recommend is history to universal regard:

In sum, we have seen with what prudence and becoming moderation Luther conducted himself in the first steps of his opposition, notwithstanding his zeal and heat of temper: we have seen how he addressed himself to those of power and influence, on the subject of indulgences, and laid before them a representation of the shameful tenets, and the no less shameful lives of those who published them. When such application was ineffectual, he afterwards spoke more openly against these scandalous doctrines; which every honest man might well have done, and which multitudes did as well as he. He then proposed a disputation on the theses or positions in which he had comprised his sentiments: and when he did so, he acted in the character of a man of learning, and suitably to the duty of his station. But his adversaries thought it more proper, as it was surely less difficult, to sound the alarm of heresy, to calumniate boldly, and to threaten severely, rather than to confute his reasonings, and to overthrow his conclusions. He laid the whole matter before the Pope, to whom he sent his book, together with a letter expressing the greatest respect, and submission. What was the effect? Did he attend to this affair in a suitable manner? Did he enter into an examination of particulars, as he ought to have done, and as Luther had humbly requested? Did he shew any the least inclination to restrain the licentious doctrines and behaviour of those who spread his indulgences, and to correct what all good men were ashamed of? Was this his conduct? Was there any ground to hope that it would be his conduct? Quite the reverse. Nothing of this spirit is to be discerned in *him*, or in the councils of his court. Instead of acting this part, instead of attending to the just complaints that were made against those heralds of the indulgences, instead of giving check to the doctrines and enormities of these miscreants; this same sceptical and applauded Pontiff, unwilling to punish or to censure them, displeased with such addresses, and extremely offended at those who seemed to call in question his authority, and to doubt the efficacy of his pardons, thought fit to assume the air and style of haughty bigotry; to speak of himself as the successor of St Peter, and the vicar of Christ upon earth; to assert his own plenitude of apostolic power, and the validity of his indulgences to the dead and living; and peremptorily to injoin all Christians to believe accordingly. Here was a speedy and a full decision of the matter; at least so far as his declaration and authority could decide it: and this bull was but a prelude to the more severe and sanguinary one, which was published soon after. Where now is the boasted "just sense of freedom;" what is become of "the generous and enlarged sentiments of religion," from which the most happy effects should have been derived? Are there any traces of the spirit of liberty and moderation in all this conduct? any marks of regard to faith and religion, to justice and probity, to equity and candour? Or rather, whatever might be his own sceptical principles, did he not act in the spirit of pride and ecclesiastical tyranny? Jealous of incroachments upon the power which he claimed, and tenaciously adhering to the principles which tended to confirm it, he could not bear with any thing that was repugnant to one or the other: in a word, he discovered the true spirit of a Roman Pontiff. He seems at first to have thought, and his whole court was willing to think, that the opposition which was made by Luther and some others was of little consequence; and that persons of no great note in the world might be easily crushed by the weight of his power. But the goodness of their cause, the truth of their sentiments, the clearness of their reasonings, and the great importance of their doctrines, gave them a strength which soon became formidable to their adversaries, and weakened the foundations of that fabric, which had been reared upon the ruins of truth, and the rights and liberties of mankind.

Judge now, my friend, to whom the epithets "furious and enraged" do rightly appertain: what pity it is, that the conduct of a Pope, who is said to have been a freethinker, and the counsels of a court, where sceptical principles are thought to have been held in no small repute; – what pity, that the counsel and conduct of those men, from whom better things might have been expected, should be so justly liable to the reproach of violence and rage! May not our author's style then be inverted on this subject? At any rate, might he not have sometimes applied these epithets where they are unquestionably most proper, and have softened them where they are least so? They are, however, reserved (and perhaps it better answered his design that they should be reserved) to be poured out on some great and worthy names. As to Luther, in particular, whose conduct we have been considering; he was certainly an eminent, an honest, and a good man; and was distinguished from his fellow-labourers not so much by superior endowments of mind, as by his peculiar firmness and intrepidity in the cause of religion, to which he bore the highest affection. His zeal to maintain its interests, seems to have been strengthened in proportion to his increasing knowledge of its doctrines, and of the complicated errors of Popery. That he was a man of a warm temper; that he sometimes wrote and acted with too much heat against his adversaries; and in general that the weakness and perturbation of human passions were sometimes mingled with his honest zeal; all this, I say, I have already acknowledged in the preceding letter, and have there added an apology, to which I now refer. Let it be remembered too, what moderation he shewed in the first steps of his conduct, of which some account has been given in the short sketch of history that I have laid before you. With pleasure could I make some remarks upon his behaviour before the illustrious assembly at Worms, which, I think, was truly noble. But this letter is already drawn out to a great length; and therefore to all that I have said of him, I shall now only subjoin the honourable testimony that is given to the purity of his life and manners, by one who was no friend of his; I mean Erasmus. "Hominis vita," says he, in one of his letters, "magno omnium consensu probatur. Jam id non leve præjudicium est, tantam esse morum integritatem, ut nec hostes reperiant, quod calumnientur."

I am, &c.

LETTER V.

The remaining points are of less importance than those we have already considered. But as we have proposed to give due attention to all that our author has said upon this subject, let us now go on to speak of the objection against the reformation, as premature, which lies first in our way. It is insinuated, that the season proper for it was not yet come, and that it would have been better to have waited for some happy event, "which might repress the exorbitant power of the clergy all over Europe, and put an end to the unbounded usurpations and pretensions of the Roman Pontiff."

But how long, pray, was the Christian world to wait for such event? and how often had events, which seemed to have the most favourable aspect on the restraint of papal tyranny, (for only this part of the subject is in his eye, and to it I shall now confine myself); how often, I say, had such events passed without producing any effect, whilst men either dared not to improve them, or had ventured to do so, without success? Nay, further, at what time soever like events should happen, was it not still to be expected, that a like formidable opposition should be made to all attempts towards improving them? We are not to think, that an unlimited submission was every where paid to the arbitrary dictates of pontifical authority, even when it was at its greatest height; far less when it was in a state of progression. Remonstrances were made in every age; and some princes now and then made a bold stand against its incroachments; the consequence of which, for the most part, was only this, that they protracted the date of their entire subjection. If I am not mistaken, it may be demonstrated, that the depravations of Christian doctrine kept pace with the progress of the spiritual monarchy; and it would be no unentertaining speculation to trace their unhappy connection and mutual influence. But as they who cannot reason can however feel, so in the darkest ages, from the eleventh century downwards, no small resistance was made to the ambition, the exactions, and oppressions of the Roman see.

During the course of these ages, it was almost impossible, that many events conducive to the purpose that I now speak of, should not have happened. With some of them we are well acquainted. For instance, was there not a concurrence of many favourable circumstances at the time when the council of Constance was assembled, towards the beginning of the fifteenth century? The greatest confusions had long prevailed in the church; the world was fully sensible of them; three Popes were contending with each other; there was much talk in the council about "the reformation of the church in its head and members," the necessity of which was pleaded by many amongst themselves; the Emperor Sigismund, who was protector of the council, and several other princes, required it of them, and good men every where anxiously longed for it. What was the result of all? – The acts of that council will inform us. In a word, little change to the better was effected; and the Pope whom they chose, soon found means to hinder the progress of that design, and even to render insignificant some concessions and regulations that had been made before his election. The solemn decree too, which appointed that general councils should be assembled every tenth year, and with which many had been amused, was in a little time totally disregarded. I need not speak of the council of Basil, or of the proceedings of that other which met at Pisa, under the protection of Lewis XII. of France. There was, it is true, no small noise in both about gross abuses and enormities in the government of the church, and about the universal corruption of discipline and manners: but their schemes were counteracted by the power, and eluded by the artifice of the court of Rome; and it might well be expected, that this would be ever the fate of all such designs. As piety, self-denial, purity of life, and humility were not often to be met with *there*, so they were qualifications not at all to be looked for in the Popes themselves: they had indeed, for ages past, ceased to be the qualifications of those who called themselves the successors of St. Peter.

But, perhaps, if the first reformers had proceeded more slowly, and if their demands had been more moderate, much might have been obtained even from the papal court. "When the doctrine of Luther was promulgated, they were somewhat alarmed at the sharpness of the remedy," &c. We have had occasion already to remark what it was that he first complained of, in what manner he behaved himself, how unworthily he was treated, and how suddenly the displeasure of Leo was stirred against him, and against the sentiments which he then entertained, though they were far from being subversive of his authority. His own jealousy, and that of his counsellors, was awakened, and their *offensive* zeal was roused, the efforts of which were vehement and formidable. But, through the direction of a wisdom infinitely superior to theirs, some of those means made use of to check the reformation, became subservient to its best interests.

The utter aversion of the rulers of the church from any design of reformation was further apparent, in the extreme uneasiness which they shewed at the proposal of calling a general council, in the various artifices they put in practice on this occasion, and in the reluctance with which they at last yielded to the request that had been so often renewed by the Catholic princes. When this importunity of theirs had prevailed, and a council was assembled, were they not to the utmost degree solicitous to obtain the direction of it, and to obstruct any measures of reformation that were, or that might be propounded? and was not every method contrived, and all that was within the compass of human policy practised, that could be of any influence in this matter? If we read Father Paul's history of the council of Trent, or even that other which was writ by Pallavicini, we shall find that they were so; and that the wished for success attended them.

Let me be allowed to suppose, that any one of the dignified prelates of that church, in compliance with the dictates of his conscience, had honestly resolved to exert his authority within the bounds of his own jurisdiction, for the correction of what was extremely amiss, and for promoting true Christian knowledge. Let it be further supposed, that the plan of reformation had been carried on slowly, in the most regular manner, without impugning the authority of the Pope, nay even without intending any great incroachment on the wealth and power of the clergy. Yet in the case I have now put, and notwithstanding all the moderation of this scheme, it is, I think, most probable, that this worthy man would have met with the greatest obstacles in prosecuting his resolution. Perhaps he might have been urged for some time to quit his purpose; but if he had refused to comply, the character of heretic, of an obstinate heretic, would have been affixed to him, and a condemnatory sentence pronounced, which the Catholic princes would have been incited to execute.

An imaginary case, you will be ready to say. Not altogether so, my friend. There is at least one instance of it in the annals of the sixteenth century. Herman de Wida the Elector of Cologn, in the year 1536, held a council of his suffragan bishops, in which were passed many decrees of reformation relative to discipline and manners. About seven years after, in an assembly of the nobility and clergy, he proceeded to establish articles of reformation in matters of faith and worship, without any mention of the Pope on the one hand, or of the Lutherans on the other. But his measures were not at all acceptable to the bigoted part of the laity, and were exceedingly unacceptable to most of the clergy. The good Archbishop published a manifesto, wherein he declared, that he could not abandon a cause in which the purity of religion, the glory of God, and the interests of his church were so nearly concerned; and that he had nothing to do with the sentiments of the Lutherans, or of any other persons, but with the truths of holy writ, to which his doctrines were conformable. The Pope was irritated at his steadiness, and pronounced sentence against him, declaring him an heretic; depriving him of his archbishoprick, and of all his ecclesiastical rights; absolving his subjects from their oath of fidelity; and affirming that he had incurred the censures of Leo's bull against Luther and his adherents, by embracing their opinions, which were contrary to the doctrines and rules of the church. The next thing that followed of course, was to solicit the Emperor to render this sentence effectual; who, for political reasons, declined the service for some time; but at length he set about it. The states of the province were assembled; they were ordered to swear allegiance to the person who had been heretofore coadjutor to the Archbishop: the ecclesiastics readily obeyed; but the nobility, and the deputies of the towns, were reluctant, declaring, that they would not throw off that allegiance to their prince, to which they were bound by solemn oaths. As they persisted in this sentiment and resolution, the clouds began to gather around them. But when the good old man perceived, that he could no longer promote the purpose he had so much at heart, moved with compassion for his friends, and for a people, who, on account of their affection and fidelity to him, were about to be involved in the desolations of war, he yielded to the violence of his enemies with a becoming dignity; and generously renouncing the electorate, he set all his subjects free from their bonds of allegiance. After which, he retired from the world, and spent the remainder of his days in a manner worthy of the Christian profession, and the hope of immortality.

Say then, my friend, is not all this treatment of a person of such high rank and merit most proper to confirm what I have asserted concerning the aversion of the court of Rome to any sort of change that deserved the name of *reformation?* A thorough one, they might easily perceive, would nearly affect those interests which were very dear to them; and if once a reformation was set on foot, they could not know to what a length it might proceed. That its beginnings therefore were to be withstood, they seem to have laid down as a capital rule, whose direction indeed they followed pretty uniformly. Even this illustrious prelate is proscribed, notwithstanding the mildness of his sentiments, and the moderation of his plan. So unquestionably certain is it, that every attempt of a reformation was abhorred, in whatever manner the purpose might be prosecuted.

"The Roman Pontiff," says our historian, "not armed with temporal force sufficient for his defence, was obliged to point anew all his spiritual artillery, and to propagate the doctrine of rebellion, and even of assassination, in order to subdue or terrify his enemies." And what pray is this *obligation?* Is any thing that binds the conscience to be understood by it? any thing that is derived from the principles of virtue and religion? Or rather, is it not that sort of obligation, which every ambitious and wicked tyrant has been under to maintain his usurped and oppressive power in every age of the world? that sort of obligation, which can never be pleaded in apology for the violation of the natural and acquired rights of men, or for the enormous acts of injustice and cruelty which have been any where perpetrated by the most corrupt and flagitious of the human race, in prosecution of their favourite schemes of wealth and dominion? Such is the nature of that obligation which lay upon the Roman Pontiff; and in consequence of it, the ancient system was to be retained in all its parts, and the papal monarchy to be upheld, in all its strength and wide extent of authority. But was it not an usurped authority? Were not its grounds, when they were inquired into, discovered to be extremely weak? and had not its exercise been destructive of the interests of religion and liberty, during a very long period of time? Yet it was to be upheld. And in what manner? "The Roman Pontiff – was obliged to point anew all his spiritual artillery, and to propagate the doctrine of rebellion, and even of assassination, in order to subdue or terrify his enemies." Hence indeed those "tumults of war" that were raised in some countries, particularly in France, which felt severely their dreadful effects.

"Priests jealous and provoked," adds our author, "timorous and uncontrolled, directed all the councils of that sect, and gave rise to such events as seem astonishing amid the mildness and humanity of modern manners." Well may he say so. But how cool and languid is the sentiment and expression of the next paragraph? "The massacre of Paris, that of Ireland, the murder of the two Henrys of France, the gunpowder-conspiracy in England, are memorable, though temporary instances" – of what? – "of the bigotry of that superstition." Indeed? And is this all? Are we to talk of this direful subject, as if we were speaking of some common effects of blind prejudice and foolish zeal? Is *bigotry* the characteristic of these acts of infernal wickedness; of these deeds of deliberate and detestable cruelty unknown to savage Tartars? And shall we affirm, as this author seems to do, that all those of the Roman-Catholic communion were animated by this spirit? No. In justice to truth, in justice to mankind, let it be acknowledged, that humanity itself reclaimed; and that thousands who belonged to that communion, abhorred those scenes of massacre and butchery: – "et factum execrantes, sic judicabant, nullum similis fævitiæ exemplum in tota antiquitate, evolutis gentium annalibus, reperiri." 'Tis the Presidente de Thou who speaks. He speaks of a great number of Catholics, and of the sentiments they entertained, concerning the massacre which begun in Paris, which spread from thence through all the provinces of France (*anno*1572), and in which twenty-five thousand persons are said to have perished. – "Ita plerique disputabant, sicque existimabant, facti hujus ratione nomen Gallicum olim invidia atque adeo infamia laboraturum, tantæque indignitatis posteritatem non immemorem futuram. Tunc etiam, ne quid ad summam insaniam deesset, æmulatione veterum imperatorum laus in tam detestando facinore quæsita: nam cusi nummi argentei et aurei, regique tertio non. Septembris oblati; in quorum antica parte regis in throno sedentis effigies depicta erat, cum inscriptione, *Virtus in rebelles*; in postica duæ columnæ, quod erat regis insigne, cum inscriptione, *Pietas excitavit justitiam*." – "Pietas excitavit justitiam!" – Thus it is that impious and bloody wretches have dared to profane the venerable names of *piety* and *justice*.

Our author's last paragraph relates to the court of inquisition, which he justly calls a "dreadful tribunal." And I would only further observe, on the whole of this subject, that, according to the strain of the above paragraphs, one would be apt to think, if he knew no better, that the tribunal of the inquisition, the doctrine of rebellion, and the merciless principles of persecution, together with all their shocking consequences, had been then first known in the church of Rome; and that these horrible engines of manifold desolation were then first set in motion, when the reformation was likely to prevail in many parts of Europe. But the truth is, persecution in every shape, and the doctrines of cruelty and tyranny in their full extent, had been long before that time but too well known, and, alas! but too often practised in the Christian world; more especially, after the famous decree of the Lateran council, towards the beginning of the thirteenth century, which ordained, that all heretics should be delivered into the hands of the civil magistrate, in order to their suffering that sort of death which was adjudged to heresy. Ecclesiastical domination and persecution have been always found inseparably united, and according to the growth of the former has the strength of the latter been powerfully exerted in its support.

The thunder of papal excommunication also had been often heard, and had been often terrible. In the end of the eleventh century, the Roman Pontiff began to pronounce his anathemas and sentences of deposition against monarchs, to absolve their subjects from their allegiance, and to give up their kingdoms to the spoil of the first invader. The infamous example was frequently and fully imitated in succeeding times; and almost all the western parts of Europe felt, in their turns, the consequences of this licentious tyranny. – Although the joint influence of bigotry and ignorance, of craft and power, did strongly counterwork the reformation, yet was its success great. And in consequence of its establishment in different countries, and of the principles of knowledge and liberty which it hath diffused, even those nations which compose the Roman church have their burden lightened; while the papal court finds it necessary to treat them in a manner very different from that of its ancient pretensions and exercise of paramount authority. – But this reminds me of what our author has said about the state of learning, in the age of the reformation.

"At the same time that she employed the stake and gibbet against her avowed enemies, she extended her jealousy even towards learning and philosophy, whom, in her supine security, she had formerly overlooked as harmless and inoffensive. Hence the severe check which knowledge received in Italy: hence its total extinction in Spain: and hence the slow progress which it made in France, Germany, and England. From the admiration of ancient literature, from the inquiry after new discoveries, the minds of the studious were every where turned to polemical science; and in all schools and academies, the furious controversies of theology took place of the calm disquisitions of learning."

Learning and philosophy, it seems, had been hitherto indulged; but the indulgence was now to cease. It had never, I doubt, been very extensive; and the world had never reaped much of its fruit. One thing is certain, that freedom of thought in general had been of old regarded with an evil eye by the church of Rome; and that if any one was known to embrace any tenets different from those commonly received, if he did not keep exactly within the magic circle, if he advanced but a few steps beyond it, his progress was soon checked, and himself made sensible of his danger. Such freedom of inquiry had been formerly not a little perilous; but it became so to a high degree, after the erection of the court of inquisition, whose authority was unlimited, and was so severely exercised in the southern regions of Europe. Now the date of its erection preceded the æra of the reformation by three hundred years: and it is surely unnecessary to add, (for who does not know it?), that as its settled rules of procedure are the reverse of justice and humanity, so its principal and steady aim has always been, to inforce a blind submission to the established system, to guard against all innovations, and every thing that might introduce them; by consequence, to repress all generous freedom of sentiment among men. With the goodwill of those at Rome would this tribunal have been every where erected; but happily for mankind, the design proved abortive. – "She extended her jealousy even towards learning and philosophy. – Hence the severe check which knowledge received in Italy: hence its total extinction in Spain," &c. It would have been well, if this author had informed us what was that philosophy which had been "formerly overlooked as harmless," and was now severely checked in Italy; which was heretofore known, and was now extinguished in Spain. For my own part, I never heard of any kind of philosophy in Spain that is not yet to be found there; nor of any very severe check that true philosophy met with in Italy, unless in the instance of Galileo. To say truth, in the ages preceding the reformation, and even during the sixteenth century itself, the church of Rome had not much occasion to interrupt the progress of true philosophy; for this plain reason, because what was then called by that name did not at all deserve it. No great genius had as yet arisen in Europe, to open the path of philosophy, to give a general survey of its different regions, and to disclose the right method of philosophising. This was an honour reserved to an English name; to the rich, the penetrating, and creative genius of a Bacon; from whom, and from whose age true philosophy may date at least her restoration: or, to change the metaphor, by whom the foundations of that structure were laid, which has been carried on with surprising strength and beauty, by those great master-builders that have appeared since his time, and in particular in his own country.

There is indeed a spurious kind of philosophy, which was formerly, and is to this day, reputed in the church of Rome quite "harmless and inoffensive;" the old Aristotelian system I mean; of which, together with an infusion of the subtilty of the Arabians, who revived it in Europe in the twelfth century, is made up what is called the philosophy of the schools. The voluminous commentaries too of those termed angelical and seraphic doctors, are not to be forgotten. This is the philosophy that has been much favoured, and has long flourished amongst them, without receiving any the least check or controul, so far as I remember: whose principles, such as they are, and whose dialectic art and metaphysical jargon have been so often employed in defence of a corrupt and irrational theology. This is the chimerical learning and bewildering philosophy, which, for political reasons, has not only been indulged, but all along countenanced by the Popish church. The progress of true philosophy too, in some of its branches, may be connived at in one nation, where the papal yoke is less burdensome. But the advancement of sound knowledge must be always dreaded; and its controul is truly connatural to the dark, the bigoted, and servile spirit of Popery.

The following paragraph concludes our author's speculations on this subject. "From the admiration of ancient literature, from the inquiry after new discoveries, the minds of the studious were every where turned to polemical science; and, in all schools and academies, the furious controversies of theology took place of the calm disquisitions of learning." We have just now said what sort of philosophy flourished at that time; and I would desire this historian to name but one university, any one school of learning in Europe, where any thing different was then to be found. As the knowledge of ancient literature was beginning to be revived, so the state of things made it necessary for its friends to apply much of their labour to the subordinate services of criticism and philosophy, while they endeavoured to pave the way to the study of the Greek and Roman writers. And in all the parts of this work, the Protestants very early and very largely assisted. Nay, these same "controversies of theology," with which this author is so much offended, quickened the progress of erudition; which, without them, I doubt, would have been exceedingly slow. They did, in truth, interrupt those "disquisitions of learning" which were carried on (though, by the way, not always in the calmest manner) by the ingenious professors of metaphysics, and the reverend doctors of the canon law, in their universities. What a piteous case, that they should have been roused from their peaceful lethargy! or else, obliged to quit the study of those momentous questions in which they were engaged, and to transfer their thoughts to the consideration of doctrines relative to the faith, the worship and practice of Christians! – If their debates were managed in a "furious," or even in any indecent way, – the fault was *theirs*.

Thus, my friend, have I gone through all that is contained in this remarkable passage of Mr Hume's history, (a short hint concerning the influence of learning in ancient Greece excepted); and have made such observations on it as appeared to me well founded. As you will, by this time, pretty fully know them, it is unnecessary for me any further to declare, what are my sentiments about the strain of the narrative, the history of facts, the exhibition of characters, the oblique hints, the reasonings, and conclusions which we find in it. The subject is of importance: his misrepresentations, I think, are gross: and my remarks are before you.

   – After all this attention to church-history, I shall leave you to relax yourself for some time in studies of a more agreeable kind, and shall take my leave with subscribing myself, &c.

LETTER VI.

The revival of learning in Europe had surely great influence in diffusing the knowledge of true religion: but the friends of ancient superstition were not a little solicitous to weaken this influence and to defeat the purpose of the reformation. The same zeal hath been ever since exerted in Popish countries; where, as I had occasion already to observe, too many things concur to maintain the empire of ignorance and bigotry over the minds of multitudes. In like manner, a variety of circumstances concurred of old, in the Heathen world, for the support of idolatry, which prevailed in the civilized nations, no less than in those uncultivated by arts and letters. The public religion and the civil polity both of the Greeks and Romans were closely united, and formed a system whose several parts had a mutual dependence on each other. The principles and practice of idolatry obtained every where; neither could the doctrines of philosophy produce any important change: another and higher interposition was requisite, and was in due time afforded.

I have said, in the close of my last letter, that in one of our author's paragraphs, there was a hint at the influence of philosophy in ancient Greece, which I have not yet considered. We find it in the passage following. "It might have been hoped, that learning and knowledge, as of old in Greece, stealing in gradually, would have opened the eyes of men, and corrected such of the ecclesiastical abuses as were the grossest and most burdensome." To render the parallel complete, he should have told us, what were those "burdensome abuses that were corrected of old in Greece," by the gradual introduction of learning; and who were the persons among the Heathen priests that exercised a civil tyranny, and laid claim to an "exorbitant power," in that country; whether, for instance, the high priest of Jupiter at Elis, or some one of his brethren elsewhere. The subject of which he treats, and the whole train of his ideas, would naturally lead our thoughts to such inquiries; but we may soon perceive that all this is an imaginary scene. We are therefore obliged to conclude that something else is intended: and indeed he seems to me to affirm, that when learning spread through Greece, the folly of idolatry was discovered, and its empire broken; and that it was reasonable to look for a similar effect from a similar cause, in relation to the gross superstitions of Popery. But then you will observe, that a more enlarged view of the reformation is thus opened to us, than our author is willing to give in his general description of it; a view which is not confined to the redress of ecclesiastical abuses, and the repression of papal domination, but which reaches to the concerns of faith and religion.

Now, though it is not essential to the general purpose of these letters, you will give me leave to enter a little into this subject, and to inquire into the influence of philosophy upon the established religion of Greece: a digression, I hope, which will not be unentertaining.

In this research we need not go higher than the age of Pythagoras; as before his time philosophy was but little known in Greece. That nation had received from Syria and Egypt the system of idolatry; which, by their additions and various infusions, became still more perplexed and irrational. The original scheme contained in it the worship of sun, moon, and stars; and to this they superadded the worship of their deceased lawgivers and princes, whom they called heroes. Some of these were honoured with the names of this and the other deified part of nature. The stories of the former were mingled with the operations of the latter. Thus were they blended in the writings of the poets; and all this medley composed the popular religion of the Greeks. The knowledge of the ancient system was probably preserved in the Eleusinian and Samothracian mysteries; but this was a recondite theology, known only to a few, while others blindly revered the public tenets and rites of superstition. It was impossible, that they who merited the name of philosophers, should approve of these in their own thoughts, however they might decline to express their dissent and displeasure. Besides, even but a slight regard to virtue must have rendered them averse from those doctrines and tales, by which vice in its different forms was countenanced and patronised. But the whole scheme was highly acceptable to the gross understandings and corrupt passions of men, whilst, through all this chaos of deplorable ignorance, philosophy shed but a glimmering and feeble light.

Many excellent things are to be met with in the Pythagoric doctrine and precepts. At present we have to do only with the tenets which concern religion. It is disputed, whether this philosopher held matter to be an eternal principle; but that he ascribed the formation of the world to the self-existent God, the Lord of earth and heaven, is beyond all dispute. He likewise professed his belief of subordinate deities, to whom he injoined religious worship to be paid. "The supreme God," says one of his disciples, "is not to be perceived by sight, but by mind alone: yet his works, and the effects of his energy, may be discerned and felt by all mankind. There is indeed one God most high, who ruleth over all: and many other gods besides subordinate to him, who is their Lord, and is supreme in power, majesty, and moral excellence." [12] This also is the doctrine of Timæus Locrus, who thus expresses himself. "By mind alone can we discern the eternal God, the Lord and Father of all things; and with our bodily eyes we see his works, this world, and all its parts." He proceeds to speak of the sun, moon, earth, and stars; and concludes with asserting, that the government of the universe is carried on by the inferior deities in subordination to him, who is the supreme and almighty Lord. [13]

---

[12] [Greek quotation removed.] Onatus ap. Stobæum, lib. 1.

[13] [Greek quotation removed.] Timæus Locrus de anima mundi.

Accordingly, the first direction that is given in the golden verses of Pythagoras, relates to the worship of the immortal gods and heroes.[14]

Anaxagoras, who was of the Ionic sect, seems to have entertained very different thoughts, while he spoke of the self-existent God as the creator and governor of the world, without mentioning either celestial or terrestrial gods. But on this account he was charged with Atheism; and neither his own great character, nor the power of Pericles could save him from the resentment of the Athenians, who imposed on him a fine, and pronounced a sentence of banishment against him.[15]

They went further, you know, in the case of Socrates. That eminent person shewed his zeal at all times against the principles of irreligion. His two illustrious disciples, Plato and Xenophon, have fully opened this part of his character. How beautiful, for instance, is his discourse with Aristodemus in the writings of Xenophon? He leads him on gradually to the acknowledgment of a Deity, and a providence, by setting before him the marks of divine wisdom, goodness, and power, impressed on all his works; and which may be particularly discerned in the structure of the human body, and in the use and arrangement of its various senses and members. He goes on to speak of the soul and its faculties; the attentive consideration of which naturally directs our thoughts upwards to the source of all intelligence and wisdom. But the supreme God is unrevealed to mortal eye, and we do not see the ministers of his providence; –

"neither do we see these souls of ours, which animate our bodies, and whose agency we feel every moment. Learn therefore," adds he, "that as your mind directs the motions of the body according to its pleasure, so the sovereign wisdom, which presides over the world, regulates all things therein, according to its counsels. If your eye can reach to objects at a great distance, why will you not allow that the eye of God can reach at once through the whole creation? As you can attend to the concerns of the Greeks both at home and abroad, may you not well admit, that the wisdom of God is abundantly sufficient to take care of all things in this great universe? If you follow after piety, you shall soon be persuaded, that such plenitude of perfection belongs to the Divinity, as that he sees all things, hears all things, is present in all places, and superintendeth all events."[16]

These doubtless are rational and worthy sentiments, which he uniformly inculcated. Xenophon tells us, that he was present at a conversation of his with

---

[14] [Greek quotation removed.] Aur. carm.

[15] Diog. Laert. in vita Anaxag. – Plutarch in Pericle. – Plat. de leg. lib. 10. – Epin. p. 1010.

[16] [Greek quotation removed.] Xen. mem. Socr. lib 1.

one Euthydemus, in which he laboured to establish the truth of divine providence. He set before him the various effects of heavenly bounty in the vicissitude of day and night, in the regular return of seasons, in the destination of animals to the use of man, in our being formed for society and its pleasing intercourse; and, in general, from the survey of the effects of goodness and wisdom he would raise his mind to the contemplation of the original Author. He then speaks of subordinate deities, and of the honour and worship to be paid them. "They," adds he,

> "are our benefactors, though we see them not; and he who framed, and who maintains the mundane system in its harmonious order, is visible in his administration, though in his essence unseen. Even the sun, who appears conspicuous to all, will not permit us steadily to gaze upon his light. – The human mind, which has in it something divine, and whose energy we experience, is in itself invisible: thus also with regard to wind and thunder, whose amazing force we plainly perceive. And if one considers all this attentively, he will not be apt to disregard those things which are unseen; but, by the sensible effects of power and goodness, will be excited to the acknowledgment and worship of Deity."[17]

This is the train of his reasoning; and thus did he inculcate the fundamental truths of religion on the minds of those with whom he conversed. Neither were his ideas of the divine government confined to this life; they reached forward to a future state of rewards and punishments. That the soul survived the dissolution of the body, and would enter into that state after death, was a point on which he laid great stress: and he endeavoured to confirm it by a variety of arguments deduced from the nature of the soul, from the perfections of God, and from the justice and benignity of his administration. His sentiments on morals are well known; on justice, temperance, honesty, benevolence, and, in general, on the virtues and duties of the social life. And let it be remarked by the way, that the principles of piety not only entered into his system of morals, but were closely interwoven with its several branches. There indeed we find no such unnatural disjunction of virtue and religion, as is to be seen in certain schemes of philosophy published, heretofore and of late, for the instruction of the Christian world, and which, in many instances, fall far below the standard of Pagan morals.

It is plain too, that Socrates was extremely offended at the ancient poets, on account of their monstrous tales concerning their gods, which were so favourably received by the multitude, and on which so many public rites of superstition had been grafted. He frequently and openly declared his opinion

---

[17] [Greek quotation removed.] Id. lib. 4.

on this subject; and thereby gave his adversaries an advantage against him, which they failed not to improve. It must however be acknowledged, that he did not reject the notion of subordinate deities; or rather, that he warmly adhered to it. This is every where manifest in the writings of Xenophon and Plato. As to the gods whose worship was publicly established, he certainly had opinions very different from those of poetic tradition, and popular belief. But it is likewise true, that he joined in their worship according to its prescribed rites, and recommended the same practice to his friends; approving the oracle of the Pythian Apollo, which ordains the gods to be honoured in the manner appointed by the law of the country.[18] Let us suspend our reflections for a little, till we have spoken of his disciple Plato, who gave name to the most celebrated sect of philosophy among the Greeks.

His general principles of theology were the same with those now mentioned. He appears anxious to support the essential articles of natural religion, and with just ardor does he every where declare against the tenets of impiety. When we attend to many passages which relate to the existence, the perfections, the providence, and government of God, we must allow, that in them he has thought and spoke worthily of these exalted themes. The existence of a first and intelligent cause is proved from the frame of nature, from the passive inactivity of matter, from the astonishing effects of consummate wisdom and power discernible through all his works, from the nature of the human mind, and from the consent of all nations to this fundamental truth.[19] His ideas of the divine excellency may be seen in the following expressions.

"It can be said only of God, that he is wise. – He is the sovereign of heaven and earth. – The maker and father of the universe, – who gave being to the earth, the heavens, and all things in the visible and invisible regions. – The eternal God. – Almighty. – Perfect in knowledge and wisdom, – by whose will and power, all nature, even the highest order of beings, is upheld. – Just. – Good – Good in the highest degree. – The source of all good, – and for whom are all things."[20]

In the dialogue intitled *Timæus*, he speaks of the generation of this world, and of its having been raised out of a chaos; of that goodness which prompted the Deity to call it into being; and of the glorious exertion of his power and

[18] [Greek quotations removed.] Xenoph. Apol. Soc. ... Id. lib. 1.

[19] Plat. Philebus, p. 381. ed. Ficini. – Epinomis, p. 1009. – Repub. lib. 7. p. 702. – De leg. lib. 10. p. 945.-951. – De leg. lib. 12. p. 998, 99. Et alibi.

[20] [Greek quotations removed.] Pædrus, p. 1243. ... Phileb. p. 381. ... Tim p. 1047. ... Rep. lib 10. p. 749 ... Cratyl. p. 283. ... Rep. lib 7. p. 702 ...Epin. p. 1011. ... Tim. p. 1054. ... Tim. p. 1047. Rep. lib. 2. p. 605. Epin. p. 1006. Ep. 2. ... Ib. et Epin. 1011.

wisdom in its production, and in the arrangement of all its parts, according to the perfect plan which he had formed. He goes on to represent the world as animated, and to talk of superior intelligences, which are supposed to have been employed as ministers to the supreme, in some portions of the workmanship of nature: and on him they are absolutely dependent.

There are many noble passages in his works relative to the divine government. Mankind is considered as in a degenerate state. – Plato's doctrine concerning the pre-existence of souls is known to all. – The individuals of our race are regarded as intelligent creatures, subjects of moral government, capable of virtue and vice, not bound up by fate or strong necessity, but endowed with a freedom of will or power of choice; and therefore, who are accountable for all their actions, and may expect a proper retribution from the wise, the just, and good ruler of the universe. They may behave extremely amiss, and may be sometimes apt to impute their sins and their misery to him: but God is not in blame; they themselves are the guilty authors of their wickedness and ruin. From punishment, either in this or the future state, they cannot possibly escape. The wicked and unholy are unlike to God; they turn aside from the divine law, are disapproved and abandoned by him, and shall receive a punishment proportionable to the demerit of their crimes. – Not only is moral evil acknowledged, but its prevalence is lamented: the liberty of the human will, the good and bad desert of actions is affirmed, and the governing justice of the Deity is asserted, who in all his counsels and ways has ever the wisest and best ends in view.[21]

These, if I am not mistaken, are the genuine sentiments of Plato; and they were employed not only to dissuade and deter from a vitious, but likewise to recommend and enforce a virtuous conduct. It is but natural that the friends of virtue should be the friends of religion; upon whose principles the strictest and fullest moral obligation is established, and from whence too are derived motives the best adapted to operate upon the hopes and fears of mankind.

After all it must be owned, though with pain, that this philosopher embraced the scheme of subordinate gods. He speaks every where of sun, moon, and stars, as animated, and of the worship due to them; whilst he is much displeased with Anaxagoras, who was not of his sentiments in this matter.[22] He proceeds a step further, and injoins the worship of ethereal demons, who are considered as beings of inferior dignity, who attend to the actions and preside over the concerns of men; to whom therefore prayers, sacrifices, and thanksgivings were to be offered. And this worship, in its full extent, is admitted into his speculative plan of a well-constituted republic. Nay, he there appoints, that each day in the year should be dedicated to one or other of the celestial gods, or

---

[21] [Greek quotations removed.] De rep. lib. 10. p. 763. ... Ib. p. 764. ... But the proud, the ambitious, and the sensual man ... De leg. lib. 4. p. 831.

[22] De leg. lib. 10. P. 946. Epin. P. 210. Apol. Soc. P. 21.

ethereal and terrestrial demons; to whom sacrifices were to be daily presented by the magistrate, who was to pray for himself, his citizens, and the interests of the state.

Now, the result of all this is plainly no other, than that the doctrines of this philosophy, which, upon the whole, was the best that ever the Greeks knew, were not at all unfavourable to idolatry and superstition; on the contrary, they tended to maintain them. True indeed, that it despised the stories of the poets, that it abhorred their literal sense, and would have them considered either as false and foolish, or as the corruptions of ancient mythology; but the general principles were espoused, on which the system of idolatry was founded.

It has been often said, that the light of philosophy could be but of little effect on the national religion of the Greeks; because whatever might be their opinions, yet the philosophers did not much differ from others in their practice, and complied with all public rites. The reasoning is good, but the facts are not stated, as I think, with sufficient precision; and the characters of these men are, in one respect, more exposed to censure than they seem to deserve. Had they been of opinion, that it was folly to talk of celestial and ethereal deities, and of erecting temples and offering up to them prayers and sacrifices, undoubtedly their compliance with the religion of their country in its external forms, would have been, in that case, downright hypocrisy. And whilst some imputed this behaviour of theirs to pusillanimity, as though they had been afraid to avow the truth; others, willing to judge more mildly, might have ascribed it to a general reverence of religion, and the laws of their country, mingled with a persuasion that the vulgar were not susceptible of a more pure and rational model of worship. But, in my apprehension, this imputation, and this apology, have been carried a great deal too far. Socrates, Xenophon, Plato, and all the disciples of the Socratic or Platonic school, gave their assent to the doctrine of inferior gods, and thought worship due to them, according to their several degrees of dignity and beneficence. They professed this opinion; and they did so without the least degree of dissimulation. As to the worship of ethereal demons, and terrestrial gods, (the souls of men departed, who had been princes and lawgivers); they were certainly highly shocked at the fables of Orpheus, Homer, and Hesiod, concerning them; which they considered not only as unseemly and absurd, but as of the most pernicious influence on the morals of those who unhappily entertained them. They wished for a proper correction of these; and that nothing mean, unjust, exorbitant, or cruel, should be imputed to those beings who were the objects of their veneration. This was the change at which they aimed; and if this had been obtained, they would not have been displeased, in all appearance, with the remaining idolatrous fabric. Some of them possibly kept off from those particular ceremonies which were grounded on the literal meaning of fabulous story; and perhaps, in the worship of their national gods, they affixed to them ideas and characters quite different from those which were framed and received by the bulk of mankind: but still they cannot, I doubt, be entirely acquitted of dissimulation in their compliance with established rites. How far this may admit of an apology, from what has been mentioned above, I shall not now inquire. One thing is certain, that from these principles, and this practice, no great change in the frame of their national religion was to be expected. It had been all along interwoven with their civil polity; its antiquity spread around it an air of reverence; it was adapted to the superstitious bias of the minds of men; was highly recommended by its splendid ceremonies and numerous festivals; and was further guarded by the authority and sanctions of their laws. For even these Greeks, with all their noble sense of liberty, and at that period of time in which they had the warmest sense of it, would not however suffer anyone to condemn the public system; and far less, openly to spread the tenets of Atheism; or if he ventured to do so, it was at his extreme peril.

All these things considered, it would seem most probable, that although the doctrines of philosophy had been, what they cannot be said to have been, of the purest kind, yet they would have produced no considerable change in the general state of religion. Need I say how ineffectual its precepts were for the reformation of a corrupt world? On many accounts they were not, they could not be of much influence here. But what no human means could possibly do, was effected by the interposition of heaven, and by the light and grace of Christianity. By these was the rule of ignorance and idolatry overthrown: by means of these was an unexpected, a salutary and important change produced; while multitudes in different regions became the willing subjects of the kingdom of truth and righteousness: so mightily grew the word of God, and prevailed; and by its blissful effects, and marvellous progress, was its heavenly original ascertained. – But to return. – Having said so much of the Platonic, I need not spend many words about the Aristotelian, and the Stoical philosophy; to both which what has been now observed, is fully applicable. The Stoics, in particular, laboured to affix the mythological sense to the tales concerning Saturn, Jupiter, Neptune, and the rest of their gods, as though these were expressive of the relations, energies, and mutual dependence of the several parts of nature. In this allegorical manner did they explain them; and with this correction the system of polytheism was perfectly consonant to the principles of their theology.

But there is another sect of philosophy that has not been yet mentioned, whose prevalence was likely to overturn that system. "It might have been hoped, that learning and knowledge, as of old in Greece, stealing in gradually, would have opened the eyes of men, and corrected," &c. I am unwilling to think, that our historian had his eye upon that particular sect at which I now point; as indeed it would appear ridiculous for one to speak of the introduction of "learning and knowledge," and to mean the gradual progress of the Epicurean philosophy, or the scheme of Atheism. The dreaming dotage of Democritus, from whom Epicurus derived his monstrous plan, had been formerly arraigned by true philosophy, and condemned as equally irrational and impious. Self-existent matter fortuitously moved, – hence the entire separation of some of its parts, and the endless combination of the rest, – and from all the inconceivable medley this universe *somehow* broke forth in its glorious form and perfect order, not by the energy and direction of mind and counsel, but by the operations of nature and chance. – This is the short view which Plato gives of that scheme, in his tenth book of laws. And is this what one would call an account of the origin of this great world? a philosophical account of the birth of nature? And could one gravely pour out such miserable stuff, and dignify it with the name of philosophy? What an insult on the human understanding! Fortuitous motions, secretions, combinations – Uniformity, beauty, and order, springing up, one does not know *how* nor *why*: If this is sense and philosophy, what then is extravagance and folly? "Does he merit the name of man, who, after having viewed the stated and invariable motions of the heavens, the regular arrangements of the stars, and the nice connection and harmony which reign throughout the universe, shall notwithstanding maintain, that all this is the effect of blind chance, and not the work of reason; though the wisdom by which they are conducted, far exceeds the power of the human mind to comprehend?"[23] The Roman philosopher, who speaks in the name of Balbus the Stoic, in the passage referred to, goes on to refute the impious scheme, and to urge the irrefragable proofs of divine wisdom and providence.

The very name of philosophy is disgraced, when those persons pretend to be her disciples, whose avowed tenets are not only subversive of the first principles of reason, but lead to the extinction of all religion, and spread a mournful gloom over the mind of man, and indeed over the whole face of nature. The corruption of mankind is great: yet the atheistical principle cannot prevail. There is something in the human soul which strongly opposes its entrance: it has always been, and ever will be so. Thus it was even amidst all the dismal darkness of the Heathen world; and I doubt whether it be possible to destroy the *innate feeling*. It may be weakened, but cannot, I believe, be extirpated. At any rate, upon supposition that the Epicurean or irreligious scheme had prevailed amongst the Greeks, we could only have deplored their wretched state, who had rushed from one extreme into another, from idolatry and superstition into the still more absurd tenets, and melancholy prospects of Atheism. But this must have been in consequence of the extinction of all true learning and wisdom, whose conclusions must be ever favourable to the grand truths and interests of religion. And with these truths and interests the doctrine and practice of sound morals are intimately connected: they stand or fall together.

---

[23] "Quis enim hunc hominem dixerit, qui cum tam certos cœli motus, tam ratos astrorum ordines, tamque omnia inter se connexa et apta viderit, neget in his ullam inesse rationem, eaque casu fieri dicat, qua quantoconsilio gerantur, nullo consilio assequi possumus?" *Cic. de nat. deor. lib.* 2. The sense of this passage is expressed in the words of a late translation.

It was heretofore observed by Plato, that the irreligious plan was peculiarly acceptable to men of profligate manners, whose vitious and debauched disposi- tions powerfully stimulated them to embrace it.[24] From this quarter indeed has its highest recommendation been all along derived, as libertine principles will always give full indulgence to licentious morals. The confederacy is of ancient date, and it still subsists. – When there is a strong bias in the soul to one side of a question, even a slight difficulty may be made to assume the form of an important objection. A few of these put together, and frequently reviewed, will still more darken the subject, till at length the mind may be unhappily seduced into such a state of uncertainty, even as to the plainest and most momentous truths, as shall be, in its nature and effects, but little different from the total rejection of them. Purity of manners in some degree, together with a sincere love of truth, and a diligent attention to it, were qualifications required of the disciples in the Pythagoric and Platonic schools, by their illustrious founders; for they well judged, that the opposite character and temper were inconsistent with the right study of religion and morality. Happy they, whose aims are wise and good, and whose researches are properly conducted. May this happiness, my friend, be ours. Our holy religion invites to a free and full, but let it be likewise an unprejudiced and candid inquiry. It cannot surely be expected, that less should be required of us, than was required of those who purposed of old to enter upon the study of philosophy: and we are assured, from the highest authority, that the best prepar- ative for the knowledge of religious truth, is an upright desire of conformity to its dictates. True religion also must ever disclaim an alliance with ignorance and implicit belief. These may be made use of as the pillars of idolatry and super- stition; and too long did they uphold the unwieldy fabric in the Christian church. The Protestant faith, in distinction from the Popish scheme, would lean on no such support: on the contrary, as it is grounded on the right of private judgment, so it tends to advance the interests of truth and learning in the world. And as that which formerly deserved the name of philosophy, may be considered as a mean betwixt the system of impiety and that of gross popular superstition; so the Protestant faith interposes betwixt the manifold corruptions of true religion in the Popish plan on the one hand, and the uncomfortable and unnatural principles of infidelity on the other. If we consider things in this light, we shall have no improper view of the reformed religion; and at the same time, several reflections will readily occur, that are little honourable either to the partisans of Popery, or to the friends and patrons of modern infidelity.

I am, &c.
Quotations that refer to p. 165. –176.[25]

---

[24] [Greek quotation removed.] De leg. lib. 10. p. 945. et alibi.

[25] [Greek quotations removed.]

Xen. mem. Socr. lib. 1. ... Id. lib. 4. ... De repub. lib. 10. p. 760. et De leg. lib. 5. p. 842. ... Phædo, p. 84. ... Gorg. p. 356. ... Epin.p. 1003. Hip. maj. p. 1255. ... De rep. lib. 2. p. 605. These passages (and there are many to the same purpose) have a plain and determinate meaning; according to which some others that are difficult and intricate ought to be explained. ... Epin. p. 1010. Conviv. p. 1194. De leg. lib. 4. p. 832. ... De leg. lib. 4. p. 832. ... Ib. et lib. 11. p. 975. ... De leg. lib. 8. p. 905. ... De leg. lib. 7. p. 901.

LETTER VII.

You are pleased to express a particular desire to have my sentiments upon what Mr HUME has affirmed concerning the different denominations of Protestants, and concerning the tumults of war in the sixteenth century. This, my friend, would lead us into a wide field of history and reasoning: you must therefore be so good as to accept of a few remarks on some things most considerable.

"The Protestants," says this author, "carried the tumults of war through every part of Christendom." A formidable charge indeed, if it were well founded. But were they really so fond of the Mahometan principle, and so universally prone to propagate religion by force of arms? If we take but a transient survey of the history of the sixteenth century, we shall soon perceive what answer is to be made to this question, and what we are to think of the above assertion. – Into England, Denmark, Sweden, and some electorates and principalities of Germany, the reformation was introduced with the full concurrence of the princes of these several states, which felt no violent internal convulsions arising from it. In Scotland the nobility and barons were obliged to enter into a bond of association for mutual defence in 1558; and after a state of confusion for about two years, the Popish religion was suppressed by acts of parliament.

The Low countries were long the seat of a desolating war: but was it not kindled by the tyranny of Phillip II. of Spain, who meant to despoil these provinces of their ancient rights, to reduce them into a state of servitude, nay further, to subject them to the dreadful authority of the inquisition? The Catholics and Protestants joined together in defence of their rights, which were about to be wrested from them, and in opposition to the plan of civil and ecclesiastical despotism that was mediated against them. In the progress of the war seven of the provinces embraced the profession of the Protestant religion, and formed themselves into an united state. England and France supported by turns the interests of the rising republic.

If we consider the characters of the Emperor Charles V. and of Francis I. the former of which monarchs could not bear a rival, nor the latter a superior in power; and if we reflect on their jealousy and hatred of each other, we can be at no loss to discover the true causes of those great wars which were carried on, during almost the whole course of their lives. As they adhered to the Roman-Catholic communion, the disputes about the reformation could have but little influence on their quarrel. The Protestant princes of Germany were indeed, sometimes, in no small danger of being overwhelmed by the power of the Emperor. This power was once and again very strenuously exerted against them, particularly in the year 1547, when that illustrious prince Frederick the Elector of Saxony was taken prisoner in a decisive battle, which he lost. His dominions were torn from him, and transferred to his cousin Maurice; and after his death, to Maurice's brother Augustus, whose descendents have ever since retained that electorate; the duchy of Saxe-Gotha being assigned to Frederick's family, which has in this age blessed the British isles with a princess universally esteemed, and of the most distinguished merit. But though Charles the Emperor so far prevailed against this *magnanimous* prince and his allies, yet his general scheme was frustrated; and in a few years after, he was pleased to enter into terms of peace with the Protestants. As they acted upon the defensive, the "tumults of war" cannot justly be imputed to them.

It will not, I think, be denied by those who attentively review the history of France, during the latter half of the sixteenth century, that the dreadful cruelty of the Catholics, the daring ambition of the house of Guise, the violent contentions for power betwixt them and the princes of the blood, and the crafty designs of Philip upon that crown, were, in truth, the chief causes of those destructive wars which raged in that kingdom. The massacre of Vitri, and afterwards the more horrible one of Paris, ushered in their civil wars; which, after some intermission, broke out again with greater fury upon the assassination of Henry III. The Protestants of that country unanimously concurred in supporting the right of Henry IV. and bore a large share in the dangers and toils of the unequal war, which that gallant prince sustained against his numerous and powerful enemies, who were united against him in what was called the holy league, at the head of which was the ambitious and bigoted monarch of Spain. Henry's gratitude towards the Protestants of his kingdom was expressed in his granting them the famous edict of Nantz, and in the public toleration which was by it afforded to all of that communion; which edict of his, ratified in the most solemn manner, was basely violated by his grandson Lewis XIV. The remarkable circumstances of outrage and cruelty which accompanied the repeal of this edict, might have furnished out to our author another of those "memorable, though temporary instances of the bigotry of the Romish superstition," which may "seem astonishing amid the mildness and humanity of modern manners;" and the more astonishing, as it is a late instance, and to be met with in a voluptuous court, where the utmost refinement of modern manners was affected. – "The doctrines of peace," and "the tumults of war," form a pretty antithesis enough; but unhappily the assertion in that paragraph is not at all consistent with historical truth.

I am far from being inclined to meddle with those particular points, by which the different denominations of Protestants are distinguished from each other. Neither would it be proper to enter upon the consideration of these, in our animadversions on this writer. It is his manner, to comprise his "enlarged sentiments" of things in a few general propositions and distinctions, which, when they are ingeniously applied, are thought sufficient to reflect a new light on every subject he treats. We may therefore well expect to meet with something of this kind in his accounting for the different sentiments and practice of Protestants, with respect to ceremonies, an established liturgy, and the form of church-government. *Enthusiasm* and *superstition*, these favourite terms, are again pressed into the service. They had been heretofore made use of for fixing a characteristical mark of distinction upon the Roman-Catholic and Protestant churches; and we had been told, that "these two species of religion, the superstitious and fanatical, stand in diametrical opposition to each other." That he should talk of higher and lower degrees of fanaticism, when he has occasion, or takes occasion to speak of the reformed churches, is quite consistent with all this: and it is sometimes his style. – "The more fanatical churches.[26] – As the Lutheran establishments were subjected to Episcopal jurisdiction, their fanatical genius gradually decayed.[27] – The spirit of enthusiasm was somewhat tempered by a sense of order;"[28] and so in other passages. But how does it come about, that this "fanatical genius" should be represented, at other times, as in alliance with that which is said to be "diametrically opposite" to it? In describing "the genius of the church of England," he speaks of its affinity to the tame superstition of the Catholics."[29] – "The English church," says he, in another place, "had retained a share of Popish superstition;"[30] again, Popery and Prelacy, alone, whose genius verged towards superstition, the Independents were inclined to treat with rigor."[31] And concerning Archbishop Laud, he thus expresses himself. "It must be confessed, that though Laud deserved not the appellation of Papist, the genius of his religion was, though in a less degree, yet the same with that of the Romish."[32] Whether these things are true or false, is not the present question; but whether such sentiments and expressions are consistent with what he has affirmed in

[26] Page 8.

[27] Page 40.

[28] Page 8.

[29] Page 81.

[30] Page 396.

[31] Page 382.

[32] Page 201.

relation to the stated distinction betwixt the Protestant and Popish churches, and the direct opposition of fanaticism to superstition.

However, in consequence of this supposed affinity to Catholic superstition, he represents the church of England as well inclined to the plan of arbitrary power, and ever favourable to it. Is this indeed the truth; and is this general position verified in history? Is there no distinction to be made, betwixt defending certain prerogatives of the crown, and the giving up all the rights of a great nation into the hands of an arbitrary monarch? Are the excesses of the members of that communion in past times, and the bigoted prejudices of too many in the present age to be imputed to all? And is an inseparable connection to be established betwixt two points that are in themselves manifestly distinct? Is it not possible for one to believe that Episcopacy is of apostolical institution, without declaring, at the same time, his implicit submission to all that a bishop dictates, or that a monarch, who approves that government, prescribes? And will the wise and moderate of that communion, – will any of them, who are friends to the interests of liberty and the British constitution, be well pleased with our author's speculations on this subject? In speaking of the arbitrary measures of James I.

> "The same alliance," says he, "which has ever prevailed betwixt kingly power and ecclesiastical authority, was now fully established in England; and while the prince assisted the clergy in suppressing schismatics and innovators, the clergy, in return, inculcated the doctrine of an unreserved submission and obedience to the civil magistrate. The genius of the church of England, so kindly to monarchy, forwarded the confederacy; its submission to Episcopal jurisdiction; its attachment to ceremonies, to order, and to a decent pomp and splendor of worship; and, in a word, its affinity to the tame superstition of the Catholics, rather than to the wild fanaticism of the Puritans."[33]

To the honour of that church let it be ever remembered by all Protestants, that in extremely difficult and dangerous times, many of its most distinguished members confuted this doctrine by their practice; and made a noble stand for our religious and civil rights, in opposition to the bold incroachments of Popery, and the daring efforts of arbitrary power. While some maintained the cause of the Protestant religion in writings which give a lustre to their names, and with such sense and sound learning as their adversaries could not withstand; others were active in concerting and pursuing proper measures for saving the nation from that complicated ruin which was impending over it. Happily for us, happily for the concerns of religion and liberty in the British islands, their generous endeavours were crowned with success. And ever since

---

[33] Id. p.81.

the memorable æra of the revolution, they who have approved themselves the best friends of the church of England, have acted in support of a free constitution, or of a limited monarchy.

Is it not also well known, that the Presbyterians in Scotland have zealously concurred in the same noble aim, and have steadily adhered to it? Determined enemies of despotism, I will admit, they have always been, and I hope will ever be; but hearty friends to the Protestant succession, to the present establishment, to the mildest and best government that ever was known in these islands. They have shewn themselves its friends in circumstances of peculiar danger; their avowed principles must lead them to such a conduct; and were it not for this, many of those, perhaps, who now bear them no extraordinary good-will, would be affected towards them in a very different manner.

But let us next consider what Mr HUME has remarked concerning the erection of the different forms of church government in Protestant countries.

"In the electorates of Germany, in Denmark, and in Sweden, where the monarch was early converted, and, by putting himself at the head of the reformers, acquired authority amongst them; as the spirit of enthusiasm was somewhat tempered by a sense of order, Episcopal jurisdiction, along with a few decent ceremonies, was preserved in the new establishment. In Switzerland and Geneva, which were popular governments; in France, Scotland, and the Low Countries, where the people reformed themselves in opposition to the prince, the genius of fanaticism displayed itself in its full extent, and affected every circumstance of discipline and worship. A perfect equality was established among the ecclesiastics; and their inflamed imagination unconfined by any forms of liturgy," &c.[34]

It is somewhat unlucky that he has not been sufficiently exact in his inquiry into facts, ere he proceeded to his speculations about them; as a mistake in point of fact has often produced a very remarkable error in speculation. Was it indeed the case, that in all those countries where the princes embraced and promoted the reformation, Episcopal jurisdiction and a public liturgy were established; while in others the Presbyterian government, without a liturgy, prevailed? In the Palatinate, in Brandenburg, and the principality of Hesse, not to mention states of inferior note in Germany, where the princes "put themselves at the head of the reformers," the ecclesiastical government was carried on by presbyters and superintendents. The latter had certain degrees of power, and a general inspection of ecclesiastical affairs assigned to them; but without the idea of a distinction or superiority of order. If our author should tell us, that this is a sort of Episcopal jurisdiction sufficient for his purpose, it

[34] P. 8.

may be granted for once; but then let it be remembered, that superintendents were in like manner established elsewhere among Presbyterians, particularly in Scotland, immediately after the reformation. But if it is his opinion, that super-intendents, and their precarious jurisdiction, are very different from bishops, and their settled authority; then what becomes of his assertion concerning the establishment of Episcopal jurisdiction in those countries where the princes declared for the Protestant religion? In either way, you see, we meet with no inconsiderable mistake. – And might not princes have had different views of this matter in a political light, as well as the clergy had in a religious one, when they formed their opinions about it? The debate itself turns chiefly upon the resolution of two questions, in point of fact; namely, Whether there is a clear distinction in scripture betwixt bishop and presbyter? and, Whether diocesan episcopacy obtained in the apostolic age, and therefore may be concluded to be of apostolic institution? And may not a man of the coolest head determine for the negative side of both these questions? Even the reformers in England did so determine as to the first of them. These worthy men entertained sentiments in relation to ecclesiastical government not a little different from those which began to be espoused about the end of James's reign, and were afterwards zealously maintained by Archbishop Laud and his friends. Our author himself, it would appear, has thought it worth while to inquire into this subject; and, which is somewhat extraordinary, his opinion is favourable to their principles, against whom he seems to have been heated, and upon whom he pours out such reproachful terms through the whole of his history. "The hierarchy," he tells us,

> "had been established in England ever since the reformation: the Romish church, in all ages, had carefully maintained that form of ecclesiastical government: The antient fathers too bore testimony to Episcopal juris-diction: And tho' parity seems at first to have had place among Christian pastors, the period, during which it prevailed, was so short, that few undisputed traces of it remained in history. The bishops and their more zealous partisans inferred thence the divine indefeizable right of prelacy: Others regarded that institution as venerable and useful."[35]

You see then to whose sentiments he inclines; and I dare say none will suspect that he was led to this opinion by any the least influence of enthusiasm.

It might be likewise observed, with respect to public liturgies, or forms of prayer, that they were, in some measure, to be found in other countries, as well as in those where the monarch concurred with the reformation; nay as much in them, as in most of the German states; and that even where established forms

---

[35] Mr Hume's history, p. 251.

were in use, yet the ministers of religion were not entirely restrained from prayers of their own composure, in their public ministrations, far less in their discharging the private duties of their office. But I am averse from entering far into the consideration of these matters of less importance, which found the distinction between the two denominations of Protestants. Neither would this be at all proper, (I repeat it,) in one's animadversions upon this historian, who surely will not be chosen umpire betwixt them. They differ in their sentiments about points which are far removed from the essentials of religion; and genuine Christianity breathes a spirit of candour and moderation, which is extended to all good men with diffusive charity. Never ought they to be regarded as friends to its interests, who would inculcate a warm zeal for the circumstantials of religion; and far less they who would wish to keep alive the flame of contention, and to set the true disciples of our Lord and Saviour at a greater distance from each other. How amiable is the spirit of benevolence to *all that love our Lord Jesus Christ in sincerity?* Men may give vent to their pride and ignorance, their spleen, their bigotry and heat of temper; but it is pity that these should have so often put on the semblance of religion, and have met with so kind a reception under this disguise. As the enemies of our holy faith have sufficiently availed themselves of this objection, it is high time for its friends effectually to refute it, and to bestow their attention and zeal upon matters of another kind, and of far other importance.

Our author's account of Queen Elisabeth's treatment of the Puritans, is the last point that is before us, and with which he concludes his speculations on the subject of the Protestant religion, in the 8th page of his history. His words are these.

"But after the persecutions of Mary had chased abroad all the most obstinate reformers, who escaped her fury; they had leisure to imbibe a stronger tincture of the enthusiastic genius; and when they returned, upon the accession of Elisabeth, they imported it, in its full force and virulence, into their native country. That renowned Princess, whose good taste gave her a sense of order and decorum, and whose sound judgment taught her to abhor innovations, endeavoured, by a steddy severity, to curb this obstinate enthusiasm, which, from the beginning, looked with an evil aspect, both on the church and monarchy. By an act of parliament in 1593, all persons above the age of sixteen, who were absent from church a month, or who, by word or writing, declared their sentiments against the established religion, were to be imprisoned, till they made an open declaration of their conformity. This if they refused during three months, they were to abjure the realm; and if they either refused such abjuration, or staid in England beyond the time limited, they were to suffer as felons, without benefit of clergy. To such extreme rigor was the severity pushed of Elizabeth's administration."

Severe indeed were the measures of her administration; and they were completed in this extraordinary act. When persecution is once let loose, it is but natural that it should proceed from one degree to another; and it is impossible to ascertain the bounds within which false politics, wrath, or bigotry, may think fit to restrain its violence. This spirit is manifestly in itself irrational, antichristian, inhuman; at all times subversive of the natural rights of men, as it is surely of the most noxious influence on true religion. But may not the iniquity of its acts, and our abhorrence of them, be sometimes heightened by particular circumstances? when we consider who they are that are animated by it, what those persons are who become the objects of its resentment, on what account they are liable to its outrage, and what is the excess of severity and cruelty they are made to feel. That Protestants should deal in this manner by their brethren! that they should ever have done so! and on account of things that are either confessedly of human institution, or at most are far distant from the fundamentals of religion! *Pudet hæc opprobria.* – And will any one rise up in our age to form an apology for such a conduct? nay, to ascribe it, in a great measure, to "good taste and sound judgment" in a monarch? Shall this be done by an historian, who professes to look into all that concerns religion with a calm and philosophic eye? Is it consistent with candour, to admit of no excuse for what may be blameable on the one hand, while on the other every favourable circumstances is mentioned, nay, even false colouring is applied to disguise blemishes, and to conceal deformity? Is it to be thought, that he may perhaps be prompted to this, by a good-will to those principles of civil government, which, as he asserts, were so agreeable to the one side, or by a tacit aversion to those different principles which were espoused by the other? Or is this bias to be imputed to some other cause?

But, conjecture apart, what was it that drew down upon the Puritans in Queen Elisabeth's time all that extremely severe usage? and what was their behaviour that could in any measure justify such treatment? Numerous quotations might be produced, to shew, that many of the most eminent members of the church of England did, at that time, highly disapprove of these violent proceedings; and I would hope that their numbers in our age were not great, who do not heartily subscribe to the same generous sentiment. Even they who are of opinion, that the Puritans were by much too zealous in the matter of *habits* and *ceremonies*, may be free to acknowledge, that too much rigour was exercised in the imposition of them, and in the punishment of all who did not exactly comply with them. Put the case, that they were in the wrong who refused to wear the habits which were in use in the church of Rome, and who wished that any other decent garb might be substituted in their room; a hat and a gown, for instance, instead of a hood and a surplice: yet was this a matter upon which such severities ought to have been founded? upon which clergymen of merit, against whom nothing else could be objected, were to be harassed and imprisoned, degraded and banished? Was it reasonable, first to create a necessity, and then to plead it? peremptorily to injoin the strictest conformity, and in the next place severely to punish the least violation of it? Allow me to say, in behalf of those who scrupled to use these habits, that the general principle on which they proceeded was the same, which had rightly influenced the conduct of the reformers in other instances; for example, in their removing the altars out of churches, and setting up tables in place of them. "Ridley, Cranmer, Latimer, and the rest of the English reformers, were unanimously of opinion," says a late historian, "that the retaining altars would serve only to nourish in people's minds the superstitious opinion of a propitiatory mass, and would minister an occasion of offence and division."[36] A like argument, in relation to the ancient habits, was urged by Bishop Hooper, so early as the year 1550; and it was thought of weight in the 1562, by one half of the lower house of convocation.[37] It is easy to throw out a little wit on this subject, as our author has somewhere done; but if we look back to these times, perhaps it will appear that this affair was not quite so frivolous. All these habits, from the scarlet robe downwards to the white surplice, had mystical significations affixed to them by the church of Rome: they were judged indispensably requisite in the ministrations of the clergy; and it was a prevailing notion among the people, that without these sacerdotal garments their ministrations were ineffectual. In the judgment therefore of many, it appeared more advisable to lay aside the Popish habits, and to prescribe some other decent garb; nay, the greatest part of the bishops and clergy seemed to have been of this opinion; but the Queen's authority turned the scale against them. By the act of *supremacy*, in the first year of her reign, and by an important clause of the act of *uniformity*, which was passed in the second, that princess was invested with extensive, and almost unlimited power, in all ecclesiastical matters. This power she exerted, in a very severe manner, by the court of *high commission*, during the course of her reign; nay, she was apt to be extremely offended, when the parliament, at different times, meant to correct its harsh measures, and to circumscribe that authority which themselves had bestowed. Any attempts of this kind were by her considered as an invasion of her prerogative, and were resented accordingly. During the first ten or twelve years of her reign, the zeal of her ecclesiastical commissioners was chiefly exercised about the *ancient habits:* and it will not be contested by those who have any regard to the natural rights of mankind, that matters were strained to a pretty high pitch, when these commissioners ordained, that every clergyman "should swear obedience to the Queen's injunctions and letters-patent, to all letters from the lords of the privy council, and to the articles and injunctions of their

---

[36] Neal's history of the Puritans, vol. 1. p. 66.

[37] Ib. p. 182.

metropolitan, of the bishop, archdeacon, and chancellors."[38] Yet these were their orders in the year 1565; and suspension, imprisonment, and deprivation, were the fatal effects of them.

It is not necessary to prosecute the history of those differences, and of the unrelenting behaviour of the commissioners towards the nonconformists, by which they became alienated from the church. In Archbishop Whitgift's primary visitation, we are told, more than two hundred ministers were suspended; and forty-nine were at once deprived.[39] Of the former a great number supplicated the lords of council, "declaring their readiness to subscribe the doctrinal articles of the church, – professing their reverence for the established church, and their esteem for the book of common prayer, so far as that they saw no necessity of separating from the unity of the church on that account:"[40] and they conclude with praying for indulgence. But these requests had little effect: nay, about this time the Queen extended the powers of the court of *high commission*; and, among other things, they are authorised and appointed to proceed in their inquiries into matters that fell under their jurisdiction,

"as well by the oaths of twelve good and lawful men, as also by witnesses, and all other ways and means they could devise: – And further, we do empower you," (they are the words of the commission), "or any three of you, to call before you all persons suspected of any of the premises, – and to examine them, on their corporal oaths, for the better trial and opening of the truth; and if any persons are obstinate and disobedient, either in not appearing at your command, or not obeying your orders and decrees, then to punish them by excommunication, or other censures ecclesiastical, or by fine according to your discretions; or to commit the said offenders to ward, there to remain till he or they shall be by you, or three of you, enlarged or delivered."[41]

What rigorous procedure was to be expected from a court that was constituted by such a commission? some clauses of which had so near an affinity with the style of the court of *inquisition*. There were twenty-four questions or articles framed by the Archbishop on that occasion; and of what nature they were, you may judge by a letter which the Lord Treasurer Burleigh thought proper to write on this subject. It breathes such a spirit of sense and freedom, that one

---

[38] Neal's hist. vol. 1. p. 218.

[39] Neal's hist. vol. 1. p. 400, *anno* 1584.

[40] Ib. p. 405.

[41] Neal's hist. vol. 1. p. 410.–413.

must read it with pleasure. He addresses the Archbishop in the following terms.

"It may please your Grace, I am sorry to trouble you so oft as I do; but I am more troubled myself, not only with many private petitions of sundry ministers, recommended for persons of credit, and peaceable in their ministry, who are greatly troubled by your Grace, and your colleagues in commission; but I am also daily charged by counsellors and public persons, with neglect of my duty, in not staying your Grace's vehement proceedings against ministers, whereby Papists are greatly encouraged, and the Queen's safety endangered. – I have read over your twenty-four articles, found in a Romish style, of great length and curiosity, to examine all manner of ministers in this time, without distinction of persons, to be executed *ex officio mero:* – and I find them so curiously penned, so full of branches and circumstances, that I think the inquisition of Spain used not so many questions to comprehend and to trap their priests. I know your canonists can defend these with all their particles; but surely, under correction, this judicial and canonical sifting poor ministers is not to edify or reform. And, in charity, I think they ought not to answer to all these nice points, except they were notorious Papists or heretics. I write with the testimony of a good conscience. I desire the peace and unity of the church. I favour no sensual and wilful recusant; but I conclude, according to my simple judgment, this kind of proceeding is too much favouring of the Romish inquisition; and is a device rather to seek for offenders than to reform any. – It is not charitable, to send poor ministers to your common register to answer upon so many articles at one instant, without a copy of the articles or their answers. – I pray your Grace bear with this one (perchance) fault, that I have willed the ministers not to answer these articles, except their consciences may suffer them."[42]

Such was the humane and Christian spirit of this great man's letter. The lords of council too wrote to the same purpose. But the zealous prelate, and some of his brethren in commission with him, would not desist. The very harsh measures which they pursued, stirred in the breasts of many nonconformists a further dislike of those things which were so rigorously imposed, and a disaffection to the ecclesiastical government itself. Some of the Puritan clergy began to think of a total separation from the established church, and to hold separate assemblies, about the year – eighty-six. The rest remained in its communion; and would have remained in it, if an exact conformity, without the least abatement, had not been demanded of them. I need not say what loyalty towards the Queen, and zeal for the Protestant religion, was shewn by

---

[42] Neal's hist. vol. 1. p. 425.

the Puritans at the time of the Spanish invasion. Soon after they addressed the parliament for relief; and the house of Commons was not unwilling to comply with their request: but as the Queen obstructed it, they could obtain no redress. They were still prosecuted; and some of them wrote satirical pamphlets, which, though they were condemned by wise men amongst them, yet raised strong prejudices against them all. At last, as her Majesty urged the two houses of parliament to compel recusants to attend the service of the church, they yielded to her message, and passed an act, intitled, "An act for the punishment of persons obstinately refusing to come to church, and persuading others to impugn the Queen's authority in ecclesiastical causes;" in which it is enacted,

"That if any person above the age of sixteen shall obstinately refuse to repair to some church, chapel, or usual place of common prayer, to hear divine service, for the space of one month, without lawful cause; or shall, at any time, forty days after the end of this session, by printing, writing, or express words, go about to persuade any of her Majesty's subjects to deny, withstand, or impugn her Majesty's power or authority in causes ecclesiastical; or shall dissuade them from coming to church, to hear divine service, or receive the communion according as the law directs; or shall be present at any unlawful assembly, conventicle, or meeting, under colour or pretence of any exercise of religion; that every person so offending, and lawfully convicted, shall be committed to prison without bail, till they shall conform, and yield themselves to come to church, and make a declaration of their conformity. – But in case the offenders against this statute, being lawfully convict, shall not submit, and sign the declaration within three months, then they shall abjure the realm, and go into perpetual banishment. And if they do not depart within the time limited by the quarter-sessions, or justices of peace, or if they return at any time afterwards without the Queen's license, they shall suffer death without benefit of clergy."[43]

What a spirit of bigotry and violence is here? Well might it be termed by a late author, "one of the severest acts of oppression and cruelty, that ever was made by the representatives of a Protestant nation and a free people." Never once, it seems, did it enter into his thoughts, and there are few into whose thoughts it would have entered, that all this was, in a great measure, the effect of the "good taste and sound judgment" of the Queen. One would be apt to imagine, that the nonconformists had been guilty of some atrocious crimes, which drew down upon them this severe resentment. But in vain will you seek for these, unless great guilt be imputed to them on account of their sentiments, or, if you will, their refractory behaviour with respect to the discipline and rites of the church; for in matters relative to the state they were entirely innocent.

[43] Neal's hist. vol. 1. p. 542.

The "sound judgment of that Princess taught her to abhor innovations." He might have added at least an exception as to those which herself approved. In the beginning of her reign, you know, all the laws of her sister Mary were abrogated, and the Popish system was overturned. And would any detriment to the Protestant religion have ensued, although matters had been so settled as that some indulgence might have been shewn in relation to external forms, and a few things of less importance? Was there any necessity of defining these so minutely, and of urging an exact conformity to them? And why were such rigorous methods put in practice to enforce it? Such a conduct may well be ascribed to other causes; but can never, I think, be referred to true wisdom and just policy. That Queen's sound judgment and shining talents were nobly displayed in other scenes: but these now before us tend rather to blemish than to adorn her character, in the eyes of all who have any regard to the religious rights of mankind, and are void of the spirit of bigotry and party-zeal. So late as the year 1592, some of the most eminent amongst the Puritan clergy solemnly declared, in a supplication which they addressed to her, that they did not think it lawful to make a schism in the church, on account of what might need to be revised and further removed. "Our whole life," add they,

"may shew the evident proof hereof; for always before the time of our trouble we have lived in the daily communion of it, not only as private men, but at the time of our restraint (as many years before) preached, and exercised our ministry in the same; and at this present most earnestly beseech all in authority over us, especially your excellent Majesty, that we may so proceed to serve God and your Highness all the days of our life."

Yet these are the men whose spirit and tenets are said "from the beginning, to have looked with an evil aspect, both on the church and monarchy." If it be once laid down as a maxim, That a "sound judgment will teach a monarch to abhor innovations," and if his power be but little subject to control, one does not know to what lengths it might proceed, so as to be exerted not only in matters of church-government, but likewise perhaps against those who would introduce "enlarged," or rather *libertine* "sentiments" about religion. Such persons, I doubt, would soon give up with the wisdom and equity of this maxim concerning innovations, if they were in danger of having the concluding sanction of the above act of Elisabeth put in execution against them.

But let me state a plain case, and with it put an end to this letter. Do but suppose that any particular monarch was a true friend of the Roman-Catholic church, and that the question respected the Popish and Protestant doctrines. The monarch has a great reverence for the superstitious and pompous service of that church; he is afraid of the Protestant spirit, as breathing too much of liberty; he sees plainly that its principles lead to great innovations, which "his sound judgment teaches him to abhor;" and in consequence of "his good taste and sound judgment," he will endeavour, by a steddy severity, to curb this obstinate enthusiasm, which looks with an evil aspect both on the church and monarchy." Therefore he will imprison, banish, proscribe, and put to death his subjects, who cannot be charged with any criminal or disloyal behaviour; and after all we need not be much surprised that he acts in so outrageous a manner. Our impartial historian is so good as to furnish out an apology for this absurd and inhuman violence: but nature and religion reclaim.

I am, &c.

LETTER VIII.

In the preceding letters I have gone through what was chiefly in view when I began this correspondence, and transcribed two remarkable passages relative to the Protestant religion, and to the characters of the first reformers. Having got thus far, I shall add two letters more upon some other points. – An accurate examination of this author's historical narrative, and of his political sentiments and reflections, which are every where interspersed, would lead us into too long a detail. Let us therefore content ourselves with a general view of some things most important, whilst we attend to what he has said concerning the rise of the calamitous civil wars, and the original grounds of difference betwixt King Charles and his parliaments. This, doubtless, is a subject of which an historian ought to have very clear and determinate ideas. And it may well be expected that his sentiments, whatever they are, should be at least uniform. As I am to lay before you the ideas and sentiments of this writer in his own words, I shall be obliged in this letter to transcribe several passages of the history.

To begin with his account of the complexion of the house of Commons, in the first parliament of Charles's reign: He had been assigning some causes of their granting only two subsidies to the King, who stood in need of a much larger supply, and he proceeds in the following manner.

"To all these causes we must yet add another of considerable moment. The house of commons, we may observe, were almost intirely governed by a set of men of the most uncommon capacity and the largest views: men, who were now formed into a regular party, and united, as well by fixed aims and projects, as by the hardships, which they had, many of them, undergone in prosecution of them. Among these we may mention the names of Sir Edward Coke, Sir Edwin Sandys, Sir Robert Philips, Sir Francis Seymour, Sir Dudley Diggs, Sir John Eliot, Sir Thomas Wentworth, Mr Selden, Mr Pym. Animated with a warm regard to liberty, these men saw, with regrete, an unbounded power exercised by the crown, and were resolved to seize the opportunity, which the King's necessities offered them, to reduce the prerogative within more reasonable compass. Tho' their ancestors had blindly given way to practices and precedents favourable to kingly power, and had been able, notwithstanding, to preserve some remains of liberty; it would be impossible, they thought, when all these pretensions were methodised and prosecuted by the increasing knowledge of the age, to maintain any shadow of popular government, in opposition to such unlimited authority in the sovereign. 'Twas necessary to fix a choice: Either to abandon intirely the privileges of the people, or to secure them by firmer and more precise barriers than the constitution had hitherto provided for them. In this dilemma, men of such aspiring genius and such independent fortune could not long deliberate: They generously embraced the side of freedom, and resolved to grant no supplies to their necessitous prince, without extorting concessions in favor of civil liberty."[44]

This historian well knows, that in the famous petition of right, which both houses of parliament offered to the King three years after, they quoted many ancient statutes to prove the illegality of such an arbitrary manner of imprisonment as had been of late practised, and of imposing taxes, under what name soever, upon the subject, without consent of parliament. After having mentioned some other measures of absolute government, they conclude with these words.

"All which they most humbly pray of your Most Excellent Majesty, as their rights and liberties according to the laws and statutes of this realm; and that your Majesty would also vouchsafe to declare, that the awards, doings, and proceedings to the prejudice of your people, in any of the premises, shall not be drawn hereafter into consequence or example."

To all which his Majesty, though somewhat ungracefully, at last agreed. What in the above paragraph our historian calls "concessions in favor of civil liberty," is by both houses considered in a quite different light, and as a just recognisance of their ancient rights and liberties, which were contained in the established laws of the kingdom. He seems to speak of the general aim of these patriots with approbation, though in a turn of expression remarkable enough. "They *generously* embraced the side of freedom, and resolved to grant no supplies to their *necessitous* prince, without extorting concessions in favor of civil liberty." How unhappily is a generous purpose here connected with an ungenerous act? and in what an extraordinary manner is the former assigned as the cause of the latter? He goes on to speak of the King's sentiments and views:

---

[44] Mr Hume's history, p. 147.

"Those lofty ideas of monarchical power, which were very commonly adopted during that age, and to which the ambiguous nature of the English constitution gave so plausible an appearance, were firmly riveted in Charles; and however moderate his temper, the natural illusions of self-love, joined to his education under James, and to the flattery of courtiers and church-men, had represented his political tenets as certain and uncontroverted. Taught to regard even the antient laws and constitution more as lines to direct his conduct, than barriers to withstand his power; a conspiracy to erect new ramparts, in order to straiten his authority, appeared but one degree removed from open violence and rebellion."[45]

The consequence was, that the two parliaments which had been called in the first and second years of his reign, were both of them hastily dissolved; and that he proceeded to raise money by different means; the last of which was a general loan that he extorted from his subjects.

"The *new councils*, which Charles had mentioned to the parliament, were now to be tried, in order to supply his necessities. Had he possessed any military force, on which he could depend, 'tis likely, that he had, at once, taken off the mask, and governed without any regard to the antient laws and constitution: so high an idea had he imbibed of kingly prerogative, and so contemptible a notion of the privileges of those popular assemblies, from which, he thought, he had met with such ill usage." But as he had not this military force, "it behoved him to proceed cautiously, and to cover his enterprises under the pretext of antient precedents; tho' it must be confessed, the veil could not possibly be thinner and more transparent."[46]

All this is not a little unfavourable to the monarch, and is indeed no other than what he was charged with by his greatest enemies.

As they who refused to give money, on this demand of a *general loan*, were to have several questions put to them upon oath, their answers to which they were peremptorily injoined not to disclose, our author expresses himself on this subject in the following words.

"So violent an inquisitorial power, so absurd an attempt at secrecy, were the objects equally of indignation and ridicule. That speculative despotism," adds he, "might lend assistance to practical, and religious tyranny support civil, sermons were preached by Sibthrope and Manwaring, in favor of the general loan; and the court very industriously spread them over the kingdom. Passive

---

[45] Mr Hume's history, p. 148.

[46] Mr. Hume's history, p. 159.

obedience was there recommended in its full extent, the whole authority of the state was represented as belonging to the King alone, and all limitations of laws and constitutions were rejected as seditious and impious. So openly was this doctrine espoused by the King, that Archbishop Abbot, a popular and virtuous prelate, because he would not license Sibthrope's sermon, was banished from London, and confined to one of his country-seats."[47]

In some following pages MR HUME seems all awake to the noble sentiments of liberty and social rights. "Tho' the nation was thus treated like a conquered province, its spirit was far from being subdued. thro'-out all England, many refused these loans, and some were even active in encouraging their neighbors to insist upon their common rights and privileges." Imprisonment was the consequence. While some patiently submitted to confinement, and others petitioned the King, "five gentlemen alone had spirit enough, at their own hazard and expence, to defend the public liberties, and to demand releasement, not as a favor from the court, but as their due by the laws of their country." The question was brought to a solemn trial before the king's-bench, and,

"by the debates on this subject, it appeared, beyond controversy, to the whole nation, that their ancestors had been so jealous of personal liberty, as to secure it against arbitrary power in the crown, by six several statutes, and by an article of the *great charter* itself, the most sacred foundation of the laws and constitution. But the kings of England, who had not been able to prevent the enacting of these laws, had sufficient authority, when the tide of liberty was spent, to hinder their regular execution."[48]

The judges did not think fit to decide the general question:

"The nation, they saw, were already, to the last degree, exasperated. Their chains were now held up to them. And the most invidious prerogative of the crown, that of imprisoning the subject, was here, openly, and solemnly, and in numerous instances, exercised for the most invidious purpose, in order to extort loans, or rather subsidies, without consent of parliament. But this was not the only hardship, of which the nation then found reason to complain." –

He proceeds to mention some others; and, upon the whole, he thus concludes.

"It may safely be affirmed, that, except a few prostituted courtiers or bigoted ecclesiastics, all men were highly discontented with this complication of

[47] Mr Hume's history, p. 160.
[48] Mr Hume's history, p. 161.

grievances, under which the nation labored. Tho' antient precedents were pleaded, in favor of the King's measures; a great difference, upon comparison, was observed betwixt the cases. Acts of power, however irregular, might casually, and at intervals, be exercised by a prince, for the sake of dispatch or expediency; and yet liberty still subsist, in some tolerable degree, under his administration. But where all these were reduced into a system, were exerted without interruption, were studiously sought for, in order to supply the place of laws, and subdue the refractory spirit of the nation; it was necessary to find some speedy remedy, or finally to abandon all hopes of preserving the antient freedom of the constitution. Nor could moderate men esteem the provocation, which the King had received, tho' great, sufficient, in any degree, to warrant all these violent measures. The Commons, as yet, had no way invaded his authority: They had only exercised, as best pleased them, their own privileges. Was he excusable, because, from one house of parliament, he had met with some harsh and unkind treatment, to make, in revenge, an unjust and illegal invasion on the rights and liberties of the whole nation?"[49] –

Elsewhere: "A more submissive nation than the English would have showed symptoms of discontent at these multiplied violences and disasters. Their liberties were, in a manner, ravished from them; illegal taxes extorted," &c.[50] He goes on to speak of the ruin of trade, and of Buckingham's unsuccessful expedition to the isle of Rhé. When things were in this situation, a new parliament was called: orders were given to release the gentlemen, to the number of seventy-eight, who had been imprisoned for refusing to pay the loan-money; and twenty-seven of them were chosen members of parliament.[51]

"When the Commons assembled, they appeared to be men of the same independent spirit with their predecessors, and possessed of such riches, that their property was computed to surpass three times that of the house of Peers; they were deputed by burroughs and counties, inflamed, all of them, by the late open violations of liberty; many of the members themselves had been cast into prison, and had suffered by the arbitrary measures of the court; yet, notwithstanding all these circumstances, which might prompt them to embrace violent resolutions, they entered upon business with perfect temper and decorum."[52]

---

[49] Mr Hume's history, p. 163.

[50] Ib. p. 167.

[51] Rushworth, quoted by Rapin, vol. 2. book 19.

[52] Mr Hume's history, p. 168.

They drew up the famous bill called *the petition of right*, which having gone through both houses of parliament, was at length assented to by the King, and passed into a law. MR HUME talks of "the extreme rigor of the Commons towards Charles" on this occasion. And was it indeed so very hard a case, to have his assent requested to a petition, every tittle of which was conformable to the laws of the kingdom, and grounded on the plainest statutes? and that the Commons should give this petition of right the preference to a bill of supply? However, even although their conduct had been liable to the imputation of "extreme rigor," yet he thinks it may allow of an apology.

"There is nothing, which tends more to excuse, if not to justify, the extreme rigor of the Commons towards Charles, than his open encouragement and avowal of such general principles, as were altogether incompatible with a limited government. Manwaring had preached a sermon, which the Commons found, upon inquiry, to be printed by special command from the King; and when this sermon was looked into, it contained doctrines subversive of all civil liberty."[53]

This person was punished by the parliament; but, after their dissolution, was pardoned and promoted by the King.

"The interval, betwixt the second and third parliament, was distinguished by so many open and flagrant violations of public liberty, that men had little leisure to attend to the affair of tonnage and poundage. – But after the Commons, during the precedent session, had remedied all these grievances by means of their petition of right, which was become so necessary; they afterwards proceeded to take this matter into consideration."[54]

A remonstrance was framed against levying tonnage and poundage without consent of parliament; but the King, unwilling to receive it, put an end to that session by a prorogation; and as this important affair was again taken up at their next meeting, the parliament was dissolved (March 1629).
"The discontents of the nation," says this historian,

"ran extremely high, on account of this violent rupture betwixt King and parliament. These discontents Charles very imprudently inflamed by his affectation of a severity, which he had not power, nor, probably, will, to carry to extremity. – Sir John Elliot, Holles, and Valentine, were summoned to their trial in the king's bench, for seditious speeches and behavior in

---

[53] Mr Hume's history, p. 181.

[54] Ib. p. 190.

parliament; but refusing to answer before an inferior court for their conduct, as members of a superior, they were condemned to imprisonment during the King's pleasure, to find sureties for their good behavior, and to be fined, the two former a thousand pound a-piece, the latter five hundred. This illegal sentence, procured by the influence of the crown, served only to show the King's disregard to all the privileges of parliament, and to acquire an immense stock of popularity to the sufferers, who had so bravely, in opposition to arbitrary power, defended the liberties of their native country."[55]

The King continued for several years to rule without a parliament; and in what manner, we are informed in the following paragraph.

"The principles, which exalted prerogative, were not entertained by the King, merely as soft and agreeable to his royal ears: They were also put in practice during all the time, when he ruled without parliament. Tho' frugal and regular in his expences, he wanted money for the support of government; and he levied it, either by the revival of obsolete laws, or by violations, some more open, some more disguised, of the privileges of the nation. tho' humane and gentle in his temper, he gave way to severities in the star-chamber and high commission, which seemed requisite, in order to support the new model of administration, and repress the rising spirit of liberty throughout the kingdom."[56]

In almost all these passages this historian, it would appear, declares against the King's arbitrary principles and manner of government, and in favour of those who endeavoured to oppose them. But his style rises a little higher, and seems to be animated with the full spirit of liberty, when he declaims against the tax of ship-money.

"The imposition of ship-money is apparently the most avowed and most dangerous invasion of national privileges, not only which Charles was ever guilty of, but which the most arbitrary Princes in England, since any liberty had been ascertained to the people, had ever ventured upon. In vain, were precedents of antient writs produced: – how wide were these precedents from a power of arbitrarily obliging the people, at their own charge, to build new ships, to victual and pay them, for the public; nay to furnish money to the crown for that purpose? What security either against the farther extension of this claim, &c.? – Notwithstanding all these reasons, the prostituted

[55] Mr Hume's history, p. 195.

[56] Mr Hume's history, p. 205.

judges, four excepted, gave sentence in favor of the crown. Hambden, however, obtained by the trial the end, for which he had so generously sacrificed his safety and his quiet: The people were rouzed from their lethargy, and saw plainly the chains, which were prepared for them."[57]

Upon the whole, then, would not all this seem fully sufficient to ascertain our author's political sentiments, and to fix them on the side of liberty and the constitution? In these and several other passages, the King's "lofty ideas of monarchical power" are acknowledged, and his arbitrary measures of government arraigned: the names of "practical despotism" and "civil tyranny" are bestowed upon them. – "The nation was treated like a conquered province," and "labored under a complication of grievances: – Their chains were held up to them; and the most invidious prerogative of the crown, that of imprisoning the subject, was openly, and solemnly, and in numerous instances, exercised for the most invidious purpose: The antient freedom of the constitution" was in the greatest danger of being overturned: – "A more submissive nation than the English would have showed symptoms of discontent, at these multiplied violences and disasters. Their liberties were in a manner ravished from them, and illegal taxes extorted: – The interval betwixt the first and second parliament was distinguished by many open and flagrant violations of public liberty: – The King gave way to severities in the star-chamber and high commission: – The principles which exalted prerogative were put in practice during all the time, when he ruled without parliament;" (notwithstanding his solemn consent to the petition of right). – "Their violations of law," (he speaks of the monarchs James and Charles), "particularly those of Charles, are palpable and obvious.[58] – The most unpopular of all Charles's measures, the most impolitic, the most oppressive, and even, excepting ship-money, the most illegal, was the revival of monopolies, so solemnly abolished, after re-iterated endeavors, by a recent act of parliament.[59] – The law, in many instances, was openly violated."[60] The tax of ship-money is strongly condemned: Hambden's spirit in opposing it is applauded: the judges who gave sentence in favour of the crown are branded with a very ignominious epithet: and "the people," we are told, "saw plainly the chains which were prepared for them."

These sentiments, one would be apt to think, might naturally issue in a pretty full vindication of the general conduct of King Charles's four parlia-

---

[57] Mr Hume's history, p. 218.

[58] Mr Hume's history, p. 245.

[59] Ib. p. 257.

[60] Ib. p. 259.

ments, nay of the fifth also, at least before the commencement of the civil war. But no such thing, it is evident, is intended by this historian. In other passages of the history very different ideas and sentiments are exhibited; of which I shall now give you a specimen. Immediately after his warm declamation against ship-money, and his representation of the miserable state of things in the kingdom, see the cool, the unexpected and surprising exordium of the following chapter. "The grievances under which the English labored, when considered in themselves, scarce deserve the name." How? Even though they were "treated like a conquered province; had their liberties in a manner wrested from them;" were subjected to "illegal imprisonments, illegal taxes, to the severities of the star-chamber and high commission," and to the other effects of civil tyranny?" – "The grievances under which the English labored, when considered in themselves, scarce deserve the name; nor were they either burthensome on the people's revenues, or any way shocking to the natural humanity of mankind." (Can you imagine yourself to be reading the same author?) "Even the taxation of ship-money, independent of the consequences, was rather an advantage to the public, by the judicious use, which the King made of the money, levied by that expedient. – Peace too, industry, commerce, opulence, along with *justice and lenity of administration:* all these were fully enjoyed by the people; and every other blessing of government, except liberty, or rather the present exercise of liberty, and its proper security."[61]

Our author had spoke of the intention of the leaders of the house of Commons to oppose arbitrary power, and to defend the liberties of their native country: their design is said afterward to have been, to "reduce the crown to necessities; – and by multiplying these necessities, it was foreseen, that his prerogative, undermined on all sides, must, at last, succumb, and be no longer dangerous to the privileges of the people."[62]

He often talks of "statute laws, of limited government, and of the antient constitution:" by and by, this constitution is represented as ambiguous, and the most important laws as transitory efforts of popular liberty. It is allowed, that personal liberty was secured by many ancient statutes against arbitrary power in the crown; and yet much may be said in support of its exercise, and "the subject is not without its difficulties."[63] – "Had the house of Commons been always disposed to make the precedents of that reign" (meaning Elizabeth's) "the rule of their conduct, they needed never have had any difference with any of their monarchs."[64] MR HUME should have told us, when it was that the

---

[61] Mr Hume's history, p. 220.

[62] Mr Hume's history, p. 238.

[63] Ib. p. 174.

[64] Ib. p. 30.

extorted loans, and levied taxes without consent of parliament; and what those taxes were. – "The turbulent government of England, ever fluctuating betwixt privilege and prerogative, would afford a variety of precedents, which might be pleaded on both sides."[65] Because the limits betwixt prerogative and privilege had not been settled, is it to be thought a doubtful point, whether the parliament had any privileges, or the nation any rights or constitution at all? The whole history of England demonstrates, that it was never an absolute, but a mixed monarchy; and that the royal authority was indeed more or less limited, but still limited in all ages. It follows, therefore, that the principles of arbitrary government, which were openly espoused and put in practice by Charles and his father, were perfectly inconsistent with the English constitution, and with its most sacred and fundamental laws. Nay, this writer upon some occasions seems inclined to allow that they were so: at other times he endeavours to spread a thick mist over all this subject. I shall transcribe but one passage, out of many, to this purpose.

'That these principles of government" (he had been speaking of arbitrary ones, which prompted the King to impose the tax of ship-money) "were derived from the uniform tenor of the English laws, it would be rash to affirm." Doubtless it would; especially as himself elsewhere affirms, that ancient laws opposed them; and that acting according to them in the ship-money tax was a "most avowed and dangerous invasion of national privileges." He goes on:

"The fluctuating nature of the constitution, the impatient humor of the people, and the variety of events, had, no doubt, in different ages, produced many exceptions and contradictions. These observations only may be established on both sides, *that* the appearances were sufficiently strong in favor of the King to apologize for his following such maxims, and *that* public liberty must be so precarious under this exorbitant prerogative as to render an opposition not only excusable, but laudable, in the people."[66]

So very moderate and cautious, and so consistent too are the sentiments and conclusions of this historian.

The same caution and consistency are to be met with in his general remarks on the conduct of both parties towards the beginning of the dismal and desolating civil war. Here I cannot help observing, that, in my judgment, he has done injury to that cause which, it would appear, he meant to support; by attempting an apology for the principles and acts of arbitrary power, which were avowed and exerted by the ill-advised and unfortunate monarch. Is it not far more proper, to rest the defence of the royal cause against the parliament,

---

[65] Mr Hume's history, p. 91.

[66] Mr Hume's history, p. 211.

upon the grounds laid down by Lord Clarendon and some other historians? and to assert, that after his Majesty had passed the triennial bill, that other for the abolition of the star-chamber and high commission, and had assented to many excellent and important acts, in order to the security of personal and the ascertaining of public liberty, the parliament ought to have been satisfied, and should not have urged things further, far less to such an extremity? It would have been better, perhaps, for our author to have followed this general plan, without deviating into other and more dangerous paths.

His opinion of the Earl of Strafford's conduct, and his character of Archbishop Laud, are not unworthy of our attention. "The house of Commons," says he, in speaking of the long parliament which met November 3. 1640,

"was never observed to be, from the beginning, so numerous and frequent. Without any interval, they immediately entered upon business, and by unanimous consent they struck a blow, which may, in a manner, be regarded as decisive. The Earl of Strafford was considered as chief minister of state, both on account of the credit, which he possessed with his master, and of his own great and uncommon vigor and capacity. By a concurrence of accidents, this man labored under the severe hatred of all the three nations, which composed the British monarchy.[67] – After several hours spent in bitter invective, it was moved – that Strafford should immediately be impeached of high treason. This motion was received with universal approbation; – Pym was chosen to carry up the impeachment, and most of the house accompanied him on so agreeable an errand."[68]

It was charged against him, that he had endeavoured to subvert the fundamental laws of England and Ireland, and to introduce an arbitrary and tyrannical government: this was what the Commons laboured to prove by a variety of facts contained in the articles of impeachment.

"These," says our historian,

"regarded his conduct, as president of the council of Yorke, as deputy or lieutenant of Ireland, as counsellor or commander in England. But tho' four months were employed by the managers in framing the accusation, and all Strafford's answers were extemporary; it appears from comparison, not only that he was free from the crime of treason, of which there is not the least appearance, but that his conduct, making allowance for human infirmities, exposed to such severe scrutiny, was innocent, and even laudable."[69]

---

[67] Mr Hume's history, p. 252.

[68] Ib. p. 255.

[69] Mr Hume's history, p. 273.

It is not enough to acquit him of all blame; his conduct, it seems, is intitled to our strong approbation. He had been a favourite minister, at the head of his Majesty's councils, for more than eight years. During that space of time, "the principles which exalted prerogative were put in practice;" money was levied, "either by the revival of obsolete laws, or by violations, some more open, some more disguised, of the privileges of the nation; oppressive and illegal measures" were pursued; "the law, in many instances, was openly violated; and the people saw plainly the chains which were prepared for them:" yet, after all, the conduct of the prime minister and favourite, who abetted all these illegal and arbitrary measures, and who copied after them so exactly in his government of Ireland, must be now declared to be not only "innocent," but "laudable." They did not however appear so to any one person in the house of Commons. The Lords Falkland and Digby, Mr Hyde, afterwards Lord Clarendon, and the other patriot royalists, zealously concurred in Strafford's prosecution. One of these Honourable Lords said of him, that

> "he committed so many mighty and so manifest enormities and oppressions in the kingdom of Ireland, that the like have not been committed by any governor, in any government, since Verres left Sicily; and after his Lordship was called over from being deputy of Ireland, to be in a manner deputy of England, he and the junto gave such counsels, and pursued such courses, as 'tis hard to say, whether they were more unwise, more unjust, or more unfortunate."

And it was the steady opinion of Lord Digby,

> "that the Earl of Strafford was the most dangerous minister, and the most insupportable to free subjects; and that his practices in themselves had been as high and tyrannical as any subject ever ventured upon."[70]

Nay his Majesty himself, who had been present during the whole trial, declared, in his speech to both houses of parliament, that "tho' he could not condemn him of high treason, yet as to matters of misdemeanours, he was so clear in that, that he did not think my Lord Strafford fit hereafter to serve him or the commonwealth in any place of trust, no not the meanest." Such was the opinion of the Lords Falkland and Digby, of the whole house of Commons, and of the King himself, concerning the Earl of Strafford, whose conduct is by this historian said to have been, not only "innocent," but "laudable."

In drawing the character of Archbishop Laud, he tells us, among other things, that

---

[70] Parliament. history, vol. 9. p. 217.

"His zeal was unrelenting in the cause of religion; that is, in imposing, by the most rigorous measures, his own tenets and pious ceremonies on the obstinate Puritans, who had profanely dared to oppose him. In prosecution of his holy purposes, he overlooked every human consideration; or, in other words, the heat and indiscretion of his temper made him neglect all views of prudence, and all rules of good manners. He was, in this respect, happy, that all his enemies were also declared enemies to loyalty and true piety, and that every exercise of his revenge, by that means, became a merit and a virtue. This was the man, &c."[71]

He was not so "happy" in every period of his life, even according to MR HUME'S own account; who, in talking of the procedure of the house of Commons against Strafford, Laud, and some others, informs us, that "there was an intire concurrence and unanimity" amongst them; and that "men of the most moderate tempers, and the most attached to the church and monarchy, exerted themselves with the utmost vigor in the redress of grievances, and in prosecuting the authors of them."[72] The truth is, the Puritans were not the only persons who condemned the conduct of this prelate. Very many of the church's best friends, and who were all along conformists to its government and liturgy, were highly displeased with some of his innovations, with the superstitious spirit that was discovered in them, and with the haughty and arbitrary manner of their imposition. But though it had been otherwise, why should they be styled "enemies to true piety," who opposed these, and who entertained harsh, or perhaps mean thoughts of the person who acted this part? Has not this historian himself poured out a sufficient portion of ridicule on "the superstitious prelate," in two or three following pages? where he talks of those "insignificant ceremonies," of which he was so fond, and of "that mechanical devotion, which was proposed to be raised in his model of religion." Is it owing to inadvertency, or to something worse, that what is termed "mechanical devotion" in one paragraph, should be called "true piety" in another? Is he to be understood as giving his own opinion in the one sentence, and in the other that of the Archbishop? Or, are we to conclude that there are certain words, which our author sometimes uses, without having affixed any determined ideas to them? However that may be, as the Puritans appear to be the objects of his constant and violent aversion, on account both of their religious and civil principles, it is not enough to say that they were "enemies, declared enemies to true piety;" they are also, all of them, without exception, to be considered as downright rebels, and "declared enemies to loyalty."

---

[71] Mr Hume's history, p. 200.

[72] Mr Hume's history, p. 259.

Thus the Puritans in England have the same character bestowed upon them, which, with equal truth and candor, he had before conferred on their brethren in Scotland,[73] when he called them "determined enemies to monarchy, by principle as well as inclination." When he is in a warm fit of zeal against them, he uses this language; but in his cooler moments he is inclined to change his style, as when he speaks of King James, "He frequently inculcated a maxim, which tho' it has some foundation, is to be received with great limitations, No Bishop, no King;[74] and again, "The Presbyterians were, by their principles, the least averse to regal authority; – the Independents were resolute to lay the foundations of a republican government;"[75] once more, he thus characterises one of the three parties in Scotland, in the year 1648; "The moderate Presbyterians, who endeavoured to reconcile the interests of religion and the crown, and hoped, by supporting the Presbyterian party in England, to suppress the Sectarian army, and re-instate the parliament, as well as King, in their just freedom and authority: The two brothers, Hamilton and Laneric, were leaders of this party;" and every one knows that they made a bold effort to accomplish their design. But to return:

What shall we make of the latter part of the above remarkable paragraph? "He was, in this respect, happy, that all his enemies were also declared enemies to loyalty and true piety, and that every exercise of his revenge, by that means, became a merit and a virtue." Is this his own conclusion? or was it that of the Archbishop? Be whose conclusion it will, the sentiment is thoroughly bad; and perfectly similar to the maxim of depraved casuists, and dishonest politicians, which teaches, That the means are sanctified by the end, or that base and

---

[73] Upon the slightest attention to his history, any one must perceive in what an extraordinary manner he has strained every thing against them. See, for instance, how he speaks of the ancient confession of faith, in which the tenets of Popery were condemned. "This famous covenant consisted first of a renunciation of Popery, formerly signed by James in his youth, and composed of the most furious and most virulent invectives, with which any human beings had ever inflamed their breast to an unrelenting animosity against their fellow-creatures," p. 227. High sounding words these, which might have been reserved to a more proper place, as there was surely no sort of occasion for them in talking of a confession of faith, which renounced the errors and corruptions of the Roman church. – Again, concerning the ecclesiastical government in Scotland, "Without accuser," says he, "without summons, without trial, any ecclesiastical court, however inferior, could, in a summary manner, pronounce a sentence of excommunication, for any cause, and against any person, even tho' he lived not within the bounds of their jurisdiction. And, by this means, the whole tyranny of the inquisition, tho' without its order, was introduced into the kingdom," p. 64. An establishment this which, I believe, was never heard of till this time. In short, these and the like passages may be well referred to that species of history commonly called *romance writing*.

[74] Mr Hume's history, p. 10.

[75] Ib. p. 416.

unworthy actions may be justified by a good intention. Thus vice and virtue may lose their names; and the exercise of revenge, or of any other criminal passion, may be not only favoured with the appellation of *virtue*, but be also dignified with the title of *merit*. And could one who meant to reflect a dishonour on the King, have done it more effectually, than by subjoining the following sentence to the character he had given of this prelate? "This was the man, who acquired so great an ascendant over Charles, and led him, by the superstition of his temper, into a conduct, which proved so fatal to himself and to his kingdoms."

There is but one other passage of this history, upon which I would at present offer a few reflections. We have seen Mr HUME'S account of the original grounds of dissension betwixt the King and the parliament; in which he has taken notice of the illegal and arbitrary measures which had been carried on during the space of fourteen years, and of the general intention of the parliament to redress past grievances, and to provide a barrier against the irruption of arbitrary power in time to come: and thus the struggle betwixt liberty and prerogative gave rise to the civil war.

"Their violations of law, particularly those of Charles, are palpable, and obvious, and were, generally speaking, transgressions of a plain limit, which was marked out to royal authority. But the encroachments of the Commons, though less positive and determinate, are no less discernible by good judges, and were equally capable of destroying the just ballance of the constitution. While they exercised the powers, transmitted to them, in a manner more independent, and less compliant, than had ever before been practised; the kings were, imprudently, but, as they imagined, from necessity, tempted to assume powers, which had scarce ever been exercised or claimed by the crown. And from the shock of these opposite pretensions arose all the factions, convulsions, and disorders, which attended that period."[76]

The sense of all this is perfectly plain. How surprising then to have this subject presented to us, in so very different a light, by the same author, in the following paragraph?

"It may be worth observing," says he, "that all the historians, who lived near that age, or what is perhaps more decisive, all authors, who have casually made mention of those public transactions, still represent the civil disorders and convulsions as proceeding from religious controversy, and consider the political disputes about power and liberty as intirely subordinate to the other. – Disuse of parliaments, imprisonment and prosecution of

[76] Mr Hume's history, p. 245.

members, ship-money, an arbitrary and illegal administration; these were loudly, and not without reason, complained of: But the grievances, which tended chiefly to enflame the parliament and nation, especially the latter, were, the surplice, the rails placed about the altar, the bows exacted on approaching it, the liturgy, the breach of the Sabbath, embroidered copes, lawn-sleeves, the use of the ring in marriage, and of the cross in baptism. On account of these, were both parties contented to throw the government into such violent convulsions; and to the disgrace of that age and of this island, it must be acknowledged, that the disorders in Scotland intirely, and those in England mostly, proceeded from so mean and contemptible an origin."[77]

But let us consider this matter a little, without being afraid of the peremptory assertion concerning the universal agreement of historians; which, by the way, our author himself should have remembered on other occasions, and particularly when he wrote the paragraph which I quoted to you immediately before this last. – One would be apt to think, that the dispute about the habits, which make so good a figure in this passage, had now become a matter of the highest consequence, and had been warmly agitated betwixt the King and parliament, so that we should meet with it every where in the papers that passed on both sides. But, for my part, I doubt whether it is to be once found in any one of them, so far is it from being an important ground of difference and animosity. – The Archbishop's superstitious innovations were indeed condemned by the Commons; neither were they defended by the King. – As little did he adhere to the *book of sports*, about which the zeal of the high-church clergy had been heretofore so strenuously exercised. James's "declaration to encourage recreations and sports on the Lord's day," was renewed by his son in the year 1633; who says in his proclamation, that, "out of a like pious care for the service of God, and for suppressing of those humors that oppose truth, and for the ease, comfort and recreation of his Majesty's well deserving people, he doth ratify his *blessed father*'s declaration." This ratification, however, was attended with fatal effects to multitudes of the clergy, who would not violate their consciences by reading a declaration which they accounted sinful, as it licensed the profanation of the Lord's day, and tended to efface a sense of religion, and to introduce a general dissolution of manners among the vulgar. Was this a proper subject on which severities should have proceeded against the ministers of religion; and in the courts of bishops too? where they were suspended, deprived, excommunicated. No less than thirty within the bounds of the diocese of Norwich met with this treatment. So very warm was the zeal of ecclesiastical courts in so very shameful a cause.

[77] Mr Hume's history, p. 266.

The liturgy then is the only remaining article that is of any consequence; concerning which, the house of Commons petitioned, that it should be reformed. This was a part of one of the nineteen propositions which they sent to the King in June 1642, two months before the war broke out: neither did he altogether reject the request. – The two last articles of his paragraph, "the ring in marriage, and cross in baptism," are put in, I suppose, merely to heighten the ridicule and contempt which he intends to excite. But how has it happened, that, in all this enumeration of particulars, he should have forgot the most important point of all, namely, the dispute about the hierarchy or Episcopal government? concerning which, I could almost venture to affirm, that all historians who mention the differences relative to the church, lay most stress upon this article, which he has entirely omitted: and therefore he can by no means plead their authority in support of what he now avers.

But let us take no advantage of his omitting to speak of the hierarchy; and let us suppose that he has taken notice of it, as he ought to have done: I will proceed to assert, that the differences about church-government and the liturgy were not the chief causes of the unhappy breach betwixt the King and parliament, which issued in a civil war; that "the political disputes about power and liberty" were not considered "as entirely subordinate" to those other matters; and that they are not so represented even by those historians who most favour the royal cause.

Without multiplying quotations, let these points be referred to the decision of an author who must be reckoned unexceptionable on this subject, to the Noble historian of the civil wars. Does his Lordship "represent the civil disorders and convulsions as proceeding from religious controversy?" and does he "consider the disputes about power and liberty," about the arbitrary power which had been so uniformly exercised by the crown, to the violation of the laws and liberties of the subject, "as intirely subordinate to the other?" Lord Clarendon's sense of things will be known, by attending to a few passages of his history.

In his entry on the history of the long parliament, in the third book, his words are these.

"In the house of Commons were many persons of wisdom and gravity, who being possessed of great and plentiful fortunes, tho' they were undevoted enough to the court, had all imaginable duty for the King, and affection to the government established by law or antient custom; and without doubt the major part of that body consisted of men who had no mind to break the peace of the kingdom, or to make any considerable alteration in the government of church or state."[78]

---

[78] Clarendon's history, b. 3. p. 184. (ed. 1705.)

And indeed, in about a fortnight after their meeting, it was resolved, that none should fit in their house, but such as would receive the communion according to the usage of the church of England. When the civil war broke out, many of them went to join the King; yet Lord Clarendon says, in relation to the temper of the house, in the beginning of the year 1643, that "very much the major part even of those members who still continued with them, were cordially affected to the (church) government established, at least not affected to any other."[79] His Lordship has drawn the characters of those who were most distinguished in both houses of parliament, in which I cannot discern the least vestige of those ideas which Mr HUME has suggested to us.

"The Earl of Bedford had no desire that there should be any alteration in the government of the church. – The Earl of Essex was rather displeased with the person of the Archbishop, and some other bishops, than indevoted to the function; – and he was as much devoted as any man to the book of common prayer, and obliged all his servants to be constantly present with him at it; his household chaplain being always a most conformable man, and a good scholar.[80] – In truth," adds he, "in the house of Peers there were only at that time taken notice of the Lords Say and Brooke, as positive enemies to the whole fabrick of the church, and to desire a dissolution of that government; the Earl of Warwick himself having never discovered any aversion to Episcopacy, and much professed the contrary. In the house of Commons, though of the chief leaders, Nathaniel Fiennes, and young Sir Harry Vane, and shortly after Mr Hambden, who had not before owned it, were believed to be for root and branch; which grew shortly after a common expression, and discovery of the several tempers; yet Mr Pym was not of that mind, nor Mr Hollis, nor any of the northern men, or those lawyers who drove on most furiously with them; all who were pleased with the government itself of the church."

His Lordship proceeds to inform us, that

"the first design that was entertained against the church, and which was received in the house of Commons with a visible countenance and approbation of many, who were neither of the same principles nor purposes, was a short bill that was brought in, to take away the bishops votes in parliament, and to leave them out in all commissions of the peace, or that had relation to any temporal affairs. This was contrived with great deliberation and

[79] Ib. b. 6. p. 117.
[80] Clarendon's history, b. 3. p. 233. 234. &c.

preparation, to dispose men to consent to it: and to this many of the house of Peers were much disposed; and amongst them, none more than the Earl of Essex, and all the popular lords, who observed, that they seldom carried any thing which directly opposed the King's interest, by reason of the number of the bishops, who, for the most part, unanimously concurred against it, and opposed many of their other designs: and they believed, that it could do the church no harm, by the bishops having fewer diversions from their spiritual charges. In the house of Commons they used that, and other arguments, to remove the prejudice from it."

Thus far his Lordship: with whose representation other writers agree. (I do not say *all*; as I cannot pretend to have read "all the historians who lived near that age," and far less "all authors who have casually made mention of those public transactions.") And according to this account, the house of Commons, so far from having been inflamed with zeal against the ecclesiastical government and liturgy, was generally well affected towards both; so that the question relative to the exclusion of bishops from their seats in parliament, was considered as subordinate to those which regarded the interests of the state. – The Commons had early expressed their displeasure with the canons of the late convocation, which continued to sit after the dissolution of the preceding parliament. "The new canons," says Lord Clarendon, "were insisted on, as a most palpable invasion by the whole body of the clergy, upon the laws and liberty of the people;" so that the house of Commons declared, "that these canons contained in them matter of sedition, and reproach to the regal power; prejudicial to the liberty and property of the subject, and to the privileges of parliament."[81] This was the light in which they viewed them; and their resolutions against them were unanimous. They were likewise extremely offended at the various oppressions and severities which, for some time past, had been exercised by the ecclesiastical courts: but many declared with warmth against these, who, notwithstanding, firmly adhered to Episcopal government. The great Lord Falkland, for instance, even in that famous speech of his, in which he concludes for the continuance of this government, talks in the following manner of the conduct of those who had the management of church-affairs; "who," says his Lordship,

"have brought in superstition and scandal under the title of decency, – and have been less eager on those who damn our church, than on those who on weak conscience, and, perhaps, as weak reason, only abstain from it. Nay, it has been more dangerous for men to go to a neighbouring parish, when they had no sermon in their own, than to be obstinate and perpetual

---

[81] Clarendon's history, b. 3. p. 204. 206.

recusants. While mass has been said in security, a conventicle has been a crime; and which is yet more, the conforming to ceremonies has been more exacted than the conforming to Christianity. – The truth is, as some ministers in our state first took away our money, and afterwards endeavoured to make our money not worth taking, by depraving it; so these men first depressed the power of preaching, and then laboured to make it such, as the harm had not been much, if it had been depressed; the chief subjects of their sermons being the *jus divinum* of bishops and tithes, the sacredness of the clergy, the sacrilege of impropriations, the demolishing of Puritanism, the building up of the prerogative, &c. In short, their work has been to try how much of the Papist might be brought in without Popery; and to destroy as much as they could of the gospel, without bringing themselves in danger of being destroyed by the law."

His Lordship mentions the injury they had done to the rights and liberties of the nation; and then he adds, "I have represented no small quantity, and no mean degree of guilt; but this charge does not lie against episcopacy, but against those who have abused that sacred function." He gives his opinion for that form of government, speaks of some bishops with honour, is for retrenching a part of their power, and agrees, "that no ceremonies, which any number count unlawful, and no man counts necessary, should be imposed upon them."[82] Such was his Lordship's sense of things; in which other patriot royalists in the house concurred, who aimed at a redress of grievances, without overturning the constitution of the church. And upon all this matter a late accurate historian has given his judgment in these words.

"It appears to me, that there was no formed design as yet (in the year 1641), either in the house of Commons, or among the Puritan clergy, to subvert the hierarchy, and erect the Presbyterian government upon its ruins. – So that what was done in the house of Commons afterwards, was the result of the situation of their affairs, and not of any formed design: as *that* changed, so did their councils and measures."

The result of all this is, that the debate about the government of the church, which, however, is not mentioned by Mr HUME in the paragraph above quoted, was not the chief cause of the fatal breach betwixt the parliament and the King, in the year 1642; and that in talking of this breach he had but little occasion to reckon up the most part of the particulars there inserted; such as, the Archbishop's innovations, which had been suppressed; what concerned the book of sports, which was not insisted in; and the habits of clergymen, which

---

[82] Rushworth, quoted by Neal, vol 2. p. 423.

were hardly, if at all, named. Nay, after the canons of the convocation had been rendered ineffectual, after the suppression of the high commission, and putting an end to the arbitrary severities of the ecclesiastical courts; and even after the act had passed, which excluded the bishops from a seat in the house of peers, and the rest of the clergy from any temporal jurisdiction; yet, after all, the civil discords still continued, which issued in the calamities of war. The causes of this you will find in every history; perhaps in few more imperfectly than in that of our author. Let me quote one passage more from Lord Clarendon, in which he discloses the state of things at that period, in his assigning reasons for his Majesty's soft answer to the declaration of the two houses, which, in February 1642, was presented to him.

"But they again," says his Lordship,

"who consider and remember that juncture of time; the incredible disadvantage his Majesty suffered, by the misunderstanding of his going to the house of Commons, and by the popular mistake of privilege of parliament, and consequently of the breach of those privileges: and, on the contrary, the great height and reputation the factious party had arrived to, the stratagems they used, and the infusions they made into the people, of the King's disinclination to the laws of the land; and especially, that he had consented to all those excellent laws made this parliament, of which the people were possessed, very unwillingly, and meant to avoid them: that the Queen had an irreconcileable hatred to the religion professed, and to the whole nation, and that her power was unquestionable: that there was a design to send the Prince beyond the seas, and to marry him to some Papist: above all, (which the principal of them, with wonderful confidence, in all places avowed to be true), that the rebellion in Ireland was fomented, and countenanced at least, by the Queen, that good terms might be got for the Catholics in England: I say, whoever remembers all this – will conclude, that it concerned his Majesty by all gentleness and condescension to undeceive, and recover men to their sobriety and understanding," &c.[83]

A great deal more might be quoted: but the subject is so plain, and so well known, that more, I think, is unnecessary; as it is likewise to add any further reflections on our author's scheme in the above passage. Only read it again, and then decide concerning it.

"It may be worth observing, that all the historians, who lived near that age, or what perhaps is more decisive, all authors who have casually made mention of those public transactions, still represent the civil disorders and

---

[83] Clarendon's history, b. 5. p. 465.

convulsions as proceeding from religious controversy, and consider the political disputes about power and liberty as intirely subordinate to the other. – But the grievances, which tended chiefly to enflame the parliament and nation, especially the latter, were, the surplice, the rails placed about the altar, the bows exacted on approaching it, &c. On account of these, were both parties contented to throw the government into such violent convulsions; and to the disgrace of that age and of this island, it must be acknowledged, that the disorders in Scotland intirely, and those in England mostly, proceeded from so mean and contemptible an origin."

He may for himself acknowledge what he pleases, and may thence draw what conclusion he thinks proper; but let him not impose a necessity on others, who, as they see no reason for such acknowledgement, cannot subscribe to his conclusion.

Let us now talk a little, and but a little, of the state of things in Scotland at that time. It is fully represented by several authors, particularly by Bishop Burnet in his memoirs of the Dukes of Hamilton; whose testimony I might make use of on this occasion. But as I am always best pleased with what assistance may be had from Mr HUME himself, and as this is the shorter method, I shall go on to prove, from his own account of the matter elsewhere, that "the disorders in Scotland did not intirely proceed from that origin," to which he now refers them.

With regard to the first commotions in Scotland in the year 1637, he acquaints us, that the nobility were exceedingly offended at the King's increasing the power of the bishops, and his raising them to the chief dignities of the state; so that

"interest joined itself to ambition, and begot a jealousy, lest the Episcopal sees, which, at the reformation, had been pillaged by the nobles, should again be enriched at their expence. – The King too, warranted by antient law and practice, had declared for a general resumption of all crown-owned lands alienated by his predecessors. – A new oath was arbitrarily exacted of intrants [into the military], in which they swore to observe the articles of Perth, and submit to the liturgy and canons. And in a word, the whole system of church-government, during a course of thirty years, had been changed, by means of the innovations introduced by James and Charles."[84]

Then he talks of the general fear of Popery, and of the suspicions which were entertained in relation to the tendency of these innovations.

---

[84] Mr Hume's history, p. 221. 222.

"Amidst these dangerous complaints," adds he,[85] "and terrors of religious grievances, the civil and ecclesiastical privileges of the nation were imagined, and with some reason, not to be altogether free from invasion. The establishment of the high commission by James, without any authority of law, was an evident and a very considerable encroachment of the crown; and erected the most dangerous and arbitrary of all courts, in a manner equally dangerous and arbitrary. All the steps towards the settlement of Episcopacy had indeed been taken with consent of parliament: The articles of Perth were confirmed in 1621: In 1633, the King had obtained a general ratification of every ecclesiastical establishment: But all these laws had less authority with the nation, that they were known to have passed contrary to the sentiments even of those who voted for them, and were in reality extorted by the authority and importunity of the sovereign. The means, however, which both James and Charles had employed, in order to influence the parliament, were intirely regular;" [How? *were intirely regular*; when in the very preceding sentence he had said that "these laws were extorted by the authority and importunity of the sovereign." According to Bishop Burnet's account, the most important of them passed in a way that was yet a little more shameful];[86] "and no reasonable pretext had been afforded for representing these laws as null or invalid."

A little after he says,

"The canons for establishing ecclesiastical jurisdiction were promulgated in 1635; and by the nation were received, tho' without much appearing opposition, yet with great inward discontent and apprehension. Men felt

---

[85] Ib. p. 223.

[86] "In this act of 1633, these acts of 1606, and 1609, were drawn into one. To this great opposition was made by the Earl of Rothes, who desired the acts might be divided: but the King said, It was now one act, and he must either vote for it or against it. He said, he was for the prerogative as much as any man, but that addition was contrary to the liberties of the church, and he thought no determination ought to be made in such matters without the consent of the clergy, at least, without their being heard. The King bid him argue no more, but give his vote: so he voted, Not content. Some few lords offered to argue; but the King stopped them, and commanded them to vote. Almost the whole Commons voted in the negative: so that the act was indeed rejected by the majority: which the King knew; for he had called for a lift of the members, and, with his own pen, had marked every man's vote: yet the clerk of register, who gathers and declares the votes, said it was carried in the affirmative. The Earl of Rothes affirmed it went for the negative: but the King said, The clerk of register's declaration must be held good, unless the Earl of Rothes would go to the bar, and accuse him of falsifying the record of parliament, which was capital: and in that case, if he should fail in the proof, he was liable to the same punishment: so he would not venture on that. Thus the act was published, though in truth it was rejected. The King expressed a high displeasure at all who had concurred in that opposition," &c. *Burnet's summary of affairs before the restoration.*

displeasure, at seeing the royal authority so highly exalted by them, and represented as absolute and uncontrollable. They saw these speculative principles of despotism reduced to practice, and a whole body of ecclesiastical laws established, without any previous consent either of church or state: They dreaded, that, by a parity of reason, like arbitrary authority, from like pretexts and principles, would be assumed in civil matters."[87]

And in a following page, he thus concludes: "In short, religion mingling with faction, private interest with the spirit of liberty, symptoms appeared, on all hands, of the most dangerous insurrection and disorder."[88]

Upon the whole, then, it may be deduced from his own narrative, that a combination of circumstances very different in their nature, gave rise to the first commotions in Scotland: and a proper attention to these might have checked his career of insult, and disposed him to a milder strain with respect to his countrymen, than is to be found in the sentence transcribed above, and in many other passages of this history. I know no one who pretends to justify all the counsels and measures of those times: but no candid reader can approve of such partial representations, and far less, of such abusive and reproachful language, as is only to be matched by the style of certain anniversary declamations. The following reflection of Bishop Burnet must needs appear extremely just, when he finishes his short summary of history on this subject in these words: "The violence with which that kingdom did almost unanimously engage against the administration, may easily convince one, that the provocation must have been very great, to draw on such an entire and vehement concurrence against it."

But I have gone further in this letter than I had at first intended, though I have confined myself to things most material, and chiefly to Mr HUME's speculations on the English government, and on the general grounds of difference between the King and parliament, from the beginning of his reign to the eve of the civil war. As to the manner in which it was carried on, and the various changes in the public counsels, till the army of the Sectaries put an end to the power of the house of Commons, and their leaders formed the daring design of bringing the King to a public trial, and executed the sentence, which in their extraordinary court of judicature they had pronounced against him; I shall not enter at all into any part of this subject, nor into an examination of our author's narrative, and sentiments about it. The nation was reduced to a dismal state; and the hypocrisy, the fanaticism and fury of these latter times, may be described in what terms our author pleases. But still the distinction betwixt the prior and latter counsels and views, ought to have been, all along, carefully maintained; neither should the intentions of those in one period be imputed to all who had joined with them in another.

[87] Mr Hume's history, p. 224.

[88] Mr Hume's history, p. 226.

The character that Mr HUME has drawn of King Charles appears to be as little shaded as possible; perhaps rather less so than would have been expected from some parts even of this history. He had formerly said of him, that "in every other age, or nation, this monarch had been secure of a prosperous and happy reign,"[89] though in the beginning of a preceding chapter he had told us, that "a more submissive nation than the English, would have showed symptoms of discontent at those multiplied violences and disasters,"[90] which he there mentions. In like manner, near the end of the history, he thus expresses himself concerning the King.

"Some historians have rashly questioned his good faith: But, for this reproach, the most malignant scrutiny of his conduct, which, in every circumstance, is now thoroughly known, affords not any reasonable foundation. On the contrary, if we consider the extreme difficulties, to which he was so frequently reduced, and compare the sincerity of his professions and declarations; we shall avow, that probity and honor ought justly to be placed among his most shining qualities. In every treaty, those concessions, which, he thought, in conscience, he could not maintain, he never could, by any motive or persuasion, be induced to grant."[91]

So he now assures us; but elsewhere he had affirmed what follows. "But this concession" (he speaks of the King's agreeing to rescind the canons, the liturgy, and high commission in Scotland, in the year 1639) "was gained by the utmost violence, which he could impose on his disposition and prejudices: He even secretly retained an intention of seizing favourable opportunities, in order to recover the ground, which he had lost;"[92] and again, in relation to his employing Papists in higher or lower offices of trust, "In this particular, they [the Commons] had, no doubt, some reason to blame the King's conduct. He had promised to the last house of Commons a redress of this religious grievance: but he was too apt, in imitation of his father, to consider these promises as temporary expedients; which, after the dissolution of the parliament, he was not any farther to regard."[93] It is quite unnecessary to add any reflections on such passages as these, of which a pretty deal, you see, is to be found in this history.

I am, &c.

[89] Mr Hume's history, p. 199.

[90] Mr Hume's history, p. 167.

[91] Ib. p. 469.

[92] Mr Hume's history, p. 235.

[93] Ib. p. 156.

LETTER IX.

A late eminent patron of infidelity has thought fit to express his contempt of their understanding, who do not acknowledge a first and supreme cause; and who, in a survey of the works of nature, do not perceive the signatures of divine wisdom and power imprinted *there*. Some of his Lordship's predecessors in free-thinking, Tindal, for instance, would probably have talked in like manner of those who, in the same obvious train of reflection, were not led on to the ideas of goodness and justice, and of the moral government of God. If these are excluded from the mind, vain to all the purposes of religion and morality, is the mere speculative idea of a first cause. The foundations of piety are overturned by his Lordship's philosophy, as much as by the tenets of the Epicurean sect. This any one, I think, must acknowledge, who attentively considers both. There is certainly something unnatural in that zeal which is shewn for promoting the principles of irreligion. Can it arise from a steady persuasion of their truth and excellence? Impossible. Can it flow from a love of virtue and of mankind? Surely it cannot: for the irreligious scheme is manifestly subversive of the interests of the former, and of the peace and happiness of the latter. Shall this be attributed to pride, and an affectation of superior parts? It may indeed: but the end that is thus in view, can hardly be attained by their writings and speculations about what they may call the *first philosophy*. On the contrary, in attention to these, many are apt to be surprised at the weakness and dotage of understanding, into which a reputed genius may fall, even in those dissertations and tracts, in which he would pour reproach on the worthiest names, on the most sacred truths, and on human reason itself. The vitious and debauched may be strongly inclined to take sanctuary within the precincts of irreligion: but there is nothing in virtuous minds that can direct them thither. "What would I have to do in a world devoid of a Deity, and devoid of a Providence?"[94] This was the language of a philosophic prince of old: it is the language of wisdom and virtue.

The principles of true piety do undoubtedly demand our regard on account of their native excellence and blissful effects. The devout character includes in it such a sense of the power, goodness, and wisdom of God, of his government and supreme authority, of our entire dependence on him, of his inspection of our conduct, of his numberless benefits and overflowing mercy, as effectually sways the soul to the fear and love of its creator and benefactor, to a willing subjection to his authority, to an ardent desire of his favour, and a full resignation to his disposal, mingled with humble trust, and with the animating prospects of a future state. This in general is true piety; and these are its natural effects. External worship and obedience flowing from such senti-

---

[94] [Greek quotation removed.] Marc. Anton. lib. 2.

ments and dispositions, – this is the service, the reasonable service which God requires.

It has often given me pleasure to observe the regard that is shewn to piety in some of the writings of ancient philosophy; whilst men were directed to acknowledge a presiding providence, at all times, and in all their concerns, and to acquiesce in the divine administration;[95] to ask the aid of heaven in all their undertakings;[96] and to render thanks for their success, for their deliverance from dangers, and for all the good things they enjoyed.[97] They were further told, that it ought to be their general aim in life, to follow God, to consent to his will;[98] and to study a conformity to him, in their becoming just, wise, and holy.[99] They were put in mind, that the divine presence was ever with them, and they were called to act as under a sense of it,[100] and so to fear the Deity, as neither to perpetrate nor devise what was impious and wicked.[101] "Delight thyself in this one thing," says the virtuous Emperor, "and rest in it; to be going on from one kind social action to another, with remembrance of God:[102] – for neither will you rightly discharge any duty to men, nor any duty to God, if at the same time you regard not the connection between things human and divine.[103] – The soul is formed for piety toward God, no less than for justice;"[104] and so in many other passages. The same spirit breathes in the following expressions of a celebrated philosopher, who lived at Rome in the age of the Apostles:

"Looking up to God in all that you do.[105] – I attend to what men say, and how they act; – and I turn in to my self, to see if I too commit the same faults. – If I was formerly liable to them, and am not now, to God I give the

[95]   [Greek quotation removed.] Pythag. in Jamblichi vit. Pythag. c. 32. – Plato et Xenophon. passim de providnetia. ... Plat. Crito, et Epict. enchir. c. 79. ... Arrian. Epictet. l. 2. c. 17. ... Id. l. 2. c. 16. ... Id. l. 3. c. 26.

[96]   [Greek quotation removed.] Xenoph. de provent. ... Id. mem. Socr. l. 5. ... Marc. Anton. l. 6. § 23.

[97]   [Greek quotation removed.] Xenoph. de Agesilao, et sic ubique. Vid. etiam M. Ant. l. 1. § 14. Arrian. Epictet. l. 1. c. 16. et alibi.

[98]   [Greek quotation removed.] Pythag. in Jamblichi vita Pythag. c. 28.

[99]   [Greek quotation removed.] Plat. Theætet. p. 129. ... Id. de repub. lib. 10. p. 760. ... M. Ant. l. 10. § 8.

[100]   [Greek quotation removed.] Arrian. Epictet. l. 1. c. 14. Plato l. 10. de rep. p. 760. et alibi.

[101]   [Greek quotation removed.] Xenoph. Cyrop. l. 8.

[102]   [Greek quotation removed.] M. Ant. l. 6. § 7.

[103]   [Greek quotation removed.] M. Ant. l. 3. § 13.

[104]   [Greek quotation removed.] Id. l. 11. § 20.

[105]   [Greek quotation removed.] Arrian. Epictet. l. 2. c. 19.

praise.[106] – Stay, mortal: be not rash. The combat is great; the attempt godlike. It is for sovereignty, for liberty, for a current of life clear and unruffled. Call to mind the Deity. Invoke him to be your assistant and supporter.[107] – I know to whom I owe subjection and obedience; it is to God."[108]

And to mention but one passage more:

"Had we understanding, what else ought we to do, both in public and private, but to praise God, and to pour out our thanks before him? Ought we not, while either digging, ploughing, or at our meals, to sing this hymn to God; *Great is God!* who hath given us hands, and organs for swallowing and digesting, and who makes us grow up insensibly, and breathe even while asleep. For each of these things we ought thus to bless him. – What then? Since you the multitude are blind, ought there not to be some one to perform this duty in your place; and pay this hymn to God for you all? – Were I a nightingale, I would do the business of a nightingale: – now that I am a rational creature, I ought to hymn the Deity. This is my business: this I perform: this is my post; and, while I am allowed, I will never leave it. And you I will exhort to join with me in this my song."[109]

Such, my friend, were the sentiments of some Pagan philosophers: thus did they honour the pious principle and disposition. To them, therefore, might we appeal on this subject: and this appeal, it would seem, ought to have influence on not a few in our age, who may be, I don't know how, more inclined to regard the sentiments of an ancient philosopher, than the dictates of our holy religion, and the words of an apostle of Christ.

But I was about to say somewhat concerning a few passages of Mr HUME'S history, relative to the worship of God. – Let one of them suffice for a specimen of this author's turn of mind, and manner of expression. It is taken from the 396th page.

"Whatever ridicule to a philosophic mind," says he, "may be thrown on pious ceremonies, it must be confessed, that, during a very religious age, no

---

[106] [Greek quotation removed.] Arrian. Epictet. l. 4. c. 4.

[107] [Greek quotation removed.] Arrian. Epictet. l. 2. c. 18.

[108] [Greek quotation removed.] Id. l. 4. c. 12.

[109] [Greek quotation removed.] Arrian. Epictet. l. 1. c. 16. In like manner, l. 2. 23. The above quotations are rendered for the most part in the words of a late translation.

institutions can be more advantageous to the rude multitude, and tend more to mollify that fierce and gloomy spirit of devotion, to which they are so subject. Even the English church, tho' it had retained a share of Popish superstition, may justly be thought too naked and unadorned, and still to approach too near the abstract and spiritual religion of the Puritans. Laud and his associates, by reviving a few primitive institutions of this nature, corrected the error of the first reformers, and presented, to the affrightened and astonished mind, some sensible, exterior observances, which might occupy it during its religious exercises, and abate the violence of its disappointed efforts. The thought, no longer bent on that divine and mysterious Essence, so superior to the narrow capacities of mankind, was able, by means of the new model of devotion, to relax itself in the contemplation of pictures, postures, vestments, buildings;" only Laud "did not conduct this scheme with the enlarged sentiments and cool disposition of a legislator, but with the intemperate zeal of a sectary." The meaning of all this is but too manifest: and thus at length these same "insignificant ceremonies," whose "very insignificancy recommended them to the superstitious prelate,"[110] are to be held as "primitive institutions," which are to be considered as of no small consequence, and worthy the attention of a wise legislator; and "the mechanical devotion which was proposed to be raised by them,"[111] must be understood to be recommended to our regard.

But did this writer think of what he was about, when he ventured to talk, as he hath too often, in a manner so irreligious, as would have been shocking to the sense of a sober Heathen? Here, my friend, I am at a loss how to proceed. Shall I speak of impiety covered with a thin veil? of an attempt, a weak and foolish one indeed, to resolve all piety into superstition or enthusiasm, that it may be thus exposed to reproach and ridicule? Must it not very sensibly affect every virtuous and good man, to see religion so insulted, and its sacred principles treated with profane irreverence? Shall I talk of the awful guilt that is thus contracted? and of the deplorable and horrible state of things, in every light, if the spirit of impiety should spread and prevail? Licentious as are the manners of the age, impiety, I trust, is not its characteristic. Some efforts indeed have been made to propagate its absurd and pernicious tenets, which even many of those whose morals are not irreproachable, shew themselves disposed to look upon with merited indignation and contempt. How dreadful a thing for any one to go about, by opposing the essential truths of religion, to weaken the foundations of human happiness and hope; nay of society itself, and of all truth, justice, and probity among men. And how mean, how sordid

[110] Mr Hume's history, p. 201.

[111] Ib. p. 203.

the aim, to sink our nature to a level with that of the animal creation? Guilty and unhappy men! who are so affected, and so prompted. God grant they may be brought to serious reflection, and to a sober mind, ere the heavy pressure of affliction be upon them, and death draw nigh.

But it is not enough for us to abhor the irreligious scheme: it is of the utmost consequence, that we have a lively sense of the worth and excellency of true piety; which surely doth not consist in abstract speculations, is far different even from a full assent of the understanding to the fundamental articles of religion, and comprehends in it, as I have before observed, many noble dispositions of the heart. What Mr HUME, in one place, calls "the abstract and spiritual religion of the Puritans," is elsewhere defined to be "a mode of worship, – that borrowed nothing from the senses, but reposed itself intirely on the contemplation of that divine essence, which discovers itself to the understanding only. This species of devotion, so suitable to the supreme Being, but so little suitable to human frailty,"[112] &c. Thus will men talk of subjects, to which they are perfect strangers, even in idea; while they speak of the imagination, instead of the understanding and will; and of contemplation and abstract speculation, instead of the rational aims, desires and affections of the soul.

Were it worth while, I might observe upon this author's representing astonishment and terror as ingredients in the devotion of those whom he would have us to consider as enthusiasts; since, according to all his ideas, these emotions should belong to the superstitious character. But, in truth, he seems to speak of them as ingredients of devotion in general. I could wish that this writer would bethink himself a little. Does he point at a dejection and anguish of a guilty mind, and at the contrition of a penitent and humble spirit? I could almost beseech him, not to talk lightly or ludicrously of this home-felt subject. Is it possible for one in a sober and vacant hour; or, it may be, when solitude and silence are forced upon him by some painful distress; – is it possible for him to look back on a life spent in folly and vice, and on some of its more guilty scenes, without the sensation of remorse and anguish? Can the reflections of conscience be warded off as heretofore, or its judgment and condemnation be evaded, or overawed? Do not these naturally direct our thoughts upward to God, and forward to futurity? Does not one then know and feel himself to be a subject of the divine government? And must he not discover one irrefragable proof of his righteous moral government, in these inward perceptions of the immediate dismal consequences of guilt? Is not this according to the general order and constitution of things, which the God of nature hath established? and according to that fundamental law of his administration, which allots present and future punishment to *the workers of iniquity?* Is not this administration here begun? Is it not felt in the breasts of the wicked, as well as exhibited in the melancholy

---

[112] Mr Hume's history, p. 62.

effects of many base and vitious acts? May not this be appealed to the experience and observation of all mankind? Unhappy those persons who have most tasted of the bitter fruits of wickedness; unless these have been to them blessed of God, I say, blessed of God, to become the salutary medicine of their souls, the means of their being restored to spiritual health, and, by consequence, to inward tranquillity. In those who have the use of their reason, remorse and fear are, in some degree or other, the attendants of heinous guilt. And when one is thus pained and dejected, whither shall he betake himself for deliverance and peace? Whither indeed, but to that *Father of mercies* against whom he hath offended, whose laws he hath violated, whose mercies he hath abused, and whose righteous displeasure he hath incurred? Deeply sensible that he has to do with God, in the spirit of humility and contrition he will pour out his requests before him, and ardently implore forgiveness. The anguish of true repentance is softened with the hope of mercy: the riches of divine compassion toward penitent offenders is an amiable and delightful subject. How fully disclosed in the Christian revelation, in its essential doctrines, and in the whole plan of our redemption by the Son of God? In it we are assured, that "God is in Christ reconciling the world unto himself, not imputing their trespasses unto them." Whosoever in faith and submission hearkens to this doctrine, and with the spirit of a true penitent returns to his heavenly Father, is accepted in our Redeemer, and blessed in his salvation. How divinely excellent and truly god-like is all this grace? How is it suited to pour light, comfort, and joy, into the dark, the doubtful and disconsolate spirit? Thoughts of God as the great legislator and governor of the world, may well create dismay and dread in their minds of the guilty and polluted, who know the demerit of wickedness, and feel the misery of internal disorder. But as their recovery is begun, when the sentiments of Christian faith, and the purposes of genuine repentance, have fully entered into the soul, so these are blended with hope, and with the pleasing views of mercy and acceptance in our Lord. – These, my friend, are not light concerns: undoubtedly they are not: our present peace, our support in trouble, our hopes beyond the grave, and our everlasting felicity are included here. Reason and religion conspire to dictate the important truth; which must be assented to by all who believe in God, who regard him as the supreme ruler of the intellectual world, who think worthily of him and of their own rational natures, and who deem themselves to be of a rank of beings superior to the brutes that perish.

But let us take a view of piety or internal worship in its full extent. It supposes the knowledge and belief of the prime articles of religion, and it includes in it every becoming affection of soul toward the most high God in all his glory and grace, and in all the relations which he bears to us, as our creator, preserver, benefactor, our redeemer, lawgiver, and judge.

Do we naturally admire what is great, and love what is good, and esteem what is excellent? and should not this admiration, esteem, and love rise up to delightful reverence and adoration, whilst we think of the self-existent Jehovah, the almighty maker of heaven and earth, whose works proclaim his power, intelligence, and goodness, and who is glorious in holiness, justice, and truth?

Do we rightly regard him as the parent of nature, whose energy is ever exerted on the material world, who upholds all things by the word of his power, who directs the motions of the hosts of heaven in their comely array, whose providence is universal, whose goodness is diffusive, and *who opens his hand liberally, and satisfieth the desire of every living thing?* and is no tribute of adoration to be paid, no incense of praise to ascend upward from this lower world, from the rational creation, which is alone capable of such noble acts of gratitude and religious worship? Or should we not rather join in the beautiful and lofty hymn of praise, which the great poet puts into the mouths of our first parents in paradise?

> *These are thy glorious works, Parent of good,*
> *Almighty, thine this universal frame,*
> *Thus wondrous fair; thyself how wondrous then!*
> *Unspeakable, who sitt'st above these heavens,*
> *To us invisible, or dimly seen*
> *In these thy lowest works: yet these declare*
> *Thy goodness beyond thought, and pow'r divine.*
> *Speak ye who best can tell, ye sons of light,*
> *Angels, for ye behold him, and with songs*
> *And choral symphonies, day without night,*
> *Circle his throne rejoicing; ye in heaven,*
> *On earth join all ye creatures to extol*
> *Him first, him last, him midst, and without end. –*
> *Hail universal Lord, be bounteous still*
> *To give us only good.*[113] –

What an elevation of sentiment and language, which flow from a sacred source? What a dignity of devotion is here; worthy of our first parents, worthy of a state of innocence? But to proceed:

Do we think of God as "the Father of our spirits, in whose hand is our breath and life, and whose are all our ways; who holdeth our souls in life, and suffereth not our feet to be moved?" – Do we consider ourselves as indeed unworthy of his regard, and yet the objects of his benignity, in a thousand instances, from day to day? – Do we reflect on the gifts and care of his providence; on our being preserved in health or relieved in sickness, shielded from dangers, delivered from impending evils, blessed in our families, our friends and worldly interests? – Do we attend to all the effects of his munificence and

---

[113] [John Milton, *Paradise Lost*, Book 5.]

paternal care? – And must not the soul be penetrated with a lively sense of his infinite goodness, and the tribute of a grateful heart be offered up with sacred delight? Do we abhor the thought of stupid insensibility or of base ingratitude towards a benefactor, a friend, a parent on earth? and can we think lightly of an habitual disregard of God, and of aggravated ingratitude towards our divine benefactor, our heavenly Father? Are we so highly indebted to his bounty, and do we deny him the honour that is due to his name? Is it reasonable, is it fit that it should be so? The mind and heart recoil from the thought as impiously absurd.

"Oh bless our God, ye people; and make the voice of his praise to be heard. – Give thanks unto the Lord, for he is good; for his mercy endureth for ever. Who can utter the mighty acts of the Lord? who can shew forth all his praise? – Great and marvellous are thy works, Lord God Almighty; just and true are thy ways, thou King of saints. Who shall not fear thee, O Lord, and glorify thy name? for thou only art holy. – Thine O Lord, is the greatness, and the power, and the glory, and the majesty: for all that is in the heaven and in the earth, is thine; thine is the kingdom, O Lord, and thou art exalted as head above all. – Justice and judgment are the habitation of thy throne: mercy and truth go before thy face. – I will extol thee, my God, O King, and I will bless thy name for ever and ever. Every day will I bless thee, and I will praise thy name for ever and ever. Great is the Lord, and greatly to be praised; and his greatness is unsearchable. One generation shall praise thy works to another, and shall declare thy mighty acts. – They shall abundantly utter the memory of thy great goodness, and shall sing of thy righteousness. The Lord is good to all: and his tender mercies are over all his works. – The Lord preserveth all them that love him: but all the wicked will he destroy. My mouth shall speak the praise of the Lord: and let all flesh bless his holy name for ever and ever. – Bless ye the Lord, all ye his hosts, ye ministers of his that do his pleasure. Bless the Lord, all his works in all places of his dominion: bless the Lord, O my soul."

What an assemblage of amiable and august ideas is here presented to us? Well may the mind be enlightened and the heart warmed by such just and sublime conceptions, which are mingled with the sacred energy of devotion.

And does Jehovah reign? the blessed and only potentate, the King of kings, and Lord of lords, whose dominion endures unto all generations. Reverence therefore and submission are due to him in this venerable character: whilst, as the loyal subjects of his kingdom, we yield a willing obedience to his authority, which is supreme, and to his laws, which are holy, wise, just, and good.

Resignation to the divine will must ever be regarded as a comely disposition of mind, and an essential part of true piety. That his providence superintends all the affairs of this great world, and that good men are the objects of the peculiar care of heaven, is to them a doctrine full of comfort and joy. Without it what a wide waste must this world appear to us, and how very desolate the condition of human life? The view of a presiding, of a particular providence, is as a friendly guide to direct and support the weary traveller in a strange country, where he is encompassed with dangers, and about to be involved in darkness. Well may full resignation and humble affiance be united in the minds of the servants of God; whilst they consider themselves as in his hands, who does all things wisely and well, who alone knows what is best for them, who will never forsake them, who is now training them up for an unseen and eternal state, who hath invited them to place their confidence in him, and who "will make all things to work together for good to them that love him." Resignation and serenity of soul are the consequences of such delightful views and hopes.

I have already spoke of the sentiments and disposition of a humble penitent, when he earnestly implores the divine mercy, and fully assents to those important truths which unfold the wisdom and grace of the mediatorial scheme. In it there is a firm foundation laid, not only for our present inward peace, but likewise for every exalting and ennobling hope. Thus too are we brought under new and endearing obligations to the service of our God and Saviour, which must be ever suitably regarded by all who are interested in the blessings of the redemption which is in Christ Jesus, and who would approve themselves his faithful disciples.

In the survey of the wondrous scene of infinite goodness that is exhibited to us in the gospel, must not the pious principle of gratitude be still more cherished in our spirits? whilst we attend to the display of adorable wisdom and love for our recovery from a state of sin and death, and our being called to the hope of life and glory, through Jesus our Lord. He must be considered as devoid of the spirit of a Christian, who is not affected in this manner. In all the acts of piety too are we to be encouraged by those peculiar doctrines of our holy faith, which lead us to consider Jesus the Saviour as our mediator and intercessor, through whom we are invited to draw nigh to God, and in whose prevailing name the humble and the upright are accepted. An important idea this, which must run through all the acts of Christian worship.

Further, Is it possible for us to reflect but ever so little on ourselves, and on our present state, without perceiving that we are, in truth, weak, indigent, and dependent creatures? And is it not most proper for us, in every respect, to cultivate in our minds a sense of our absolute dependence on God? Thus are we taught to acknowledge him in all our ways, to ask the supply of all our wants, and to commend ourselves at all times to his guardianship and guidance. They who fear and serve him, may indeed be persuaded, that his power, goodness, and wisdom will not be inactive, but will be exerted in their behalf, not only with regard to the concernments of this transient state, but also with respect to those of another and a better world. Thus may they hope to grow in grace and goodness, to be delivered from the dangerous snares of sin, to be guided and animated in the paths of righteousness and religion, and to be fitted for entering into that pure and perfect state, to which they now look forward, and whither their desires, their aims, and affections are now to be directed. He who formed the spirit of man, well knows every way of access to it, and in what manner it may be influenced. Is it the language both of religion and of true philosophy, that we are dependent creatures; and shall this dependence be acknowledged in our less important interests, and the thought of it be rejected with relation to those of the highest moment? Is the divine agency confessed in the material world, and shall it be denied in the intellectual? Would a rational creature of God, sensible of internal maladies and weakness, aspire after spiritual health and purity, and lift up his supplications for divine aid; and will these be disregarded by our heavenly Father? Are we naturally prompted to look upwards, in every season of distress and need; and shall the upright and pious do so in vain? "If ye being evil," says the Redeemer of men, "know how to give good gifts unto your children, how much more shall your Father which is in heaven give the Holy Spirit, and all good things, to them that ask him?" The doctrine of divine assistance is in itself most rational, and is well suited to our ideas of the goodness of God, and of the illustrious manifestation of it in the Christian scheme; in which the clearest promises of his abundant grace are contained. It must be acknowledged, 'tis true, that this doctrine hath been too oft perverted to the purposes of sloth and presumption on the one hand, and of wild enthusiasm on the other. But is there any thing new, any thing extraordinary in all this? The wisest doctrines and the most salutary truths have in every age been liable to the misrepresentations of ignorance, and to the perversions of vice and folly.

Let me likewise remind you, that a sacred regard to God as ever present with us, and an habitual study to approve ourselves to him, are essential ingredients in true piety, and of the most commanding influence on the heart and life.

Upon the whole, Is there any thing in all this subject that is not perfectly agreeable to the dictates of our purest reason? Is not all veneration due to the eternal God, the Creator of the world, the Father of our spirits, glorious in holiness and goodness, supreme in authority and power? Is not our lively gratitude, though a poor, yet a proper return to his benignity, his munificence and mercy to the children of men? Do we not owe all subjection to his authority, and an unlimited resignation to his will? Is it not most fit, and does it not tend to our greatest good, to cherish the thoughts of our entire dependence on him in all regards, and humbly to commit ourselves to his grace and protection? As the Christian revelation has given us some new discoveries of the glory of God, and of the relations which he bears to us, does it not become us to attend diligently to these, and to be suitably affected by them? If conscious of guilt, if truly penitent on account of it, and earnestly concerned for remission; should we not pour out our desires before him, who has mercifully invited us to draw nigh in Jesus our Lord? Are we ever in his presence, and should we not revere it? Are we accountable to him for our conduct; and should we not study now to be accepted, that we may be for ever blessed?

All this is true piety: this is the worship of the mind and heart: these are sentiments and dispositions strictly rational and truly excellent, which are obviously founded in right apprehensions of ourselves, and of God. What shall we think of the state of an intelligent creature who is wholly a stranger to them, and who lives "without God in the world?" Is not this a base and unworthy habit of soul, which we must strongly condemn? and is not such a one engaged in an ungrateful, a criminal, and impious, nay in a sordid and contemptible course of life, that is separated from all noble views, when he so behaves, and so persists? The reasonableness, the worth, the amiableness and excellency of true piety are so perspicuous to an attentive mind, that it would seem they must be acknowledged in theory by all who believe in God, even by those who have never felt its benign influence in their own spirits. – External acts of worship are the proper expressions of devout dispositions. If these are felt, they will be expressed: and the frequency of such acts tends to confirm the pious habit. As the spirit of diffusive benevolence is the true Christian spirit, so it will enter into our private and social worship; whilst we render thanks to our God for the various gifts of his bounty and love, not only to ourselves, but to our fellow Christians, and all our brethren of mankind; and earnestly pray for their good, for their greatest good in the advancement of the interests of the kingdom of God upon earth. In short, true piety, in all its parts, in all its acts, has a manifest tendency to strengthen every virtuous principle, to cherish every noble aim, to purify and elevate the soul, to encourage and to animate us in the path of our duty, and to lead us onward through every stage of life, to its concluding period, with serenity and hope.

I have done, Sir; and shall not take any further notice of the loose and irreligious sneers which Mr HUME has not been afraid to throw out on a subject of the highest dignity, and of infinite importance. We have had enough of his confused ideas and speculations about superstition and enthusiasm. Rational and manly piety disclaims an affinity with both. They may indeed borrow her venerable name, and may disparage it in the eyes of those who are unacquainted with her native worth and heavenly original. But true wisdom will teach us to mark the great disparity, and to be on our guard against deceitful appearances. May this be the concern of the friends of religion; whilst at the same time they study to shew the mild, the pure, and salutary influence of genuine piety, in an uniform worthy behaviour. Thus would its sacred honours be retrieved, and its sentiments and dispositions be recommended to the esteem and love of all around them. – Piety, virtue, and sound knowledge are in themselves nearly allied; and they will ever produce the happiest effects when they are united in the minds of men.

I am, &c.

THE END

5
TOBIAS SMOLLETT,
THE CRITICAL REVIEW

[Tobias Smollett], review of *The History of Great Britain. Vol. 2. Containing the Commonwealth and the Reigns of Charles II and James II*, in *The Critical Review*, December 1756, Vol. 2, pp. 385–404.
Complete review.

The *Critical Review* was founded in 1756 by Scottish novelist and historian Tobias Smollett (1721–1771) and printer Archibald Hamilton. Smollett previously reviewed for the *Monthly Review* – which had been in publication since 1749 – and he modelled his new journal after the successful format of the *Monthly*. For the next half-century, the two journals competed with each other for dominance, although the *Monthly Review* was always slightly in the lead in terms of sales. Like the *Monthly* and virtually all early review journals, reviews in the *Critical* appeared anonymously. However, Hamilton's personal copy of the journal contains annotations indicating authorship.[1] According to Hamilton's notes, the reviewer of Volume 2 of Hume's *History* was Smollett, who around this time was composing his own multi-volume history of England. Smollett had earlier reviewed Daniel MacQueen's *Letters on Mr. Hume's History of Great Britain* (1756) in the *Critical Review*, and concluded that MacQueen impartially and successfully refuted Hume's view of Protestant fanaticism at the time of the Reformation (for quotations from Smollett's review, see the entry on MacQueen earlier in this collection).

Smollett's review of Hume's second volume of the *History* is the opening article in the December 1756 issue of the journal. According to Smollett, it is "one of the best histories which modern times have produced." He gives Hume high marks for organization, clarity, and reflection. In spite of such praise, though, much of the review exposes problems – or "little blemishes" as he calls them. There are problems with some historical speculations, such as Hume's observations about the strategic disadvantage of castles that are located on the water's edge; Hume removed that entire discussion in later editions of

---

[1] Smollett's own contributions to the *Critical Review* are catalogued in James G. Basker's *Tobias Smollett: Critic and Journalist*, (Newark: University of Delaware Press, 1988).

144

the *History*. There are additional problems with verbosity, Scotticisms, and ambiguous expressions; Hume again modified several of these passages in later editions. As to Hume's account of battle scenes, Smollett suggests that "Mr. *Hume's* genius shines more in speculation than in description." He concludes the article with extended quotations regarding Montrose and Cromwell, which he thinks show Hume at his best.

Although Hume believed that the sale of Smollett's own *History* negatively impacted on the sale of his own, the two authors nevertheless developed a friendship. Smollett acquired a notorious reputation as a libeller, and, facing exile near the close of his life, he wrote to Hume for help in obtaining employment. In one such letter he writes, "In whatever part of the earth it may be my Fate to reside, I shall always remember with pleasure, & recapitulate with pride, the friendly intercourse I have maintained with one of the best men, & undoubtedly, the best writer of the age" (Smollett to Hume, August 31, 1768). Hume responded shortly after, "I am sensible of your great partiality, in the good opinion you express towards me; but it gives me no less pleasure than if it were founded on the greatest truth, for I accept it as a pledge of your good will and friendship" (Hume to Smollett, September 21, 1768). By that time, Smollett's reputation was so marred that Hume was unable to find him employment. He once reportedly said of Smollett and his volatile disposition that "he was like a cocoa-nut, the outside was the worst."[2] As Hume's *History* increased in popularity in the decades after his death, several editions inserted supplemental narrative from Smollett's *History*, covering the more recent periods of English history not dealt with by Hume.

ARTICLE I.

The History of Great Britain. Vol. II. Containing the Commonwealth, and the Reigns of Charles II. and James II. By David Hume, Esq; 4to. Price 14s. in Boards. Millar.

This is one of the few performances of modern authors, which we can read with satisfaction and commend with pleasure. The materials are well arranged; the facts are, in general, related with perspicuity and precision; new lights are thrown upon many occurrences which were not well understood before: the connections of states, and politics of princes, are judiciously explained and unravelled: the paroxysms of the *English* constitution carefully noted and diligently described: the characters accurately delineated, and the reflections just and pertinent. The author seems to be master of his subject: his language is

---

[2] Henry Grey Graham, *Scottish Men of Letters*, London: Adam and Charles Black, 1908, p. 317.

copious, and his diction correct. Yet with all this merit, the work may not be altogether without imperfections.

We do not, however, by way of reproach, observe, that the historian seems to have begun his performance with a warm (not to call it a weak) side towards those princes of the *Stuart* family who have sat upon the throne of *England*, and a pique, of education, against the Protestant Dissenters. Without such prepossessions, perhaps, no writer ever assumed the pen; and we have the less reason to impute them as capital defects to Mr. *Hume*, as they do not seem to have warped him from the truth in any part of the narration: on the contrary, we think we can perceive, in the course of his production, those prejudices vanishing before the power of historical credit, operating upon the natural candour and good sense of the author.

Were we disposed to find fault, we should disapprove of the numerous reflections which occur in every page, and instead of elucidating the subject not only perplex the reader, but also serve to fix upon the historian the charge of vanity, singularity, and affectation. This rage of reflecting, and even of dogmatizing, seems to have possessed all the late compilers, in this as well as in other countries of *Europe*. Histories are metamorphosed into dissertations; the chain of events is broken, the reader's attention diffused; and his judgment anticipated: peculiar incidents that distinguish the complexion of times, and form the features of the most remarkable individuals, are overlooked and omitted, and all character distorted into grotesque figures made up of conceit and antithesis. – This, however, is not the case with Mr. *Hume*. His reflections are, for the most part, just, tho' sometimes superfluous; and as we have already observed, his characters distinctly marked. Not but that, sometimes, his reflections will admit of dispute. In page 61 he says, 'A government totally military and despotic, is sure, after some time, to fall into impotence and languor.' – We should imagine that a military government is, of all others, the least subject to languor, because it is in continual action. – It may be overheated by exercise and enterprise, so as to burst into anarchy; but surely it is not so apt to flag or grow impotent as a merely civil institution. – Speaking of *Blakes's* atchievements, he says, (p. 67.)

'The castles which at that time guarded the entrance into harbours were commonly built on the brink of the water: if they were raised to any height, their shot passed over the ships, and they were themselves soon destroyed by the superior fire of the vessels; if low, the small arms of the seamen, who overlooked them, rendered it impossible for the soldiers to stand to their guns. At present the castles are removed to some distance, and sunk to a level with the water; which renders such enterprises as those of *Blake*, in reality as impracticable, as before his time they were universally esteemed.'

In one case then, the seamen had an advantage over the landmen by being above them; and in the other, the landmen have the better of the seamen, by being below them. With submission to Mr. *Hume's* philosophy and observation, we apprehend it is as easy for a man to fire up as to fire down; that modern fortifications are not placed at a distance from the water's edge; and that wheresoever they may be placed, they can have no advantage over ships of war provided with the same number and weight of metal; but that the contrary is true.

In the 118th page we are told, 'that the Presbyterians and Independents esteemed bear-baiting heathenish and unchristian: the sport of it, not the inhumanity, gave offence.' How does that appear? – Colonel *Hewson*, from his pious zeal, marched into the city, and destroyed all the bears that were kept for the diversion of the citizens. – Certes, he was not the more a bear for that reason. – There is a difference between killing an animal outright, and torturing it to death. Besides, he might think such diversions serve only to render the spectators barbarous and cruel. It is a national reproach. Nevertheless, we cannot believe that colonel *Hewson* destroyed all the bears in the city; though we approve of the massacre, if it was for no other reason than that it gave rise to the facetious and witty production known by the name of *Hudibras*. He, in the same page, remarks, 'that religious hypocrisy is of a singular nature; and being generally unknown to the person himself, implies less falshood than other species of insincerity.' We always imagined that dissimulation was an ingredient in hypocrisy; and that dissimulation was a voluntary effort. How then can a man be a hypocrite without knowing himself false; or dissemble without insincerity?

He gives us to understand (p. 144.) that 'the power of the sword had, in all ages, been allowed to be vested in the crown; and though no law conferred this prerogative, every parliament, till the last of the preceding reign, had willingly submitted to an authority more antient, and therefore more sacred than that of any positive statute.' – That it was more ancient than any positive statute may be doubted. Those who imagine all the liberty of the subject is the gift of the sovereign, may be of that opinion. We can conceive original monarchies formed by a compact between king and people, and in that case the sovereign could have no authority but what he derived from that compact. The princes among the antient *Germans* never declared war without the consent of the people. Neither do we think the antiquity of any custom renders it the more sacred. Were customs to be sanctified in that manner, we should have retained to this day, many barbarous practices which are now happily laid aside and forgotten.

Our historian after having given an account of the treaty of *Nimeguen*, observes, (p. 265.) that '*Lewis XIV. of France* had, during some years, a real and near prospect of attaining the monarchy of *Europe*, and of exceeding the empire of *Charlemagne*, perhaps equalling that of antient *Rome*, had *England* continued much longer in the same condition, and under the same government, it is not easy to conceive that he could have failed of his purpose.' – When we consider the powers that would have opposed him, we cannot conceive how he could accomplish that purpose, even though *England* had been annihilated. The prince of *Orange* had already, in a good measure, checked the progress of the *French* conquests. The whole house of *Austria* in *Spain* and *Germany* would have exerted itself to oppose them; and doubtless the northern crowns would have joined in the alliance, had they thought the liberties of *Europe* in such imminent danger.

We think Mr. Hume_is too severe on the character and abilities of *Milton*. He says, (p. 125.) 'he prostituted his pen in factious disputes, and in justifying the most violent measure of his party.' – We have a better opinion of *Milton*. – He was an enthusiast; but, surely no prostitute. Neither do we find his prose writings disagreeable; nor any of his poetical performances flat and insipid. We cannot think that near one third of his *Paradise Lost* is devoid of harmony, elegance, and vigor of imagination. – In comparing him with *Homer, Lucretius, and Tasso*, he affects to overlook the *Mantuan* Swan, and *il divino Ariosto*. – *Lucretius* is a didactic poet, and therefore we apprehend, bears little affinity with the *Paradise Lost*, which is an heroic poem. There are indeed in both, harmonious verses and noble description; but these we expect to meet with in all poems, let them be never so different in their natures. – Ου゚ δεν δε κοινόν ἐστι ʹΟμήρω καὶ Εμῶεδοκλει, ὦλὴν τὸ μετρον· δὶ ὅ τὸν μεν ποιητὴν δίκαιον καλεῖν, τὸν δε Ρυσιολὰγον μᾶλλον ἤ ὦοιητὴν. For, *Homer* and *Empedocles* have nothing in common but the measure; therefore the first ought to be called a poet, and the other a philosopher.

Mr. *Hume*, after having convicted *Charles* II. of ingratitude to his friends; repeated breach of faith to his parliament; corruption, cruelty, and oppression; in summing up his character, says, 'All his enormities, if fairly and candidly examined, may be imputed, in a great measure, to the indolence of his temper; a fault, which, however unfortunate in a monarch, it is impossible for us to regard with great severity.' – His want of œconomy, his being dead to glory, his neglecting the interest of the nation, as well as the good offices of his friends, might be owing to that natural infirmity: but schemes of perfidy and corruption, cruel executions, and efforts of revenge, must have been produced from more active principles.

The character of his brother *James* is, we conceive, treated with the same overstrained tenderness.

'Thus ended the reign of a prince (*says he, p.* 434.) whom, if we consider in his personal character rather than his public conduct, we may safely pronounce to have been more unfortunate than criminal. He had many of those qualities that form a good citizen: even some of those which, had not they been swallowed up in bigotry and arbitrary principles, serve to compose a good sovereign. In domestic life, his conduct was irreproachable, and is intitled to our approbation. Severe, but open in his enmities, steady in his councils, diligent in his schemes, brave in his enterprises, faithful, sincere, and honourable in his dealings with all men.' –

We shall see how far this character corresponds with his conduct and administration, even as it is described by our historian.

The first act of his reign was to declare his resolution to maintain the established government, both in church and state, p. 376. – The customs and the greater part of the excise had been voted, by parliament, during the late king's life: the grant was now expired; nor had the successor any right to levy these branches of the revenue. But *James* issued a proclamation, ordering the customs and excise to be paid as before; and this exertion of power he would not deign to qualify by the least act, or even appearance of condescension. – The king likewise went openly, and with all the ensigns of his dignity, to mass, an illegal meeting. He even sent *Caryl* as his agent to *Rome*, to make submissions to the pope, and to pave the way for a solemn re-admission of *England* into the bosom of the catholic church. – So much for his sincerity and honourable dealing. – Next for his irreproachable conduct in domestic life.

'The king however (p. 378.) had another attachment, seemingly not very consistent with this devoted regard to his queen and to his priests: it was to Mrs. *Sedley*, whom he soon after created countess of *Dorchester*, and who expected to govern him with the same authority, which the duchess of *Portsmouth* had possessed during the former reign. But, the king, who had entertained the ambition of converting his people, was told, that the regularity of his life ought to correspond to the sanctity of his intentions; and he was prevailed with at first to remove Mrs. *Sedley* from court: a resolution in which he had not the courage to persevere.' –

We would ask, is the open and avowed practice of adultery irreproachable, even in a king? We shall pass by the outrageous cruelties committed in the west by *Kirke* and *Jefferies*, with his approbation; and consider how far he was brave in his enterprises. Mr. *Hume* owns that his courage was questioned in the *Dutch* war, though we really think that was a malicious imputation. But let us see how he behaved after the landing of the prince of *Orange*. P. 428. "He embraced a sudden resolution of drawing off his army, and retiring towards *London*: a measure which could serve only to betray his fears, and provoke farther treachery. – He seemed in this emergence as much depressed with adversity, as he had before been vainly elated with prosperity. – The news which the king received from all quarters, helped to continue the panic into which he was fallen. – Impelled by his own fear and those of others, he precipitately embraced the resolution of withdrawing into *France*. – He himself shewed not any symptoms of spirit, nor discovered any intention of resuming the reins of government which he had once thrown aside. His authority was not plainly expired; and if he had exercised his power, while possessed of it, with very precipitant and haughty councils, he relinquished it by a despair equally precipitant and pusillanimous." With respect to the steadiness of his councils, in page 424, we find the following paragraph.

'While the king was dismayed with these symptoms of general disaffection, he received a letter from the marquiss of *Albeville*, his minister at the *Hague*; which informed him with certainty that he was soon to look for a powerful invasion from *Holland*, and that pensionary *Fogel* had at last acknowledged, that the scope of all the *Dutch* preparations was to transport forces into *England*. Though *James* could reasonably expect no other intelligence, he was astonished at the news: He grew pale, and the letter dropped from his hand: His eyes were now opened, and he found himself on the brink of a frightful precipice, which his delusions had hitherto concealed from him. His ministers and counsellors, equally astonished with himself, saw no recourse but in a sudden and precipitant retraction of all those fatal measures, by which he had created himself so many enemies, foreign and domestic. He paid court to the *Dutch*, and offered to enter into any alliance with them for common security: He replaced in all the counties the deputy-lieutenants and justices, who had been deprived of their commissions for their adherence to the test and the penal laws: He restored the charters of *London* and of all the corporations: He annulled the court of ecclesiastical commission: He took off the bishop of *London's* suspension: He re-initiated the expelled president and fellows of *Magaelen* college: And he was even reduced to caress those bishops, whom he had so lately prosecuted and insulted. All these measures were regarded as symptoms of fear, not of repentance. The bishops, instead of promising succour, or suggesting comfort, recapitulated to him all the instances of his mal-administration, and advised him thenceforwards to follow more salutary council. And as intelligence arrived of a great disaster, which had befallen the *Dutch* fleet, it is commonly believed, that the king recalled, for some time, the concessions, which he had ordered to be made to *Magdalen* college: A very bad sign of his sincerity in his other concessions. Nay so prevalent were his unfortunate prepossessions, that, amidst all his present distresses, he could not forbear, at the baptism of the young prince, from appointing the pope to be one of the godfathers.'

On the whole, when we consider this king's breach of faith to his parliament; his arbitrary exactions; his cruelty and revenge upon those who were supposed to favour *Monmouth*; his efforts to establish the dispensing power; his reviving the court of high commission; his suspending the penal laws; his patronizing the furious *Tyrconnel*, in practising the most outrageous violence and injustice against the Protestants of *Ireland*; his embassy to *Rome*; his attempt upon *Magdalen* college in *Oxford*, his imprisoning the bishops for having presented an humble and dutiful petition; and his tampering with corporations to pack a parliament; we are apt to think he took some pains to render himself odious to his people, by a continued succession of the most provoking measures, without the intervention of one popular act; and as we do not find one single instance of his generosity, clemency, or any active virtue, on record, we cannot think he deserves the least historical praise either as a monarch or a man. Mr. *Hume*, indeed, when he delineates his character, says, 'Such it was when as duke of *York* he mounted the throne of *England*.' But, if he thought his character changed with his condition, he ought to have mentioned the alteration.

We come now to make a few animadversions upon the stile of this history, which we think in some few places inflated or affected; and in others incorrect; perhaps it is, in the main, deficient in weight and simplicity. He seems to be superstitiously fond of the word *fanaticism*, and indeed singular in the interpretation thereof. *Oliver Cromwell* never appears unimcumbered of the epithet *embarrassed*; and *Foster* seems to be a pampered favourite that struts forth in every page. We complain of affectation and periphrasis in the following sentences. Page 119, speaking of the quakers, he says, 'Instead of that affected adulation introduced into modern tongues, of speaking to individuals as if they were a multitude, they returned to the simplicity of ancient languages; and *thou* and *thee* were the only expressions, which, on any consideration, they could be brought to employ.' – Instead of this long diffuse period, he might have expressed his meaning in a few words. *They used the simple appellatives* thou *and* thee *even to persons of the most distinguished rank.* His sentence is not only diffuse, but perplexed and incorrect. 'Instead of speaking to individuals as if they were a multitude.' A multitude is certainly composed of individuals. – Whoever spoke to individuals, must have spoke to more than one person, and if he spoke to more than one person, he might have spoke to the whole multitude. His meaning is, *instead of speaking to an individual as if he was a multitude.* He affirms that '*thou* and *thee* were the only expressions, which, on any consideration, they could be brought to employ.' – What had they reduced the whole language to these two words? At that rate, had any man asked a quaker, 'Who shall lie with your wife to night?' he would have answered, '*thou*.' If an attorney had been called to write his will, and demanded, 'Whom do you constitute sole heir of your estate?' the reply would have been, '*thee*.' We thought the quakers had been as tenacious of *meum* as of *tuum*.

We meet with another affected mode of expression in page 144. 'To maintain that the long parliament is not dissolved, or that either, or both houses, without the king, are possessed of legislative authority, or that the covenant is binding; whoever defended these dangerous positions, was made liable to the penalty of a premunire.' Our language does not require such *Latin* idioms. Nor is it necessary to use the *Roman* orthography in spelling words derived from the *Latin*, such as *favour, labor, honor, order, etc.* which appear like aliens in an *English* production. If we adopt foreign words, it is but reasonable that we should alter them according to the genius and fashion of our own language. Had we occasion to inlist a number of *Persian* recruits, we should not allow them to wear their long cloaths and turbans, Besides, we did not derive those words, immediately from the *Latin*; but borrowed them at second-hand from the *French*. – In such cases, we think, custom ought to determine: and therefore we do not approve of *emergence* and *inconsistence*, which Mr. *Hume* uses for emergency and inconsistency. *Verba valient usu.*

Some few, and but few *Scoticisms* have escaped our author. In page 137. we meet with the following expression: 'And any attempt of the parliament, by new acts, to give the superiority to presbyterianism, *had been* (instead of *would have been*) sufficient to involve again the nation in blood and confusion.' This we mention because it may mislead the reader, and make him imagine that some such attempts had been made. We find the words *rescind, succumb*; the phrases of *deliberating what use; prevent like confusions* WITH *those*. We perceive likewise some ill sustained metaphors, such as *a torrent irritated, territories in motion, immeasurable ardor*; with a few inaccuracies, as *a library of medals, every order were, came* (instead of *went*) *over to Spaw; the convention passed a bill, where, etc.* lord Dumblaine, *son to the earl of* Danby, *being master of an independent frigate.* – We cannot suppose this nobleman was reduced to the condition of a shipmaster; nor can we conceive what he means by an *independent frigate.* Did the vessel belong to the sect of independents? Or does the author mean that lord *Damblaine* sailed in a ship of his own.

Mr. *Hume* has not (in our opinion) been very happy in his manner of relating some private incidents; such as the adventure of king *Charles* II. and the presbyterian minister in *Scotland*; the gallantry of captain *Douglas* in the river *Medway*, when he was attacked by the *Dutch*; and some other anecdotes which he has endeavoured to throw in by way of sudden apostrophe, in imitation of *Voltaire.* We likewise wish he had omitted mentioning the ballad of *Lilliballero*, a circumstance, as we apprehend, unworthy of a place in the text of such a dignified performance. That and several other particulars would have appeared with more propriety in notes.[3] The battles of *Dunbar, Worcester*, and those fought at sea during the *Dutch* wars, are but tamely represented. Nothing is more agreeable to an *English* reader, than a battle well told. Such pictures must please, warm, and animate every reader of sensibility. They leave agreeable impressions on the memory, and these serve as land-marks to those who embark in the voyage of History. Mr. *Hume's* genius shines more in speculation than in description.

---

[3] We cannot help mentioning the translation of the third ode of the third book of *Horace*, which we find in the notes, p. 304. as the most elegant version we have seen.

Having thus finished the disagreeable part of criticism, we shall entertain the reader with some quotations, which will give a much more advantageous idea of this author's ability. The state of *England*, immediately after the death of *Charles* I. he has thus explained in a concise, distinct, masterly manner.

'The confusion, which overspread *England* after the murder of the king, proceeded, as well from the spirit of refinement and innovation, which agitated the ruling party, as from the dissolution of all that authority, both civil and ecclesiastical, by which the nation had ever been accustomed to be governed. Every man had framed the model of a republic; and, however new or fantastical, he was eager of recommending it to his fellow-citizens, or even of imposing it by force upon them. Every man had adjusted a system of religion, which, being derived from no traditional authority, was peculiar to himself; and being founded on supposed inspiration, not on any principles of human reasoning, had no means, besides cant and low rhetoric, by which it could recommend itself to others. The levellers insisted on an equal distribution of property and power, and declaimed all dependance and subordination. The *Millenarians* or fifth-monarch-men required, that government itself should be abolished, and all human powers be laid in the dust, in order to pave the way for the dominion of Christ, whose second coming on earth they suddenly expected. The *Antinomians* even insisted, that the obligations of morality and natural law were suspended, and that the elect, guided by internal principle, more perfect and divine, were superior to the *beggarly elements* of justice and humanity. A considerable party declaimed against tithes and a hireling priesthood, and were resolved, that the magistrate should not support by power or revenue any ecclesiastical establishment. Another party inveighed against the law and its professors; and under pretext of rendering more simple the distribution of justice, were desirous of abolishing the whole system of *English* jurisprudence, which seemed interwoven with monarchical government. Even those among the republicans, who adopted not such extravagancies, were so intoxicated with their saintly character, that they supposed themselves possessed of peculiar privileges; and professions, oaths, laws, and engagements had, in a great measure, lost their influence over them. The bands of society were every where loosened; and the irregular passions of men were encouraged by speculative principles, still more unsocial and irregular.

The royalists, consisting of the nobles and more considerable gentry, being degraded from their authority and plundered of their property, were inflamed with the highest resentment and indignation against those ignoble adversaries, who had reduced them to subjection. The presbyterians, whose credit had first supported the arms of the parliament, were enraged to find, that, by the treachery of superior cunning of their associates, the fruits of all their successful labours were ravished from them. The former party, from inclination and principle, zealously attached themselves to the son of their unfortunate monarch, whose memory they respected, and whose tragical death they deplored. The latter cast their eyes towards the same object; but they had still many prejudices to overcome, many fears and jealousies to be allayed, ere they could cordially entertain thoughts of restoring that family, whom they had so grievously offended, and whose principles they regarded with such violent abhorrence.

The only solid support of the republican independent faction, which, though it formed so small a part of the nation, had violently usurped the government of the whole, was a numerous army of about fifty thousand men. But this army, formidable from its discipline and courage, as well as its numbers, was actuated by a spirit, that rendered it extremely dangerous to the assembly, which had assumed the command over it. Accustomed to indulge every chimera in politics, every frenzy in religion, the soldiers knew little of the subordination of citizens, and had only learned, from apparent necessity, some maxims of military obedience. And while they still maintained, that all those enormous violations of law and equity, of which they had been guilty, were justified by the success with which providence had blessed them; they were ready to break out into any new disorders, where-ever they had the prospect of a like sanction and authority.

What alone gave some poize and stability to all these unsettled humours, was the great influence, both civil and military, acquired by *Oliver Cromwel*. This man, suited to the age in which he lived, and to that alone, was equally qualified to gain the affection and confidence of men, by what was mean, vulgar, and ridiculous in his character; as to command their obedience by what was great, daring, and enterprizing. Familiar even to buffoonery with the meanest centinel, he never lost his authority: transported to a degree of madness with religious extasies, he never forgot the political purposes, to which they might serve. Hating monarchy, while a subject; despising liberty, while a citizen; though he retained for a time all orders of men under a seeming obedience to the parliament; he was secretly paving the way, by artifice and courage, to his own unlimited authority.

The parliament, for so we must call henceforth a small and inconsiderable part of the House of Commons, having murdered their sovereign with so many appearing circumstances of solemnity and justice, and so much real violence and even fury, began to assume more the air of a civil, legal power, and to enlarge a little the narrow bottom, upon which they stood. A few of the excluded and absent members, such as were liable to least exception, they admitted; but on condition, that they should sign an approbation of whatever had been done in their absence with regard to the king's trial: And some of them were willing to acquire a share of power on such terms: The greatest part disdained to lend their authority to such apparent usurpations. Some writs they issued for elections, where they hoped to have interest enough to bring in their own friends and dependents. They named a council of state to the number of thirty-eight, to whom all addresses were made, who gave orders to all generals and admirals, who executed the laws, and who digested all business before it was introduced into parliament.[4] They pretended to employ themselves entirely in adjusting the laws, forms, and methods of a new representative; and as soon as they should have settled the nation, they professed their intention of restoring the power to the people, from whom, they acknowledged, they had entirely derived it.'

The fate of the gallant marquiss of *Montrose*, is pathetically related (p. 17.)

'All the insolence which success can produce in ungenerous minds, was exercised by the covenanters against *Montrose*, whom they so much hated and so much dreaded. Theological antipathy farther increased their indignities towards a person, whom they regarded as execrable on account of the excommunication, which had been pronounced against him. *Lesley* led him about for several days in the same low habit, under which he had disguised himself. The vulgar, wherever he passed, were instigated, tho' sometimes with reluctance, to reproach and vilify him. When he came to *Edinburgh*, every circumstance of elaborate rage and insult was put in practice by the order of the parliament. At the eastern gate of the city, he was met by the magistrates, and put into a new cart, purposely made with a high chair or bench, where he was placed, that the people might have a full view of him. He was bound with a cord, drawn over his breast and shoulders, and fastened thro' holes made in the cart. When in this posture, the hangman took off the hat of the noble prisoner, and rode himself before the cart in his livery and with his bonnet on; the other officers, who were taken prisoners along with the marquiss, walking two and two before them.

The populace more generous and humane, when they saw so mighty a change of fortune in this great man, so lately their dread and terror, into whose hands the magistrates, a few years before, had on their knees delivered the keys of the city, were struck with compassion, and viewed him with silent tears and admiration. The preachers, next *Sunday*, exclaimed against these movements of rebel nature, as they expressed it; and reproached the people with their profane tenderness towards this capital enemy of all piety and religion.

---

[4] Their names were, the earls of *Denbigh, Mulgrave, Pembroke, Salisbury*, lords *Grey, Fairfax*, lord *Grey of Groby*, lord *Lisle, Rolles, St. John, Wilde, Bradshaw, Cromwel, Skippon, Pickering, Massam, Haselrig, Harrington, Vane* jun, *Danvers, Armine, Mildmay, Constable, Pennington, Wilson, Whitlocke, Martin, Ludlow, Stapleton, Hevingham, Wallop, Hutchinson, Bond, Popham, Valentine, Walton, Scot, Purefoy, Jones.*

Montrose himself, tho' passionately fond of true glory, knew to despise unmerited ignominy, and, wherever he was carried, received with manly scorn and indifference the insults of his enemies: their ignoble behaviour he considered as sufficient vengeance for all their injuries. In the road, he had passed by the earl of *Southesk's* house, his father in law, and was allowed to see his children, who lived there: Not even the tenderness of this last adieu could disturb the even tenor of his heroic mind, or extort a complaint against the injustice of men or the cruelty of fortune.

When he was carried before the parliament, which was then sitting, *Loudon*, the chancellor, in a violent declamation, reproached him with the breach of the national covenant, which he had subscribed; his rebellion against God, the king, and the kingdom; and the many horrible murders, treasons, and impieties, for which he was now brought to condign punishment. *Montrose* in his answer maintained the same superiority above his enemies, to which, by his fame and great actions, as well as by the conscience of a good cause, he was justly entitled. He told the parliament, that since the king, as he was informed, had so far avowed their authority as to enter into treaty with them, he now appeared uncovered before their tribunal; a respect, which, while they stood in open defiance to their sovereign, they would in vain have required of him. That he acknowledged with infinite shame and remorse the errors of his early conduct, when their plausible pretexts had seduced him to tread with them the paths of rebellion, and bear arms against their prince and country. That his following services, he hoped, had sufficiently testified his repentance, and his death would now atone for that guilt, the only one with which he could justly reproach himself. That in all his warlike enterprizes he was warranted by that commission, which he had received from his and their master, against whose lawful authority they had erected their standard. That to venture his life for his sovereign was the least part of his merit: he had even thrown down his arms in obedience to the sacred commands of the king; and had resigned to them the victory, which, in defiance of all their efforts, he was still enabled to dispute with them. That no blood had ever been shed by him but in the field of battle; and many persons were now in his eye, many now dared to pronounce the sentence of death upon him, whose life, forfeited by the laws of war, he had formerly saved from the fury of the soldiers. That he was sorry to find no better testimony of their return allegiance than the murder of so faithful a subject, in whose death the king's commission must be at once so highly injured and affronted. That as to himself they had in vain endeavoured to vilify and degrade him by all their studied indignities: the justice of his cause, he knew, would ennoble any fortune; nor had he other affliction than to see the authority of his prince, with which he was invested, treated with so much ignomy. And that he now joyfully followed, by a like unjust sentence, his late sovereign; and should be happy, if, in his future destiny, he could follow him to the same blissful mansions, where his piety and humane virtues had already, without doubt, secured him an eternal recompence.

Montrose's sentence was next pronounced against him, "That he, *James Graham*" (for this was the only name they vouchsafed him) "should next day be carried to *Edinburgh* cross, and there be hanged on a gibbet, thirty foot high, for the space of three hours; then be taken down, his head be cut off upon a scaffold, and affixed to the prison: his legs and arms be stuck up on the four chief towns of the kingdom: his body be buried in the place appropriated for common malefactors; except the church, upon his repentance, should take off his excommunication."

The clergy, hoping that the terrors of immediate death had now given them an advantage over their enemy, flocked about him, and insulted over his fallen fortunes. They pronounced his damnation, and assured him, that the judgement, which he was so soon to suffer, would prove but an easy prologue to that which he must undergo hereafter. They next offered to pray with him: but he was too well acquainted with those forms of imprecation, which they called prayers. "Lord, vouchsafe yet to touch the obdurate heart of this proud incorrigible sinner; this wicked, perjured, traitorous, and profane person, who refuses to hearken to the voice of thy church." Such were the petitions, which, he expected, they would according to custom, offer up for him. He told them, that they were a miserable, deluded and deluding people; and would shortly bring their country under the most insupportable servitude, to which any nation had ever been reduced. "For my part, added he, I am much prouder to have my head affixed to the place where it is sentenced to stand, than to have my picture hang in the king's bed-chamber. So far from being sorry, that my legs and arms are to be sent to four cities of the kingdom, I wish I had limbs enough to be dispersed into all the cities of Christendom, there to remain as testimonies in favour of the cause, for which I suffer." This sentiment, that very evening, while in prison, he threw into verse. The poem remains; a signal monument of his heroic spirit, and no despicable proof of his poetical genius.

Now was led forth, amidst the insults of his enemies and the tears of the people, the man of the most illustrious birth and greatest renown of the nation, to suffer, for his adherence to the laws of his country and the rights of his sovereign, the ignominious death destined to the meanest malefactor. Every attempt, which the insolence of the governing party had made to subdue his gallant spirit, had hitherto proved fruitless: they made yet one effort more, in this last and melancholy scene, when all enmity, arising from motives merely human, is commonly softened and disarmed. The executioner brought that book, which had been published in elegant Latin of his truly heroic actions, and tied it by a cord about his neck. *Montrose* smiled at this new instance of their malice. He thanked them, however, for their officious zeal; and said, that he bore this testimony of his bravery and loyalty with more pride than he had ever worne the garter. Having asked, whether they had any more indignities to put upon him, and renewing some devout ejaculations, he patiently endured the last act of the executioner.

Thus perished in the thirty-eighth year of his age, the gallant marquiss of *Montrose*; the man whose military genius, both by valor and conduct, had shone forth beyond any, which, during these civil disorders, had appeared in the three kingdoms. The finer arts to, in his youth, he had successfully cultivated; and whatever was sublime, elegant, or noble touched his great soul. Nor was he insensible to the pleasures either of society or of love. Something, however, of the *vast* and *unbounded* characterized his whole actions and deportment; and it was merely by an heroic effort of duty, that he brought his mind, impatient of superiority and even of equality, to pay such unlimited submission to the will of his sovereign.'

We shall conclude with his observations on the character of *Cromwel*, which, in our opinion, are equally judicious and uncommon, and serve to demonstrate the author's intimate acquaintance with the human mind.

'It seems to me, that the occurrence of *Cromwel's* life, where his abilities are principally discovered, is his rising from a private station, in opposition to so many rivals so much advanced before him, to a high command and authority in the army. His great courage, his signal military talents, his eminent dexterity and address, were all requisite for this important acquisition. Yet will not this promotion appear the effect of supernatural abilities, when we consider, that *Fairfax*, himself a private gentleman, who had not the advantage of a seat in parliament, had, thro' the same steps, attained even a superior rank, and, if endued with common capacity and penetration, had been able to retain it. To incite such an army to rebellion against the parliament, required no uncommon art or industry: to have kept them in obedience had been the more difficult enterprise. When the breach was once formed betwixt the military and civil powers, a supreme and absolute authority, from that moment, is devolved on the general; and if he is afterwards pleased to employ artifice or policy, it may be regarded, on most occasions, as great condescension, if not as a superfluous caution. That *Cromwel* was ever able really to blind or over-reach, either the king or the republicans, does not appear: as they possessed no means of resisting the force under his command, they were glad to temporize with him, and, by seeming to be deceived, wait for opportunities of freeing themselves from his dominion. If he seduced the military fanatics, it is to be considered, that their interest and his evidently concurred, that their ignorance and low education exposed them to the grossest imposition, and that he himself was at bottom as frantic an enthusiast as the worst of them, and, in order to obtain their confidence, needed but display those vulgar and ridiculous habits, which he had early acquired, and on which he set so high a value. An army is so forcible, and at the same time so coarse a weapon, that any hand, which wields it, may, without much dexterity, perform any operation, and attain any ascendant in human society.

The domestic administration of *Cromwel*, tho' it discovers great ability, was conducted without any plan either of liberty or arbitrary power: perhaps, his difficult situation admitted of neither. His foreign enterprises, tho' full of intrepidity, were pernicious to national interest, and seem more the result of impetuous fury or narrow prejudices, than of cool foresight and deliberation. An eminent personage, however, he was in many respects, and even a superior genius; but unequal and irregular in his operations. And tho' not defective in any talent, except that of elocution, the abilities, which in him were most admirable, and which most contributed to his marvellous success, were the magnanimous resolution of his enterprises, and his peculiar dexterity in discovering the characters, and practicing on the weaknesses of mankind.

If we survey the moral character of *Cromwel* with that indulgence, which is due to the blindness and infirmities of the human species, we shall not be inclined to load his memory with such violent reproaches as those which his enemies usually throw upon it. Amidst the passion and prejudices of that time, that he should prefer the parliamentary to the royal cause will not appear very extraordinary; since, even at present, many men of sense and knowledge are disposed to think, that the question with regard to the justice of the quarrel may be regarded as very doubtful and ambiguous. The murder of the king, the most atrocious of all his actions, was to him covered under a mighty cloud of republican and fanatical illusions; and it is not impossible; that he might believe it, as many others did, the most meritorious action, which he could perform. His subsequent usurpation was the effect of necessity, as well as of ambition; nor is it easy to see, how the various factions could at that time have been restrained, without a mixture of military and arbitrary authority. The private deportment of *Cromwel*, as a son, a husband, a father, a friend, is exposed to no considerable censure, if it does not rather merit praise, and, upon the whole, his character does not appear more extraordinary and unusual by the mixture of so much absurdity with so much penetration, than by his tempering such violent ambition and such enraged fanaticism with so much regard to justice and humanity.'

We have carefully perused this performance, comparing it with other productions on the same subjects, and notwithstanding the little blemishes on which we have animadverted, we will venture to pronounce it one of the best histories which modern times have produced.

6

WILLIAM ROSE,
THE MONTHLY REVIEW

[William Rose], review of *The History of Great Britain. Vol. 2. Containing the Commonwealth and the Reigns of Charles II and James II*, in *The Monthly Review*, January 1757, Vol. 16, pp. 36–50.
Complete review.

According to Nangle's catalogue of reviewers for the *Monthly Review*, the article on Volume 2 of Hume's *History* was authored by William Rose (1719–1786). A Scotsman and proprietor of a school in Chelsea, Rose regularly reviewed philosophy books for the journal and is responsible for reviewing seven of Hume's works in the *Monthly*. His assessment here is mixed. He is pleased to see that this volume lacks the overt anti-religious elements of the previous one, and he finds Hume's treatment of the Commonwealth to be a "masterly performance." However, he believes that Hume lacks the impartiality that is necessary for historians to possess. Rose excerpts some of the more problematic passages that he finds in this volume. He reproduces a footnote in which Hume defends his treatment of religion in the former volume – a footnote which Hume removed from later editions of the *History*. He also presents Hume's critical discussion of Milton, the somewhat partial character portrayals of Charles II and James II, and the account of manners, arts and sciences during this period.

The History of Great Britain. Vol. 2d. Containing the Commonwealth, and the Reigns of Charles II. and James II. By David Hume Esq; 4to. 14s. *in boards.* Millar.

Having, in the Review for March 1755, delivered our sentiments concerning the first volume of Mr. Hume's History, we shall, without further introduction, proceed to lay before our Readers a short account of his second volume; which, we freely acknowlege, has given us more pleasure than we received from the perusal of the first. In that part of his work now before us, we have none of those indecent excursions on the subject of religion, which are to be met with in his first volume, and which must, no doubt, have given offence to every candid Reader.

Whether his restraining the wantonness of his invective, against every denomination of Christians, be owing to a change of sentiments, or to prudential considerations, we shall not stop here to enquire; but there are several passages in his work that may greatly assist the attentive Reader, in forming a judgment, as to this circumstance: However, let him be heard in vindication of what he had formerly advanced upon the subject.

'This sophism,' says Mr. Hume,

'of arguing from the abuse of any thing against the use of it, is one of the grossest, and, at the same time, the most common, to which men are subject. The history of all ages, – offers us examples of the abuse of religion; and we have not been sparing in this volume, more than in the former, to remark them: but whoever would thence draw an inference to the disadvantage of religion in general, would argue very rashly and erroneously. The proper office of religion, is, to reform mens lives, to purify their hearts, to enforce all moral duties, and to secure obedience to the laws and civil Magistrate. While it pursues these salutary purposes, its operations, tho' infinitely valuable, are secret and silent, and seldom come under the cognizance of history. That adulterate species of it alone, which inflames faction, animates sedition, and prompts rebellion, distinguishes itself on the open theatre of the world, and is the great source of revolutions and public convulsions. The Historian, therefore, has scarce occasion to mention any other kind of religion; and he may retain the highest regard for true piety, even while he exposes all the abuses of the false. He may even think, that he cannot better shew his attachment to the former, than by detecting the latter, and laying open its absurdities, and pernicious tendency.

It is no proof of irreligion in an Historian, that he remarks some fault or imperfection in each sect of religion, which he has occasion to mention. Every institution, however divine, which is adopted by men, must partake of the weakness and infirmities of our nature; and will be apt, unless carefully guarded, to degenerate into one extreme or the other. What species of devotion so pure, noble, and worthy the Supreme Being, as that which is most spiritual, simple, unadorned, and which partakes nothing either of the senses, or imagination? Yet is it found by experience, that this mode of worship does very naturally, among the vulgar, mount up into extravagance and fanaticism. Even many of the first reformers are exposed to this reproach; and their zeal, tho', in the event, it proved extremely useful, partook strongly of the enthusiastic genius. Two of the Judges in the reign of Charles the second, scrupled not to advance this opinion, even from the bench. Some mixture of ceremony, pomp, and ornament, may seem to correct the abuse; yet will it be found very difficult to prevent such a form of religion from sinking sometimes into superstition. The Church of England itself, which is, perhaps, the best medium among these extremes, will be allowed, at least during the age of Archbishop Laud, to have been somewhat infected with a superstition, resembling the popish; and to have paid a higher regard to some positive institutions, than the nature of the things, strictly speaking, would permit. It is the business of an Historian to remark these abuses of all kinds; but it belongs also to a prudent Reader, to confine the representations, which he meets with, to that age alone, of which the Author treats. What absurdity, for instance, to suppose, that the Presbyterians, Independents, Anabaptists, and other sectaries of the present age, partake of all the extravagancies, which we remark in those, who bore these appellations in the last century? The inference, indeed, seems juster, where sects have been noted for fanaticism during one period, to conclude, that they will be very moderate and reasonable in the subsequent. For, as it is the nature of fanaticism, to abolish all slavish submission to priestly power; it follows, that as soon as the first ferment is abated, men are naturally in such sects left to the free use of their reason, and shake off the fetters of custom and authority.'

We shall leave our Readers to their own reflections on this, and proceed to lay before them a few extracts, added to our former account, sufficient to give them a just idea of our Historian: for as the ground-work and materials, of his history are well known, it is altogether unnecessary to give a particular account of the facts it contains.

He introduces his second volume with a very clear and distinct account of the state of England, immediately after the death of Charles I. and, indeed, his whole history of the Commonwealth, appears to us, a masterly performance: his narrative is succinct and animated, his diction, in general, flowing yet correct, and his reflections pertinent, and such as naturally arise from the subject.[1]

Speaking of Oliver's character, he expresses himself in the following manner. –

'It seems to me, that the occurrence of Cromwel's life, where his abilities are principally discovered, is his rising from a private station, in opposition to so many rivals, so much advanced before him, to a high command and authority in the army. His great courage, his signal military talents, his eminent dexterity and address, were all requisite for this important acquisition. Yet will not this promotion appear the effect of supernatural abilities,

---

[1] Some few marks of inaccuracy and inattention, indeed, are to be met with: one instance of which we have in the character of Cromwell: Mr. Hume tells us, page 80, that the great defect of Oliver's speeches consisted, not in his want of elocution, but in his want of ideas: and, page 90, he says, that he was not defective in any talent, except that of elocution. There are other slips of the same kind, which an attentive Reader may easily discover.

when we consider, that Fairfax, himself a private Gentleman, who had not the advantage of a seat in Parliament, had, through the same steps, attained even a superior rank, and if endued with common capacity and penetration, had been able to retain it. To incite such an army to rebellion against the parliament, required no uncommon art or industry: to have kept them in obedience, had been the more difficult to enterprize. When the breach was once formed betwixt the military and civil powers, a supreme and absolute authority, from that moment, is devolved upon the General; and if he is afterwards pleased to employ artifice, or policy, it may be regarded, on most occasions, as great condescension, if not as a superfluous caution. That Cromwell was ever able really to blind, or over-reach, either the King or the Republicans, does not appear: as they possessed no means of resisting the force under his command, they were glad to temporize with him, and, by seeming to be deceived, wait for opportunities of freeing themselves from his dominion. If he seduced the military Fanatics, it is to be considered, that their interest and his evidently concurred, that their ignorance, and low education, exposed them to the grossest imposition, and that he himself was at bottom as frantic an Enthusiast as the worst of them; and, in order to obtain their confidence, needed but display those vulgar, and ridiculous habits, which he had early acquired, and on which he set so high a value. An army is so forcible, and, at the same time, so coarse a weapon, that any hand which wields it, may, without much dexterity, perform any operation, and attain any ascendant, in human society.

The domestic administration of Cromwel, tho' it discovers great ability, was conducted without any plan of liberty or arbitrary power; perhaps, his difficult situation admitted of neither. His foreign enterprizes, tho' full of intrepidity, were pernicious to national interest, and seem more the result of impetuous fury, or narrow prejudices, than of cool foresight and deliberation. An eminent personage, however, he was in many respects, and even a superiour genius; but unequal and irregular in his operations. And tho' not defective in any talent, except that of elocution, the abilities, which in him were most admirable, and which most contributed to his marvellous success, were the magnanimous resolution of his enterprizes, and his peculiar dexterity in discovering the characters, and practising on the weaknesses of mankind.

If we survey the moral character of Cromwel, with that indulgence which is due to the blindness and infirmities of the human species, we shall not be inclined to load his memory with such violent reproaches, as those which his enemies usually throw upon it. Amidst the passion and prejudices of that time, that he should prefer the parliamentary to the royal cause, will not appear very extraordinary; since, even at present, many men of sense and knowlege, are disposed to think, that the question, with regard to the justice of the quarrel, may be regarded as very doubtful and ambiguous. The murder of the King, the most atrocious of all his actions, was to him covered under a mighty cloud of republican and fanatical illusions; and it is not impossible, that he might believe it, as many others did, the most meritorious action, which he could perform. His subsequent usurpation was the effect of necessity, as well as of ambition; nor is it easy to see, how the various factions could at that time have been restrained, without a mixture of military and arbitrary authority. The private deportment of Cromwell, as a son, a husband, a father, a friend, is exposed to no considerable censure, if it does not rather merit praise. And, upon the whole, his character does not appear more extraordinary and unusual, by the mixture of so much absurdity with so much penetration, than by his tempering such violent ambition, and such enraged fanaticism, with so much regard to justice and humanity.'

Mr Hume concludes the History of the Commonwealth, with a general survey of that age, so far as regards manners, finances, arms, commerce, arts and sciences. The chief use of history, he observes, is, that it affords materials for disquisitions of this kind; and that it is the duty of an Historian, to point out the proper inferences or conclusions. There are several striking observations in this part of his work, tho' some of the characters he gives of those persons who were most distinguished, at that time, for their literary merit, are very exceptionable; particularly his character of Milton.

'It is, however, remarkable,' says Mr. Hume,

'that the greatest genius by far, which shone forth in England, during this period, was deeply engaged with these Fanatics, and even prostituted his pen in theological controversy, in factitious disputes, and in justifying the most violent measure of the party. This was John Milton, whose poems are admirable, tho' liable to some objections; his prose writings disagreeable, tho' not altogether *devoid*[2] of genius. Nor are all his poems equal: his Paradise Lost, his Comus, and a few others, shine out amidst some flat and insipid compositions: even in the Paradise Lost, his capital performance, there are very long passages, amounting to near a third of the work, almost wholly *devoid* of harmony and elegance, nay, of all vigour of imagination. The natural inequality in Milton's genius, was much increased by the inequalities in his subject; of which some parts are of themselves the most lofty that can enter into human conception; others would have required the most laboured elegance of composition to support them. It is certain, that this Author, when in a happy mood, and employed on a noble subject, is the most wonderfully sublime of any poet in any language; Homer, and Lucretius, and Tasso, not excepted. More concise than Homer, more simple than Tasso, more nervous

---

[2]   This ill sounding word seems to be a peculiar favourite with our Author.

than Lucretius; had he lived in a latter age, and learned to polish some rudeness in his verses; had he enjoyed better fortune, and possessed leisure to watch the returns of genius in himself; he had attained the pinnacle of human perfection, and borne away the palm of epic poetry.'

We shall not anticipate the objections that will be made to what is here said of Milton, by the admirers of that immortal genius; but proceed to lay before our Readers Mr. Hume's character of Charles the second.

'If we survey the character of Charles the second, in the different lights which it will admit of, it will appear very various, and give rise to different, and even opposite sentiments. When considered as a companion, he appears the most amiable and engaging of men; and, indeed, in this view, his deportment must be allowed altogether unexceptionable. His love of raillery was so tempered with good breeding, that it was never offensive: his propensity to satire was so checked with discretion, that his friends never dreaded their becoming the object of it: his wit, to use the expression of one who knew him well, and who was himself an exquisite judge, (Marquis of Halifax) could not be said so much to be very refined or elevated, qualities apt to beget jealousy, and apprehension, in company, as to be a plain, gaining, well-bred, recommending kind of wit. And tho', perhaps, he talked more than strict rules of behaviour might permit, men were so pleased with the affable, communicative deportment of the monarch, that they always went away contented, both with him and with themselves. This, indeed, is the most shining part of the King's character; and he seems to have been sensible of it: for he was fond of dropping the formality of state, and of relapsing every moment into the companion.

In the duties of private life, his conduct, tho' not free from all exception, was, in the main, laudable. He was an easy generous lover, a civil obliging husband, a friendly brother, an indulgent father, and a good-natured Master. The voluntary friendships, however, which this Prince contracted, nay even his sense of gratitude, were feeble; and he never attached himself to any of his Ministers or Courtiers; with a very sincere affection. He believed them to have no more motive for serving him but self-interest, and he was still ready, in his turn, to sacrifice them to present ease of convenience.

Here we must set bounds to our Panegyric on Charles. The other parts of his conduct may admit of some apology, but can deserve small applause. He was, indeed, so much fitted for private life, preferably to public, that he even possessed order, frugality, œconomy in the former: was profuse, thoughtless, negligent, in the latter. When we consider him as a Sovereign, his character, tho' not altogether *devoid* of virtues, was, in the main, dangerous to his people, and dishonourable to himself. Negligent of the interests of the nation, careless of its glory, averse to its religion, jealous of its liberty, lavish of its treasure, sparing only of its blood; he exposed it by his measures, tho' he appeared ever but in sport, to the dangers of a furious civil war, and even to the ruin and ignominy of a foreign conquest. Yet may all these enormities, if fairly and candidly examined, be imputed, in a great measure, to the indolence of his temper; a fault, which, however unfortunate in a Monarch, it is impossible for us to regard with great severity.

It has been remarked of this King, that he never said a foolish thing, nor ever did a wise one; a censure, which, tho' too far carried, seems to have some foundation in his character and deportment.

If we reflect on the appetite for power, inherent in human nature, and add to it, the King's education in foreign countries, and among the Cavaliers, a party which would naturally exaggerate the usurpations of popular assemblies upon the rights of Monarchy; it is not surprising, that civil liberty should not find in him a very zealous patron. Harrassed with domestic factions, weary of calumnies and complaints, oppressed with debts, straitened in his revenue; he sought, tho' with feeble efforts, for a form of government, more simple in its structure, and more easy in its management. But his attachment to France, after all the pains which we have taken, by enquiry and conjecture, to fathom it, contains still something, it must be confessed, mysterious and inexplicable. The hopes of rending himself absolute, by Lewis's assistance, seem so chimerical, that they could scarce be retained with such obstinacy by a Prince of Charles's penetration; and as to pecuniary subsidies, he surely spent much greater sums in one season, during the second Dutch war, than were remitted from France during the course of his whole reign. I am apt, therefore to imagine, that Charles was, in this particular, guided chiefly by inclination, and by a prepossession in favour of the French nation. He considered that people, as gay, sprightly, polite, elegant, courteous, devoted to the Prince, and attached to the Catholic Faith. And for these reasons he cordially loved them. The opposite character of the Dutch, had rendered them the objects of his aversion; and even the uncourtly humours of the English, made him very indifferent towards them. Men's notions of interest are much warped by their affections; and it is not altogether without example, that a man may be guided by national prejudices, who have ever been little biassed by private and personal friendship.

The character of this Prince has been very elaborately drawn by two great masters, perfectly well acquainted with him, the Duke of Buckingham, and the Marquis of Halifax; not to mention several elegant strokes given by Sir William Temple. Dr. Welwood likewise, and Bishop Burnet, have employed their pencil on the same subject; but the former is somewhat partial in his favour; as the latter is by far too harsh and malignant. Instead of finding an exact parallel betwixt Charles the second and the Emperor Tiberius, as that Prelate pretends, it would be more just to remark a full contrast and opposition. The Emperor seems as much to have surpassed the King in abilities, as he falls short of him in virtue. Provident, wise, active, jealous, malignant, dark, sullen, unsociable, reserved, cruel, unrelenting, unforgiving; these are the lights under which the Roman tyrant has been transmitted to us. And the only circumstance in which, it can justly be pretended, he was similar to Charles, is his love of women; a passion, which is too general to form any striking resemblance.'

Such is the character our Historian draws of Charles the second; a character, which, by those who look upon vice, and vicious manners, with a severer eye, will be thought to bear upon it strong marks of partiality. The portrait he gives us of James the second too, is far from appearing to be drawn by the pencil of truth; hear what he says of him.

James, he tells us, was

'a Prince, whom, if we consider his personal character, rather than his public conduct, we may safely pronounce to have been more unfortunate than criminal. He had many of those qualities which form a good citizen: even some of those, which, had they not been swallowed up in bigotry and arbitrary principles, serve to compose a good Sovereign. In domestic life, his conduct was irreproachable, and is entitled to our approbation. Severe, but open in his enmities, steddy in his councils, diligent in his schemes, brave in his enterprizes, faithful, sincere, and honourable in his dealings with all men: Such was the character with which the Duke of Yorke mounted the throne of England. In that high station his frugality of public money was remarkable, his industry exemplary, his application to naval affairs successful, his encouragement of trade judicious, his jealousy of national honour laudable; what then was wanting to make him an excellent Sovereign? A due regard and affection to the religion and constitution of his country. Had he been possessed of this essential quality, even his midling talents, aided by so many virtues, would have rendered his reign honourable and happy. When it was wanting, every excellency, which he possessed, became dangerous and pernicious to his kingdom.

The sincerity of this Prince (a virtue on which he highly valued himself) has been much questioned in those re-iterated promises, which he made of preserving the liberties and religion of the nation. It must be confessed, that this reign was one continued invasion of both; yet is it known, that to his last breath, he persisted in asserting, that he never meant to subvert the laws, or procure more than a toleration, and an equality of privileges to his catholic subjects. This question can only affect the personal character of the King; not our judgment of his public conduct. Tho' by a stretch of candour we should admit of his sincerity in these professions, the people were equally justifiable in their resistance of him. So lofty was the idea which he had entertained of his *legal* authority, that it left his subjects little or no right to liberty, but what was dependent on his sovereign will and pleasure. And such was his zeal of proselytism, that whatever he might have intended, he plainly stopped not at toleration and equality: he confined all power, encouragement, and favour to the Catholics. Converts, from interest, would soon have multiplied upon him: if not the greatest, at least the best part of the people, he would have flattered himself, were brought over to his religion: and he would, in a little time, have thought it just, as well as pious, to bestow on it all the public establishments. Rigors, and persecutions against Heretics, would speedily have followed; and thus liberty, and the Protestant religion, had, in the issue, been totally subverted; tho' we should not suppose, that the King, on the commencement of his reign, had seriously formed a plan for that purpose. And on the whole, allowing that Prince to have possessed good qualities, and good intentions, his conduct serves only, on that very account, as a stronger proof, how dangerous it is to allow any Prince, infected with the superstition, to wear the crown of these kingdoms.'

Every Reader, who has impartially considered the character and conduct of this Prince, must, we imagine, be sensible, that there are but few features of the original in the picture our Historian has drawn of him. The account, indeed, which Mr. Hume himself gives of his administration, shews plainly, that he was cruel, revengeful, pusillanimous, and perfidious. What then are we to think of our Author's impartiality? But we must not enlarge, and shall therefore close these extracts with inserting part of what Mr. Hume advances under the article of Manners, Arts and Sciences.

'Amidst the thick cloud of bigotry and ignorance,' says he,

'which overspread the nation, during the Commonwealth and Protectorship, there were a few sedate Philosophers, who, in the retirement of Oxford, culti-vated their reason, and established conferences for the mutual communi-cation of their discoveries in Physics and Geometry. Wilkins, a Clergyman, who had married Cromwell's sister, and was afterwards created Bishop of Chester, promoted these philosophical conversations. Immediately after the Restoration, these men procured a patent, and having enlarged their number, were denominated the *Royal Society*. But this patent was all they obtained from the King. Tho' Charles was a great lover of the sciences, particularly Chymistry and Mechanics, he animated them by his example alone, not by his bounty. His craving Courtiers and Mistresses, by whom he was perpet-ually surrounded, engrossed all his expence, and left him neither money nor attention for literary merit. His contemporary Lewis, who fell short of the King's genius and knowlege in this particular, much exceeded him in liber-ality. Besides, pensions conferred on learned men throughout all Europe, his academies were directed by rules, and supported by salaries; a generosity which does great honour to his memory; and in the eyes of all the ingenious part of mankind, will be esteemed an atonement for many of the errors of his reign. We may be surprised, that this example should not be more followed by Princes; since it is certain, that this bounty, so extensive, so beneficial, and so much celebrated, cost not that Monarch so great a sum as is often conferred on one single, useless, over-grown Favourite or Courtier.

But tho' the French Academy of Sciences was directed, encouraged, and supported by the Sovereign, there arose in England, some men of superior genius, who were more than sufficient to cast the ballance, and who drew on themselves, and on their native country, the regard and attention of all Europe. Besides Wilkins, Wren, Wallis, eminent Mathematicians, Hooke, an accurate observer by microscopes, and Sydenham, the restorer of true physic; there flourished during this period, a Boyle, and a Newton; men who trod with cautious, and therefore the more secure, steps, the only road which leads to true philosophy.

Boyle improved the pneumatic engine, invented by Otto Guerieke, and was thereby enabled to make several new and curious experiments on the air, as well as on other bodies; his Chemistry is much admired by those acquainted with that art: his Hydrostatics contain a greater mixture of reasoning and invention, with experiment, than any other of his works; but his reasoning is still remote from that boldness and temerity which had led astray so many Philosophers. Boyle was a great partizan of the mechanical philosophy; a theory, which, by discovering some of the secrets of nature, and allowing us to imagine the rest, is so agreeable to the natural vanity and curiosity of men.

In Newton this island may boast of having produced the greatest and rarest genius that ever arose for the ornament and instruction of the species. Cautious, in admitting no principles but such as were founded on experiment; but resolute to adopt every such principle, however new or unusual; from modesty, ignorant of his superiority above the rest of mankind; and thence, less careful to accommodate his reasonings to common apprehensions: more anxious to merit than acquire fame: he was from these causes long unknown to the world; but his reputation at last broke out with a lustre, which scarce any writer, during his own lifetime, had ever before attained. While Newton seemed to draw off the veil from some of the mysteries of nature, he shewed, at the same time, the imperfections of the mechanical philosophy; and thereby restored her ultimate secrets to that obscurity in which they ever did, and ever will remain.

This age was far from being so favourable to polite literature as to the sciences. Charles, tho' fond of wit, tho' possessed himself of a considerable share of it, tho' his taste of conversation seems to have been sound and just; serve rather to corrupt than improve the poetry and eloquence of his time. When the theatres were opened at the restoration, and freedom was again given to pleasantry and ingenuity, men, after so long an abstinence, fed on these delicacies with less taste than avidity; and the coursest and most irregular species of wit was received by the court as well as by the people. The productions at that time represented on the theatre, were such monsters of extravagance and folly; so utterly *devoid* of all reason, or even common sense, that they would be the disgrace of English literature, had not the nation made atonement for its former admiration of them, by the total oblivion to which they are now condemned. The Duke of Buckingham's Rehearsal, which exposed these wild productions, seems to be a piece of ridicule carried to excess; yet, in reality, the copy scarce equals some of the absurdities which we meet with in the originals.

This severe satire, together with the good sense of the nation, corrected, after some time, the extravagancies of the fashionable wit; but the productions of literature still wanted much of that correctness and delicacy which we so much admire in the antients, and in the French writers, their judicious imitators. It was, indeed, during this period chiefly, that that nation left the English behind them in the productions of poetry, eloquence, history, and other branches of polite letters; and acquired a superiority, which the efforts of English writers, during the subsequent age, did more successfully contest with them. The Arts and Sciences were imported from Italy into this island, as early as into France; and made at first more surprising advances. Spencer, Shakespear, Bacon, Johnson, were much superiour to their contemporaries, who flourished in that kingdom. Milton, Waller, Denham, Cowley, Harvey, were at least equal to their contemporaries. The reign of Charles the second, which some preposterously represent as our Augustan age, retarded the progress of polite literature in this island; and it was then found, that the immeasurable licentiousness which was indulged, or rather applauded at court, was more destructive to the refined arts, than even the cant, nonsense, and enthusiasm of the preceding period.

Most of the celebrated writers of this age remain monuments of genius, perverted by indecency and bad taste; but none more than Dryden, both by reason of the greatness of his talents, and the gross abuse which he made of them. His plays, excepting a few scenes, are utterly disfigured by vice, or folly, or both; his translations appear too much the offspring of haste and hunger; even his fables are ill chosen tales, conveyed in an incorrect, tho' spirited, versification. Yet amidst this great number of loose productions, the refuse of our language, there are found some small pieces, his Ode to St. Cecilia, the greatest part of Absalom and Achitophel, and a few more, which discover so great genius, such richness of expression, such pomp and variety of numbers, that they leave us equally full of regret and indignation, on account of the inferiority, or rather great absurdity, of his other writings.

The very name of Rochester is offensive to modest ears; yet does his poetry discover such energy of stile, and such poignancy of satire, as give ground to imagine what so fine a genius, had he fallen in a more happy age, and followed better models, was capable of producing. The ancient Satirists often used great liberty in their expressions; but their freedom no more resembles the licence of Rochester, than the nakedness of an Indian does that of a common prostitute.

Wycherley was ambitious of the reputation of Wit and Libertinism; and he attained it; he was probably capable of reaching the fame of true comedy, and instructive ridicule. Otway had a genius finely turned to the pathetic; but he neither observes strictly the rules of the drama, nor the rules, still more essential, of propriety and decorum. By one single piece the Duke of Buckingham did both great service to his age and honour to himself. The Earls of Mulgrave, Dorset, and Roscommon, wrote in a good taste; but their productions are either feeble or careless. The Marquis of Halifax discovers a refined genius; and nothing but leisure, and an inferior station, seem wanting to have procured him great eminence in literature.

Of all the considerable Writers of this age, Sir William Temple is almost the only one who kept himself altogether unpolluted by that inundation of vice and licentiousness, which overwhelmed the nation. The stile of this Author, tho' extremely negligent, and even mixed with foreign idioms, is agreeable and interesting. That mixture of vanity which appears in his works, is rather a recommendation to them. By means of it, we enter into acquaintance with the character of the Author, full of honour and humanity; and fancy that we are engaged, not in the perusal of a book, but in conversation with a companion.

Tho' Hudibras was published, and probably composed, during Charles's reign, Butler may justly, as well as Milton, be thought to belong to the foregoing period. No composition abounds so much as Hudibras in strokes of just and inimitable wit; yet are there many performances, which give as great, or greater entertainment, on the whole perusal. The allusions are often dark and far-fetched; and tho' scarce any Author was ever able to express his thoughts in so few words, he often employs too many thoughts on one subject, and thereby becomes prolix, after an unusual manner. It is surprizing how much erudition Butler has introduced, with so good a grace, into a work of pleasantry and humour. Hudibras is, perhaps, one of the most learned compositions that is to be found in any language. The advantage which the royal cause received from this poem, in exposing the fanaticism, and false pretences of the former parliamentary party, was prodigious. The King himself had so good a taste, as to be highly struck with the merit of the work, and had even got a great part of it by heart: yet was he either so careless in his temper, or so little endowed with the virtue of liberality, or, more properly speaking, of gratitude, that he allowed the Author, who was a man of virtue and probity, to live in obscurity, and die in want. Dryden is an instance of a negligence of the same kind. His Absalom sensibly contributed to the victory which the Tories obtained over the Whigs, after the exclusion Parliaments: yet could not this merit, aided by his great genius, procure him an establishment, which might exempt him from the necessity of writing for bread. Otway, tho' a professed royalist, could not even procure bread by his writings: and he had the singular fate of dying literally of hunger. These incidents threw a great strain on the memory of Charles, who had discernment, loved genius, was liberal of money, but attained not the praise of true generosity.'

Having thus finished our extracts, we shall conclude this article with a few observations.

And first, we readily acknowlege, that the perusal of our Author's History has afforded us no small entertainment. He does not perplex the minds, nor overload the memories of his Readers, with a circumstantial detail of minute incidents, or eternal references to dates and authorities; but presents them with comprehensive, and, in general, distinct views of things, interspersed with lively descriptions, and acute reflections. His language too, excepting a few inaccuracies, is perspicuous and correct; his narrative animated, his materials well arranged, and the peculiar features of the times he describes, strongly marked. But here we must set bounds to our panegyric on Mr. Hume. In regard to impartiality, and an inviolable respect to truth, the indispensable and essential qualifications of an Historian, he appears to us greatly deficient. There are many facts, which he either totally conceals, or partially exhibits; which ought to have been set before his Readers in a full and clear light; and though his delineation of characters is generally pleasing and spirited, yet is it far from being always just and faithful. In some of them there appears too much refinement; in others we find our Historian censuring with too much alertness those whom he chuses to depreciate; or artfully endeavouring to give agreeable pictures of very disagreeable originals. As to religion, in general, and the different professions of Christianity, in particular, he is far from appearing to have too zealous an attachment to any. In speaking of Hobbes, he tells us, that he was as positive and dogmatical, as if *human reason* could attain a thorough *conviction on* religious subjects: whence it should seem, that our Author thinks human reason incapable of investigating any principles and obligations of religion; – which, by the bye, whatever Mr. Hume might intend, is carrying the grand scheme of Popery further than it is carried by the Papists themselves; whose capital doctrine of the necessity of an *infallible guide* rests upon this foundation: – and it is observable, that Popery has ever gathered the most plenteous harvests in the fields of Scepticism.

7
RICHARD HURD

[Richard Hurd], *Moral and political dialogues, being the substance of several conversations between divers eminent persons of the past and present age: digested by the parties themselves, and now first published from the original mss with critical and explanatory notes*. London: printed for A. Millar; and W. Thurlborne and J. Woodyer at Cambridge, 1759, [2], xii, 304, 283–289, [1] p.
Complete Postscript from 1759 edition and selections from Dialogue 6 from *The Works of Richard Hurd*, 1811, Vol. 4.

Born in Congreve, Staffordshire, Richard Hurd (1720–1808) was educated at Cambridge and ordained Anglican priest in 1744. He became Bishop of Litchfield and Coventry in 1775 and was translated to Worcester in 1781. Hurd was a prolific writer in theology, classics and literature, and is most known in Hume scholarship for his work with close friend William Warburton on *Remarks on Mr. David Hume's Essay on the Natural History of Religion* (1757). In 1759 he anonymously published *Moral and Political Dialogues*, which covers the topics of sincerity in commerce, retirement, the age of Queen Elizabeth, and the English constitution. At the last minute, he included the Postscript to that work, after reading the 1759 instalment of Hume's *History* on the House of Tudor and its attack on civil liberty. To justify the absolute rule of the Stuart monarchs, Hume argued that they were simply following the precedent of royal prerogative established under Elizabeth. Hurd, in response, says that the issue should not be based on immediate precedent, but instead on what is right and whether the Stuarts' absolutism was consistent with the earlier English history. Hurd removed this Postscript in later editions of his work and in its place, inserted a footnote that discusses the same general issue, although more diplomatically. The note appears in Dialogue 6, in which he argues that English liberty is grounded in its feudal laws. He specifically attacks Hume's view that no nation ever has or will have a free constitution. He suggests that if Hume "had begun his work at the right end," the thread of English freedom would be more evident. He laments Hume's defence of the Stuarts, but nevertheless feels that his *History* is the best available general account of English history.

The *Critical Review* offered a mixed evaluation of Hurd's *Dialogues*, praising its style, but faulting its insight into human nature:

The dialogues before us seem to have been written by an author who has studied men, a great deal more from books, than from life. In point of erudition and stile they are only exceptionable, in shewing more of both than many of his dead interlocutors ever possessed, when alive. His manner of introducing his dialogues, is no unhappy imitation of that of Cicero upon old age.... [*Critical Review*, June 1759, Vol. 7. pp. 471–483]

The reviewer concludes, "Upon the whole, the book is a very good gentleman's book, but the author seems to be fitted more for works of genius than of learning." Writing for the *Monthly Review*, Owen Ruffhead criticizes Hurd's writing style, but feels that he shed fresh light on his subject matter:

... the Writer of the Dialogues before us, though evidently a man of learning and distinguished talents, does not appear to such an advantage as might be expected: and that, in the *preface* particularly, he sinks greatly beneath himself.

The subjects he has chosen to discuss in six dialogues have been so often agitated, that there is little room for new or striking observations: yet the dialogues on the constitution of the English government, afford some fresh lights, and place the points of controversy, though not in a new, yet in a more clear and distinct point of view, than any in which that subject has been hitherto examined. [*Monthly Review*, July 1759, Vol. 21, pp. 35–46]

Regarding the Postscript on Hume, Ruffhead states that "The Reader will find the substances of these censures [on Hume] in our account of that History" – namely, in Ruffhead's own 1759 review of the third instalment of Hume's *History*.

Hume already had a low opinion of Hurd as a result of the *Remarks* on Hume's "Natural History of Religion," published two years earlier. He read Hurd's latest attack in the *Moral and Political Dialogues* and wrote the following to Adam Smith: "You have probably seen Hurd's Abuse of me. He is of the Warburtonian School; and consequently very insolent and very scurrilous; but I shall never reply a word to him. If my past Writings do not sufficiently prove me to be no Jacobite, ten Volumes in folio never would" (July 28, 1759). Hurd's *Dialogues* is favourably mentioned by Joseph Towers in his *Observations on Mr. Hume's History of England* (1778), in the anonymous article "On Mr. Hume's Political Inconsistency as an Historian" (1821) and Francis Jeffrey in his 1824 review of Brodie's *History*, contained later in this collection. In *The Life of Samuel Johnson* (1791), James Boswell commented on Hurd's move towards political moderation in successive editions of the *Dialogues*:

That learned and ingenious Prelate, it is well known, published at one period of his life *Moral and Political Dialogues*, with a woefully whiggish cast.

Afterwards, his Lordship having thought better, came to see his errour, and republished the work with a more constitutional spirit. Johnson, however, was unwilling to allow him full credit for his political conversion.

In his unpublished manuscripts, Hurd himself offers a candid and sometimes critical evaluation of his *Dialogues*.[1] The *Dialogues* were republished eight times during his life and also appeared in his posthumous 1811 *Works*. The following is from the 1759 Postscript, which is followed by the footnote as appears in Hurd's *Works*.

POST-SCRIPT.

While these sheets were in the press, and when the greater part of them had been printed off, the new *history of England under the house of Tudor* came forth, and chanced to fall into the hands of the editor. It was amusing to him to observe, in this work ,a design carried on, with no small art, to advance that very system of policy which the concluding dialogues in this collection seemed effectually to have overthrown.

It is true, no part of this amusement arose from the historian's usual art, which, like that of Bays, is *to surprize and elevate*; the editor easily recollecting, that the foundations of this writer's system had been laid before in his *history of England under the house of Stuart*. For it is to be noted, that the method observed by him in these histories is as singular as his view in composing them. For having undertaken to conjure up the spirit of absolute power, he judged it necessary to the charm, to reverse the order of things, and to evoke this frightful spectre by writing (as witches use to say their prayers) *backwards*.

However the end should, in all reason, attone for the perverseness of the *means*. Accordingly, while one half of his pains is laid out in exposing the absurdities of *reformed religion*, the other half is suitably employed in discrediting the cause of *civil liberty*.

With his sentiments of religion, the editor of these dialogues hath nothing to do. But this injurious treatment of the *state* is so offensive to the civil zeal of the public, that, had the history appeared in due time, he should hardly have failed, in his office of annotator, to bestow some occasional animadversions upon it.

As it is, he contents himself, for the present, with one word on the historian's *system*, and on the *conclusion* he would have us draw from it.

His SYSTEM is, "That the high prerogative of the crown, so much pretended to, and so warmly opposed, in the reigns of the house of Stuart, was the

---

[1] See M.A. Stewart, "Richard Hurd," *Dictionary of Eighteenth-Century British Philosophers*, (Bristol: Thoemmes Press, 1999).

antient, the hereditary, the rightful patrimony of our English monarchs:" And he builds it on this foundation, "That such prerogative was exercised by the princes of the Tudor family, and that their administration was, in the highest degree, imperious, arbitrary, and despotic.

This point indeed the historian labours through all the volumes of his history, but more especially in those just given to the public. He hath his reasons for laying the utmost stress upon it, of which ONE, we may suppose is, that he takes it for a sort of *discovery*, which the zeal of our late writers in politics, or rather their profound ignorance[2] of the English history, prevented them from making.

Now here it must be a satisfaction to the systematic historian to find this favourite point, not only wholly conceded to him, but, as the editor presumes to think, fully and fairly accounted for, in the preceding dialogues *on the constitution*.

His CONCLUSION follows, in due form, "That therefore the patriots, to whom we owe our present and, it seems, lately usurped liberties, are little deserving of those praises which have been so largely bestowed upon them; and that the memory of the house of Stuart, from whom they were usurped, cannot be fostered with too much tenderness and compassion." I hardly mistake his meaning; but his own words, as decency required, are something softer. – "The praise, which we bestow on those patriots, to whom we are indebted for our privileges, ought to be given *with some reserve*, and surely *without the least rancour* against those who adhered to the antient constitution."[3]

But though his apology for the unhappy Scotish line be very generous, every one may not be brought to feel the force of his conclusion. For how does it follow that, because the arbitrary government of one family was born with the people, in certain critical conjunctures, or was necessary to be complied with for certain temporary and political ends, *therefore* they should suffer another family to confirm and perpetuate that tyranny; when their own more antient privileges, not to say the genius of their constitution, reclaimed against it; and when all the reasons had now ceased, which had procured and seemed to merit that indulgence?

We are told indeed that "in the particular exertions of power, the question ought never to be forgot, *what is best?* But in the general distribution of power among the several members of a constitution, there can seldom be admitted any other question, than *what is usual?*"[4]

---

[2]   "The party amongst us who have distinguished themselves by their adherence to liberty and a popular government, have long indulged their *prejudices* against the succeeding race of princes, by bestowing unbounded panegyrics on the virtue and wisdom of Elizabeth. *They have even been so extremely ignorant* of the transactions of this reign as to extoll her, &c." Hist. of England. *Elizabeth*, p. 716 [Appendix III.]

[3]   Ibid.

[4]   Ibid.

Were this true, is that *use* to be estimated only from the immediately preceding times? And is it presumption to inquire, not only, as K. James said, what the reigning prince may do in the plenitude of his power, but what his predecessors had been *accustomed* to do, and what indeed they were *required* to do by the constituent principles of the monarchy? Above all, shall a great people be also freely censured for looking back into their old characters; and, when so mighty a cause as that of liberty is pleading, shall they be rigorously tied up to the precedents of two or three reigns, when they could so easily defend themselves by alleging their elder usages, and by opposing to these novel encroachments the more reverend prescription of ages?

At this rate I desire to know how a free constitution could ever subsist, or at least preserve itself in any country? Ambition, intrigue, expediency, neglect, and even chance itself are constantly introducing, and for a time will frequently continue, infringements of a people's rights. And shall usurpation under the name of *use* be presently pleaded against the resumption of them?

"But whether these patriots were to blame, or no, for opposing *what was usual,* surely that family who followed so reasonable a rule, or, in the historian's language, *who adhered to the antient constitution*, can be thought deserving of no great censure."

What, not for endeavouring to rivet those chains of servitude, which their predecessors had perhaps been kindly forging, on the necks of their subjects? Not, for endeavouring to turn irregularities into precedent, and extravagancies into system, and so to enslave a mighty people beyond all hopes of redemption; a people, that had just before unanimously called this family to the throne, and whose liberties had been respected even in the highest exertions of former tyranny? The *cause regnandi*, which tyrants magnify so much, must surely, in the opinion of this political casuist, be a powerful excuse, to justify these enormous attempts, and to cover the infamy of entailing so pestilent a mischief, as that of CIVIL SERVITUDE, on the souls and bodies of their good subjects.

"Few examples, he observes, occur of princes, who have willingly resigned their power. None of those who have, without struggle, allowed it to be extorted from them."[5] It may be so; and, for the credit of princes, I am sorry for it. But what glory then had the Stuart line acquired to themselves by pursuing so just a conduct without, and beyond example? "It was not to be expected, he will say with much ease, for that *antient practice* ought to be followed, and that, in exercising an arbitrary dominion, they did but adhere to *the antient constitution.*

But here I suspect the historian to be playing tricks with us. For what, might one ask him, is this *antient practice*, and *antient constitution*? He is something shy of answering this question, and it is well we can do it ourselves by reflecting

---

[5] Ibid.

on what he hath casually, as it may seem, but not improvidently dropped elsewhere, in the former part of this history;[6] where he warns us *against the curiosity of looking farther back into the English affairs than the accession of the Tudor family*, that is, of that very family, which had set the example of this *antient practice*, and had given birth to this *ancient constitution*.

This warning to the reader was very kind, but, I doubt, will hardly be taken by those for whose sake it is intended; the friends of liberty knowing very well (at least the most *ignorant* of them may now know from the perusal of these dialogues) that the English constitution was formed and even fixed on immoveable principles of public freedom long before the accession of the house of Tudor. So that to interdict our researches into the remoter parts of our history, is, in effect, to bid us shut our Eyes, and swear against day light. It is just as reasonable as to say that, to judge of the Greek and Roman constitutions, there is no need of going farther back in our reading than to the reign of PISISTRATUS, or the dictatorship of SYLLA, for that all before those æras contributeth nothing to a knowledge of the thing in question. But in the basest times of Greece and Rome we shall not find an Historian of either nation base enough to give this council to his fellow citizens.

Yet this advice, as much as we may resent it, was perfectly suited to the writer's views of conciliating our esteem for his *antient practice* and *antient constitution*. For that *practice* must needs appear antient, beyond which nobody knows of any thing further; and that *constitution* may well deserve to be respected for it's age, which commenced with the earliest instructions of our history.

This much I have taken upon myself to say, as editor of these dialogues on the *constitution of the English government*; which are luckily so compounded as to afford a seasonable antidote to the poison of this new history. For if it be true, as the *first* of them pretends, "That we had a *free constitution* for ages before it suffered an interruption under the baleful influence of the Tudors;" and a reasonable account be given, in the *second*, "Why the nation was contented to repose itself for a time under the shade of despotism, while the vestal fires of liberty burnt faintly indeed, but were not extinguished;" The reader is left to himself to answer that insulting question, "*Whether it was the people, who encroached upon the sovereign, or the sovereign, who attempted to usurp on the people.*"[7]

To conclude, though such a history as this may be looked upon as an inexpiable prodigy, in these golden days of *British* freedom, yet warmed, as the

---

[6] Hist. of Eng. HEN. VII. p. 67.

[7] "I shall only ask, whether it be not sufficiently clear from all these transactions, that in the two succeeding reigns [of James and Charles] it was the people who encroached upon the sovereign; not the sovereign, who attempted, as is pretended, to usurp upon the people?" Hist. of Eng. ELIZ. p. 611 [Chapter 42, Note.]

editor is, with the spirit of old Maynard, he cannot help taking one comfortable presage from it. It is, "That Britons will never hereafter suffer the least encroachment on their (now, at least) constitutional rights and privileges; lest not only that indulgence should favour the introduction of tyranny, but (which is more provoking, tho' less terrible) lest it give a handle to thankless men, grown wanton in the abuse of liberty, to calumniate the friends and benefactors of mankind, and to plead the cause of tyrants."

———

DIALOGUE VI.
On the Constitution of the English Government.

...

Such was the issue of this desperate conflict between prerogative and liberty. The wonder was, that this fatal experience should not have rectified all mistakes, and have settled the government on a sure and lasting basis at the Restoration. The people were convinced, that nothing more was requisite to their happiness, than the secure possession of their ancient legal constitution. The re-called family were not so wise. And in their attempts to revive those old exploded claims, which had succeeded so ill with their predecessors, they once more fell from the throne, and left it to the possession of that glorious prince whom the greatly injured nation has now called to it.

This then will be considered by grateful posterity as the true æra of *English* liberty. It was interwoven indeed with the very principles of the constitution. It was inclosed in the ancient trunk of the feudal law, and was propagated from it.

{[Note:] This appears even from Mr. HUME'S own account of the feudal times; incomparably the best part of his *History of England*. And it is to be presumed that, if so ingenuous a writer had begun his work at the right end, he would have been led, by the evidence of so palpable a truth, to express himself more favourably, indeed more consistently, of the *English* constitution. But having, by some odd chance, written the history of the STUARTS first, and afterwards of the TUDORS, (in both which he found it for his purpose to adopt the notion of a despotic independent spirit in the *English* monarchy), he chuses in the last part of his work, which contains the history of *England from* JULIUS CÆSAR *to* HENRY VII. to abide by his former fancy; on this pretence, that, in the administration of the feudal government, the liberty of the subject was incomplete and partial; often precarious and uncertain; a way, in which the learned historian might prove, that no nation under heaven ever was, or ever will be, possessed of a FREE CONSTITUTION.

By FREE CONSTITUTION of the *English* monarchy, every advocate of liberty, that understands himself, I suppose, means, that limited plan of policy, by which the supreme legislative power (including in this general term the power of levying money) is lodged, not in the prince singly, but jointly in the prince and people; whether the *popular* part of the constitution be denominated *the king's* or *kingdom's great council*, as it was in the proper feudal times; or *the parliament*, as it came to be called afterwards; or, lastly, *the two houses of parliament*, as the style has now been for several ages.

To tell us, that this constitution has been different at different times, because the regal or popular influence has at different times been more or less predominant, is only playing with a word, and confounding *constitution* with *administration*. According to this way of speaking, we have not only had *three or four*,[8] but possibly three or four score, different constitutions. So long as the great distribution of the supreme authority took place (and it has constantly and invariably taken place, whatever other changes there might be, from the *Norman* establishment down to our times) the nation was always enabled, at least *authorized*, to regulate all subordinate, or, if you will, supereminent claims and pretensions. This it effectually did at the *Revolution*, and, by so doing, has not created a *new plan of policy*, but perfected the old one. The great MASTER-WHEEL of the *English* constitution is still the same; only freed from those checks and restraints, by which, under the specious name of *prerogatives*, time and opportunity had taught our kings to obstruct and embarrass its free and regular movements.

On the whole, it is to be lamented that Mr. HUME'S too zealous concern for the honour of the house of STUART, operating uniformly through all the volumes of his history, has brought disgrace on a work, which, in the main, is agreeably written, and is indeed the most readable *general* account of the *English* affairs, that has yet been given to the public.}

---

[8] Mr. HUME'S Hist. vol. v. p. 472, *n.* ed. 8vo, 1763.

8
TOBIAS SMOLLETT,
THE CRITICAL REVIEW

[Tobias Smollett], review of *The History of England, under the House of Tudor*, in *The Critical Review*, April 1759, Vol. 7, pp. 289–303. Complete review.

Tobias Smollett (1721–1771) authored the *Critical Review* article on the 1757 volume of Hume's *History*, contained earlier in this collection. His review here is the opening item in the April 1759 issue of the journal. As with his 1757 review, Smollett gives a highly favourable review of the 1759 instalment of Hume's *History*, and praises its engaging style. He nevertheless points out some stylistic problems, several of which Hume altered in later editions. He also lists factual mistakes, which Hume similarly altered. For example, Smollett writes,

> We are at a loss to understand our author, page 16, where he says, 'That the marquis of Dorset, brother to the queen-regent was confined by the command of Henry.' It is probable that *regent*, by a slip of the pen or error of the press, is put for dowager. But our author is still mistaken in point of fact; for the marquis of Dorset was not brother to the queen-dowager, but her son by a former marriage.

We find the above-quoted passage revised as follows in subsequent editions of the *History*: "He confined the marquis of Dorset, who, he suspected, would resent the injuries suffered by his mother." Smollett presents extended quotes pertaining to Lambert's and Cranmer's executions, and shorter excerpts on the characters of Wolsey, Mary Queen of Scots, and Elizabeth.

ARTICLE I.

The History of England, *under the House of* Tudor. *In Two Vols.* 4to. *By* David Hume, *Esq; Pr.* 1*l.* 1*s.* Millar.

This writer is already well known to the public by his many ingenious performances; and his talents for historical composition in particular have appeared in two volumes of the British History, which are a continuation of his present subject. The reasons which have induced him to reverse the order of history in his publications are not very material to his readers. Tacitus, it appears, wrote his History before the Annals; and it is probable, that these writers have fallen into this piece of irregularity, by the same accident, their having written the history of a later period before they thought of undertaking that of the former.

It is perhaps unnecessary for the information of our readers, to enter minutely into the particulars of this author's stile, as we have not been able to remark any great variation from his former manner. We find, indeed, fewer examples of those forced inversions, and uncommon terms which, in his preceding volumes, were liable to considerable objections. With the advantage of more ease and simplicity, he has, in our opinion, supported the former elegance of his composition, and produced a work so much the more agreeable to a sound taste, that he has not, in every instance, discovered the same attention to polish and refine, by departing from the ordinary forms of expression.

Errors of this kind now seldom occur, though we must observe that they are, perhaps, not altogether avoided; and that we sometimes meet with words of a doubtful authority, which it would have become so correct and elegant writer to have shunned.

Delate, which our author makes use of in the sense of informing and accusing, is a Scotch expression.

Insurgents, which frequently recurs, is a new word, of doubtful authority, and not very pleasing to the ear. Such a word may be convenient on many occasions, where rebel or malecontent are improper: but if this reason were admitted for the coining of new words, we should hardly have any standard of language remaining.

The author, page 475, is not aware, that in England we say that the jury gives the verdict, the judge pronounces the sentence.

How a criminal, page 62, can be punished capitally for more offences than one, we are at a loss to imagine. We are put in mind of a judge, who, having dismissed a criminal from his bar, declared, that if ever he was brought there again for a like offence, he should lose his ears *toties quoties*.

Whilst we do our author the justice to acknowledge that he has discovered great sagacity in clearing up some doubtful and controverted parts of history, and is, in general, exact in the minute circumstances of his narration, we are, in justice to our task, obliged to make some remarks where we think him mistaken.

The patent, page 2, obtained by the Duke of Lancaster for the legitimation of his natural children is not silent, as this historian supposes, upon the point of the succession to the crown. Had he consulted the patent itself in the Foedera, Tom. VII. p. 849, he would have found, that the right of succession to the crown is positively excluded from the privileges which the duke of Lancaster's children were to enjoy in consequence of their legitimation. Sir Edward Coke, in his Institutes, 4th Instit. Part I. ch. i. p. 37. gives a copy of the patent containing the same clause.

We are at a loss to understand our author, page 16, where he says, 'That the marquis of Dorset, brother to the queen-regent was confined by the command of Henry.' It is probable that *regent*, by a slip of the pen or error of the press, is put for dowager. But our author is still mistaken in point of fact; for the marquis of Dorset was not brother to the queen-dowager, but her son by a former marriage.

He seems, page 41, to have mistaken the force of Poyning's law, in alledging, that the government of England was, by this statute, empowered to make laws for Ireland. The intention of that act was, in reality, to make the laws then established in England of force likewise in that part of his majesty's dominions.

Page 475, our author speaks of Sir James Balfour as governor of the castle of Edinburgh; but this is certainly a mistake, as both Keith and Anderson agree, that Bothwell himself obtained the government of that fortress: it is not therefore surprising, that a creature of his was trusted with the immediate care of it in the character of his deputy.

It appears by comparing the Latin with the English edition of lord Bacon's history, that our author has been precipitant in charging his lordship with a mistake. The pope indeed, as lord Bacon observes in the Latin edition, enjoyed before the reign of Henry VIII. the emolument of vacant sees; but our kings were in the practice of compounding for that occasional revenue; and as they satisfied the court of Rome at an under-value, they still had so much profit in the bargain as tempted them to prolong the vacancies.

Notwithstanding any errors or inaccuracies of this nature, we gladly acknowledge the general merit of our author's performance, which, by the elegance, variety, and force of his elocution, is certainly an accession of great lustre to the English literature. Rapid and interesting in his narration, easy and natural in his transitions; profound in his reflections; ingenious, copious, and eloquent, in urging the reasons of a measure, or in stating the arguments which favour the views of contending parties, he has offered to the public a work highly instructive and entertaining, in which not only affairs of state, but the passions, characters, and reasonings of men, are laid open with a masterly, a skilful, and impartial hand.

He has indeed in this, as well as in the following part of the history, bent the force of his genius, more than that single object deserved, to prepare in his readers the ground of that compassion which he himself had felt for a prince who became the sacrifice of liberty, and perished in the flames, by which our constitution has been refined.

Impressed with a regard for public order and national tranquillity, he has maintained a great reserve on the principles of resistance and opposition, amidst acknowledgments of their just foundation, and a sense of the benefits which arise to mankind from their seasonable operation.

When we consider the blessings which redound to our country from the change of religion, which took place in this period, we shall wish perhaps to find the merit of our first reformers, in many places, treated with more of that respect, which was due, at least to the vigour, resolution, and integrity of the part they acted, if not to the correctness of their apprehension, or the propriety of their measures on many occasions; but must, at the same time, acknowledge, that a historian wading through the torrents of violence, bigotry, and faction, which over-ran the ages of which he wrote, could not retain the air of impartiality, without setting in their proper light the faults, and even the ridicule of opposite parties, who were equally ready to make religious belief a matter of compulsion, nor of amicable persuasion, and friendly information. If in such a representation the patrons of truth itself fall under occasional censure, we are not to confound the merits of their cause with the errors of their conduct; nor interpret the blemishes of that zeal which becomes a principle of contention, hostility, and outrage, among parties, as a ground of censure against the sacred tenets which are calculated to pacify and reconcile, not to exasperate, mankind.

Although our author does not depart from the business of an historian, to enter into the merits of any controversial difference, he has made free with the vices of every party; and if we examine the bent of his censures, as they are pointed at different extremes, his representation upon the whole has done honour to the English reformation, and the subsequent establishment. A patron of toleration, in opposition to the violence of different factions, he has, with great depth, observed, the circumstances which hindered even the reformed of that age from adopting this prudent and charitable policy. And in the character of Edward, p. 345, he has justly remarked, *that the bigotry of Protestants, less governed by priests, lies under more restraints than that of the Catholics, and that the effects of this malignant quality are in the former less to be apprehended.*

When we take still a more general view of the work before us, we find an attempt to comprehend all the objects of history, not only the great and interesting transactions of each reign, with whatever may characterize the persons engaged in public life, or delineate the state of the constitution in different periods; but, in order to point out the progress of the nation in political, commercial, or literary improvements, the regulations which relate to police, commerce, or the revenue, are minutely observed, and the essays of genius are considered. And we must, upon the whole, applaud the skill with which our author has involved the reflections of a philosophical historian in the detail of his facts, in a manner which throws a light upon every subject, without sensibly interrupting the course of the narration.

The reader will be able to observe the variety of his stile, and the genius of his narration in the following passages, where the ridicule and the lamentable bigotry of those ages are equally exposed to his view.

'There was one Lambert, a schoolmaster in London, who had been questioned for unsound opinions by archbishop Warham; but, upon the death of that prelate, and the changing of councils at court, he had been released. Not terrified with the danger which he had incurred, he still continued to promulgate his tenets; and having heard Dr. Taylor, afterwards bishop of Lincoln, defend in a sermon the corporal presence, he could not forbear expressing to Taylor his dissent from that doctrine; and he drew up his objections under ten several heads. Taylor carried the paper to Dr. Barnes, who happened to be a Lutheran, and who maintained, that, though the substance of bread and wine remained in the sacrament, yet the real body and blood of Christ were there also, and were, in a certain mysterious manner, incorporated with the material elements. By the present laws and practice, Barnes was no less exposed to the stake than Lambert; yet such was the persecuting rage which prevailed, that he was determined to bring this man to condign punishment; because, in their common departure from the ancient faith, he had dared to go one step farther than himself. He engaged Taylor to delate Lambert to Cranmer and Latimer, who, whatever their private opinion might be on these points, were obliged to conform themselves to the standard of orthodoxy established by Henry. When Lambert was cited before these prelates, they endeavoured to bend him to a recantation; and they were surprized, when, instead of compliance, he ventured to appeal to the king.

The king, not displeased with an opportunity, where he could at once exert his supremacy, and display his learning, accepted the appeal; and was determined to mix, in a very unfair manner, the disputant with the judge. Public notice was given, that he intended to enter the lists with this schoolmaster: scaffolds were erected in Westminister-hall, for the accommodation of the audience: Henry appeared on this throne, accompanied with all the ensigns of majesty: the prelates were placed on his right hand: the temporal peers on his left. The judges and most eminent lawyers had a place assigned them behind the bishops: the courtiers of greatest distinction behind the peers: and in the midst of this splendid assembly was produced the unhappy Lambert, and he was required to defend his opinions against his royal antagonist.

The bishop of Chichester opened the conference, by saying, that Lambert, being charged with heretical pravity, had appealed from his bishop to the king; as if he expected more favour from this application, and as if the king could ever be induced to protect a heretic: that though his majesty had thrown off the usurpations of the see of Rome; had disincorporated some idle monks, who lived like drones in a beehive; had remedied the idolatrous worship of images; had published the Bible in English, for the instruction of all his subjects; and had made some lesser alterations, which every one must approve of; yet was he determined to maintain the purity of the catholic faith, and to punish with the utmost severity all departure from it: and that he had taken the present opportunity, before so learned and grave an auditory, of convincing Lambert of his errors; but if he still persevered obstinately in them, he must expect the most condign punishment.

After this preamble, which was not very encouraging, the king asked Lambert, with a stern countenance, what his opinion was of Christ's corporal presence in the sacrament of the altar; and when Lambert began his discourse with some compliment to his majesty, he rejected the praise with disdain and indignation. He afterwards pressed Lambert with some arguments, drawn from scripture and the schoolmen: the audience applauded the force of his reasoning, and the extent of his erudition: Cranmer seconded his proofs by some new topics: Gardiner entered the lists as a support to Cranmer: Tonstal took up the argument after Gardiner: Stokesley brought fresh aid to Tonstal: six bishops more appeared successively in the field after Stokesley. And the disputation, if it deserves the name, was prolonged for five hours; till Lambert, fatigued, confounded, brow-beaten, and abashed, was at last reduced to silence. The king then, returning to the charge, asked him whether he was convinced; and he proposed, as a concluding argument, this interesting question, whether he was resolved to live or die? Lambert, who possessed that courage which consists in obstinacy, replied, that he cast himself wholly on his majesty's clemency: the king told him, that he would be no protector of heretics; and therefore, if that was his final answer, he must expect to be committed to the flames. Cromwell, as vicegerent, read the sentence against him.

Lambert, whose vanity had probably incited him the more to persevere on account of the greatness of this public appearance, was not daunted by the terrors of that punishment, to which he was condemned. His executioners took care to make the sufferings of a man who had personally opposed the king, as cruel as possible: he was burned at a slow fire; his legs and thighs were consumed to the stumps; and when there appeared no end of his tortures, some of the guards, more merciful than the rest, lifted him on their halberts, and threw him into the flames, where he was consumed. While they were employed in this friendly office, he cried aloud several times. *None but Christ, none but Christ*; and these words were in his mouth when he expired.

An act of barbarity was this year exercised in England, which, added to many other instances of the same kind, tended to render the government extremely unpopular. Cranmer had long been detained a prisoner; but the queen was now determined to bring him to punishment; and in order the more fully to satiate her vengeance, she resolved to punish him for heresy, rather than for treason. He was cited by the pope to stand his trial at Rome; and though he was known to be kept in close custody at Oxford, he was, upon his not appearing, condemned as contumacious. Bonner, bishop of London, and Thirleby of Ely, were sent down to Oxford to degrade him; and the former executed that melancholy ceremony with all the joy and exultation, which suited his savage nature. The revenge of the queen, not satisfied with the eternal damnation of Cranmer, which she believed inevitable, and with the execution of that dreadful sentence to which he was condemned, prompted her also to seek the ruin of his honour, and the infamy of his name. Persons were employed to attack him, not in the way of disputation, against which he was sufficiently armed, but by flattery, insinuation and address; by representing the dignities to which his character still entitled him, if he would merit them by a recantation; by giving hopes of long enjoying those powerful friends, whom his beneficent disposition had attached to him during the course of his prosperity. Overcome by the fond love of life, terrified by the prospect of those tortures which awaited him, he allowed, in an unguarded hour, the sentiments of nature to prevail over his resolution, and he agreed to sign a paper, in which he acknowledged the doctrines of the papal supremacy and of the real presence. The court, equally perfidious and cruel, were determined, that this recantation should avail him nothing; and they sent orders, that he should be required to acknowledge his errors in church before the whole people, and that he should thence be immediately led to execution. Cranmer, whether that he had received a secret intimation of their design, or had repented of his weakness, surprized the audience by a contrary declaration. He said, that he was well apprized of the obedience which he owed his sovereign and the laws, but this duty extended no farther than to submit patiently to their commands, and to bear, without resistance, whatever hardships they should impose upon him: that a superior duty, the duty which he owed his Maker, obliged him to speak truth on all occasions, and not to relinquish, by a base denial, the holy doctrine which the supreme being had revealed to mankind: that there was one miscarriage in his life, of which, above all others, he severely repented; the insincere declaration of faith to which he had the weakness to consent, and which the fear of death alone had extorted from him: that he took this opportunity of attoning for his error, by a sincere and open recantation; and was willing to seal with his blood that doctrine which he firmly believed to be communicated from heaven: and that as his hand had erred by betraying his heart, it should first be punished, by a severe but just doom, and should first pay the forfeits of its offences. He was thence led to the stake amidst the insults of the catholics; and having now summoned up all the force of his mind, he bore their scorn as well as the torture of his punishment with singular fortitude. He stretched out his hand, and without betraying, either by his countenance or motions, the least sign of weakness or even of feeling, he held it in the flames till it was entirely consumed. His thoughts seemed entirely occupied with reflections on his former fault; and he called aloud several times, *This hand has offended.* Satisfied with that attonement, he then discovered a serenity in his countenance; and when the fire attacked his body, he seemed to be wholly insensible of his outward sufferings, and by the force of hope and resolution to have collected his mind altogether within itself, and to repel the fury of the flames. It is pretended, that, after his body was consumed, his heart was found entire and untouched among the ashes; an event, which, as it was the emblem of his constancy, was fondly believed by the zealous protestants. He was undoubtedly a man of merit; possessed of learning and capacity; and adorned with candour, sincerity and beneficence, and all those virtues, which were fitted to render him useful and amiable in society. His moral qualities procured him universal respect; and the courage of his martyrdom, though he fell short of the rigid inflexibility observed in many, made him the hero of the protestant party.'

In order to give some idea of the depth with which our author treats the particulars of his subject as they occur, we refer to the following reflections:

'The power of the kings of England had always been somewhat irregular or discretionary; but was scarce ever so absolute during any reign as during that of Henry. Besides the personal character of the man, full of vigour, industry, and severity, deliberate in all projects, steady in every purpose, and attended with caution, as well as good fortune, in each enterprize; he came to the throne after long and bloody civil wars, which had destroyed all the great nobility, who alone could resist the encroachments of his authority: the nation was tired with discord and intestine convulsions, and willing to submit to usurpations, and even injuries, rather than plunge themselves anew into like miseries: the fruitless efforts made against him served always, as is usual, to confirm his authority: as he ruled by a faction, and the lesser faction, all those on whom he conferred offices, sensible that they owed every thing to his protection, were content to support his power, though at the expence of justice and national privileges: these seem the chief causes which at this time bestowed on the crown so considerable an addition of prerogative, and rendered the present reign a kind of epoch in the English constitution.

This prince, though he exalted his own prerogative above law, is celebrated by his historian for many good laws, which he caused to be enacted for the government of his subjects. Several considerable regulations, indeed, are found among the statutes of this reign, both with regard to the police of the kingdom, and its commerce: but the former are commonly contrived with much better judgment than the latter. The more simple ideas of order and equity are sufficient to guide a legislator in every thing that regards the internal administration of justice: but the principles of commerce are much more complicated, and require long experience and deep reflection to be well understood in any state. The real consequence of a law or practice is there often contrary to first appearances. No wonder, that during the reign of Henry the Seventh, these matters were often misunderstood; and it may safely be affirmed, that even in the age of lord Bacon, very imperfect and erroneous ideas were formed on that subject.'

From this reign we may observe our author dates that change in the antient constitution which gave the government of England, under the house of Tudor, more the air of a settled despotism than that of a Gothic monarchy. And, indeed, the general tenor of this history prepares us to expect those struggles for liberty which commenced under the following reigns; and may prevent our surprize at the irreconcilable differences which arose between a court for some time accustomed to discretionary measures, and a people roused to the love of liberty, and desirous of legal government.

The age of Henry the Seventh was remarkable for many innovations, which were then introduced in Europe. The reader may be pleased to see how our author assembles these particulars into one view, at the conclusion of this reign.

'But though this improvement of navigation, and the discovery of both the Indies, was the most memorable incident that happened during this or any other period, it was not the only great event by which the age was distinguished. In 1453 Constantinople was taken by the Turks; and the Greeks among whom some remains of learning were still preserved, being scattered by these Barbarians, took shelter in Italy, and imported, together with their admirable language, a tincture of their science and their refined taste in poetry and eloquence. About the same time, the purity of the Latin tongue was revived, the study of antiquity became fashionable, and the esteem for literature gradually propagated itself through every nation of Europe. The art of printing, invented about that time, facilitated extremely the progress of all these improvements: the invention of gunpowder changed the whole art of war: mighty innovations were soon after made in religion, such as not only affected those states that embraced them, but even those that adhered to the antient faith and worship: and thus a general revolution was made in human affairs throughout this part of the world; and men attained that situation with regard to commerce, arts, sciences, government, police, and cultivation, in which they have ever since persevered. Here therefore commences the useful, as well as agreeable part of modern annals; certainty has place in all the considerable, and even most of the minute parts of historical narration; a great variety of events, preserved by printing, give the author the power of selecting, as well as adorning, the facts, which he relates; and as each incident has a reference to our present manners and situation, instructive lessons occur every moment during the course of the narration. Whoever carries his anxious researches into preceding periods is moved by a curiosity, liberal indeed and commendable; not by any necessity for acquiring a knowledge of public affairs, or the arts of civil government.'

Although our author is inferior, perhaps, to no historian in the talent of characterising eminent men, by the short glances of a penetrating reflection, which are thrown upon their conduct in the course of his narration; yet he has, in our opinion, greatly adorned his history, by the professed characters he has drawn. Such pictures serve either to give the first notice of a remarkable person, and prepare the reader for that part he is to act, or close the account of his life, by a very natural recollection of his principal features, and a judgment of his merits or defects. Of the former kind is the character for Wolsey, p. 86.

'Henry entered into all the views of Wolsey; and finding no one so capable of executing this plan of administration as the person who proposed it, he soon advanced his favourite, from being the companion of his careless hours, to be a member of his council; and from being a member of his council, to be his sole and absolute minister. By this rapid advancement and uncontrouled authority, the character and genius of Wolsey had full opportunity to display itself. Insatiable in his acquisitions, but still more magnificent in his expence: of extensive capacity, but still more unbounded enterprize: ambitious of power, but still more desirous of glory: insinuating, engaging, persuasive; and, by turns, lofty, elevated, commanding: haughty to his equals, but affable to his dependants; oppressive to the people, but liberal to his friends; more generous than grateful; less moved by injuries than by contempt; he seemed framed to take the ascendant in every intercourse with others, but exerted this superiority of *nature* with such ostentation as exposed him to envy, and made every one willing to recall the original inferiority or rather meanness of his *fortune*.'

For a specimen of the latter kind, the reader may consider the characters of the rival queens, that of Mary, p. 622.

'Thus died, in the forty-sixth year of her age, and the nineteenth of her captivity in England, Mary queen of Scots; a princess of great accomplishments both of body of mind, natural as well as acquired,; but unfortunate in her life, and during one period, very unhappy in her conduct. The beauties of her person, and of her air, combined to make her the most amiable of women; and the charms of her address and conversation added the impression which her lovely figure made on the hearts of all beholders.

Ambitious and active in her temper, yet inclined to chearfulness and society: of a lofty spirit, constant and even vehement in her purpose; yet polite, and gentle, and affable in her demeanor; she seemed to partake only so much of the male virtues as to render her estimable, without relinquishing those soft graces which compose the proper ornaments of her sex. In order to form a just idea of her character, we must set aside one part of her conduct, while she abandoned herself to the guidance of a profligate man; and must consider these faults, whether we admit them to be imprudences or crimes, as the result of an inexplicable, though not uncommon, inconstancy in the human mind, of the frailty of our nature, of the violence of passion, and of the influence which situations, and sometimes momentary incidents, have on persons whose principles are not thoroughly confirmed by experience and reflection. Enraged by the ungrateful conduct of her husband, seduced by the treacherous counsels of one in whom she reposed confidence, transported by the violence of her own temper, which never lay sufficiently under the guidance of discretion; she was betrayed into actions, which may, with some difficulty, be accounted for, but which admit of no apology, nor even of allevation. An enumeration of her qualities might carry the appearance of a panegyric; an account of her conduct must, in some parts, wear the aspect of a severe satire and invective.

Her numerous misfortunes, the solitude of her long and tedious captivity, and the persecutions to which she had been exposed on account of her religion, had wrought her up to a degree of bigotry during her latter years; and such was the prevalent spirit and principles of that age, that it is the less wonder, if her zeal, her resentment and her interest uniting, induced her to give consent to a design, which conspirators, actuated only by the first of these motives, had formed against the life of Elizabeth.'

To the death of Elizabeth is subjoined the following character of that celebrated princess:

'Such a dark cloud overcast the evening of that day, which had shone out with a mighty lustre in the eyes of all Europe. There are few great personages in history who have been more exposed to the calumny of enemies, and the adulation of friends, than queen Elizabeth; and yet there scarce is any, whose reputation has been more certainly determined, by the unanimous consent of posterity. The unusual length of her administration, and the strong features of her character, were able to overcome all prejudices; and obliging her detractors to abate much of their invectives, and her admirers somewhat of their panegyrics, have, at last, in spite of political factions, and what is more, of religious animosities, produced an uniform judgment with regard to her conduct. Her vigour, her constancy, her magnanimity, her penetration, vigilance, address, are allowed to merit the highest praises, and appear not to have been surpassed by any person who ever filled a throne: a conduct less rigorous, less imperious, more sincere, more indulgent to her people, would have been requisite to form a perfect character. By the force of her mind, she controuled all her more active and stronger qualities, and prevented them from running into excess: her heroism was exempt from all temerity, her frugality from avarice, her friendship from partiality, her enterprize from turbulency and a vain ambition: she guarded not herself with equal care of equal success from lesser infirmities; the rivalship of beauty, the desire of admiration, the jealousy of love, and the sallies of anger.

Her singular talents for government were founded equally on her temper and on her capacity. Endowed with a great command over herself, she soon obtained an uncontrouled ascendant over her people; and while she merited all their esteem by her real virtues, she also engaged their affection by her pretended ones. Few sovereigns of England succeeded to the throne in more difficult circumstances; and none ever conducted the government with such uniform success and felicity. Though unacquainted with the practice of toleration, the true secret for managing religious factions, she preserved her people, by her superior prudence, from those confusions in which theological controversy had involved all the neighbouring nations; and though her enemies were the most powerful princes of Europe, the most active, the most enterprising, the least scrupulous, she was able by her vigour to make deep impressions on their state: her own greatness mean-while remained untouched and unimpaired.

The wise ministers, and brave warriors, who flourished during her reign, share the praise of her success; but instead of lessening the applause due to her, they make great addition to it. They owed, all of them, their advancement to her choice; they were supported by her constance; and with all their ability, they were never able to acquire any undue ascendant over her. In her family, in her court, in her kingdom, she remained equally mistress: the force of the tender passions was great over her, but the force of her mind was still superior; and the combat which her victory visibly cost her, serves only to display the firmness of her resolution, and the loftiness of her ambitious sentiments.

The fame of this princess, though it has surmounted the prejudices both of faction and of bigotry, yet lies still exposed to another prejudice, which is more durable because more natural, and which, according to the different views in which we survey her, is capable either of exalting beyond measure, or diminishing the lustre of her character. This prejudice is founded on the consideration of her sex. When we contemplate her as a women, we are apt to be struck with the highest admiration of her great qualities and extensive capacity; but we are also apt to require some more softness of disposition, some greater lenity of temper, some of those amiable weaknesses by which her sex is distinguished. But the true method of estimating her merit, is to lay aside all these considerations, and to consider her merely as a rational being, placed in authority, and entrusted with the government of mankind. We may find it difficult to reconcile our fancy to her as a wife or a mistress; but her qualities as a sovereign, though with some considerable exceptions, are the object of undisputed applause and approbation.'

Our author concludes the whole with a review of the government, an account of the revenues, the military force, the commerce, the arts, and the learning of England, during this period, from which it appears how greatly the nation is changed or improved in these several respects.

After running over the different particulars which indicate an arbitrary or a dangerous power in the crown, the servility of parliaments, the acknowledged authority of proclamations, the dispensing power, the arbitrary courts which exercised the jurisdiction of the crown, and the irregular methods of raising contributions from the subject, he concludes the article of government with the following remark:

'On the whole, the English have no reason, from the example of their ancestors, to be in love with the picture of absolute monarchy; or to prefer the unlimited authority of the prince, and his unbounded prerogatives, to that noble liberty, that sweet equality, and that happy security, by which they are at present distinguished above all nations of the universe. The utmost that can be said in favour of the antient government (and perhaps it may be said with truth) is, that the power of the prince, thought really unlimited, was exercised after the European manner, and entered not into every part of the administration; that the instances of a high exerted prerogative were not so frequent as to render property sensibly insecure, or reduce the people to a total servitude; that the freedom from faction, the quickness of execution, and the promptitude of those measures, which could be taken for offence or defence, made some compensation for the want of a legal and determined liberty; that as the prince commanded no mercenary army, there was a tacit check on him, which maintained the government in that medium, to which the people had been accustomed; and that this situation of England was in reality more remote, though seemingly it approached nearer, a despotic and eastern monarchy, than the present government of that kingdom, where the people, though guarded by multiplied laws, are totally naked, defenceless, and disarmed.'

We cannot extend quotations of this nature, without exceeding the necessary limits of our paper: and although we dwell with pleasure on a work, of which every page deserves a particular attention, yet we have found difficulty in the choice of quotations, from a work which is sustained in every part, and where we are not assisted in our choice by remarkable inequalities, on which to ground any heavy censure or peculiar approbation.

9
OWEN RUFFHEAD,
THE MONTHLY REVIEW

[Owen Ruffhead], review of *The History of England, under the House of Tudor*, in *The Monthly Review*, April and May 1759, Vol. 20, pp. 344–364, 400–417. Complete review.

Owen Ruffhead (1723–1769) was a barrister, prolific author of political pamphlets, and editor of *The Life of Alexander Pope* (1769) and the multi-volume *Statute at Large*. He authored around 200 articles for the *Monthly Review* between 1757 and 1769. Ruffhead gives a generally favourable review of this instalment of Hume's *History*, stating that "The stile is copious and manly; the reflections are pertinent and poignant: and the conclusions, in general, are judicious." He does, however, contest Hume on several points, and in subsequent editions of the *History* Hume altered many of the passages accordingly. Specifically, Hume reworked his accounts of Henry VIII's views of marriage, Anne Boleyn's diminishing protestations of innocence, the importance of following "ancient" practices, and the impact of changing manners on the power of the barons. In his objections, Ruffhead italicized specific phrases that he found problematic, and, invariably, these are the phrases that Hume later changed. Footnotes at the appropriate locations below present Hume's modified wording. However, he was not apparently moved to make all the corrections that Ruffhead suggests. For example, regarding Hume's claim that the rise of the arts helped usher in the decline of the feudal system, Ruffhead argues that in fact laws aimed at dismantling feudalism created a climate for arts. Regarding Hume's view that industry and diligence among the clergy perverts even true religion, Ruffhead holds that industry helps ward off fanaticism. Also, he challenges Hume's speculation that the publishing of the King James Bible bred fanaticism and led people away from more ancient and secure Christian establishments. Ruffhead's review contains extended quotes from Hume's account of religious persecution at the time of Queen Mary, the tension between Elizabeth and Mary Queen of Scots, and Elizabeth's character. In later years Hume became aware that Ruffhead had written reviews of the *History*, and Hume accordingly expressed his gratitude (see Ruffhead's 1763 letter to Hume, included later in this collection).

The History of England, Under the House of Tudor. Comprehending the Reigns of K. Henry VII. K. Henry VIII. K. Edward VI. Q. Mary, and Q. Elizabeth. By David Hume, *Esq;* In two volumes. 4to. 1l. 1s. *in boards.* Millar.

This learned and liberal writer, who has already obliged the publick with the History of Great-Britain during the reigns of some of our later kings,[1] has, in the volumes before us, traced the history of England further back; and with great diligence and ingenuity, recorded the transactions of more remote, though not less interesting periods. Whether choice or accident induced the author to write backward, we are at a loss to determine; but we may venture to say, that it is by no means the most natural or intelligible method of connecting historical matter.

The writer, however, is to be commended for having confined himself to detached reigns, instead of venturing at once upon a general history. The annals of seventeen or eighteen centuries, compiled, perhaps, in little more than as many months, can expect little credit or favour from the judicious. A work of such extent, if properly executed, is sufficient to engage almost all the years of mature judgment, with which nature has indulged the strongest faculties.

In selecting detached periods of history, the historian has leisure to be particularly copious and accurate in his narrative. He is supposed to examine the facts he relates, as far as possible, by original vouchers, which alone is a work of great labour and time. It is expected, that he should endeavour to investigate the causes of the events he commemorates, but more especially to trace their effects; and by the acuteness and solidity of his reflections, to explain, illustrate, and adorn the passages of history.

The reigns comprized in these volumes, are of the utmost importance to those who would gain a thorough knowledge of our government; and it requires an intimate acquaintance with the antient Constitution of this kingdom, that is, the feudal system; to treat of them with judgment and perspicuity. Within this period, Henry the seventh laid the basis of civil liberty; and in our review of the history before us, we shall take occasion to controvert the writer's insinuation to the contrary.

This shrewd prince first undermined that barbarous system, under which brutal violence had so much the ascendancy in civil administration, that mankind, during that time, can scarce be considered as connected in a state of society. The alterations which he made in civil polity however, though they were the foundation of the freedom we now enjoy, were, nevertheless, as we shall shew in the course of our animadversions, the occasion of that tyranny, which was exercised by his more immediate successors.

---

[1]   Mr. Hume has published the History of Great Britain, in two Vols. quarto. Containing the Reigns of James I. Charles I. the Commonwealth, Charles II. and James II. See Review, vol. XII. p. 206. and vol. XVI. p. 36.

The reformation, which dawned in the reigns of Henry VIII. and Edward VI. with the violent measures taken by the former in the abolition of the religious houses, and the conversion of the sacred plunder, contributed greatly to enlarge and improve the popular plan of freedom, which his predecessor concerted, perhaps, without foreseeing the consequences. Though the bloody disposition and blind bigotry of Mary, endangered a fatal change, yet the spirit and prudence of Elizabeth in completing the reformation, rekindled the smothered sparks of political liberty; and even the tyranny of that princess, served to strengthen the hands of the people, by abasing the nobility.

It is but just to acknowledge, that the historian, in recounting the revolutions of this period, has, upon the whole, proceeded with great freedom of inquiry, and impartiality of judgement. He has occasionally done justice to all sects, and all parties: he does not appear to be in the least tinctured with that bigotry, which disposes men to adopt particular received tenets and opinions in religion and politics. But though he is free from all slavish zeal for the systems of others, he is not exempt from a frailty scarce less dangerous, which is a passion for singularity. If, in the course of this history, he has inadvertently fallen into inconsistencies and improprieties, his errors are to be imputed to this source: and it should be considered, that though the reputation he has deservedly acquired in the literary world, may hide his defects from those who are content to take facts and sentiments upon trust, yet by such means they become more striking and observable to men, who are detached from personal prepossessions: and it becomes more immediately their duty, to obviate the impressions which error may make under the sanction of such acknowledged merit.

The first volume begins with the accession of Henry VII. to the crown of England. The historian states the several titles on which that prince founded his right to the throne, and among the rest, takes notice of the act of settlement by parliament. He then observes, that after all the king's precautions,

'He was so little satisfied with his own title to the crown, that, in the following year, he applied to Rome for a confirmation of it; and as that court gladly laid hold of all opportunities which the imprudence, weakness, or necessity of princes afforded it to extend its authority. Innocent the eighth readily granted a bull, in whatever terms the king was pleased to desire. All Henry's titles by succession, marriage, parliamentary choice, even conquest, are there enumerated; and to the whole the sanction of religion is added; excommunication is denounced against every one who should either disturb him in the present possession, or the heirs of his body, in their future succession to the crown; and from this penalty no criminal, except in the article of death, can be absolved but by the pope himself, or his special commissioners.'

It is difficult to imagine, says the writer, that the security derived from this bull could be a compensation for the defect which it betrayed in Henry's title, and to the danger of thus inviting the pope to interpose in these concerns. We must confess, however, that we do not view this measure of Henry's in the same light with the historian. As to the defects in Henry's title, they were so extremely obvious, and all his claims were liable to such insuperable objections, that he could run no risk of betraying defects which were so generally notorious. If, on the other hand, we reflect on the extreme bigotry and superstition of those times, and consider how powerfully the pope's authority and the dread of excommunication operated, we may easily conceive that the advantages which Henry might reasonably propose to himself from this bull of the pope's, were greater than the danger he might apprehend from the interposition of his holiness. Not to mention, that by this scheme he might hope to gain the ecclesiastics, who, at that time, both in number and power, constituted so great a part of the kingdom, and whose favour he always courted, by promoting them to the highest offices of state, to the exclusion of the nobility and laity from the administration.

The historian then proceeds to recount the unpopular measures of Henry's government, which, in some degree, occasioned those insurrections that troubled his reign. We must observe, that the many imprudent steps which Henry pursued, particularly his violent oppression of the house of York, do by no means correspond with that consummate wisdom and policy for which he is celebrated by historians. But we are too apt to judge of men, especially of princes, from a few *successful* incidents, without regard to the general tenor of their conduct, which is the only just criterion by which to determine their character.

Having gone through the transactions of this reign with great spirit and accuracy, the historian sums up the character of Henry in the following words.

'The reign of Henry the seventh was, in the main, fortunate for his people at home, and honourable abroad. He put an end to the civil wars with which the nation had been long harassed, he maintained peace and order in the state, he depressed the former exorbitant power of the nobility, and, together with the friendship of some foreign princes, he acquired the consideration and regard of all. He loved peace without fearing war; though agitated with continual suspicions of his servants and ministers, he discovered no timidity either in the conduct of his affairs, or in the day of battle; and though often severe in his punishments, he was commonly less actuated by revenge than by the maxims of policy. The services which he rendered the people, were derived from his views of private interest, rather than the motives of public spirit; and where he deviated from selfish regards, it was unknown to himself, and ever from the malignant prejudices of faction, or the mean projects of avarice; not from the sallies of passion, or allurements of pleasure; still less, from the benign motives of friendship and generosity. His capacity was excellent, but somewhat contracted, by the narrowness of his heart; he possessed insinuation and address, but never employed these talents, except where some great point of interest was to be gained; and while he neglected to conciliate the affections of his people, he often felt the danger of resting his authority on their fear and reverence alone. He was always extremely attentive to his affairs, but possessed not the faculty of seeing far into futurity; and was more expert at providing a remedy for his mistakes than judicious in avoiding them. Avarice was on the whole his ruling passion; and he remains an instance, almost singular, of a man, placed in a high station, and possessed of talents for great affairs, in whom that passion predominated above ambition. Even among private persons, avarice is commonly nothing but a species of ambition, and is chiefly incited by the prospect of that regard, distinction, and consideration which are derived from riches.

The power of the kings of England had always been somewhat irregular or discretionary; but was scarce ever so absolute during any reign as during that of Henry. Besides the personal character of the man, full of vigour, industry, and severity, deliberate in all projects, steady in every purpose, and attended with caution, as well as good fortune, in each enterprize; he came to the throne after long and bloody civil wars, which had destroyed all the great nobility, who alone could resist the encroachments of his authority; the nation was tired with discord and intestine convulsions, and willing to submit to usurpations, and even injuries, rather than plunge themselves anew into like miseries: the fruitless efforts made against him served always as is usual, to confirm his authority: as he ruled by a faction, and the lesser faction, all those on whom he conferred offices, sensible that they owed every thing to his protection, were content to support his power, though at the expence of justice and national privileges; these seem the chief causes which at this time bestowed on the crown so considerable an addition of prerogative, and rendered the present reign a kind of epoch in the English constitution.'

This appears to be a faithful and lively portrait of that celebrated monarch: but the historian does not seem to have done the same justice to his particular institutions, which he has paid to his general character; for he observes, that Henry's system of policy acquired him more praise than his institutions, strictly speaking, deserve, on account of any profound wisdom attending them. In enumerating the laws of this prince, he takes particular notice of three or four, perhaps the most important in their consequences.

'There scarce, says the historian, passed any session during this reign, without some statute against engaging retainers, and giving them badges or liveries; a practice by which they were, in a manner, enlisted under some great lord, and were kept in readiness to assist him in all wars, insurrections, riots, violences, and even in bearing evidence for him in courts of justice. This disorder, which had arisen during turbulent times, when the law could give little protection to the subject, was then deeply rooted in England; and it required all the vigilance and rigour of Henry to extirpate it. There is a story of his severity against the abuse, which seems to merit praise, though it is commonly cited as an instance of his avarice and rapacity. The earl of Oxford, his favourite general, in whom he always reposed great and deserved trust, having splendidly entertained him at his castle of Henningham, was desirous of making a shew of his magnificence at the departure of his royal guest; and ordered all his retainers, with their liveries and badges, to be drawn up in two lines, that their appearance might be more gallant and splendid. "My Lord, said the King, I have heard much of your hospitality, but the truth far exceeds the report. These handsome gentlemen and yeomen, whom I see on both sides of me, are surely your menial servants." The earl smiled, and confessed that his fortune was too narrow for such magnificence. "They are most of them, subjoined he, my retainers, who are come to do me service at such a time, when they knew I was honoured with your majesty's presence." The king started a little, and said "By my faith, my lord, I thank you for my good cheer, but I must not allow my laws to be broken in my sight. My attorney must speak with you." – Oxford is said to have paid no less than fifteen thousand marks, as a composition for his offence.'

'The encrease of the arts, adds our historian, more effectually than all the severities of laws, put an end to this pernicious practice.' Here we must differ from the writer, who, in our judgment, seems, in some degree, to mistake an effect for a cause. We are so far from thinking that the encrease of the arts had the influence he supposes, that we rather conclude the foregoing law, with others which followed, to have contributed to the encrease of the arts, by abolishing that pernicious practice of retaining, and changing the course of property.

The subsequent laws we allude to, are those which enabled the nobility and gentry to bar the antient entails, and to alienate their estates without paying fines.[2] By the co-operation of these statutes, the principles of the old feudal system were destroyed, the power of the nobility was weakened, and that of the commons strengthened, by the landed property which was shared among them.[3]

---

[2] These laws were made nearly about the same time with those against retaining.

[3] The laws for barring entails, and empowering the nobility, etc. to alienate their estates, though not directly levelled against retaining, yet they eventually operated to that end; for by preventing the perpetuity of estates, and insensibly drawing property out of the hands of the nobility, they deprived them of the power, had they retained the inclination to transgress, by keeping retainers.

Before these regulations took place, there was little encouragement to cultivate the arts. There were, at that time, no moneyed funds, and to what end could men labour to amass property, which they had no means of realizing, or employing to any certain advantage. Besides, by these institutions, men were set free from a slavish dependance on their superiors, and left at liberty to cultivate the arts, which, in their state of indolent dependance, they had neither inclination or opportunity to pursue.

It is observable, that the historian himself has adopted this latter argument, without perceiving its force. Speaking of the statutes concerning retainers, he says, 'The common people,[4] no longer maintained in a vicious idleness by their superiors, were obliged to learn some calling or industry, and became useful both to themselves and others.' It is strange that he should not discover how forcibly this observation militates against his own proposition. Certainly, the obligation to industry, which, as he justly observes, these statutes enforced, is a proof that the laws, by suppressing the mischief of retaining, furnished hands for the improvement of the arts; and *that* custom must have been effectually abolished, before the arts could flourish to a degree sufficient to extend their influence over prevailing habits and manners.

There were other institutions, however, which contributed to depress the nobility, and raise the people; those of population for instance. Our historian says, that 'the law against inclosures, and for the keeping up farm-houses, scarce deserves the high praises bestowed on it by lord Bacon.' Whether lord Bacon's eulogy is exaggerated or not, is a matter not worth disputing. But the law itself appears to have been wisely framed, and to correspond with the other institutions, so as to form together one consistent plan of policy. By this law the strength of the kingdom was more equally distributed; landed property was thrown into the hands of the middle people, who being free from servile subjection on the lords, became, as lord Bacon observes, most excellent and independent infantry. The historian adds, that 'all methods of supporting populousness, except by the interest of the proprietors, are violent and ineffectual.' This, in one sense, is undoubtedly true: but there it often happens, that proprietors pursue a partial and present interest, to the neglect of the general and lasting benefit, which in the end, indeed, is their own true interest. Upon the whole, whether Henry foresaw all the consequences of this policy, we will not undertake to determine. We rather think, with Harrington, that he did not; but that he acted upon the narrow and selfish principle of depressing the nobility, to secure himself upon the throne. This, indeed, is mere matter of conjecture: but however limited his motives were, his institutions were wise in themselves, extensive in their consequences; and our author's opinion to the

---

[4] Though the historian speaks of these retainers as *common people*, there were many of them, nevertheless, younger brothers of good families.

contrary, appears to be singular and erroneous. As we shall have occasion to consider these matters farther in our review of the second volume, we leave them for the present, and proceed with our historian to the transactions of the succeeding reign.

Our historian's reflections on the ecclesiastical state in this reign, are, in general, too ingenious and solid to be passed over in silence. We are concerned that our limits will not allow us to be more liberal in our extracts; but the following specimen will be sufficient to engage the curious and intelligent reader to refer to the work itself.

'Most of the arts and professions in a state are of such a nature, that, while they promote the interests of the society, they are also useful or agreeable to some individuals; and in that case, the constant rule of the magistrate, except, perhaps, on the first introduction of any art, is, to leave the profession to itself, and trust its encouragement to the individuals, who reap the benefit of it. The artizans, finding their profits to rise by favour of their customers, encrease, as much as possible, their skill and industry; and as matters are not disturbed by any injudicious tampering, the commodity is always sure to be at all times, exactly proportioned to the demand.

But there are also some callings, which, though useful and even necessary in a state, bring no advantage nor pleasure to any individuals; and the supreme power is obliged to alter its conduct with regard to the retainers of those professions. It must give them public encouragement in order to their subsistence; and it must provide against that negligence, to which they will naturally be subject, either by annexing particular honour to the profession, by establishing a long subordination of ranks and a strict dependance, or by some other expedient. The persons employed in the finances, armies, fleets, and magistracy are instances of this order of men.

It may naturally be thought, at first view, that the ecclesiastics belong to the first class, and that their encouragement, as well as that of lawyers and physicians, may safely be trusted to the liberality of individuals, who are attached to their doctrines, and who find benefit or consolation from their spiritual ministry and assistance. Their industry and vigilance will, no doubt, be whetted by such an additional motive; and their skill in the profession, as well as their address in governing the minds of the people, must receive daily encrease, from their encreasing practice, study, and attention.

But if we consider the matter more closely, we shall find, that this interested diligence of the clergy is what every wise legislator will study to avoid; because in every religion, except the true, it is highly pernicious, and has even a natural tendency to pervert the true, by infusing into it a strong mixture of superstition, folly, and delusion. Each ghostly practitioner, in order to render himself more precious and sacred in the eyes of his retainers, must inspire them with the most violent abhorrence against all other sects, and continually endeavour, by some novelty, to excite the languid devotion of his audience. No regard will be paid to truth, morals, or decency in the doctrines inculcated. Every tenet will be adopted, that best suits the disorderly affections of the human frame. Customers will be drawn to each conventicle, by new industry and address in practising on the passions and credulity of the populace. And in the end, the civil magistrate will find, that he has paid dearly for his pretended frugality, in saving a settled foundation for the priests; and that in reality the most decent and advantageous composition, which he can make with the spiritual guides, is to bribe their indolence, by affixing stated salaries to their profession, and rendering it superfluous for them to be farther active, than merely to prevent their flock from straying in quest of new pastures. And in this manner ecclesiastical establishments, though commonly they arose at first from religious views, prove in the end advantageous to the political interest of society.'

Daily experience justifies the truth and propriety of these reflections. The interested diligence of the clergy is certainly of disadvantage to all religions, except the true. We think, however, that our author is too hasty, when he concludes, that it has even a natural tendency to pervert the true. The clergy of a true religion surely may exert themselves with diligence, without giving way to superstition, folly, and delusion: and we are of opinion, that if our divines (whose indolence needs no bribe) had exercised their function with more industry, we should not have been pestered with so many fanatical sectaries, who are a disgrace to religion, and a detriment to civil government.

The historian then proceeds to shew the origin of the reformation, which he traces with equal skill and diligence. His reflections likewise, on Henry's divorce from his queen Catherine, are extremely acute and observable; but are to be read, however, with great attention and caution. They are, indeed, of a most liberal nature; yet it should be remembered throughout, that acts which may be justifiable from necessity, are, nevertheless, illicit and unnatural, when made a matter of choice.

'Had the question of Henry's marriage with Catherine,' says the Historian, 'been examined by the principles of sound philosophy, exempt from superstition, it seemed not liable to much difficulty. The natural reason, why marriage in certain degrees is prohibited by the civil laws, and condemned by the moral sentiments of all nations, is derived from men's care to preserve purity of manners; while they reflect, that if a commerce of love were authorized between the nearest relations, the frequent opportunities of intimate conversation, especially during early youth, would introduce an universal dissoluteness and corruption. But as the customs of countries vary considerably, and open an intercourse, more or less restrained, between different families, or between the several members of the same family, so we find, that the moral precept, varying with its cause, is susceptible, without any inconvenience, of very different latitude in the several ages and nations of the world. The extreme delicacy of the Greeks, permitted no converse between persons of the two sexes, except where they lived under the same roof; and even the apartments of a step-mother, and her daughters, were almost as much shut up against visits from the husband's sons, as against those from any strangers or more remote relations: hence in that nation it was lawful for a man to marry, not only his niece, but his half-sister by the father: a liberty unknown to the Romans, and other nations, where a more open intercourse was authorised between the sexes. Reasoning from this principle, it would appear, that the ordinary commerce of life among great princes, is so obstructed by ceremony, and numerous attendants, that no ill consequence would result among them, from the marriage of a brother's widow; especially if the dispensation of the sovereign priest is previously required, in order to justify what may in common cases be condemned, and to hinder the precedent from becoming too common and familiar. And as strong motives of public interest and tranquillity may frequently require such alliances between the sovereign families, there is less reason for extending towards them the full vigour of that rule which has place among individuals.'[5]

In the history of this reign, Henry's foreign and domestic conduct is stated in a clear and impartial light; and illustrated with observations always striking, and generally judicious. That monarch's variable system of politicks, between the emperor, and the French, is, by our historian, in some instances, attributed to the eagerness of Henry's passions, and the undue influence of his favourite Wolsey. Sir Robert Cotton the antiquarian, however, with other eminent men,[6]

---

[5] 'Even judging of this question by the scripture, to which the appeal was every moment made, the arguments of the King's cause appear but lame and imperfect. Marriage in the degree of affinity which had place between Henry and Catherine, is, indeed, prohibited in Leviticus; but it is natural to interpret that prohibition as a part of the Jewish ceremonial or municipal law: and though it is there said, in the conclusion, that the gentile nations, by violating these degrees of consanguinity, had incurred the divine displeasure, the extension of this maxim to every precise case before specified, is supposing the scriptures to be composed with a minute accuracy and precision, to which, we know with certainty, the sacred penmen did not think proper to confine themselves. The descent of mankind from one common father, obliged them in the first generation to marry in the nearest degrees of consanguinity: instances of a like nature occur among the patriarchs: and the marriage of a brother's widow was, in certain cases, not only permitted, but even enjoined as a positive precept by the Mosaical law. It is in vain to say, that this precept was an exception to the rule; and an exception confined merely to the Jewish nation. The inference is still just, that such a marriage can contain no natural or moral turpitude; otherwise God, who is the author of all purity, would never, in any case, have enjoined it.'

[6] A famous speaker in the long parliament, either Pym or Rutherford, has been very lavish in his eulogy on Henry on this account.

have complimented Henry, by supposing his fluctuating measures to have been the result of deep sagacity and profound policy. But we can judge of effects with authority, where it is often presumption to decide concerning motives. From whatever principle the king acted, whether from passion or policy, his measures, by which he balanced the two powers, were for the good of the kingdom and Europe in general: though it must be confessed, that had he been more early in his opposition to the emperor Charles, he might have saved a great deal of blood and treasure, which was lost by temporizing.

The violent innovations in religion, in consequence of Henry's quarrel with the pope, which occasioned the suppression of the religious houses, and in the end produced the reformation, are related by our historian with peculiar spirit and judgment. It is observable, that the pope was at first inclined to grant Henry's request in the matter of the divorce; and had not his holiness been over-awed with compliance by fear of the emperor, this kingdom might still, humanly speaking, have groaned under the yoke of Rome. Mr. Hume observes, that nothing, during this revolution, ensured publick tranquillity so much, as the decisive authority acquired by the king; but we may add, that it was not the interest of the great men to oppose these innovations, as they might hope to participate of the spoils, which they actually shared among them:[7] and an insurrection of the populace, without powerful leaders, is not greatly to be apprehended. On the whole, says the historian, the king suppressed six hundred and forty-five monasteries. The whole revenue of these establishments is computed at one hundred and sixty one thousand one hundred pounds. He adds, that the whole lands and possessions of England had, a little before this period, been rated at three millions a year; so that the revenues of the monasteries did not really much exceed the twentieth part of the national income: a sum vastly inferior to what is commonly apprehended.

Among the impostures discovered in these monasteries, the historian relates one very remarkable.

'At Hales, says he, in the country of Glocester, had been shewn, during several ages, the blood of Christ brought from Jerusalem; and it is easy to imagine the veneration with which such a relic was regarded. A miraculous circumstance also attended this miraculous relict; the sacred blood was not visible to any one in mortal sin, even when set before him; and till he had performed good works sufficient for his absolution, it would not deign to discover itself to him. At the dissolution of the monastery the whole contrivance was discovered. Two of the monks, who were let into the secret,

---

[7] Some of inferior rank shared in the plunder, and Henry was so profuse, that he is said, adds our historian, to have given a woman the whole revenues of a convent, as a reward for making a pudding, which happened to gratify his palate.

had taken the blood of a duck, which they renewed every week; they put it into a phial, one side of which consisted of thin and transparent crystal, the other of thick and obscure. When any rich pilgrim arrived, they were sure to shew him the dark side of the phial, till masses and offerings had expiated his offences; and then finding his money, or patience, or faith, near exhausted, they made him happy by turning the phial.'

The deliberations concerning a new translation of the bible, as related by our historian, are too interesting to be suppressed. 'Tindal', says he,

'had formerly given a translation, and it had been greedily read by the people; but as the clergy complained of it, as very inaccurate and unfaithful, it was now proposed that they should themselves publish a translation, which would not be liable to those objections. The friends of the reformation asserted, that nothing could be more absurd than to conceal, in an unknown tongue, the word itself of God, and thus to counteract the will of heaven, which, for the purpose of universal salvation, had published that salutary doctrine to all nations; that if this practice was not very absurd, the artifice at least was very barefaced, and proved a consciousness, that the glosses and traditions of the clergy stood in direct opposition to the original text, dictated by Supreme Intelligence: that it was now necessary for the people, so long abused by interested pretentions, to see with their own eyes, and to examine whether the claims of the ecclesiastics were founded on that charter, which was on all hands acknowledged to be derived from heaven; and that as a spirit of research and curiosity was happily revived, and men were now obliged to make a choice among the pretensions of different sects, the proper materials for decision, and above all, the holy scriptures, should be set before them, and the revealed will of God, which the change of language had somewhat obscured, be again, by their means, revealed to mankind.

The favourers of the ancient religion maintained, on the other hand, that the pretence of making the people see with their own eyes, was a mere cheat, and was itself a very barefaced artifice, by which the new preachers hoped to obtain the guidance of them, and seduce them from those pastors, whom the laws, whom ancient establishments, whom heaven itself had appointed for their spiritual direction: that the people were, by their ignorance, their stupidity, their necessary avocations, totally unqualified to choose their own principles, and it was a mockery to set materials before them, of which they could not possibly make any proper use: that even in the affairs of common life, and in their temporal concerns, which lay more within the compass of human reason, the laws had, in a great measure, deprived them of the right of private judgment, and had, happily, for their own and the public interest, regulated their conduct and behaviour: that theological questions were placed much beyond the sphere of vulgar comprehension; and ecclesiastics themselves, though assisted by all the advantages of education, erudition, and an assiduous study of the science, could not be fully assured of a just decision; except by the promise made them in scripture, that God would be ever present with his church, and that the gates of hell should not prevail against her: that the gross errors adopted by the wisest heathens, proved how unfit men were to grope their own way, through this profound darkness; nor would the scriptures, if trusted to every man's judgment, be able to remedy; on the contrary, they would much augment, these fatal illusions: that sacred writ itself was involved in so much obscurity, was exposed to so many difficulties, contained so many appearing contradictions, that it was the most dangerous weapon which could be intrusted into the hands of the ignorant and giddy multitude: that the poetical spirit, in which a great part of it was composed, at the same time that it occasioned uncertainty in the sense, by its multiplied tropes and figures, was sufficient to kindle the zeal of fanaticism, and thereby throw civil society into the most furious combustion: that a thousand sects must arise, which would pretend, each of them, to derive its tenets from the scripture; and would be able, by specious arguments, or even without specious arguments, to seduce silly women, and ignorant mechanics, into a belief of the most monstrous principles: and that if ever this disorder, dangerous to the magistrate himself, received a remedy, it must be from the tacit acquiescence of the people in some new authority; and it was evidently better, without farther context of enquiry, to adhere peaceably to ancient, and therefore the more secure establishments.'

The arguments against the translation are very copious and ingenious; but we must make allowances for the historian's embellishments. The reasoning he makes use of is drawn from events within his own observation, and which probably were not foretold at the time of these deliberations. The author, however, is not to be censured for this liberty of amplification upon a point merely speculative.

Nevertheless, his reflections on some passages in this reign, are liable to great exception. In describing the decline of Henry's affection for Anne Boleyn, and his growing attachment of Jane Seymour, he observes, that the king 'was determined to sacrifice every thing to the gratification of his new appetite. Unlike to most monarchs, says he, who judge lightly of the crime of gallantry, and who deem the young damsels of the court rather honoured than disgraced by their passion, *he never thought of any other attachment than that of marriage*; and in order to attain this end, he underwent more difficulties, and committed greater crimes, than those which he sought to avoid by forming that legal connexion.'

Here the historian forgets that Henry had an intrigue with Elizabeth Blunt, afterwards Lady Talsboyse, by whom he had a son, named Henry Fitzroy, afterwards created duke of Richmond and Somerset. This circumstance proves that Henry was not so scrupulous in the point of gallantry, as the writer would represent him.[8]

His observations likewise on Anne Boleyn's behavior, previous to her execution, appear unnatural. 'The queen', says he,

> 'prepared for suffering that death to which she was sentenced. She sent her last message to the king, in which she renewed the protestations of her innocence, and recommended her daughter to his care. Before the lieutenant of the Tower, and all who approached her, she made the like declarations, and continued to behave herself with her usual serenity, and even with chearfulness. "The executioner," she said to the lieutenant, "is, I hear, very expert; and my neck is very slender:" upon which she grasped it in her hand, and laughed heartily. When brought, however, to the scaffold, says the historian, she softened her tone a little with regard to her protestations of innocence. *She reflected*, that the obstinacy of queen Catherine, and her resistance to the king's will, had much alienated him from the lady Mary; and her maternal concern, therefore, for Elizabeth, prevailed in these last moments over that indignation, which the unjust sentence, by which she suffered, naturally excited in her.'

This eager desire of penetrating into the human heart, and opening the secret springs of action, often betrays historians into excess of refinement. By endeavouring to account for every change of conduct, they often excite doubts, instead of solving difficulties; forgetting that there are transitions of passion in the human mind, which are as unaccountable as involuntary. To us it seems highly improbable, that the alteration in Anne's behavior proceeded from the cause mentioned by our historian, or that she entertained the reflections which he has so positively ascribed to her; as we can discover no evidence, that she ever made any declaration of her sentiments to that effect. It seems unnatural to suppose, that her maternal concern for Elizabeth did not take place till her last moments; and we would rather think, that she was inclined to moderate her resolution from some more immediate apprehension. Might we, without falling into the excess we condemn, hazard a conjecture in this case, we should imagine, that her flexibility was owing, perhaps, to the dread of suffering the utmost severity of her sentence; for we find, that the menace of executing it against her in its greatest rigour, had before extorted a confession from her of some lawful impediment to her marriage with the king: by which, as far as her declaration could operate, she acknowledged Elizabeth to be illegitimate.[9]

[8] [In later editions of the *History* Hume altered the above quotation to read "he seldom thought of any other attachment than that of marriage."]

[9] [In later editions of the *History* Hume altered "she reflected" to "she probably reflected."]

In the succeeding part of this history, Henry's cruel persecution of the non-conformists, with the extreme fortitude of the unhappy sufferers, is related in the most affecting terms of description. The king's caprice and inconsistency in points of religion[10] are clearly exposed, and censured with becoming spirit. But, as we have not room to be further particular, we hasten to the historian's masterly protraiture of this tyrannical monarch.

'It is difficult,' says he, 'to give a just summary of this prince's qualities; he was so different from himself in different parts of his reign, that, as it is well remarked by lord Herbert, his history is his best character and description. The absolute, uncontrouled authority which he maintained at home, and the regard which he acquired among foreign nations, are circumstances which entitle him to the appellation of a great prince; while his tyranny, and cruelty, seem to exclude him from the character of a *good* one. He possessed, indeed, great vigour of mind, which qualified him for exercising dominion over men; courage, intrepidity, vigilance, inflexibility: and though these qualities lay not always under the guidance of a regular and solid judgment, they were accompanied with good parts, and an extensive capacity; and every one dreaded a contest with a man who was known never to yield, or to forgive, and who, in every controversy, was determined, either to ruin himself or his antagonist. A catalogue of his vices would comprehend many of the worst qualities incident to human nature; violence, cruelty, profusion, rapacity, injustice, obstinacy, arrogance, bigotry, presumption, caprice: but neither was he subject to all these vices in the most extreme degree, nor was he, at intervals, altogether devoid of virtues: he was sincere, open, gallant, liberal, and capable at least of a temporary friendship and attachment. In this respect he was unfortunate, that the incidents of his times served to display his faults in their full light: the treatment which he met with from the court of Rome, provoked him to violence; the danger of a revolt from his superstitious subjects, seemed to require the most extreme severity. But it must, at the same time, be acknowledged, that his situation tended to throw an additional lustre on what was great and magnanimous in his character: the emulation between the emperor and the French king, rendered his alliance, notwithstanding his impolitic conduct, of great importance in Europe: the extensive powers of his prerogative, and the submissive, nor to say slavish, disposition of his

[10] The historian has, in a note, preserved the following facetious anecdote. The duke of Norfolk, soon after the act was passed imposing celibacy on the clergy, meeting one of his chaplains, who was suspected of favouring the reformation, said to him, 'Now, Sir, what think you of the law to hinder priests from having wives?' 'Yes, my lord, replies the chaplain, you have done that; but I will answer for it, you cannot hinder men's wives from having priests.'

parliament, made it the more easy for him to assume and maintain that entire dominion by which his reign is so much distinguished in the English history.

'It may seem a little extraordinary, that notwithstanding his cruelty, his extortion, his violence, his arbitrary administration, this prince not only acquired the regard of his subjects; but never was the object of their hatred: he seems even in some degree to have possessed, to the last, their love and affection. His exterior qualities were advantageous, and fit to captivate the multitude: his magnificence and personal bravery rendered him illustrious in vulgar eyes: and it may be said, with truth, that the English in that age, were so thoroughly subdued, that, like eastern slaves, they were inclined to admire even those acts of violence and tyranny, which were exercised over themselves, and at their own expence.

'With regard to foreign states, Henry appears long to have supported an intercourse of friendship with Francis, more sincere and disinterested than usually takes place between neighbouring princes. Their common jealousy of the emperor Charles, and some resemblance in their characters, (though the comparison is extremely to the advantage of the French monarch) served as the cement of their mutual amity. Francis is said to have been affected with the king's death, and to have expressed much regret for the loss. His own health began to decline: he foretold, that he should not long survive his friend: and he died in about two months after him.'

The writer then proceeds to give a summary of the laws passed in this reign, upon most of which he makes very pertinent and politick observations. He mentions one, by which all foreign artificers were prohibited having above two foreigners in their house, either journeymen or apprentices; and another, by which all denizens were obliged to pay the duties impose[d] upon aliens. Of these laws, he judiciously observes, that the parliament had done better to have encouraged foreign merchants and artisans to come over to England; which might have excited the emulation of the natives, and improved their skill.

The succeeding reign, with the short-lived royalty of lady Jane Gray, afford no great subject for historical comment, or political speculation. It is but just to observe, however, that the character of the unhappy lady Jane is placed in so amiable a light by our historian, and her deplorable fate is so pathetically described, that a reader of any feeling cannot peruse the description without dissolving in tears of sympathy.

The reign of the bigotted Mary is chiefly distinguished by the many instances of almost incredible cruelty and inhumanity. As the historian is particularly happy in his power of description, his pen aggravates the horror of these shocking scenes of barbarity. Previous to this cruel persecution, a debate was had before the queen and council, between the two ecclesiastics, Pole and Gardiner; when the arguments for and against toleration were canvassed. The historian has obliged us with the topics by which each side supported, or, as he says, might have supported, their schemes of policy.

'The practice of persecution, said the defenders of Pole's opinion, is the scandal of all religion; and the theological animosity, so fierce and violent, far from being an argument of men's conviction in their opposite tenets, is a certain proof, that they have never reached any serious persuasion with regard to these remote and sublime subjects. Even those who are the most impatient of contradiction in other controversies, are mild and moderate in comparison of polemical divines; and wherever a man's knowledge and experience give him a perfect assurance of his own opinion, he regards with contempt, rather than anger, the opposition and mistakes of others. But while men zealously maintain what they neither clearly comprehend, nor entirely believe, they are shaken in their imagined faith, by the opposite persuasion, or even doubts of other men; and vent on their antagonists that impatience which is the natural result of so disagreeable a state of the understanding. They then embrace easily any pretence for representing opponents as impious and prophane; and if they can also find a colour for connecting this violence with the interests of civil government, they can no longer be restrained from giving uncontrouled scope to vengeance and resentment. But surely never enterprize was more unfortunate than that of founding persecution upon policy, or endeavouring, for the sake of peace, to settle an entire uniformity of opinion, in questions which, of all others, are least subject to the criterion of human reason. The universal and uncontradicted prevalence of one opinion in religious subjects, can only be owing at first to the stupid ignorance and barbarism of the people, who never indulge themselves in any speculation or enquiry; and there is no other expedient for maintaining that uniformity, so fondly sought after, but by banishing for ever all curiosity and all improvement in science and cultivation. It may not, indeed, appear difficult to check, by a steddy severity, the first beginnings of controversy; but besides that this policy exposes for ever the people to all the abject terrors of superstition, and the magistrate to the endless encroachments of ecclesiastics, it also renders men so delicate, that they can never endure to hear of opposition; and they will sometime pay dearly for that false tranquillity in which they have been so long indulged. As healthful bodies are ruined by too nice a regimen, and are thereby rendered incapable of bearing the unavoidable incidents of human life; a people who never were allowed to imagine, that their principles could be contested, fly out into the most outrageous violence when any event (and such events are common) produces a faction among their clergy, and gives rise to any difference in tenet or opinion. But whatever may be said in favour of suppressing, by persecution, the first beginnings of heresy, no solid argument can be alledged for extending severity towards multitudes, or endeavouring, by capital punishments, to extirpate an opinion, which has diffused itself through men of every rank and station. Besides the extreme barbarity of such an attempt, it proves commonly ineffectual to the purpose intended; and serves only to make men more obstinate in their persuasion, and to encrease the number of their proselytes. The melancholy with which the fear of death, torture, and persecution inspires the sectaries, is the proper disposition for fostering religious zeal: the prospect of eternal rewards, when brought near, overpowers the dread of temporal punishment: the glory of martyrdom stimulates all the more furious zealots, especially the leaders and preachers: where a violent animosity is excited by oppression, men pass naturally from hating the persons of their tyrants, to a more violent abhorrence of their doctrine: and the spectators, moved with pity towards the supposed martyrs, are naturally induced to embrace those principles which can inspire men with a constancy that appears almost supernatural. Open the door to toleration, the mutual hatred relaxes among the sectaries; their attachment to their particular religion decays; the common occupations and pleasures of life succeed to the acrimony of disputation; and the same man, who, in other circumstances, would have braved flames and tortures, is engaged to change his religion from the smallest prospect of favour and advancement, or even from the frivolous hopes of becoming more fashionable in his principles. If any exception can be admitted to this maxim of toleration, it will only be where a theology altogether new, no way connected with the ancient religion of the state, is imported from foreign countries, and may easily, at one blow, be eradicated, without leaving the seeds of future innovations. But as this instance would involve some apology for the ancient pagan persecutions, or for the extirpation of christianity in China and Japan; it ought surely, on account of this detested consequence, to be rather buried in eternal silence and oblivion.

Though these arguments appear entirely satisfactory, yet such is the subtility of human wit, that Gardiner, and the other enemies to toleration, were not reduced to silence, and they still found topics on which to support the controversy. The doctrine, said they, of liberty of conscience is founded on the most flagrant impiety, and supposes such an indifference among all religions, such an obscurity in theological doctrines, as to render the church and magistrate incapable of distinguishing, with certainty, the dictates of heaven, from the mere fictions of human imagination. If the Divinity reveals principles to mankind, he will surely give a criterion by which they may be ascertained; and a prince, who knowingly allows these principles to be perverted, or adulterated, is infinitely more criminal than if he gave permission for the vending of poison, under the shape of bread, to all his subjects. Persecution may, indeed, seem better calculated to make hypocrites than converts; but experience teaches us, that the habits of hypocrisy often turn into reality; and the children at least, ignorant of their parents dissimulation, may happily be educated in more orthodox tenets. It is absurd, in opposition to considerations of such unspeakable importance, to plead the temporal and frivolous interests of civil society; and if matters be thoroughly examined, even that topic will not appear so certain and universal in favour of toleration as by some it is represented. Where sects arise, whose fundamental principle on all sides, is to execrate, and abhor, and damn, and extirpate each other; what choice has the magistrate left but to take party, and by rendering one sect entirely prevalent, restore, at least for a time, the public tranquillity? The political body, being here sickly, must not be treated as if it were in a state of sound health, and an affected neutrality in the prince, or even a cool preference, may serve only to encourage the hopes of all the sects, and keep alive their animosity. The protestants, far from tolerating the religion of their ancestors, regard it as an impious and detestable idolatry; and during the late minority, when they were entirely masters, enacted very severe, though not capital, punishments against all exercise of the catholic worship, and even against such as barely abstained from their profane rites and sacraments. Nor are instances wanting of their endeavours to secure an imagined orthodoxy by the most rigorous executions: Calvin has burned Servetus at Geneva: Cranmer brought Arians and Anabaptists to the stake: and if persecution of any kind is to be admitted, the most bloody and violent will surely be allowed the most justifiable, as the most effectual. Imprisonments, fines, confiscations, whippings, serve only to irritate the sects, without disabling them from resistance: but the stake, the wheel, or the gibbet, must soon terminate in the extirpation or banishment of all the heretics, who are inclined to give disturbance, and in the entire silence and submission of the rest.'

In the state of this argument, the writer displays great depth of thought, strength of reasoning, and energy of expression. It must, indeed, be acknowledged, that the history of these reigns, upon the whole, affords such evident marks of conspicuous merit in the historian, as cannot fail to engage the approbation of the intelligent and discerning reader. Though we have, in some instances, reluctantly pointed out the author's defects, and controverted his opinions, nevertheless, we are not blind to his excellencies, or backward to commend them. We are actuated by the spirit of free inquiry, not the malevolence of criticism; and it is with pleasure we observe, that even his errors are generally the mistakes of genius, ever ambitious to be singular. The second volume affords us more striking instances of this singularity; and in that, we shall have occasion to take our historian's political principles into farther consideration.

—

Conclusion of HUME's *History of England, under the House of Tudor.*

It is seldom that writers perform more than they undertake; but in the volume before us the learned historian has, in fact, exceeded his engagements. It not only contains the history of England, under the reign of Elizabeth; but actually comprises that of Scotland likewise, during that period.

The affairs of England, indeed, were, during this reign, so implicated with those of the sister kingdom, that it is impossible to have a clear conception of the one, without an intimate knowledge of the other: which made it necessary for our author to relate the latter, with a minuteness which might otherwise, perhaps, have been liable to censure.

The imminent dangers which this nation escaped, and the great advantages which accrued to it, during Elizabeth's reign, render it uncommonly interesting and remarkable. Her conduct abroad was wise and spirited, her administration at home prudent, though arbitrary. The time, at which she took the reins of government in her hands, was extremely critical. Within, the kingdom was torn to pieces by the zeal of theological controversy, and raged with all the horrors of religious persecution. Abroad, the nation was engaged in an unsuccessful war against France. The Dauphin, soon after king, was married to the queen of Scots, who laid claim to the crown of England, openly assumed the title, and quartered the English arms. On the side of Scotland, every thing was to be apprehended from that neighbouring kingdom, thus strengthened by the French alliance.

In this nice situation the queen conducted herself with equal prudence and skill. At home, she pacified the rage of religious animosities by her moderation and magnanimity. She buried all past offences in oblivion, and even gave a kind reception to those who had treated her with the greatest enmity. She opened the way for the reformation by a gradual and cautious progress,[11] and took all occasions to insinuate herself into the affections of her subjects, by public marks of favour and condescension.

In her conduct with regard to foreign affairs, she discovered equal address. She concluded a peace with France; and secured herself against any apprehensions from Scotland, by secretly fomenting civil discord and commotions in that kingdom. The religious dissentions among the Scotch, occasioned by the reformation which was then in its infancy there, afforded Elizabeth a favourable

---

[11] The first step she took, was to recall those who were exiled in the last reign; and to give liberty to the prisoners who were confined on account of religion. On this occasion, says the historian, we are told of a pleasantry of one Rainsford, who said to the queen, that he had a petition to present to her in behalf of other prisoners, Matthew, Mark, Luke, and John: she readily replied, that it behooved her first to consult the prisoners themselves, and to learn of them whether they denied that liberty, which he demanded for them.

opportunity of dividing that nation, by giving private aid and encouragement to the reformers.

The historian's account of the Scotch civil wars is extremely animated. His reflections on the league and other transactions of the fanatics, are liberal and judicious. But we shall take less notice of what relates to the concerns of Scotland, since we presume that those circumstances are still fresh in the reader's mind, from what has been said concerning the late history of that kingdom.[12] We shall therefore only mention such memorable particulars as do not occur in that work.

Having taken a Review of the Scotch affairs, our historian turns his eye towards France, where Mary queen of Scots, upon the death of her husband the French king, was preparing to return into England. Previous to her departure, she applied to Elizabeth by D'Oisel, for liberty to pass through England. But she received for answer, that till she had given satisfaction, by ratifying the treaty of Edinburgh, she could expect no favour from a person whom she had so much injured. This denial excited her resentment; and she made no scruple of expressing her sentiments to Throcmorton, when he reiterated his applications to gratify his mistress in a demand, which he represented as so reasonable. Having cleared the room of all her attendants, she said to him, "How weak I may prove, or how far a woman's frailty may transport me, I cannot tell: however, I have no mind to have so many witnesses of my infirmity, as your mistress had at her audience of my ambassador, D'Oisel. There is nothing disturbs me so much, as the having asked, with so much importunity, a favour which it was of no consequence for me to obtain. I can, with God's leave, return to my own country without her leave; as I came to France, in spite of all the opposition of her brother, king Edward: neither do I want friends, both able and willing to conduct me home, as they have brought me hither; though I was desirous rather to make an experiment of her friendship than of the assistance of any other person. I have often heard you say, that a good correspondence between her and myself would conduce much to the security and happiness of both our kingdoms; but were she well convinced of this truth, she had hardly denied me so small a request. But, perhaps, she bears a better inclination to my rebellious subjects than to me, their sovereign, her equal in royal dignity, her near relation, and the undoubted heir of her kingdoms. Besides her friendship, I ask nothing at her hands: I neither trouble her, nor concern myself in the affairs of her kingdom: not that I am ignorant, that there are now in England a great many malecontents, who are no friends

---

[12] See Robertson's History of Scotland, Review for Feb. and March last. It is observable that Mr. Hume differs from Dr. Robertson, with regard to the infringement of the capitulation of Perth. For the former is of opinion, that the Queen Regent made no promise to the malecontents, that nothing should be done to their prejudice.

to the present establishment. She is pleased to upbraid me as a person little experienced in the world: I freely own it; but age will cure the defect. However, I am old enough to acquit myself honestly and courteously to my friends and relations, and to encourage no reports of her, which would misbecome a queen and her kinswoman. I would also say, by her leave, that I am a queen as well as she, and not altogether friendless: and, perhaps, I have as great a soul too; so that methinks we should be upon a level in our treatment of each other. As soon as I have consulted the states of my kingdom, I shall be ready to give a reasonable answer; and I am the more intent on my journey, that I may be able to make the quicker dispatch in this affair. But she, it seems, intends to stop my journey; so that either she will not let me give her satisfaction, or is resolved not to be satisfied; perhaps, on purpose to keep up the disagreement betwixt us. She has often reproached me with my being young; and I must be very young, indeed, and as ill advised, to treat of matters of such great concern and importance, without the advice of my parliament. I have not been wanting in any friendly offices to her; but she disbelieves or overlooks them. I could heartily wish, that I was as near allied to her in affection as in blood: for that, indeed, would be a most valuable alliance."

Making allowance for the elegant dress in which these sentiments appear, it must be confessed, that nothing can be readily conceived more noble, spirited, and majestic than these remonstrances of Mary. It must be acknowledged, however, that her resentment does not appear to be altogether justly grounded. Considering her refusal to ratify the treaty of Edinburgh, and her public assumption of the arms and title of queen of England, she had little reason to expect a friendly passage through a kingdom, where she had claimed the crown – Less still, to hope that the queen, whose title she impeached, would pay her such a compliment.

On Mary's arrival in Scotland, though she placed her confidence in the leaders of the reformed party, yet her being a papist soon exposed her to the insults of these men; who, as our historian observes, filled her whole life with bitterness and sorrow. The rustic apostle Knox, says he, scruples not, in his history, to inform us, that he once treated her with such severity, that she lost all command of her temper, and dissolved into tears before him: yet so far from being moved with youth and beauty, and royal dignity reduced to that condition, he persevered in his insolent reproofs; and when he relates this incident, he even discovers a visible pride and satisfaction in his own conduct. The pulpits, adds our author, had become nothing but scenes of railing against the vices of the court; among which was always noted as the principal, feasting, finery, dancing, balls, and whoredom their necessary attendant. Some ornaments, which the ladies at that time wore upon their petticoats, excited mightily the indignation of the preachers, and they affirmed, that such vanity would provoke God's vengeance, not only against these foolish women, but against the whole realm. To the harsh and preposterous usage which this princess met with, may, in part, says our historian, be ascribed those errors of her subsequent conduct, which seemed to be so little of a piece with the general tenor of her actions. He shrewdly adds, that the reformed clergy in Scotland had, at that time, a very natural reason for their ill humour; viz. the poverty, or rather beggary, to which they were reduced. Nothing, we will add, is more common than for men to declaim against those things which they are not in a capacity to enjoy. Perhaps, the circumstances of age, health, and fortune, vary the taste and regulate the appetites of mankind, more than reason and reflection. Had these fanatical censors, who were provoked at the ornaments of the ladies petticoats, beheld our modern belles, who scarce wear any petticoats at all, how would their indignation have risen! How would they have exclaimed against our lovely virgins, who lay traps for the glances of concupiscence, by shading their snowy beauties with transparent gauzes, which are but apologies for nakedness! How would they have railed against the *Coas Vestes* of our liberal *Iphigenias*! But to what a pitch of chaste zeal would they have been transported, had they seen the British fair ones in full dress, who exhibit their persons, like the empress in Juvenal, *nudis papillis*!

If female vanity, however, was conspicuous in the queen of Scots, we may learn from our historian, that it was not less predominant in the British queen. A difference having arisen between them, on account of the artifices which Elizabeth practised to prevent Mary from marrying, the latter dispatched Sir James Melvil to London to make up the breach. The subject of the conferences between Elizabeth and that ambassador is highly curious and entertaining; and places this queen's vanity in the most glaring and ridiculous light.

'Melvil was an agreeable courtier, a man of address and conversation; and it was recommended to him by his mistress, that, besides grave reasonings concerning politics and state-affairs, he should introduce more entertaining topics of conversation, suitable to the sprightly character of Elizabeth; and should endeavour by that means to insinuate himself into her confidence. He succeeded so well, that he threw that artful princess entirely off her guard, and brought her to discover the bottom of her heart, full of all those levities and follies and ideas of rivalship, which possess the youngest and most frivolous of her sex. He talked to her of his travels, and forgot not to mention the different dresses of the ladies in different countries, and the more advantages of each, in setting off the beauties of the shape and person. The queen said that she had dresses of all countries, and she took care thenceforth to meet the ambassador every day apparelled in a different habit: sometimes she was dressed in the English garb, sometimes in the French, sometimes in the Italian; and she asked him, which of them became her most. He answered, the Italian; a reply, that he knew would be agreeable to her, because that mode showed her flowing locks, which, he remarked, though they were more red than yellow, she fancied to be the finest in the world. She desired to know of him what was reputed to be the best colour of hair: she asked whether his queen's hair or hers was the best: she even inquired which of them he esteemed the fairest person: a very delicate question, and which he prudently eluded, by saying that her majesty was the fairest person in England, and his mistress in Scotland. She next demanded which of them was tallest: he replied, his queen; then, said Elizabeth, she is too tall: for I myself am of a just stature. Having learned from him, that his mistress sometimes recreated herself by playing on the harpsichord, an instrument at which she herself excelled, she gave orders to lord Hunsdon, that he should lead him, as it were casually, into an apartment, where he might hear her performance; and when Melvil, as if ravished with the harmony, broke into the queen's apartment, she pretended to be displeased at his intrusion; but still took care to ask whether he thought Mary or her the best performer on that instrument. From the whole of her behaviour, Melvil thought he might, on his return, assure his mistress that she had no reason ever to expect any cordial friendship from Elizabeth, and that all her professions of amity were full of falshood and dissimulation.'

But whatever jealousy Elizabeth entertained towards Mary, yet when the latter was made captive, and severely treated by her rebellious subjects, the British queen interposed earnestly in her behalf. She empowered her ambassador to tell the lords associated against Mary, that whatever blame she might throw on Mary's conduct, any opposition to their sovereign was totally unjustifiable, and incompatible with all good order and good government: that it belonged not to them to reform, much less to punish, the mal-administration of their prince; and that the only arms which subjects could, in any case, lawfully employ against the supreme authority, were entreaties, councils, and representations; that if these expedients failed, they were next to appeal by their prayers to heaven; and to wait with patience till the Almighty, in whose hands are the hearts of princes, should be pleased to turn them to justice and to mercy.

This slavish doctrine is only worthy of an arbitrary prince, who finds an interest in its observance. When princes, who are entrusted with government for the good of the community violate the rights of their subjects, they may lawfully be resisted. Obedience can only be demanded in consequence of protection; much less can it be exacted in return for usurpation. Neither reason or religion enjoin us to be passive under the hands of rapine and oppression. The law of nature, which dictates self-preservation, directs us to repel the invaders; and though we ought to prefer our prayers to the Almighty, that he would be pleased to incline them to justice, yet we ought at the same time to exert all temporal means of compelling them to be just.

But Elizabeth was upon all occasions extremely jealous of that arbitrary and boundless authority which she exercised, under the motion of *prerogative*. Of which there cannot be a stronger instance, than the lawless severity with which she suppressed the freedom of parliamentary debate. Our historian has related a memorable event which happened in a session of parliament summoned in the year 1576, where debates were started which may appear somewhat curious and singular; and from whence we may perceive how the spirit of liberty dawned during the period, and how it was suddenly eclipsed by the interposition of the rude hand of tyranny.

'Peter Wentworth, says he, a puritan, who had signalized himself in former parliaments, by his free and undaunted spirit, opened this session with a premeditated harangue, which drew on him the indignation of the house, and gave great offence to the queen and the courtiers. As it seems to contain the first rude sketch of those principles of liberty which happily gained afterwards the ascendant in England, it may not be improper to give, in a few words, the substance of it. He premised, that the very name of liberty is sweet; but the thing itself is precious beyond the most inestimable treasure: and that it behooved them to be careful, lest, contenting themselves with the sweetness of the name, they forego the substance, and abandon what of all earthly possessions was of the highest value to the kingdom. He then proceeded to observe, "that freedom of speech in that house, a privilege so useful both to sovereign and subject, had been formerly infringed in many essential articles, and was, at present, exposed to the most imminent danger: that it was usual, when any subject of importance was handled, especially if it regarded religion, to surmise, that these topics were disagreeable to the queen, and that the farther proceeding in them would draw down her indignation upon their temerity: that Solomon had justly affirmed, the king's displeasure to be a messenger of death; and it was no wonder that men, even though urged by motives of conscience and duty, should be inclined to stop short, when they found themselves exposed to so severe a penalty: that by employing this argument, the house was incapacitated from serving their country, or even from serving the queen herself; whose ears, besieged by pernicious flatterers, were thereby rendered inaccessible to the most salutary truths: that it was a mockery to call an assembly a parliament, and yet deny them that privilege, which was so essential to their being, and without which they must degenerate into an abject school of servitude and dissimulation: that as the parliament was the great guardian of the laws, they ought to have liberty to discharge their trust, and to maintain that authority whence even kings themselves derive their being: that a king was constituted such by law, and though he was not dependent on man, yet was he subordinate to God and the law, and was obliged to make their prescriptions, not his own will, the rule of his conduct: that even his commission, as God's vicegerent, enforced, instead of loosening, this obligation; since he was thereby invested with authority to execute on earth the will of God, which is nothing but law and justice; that though these surmises of displeasing the queen by their proceedings, had impeached, in a very essential point, all freedom of speech, a privilege granted them by a special law; yet was there a more express and more dangerous invasion made on their liberties, by frequent messages from the throne: that it had become a practice, when the house were entering on any question, either ecclesiastical or civil, to bring an order from the queen, prohibiting them absolutely to treat of such matters, and barring them all farther discussion of these momentous articles: that the prelates, emboldened by her royal protection, had assumed a decisive power in all questions of religion, and required that every one should implicitly submit his faith to their arbitrary determinations: that the love which he bore his sovereign, forbad him to be silent under such abuses, or to sacrifice, on this important occasion, his duty to servile flattery and complaisance: and that, as no earthly creature was exempt from fault, so neither was the Queen herself; but in imposing this servitude on her faithful Commons, had committed a great, and even dangerous, fault, against herself and the whole realm.'

From this speech, as our Historian justly remarks, it is easy to observe, that the parliamentary stile was then crude and unformed; and that the proper decorum of attacking ministers and counsellors, without interesting the honour of the crown, or mentioning the person of the Sovereign, was not yet entirely established. Mr. Wentworth, at the issue of this affair, underwent a month's confinement for the liberty he had taken in this debate.

Nevertheless, the severe treatment he met with, did not abate the zeal of that bold patriot; for, some years after, as appears from our Historian,

'he delivered to Mr. Speaker certain articles, which contained questions concerning the liberties of the house, and to some of which he was to answer, and desired they might be read. Mr. Speaker desired him to spare his motion, but Mr. Wentworth would not be satisfied, but required that his articles might be read. Mr. Wentworth introduced his queries by lamenting, that he, as well as many others, were deterred from speaking by their want of knowlege and experience in the liberties of the house; and the queries were as follows – Whether this council were not a place for any member of the same, here assembled, freely, and without controul of any person, or danger of laws, by bill or speech, to utter any of the griefs of this commonwealth whatsoever, touching the service of God, the safety of the Prince and this noble realm? Whether that great honour may be done unto God, and benefit and service unto the Prince and state, without free speech in this council that may be done with it? Whether there be any council which can make, add, or diminish from the laws of the realm, but only this council of Parliament? Whether it be not against the orders of this council, to make any secret or matter of weight, which is here in hand, known to the Prince, or any other, concerning the high service of God, Prince, or state, without the consent of this house? Whether the Speaker, or any other, may interrupt any member of this council in his speech used in this house, tending to any of the forenamed services? Whether the Speaker may rise when he will, any matter being propounded, without the consent of the House, or not? Whether the Speaker may over rule the House in any matter or cause there in question, or whether he is to be ruled or over-ruled in any matter or not? Whether the Prince and State can continue and stand, and be maintained, without this council of Parliament, not altering the government of the State?'

In consequence of these queries, Mr. Wentworth, with others who were thought to have spoken too freely, was sent to the Tower, and detained in custody, till the Queen thought fit to release them. Upon this passage, our Historian makes the following query – 'I shall only ask,' says he, 'Whether it be not sufficiently clear, from all these transactions, that in the two succeeding reigns, it was the people who encroached upon the sovereign; *not the sovereign who attempted, as is pretended, to usurp upon the people?*'

This query comes with an ill grace, from a Writer of our Author's liberal cast of mind. These transactions do by no means make it evident, that, in the two succeeding reigns, the sovereign did *not usurp* upon the people. If precedents, abstractedly considered, are admitted as pleas in justification of regal mal-administration, there is scarce an instance of oppression and tyranny, which may not be vindicated on that footing. But when we consider whether acts of government are founded on *right*, or exercised by way of *usurpation*, we must examine them on the grounds of *general* usage, supported by fundamental principles, and constitutional maxims. From this mode of examination it will appear, that these transactions of Elizabeth were clearly usurpations in *her*, and her *immediate* predecessors, and consequently could not change their nature in her successors. The liberty she took of silencing members in the course of their debates on religious and civil matters, was manifestly *usurped*: because whether we consider the antient practice in such cases, or the nature of Parliaments, or lastly, the form of the old writ of election; it will appear that the Parliament had not only a right of discussing such points, but that it was their duty, and the chief end of their meeting.

With regard to antient practice, it is past all doubt that the Kings of England used to ask, and graciously receive, the advice of their parliaments, on important occasions. Evidences of this sort may be copiously collected from Sir Robert Cotton, who has produced many instances of this purpose from the time of King John, to the reign of the Queen of whom we are now speaking. Even that inconsistent tyrant Henry the Eighth, courted and received council from his Parliament, both in religious and civil affairs. We find them not only giving, but often obtruding their advice, nay, interposing their authority; and this, too, even in the King's domestic concerns. Thus in the time of Edward the Second, and Third, Richard the Second, Henry the Fourth and Sixth, and others, the King's household was regulated by parliament. In Richard the Second's time, a commission was granted, at the petition of the Commons, to survey and abate the household.

With respect to the nature of Parliaments, not to enter into the old dispute at what time the Commons became a part of that assembly, it is manifest that they were from the beginning summoned to debate of the public affairs of the kingdom: and their jurisdiction antiently was extremely extensive, they having an original judicial authority in many cases which they have since lost.

With relation to the old writ of election, the words of it are an incontestible proof of the Parliament's right of free debate: for it antiently recited, "That whereas the king was desirous to have a conference and treaty with the Barons, and other great men of the kingdom, to provide remedies against the dangers of the kingdom; that therefore the Sheriff command the Knights, Citizens, etc. to be at Westminster, to *treat, ordain, and do*, so as these dangers may be prevented." But, indeed, the very derivation of the word *Parliament*, in itself implies an uninterrupted freedom of debate. Therefore, from all these circumstances, it appears, that these transactions of the Queen, respecting the liberty of debate, were usurpations; and consequently were such in her successors, though they were not original ones in them, or perhaps in her. But admitting that their usurpations may in these particulars be palliated by these bad precedents, yet they were guilty of other *original* acts of arbitrary power: and the unhappy Charles, after he had solemnly acknowleged particular rights of his people, by which acknowlegement he resigned all plea of prerogative, and all advantage from precedents; yet, nevertheless, did not scruple to renew his violation of those rights: which violation, by means of the new contract he had signed with his people, became an original usurpation in him. Upon the whole, the conduct of these two monarchs, especially of the latter, admits of no vindication. But it is time to return to our Historian, who relates a curious incident, which sets Mary's extreme animosity against Elizabeth, on account of the rigorous treatment she met with from the latter, in a very strong light.

While the former Queen was kept in custody by the Earl of Shrewsbury, she lived during a long time in great intimacy with the Countess; but that lady entertaining a jealousy of an amour between her and the Earl, their friendship was converted into enmity, and Mary took a method of revenge, which at once gratified her resentment against the Countess and Elizabeth. She wrote to the Queen, informing her of all the scandalous stories, which, she said, the Countess of Shrewsbury had reported of her. – That Elizabeth had given a promise of marriage to a certain person whom she afterwards often admitted to her bed; that she had been equally indulgent to Simier, the French agent, and the Duke of Anjou. – That Hatton was one of her paramours, who was even disgusted with her excessive love and fondness: that she spared no expence in gratifying her amorous passions: that notwithstanding her licentious amours, she was not made like other women; and that all those who courted her, would in the end be disappointed: that she was so conceited of her beauty, as to swallow the most extravagant flattery from her courtiers. She pretended, that the Countess had represented her as no less odious in her temper, than profligate in her manners, and absurd in her vanity: that she had so beaten a young woman of the name of Scudamore, as to break that lady's finger: and that she had cut across the hand with a knife. How far, says our Historian, all these imputations against Elizabeth can be credited, may, perhaps, appear doubtful. But he observes that her extreme fondness for Leicester, Hatton, and Essex, not to mention Mountjoy, and others, with the curious passages between her and Admiral Seymour, contained in Haynes, render her chastity very suspicious. Her self-conceit, says he, with regard to beauty, we know, from other undoubted authority, to have been extravagant. Her passionate temper, he adds, may also be proved from many lively instances. It was not unusual with her to beat her maids of honour: and the blow she gave to Essex, before the privy council, is another remarkable instance.

Our Historian takes notice, that this imprudent and malicious letter was wrote a very little before the detection of Queen Mary's conspiracy; and contributed, as he observes, no doubt, to render the proceedings against her more rigorous. The event of those proceedings, is well known. The unfortunate Queen of Scots lost her life by the hands of the executioner. Her character, as drawn by our Historian, must not be omitted. It is short, just, and spirited.

'Thus died, in the forty-sixth year of her age, and the nineteenth of her captivity in England, Mary Queen of Scots; a princess of great accomplishments, both of body and mind, natural as well as acquired; but unhappy in her life, and during one period, very unfortunate in her conduct. The beauties of her person, and of her air, combined to make her the most amiable of women; and the charms of her address and conversation, aided the impression which her lovely figure made on the hearts of all beholders. Ambitious and active in her temper, yet inclined to chearfulness and society; of a lofty spirit, constant, and even vehement in her purpose; yet polite and gentle, and affable in her demeanor, she seemed to partake only so much of the male virtues as to render her estimable, without relinquishing those soft graces which compose the proper ornaments of her sex. In order to form a just idea of her character, we must set aside one part of her conduct, while she abandoned herself to the guidance of a profligate man; and must consider these faults, whether we admit them to be imprudences or crimes, as the result of an inexplicable, though not uncommon, inconstancy in the human mind, of the frailty of our nature, of the violence of passion, and of the influence which situations, and sometimes momentary incidents, have on persons whose principles are not thoroughly confirmed by experience and reflection. Enraged by the ungrateful conduct of her husband, seduced by the treacherous counsels of one in whom she reposed confidence, transported by the violence of her own temper, which never lay sufficiently under the guidance of discretion, she was betrayed into actions, which may, with some difficulty, be accounted for, but which admit of no apology, nor even of alleviation. An enumeration of her qualities might carry the appearance of a panegyric; an account of her conduct must, in some parts, wear the aspect of a severe satire and invective.' –

We shall close our extracts with the Historian's character of Elizabeth, and his reflections on her government.

'There are few great personages in history, who have been more exposed to the calumny of enemies, and the adulation of friends, than Queen Elizabeth; and yet there scarce is any, whose reputation has been more certainly determined, by the unanimous consent of posterity. The unusual length of her administration, and the strong features of her character, were able to overcome all prejudices; and obliging her detractors to abate much of their invective, and her admirers somewhat of their panegyrics, have at last, in spite of political factions, and what is more, of religious animosities, produced an uniform judgment with regard to her conduct. Her vigour, her constancy, her magnanimity, her penetration, vigilance, address, are allowed to merit the highest praises, and appear not to have been surpassed by any person who ever filled a throne: A conduct less rigorous, less imperious, more sincere, more indulgent to her people, would have been requisite to form a perfect character. By the force of her mind, she controuled all her more active and stronger qualities, and prevented them from running into excess: her heroism was exempt from all temerity, her frugality from avarice, her friendship from partiality,[13] her enterprize from turbulency and a vain ambition: she guarded not herself with equal care, or equal success, from lesser infirmities; the rivalship of beauty, the desire of admiration, the jealousy of love, and the sallies of anger.

Her singular talents for government were founded equally on her temper, and on her capacity. Endowed with a great command over herself, she soon obtained an uncontrouled ascendant over her people; and while she merited all their esteem by her real virtues, she also engaged their affection by her pretended ones. Few sovereigns of England succeeded to the throne in more difficult circumstances; and none ever conducted the government with such

[13] Perhaps, however, the Historian pays her too great a compliment when he says, 'her friendship was exempt from partiality.' Her trusting Leicester with such an important command, at the time of the Spanish Invasion, when the nation was in such imminent danger, is a proof to the contrary. He had given so many frequent and flagrant instances of his incapacity, that nothing but her extreme fondness for him, could determine her to place such a confidence in a man who so little deserved it.

uniform success and felicity. Though unacquainted with the practice of toleration, the true secret for managing religious factions, she preserved her people, by her superior prudence, from those confusions in which theological controversy had involved all the neighbouring nations: and though her enemies were the most powerful princes of Europe, the most active, the most enterprizing, the least scrupulous, she was able by her vigour to make deep impressions on their state: her own greatness mean while remained untouched, and unimpaired.

The wise ministers, and brave warriors, who flourished during her reign, share the praise of her success; but instead of lessening the applause due to her, they make great addition to it. They owed, all of them, their advancement to her choice; they were supported by her constancy: and with all their ability they were never able to acquire any undue ascendant over her. In her family, in her court, in her kingdom, she remained equally mistress: the force of the tender passions was great over her, but the force of her mind was still superior; and the combat which her victory visibly cost her, serves only to display the firmness of her resolution, and the loftiness of her ambitious sentiments.

The fame of this princess, though it has surmounted the prejudices both of faction and of bigotry, yet lies still exposed to another prejudice, which is more durable because more natural, and which, according to the different views in which we survey her, is capable either of exalting beyond measure, or diminishing the lustre of her character. This prejudice is founded on the consideration of her sex. When we contemplate her as a woman, we are apt be struck with the highest admiration of her great qualities and extensive capacity; but we are also apt to require some more softness of disposition, some greater lenity of temper, some of those amiable weaknesses by which her sex is distinguished. But the true method of estimating her merit, is to lay aside all these considerations, and to consider her merely as a rational being, placed in authority, and entrusted with the government of mankind. We may find it difficult to reconcile our fancy to her as a wife or a mistress; but her qualities as a sovereign, though with some considerable exceptions, are the object of undisputed applause and approbation.'

It must be allowed, that this portraiture is drawn with a masterly hand. It is, indeed, *pictura loquens*. The whole cast of the features is just, animated, and expressive. But in his reflections on her government, the Historian has advanced sentiments which are extremely singular and exceptionable.

'The party amongst us,' says he, 'who have distinguished themselves by their adherence to liberty, and a popular government, have long indulged their prejudices against the succeeding race of princes, by bestowing unbounded panegyrics on the virtue and wisdom of Elizabeth. They have even been so extremely ignorant of the transactions of this reign, as to extol her for a quality which, of all others, she was the least possessed of; a tender regard for the constitution, and a concern for the liberties and privileges of her people. But as it is scarce possible for the prepossessions of party to throw a veil much longer over facts so palpable and undeniable, there is danger lest the public should run into the opposite extreme, and should entertain an aversion to the memory of a princess, who exercised the royal authority in a manner so much contrary to all the ideas which we at present entertain of a legal constitution. But Elizabeth only supported the prerogatives which were transmitted to her by her immediate predecessors: she believed that her subjects were entitled to no more liberty than their ancestors enjoyed: she found that they entirely acquiesced in her arbitrary administration: and it was not natural for her to find fault with a form of government, by which she herself was invested with such unlimited authority. In the particular exertions of power, the question ought never to be forgot, *What is best?* But in the general distribution of power among the several members of a constitution, there can seldom be admitted any other question, than *What is usual?* Few examples occur of Princes, who have willingly resigned their power: none of those who have, without struggle, allowed it to be extorted from them. If any other rule than antient practice be followed, factions and dissentions must multiply without end: and though many constitutions, and none more than the British, have been improved even by violent innovations, the praise which we bestow on those patriots, to whom we are indebted for our privileges, ought to be given with some reserve, and surely without the least rancour against those who adhered to the antient constitution.'

That Elizabeth only supported the prerogatives which were transmitted to her by her *immediate* predecessors, we will not dispute; but we deny, that in the general distribution of power, no other question can be admitted than *what is usual?* From our Historian's reasoning on the subject of prerogative, one might be apt to conclude, that he considered it as an inherent and independent privilege annexed to royalty; and as something intended to gratify the personal pride, pleasure, or interest of Kings. Whereas, in fact, the prerogative of Princes are not rights absolutely and irrevocably vested in them, but only entrusted with them during such time as they shall be judged necessary to support their administration for the good of the people. The same power which conferred those privileges on them, may undoubtedly modify or revoke them, whenever the changes of time or accident shall make new regulations necessary in the state, for the benefit of the community. The rights of princes are but the rights of the people reflected, and the former cannot in reason be entitled to any other prerogatives, than such as are necessary to maintain their dignity and authority for the common interest.

Our Historian observes, that 'if any other rule than *antient practice* be followed, factions and dissentions must multiply without end.' To which we answer, that Princes who govern with prudence, justice, and lenity, will not be guided by bad precedents, but good principles. We may add, that whatever practices sovereigns pursue, be they constitutional or arbitrary, yet the people will never be factious, while they perceive the general tenor of the Prince's administration to be just, prudent, and profitable for the whole. But when they find the government throughout to be oppressive and injurious, it is natural and reasonable to oppose practices, which tend to their general prejudice. It is observable, that in this sentence our Historian speaks of *antient* practice, where as he had before acknowleged, that 'Elizabeth only supported the prerogatives which were transmitted to her by her *immediate* predecessors.' With regard to those recent precedents transmitted by her *immediate* predecessors, they may, as appears from what we have said before, more properly be called *innovations*: and even as to *antient* practice, though it may serve as an apology for the tyrant, it lays no obligation on his oppressed subjects to submit to tyranny, be it ever so *antient*, when they are in a capacity to resist. We agree with the Historian, however, that the praise we bestow on those patriots to whom we are indebted for our privileges, ought to be given with reserve. They who temper zeal with discretion, rather commend actions than applaud men. It is not within human penetration to pry into the heart, and discover the secret springs and motives which actuate individuals. But on what ever principles these patriots founded their opposition, the opposition itself, though in many respects wrong conducted, cannot be too highly extolled.[14]

After all, as to Elizabeth, it must be confessed, that her usurpation was the more tolerable, since, though the mode of her government was tyrannical, yet the end was truly patriotic. The tyranny of her reign, and those immediately preceding, was the result, as we hinted in the introduction to our review of the first volume, of the institutions framed by Henry VII. He depressed the nobility by his policy, awed them by his wisdom and vigour, so that they were not in a capacity to resist his encroaching power: and the Commons, in his and the reigns immediately subsequent, had not acquired strength sufficient for opposition. In this Queen's reign, by the assistance of commerce and arts,[15] which necessarily enlarged their property, and consequently their power, they seem to have had ability for resistance, but, generally speaking, they had no

---

[14] [In later editions of the *History* Hume changed the phrase "antient practice" to "established practice".]

[15] This increase, as we suggested in our last, was owing to the institutions of Henry VII. who disengaged a number of idle hands from military dependence, and threw them into commerce, &c.

inclination. Though she was frequently imperious, yet she knew how to practice affability, and flatter the people by professions of love and confidence. If she infringed the constitution, by raising money in an illegal manner, with other acts of arbitrary power; on the other hand, she repaired those breaches, by refusing money when it was offered her, and *by discharging her predecessors debts*, to the amount of *four millions*, an incredible sum for that age.[16] By these acts of public justice, and by many obliging points of condescension, she softened the rigour of her absolute sway. In short, she used all methods to assure and convince the people, that whatever she did, was for the general good. We may add to this, that her sex, perhaps, inclined them to bear her imperious and arbitrary conduct, with more patience than they would have endured it under a King. The troublesome state of the nation likewise, which, during a long time, was in imminent danger from Spain and other parts, was a further circumstance which favoured her oppression: the people's apprehensions from foreign invasions, rendered them less attentive to the evil of domestic encroachments. But under her successors, these incidents did not concur. James and Charles were not content to *be* absolute, but would *seem* so. They behaved with the imperious carriage of Elizabeth, and pursued her absolute measures; but did not practise her occasional affability and condescension; or imitate her examples of generosity and justice: by which means the latter of those Kings provoked the people, secure in peace, and wanton with prosperity, to exert their power of opposition.

In the conclusion of this history, the Writer takes a review of the manners, commerce, arts, and learning, during the period he treats of. In discussing these heads, he displays, upon the whole, great penetration, and political knowlege. Nevertheless, his sentiments, in some respects, are controvertible; but we shall confine our animadversions to the following passage, where he tells us, as he had intimated before, that 'the laws of Henry the Seventh contributed very little towards the great revolution which happened about this period in the English constitution. The practice of breaking entails by a fine and recovery, he says, had been introduced in the preceding reigns; and this Prince only gave indirectly a legal sanction to the practice, by reforming some abuses which attended it. But,' he subjoins, 'the change of manners was the chief cause of the secret revolution of the government, and subverted the power of the Barons.'

Here, as we remarked in our review of the first volume, the Historian seems to mistake an effect for a cause. The institutions of Henry certainly contributed to the increase of commerce and arts, by providing hands to cultivate them, which before rested in indolent dependence. Besides the retrenchment of the antient country hospitality, by the diminution of retainers; drew the noblemen

---

[16] The Historian doubts of this, and thinks 300,000 the most likely sum. But the act, not the sum, is matter of illustration.

to town, where they devised new modes of luxury: and all together contributed to operate a change in the manners of the people.[17]

With respect to what our Historian says, concerning the practice of breaking entails, he is clearly mistaken. Henry did more than he is willing to allow: for though the practice of barring entails, as to persons in remainder, was in use before his time,[18] yet the practice of cutting off the issues, was first introduced in his reign.

This article having already drawn us to the full extent of our bounds, we shall conclude with observing, that notwithstanding some peculiarities in sentiment, and a few slight inaccuracies, this history may reasonably hope for a favourable reception from all parties. The stile is copious and manly; the reflections are pertinent and poignant: and the conclusions, in general, are judicious.

[17] [In later editions of the *History* Hume altered the above passage in question (i.e., "the change of manners...") to read as follows: "But the settled authority, which he acquired to the crown, enabled the sovereign to encroach on the separate jurisdictions of the barons, and produced a more general and regular execution of the laws."]

[18] It was in use in the Time of Edward IV. [Hume revised this portion of the text in later editions; a footnote to Chapter 26 directly addresses Ruffhead's point: "The practice of breaking entails by means of a fine and recovery was introduced in the reign of Edward the IVth; But it was not, properly speaking, law, till the statute of Henry the VIIth; which, by correcting some abuses that attended that practice, gave indirectly a sanction to it."]

10
WILLIAM TYTLER

[William Tytler], *An historical and critical enquiry into the evidence produced by the Earls of Murray and Morton, against Mary Queen of Scots. With an examination of the Rev. Dr. Robertson's Dissertation, and Mr. Hume's History, with respect to that evidence.* Edinburgh: printed by. W. Gordon, and sold by him and the other booksellers; and at London by W. Owen, T. Longman, J. Scott, Davie and Law, 1760, [2], viii, 262, 31, [1] p.
Selections from Preface, Chapters 1, 2, 3, 4, 6 (1760 edition) and complete Postscript (1772 edition).

Born in Aberdeen and educated at the University of Edinburgh, William Tytler (1711–1792) was by profession a solicitor. He also actively wrote on Scottish history, music and poetry, and was editor of the *Poetical Remains of James I. of Scotland* (1783). He was perhaps best known for his *Historical and Critical Enquiry*, in which he defends the innocence of Mary Queen of Scots (for background on the Queen Mary controversy, see the general introduction to this collection). Tytler draws heavily on the earlier defence of Mary published by his friend Walter Goodall, entitled *Examination of the Letters said to be Written by Mary, Queen of Scots* (1754). Goodall argued that the incriminating love letters allegedly written by Mary were in fact forged; specifically, he holds that there was no original French manuscript of her letters – as her enemies maintained – and the existing Latin and French copies were in fact translated from an original forged Scottish version. In Chapter 1 Tytler criticizes several of Hume's contentions, most importantly Hume's statement that Mary refused to answer the charges brought against her. In Chapter 2, he considers Robertson's and Hume's arguments against Goodall's case. Hume argues that there must have been a French original since the Scottish text contains words of French origin. Tytler argues that at the time of Mary, the Scottish language abounded with French idioms. In Chapter 3 he criticizes Hume's view that the casual marginal notes on Mary's letters are proof of their authenticity. In Chapter 4 Tytler counters Hume's view on the credibility of Hubert's dying confession. In Chapter 6, contrary to Hume and Robertson, he supports Mary's accusation that Murray, Morton, and Lethington were behind King Darnley's murder.

After the *Enquiry* appeared in 1760, Hume expressed dissatisfaction with Tytler's analysis, and an anecdote relates that Hume would even walk out of a room if he found Tytler there.[1] Hume offers his assessment of Tytler in the following letter:

> I ran over the Enquiry [by Tytler], which he mentions; and really found nothing new in it, nor anything capable in the least to shake my former Opinion: This perhaps proceeded from my Opinions being already fixt; and Mr Campbel, being a Neuter, must be the better Judge. The Enquirer's Learning on this Subject seems all to lie within a few Pages of Goodall; and these, according to the usual Artifice of controversial Writers, he has perverted, misrepresented, & curtaild at his Pleasure. [Hume to Alexander Dick, Edinburgh Aug. 26 1760]

Among Hume's manuscripts is a draft of another letter, probably written around 1760 to Lord Elibank, in which he also discusses Tytler's *Enquiry*. We do not know if Hume sent any version of this communication to Elibank. It opens as follows:

> As I am told, that Dr Robertson has wrote a few Remarks, which he communicated to your Lordship, on our common Answerer [i.e. Tytler] about the Affair of Q. Mary, and has endeavourd to show you, that it was Contempt, & not Inability, which kept him from making a public Reply; I thought it wou'd not be amiss for me to imitate his Example: And I did not indeed know a properer Person nor a more equal Judge than your Lordship, to whom I coud submit the Cause....

The letter continues with a detailed critique of Goodall, and concludes with the following attack on Tytler – which in the original is marked out with two lines:

> It is an old Proverb, *Love me, love my Dog*: But certainly it admits of many Exceptions: I am sure, at least, that I have a great Respect for your Lordship; yet have none at all for this Dog of Yours [i.e., Tytler]. On the contrary, I declare him to be a very mangey Cur: Entreat your Lordship to rid your hands of him as soon as possible: And think a sound beating or even a Rope too good for him. [Hume to Elibank, c. 1760]

In spite of his animosity towards Tytler, Hume revised his *History* based on some of Tytler's comments.

---

[1]   John William Burgon, *The Portrait of a Christian Gentleman. A Memoir of Patrick Fraser Tytler*, London, Murray, 1859, p. 69.

In the 1770 edition of his *History*, Hume included a note, sternly criticizing Tytler's treatment of him. He accuses Tytler of taking passages out of context and charges that the "whole Enquiry, from beginning to end, is composed of such scandalous artifices" (Tytler reproduces the relevant parts of Hume's note in the selection below). Tyler responded in a Postscript added to the 1772 edition of his *Enquiry*. He condemns the harshness of Hume's rebuke and defends himself against the specific example that Hume gives in his note. Tytler also mentions two specific passages that Hume revised in subsequent editions of his *History* based on Tytler's criticisms in the first edition of the *Enquiry*. For Tytler, Hume's account of Mary reflects a "systematic perversity" and the portrait he paints of her is "a false, hideous, and unnatural caricatura." He concludes by considering how Hume might react from a similarly harsh verbal attack. Hume made no changes to his note against Tytler in subsequent editions of the *History*.

The first edition of Tytler's *Enquiry* was favourably reviewed in several journals. Writing for the *Monthly Review*, Owen Ruffhead applauds Tytler's even-handed treatment of Hume and Robertson:

> We do not scruple to declare that, in our judgement, the Author of this very sensible enquiry, has acquitted himself with great moderation and impartiality. He does not set out like a furious knight errant, to rescue beautiful and accomplished innocence from a load of infamy: on the contrary he appears in the light of a cool, discerning, acute, and judicious examiner. He weighs the evidence on each side with temper and candor; and though he widely differs from Mr. Hume and Dr. Robertson, yet he never treats those respectable Writers with any degree of acrimony or indecency.

He praises Tytler's ability to defend Mary, but finds him much weaker as a critic of Mary's adversaries:

> In our opinion, indeed, the Author had done much better to have stopped at his vindication of Mary; after he had so ably invalidated the presumptive evidence against her, it was injudicious to build a charge against her accusers, on presumptions equally weak. But we must observe, that our Author's talents seem fitter for defence, than attack: for though, he is very quick in discovering any opening which his adversary makes, yet he does not always pursue the discovery to the best advantage. He is sometimes apt to be too refined, and now and then lessens the force of his arguments, by endeavouring to prove too much. In some places, likewise, he violates the rules of rhetoric, by setting out with his strongest proofs; and here and there, from an over anxiety to enforce his remarks, he gives way to repetitions, and breaks into the order of his discourse. Upon the whole, however, he appears in the light of an able critic, ad judicious reasoner: he seems to have fully

exculpated Mary from the presumption of her having been accessory to the murder of her husband, though he has not been able to establish the innocence of hr conduct in general. [*Monthly Review*, July 1760, Vol. 23, pp. 30–40]

The *Critical Review* calls Tytler a "sensible writer" as he generously tries to "rescue from a load of infamy the memory of the beautiful, accomplished, and, perhaps, the rather unfortunate than criminal Mary queen of Scotland." The reviewer censures Hume's biased account of the letters:

> It must be confessed, however, that the above account of the letters, and of Elizabeth's conduct, attested by the express words of the records, varies so much from Mr. Hume's relation, that we are astonished to see a writer so ingenious, so learned, and so penetrating, fall into such prejudices, so inconsistent with charity and good nature; virtues which we never heard denied him. [*Critical Review*, June 1760, Vol. 9, pp. 421]

The review concludes, "In a word, our author has in general acquitted himself with great ability and address; he has invalidated the evidence against Mary, but he has not fully established her innocence."

Samuel Johnson reviewed Tytler's *Enquiry* in *Gentleman's Magazine*, stating that Tytler shows a "zeal for truth, a desire of establishing right, in opposition to fashion." After presenting an objective summary of the book, Johnson concludes, "That the letters were forged is now made so probable, that perhaps they will never more be cited as testimonies" (*Gentleman's Magazine*, October 1760, Vol. 30, pp. 453–456). Some years later, in his *Life of Samuel Johnson* (1791) James Boswell said that this review showed "the generosity of Johnson's feelings;" Boswell himself called Tytler's *Enquiry* "acute and able." The article in the *Annual Register* – possibly penned by editor Edmund Burke – agrees with Tytler that Hume and Robertson were not sufficiently impartial in their treatment of Mary:

> The two respectable names our author uses in his title-page, are not more esteemed as good writers than good citizens. They are both men of too enlarged understanding to be actually circumscribed in the narrow limits of this or that party; and yet possibly we must so far agree with the author before us, as to suspect that they are not quite indifferent in the question of Mary's guilt or innocence, and have not here perhaps observed that exact impartiality, which we thought one of the valuable and uncommon qualities of these two able and elegant historians. [*Annual Register* December 1761, Vol. 4, pp. 305–316]

Some decades later, the *European Magazine and London Review* presented a biographical sketch of Tytler in which they state that he was victorious over Hume and Robertson, and that Hume's reputation suffered because of the harshness of his attack on him in the 1770 note in the *History*:

> When Mr. Hume and Dr. Robertson reviled the character of Mary Queen of Scots, and abused Mr. Goodal as an idle panegyrist of her virtues, he thought himself bound to take the field against them. It was not, however, for his friend Mr. Goodal, that he was interested to buckle on his armour. He drew his pen in the cause of innocence and virtue. This work he intitled, 'An Inquiry, Historical and Critical....' It was received with avidity by the public; and he pressed his opponents with such strength of argument, that they were fairly beat from their ground. Mr. Hume was so enraged with his strictures, that he lost all temper; and vented himself with a degree of passion, peevishness, and spleen, which utterly overset him in the opinion of men of probity and candor.
>
> To this violent declaimer, Mr. Tytler took the trouble to reply; and in a postscript to the third edition of his 'Inquiry,' he afforded him a refutation so just, so complete, and so convincing, that it cannot be read without admiration and applause. It would exceed, however, our purpose to lay it at this time before our readers.
>
> With regard to Dr. Robertson, he was more prudent than Mr. Hume. He, doubtless, perceived that Mr. Tytler was an overmatch for him; and he therefore carefully abstained from giving any answer to his observations. [*European Magazine and London Review*, October 1783, Vol. 4, pp. 284–285]

Tytler is discussed in John Whitaker's *Mary Queen of Scots Vindicated* (1760), David Dalrymple's *Miscellaneous Remarks on "The Enquiry"* (1784), and Francis Garden's *Miscellanies in Prose and Verse* (1791), selections from which are contained later in this collection. Revised editions of Tytler's *Enquiry* appeared in 1767, 1772, and 1790, and the work was translated into French in 1772 and 1860. The chapter selections below are from the 1760 first edition, which sparked Hume's initial reaction. The Postscript is from the 1772 third edition. The 1772 edition also includes some passages critical of Hume that do not appear in that of 1760. I have included two of these at the appropriate spot, within curly brackets. Other bracketed comments in the body of the text below are Tytlers. Bracketed comments in the footnotes are mine.

THE
PREFACE.

The history of Scotland, during the unfortunate reign of queen Mary, has always been looked upon as one of the most interesting periods of modern history. Of late, it has become a fashionable part of reading, having been treated of by two eminent writers, whose works make a considerable figure in the republic of letters; I mean, the Rev. Doctor Robertson, and David Hume, Esq;

These two gentlemen, tho' differing considerably in the character given by them of the princess, yet seem to agree in their sentiments with respect to the evidences of her knowledge of, and accession to, the murder of the lord Darnley her husband; and particularly as to the genuineness of the letters said to have been written by her to the earl of Bothwell. These letters have indeed been always regarded, by the discerning class of readers, as the principal point of controversy between queen Mary and her accusers, the earls of Murray and Morton. If we suppose that the letters are genuine, the advocates of Mary will labour in vain to convince the world of her innocence. If, on the other hand, the letters can be proved to be spurious and forged, Mary not only stands absolved, but these letters must become a direct evidence of the guilt of Murray and Morton, who produced them against her.

A late author, Mr. Goodall, keeper of the advocates library in Edinburgh, from an accurate examination of the letters, together with several other collateral evidences found among the records, has made many ingenious discoveries, tending to prove, that these letters are spurious. On the other hand, Mr. Hume, and Dr. Robertson in the dissertation annexed to his history, have laboured to prove these letters to be genuine, in opposition to Mr. Goodall's proofs to the contrary.

Truth and falshood must ever take opposite sides. To discover the one from the other, is often a difficult task. Curiosity, and a strong desire to find out the truth, were inducements to the author of the following treatise to try, if, amidst so many mazes and perplexed windings, some path might not be fallen upon that could lead to truth in her retreat.

His plan was to trace these letters, step by step, from their very first appearance in the hands of the earl of Morton, and to remark with care and candour every circumstance that attended them thro' the whole procedure of the conferences in England, before queen Elizabeth and her council and commissioners.

Towards this plan Mr. Goodall had smoothed the way, by the valuable collection of original papers contained in the second volume of his work; by which he has united the chain of procedure in those conferences, and supplied us with such papers as Anderson, in his four volumes of collections, has, with too much partiality, suppressed.

In proceeding upon this plan, the author was soon sensible of the light gradually breaking in, by the beams of which he has been directed in his search.

For the sake of perspicuity, he has divided his examination into the following Chapters.

In the *First* is contained the history of the letters from their discovery by the earl of Morton, their being produced against queen Mary, and their several appearances in England before queen Elizabeth and her commissioners, until they were finally delivered back again to the earl of Morton.

The *Second* Chapter contains a short abstract of Mr. Goodall's arguments for proving the letters to be spurious and forged; and of Dr. Robertson and Mr. Hume's objections by way of answer to Mr. Goodall, with critical observations on these authors.

Chapter *Third* contains an examination of the arguments of Dr. Robertson and Mr. Hume, in support of the authenticity of the letters.

Chapter *Fourth* contains an examination of the confession of Nicholas Hubert, commonly called French Paris, with observations showing the same to be a forgery.

The *Fifth* Chapter contains a short recapitulation or summary of the arguments on both sides of the question. And,

The *Last* Chapter is an historical collection of the direct or positive evidence, still on record, tending to show what part the earls of Murray, and Morton, and secretary Lethington, had in the murder of the lord Darnley.

In treating this subject, as the author disdains the name of a party writer, he is conscious of no design to mislead the reader; he has asserted nothing without giving good authority, he generally quotes the very words of the records, and leaves the reader to give his own judgment. If he has differed either in point of fact or argument, from any of the latest writers on this subject, he has given his reasons; and hopes he has done so, with the deference which is due to the public, and with that temper and good manners which every gentleman has a right to expect. In the course of argument, it is scarce possible for one, who thinks he has conviction on his side, to remain at all times cool and unconcerned. If, in some passages, he may have exceeded the moderation of a critic, he did not mean to offend, and hopes that he will not often stand in need of an indulgence on that account. ...

CHAP. I.

The Letters said to have been written by Mary Queen of Scots to the Earl of Bothwell, have been the subject of much dispute among the writers of the history of those times. Much virulence and invective have been thrown out from both sides; at the same time that the bulk of the arguments used by either party has been rather conjectural than founded upon facts. The adversaries of that princess have always regarded these letters as an invincible proof of her knowledge and participation of the crimes laid to her charge: And indeed, allowing them to have been genuine, there is no resisting the force of such a conclusion. It is my design, by tracing the history of those letters from their very first appearance, to detach them from that confused heap of rubbish under which they have artfully been buried, to produce them into light, stript of their false colouring; and, by coolly and dispassionately considering the arguments on both sides of the question, endeavour to investigate the truth.

The way and manner by which these letters came into the possession of the Queen's enemies, is conveyed to us by a Memorandum, published along with Buchanan's detection in these words:

Memandorum.

"That in the castell of Edinburgh thair was left to the Erle of Bothwell, before his fleeing away, and was send for be ane George Dalgleish, his Servand, who was taken be the Erle of Mortoun, ane small gylt coffer, not fully ane fute lang, garnisht in sindrie places with the Roman Letter F. under ane king's crowne; wharin were certane letteris and writings weel knawin, and be aithis to be affirmit to have been written with the Quene of Scottis awin hand to the Erle."

...

Upon the 15th day of December, ten days after the above act of secret council, the earl of Murray's first parliament met, where an act is passed concerning the queen's detention, which is almost a transcript of the above act of their secret council, justifying the queen's imprisonment from "her awin default, in sa far as be divers her previe letters, WRITTEN HALELIE [*i.e.* wholly] *with her awin hand*,[2] and send be her to James earl of Bothwell, &c. it is certain she was privy art and part of the king's murder."

Upon comparing the words of these two acts together, relating to the letters, it is plain, that an ugly jarring betwixt them appears: The act of secret council asserting the letters to be "*written and subscrivit* with the queen's awin hand;" whereas the act of parliament declares them only to be "*written halelie* with her awin hand." From whence could so strange a discordance arise, in two such solemn deeds, and in so very material a point? The additional word *halelie* in the act of parliament, which is substituted in the place of the words *and subscrivit*, in the act of council, is pretty convincing that this variation was owing to no inadvertency in the compiler.

The only person who has attempted to explain this jarring betwixt the two records, is the ingenious David Hume, Esq; who thinks there is no difficulty

---

[2] Ander. vol. 2. p. 211. Goodall, vol. 2. p. 67.

in the matter. As his remark is singular, I choose to cite his own words: *Hist. of England, vol.* 2. *p.* 500. In the notes, after mentioning the objection arising from the jarring of the two records, he says, *But it is not considered that this circumstance is of no manner of force*; there were certainly letters , true or false, laid before the council; and whether the letters were true or false, this mistake proceeds equally from the inaccuracy or blunder of the clerk. The mistake is easily accounted for: The letters were only *wrote* by her, the second contract with Bothwell was only *subscribed*. A proper accurate description was not made, and they are all said to be *wrote and subscribed.*"

The proper reply to be made to this solution of the above difficulty, is only to desire the reader to compare the words in the two records before cited: The express words are, *The previe letteris written and sent by the queen to* James *earl of* Bothwell. I scarce think that Mr. Hume will perswade any man, notwithstanding the precision in which he gives judgment, that these words can be applied to a contract, which can neither be said to have been written or sent by the queen to Bothwell, or to any other writings whatever but the letters: Far less could this jarring happen in the words of the two records from any mistake or inaccuracy of a clerk. He must be no sceptic indeed, who can believe, that, in so important a matter, the wise heads of Murray, Morton, and secretary Lethington, would have trusted the compiling of these two acts to a blundering clerk, or let such an obvious blunder escape them.

If the letters, first produced by Murray and Morton in their secret council, were signed by the queen, certain it is, that the letters produced before the parliament had no subscription, but were only asserted to be *halelie*, or wholly written by the queen's own hand. If these letters are genuine, I own, I cannot see how so strange a discordance can be accounted for: If we suppose them spurious and forged, a reason, I think, for this strange conduct may be given. ...

{[1772 edition:] Mr Hume is pleased to say, that "bishop Lesly expressly declined comparing the hands, (in the letters), as not being a legal proof." Let us examine what authority Mr Hume has for this assertion. We have seen from the record of 6th December, that queen Elisabeth, in answer to Mary's supplication, tells her commissioners, that she is to call upon Murray, and receive the proofs of his accusation against their Queen, that is, the letters. In a paper drawn up by the Bishop of Ross upon that occasion, he uses the following argument. "If they, Murray and Mortoun, wald press to verify their accusation by comparison of letters, the samen is na ways sufficient; *cum, de jure, fallacissimum genus probandi sit per comparationem literarum.*" The above authority from the Roman law, that a proof *comparatione literarum* is the most fallacious of all proof, is certainly just; especially in absence of the party accused. But does it follow from this, that the Bishop, by using this argument, expressly declined comparing the hands, as Mr Hume is pleased to assert? With submission, the contrary of this appears; and that Queen Mary repeatedly, as we shall see, instructs her commissioners to see and inspect the original letters; but in vain;

this reasonable and necessary demand, though often insisted on by them, they never did obtain. But to proceed. ...}

The defect of having some other impartial and unsuspected witnesses to have concurred with Morton, as to the discovery and seizure of the box and letters, and his remarkable shyness in interrogating Dalgleish on this point, have already been observed. But it perhaps will be said, that, at the time of Dalgleish's trial, this was an oversight which escaped even the sagacity and penetrating genius of Morton, and the whole party. The man was hanged, and he cannot now be called from the grave to answer questions. It is to be observed, however, that, at this very time, December 1568, they had in their custody a very material and living evidence, who had a part in the letters. The second letter mentions, by name, one Paris, or Nicholas Hubert a Frenchman, servant of Bothwell, who, it is said, was the person intrusted to carry the letters from the queen to Bothwell. This man had been kept in close confinement in St. Andrews during all this time. Now when one sees the remarkable care and attention of the party in collecting every circumstance which they supposed could be matter of proof against the queen, in support of their accusation, their penury of proof notwithstanding, and the pinching necessity of supporting the only evidence they had (that of the letters) by the bare and single affirmation of Morton himself, the queen's accuser, and most inveterate enemy; it is impossible to overlook, without the strongest suspicion, their omitting to have produced so very material an evidence as this Frenchman, in person, to have answered to questions of Mary, or her commissioners, before the English council, and to the part assigned to him in the letters themselves.

Mr. Hume, who has omitted nothing that he thought was evidence against the queen, has been very sensible of this defect of Murray's, in not calling upon Paris, and he endeavours to supply it in a pretty extraordinary manner: "On the giving in the letters, (says he) Murray fortified this evidence by some testimonies of corresponding facts; and he added, sometime after, the dying confession of Hubert, or French Paris, a servant of Bothwell, who had been executed for the king's murder, and who directly charged the queen with being accessory to that criminal interprise."[3] He afterwards adds: "It is in vain at present to seek for improbabilities in this confession: It was certainly a regular judicial paper, given in regularly and judicially, and ought to have been canvassed at the Time."[4] From this account Mr. Hume would make one believe, that that piece of evidence, Paris's confession, had been given in by Murray within a few days after the letters, at least whilst the conferences subsisted; yet nothing can be more false. The conferences broke up, and the earl

[3] Hume, vol. 2. p. 497.

[4] Ibid. p. 500.

of Murray and his party got licence from queen Elizabeth to return home to Scotland, in January 1568–9. Paris, after lying in close prison till August 1569, was then put to death; at which time it is pretended he made these confessions against the queen. But I shall hereafter have occasion more particularly to examine this pretended confession by itself. ...

In this manner, did Murray and Morton, with their box and letters, withdraw from the conferences in England. What afterwards became of the letters we know not. They are now lost, or have been destroyed, no body knows how. This we are certain of, and have seen, that queen Mary, notwithstanding her frequent assertions, that they were forged by her accusers, and her repeated earnest supplications, both under her hand, and by the mouth of her commissioners, to see the letters, to answer them, and prove the forgery upon Murray and Morton, could not prevail in so reasonable a request. And to her dying hour, these very letters, upon which only, at this day, her enemies pretended to found any proof of her guilt, were most industriously hid from her, and at last buried for ever in the same pit of darkness from which they at first emerged.

The preceeding account of the several steps of the conferences relating to the letters, from the very words of the records themselves, is so very different from, and so contradictory to Mr. Hume's relation, in his late history, that I think it incumbent upon me, in justice to the public, to set down a short abstract of his account, so that upon a comparison, the impartial reader may, from his own eye-sight, judge, how far that Gentleman has been directed by truth, in his representation of this affair.

"When the charge, (says Mr. Hume) or accusation against Mary was given in, and copies of it transmitted to the bishop of Ross, lord Herries, and her other commissioners, they absolutely refused to return any answer; and they grounded their silence on very extraordinary reasons: They had orders, they said, from their mistress, if any thing was advanced that might touch her honour, not to make any defence, as she was a sovereign princess, and could not be subject to any tribunal; and they required, that she should previously be admitted to Elizabeth's presence. They forgot that the conferences were at first begun, and were still continued, with no other view than to clear her from the accusations of her enemies; that Elizabeth had ever pretended to enter into them *only as her friend, by her own consent*, without assuming any superior jurisdiction over her. – As the queen of Scots refused to give in any answer to Murray's charge, the necessary consequence seemed to be, that there could be no farther proceedings in the trial."[5]

---

[5]   Hume, vol. 2. p. 496.

If this was a necessary consequence of Mary's refusing to answer, (unless in person, Mr. Hume should have added) it may be asked, How came Elizabeth, notwithstanding, to proceed in the trial, in absence of both Mary and her commissioners? Was not this the height of partiality, in this pretended friend of Mary, to hear her enemies by themselves, or to receive any thing from their hands as sufficient proof against her, upon their word only? And when she did so, ought she not, in common justice, to have communicated the same to Mary? But to go on with this author's account:

"Elizabeth and her ministers desired to have in their hands the proofs of her guilt: – Murray made no difficulty in producing the proofs of his charge against the queen of Scots, and among the rest, some love letters and sonnets of her's to Bothwel, wrote all in her own hand, and two promises of marriage to him. – They contained incontestible proofs of Mary's criminal correspondence with Bothwel, of her consent to the king's murder, and of her concurrence in that rape, which Bothell pretended to commit upon her. Murray fortified this evidence, by some testimonies of corresponding facts; and he added, sometime after, the dying confession of one Hubert, or French Paris, a servant of the earl of Bothwel, *who had been* executed for the king's murder, and who directly charged the queen with her being accessory to that criminal enterprize."[6]

Would not any one believe from this account, that Hubert had been hanged before the time here spoken of by Mr. Hume, and that his confession was produced during the conferences; and yet we have seen that Hubert was alive all the time of the conferences, and no confession from him, nor the least mention of his name made for ten months after they broke up.

"Mary's commissioners (continues our author) had used every expedient to ward this blow, which they saw coming upon them. – And finding that the English commissioners were still determined to proceed, in the method which had been projected, *they finally broke off* the conferences, and *never* would make any *reply*. These papers have all of them been since published. The objections made to their validity, are in general of small force: But were they ever so specious, they cannot now be hearkened to; since Mary, at the time when the Truth could have been fully cleared, did, in effect, ratify the evidence against her, by recoiling from the enquiry at the very critical moment, and *refusing to give any answer* to the accusation of her enemies."[7]

Let us, by way of answer, now compare the words of the record, with this gentleman's account:

---

[6]   Hume, vol. 2. p. 497.

[7]   Hume, vol. 2. p. 498.

"Hampton-court, 25th day of December 1568: The quhilk day the bishop of Ross and lord Herries came to Hampton-court, whair, in the council chamber, thay declarit, that thay had special command sent to thame fra the quene thair maistres, to declair, That being advertisit of the unnatural and ungrate dealing of hir disobedient subjectis and rebelis, could not suffer thair blasphemous and sklanderous accusatiounis to pas over with silence *unanswerit*; quhan thay thamselfis quha did accuse hir, wer the authoris, and inventeris, and, sum of thame, executouris of the murthour: And thairfoir *wald answer* to thair accusatioun, in defence of hir awin innocence, and accusatioun of thame, as the authoris thameselfis of the king's murthour. And the said commissionaris producit their writingis and instructiounis, sent be thair maistres to thame to that effect. Quhilk being read befoir hir majestie, and hir counsall, thay maist humblie desyrit hir majestie to cause thame have sic writingis, as wer producit againis thair maistres be hir adversaris."[8]

The account that this historian has given of the queen's conduct, is directly contradicted almost in every sentence by the records, which, it appears, he has himself perused. At the same time it is easy to perceive the poor evasion that our author pretends to make for this so strange a detail, *viz.* 1*st*, That Mary had insisted to confront, personally, Murray and Morton her accusers, in presence of Elizabeth, the whole English nobility, and foreign ambassadors; which Mr. Hume is pleased to say, was such a request as could not be granted:[9] And 2*dly*, That this request being refused, Mary's commissioners had protested against all further procedure, on the 9th of December; the conferences, therefore, according to Mr. Hume, were from that minute, as he has said above, finally broke off. But this is a pitiful shift, in which our author has followed Anderson, who breaks off his collections, and gives us no more of the proceedings of the English council after the 16th of December 1567.[10] Let it be asked, what was the basis of these conferences, and the design of the parties by entering into them? Mr. Hume himself has told us above, that the conferences were at first begun, and were still continued with no other view than to clear Mary from the accusations of her enemies: "Elizabeth, says he, had only entered into them *as her friend, by her own consent*, not assuming any jurisdiction over her." This I agree was truly the footing the conferences were on: Mary demands to be heard personally upon her defence; to confront and interrogate her accusers in presence of all the world: A demand, that, without regard to Mr. Hume's opinion, will, I presume, be thought a most just and necessary one. Elizabeth refuses it: Mary's commissioners, on so manifest a

---

[8]   Cot. lib. Good. vol. 2. p. 281.

[9]   Dr. Robertson is of a quite different opinion from Mr. Hume, vol. 1. p. 413.

[10] Ander. vol. 4. p. 179. As we have already observed p. 26th.

partiality, protest against all further procedure in the matter. What follows: Let me ask, Do the conferences finally break up? No, 'tis quite otherwise: On the 16th of December 1567, Elizabeth "wald not be content that ony of thame (the Scots commissioners) should depart into Scotland before the end of this conference."[11] She allowed Murray and his associates to proceed to produce the proof of their accusation, and twelve days after the protest she wrote to Mary, and advised her to make answer.[12] This Mary had determined to do, before the date of Elizabeth's letter of the 21st of December; and had already written her resolution to her commissioners, on the 19th of that month, to have inspection of Murray's proof, and doubles of all the writings, "and with God's grace, (says she) I sall mak sic answer to thair accusatioun, as my innocence sall appear, and thair guilt."[13] It is plain therefore, that, as the conferences were intirely founded on the consent of parties, allowing that Mary's commissioners, or that even she herself had broke them off, yet as Murray and his associates, on their part, were still going on before the English council, it was still in Mary's power to resume her defence, as Elizabeth herself desired she should do; and which she did accordingly, in the strongest manner, by letters under her hand and signet.

Upon the whole, I shall leave it to every impartial reader, to make his own reflections on our historian, as invective or personal abuse is neither my talent nor design.

{[1772 edition:] Upon the whole, I leave it to every impartial person, to judge, with what justice our historian has given sentence in favour of the evidence against Queen Mary, and to make his own reflections. At the same time, I think myself intitled to lay hold of the gentleman's own argument, and turn it against himself, by maintaining, That Queen Elisabeth, by refusing to Mary and her commissioners inspection of the evidence against her, or to give so much as a copy of the letters, "did recoil from the inquiry at the very critical minute when a scrutiny was demanded of that evidence, and when the truth could have been fully cleared; and therefore has ratified every argument and proof of forgery that is now brought against them;"[14] – and, in fine, has left an indelible stain upon the justice of the whole procedure in that affair.}

[11] Good. vol. 2. p. 269.

[12] Ander. vol. 4. p. 179. Good. vol. 2. p. 269.

[13] Cot. lib. Good. vol. 2. p. 289. Page 26th of this.

[14] [This quotation is modeled after the following by Hume in Chapter 39: "The objections, made to their authenticity, are in general of small force: But were they ever so specious, they cannot now be hearkened to; since Mary, at the time when the truth could have been fully cleared, did, in effect, ratify the evidence against her, by recoiling from the enquiry at the very critical moment, and refusing to give an answer to the accusation of her enemies."]

CHAP. II.

The conferences in England being ended, the original letters, said to have been written by the Queen to the Earl of Bothwell, were never afterwards exposed to light. Queen Elisabeth having attained the double end, of blackening Queen Mary, and securing the dependency of Murray's faction, broke off all further inquiry. That copies of the letters were soon after spread abroad, is notorious; after being in the hands of Elisabeth and her council, whose great aim, through the course of their proceedings, as has been shown, was, to load Mary with the crimes imputed to her by her rebellious subjects, to countenance and support them in their usurpation, and to give a specious pretence for detaining that princess a prisoner in England; it will scarce be imagined that Elisabeth would lose the fruit of her labour, which she had, by so much industry and care, brought to maturity, by keeping locked up from the publick, those pretended evidences of Mary's guilt, *her love letters and sonnets.*

The originals produced were written in French, a language then as generally understood at the court of England, as it is at this day. What a fund this, of court-scandal! How delicious to Elisabeth, to mortify so hated a rival, to her genius, to her beauty, to her kingdom! It will obviously occur, that Mary, by this time, when those letters must have been in every body's hands, could easily have procured copies, and made answer to them. I own, it is not to be doubted but she must have got copies of them; but, as has been already observed, a forgery cannot be detected from a copy, and the inspection of the originals had constantly been refused to her. What answer then could she make? An answer, however, she did make. The Bishop of Ross, the very same year 1569, published her defence.[15]

As to the letters, they are asserted to be forged; and that it was notoriously known, that persons about the Queen had often been in the practice of forging letters in her name. They had neither date, address, seal, nor subscription. That, as they had only been collated by the Queen's accusers, there was no proof that they were of her hand-writing. The person (says the Bishop) who was surmised to be the bearer, (Nicholas Hubert, or French Paris), "at the time of his execution, took it upon his death, as he should answer before God, that he never carried any such letter, nor that the Queen was participant, nor of council in the cause."[16] We see then, that tho' the Queen was denied a sight of the original letters; yet, under that disadvantage, she made a good an answer.

There is no mention made of the letters after this, until the year 1571, when Buchanan published his libel, called *The detection of the doings of Mary*, both

---

[15] Ander. vol. 1. part 2. preface v.

[16] Ander. vol. 1. part 2. p. 19.

in Latin and in the Scotish dialect. Secretary Cecil immediately took care to have it printed in England, that same year 1571. The Latin copy had affixed to it, the first three letters of Mary, translated by Buchanan into that language; and the Scottish copy contained eight letters and the love verses.[17]

In the beginning of the year 1572, at the time of the duke of Norfolk's trial, a French translation of Buchanan's detection was printed at London, to which were subjoined seven of these French letters, and the love sonnets in verse: the title page bears that it was printed *à Edinbourg le* 13 *de Fevrier* 1572, *par Thomas Waltam.* But there never was a printer in Scotland of that name.

The original letters themselves, with the silver box, delivered back to Morton, being long ago lost, this French copy of the detection, with seven of the letters annexed to it, and the love sonnet in rhyme, has, now for these 200 years, been looked upon, by all parties, as true copies of the originals, and underwent several editions as such.

The late writer, Mr. Walter Goodall, keeper of the advocates library at Edinburgh, who had made it his study to collect materials for the history of those times, a few years ago, published a critical examination of the letters: By comparing the three different copies of them together, he has very ingeniously shown that those pretended letters, said to be written in French by queen Mary to the earl of Bothwell, must be spurious. His arguments may be reduced to this proposition.

The letters said to be written in French by the queen, as now extant, have, by all parties, been held for true copies of the originals produced by Morton, and have, down to this time, passed uncontested as such.

Buchanan, the confident of Murray and Morton, who attended them both at York and London, had the letters in his custody, and was so much master of their contents, that he was employed by Murray to show and explain them to the English commissioners at York, and translated the three first of them into Latin.

If then it can be shown, that, in place of the French being the originals, the Scotch copies are the true originals, and that the French are apparently translations from Buchanan's Latin, the conclusion fairly follows, that these French pretended originals are spurious. This Mr. Goodall has done.

By comparing the letters, as they stand in the three different languages, he has, to a demonstration, shown, that, in place of the Scotch and Latin being translated from the French originals, these last are palpably a version from the Latin, and the Latin again a version from the Scotch. The Scotch is apparently

---

[17] Vide Alexander Hay's letter to John Knox, dated the 14th December 1571; and an anonymous letter, published at that time in England, to give credit to Buchanan's book. Goodall, vol. 2. p. 371 and 377. – Vide also a letter from Cecil to Walsingham in Digges's ambassador, p. 151; Good. vol. 1. p. 106.

original: The thoughts therein are naturally and sententiously turned, and abounding in phrases and proverbs peculiar to that language. – These are servilely expressed in the Latin, and sometimes erroneously: And, as often as that happens, the French always follows these errors of the Latin. As Mr. Goodall's book is common, I shall not tire my reader with going through ingenious remarks, I shall only quote two or three examples from the first letter,[18] and refer to his book for the rest.

1. The Scotch copy says proverbially, in letter first, "thair's no receipt (meaning a medical prescription of a physic) can serve againis feir." The Latin has, "nullam adversus timorem esse medicinam."

And the French is, "qu'il n'y avoit point de remede contre la crainte."

2. Scotch, "ze have *fair* going to see *seik* folk." Another proverbial saying.

The Latin translator has here committed no less than two blunders, he mistook the word *fair* (or fore) for *fair*, and the word *seik* for *sic* (or such) and has translated them both erroneously in the last sense: "Bella *hujusmodi* hominum visitatio."

And the French copies him thus: "voyla une *belle* visitation de *telles* gens."

3. The queen is made to say, that she was going to seek her rest till to-morrow, "quhen (says she) I fall end my *bybill*," in place of her *bylle* (or bill) a word used commonly at that time for any sort of writing. The transcriber, from the resemblance of the two words, made it *bybill*; the Latin follows him in this absurdity, "ego eo ut meam quietem inveniam in crastinum, ut tum mea *biblia* finiam;" and the French follows him thus: "je m'en vay pour trouver mon repos jusques au lendemain, afin que je finesse icy ma *bible*."

I shall not trouble my reader with any more of these quotations, whereby Mr. Goodall has proved, undeniably, that the French letters, in place of being the originals, are, to a demonstration, translations from Buchanan's latin, and from the Scotch copies of the letters. This he has made so evident, that Mr. Hume, and likewise doctor Robertson in the dissertation on the murder of King Henry Darnley, annexed to his history, who both labour to vindicate the authenticity of the French letters produced by Murray and Morton, have been obliged *fairly to acknowledge*,[19] that the French letters, now extant are palpable translations from Buchanan's Latin and Scotch copies of these letters. A concession the more remarkable, that it was never made before by any individual on their side of the question, the present French copy being always held to be the original from the year 1572, until the day that Mr. Goodall published his detection of this pretended original, and exposed the imposture.

Mr. Hume, and his ingenious friend the author of the Dissertation, make light of this discovery of Mr. Goodall, and endeavour to evade the force of it, in the

[18] Good. vol. 2. p. 1.

[19] Hume, vol. 2. p. 499. Robertson, vol. 2. p. 25.

following manner. The original letters (say they) are now lost, and we know nothing of them. I shall cite the learned Dissertator's words, in his answer to Mr. Goodall: "All this author's (Goodall's) premises may be granted, and yet his conclusions will not follow, unless he likewise prove, that the French letters, as we now have them, are a true copy of those which were produced by Murray and his party in the Scots parliament, and at York and Westminster: but this he has not attempted."[20] ...

I believe it will be readily granted, that, in the above instances, there is a much easier turn of phrase in the French translation, than in the Latin: which proves no more than what is said above, that, in some scattered sentences, a poor and low translation may express the thought better than the original. Mr. Goodall's critical observations on the letters, are, however, quite of another sort: He has shown, by many instances, that the Scotch are the real originals; that in transcribing them, some errors, such as *byble* for *bylle*, have been made, which followed the Latin translator, who makes it *biblia*, and the French, said to be the original of all, following the error of the Latin, translates it *bible*.[21]

In the same manner, the Scotch word *irkit* (i. e. *weary*) has been erroneously, from its similarity, read *nakit*, translated *nudata* in the Latin, and by the French *nue*, after the Latin, tho' it makes the sentence apparently nonsense. But I need not tire the reader with more on this subject; since both our author, and Mr. David Hume, the other combatant for the authenticity of the letters, do plainly acknowledge that Mr. Goodall has proved the present French letters to be direct translations from the Latin, which is sufficient for my present purpose.[22]

I have only one argument more to answer, which is used by Mr. Hume: The present French letters, he acknowledges, are professedly done from the Latin; no body can dispute, I think, that the Latin is a translation from the Scotch: "But (says Mr. Hume) it appears, that the Scotch itself is only a translation from some other French original, which we have now lost." What a strange process have we here? all to show, that the publisher of the present French letters could not, for his heart, procure so much as a copy of the original French letters to print with his book, although these pretended originals must have been in every body's hand at the time; and therefore, to supply that defect, he translated his French letters from the Latin, which was a translation from the Scotch, which last was again a translation from a certain French original, which, according to this hypothesis of Mr. Hume, is lost, and we know nothing about it. Mr.

---

[20] Robertson, vol. 2. Dissertation, p. 25.

[21] Good. vol. 2. Appendix, No 1.

[22] "It is probable (says the dissertator, p. 29.) that Buchanan made his translation, not from the French, but from the Scotch copy. Were it necessary, (continues he) "several proofs of this might be produced."

Hume's proof of all this, to wit, that the Scotch is not the original, as Mr. Goodall affirms, is, because this Scotch copy of the letters, says he, abounds with Gallicisms, and French words: Such as, "make fault, *faire des fautes*; – make it seem that I believe, *faire semblant de la croire*; – this is my first journay, *c'est ma premiere journee*," *&c.* From these instances he infers, in a very decisive manner, that the Scotch letters are not originals, but translations from a French original.[23]

The answer to this is, that any person conversant with the language and writings in queen Mary's time, and even after that period, will see, that from the long and continued intercourse and connection between the Scotch and French nations at that time, the Scotch language abounded with Gallicisms, and even with French words; some of which, tho' now almost worn out in our writings, yet remain to this day in our language, especially among the vulgar. Mr. Hume himself, and every other Scotchman, knows well what the vulgar mean by giving a *bonaillie, bonneallee*, or departing pint; also, in the same sense, giving one's *foy*. – To give a *benison*, or blessing, is still a vulgar phrase; and the *Beggars Benison*, which gives title to a very numerous society in Scotland. Old people still give the name of *montre* to a watch; and a *jardelou*, or *gar de l'eau*, I believe, is pretty well known in Edinburgh, even at this very day. I shall also give a few instances from the writings of those times. In the Earls of Huntly and Argyle's protestation Lethington says, "tak you na care, we sal fynd an *moyen* to make her quit of him." – Queen Mary, in answer to Murray and Morton's accusations against her, says, "they have *meschantlie* sclanderit her." – Secretary Lethington, confessedly the best Scotch writer of that time, in his letter to Cecil, the English secretary, useth the word *appuy*, for support[24] – Sir James Melvil's memoirs, p. 184. "others of the *finest* of them perswaded the regent." By the word *finest*, in this place, is meant the most subtile, cunning, or penetrating genius, from the French words *fin*, and *finet*, a cunning or subtile man: a word not known or used, either in writing or in common speech, at this day. – In the very next page of Melvil: "He desired the accusation to be *rendered* up to him again." – And secretary Cecil useth this phrase, "and because it was *bruited*," i.e. rumoured. See page 35.

These are a few of many instances[25] that easily occur, which may be sufficient to show Mr. Hume, that Gallicisms and French words abounded in the language; and also in the original Scotch writings in those days, as well as in

[23] Hume, vol. 2. p. 499.

[24] Keith, p. 233.

[25] We may observe too, that some of the Gallicisms he unluckily pitches on, are standard words, and daily used in the English language; as *Journey* is the usual words in England for a day's work of a labourer; *Journey-man*, a day-labourer, and *Journey-work* the work of a day labourer.

the letters he mentions. Whence the inference he is pleased to make, that the Scotch letters are, for that reason, no originals, but translations from some other French originals, must fall to the ground.

But further, as far as I can judge, there appears, in the Scotch copy of the letters, a spirit, and so happy a turn of phrase, altogether peculiar to that language, and so very different from the languor, baldness of expression, and servility of both the French and Latin copies, that plainly denotes the first to be altogether original in every sense. To show this, I shall take a few phrases from the first letter only.[26]

"A gentleman of the earl of Lennox came and *made his commendatiouns* to me." This phrase is still used in the Scotch language, to signify, he presented his compliments.

"This speech was *of his awin head*, without ony commission."

"There is na receipt can serve againis feir." – A proverb.

"He hes ever the teir in his eye."

"Fals race – they hae bene at achullis togidder."

"He hes almaist slane me with his braith."

"Ye have fair going to see seik folk."

"He gave me a check in the quick."

"Excuse that thing that is scriblit."

These few examples of proverbial sentences and phrases, peculiar to the Scotch language, and to which the French have nothing similar in their language, are sufficient to show, that this Scotch copy of the letters, is not only the original of the three copies of the letters still extant, but likewise, that it is not a translation at all, but a true original in every sense. Both Mr. Hume and the dissertator have fairly acknowledged, that the Scotch is the original of the three copies extant of these letters. If, notwithstanding, Mr. Hume will still maintain, that this Scotch copy may, for all this, be a translation from some other French original, with submission, it is incumbent upon that gentleman to produce that original; or, at least, to show us, that there ever existed any other French letters besides the present copy, and how this other supposed original came to be lost, after being in every body's hands, both in Scotland and England, otherwise his bare assertion must go for nothing.

I have now gone through this tiresome piece of criticism. The necessity of stating Mr. Goodall's examination of the letters, the arguments and objections on the other side made to him, and of giving some observations of my own, in answer to these objections, will, I hope, be an excuse for me. How far the answer is satisfactory or not, I leave to others to determine.

[26] Appendix, No. 1.

CHAP. III.

... Upon this passage of the memorandums, Mr. Hume makes a very strange observation: "In this letter, (says he) which she penned late at night, her paper failed her, and she takes down a memorandum of what she intended to add next morning; and it is added accordingly: A circumstance (continues he) not likely to occur to a forger." In answer to this, I only desire the reader to look into that part of the letter which follows this memorandum, in which there is not one word that has relation to these memorandums, except the last respecting Livingston. One would think, that this gentleman had fondly adopted the dissertator's conceit, without giving himself the trouble to examine the evidence.

CHAP. IV.

... Before we conclude, we must again beg leave to take notice of Mr. Hume's arguments in support of this noted piece of evidence of Paris: "It is in vain (says he) at present to seek for improbabilities in Nicholas Hubert's dying confession, and to magnify the smallest difficulties into a contradiction. It was certainly a *regular judicial* paper, given in regularly and judicially, and ought to have been canvassed at the time, if the persons, whom it concerned, had been assured of their innocence."[27]

Here we see a short, but very positive decision against all and every objection that possibly can be brought against Paris's confession. But upon what does this author ground his sentence? Upon two very plain reasons, *first*, That the confession was a judicial one, that is, taken in presence, or by authority of a judge. And *secondly*, That it was regularly and judicially given in; that must be understood during the time of the conferences before queen Elizabeth and her council, in presence of Mary's commissioners; at which time she ought to have canvassed it, says our author, if she knew here innocence.

That it was not a judicial confession, is evident: The paper itself does not bear any such mark; nor does it mention that it was taken in presence of any person, or by any authority whatsoever; and, by comparing it with the judicial examinations of Dalgleish, Hay, and Hepburn, in page 146, it is apparent, that it is destitute of every formality requisite in a judicial evidence. In what dark corner, then, this strange production was generated, our author may endeavour to find out, if he can.

As to his second assertion, that it was regularly and judicially given in, and therefore ought to have been canvassed by Mary during the conferences. We

[27] Hume, vol. 2. p. 500.

have already seen that this likewise is not fact: The conferences broke up in February 1569: Nicholas Hubert was not hanged till August thereafter, and his dying confession, as Mr. Hume calls it, is only dated the 10th of that month. How then can this gentleman gravely tell us that this confession was judicially given in, and ought to have been at the very time canvassed by queen Mary and her commissioners? such positive assertions, apparently contrary to fact, are unworthy the character of an historian, and may very justly render his decision, with respect to evidences of a higher nature, very dubious. In answer then to Mr. Hume: As the queen's accusers did not chuse to produce this material witness, Paris, whom they had alive, and in their hands, nor any declaration or confession from him at the critical and proper time for having it canvassed by the queen, I apprehend our author's conclusion may fairly be used against himself; That it is in vain at present to support the improbabilities and absurdities in a confession, taken in a clandestine way, no body knows how; and produced after Paris's death, by no body knows whom; and from every appearance destitute of every formality requisite and common to such sort of evidence: For these reasons, I am under no sort of hesitation to give sentence against Nicolas Hubert's confession, as a gross imposture and forgery.

CHAP. VI.

Having examined the evidences that were produced by the earls of Murray and Morton, and secretary Lethington, for proving queen Mary guilty of the crimes with which that Confederacy accused her; we have attempted to prove, that these evidences, so far from being sufficient to make out the accusation, were themselves false and forged. This, if we have succeeded in, according to the judgment of monsieur Bayle (a judge, who has shewn himself, by his writings, no ways prejudiced in favour of Mary) should determine the question, not only that the queen is innocent, but moreover that her accusers themselves must be guilty. Plain however as this consequence is, let us, to please the curious, go a step further, and try, if it is possible, even at this day, by direct evidence, to trace the footsteps of any of those dark, daring, and subtle geniuses, in the bloody scene of Darnley's death, thro' the thick cloud in which they have enveloped themselves.

The queen's accusation against her bastard brother the earl of Murray, and his confederates, was, in general, "That they themselves were the inventors, conspirators, and some of them the executors of the murder of the king."[28]

Now, before we enter into the defence made to this accusation, the following two points, which I think do both naturally result from the queen's accusation, will, I hope, be readily granted.

---

[28] Cot. lib. Good., vol. 2. p. 298.

First, That if the queen had made good this accusation, and proved, that the accusers themselves, Murray, Morton, and Lethington, had been in the conspiracy and execution of the king's murder: In that case, she herself could not have been in that confederacy, or guilty of the murder. This I take to be consistent with common sense and reason.[29]

Secondly, I presume it will likewise be granted, that as this triumvirate, Murray, Morton, and Lethington, had been from the beginning, equally embarked in the same cause; as they had with one voice publicly accused their sovereign of the above crimes, and pretended to bring proof of their accusation; and as they had, by that means, deprived her of her crown, and possessed themselves of the government of her kingdom: If, I say, the queen could have proved that these joint accusers, or any of them, had themselves been the authors or contrivers of the King's death, in that case the whole triumvirate, as *socii criminis,* must one and all of them be deemed guilty, as accessories to the murder.

These two points being allowed, let us now turn to the other side, and hear what defence Murray and his associates have made for themselves, and what has been said for them by the writers upon their side, in answer to the queen's accusation.

The answer made by Murray and his associates to the queen's accusation, was in these general terms: "That they deny they were culpable thereof."

Mr. Hume argues thus in their defence against the above accusation:

"The queen's accusation coming so late, can only be regarded as an angry retaliation upon her enemy: Unless (adds this gentleman) we take this angry accusation of Mary's to be an argument of Murray's guilt, *there remains not the least presumption,* which should lead us to suspect him to have been an accomplice in the crime. – Murray could have had no motives to commit that crime. – The king's murder, indeed, procured him the regency; but much more queen Mary's ill conduct, which he could not foresee."[30]

The dissertator argues thus on the same side:

"Murray, on the queen's return to Scotland, served her with great fidelity, and, by his prudent administration, rendered her so popular, and so powerful, as enabled her with ease to crush a formidable insurrection raised by himself in the year 1565. What motive could induce Murray to murder a prince, without capacity, without followers, without influence? It is difficult

[29] Dr. Robertson uses the very same argument in his vindication of the Earl of Murray. Diss. p. 4.

[30] Hume, vol. 2. p. 500.

to conceive what Murray had to fear from the King's life. It is no easy matter to guess what he could gain by his death.[31] – If Murray had instigated Bothwell to commit the crime, or had himself been accessory to it, what hopes was there, that Bothwell would silently bear, from a fellow-criminal, all the persecutions which he suffered, without retorting upon him the accusation, or revealing the whole scene of iniquity?[32] Or, is it probable that Murray would first raise Bothwell to supreme power, in hopes that afterwards he might crush him?"[33]

Such is the answer, such the defence made by the writers on Murray's side of the question to the queen's general accusation of him and his associates.

We are here amused with fine-spun arguments *a priori*, endeavouring to overturn facts by inferences, from the unreasonableness of the motives productive of these facts. Were the certainty of events to be determined only by an induction of probable causes, there must be an end of all historical faith, we must doubt of every thing that does not fall under the direct conviction of our own eyes. Dr Robertson asks, What motive could induce Murray to murder Darnley? His friend Mr. Hume shall answer him, *It was to procure himself the regency.* But after all, this sort of reasoning by inference, can have no place here. It is by direct evidence, that we are to endeavour to prove the queen's accusation against Murray and his confederates, Morton and Lethington; and in the same way only, must the advocates for them be allowed to make their defence. ...

POSTSCRIPT.

Mr Hume, in the last edition of his History of England, published within these few months, has made the following attack upon the Inquirer.[34]

"I believe" (says the Historian) "there is no reader of common sense, who does not see, from the narrative, in the text, that the author means to say, that Queen Mary refuses constantly to answer before the English commissioners, but offers only to answer in person before Q. Elizabeth in person, contrary to her practice during the whole course of the conference, till the moment the evidence of her being an accomplice in her husband's murther

---

[31] Strange reasoning this, when we shall see by and by, that Murray's insurrection in the 1565, was to murder Darnly, and to imprison the queen for life.

[32] We shall afterwards show in what manner Bothwell was allowed to escape, for fear of revealing the black scene against his accomplices.

[33] Dissertation, p. 3.

[34] Hume's history, quarto edition, 1770, vol. 5. p. 152. note, p. 533.

is unexpectedly produced. It is true, the author having repeated four or five times an account of this demand of being admitted to Elizabeth's presence, and having express'd his opinion, that, as it had been refused from the beginning, even before the commencement of the conferences, she did not expect it would now be complied with; thought it impossible his meaning could be misunderstood, (as indeed it was impossible,) and not being willing to tire his reader with continual repetitions, he mentions in a passage or two, simply, that she had refused to make any answer. I believe also, there is no reader of common sense who peruses Anderson or Goodall's collections, and does not see, that, agreeably to this narrative, Q. Mary insists unalterably and strenuously on not continuing to answer before the English commissioners, but insists to be heard in person, by Q. Elizabeth in person; though once or twice, by way of bravade, she says simply, that she will answer and refute her enemies, without inserting this condition, which still is understood. But there is a person, that has wrote an *Enquiry historical and critical into the evidence against Mary Queen of Scots*, and has attempted to refute the foregoing narrative. *He quotes a single passage* of the narrative in which Mary is said simply to refuse answering; and then a *single passage from Goodall*, in which she boasts simply that she will answer; and he very civilly and almost directly calls the author a lyar, on account of this pretended contradiction. That whole Enquiry, from beginning to end, *is composed of such scandalous artifices; and from this instance*, the reader may judge of the *candour, fair dealing, veracity, and good manners of the Enquirer*."

This is a very heavy impeachment against the Inquirer, and delivered in terms very inconsistent with Mr Hume's complaint upon the head of incivility and good manners, or with that treatment which one gentleman ought to expect from another. If the Inquirer has, in these respects, been deficient to Mr Hume, (of which he is not at all sensible), that gentleman has now very amply retorted upon him. Who could have suspected the cool Philosopher to be so conversant in terms of the grossest and most illiberal abuse?

This small Essay took its rise from notes which the author, in the course of his reading, had made, with no other view than for his own amusement, and to enable him to form a judgement of a point which he had considered as a historical problem. When he was induced to put these strictures into their present form, and to allow them to be made public, he was sensible of the difficult task he had undertaken. To canvass a disputed point, which perhaps, even at this day, with some narrow minds, involved a notion of party-spirit, was not his greatest embarrassment. He found himself obliged to examine, with freedom, the opinion of authors of weighty authority; of living authors. He imagined he saw sufficient reasons to differ widely in sentiment from these authors; to believe, that even a writer, generally unquestioned in candour, might, in the ardour of supporting a favourite and popular side of a question, have shut his eyes against the light. Here was the Inquirer's difficulty. The love of truth demanded, that nothing should be palliated in an investigation of this kind; at the same time, he knew well, that, from the weakness of human nature, there was scarce a disputant who could separate the idea of an antagonist from that of a foe, or who could coolly suffer even the apprehension of losing any part of that universal deference which he was persuaded he merited. This consideration was an incitement to the Inquirer, to consider well the grounds of the controversy, to review his own arguments, and to be cautious even in the manner of dressing and advancing them. This caution he flattered himself he had never departed from; and indeed the indulgent approbation of the public had almost set his mind at ease upon that score. – He now, however, at this late period, finds he has been mistaken; and that his early fears were but too well grounded.

The author of the History of England, so often mentioned in this Inquiry, has now for many years, with regard to this Essay, preserved a profound silence. But it would seem, that all this while he has been meditating vengeance: he has now stept out into the world, and aimed a deadly thrust at the Inquiry and its author.

The whole book, says the Historian, from beginning to end, is composed of scandalous artifices, foul dealing, want of candour, veracity, and good manners.

After a sentence of this kind, what remains for the Inquirer? This supreme judge of literary merit, has pronounced sentence with that confidence which mocks all appeal.

The Inquirer, however, believes his cause to be subjected to another, and rather a higher tribunal, than this author's court of judicature. Let not that gentleman, intoxicated as he seems to be with popular applause, assume the character and style of infallible director of opinion, nor presume to wrest from that public, to whose indulgent favour he owes the credit he has obtained, the right which they have of judging for themselves. Had the Historian's judgement of the Inquiry been equitable, he would have found his opinion long ere now justified by the concurring sentiments of the public on his side: but that these sentiments have not concurred with him he seems tacitly to acknowledge, when now, at the distance of a dozen of years since the offence, he deigns (contrary to his conduct with his other opponents) to take the offender out of the hands of the public, and to pronounce sentence himself.

To the impartiality of that public the Inquirer now enters his appeal; and to their judgement he shall submit the examination of this late manifesto of the Historian, leaving them to apply the above heavy epithets of *scandalous artifice, want of candour, veracity, and good manners*, to whom they shall be found properly to belong.

And now as to Mr Hume's manifesto:

There is no reader of common sense, says he, who does not see from his narrative in the text, that the Historian means to say, that Queen Mary constantly refuses to answer before the English commissioners, but offers to answer only in person before Queen Elizabeth in person. – That the Historian, continues he, having often repeated Queen Mary's demand of being admitted to Queen Elisabeth's presence, – and being unwilling to tire his reader with continual repetitions of this demand, mentions in a *passage or two simply*, that she refused to make any answer.

Upon this, says our Historian, the author of the Inquiry has attempted to refute his narrative, by *quoting* the above *single passage* from his history, in which Queen Mary is said simply to refuse answering; – and in opposition to that, quoting a *single passage* from Goodall, in which she boasts simply, that she will answer; and on account of this contradiction, the author of the Inquiry almost directly calls him a lyar. – This is the charge against the Inquirer.

One would have thought, that when the Historian ventured thus to pledge his credit with the public, by taking upon him to condemn a book, as composed of *scandalous artifices*, and destitute of *candour* and *truth*, from one single instance, in which he asserts, upon his own word, that the author had not quoted him fairly; – one would have thought, that the Historian should undoubtedly have been sure of the fact. Is the fact then so as he is pleased to aver? – Has the Inquirer taken hold of this single passage from Mr Hume's history, wherein he says Queen Mary refused simply to answer, without repeating her request of being admitted to Queen Elisabeth's presence? – The Inquirer does aver, that it is not so.

He has not quoted a single or detached passage from him; on the contrary, he has quoted almost the whole of the Historian's narrative concerning Queen Mary's refusal to answer, and likewise her request to be present at the trial of her cause, and that, too, in the Historian's own words. In his quotation, he particularly mentions the grounds upon which that author says Queen Mary's commissioners founded their refusal to answer. The reader is referred to the whole quotation; part of which shall here be repeated. –

"When the charge," says Mr Hume, "or accusation against Queen Mary was given in, – her commissioners absolutely refused to return any answer; and they grounded their silence on very extraordinary reasons. They had orders, they said, from their mistress, if any thing was advanced that might touch her honour, not to make any defence, as she was a sovereign princess, and could not be subject to any tribunal; *and they required that she should previously be admitted to Elizabeth's presence.*"[35] –

Thus runs the quotation through every edition of the Inquiry.

The Inquirer shall now proceed to show in what manner Mr Hume's narrative, as above, was opposed.

[35] p. 65. of this Inquiry.

In the first edition of the Inquiry, to the Historian's narrative was opposed verbatim the declaration of Queen Mary's commissioners on the 25th of December 1568; wherein they declare, by her special command, That she would answer to Murray's accusation; and for that purpose, they desire to have the writings that he had produced against her: and neither the Queen in her letter, nor the commissioners, mention any request from her of being admitted to Queen Elisabeth's presence. This, the Historian is pleased to say, was only a bravade of Mary. – It may be so: but this is only his conjecture; it might as probably have been otherwise; that could only have been determined by Queen Mary herself, as it lay in her own breast. But it is to be observed, on the other hand, that the letter, containing the above declaration, was the very last which Queen Mary wrote during the conferences. This, the author of the Inquiry apprehends, was a fair authority, and, for the above reason, might very properly be quoted against Mr Hume. However, to give full scope to the Historian's argument, the Inquirer, in his second, and in this edition, has omitted the above declaration: and he opposes the Historian's narration, by referring the reader to the abstract of the whole procedure in the conferences,[36] which he had recently, and in the immediately preceding pages, given. What must show to the conviction of every reader the candid intention of the Inquirer, and that he had not the most remote design of concealing any part of the Historian's argument, (as indeed he had no reason), he, immediately after the above general reference, fully and fairly states the whole of his argument, and every branch of it;[37] a part of which he shall here repeat. –

"Mr Hume's evasion is, 1*st*, That Mary had insisted to confront, personally, Murray and Morton, her accusers, in presence of Elisabeth, the whole English nobility, and foreign ministers; which," Mr Hume is pleased to say, "was such a request as could not be granted: 2*dly*, That this request being refused, Mary's commissioners had protected against all further procedure," &c.

The author of the Inquiry hopes he hath sufficiently vindicated himself from Mr Hume's accusation, by disapproving his averment: On that averment, and the gross abuse attending it, the Inquirer shall make no reflections, but leave it to the public to determine who is best intitled to bring the accusation of want of fair dealing and good manners.

The author of the Inquiry shall now, in his turn, enter a little more minutely into the examination of the Historian's proposition; from which he has inferred,

---

[36] Inquiry, p. 69.

[37] Ibid. p. 70. & 71.

that Queen Mary *absolutely refused* to answer Murray's accusation, and recoiled from the inquiry.

Queen Mary's commissioners, our Historian says, absolutely refused to return an answer to Murray's charge or accusation; and they required, that she should previously be admitted to Elizabeth's presence; to whom, and to alone, she was determined to justify her innocence; – and that they finally broke off the conferences, and never would make any reply.

Here I beg leave to stop him, to tell him civilly, that he is in a mistake. Queen Mary, it is granted, at first, sensible of Elisabeth's gross partiality, did refuse to answer the charge or accusation. But she thought better on it; and afterwards, not only offered to answer the charge conditionally as above, but actually did give in her answer; to which I beg leave to refer the reader, Inquiry, p. 44.

The Historian perhaps will say, that Queen Mary refused to answer to the *proof* of the charge, that is, *the letters*. – How could she, unless she was allowed to see them? She often requested to *see these writings*, for the express purpose of answering them.

But, it is said, she annexed to her offer to answer, a demand which, she was sensible, could not be granted. – For what reason could not her demand be granted? Was it impossible? – It shall be allowed, that an offer to perform a thing under a condition which is impossible, resolves into an absolute refusal. But is this the case of Queen Mary's conditional demand, of being admitted to Queen Elisabeth's presence, as her accusers had been? Was this impossible? Was it even unreasonable? On the contrary, I apprehend it was absolutely necessary. What was the meaning of Queen Mary's demand? She was accused of very high crimes, which were offered to be proved by letters said to be of her own hand-writing. Her demand was, to appear personally, in defence and vindication of what was more valuable to her than life, her honour and reputation, not to mention her kingdom. Was it ever heard of in the annals of any civilized nation, that a person could be tried for life or property in absence? – When Queen Mary demanded that she might be present, what was she to do? Why, to hear, and see with her own eyes, what evidence her accusers were to produce against her; to have inspection of these letters, which she exclaimed to the whole world were forged by these very accusers. – Letters, it is true, may be compared, and the similarity of hand-writings guessed at, by third parties; but will it be maintained, that any person could supply the place of Mary herself for detecting forged letters said to be written by herself?

But, says our Historian, Queen Mary had before this time made the same request to come before Elizabeth, and was refused;[38] and thence it is inferred, that she had no reason to think, that Elizabeth would alter her resolution. –

---

[38] Hume's Hist. vol. 2. p. 496.

Why not? When Mary, upon Queen Elisabeth's proposal, consented to have her cause treated in the way of conference, as she herself was not allowed to see Elizabeth, she insisted with that princess, and got her "promise, that during this conference the Erle of Murray, principal of the rebels, should not come in to the presence of Queen Elisabeth, no more than Queen Mary; and yet, (complains Mary), on the contrair, he is received and welcomed by her, and we, ane free princess, have not access to answer for ourselves, as he and his accomplices."[39]

But again: It was said by Queen Elisabeth, that it was inconsistent with her honour to admit Mary to her presence till she could clear herself of the crimes imputed to her.[40] – This was surely very squeamish in this virgin Queen: but where was her delicacy, nay, let me ask, what became of her honour, and her honesty, when she broke through a solemn promise, and admitted into her presence, both publicly and in private, the declared rebels, and usurpers of the crown of her sister Queen? When she cherished persons accused of the murder of their King? And of which crime two of them, Morton and Lethington, were afterwards tried and convicted by their peers. Such were the persons whom this high and mighty Queen, of such punctilious honour, such nice and delicate feelings, exerted her utmost endeavours, by threats and promises, even when the matter in dispute was submitted to her as a judge, to incite and instigate, from being at first defendants, on Queen Mary's complaint against them, as rebels and usurpers, to turn accusers against her. Fy upon it! Fy upon it!

I shall now conclude, by bringing the argument to a very narrow point.

Let me suppose, that Queen Mary's request, to be admitted to Queen Elisabeth's presence, had appeared unreasonable or improper, and therefore was refused. Was that a good reason for refusing her request to see the letters? If, after inspecting the evidence against her, Queen Mary had remained silent, and made no answer, the consequence is plain, the letters must have been held as genuine, and she stood convicted to Queen Elisabeth, and the whole world, by her own letters. On the other hand, I apprehend, unless a good reason can be shown for refusing Mary's request to see the letters, that refusal is equally decisive of the question in her favour. I call upon Mr Hume, therefore, and desire him, with all his ingenuity, to give me a solid reason for Elisabeth's refusing to allow Queen Mary to see these letters. I will venture to say, that only one reason, consistent with common sense, can be given, which is this, That Queen Elisabeth, and the penetrating Cecil, saw or suspected a forgery; and by the many shifts which, through the whole course of the conferences, were devised to elude a scrutiny, and inspection of these letters, it is apparent they

[39] Goodall, vol. 2. p. 184.

[40] Hume's Hist. vol. 2. p. 501.

were resolved to guard against a detection: and to close the scene, and to prevent Queen Mary from ever getting a sight of this forged evidence, they took a very effectual way, by dismissing Murray, and them together, from the conferences. To this let me join the proof which has lately been brought by Goodall against the letters, which, I am warranted to say, in the opinion of many of the first critics of the age, does clearly demonstrate the forgery.

In short, I make no scruple to affirm, that our Historian's proposition, upon which he condemns Queen Mary, as recoiling from the inquiry, is false, that it has not a foot to stand on, and therefore must fall to the ground. I shall not, in Mr Hume's language, very unbecoming a gentleman, call it *foul dealing*, and a *scandalous artifice*; but I will venture to say, that, by as glaring a sophism as ever was used, he has converted a positive offer, under a condition reasonable, equitable, and necessary, into an absolute refusal.

As to the veracity and candour of the Historian, the Inquirer, without going beyond the subject in hand for examples, shall mention a few facts, and leave the reader to make his own reflections.

In the first place, The Inquirer does say, That the detail which our Author has given of the conferences is contradicted by the records, almost in every line. – The Inquirer shall not speak without book.

Queen Mary, says our Historian, absolutely refused to make answer to Murray's accusation. – See the answers given in by her to the English commissioners, p. 44. of this Inquiry.

Queen Mary's commissioners, says he, finally broke off the conferences, and never would make any reply.[41] – See a confutation of this, and the procedure of the parties after the protest of Mary's commissioners of the 3rd of December, pages 29. and 30 of this Inquiry; and continuation of the conferences, from the 25th of December, when Queen Mary's commissioners resumed them, pages 41. 42. and 43. to the 13th of January, which were frequent and full, until Murray and his accomplices withdrew themselves.

And, lastly, According to the Historian, Mary's accusation of Murray and his party was made by her, after all the conferences were broke off, and was only an angry retaliation, extorted from her by Murray's complaint.[42] – Did not the Author's prejudice blind him, he might with greater reason and truth have said, that Murray's accusation was extorted from him after Mary had exposed his rebellious practices before the commissioners at York, and refuted every argument offered in his defence, even according to our Author's own opinion.[43] But as to the point of fact asserted by our Author, That Mary's accusation of Murray and his party was made by her after all the conferences

---

[41] Hume's history, vol. 2. p. 498. first edit.

[42] Hume's history, vol. 2. p. 501. first edit.

[43] Ibid. p. 494.

were broke off: It is denied. Perhaps our Author will say, this is almost directly saying, it is a lie. I shall not say so: but if the records directly contradict his assertion, who is to blame? – Let us see how the facts as to this stands.

On Murray's accusation being given in on the 26th of November, and a copy given to Mary's commissioners, they, upon the 1st of December, assert, "That Murray and his partisans had invented this accusation for maintenance of their own treason; and that, when the cause should be farther tried, it would be proved, that some of the accusers were the inventors, and privy to the making bonds for the conspiracy of the death of the Lord Darnley; – and they begged, that the accusers might be arrested until the end of the cause."[44]

After this, we see Queen Mary herself, in almost every paper, and her commissioners, in her name, to the very end of the conferences, in January, insisting in her accusation of Murray and his party; and that, if time were allowed her, she would prove that accusation.

So much on the point of veracity. – With regard to the candour of our Historian, the Inquirer submits the following instances.

Our Author, in arguing in support of the letters as genuine, has this remark: – "In writing the first letter, which," says he, "was penned by the Queen, late at night, her paper failed her, and she takes down a memorandum of what she intended to add next morning; and it is accordingly added. – This," says he, "is a circumstance very particular, and not likely to occur to any person who would forge these letters."[45]

The Inquirer, in the first edition of his book, challenged this observation of our Author as contrary to fact; and he proved, that the passage in the Queen's letter referred to, did not contain one word which had the least relation to the memorandums, unless in one particular.

The Historian, sensible that he had no ground for his assertion, was pleased, in his second and after editions, to drop the whole of this argument, by leaving it out altogether. Was that sufficient? Ought he not to have acknowledged his error, to call it no worse?

In support of Hubert's confession, the Historian, in his first edition, asserted, 1*st*, That it was certainly a regular judicial confession, i.e. taken in the presence of a judge; – 2*dly*, That it was produced by Mary's accusers judicially against her: From which he concluded, that Queen Mary, if she was innocent, ought, at the time that it was judicially produced, to have canvassed this confession.[46]

The Inquirer, in the first edition of his book, detected the above assertions of our Author, and brought a full proof of their falsity, – and that the Queen never saw this confession. – What was the consequence? Let the boasted

---

[44] See p. 25. of the Inquiry.

[45] Hume's history, vol. 2. first edit. 4to, p. 498.

[46] History of England, first edition, 4to, p. 500.

candour of our Historian now speak out? No! his candour was asleep on this occasion. He chose silently to withdraw the whole of these assertions in his future editions. But let me ask, although the pride of an author would not suffer him to acknowledge those errors to the person who had detected them, in consistency with honour, was not something due to the public, and to the possessors of his first edition?

Upon this head, it might be asked of our Author, whether he himself seriously believes, that Hubert's confession is really genuine? But as it is not expected that he will answer this question, we refer the reader to the detection of that forged evidence in chap. 3. of the foregoing sheets.

Indeed the whole of our Author's plan for condemning Queen Mary unheard, is most uncandid, to say no worse of it. – Because she, in the beginning, sensible of Elisabeth's partiality, broke off the conferences; yet although she resumed them, our Author, taking her at her first word, rejects her remonstrances, and stifles the whole procedure after this on Mary's part, while he takes care to give a minute detail of the evidence poured in against her on the other side; and from thence draws a conclusion, which, in my humble opinion, does very little credit, either to his moral sentiments of equity as a judge, or to his feelings as a man. – Were Queen Mary's objections, says he, to the evidence produced against her, ever so specious, they cannot *now* be hearkened to, "since she did in effect ratify the evidence, by recoiling from the inquiry, at the critical moment, and refusing to given an answer to the accusation of her enemies."

Unfortunate Mary! Hard has been thy fate: condemned at first unheard, upon evidence which thou wert not allowed to see! And now a second time brought to trial, and condemned for not answering to that evidence! – Hard is thy fate on another account. – Had those talents, and that ingenuity, which have of late been displayed against thee, been as forcibly exerted *in thy favour*, how would thy cause have shone forth, and, like lightning, blasted all opposition? – Let not, however, the injured Mary be dismayed, nor sink under the dread of her formidable opponents; weak as her present advocate may be, she has a much more powerful one, Truth! Truth may for a time be overpowered, but at length will prevail; and although, according to the old sage, she often lies buried at the bottom of a well, yet Time will find her out, and usher her into light.

The Inquirer, after all, shall not, according to the manner of our Historian, say, that his history, from beginning to end, is of a piece. He is far from thinking so: although the Inquirer, by taking another period of it in hand, might perhaps shew the same systematic perversity in our Author; yet it is sufficient to the present purpose to say, that of the unfortunate Queen Mary he has painted a most foul picture. He has thrown out almost every grace from his canvas, and overcharged and distorted every feature. In place of a portrait, he has given us a false, hideous, and unnatural caricatura.

To conclude: The Inquirer hopes he has sufficiently vindicated himself from the violent attack and illiberal abuse thrown out against him by the Historian. – He is pleased to say, That the Inquirer almost directly called him a lyar. The Inquirer appeals to his book for the contrary. If many of the facts advanced by the Historian are contradicted by the authorities cited by the Inquirer, who is in the fault? Was he to compliment him at the expence of truth? He has kept strictly to his plan through the whole of his book, and he has not gone a foot out of his way to attack Mr Hume: he has studied to avoid abuse; sensible, that where-ever recourse is had to this weapon, it is a certain sign of a tottering cause. The Historian, if he chuses, may apply this to himself. He has on many occasions pleaded the cause of liberty against intolerant principles; of the freedom of attack even of first principles: But let us ask him, Had any of his opponents attacked him in the same abusive and illiberal way he now does the Inquirer, in what contempt would he have held him? what airs of superiority would he have given himself? – The Inquirer does not assume the high tone either of Historian or Philosopher: all he pretends to is that of a reader, who may, and will, think for himself. He wrote neither for money nor for applause. – If the Historian shall point out to him any one circumstance in which he is wrong, either in fact or argument, he will, with great frankness, retract and acknowledge his error: but as he is a free subject, – *no man's heir or slave*, – our Author will find it not so easy a matter to convince him in any other way.

Edinburgh, September 1771.

11
ANNUAL REGISTER

Review of Hume's *History of England* in *Annual Register for the year 1761*, December 1761, Vol. 4, pp. 301–304.
Selections.

The *Annual Register* was a yearly serial publication initiated in 1758 by publisher Robert Dodsley at the suggestion of Irish-born philosopher and statesman Edmund Burke (1729–1797). For several years Burke was the editor and principal contributor. It appeared in two volumes each year; the first summarized historical events of the previous year, and the second discussed a range of popular topics and included some book reviews. The *Annual Register* for the year 1761 contains a review of the final instalment of Hume's *History*. The reviewer – possibly Burke himself – praises the earlier volumes of Hume's *History* and says that it has elevated British history writing to the level of the French, and he finds a natural flow to the various volumes of the work in the reverse-chronological order in which they appeared. "No man," says the reviewer, "perhaps has come nearer to that so requisite and so rare a quality in an historian of unprejudiced partiality." The remainder of the review is a quotation from Hume's narrative of Becket. Included below is the entirety of the reviewer's comments; Hume's narrative of Becket is omitted, except for the beginning and ending sentences. For a discussion of Burke's assessment of Hume see the entry on Robert Bisset's 1798 *Life of Edmund Burke*, contained later in this collection.

The history of England, from the invasion of Julius Cæsar to the Accession of Henry VII. In two vols. By David Hume. Printed for A. Millar.

Our writers had commonly so ill succeeded in history, the Italians and even the French had so long continued our acknowledged superiors, that it was almost feared that the British genius, which had so happily displayed itself in every other kind of writing, and had gained the prize in most, yet could not enter the lists in this. The historical work Mr. Hume first published, discharged our country from this opprobrium.

This very ingenious and elegant writer is certainly a very profound thinker. The idea of the growth, as I may call it, of our present constitution seems to be the principle of the whole work compleated by the part now published, which is written in the same bold masterly manner as the two formerly published; and though in point of time it precedes them, is possibly, in reason, but a consequence of the other two; and the three parts, we imagine, may with propriety enough be read in the order the ingenious author has chosen to publish them.

It is natural that the line, which is always kept to its utmost length, must break at last; and probably in its recoil hurt them who endeavour to keep it at full stretch; and so it fared with the Stuarts, who, we imagine with this ingenious author, erred not so much in extending the prerogative, as in not having had sagacity enough to see that they had fallen in the times, when, from the opinions and fashions of the age, it behoved them to slacken and remit of the authority exercised by their predecessors.

The second work, which appeared, certainly shewed that the Tudors had not left it in the power of any other family to carry the prerogative higher than they had done. They left it to their successors, adorned and supported with every sanction, which custom, and which, in many cases, legal institution, could give it.

The third part seems to evince, that this pitch, which the prerogative had attained, was not the effect of the abilities, or the violence, of this or that family, so much as the natural course of things.

If the periods of the history first published interested our passions more, the curiosity of the learned will be more gratified in that now before us. It will be curious to observe from what a strange chaos of liberty and tyranny, of anarchy and order, the constitution, we are now blessed with, has at length arisen: in his appendixes is much curious matter of some things, as the odd fines paid the crown for protection to great men in palpable injustices, which the author might think did not suit the dignity of history, and has therefore thrown them into an appendix. Yet, with deference to so learned and sensible a writer, we think some matters, as the history of the Wittangemot, might in his hands have appeared to advantage in the text, and have relieved the reader in a period, where the recital of uninteresting facts seems to demand some argumentative or discussive matter to engage the attention, and so perhaps might the origin of the feudal law.

No man perhaps has come nearer to that so requisite and so rare a quality in an historian of unprejudiced partiality. As a strong instance of this, as well as a specimen of our author's fine writing, we insert the dispute of Henry II. with Thomas a Becket.

"Becket waited not till Henry should commence those projects against the ecclesiastical power, which, he knew, had been formed by that prince: He was himself the aggressor; and endeavoured to overawe the king by the intrepidity and boldness of his enterprizes. ...

... Henry therefore deemed it necessary to define with the same precision the limits of the civil power; to oppose his legal customs to their divine ordinances;

to determine the exact boundaries of the rival jurisdictions; and, for this purpose, he summoned a general council of the nobility and prelates at Clarendon, to whom he submitted this great and important question."

12
OWEN RUFFHEAD,
THE MONTHLY REVIEW

[Owen Ruffhead], review of *The History of England, from the Invasion of Julius Caesar to the Accession of Henry VII*, in *The Monthly Review*, December 1761, Vol. 25, pp. 401–414, and February 1762, Vol. 26, pp. 81–95. Complete review.

Owen Ruffhead (1723–1769) authored the *Monthly Review* article on Hume's 1759 instalment of the *History*. His review here, which opened the December 1761 and February 1762 issues, is equally flattering. He notes that, in previous volumes, Hume's "free and liberal cast of mind" has offended readers on all sides of the religious and political spectrum. However, Ruffhead feels that the remote periods covered in these volumes will "afford little matter to inflame zeal." Ruffhead criticizes Hume on several issues, and in several of these instances Hume altered subsequent editions of his *History*; footnotes at the appropriate locations below present Hume's modified wording. He concludes stating that these two volumes of Hume's *History* contain "the most just and masterly account of the reigns of our early Kings, that has hitherto been penned." One year after this review appeared, Ruffhead sent a letter to Hume with two detailed criticisms, one of which expands on a point that he makes in this review. In later years Hume was alerted to Ruffhead's authorship of reviews of the *History*, and Hume expressed his appreciation (see Ruffhead's 1763 letter to Hume included later in this collection).

The History of England, from the Invasion of Julius Caesar to the Accession of Henry VII. Vol. I. Containing the Reigns of the Princes before the Conquest, William the Conqueror, William Rufus, Henry I. Stephan, Henry II, Richard I, and John. By David Hume, Esq; 4to. Millar.[1]

This spirited and intelligent Writer has at length finished his retrograde progress, and has compleated the History of England from the invasion of

---

[1] Price of the two volumes, 1 l. 10 s. in boards.

Julius Caesar, to the reign of James II, inclusive.[2] In the preceding volumes, which comprized the reigns of the houses of Tudor and Stuart, our Historian had many difficulties to encounter, from the political prejudices, the party divisions, and the religious bigotry, which have occasioned such a contrariety of opinions, with regard to the transactions of those interesting periods. The reformation in religion, which took place under the Tudors, the frequent and important revolutions in government, which happened under the Stuarts, were events which have bred endless divisions and animosities among religious and political zealots: and Mr. Hume's free and liberal cast of mind, was ill adapted to reconcile their discordant principles. Little biassed by prejudice, a slave to no sect or party, he attacked both Papists and Protestants, Royalists and Republicans, who, each in their turns, suffered from the acuteness of his reflections, and the severity of his censures. Consequently, he has given frequent, and sometimes reasonable, cause of disgust to both sides, who, although obliged to confess the talents of the Writer, have joined in condemning the Historian.

But the passions and prejudices of the Reader are but slightly affected by the strange disorders and revolutions of those early ages, which furnish the contents of the present volumes; and which, though they yield abundant store to gratify curiosity, afford little matter to inflame zeal. They, however, who covet instruction as well as entertainment, will find it of the utmost importance to have studied these areas of the English History with care and attention. In these dark and remote periods, they will discover the substrata, whereon, by degrees, was established that firm basis, which upholds private property and supports personal freedom.

To throw light on the obscure pages of Antiquity, required all the knowlege and penetration by which our Author is distinguished. In explaining and unfolding the first rude principles of the constitution, he might, without offence, push the freedom of enquiry, and indulge that propensity to refinement, which is too frequently the failing of a bold and speculative mind. It must be observed, nevertheless, that the love of singularity has sometimes led him to oppose the concurrence of the best authorities; and, at others, to adopt hasty and peremptory conclusions, in some cases which are extremely dubious. We shall point out these instances with the less reserve, as we are persuaded that he has too just a sense of fame, to be flattered by undistinguished praise, and too much generosity to be offended at candid criticism.

Our Historian briefly relates the events attending the Roman conquest of this island, and hastens through the obscure, and what he, in our opinion, improperly calls uninteresting period of Saxon annals. He stops, however, very properly, to expatiate on the reign of Alfred the Great; and he has described the character and policy of that brave, wise and patriot Prince, with

---

[2] See Review, Vol. XII. p. 206. – Vol. XVI. p. 36. – Vol. XX. p. 344–400.

such a judicious and masterly pen, that we are sorry his reflections on this subject cannot be admitted without exceeding our limits.

Having gone through the reigns of the Saxon and Danish Princes, he gives, in an Appendix, a very curious, and in general just account of the Anglo-Saxon government and manners. His reflections, however, on the Saxon *Wittenagemot* seem liable to some objections.

"The Members, he observes, are almost always called the *Principes, Satrapae, Optimates, Magnates, Procures*; terms which seem to suppose an aristocracy, and to exclude the Commons. The boroughs also, from the low state of commerce, were so small and poor, and the inhabitants lived in such dependance on the great men, that it seems nowise probable they would be admitted as a part of the national councils. The Commons are well known to have had no share in the governments established by the Franks, Burgundians, and other northern nations; and we may conclude, that the Saxons, who remained longer barbarous and uncivilized than those tribes, would never think of conferring such an extraordinar privilege on trade and industry. The military profession alone was honourable among all those conquerors. The warriors subsisted by their possession in land; they became considerable by their influence over their vassals, retainers, tenants, and slaves: and it had need of strong proofs to convince us, that they would admit any of a rank so much inferior as the burgesses, to share with them in the legislative authority. Tacitus indeed affirms, that, among the antient Germans, the consent of all the members of the community was required in every important deliberation; but he speaks not of representatives; and this antient practice, mentioned by the Roman Historians, could only have place in small tribes, where every citizen might, without inconvenience, be assembled upon any extraordinarily emergency. After principalities became more extensive; after the difference of property had formed distinctions, more important than those arising from personal strength and valour; we may conclude, that the national assemblies must have been more limited in their number, and composed only of the more considerable citizens.

But though we must exclude the burgesses or commons from the Saxon Wittenagemot, there is some necessity for supposing, that this assembly consisted of other members beside the Prelates, Abbots, Aldermen, and the Judges or Privy Council. For as all these, excepting some of the Ecclesiastics, were antiently appointed by the King, had there been no other legislative authority, the royal power had been in a great measure despotic, contrary to the tenor of all the Historians, and to the practice of all the northern nations. We may therefore conclude, that the more considerable proprietors of land were, without any election, constituent members of the national assembly; and there is reason to think, that forty hides, or about four or five thousand acres, was the estate requisite for entitling the possessor to this honourable privilege. There is a passage of an antient Author from which it appears, that a person of very noble birth, even one allied to the crown, was not esteemed a *Princeps*, (the term usually employed by antient Historians when the Wittenagemot is mentioned) till he had acquired a fortune of that extent. Nor need we imagine, that the public Council would become disorderly or confused by admitting so great a multitude. The landed property of England was properly in few hands during the Saxon times; at least, during the latter part of that period: and as men had small ambition of attending these public Councils, there was no danger of the assembly's becoming too numerous for the dispatch of the little business which was brought before them."

It must be confessed, that Mr. Hume assigns very plausible reasons for supposing that the commons were excluded from the Saxon Wittenagemot, but they do not appear to us in any wise conclusive. He admits, that considerable proprietors of land were constituent members, without election; and he imagines, that forty hides of land was an estate requisite for this privilege. As our Historian does not cite any authority for this supposition, we are at a loss to conjecture on what ground he rests his opinion. A proprietor of forty hides must indeed have been a considerable landholder, since even five hides, held of the King himself, by personal attendance, was sufficient to gain the holder the honorary title of *King's Thane*. But we are not to conclude that none but the considerable proprietors were admitted to the Wittenagemot; neither are we to suppose, that the word *Thane* always implies nobility.[3] There were among the Saxons a species of tenants, called *middle Thanes*, otherwise *Vavasours*, who held their lands by a tenure which was of a feudal nature, but not honorary; and their lands, or vavasories, were held of some mesne Lord, and not immediately of the King. These *middle Thanes* seem to have been a distinct order from the *lesser Thanes*, who were a kind of honorary tenants, holding a certain quantity of land, together with some office in the King's court; the *greater Thanes*, being the Aldermen or Earls, who held of the King in chief, by a kind of grand serjeantry.[4] Now, it is probable, that the number of these *middle Thanes* was great; and that they made a part of the *Wittenagemot*, either personally, or, more probably, by their representatives. Our Historian's conclusion, that because the Saxons remained longer barbarous than other northern tribes, that therefore they must have excluded the Commons from a share in the government, is somewhat singular: since it is clear, from Tacitus,

[3] *Thane* sometimes denotes a Freeman, sometimes a Magistrate, and more properly an officer of the King.

[4] The King's Thanes had the power of holding courts, which were called Halymoots, which, at this day, are termed Courts Baron. We wonder our Historian, in speaking of the Saxon Courts, should have omitted taking notice of these Halymoots.

that in their most uncivilized state, the Commons among them had the chief share in government; and some well-known passages, in the Roman Historian, might almost justify our concluding, that they had the *sole legislative* power. Now, it is not probable, that a people, who were so free and important at home, would readily submit to such an exclusion in a country which they had helped to subdue; though it is likely, indeed, that their victorious leaders, when they had secured their conquests, might gradually advance prerogative above privilege. As to Mr. Hume's objection, that the boroughs were too small and poor to be admitted as a part of the national Councils, though it may serve to shew the weakness of their influence, it has very little weight to prove their total exclusion. Beside, this account of the state of the boroughs is not altogether consistent with what he advances in a note to the second Appendix, where he observes, on the authority of Brady, "That almost all the boroughs of England had suffered in the shock of the Conquest, and had *decayed extremely*, between the death of the Confessor, and the time when Doomsday was framed." From this note we may collect, that the boroughs among the Anglo-Saxons were not so poor as our Historian above represents them; at least, they were not inconsiderable enough to account for the exclusion of the Commons. But, in our opinion, there is an argument, which, though insisted on by an over zealous Republican, appears, among others which might be urged, to have great weight in proving the admission of the Burgesses among the Saxons: it being well known that there are many boroughs that send Members to Parliament, which cannot be shewn to have been of any repute since the Conquest, much less to have obtained any such privilege by the grant of any succeeding King; wherefore, their right must have accrued before the Conquest. But however we may differ from our Historian in this, and some other particulars[5] too minute for animadversion, it is with pleasure we acknowlege, that no account of the Anglo-Saxons, hitherto published, is so clear, intelligible and satisfactory, as this succinct Appendix, which treats of the first Saxon Government, – Succession of the Kings, – the Wittenagemot, – the Aristocracy, – the several Orders of Men, – Courts of Justice, – Criminal Law, – Rules of Proof, – Military Force, – Public Revenue, – Value of Money, – and lastly, of Manners.

Our Historian proceeds next, in order, to the reign of William the Conqueror, whom he thus characterizes:

"Few Princes have been more fortunate than this great Monarch, or were better entitled to grandeur and prosperity, from the abilities and the vigour

---

[5] For instance, we question our Historian's authority, when he says, that there is no mention of leases among the Saxons; for we read of leases among them, and of long terms too, not less than one hundred years. [In future editions of the *History* Hume altered the relevant sentence to read as follows: "For there is little mention of leases among the Anglo-Saxons...."]

of mind which he displayed in all his conduct. His spirit was bold and enterprising, yet guided with prudence. His ambition, which was exorbitant, and
lay little under the restraint of justice, and still less under that of humanity,
still submitted to the dictates of reason and sound policy. Born in an age
when the minds of men were intractable, and unacquainted with submission,
he was yet able, to direct them to his purposes; and partly from the ascendant
of his vehement character, partly from art and dissimulation, to establish an
unlimited authority. Though not insensible to generosity, he was hardened
against compassion; and he seemed equally ostentatious and ambitious of
eclat in his clemency and in his severity. The maxims of his administration
were austere; but might have been useful, had they been solely employed in
preserving order in an established government: they were ill calculated for
softening the rigours, which, under the most gentle management, are inseparable from conquest. His attempt against England was the last great enterprize of the kind, which, during the course of seven hundred years, has fully
succeeded in Europe; and the greatness of his genius broke through those
limits, which first the feudal institutions, then the refined policy of Princes,
have fixed to the several states of Christendom. Though he rendered himself
infinitely odious to his English subjects, he transmitted his power to his
posterity, and the throne is still filled by his descendants: a proof, that the
foundations which he laid were firm and solid, and that, amidst all his
violences, while he seemed only to gratify the present passion, he had still an
eye towards futurity."

This character of the Conqueror is bold, striking, and, upon the whole, just:
nevertheless, we are of opinion, that it is more owing to accident than the result
of policy, that the foundations laid by the Conqueror have proved firm and
solid. For it is certain that the Barons wars, which happily opened the road to
Liberty, were owing to his imprudent allotment of such immense possessions
to his followers.

But we must not omit our Historian's sentiments, with respect to William's
right to the title of Conqueror, as they are somewhat singular, and repugnant
to the most respectable authorities.

"Some Writers, says he, have been desirous of refusing to this Prince the title
of Conqueror, in the sense in which it is commonly understood; and under
pretence, that that word is sometimes, in old books, applied to such as
make an acquisition of territory by any means, they are willing to reject
Williams's title, by right of war, to the crown of England. It is needless to
enter into a controversy, which, by the terms of it, must necessarily degenerate into a dispute of words. It suffices to say, that the Duke of Normandy's
first invasion of the island was hostile; that his subsequent administration was
entirely supported by arms; that in the very frame of his laws he made a

distinction between the Normans and English, to the advantage of the former; that he acted, in every thing, as absolute master over the natives, whose interests and affections he totally disregarded; and that if there was an interval, when he assumed the appearance of a legal Magistrate, the period was very short, and was nothing but a temporary sacrifice, which he, as has been the case with most Conquerors, was obliged to make of his inclination to his present policy. Scarce any of those revolutions, which, both in history and in common language, have always been denominated conquests, appear equally violent, or have been attended with so sudden an alteration both of power and property. The Roman state, which spread its dominion over Europe, left the rights of individuals, in a great measure, untouched; and those civilized Conquerors, while they made their own country the seat of empire, found, that they could draw most advantage from the subject provinces, by bestowing on the natives the free enjoyment of their own laws and of their private possessions. The barbarians, who subdued the Roman empire, though they settled in the conquered countries, yet being accustomed to a rude uncultivated life, found a small part of the land sufficient to supply all their wants; and they were not tempted to seize extensive possessions, which they neither knew how to cultivate nor employ. But the Normans, and other foreigners, who followed the standard of William, while they made the vanquished kingdom the seat of empire, were yet so far advanced in arts as to be acquainted with the advantages of a large property; and having totally subdued the natives, they pushed the rights of conquest (very extensive in the eyes of avarice and ambition, however narrow in those of reason) to the utmost extremity against them. Except the former conquest of England by the Saxons themselves, who were induced, by peculiar circumstances, to proceed even to the extermination of the natives, it would be difficult to find in all history a revolution more destructive, or attended with a more compleat subjection of the antient inhabitants. Contumely seems even to have been wantonly added to oppression; and the natives were universally reduced to such a state of meanness and poverty, that the English name became a term of reproach, and several generations elapsed before one family of Saxon pedigree was raised to any considerable honours, or could so much as attain the rank of Barons of the realm. These facts are so apparent from the whole tenor of the English History, that none would have been tempted to deny or elude them, were they not heated by the controversies of faction; while one party were *absurdly* afraid of those *absurd* consequences, which they saw the other party inclined to draw from this event. But it is evident, that the present rights and privileges of the people, who are a mixture of English and Normans, can never be affected by a transaction, which passed seven hundred years ago; and as all antient Authors, who lived nearest the time, and knew best the state of the country, unanimously speak of the Norman dominion as a conquest by war and arms, no reasonable man, from the fear of imaginary consequences, will ever be tempted to reject their concurring and undoubted testimony."

We agree with our Historian, that no reasonable man will reject these testimonies, through fear of any consequences which may affect present rights and privileges; nevertheless, this is no pretence for admitting them, unless they deserve credit from their own weight; which, in our opinion, they do not. There is a material difference, as Lord Hale observes, between a conquest over the King and a conquest over the kingdom. William either had, or pretended to, a right of succession, from the Confessor, consequently could make no pretence to a conquest over the kingdom. As to his cruel treatment of the natives, he punished them in their persons and properties, not as enemies, but as rebels. It is plain that he did not pretend to acquire any thing *jure belli*; he confirmed the laws of the Confessor, and soon after the Conquest the charters of the antient Saxon Kings were pleaded and allowed. The famous records of Pinnenden and Sharbonne are, among others, proofs of such allowance. Though Mr. Hume, with regard to the latter, says that this paper, which was able to impose on such great Antiquarians as Spellman and Dugdale, is proved by Dr. Brady to have been a forgery.[6] But William likewise made several grants and charters for restoring the lands and goods which had been taken from the Bishopricks and Abbies; and it is evident from many authorities, that he never pretended any title to the lands of neuters: neither did William tyrannically and arbitrarily subject the nation to a feudal dependence. And this alteration which he made, so far from proving his right of conquest, shews the contrary: for the law which, in effect, introduces the feudal law runs thus: *Statuimus ut omnes liberi homines fœdere et sacramento affirment quod intra et extra universum regnum Angliæ,* WILLIELMO SUO DOMINO *fideles esse volunt,* &c. The terms of this law are absolutely feudal; and, as Wright takes notice, in his Tenures, the manner of penning it is observable: for it is penned as if the King was merely passive, the more clearly and fully to express the consent of the *Commune Consilium* to so considerable an alteration. In the language of the other laws of this King, it would have run, *Quod* NOBIS *fideles esse volunt,* &c. As to the Monkish Writers, though they evidently prove too much, consequently deserve little credit, when they say, speaking of the English, NEC UNUM *de illis pristina potestate uti permissum*; yet, admitting their relations of William's cruelty and oppression in their utmost extent, they by no means prove a right of conquest. If every Tyrant, Oppressor and Usurper, may

---

[6] This paper, if a forgery, imposed on others besides Spelman and Dugdale. See Hale's Hist. of Common Law; Wright's Tenures, Wilkin's Leg. Anglo-Sax. Bacon's Hist. of Eng. Gov. and Taylor's Hist. of Gov. Perhaps, it may be thought too hasty to reject such authorities on a single testimony: especially, as Brady is a professed Answerer, and, as such, partial and systematical.

be stiled a Conqueror, many of our early Kings have a claim to that title. On this foundation, Henry the IVth, Edward the IVth, and others, may be deemed Conquerors, as they exercised several acts of tyranny, cruelty and oppression, on those whom they subdued, and indeed over others. But not to insist farther on this point, we with pleasure return to our Historian: and as our limits will not allow us to attend him, in the order we could wish, we pass on to the reign of Henry the IId, where we find the following judicious and manly reflections on the murder of Becket.

"The Clergy, meanwhile, though their rage was happily diverted from falling on the King, were not idle in magnifying the sanctity of Becket; in extolling the merits of his martyrdom; and in magnifying him above all that devoted tribe, who, in several ages, had, by their blood, cemented the fabric of the Temple. Other Saints had only borne testimony, in their sufferings, to the general doctrines of Christianity; but Becket had sacrificed his life to the power and privileges of the Clergy; and this peculiar merit challenged, and not in vain, a suitable acknowledgment to his memory. Endless were the panegyrics on his virtues; and the miracles, operated by his relicts, were more numerous, more nonsensical, and more impudently attested, than those which ever filled the legend of any Confessor or Martyr. Two years after his death, he was canonized by Pope Alexander; a solemn jubilee was established for celebrating his merits; his body was removed to a magnificent shrine, enriched with presents from all parts of Christendom; pilgrimages were performed to obtain his intercession with heaven; and it was computed, that, in one year, above an hundred thousand pilgrims arrived in Canterbury, and paid their devotions at his tomb. It is indeed a mortifying reflection to those who are actuated by the love of fame, so justly denominated the last infirmity of noble minds, that the wisest legislator and most exalted Genius, that ever reformed or enlightened the world, can never expect such tributes of praise, as are lavished on the memory of a pretended Saint, whose whole conduct was probably, to the last degree, odious or contemptible, and whose industry was entirely directed to the pursuits of objects pernicious to mankind. It is only a Conqueror, a personage no less intitled to our hatred, who can pretend to the attainment of equal renown and glory."

These bold, and at the same time, just sentiments are worthy the pen of a Livy or a Tacitus; and they display that liberality and benevolence of mind, which must render the Author respectable in the opinion of every one, who dares to think freely, and who has strength to break asunder the fetters of religious and political bigotry. His reflection on Conquerors is keen and just, for in the eye of true wisdom, military heroism, so far from being a proof of magnanimity, is rather an indication of a narrow mind, which, for want of a more exalted sense of greatness, meanly places its glory in inhuman triumphs and savage skill. – Omitting the intermediate King, we proceed next to the reign of John.

Every one, the least acquainted with the English history, knows to what extremities King John was reduced by his struggle with the Pope, which at last brought on a heavy interdict on the kingdom. John for a long time remained obstinate, and the measures he took in opposition to the Pope are described by our Historian in the following lively and entertaining strain.

"The King, that he might oppose *his* temporal to *their* spiritual terrours, immediately, from his own authority, confiscated the estates of all the clergy who obeyed the interdict, banished the prelates, confined the monks to their convent, and gave them only such a small allowance from their estates, as would suffice to provide them in food and rayment. He treated with the utmost rigour all Langton's adherents, and every one that shewed any disposition to obey the orders of Rome: and that he might distress the clergy in the tenderest point, and at the same time expose them to reproach and ridicule, he threw into prison all their concubines, and required high fines and confiscations as the price of their liberty.

"After the canons, which established the celibacy of the clergy, were, by the zealous endeavours of Archbishop Anselm, more rigorously executed in England, the ecclesiastics gave, almost universally and avowedly, into the use of concubinage; and the court of Rome, which had no interest in prohibiting this practice, made a very slight opposition to it. The custom was become so prevalent, that some German synods, before the reformation, not only permitted, but, to avoid scandal, enjoined the use of concubines to the younger clergy; and it was usual every where for priests to apply to their ordinary, and obtain from him a formal liberty for this indulgence. The bishop commonly took care to prevent this practice from degenerating into licentiousness; he confined the priest to the use of one woman, required him to be constant to her bed, obliged him to provide for her subsistence and that of her children; and though the offspring was, in the eyes of the law, deemed illegitimate, this commerce was really a kind of inferior marriage, such as is still practised in Germany among the nobles, and may be regarded by the candid as an appeal, from the tyranny of civil and ecclesiastical institutions, to the more virtuous and more unerring laws of nature."

It must be allowed, that the Popes in these ages were, and still are, *for a valuable consideration*, very indulgent to their own, and to all orders of men: and, perhaps, among the rigid, our Historian may be deemed as liberal in principle, as the Romish church is in practice. He will probably meet with few who can conceive that the Laws of Nature can be "virtuous and unerring," when repugnant to civil and cannon discipline. But without farther comment on this passage, we will only observe, that the inferior marriages in Germany to which Mr. Hume alludes, are there called Left-handed marriages, and that there is this material difference between them and the ecclesiastical concubinage here spoken of. – That the children born of a German left-handed marriage are lawful, and entitled to all the rights of cognation, though not of agnation. These appear to be whimsical expedients of sacrificing natural affection and moral sentiment, to worldly views and political interests.

The contest between the king and the pope, it is well known turned out to the loss and dishonour of the sovereign, who finished an oppressive and inglorious reign of more than sixteen years, in the forty-ninth year of his age. His character is described by our Historian in strong and glowing colours. "The character of this prince is nothing but a complication of vices, equally mean and odious; ruinous to himself, and destructive to his people. Cowardice, inactivity, folly, levity, licentiousness, ingratitude, treachery, tyranny, and cruelty; all these qualities appear too evidently in the several incidents of his life, to give us any room to suspect that the disagreeable picture has been anywise overcharged by the prejudice of the antient Historians. It is hard to say, whether his conduct to his father, his brother, his nephew, or his subjects, was most culpable; or whether his crimes in these respects were not even exceeded by the baseness, which appeared in his transactions with the king of France, the pope, and the barons. His dominions, when they devolved to him by the death of his brother, were more extensive than have, ever since his time, been ruled by any English monarch; but he first lost by his misconduct the flourishing provinces in France, the antient patrimony of his family: he subjected his kingdom to a shameful vassalage under the see of Rome; he saw the prerogatives of his crown diminished by law, and still more reduced by faction; and he died at last, when in danger of being totally expelled by a foreign power, and of either ending his life miserably in prison, or seeking shelter as a fugitive from the pursuit of his enemies.

"The prejudices against this prince were so violent, that he was believed to have sent an embassy to the miramoulin or emperor of Morocco, and to have offered to change his religion and become Mohometan, in order to purchase the protection of that monarch. But though that story is told us, on plausible authority, by Matthew Paris, it is in itself utterly improbable, except that there is nothing so incredible as may not become likely from the folly and wickedness of John.

The monks throw great reproaches on this prince for his impiety and even infidelity; and as an instance of it, they tell us, that having, one day, caught a very fat stag, he exclaimed, *How plump and well fed is this animal, and yet I dare swear he never heard mass.* This sally of wit, upon the usual corpulency of the priests, more than all his enormous crimes and iniquities, made him pass with them for an atheist."

It is no wonder that in those days of superstition the clergy should deem this sarcasm atheistical; since, even in these enlightened times, *some* do not scruple to confound the cause of religion with the interests of their own order.

This volume concludes with a second appendix, concerning the fœdal and Anglo-Norman government and manners, under the following heads: – Origin of the feudal law. – Its progress. – Feudal government of England. – The feudal parliament. – The commons. – Judicial power. – Revenue of the crown. – Commerce. – The church. – Civil law. – Manners.

It required all the abilities of our Historian to furnish any thing new and entertaining on a subject, which has been so lately exhausted by writers of eminent talents, whom Mr. Hume mentions with all the generosity of true genius, which can distinguish between emulation and envy. To enter into a comment on this Appendix would lead us into too large a field for criticism; and, as disquisitions of this sort are chiefly calculated for the studious, would probably prove unentertaining to the generality of our Readers. Let it suffice to observe, that it contains a brief, ingenious, and intelligent account of the feudal system; though, in some particulars, liable to exception. We conceive, for instance, that he is mistaken, where he says that "The land was apprehended to be a species of *benefice*, which was the *original* conception of a feudal property." On the contrary, we may venture to assert, on the authority of Sir H. Spelman, that feuds did not take the denomination of *benefices*, till they were granted for life. At first they were given at will, and were called *Munera*, which seems more properly to be the original conception of feudal property.[7]

As to our Historian's style, it is so well known and so deservedly approved, that it is almost needless to say, it is close, nervous, and correct; though we may sometimes meet with those *maculae*, which, *incuria fudit*, and from which no human production is exempt. Thus when we read that PRINCE-OFFA made a vow of *virginity*, we apprehend that *continence* would be a more proper expression: as virginity is usually appropriated to denote maiden chastity.[8] We reserve the consideration of the next volume to the ensuing month.

—

The History of England, from the invasion of Julius Caesar, to the Accession of Henry VII. *Vol.* II. *Containing the reigns of Henry* III. *Edward* I. *Edward* II. *Edward* III. *Richard* II. *Henry* IV. *Henry* V. *Henry* VI. *Edward* IV. *Edward* V. *and Richard* III. By David Hume, Esq; 4to. Millar.

---

[7] [Hume revised this sentence in later editions to read "The land was still apprehended to be a species of benefice...."]

[8] [Hume revised this sentence in later editions to read "This last prince, having made a vow of chastity...."]

Having, in our account of the preceding volume,[9] delivered our sentiments concerning the manner of Mr. Hume's treating this early part of our History, we now with pleasure proceed to the consideration of the second volume, which opens with the reign of Henry III.

To the speculative and intelligent, the history of the reigns included in this volume, will prove extremely curious and interesting; though perhaps to the generality of readers it may appear dry and un-entertaining, in comparison with the reigns of the Tudors and the Stuarts, which, as they approach nearer to the present manners and customs, are more generally understood, and consequently more agreeable.

To enter into the rude policy of the feudal reigns, and to discover the principles which influenced the civil and military operations of our brave and unpolished ancestors, requires a deeper insight into antiquity, and a closer degree of application, than falls to the lot of our modern students, who delight in the flimsy productions of prostituted genius, constrained by necessity, or seduced by vanity, to flatter the prevailing depravity of taste, which seems to forebode the decline of literature.

If however, the admirers of modish ease and elegance, can for once bend their attention to subjects which require strength and solidity of judgment, they will find their labour amply repaid in the perusal of this history, wherein Mr. Hume has given a very clear and accurate account of the religion, laws, manners, and customs of those early times, with the state of trade and commerce, the value of money, and price of commodities, with such shrewd and suitable reflections upon the whole, at the end of each reign, as may enable the attentive reader to trace the gradual advances, by which we rose from a condition of hospitable[10] barbarism, to our present imperfect state of modern refinement.

The wars which Henry III waged against his Barons, and the consequences they produced, are well known. The King being defeated, was obliged to confirm the Great Charter, the corner stone of our liberties. The contest however between the King and his Nobles, seems to have been merely whether there should be one or many tyrants; for the people were alike oppressed by both; and though it is true, that the Great Charter contained some provisions in their favour, yet in those days, when power was the measure of right, they were not in a condition to render those provisions effectual. In short, this reign is almost a continued scene of tyranny, rapine, and violence: even the courtiers of the King's household, and men of title, were public robbers, and being

---

[9] See Rev. Dec. 1761.

[10] We say hospitable, because in those early times the doors of the nobility were in a manner open to all comers, and the member of their retainers, &c. is incredible. But this hospitality proves the dependence of the people, who in return for their subsistence, were in the most abject subjection to their lords.

convicted, said in their excuse, that "they received no wages from the King, and were obliged to rob for a maintenance." But no people were more cruelly oppressed at this time than the unhappy Jews.

"Interest," says our Historian, "had in that age mounted to an enormous height, as might be expected from the barbarism of the times and mens ignorance of commerce. There are instances of fifty per cent. paid for money. Such profits tempted the Jews to remain in England, notwithstanding the grievous oppressions to which they were continually exposed from the prevalent bigotry and rapine of the age. It is easy to imagine how precarious their state must be under an indigent prince, somewhat restrained in his tyranny over his native subjects, but who possessed an unlimited authority over them, the sole proprietors of money in the kingdom, and hated on account of their riches, their religion, and their usury: Yet will our ideas scarce come up to the extortions which in fact we shall find to have been practiced upon them. In the year 1241, 20,000 marks were exacted from them: two years after money was again extorted, and one Jew alone, Aaron of York, was obliged to pay above 4000 marks: in 1250, Henry renewed his oppressions; and the same Aaron was condemned to pay him 30,000 marks upon an accusation of forgery: the high penalty imposed upon him, and which, it seems, he was thought able to pay, is rather a presumption of his innocence than of his guilt. In 1255, the King demanded 8000 marks from the Jews, and threatened to hang them, if they refused compliance. They now lost all patience, and desired leave to retire with their effects out of the kingdom. But the King replied, 'How can I remedy the oppressions you complain of? I am myself beggared. I am despoiled, I am stripped of all my revenues: I owe above 200,000 marks; and if I had said 300,000, I should not exceed the truth: I am obliged to pay my son, prince Edward, 15,000 marks a year: I have not a farthing; and I must have money, from any hand, from any quarter, or by any means.' He then delivered over the Jews to the earl of Cornwal, that those whom the one brother had flead, the other might embowel, to make use of the words of the historian.[11] King John, his father, once demanded 10,000 marks from a Jew of Bristol; and on his refusal, ordered one of his teeth to be drawn every day till he should consent. The Jew lost seven teeth, and then paid the sum required of him."

The barbarity exercised toward this race of men, will not so greatly surprize us, when we consider the severity of the antient law of England, by which, if a christian man married a woman who was a Jewess, or a christian woman did marry with a Jew, it was felony, for which the offending party was to be

---

[11] Matthew Paris.

burned alive. This strange and inhuman law was made in the infancy of christianity, and we might almost doubt its real existence, did we not consider that
zealots have ever been forward to violate the dictates of reason and humanity,
in defence of a new and favourite system, against an opposite sect.

The reign of Edward I, who has been celebrated as the English Justinian,
affords abundant matter of speculation. Under this prince, the English constitution acquired some tolerable consistence. Knights, citizens, and burgesses
were now more regularly summoned to parliament, and the commons beheld
the gladsome dawn of independence. It suffered many eclipses however, before
it rose so near to the meridian as it has since advanced. Our Historian makes
a digression in this reign, in which he gives a succinct and ingenious account
of the progress of the commons' authority. Nevertheless it is too long for us
to give it entire, and to select any particular part, would be injustice to the
whole. We will only observe therefore, that Mr. Hume seems to rely too much
on the authority of Brady, who, though very ingenious and intelligent, is, in
many instances hasty and partial: and we are by no means persuaded by the
authorities he cites, that the knights originally sat apart from the commons, and
that the latter, even in the reign of Henry IV. had not any legislative authority.
Were we however to enter into a regular confutation of these propositions, it
would carry us too far into the cobwebs of antiquity, wither few of our readers,
perhaps, would chuse to follow us. We therefore refer the examination of these
niceties to the learned and curious.

It would be needless to enter into the military exploits of this prince in
France and Scotland, against the latter of which he was actuated more by
principles of policy than justice, having violated the confidence reposed in his
friendly arbitration, to promote an usurped dominion. The civil government
of this reign is most worthy of our attention, and is indeed well described by
our Historian. Here however he is clearly mistaken, when he says, that
"Edward seems to have been the first Christian Prince, who passed a statute
of mortmain;" for this was one of the articles of the Great Charter passed in
his father's time.

Our Historian's reflections on the reign of that weak and unfortunate Prince,
Edward II. are well worthy of observation. Mr. Hume has softened the
character of this unhappy Monarch, and takes notice, that it is a shameful
delusion in modern historians, to imagine that all the antient Princes who were
unfortunate in their government, were also tyrannical in their conduct. This
reflection is certainly just: but we must add, that if a prince is ever so innocent
and inoffensive in himself, yet his weak attachment to a tyrannical and
oppressive minion, is as reasonable a ground for opposing his authority, as if
the tyranny was personal in himself. It must be confessed nevertheless, that "the
facility and weakness of this Prince, more than his violence, threw every thing
into confusion;" and these considerations, more than any real grievances, gave
birth to the sedition of the turbulent Barons; whose conduct and influence is

admirably described in the following extract, which opens with some curious particulars, relative to the elder Spenser, father to Edward's favourite.

"The petition of the elder Spencer to parliament, complaining of the devastation committed on his lands by the barons, contains several particulars, which are curious, and discover the manners of the age. He affirms, that they had ravaged sixty three manors belonging to him, and he makes his losses amount to 46,000 pounds; that is, to 138,000 of our present money. Among other particulars, he enumerates 28,000 sheep, 1000 oxen and heifers, 1200 cows with their breed for two years, 560 cart horses, 2000 hogs, together with 600 bacons, 80 carcasses of beef, and 600 muttons in the larder; ten tuns of cyder, arms for 200 men, and other warlike engines and provisions. The plain inference is, that the greatest part of Spenser's vast estate, as well as that of the other nobility, was farmed by the landlord himself, managed by his stewards or bailiffs, and cultivated by his villains. Little or none of it was let on lease to husbandmen: its produce was consumed in rustic hospitality by the baron or his officers: a great number of idle retainers, ready for any disorder or mischief, were maintained by him: all who lived upon his estate were absolutely at his disposal: instead of applying to courts of justice, he usually sought redress by open force and violence: the great nobility were a kind of independent potentates, who, if they submitted to any regulations at all, were less governed by the municipal law, than by a rude species of the laws of nations. The method in which we find they treated the King's favourites, and ministers, is a proof of their usual way of dealing with each other. A party, which complains of the arbitrary conduct of ministers, ought naturally to affect a great regard for the laws and constitution, and maintain at least the appearance of justice in their proceedings: yet these barons, when discontented, came to parliament with an armed force, constrained the King to assent to their measure, and without any trial or witness or conviction, passed, from the pretended notoriety of facts, an act of banishment or attainder, against the minister, which, on the first revolution of fortune, was reversed by like expedients. The parliament, during factious times, was nothing but the organ of present power. Tho' the persons of whom it was chiefly composed, seemed to enjoy great independence, they really possessed no true liberty; and the security of each individual among them, was not so much derived from the general protection of law, as from his own private power and that of his confederates. The authority of the monarch, tho' far from absolute, was very irregular, and might often reach him: the current of a faction might easily overwhelm him; a hundred considerations, of benefits and injuries. friendships and animosities, hopes and fears, were able to influence his conduct, and amidst these motives a regard to equity and law and justice was commonly, in those rude ages, of little moment. Nor did any man entertain thoughts of opposing present power, who did not deem himself strong enough to dispute the field with it by force, and was not prepared to give battle to the sovereign or the ruling party."

We are here presented with a very just and lively picture of the manners of these times, and this may serve as a key for the more perfect understanding of the disorderly and violent transactions of these reigns. Such comments display the true characteristics of an Historian.

The reign of Edward III. affords little more than a romantic scene of chivalry. The much celebrated victories of Crecy and Poictiers, only serve, among other instances, to prove that heedless temerity frequently triumphs over supine confidence. The treatment however, which John, the captive King of France received from the Black Prince, his conqueror, displayed a noble generosity and humanity, which shewed the Prince to have possessed a mind superior to the little ambition of false heroism. The military exploits of this reign have ever been the theme and boast of vulgar admiration, but we find little improvement in civil polity, which is more worthy of attention. The government, as our Historian observes,

"at best, was only a barbarous monarchy, not regulated by any fixed maxims, not bounded by any certain undisputed rights, which were in practice regularly observed. The King conducted himself by one set of principles; the barons by another; the commons by a third; the clergy by a fourth. All these systems of government were contrary and incompatible: each of them prevailed according as incidents were favourable to it: a great Prince rendered the monarchical power predominant; the weakness of a King gave the reigns to aristocracy; a superstitious age saw the clergy triumphant: the people, for whom alone government was instituted, and who alone deserve consideration, were commonly the weakest of the whole. But the commons, little obnoxious to any other order, though they sunk under the violence of tempests, silently reared their head in more peaceable times; and while the storm was brewing, were courted by all sides, and thus received still some accession to their privileges, or, at worst, some confirmation of them."

The reign of that weak Prince, Richard II. affords little matter worthy of commemoration. Our Historian, though he warns the reader not to give entire credit to writers who composed their works during the reigns of the Lancastrian Princes, acknowledges nevertheless, that, "he was a weak Prince, and unfit for government, less for want of natural parts and capacity, than of solid judgment, and of a good education. He was violent in his temper, profuse in his expences; fond of idle shew and magnificence; devoted to favourites, and addicted to pleasure; passions, all of them, the most inconsistent with a prudent œconomy, and consequently dangerous in a limited and mixed government."

The ensuing reign, though busy and active, was chiefly employed in defending a bad title to the crown, so that Henry IV. had little leisure to look abroad, or perform any actions which might redound to the honour or advantage of the nation. "It must be owned however," adds our Historian, "that his prudence and vigilance and foresight, in maintaining his power, was admirable: his command of temper remarkable: his courage, both military and political, without blemish: and he possessed many qualities, which fitted him for his high station, and which rendered his usurpation of it, though pernicious in after times, rather salutary, during his own reign, to the English nation." We confess that we cannot readily subscribe to the propriety of this concluding sentiment. It is difficult to conceive, in what respect Henry's usurpation was salutary to the kingdom, even during his own reign: neither does such a reflection seem consistent with what our Historian had before acknowledged, viz. "That Henry had little leisure to perform any actions, which might redound to the honour or advantage of the nation."

His son however raised the nation to the highest pitch of honour to which martial merit and success could exalt it. This conqueror of France, it is well known, was, while Prince of Wales, wild and dissolute to a shameful excess; and his extravagance is thus, not improbably, accounted for by our Historian.

"The many jealousies, to which Henry IV's situation naturally exposed him, had so infected his temper, that he had been persuaded to entertain unreasonable suspicions with regard to the fidelity of his eldest son; and during the latter years of his life, he had excluded that Prince from all share in public business, and even displeased to see him at the head of armies, where his martial talents, though useful to the support of government, acquired him a renown, which he thought, might prove dangerous to his own authority. The active spirit of young Henry, restrained from its proper exercise, broke out in extravagancies of every kind; and the riot of pleasure, the frolics of debauchery, the outrage of wine, filled the vacancies of a mind, better adapted to the pursuits of ambition, and the cares of government. This course of life threw him among companions, whose disorders, if accompanied with spirit and humour, he seconded and indulged; and he was detected in many sallies, which, to severe eyes, appeared totally unworthy of his rank and station. There even remains a tradition, that, when heated with liquor and jollity, he scrupled not to accompany them in attacking the passengers on the streets and highways, and despoiling them of their goods; and he found an amusement in the incidents, which the terror and regret of these defenceless people produced on such occasions. This extreme of dissoluteness proved equally disagreeable to his father, as that eager application to business, which had at first given him occasion of jealousy; and he saw in his son's behaviour the same neglect of decency, the same attachment to low company, which had destroyed the personal character of Richard, and which, more than all his errors in government, had tended to overturn his throne. But the nation in general considered the young prince with more indulgence; and observed so many gleams of generosity, spirit, and magnanimity, breaking continually through the cloud, which a wild conduct threw over his character, that they never ceased hoping for his amendment, and ascribed all the weeds, which shot up in that rich soil, to the want of proper culture and attention in the King and his ministers. There passed an event which encouraged these agreeable views, and gave much occasion for favourable reflections to all men of sense and candor. A riotous companion of the prince's had been indicted before Gascoigne, the chief justice, for some disorders; and Henry was not ashamed to appear at the bar with the criminal, in order to give him countenance and protection. Finding, that his presence had not over-awed the chief justice, he proceeded to insult that magistrate on his tribunal; but Gascoigne, mindful of the character which he then bore, and the majesty of the sovereign and of the laws, which he sustained, ordered the Prince to be carried to prison for his rude behaviour. The spectators were agreeably disappointed, when they saw the heir of the crown submit peaceably to this sentence, make reparation for his error by acknowledging it, and check his impetuous nature in the midst of its extravagant career."

These sentiments may, to some, appear overstrained and too refined: but they who have accurately examined the human heart, who can make allowances for the frailties of mortality, and who know how nearly the greatest virtues border on the opposite vices, will withhold their censure of this apology for the Prince's strange irregularities. As it is essentially necessary for an historian, among other requisites, to be a philosopher; so philosophers only are capable of forming a right judgment of history.

The character of this Prince, who died in the flower of his age, is painted in the following strong and glowing colours.

"This Prince possessed many eminent virtues; and if we give indulgence to ambition in a monarch, or rank it, as the vulgar are inclined to do, among his virtues, they were unstained by any considerable blemish. His abilities appeared equally in the cabinet and in the field; the boldness of his enterprizes has no less remarkable than his personal valour in conducting them. He had the talent of attaching his friends by affability, and of gaining his enemies by address and clemency. The English, dazzled by the lustre of his character, still more than by that of his victories, were reconciled to the defects of his title: the French almost forgot that he was an enemy; and his care of maintaining justice in his civil administration, and preserving discipline in his armies, made some amends to both nations for the calamities inseparable from those wars, in which his short reign was almost entirely occupied. That he could forgive the earl of Marche, who had a better right to the throne than himself, is a sure proof of his magnanimity; and that the earl relied so entirely on his friendship is no less a proof of his established character for candor and sincerity. There remain in history few instances of such mutual trust; and still fewer where neither party found reason to repent it."

After all however, it must be confessed, that he owed the splendor of his military character to a fortunate rashness, and the most destructive and fatal consequences might reasonably have been expected from his daring and indiscreet enterprizes. Indeed Mr. Hume acknowleges, that "nothing in appearance could be more unequal than the battle of Azincourt, upon which all his safety and his fortunes depended. His situation was exactly similar to that of Edward at Cressy, and that of the Black Prince at Poictiers; and the French confidence, notwithstanding past experience, in like manner proved their ruin; so that in the end, their enemies, by their misconduct, derived immortal glory from a temerity which portended inevitable destruction."

The reign of Henry VI. is a farther proof, that every weak Prince will, in a limited and mixed government, be unhappy. This King had the misfortune to lose most of the territories which his father had conquered from France, and had the farther mortification to have them, in fact, ravished from him by a General in petticoats, that is, the famous Joan d'Arc, known by the name of the Maid of Orleans. Of this wonder girl, our Historian gives the most accurate account we remember to have met with.

"In the village of Domremi, near Vaucoulerus, on the borders of Lorraine, there lived a country girl of twenty-seven years of age, called Joan d'Arc, who was servant in a small inn, and who in that station had been accustomed to tend the horses of the guests, to ride them without a saddle to the watering place, and to perform other offices, which, in well frequented inns, commonly fall to the share of the men servants. This girl was of an irreproachable life, and had not hitherto been remarked for any singularity; whether that she had met with no occasion to excite her genius, or that the unskilful eyes of those, who conversed with her, had not been able to discern her uncommon merit. It is easy to imagine, that the present situation of France was an interesting object, even to persons of the lowest rank, and would become the frequent subject of their conversation: a young Prince, expelled his native throne, by the sedition of subjects and by the arms of strangers, could not fail to move the compassion of all his people, whose hearts were uncorrupted by faction; and the peculiar character of Charles, so strongly inclined to friendship and the tender passions, naturally rendered him the hero of that sex, whose generous minds knew no bounds in their affections. The siege of Orleans, the progress of the English before that place, the great distress of the garrison and inhabitants, the importance of saving the city and its brave defenders, had turned thither the eyes of all the world; and Joan, inflamed by the general sentiment, was seized with a wild desire of bringing relief to her sovereign in his present distresses. Her unexperienced mind, working day and night on this favourite object, mistook the impulses of her passion for heavenly inspirations; and she fancied, that she saw visions and heard voices, exhorting her to re-establish the throne of France, and to expel the foreign invaders. An uncommon intrepidity of temper made her overlook all the dangers, which might attend her in such a path; and thinking herself destined by heaven to this office, she threw aside that bashfulness and timidity, which would naturally adhere to her sex, her years, and her low station. She went to Boudricourt, governor of Vacouleurs; procured admission to him; informed him of her inspirations and intentions; and conjured him not to neglect the voice of God, who spoke thro' her, but to second those heavenly revelations, which impelled her to this glorious enterprize. Baudricourt treated her at first with some neglect; but on her frequent returns to him, and importunate solicitations, he began to remark something extraordinary in the maid, and was inclined, at all hazards, to make so easy an experiment. It is uncertain, whether this gentleman had discernment enough to perceive, that great use might be made with the vulgar of so uncommon an engine; or, what is more likely in that credulous age, was himself a convert to this visionary: but he adopted at last the scheme of Joan; and he gave her some attendants, who conducted her to the French court, which at that time resided at Chinon.

It is the business of history to distinguish between the *miraculous* and the *marvellous*; to reject the first in all narrations merely profane and human; to scruple the second; when obliged by undoubted testimony, as in the present case, to admit of something extraordinary, to receive as little of it as is consistent with the known facts and circumstances. It is pretended, that Joan, immediately on her admission, knew the King, tho' she had never seen his face before, and tho' he purposely kept himself in the crowd of courtiers, and had laid aside every thing in his dress and apparel, which might distinguish him; that she offered him, in the name of the supreme Creator, to raise the siege of Orleans, and conduct him to Rheims to be there crowned and anointed; and on his expressing some doubts of her mission, revealed to him, before some sworn confidents, a secret, which was unknown to all the world but himself, and which nothing but a heavenly inspiration could discover to her: and that she demanded, as the instrument of her future victories, a particular sword, which was kept in the church of St. Catherine de Fierbois, and which, tho' she had never seen it, she described by all its marks, and by the place in which it had long been laid and neglected. This is certain, that all these miraculous stories were spread abroad, in order to catch the vulgar. The more the King and his ministers were determined to give into the illusion, the more scruples they pretended. An assembly of grave doctors and theologians cautiously examined Joan's mission, and pronounced it undoubted and supernatural. She was sent to the parliament, then residing at Poictiers; and was interrogated before that assembly: the presidents, the counsellors, who came persuaded of her imposture, went away convinced of her inspiration. A ray of hope began to break thro' that despair, in which the minds of all men were before enveloped. Heaven had now declared itself in favour of France, and had laid bare its outstretched arm to take vengeance on her invaders. Few could distinguish between the impulse of inclination and the force of conviction; and none would submit to the trouble of so disagreeable a scrutiny."

The merit of these reflections must be acknowleged by every reader, who has the least portion of that manly and liberal spirit which distinguishes our author. An Historian above all others, should never be a dupe to credulity: and he ought not only to reject incredibilities himself, but it is his duty likewise to warn his readers against crediting phantastic relations, which often give a wrong bias to enthusiastic minds, and render them ridiculous to the wise, and dangerous to the weak.

Henry's losses and misfortunes abroad, naturally produced discontents at home, which at length broke out into open rebellion, and made way for the line of York in the person of Edward IV. His throne however tottered for some time, but the victory over Henry's forces at the battle of Hexham, seemed to have extinguished the hopes of the Lancastrian family. The consequences of this battle are described in a very affecting manner.

"The fate of the unfortunate royal family, after this defeat, was very singular. Margaret, flying with her son into a forest, where she endeavoured to conceal herself, was beset, during the darkness of the night, by robbers, who either ignorant or regardless of her quality, despoiled her of her rings and jewels, and treated her with the utmost indignity. The partition of this rich booty raised a quarrel among them; and while their attention was thus engaged, she took the opportunity of making her escape with her son into the thickest of the forest, where she wandered for some time, over-spent with hunger and fatigue, and sunk with terror and affliction. While in this wretched condition, she saw a robber approach with his naked sword; and finding that she had no means of escape, she suddenly embraced the resolution of trusting entirely for protection to his faith and generosity. She advanced towards him, and presenting to him the young prince, called out to him, *Here, my friend, I commit to your care the safety of your King's son.* The man, whose humanity and generous spirit had been obscured, but not entirely lost, by his vicious course of life, was struck with the singularity of the event, and charmed with the confidence reposed in him; and he vowed, not only to abstain from all injury against the princess, but to devote himself entirely to her safety and protection. By his means she dwelt some time concealed in the forest, and was at last conducted to the sea-coast, whence she made her escape into Flanders. She passed thence into her father's court, where she lived several years in privacy and retirement. Her husband was not so fortunate or so dexterous in finding the means of his escape. Some of his friends took him under their protection, and conveyed him into Lancashire, where he remained concealed during a twelvemonth; but he was at last detected, delivered up to Edward, and thrown into the Tower. The safety of his person was owing less to the generosity of his enemies, than to the contempt which they had entertained of his courage and his understanding."

Distress, like this, must move our pity, even though the sufferers were in the meanest station. But when we consider it as the lot of an unfortunate pair, accustomed to the pomp of royalty, and softened by all the blandishments of ease and luxury, then our compassion increases in proportion as the extreme reverse of fortune must make their sense of misery the stronger.

The unfortunate Henry, however, was afterwards restored, and in a short time fell again into the hands of Edward, to experience still farther calamities, which not long after put an end to the days of this weak but pious prince; though some incline to think that he died a violent death.

All the glories of Edward's reign, Mr. Hume observes, terminated with the civil wars, where his laurels too were extremely sullied with blood, violence, and cruelty. His spirit seems afterwards to have been sunk in indolence and pleasure, or his measures were frustrated by imprudence and want of foresight. His character is summed up in these few words: He was "a prince more splendid and showy, than either prudent or virtuous; brave, though cruel; addicted to pleasure, though capable of activity in great emergencies; and less fitted to prevent ills by wise precautions, than to remedy them after they took place by his vigour and enterprize."[12]

We shudder as we pass through the short reign of Edward V. which is full of the butcheries of that inhuman monster the Duke of Gloucester, who murdered the young King with his brother the Duke of York, and stepped to the throne through the blood of his slaughtered kinsmen, under the title of Richard III. Happily, however, this strain to humanity did not long disgrace the diadem; he was killed at the battle of Bosworth, and fell by too mild a fate. Mr. Hume, who by many, perhaps, will be thought to have been too indulgent

---

[12] Mr. Hume seems to be mistaken, when he says that the *Benevolence* attempted to be levied by this prince, was "a sort of exaction, which, except during the reign of Henry III. had scarce ever been practised in former times." They appear to have been more frequently raised than he supposes: they were even levied in the preceding reign; and the instructions to the commissioners employed in procuring a benevolence in the 20th of Henry VI. speak the language of an arbitrary prince. [In later editions of the *History*, Hume modified this sentence as follows: "he attempted to levy money by way of *benevolence*; a kind of exaction, which, except during the reigns of Henry III. and Richard II. had not much been practised in former times...."]

to the characters of our weak and wicked princes, does not attempt to palliate that of Richard. "The Historians (says he) who favour Richard, (for even he has met with partizans among the late Writers) maintain that he was well qualified for government, had he legally obtained it; and that he committed no crimes but such as were necessary to procure him possession of the crown: but this is a very poor apology, when it is confessed that he was ready to commit the most horrid crimes, which appeared necessary for that purpose. And it is certain that all his courage and capacity, qualities in which he really seems not to have been deficient, would never had made compensation to the people for the danger of the precedent, and for the contagious example of vice and murder, exalted upon the throne."

"Thus (says our Historian) we have pursued the History of England through a series of many barbarous ages, till we have at last reached the dawnings of civility and science, and have the prospect, both of greater certainty in our historical narrations, and of being able to present to the Reader a spectacle more worthy of his attention." Mr. Hume concludes with a kind of recapitulation, wherein he gives an abstract of the antient system of government, and its successive changes in these remote times; but our limits will not allow us to extend our extracts any farther.

Upon the whole, we do not scruple to commend these Volumes, as containing the most just and masterly account of the reigns of our early Kings, that has hitherto been penned. The attentive Reader will find that philosophy and jurisprudence constantly go hand in hand with History: and we hope that as Mr. Hume has with such success gone backwards as far as probability can warrant relation, that he will now continue the History of this kingdom, from the period at which he left off, on the publication of the first two Volumes.

13
CRITICAL REVIEW

Review of *The History of England, from the Invasion of Julius Caesar to the Accession of Henry VII*, in *The Critical Review*, January and February 1762, Vol. 13, pp. 58–65, 81–93.
Complete review.

The final volumes of Hume's *History* were reviewed in two parts by the *Critical Review*, both of which lavish praise on the work. In the first part the reviewer presents comparatively few quotations from the *History*, and instead reflects on the nature of history writing and how Hume fares in terms of writing style, reflection, and historical accuracy. He commends Hume, Smollett, and Robertson for elevating the quality of British history writing to the level of historians in other European countries. The second part was the opening article in the *Critical Review* for February 1762. The earlier part apparently sparked the criticism that it was written by a friend of Hume's, thus explaining its almost excessive level of praise. The reviewer, though, contends that "The author of that article is an intire stranger to the person of the historian." As an example of Hume's ability, the reviewer quotes the final paragraphs of Chapter 23, which describe the progress of learning during the middle ages.

ART. IX. *The History of* England, *from the Invasion of* Julius Caesar *to the Accession of* Henry VII. *In Two Volumes. 4to. Pr. 1l. 10s. Millar.*

At a period when learning is ready to sink beneath its own weight, and books multiply without the display of genius, or progression of knowledge, the publication of a work, not unworthy of the Augustan age, must afford satisfaction to every reader of true taste and discernment, and to every sincere friend of literature. Mr. Hume is one of those few writers, whose fame will increase in the same proportion that the human understanding is cultivated; his abilities have already contributed eminently to wipe off the reproach too long urged by foreigners, that the genius of the British nation was either averse or unequal to historical composition. France, Spain, Italy, Holland, and even the more uncivilized nations of the North, have their historians, who rival the most celebrated writers of antiquity. Great Britain hath, for centuries past, had a principal share in the wars, politics, and erudition of Europe; the freedom of her happy constitution admits of the full display of talents; her inhabitants are celebrated among strangers for their national pride, ferocity, spirit, reflection, and judgment; and her language is confessed to be manly, nervous, and copious; nevertheless, our author's history of the houses of Stuart and Tudor, Dr. Smollett's Complete History of England, and Dr. Robertson's History of Scotland, are perhaps the only instances which can be produced to the credit of the nation, in this species of composition, unless we except the historical pieces of Buchanan, Bacon, and the earl of Clarendon; the first, celebrated for the elegance of his Latinity; the second, for his refinement in the knowledge of the human heart; and the third, for the beauty of his characters.

From the peculiar circumstances of this island, it might naturally be imagined that history is the province particularly adapted to the genius and disposition of the people. The very nature of the government, the constitutional necessity of canvassing publicly in the senate every measure of general importance, the extraordinary revolutions which have been effected in church and state, the vast extension of commerce, naval power, arts, luxury, and refinement, and, lastly, the sure establishment of national liberty on its present solid basis, all furnish the greatest advantages to an historian, and open an unbounded field for the display of genius, sentiment, sagacity, stile, and every beauty of fine composition.

Till of late years the elaborate work of M. Rapin de Thoyras was considered as the only regular, complete, and well digested annals of the transactions of this country. The success of his undertaking would seem to have animated divers learned natives to run the same course. They pretended to hold the Frenchman in the light of a mere painful compiler of materials, who had dug from the mine the ore which they were to purify and refine; they professed to correct his errors, soften his prejudices, retrench his superfluities, and polish and enliven his narrative; but the public expectation raised high by vast promises, was disappointed, our rivals in arms and arts had fresh cause of triumph, and all the world joined in the same opinion, that our island produced excellent critics and politicians, but very indifferent historians. Rapin was, indeed, detected in a variety of gross blunders; the principles of liberty were well explained, and every minute wheel of the political machine accurately described; but the elegant uniformity of texture, the chaste simplicity of diction, the flowing harmony of composition, the unruffled rapid narrative, in a word, the soul and spirit of true history were wanting; and those enormous folios were treasured up in the libraries of the curious, as useful repositories of facts, and monuments rather of the industry and erudition than of the genius of the authors.

Such was the state of the British history, when Mr. Hume exhibited the first specimen of the work now completed by a retrogressive progress, and confirmed the general opinion entertained of his learning and capacity. There was something so original, refined, and masterly in his sentiments, that even those who dissented from his principles confessed his merit. His severe strictures on the hierarchy, the boldness of his religious, moral, and political reflections; his sometimes paradoxical positions, extreme refinement, and philosophising talent, gave offence; but at the same time commanded respect, and, in the end, triumphed over opposition. No writer hath more fortunately hit upon the method of rendering history instructive than our ingenious author, whose work may be regarded as a table of the human passions, stripped of all disguise, laid naked to the eye, and dissected by the masterly hand of a curious artist. We see actions traced up to their first springs and actuating principles, in so natural a manner, that we cannot avoid giving our assent to Mr. Hume's conclusions, even when they disagree with those we should have formed from a perusal of the simple facts. He compares circumstances so accurately, pierces with so keen a glance into the darkest recesses of the heart, and disposes every part of the same object in so collective, just, and striking a point of view, that the judgment immediately acquiesces, because the imagination is strongly captivated, and the persuasion as irresistible as the arguments are convincing. He appears not only the philosopher and politician, but in many instances the orator, although his stile be sometimes tinctured with impurity. Little indelicacies of diction offend extreme sensibility; but they are, in general, absorbed in the torrent of nervous elocution and rapid sentiment. Mr. Hume, however, scarce ever ventures upon figure or metaphor, which always distinguishes a warm imagination, and when introduced with discretion, and sustained with propriety, imparts great beauty and classical elegance to historical narration. Of this we have a striking instance in the Complete History of England, now publishing, by a contemporary writer, to whose merit we have had frequent occasion to pay the tribute of applause. His stile is less close, energic, and pointed, than that of our author; but it is more chaste, flowing, sublime, and descriptive. He would seem to have imitated the engaging manner of Paterculus, while Mr. Hume's genius led him into the path marked out by the manly Tacitus; and we must confess, under correction of the critics, that we think the former superior to the latter in point of historical composition. In a long course of narrative, the ear tires with short uniform periods, which give an air of stiffness, and laboured correctness, to what ought especially to appear smooth, easy, and variegated. Had Seneca wrote a history, it would have been like his philosophy, disagreeably sententious; and if we may be allowed to speak our own opinion, we should imagine that this elaborate diction ought to be wholly confined to reflection, and subjects where abundance of matter is necessarily crowded within a small compass.

Antithesis too is a fault into which Mr. Hume hath been seduced, contrary to his better judgment. A rhetorician, and even an historian, may sometimes shade opposite qualities by contrasting them; but a play of words or thoughts is puerile, and much beneath the dignity of any historical subject. Voltaire's sprightly wit and satirical genius, hath frequently led him into this trespass against the laws of grave narrative; but no man ever set up that ingenious French writer as a model of historical excellence, though no biographer ever furnished more entertainment to the public. Nor should the example of Cicero have greater weight, though he frequently introduces this mode of smartness into his finest pieces of eloquence. It ought to be considered that he is pleading before an audience, whose passions and good opinion it is his business to engage at the expence of just composition.

As to our author's disposition, it is clear, natural, and demonstrative of a distinct arrangement of ideas. The parts are well combined; they glide gently into each other, like the lights and shades in painting, and no new subject is introduced before the reader is sufficiently prepared. Hence it is, that the memory will be supplied with greater store of useful facts from a single perusal of the concise history before us, than from the eternal study of the numerous immense folios published upon the same subject; for there cannot be a greater obstacle to retention than want of method, nor a stronger proof that the writer had not fully digested his materials.

In point of reflection Mr. Hume is excelled by no writer that we know, whether we consider the propriety, novelty, depth, or energy of his sentiments. In the two preceding publications of this history, he evinced himself the friend only of virtue. Attached to no party, swayed by no prejudices, he boldly attacked vice, and unmasked hypocrisy, whether in a monarch or a subject, without regard to the sect, the principles, or the religion of the object; nor was his praise distributed with less impartiality; even Cromwell's self was allowed the just tribute.

We find our historian now engaged in a scene more remote, and consequently less trying to the passions. Zeal cannot be greatly inflamed, nor prejudice deeply interested in the revolutions of a barbarous period; it therefore requires all the powers of genius to sustain the subject, and keep awake the attention, through so long a narrative of transactions with which we are little affected. Mr. Hume hath enlivened it by the finest remarks on characters, manners, customs, laws, policy, the human heart, and the progress of arts, science, and the understanding. Were we to close in with the opinion of those critics who affirm that all reflection ought to be left to the mind of the reader, as being foreign to the business of the historian, we should deprive ourselves of abundance of entertainment and instruction. The heart may be affected by pathetic narratives but the mind will always be improved by solid reflection. The finest writers of antiquity are no less admirable for the beauty of their narrative, than for the richness of their imagination, force, and propriety of reflection. Livy and Velleius Paterculus, animate and affect by the strength of painting, and height of colouring: they have possibly carried poetical beauty to excess; while Tacitus, and even Sallust, open and enlarge the understanding by the reflective powers. If close imitation of the fine writers of antiquity be the test of modern composition, how shall we judge by this standard, while those writers differ from each other? The truth is, perfection may be found in all or in neither, just as they happen to excel in their several kinds; and the modern historian, who equals Livy or Paterculus, must be deemed on a footing with him who is the exact copy of Sallust or Tacitus, until the several pretentions of these classics to superior merit be finally adjusted. It would be as difficult for a philosopher, or politician, to acquire eminence in description, as for a poet to excel in refinement, subtlety, and argument.

The view which our author presents of the state of ancient Britain, and of the Roman conquest, is extremely concise, because he chuses to refer us to the Latin and Greek writers, from whom we must deduce all our knowledge of this period. Cæsar, Tacitus, Dio, Herodian, and other writers, may be consulted with as much satisfaction and advantage as the best compilation. It is otherwise with respect to the succeeding Saxon period, during which learning was more cultivated than taste, and every emotion of the heart was absorbed in super-stition. Besides, the total revolution effected by this people in genius, manners, and government, required the strictest attention, as nothing more is exhibited by the rude historians of that age, than facts, in the relation of which they frequently disagree. Sensible that modern writers have borrowed implicitly from each other, without giving themselves the trouble of consulting ancient documents, Mr. Hume has recourse to the original sources of intelligence, whence it is that he has, in our opinion, thrown new light upon the Saxon civil and political constitution. His review of the military exploits, and civil insti-tutions of the great Alfred, set the character of that extraordinary monarch in the most satisfactory light. We cannot, indeed, sufficiently admire the genius, judgment, and erudition, displayed by the masterly author, upon an apparently favourite topic; and we conclude the history of this glorious reign, with senti-ments of equal esteem for the virtues of the prince, and the talents of the historian. In the appendix annexed to the Saxon history, the author descends to a very particular account of the Anglo Saxon government, laws of succession, national assemblies, nobility, courts of justice, criminal law, and other peculiar-ities of those people, in which he evinces his deep knowledge in the antiquities of this country; advances some disputable assertions, and supports them with extremely ingenious, though not always conclusive arguments. To enter upon a discussion of these points, would demand more space and leisure than we have to bestow: however, the reader who is curious to obtain a knowledge of the peculiar notions of our author, may compare him with Rapin's account of the Wittenagemot, or Saxon parliament, and Mr. Guthrie's second and third dissertations subjoined to the second volume of his history, without taking the labour of turning over all that antiquaries have advanced on the subject. We could wish he had enlarged more upon that long-disputed question, 'whether the crown of Scotland was at any period of time dependent on that of England, or at least as early as the Saxon government?' This question, indeed, is rather curious than useful; but as it still furnishes matter of debate, it would afford satisfaction to see it discussed by so able and impartial a writer. – Prudence, indeed, and the fear of reviving ancient animosities, may possibly have occasioned Mr. Hume's silence.

A point of less consequence, in our opinion, hath employed all our author's talents. What avails it to the present generation, whether William duke of Normandy succeeded to the crown of England by the will of Edward, in consequence of private compact, or by right of conquest? The principal argument brought in proof, that William was actually the conqueror of England, is adduced from the despotism of his government; but Mr. Hume ought to have reflected, that tyranny may be exerted under certain circumstances even in a limited government, where the prince has succeeded by election or the right of inheritance. However, though we must dissent from his conclusions, we must in justice acknowledge, that the whole argument is treated with great ability and candour. Perhaps he may be accused of softening the features of this arbitrary prince beyond what historical truth admits.

'Few princes (says he) have been more fortunate than this great monarch, or were better entitled to grandeur and prosperity, from the abilities and the vigour of mind which he displayed in all his conduct. His spirit was bold and enterprising, yet guided with prudence: his ambition, which was exorbitant, and lay little under the restraint of justice, and still less under that of humanity, still submitted to the dictates of reason and sound policy. Born in an age when the minds of men were intractable and unacquainted with submission, he was yet able, to direct them to his purposes; and partly from the ascendant of his vehement character, partly from art and dissimulation, to establish an unlimited authority. Though not insensible to generosity, he was hardened against compassion; and he seemed equally ostentatious and ambitious of eclat in his clemency and in his severity. The maxims of his administration were austere; but might have been useful, had they been solely employed in preserving order in an established government: they were ill calculated for softening the rigours, which, under the most gentle management, are inseparable from conquest. His attempt against England was the last great enterprize of the kind, which, during the course of seven hundred years, has fully succeeded in Europe; and the greatness of his genius broke thro' those limits, which first the feudal institutions, then the refined policy of princes, have fixed to the several states of Christendom. Though he rendered himself infinitely odious to his English subjects, he transmitted his power to his posterity, and the throne is still filled by his descendants; a proof, that the foundations which he laid were firm and solid, and that, amidst all his violences, while he seemed only to gratify the present passion, he had still an eye towards futurity.'

He is no less partial to the character of Henry I. who is celebrated as the most accomplished monarch who had ever worn the English diadem; whereas, if we credit other historians, Henry indeed was learned, able, and brave; but he was rigid, vindictive, cruel, incontinent, and inexorable.

According to Mr. Hume, he

'possessed all the qualities both of body and mind, natural and acquired, which could fit him for the high station to which he attained. His person was manly, his countenance engaging, his eyes clear, serene, and penetrating. The affability of his address encouraged those who might be overawed by the sense of his dignity or of his wisdom; and tho' he often indulged his facetious humour, he knew how to temper it with discretion, and ever kept at a distance from all indecent familiarities with his courtiers. His superior eloquence and judgement would have given him an ascendant even had he been born in a private station; and his personal bravery would have procured him respect, even though it had been less supported by art and policy. By his great progress in literature, he acquired the name of Beau-clerc, or the scholar; but his application to these sedentary pursuits abated nothing of the activity and vigilance of his government; and though the learning of that age was better fitted to corrupt than improve the understanding, his natural good sense preserved itself untainted both from the pedantry and superstition, which were then so prevalent among men of letters. His temper was very susceptible of the sentiments as well of friendship as of resentment; and his ambition, though high, might be esteemed moderate and reasonable; had not his conduct towards his brother and nephew showed that he was too much disposed to sacrifice to it all the maxims of justice and equity. But the total incapacity of Robert for government afforded his younger brother a reason or pretence for seizing the scepter both of Normandy and England; and when violence and usurpation are once begun, necessity obliges a prince to continue in the same criminal course, and engages him in measures, which his better judgment and sounder principles would otherwise have induced him to reject with warmth and indignation.'

Doth not the latter part of this description seem a mere apology in favour of vices that admit of no extenuation; for with such acquirements and natural talents as Henry certainly possessed, his foibles were inexcusable.

To particularize all the instances in which Mr. Hume dissents from other modern historians, would appear a dry and uninteresting critique to our readers. In general, he hath drawn his characters from facts, though he sometimes gives play to his fancy, and indulges in peculiarity. Wherever he finds any opportunity for advancing novel opinions, Mr. Hume embraces it, and seldom fails of giving entertainment, and encreasing our idea of his capacity; but we postpone our farther remarks to a future article, and close this with observing, that the diction is so nervous, the disposition so clear, the reflections so original and energic, the characters so strikingly marked, without being overcharged; and the writer's candour, penetration, and good sense so conspicuous, that we may safely venture to pronounce Mr. Hume's performance, at least, upon a footing with the best modern historical productions in any language.

———

The History of England, *from the Invasion of* Julius Caesar *to the Accession of* Henry VII. *In Two Volumes.* 4to. *Price* 1l. 10s. Millar. [Concluded.]

It is with pleasure we hear that our judgment of the ingenious Mr. Hume's historical abilities is confirmed by the public approbation; and that, although we recommended with warmth, we have not been accused of partiality. In truth, there could be nothing more unjust than any insinuation that we have been seduced into panegyric by the ties of private connection. The author of that article is an intire stranger to the person of the historian; and he was actuated to applaud by no other motives than the satisfaction of giving expression to his feelings, of acknowledging the respect which only little minds can deny to superior genius, and of extending the reputation of a work equally productive of utility to individuals, and the republick of letters, and of honour to Great Britain in general. It merits attention, because it hath been asserted by some very ingenious gentlemen, that the easiest method of acquiring literary fame, is to write history after the materials have been thoroughly examined, digested, and embellished by the labour of preceding writers; the sole meaning of which observation is to detract from the reputation of three contemporary historians, whose extraordinary success appears to have given umbrage. The very reverse of this opinion we believe to be true. It demands all the powers of genius to give novelty and originality to an exhausted subject, without which a writer is nothing better than a transcriber and plagiary; and the more excellence we attribute to any preceding historian, in the same proportion we must grant, that the succeeding writer who pursues the same course, must possess uncommon talents before he can rise to eminence and be distinguished by the public. In every other branch of human knowledge the case is similar. Should any philosopher of the present age attempt to demonstrate the general laws of nature, upon the same strict geometrical principles as Newton, he must surpass the abilities of that extraordinary genius, before he could acquire the same degree of reputation. We shall endeavour to support the truth of this remark by examples.

There is not a reign from the conquest to the present times, nor an important character that hath not been delineated with all the force of painting, and strength of colouring; yet in Mr. Hume's performance, we behold persons and actions in a point of view extremely different, yet equally just and striking. How uncommon and seasonable is the reflection with which he enters upon the reign of Henry II.

'The extensive confederacies (says he) by which the European potentates are now at once united and set in opposition to each other, and which, tho' they diffuse the least spark of dissention thro' the whole, are at least attended with this advantage, that they prevent any violent revolutions or conquests in particular states, were totally unknown in ancient ages; and the theory of foreign politics, in each kingdom, formed a speculation much less complicate and involved than at present: Commerce had not yet bound the most distant nations together in so close a chain: Wars, finished in one campaign, and often in one battle, were little affected by the movements of remote states: the imperfect communication among the kingdoms, and their ignorance of each other's situation, made it impracticable for a great number of them to combine in any one project or effort: and above all, the turbulent spirit and independent situation of the barons or great vassals in each state, gave so much occupation to the sovereign, that he was obliged to confine his attention chiefly to his own system of government, and was more indifferent about what passed among his neighbours. Religion only, not politics, carried abroad the views of princes; and either fixed their thoughts on the Holy Land, whose conquest and defence was deemed a point of common honour and interest, or engaged them in intrigues with the court of Rome, to whom they had yielded the direction of ecclesiastical affairs, and who was every day assuming more authority than they were willing to allow her.

Before the conquest of England by the duke of Normandy, this island was as much separated from the rest of the world in politics as in situation; and except from the inroads of the Danish pirates, the English, happily confined at home, had neither enemies nor allies on the continent. The foreign dominions of William connected them with the kings and great vassals of France; and while the opposite pretensions of the pope and emperor in Italy produced a continual intercourse between Germany and that country, the two great monarchs of France and England formed, in another part of Europe, a separate system, and carried on their wars and negotiations, without meeting either with opposition or support from the others.'

The whole recital of this busy reign is entertaining and masterly. After the above reflection, the historian enters upon a comparative view of the different situations of France and England, previous to the war that broke out between the monarchs, in which we can discern great depth of political sagacity and sound observation. Having related the progress of the war, he makes the reader acquainted with all the circumstances of the life of the famous Thomas a Becket, and then proceeds to that celebrated dispute between the king and the archbishop, which had almost terminated in the destruction of civil government. We have not seen the particulars of this affair so minutely, accurately, and satisfactorily related. A variety of little anecdotes and reflections are disseminated through every part of the narrative, to elucidate the characters of the primate and the monarch, inform the understanding, and engage the passions.

'One day (says Mr. Hume) as the king and chancellor (Becket) were riding together in the streets of London, they observed a beggar, who was shivering with cold. Would it not be very praise-worthy, said the king, to give that poor man a warm coat in this severe season? It would, surely, replied the chancellor; and you do well, Sir, in thinking of such good actions: then he shall have one presently, cried the king: and seizing the skirt of the chancellor's coat, began to pull it violently. The chancellor defended himself for some time; and they had both of them like to have tumbled off their horses in the street, when Becket, after a vehement struggle, let go his coat; which the king bestowed on the beggar, who, being ignorant of the quality of the persons, was not a little surprised with the present.'

Speaking of the necessity Henry was under of retrenching the exorbitant power of the clergy, the historian adds:

'The union of the civil and ecclesiastical powers serves extremely, in every civilized government, to the maintenance of peace and order; and prevents those mutual incroachments, which, as there can be no ultimate judge between them, are often attended with the most dangerous consequences. Whether the supreme magistrate, who unites these powers, receive the appellation of prince or prelate, is not material: the superior weight, which temporal interests commonly bear in the apprehension of men above spiritual, renders the civil part of his character most prevalent; and in time prevents those gross impostures and bigotted persecutions, which, in all false religions, are the chief foundation of clerical authority. But during the progress of ecclesiastical usurpations, the state, by the resistance of the civil magistrate, is naturally thrown into convulsions; and it behooves the prince, both for his own interest, and for that of the public, to provide in time sufficient barriers against so dangerous and insidious a rival. This precaution had been hitherto much neglected in England, as well as in other catholic countries; and affairs at last seemed to have come to a dangerous crisis: a sovereign of the greatest abilities was now on the throne: a prelate of the most inflexible and intrepid character was possessed of the primacy: the contending powers appeared to be armed with their full force, and it was natural to expect some extraordinary event to result from their rencounter.'

In course of the contest between the spiritual and civil powers, Mr. Hume illustrates, in the most ingenious manner, the extent of the regal government at that period; he cites the constitutions of Clarendon, to which the clergy had swore, and in the very relation proves, that Henry had extended the royal prerogative, by the most arbitrary, though necessary and salutary exertion of his popularity and power. After the recital of the archbishop's death, he subjoins the following character of Becket, and of the age:

'This was the tragical end of Thomas a Becket, a prelate of the most lofty, intrepid, and inflexible spirit, who was able to cover, to the world and probably to himself, the enterprize of pride and ambition, under the disguise of sanctity and of zeal for the interests of piety and religion: an extraordinary personage, surely, had he been allowed to remain in his first station, and had directed the vehemence of his character to the support of law and justice; instead of being engaged, by the prejudices of the times, to sacrifice all private duties and public connexions to tyes, which he imagined, or represented, as superior to every civil and political consideration. But no man, who enters into the genius of that age, can reasonably doubt of this prelate's sincerity. The spirit of superstition was so prevalent, that it infallibly caught every careless reasoner, much more every one whose interest, and honour, and ambition, were engaged to support it. All the wretched literature of the time was inlisted on that side: some faint glimmerings of common sense might sometimes pierce through the thick cloud of ignorance, or what was worse, the illusions of perverted science, which had blotted out the sun, and enveloped the face of nature: but those who preserved themselves untainted from the general contagion, proceeded on no principles which they could pretend to justify: they were beholden more to their total want of instruction, than to their knowledge, if they still retained some share of understanding: folly was possessed of all the schools as well as all the churches; and her votaries assumed the garb of philosophers together with the ensigns of spiritual dignities. Throughout that large collection of letters, which bears the name of St. Thomas, we find, in all the retainers of that aspiring prelate, no less than in himself, a most entire and absolute conviction of the reason and piety of their own party, and a disdain of their antagonists; nor is there less cant and grimace in their stile, when they address each other, than when they compose manifestos for the perusal of the public. The spirit of revenge, violence, and ambition, which accompanied their conduct, instead of forming a presumption of hypocrisy, are the surest pledges of their sincere attachment to a cause, which so much flattered these domineering passions.'

The genius of the painter is visible in every stroke of the picture of Henry, drawn by Mr. Hume.

'Thus died (says he) in the fifty-eighth year of his age, and thirty-fifth of his reign, the greatest prince of his time for wisdom, virtue, and ability, and the most powerful in extent of dominion of all those that had ever filled the throne of England. His character, both in public and private life, is almost without a blemish; and he seems to have possessed every accomplishment both of body and mind, which makes a man either estimable or amiable. He was of a middle stature, strong and well proportioned; his countenance was lively and engaging; his conversation affable and entertaining; his elocution easy, persuasive, and ever at command. He loved peace, but possessed both bravery and conduct in war; was provident without timidity; severe in the execution of justice, without rigour; and temperate without austerity. He preserved health, and kept himself from corpulency, to which he was somewhat inclined, by an abstemious diet, and by frequent exercise, particularly hunting. When he could enjoy leisure, he recreated himself either in learned conversation or in reading; and he cultivated his natural talents by study, above any prince of his time. His affections, as well as his enmities, were warm and durable; and his long experience of the ingratitude and infidelity of men never destroyed the natural sensibility of his temper, which disposed him to friendship and society. His character has been transmitted to us by many writers, who were his contemporaries; and it resembles extremely, in its most remarkable strokes, that of his maternal grandfather Henry I. excepting only that ambition, which was a ruling passion in both, found not in the first Henry such unexceptionable means of exerting itself, and pushed that prince into measures, which were both criminal in themselves, and were the cause of farther crimes, from which his grandson's conduct was happily exempted.'

Our author has thrown together, at the close of every reign, a collection of miscellaneous transactions, which are extremely entertaining, though of too little importance to be introduced into the texture of his narrative. We could with pleasure, however, quote some of these particulars, many of which are intirely omitted by the bulk of modern historians; but that the limits of our paper oblige us to refrain from making extracts of still more utility to our readers. In order therefore to compensate this deficiency, to convey a just idea of Mr. Hume's talents, we shall exhibit a summary of the progression of the human understanding, from the extinction of the Saxon government to the accession of the house of Tudor. This single specimen will be sufficient, we imagine, to confirm the judgment we have given of this performance, and impress the reader with the same exalted sentiments of Mr. Hume's merit, that we ourselves entertain.

'Thus have we (says the historian at the close of the reign of the third Richard) pursued the History of England through a series of many barbarous ages; till we have at last reached the dawnings of civility and science, and have the prospect, both of greater certainty in our historical narrations, and of being able to present to the reader a spectacle more worthy of his attention. The want of certainty, however, and of circumstances, is not alike to be complained of throughout every period of this long narration. This island possesses many ancient historians of good credit, as well as many historical monuments; and it is rare, that the annals of so uncultivated a people, as were the English as well as the other European nations, after the decline of Roman learning, have been transmitted to posterity so complete, and with so little mixture of falsehood and of fable. This advantage we owe entirely to the clergy of the church of Rome; who, founding their authority on their superior knowlege, preserved the precious literature of antiquity from a total extinction; and under shelter of their numerous privileges and immunities, acquired a security, by means of the superstition, which they would in vain have claimed, from the justice and humanity of those turbulent and licentious ages. Nor is the spectacle altogether unentertaining and uninstructive, which the history of those times presents to us. The view of human manners and actions, in all their variety of appearances, is both profitable and agreeable; and if the aspect in some periods seems horrid and deformed, we may thence learn to cherish with the greater anxiety that science and civility which has so close a connexion with virtue and humanity, and which, as it is a sovereign antidote against superstition, is also the most effectual remedy against vice and disorders of every kind.

The rise, progress, perfection, and decline of art and science, are curious objects of contemplation, and intimately connected with a narration of civil transactions. The events of no particular period can be fully accounted for, but by considering the degrees of advancement, which men have reached in those particulars.

Those who cast their eye on the general revolutions of society, will find, that as all the improvements of the human mind had reached nearly to their state of perfection about the age of Augustus, there was a sensible decline from that point or period; and men thenceforth relapsed gradually into ignorance and barbarism. The unlimited extent of the Roman empire, and the consequent despotism of the monarchs, extinguished all emulation, debased the generous spirits of men, and depressed that noble flame, by which all the refined arts must be cherished and enlivened. The military government, which soon succeeded, rendered even the lives and properties of men insecure and precarious; and proved destructive to those vulgar and more necessary arts of agriculture, manufactures, and commerce; and in the end, to the military art, and genius itself, by which alone the immense fabric of the empire could be supported. The irruption of the barbarous nations, which soon followed, overwhelmed all human knowledge, which was already far in its decline; and men sunk every age deeper into ignorance, stupidity, and superstition; till the light of ancient science and history had very nearly suffered a total extinction in all the European nations.

But there is an ultimate point of depression, as well as of exaltation, from which human affairs naturally return in a contrary progress, and beyond which they seldom pass either in their advancement or decline. The period, in which the people of Christendom were the lowest sunk in ignorance, and consequently in disorders of every kind, may justly be fixed at the eleventh century, about the age of William the Conqueror; and from that æra, the sun of science, beginning to re-ascend, threw out many gleams of light, which preceded the full morning, when letters were revived in the fifteenth century. The Danes and other northern people, who had so long infested all the coasts, and even the inland parts of Europe, by their depredations, having now learned the arts of tillage and agriculture, found a settled subsistence at home, and were no longer tempted to desert their industry, in order to seek a precarious livelihood by rapine and by the plunder of their neighbours. The feudal governments also, among the more southern nations, were reduced to a kind of system; and though that strange species of civil polity was ill fitted to ensure either liberty or tranquility, it was preferable to the universal licence and disorder, which had every where preceded it. But perhaps there was no event which tended farther to the improvement of the age, than one, which has not been much remarked, the accidental finding a copy of Justinian's Pandects, about the year 1130, in the town of Amalfi in Italy.

The ecclesiastics, who had leisure, and some inclination to study, immediately adopted with zeal this excellent system of jurisprudence, and spread the knowledge of it in every part of Europe. Besides the intrinsic merit of the performance, it was recommended to them by its original connexion with the imperial city of Rome, which, being the seat of their religion, seemed to acquire a new lustre and authority, by the diffusion of its laws over the western world. In less than ten years after the discovery of the Pandects, Vacarius, under the protection of Theobald, archbishop of Canterbury, read public lectures of civil law in the university of Oxford; and the clergy every where, by their example as well as exhortation, were the means of spreading the highest esteem for this new science. That order of men, having large possessions to defend, were in a manner necessitated to turn their studies towards the law; and their properties being often endangered by the violence of the princes and barons, it became their interest to enforce the observance of general and equitable rules, from which alone they could receive protection. As they possessed all the knowledge of the age, and were alone acquainted with the habits of thinking, the practice as well as science of the law, fell mostly into their hands: and though the close connexion, which without any necessity they formed between the canon and civil law, begot a jealousy in the laity of England, and prevented the Roman jurisprudence from becoming the municipal law of the country, as was the case in many states of Europe, a great part of it was secretly transferred into the practice of the courts of justice, and the imitation of their neighbours, made the English gradually endeavour to raise their own law from its original state of rudeness and imperfection.

It is easy to see what advantages Europe must have reaped by its inheriting at once from the ancients, so complete an art, which was of itself so necessary for giving security to all other arts, and which, by refining, and still more, by bestowing solidity on the judgment, served as a model to farther improvements. The sensible utility of the Roman law both to public and private interest recommended the study of it, at a time when the more exalted and speculative sciences carried no charms with them; and thus the last branch of ancient literature, which remained uncorrupted, was happily the first transmitted to the modern world. For it is remarkable, that in the decline of Roman learning, when the philosophers were universally infected with superstition and sophistry, and the poets and historians with barbarism, the lawyers, who in other countries are seldom models of science or politeness, were yet able, by the constant study and close imitation of their predecessors, to maintain the same good sense in their decisions and reasonings, and the same purity in their language and expression.

What bestowed an additional merit on the civil law, was the extreme ignorance and imperfection of that jurisprudence, which preceded it among all the European nations, especially among the Saxons or ancient English. What absurdities prevailed at that time in the administration of justice, may be conceived from the authentic monuments which remain of the ancient Saxon laws; where a pecuniary commutation was received for every crime, where stated prices were fixed for men's lives and members, where private revenges were authorized for all injuries, where the use of the ordeal, corsnet, and afterwards of the duel, was the received method of proof, and where the judges were rustic freeholders, assembled of a sudden, and deciding a cause from one debate or altercation of the parties. Such a state of society was very little advanced beyond the rude state of nature: violence universally prevailed, instead of general and equitable maxims: the pretended liberty of the times, was only an incapacity of submitting to government: and men, not protected by law in their lives and properties, sought shelter, by their personal servility and attachments, under some powerful chieftain, or by voluntary combinations.

The gradual progress of improvement, raised the Europeans somewhat from this uncultivated state; and affairs, in this island particularly, took very early a turn, which was more favourable to justice and to liberty. Civil employments and occupations soon became honourable among the English: the situation of that people rendered not the perpetual attention to wars so necessary as among their neighbours, and all regard was not confined to the military profession: the gentry, and even the nobility, began to deem an acquaintance with the law, a requisite part of education: they were less diverted than afterwards from studies of this kind by other sciences; and in the age of Henry VI. we are told by Fortescue, there were in the inns of court about two thousand students, most of them men of honourable birth, who gave application to this branch of civil knowledge. A circumstance which proves, that a considerable advance was already made in the science of government, and which prognosticated still a greater.

One chief advantage, which resulted from the introduction and progress of the arts, was the introduction and progress of freedom; and this consequence affected men both in their personal and civil capacities.

If we consider the ancient state of Europe, we shall find, that the far greater part of the society were every where bereaved of their personal liberty, and lived entirely at the will of their masters. Every one, that was not noble, was a slave: the peasants were sold along with the land: the few inhabitants of cities were not in a better condition: even the gentry themselves were subjected to a long train of subordination under the greater barons or chief vassals of the crown; who, though seemingly placed in a high state of splendor, yet, having but a slender protection from the law, were exposed to every tempest of state, and by the precarious condition, in which they lived, paid dearly for the power of oppressing and tyrannizing over their inferiors. The first incident which broke in upon this violent system of government, was the practice, begun in France, of erecting communities and corporations, endowed with privileges and a separate municipal government, which gave them protection against the tyranny of the barons, and which the prince himself deemed it prudent to respect. The relaxation of the feudal tenures, and an execution, somewhat stricter, of the public law, bestowed an independence on vassals, which was unknown to their forefathers. And even the peasants themselves, though later than other orders of the state, made their escape from those bonds of villenage or slavery, in which they had formerly been retained.

It may appear strange, that the progress of the arts, which seems, among the Greek and Romans, to have daily encreased the number of slaves, should, in later times, have proved so general a source of liberty: but this difference of the events proceeded from a great difference in the circumstances, which attended those institutions. The ancient barons, being obliged to maintain themselves continually in a military posture, and little emulous of elegance or splendor, employed not their villains as domestic servants, much less as manufacturers, but composed their retinue of free-men, whose military spirit rendered the chieftain formidable to his neighbours, and who were ready to attend him in every warlike enterprize. The villains were occupied entirely in the cultivation of their master's land, and paid their rents either in corn and cattle and other produce of the farm, or in servile offices, which they performed about the baron's family, and upon the farms which he retained in his own possession. In proportion as agriculture improved, and money encreased, it was found, that these services, though extremely burthensome in the villain, were of little advantage to the master; and that the produce of a large estate could be much more conveniently disposed of by the peasant himself, who raised it, than by the landlord or his bailiff, who were formerly accustomed to receive it. A commutation was therefore made of rents for services, and of money rents for those in kind; and as men, in a subsequent age, discovered, that farms were better cultivated where the farmer enjoyed a security of possession, the practice of granting leases to the peasant began to prevail, which entirely broke the bonds of servitude, already much relaxed from the former practices. Thus villenage went gradually into disuse through the more civilized parts of Europe: the interest of the master, as well as that of the slave, concurred in this alteration. The latest laws which we find in England for the enforcing or regulating this species of servitude, were enacted in the reign of Henry VII. And though the ancient statutes on this subject remain still unrepealed by parliament, it appears, that, before the reign of Elizabeth, the distinction of villain and freeman was totally, though insensibly abolished, and that no person remained in the state to whom the former laws could be applied.

Thus personal freedom became almost general in Europe; an advantage which paved the way for the encrease of political or civil liberty, and which, even where it was not attended with this salutary effect, served to give the members of the community some of the most considerable advantages of it.

The constitution of the English government, ever since the invasion of this island by the Saxons, may boast of this preeminence, that in no age the will of the monarch was ever entirely absolute and uncontrouled: but in other respects the balance of power has extremely shifted among the several orders of the state; and this fabric has experienced the same mutability, which has attended all human institutions.

The antient Saxons, like the other German nations, where each individual was enured to arms, and where the independence of men was secured by a great equality of possessions, seem to have admitted a considerable mixture of democracy into their form of government, and to have been one of the freest nations, of which there remains any account in the records of history. After this tribe was settled in England, especially after the dissolution of the heptarcy, the great extent of the kingdom produced a great inequality in property; and the balance seems to have inclined to the side of the Aristocracy. The Norman conquest threw more authority into the hands of the sovereign, which, however, admitted of great controul; though derived less from the general forms of the constitution, which were inaccurate and irregular, than from the independent power enjoyed by each baron in his particular district or province. The establishment of the great charter exalted still higher the Aristocracy, imposed regular limits on royal power, and gradually introduced some mixture of Democracy into the constitution. But even during this period, from the accession of Edward I. to the death of Richard III. the condition of the commons was nowise desirable; a kind of Polish Aristocracy prevailed; and tho' the kings were limited, the people were as yet far from being free. It required the authority almost absolute of the sovereigns, which took place in the subsequent period, to pull down these disorderly and licentious tyrants, who were equal enemies to peace and to freedom, and to establish that regular execution of the laws, which, in a following age, enabled the people to erect a regular and equitable plan of liberty.

In each of these successive alterations, the only rule of government, which is intelligible or carries any authority with it, is the established practice of the age, and the maxims of administration, which are at that time prevalent, and universally assented to. Those who, from a pretended respect to antiquity, appeal at every turn to an original plan of the constitution, only cover their turbulent spirit and their private ambition under the appearance of venerable forms; and whatever period they pitch on for their model, they may still be carried back to a more ancient period, where they will find the measures of power entirely different, and where every circumstance, by reason of the greater barbarity of the times, will appear still less worthy of imitation. Above all, a civilized nation, like the English, who have happily established the most perfect and most accurate system of liberty, that ever was found compatible with government, ought to be cautious of appealing to the practice of their ancestors, or regarding the maxims of uncultivated ages as certain rules for their present conduct. An acquaintance with the history of the remote periods of their government is chiefly useful by instructing them to cherish their present constitution from a comparison or contrast with the condition of those distant times. And it is also curious, by showing them the remote, and commonly faint and disfigured originals of the most finished and most noble institutions, and by instructing them in the great mixture of accident which commonly concurs with a small ingredient of wisdom and foresight, in erecting the complicated fabric of the most perfect government.'

To close the article, we must congratulate our countrymen on this accession to their literary fame; we must exhort Mr. Hume to continue those exertions of genius, so respectable to himself, and useful to the community; and we beseech our readers, not to ascribe to partial attachments the warm applause which we bestow wholly upon merit. The proofs are before them; let these be the tests of our candour.

14
OWEN RUFFHEAD

Owen Ruffhead, letter to Hume, March 1, 1763.
Complete letter; from *Letters of Eminent Persons addressed to David Hume*
(1849).

Owen Ruffhead (1723–1769) was the author of the *Monthly Review* articles on the 1759 and 1762 instalments of Hume's *History*, contained earlier in this collection. Quotations from his reviews of Richard Hurd's *Moral and Political Dialogues* (1759) and William Tytler's *Historical and Critical Enquiry* (1760) are also included earlier. In this letter to Hume – written a little over a year after the 1761 review – he again expresses the same admiration that we see in both of his reviews. He then criticises two passages in the 1762 volumes of Hume's *History*; in both cases Ruffhead opposes Hume's view that the Commons during Saxon times had very little political power. The first regards Hume's characterisation of the Saxon Witenagemot, and is similar to Ruffhead's criticism in his 1761 review. In later editions of the *History* Hume removed both of these passages. Ruffhead sent his letter to Hume by way of their common friend, Andrew Millar. In a correspondence now lost, Millar apparently informed Hume that Ruffhead authored earlier reviews of Hume's *History*. In a letter of response to Millar, Hume expressed gratitude to Ruffhead and enclosed a reply to Millar to deliver to him: "I reckon myself much beholden to Mr Ruffhead for his Letter, and, as I conjecture from yours, for his favourable Opinion, expressed on other Occasions. I beg of you to send him the enclosd" (Hume to Andrew Millar, March 10, 1763). Hume's note to Ruffhead has not yet surfaced. The following is as appears in John Hill Burton's *Letters of Eminent Persons addressed to David Hume* (1849). A comparison of Burton's version with the original indicates only minor modifications in spelling and punctuation, but no omissions or alterations in wording. I have reintroduced some paragraph breaks omitted by Burton.

Sir,

In a conversation which I had the pleasure to hold with your very worthy friend, Mr. Millar, concerning your History of England, I had occasion to take notice of some inaccuracies in the volume last published; and I am indebted to his kind intervention for this opportunity of submitting my remarks to your candid consideration. You are sensible, sir, that they who most sincerely admire the whole, are most free in animadverting on particular parts. I shall therefore make no apology for the liberty I take, since it is a proof of the respect I pay to your merit. Was you less liberal and ingenuous, I should be more scrupulous and reserved.

I am persuaded, sir, that you are above the little pride of being flattered by the applause of admiration of readers, who do not examine and think for themselves. Had I, however, been of a disposition to resign myself to authority implicitly, yet being engaged in a pursuit wherein I thought it a duty to take nothing upon trust, I found myself under a necessity of comparing some passages, in your History, with the originals you refer to; and, upon collation, I am induced to doubt whether they warrant the use you make of them.

Speaking of the Saxon constitution, you observe, with your usual sagacity, that there is some necessity for supposing that the Saxon *Wittenagemot*, (from which you exclude the Burgesses or Commons) consisted of other members besides the ecclesiastics and aldermen. You therefore conclude that the more considerable proprietors of land were, without any election, constituent members of the national assembly; and you suppose that *forty* hides was the estate requisite for entitling the possessor to his honourable privilege. In support of this opinion, you refer to a passage in Hist. Eliensis, chap. 36, 40, from whence, you say, it appears that a person, even though allied to the crown, was not esteemed a *princeps* till he had acquired a fortune of that extent; and you add, that this passage is remarked by Dugdale, (Pref. to his Baron. vol. i.,) and that "he draws the same inference from it."

Now, sir, upon reference to Dugdale, I have not been able, after the most diligent scrutiny, to find any thing which justifies the use you make of his authority. All that Dugdale seems to conclude from the ancient history is, that, in the *Conqueror's* time, he who had not *forty* hides of land was not reputed a *baron*; which, you will admit, is in no degree applicable to the qualification of a *Princeps* in the Saxon *Wittengemot*. Besides, with due deference to your judgment, I cannot think it probable that *forty* hides should be the requisite estate to constitute the possessor a member of the national assembly, when it is evident, from the best authorities, that *five* hides only were sufficient to advance the proprietor to the dignity of a *Thane*.

Again, sir, in another part of your History, you refer to a record in Cotton's Abridgment, where the King "told the Commons that they were only *petitioners*, that is," you add, "*they had not any proper* legislative *authority*."

But, considering the occasion of the King's answer, and taking the whole sentence together, I am inclined to think that your conclusion is too hastily drawn. Upon examining the preceding record, we find a petition from some of the relations of the Archbishop of Canterbury, praying that the Archbishop might recover against *Roger Waldon* for *waste* done in the archbishopric, which the King granted. Against this the commons preferred their petition, praying that, "Forasmuch as they were not made privy to the *judgment* aforesaid, that no record be made to charge, or make them parties thereunto;" whereupon the Archbishop of Canterbury, by the King's command, answered, "That the commons were only *petitioners*, and that all *judgments* appertain to the King, and to the lords, *unless* it were on *statutes*, grants," &c.

Thus it appears, from the whole context, that the grounds of the commons' petition concerned a matter of mere judicial cognizance; and that, though the King denies their *judicial* authority, yet he expressly confirms and saves their *legislative* right, by these words of exception, "*Unless* it were on *statutes*," &c.

In these instances, sir, I apprehend that, in the rapidity of composition, you have too slightly regarded the pages of antiquity. If I am right in my objections, I dare say that you will be candid enough to rectify these inaccuracies in some future edition; if I am wrong, I trust that you will be kind enough to correct my errors.

Should it, however, be confessed that there are inaccuracies, we may say of them, as Addison says of Milton's blemishes: and I cannot release you from this tedious interpretation, without expressing the obligations which I, in particular, owe to you for your excellent History, which I have read with no less pleasure than profit.

I am, with perfect sincerity and well-grounded esteem,
Your most obedient servant,
Owen Ruffhead.

1. March 1763.
Middle Temple.

15
ARCHIBALD MACLAINE

Archibald Maclaine, *An ecclesiastical history, antient and modern, from the birth of Christ, to the beginning of the present century: ... By the late learned John Lawrence Mosheim, ... Translated from the original, ... by Archibald Maclaine, ... In two volumes.* London: printed for A. Millar, 1765, 2 v. Note and complete Appendix 2; from 1826 edition, vols. 4 and 6.

Born in Monaghan, Ireland, Archibald Maclaine (1722–1804) was son of a Presbyterian minister, and brother of James Maclaine, the "gentleman highwayman." He was a student of Francis Hutcheson at the University of Glasgow, and in 1747 became minister of the English church at The Hague. He authored several theological works and was best known for his translation of the Latin *Institutiones historiae Christianae* by Johann Lorenz Mosheim (1694?–1755). In a footnote to Mosheim's account of Luther, Maclaine attacks Hume's discussion of indulgences. In particular, he challenges Hume's view that Luther spitefully opposed indulgences because his Augustinian order was not at that time granted the lucrative commission to sell them. In the 1768 second edition of this work Maclaine added several appendices, one of which attacks Hume's claim in the *History* that the reformers were incited by enthusiasm. Maclaine first contests Hume's view that superstition and enthusiasm are diametrically opposed to each other – superstition being linked with Catholicism, and enthusiasm being linked with the Protestant reformers. First, Maclaine argues, philosophically inclined people will see that "they lend, on many occasions, some strength and assistance to each other." Second, those versed in church history will see that Catholicism has a long record of fanaticism, and not just superstition. Third, Protestents will be puzzled by Hume's apparent pronouncement against all reformers; although some were indeed fanatical, others were not. Maclaine notes that Hume's comments on Protestant enthusiasm are scattered throughout his *History*, and "gradually unite their influence on the imagination of an uninstructed and unwary reader." Maclaine cautiously suggests that religious fanaticism is justified when all other measures of reform fail, and the Protestant reformation was a case in point.

Writing for the *Monthly Review*, William Rose commends "the ingenious and learned Translator, who has added many useful and judicious notes, which do honour to his abilities and taste, and render the translation much more valuable than the original. Regarding Maclaine's note on Hume's account of indulgences, Rose writes that Maclaine "has, in a very judicious manner, set the matter in a true light." Maclaine's translation of Mosheim was also favourably received by the *Critical Review*.[1]

Shortly after the *Ecclesiastical History* was published, Maclaine wrote Andrew Millar (Hume's and Maclaine's bookseller) concerning the recent controversy between Hume and Rousseau:

> Everybody, however, except a few foaming partisans of Rousseau, is perswaded that Mr Hume has been ill repaid for his generosity and friendship…. For my own part I am of this way of thinking, tho at the same time, I cannot say it was highly prudent in Mr Hume to bring wt him such an *ouran-outang* into England…. [as quoted by Andrew Millar in an October 4, 1766 letter to Hume]

Hume responded to Millar, "I fancy Mr Macleane's Questions are by this time answerd to his Satisfaction" (October 21, 1766). Maclaine is favourably mentioned in Joseph Towers's *Observations on Mr. Hume's History of England* (1778), contained later in this collection. Maclaine's translation of Mosheim was published numerous times throughout the 18th and 19th centuries. The following is from the 1826 edition.

HISTORY OF THE REFORMATION
SECTION I.
CHAPTER II.

III. … At this, Luther, unable to repress his just indignation, raised his warning voice, and, in ninety-five propositions (maintained publicly at Wittenberg, on the 30th of September, 1517), censured the extravagant extortion of these quæstors, and plainly pointed out the pontiff as a partaker of their guilt, since he suffered the people to be seduced, by such delusions, from placing their principal confidence in Christ, the only proper object of their trust. This was the commencement and foundation of that memorable rupture and revolution in the church, which humbled the grandeur of the lordly pontiffs, and eclipsed so great a part of their glory.

{[Note:] Dr. Mosheim has taken no notice of the calumnies invented and propagated by some late authors, in order to make Luther's zealous opposition

---

[1]   *Monthly Review*, 1765, Vol. 33, August pp. 89–107, November pp. 329–342, December pp. 430–444; *Critical Review*, 1765, Vol. 19, pp. 401–410, Vol. 20, pp. 1–8, 81–93.

to the publication of indulgences appear to be the effect of selfish and ignoble motives. It may not, therefore, be improper to set that point in a true light; not that the cause of the reformation (which must stand by its own intrinsic dignity, and is in no way affected by the views or characters of its instruments) can derive any strength from this inquiry; but as it may tend to vindicate the personal character of a man, who has done eminent service to the cause of religion.

Mr. Hume, in his history of the reign of Henry VII., has thought proper to repeat what the enemies of the reformation, and some of its dubious or ill-informed friends, have advanced, with respect to the motives that engaged Luther to oppose the doctrine of indulgences. This elegant historian affirms, that the

"Augustin friars had *usually* been employed in Saxony to preach indulgences, and from this trust had derived both profit and consideration; that Arcemboldi gave this occupation to the Dominicans; that Martin Luther, an Augustin friar, professor in the university of Wittenberg, *resenting the affront put upon his order,* began to preach against the abuses that were committed in the sale of indulgences, and being provoked by opposition, proceeded even to decry indulgences themselves."

It is to be wished, that Mr. Hume's candor had engaged him to examine this accusation better, before he had ventured to repeat it. In the first place, it is not true, that the Augustin friars had been usually employed in Saxony to preach indulgences. It is well known, that the commission had been offered alternately, and sometimes jointly, to all the Mendicants, whether Augustin friars, Dominicans, Franciscans, or Carmelites. From the year 1229, that lucrative commission was principally entrusted to the Dominicans;[2] and in the records which relate to indulgences, we rarely meet with the name of an Augustin friar, and not a single act by which it appears, that the Roman pontiff ever named the friars of that order to the office under consideration. More particularly it is remarkable, that for half a century before Luther, (i.e. from 1450 to 1517) during which period indulgences were sold with the most scandalous marks of avaricious extortion and impudence, we scarcely find an Augustin friar mentioned as being employed in that service; if we except a monk named Balzius, who was no more than an underling of the papal quæstor Raymond Peraldus; so far is it from being true, that the Augustin monks were exclusively, or even usually, engaged in that service.[3] Mr. Hume has built his assertion upon

[2] See Weisammi Memorabilia Historiæ Sacræ N.T. p. 1051.

[3] See Harpii Dissertat. de Nonnullis Indulgentiarum (Sæc. xiv. et xv.) Quæstoribus, p. 384, 387.

the sole authority of a single expression of Paul Sarpi, which has been abundantly refuted by De Priero, Pallavicini, and Grawson, the mortal enemies of Luther. – But it may be alleged, that even supposing it was not usual to employ the Augustin friars alone in the propagation of indulgences, yet Luther might be offended at seeing such an important commission given to the Dominicans exclusively, and that, consequently, this was his motive in opposing the propagation of indulgences. To shew the injustice of this allegation, I observe, secondly, that, in the time of Luther, the preaching of indulgences had become very odious and unpopular; and it is therefore far from being probable, that Luther would have been solicitous about obtaining such a commission, either for himself or for his order. The princes of Europe, with many bishops, and multitudes of learned and pious men, had opened their eyes upon the turpitude of this infamous traffic; and even the Franciscans and Dominicans, toward the conclusion of the fifteenth century, opposed it publicly, both in their discourses and in their writings.[4] The very commission, which is supposed to have excited the envy of Luther, was offered by Leo to the general of the Franciscans, and was refused both by him and his order,[5] who gave it over entirely to Albert, bishop of Mentz and Magdeburg. Is it then to be imagined, that either Luther, or the other Augustin friars, aspired after a commission of which the Franciscans were ashamed? Besides, it is a mistake to affirm, that this office was given to the Dominicans in general; for it was given to Tetzel alone, an individual member of that order, who had been notorious for his extortion, profligacy, and barbarity.

But that neither resentment nor envy were the motives that led Luther to oppose the doctrine and publication of indulgences, will appear with the utmost evidence, if we consider, in the third place, that he was never accused of any such motives, either in the edicts of the pontiffs of his time, or amidst the other reproaches of the contemporary writers, who defended the cause of Rome, and who were generally very prodigal of their invectives and calumnies. All the contemporary adversaries of Luther are absolutely silent on this head. From the year 1517 to 1546, when the dispute about indulgences was carried on with the greatest warmth and animosity, not one writer ever ventured to reproach Luther with these ignoble motives of opposition now under consideration. I speak not of Erasmus, Sleidan, De Thou, Guicciardini, and others, whose testimony might be perhaps suspected of partiality in his favor; but I speak of Caietan, Hoogstrat, De Priero, Emser, and even the infamous John Tetzel, whom Luther opposed with such vehemence and bitterness. Even Cochlæus was silent on this head during the life of Luther, though, after the

---

[4] See Walch. op. Lutheri, tom. xv. p. 114, 238, 312, 349. – Seckendorf. Hist. Lutheranismi, lib. i. sect. vi. p. 13.

[5] See Walch. loc. cit. p. 371.

death of that great reformer, he broached the calumny I am here refuting. But such was the scandalous character of this man, who was notorious for fraud, calumny, lying, and their sister vices,[6] that Pallavicini, Bossuet, and other enemies of Luther, were ashamed to make use either of his name or testimony. Now may it not be fairly presumed, that the contemporaries of Luther were better judges of his character, and of the principles from which he acted, than those who lived in after-times? Can it be imagined, that motives to action, which escaped their prying eyes, should have discovered themselves to us who live at such a distance of time from the scene of action, to M. Bossuet, to Mr. Hume, and to other abettors of this ill-contrived and foolish story. Either there are no rules of moral evidence, or Mr. Hume's assertion is entirely groundless.

I might add many other considerations to shew the unreasonableness of supposing that Luther exposed himself to the rage of the pontiff, to the persecutions of an exasperated clergy, to the severity of such a potent and despotic prince as Charles V. and to the risque of death itself, from a principle of avarice and ambition. But I have said enough to satisfy every candid mind.}

THE SECOND APPENDIX,
BY DR. MACLAINE;

Concerning the Spirit and Conduct of the first Reformers, and the Charge of enthusiasm (*i.e. Fanaticism*) that has been brought against them by a celebrated Author.

The candor and impartiality, with which Dr. Mosheim represents the transactions of those who were agents and instruments in bringing about the Reformation, are highly laudable. He acknowledges that imprudence, passion, and even a low self-interest, mingled sometimes their rash proceedings and ignoble motives in this excellent cause; and, in the very nature of things, it could not be otherwise. It is one of the inevitable consequences of the subordination and connexions of civil society, that many improper instruments and agents are set to work in all great and important revolutions, whether of a religious or political nature. When great men appear in these revolutions, they draw after them their dependents; and the unhappy effects of a party spirit are unavoidably displayed in the best cause. The subjects follow their prince; the multitude adopt the system of their leaders, without entering into its true spirit, or being judiciously attentive to the proper methods of promoting it; and thus irregular proceedings are employed in the maintenance of truth. Thus it happened in the

---

[6]   Sleidan de Statu Rel. et Reip. in Dedic. Epist. ad August. Electorem.

important revolution that delivered a great part of Europe from the ignomnious yoke of the Roman pontiff. The sovereigns, the ecclesiastics, the men of weight, piety, and learning, who arose to assert the rights of human nature, the cause of genuine Christianity, and the exercise of religious liberty, came forth into the field of controversy with a multitude of dependents, admirers, and friends, whose motives and conduct cannot be entirely justified. Besides, when the eyes of whole nations were opened upon the iniquitous absurdities of popery, and upon the tyranny and insolence of the Roman pontiffs, it was scarcely possible to set bounds to the indignation of an incensed and tumultuous multitude, who are naturally prone to extremes, generally pass from blind submission to lawless ferocity, and too rarely distinguish between the use and abuse of their undoubted rights. In a word, many things, which appear to us extremely irregular in the conduct and measures of some of the instruments of our happy reformation, will be entitled to a certain degree of indulgence, if the spirit of the times, the situation of the contending parties, the barbarous provocations of popery, and the infirmities of human nature, be duly and attentively considered.

The question here is, what was the spirit which animated the first and principal reformers, who arose in times of darkness and despair to deliver oppressed kingdoms from the dominion of Rome, and upon what principles a Luther, a Zuingle, a Calvin, a Melanchthon, a Bucer, &c. embarked in the arduous cause of the Reformation? This question, indeed, is not at all necessary to the defence of the Reformation, which rests upon the strong foundations of Scripture and reason, and whose excellence is absolutely independent of the virtues of those who took the lead in promoting it. Bad men may be, and often are, embarked in the best causes, as such causes afford the most specious mask to cover mercenary views, or to disguise ambitious purposes. But until the more than Jesuitical and disingenuous Philips resumed the trumpet of calumny,[7] even the voice of popery had ceased to attack the moral characters of the leading reformers.

These eminent men were indeed attacked from another quarter, and by a much more respectable writer. The truly ingenious Mr. Hume, so justly celebrated as one of the first favorites of the historic muse, has, in his history of England, and more especially in the history of the houses of Tudor and Stuart, represented the character and temper of the first reformers in a point of view, which undoubtedly shews, that he had not considered them with the close and impartial attention that ought always to precede personal reflexions. He has laid it down as a principle, that *superstition* and *enthusiasm* are two

---

[7] See the various answers that were made to this biographer by the ingenious Mr. Pye, the learned Dr. Neve, and other commendable writers who have appeared in this controversy.

species of religion that stand in diametrical opposition to each other; and seems to establish it as a fact, that the former is the genius of popery, and the latter the characteristic of the Reformation. Both the principle and its application must appear extremely singular; and three sorts of persons must be more especially surprised at it.

In the first place, persons of a philosophical turn, who are accustomed to study human nature, and to describe with precision both its regular and eccentric movements, must be surprised to see superstition and fanaticism[8] represented as opposite and jarring qualities. They have been often seen together, holding with each other a most friendly correspondence; and indeed if we consider their nature and their essential characters, their union will appear, not only possible, but in some cases natural, if not necessary. *Superstition*, which consists in false and abject notions of the Deity, in the gloomy and groundless fears of invisible beings, and in the absurd rites, that these notions and there fears naturally produce, is certainly the root of Various branches of fanaticism. For what is *fanaticism*, but the visions, illuminations, impulses, and dreams of an over-heated fancy, converted into rules of faith, hope, worship, and practice? This fanaticism, as it springs up in a melancholy or a cheerful complexion, assumes a variety of aspects, and its morose and gloomy forms are certainly most congenial with superstition, in its proper sense. It was probably this consideration that led the author of the article *Fanaticism*, in the famous Dictionnaire Encyclopedique, to define it[9] as "a blind and passionate zeal, which arises from superstitious opinions, and leads its votaries to commit ridiculous, unjust, and cruel actions, not only without shame, but even with certain internal feelings of joy and comfort;" from which the author concludes, that "fanaticism is really nothing more than superstition set in motion." This definition unites perhaps too closely these two kinds of false religion, whose enormities have furnished very ill-grounded pretexts for discrediting and misrepresenting the true. It is, however, a testimony from one of the pretended oracles of modern philosophy, in favor of the compatibility of fanaticism with superstition. These two principles are evidently distinct; because superstition is, generally speaking, the effect of ignorance, or of a judgement perverted by a sour and splenetic temper; whereas fanaticism is the

---

[8] I use the word *fanaticism* here, instead of *enthusiasm*, to prevent all ambiguity; because, as shall be shewn presently, Mr. Hume takes *enthusiasm* in its worse sense when he applies it to the reformers; and in that sense it is not only equivalent to, but is perfectly synonymous with, fanaticism. Besides, the latter term is used indiscriminately with enthusiasm, by this celebrated historian, in characterising the Reformation.

[9] The words of the original are, "Le fanatisme est un zele aveugle et passionné, qui nait des opinions superstitiouses, et fait commettre des actions ridicules, injustes et cruelles, non seulement sans honte, mais avec une sorte de joye et de consolation. Le fanatisme donc n'est que la superstition mise en mouvement."

offspring of an inflamed imagination, and may exist where there is no super-stition, *i.e.* where no false or gloomy notions of the divinity are entertained. But, though distinct, they are not opposite principles; on the contrary, they lend, on many occasions, some strength and assistance to each other.

If persons accustomed to philosophical precision will not relish the maxim of the celebrated writer which I have been now considering, so neither, in the second place, can those who are versed in ecclesiastical history look upon super-stition as a more predominant characteristic of popery than fanaticism; and yet this is a leading idea, which is not only visible in many parts of this author's excellent History, but appears to be the basis of all the reflexions he employs, and of all the epithets he uses, in his speculations upon the Romish religion.

And nevertheless it is manifest, that the multitudes of fanatics, which arose in the church of Rome before the Reformation, are truly innumerable; and the operations of fanaticism in that church were, at least, as visible and frequent, as the restless workings of superstition; they went, in short, hand in hand, and united their visions and their terrors in the support of the papacy. It is, more especially, well known, that the greatest part of the monastic establishments (that alternately insulted the benignity of Providence by their austerities, and abused it by their licentious luxury), were originally founded in consequence of pretended illuminations, miraculous dreams, and other wild delusions of an overheated fancy. Whenever a new doctrine was to be established, that could augment the authority of the pope, or fill the coffers of the clergy; whenever a new convent was to be erected, there was always a vision or a miracle ready to facilitate the business; nor must it be imagined, that forgery and imposture were the only agents in this matter; – by no means; – imposture there was; and it was frequently employed: but impostors made use of fanatics; and in return fanatics found impostors, who spread abroad their fame, and turned their visions to profit. Were I to recount with the utmost simplicity, without the smallest addition of ludicrous embellishment, the ecstasies, visions, seraphic amours, celestial apparitions, that are said to have shed such an odor of sanctity upon the male and female saints of the Romish church; were I to pass in review the famous conformities of St. Francis, the illuminations of St. Ignatius, and the enormous cloud of fanatical witnesses that have dishonored humanity in bearing testimony to popery, this dissertation would become a voluminous history. Let the reader cast an eye upon Dr. Mosheim's account of those ages which more immediately preceded the Reformation, and he will see what a number of sects, *purely fanatical*, arose in the bosom of the Romish church.

But this is not all – for it must be carefully observed, that even those extrav-agant fanatics, who produced such disorders in Germany about the commencement of the Reformation, were nursed in the bosom of popery, were professed papists before they adopted the cause of Luther; and that many of them even passed directly from popery to fanaticism, without even entering into the outward profession of Lutheranism. It is also to be observed, that beside the fanatics, who exposed themselves to the contempt of the wise upon the public theatre of popery, Seckendorf speaks of a sect that merits this denomination, which had spread in the Netherlands, before Luther raised his voice against popery, and whose members were engaged, by the terror of penal laws, to dissemble their sentiments, and even affected a devout compliance with the ceremonies of the established worship, until religious liberty, introduced by the reformation, encouraged them to pull off the mask, and propagate their opinions, several of which were licentious and profane.

But, in the third place, the friends of the Reformation must naturally be both surprised and displeased to find enthusiasm, or fanaticism, laid down by Mr. Hume, as the character and spirit of its founders and abettors, without any exception or distinction in favor of any one of the reformers. That fanaticism was visible in the conduct and spirit of many who embraced the Reformation, is a fact which I do not pretend to deny, and it may be worthy of the reader's curiosity to consider, for a moment, how this came to pass. That religious liberty, which the Reformation introduced and granted (in consequence of its essential principles) indiscriminately to all, to the learned and unlearned, rendered this eruption of enthusiasm inevitable. It is one of the imperfections annexed to all human things, that our best blessings have their inconveniences, or, at least, are susceptible of abuse. As liberty is a natural right, but not a discerning principle, it could not open the door to truth without letting error and delusion come with it. If reason came forth with dignity, when delivered from the despotism of authority, and the blind servitude of implicit faith; imagination, also set free, and less able to bear the prosperous change, came forth likewise, but with a different aspect, and exposed to view the reveries which it had been long obliged to conceal.

Thus many fanatical phantoms were exhibited, which neither arose from the spirit of the Reformation, nor from the principles of the reformers, but which had been engendered in the bosom of popery, and which the fostering rays of liberty had disclosed; similar in this, to the enlivening beams of the sun, which fructify indiscriminately the salutary plant in the well-cultivated ground, and the noxious weed in a rank and neglected soil. And as the Reformation had no such miraculous influence (not to speak of the imperfection that attended its infancy, and that has not entirely been removed from its more advanced stages) as to cure human nature of its infirmities and follies, to convert irregular passions into regular principles, or to turn men into angels before the time, it has still left the field open, both for fanaticism and superstition to sow their tares among the good seed; and this will probably be the case until the end of the world. It is here, that we must seek for the true cause of all that condemnable enthusiasm which has dishonored the Christian name, and often troubled the order of civil society, at different periods since the Reformation; and for which the reformation is no more responsible, than a free government is for the weakness or corruption of those who abuse its levity and indulgence. The Reformation established the sacred and inalienable right of private judgement; but it could not hinder the private judgement of many from being wild and extravagant.

The Reformation, then, which the multiplied enormities of popery rendered so necessary, must be always distinguished from the abuses that might be, and were often made, of the liberty it introduced. If you ask, indeed, what was the temper or spirit of the first heralds of this happy Reformation, Mr. Hume will tell you, that they were universally inflamed with the highest enthusiasm. This assertion, if taken singly, and not compared with other passages relating to the reformers, might be understood in a sense consistent with truth, and even honorable to the character of these eminent men. For, if by enthusiasm we understand that spirit of ardor, intrepidity, and generous zeal, which leads men to brave the most formidable obstacles and dangers in defence of a cause, whose excellence and importance have made a deep impression upon their minds, the first reformers will be allowed by their warmest friends to have been enthusiasts. This species of enthusiasm is a noble affection, when fitly placed and wisely exerted. It is this generous sensibility, this ardent feeling of the great and excellent, that forms heroes and patriots; and, without it, nothing difficult and arduous, that is attended with danger, or prejudice to our temporal interests, can either be attempted with vigor, or executed with success. If this ingenious writer had even observed, that the ardor of the first reformers was more or less violent, that it was more or less blended with the warmth and vivacity of human passions, candor would be obliged to avow the charge.

But it is not in any of these points of view, that our eminent historian considers the spirit, temper, and enthusiasm of the first reformers. The enthusiasm he attributes to them is fanaticism in its worst sense. He speaks indeed of the 'inflexible intrepidity, with which they braved dangers, torments, and even death itself;' but he calls them 'the fanatical and enraged reformers;' he represents fanaticism, through the whole course of his history, as the characteristic of the Protestant religion and its glorious founders: the terms, 'Protestant fanaticism – fanatical churches' – are interspersed in various parts of his work; and we never meet with the least appearance of a distinction between the rational and enthusiastic, the wise and indiscreet friends of the Reformation. In short, we find a phraseology constantly employed upon this subject, which discovers an intention to confound Protestantism with enthusiasm, and to make *reformers* and *fanatics* synonymous terms. We are told, that, while absurd rites and burthensome superstitions reigned in the Romish church, the reformers were 'thrown, by a spirit of opposition, into an enthusiastic strain of devotion;' and, in another place, that the latter 'placed all merit in a mysterious species of faith, in inward vision, rapture, and ecstasy.' It would be endless to quote the passages in which this representation of things is repeated in a great variety of phrases, and artfully insinuated into the mind of the reader, by dexterous strokes of a seducing pencil; which, though scattered here and there, yet gradually unite their influence on the imagination of an uninstructed and unwary reader, and form, imperceptibly, an unfavorable impression of that great event, to which we owe at this day our civil and religious liberty, and our deliverance from a yoke of superstitious and barbarous despotism. Protestants, in all ages and places, are stigmatised by Mr. Hume with very dishonorable titles; and it struck me particularly to see even the generous opposers of the Spanish inquisition in Holland, whose proceedings were so moderate, and whose complaints were so humble, until the barbarous yoke of superstition and tyranny became intolerable; it struck me, I say, to see these generous patriots branded with the general character of *bigots*. This is certainly a severe appellation; and were it applied with much more equity than it is, I think it would still come with an ill grace from a lover of freedom, from a man who lives and writes with security under the auspicious shade of that very liberty which the Reformation introduced, and for which the Belgic heroes (or *bigots* – if we must call them so) shed their blood. I observe with pain, that the phraseology and mode of expression, employed perpetually by Mr. Hume, on similar occasions, seem to discover a keen dislike of every opposition made to power in favor of the Reformation. Upon the too general principle which this eminent writer has diffused through his history, we shall even be obliged to brand, with the opprobrious mark of fanaticism, those generous friends of civil and religious liberty, who, in the revolution of 1688, opposed the measures of a popish prince and an arbitrary government, and to rank the Burnets, Tillotsons, Stillingfleets, and other immortal ornaments of the Protestant name, among the enthusiastic tribe; it is a question, whether even a Boyle, a Newton, or a Locke, will escape a censure which is lavished without mercy and without distinction. – But my present business is with the first reformers, and to them I return.

Those who more especially merit that title were Luther, Zuingle, Calvin, Melanchthon, Bucer, Martyr, Bullinger, Beza, Œcolampadius, and others. Now these were *all* men of learning, who came forth into the field of controversy (in which the fate of future ages, with respect to liberty, was to be decided) with a kind of arms that did not at all give them the aspect of persons agitated by the impulse, or seduced by the delusions of fanaticism. They pretended not to be called to the work they undertook by visions, or internal illuminations and impulses; – they never attempted to work miracles, or pleaded a divine commission; – they taught no new religion, nor laid claim to any extraordinary vocation; – they respected government, practised and taught submission to civil rulers, and desired only the liberty of that conscience which God has made free, and which ceases to be conscience if it be not free. They maintained, that the faith of a Christian was to be determined by the word of God alone; they had recourse to reason and argument, to the rules of sound criticism, and to the authority and light of history. They translated the

Scriptures into the popular languages of different countries, and appealed to them as the only test of religious truth. They exhorted Christians to judge for themselves, to search the Scriptures, break asunder the bonds of ignorant prejudice and lawless authority, and assert that liberty of conscience to which they had an inalienable right as reasonable beings. Mr. Hume himself acknowleges, that they offered to submit 'all religious doctrines to private judgement, and exhorted every one to examine the principles formerly imposed upon him.' In short, it was their great and avowed purpose to oppose the gross corruptions and the spiritual tyranny of Rome,[10] of which Mr. Hume himself complains with a just indignation, and which he censures in as keen and vehement terms as those which were used by Luther and Calvin in their warmest moments.

I have already insinuated, and I acknowlege it here again, that the zeal of the reformers was sometimes intemperate; but I cannot think this circumstance sufficient to justify the aspersion of *fanaticism*, which is cast both on the spirit of the Reformation, and the principal agents concerned in it. A man may be over-zealous in the advancement of what he supposes to be the true religion, without being entitled to the denomination of a fanatic, unless we depart from the usual sense of this word, which is often enough employed to have acquired, before this time, a determinate signification. The intemperate zeal of the reformers was the result of that ardor, which takes place in all divisions and parties that are founded upon objects of real or supposed importance; and it may be affirmed, that, in such circumstances, the most generous minds, filled with a persuasion of the goodness of their end, and of the uprightness of their intentions, are the most liable to transgress the exact bounds of moderation, and to adopt measures, which, in the calm hour of deliberate reflexion, they themselves would not approve. In all great divisions, the warmth of natural temper, – the provocation of unjust and violent opposition, – a spirit of sympathy, which connects, in some cases, the most dissimilar characters, renders the mild violent, and the phlegmatic warm; – and frequently the pride of conquest, which mingles itself, imperceptibly, with the best principles and the most generous views, – produce or nourish an intemperate zeal; and this zeal is, in some cases, almost inevitable. On the other hand, it may be suspected, that some writers, and Mr. Hume among others, may have given too high colors to their descriptions of this in temperate zeal. There is a passage of Sir Robert Cotton, that has much meaning. "Most men (*says he*) grew to be frozen in zeal and benumbed, so that whosoever pretended a little *spark of earnestness*, seemed no less than red-fire hot, in comparison of the other."

---

[10] See the sensible and judicious Letters on Mr. Hume's History of Great Britain, that were published at Edinburgh in 1756, and in which some points, which I have barely mentioned here, are enlarged upon and illustrated, in an ample and satisfactory manner.

Nothing can be more foreign from my temper and sentiments, than to plead the cause of an excessive zeal; more especially, every kind of zeal that approaches to a spirit of intolerance and persecution ought to be regarded with aversion and horror by all who have at heart the interest of genuine Christianity, and the happiness of civil society. There may be, nevertheless, cases, in which a zeal (not that breathes a spirit of persecution, but) that mounts to a certain degree of intemperance, may be not only inevitable, but useful; and not only useful but necessary. This assertion I advance almost against my will, because it is susceptible of great and dangerous abuse; the assertion, however, is true, though the cases must be singularly important and desperate to which such zeal may be applied. It has been observed, that the reformation was one of these cases, and, all things attentively considered, the observation appears to be entirely just; and the violence of expression and vehement measures employed by some of the reformers *might have been* (I do not say that they *really were*) as much the effect of provident reflexion, as of natural fervor and resentment. To a calculating head, which considered closely, in those times of corruption and darkness, the strength of the court of Rome, the luxury and despotism of the pontiffs, the ignorance and licentiousness of the clergy, the superstition and stupidity of the people; in a word, the deep root which the papacy had gained through all these circumstances combined, – what was the first thought that must naturally have occurred? No doubt, it was this – the improbability that cool philosophy, dispassionate reason, and affectionate remonstrances, would ever triumph over these multiplied and various supports of popery. And, if a calculating head must have judged in this manner, a generous heart, which considered the blessings that must arise upon mankind from religious liberty and a reformation of the church, would naturally be excited to apply even a violent remedy, if that were *necessary*, to remove such a desperate and horrible disease. It would really seem that Luther acted on such a view of things. He began mildly, and did not employ the fire of his zeal, before he saw that it was essential to the success of his cause. Whoever looks into Dr. Mosheim's history, or any other impartial account of the sixteenth century, will find, that Luther's opposition to the infamous traffic of indulgences, was carried on at first in the most submissive strain, by humble remonstrances addressed to the pope, and the most eminent prelates of the church. These remonstrances were answered not only by the despotic voice of authority, but also by opprobrious invectives, perfidious plots against his person, and the terror of penal laws. Even under these he maintained his tranquillity; and his conduct at the famous diet of Worms, though resolute and steady, was nevertheless both respectful and modest. But, when all moderate measures proved ineffectual, then, indeed, he acted with redoubled vigor, and added a new degree of warmth and impetuosity to his zeal; and (I repeat it) reflexion might have dictated those animated proceedings, which were owing, perhaps, merely to his resentment, and the natural warmth of his temper inflamed by opposition. Certain it is at least, that neither the elegant satires of Erasmus (had he even been a friend to the cause of liberty), nor the timid remonstrances of the gentle Melanchthon (who was really such), would ever have been sufficient to bring about a reformation of the church. The former made many *laugh*, the latter made some *reason*; but neither of the two could make them act, or set them in motion. At such a crisis, bold speech and ardent resolution were necessary to produce that happy change in the face of religion, which has crowned with inestimable blessings one part of Europe, and has been productive of many advantages even to the other, which censures it.

As to Calvin, every one, who has any acquaintance with history, knows how he set out in promoting the Reformation. It was by a work composed with a classic elegance of style: and which, though tinctured with the scholastic theology of the times, breathes an uncommon spirit of good sense and moderation. This work was the Institutes of the Christian religion, in which the learned writer shews, that the doctrines of the reformers were founded in Scripture and reason; and one of the designs of this book was to shew, that the reformers ought not to be confounded with certain fanatics, who, about the time of the Reformation, sprang from the bosom of the church of Rome, and excited tumults and commotions in several places. The French monarch (Francis I.) to cover with a specious pretext his barbarous persecution of the friends of the Reformation, and to prevent the resentment of the Protestants in Germany, with whom it was his interest to be on good terms, alleged that his severity fell *only* upon a sect of enthusiasts, who, under the title of Anabaptists, substituted their visions in the place of the doctrines and declarations of the Scriptures. To vindicate the reformers from this reproach, Calvin wrote the book now under consideration: and though the theology that reigns in it be chargeable with some defects, yet it is as remote from the spirit and complexion of fanaticism, as any thing can be. Nor indeed is this spirit visible in any of the writings of Calvin that I have perused. His commentary upon the Old and New Testament is a production that will always be esteemed, on account of its elegant simplicity, and the evident marks it bears of an unprejudiced and impartial enquiry into the plain sense of the sacred writings, and of sagacity and penetration in the investigation of it.

If we were to pass in review the writings of the other eminent reformers, whose names have been already mentioned, we should find abundant matter to justify them in the same respect. They were men of letters, and some of them were even men of taste for the age in which they lived; they cultivated the study of languages, history, and criticism, and applied themselves with indefatigable industry to these studies, which, of all others, are the least adapted to excite or nourish a spirit of fanaticism. They had, indeed, their errors and prejudices; nor perhaps were they few in number; but who is free from the same charge? We have ours too, though they may turn on a different set of objects. Their theology savored somewhat of the pedantry and jargon of the schools; – how could it be otherwise, considering the dismal state of philosophy at that period? The advantages we enjoy above them, give them, at least, a title to our candor and indulgence; perhaps to our gratitude, as the instruments who prepared the way through which these advantages have been conveyed to us. To conclude, let us regret their infirmities; let us reject their errors; let us even condemn any instances of ill-judged severity and violence with which they may have been chargeable; but let us never forget, that, through perils and obstacles almost insurmountable, they opened the path to that religious liberty, which we cannot too highly esteem, nor be too careful to improve to rational and worthy purposes.

16
HENRI GRIFFET

Henri Griffet, *Nouveaux éclaircissements sur l'histoire de Marie, reine d'Angleterre* (1766)
Selections; from *New lights thrown upon the history of Mary Queen of England, eldest daughter of Henry VIII. Addressed to David Hume, Esq; author of The history of the Plantagenets, the Tudors, and the Stuarts. Translated from the French.* London: printed for J. Wilkie, 1771, vii, [1], 111, [1] p.
Selections; from 1771 edition.

French priest Henri Griffet (1698–1771) authored several theological and historical works, and was best known for his 18 volume *L'Année du Chrétien* (1747). His *Nouveaux éclaircissements* first appeared anonymously in 1766, and in 1771 was published anonymously in English. The work presents extracts from correspondence by French officials, which he believes vindicates Mary Queen of Scots and places blame on Elizabeth. Addressing his work to Hume, he requests that Hume revise his *History* in view of recently disclosed dispatches of de Noailles, French ambassador to the English court. In the Preface, the anonymous translator, who takes Hume's side on the position of Mary's guilt, concedes that the letters cited by Griffet do help Mary's case; however, he conjectures that there may be other statements in these letters that support Elizabeth. Griffet opens noting that Hume's account of John Dudley, Duke of Northumberland, could be illuminated by statements made by de Noailles. Griffet also attempts to clarify a vagueness in Hume's statement in Chapter 35 concerning Mary that, "Dreading farther violence, she endeavoured to make an escape to her kinsman Charles; but her design was discovered and prevented."

The English translation of Griffet's work was praised by the *Critical Review*:

We do not hesitate to recommend this interesting and well-translated pamphlet to the perusal of our readers; and hope when Mr. Hume shall be disposed to attempt a revisal of that part of his history to which these anecdotes belong, that he will take the pains to enquire into the value of the credentials which have furnished our French writer with his accounts. [*Critical Review* 1771, Vol. 31, pp. 151–153]

However, writing for the *Monthly Review*, Gilbert Stuart argued that Griffet's work is uninformed:

> As this publication has imposed upon its Translator, and as it may fall into the hands of Readers who have little acquaintance with the English history, we think it or duty to expose its defects, and to point out its general scope and intention.
>
> Instead of throwing any light on the transactions of Mary's reign, it serves to involve them in confusion; and from the censure which it has profusely lavished on a celebrated historian, we can only learn, that its Author is totally uninformed concerning the subject which he has endeavoured to illustrate.

As to the passage regarding Mary's attempted escape with Charles, Stuart defends Hume's account:

> In the reign of Edward VI. when Somerset resigned the protectorship, the administration of affairs was conducted by the Duke of Northumberland, who promoted the principles of the reformation; and among other steps which were then taken for the suppression of popery, it was determined, that the Princess Mary should no longer be suffered to adhere to the mass, and to reject the new liturgy. She was, therefore, remonstrated with on this subject; and her two chaplains were thrown into prison. In this situation, dreading farther violence, "she endeavoured, says Mr. Hume, to make her escape *to* her kinsman Charles; but her design was discovered and prevented." That she made this attempt is sufficiently ascertained by authentic proofs, and by the consequences it produced. For when Charles found that she was detained in England, he threatened hostilities if liberty of conscience was refused her; and the young King, who lamented his sister's obstinacy, was prevailed with to allow her to continue in the Romish faith. But our Author, while he is unacquainted with the terms in which Mr. Hume has expressed himself, with regard to the design, has also asserted, that he is mistaken in relation to the period of time when Mary formed the project of her flight. M. de Noailles, he observes, places this circumstance in the short interval between Edwards death and Mary's advancement to the throne. It is not, however, to this circumstance that M. de Noailles has alluded; and if our Author had given himself the trouble to consult the English historians, he might have learned, that Mary had, at *different times*, conceived an intention of abandoning the kingdom. At the time referred to in the dispatches of M. de Noailles, she thought of flying into a foreign country, in order to escape the vigilance of the duke of Northumberland, whose criminal ambition had induced him to plot against her life, that he might secure to lady Jane Grey the succession to the crown of England.

In a footnote to the italicized word "*to*" in the above paragraph, Stuart writes,

> Not *with*. The error of the French translator is ascribed to Mr. Hume. It is perfectly ridiculous to put the question, *Who is this kinsman Charles?* Had Mary any other kinsman of that name besides the Emperor Charles to whom she should think of flying for protection?

Stuart concludes that Griffet's work is inaccurate and biased in favour of Catholicism:

> The ignorance and inaccuracy so apparent in the extract we have given from this performance, are no less conspicuous in the other observations which it contains. It appears to be the production of a rigid papist; and its general tendency is to vindicate the character of Mary from the just reproaches that have been thrown upon it by the protestant historians. It is a panegyric on a queen, who joined to great weakness of understanding, the most obstinate bigotry and the utmost malignity of disposition. [*Monthly Review*, April 1771, Vol. 44, pp. 277–279]

The following is from the 1771 and only English edition of Griffet's *Nouveaux éclaircissements*.

PREFACE,
By the TRANSLATOR.

The following sheets were printed at Amsterdam in 1766, and lately received from Paris: but whether yet imported by any bookseller, is unknown to the Translator.

As it contains some strictures on our celebrated Historian, and indeed on all Protestants that have written the history of the period here treated of, it is thought proper to make it more publickly known, that those accused of partiality may, if they judge it worth their labour, vindicate themselves from the imputation.

The apparent design of the author is to remove, or at least extenuate, the charge of cruelty, so universally ascribed to Queen Mary, and to fix an odium upon the Princess Elizabeth, whose memory all true Englishmen and good Protestants have so much reason to revere and hold sacred.

The authenticity of the extracts from the dispatches and letters of the Imperial and French ambassadors, now published, cannot be doubted of, as he refers to dates and volumes: but it is not improbable the same source might furnish other extracts sufficient to counterballance what he has produced.

The cause of Protestantism, and the high reputation of Queen Elizabeth, stand in no need of falshood, and misrepresentation of facts, for its support.

There are many circumstances brought to light in this performance, that are unnoticed by other historians, and particularly what relates to Bishop Gardner, who is here painted in colours very different from what he appears in other writers.

NEW LIGHTS
THROWN UPON THE
HISTORY
OF MARY Queen of ENGLAND,
Eldest Daughter of HENRY VIII.

SIR

You are sensible that History is a country wherein fresh discoveries may be continually made, from the appearance of original pieces, long buried in oblivion, which inform us of indisputable facts, that either contradict the testimony, or supply the defects of historians.

The exact and complete collection of the Dispatches of M. de Noailles, the French ambassador at the English court, towards the end of the reign of Edward VI. and in some part of Mary's reign, furnishes us with a proof of this observation.

In this collection is found a great variety of important particulars, which cannot be called in question, and are such as have been either omitted or misrepresented by historians.

Of this, Sir, you will judge by the remarks I have extracted from these dispatches, in comparing them with the account given by the most celebrated writers of the English history.

My motive for addressing these extracts to you, will be easily comprehended, as every thing relating to the history of the English nation is in some sort a part of your province, from the high reputation you have acquired in that species of learning.

If the important business you are at present engaged in will permit you to cast an eye upon this letter, you will perhaps be sorry you had not an opportunity of consulting these dispatches of M. de Noailles, while you were writing the reigns of Edward VI. and Mary.

The public will certainly regret that the particular facts therein contained, were not brought to light under your masterly hand.

[I.] In the first place, historians inform us that young Edward, being seized with the disorder that carried him off,

"was imprudent enough to dismiss his physicians, by the advice of the Duke of Northumberland, and the Council, and to entrust his life to the quackery of an ignorant woman, who pretended to perform an immediate cure; but that he had no sooner taken her prescription than the most alarming symptoms returned with redoubled force." (History of Tudor, vol. I. p. 424)

You will observe, that on the 16th of June, 1553, and consequently three weeks before Edward's death; M. de Noailles writes to the Constable Montmorenci that the Prince's life was absolutely despaired of; and that one of his physicians had told him, that

"he and two others were of opinion he would not out-live the month of August, and even during that interval he was in the utmost danger of dying at a moment when least expected." (Vol. II. p. 31.)

His physicians were not therefore dismissed the 16th of June, when they so positively fixed the duration of his life; and if they were afterwards sent away, the Duke of Northumberland, and the Council, did no more than what is still done, and will be always practised on a similar occasion.

It is not construed an act of imprudence to call in an Empiric to the assistance of a patient, when the regular physicians peremptorily declare they see no means of saving him either by the help of their art, or the strength of nature.

II. The histories you have published are much admired for the exactness of the portrait. No writer can exceed you in drawing true characters of every one concerned in the great events you treat of. What use would you not have made of various facts furnished by M. de Noailles's letters, to give a natural picture of the Duke of Northumberland, who had the lead in the Council of Regency, and who governed England in an absolute manner during the last years of Edward's reign?

Historians make us sufficiently acquainted with his unbounded ambition, his bold and violent spirit; but they hardly take any notice of that cunning and dissimulation he so often made use of to conceal his views and designs.

M. de Noailles mentions many instances of his dexterity in this art which may serve to give a perfect idea of his character. ...

III. In the first volume of the French translation of your history of the Tudors, we read, that during the reign of Edward VI. the Princess Mary his sister, *attempted to escape with Charles her kinsman to avoid greater persecutions, but that her design was discovered and prevented.* This expression ought certainly to be explained: first, who is this kinsman Charles, with whom she attempted to escape? Was it Charles V. her cousin-german? If it was him, it should have been said that she attempted to withdraw, and take refuge with Charles her relation; for certainly that Emperor did not then come into England to assist in her escape. What steps did she take in order to leave England (for the word *attempt* implies some action and effort) and what was done to hinder her flight? Had she set out in order to embark, or had any vessel been prepared to receive her? Was she stopped upon the road before she reached the sea-shore, or was any one measure taken to deprive her of the ship engaged for her transportation? One might reasonably expect something would have been offered to obviate such doubts as must naturally arise in the mind of an attentive, and intelligent Reader.

M. de Noailles places this project of a flight to have happened in the short interval between Edward's death and her advancement to the throne. He says, the Princess had some thoughts of crossing the sea after the death of her brother, to which she was advised by several persons, in order to secure her life and liberty; and adds, that if she had then quitted England, she would not have found one friend to support her interest, or contribute to her return. It is very probable she relinquished this design so soon as she perceived her party was stronger, and more numerous than was at first imagined; and instead of abandoning her hopes to the impulse of fear and distrust, she found herself in a condition to render her power respectable.

IV. You have taken great care to remark in your History the frequent changes that happened in the manners and customs of the English nation. But there is one circumstance that does not seem to have been sufficiently attended by Historians. – the new Sectaries that governed England during the minority of Edward VI. not contented with depriving the Church of all the pomp of her ceremonies, and splendor of her worship, had also attempted, as a step towards a reformation, to reduce the womens dress to the same simplicity. They were forbidden to wear any kind of lace or embroidery, and even any thing of colours. – Mary immediately took off this restraint; and M. de Noailles, being at Court, was much surprized to see this Princess, and all the ladies about her, ornamented with *gold lace and embroidery, and dressed in the French fashion with gowns and long sleeves.* ...

V. It must be acknowledged, Sir, that the Protestant Historians, were either unacquainted with the merits of this Princess, or determined not to do her justice. You will be fully convinced of this, if you compare her picture drawn by them, with the report of ambassadors who had the honour of frequently treating immediately with her. – These Historians, soured by the vigorous punishments inflicted upon the principal leaders of their party, have represented her as an "obstinate, superstitious, violent, cruel, malicious, vindictive, tyrannical woman, the whole of whose inclinations and actions bore evident marks of the depravity of her natural disposition, and the narrow limits of her understanding." This is, as you perceive, a frightful picture; and stronger colours could not be employed, if a fury, or Medea, were to be painted. – But is this representation exactly conformable to truth? and is there no exaggeration in the portrait?

Mary undoubtedly had faults, and, if you please, great faults; but were they not compensated by any virtue? Was she born an idiot, without any talent? and was her reign nothing but a series of horror and folly, and her character a composition of every vice?

Let us judge without passion and partiality; let us attend to the evidence of such as knew her well, and who had opportunities to examine her words and actions. Perhaps we shall find much excess in the reproaches cast upon her, and that upon a more impartial and mature examination, some qualities may be discovered deserving praise. ...

XLIX. ... I am persuaded, Sir, that, should you be disposed to a revision of that part of your history of the Tudors, you would begin by consulting these valuable monuments, from whence you would gather many lights that may have escaped my observation, and to which the elegance of your style, joined to the force and solidity of your reflections, would add a beauty of value that I am not capable of giving them.

I have the honour to be,

SIR,
Your most humble, and
most obedient Servant,

* * * *

17
JOSEPH PRIESTLEY

Joseph Priestley, *The rudiments of English grammar, adapted to the use of schools; with notes and observations, for the use of those who have made some proficiency in the language. By Joseph Priestley, LL.D. F.R.S.* London: printed for T. Becket and P.A. De Hondt, and J. Johnson, 1768, xxiii, [1], 200, [4] p. Selections from "Notes and Observations"; from *Theological and Miscellaneous Works* (1817–1832), Vol. 23, pp. 87–102.

Born in Fieldhead, Yorkshire, Joseph Priestley (1733–1804) was a dissenting minister, an influential scientist, and a prolific author of philosophical, theological, and educational books. Many of Priestley's writings contain references to and critical discussions of Hume. His *Rudiments of English Grammar* first appeared in 1761, and in a revised edition of 1768 he doubled its size by adding "Notes and Observations," which provide hundreds of examples of stylistic flaws in famous publications. Hume is chief among the writers that he cites, particularly his *History*, but also his *Essays*. In the Preface he states that he was "harder upon Mr. Hume than upon any other living author." In his article in the *Monthly Review*, Andrew Kippis praised the expanded edition of Priestley's *Rudiments* and comments on the attention that Priestley paid to Hume:

Without entering into a dispute concerning the truth of these observations [about publicly exposing the stylistic errors of living authors], we will venture to assert, that it can afford no satisfaction to Mr. Hume, to be found guilty of such a number of improprieties in expression, as he is actually convicted of, in the work before us. It was, however, right that they should be exhibited to a public view, to prevent the bad effects that might proceed from the example and imitation of so eminent an author. At the same time, every person of true taste will be ready to acknowledge, that Mr. Hume excels in accuracies and elegancies of a higher kind, which justly entitle him to be reckoned among our best writers. [*Monthly Review*, September 1768, Vol. 39, pp. 184–186]

The *Rudiments* was also favourably received in the *Critical Review*, which excerpted many of Priestley's comments on Hume. The reviewer concludes, "This work is a valuable addition to that of the accurate and judicious Dr.

Lowth; and, we hope, will contribute to the refinement of the English language" (1768, Vol. 26, pp. 101–106).

When reading the *Rudiments* Hume took offence at many of Priestley's critical observations:

> Have you seen Priestly's Grammar? In his Censure of me, he is wrong nine times in ten, as I am assurd by consulting the best Judges; and his Friend, [Samuel] Johnson, is even commonly against him; so negligently did he write. However, you may look into it. The People in this Country wou'd wish to be hypercritical on these points, if they knew how. [Hume to William Robertson, November 27, 1768]

In spite of Hume's immediate negative reaction, he took Priestley's comments to heart. Woodhouselee reports that Hume was "made sensible of the gallicisms and peculiarities of his style by reading this Grammar" as "he acknowledged to Mr. Griffith, the bookseller."[1] In his *Lectures on History and General Policy* (1788), Priestley supplies his own anecdote to the same effect: "To a common friend [i.e., Benjamin Franklin] he acknowledged the justness of my remarks [in the *Rudaments*], and promised to correct his style in future editions of his work; and I believe he has in a great measure done it."[2] In fact, Hume either altered or deleted most of the passages that Priestley critiques; when possible, I have inserted footnotes at the appropriate locations below that contain Hume's altered wording.

In the decades ahead, Priestley critiqued Hume's philosophical views in *Institutes of Natural and Revealed Religion* (1772–1774) and *Letters to a Philosophical Unbeliever* (1780). In his 1788 *Lectures on History and General Policy*, Priestley assesses Hume's *History*:

> A more entertaining history of the same period, and much superior in point of composition [to Rapin's], is that of Mr. Hume. For a judicious choice of materials, and a happy disposition of them, together with perspicuity of style in recording them, this writer was hardly ever exceeded; especially in the latter part of his work, which is by far the most elaborate. The earlier part

---

[1] Lord Woodhouselee, Alexander Fraser Tytler, *Memoirs of the life and writings of the honourable Henry Home of Kames....* 1807, Edinburgh, W. Creech; London, T. Cadell and W. Davis, 2 Vol; vol. 1, pp. 236–237.

[2] In their review of Priestley's *Lectures on History*, the *Analytical Review* makes the following comment on Priestley's comment here and Hume's stylistic revisions in the *History*: "He has so [i.e., revised his *History*]. It was his constant method to relabour his style in every new edition. We have seen in the possession of Mr. Herbert Croft, a most curious collation of the last edition of the *History of England* with the first in quarto; and there is hardly a page of the former, in which there occurs not some grammatical correction or improvement" (*Analytical Review*, 1788, Vol. 1, p. 296).

of his history is too superficial. He has endeavoured to trace the progress of our constitution, and has descended more into the internal state of the nation, in exhibiting a view of the manners and sentiments of each age, the state of property and personal security, with the improvements in the conveniences of life, than most other writers; but he has misrepresented the ancient government as much more arbitrary than it really was, as will appear by the much more accurate accounts of Dr. Sullivan, and especially Mr. Millar, whose work on the English Constitution I cannot too strongly recommend. Some great faults in Mr. Hume's history were very well pointed out by Dr. Towers. Mr. Hume is also thought by many to have given too favourable an idea of the characters of our princes of the Stewart family, by omitting to mention those particulars in their conduct which have been most objected to; and it was probably with a view to exculpate them that he has taken so much pains to give the colour that he has done to the preceding periods of our history. A good antidote to what is unfavourable to liberty in Mr. Hume will be found in the very masterly history of Mrs. Macaulay. Though the style of Mr. Hume is upon the whole excellent, yet he has departed more than any other writer of the present age from the true English idiom, and leaned more to that of the French.

Priestley's *Rudiments* is favourably mentioned in Joseph Towers's *Observations on Mr. Hume's History of England* (1778) and Francis Palgrave's "Hume and his Influence upon History" (1826), contained later in this collection. The *Rudiments* was republished seven times during the 18th century, it was also translated into French in 1798. In the "Notes and Observations," Priestley makes over one hundred references to Hume. I have excerpted his comments on Hume from a 15–page portion of the text, in which the criticisms appear with frequency. The following is from the *Theological and Miscellaneous Works*, which in turn is based on the 1798 edition. In the *Works*, citations to Hume's publications appear in footnotes; I have moved them into the body of the text and modified some for clarity and consistency.

PREFACE

...

I make no apology for the freedom I have taken with the works of living authors, in my collections. Except a very few pages in *Swift*, I read nothing with an immediate view to them. This was always a secondary consideration; but if any thing of this kind struck me in the course of my reading, I did not fail to note it. If I be thought to have borne harder upon Mr. Hume than upon any other living author, he is obliged for it to the great reputation his writings have justly gained him, and to my happening to read them at the time that I did; and I would not pay any man, for whom I have the least esteem, so ill a compliment, as to suppose, that exactness in the punctilios of grammar was an object capable of giving him the least disturbance. This is the smallest point of excellence, even with respect to style; and style, in its whole extent, is but a very small object in the eye of a philosopher. I even think a man cannot give a more certain mark of the narrowness of his mind, and of the little progress he has made in true science, than to shew, either by his vanity with respect to himself, or the acrimony of his censure with respect to others, that this business is of much moment with him. We have infinitely greater things before us; and if these gain their due share of our attention, this subject, of grammatical criticism, will be almost nothing. The noise that is made about it, is one of the greatest marks of the frivolism of many readers, and writers too, of the present age. ...

NOTES
AND
OBSERVATIONS
FOR THE USE OF THOSE WHO HAVE MADE SOME PROFICIENCY
IN THE LANGUAGE

SECTION VII.
Of the Composition and Derivation of Words.

... The hyphen is also sometimes used to connect particles to other words, in order to compound the ideas: "as *unherard-of* restraint (*Hume's Hist.* VII. p. 459) ...

Notwithstanding the rules of the composition and derivation of words be ever so well fixed, custom prescribes how far we may take advantage of them; and the force of association of ideas is hardly any where more evident, than in the disagreeable sensation excited by words, which, though perfectly intelligible, have not happened to be adopted by the generality of writers; and especially when easier words have happened to supply their places. A few examples will make this remark striking. ... "Among other *informalities*" (*Hume's Hist.* IV. p. 401). "It would be such a *disobligation* to the prince" (*Hume's Hist.* VI. p. 74). ... "Without any *circuity*" (*Hume*). Instead of precipitate *and* precipitately, Mr. Hume writes "precipitant" and "precipitantly" (*Hume's Hist.* p. 291). Also instead of *consultation*, he uses "consult" (*Hume's Hist.* VIII. p. 65). ...

When there are two derivatives from the same word, they are apt to slide, by degrees, into different meanings; a custom which tends greatly to enrich a language. Thus we use the word *adhesion* in a literal sense; as, when we speak of the adhesion of the lungs to the pleura; and we use the word *adherence* in a figurative sense only; as, when we speak of the adherence of a people to their prince, or to a cause. We also use the word *exposure* in a literal sense, and *exposition* in a figurative one; yet Mr. Hume says, "a fountain which has a north *exposition*" (*Political Essays, p.* 219).[3]

Though both the words *proposal* and *proposition* be derived from the verb *propose*, we now use the word *proposal* to denote a thing that is proposed to be done, and *proposition* for an assertion proposed to be proved. Some writers, however, and particularly Mrs. Macaulay, in conformity, perhaps, to the French idiom, use the latter in the sense of the former. "This observation was followed by a *proposition*, which had been at first suggested, and was immediately consented to by the commissioners" (*Hume's Hist.* IV. p. 312.)

The Latin word *extempore* is often used without any change, as an English word. Mr. Hume writes "*extemporary.*" ...

SECTION VIII.
Of Articles.

... The article *a* is made more emphatical by the additions of the adjective *certain*.... "At last, a *certain* Fitzgerald appeared" (*Hume's Hist*, VIII. p. 161)....

In general, it may be sufficient to prefix the article to the former of two words in the same construction; though the French never fail to repeat it in this case. ... And, for the sake of emphasis, we often repeat the article in a series of epithets. "He hoped, that this title would secure him a perpetual, and *an* independent authority" (*Hume's Hist.* III. p. 326). ...

A is sometimes put for *every*; as in such phrases as these, *a hundred* a year, that is, *every year*; or for *one*, as when we say, *so much a dozen*, a *pound*, &c. "A hundred men *a* day died of it" (*Hume's Hist.* V. p. 80). ...

In applying the ordinal numbers to a series of kings, &c., we generally interpose the article *the* between the name and the adjective expressing the number, as "Henry *the* First, Charles *the* Second:" but some writers affect to transpose these words, and place the numeral adjective first. "The *First* Henry" (*Hume's Hist.* I. p. 497). This construction is common with this writer, but there seems to be a familiarity and want of dignity in it. ...

When a word is in such a state, so that it may, with very little impropriety, be considered either as a proper or a common name, the article *the* may be prefixed to it, or not, at pleasure. "The Lord Darnly was *the* person in whom most men's wishes centered" (*Hume's Hist.* V. p. 87). *Lord Darnly* would have read just as well; and this form is more common, the word *Lord* being generally considered as part of the proper name. ...

In many other cases, the articles seem to be omitted where we can discover nothing but a mere ellipsis; as no reason can be seen for the omission, except

---

[3] [In later editions Hume altered this to read "a fountain that has a north exposure" ("Of the Populousness of Ancient Nations").]

that it has a little more conciseness or energy. Thus we say, have you *trout* in this river? that is, *have you any of that species of fish which is called trout?* "Nothing is so dangerous, as to unite two persons so closely, in all their interests and concerns, as *man and wife*, without rendering the union entire and total" (*Hume's Essays*, p. 259). ... In the former of these sentences, the words *a man and his wife* would have conveyed the same idea, and in the same extent, as *man and wife*: for the meaning of both is precisely, *any man and his wife*. ...

In the following sentence an universality seems to be aimed at by the omission of the article, which the sense hardly requires. "The pope found himself entitled to the possession of England and Ireland, on account of the heresy of *prince and people.*" *Of the prince* would have been better. In some cases, however, there seems to be a peculiar elegance in adopting the universal sense of the word, by omitting the article when it might have been used with propriety enough. "If the young man who appeared in Flanders was really *son* to king Edward, he never would bear arms against him" (*Hume's Hist.* III. p. 383). ...

In many cases, articles are omitted in common conversion, or in familiar style, which seem to have a propriety in writing, or in grave style. "*At worst,* time might be gained by this expedient" (*Hume's Hist.* VI. p. 435). *At the worst* might have been better in this place. ...

SECTION IX.
Of the Use of Prepositions.

All that I have done in this difficult part of grammar, concerning the proper use of prepositions, has been to make a few general remarks upon the subject; and then to give a collection of the instances that have occurred to me of the improper use of some of them. ...

In some cases, it is not possible to say to which of two prepositions the preference is to be given, as both are used promiscuously, and custom has not decided in favour of either of them. We say, expert *at* and expert *in* a thing. "Expert *at* finding a remedy for his mistakes" (*Hume's Hist.* IV. p. 417). ...

When prepositions are subjoined to nouns, they are generally the same which are subjoined to the verbs, from which the nouns are derived. "John, shewing the same disposition *to tyranny over* his subjects" (*Hume's Hist.* I. p. 74); that is, *to tyrannize over his subjects.*

When a word ending in *ing* is preceded by an article, it seems to be used as a noun, and therefore ought not to govern another word, without the intervention of a preposition. "By blackening his fame, had that injury been in their power, they formed a very proper prelude to *the murdering* his person" (*Hume's Hist.* VII. p. 117).

Many writers affect to subjoin to any word the preposition with which it is compounded, or the idea of which it implies, in order to point out the relation of the words in a more distinct and definite manner, and to avoid the more indeterminate prepositions *of* and *to*; but general practice, and the idiom of the English tongue, seem to oppose the innovation. ... "The abhorrence *against* all other sects" (*Hume's Hist.* IV. p. 34). But other writers use averse *to* it, which seems more truly English.[4] ...

Of the Preposition of.

Several of our modern writers have leaned to the French idiom in the use of the preposition *of*, by applying it where the French use *de*, though the English idiom would require another preposition, or no preposition at all in the case; but no writer has departed more from the genius of the English tongue, in this respect, than Mr. Hume. "Richlieu profited *of* every circumstance which the conjuncture afforded" (*Hume's Hist.* IV. p. 251). We say profited *by*. "He remembered him *of* the fable" (*Hume's Hist.* V. p. 185). "The great difficulty they find *of* fixing just sentiments" (*Hume's Hist.*). "The king of England provided *of* every supply" (*Hume's Hist.* I. p. 206). In another place he writes, "provide them *in* food and raiment" (*Hume's Hist.* II. p. 65). The true English idiom seems to be to provide *with* a thing. "It is situation chiefly which decides *of* the fortunes and characters of men" (*Hume's Hist.* VI. p. 283). That is, *concerning*. "He found the greatest difficulty *of* writing" (*Hume's Hist.* I. p. 401); that is, *in*. "*Of* which he was extremely greedy, extremely prodigal, and extremely necessitous" (*Hume's Hist.* IV. p. 12). "He was eager *of* recommending it to his fellow-citizens" (*Hume's Hist.* VII. p. 161). "The good lady was careful of serving me *of* every thing." In this example *with* would have been more proper.

It is agreeable to the same idiom, that *of* seems to be used instead of *for* in the following sentences. ... "The esteem which Philip had conceived *of* the ambassador" (*Hume's Hist.* VI. p. 90). ... "Youth wandering in foreign countries, with as little respect *of* others, as prudence of his own, to guard him from danger. An indemnity *of* past offences" (*Hume's Hist.* V. p. 29).

In the following sentences, *on* or *upon* might very well be substituted for *of*. "Was totally dependent *of* the papal crown" (*Hume's Hist.* II. p. 71). "Laid hold *of*" (*Hume's Hist.* I. p. 292). We also use *of* instead of *on* or *upon*, in the following familiar phrases, which occur chiefly in conversation; "to call *of* a person," and "to wait *of* him."

In some cases, a regard to the French idiom hath taught us to substitute *of* for *in*. "The great difficulty they found *of* fixing just sentiments" (*Hume's Hist.* VI. p. 63.)

---

[4] [In later editions Hume altered the passages in the above section to the following: "the same disposition to tyrannize over his subjects" (Chapter 11); "they formed a very proper prelude to the executing of violence on his person" (Chapter 59); "abhorrence of all other sects" (Chapter 29).]

In a variety of cases, the preposition *of* seems to be superfluous in our language; and in most of them, it has been derived to us from the French. "Notwithstanding *of* the numerous panegyrics on the ancient English liberty" (*Hume's Essays*, p. 81); "Notwithstanding *of* this unlucky example" (*Hume's Essays*, p. 78).[5] Awkward as this construction is, it is generally used by several of our later writers. This preposition seems to be superfluous, when it is prefixed to a word which is only used to shew the extent of another preceding word.... It also seems to be superfluous after several adjectives, which are sometimes used as substantives: "a dozen *of* years" (*Hume's Essays*, p. 258).

In the following instances, it may be a matter of indifference whether we use this preposition or not. "To one who considers coolly *of the subject*" (*Hume's Political Essays*, p. 141). ... "It is worthy observation" (*Hume's Hist.*). I should choose to make use of it in this case. ...

Of is frequently ambiguous, and would oftener be perceived to be so, did not the sense of the rest of the passage in which it occurs prevent that inconvenience: and this it will often do, even when this part of the sentence, singly taken, would suggest a meaning the very reverse of what is intended. "The attack *of* the English" naturally means *an attack by the English upon others;* but in the following sentence, it means an attack made upon the English. "The two princes concerted the means of rendering ineffectual their common attack *of* the English" (*Hume's Hist.* III. p. 114). "The oppression of the peasants seemeth great" (*Hume's Hist.* III. p. 152), is in itself quite ambiguous, but the same sense of the passage makes the peasants to be the oppressed, not the oppressors.[6]

[5] [In later editions Hume altered the passages in the above section to the following: "He reminded them of the fable of the hare" (Chapter 40); "the greater difficulty they found in fixing just sentiments"; (Chapter 48) "the king of England, in his own country, beloved by his subjects, provided with every supply" (Chapter 3); "provide them with food and rayment" (Chapter 11); "of which he was very greedy, very prodigal, and very indigent" (Chapter 28); "he was eager in recommending it to his fellow citizens" (Chapter 60); "the greater difficulty they found in fixing just sentiments" (Chapter 48); "notwithstanding the numerous panegyrics on ancient ENGLISH liberty" ("That Politics may be Reduced to a Science"); "Notwithstanding this unlucky example" ("Whether the British Government Inclines More to Absolute Monarchy, or to a Republic").]

[6] [In later editions Hume altered the passages in the above section to the following: "deciding law-suits in the northern counties" (Chapter 31); "a great change for the better" ("Of Civil Liberty"); "his abhorrence of that superstitious figure" (Chapter 54); "they stole his gibbet, paid the same veneration to it as to the cross" (Chapter 10); "a dozen years" ("Of the Original Contract"); "But to one who considers coolly on the subject" ("Of the Populousness of Ancient Nations"); "It is worthy of observation" (Chapter 31); "their common attack on the English" (Chapter 19).]

Of the Prepositions to *and* for.

Agreeably to the Latin and French idioms, the preposition *to* is sometimes used in conjunction with such words as, in those languages, govern the dative case; but this construction does not seem to suit the English language. ...

To seems to be used instead of for in the following sentences. "Deciding lawsuits *to* the northern countries" (*Hume's Hist*. IV. p. 191). "A great change to the better" (*Hume's Essays*, p. 133). At least *for* is more usual in this construction.

To seems to be used improperly in the following sentences. "His abhorrence *to* that superstitious figure" (*Hume's Hist*. VI. p. 323, i.e., *of*. ...

In several cases, *to* may be suppressed; but if there be two clauses of a sentence, in the same construction, it should either be omitted, or inserted in both alike. "The people stole his gibbet, and paid it the same veneration, as *to* his cross" (*Hume's Hist*. II. p. 39). ...

Of the Prepositions with *and* upon.

The preposition *with* seems to be used where *to* would have been more proper in the following sentences. "Reconciling himself *with* the king" (*Hume's Hist*. IV. p. 176). ...

Other prepositions had better have been substituted for *with* in the following sentences. ... "They could be prevailed *with* [*upon*] to retire. (*Hume's Hist*. IV. p. 10). ...

The preposition *on* or *upon* seems to be used improperly in the following sentences. "His reason could not attain a thorough conviction *on* those subjects" (*Hume's Hist*.VII. p. 355). "A greater quantity may be taken from the heap, without making any sensible alteration *upon* it" (*Hume's Political Essays*, p. 12), i.e. *in*. ...

This preposition seems to be superfluous in the following sentence. "Their efforts seemed to anticipate *on* the spirit, which became so general afterwards" (*Hume's Hist*. III. p. 5).

We say, *to* depend upon *a thing*, but not *to* promise upon it. "But this effect we may safely say, no one could beforehand have *promised upon*" (*Hume's Hist*. Vol. VIII. p. 75). It might have been, *have promised themselves*.[7]

---

[7] [In later editions Hume altered the passages in the above section to the following: "reconciling herself to the king" (Chapter 31); "they could be prevailed on to retire" (Chapter 28); "is as positive and dogmatical as if human reason, and his reason in particular, could attain a thorough conviction in these subjects" (Chapter 62); "the greater quantity may be taken from the heap, without making any sensible alteration in it" ("Of Commerce"); "their efforts against the church were still more extraordinary, and seemed to anticipate very much the spirit which became so general in little more than a century afterwards" (Chapter 18); "But this effect, we may safely say, no one could before-hand have expected" (Chapter 67).]

Of the Prepositions in, from, *and others.*

The preposition *in* is sometimes used where the French use their *en*, but where some other preposition would be more agreeable to the English idiom. Some of the following sentences are examples of this. "He made a point of honour *in* (*of*) not departing from his enterprize" (*Hume's Hist.* I. p. 402). ... In some of these cases, *in* might with advantage be changed for *to* or *into*. "Painters have not a little contributed to bring the study of medals *in* vogue" (*Addison*). On the other hand, I have found *into* put for *in*: "engaged him *into* attempts" (*Hume's Hist.* V. p. 162). ...

It is agreeable to the French idiom, that *in* is sometimes put for *with*. "He had been *provided in* a small living by the duke of Norfolk" (*Hume's Hist.* VIII. p. 68).

In some similar cases, there is an ellipsis of this preposition. "It was esteemed *no wise* probable" (*Hume's Hist.* VII. p. 315) but this construction hardly suits grave style. ...

The preposition *from* had better be changed in the following sentences. "The estates of all were burthened by fines and confiscations, which had been levied *from* them" (*Hume's Hist.* VII. p. 315). ... "Could he have profited *from* (*by*) repeated experiences" (*Hume's Hist.* VIII. p. 259).

From seems to be superfluous after *forbear*. "He could not forbear *from* appointing the pope to be one of the god-fathers" (*Hume's Hist.* VIII. p. 282).

The preposition *among* always implies a number of things; and therefore cannot be used in conjunction with the word *every*, which is in the singular number. "Which is found *among every* species of liberty" (*Hume's Essays*, p. 92). "The opinion of the advance of riches in the island seems to gain ground *among every* body" (*Hume's Political Essays*, p. 71).[8]
...

---

[8]   [In later editions Hume altered the passages in the above section to the following: "he made it a point of honour not to depart from his enterprize" (Chapter 8); "engaged him in attempts (Chapter 40); "he had been settled in a small living by the duke of Norfolk" (Chapter 67); "The estates of all were burthened by the fines and confiscations, which had been levied upon them" (Chapter 62); "Could he have profited by repeated experience" (Chapter 70); "he could not forbear, at the baptism of the young prince, appointing the pope to be one of the godfathers" (Chapter 71); "that opinion of the advance of riches in IRELAND, which gave the Doctor so much indignation, seems still to continue, and gain ground with every body" ("Of the Balance of Trade").]

18
HORACE WALPOLE

Horace Walpole, *Historic doubts on the life and reign of King Richard the Third. By Mr. Horace Walpole*. London : Printed for J. Dodsley, 1768, xv, [1], 134, [2] p.
Selections; from 1768 London edition.

Born in London, youngest son of Prime Minister Robert Walpole, Horace Walpole (1717–1797) was educated at King's College, Cambridge, and in 1741 became a member of Parliament. Among his varied literary contributions are a Gothic romance novel titled *The Castle of Otranto* (1765) and over 3,000 private letters. He occasionally corresponded with Hume, with early letters dating from around 1758. In 1766 Walpole composed a satirical letter which triggered a dispute between Hume and Rousseau (see *Early Responses to Hume's Life and Reputation*), and the two corresponded on the controversy. Walpole's attitudes towards Hume's *History* were mixed, sometimes praising it and other times ridiculing it as incompetent (see "Miscellaneous Comments on Hume's *History*" later in this collection). In 1768 Walpole published *Historic Doubts on the Life and Reign of King Richard the Third*, a work which challenged the prevailing view that Richard III was behind the murders of Henry VI and Richard's own two nephews. Walpole here criticizes Hume's account of the story in the *History*, charging Hume with relying on questionable authorities and being influenced by recent biased accounts of Richard. Hume wrote a critique of Walpole's *Historic Doubts*, to which Walpole responded (see Walpole's *Supplement* later in this collection).

HISTORIC DOUBTS
ON THE
LIFE and REIGN of King RICHARD III

... Henry was so afraid of not ascertaining a good foundation of Perkin's English accent, that he makes him learn the language twice over. "Being sent with a merchant of Turney, called Berlo, to the mart of Antwerp, the said Berlo set me," says Perkin, "to borde in a skinner's house, that dwelled beside the house of the English nation. And after this the said Berlo set me with a

343

344 Early Responses to Hume's History of England

merchant of Middleborough to service for *to learne the language,* with whom I dwelled from Christmas to Easter, and then I went into Portyngale." One does not learn any language very perfectly and with good, nay, undistinguishable accent, between Christmas and Easter; but here let us pause. If this account was true, the other relating to the duchess Margaret was false; and then how came Perkin by so accurate a knowledge of the English court, that he did not faulter, nor could be detected in his tale? If the confession was *not* true, it remains that it was trumped up by Henry, and then Perkin must be allowed the true duke of York.

But the gross contradiction of all follows: "It was in Ireland," says Perkin, in this very narrative and confession, "that against my will they made me to learne English, and taught me what I should do and say." Amazing! What forced him to learn English, after, as he says himself in the very same page, he had learnt it at Antwerp! What an impudence was there in royal power to dare to obtrude such stuff on the world! Yet this confession, as it is called, was the poor young man forced to read at his execution – no doubt in dread of worse torture. Mr. Hume, though he questions it, owns that it was believed by torture to have been drawn from him. What matters how it was obtained, or whether ever obtained; it could not be true: and as Henry could put together no more plausible account, commiseration will shed a tear over a hapless youth, sacrificed to the fury and jealousy of an usurper, and in all probability the victim of a tyrant, who has made the world believe that the duke of York, executed by his own orders, had been previously murdered by his predecessor.[1]

I have thus, I flatter myself, from the discovery of new authorities, from the comparison of dates, from fair consequences and arguments, and without straining or wresting probability, proved all I intended to prove; not an hypothesis of Richard's universal innocence, but this assertion with which I set out, that we have no reasons, no authority for believing by far the greater part of the crimes charged on him. I have convicted historians of partiality, absurdities, contradictions, and falsehoods; and though I have destroyed their credit, I have ventured to establish no peremptory conclusion of my own. What did

---

[1] Mr. Hume, to whose doubts all respect is due, tells me he thinks no mention being made of Perkin's title in the Cornish rebellion under the lord Audeley, is a strong presumption that the nation was not persuaded of his being the true duke of York. This argument, which at most is negative, seems to me to lose its weight, when it is remembered, that this was an insurrection occasioned by a poll-tax: that the rage of the people was directed against archbishop Morton and Sir Reginald Bray, the supposed authors of the grievance. An insurrection against a tax in a southern county, in which no mention is made of a pretender to the crown, is surely not so forcible a presumption against him, as the persuasion of the northern counties that he was the true heir, is an argument in his favour. Much less can it avail against such powerful evidence as I have shown exists to overturn all that Henry could produce against Perkin.

really happen in so dark a period, it would be rash to affirm. The coronation and parliament rolls have ascertained a few facts, either totally unknown, or misrepresented by historians. Time may bring other monuments to light:[2] but one thing is sure, that should any man hereafter presume to repeat the same improbable tale on no better grounds that it has been hitherto urged, he must shut his eyes against conviction, and prefer ridiculous tradition to the skepticism due most points of history, and to none more than to that in question.

I have little more to say, and only on what regards the person of Richard and the story of Jane Shore; but having run counter to a very valuable modern historian and friend of my own, I must both make some apology for him, and for myself for disagreeing with him. When Mr. Hume published his reigns of Edward the Fifth, Richard the Third, and Henry the Seventh, the coronation roll had not come to light. The stream of historians concurred to make him take this portion of our story for granted. Buck had been given up as an advancer of paradoxes, and nobody but Carte had dared to controvert the popular belief. Mr Hume treats Carte's doubts as whimsical: I wonder, he did; he, who having so closely examined our history, had discovered how very fallible many of its authorities are. Mr. Hume himself had ventured to contest both the flattering picture drawn of Edward the First, and those ignominious portraits of Edward the Second and Richard the Second. He had discovered from the Foedera, that Edward the Fourth, while said universally to be prisoner to archbishop Nevil, was at full liberty and doing acts of royal power. Why was it whimsical in Carte to exercise the same spirit of criticism? Mr. Hume could not but know how much the characters of princes are liable to be flattered or misrepresented. It is of little importance to the world, to Mr. Hume, or to me, whether Richard's story is fairly told or not: and in this amicable discussion I have no fear of offending him by disagreeing with him. His abilities and sagacity do not rest on the shortest reign in our annals. I shall therefore attempt to give answers to the questions on which he pins the credibility due to the history of Richard.

The questions are these. 1. Had not the queen-mother and the other heads of the York party been fully assured of the death of both the young princes, would they have agreed to call over the earl of Richmond, the head of the Lancastrian party, and marry him to the princess Elizabeth? – I answer, that when the queen-mother could recall that consent, and send to her son the marquis Dorset to quit Richmond, assuring him of king Richard's favour to him and her house, it is impossible to say what so weak and ambitious a woman would not do. She wanted to have some one of her children on the throne, in order to recover her own power. She first engaged her daughter to Richmond

---

[2] If diligent search was to be made in the public offices and convents of the Flemish towns in which the duchess Margaret resided, I should not despair of new lights gained to that part of our history.

and then to Richard. She might not know what was become of her sons; and yet that is no proof they were murdered. They were out of her power, whatever was become of them; and she was impatient to rule. If she was fully assured of their deaths, could Henry, after he came to the crown and had married her daughter, be uncertain of it? I have shown that both Sir Thomas More and lord Bacon own it remained uncertain, and that Henry's account could not be true. As to the heads of the Yorkists;[3] how does it appear they concurred in the projected match? Indeed who were the heads of that party? Margaret duchess of Burgundy, Elizabeth duchess of Suffolk and her children; did they ever concur in that match? Did not they to the end endeavor to defeat and overturn it? I hope Mr. Hume will not call bishop Morton, the duke of Buckingham, and Margaret countess of Richmond, chiefs of the Yorkists. 2. The story told constantly by Perkin of his escape is utterly incredible, that those who were sent to murder his brother, took pity on him and granted him his liberty. – Answer. We do not know but from Henry's narrative and the Lancastrian historians that Perkin gave this account.[4] I am not authorized to believe he did, because I find no authority for the murder of the elder brother; and if there was, why is it utterly incredible that the younger brother should have been spared? 3. What became of him during the course of seven years from his supposed death till his appearance in 1491? – Answer. Does uncertainty of where a man has been, prove his non-identity when he appears again? When Mr. Hume will answer half the questions in this work, I will tell him where Perkin was during

---

[3] The excessive affection shown by the Northern counties, where the principle strength of the Yorkists lay, to Richard the Third while living, and to his memory when dead, implies two things; first, that the party did not give him up to Henry; secondly, that they did not believe he had murdered his nephews. Tyrants of that magnitude are not apt to be popular. Examine the life of the chiefs in Henry's army, as stated by the Chronicle of Croyland, p. 574. and they will be found Lancastrians, or very private gentlemen, and but one peer, the earl of Oxford, a noted Lancastrian.

[4] Grafton has preserved a ridiculous oration said to be made by Perkin to the king of Scotland, in which this silly tale is told. Nothing can be depended upon less that such orations, almost always forged by the writer, and unpardonable, if they pass the bounds of truth. Perkin, in the passage in question, uses there words, "And farther to the entent that my life might be in a suretie he (the murderer of my elder brother) appointed one to convey me into some straunge countrie, where, when I was furthest off, and had most neede of comfort, he then forsooke me soudainly (I think he was so appointed to do) and left me desolate alone without friend or knowledge of any reliefe or refuge, &c." Would not one think one was reading the tale of Valentine and Orson, or any legend of a barbarous age, rather than the history of England, when we are told of straunge countries and such indefinite ramblings, as would pass only in a nursery? It remains not only a secret but a doubt, whether the elder brother was murdered. If Perkin was the younger, and knew certainly that his brother was put to death, our doubt would vanish: but can it vanish on no better authority than this foolish oration? Did Grafton hear it pronounced? Did king James bestow his kinswoman on Perkin, on the strength of such a fable?

those seven years. 4. Why was not the queen-mother, the duchess of Burgundy, and the other friends of the family applied to, during that time, for his support and education? – Answer. Who knows that they were not applied to? The probability is, that they were. The queen's dabbling in the affair of Simnel indicates that she knew her son was alive. And when the duchess of Burgundy is accused of setting Perkin to work, it is amazing that she should be quoted as knowing nothing about him. 5. Though the duchess of Burgundy at last acknowledged him for her nephew, she had lost all pretense to authority by her former acknowledgement and support of Lambert Simnel, an avowed impostor. – Answer. Mr. Hume here makes an unwary consession by distinguishing between Lambert Simnel, an avowed impostor, and Perkin, whose imposture was problematic. But if he was a true prince, the duchess could only forfeit credit for herself, not for him: nor would her preparing the way for her nephew, by first playing off and feeling the ground by a counterfeit, be an imputation on her, but rather a proof of her wisdom and tenderness. Impostors are easily detected; as Simnel was. All Henry's art and power could never verify the cheat of Perkin; and if the latter was astonishing adroit, the king was ridiculously clumsy. 6. Perkin himself confessed his imposture more than once, and read his confession to the people, and renewed his confession at the foot of the gibbet on which he was executed. – Answer. I have shown that this confession was such an awkward forgery that lord Bacon did not dare adhere to quote or adhere to it, but invented a new story, more specious, but equally inconsistent with probability. 7. After Henry the Eighth's accession, the titles of the houses of York and Lancaster were fully confounded, and there was no longer any necessity for defending Henry the Seventh and his title; yet all the historians of that time, when the events were recent, some of these historians, such as Sir Thomas More, of the highest authority, agree in treating Perkin as an impostor. – Answer. When Sir Thomas More wrote, Henry the Seventh was still alive; that argument therefore falls entirely to the ground: but there *was* great necessity, I will not say to defend, but even to palliate the titles of both Henry the Seventh and Henry the Eighth. The former, all the world agrees now, had no title:[5] the latter had none from his father, and a very defective one from his mother. If she had any right, it could only be after her brothers; and it is not to be supposed that so jealous a tyrant as Henry the Eighth would suffer it to be said that his father and mother enjoyed the throne to the prejudice of that mother's surviving brother, in whose blood the father had imbrued his

---

[5] Henry was so reduced to make out any title to the crown, that he catched even at a quibble. In the act of attainder, passed after his accession, he calls himself a nephew of Henry the Sixth. He was so, but it was by his father, who was not of royal blood. Catherine of Valois, after bearing Henry the Sixth, married Owen Tudor, and had two sons, Edmund and Jasper, the former of which married Margaret, mother of Henry the Seventh, and so he was half nephew of Henry the Sixth. On one side he had no royal blood, on the other only bastard blood.

hands. The murder therefore was to be fixed on Richard the Third, who was to be supposed to have usurped the throne, by murdering, and not, as really was the case, by bastardizing his nephews. If they were illegitimate, so was their sister; and if she was, what title had she conveyed to her son Henry the Eighth? No wonder that both Henrys were jealous of the earl of Suffolk, whom one bequeathed to slaughter, and the other executed; for if the children of Edward the Fourth were spurious, and those of Clarence attainted, the right of the house of York was vested in the duchess of Suffolk and her descendants. The massacre of the children of Clarence and the duchess of Suffolk show what Henry the Eighth thought of the titles both of his father and mother.[6] But, says Mr. Hume, all the historians of that time agree in treating Perkin as an impostor. I have shown from their own mouths that they all doubted of it. The reader must judge between us. But Mr. Hume selects Sir Thomas More as the highest authority; I have proved that he was the lowest – but not in the case of Perkin, for Sir Thomas More's history does not go so low; yet happening to mention him, he says, the man, commonly called Perkin Warbeck, was, as well with the princes as the people, held to be the younger son of Edward the Fourth; and that the deaths of the young king Edward and of Richard his brother had come so far in question, as some are yet in doubt, *whether they were destroyed or no in the days of king Richard.* Sir Thomas adhered to the affirmative, relying as I have shown on very bad authorities. But what is a stronger argument ad hominem, I can prove that Mr. Hume did not think Sir Thomas More good authority; no, Mr. Hume was a fairer and more impartial judge: at the very time he quotes Sir Thomas More, he tacitly rejects his authority; for Mr. Hume, agreeably to truth, specifies the lady Eleanor Butler as the person to whom king Edward was contracted, and not Elizabeth Lucy, as it stands in Sir Thomas More. An attempt to vindicate Richard will probably no longer be thought whimsical, when so very acute reasoner as Mr. Hume could find no better foundation than these seven queries on which to rest his condemnation.

---

[6] Observe, that when lord Bacon wrote, there *was* great necessity to vindicate the title even of Henry the Seventh, for James the First claimed from the eldest daughter of Henry and Elizabeth.

19
HORACE WALPOLE

Horace Walpole, *Supplement to the Historic doubts on the life and reign of King Richard III. With remarks on some answers that have been made to that Work* (1769).
Selections; from *The Works of Horatio Walpole*. London, G.G. and J. Robinson, 1798, Vol. 2, pp. 185–220.

Horace Walpole (1717–1797) was the author of *Historic Doubts* (1768), excerpted earlier in this collection. Hume wrote a critique of that work titled "Sixteen notes on Walpole's *Historic Doubts*," which in 1769 appeared in French in a periodical titled *Mémoires littéraires de la Grande Bretagne*. The editors were Edward Gibbon and George Deyverdun, the latter being a clerk in the Secretary of State's office, Northern Department, while Hume was working there. Hume later incorporated his "Sixteen Notes" into a lengthy Note to Chapter 26 of his *History of England*. Walpole heard about – and perhaps viewed – Hume's forthcoming critique, and wrote to a friend, "Mr. Hume shall publish a few remarks he has made on my book: they are very far from substantial; yet still better than any other trash that has been written against it, nothing of which deserves an answer" (Walpole to Cole, April 16, 1768). Walpole's reaction, though, was more negative after Hume's comments appeared in print. In the *Supplement*, composed in 1769, Walpole defends his original contentions against all of Hume's arguments, and accuses Hume of relying on questionable historical sources, particularly those by Thomas More and Francis Bacon. Although the *Supplement* seems to have been intended for publication as a pamphlet, it remained unpublished until a year after Walpole's death, when it appeared in a five-volume collection of his works. Upon its appearance, reviewers commented on the vehemence of Walpole's response to Hume and other critics of *Historic Doubts*. Three of these are as follows:

[T]he contempt with which he treats every one who thinks differently from himself, on a speculative question of little consequence to any of the great interests of society, is very aristocratic. [Charles Burney, *Monthly Review*, July 1798, Vol. 26, pp. 323–327, September, Vol. 27, pp. 51–66, October, pp. 171–189, November, pp. 271–289]

Some meaner opponents are quickly dispatched: ranks are with little ceremony overwhelmed in his career; but he meets two champions worthy of particular notice; Mr. Hume, who had considered the Historic Doubts at the end of a criticism in M. d'Yverdun's journal, and Dr. Milles, the late president of the Antiquarian Society. To Mr. Hume, he is apparently respectful; but it is the respect of Henry of Bolingbroke to Richard II. or that of the duke of Glocester to his nephews: he can 'bear no rival near his throne.' [*Critical Review*, 1798, Vol. 23, pp. 121–132, 248–256, Vol. 24, pp. 130–141]

To the *"Historic Doubts on the Life and Reign of Richard III."* is now subjoined a supplement, in which the author considers, with great acuteness, and with more warmth than appears in the principal work, the observations made upon it by Mr. Guthrie and Mr. Hume. [*New London Review*, 1799, Vol. 1, p. 113–120, 220–227, 319–326, 454–460]

The following is from the 1798 edition of Walople's *Works.*

SUPPLEMENT
TO THE
HISTORIC DOUBTS
ON THE
Life and Reign of King Richard III.
With REMARKS on some ANSWERS that have been made to that Work.

...

After the first gush of opponents whom I have mentioned, my Doubts seemed to have nothing farther to fear but oblivion. I thought my work was much forgotten, as I had forgot my adversaries. I neither cared about them nor king Richard. How was I surprised the other day on receiving a present of a French Swiss journal from the learned author[1] himself, in which the first thing in the book was a criticism of my Doubts. – I call it criticism in deference to the author, though the whole, like other reviews, is chiefly composed of extracts from my work; and, unlike other reviews, of such a torrent of encomiums on myself, as made me blush for the mistaken good nature of the author, and for my own demerit, which is ill entitled to such incense. Indeed, any vanity I might have conceived from this panegyric was greatly lowered by a passage at the end of the book, in which the author modestly owns that he does not much admire the works of doctor Swift. Could I be greatly flattered with the approbation of a gentleman who has so little taste as to dislike

---

[1]   Mons. Diverdum, author of Mémoires litteraires de la Grande Bretagne pour les années 1767, 1768.

doctor Swift and to admire me? How qualified is this kind person to sit in judgment on books, who gives such a criterion of his distinguishing faculties!

If I found myself overwhelmed with praise, I was not less astonished to find at the end of his criticism two or three pages drawn up by Mr. Hume in answer to my Doubts, and bestowed on the journalist to help him in pronouncing sentence. He pronounces it accordingly, and declares me guilty of specious but false reasoning, and decides the victory in favour of Mr. Hume on the evidence collected from the latter's own notes.

The notes thus crept into the world are in French. Many months ago Mr. Hume gave me a sight of them in English, and I then told him what I must repeat now, that I thought I never saw more unsubstantial arguments. As he is of a different opinion, and as I am now at liberty to take them to pieces, I shall make bold to show, that they are not only no answer to my reasonings, which remain in full force, but that, if they are the best confutation Mr. Hume can make of my book, it had been wiser to let it sink or swim as it could, instead of heaping conjectures on improbabilities, and thereby leading our readers to see, that he not only avoided giving answers to my strongest arguments, but had rashly taken up an idle story without examination, and now is at a loss how to defend it.

Before I enter on the discussion of Mr. Hume's notes, I must make one or two short observations. Having remarked how shallow the authorities were on which the history of Richard is built, I thought myself warranted to call much of it in question. Buck, Carte, and it seems Mr. Guthrie, had preceded me in rejecting the received account. Some new lights had accidentally flowed in. Still I proposed my sentiments but as *doubts* – and yet have been told that I have not *proved* my hypothesis. If I had *proved* it, I should not have *doubted*. My adversaries on the other side seem to think that assertions and repetitions will serve for proofs, where facts and reasons are wanting. The best reasoner and greatest sceptic amongst them has for once listed under such mob-banners, and cooly retails the very same kind of logic against me, that has so often been wasted in vain against himself. I own there is much difference between us; our abilities are as unequal as our bodily prowess: a feather may fell me; he can resist a broad-sword.

My next observation is, that Mr. Hume rests the whole of his confutation on the single fact, the murder of the children. Whether he allows that I have cleared Richard's character from the other murders, he leaves me uncertain. What does this silence imply? Am I to infer from it that he gives up all the rest, though he had adopted into his history many of those idle tales? Or am I to conclude that he despises my arguments? But so he does with regard to Perkin Warbeck. He endeavours to establish that imposture, but does not attempt to refute the reasons I have brought to support Perkin's being the true duke of York. I challenged him to reconcile the contradictions in the story: he reverts to great names, as if names were arguments. Are all the murders charged on Richard supported by one and the same authority? Does Mr. Hume think that, if he proves one, all the rest follow of course? Or does he hope to rehabilitate the credit of his history, by attempting to show that in one point he has not been mistaken or lightly credulous? I must leave it to his own candour to answer these questions – and shall now show, that if he has no better arguments in store than what he has bounteously bestowed on his friend the journalist, or thought good enough for both him and me, the assumption of Perkin Warbeck being the true son of Edward the fourth, will gain new strength by the trifling arguments so great a man as Mr. Hume has been reduced to bring on the contrary side of the question.

The first note says that, *in general there reigns a great obscurity in the circum-stances of the wars between the two roses.* I allow it. My doubts sprung from that obscurity. *But,* continues he, *the narrative of sir Thomas More throws great light over all the transactions of the reign of Richard, and over the murder of the two young princes his nephews.* This begging the very question in dispute. *The magnanimity, the probity and the great sense of that author confirm his testimony; and there is no historian ancient or modern who ought to have more weight.* I must here stop in the middle of this note. In the first place I do not precisely know the meaning of *magnanimity.* It is a pompous but empty word, often employed by another modern historian[2] in lieu of qualities more easily to be defined. When Henry the second had been over-reached, bubbled, baffled, humbled by Becket, and consequently could no longer pass for wise, provident or firm, his panegyrist salves all with that bombast and vague epithet, *magnan-imous:* happen what would, his magnanimity was invulnerable. But if *magna-nimity* is ridiculous in the mouth *of* an historian, it is still more absurd when applied *to* an historian. What has *magnanimity* to do with that character? And in what sense does it confirm his testimony? Sir Thomas More's *probity* will prove as little, if I have shown that he has given false evidence. Let Mr. Hume, before he quotes sir Thomas's probity, refute the charge that I have brought against him from facts. A man cannot be a faithful historian if he perverts wilfully, or mistakes facts ignorantly: nor, I should think, would Mr. Hume allow in general that the *probity* of a bigot qualifies him for a sincere historian. Where was sir Thomas's *probity,* or his *great sense,* when he was the dupe of the holy maid of Kent? Mr. Hume too, now become fond of authority, amasses all sir Thomas's great qualities in the various parts of his life, to support a history which More wrote in the very early part of his life, at twenty-eight. I had remarked this; but Mr. Hume did not choose to make the distinction. By a flourish, and tacitly sinking the æra of the composition, he would lead his readers to believe, that the story of Richard the third was written by More in the grave and sedate part of his life, and bequeathed to posterity with all the sanction that the impress of the statesman and martyr could bestow on it. Young Mr. More, under sheriff of London, is the historian Mr. Hume equals with Tacitus, Davila, Thuanus, and

---

[2]   Lord Lyttelton.

all the standard authors of ancient and modern ages! Yet, still the question is not whether sir Thomas lived near the time, but whether his narrative is a competent and probable account. I have questioned his competency, and proved him guilty of ignorant or wilful mistakes. Is it an answer worthy of an able reasoner to tell us, that sir Thomas More lived at or near the time, and that as we have no better account we must believe his? Does Mr. Hume then believe all improbabilities because delivered by cotemporaries, and because he can find no better? Is he under such a necessity, has he such an alacrity of believing, that absurdities are with him preferable to doubting? Must he have an unbroken chain of history reposited in his head, be that history what it will, true or false, marvellous or rational? In theological controversy divines often repeat, that where you have no better testimony, you must take up with what you have. Does Mr. Hume allow this doctrine? I thought he knew that the accuracy of modern criticism had established two kinds of evidence, the *external* and the *internal*; and that the former, however respectable, is often called in question, when repugnant to the latter. But were Mr. Hume's still newer standard of authority to take place, we should be compelled to believe the origin of Rome, with its Mars, Rhea and the wolf, the marvels of Herodotus, and the fables of ancient Egypt: and in that case I doubt Mr. Hume would be embroiled with Voltaire, the patriarch of modern sceptics, who has called in question a mob of assassinations and poisonings far more credible than those imputed to Richard the third.

Mr. Hume continues: *We may justly regard him* (sir Thomas More) *even as a cotemporary; for though he was but five years old when the two princes were massacred, he lived and was brought up among the chief actors of Richard's reign; and one sees clearly by his recital, which is often very circumstantial, that he received the particularities from ocular witnesses.* This is again equally vague, unfair, and void of argument. Mr. Hume avoids specifying that More received his information from archbishop Morton, who I have proved was the most partial and suspicious authority from whence More could possibly draw his materials; and yet I defy him to show the least probability that More, a retainer of Morton, was likely to converse with any other chief actor of that period. Is it better proof of an authors veracity, that he is very circumstantial? If it is, why has Mr. Hume reposed so little trust in, quoted so little from Wilson, Weldon, Burnet, and others, who give circumstantial accounts of the vices, folly, falsehood and tyranny of four Stuarts? Is there a legend in the monkish writers that is not circumstantial?

We cannot therefore, continues the note, *reject his authority, and it ought to weigh over an hundred light doubts, scruples and objections, for no solid objection has yet been brought against him, nor can he be convicted of any error.* This sentence ex cathedrâ is ridiculous, and fulminated like many bulls against those who do not acknowledge the papal authority. It is easy to say doubts and scruples are light: if they are, they are easily answered. Mr. Hume's infallibility is not more generally recognized, than that of many great men whose authority he himself has set at nought. He will excuse me therefore if I say he asserts only because he cannot answer. Mr. Guthrie and I have shown that sir Thomas More's account of Tirrel is an absolute falshood. It is proved from record that Tirrel was a great officer of the crown when More represents him as a low creature following the court, but unknown to the king, an intimate of a nameless page, and a fellow ready to be dispatched on any base and sudden assassination. Is this a light doubt, a trifling objection to More's veracity and competence? Sir Thomas adds, that Tirrell, a commissioner for executing the office of high constable in the last reign, and actually master of the horse at the period in question, or, as others say, appointed so within a month, was kept down by Ratcliffe and Catesby, neither of whom ever was Tirrel's equal, and one of whom I have proved was absent at the time. If these are trifling objections, I invite Mr. Hume to answer them – yes, and to answer sir Thomas More himself, who owns that *there was nothing so plainly and openly proved but that yet men had it ever inwardly suspect.* Mr. Hume, it seems, better informed than sir Thomas himself, knows that sir Thomas was perfectly acquainted with the fact and all the circumstances; and with equal confidence, equally unfounded, declares that *sir Thomas cannot be convicted of any error!*

It is with concern that I am forced to produce the remainder of the first note; nor can I conceive how Mr. Hume could allow himself to make such a misrepresentation of sir Thomas More's evidence in the face of sir Thomas's own words. *It is true*, says Mr. Hume, *that sir Thomas declares that the protector's partisans, in particular doctor Shaw, spread a report of a precontract between Edward the fourth and Elizabeth Lucy, while it appears from records that the parliament pronounced the children of Edward illegitimate, under pretext of a precontract with the lady Eleanor Butler. But,* continues Mr. Hume, *we must observe that no attempt was made to prove either of the contracts; and why should not the protector's flatterers and tools have spread sometimes the one, sometimes the other of those reports? More quotes both, and treats both as lightly as they deserved. Mr. Carte thinks it incredible that Richard should have engaged doctor Shaw openly to calumniate the duchess of York his mother, with whom he lived on good terms; but if in reality it is difficult to believe this, why should not we suppose that the doctor, taking the general matter of his sermon from the protector or his friends, chose himself the particulars, and chose them with very little judgment? The disgrace into which he afterwards fell seems to strengthen his supposition.*

I have translated Mr. Hume's words as fairly and faithfully as I am able; and thus I answer them. On the authority of the roll of parliament I accused sir Thomas More of ignorance or falsification in naming Elizabeth Lucy instead of lady Eleanor Butler; and Mr. Hume is forced to admit the evidence, though he would fain avoid the conclusion. This he attempts by urging that sir Thomas mentions both reports. I must own that with all my care I can find no one word in sir Thomas relative to the lady Butler, and would be much obliged to Mr.

Hume for pointing out the passage[3] to me. He also speaks of Elizabeth Lucy as a report propagated by the protector's tools and in doctor Shaw's sermon. Unfortunately sir Thomas gives us a *circumstantial* detail of a conversation between king Edward and his mother, in which that princess taxes him with a precontract with Elizabeth Lucy. Did the protector's mother spread those reports? Still farther: "The duchess, says sir Thomas, devised to disturb this marriage (with the widow Gray), and rather to help that he should marry one dame Elizabeth Lucy, whom the king had also not long before gotten with child, and openly objected his marriage, as it were in discharge of her conscience, that the king was sure to dame Elizabeth Lucy." Surely, surely, Mr. Hume, this is not a report spread by the protector's tools, but by that very mother whom Richard is accused of aspersing too – and so consistent is your circumstantial oracle, that in one place he ascribes the report to Richard, and in another to the duchess of York. And am I now unfounded in saying that sir Thomas More affirmed deliberately of Elizabeth Lucy what related to Eleanor Butler? What follows is still stronger: "By reason of which words such obstacle was made in the matter, that either the bishops durst not, or the king would not, proceed to the solemnization of this wedding, till these same were clearly purged and the truth well and openly testified. Whereupon dame Elizabeth Lucy was then sent for – and confessed they were never married." "This examination, adds sir Thomas, was solemnly taken." I ask if this proves that doctor Shaw chose the particulars without judgment? And I ask, if what is here said by More is not a wilful or mistaken falsehood? But, says Mr. Hume, no attempt was made to prove either of the contracts. – No! Does not sir Thomas here directly affirm that the bishops refused to marry the king, till the examination was solemnly taken? Which are we to believe, the infallible chancellor, or his determined advocate? Mr. Guthrie goes farther, and, relating the same story of the lady Butler, affirms, as we have seen, that she denied any precontract in open court. So clear is this whole story, after being circumstantially related by sir Thomas More from ocular witnesses! I leave this part to be adjusted as it may by sir Thomas, Mr. Hume and Mr. Guthrie; and proceed to the article of doctor Shaw, of which Mr. Hume is not much happier in his solution.

Mr. Hume, not quite clear whether Mr. Carte is in the right or the wrong, in not believing that the protector aspersed his own mother, though I produced two original papers to prove that he lived in the house with her at the very time of the supposed calumny, and continued on good terms with her, desires us to suppose that doctor Shaw was prompted by the protector general, but did not choose his materials judiciously. He has guessed that *both* the reports of Lucy

---

[3] I have heard that it is mentioned somewhere in the Biographia Britannica, that in a late edition of sir Thomas More's History Eleanore Butler is inserted instead of Elizabeth Lucy. My edition, which is of 1641, has no such correction; and a correction more recent would but prove that sir Thomas More wrote Elizabeth Lucy, and that the grossness of the mistakes induced some modern editor to restore the genuine name.

and Butler were spread by the protector's agents. This is supposing that a sensible man and artful usurper made choices of very bungling tools, because spreading both reports would have been the surest way of contradicting both reports. But on this point I have better evidence, even that of sir Thomas himself against Mr. Hume, who says, "the protector would that the matter should be *touched aslope craftily.*" *One may see clearly* (to use Mr. Hume's own words) *that sir Thomas is so circumstantial that he must have gathered his materials from the best evidence*; and thence conclude that the protector did not leave the execution of his plot to injudicious tools, but himself adjusted the whole detail of what they should say and do. This is a complete answer to Mr. Hume's supposition, which being raised in opposition to his own evidences, stands on no ground at all: and therefore, when he was reduced to his hypothesis, it is plain that he could not support so silly a story as that of Richard blackening his own mother and setting up a precontract with Elizabeth Lucy: both which I exposed; and which as Mr. Hume cannot defend from the authority of sir Thomas More, without contradicting sir Thomas More, I may fairly presume that I have confuted sir Thomas More, when Mr. Hume himself is forced to give him up, and is forced to deny that he has said what he *has* said so positively and *circumstantially*.

NOTE the Second. If we refuse to More the quality of cotemporary relatively to the protectorate of the duke of Gloucester, we cannot deny it to him with regard to the imposture of Perkin. He was then grown a man, and had all the faculties necessary for knowing, examining and deciding on the truth; so that when he assures us that Richard ordered the massacre of the duke of York, he assures us in effect in the clearest manner that Perkin, who assumed his name, was an impostor.

ANSWER. When this note is analysed, I will recommend it for as beautiful an instance of false logic as can be produced. Here is the sum of it: Sir Thomas More was a grown man when Warbeck appeared, and had all the faculties necessary for knowing, examining and deciding on the truth; *therefore* a fact that he relates which passed in his childhood when he was *not* capable of knowing, examining, &c. proves another fact that happened when he was capable of knowing and examining, but which fact he neither related nor examined. Yet even in that circumstance of age Mr. Hume is unfortunate. Sir Thomas was born in 1480; Perkin appeared in 1495, when More was fifteen. Is not that a time of life singularly qualified for knowing, examining and deciding on the truth of a state secret? But perhaps Mr. Hume refers to sir Thomas's age when he composed his history. I have shown that was in his twenty-eighth year, and when he was under-sheriff of London. Was he in a situation then of fathoming all the depths of a mystery which he himself and lord Bacon own had been sedulously involved by Henry the seventh in impenetrable obscurity? Does not sir Thomas confess that he had heard the story of the murder related in many various ways, but gave it from the mouths of those he deemed the most credible witnesses? Was this being in a situation to know, examine and decide peremptorily on so dark a story? Is this assuring us *in the clearest manner* that Richard ordered the murder of his nephews? Does Mr. Hume thing that every historian, who is a grown man at or near the time of an event, and who assures us of certain facts, ought to be implicitly received as a faithful reporter? who stands more strongly in that predicament than doctor Burnet? Who has made a more solemn appeal to heaven for his veracity? I profess I believe the general and by far the greater part of the bishop's history, because I have seen how vain the attempts have been to confute it. – But does Mr. Hume believe so too? If he does, why has he followed him so little? Why are More and Bacon competent witnesses against Richard the third, and Burnet not so against Charles the second?

NOTE the Third. This note is composed of mere declamation, and assertions unfounded in fact. It contains a pompous panegyric of lord Bacon as a genius of the first water, an excuse for the flattery he has showered on Henry the seventh, and an assumption that it was composed from original papers now lost; with other positions equally arbitrary, which I shall examine presently. I have already observed, that nothing can be weaker than to pretend to establish the credit of an historian on the extent of his understanding. I fear the contrary is more often true; and that the less bright the imagination of an historian, the more he is likely to be exact in his narrative. Many historians are admired for their art, method, style, and shrewdness, on whose fidelity the world does not bestow equal approbation. Perhaps one of the least bright of our historians, Rapin, is more generally esteemed for his veracity than many of his superiors in composition. *But lord Bacon is an upright historian, is not partial to Henry, since it is from him we have received the details of the tyrannic government of that prince. All one can reproach him with is, for not blaming the facts he relates so severely as they deserved.* As the book is in print and common enough, one can scarce conceive how Mr. Hume could give this character of it. If the worst actions are not defended and palliated throughout, if his lordship's tacit disapprobation of them may be conjectured, as it is true it sometimes may, still so timidly is it insinuated, so cautiously enveloped, that he seems to have hoped the learned prince (James the first) under whose auspices the work was composed, would not have sagacity enough to penetrate his real sentiments. But I will recur to the book itself. In the dedication to Prince Charles, lord Bacon professes *that he has endeavoured to do honour to the memory of that king,* (Henry the seventh) and the history takes care to keep the promise made by the dedication. *Besides,* continues the dedication, *the times deserve it, for he was a wise man and an excellent king.* This was the text, and we find it amply handled in the same style. I shall select a few instances, and will leave the reader to judge whether lord Bacon is solely reproachable with not having treated Henry's tyranny with due rigour, as Mr. Hume asserts; or whether, as I pretend, he has not exalted some of his worst actions into matter of panegyric: and under this head I shall forbear recapitulating the instances I have already quoted in the Historic Doubts.

Henry procured the Star-chamber, which before subsisted by the common law, to be confirmed in certain cases by act of parliament. This court, says lord Bacon, is one of the sagest and noblest institutions of this kingdom.

Recounting the reasons that moved Henry to put to death sir William Stanley, the brother of his own mother's husband, lord Bacon reckons those that were predominant in the king's nature and mind, as, *Stanley's overmerit and the glimmering of a confiscation, for he was the richest subject for value in the kingdom* – after assigning these base and scandalous motives, he adds these words: *after some six weeks distance of time, which the king did honourably interpose, both to give time to his brother's intercession and to show to the world that he had a conflict with himself what to do, Stanley was arraigned, condemned and beheaded.* This *honourable* hypocrisy is something more methinks than not treating Henry with proper severity. And these sordid motives weighed to get rid of a man, whom lord Bacon impiously compares to Jesus Christ, *as having had the benefit at once to save and crown.* p. 135.

On the inhuman murder of the young and simple earl of Warwick the noble historian is as indulgent as possible, and rather treats it as an act of political wisdom. "It happened opportunely, says he, that while the king was mediating that young prince's death, another counterfeit started up to represent the danger to the king's estate, and thereby to colour the king's severity that followed. And to shift the envy of so foul a deed from himself, the king thought good to transport it out of the land, and to lay it upon his new ally the king of Spain: for these two kings understanding one another at half a word, Ferdinand refused to give his daughter to prince Arthur, while the earl of Warwick was alive." Is it possible to palliate a shocking murder by smoother terms? And did not the sage Henry by this infamous intrigue avow that the earl of Warwick had the best title to the crown, from the illegitimacy of Henry's own queen and her sisters? In truth, among the instances of his boasted wisdom, there is scarce one in which he did not prove the dupe of his own duplicity, and of the superior cunning of others. But I should tire the reader and myself with recapitulating what the whole book demonstrates, that it is the panegyric of a knavish tyrant, and in no light deserves the rank to which Mr. Hume would prefer it. I will only observe farther, that in the end he calls him *the Solomon of England, and a wonder for wise men,* and talks of the piety, charity, morality, justice and lenity, of a tyrant who plundered his people by every act of extortion, shed innocent blood from jealousy, wrenched the laws to serve his purposes, and died mocking God by commanding his son to put to death the earl of Suffolk whom he had sworn himself to save.

Mr. Hume's next assertion in this note is, that lord Bacon composed his history from authentic papers now lost; and therefore ought always to be cited as an original writer. Lord Bacon no where pretends to have seen any such papers: it is a mere ipse dixit of Mr. Hume, who being the sole finder of those papers was certainly at liberty to lose them again if he pleased. Lord Bacon's history was rather composed like Xenophon's Cyrus, for a model to princes, than as a strict and faithful narrative. Livy, Josephus, Eusebius, and even Varilas, might by Mr. Hume's argument be equally entitled to universal credit. The first founded all his fables of the early ages of Rome on writers long since perished: and the three others pretended to have consulted authentic monuments and papers in the composition of their several works; and yet, though on that foot original writers, are now treated by all men of sense as fabulous romancers. But Mr. Hume takes great care to forget that the truth of history does not depend solely on the originality of an author. A thousand circumstances must concur to establish his credit. A cotemporary, if not an actor, is seldom well informed, and the first histories we have are generally the least true. Time brings greater evidence to light, and dissipates the clouds of party, partiality, and mistake. Why else has Mr. Hume taken the trouble of recomposing what has been so often written?

I will conclude my remarks on this note with exemplifying two more round assertions in it, as little founded as the preceding. In lord Bacon's time, says Mr. Hume, it was no longer any body's interest to blacken Richard. I have stated, and I thought clearly, that it was as unsafe in king James's time, as in king Henry's, to assert the bastardy of the children of Edward the fourth. James the first claimed from the eldest daughter of Henry and Elizabeth. In the very last years of queen Elizabeth, not twenty-five years before lord Bacon wrote his history, various claims to the crown had been set forth in opposition to that of James. The earls of Huntingdon, Derby, and others, were descended from different branches of the royal stock, whose titles were preferable to those of Henry, who had in reality no title at all, and even of his wife Elizabeth, if her mother's was not a lawful marriage. I am not surprised that Mr. Hume should overlook my arguments, but I will not wonder if I think them preferable to his assertions founded on no argument at all, and contrary to facts.

But the most strange assertion of all is, Mr. Hume's pretending, contrary to the evidence of his own eyes, that lord Bacon had no doubt of Perkin being an impostor. I have stated in the Historic Doubts various expressions of lord Bacon, which evince, that whatever pains he took to persuade others, he was by no means convinced himself. The immunity of Lambert Simnel, *which was no small argument that there was some secret in it; the king's manner of muffling the story, which has left it almost a mystery to this day;* his owning *that the king did himself no good* by the publication of the narrative – these and twenty other expressions must convince us that lord Bacon was far from having any inward conviction that Perkin was not the true duke of York; and that, if my doubts are light and trifling, Mr. Hume's assertions are so overloaded with false weight, that they will sink themselves in the mind of every impartial reader.

But without guessing at the depths of so insincere a mind as lord Bacon's, here is positive proof that he did not believe the story as he related it. He has composed a new confession for Perkin, different from and irreconcileable with that published by king Henry. This I stated before. Mr. Hume could not answer it, and consequently overlooked it – at the expence of his accuracy. I offer it to him once more thus: Lord Bacon could not compose a new confession for Perkin, without thinking that that given out by Henry was a fiction; and certainly not without knowing that what he himself composed in lieu of it, was so. Was it from these two impostures that lord Bacon believed Perkin was an impostor?

NOTE the Fourth. But if we demand, says Mr. Hume, cotemporary evidence, the strongest and least suspicious are ready with their testimony. He then musters a long list of the queen and first persons and families, who, says he, were so persuaded of the murder of the two princes, that they addressed themselves to the earl of Richmond, the mortal enemy of their family and party. Here let us pause a moment. – Mr. Hume formerly, making use of the same argument, was so unlucky as to mistake Lancastrians for Yorkists. Corrected now, though without owning his mistake, he has invented a new muster-roll of names, still without offering the least authority to inform us from whence he took them. He has dubbed them all Yorkists at once. That they all submitted afterwards to the usurper Henry, I do not doubt, especially after he had married the heiress of York. For such of them as joined to invite Richmond over, their belief or disbelief of the murder proves just nothing at all, but that they deserted the right heirs of the crown, and entered into a conspiracy to place it on the head of a bastard branch. Let Richard be what he would, his usurpation could give no title to Henry. If the princes were dead and their sisters legitimate, the latter were the next heirs. There were also many other princes and princesses living of the house of York. As it appeared afterwards that the counties in which the chief interest of that family lay, maintained their affection and attachment to that house, Mr. Hume will excuse me if I do not believe from his fictitious roll of names that the party of York did concur in general in the invitation to Henry; and though he lays great stress on illustrious names, whoever calls to mind the factions of that time and their frequent changes from interested views, and whoever has seen anything of factions at all, will not form his opinion of a cause from the behaviour of the most illustrious persons on either side. Much less will he pay regard to a second edition of names, supported, according to Mr. Hume's method, by no authority.

But, as if he was sensible of the weakness of his argument, he endeavours to prop the question he has begged, by asking the most wonderful question that I suppose was ever asked since the days of the schoolmen. They indeed used to enquire how things would have been, if they had been very different from what they were; as how Adam and Eve would have begotten children, if they had both been women? Our new Tostatus proposes the following quære in support of his imaginary host of Yorkists: *Is there one,* says he, *of these persons, who in writing the memoirs of their own time would not have assured us that Richard murdered his nephews?* – In truth, I have not such intuition into what never existed, as to know how a nothing would be, if it had ever been. Would Mr. Hume allow me that Charles the first was a tyrant and murderer, because I should assert that Bradshaw, Ireton, and Hugh Peters, who never did write his history, would have represented him as such, if they ever had written his history? How difficult is it to establish the received history of Richard, when so able a man as Mr. Hume is reduced to suppose that it would be confirmed by the writings of his bitterest enemies, if those enemies had given any account of him! A man less bright than Mr. Hume would suspect that such non-existent hypothetical authors would have been partial. His Promethean sagacity, after creating the persons, has discovered not only what they would have written, but argues from this posthumous kind of non-entities. This is a fair and fruitful addition to the stores of disputation: its latitude is unbounded: it may serve alike the cause of truth and falsehood, and does equal honour to the ingenious gentleman who invented this sort of argument, and to his friend the Swiss reviewer, who was only dazzled by my old-fashioned arguments, but was convinced by the luminous force and solidity of this new method of induction.

NOTE the Fifth, is built on Richard's supposed intention of marrying his niece. Unluckily it proves nothing at all. If the young duke of York escaped, Richard certainly did not know whether he was living or dead. If Richard designed to marry his niece, it was to prevent her espousing Richmond. These round-about ways of supposing the murder, are the shifts of one that cannot prove the imposture of Perkin. Prove that, and I will not dispute the murder. It is the strong evidence in favour of his being the true duke of York that invalidates the murder. Mr. Hume had rather do any thing than discuss that evidence. He flies from it to presumptions, fantastic bead-rolls of names, unwritten memoirs, and non-repeals of acts of parliament. With him, the *not* repealing an act of parliament is a proof that there was no ground for making it. By the same kind of logic, a repeal ought to corroborate an act of parliament.

NOTE the Sixth. In a string of propositions it is usual to increase the strength of the argument. Mr. Hume has inverted this method. The farther he advances ,the weaker his reasons, till he concludes with one that recedes the faculty of reasoning, and is calculated only for the nursery. In the note before me, after endeavouring from historians and actors to establish the murder, he has recourse to the reports spread in foreign nations. Let Mr. Hume, if he can, refute my arguments in favour of Perkin Warbeck; I willingly resign to him the sudden impression spread in France by Richard's enemies, and the recent and more mature judgment of the Swiss reviewer. Let me however observe, that the emperor of China refused to receive an embassy from a great princess on much the same plea that Charles the eighth urged against Richard's embassadors. Would Mr. Hume, his friends messieurs Dalembert and Diderot, and Voltaire, who have celebrated the tolerating and legislative spirit of that heroine, allow that the Chinese monarch's ill-breeding was a proof that the most atrocious reports were well-founded?

NOTE the Seventh. Still advancing like a lively crab in retrograde argumentation, Mr. Hume next presents us with every body's oration. Every body, says he, argued thus and thus: and then, like a good christian, sums up this harangue with a quotation from scripture. "Richard, says he, could not plead like Cain, Am I the keeper of my nephews?" I am rejoiced that saint Cain is admitted into Mr. Hume's rubric. "Richard, continues he, might have answered the accusation by producing his nephews." – What! if one or both had escaped, and were not in his power? Thus Mr. Hume supposes the very point to be proved, and wonders it is disputed, after he has taken it for granted. I have so good an opinion of his sagacity, that if he had *not* taken it for granted *before* he wrote his history, I am persuaded he would not believe it now. There is a good deal of difference in the kind of belief which a man entertains *before* he has treated a subject, and *after*.

NOTE the Eighth, is built on the evidence of Tirrel, which I have examined distinctly in my Doubts, and there challenged Mr. Hume to show how it was possible for Perkin to agree in his narrative with Tirrel and Dighton, unless he was the true duke of York; supposing Tirrel made the concession alleged, which I have shown to be most improbable. If Tirrel did *not* make that confession, there is no evidence of the murder, but the declaration of Dighton, who, says lord Bacon, *spake best for the king*, and whose testimony is invalidated by every rule of evidence. I own there is less trouble in repeating the words *Tirrel* and *Dighton*, than in answering those arguments – and Mr. Hume has chosen the easier part. Indeed I do not conceive why my book was worth answering, and not my arguments.

NOTE the Ninth. *If the duke of York had escaped*, says Mr. Hume, *the queen his other, the duchess of Burgundy, and all those attached to his family would have been made acquainted with it*. I agree with him on the two former, not at all on the rest. It was too important a secret to be confided to many. The illustrious partisans of that or any party were not, I doubt, so immaculate as to deserve a trust of such consequence. The queen and duchess probably were informed: and it is odd to hear Mr. Hume complaining that the secret was not trusted to the duchess, when she was the principal supporter of Perkin. Mr. Hume is surprised that she was not let into the secret; and presently will reject her own declaration that she knew him for her nephew. Henry's treatment of the queen dowager, and her close imprisonment with prohibition of all access, is a stronger presumption of her being privy to that fatal secret, than any Mr. Hume can bring to show that she did not know it.

NOTE the Tenth. *Our total ignorance of those who assisted the duke of York in his escape is sufficient proof of this imposture of Perkin*. If Perkin had obtained the crown, this would be something of an argument. Did not the pretender escape from Scotland, because Mr. Hume does not *know* who assisted him?

NOTE the Eleventh. *Perkin's narrative is void of all probability.* – I know it. Lord Bacon thought so, and composed a new one for him. What consequence ought to be drawn thence? Why, that we have not his genuine narrative, but such as were composed for him by Henry the seventh and the

Lancastrian historians. Mr. Hume is as unhappy in his conclusions as in his assertions.

NOTE the Twelfth. *Perkin made an entire confession of his imposture, and read it three times. We do not find the least insinuation that it was drawn from him by torture; and when he made it the last time, he had certainly nothing to fear.*

ANSWER. It would be highly unreasonable in me to take offence at Mr. Hume's forgetting all my arguments, and all the answers which I have already given to his, (for indeed he does little more than repeat what he had said before) when he takes the liberty of contradicting a person who ought to have much greater weight with him, I mean himself. In his notes on his own history he informs us, that Perkin's confession was supposed (though he questions it) to be wrung from him by torture. He now positively asserts that we do not find the least insinuation of such force being employed. This is asserting and denying to some purpose. With regard to the confession, he does not inform us to which he adheres, to Henry's or Bacon's. No matter: we cannot believe both, and both give us cause to believe neither. Henry's was rejected by the infallible Bacon, and his own substitution of another destroys that too. That Perkin had nothing farther to fear, is asserted with as little foundation. Have we never heard in arbitrary governments (such was that of England then) of men submitting on imposed conditions to a milder death, to avoid one more cruel? Who knows whether Perkin (supposing he made a confession, which is most improbable) read it in an audible voice; or whether Henry's tools and sheriffs and guards did not disperse a paper after his death, and affirm he had delivered it to them? Were the histories of those times written *circumstantially* as they are now? Indeed, which history of that time was written at the time? Sir Thomas More does not go so low: lord Bacon and the rest wrote many ears afterwards.

NOTE the Thirteenth. *If Henry had not been convinced that Perkin was a ridiculous impostor, he would not have let him live an hour after he had got him in his power. The manner in which he treated the innocent earl of Warwick gives great force to this argument.*

ANSWER. I do not presume to trouble Mr. Hume or any body else with looking over the details I have given of Henry's anxiety and suspicions on Perkin's account; and of the difference of his behaviour towards him and Lambert Simnel, who *was* a ridiculous impostor, and whom Henry treated accordingly. But if Mr. Hume does not *purposely* choose to confound this conduct on two very different subjects, I would beg him to peruse once more his infallible Bacon, and see whether Henry thought that Perkin was an object of contempt and ridicule.

The latter part of the note is as extraordinary an oversight (I will call it no more) as the former. "Had Henry been convinced that Perkin was the true duke of York, he would not have let him live an hour, but would have treated him as he did the young earl of Warwick." Henry had reigned at least nine years before Perkin appeared. The earl of Warwick was all that time in Henry's power, and it was at least two years before the latter was put to death. Perkin was not in Henry's hands as many *months*, as Warwick had been *years*, before Henry caused him to be executed. Does not Mr. Hume's argument contract, as he boasts, great force from this happy illustration?

NOTE the Fourteenth. Enter the duchess of Burgundy on the other side of the question. Just now Mr. Hume argued from her knowing nothing of her nephew; now it seems she knew too much. Like Hudibras, Mr. Hume can take up his arms, dispute,

"Confute, change sides, and still confute himself back again."

She had adopted Simnel, and therefore was not to be credited about Perkin. Mr. Hume demands that she should be acquainted with the fate of her nephew; she tells you she is. – Therefore what? Therefore do not believe her. – But I will rest contented with Mr. Hume's contradicting himself as he has done in so many instances, and shall leave the reader to judge from what I have said in the Doubts, whether Henry or Margaret set up an imposture?

But I cannot so easily abandon Mr. Carte to the attacks of that powerful *whig*-champion, Mr. Hume, who has no mercy on a poor dead man, only because he was attached to that nonsensical tenet *hereditary right*. Mr. *Carte*, says he, to blacken Henry the seventh for having no hereditary right, suppressed entirely the important fact of the duchess supporting Simnel. Is it then an irremissible crime in an historian to suppress any material fact? I do not know, nor can I take the trouble now to examine whether Mr. Carte has suppressed the negotiations between Charles the first and the pope's nuncio, so unanswerably proved upon him by the exact Mrs. Macaulay. I myself have declared that it was natural for Charles to treat with Roman catholic subjects against protestant subjects who endeavoured to dethrone him. But what becomes of his protestant piety, his martyrdom, his sincerity? Look at the concessions he made on every capital point, and the oaths he swore to conceal them. If Mr .Carte has suppressed this enormous treaty, and has still represented Charles in an amiable light, I shall indeed allow that he has stifled an important fact, and will abandon him to my whig friend – but an historian may omit less material circumstances, and not deserve the same censure. For instance: Burnet assures us that sir Edmundbury Godfrey told him that he expected to be knocked on the head. This circumstance is entirely omitted by a late masterly historian, though very material with regard to the murder that ensued: but it did not suit the hypothesis of Godfrey's murdering himself. *Vide Hume's Reign of Charles II.*

I will not wander from my subject to lay open many other errors and omissions in the history I have here quoted, though I could loosen its artful texture in variety of places with far greater facility than I have unravelled the story of Richard the third. I admire the ingenious fabrick with all its want of symmetry, and in spite of the conflict with which it is ever at war with itself, by endeavouring to separate those hearty friends the prerogative and the church, and by fruitlessly trying to exalt the former and decry the latter; an attempt that renders the whole work one beautiful contradiction.

NOTE the Fifteenth. *No proofs*, says Mr. Hume, *were produced at the time, of Perkin's being the true duke of York.* How does he know? When so much accumulative evidence in his favour, after all the labours of Henry and his partisans to destroy it, yet remains, sure the probability is, that still greater appeared at the time. From what Henry forged, we may guess at what he suppressed. We have none but Lancastrian historians: the queen was shut up, and, by lord Bacon's own confession, every thing so muffled by Henry, that it staggered every body. Mr. Hume, cutting the Gordian knot which he could not untie, asserts with the tone of an Alexander, that all Perkin's answers might have been easily suggested to him by the duchess of burgundy, by Frion, and by whoever had lived in the court at the time. I have shown to demonstration by *dates*, which Mr. Hume swallows as if they were expletives, that the duchess did *not* live in the court at any part of the time; and any man's common sense, but Mr. Hume's, will tell him, that it is absolutely impossible to instruct a stranger so thoroughly in all the passages of the court, that he would not be detected in an hour's time. If my book is not a heap of absurdities, there is no part of it less liable to be contested than the passages in which I have stated the true and obvious method of detecting such an impostor, if he was one. I have shown that the omission of such satisfaction, and the substitution of the most absurd assertions, create the strongest objections against Henry. If I have talked nonsense, it would be charity in Mr. Hume to set me right. He knows the deference I have for his understanding, and no doubt he, if he pleased, could convince me that Henrys conduct was clear, rational, and liable to no misrepresentation: that lord Bacon's account of his ambiguity is false, and yet that Lord Bacon's account ought to be implicitly relied on. Mr. Hume could certainly disprove all that I have said, and prove all that he has said himself, though as yet he has done neither. Nay, I am persuaded he could do what is still more difficult, since his eloquence has worked that miracle both on himself and his friend the reviewer, convince me by weak arguments and groundless assertions, that the authority of great names is preferable to solid reasons; and that repeating arguments that have been confuted, gives them new force. Women and drunken men make use of that kind of oratory; and perhaps Mr. Hume's example may give new weight to the practice.

The note concludes with confessing that many persons of distinction were *at first* deceived by Perkin, which he ascribes to the enthusiasm of the nation in favour of the house of York. – I thought that all the illustrious Yorkists, according to Mr. Hume's catalogue of them, knew for certainty that the children were murdered. How came they to unknow it again? *But*, says he, *many were at first deceived.* Would not one think that that persuasion had been momentary? Does Mr. Hume forget, or with the art of a disputant did he slip in the words *at first* to make his reader forget, that four of five knights of the garter and privy-counsellors to Henry were convinced Perkin was king Edward's son, and died in that persuasion? Does such attestation of their belief accord with Mr. Hume's assertion in the beginning of the note, that *no proofs* were produced at the time, of Perkin being the true duke of York? This manner of stating a fact and evading the just conclusion, I call owning the truth without allowing it: it is endeavouring to delude with a clear conscience. The poor reviewer fell into the snare – I do not believe any body else will.

NOTE the Sixteenth. The last note, which establishes the murder on the authority of the bones found in the Tower, is the only note to which I shall not presume to give an answer. Untouched let it subsist to the comfort and edification of all the good women who visit the tombs in Westminster-abbey! May those bones remain an equal proof of the crimes of Richard, and of the catholic credulity of Mr. Hume and the reviewer! In those pious lands where all the evidence of a miracle depends on showing the rotten remains of those to whom, or the spot on which it happened, such faith is often found. – In truth, I did not expect it would make its appearance in the form of an argument – but since Mr. Hume is reduced to reason from relics, he will excuse me if I leave him at the door of the sanctuary, and am still unbeliever enough to think that those bones so enshrined are no more a proof of the guilt of Richard, than they are of the piety of Charles the second.

I have thus replied to Mr. Hume's remarks; an attention certainly due to whatever falls from so superior a writer. I am not entitled to the same observance from him; nor would the public excuse me, if he wasted some of those moments in answering my objections, which he can employ so much better for their instruction and amusement. In truth, they expect greater things from him. As he has been admitted into the penetraila of the Benedictine college at Paris, and has explored the authentic secrets of the two last Stuarts, the public is impatient for the detail of those mysteries, of which he has already given them a hint: nor can the appetite which *he* has raised be satisfied with a meagre note. He has another and still greater achievement to perform, which can never be executed by so masterly a hand, and which the world eagerly demands from his; a work more worthy of his genius, than any on which it has yet been exercised. As Mr. Hume's talent certainly veers to panegyric rather than satire, it must be a grateful satisfaction to so generous a mind to bestow deserved enconmiums, instead of softening defects and excesses. The reign of king William, who expelled the tyrants of Britain and tools of France, will shine with all its lustre when treated by a philosopher and patriot, who prefers the rights, the liberty, the happiness of mankind, to the selfish politics of narrow-minded kings, and to the base adulation of venal courts. In Mr. Hume's page we shall read with pleasure the establishment and extent of our invaluable constitution, as immoveably founded on the revolution – and the excellent doctor Robertson will not remain the first of historians, who, above the little prejudices of country, party, and profession, has dared to speak of the natural rights of mankind with just boldness, and has traced the progress of despotism in such glorious glowing colours, as must warn the few free nations yet remaining on earth to watch the silent craft and undermining policy of princes and statesmen.

Having now dispatched all the straws that have been thrown in my way, may I be allowed to add to what I have formerly said, some additional confirmations of my opinion?

A very sensible gentleman, whose name I will not mix with Guthrie's and reviewers, on reading my book, sent me a small volume of notes that he had drawn up forty years ago, in which I was flattered to find very many of my own remarks, and others of great weight, which I should be proud to be at liberty to publish. This is a proof that my opinion is not singular. Indeed, Rapin, Carte, and others, had seen the objection that ought to be made to Lancastrian historians. Mr. Hume calls Carte's doubts whimsical; and mine, light scruples. With submission, they are not whimsical or light scruples, which so profound a reasoner as Mr. Hume can answer no better.

With regard to the person of Richard, the earl of Shaftesbury was so good as to inform me, that his ancestor the lady Ashley, who lived to a great age, had conversed with lady Desmond, and gave from her the same account that I have given, with this strong addition, that Perkin Warbeck was remarkably like Edward the fourth. And to prove that the print I have exhibited of Richard and his queen, which the late bishop of Carlisle believed was taken from a window in the priory of Little Malvern (destroyed by a storm some years ago), was not a fanatic picture of imagination, I shall here present the reader with two more portraits of Richard and his queen, almost minutely corresponding with Vertue's drawing, and taken from the best and most unquestionable authority. The earl of Sandwich, on reading my Doubts, obligingly acquainted me that the duke of Manchester was possessed of the most curious and original roll, containing the list, portraits and descent of all the earls of Warwick, drawn by John Rous himself, the antiquary. This singular manuscript his grace, at my desire, was so good as to lend me; and with his permission I caused ten of the last and most curious portraits to be traced off, and here present them to the public faithfully and exactly engraven.

The roll is on parchment, and is seven yards and a half long; perfectly preserved within, but by handling damaged on the outside, on which have been painted many coats of arms.

The list begins with Guthalmus, and contains the effigies of several imaginary saints and heroes, many kings of England, and the portrait of Richard the third, with whom it concludes, twice; all neatly tricked, and the habits of the most distant ages, as well as of the succeeding, judiciously observed. On the outside is written

"This roll was laburd and finishd by master John Rows of Warwick."

But perhaps the most curious part of this curiosity is the following inscription under Richard, which shows that, whatever Rous chose to say of him in compliment to Henry the seventh, he gave a very different account of him in his roll, which he left to posterity, as a monument of the earls and town to which he was so much attached. Here is the inscription as it was written by Rous's own hand:

"The moost mighty prince Richard by the grace of God kynge of Ynglond and of Fraunce and lord of Irelond, by verey matrymony, wtowt dyscontynewance or any defylynge yn the lawe, by eyre male lineally dyscendyng fro kynge Harre the second, all avaryce set asyde, rewled his subjettys in hys realme ful comendabylly, puneshynge offenders of hys lawes, specyally extorcioners and oppressers of hys comyns, and cheryshynge tho yat were vertuos, by the whyche dyscrete guydynge he gat gret thank of God and love of all hys subjettys ryche and pore, and gret lawd of the people of all othyr landys abowt hym."

Mr. Hume declares his affection to cotemporary and original authors. I beseech him to produce one more genuine, more uncastrated, less interpolated than this record, existing in the very hand writing of the author. Let him try it by his rules of originality, and compare it with the testimonies of More and Bacon. He will tell me, perhaps, that Rous in his history has said the very reverse. True, in a book dedicated to Richard's rival and successor. Lay Richard for a moment out of the question, and let Mr. Hume tell me on any indifferent point which evidence he would prefer. Would he believe Rous flattering Henry to his face; or Rous in his cell delivering his opinion of a dead king? for it is evident that in the inscription Rous speaks of Richard as one that *had* ruled.

I do not doubt but the able critics with whom I have been engaged ,would treat my conjecture as light and whimsical, if I said I believed (and yet I must avow I do believe) that the remarkable and by no means indifferent words *by very matrymony without discontinuance or any defiling in the law, by heir male lineally descending,* allude to the bigamy of Edward the fourth and the illegitimacy of his children. I firmly believe too that the subsequent words *all avarice set aside, punishing offenders of his laws, especially extorcioners and oppressors of his commons,* were a tacit satire on the usurer his successor. I have at least produced here much better authority in vindication of Richard than Mr. Hume can bring against him; for he cannot reject the testimony of Rous, without giving up those criterions of truth, which he has established as demanding our assent and trust.

I said in my Doubts, that I was ready to yield to better reasons than my own; but I did not say I would yield to worse. Still less was I ever inclined to accept of great names instead of any reasons at all. If mere authority would do, Mr. Hume would have as much weight with me as Bacon or More: but great men without their great sense strike me with no more awe than their monuments, which only exhibit their titles and cover their dust. We shed a tear over their ashes and their weaknesses, but bestow our tribute of praise on those excellencies alone which touch the heart or convince the understanding.

May 10, 1769.

FINIS.

P.S. Since the above notes were written, I have found two passages, that evidently show how vague and uncertain the reports relating to the death of Edward the fifth and his brother were even in the life-time of sir Thomas More. From that very scarce book called The Pastyme of the People, and better known by the title of Rastell's Chronicle, in the possession of Mr. John Ratcliffe of Rotherhithe, I transcribed verbatim the following paragraphs:

"But of the maner of the dethe of this yonge kynge and of his brother, there were dyvers opinyons. But the most comyn opinyon was that they were smoldery'd betwene two fetherbeddes, and that in the doynge the yonger brother escaped from under the fetherbeddes, and crept under the bedstede, and there lay naked awhyle, tyll that they had smoldery'd the yonger kyng, so that he was surely dede. And aftert. one of them toke his brother from under the bedstede and hylde his face downe to the grounde with his one hande, and with the other hande cut his throte holle a sonder with a dagger. It is a mervayle that any man coude have so harde a harte to do so cruell a dede, save onely that necessyte compelled them, for they were so charged by the duke the protectour, that if they shewed nat to hym to bodyes of bothe those chylderne dede on the morowe after they were so comaunded, that than they themselfe shulde be put to dethe. Wherefore they that were comaunded to do it were compelled to fulfyll the protectour's wyll. And after that the bodyes of these 11 chylderne as the opinyon ranne were bothe closed in a great hevy cheste, and by the meanes of one that was secrete with the protectour, they were put in a shyppe goynge to Flaunders; and whan the shyppe was in the blacke depes this man threwe bothe those ded bodyes so closed in the cheste over the hatches into the see, and yet none of the maryners nor none in the shyppe, save only the sayd man, wyst what thynge it was that was there so inclosed; which sayenge dyvers men conjectured to be trewe, because that the bones of the sayd chylderne coude never be founde buryed nother in the Towre nor in no other place."

"Another opinyon there is that they whiche had the charge to put them to dethe caused one to cry so sodaynly treason, treason, wherewith the chylderne beynge aferde, desyred to knowe what was best for them to do. And than they bad them hyde themselfe in the great cheste that no man shulde fynde them, and if any body came into the chambre, they wolde say they were nat there. And accordynge as they counsellyd them, they crepte bothe into the cheste, which anone after they locked. And than anone they buryed that cheste in a great pytte under a steyre, which cheste was after caste into the blacke depes, as is before sayd."

I shall pass over the absurdities of both the foregoing accounts; but how will they strike us, when we find from Ames's Typographical Antiquities, p. 147, that this book was printed in 1529, the twenty-first year of Henry the eighth, and from p. 141, that Rastell the compiler and printer married sir Thomas More's own sister? If sir Thomas, as Mr. Hume pretends, was so intimate with the chief persons of Richard's court or reign, how came he to suffer his brother-in-law to pass such senseless stuff on the public, in a work no doubt submitted to his inspection? for Rastell was not only his relation but printer, his very next publication being a dialogue written by More and printed in the same year with the Chronicle. Nor did sir Thomas pick up the materials for his own history *after* the appearance of Rastell's Chronicle, which was published but six years before sir Thomas's death, when the persons from whom he gained his intelligence must have been dead likewise. But do not sir Thomas's own words betray, not only doubts in his own breast, but thorough proof of the uncertainty of all the incidents relative to the murder? He tells us, that he does not relate the murder in every way he had heard it, but according to the most probable account he could collect from the most creditable witnesses. And I will ask one or two more questions, which I defy Mr. Hume or any man living to answer in a rational manner. If Dighton and Tirrel confessed the murder in the reign of Henry the seventh, how could even the outlines be a secret and uncertain in the reign of Henry the eighth? Is it credible that they owned the fact, and concealed every one of the circumstances? If they related those circumstances, without which their confession could gain no manner of belief, could sir Thomas More, chancellor to Henry the eighth, and educated in the house of the prime minister to Henry the seventh, be ignorant of what it was so much the interest of cardinal Morton to tell, and of Henry the seventh to have known and ascertained? A king and his brother are murdered (according to Henry, More, Bacon, Hume, Guthrie, and the mob), a great officer of the crown and a low groom confess themselves principals in the guilt, the first is executed, the latter suffered to live, to disperse the tale. Neither of them give the least account *how* they committed the fact; or, if they did, no man living from the prime minister to the compiler of the Chronicle could get *certain* intelligence of what they confessed, though it is impossible to assign any other reason for the impunity of Dighton, but the intention of his spreading and authenticating the story. If therefore the confessions said to be made by Tirrel and Dighton are irreconcileable to every standard by which we can judge of evidence, no evidence of the murder exists. If the attestations produced by Henry, More, and Bacon, who indubitably furnished the best they could, are inconsistent and improbable, the identity of Perkin Warbeck and the duke of York remains unshaken, Mr. Hume himself allowing and bending all the force of his argument to prove, that the strong evidence against Perkin is the certainty of the murder. If, on the contrary, the authority of historians is sufficient to pass such stuff on our credulity, I must avow I cannot see what criterion there is in human reason by which we may distinguish between truth and the most clumsy and incoherent legends.

August 6, 1769.

20
OLIVER GOLDSMITH

Oliver Goldsmith, *History of England, from the earliest times to the death of George II*. London, printed for T. Davies, 1771, 4 v.
Selections from Preface; from 1789 Dublin edition.

Born in a small village in the county of Longford, Ireland, Oliver Goldsmith (1730?–1774) was the son of a minister and the sixth of nine children. An uncle funded his schooling at Trinity College, Dublin. He later studied law and medicine and, after a series of minor jobs, he established himself as an author, first writing for periodicals, and later publishing poems, novels and historical works. Although Hume and Goldsmith were not in direct communication, their literary lives often paralleled each other. In 1757, John Home published his play *Douglas*, which Hume praised in the Dedication of *Four Dissertations*. Goldsmith gave a mixed review of *Douglas* in the *Monthly Review*, which concludes noting that Hume's flattering Dedication built up expectations that the play could not fulfil when it was produced in London (May 1757, Vol. 16, pp. 426–429). The same year Goldsmith harshly evaluated John Wilkie's *Epigoniad* in the *Monthly Review* (July 1757, Vol. 17, pp. 228–230). Shortly after, Hume wrote to his bookseller Andrew Millar, "Nothing surprises me more than the Ill Usage which the Epigoniad has receiv'd. Every body here likes it extremely" (Hume to Millar, September 3, 1757). Hume himself wrote a flattering review of Wilkie's work, which was printed in the *Critical Review* (April 1759, Vol. 7. pp. 323–334).

In 1771 Goldsmith published his four-volume *History of England*, which was compiled and abridged, as he states in the Preface, principally from "Rapin, Carte, Smollett, and Hume." Although Goldsmith praises the depth of Hume's *History*, he nevertheless criticizes Hume's views of religion and politics. In spite of Goldsmith's claim to be impartial regarding the role of the monarchy, Gilbert Stuart, in his article for the *Monthly Review*, attacks his defence of royal prerogative:

… the historian has leaned with too much partiality to the prerogative of our kings: and in a work, which is evidently addressed to young and inexperienced minds, there cannot possibly be a fault of a more destructive tendency. The first political lessons inculcated on the youth of a free state, ought not, surely, to be dependence on servility.

Stuart also criticizes aspects of Goldsmith's style:

> ... In its style it has a degree of dignity, which is perfectly suitable to historical compositions; and its periods are harmonious and flowing. It must be remarked, notwithstanding, that it is frequently deficient in grammatical precision; and that it sometimes degenerates into the insipid langour and the tawdry pettiness of romance.

He concludes with a negative assessment both of Goldsmith and his sources:

> In the task of abridging the history of England, our Author has started with very humble competitors. But we cannot justly remark, to his praise, that he has left them behind him at a great distance. [*Monthly Review*, December 1771, Vol. 45, pp. 436–444]

Goldsmith revised his abridgment in a 1774 second edition; the work was subsequently reprinted dozens of times in the 18th and 19th centuries, many of which were revisions by William Pinnock (1782–1843).

PREFACE.

...

The books which have been used in this abridgment are chiefly Rapin, Carte, Smollett, and Hume. They have each their peculiar admirers, in proportion as the reader is studious of historical antiquities, fond of minute anecdotes, a warm partizan, or a deliberate reasoner. Of these I have particularly taken Hume for my guide, as far as he goes; and it is but justice to say, that wherever I was obliged to abridge his work I did it with reluctance, as I scarce cut out a line that did not contain a beauty.

But though I must warmly subscribe to the learning, elegance, and depth of Mr. Hume's history, yet I cannot entirely acquiesce in his principles. With regard to religion, he seems desirous of playing a double part, of appearing to some readers as if he reverenced, and to others as if he ridiculed it. He seems sensible of the political necessity of religion in every state; but at the same time he would every where insinuate, that it owes its authority to no higher an origin. Thus he weakens its influence, while he contends for its utility, and vainly hopes that while free-thinkers shall applaud his scepticism, real believers will reverence him for his zeal.

In his opinions respecting government, perhaps, also, he may be sometimes reprehensible; but in a country like ours, where mutual contention contributes to the security of the constitution, it will be impossible for an historian, who attempts to have any opinion, to satisfy all parties. It is not yet decided in politics, whether the diminution of kingly power in England tends to encrease the happiness, or the freedom of the people. For my own part, from seeing the bad effects of the tyranny of the great in those republican states that pretend to be free, I cannot help wishing that our monarchs may still be allowed to enjoy the power of controlling the encroachments of the great at home. A king may easily be restrained from doing wrong, as he is but one man; but if a number of great are permitted to divide all authority, who can punish them if they abuse it? Upon this principle, therefore, and not from any empty notion of divine or hereditary right, some may think I have leaned towards monarchy. But as in the things I have hitherto written, I have neither allured the vanity of the great by flattery, nor satisfied the malignity of the vulgar by scandal, as I have endeavourd to get an honest reputation by liberal pursuits, it is hoped the reader will admit my impartiality.

21
SYLVESTER O'HALLORAN

Sylvester O'Halloran, *An introduction to the study of the history and antiquities of Ireland: in which the assertions of Mr. Hume and other writers are occasionally considered... By Sylvester O Halloran.* Dublin: printed by Thomas Ewing, 1772, [10], xx, 96, [1], 102–384 p.
Selections from 3.3 and 3.5; from 1772 Dublin edition.

Born in Limerick, Ireland, Sylvester O'Halloran (1728–1807) was a physician and author of medical works on the topics of gangrene, amputation, cataracts, and head injuries. He also authored two major books on Irish history: *An Introduction to the Study of the History and Antiquities of Ireland* (1772) and the two-volume *General History of Ireland* (1778). O'Halloran's *Introduction* defends the legendary greatness of ancient Ireland and blames the Scottish for many of Ireland's social and political problems. Throughout the work, he attacks Scottish writers such as Hume, MacPherson, and Dalrymple for misrepresenting Irish history. O'Halloran has sustained discussions of Hume in two Chapters. In 3.3 he attacks Hume's account of native Irish barbarism as "mere rhetorical flourish without the least foundation in history" and calls Hume's discussion of the English invasion of Ireland "romance." He criticizes Hume for ignoring respectable accounts of Irish history, such as that by James Ware. In 3.5 he rejects the "extremely horrid" picture of the war of 1641 drawn by Hume. According to O'Halloran, only a few Irish were excessively violent during the initial revolt, and the true violence, he believes, emerged with the British reprisal to the revolt. Further, according to O'Halloran, the Scottish were in fact responsible for the massacre, since their continuous revolts in the previous years ripened the English for a violent reproach.
 The *Critical Review* rejects O'Halloran's *Introduction* as a prejudicial and "criminal imposture" which attempts to pass absurd fables off as genuine history:

This author writes avowedly under the influence of national prejudice, a disposition of mind the most pernicious to historical inquiry, and which seems more or less to have actuated all the literary champions who have taken up the pen in defence of the antiquity and honour of their native country. Such a predilection we shall admit may be excusable, or even laudable, when indulged in speculations which have no relation to any serious exercise of the understanding; but where knowledge, truth, and science are concerned in the discussion, every candid enquirer must reject with disdain the appearance of undue partiality. In such circumstances, an attempt to mislead the public judgment deserves, in our opinion, to be considered as a criminal imposture, and it receives additional aggravation in proportion to the futility of the arguments by which it is supported. The absurd fables, respecting the Irish antiquities, have already been refuted upon the clearest evidence of probability, authentic history, and rational investigation; against which all the arbitrary opinions founded on etymology, can never be admitted to prevail. This, however, is the principal ground of determination brought by the author now before us, in favour of the legendary system of Irish antiquity. It will not be expected that we should give a particular detail of a work, in which the whole monstrous mass of Hibernian fiction is exhibited to the view. [*Critical Review*, 1773, Vol. 35, pp. 198–202]

The article for the *Monthly Review*, co-authored by William Rose and Ralph Griffiths, considers O'Halloran's *Introduction* more favourably as "a performance which, notwithstanding all the national zeal, and personal acrimony of the Writer, hath afforded us both entertainment and information." The review notes both the high and low points of the book:

We cannot, however, say that we received many new lights on some points which most wanted them: especially with regard to the state of Ireland before the introduction of Christianity into that country. Yet, in general, we have formed nearly the same opinion of it with Mr. O Halloran, but, we trust, without running into those chimeras with which he has, in the heat of a zeal that seems to have burnt up his discretion, rather weakened than strengthened his tenets on that head. While he offers the presumptions in favour of the laws and civilization of Ireland, before the Christian epoch, he is very just, and laudable; but when he comes to adopt the old Milesian and other fables, he only provokes a smile. What, too, can be more ridiculous than his assigning the cause of the first general acquiescence of the Irish, in the English laws, than their seeing, in the Scottish king, James I. a prince of the blood of Milesius? Such dreams cannot but detract from the merit of the real essential lights which, in other respects, he throws upon the subject. [*Monthly Review*, September 1773, Vol. 49 pp. 193–202]

Hume appears to have made one correction to his *History* based on O'Halloran's comments: a footnote at the appropriate location below presents Hume's modified wording. O'Halloran's *Introduction* also appeared in 1772 under a London imprint, but was not subsequently republished. The following is from the 1772 Dublin publication.

PART III.
CHAP. V.

Political distinctions, particularly ruinous to Ireland. Mr. Voltaire's censures on this nation examined, and confuted. The more severe ones of Mr. Hume considered, as well as his intemperance, and disingenuity. Visible remains of the antient state of letters yet preserved.

The very sensible remark which Mrs. Mac Auley, treating of Irish affairs,[1] makes, is too important to be here passed by. "The two factions (says she) of Papist and Protestant, more intent on thwarting each other, *than in maintaining their mutual rights,* were easy prey to the views of the ministry." In the days of popery this unhappy union was founded on principles of policy: after the reformation, religion was made the pretence. It is demonstrable, that it was their interest to keep up this spirit of political and religious rage, since by dividing, they the more triumphantly governed. It is a just observation on the British constitution, that it can only flourish by opposition. It is this that makes them great and powerful. Zealous to preserve public applause, the party in power are always careful to support public credit, and to keep trade and commerce, in the most flourishing condition. The party in opposition carefully watch their motions; and any unpopular measure, is immediately echoed through the kingdom. The national business is, by these means, sedulously attended to, and all acts of soul oppression on either side religiously avoided. But from a retrospection of Irish affairs, for near 600 years past, it becomes evident, that different interests have been always the ruin of the kingdom; and that by a firm coalition of Irishmen, *only,* can it again become respectable.

These untoward divisions, and the solicitude of each party to blacken the other, have unhappily made our country appear in the eyes of Europe, very differently from what it deserves; and scarce a writer, even of modern date, from the great Voltaire, down to Mr. Hume, who does not think he may with impunity, publish any misrepresentation of Ireland, how scandalous and false soever. Thus Voltaire, with the greatest coolness, tells us,[2] "Some nations seem formed for subjection to others. The English always had a superiority over the Irish, in genius, as well as arms and riches; nor has Ireland ever been able to shake off the yoke, *since she was first subdued by an English baron!*" But in this, as well as other instances, it will appear that m. de Voltaire took his accounts from ill-informed, if not prejudiced, writers. ...

[1] History of England, vol. ii. p. 173.

[2] Siecle de Louis XIV. T. 1.

But of all the historians that have treated of Irish affairs, Mr. Hume is the one we lie under the greatest obligations to. Others of his countrymen, as we shall shew, have for centuries endeavoured to injure us; but they seemed to have some regard to the judgment of their readers, and their own characters, by offering the best historical proofs they had. This gentleman, scorning the confined paths of his predecessors, has at once nobly bounded over all the fences of history, truth, decency, and common sense, and at one dash of a pen, represented us as the most nefarious and abandoned of the human race! "The Irish (says this writer) from the beginning of time, had been buried in the most profound barbarism and ignorance; and as they were never conquered, nor even invaded by the Romans, from whom all the western world derived its civility, they continued still in the most rude state of society, and were distinguished only by those vices, to which human nature, not tamed by education, nor restrained by laws, is ever subject:"[3] – he goes on – "the usual title of each petty sovereign was the murder of his predecessor: courage and force, though exercised in the commission of crimes, were more honoured than any pacific virtue; and the most simple arts of life, *even tillage and agriculture were almost totally unknown to them.*" He tells us, "that the incursions of the Danes and Normans, which had spread barbarism in other parts of Europe, *tended rather to improve the Irish; and the only towns which were to be found in the island, had been planted along the coasts by the free booters of Norway and Denmark.*"

As this outrageous setting off is a mere rhetorical flourish without the least foundation in history, I shall pass it over unnoticed; but as the remainder of his performance, seems to have some little allusion to record, I shall pay some attention to it, though in truth it be scarcely worthy confutation.

If, as *Tully* assures us, "History be the witness of times past, the light of truth, the life of memory, the guide of life, and the herald of antiquity," we shall find Mr. Hume, in his accounts of Ireland, rather a writer of romance, than of history: he tells us, that the Irish were converted by the English; an assertion most remotely distant from truth, as we have already shewn in the course of this work; and so careless and inaccurate is he, that in his relation of the first cause of calling in the Normans, or English, he even mistakes the names of the principal parties. Thus, he tells us, that the lady carried off by the king of Leinster, was wife to ô Rourke, king of Meath, and called Omach; whereas her real name was Dearbhorguil, the daughter of Mac Floin, king of Meath, and married to the prince of Breffni.[4] From the general character he had given of the nation, we must not be surprised at his remark on this adventure. "This

---

[3] Life of Henry II.

[4] [In later editions Hume revised this as follows: "This prince had formed a design on Dovergilda, wife of Ororic, prince of Breffny...."]

exploit (says he) *"tho' usual among the Irish,* and esteemed a proof of gallantry and spirit, provoked the husband." We have already so fully shewn that purity of blood was one of the first national objects in Ireland, and of violence offered to woman being punishable by death, that we only introduce this curious quotation, to shew how proper a master Mr. Hume is of the history of a country, he has so grosly insulted. His account of the English Invasion, and its consequences are in the true stile of romance. He tells us, that the first English adventurers, "completely armed, *a thing almost unknown in Ireland,* struck a great terror into the barbarous inhabitants, and seemed to menace them with *some great revolution!"* Is not this in the true Quixotian style? But all writers, foreign and domestic, remark the fondness the Irish had at all times for arms; and *Solinus,* in other respects as little in love with our ancestors as Mr. Hume, expressly says, "that the Irish placed their greatest pride in the beauty and splendor of their arms." Besides, the reader cannot have forgotten that the helmets and breast-plates of our nobility were inlaid with gold, and their shields of pure silver, from the earliest times. The junction of *Fitz Stephens* with *Prenderghast* and *Fitz Gerald,* this writer proceeds, "composed a force which nothing in Ireland was able to withstand! *Roderic the chief monarch of Ireland, was defeated in battle, the prince of Ossory was obliged to submit, and Diarmond aspired to the sole dominion of the island!"* What says my old friend *Farnabius,* on such occasions?

A sonitu vocis, Onomatopoeia *fingit.*
Bombalio, Clangor, Stridor, Tarantara, murmur.

This powerful kingdom, which had so bravely and successfully expelled the Danes; the part of a province of which *only,* supported a 15 years bloody war, against the power of Elizabeth, aided by a strong party of the natives; which, though divided into many different and opposite factions in the days of Charles I. kept up a fair and stout war against the Parliamentarians, for above eight years; which in the time of James II. though opposed by a very great party in the North, insurrections in the South, and a mighty army from England, headed by king William in person, yet carried on a gallant war, and fought two general engagements in the compass of a year, against the bravest troops in the world; was unable to resist 600 foreigners, (the number produced from this junction) which Mr. Hume blushes not to affirm, "composed a force that nothing in Ireland was able to withstand!"

Some works the matter may recommend, though the style be indifferent; and in others, the language and manners, tho' destitute of interesting materials, may soften the asperity of critical censure; even glaring falshoods lessen not the merit of polite language. Thus Quintilian speaking of *Clitarchus,* a Greek historian, remarks, *Clitarchi probatur ingenium, fidei infamatur,* "whilst we admire the style of Clitarchus, as a writer, we detest his want of truth, as an historian."

In relating Irish affairs it would seem that even this talent had forsaken Mr. Hume. "The exiled king of Leinster (says he) being assured of assistance, returned privately to his own state; and lurking in the monastery of Ferns, which he had founded," he adds in a parenthesis too! *"for this ruffian also was the founder of monasteries!"* – Had Mr. Hume been conversant in Irish history he would have learned from it more politeness and good manners. For though our ancestors had much more reason to detest the memory of this prince than he, yet, in our annals, the severest appellation he goes by, is, Murrough na NGall, or Murrough of the Strangers, on account of his fondness for them. Even the Dane, though a most cruel, perfidious, and barbarous enemy, we find no harsher names for than Lochlonnach, which may be rendered into English, either a *Ship Champion*, or powerful by sea, and Fear-muire, or Sea-man. Which should be deemed most barbarous, the antient Irish, who treated even their mortal enemies with manly decency, or the modern historian, who divests himself of decorum, truth, and common sense, let the reader judge!

M. Hume begins his account of the Elizabethian war, in the following *clear*, and *sensible* manner. "Though the *dominion* of the English over Ireland, had been *established* above four centuries, *it may be safely affirmed*, that their *authority* had been *hitherto but nominal*." He thus proceeds, in this chapter, which opens with so much perspicuity; "as the brutality and ignorance of the Irish were extreme, they were sunk below the reach of that curiosity, and love of novelty, by which every other people had been seized, at the beginning of that century, and which had engaged them in innovations, and religious disputes, with which they were still so violently agitated." Tho' Mr. Hume might despise the account of Irish writers of this century, though delivered by so respectable a name as Sir James Ware; and though he might not see, or even hear of Mr. Harris's edition of that valuable work in two volumes folio, yet had he taken the trouble to consult Wood,[5] and other British antiquarians, he might have saved himself the confusion of being here again detected in the most barefaced falshoods. For at this particular period, so very attentive were the natives to the literary reputation of their country, that many of them began to refute the amazing falshoods of plagiarism of Pictish writers, and to reclaim the numbers of lettered and pious Irish, whom the former had attempted to make Denizons of Pictavia! I shall concludes this chapter with one observation, to prove unquestionably how highly letters were cultivated *here, even in those days of anarchy*: The best schools then in the kingdom were in the most retired parts of it, where strangers had least access; and to this day as good classical scholars are found in the counties of Limerick, Clare, Kerry, and most parts of Connaught, as in any part of Europe; insomuch that the very common people in many places, speak correct Latin, nor is Greek unknown to them.

[5] Athen. Oxon. &c.

To this point, Mr. Smith[6] observes, "It is well known, that classical reading, extends itself, *even to a fault*, amongst the lower and poorer kind of people in this country; *many* of whom have greater knowledge in this way than some of the *better sort* in other places." And in another place he observes, "that Greek is also taught, in some of the mountainous parts of this country;" and it is worth notice, that where these schools are in greatest repute, the people have the least communication with the adjacent plains, and speak but the native Irish.

CHAP. VI.

Remarks on Mr. Hume's account of the civil war of Ireland. Character of the Irish nation before and after the breaking out of this war. Why it has been misrepresented. Irish exculpated, by the most public acts, from the very pretences to the charges of the massacres and murders. The real authors of these out-rages singled out. Present state and character of the common Irish. Lord Clarendon's severe remarks considered and exposed. Unexampled cruelties exercised on the Irish, and lord Clarendon again censured. The Scotch the real source of all the calamities of these unhappy times. Their prudent manner of carrying on the war in England and Ireland, to the selling of the king.

The picture of the war of 1641, as drawn by Mr. Hume, is so extremely horrid, that were he in earnest, we must certainly believe that he has viewed mankind thro' a medium equally false and degrading. But the man who could boldly assert that the corsairs of Denmark and Norway who spread desolation over every part of Europe, rather improved and polished the Irish, should be allowed a *charte blanche*: let us amuse ourselves with the elegant declaimer, if we cannot be instructed by the sober historian. Almost totally ignorant of Irish history, yet unwilling to appear so, what remained for Mr. Hume but to inflame the passions since he could not convince the judgment? And where is the wonder if in the darkness of ignorance, his imagination, like Falstaff's, should have multiplied his enemies?

As this war was the act of the whole Irish nation, and as the most foul and bloody deeds have been charged home on the kingdom, I shall lay down a few incontestable facts, by which my readers may form some judgment of the nature of this charge. But I shall first present the reader with a few slight sketches, of the character of our countrymen, as delivered by foreigners. We have seen them involved in a cruel Danish war above 200 years; and though the

[6]   History of Kerry.

constitution was materially affected by it, yet the principles of the people were not. The English wars, though in too many instances, *wars against humanity*, could not debauch the morals of the Irish; for say the writers of the former "they [the English] scarce observed the very laws enacted by themselves eight days after passing, yet could the Irish by no favour or affection be prevailed upon to break through theirs." Here we see, so late as the reign of Henry VIII. English evidence of the obedience of the Irish to sound legislation. In the wars of Elizabeth, while their enemies scrupled little as to the mode of offence, yet were the Irish unimpeached of any base or dishonourable retaliation. In the next reign, Sir John Davis declares, "that no nation love equal and impartial justice better than the Irish." Lord Coke, at the very period in question, affirms, from his own knowledge, that "there is no nation in the Christian world, that are greater lovers of justice; which virtue he adds, must necessarily be accompanied by many others." At the conclusion of Cromwell's wars, they were influenced by the same heroic principles: they followed the fortunes of the fugitive Charles; formed themselves into regiments, transferrable from the French to the Spanish service, as suited the interests of this inglorious exile; and from the colonel to the common soldier, they cheerfully and voluntarily gave up half their pay, to his support. In the last wars of Ireland, their bravery and generosity remained unsullied.[8] Such of them as thought they could not in honour and conscience swear allegiance to king William, chose rather to lose their ample fortunes, and embrace a voluntary exile, than to act the base part of temporizers; and those who remained at home, in all subsequent troubles that have agitated our sister countries, have not even been suspected of treasonable practices! From that period to this day, we have seen them in the most distinguished employments; places of the highest trust, in almost every state, as well in the field as the cabinet, have been committed to their charge; and all Europe proclaims their bravery, their honour, their fidelity, and their justice! Such are the people who have been represented as the most cruel and sanguinary of mankind, and *that too, at one particular time only!* But by whom have they been thus painted? By English writers, who, of all others, could do it with the worst grace, when the reader is reminded, that this very nation for near 400 years preceding the period we are now speaking of, gave murder, robbery, and theft, the sanction of the law of Ireland! And by Scotch historians, whose countrymen were the real source of all those evil and bloody actions, that disgraced the kingdom in the 17th century!

---

[7] Baron Finglass's Breviate of Ireland.

[8] At the first siege of Limerick, when the English entered the town through a breach they had made, they were gallantly beat back, even to their camp, by the Irish. In this confusion the hospital of the English by some means took fire; on this occasion the Irish shewed their generosity to be equal to their bravery, by doing their utmost to preserve from the flames their enemies.

But how shall we account for the accumulated charges laid on the Irish, for murders and massacres in the war of 1641, *and in this war only?* The truth is, without descending to particular and disagreeable proofs, that the æra in question was an age of fanaticism, of hypocrisy, and of dark and bloody doings, and those men who, after bringing their prince to the block,[9] offered to restore Sir Phelim ô Neal to his honours and estate, as well as to save a life justly forfeited by his cruelty, provided he would accuse the late king as been the source of all the disturbances in Ireland, would stick at nothing to promote their interest, or palliate their own unequalled barbarities. That they were deeply concerned, to misrepresent this kingdom, needs no proof; but we may reasonably believe that were the Irish capable of *even imagining* half the barbarities then laid to their charge, they would be at this day as free a nation as any in Europe. *Throw dirt, and some of it will stick*, is a political maxim which even the upper ranks in society have sometimes adopted; and surely there is nothing in the origin, the education, or the principles of the anti-royalists of the last century, that should lead us to believe them incapable of employing it on a useful occasion.

It is far from my intention or inclination to justify any kind of outrage against a lawful authority; but surely those gentlemen who, *from principle,* defend the measures taken by the English and Scotch, in taking up arms against their lawful sovereign, should not censure the Irish for endeavouring to preserve their liberties from the invasions of the English parliament. No one looks on oppression for religious principles in a more detestable light than I; and, upon reflection, it must appear astonishing, that the professors of a doctrine which inculcates the most humiliating and passive principles, should be the foremost to maintain it by means the least justifiable. But surely the clergy and laity of England and Scotland, who solemnly swore "to the *extirpation* of popery and prelacy in the three kingdoms, *without respect of persons,* lest they might partake in their sins, and thereby be in danger to partake of their plagues,"[10] should be the last to condemn the people of Ireland for rising in defence of their religion. These last were certainly more justifiable in defending their old opinions, than the reformers in forcing new tenets on them. ...

Mr. Hume tells us, "so great was the hatred of the Irish to every thing that was English, that they not only murdered the poor defenceless people, but fired their houses, burnt their furniture, and destroyed their very cattle, that nothing belonging to them should remain in the kingdom!" It must be owned, that altho' none shewed themselves more forward to spill the blood of the Irish than the countrymen of this historian, yet they did not carry their malice to the same extremity. However criminal the Irish appeared in their eyes, and though by

---

[9]   Dean Kerr's affidavit in Nelson's Collections.

[10]   Solemn League and Covenant.

their *covenant* they were obliged to *extirpate Popery* and *Prelacy*, yet upon reflection they concluded their goods and chattels not culpable. Whilst they destroyed the people, they rifled their goods, and sent off the cattle in large droves to Scotland. The war they carried on there, was rather that of plunderers and robbers, than of disciplined troops. Nay, to such an height did they carry their rapacity, that the chief justices in those days, iniquitous as they were, began to apprehend an universal scarcity, from these *Caledonian Tartars*. Dr. Warner[11] tells us, that Monroe, in his turn to Carrig-fergus, wasted the country, and with other effects carried off 4000 head of cattle; but the night before they were to be divided between the English and Scots, they were conveyed away, to the great discontent of the English, "who began to mutiny, and *never after cared to march with such a band of thieves.*" After this they marched into the country of Antrim, where they drove off 5000 head of cattle; and when lord Antrim invited *Monroe* to his castle where he was sumptuously entertained, and offered to unite with them to preserve the peace of this country, the return the latter made his noble host was, to seize on the cattle, and make himself a prisoner! *"in short,* (says Dr. Warner) *the Scotch general had as little honour as the banditti he commanded."* ...

---

[11] Civil Wars of Ireland, vol. i. p. 198.

22
QUAKERISM DEFENDED AGAINST FALSE REPRESENTATION

"Quakerism Defended Against False Representation," *Gentleman's Magazine*, December 1772, Vol. 42, pp. 566–570; and "Hume's Account of Quakerism Defended," *Gentleman's Magazine*, February 1773, Vol. 43, pp. 122–123. Selections.

In his essay "Of Superstition and Enthusiasm" Hume writes that "the *Quakers* are, perhaps, the only regular Body of *Deists* in the Universe, except the *Literati* or Disciples of *Confucius* in *China*." In Chapter 62 of the *History*, Hume discusses the origin and nature of the Quaker denomination, highlighting the fanaticism of their dress, doctrines, and worship practices, and even insinuating that some were mentally unbalanced. In 1772 an anonymous article appeared in *Gentleman's Magazine*, which attacked several misrepresentations of Quakerism in recent publications – including those by Hume in his essay and the *History*. Among the misrepresentations objected to is that Quakerism is founded in freethinking; the author responds by quoting from Quaker documents which run contrary to the misrepresentations. Two months later a letter of response was printed in *Gentleman's Magazine*, which defends Hume's account of Quakerism as being grounded in historical fact. The author also maintains that Quaker doctrine is in fact conceptually similar to Deism.

QUAKERISM DEFENDED AGAINST FALSE REPRESENTATION.

MR. URBAN,

Nothing in the history of this country has been more unfairly represented by modern writers than the religious principles of the people called Quakers. It were, perhaps, a breach of charity to charge all the writers who have fallen into this error with malignity. I rather believe, that most of them have been guilty of misrepresentation rather from indolence than design, and that they have copied one after the other, without taking the pains to examine the truth of what the first writers advanced, though often refuted, upon the strongest evidence of uncontrovertible facts. As Guthrie, in his treatise of geography, is the last author of credit who has characterised these people, allow me, through the extensive channel of your Magazine, to exhibit the articles with which they are charged, and to recapitulate the answers that have been made to those articles, which have never yet been contradicted.

"The Quakers, says Mr. Guthrie, form a numerous sect of dissenters in England; and, perhaps, if their profest principles were to undergo a very strict examination, they would appear to be founded in Freethinking, though they pretend to be guided by internal revelation, dictated by the Spirit of God. That revelation and that Spirit, however, are just what they please to make them; and, if they mean any thing, it is an abstraction from all sensual ideas, in treating of the Christian religion and its mysteries, for they attempt to allegorise all the facts in the gospel. This has subjected them to a charge of their denying all the fundamentals of Christianity. Though some of them have disclaimed this charge, yet they utterly deny that the outward person, who suffered his body to be crucified by the Jews, without the gates of Jerusalem, is properly the Son of God. With regard to the resurrection of the body, and the doctrines of rewards and punishments hereafter, they have not yet explained themselves authentically.

"I should here take my leave of the state of religion in England, was it not necessary to mention those who profess no religion at all. Those go under the name of freethinkers." *Guthrie's Geography.*

I really thought, at this day, our principles were so well known, and these obsolete calumnies of our adversaries so often and so plainly refuted, that these antiquated prejudices were long since quite laid aside; but this is the fourth modern publication which hath fallen in my way, giving either very mistaken or very partial accounts of us as a people. The first is an extract from *Mosheim's Ecclesiastical History*, which, in many particulars, is merely fabulous, in others his representations are very unfair; and, if he is not better informed in other subjects of his history, than he seems to have been concerning the people called Quakers, his history deserves little credit. The second is *Hume's* account of them, in his *History of England*; in which the author, too prone to hold up to ridicule all professions of religion which coincide not with his partial plan, hath selected and exaggerated whatever may appear extravagant and ridiculous in the principles or character of the first of those who went under the denomination of Quakers; and this, and this only, he gives as a history, or rather a character, of this people; a proceeding derogatory to the reputation of an historian, whose principal characteristic should be candour and impartiality. The third is that of *Smollet*, in his *History of the State of all Nations*, as well as in his *History of England*, which is mostly a transcript of *Hume's*. I hope there will be no objection to my attempt to set the public right in the points wherein this people appear to be misrepresented, especially as these are points of much importance.

The propositions or assertions I object to, as misrepresentations of this society, are these three:

1. There principles appear to be founded in freethinking.

2. They utterly deny that the outward person who suffered his body to be crucified by the Jews, without the gates of Jerusalem, is properly the Son of God.

3. With regard to the resurrection of the body, and the doctrines of rewards and punishments hereafter, and many other capital points of Christianity, they have not yet explained themselves authentically.

1. As I cannot form a precise idea of what the author intends by the word freethinking, this assertion seems too ambiguous to receive a direct answer. If he means it, according to his own explanation, professing no religion at all, it cannot, with the least propriety, be applied to the people called Quakers, even from his own account of them. "They pretend," therefore they profess, "to be guided by internal revelation, dictated by the spirit of God, by which, if they mean any thing, it is an abstraction from all sensual ideas in treating of the Christian religion and its mysteries." They do, then, profess religion, and the Christian religion, but not Deism, which denies all revelation, since they found religion in internal revelation. Of consequence, their principles are not founded in freethinking, so far as freethinking and Deism are deemed synonimous. Yet, inasmuch as I have heard, that the Quakers have been represented, by a late author before mentioned [i.e., Hume], as the most regular set of Deists, it may not be foreign to my business, to shew the contrary, from the most authentic testimony, the epistles of their yearly meeting in London. ...

———

HUME'S ACCOUNT OF QUAKERISM DEFENDED.

MR. URBAN,

Your anonymous correspondent in December, the author of Quakerism defended against false representations, sets out with a bold assertion, that, "Nothing in the history of this country has been more unfairly represented by modern writers than the religious principles of the people called Quakers." Guthrie, indeed, charges them with being Freethinkers, which your correspondent denies, if, by freethinking, Deism be meant. That Deism and Quakerism are synonimous terms, I will not pretend to say; yet I am of opinion that Deism is naturally deducible from Quaker-principles, and therefore may properly enough be denominated Enthusiastic Deism.

Hume, though represented by your correspondent as a ridiculer of religion, as a partial historian, and as one who pays no regard to truth, has represented the Quakers justly, properly, and with that regard to truth, which every historian owes to the public. He has had recourse to their first principles, which your correspondent acknowledges are extravagant and ridiculous, and from thence he has deduced his history. Had he given a modern character of that body of people, he must have deviated from his plan, and given us a strange mixture of contradictions and inconsistencies; he must have given a description of plain Quakers and gay or fashionable Quakers, and shewn the enmity that is subsisting between them.

To dissect properly the principles of the Quakers, or to say precisely what they mean, is, perhaps, the most difficult task that ever historian undertook. They found their religion upon revelation, and they make, as Guthrie says, that revelation just what they please. Had your correspondent given us a clear definition of what he means by revelation, we should then have been better qualified to determine the subject under consideration. Their preachers are influenced by the spirit of truth, and they speak as that spirit giveth utterance. This is frequently the language of Quakers, and what many have published to the world.

Now I should be glad your correspondent would give positive answers to the following questions, without equivocation, circumlocution, or quoting any authorities whatever; for authorities frequently lead men astray.

Qu. I. In what manner are Quaker preachers inspired?

Qu. II. Doth that spirit they boast of deliver to them the subject of their discourse only? or doth it deliver to them the discourse in a plain, intelligible manner, verbatimet literatim? And

Qu. III. What reason can be given why that same spirit should inspire two or three at once? Can God be the author of confusion? If candid and ingenuous answers are given to the above questions, your correspondent and I perhaps may enter more deeply into the subject; and in the interim I shall remain, Sir, yours,

SCRUTATOR.

EARLY RESPONSES TO HUME

Volume 8

Edited and Introduced by
James Fieser
University of Tennessee at Martin

THOEMMES CONTINUUM

Early Responses to Hume

Edited and Introduced by **James Fieser**
University of Tennessee at Martin, USA

Volumes 1 and 2
Early Responses to Hume's Moral, Literary and Political Writings

Volumes 3 and 4
Early Responses to Hume's Metaphysical and Epistemological
Writings

Volumes 5 and 6
Early Responses to Hume's Writings on Religion

Volumes 7 and 8
Early Responses to Hume's *History of England*

Volumes 9 and 10
Early Responses to Hume's Life and Reputation
Bibliography of Early Responses to Hume, with Indexes

EARLY RESPONSES TO HUME'S
HISTORY OF ENGLAND

Second Edition, Revised

II

Edited and Introduced by
James Fieser
University of Tennessee at Martin

thoemmes

First published by Thoemmes Press, 2003

Thoemmes Continuum
11 Great George Street
Bristol BS1 5RR, England

http://www.thoemmes.com

Early Responses to Hume
Second edition, revised, 2005
10 vols : ISBN 1 84371 114 1

Early Responses to Hume's *History of England*
Second edition, revised, 2005
2 Volumes : ISBN 1 84371 119 2

British Library Cataloguing-in-Publication Data
A CIP record of this title is available from the British Library

Printed and bound in Great Britain
by Biddles Ltd, Kings Lynn, Norfolk

23
JOHN WHITAKER

John Whitaker, *The history of Manchester. In four books.* By John Whitaker. [London]: Sold by Mess. Dodsley in Pall-Mall [et al.], 1773–1775, 2 v. Appendices; from 1773 and 1775 editions.

Native of Manchester, John Whitaker (1735–1808) was a fellow of Corpus Christi College, Oxford, and later Rector of Ruan Lanyhorne, Cornwall. He authored several books in British history, including *Mary Queen of Scots Vindicated* (1787), selections from which appear later in this collection. In 1771 the first volume appeared of his *History of Manchester* – a work which he envisioned in four books, but never went past the second. In the revised 1773 edition of this volume, Whitaker included an Appendix, which critiques the opening paragraphs of Chapter 1 of Hume's *History* (this new material was also issued in a pamphlet for the benefit of owners of the 1771 edition). The second and final volume of this work appeared in 1775, which contains a second Appendix on Hume, continuing where the first Appendix left off. The two appendices combined cover Hume's discussions of the Britons, Romans, and Saxons. Throughout, Whitaker harshly attacks Hume for having only a superficial understanding of early English history and for copying from Thomas Carte's *History of England*. He produces several examples where Hume clearly drew from Carte's narrative, but footnoted the work of a classical authority, rather than Carte. His rhetoric is especially harsh, as we see here: "Mr. Hume paces so exactly at the heels of his master [i.e., Carte], that one well-urged thrust pierces them both at once." Whitaker concludes by calling on Hume "to revise these early parts of his history immediately."

Hume's surviving letters do not mention Whitaker, and Hume made no changes to his *History* based on Whitaker's detailed critique. It is more reasonable to assume that Hume was unaware of – or did not have access to – Whitaker's text, rather than that he consciously rejected the suggestions. Several of Whitaker's observations involve transcription errors that Hume or his sources made, such as setting the departure of the Romans at 448 A.D. rather than 446. These are the kind of mistakes that Hume readily corrected when brought to his attention by critics.

The *Edinburgh Magazine and Review*, edited by Gilbert Stuart, reviewed the 1773 revision of Book one, which included the first appendix on Hume. Stuart himself was the author of the review, and he writes very approvingly of Whitaker:

> Extensive erudition, it must be allowed, and much originality of genius, distinguished what he has written. The vigour also of his diction deserves the highest commendation. It flows with uniform majesty, and discovers at all times the hand of a master.

Regarding the Appendix on Hume, Stuart concurs with Whitaker's assessment:

> In an appendix, which our historian has added to the first book, he has made remarks on the histories of Mr Carte and Mr Hume. The last he seems to have examined most attentively; and he expresses himself concerning it with the spirit which becomes an inquirer after truth. If his censure is bold, let it be acknowledged that it is decisive. It carries every where conviction along with it. We are fully disposed to allow to Mr Hume all his merits: The same justice we owe to Mr Whitaker; and we hesitate not to pronounce, that, as far as his criticism goes, the wounds he inflicts are deep and mortal. [*Edinburgh Magazine and Review*, June 1774, Vol. 2, pp. 489–490]

Stuart was angry with Hume at this point in time, which may account for his harsh assessment (for background on this see the entry on Stuart contained later in this collection). Regarding the 1775 volume of Whitaker's *History of Manchester*, Stuart comments on how few critics there have been of Hume's *History*; he then compares Whitaker's and MacQueen's respective critiques of Hume, praising the former, and attacking the latter:

> In his appendix, he has offered a variety of strictures on the histories of Messrs Carte and Hume. Those upon the last are particularly interesting; and we cannot but mention it as a circumstance somewhat remarkable, that, while the philosophy of Mr Hume has been assailed by such a number of combatants, his history, though, in many respects, exceptionable, should have been the foundation of so little animadversion. Our author, and the writer of a small book, entitled *Letters on Mr Hume's History of Great Britain*, if we rightly remember, are the only inquirers, who have endeavoured formally to censure him as n historian; and they stand in so remarkable an opposition to each other, that it may not be incurious to remark it.
>
> The quickness and penetration of Mr Whitaker qualify him in a particular manner for controversy. The other author is perhaps the most frivolous and uninformed who ever spurned at his betters; and his unpenetrating spirit should have entirely precluded him from every pursuit of literature. The one rushes to his point, uncovers the weakness he would combat, and opposes truth to error. The other approaches his adversary with a fastidious

formality, selects from him particular passages, which he interprets with little reference to the general sense of the narration, and gravely imputes to him his own want of discernment. The understanding of the one is strong and active; that of the other, weak and sluggish. Every ornament of literature distinguishes the former; the most trifling acquirements foster the vanity of the latter. The vigorous genius of the one assaults Mr Hume where he is weakest, and has neglected to exert himself; the wild pertinacity of the other attacks him where he is strongest, and where he is perpetually displaying those characteristic strokes of ability, which never mark the productions of ordinary men. The manly sense, and irrefragable argument of the former are adorned and illustrated by an expression the most eloquent and forcible; the little meaning of the latter is frittered away in a language the most prolix and vapid. The one has all the respectful gallantry of a generous enemy; the other would inflict disease and death, and every where steps aside to enjoy a victory, which it was impossible he could gain. In the performance of the former, our admiration is every where excited by knowledge and ability; in that of the latter, the disappointed reader is left to mourn over the melancholy madness of fanaticism, or to eye, with scorn, the feculent spawn of unlettered presumption. The work of the one will live for ages; that of the other, if it were possible to preserve it from oblivion, would serve, in a most admirable manner, to gratify the painful curiosity of a philosophic observer, who would mark the workings of an intellect never destined to reason; vain of powers, which it never possessed; struggling to exert them; and languishing in weakness.

In a footnote to the sentence ending "ordinary men", the reviewer criticizes MacQueen's efforts in defending the reformers:

This adversary is offended with Mr Hume's account of the reformation; a morsel of history than which, perhaps, antient and modern times can show nothing more finished and masterly. He meant possibly to do a service to religion, by extolling the characters of the reformers beyond what history or nature will permit; and it is by such well meant, but futile endeavours, that our most holy religion receives its worst wounds; the great source of infidelity being the contemptible bigotry of too many of the defenders of christianity. [*Edinburgh Magazine and Review*, April 1775, Vol. 3, pp. 257–260]

The *Critical Review* gives Whitaker high marks for content, but criticizes his writing style:

His ingenuity and learning are no less conspicuous in the present volume than in the first, and we have the pleasure to observe, that he has now avoided in great measure those blemishes arising from affectation, with which the former part of the work was somewhat disfigured. He seems, however, to be still much attracted with the charms of a flowery diction, which lead him sometimes into declamatory redundancy, and sometimes into laconic brevity. Nor can we acquit him entirely of opposing the evidence of other writers with such an air of decisiveness, as, perhaps, is not always supported by sufficient testimony; a fault which is common to authors who mix the conjectures of the antiquarian with the scrupulous narrative of history. It must be acknowledged, at the same time, that his remarks on preceding writers, discover an elaborate and minute investigation into the subject of which he treats; and that he has detected many historical errors, which have been received upon prescriptive authority. [*Critical Review*, February 1775, Vol. 39, pp. 81–91]

Writing for the *Monthly Review*, John Langhorne praises the work as a whole, but ridicules the conjectural nature of the earlier parts of this work:

Mr. Whitaker, in the volume before us, which is a second volume on the subject, though not so mentioned in the title, had strong temptations to fall into this species of conjectural history: for, treating of the Roman-British and Saxon periods, he had little more to build upon than the basis of tradition, connected with the scanty notices of a few historians of doubtful credit. With such materials, however, he has courage to venture upon the fabulous æra of King Arthur, and to attempt even a systematic history of that doughty hero. Of the style and manner in which such a narrative must run, and of the singular utility of the words *probably, perhaps*, and *would*, under such difficulties, let the following passage serve as a specimen. [*Monthly Review*, 1775, Vol. 52, June pp. 496–505, Vol. 53, August pp. 128–139, September pp. 231–240]

Apparently aware of the *Monthly Review*'s critique, The *London Review* defends Whitaker against the charge that his work is too conjectural:

It has been objected to this work, that the former part of it is in great measure *conjectural*; the ingenious Author having fabricated a history out of traditionary fables and relations unsupported by records. But these are not only the sole grounds on which the historian of so early a period could proceed; but are perhaps less foreign from the truth than many recorded facts of later date. Visionary and fanciful as may be the traditionary reports of particular facts and circumstances, the general outlines of characters and manners, may sometimes be more faithfully traced through a certain age, which the historian lies under no temptation to misrepresent, than they may be delineated through a later æra, whose historical facts and political characters are disguised or misrepresented by passion and party. The truth is, that scepticism is no where so justifiable as in historical researches. The

credulity of some writers, the prepossession of others, and the precipitancy
of all, render some of our best-written histories, even of modern date, little
better than romances, consisting of well-wrought tissue of plausible tales, and
fashionable fables. The number of errors and mistakes, which Mr. Whitaker
hath pointed out in Carte and Hume, may serve to confirm this animadversion, and, at the same time, to justify our confidence in Mr. Whitaker's
researches, and reasonings on periods of an earlier date. There is something
awkward, indeed, in his frequent use of the conditional *would be*, in cases
where a more positive and elegant writer would say *were*. But we cannot help
thinking it argues modesty in the recorder of facts, founded on mere probability, to give only a probable narrative of what he has no other evidence for;
without that modesty's arguing any diffidence of the truth of them. [*London
Review*, 1775, Vol. 1, pp. 431–439, 490–496; 1776, Vol. 2, pp. 225–228]

Boswell reports the following statement by Samuel Johnson regarding
Whitaker's *History*:

All that is really *known* of the ancient state of Britain, is contained in a *few
pages*. We can know no more than what the old writers have told us; yet
what large books have we upon it, the whole of which, excepting such parts
as are taken from those old writers, is all a dream, such as Whitaker's
Manchester. [*Life of Samuel Johnson* (1791)]

Whitaker's critique of Hume in *The History of Manchester* was favourably
mentioned in Joseph Towers's *Observations on Mr. Hume's History of
England* (1778) and by Samuel Rose in his review of John Millar's *Historical
View of the English Government* (1787), contained later in this collection.
Whitaker's *History of Manchester* did not appear again after the 1775 volume.
The following is from the 1773 and 1775 volumes.

APPENDIX.
Nº I.

I have long thought, that a regular course of remarks upon the incidents and
observations, which occur in the principal of our English historians, would be
of considerable service to historical knowledge. Our best national accounts, in
the period especially before the Conquest, call loudly, I think, for the corrective
hand of criticism. Prejudice and partiality, ignorance and inattention, dulness
and refinement, have all cooperated to throw their several false colours over
the face of our annals, and disguise their real and genuine features. And some
bolder spirit has been long wanted among us, that would dare to read, examine,
and think for himself; mount up to the fountainheads of our history, there mark

the principles that secretly colour the waters at the source, and then observe the tints that incorporate with them afterwards. Something of this nature is attempted in the present work. But it wants perhaps one addition. It should not only endeavour to open the great and unveiled truths of our history, but also point out the errours, with which the earlier part of it seems to be clouded over. The brightness of truth, like that of the sun, is most fully displayed, not merely by the radiance of its own light, but by a contrast with its opposite darkness. And the many faults that have been committed by all our recent historians, I think, and are continually gleaned by each succeeding writer from the earlier, will be the sooner avoided by being held up to the light, and our island annals more readily purged of their original falsities.

These reasons have induced me to begin here, and to think of continuing regularly in the appendix, a series of remarks, short and decisive, on our two best historians Mr. Carte and Mr. Hume, as the proper representatives of the rest. I shall remark upon them, however, only so far as their accounts run parallel in time with my own. And I shall do it with all the respect that is due to both. From this plan I foresee not a little advantage to myself; as I doubt not but I shall have frequent occasion, in animadverting upon them, to correct myself. And each volume of the History of Manchester, before it appears in publick, will be improved by the light reflected back from the appendix. The observations will, many of them perhaps, appear un-important and trifling in the detail. But all will be found serviceable, I think, as parts of a whole. And, before I finally close the subject, a regular scheme of historical criticism may be given, perhaps, for all the period of our national history before the Conquest.

At this time, I shall notice only such parts of Mr. Hume's and Mr. Carte's histories, as relate to the preceding accounts. And these are not very many. The present work has struck out a new path of history, that seldom comes near to theirs.

HUME.
Vol. I. 8vo.

P. 1–2. Mr. Hume appears in his history to be frequently seduced from the truth by pursuing a splendour of sentiment, and led away by an affectation of singularity into wildness and extravagance. And he sometimes appears adapting his sentiments to his situation, and throwing out such observations as will best serve the present purpose. And both these principles seem to have concurred in the production of his remarkable preface. There he advances a position, convenient perhaps for himself, but certainly unjust in its nature, That the history of nations in their infancy is not worthy a recital; as if the commencement of civil life, the dawn of the arts, and the rise of literature, were not incidents as important and interesting, as the posteriour account of them, their occasional eclipses or accidental illuminations. And on this false principle he proposes to run briefly over the events, which attended the Roman conquest of Britain. – He assigns also this additional reason for it, that they "belong more to Roman than British story" (p. 2). For the same reason he must as briefly run over the Saxon, the Danish, and the Norman invasions, the irruptions of the Scots into our borders, and the descents of the French upon our coasts, as belonging rather to the history of Saxony, and Denmark, Neustria, Scotland, and France. And in writing the annals of France, Scotland, or Ireland, he would take very little notice of the English transactions in those countries. – Such are the trifling arguments adduced, for giving us so short an account of the Roman history of Britain. And Mr. Hume adds, in prosecution of the former principle, what (as I have observed above) the latter would equally have led him to, That he shall also "hasten through the obscure and un-interesting period of the Saxon annals" (p. 2). By this means, that whole portion of our history, which (as I have formerly remarked) is the most important in all our annals, is consigned over to neglect and carelessness, as unworthy a man of genius for its writer, and incapable of affording entertainment and instruction to the reader. And a strong brand is fixed upon that period of our annals, which is (as I may say) the great seed-plot of our national history, as it gives us the origin and institution of all our government, all our civility, and all our religion; and is therefore fraught with infinite variety of instruction and pleasure to the man, Christian, and the critick.

The extravagance of sentiment in these positions, and, what as strongly marks them, the fastidious affectation of delicacy, must have been very manifest to a gentleman of Mr. Hume's strong and masculine judgment. And his severer reflections must have been disgusted with both. But it was not convenient for him, to travel properly through the period preceding the Conquest. And yet it was necessary in itself, in order to give a seeming and saleable compleatness to his history. In this dilemma, not furnished with the requisite knowledge, and yet obliged to engage in the work, he naturally resolved to skim lightly along the surface, and throw an air of propriety over his conduct by some general reasons at the beginning. These, however slight and flimsy in themselves, would engage attention from their novelty, and perhaps convert even a deficiency into a grace. And that this was actually the reason for the preface and the practice of Mr. Hume, is plain (I think) from the innumerable mistakes which he has made, even in his method of writing history, in the British, Roman, and Saxon periods of it. Some of these I shall now point out, and nearly transcribe the whole of his general account of the Britons.

P. 2. "All antient writers agree in representing the first inhabitants of Britain as a tribe of the Gauls or Celtæ, who peopled that island from the neighbouring continent. Their language was the same, their manners, their government, and superstition; varied only by those small differences, which time or a communication with the bordering nations must necessarily introduce."

Mr. Carte p. 7. says thus. And Mr. Hume sets out the mere abridger of him. "That they [the Britons] were a Celtic nation, and came hither from Gaule, is no longer doubted by any body: the perfect conformity between them and the old Gaulois in their manners, customs, habits, buildings, temper, warlike genius, superstitions of religion, and above all in their language, joined to the situation of the two countries, not allowing on this head the least room for dispute." And Mr. Hume appears to have judiciously compacted what had been diffusively said by Mr. Carte, and to have given us his argument in a better form. – But he has varied a little from his original, and thereby fallen into mistakes. Mr. Carte says, that the Gallick derivation of the Britons is no longer doubted by any one; and Mr. Hume, that it is unanimously asserted by all the antient writers. These are very different propositions. And the former is generally true, but the latter entirely false. There are only two antient writers, I think, that speak of the Gallick decent of the Britons. One is Cæsar, who does not agree with Mr. Hume. And the other is Tacitus, who directly opposes him. Cæsar says not, whence the great body of the islanders was derived; and he speaks only of the southern Britons as Gallick Belgæ. Britanniæ pars interior ab iis incolitur quos *natos in insulâ memoriâ proditum* dicunt; maritima pars ab iis qui – ex Belgis transierant (p. 88). And Tacitus expressly affirms the origin of the Britons to be a thing unknown. Britanniam qui mortales initio coluerint, indigenæ an advecti, ut inter barbaros, parum compertum (Agric. Vit. c. xi). He then advances several conjectures, that the Caledonians were of German origin, and the Silures of Spanish; or rather upon the whole, that they were all of Gallick. But he advances these only as conjectures, as problematical reasonings from the aspect of the men, the vicinity of the several parts of the continent, or a conformity of religious principles. "And "all the antient writers, that agree in representing the *first* inhabitants of Britain as a tribe of the Gauls," appear to be only one, who only *conjectures* that they were so, but asserts their real origin to have been utterly unknown. – I mention not this, to destroy or render dubious the Gallick origin of the old Britons. I do it, merely to vindicate the truth. The argument is a good one in itself. And I have endeavoured to improve it into a demonstration, in ch. xii. s. 4 and History of the Britons asserted p. 28–29.

– "Their language was the same, their manners, their government, their superstition; varied only by those small differences, which time and a communication with the bordering nations must necessarily introduce."
This account is evidently taken from Tacitus, though neither Tacitus nor any other historian is quoted for it. His words are these. Eorum [Gallorum] sacra deprehendas, superstitionum persuasione. Sermo haud multùm diversus; in deposcendis periculis eadem audacia, et, ubi advenerint, in detrectandis eadem formido. And Mr. Hume appears to have added to Tacitus's account, and thrown in a circumstance that is not true. Tacitus says not, that the govern-

ments of the Gauls and Britons were the same. And they were not. The Gauls had nothing but a kind of aristocratical republicks amongthem, in the days of Caesar and Strabo. And the Britons had none at all. The magistrates of the former, therefore, were always elective and generally annual; and those of the latter hereditary and for life. See Cæsar and Strabo for the Gallick republicks; Cæsar p. 2, 3, and 5 for the Helvetian, p. 9 and 34 for the Æduan, and p. 32 and Strabo p. 301 for all.

P. 3. "The Greek and Roman navigators or merchants brought back the most shocking accounts of the ferocity of the people, which they magnified, as usual, in order to excite the admiration of their countrymen. The south-east parts, however, of Britain had already, before the age of Cæsar, made the first and most requisite step towards a civil settlement; and the Britains, by tillage and agriculture, had there encreased to a great multitude (Cæsar) lib. iv)."

Where are these most shocking accounts of our ancestors to be found at present? I remember nothing but the Britannos hospitubus feros of Horace, which is not very shocking, and could not have been much magnified. And the quotation here from Cæsar is the first in the history, and is greatly misapplied. – That only the *south-eastern* parts of Britain were acquainted with tillage, is not said by Cæsar. His words are these. Britanniæ pars interior ab iis incolitur, quos natos in insulâ ipsâ memoriâ proditum dicunt; maritima pars ab iis qui – ex Belgis transierant: and, Ex his omnibus longè sunt humanissimi qui Cantium incolunt; quæ regio est maritima omnis, neque multùm a Gallicâ differunt consuetudine; interiores plerique frumenta non serunt (p. 89). Here we see, not merely the south-eastern, but all the maritime Britons, all on the southern coast of the island, expressly declared to practise agriculture. And not only these, but some of the inland tribes, are equally declared to have practised it. So grossly erroneous is this account of Mr. Hume's! And another passage in Cæsar coincides with this, and two in Tacitus and Dio confirm both. Maritima pars [Britanniæ] ab iis [incolitur] qui ex Belgis transierant, *qui omnes* bello illato ibi remanserunt, atque *agros colere coeperunt*. And we find the Britons under Boadicia, the Trinobantes, a Belgic tribe, and the Cassi and Iceni, two Aboriginal ones, and running up to the north as far as Lincolnshire at least, all well acquainted with the arts of agriculture; and the more northerly of them, the Iceni, even before their reduction by the Romans. This appears with regard to the last from the notice given us by Tacitus concerning them, That previously to their insurrection under Boadicia, and while they were meditating it, they had been serendis frugibus incuriosi (Ann. lib. xiv. c. 38). And it appears equally with regard to all from Boadicia's address to them all, That they were obliged to cultivate their lands γεωργειν, with heavy taxes upon them (1004). – Nor had the *south-eastern* Britons, merely, increased to a great multitude. Mr. Hume had before restricted to the *south-east* of Britain, what Cæsar had applied to all the southern coast, and even to some of the interiour parts of the country. And he now advances farther, and confines equally to the *south-east* what Cæsar has spoken of all the island. So inaccurate and careless is he, in merely copying the notices of Cæsar! The latter having divided the islanders more accurately than any other of his countrymen, into Belgæ and Aborigines, and assigned them their respective possessions in general; he proceeds to an account of both, and begins with this remark, That both Aborigines and Belgæ were exceedingly numerous, Hominum est infinita multitudo. And Diodorus accordingly calls Britain the well-peopled island ωολυ-ανθρωπος νησος (p. 347). – But Mr. Hume, even in the compass of this very extract, has fallen into two other inaccuracies. Cæsar's Hominum infinita multitudo he translates into "a great multitude"; words much below the standard. And this populousness he ascribes to the practice of agriculture; when the facts appear not with the smallest connexion in his author, and could not possibly have any at all. The practice of agriculture was confined to the more southerly parts of the island. And the populousness extended over the whole of it.

– "The other inhabitants of the island still maintained themselves by pasturage: they were cloathed with skins of beasts: they dwelt in huts, which they reared in the forests and marshes, with which the country was covered: they shifted easily their habitations, when actuated either by the hopes of plunder or the fear of an enemy: the convenience of feeding their cattle was even a sufficient motive for removing their seats: and being ignorant of all the refinements of life, their wants and their possessions were equally scanty and limited."

This general account of the Britons is all one accumulation of errours, formed partly by a repetition of the preceding mistakes, and partly by an addition of others. – The preceding have occasioned Mr. Hume to represent all but the south-eastern Britons, as maintaining themselves by pasturage, all but the south-eastern as cloathed with skins, and all but them as dwelling in huts reared among the forests and marshes, easily shifting their habitations, and having few wants and small possessions. And we must once more produce the often-cited passage of Cæsar, in opposition to this strange account. Interiores plerique, says he, – lacte et carne vivunt, pellibusque sunt vestiti. They were not all but the south-eastern Britons, they were not even any of the more westerly Belgæ, and they were not even some of the more inland Britons; they were only the generality of the Aborigines; who lived upon milk and flesh, and cloathed themselves in skins. – Nor did all but the south-eastern Britons dwell in huts constructed amid the forests and marshes. Strabo p. 306 informs us, that the Britons lived in cabins among the forests. But then he confines not the remark to all except the south-eastern Britons. He applies it to all the Britons of the south. He extends it to all the Britons of the inland country. And he carries it over all the island. – That all but the south-eastern Britons easily shifted their habitations and seats, is also equally false. Strabo, I think, is the only author that has been quoted by others (for Mr. Hume quotes nobody here), in proof of this opinion. And I have already shewn, that his words carry no such meaning with them. And, even if they did, they are not restricted to the south-eastern Britons, but are equally spoken of all. – Such are the many mistakes in this small extract! And there are still more.

None of the Britons shifted their habitations and seats easily, as the hope of plunder or the fear of being plundered, or as the want of pasturage for their cattle, led them. Nor were all but the south-eastern ignorant of every refinement of life. – Mr. Hume has erred throughout this whole passage, from a strange indistinctness and confusion of ideas concerning the Britons. The other inhabitants were equally with the south-eastern divided into tribes and kingdoms. Their possessions were equally fixed and known among both. They roved not, any more than these, over the face of the country, sometimes settling in one place and sometimes in another. Each tribe had its distinct territory. And some of their dominions were not scanty and narrow. When they were alarmed by the plundering inroads of their neighbours, they drove off their cattle before the invaders. And they left their houses. Many of them were also employed in looking after the herds, and the droves, and the flocks of their lords, along the woods or the heaths of the country; and gradually moved from the hills to the vallies, and from the vallies to the hills, for the sake of pasturage. But the tribe never shifted its position. And nothing but a total inattentiveness to what appears manifest upon the face of Mr. Hume's own history, the regular division of the island into principalities and kingdoms, could have seduced the author into this extravagant representation of the natives. The Britons did not live, as Mr. Hume describes them, like so many hords of Tartars or tribes of wild Indians. They were formed into regular kingdoms. They had ascertained possessions. And they were governed by stated laws. – This account will serve of itself to demonstrate the fallacy of the other assertion in Mr. Hume, That all but the south-eastern Britons were unacquainted with every refinement of life. Where a regular frame of polity had been erected, and where property was regularly ascertained, there many of the refinements must necessarily have been known. And, that they actually were among the Britons, I have already shewn in the preceding chapters. The labours of the pottery, the loom, and the furnace, were successfully practised among them. The arts of the turner, the carpenter, the miner, and the architect, were studied and known. And many of the ruling principles of mechanicks, many of the more mysterious truths of geometry, and various secrets in medicine, botany, astronomy, and religion, were familiar to the scholars of the island. And were such men ignorant of all the refinements of life? Common sense is shocked at the suggestion. And we need only appeal against it to a slight but remarkable fact, known to every reader, and of which we have demonstration remaining at present. I speak of the piles at Coway, which the Britons contrived to drive into the hard bed of the Thames, several feet under the surface of the water; and to fix so firmly in the ground, that they have continued amid all the waste of time, the violence of floods, and the plunder of interest of curiosity, the admiration of every age. And, even if Mr. Hume's representation of the Britons had been as generally true as it is false, his extension of the censure to all but the south-eastern must have destroyed the whole of it. All the *southern* Britons were equally Belgæ, equally engaged in trade, and equally conversant with foreigners. Cæsar indeed speaks of the Cantii as the most humanized tribes of the island. But Diodorus says the same of the Britons in the most south-westerly parts of it. And, even according toe Cæsar's account, agriculture particularly was practised by all the Belgæ, and also by several tribes of the Aborigines. The refinements of life, that I have shewn to have been cultivated in the island, were all cultivated equally by the Britons of the south. And most of them were known to all the Britons.

– "The Britains were divided into many small nations or tribes; and being a military people, whose sole property was their sword and their cattle, it was impossible, after they had acquired a relish of liberty, for their princes or chieftains to establish any despotic authority over them."

We have been told immediately before, that all but the south-eastern Britons roved over the country, and shifted their habitations as the hope of plundering or the fear of being plundered led them. And yet here, in the very next words, we find all the Britons as I have before represented them, formed into regular kingdoms and subject to regular governments. Both however, as I have observed above, cannot be true. Regular kingdoms and governments, in an island especially that was infinitely populous and full of buildings, necessarily involved in their ideas a permanent residence and defined possessions. And, if the point wanted any additional proof, we might remark that Mela describes Britain thus: Fert populos regisque populorum, sed, – ut longiùs a continenti absint, ita, aliarum opum ignari magis, tantùm pecore ac *finibus* dites; and, bella contrahunt, ac se frequenter invicem infestant, – studio *prolatandi* ae quæ possident (l. iii. c. 6). So inconsistent is Mr. Hume with himself, even within the compass of two succeeding sentences!

Nor was the sole property of the Britons their sword and their cattle. It was not, either as they were nations or individuals. The soil must necessarily have been property with both. And the numerous houses of the Britons must have been equally so with all. So vague and unmeaning is Mr. Hume's hypothesis, all the airy speculation of a mind that has taken a hasty view of the island, and never attended even to the consequence of his own notices and representations. – And Mr. Hume says further, That it was impossible, after the Britons had acquired a relish of liberty, for their chieftains to tyrannize over them. But how were the Britons to acquire this relish? By roving with their cattle over the country? Mr. Hume's argument plainly intimates this. And yet he cannot mean it. For this relish is attributed to all the Britons without exception: and the south-eastern are expressly excepted from the roving. And how could the rovers obtain the relish, when even they, as appears from this very quotation, were in regular communities and under regular governments? But let us suppose the Britons possest of this relish, and then see the result. It was then impossible, says Mr. Hume, for their princes to tyrannize over them. And why was it impossible? Is the Genius of liberty, like some of the knight-errants in antient story, cased by the Gods in the coat of impenetrable armour? And has that heroick spirit, which blusters and bullies in these our days, never crouched under the feet of our kings? For the safety of liberty, I wish the one could be imagined without credulity. And, for its credit with the world, I should be glad that the other could be said with truth.

– "Their governments, though monarchical, were free (Diod. Sic. l. iv, Mela lib. iii. cap. 6, Strabo lib. iv), as well as those of all the Celtic nations; and the common people seem to have enjoyed more liberty among them (Dion Cassius lib. 75), than among the nations of Gaul."

This passage is full of mistakes. And I shall endeavour to point them all out. – Mr. Hume here says, that the British government was monarchical. And yet in p. 2. he tells us, that it was the same with Gallick, which I have shewed before not to have been monarchical. – Mr. Hume also says, that the British monarchies were free governments; and quotes for it Diodorus, Mela, and Strabo. All that the last says, is this. Δυναστειαι δ' εισι παρ' αυτοις, there are many monarchies among the Britons; and immediately afterwards he speaks of their monarchs, των Δυναστων τινεσ των αυτοθι (p. 306). And here is evidently not a single syllable concerning the free nature of the British monarchies. but perhaps we may find the proper notices in Diodorus or Mela. What the former says is this; Βασιλεισ τε και Δυναστασ πολλουσ εχειν, that the island had many kings and monarchs in it (p. 347). And here therefore is as little as in Strabo, concerning the freedom of the Britons under their kings. If it is found any where, it must appear in Mela. And his words are these: Fert populos regesque populorum, there are many communities in the country under their distinct princes. All these evidences, we see, prove nothing more than the monarchical nature of the governments. And the freedom enjoyed under them, for any thing that yet appears, is all an additional touch from Mr. Hume's pencil. – But perhaps Dion Cassius, quoted afterwards for the greater freedom of the Britons than the Gauls, may at least prove the positive point. And his words seem likely to do it. Among the Caledonians and Mæatæ, says he, δημοκρατουνται ως πληθει (p. 1280); the generality of their tribes are under republican governments. This is a very extraordinary assertion. And it deserves to be considered.

The words, we see, are restricted by Dio to the Mæatæ and Caledonians, and applied by Mr. Hume to the Britons in general. But we have a testimony equal to Dio's, even his own, That the Britons in general were not under republican governments. They were, he expressly assures us in p. 957, under kingly. And therefore, as Mr. Hume has applied the words, there is a direct contradictoriness in Dio, which necessarily destroys his credibility. This takes off at once the whole weight of the testimony here. And as the one intimation, concerning the general freedom of the British monarchies, either rests upon Dio or is totally ungrounded; and the other, concerning the greater liberty of the Britons than the Gauls, is entirely built upon him; they both fall with him to the ground. – It may be proper, however, to observe in addition to this remark, That Dio speaks not of the Britons enjoying a greater share of liberty under their kings, as Mr. Hume interprets him. And, even if his account had not been superseded by himself in another place, it would not prove the point for which it is adduced by Mr. Hume. It would not shew the freedom of the monarchical government in Britain. It would only prove the existence of a popular one. And consequently, even if its testimony was of any moment, it would be in direct opposition to Mr. Hume's representation. – But Dio's account is not only contradicted by himself, but by every other writer. As applied by Mr. Hume to the whole island, it is encountered equally by the very Diodorus, Mela, and Strabo, whom Mr. Hume quotes immediately before, and by Cæsar (p. 74, 92, &c.), Tacitus (Agric. Vit. c. 15), and others. Each of these is an authority fully equal to Dio's. And the concurrence of all forms an irresistible weight of evidence against him. And, even in their natural signification, and as applied only to the generality of the Picts, the words of Dio are directly confronted by a passage in Martial; which of itself is perhaps not an inferior testimony to Dio's, and, by its coincidence with all the other accounts of the island, becomes greatly superiour to it:

Turpes, humiles, supplicesque,
Pictorum sola basiate regum.

Lib. x. E. 72.

I have gone over this extract from Mr. Hume the more circumstantially, in order fully to open the extravagance of it. I have shewn in the body of this work, that the monarchies of Britain were founded on a regular system of liberty. And so far I have asserted the interests of freedom and of man. But the spirit of the times, if not properly checked, would carry us into absurdities that disgrace the cause. We should see the Tartuffes of liberty, like those of religion formerly, throwing a discredit over it by their follies. And antient history would be gradually drest up in the cropt hair, the cloak, and the band of political puritanism. And there is the more reason for this apprehension, when we see so philosophical a spirit as Mr. Hume's carried away by the civil fanaticism of the times, and sacrificing truth at the shrine of freedom.

P. 3–4. "Each state was divided into factions within itself (Tacit. Agric.): it was agitated with emulation towards the neighbouring states: and while the arts of peace were yet unknown, wars were the chief occupation, and formed the chief object of ambition among the people."

All this implies a fixedness of possession and dominion among the Britons, which very ill agrees with the account before of their roving over the face of the island. But indeed all this description of our forefathers, short and scanty as it is, is little more than a mass of gross contradictions. And the lines are like the British kingdoms in the present extract, almost each of them in a state of hostility with its neighbour. – But that each kingdom was divided into factions within itself, is not true, as deduced from the work here quoted for it, Tacitus's Life of Agricola. That indeed proves just the reverse. *Olim*, says Tacitus, regibus parenbant, *nunc* per principes factionibus et studiis trahuntur (c. 12). – And, that the arts of peace were not unknown to the Britons, is plain from Mr. Hume's own words, which allow tillage and agriculture to have been known to the south-eastern natives; and is still plainer from Cæsar's, which shew them to have been familiar to all the southern and some of the inland Britons. And in the present work I have even shewn all the mechanical arts to have been practised in every part of the island.

So grossly inaccurate as Mr. Hume is in his general presentation of the civil state of the Britons, we cannot expect him to be commonly precise with regard to their geographical divisions. If he has erred in a plain path and at noon-day, he must be sure to deviate upon a winding one and in the shade of the evening. And to criticize upon these mistakes would perhaps be cruel; like arraigning a person for the breach of laws with which he was never acquainted. I shall therefore pas them all over. Only let me observe, that there is a capital absurdity both in Mr. Carte's and Mr. Hume's histories, which appears manifest upon the face of them. And that is the relating the military transactions of the island, without any previous information concerning the names, the position, and the power of the respective tribes in it. In this mode of writing history, the reader is introduced into a sort of fairy land, where beings arise with whom he has no previous acquaintance, and kingdoms are mentioned of which we have never yet heard the existence. Thus the Trinobantes are mentioned for the first time in p. 6 of the one, and the Iceni and Cattivellauni in p. 27 of the other, without one note of their situation and strength. And the reader is left entirely in the dark, whether they resided in Kent or Cornwall, in Middlesex or Cathness.

I have here laid open a variety of errours within the compass only of two or three pages in Mr. Hume's history. And I may subjoin one remark to the whole, That his in-accuracy and in-attention have made him give us scarcely any real information, concerning the interiour state of the island, even for the whole of the Roman period. His hastiness to discharge himself of this part of his work, has increased and multiplied his mistakes. And yet it has in all probability preserved him from more; as upon a rough road a brisk pace is frequently safer for a fine horse, than a slow one.

———

APPENDIX

HUME

Octavo p. 13. "That they might leave the island with a better grace, the Romans assisted them [the Britons] in erecting anew the wall of Severus, which was built entirely of stone, and which the Britains had not at that time artisans skillful enough to repair (Bede lib. i. Cap. 12. Ann. Beverl. p. 440)."

In all the earlier parts of our history Mr. Hume is merely the copier of Mr. Carte, escaping many of his amplified absurdities from the contracted nature of his plan, passing by some perhaps from a sense of their dangerousness, and possibly avoiding others from a conviction of their folly; but giving us, after all, the general air and features of his work in miniature. This is an observation, that forces itself upon the mind on every examination of their respective histories. And it is particularly striking in the present passage.

The wall of Antoninus, which Gildas had so ignorantly ascribed to the Britons of the fifth century, and of which Mr. Carte had more discreetly given only the reparation to them, Mr. Hume has with greater discretion or better fortune left entirely unnoticed. Candour would attribute the act to the former, if justice did not plead for the latter, by suggesting that, had discretion been the operating principle, it would equally have dropt all notice of the wall of Severus. The marvelous relation of Gildas concerning this is all adopted by Mr. Hume, though he has rejected his account of that; and, what is remarkable, has adopted it exactly in Mr. Carte's manner. Like him, he has changed the original erection into a re-edification, in order to reconcile the assertion of Gildas with history and remains. And I have sufficiently exposed the impropriety of the change before, its contradictoriness to the only authority for the general fact itself, and its persisting ir-reconcileableness to remains and to history.

Mr. Hume indeed does not refer to Gildas at all for the incident. He appeals to Bede, whose history in all this period is only a reflection from Gildas's, and to Alured of Beverley, whose annals are only the same reflection at second hand; two mock-suns, successively produced from a third. And he quotes both, when Mr. Carte is evidently his author.

Euphelia serves to grace his measure,
  But Chloe is his real flame.

This appears from the obvious circumstance, That Mr. Hume makes his wall to be Severus's, when Bede expressly distinguishes his own from it. Mr. Hume asserts his to be composed of stone, and Bede affirms Severus's to have been of turf. Murum – , *ubi et Severus quondam vallum secerat*, firmo de lapide conlocarunt: and Severus, he observes, non muro, ut quidam æstimant, sed vallo distinguendam [Britanniam] putavit; murus etenim de lapidibus, vallum verò – fit de cespitibus. And Alured has nearly the same words and absolutely the same meaning. But though Alured and Bede, to whom Mr. Hume appeals, so strikingly disagree with him in the fact, Mr. Carte, to whom he does not appeal, agrees with him exactly. "To do them still another service before their departure," he says, "they [the Romans] directed and assisted the natives in repairing the wall of Severus, which was built of stone."

– "And, having done this last good office to the inhabitants, they [the Romans] bid a final adieu to Britain, about the year 448." And in page 14 he fixes the address to Actius for succours "A.D. 448".

I have brought this passage before the reader, not to enter into any discussion of its merits, but merely to mark the humble spirit that I have noticed in Mr. Hume before. To dot he former, is wholly unnecessary; as I have already shewn the falseness of the chronology, in my observations on Mr. Carte. And to do the latter is requisite, in order to be just to Mr. Carte and Mr. Hume, and to ascertain, so far as these remarks can, the rank which the latter should hold in the scale of our national history. Mr. Carte had fixed the application to Aetius in 448, by a mistake for 446. And Mr. Hume, insensible of the errour in his author, and too indolent to consult the Fasti Consulares himself, follows him implicitly. Mr. Carte had not settled the Roman departure in the same year, but vainly fancied it to be at some distance of time before. And Mr. Hume dates the Roman departure, not *in* 448, but *about* it. So exactly does he tread in his steps, copying his accounts without examining them, and adopting his errours without knowing them.

– "The Picts and Scots, finding that the Romans had finally relinquished Britain, now regarded the whole as their prize, and attacked the northern wall with redoubled forces."

Mr. Hume's whole account of these important transactions is so lean, meager, and unmeaning, that it scarcely seems worthy of a critical examination. And I can hardly command a proper degree of attention for the purpose. The narration in Gildas, which is uncommonly lively and useful in these moments, is given us again by Mr. Hume divested of every lively particularity, and stript of every useful accompaniment. The boundaries of the empire at this period are no longer marked. The manner, in which the Caledonians invaded the province, is no longer noticed. And the real wall, which they attacked, is no longer pointed out by the circumstances. All is wrapt up in one thick mist, which now and then opens, and gives us faint and erroneous views of the objects around us, and then, closing, involves us in impenetrable darkness again.

Mr. Hume leaving the wall of Antoninus, as he supposes, ruined and dismantled many years before, and having omitted Gilda's account of its erection and Mr. Carte's of its re-edification; he found it impossible to reconcile his own ideas of the matter with the description in Gildas, of the Caledonians passing the friths into Valentia, instead of coming into it by the unguarded isthmus. And indeed apprehending with all our historians and antiquaries, that Valentia was at this time in the possession of the Picts, he found himself still more embarrassed to reconcile the whole with Gilda's general account, of the Caledonians crossing the friths, landing in Valentia, and seizing all the country quite up to the wall. Illis [Romanis] ad sua revertentibus, emergunt certatim de curicis, quibus sunt trans Tithicam vallem vecti, – tetri Scotorum Pictorumque greges, – et – omnem aquilonalem extremamque terræ partem pro indigenis muro tenus caperssunt. In this state of doubt and distraction, not having strength of mind enough to throw off the incumbering load, and to reject the common opinions with disdain, because of their plain contrariety to Gilda's testimony; he resolved to omit what he did not understand, and to leave out all that would obstruct his progress in the history. And he has accordingly given us a description – that describes nothing, telling us not from whence the Caledonians came, and whether they were settled in Valentia or to the north of the friths; or, if to the north, how they got into the province; and, if to the south, how the wall could have been re-edified a little before. And yet, with all his cautious treading upon the embers, he has actually burnt himself. He has done it, in leaving his history embarrassed by this questionable mode of regis-tering transactions. And he has also done it, by the use of a term and the intro-duction of an idea, that actually mislead his readers. He points the attack of the Caledonians at the "northern wall," when he really means the southerly one. And, in a style of boyish amplification, he gives them "redoubled forces" for the attack, equally without authority and without reason.

P. 14. "The Britains, thus rejected [by Aetius], were reduced to despair, deserted their habitations, abandoned tillage, and flying for protection to the forests and mountains, suffered equally from hunger and from the enemy."

Here are several errours crouded into this short passage, some of Mr. Carte's repeated again, and others added to them by Mr. Hume.

The *Britains*, as Mr. Hume writes the name after his original Mr. Carte, are here said in general and without any limitations to have deserted their habita-tions, abandoned their tillage, and fled to the woods and mountains. But the inroad, as I have already shewn, was confined to a very small portion of the country. And even within the real sphere of its influence, as I have equally shewn, the effects of it are greatly exaggerated. But Mr. Carte had previously used all this wild extensiveness of expression. And Mr. Hume either did not discern the absurdity of it, or, with the blind spirit of historical orthodoxy, thought himself obliged to embrace what the other had adopted, and take implicitly the creed of his master.

Even in the countries immediately affected by the inroad, the number of Britons that fled to the woods and mountains could not have been very great. To suppose, that in the very line of the incursion all the inhabitants took refuge there, is truly ridiculous. And the number of the fugitives, upon such occasions, is generally in no proportion to the remaining residents. A few of the wealthier or more timorous families, and a variety of children and women, almost always constitute the bulk of the flyers. But in an invasion, so rapidly executed as this appears to have been, many could have had no time to remove. These invaders, like genuine Highlanders, carrying their tents in their mantles, their provisions in their knapsacks, and their artillery in their hands; being incumbered with none of the clogging appendages of a modern army, and able to march forty or fifty miles a day; the inhabitants, all along the course of their progress, would find the enemy upon them nearly as soon as they received the alarm of their coming. This would be evidently the case in Valentia. And the flying to the wilds would be almost confined entirely to Maxima. There the inhabitants would have time for their removal, because of the wall that restrained the progress of the Caledonians for a few days; and be more strongly stimulated to fly, because any invasion of Maxima had been very uncommon, and would carry the greater terrour from its novelty. And Gildas accordingly confines his account of the flying to the country south of Severus's wall: relictis civitatibus muroque celso, iterum quibus [illis] fugæ, iterum dispersiones solito desperabiliores &c. The only fugitives therefore were among the Brigantes. Even of these, a few hundreds are all that we can imagine to have fled to the wilder parts of the country. And even such would be principally derived from the course of the great road to the north. So plainly does Mr. Hume's giant appear upon examination to be only a pigmy. The whole collective body of the Provincials, that he had huddled together in the forests and hills, is dwindled away into the Provincials north of the Humber, is reduced into the inhabitants of East-Valentia and East-Maxima, and is even shrunk into a few hundreds among the great road in Durham and the North-riding.

Mr. Hume says, that all this happened *because* the suit of the Britons had been rejected by Actius. But the position is grossly absurd. It is evidently so in its consequences. The effect being necessarily as extensive as the cause, it makes the flying as national as the suit, and consequently drives again all the inhabitants of all parts of the provinces to the wilds. And it is equally absurd in itself. If people run away upon an invasion of the country, it is as the invaders are advancing. The general consternation excited by their approach is more alarming to the spirits, than the actual feeling of their insolence. And the inhabitants therefore fly before the storm, and retire as they see it gathering behind them. But Mr. Hume inverts the order entirely. He supposes the Britons to have staid as the Caledonians came on, to have stood patient while they "exerted to the utmost their native ferocity, which was not mitigated by the helpless condition and submissive behaviour of the inhabitants" (p. 14): and then to have all run away from them, when they found the Romans resolved not to send them assistance. And the position is as false as it is absurd. The Britons, that "deserted their habitations, abandoned tillage, and fled for protection to the forests and mountains," are expressly declared by the only historian of the transactions to have done all this *before* the application to Aetius. They did it, as the enemy advanced upon them when they had broken through the wall. Relictis civitatibus muroque celso, iterum quibus [illis] fugæ, iterum dispersiones solito desperabiliores, item ab hoste insectationes. After this, the application was made to Aetius. *Igitur* rursum miseræ, reliquiæ mittentes epistolas ad Agitium &c. So plainly was the flying antecedent to the application, that it was partly the cause of it. And the despair, into which the refusal of Aetius threw the Britons, operated in a manner just the reverse of what Mr. Hume has described. This it will be proper to shew at full length, as there has been a great mistake made by all our writers concerning Gilda's meaning in this point.

In the time preceding the address to Aetius, Gildas says of the starving refugees in the wilds, That they came into the cultivated country by stealth, and carried off privately all the provisions that they could meet with there. Nec pro-victûs-sustentaculo miserrimorum civium latrocinando temperabant. And in the interval of the application he says, That though some of them were impelled by the want of food to go back, and throw themselves upon the mercy of the enemy, yet others still continued in the woods and mountains, and persisted the more in their practice of plundering the neighbouring inhabitants. *Inerea* – samis dira – multos eorum cruentis compellit prædonibus sine dilatione victas dare manus, – alios verò nusquam, quin potiùs de ipsis montibus, speluncis, ac saltibus, dumis consertis, continuè rebellabant. Such is plainly the import of this quotation. Its relation to the preceding one directly ascertains its meaning. And the tenour of its own narration decisively confirms it. Yet, in opposition to both these reasons, the passage has been universally understood in a much higher acceptation, and the word *rebellabant* applied to some imaginary attacks of the fugitives upon the enemy. This word, however, has obviously no peculiar significancy here, and is only equivalent to the *latroci-nando*, the *direptionibus*, and the *domesticis motibus* of the passage before: Nec pro-victûs-sustentaculo miserrimorum civium *latrocinando* temperabant, et augebantur extraneæ clades *domesticis motibus*, quò et hujusmodi tam crebris *direptionibus* vacuaretur omnis region totius cibi baculo. And, in reading Gildas or any injudicious author, we must always attend more to the course of the ideas than the precision of the words.

But, concerning the time immediately after the application to Aetius, Gildas speaks in a manner that has never been noticed, and yet acquaints us with a remarkable fact. The division of chapters in this author, and the titles prefixed to them, are as authentick as any part of his work. And his title to the 18th runs thus, DE VICTORIA, plainly referring to some considerable defeat given the Caledonians, and spoken of in the body of the chapter. There also the defeat is described in the following terms: et *tum*, after the application to Aetius, his refusal, and the other co-temporary facts recorded in the chapter preceding, *primùm* inimicis – *strages dabant,* non confidentes in homine sed in Deo, secundùm illud exemplum Philonis, "necesse est adesse divinum ubi humanum cessat auxilium." The Britons, he says, being deprived of all assistance from man by the refusal of the Romans, applied themselves to God for help; and, supported by their confidence in him, attacked the enemy, gained the first battle that they had ever obtained over them without the aid of the Romans, and made a considerable slaughter of them. This is very plainly the account of an important engagement, though it has been so utterly unnoticed by all our writers; of the first that was gained by the Britons alone; and of the great slaughter of the Caledonians in it. And the natural consequences of the victory are expressed immediately afterwards: quievit – inimicorum audacia –; recesserunt hostes. The insolence of the Caledonians was checked by the blow. And they instantly fled out of the provinces.

So far then were the Britons from flying to the woods and mountains, as Mr. Hume represents them, on the refusal of the Romans; that the army which had been raised before, in order probably to join with the Romans, now ventured to advance without them, and boldly faced the enemy in the field. And the very people, that Mr. Hume describes deserting their houses, abandoning their tillage, and flying to the hills and forests, we find actually engaging the enemy, actually defeating and slaughtering them, and actually driving them out of the kingdom.

"The barbarians themselves began to feel the pressures of famine in a country which they had ravaged; and being harrassed by the dispersed Britains, who had not dared to resist them in a body, they retreated with their spoils into their own country (Ann. Beverl. P. 45)."

This is a continuation of the preceding errours, and an addition to them.

That the Caledonians by any ravages should be able to lay the whole country waste, and diffuse a famine through every part of the provinces, is one of those monstrous incredibilities on the face of the British history, which shew both the writers and the readers to have never *thought* about it. If they had, the common principles of scepticism, that every mind is obliged to carry about with it, must ages since have revolted at the extravagance of the assertion. And it appears the more astonishing to an examiner, when he finds even the wild historian of all these events not running into the wildness of his copiers, and expressly appropriating the famine to the refugees in the woods. Interea, says he, while application was making Aetius, famis dira ac famosissima *vagis ac nutabundis* hæret. The Caledonians therefore could not possibly feel the effects of it. And Gildas very explicitly declares that they did not, as he describes several of the fugitives quitting their retirements, and surrendering themselves to the enemy, in order to be relieved from the distress. Interea famis dira ac famosissima vagis ac nutabundis hæret, quæ multos eorum cruentis compellit prædonibus sine dilatione victas dare manus, *ut pauxillun ad resocillandam animam cibi caperent.*

Nor did the Britons harrass the enemy in dispersed parties. Nor were they afraid to face them in a body. Nor did they suffer them to retire with their spoils into their own country. All these assertions are absolutely untrue. This I have already shewn with regard to the two first, in the remark immediately preceding. And the Britons appear there to have not only not harrassed the Caledonians in little bodies, but to have actually encountered them with an army. The passage of Gildas, upon which all our writers have rested, I have decisively proved, I think, to have been grossly misunderstood by them, and to speak the very reverse of the language attributed to it. Bede appears to have been the original author of the construction, who has thus confounded the order of Gilda's words and the arrangement of his ideas. Interea Britones fames sua – multos eorum coegit victas infestis prædonibus dare manus, alios verò nunquam, quin potiùs, confidentes in divinum ubi humanum cessabat auxilium, de ipsis montibus, speluncis, ac saltibus continuè rebellabant; et tum primùm inimicis – strages dare cœperunt. And he has been followed in this, as he is most implicitly in every thing, by the ridiculous historian that is cited by Mr. Hume, the weak and unthinking Alured. Only the spoils, which the Caledonians are here said to carry home with them, are the donation of Mr. Hume. And an army that is routed and flying never takes its plunder along with it.

P. 15. "The Britains, taking advantage of this interval, returned to their usual occupations; and the favourable seasons, which succeeded, seconding their industry, made them soon forget all their past miseries, and restored to them great plenty of all the necessaries of life. No more can be imagined to have been possessed by a people so rude, who had not, without the assistance of the Romans, art of masonry sufficient to raise a stone rampart for their own defence: yet the monkish historians (Gildas, Bede lib. 1. cap. 14), who treat of those events, complain of the luxury of the Britains during this period, and ascribe to this vice, not to their cowardice or improvident councils, all their subsequent calamities."

Here is a gleam of thought, such as one naturally expects from an intellect like our author's, suddenly shooting across the darkness of the history, and throwing a faint light upon it. But it is as momentary as it is faint, and serves principally to make us regret the want of the same irradiation in a thousand parts of the work besides. And his thinking but indolent mind, fatigued by this little exertion, soon retires back into her cell, and reposes as soundly as she did before.

The plenty here is made commensurate in extent with the preceding famine, and carried over all the provinces. And the one is supposed to be caused by the progress of the invasion, and the other by the termination of it. But all this has been amply refuted before. And even the plenty here spoken of has been shewn, not to relate to the Provincials in general, but to a few of the Brigantes only, not to mean any exuberant harvests, that followed even in Brigantia upon the expulsion of the Caledonians, and merely to point out the abundance, to which the starving fugitives of the wilds were now restored.

But Mr. Hume, who so justly reprobates the declamations of Gildas and of Bede against the luxury of the Provincials, has here ascribed to them an opinion, which even their folly was incapable of admitting. He makes them refer all the subsequent calamities to the luxury of the Britons, instead of charging them upon their cowardice or improvidence. And yet they are not referred to the luxury by either, and are expressly attributed to their improvidence or infatuation by both. Omnes consiliarii, says Gildas of the great and radical occasion of their miseries, unà cum – Gurthrigerno Britamorum duce *cæcantur*, ut – Saxones – intromitterentur. And placuit omnibus, says Bede with all a Mr. Hume's adherence to his author, cum suo rege Vortigerno, ut Saxonum gentem – in auxilium vocarent; quod Domini nutu dispositum esse constat, ut veniret contra improbos malum.

 – "We are not exactly informed what species of civil government the Romans on their departure had left among them [the Britons]; but it appears probable, that the great men in the different districts assumed a kind of regal, though precarious, authority; and lived in a great measure independent of each other. To this disunion of councils were also added, &c."

What idea Mr. Hume had of the provinciating spirit of the Romans in Britain, we cannot pretend to say, because he has not thought proper to inform us. But, as in p. 3 of his work he has fixed a variety of monarchical governments among the original Britons, the consistency of history required him either to notice their removal or to find their continuance. Mr. Hume's mode of writing history, however, is very different. He describes the island partitioned into a multiplicity of kingdoms, at the Roman arrival. He speaks of no alteration made in this œconomy by the Romans. And yet, at their departure, he finds not a single king in the provinces. This shews evidently the carelessness, with which he wrote his few pages of our earlier history, and the inattentiveness with which he revised them afterwards.

But, though Mr. Hume discovers no kings where only twelve pages before he had left so many, he finds something like it in appearance and yet very unlike in reality, "the great men in the different districts assuming a kind of regal authority." These were evidently the lords of the clans, the seigniors or Uchelwyrs of the states, the only nobles within them. And Mr. Hume has borrowed the thought from Mr. Carte, and added to its original impropriety by mistaking it. Throughout his whole account of the Britons, and in this part of it especially, Mr. Carte has confounded a clan and a kingdom together, and a chief of the one with a sovereign of the other. So in page 179 he observes, that "the power of the nation naturally reverted to the heirs of the British *chieftains*, who had enjoyed it before the Roman conquest –; but the pretensions of various persons to the *headship* of particular *clans and nations* could not fail of producing broils." And the same confusion appears in p. 77, 78, 80, 87, 93, &c. 189, 190, &c. A nation is an aggregate of clans. And a king is the sovereign over many chieftains. Mr. Carte however, as appears plain in the quotation above, means a kingdom by a clan and a monarch by the chief of it. But Mr. Hume in copying him has interpreted his words literally, and supposed them to mean a mere clan and a mere chieftain. And this has induced him to plant the provinces with seigniories instead of kingdoms, and to stock them with lords instead of monarchs; though the tenour of his own history before, his declarations hereafter, and the suggestions of good sense, all concurred to warn him of his errour, and should have induced him to leave the country as he found it, under a variety of distinct sovereigns.

In following the course of Mr. Carte's ideas with regard to the internal regimen of the provinces at this period, Mr. Hume falls into all the gross contradictoriness about it, that I have previously noted in his author. And, though he supposes the country not to have a single monarch within it at present, and imagines every old kingdom to be broken into a variety of seigniories, and to have entirely lost its authority over them all; yet in the course of a few lines, with an amazing absence of thought, he talks of "Vortigern the prince of Dumnonium," as in p. 24 he does of "Arthur prince of the Silures," when the Silures and the Dumnonii were each of them a multiplicity of clans united under one sovereign. According to this representation, there was not a single king in the provinces, and yet Vortigern was one and Arthur another. There were nothing but seigniories in the country, and yet the Silures and Dumnonii were both under monarchies. And, to compleat the absurdity, these lords, who had no superior over them, were in some measure dependent on each other. "The great men in the different districts assumed a kind of regal – authority, and lived in a great measure independent of each other."

But we must leave this game, in order to fly at still greater. And if we examine our author's ideas more at large, concerning the present polity of the provinces, we shall see his contradictions rising upon us equally in magnitude and in number. Here in p. 15 he says, that the Britons were disunited, and had no other government than what the great men affirmed in their different districts. But, in the page immediately following, he affirms "Vortigern, prince of Dumnonium," to have "possessed the chief authority among them." Those, who had no government over any of their numerous tribes in the provinces, by the creative power of contradiction are immediately possest of a general one over the whole. But this is not all. In p. 19 Mr. Hume cancels this cancelling declaration, and raises again his subverted opinion of p. 15; by asserting even after the coming of the Saxons, that the Britons "had not yet acquired any union among themselves." And yet in the page directly succeeding he does as he did before, and again encounters his preceding declaration. He contradicts his own contradiction, and condemns his own condemnation, by recurring to the opinion that he has twice opposed, and again asserting Vortigern to be "the British leader." And from this office he affirms him to have been afterwards "deposed" (p. 20), but on the death of Vortimer "restored to the throne" (p. 21), and to have been followed in it by Ambrosius (p. 21), Nazan leod (p. 24), and Arthur (p. 24), and all this in a country, in which he has told us there was no authority higher than that of the seignior of a clan.

– "Menaced with a foreign invasion, the Britains attended only to the suggestions of their present fears, and following the councils of Vortigern prince of Dumnonium, who, though stained with every vice, possessed the chief authority among them, they sent into Germany a deputation to invite over the Saxons for their protection and assistance."

The two great assertions here have been fully refuted before, in the criticisms upon Mr. Carte. Mr. Hume paces so exactly at the heels of his master, that one well-urged thrust pierces them both at once. And I have shewn Vortigern not to have counselled the calling in of the Saxons, more than any other of the sovereigns, and a formal deputation to Germany to be all the dream of visionary history. Mr. Hume's asserting Vortigern to be prince of Dumnonium is a singular exertion of boldness in him, in so widely departing from the line of his director, who makes him the lord of a clan among the Silures. But Mr. Hume had better have followed Mr. Carte, mistaken as he is in this particular, than have left him for the company to which he has joined himself, the impertinent fabulists and chronologers of Wales and Cornwall. He would have been much nearer to the truth, if he had, since Vortigern was not prince of Dumnonium, as those writers sometimes denominate the kingdom of the Dumnonii, but, as I have shewn in the body of the work, the sovereign of the Dimatæ, a tribe adjoining to the Silures and immediately subject to them.

This prince, who was so unfortunate in his life, has been infinitely more so in the representations that have been made of him since. He has been highly abused by each succeeding historian. And all the woes of the Provincials, which were only the result of their own situation, the general disposition of affairs in Europe, and the natural timorousness of inexperience, have been wantonly ascribed to the conduct of Vortigern. That the Provincials themselves should do this, in the agony of their own sufferings at first should be unable to discern the true cause of them, and in their ignorance of incidents afterward should refer them to an imaginary Rowena, a visionary massacre at Stonehenge, and the weakness and wickedness of Vortigern, as the cause of both; is not to be wondered at. But how comes the later historian to be agitated with their passions, and to deal in their virulence? It arises from a principle, I fear, of which we have too many proofs in the recenter parts of our history especially,[1]

---

[1] In Mrs. Macaulay, &c.

not to be well acquainted with its tendency and ashamed of its operations. The spirit of vulgarity has often stained the pages of our national annals. And the insolence of meanness is frequently discharging itself in rancour upon the heads of our unfortunate sovereigns. With both, the miserable are always guilty. But it is time for history to vindicate her own dignity, to rise superiour to the passions of the populace, and generously interpose in protection of abused innocence. And let us extend the favour even to Vortigern, and candidly examine the charges against him. Gildas is too much lost in his generalities, to be very specifick upon any point: yet, incidentally mentioning Vortigern in the course of his petty work, he calls him a *superbus tyrannus*, which in his embossed style, I apprehend, may mean either a proud tyrant or a great king. But Nennius or his enlarger is more particular and more rancorous. He represents him as under the immediate influence of the devil, and therefore falling in love with the fair daughter of Hengist, giving Kent as the marriage-present for her, and actually marrying and bedding her (c. 36). He also represents him afterwards as marrying his own daughter, having a son by her, and being excommunicated for the fact (c. 38). And he finally describes him siding with the Saxons (c. 45), and even practising magick (c. 40–43). Such are the charges produced even by the hand of malignity against him. They sufficiently bespeak their own absurdity. And yet Mr. Hume has been thoughtless enough to listen with Malmesbury (fol. 3) to these ridiculous surmises, credulous enough to adopt them in their full amount, and even so unfair as to improve upon them, and describe Vortigern as "stained with every vice."

P. 19. Hengist and Horsa "embarked their troops in three vessels, and about the years 449 or 450 carried over 1600 men, who landed in the isle of Thanet, and immediately marched to the defence of the Britains against the northern invaders."

Mr. Carte states the number of men, as *computed by some* to be 1500 (p. 192). Mr. Hume more decisively asserts it to be actually so, and by mistake puts 1600 for it. But there is no authority for either, that is worthy our attention. Mr. Hume also, like Mr. Carte (p. 193), afterwards brings over 5000 more (p. 20) with as little authority. And, if three ships contained 1500 men, eighteen, as Mr. Carte numbers them, or seventeen, to which Mr. Hume has justly reduced them, should upon every principle of proportion contain no less than 8 or 9000.

As to the Saxons marching immediately after their arrival against the enemy, I have already shewn it to be untrue. They appear to have landed before the winter, and to have marched against the Caledonians the spring or summer following; and, though I love not to quote a secondary authority upon a point that is sufficiently spoken to by a primary one, and to produce Bede, Malmesbury, or Huntingdon when Gildas or Nennius are the original historians; yet it is worth while to observe, how strikingly Malmesbury's account agrees with mine before. Venientibus Anglis, undique occursum; a rege impertitæ gratiæ, a populo effuses favor, datâ fide acceptâque, et traditâ Thanatos insulâ incolatui eorum, subventum. Accessit et pactum, ut illi invictis umbonibus sudores suos patriæ impenderent, recepturi emolumenta militiæ ab his quorum saluti vigilias prætenderent. Paululum in medio moræ, et ecce Scotos, &c.

P. 27. "The Britains under the Roman dominion, had made such advances towards arts and civil manners, that they had built twenty-eight considerable cities within their provinces, besides a great number of villages and country seats (Gildas, Bede lib. 1.). But the fierce conquerors, by whom they were now subdued, threw every thing back into antient barbarity."

To give a compleat view of Mr. Hume's ideas of the state of the provinces under the Romans, let us go back three or four centuries in the history, and see what he has observed concerning the well-known conduct of Agricola before. And he says thus of him: "He introduced laws and civility among the Britains, taught them to desire and raise all the conveniences of life," and "instructed them in letters and sciences" (p. 9–10).

These are the only parts of Mr. Hume's history, which give us any ideas concerning the introduction and the progress of civility in the provinces. So inattentive has he been throughout the whole of the British annals, to the first great business of an historian. And the distinct though general description, which he has here given us, is at once trifling in its amount, inaccurate in its narration, and contradictory to his own account before. So unjust has he been equally to himself and the truth.

I have already shewn Nennius and Gildas to be actually contemporary authors, the one writing about 550 and the other about 564. And it appears upon a collation of their notices, so far as they relate to the same transactions, that they both copied several parts of their accounts from one and the same original. Thus Nennius says of Britain, sunt – duo flumina præclariora cæteris fluminibus, Tamisia et Severna, quæ duo brachia Britanniæ, per quæ olim rates vehebantur ad deportandas divitias causâ negotiationis (c. 2); and Gildas, that it is vallata duum ostiis nobilium, Thamesis ac Sabrinæ, fluminum, per quæ eidem olim transmarinæ delitiæ ratibus vehebantur (c. 1). So all the wild account of Gildas in the 12th, 13th, 14th, and 15th chapters, is told also in the 27th and 28th of Nennius. And chapter the 1st of the latter has these words, In eâ sunt 28 civitates – cum innumeris castellis, and chapter the second of the former these, Bis denis bisque quaternis civitatibus ac nonnullis castellis – decorata. These towns, we see, are expressly denominated civitates by both, and were therefore cities or towns of superiour rank, in contradistinction to many others, which are plainly supposed to exist, and are only omitted as inferiour. And Mr. Hume has accordingly called them "considerable cities." But he has precluded himself from the interpretation that so evidently lies for his authors, by mentioning the construction of so many cities "besides villages and country seats." And he has thus fixed twenty-eight to be the number of all the real towns in the provinces. How trifling this number is in comparison with the true one, the reader will readily perceive, when he reflects on what I have observed in the preceding Book, ch. 8 sect. 1, that at the close of the first century there were no less than a hundred and forty towns betwixt the Friths and the Channel. Of these there were ninety-two pre-eminent over the rest, and thirty-three that ranked superiour to the whole (Richard p. 36). And this representation gives us some adequate idea of the great civilization of the Britons and the high cultivation of their country, while Mr. Hume's appears petty, poor, and unjust.

Mr. Hume, however, has added a number of villages and country-seats. But of these neither Gildas nor Nennius knew any thing, whatever Mr. Hume might. The former speaks of twenty-eight towns cum nonnullis castellis, and the latter, cum innumeris castellis. And Bede, who copies Gildas here with his usual obsequiousness, has also transcribed one particular of his account from Nennius, an author whom he has been hitherto supposed not to have known. Erat et civitatibus quondam viginti et octo nobilissimis insignita, præter castella innumera (c. i). Mr. Hume has translated the *innumera* of Nennius and Bede, and the *nonnulla* of Gildas, in a kind of middle way betwixt both, by the words *a great number*. And he has changed the castles of all three into villages and country-seats.

But this inaccuracy, gross as it is, is exceeded by a much grosser. And our author's declarations, concerning the state of civility among the Britons, appear in an absolute contradiction to each other. He says expressly here, that "the Britains, under the Roman dominion, had made such advances towards arts and civil manners, that they had built twenty-eight considerable cities within their province, besides a great number of villages and country-seats," when the Saxons came and threw all back into antient barbarity. And in p. 9 he observes, that Agricola "taught them to desire and raise all the conveniencies of life;" by which he means, as his author expressly specifies, the erection of temples, the construction of market-places, and the building of porticos, baths, and private houses. But he tells us in p. 15, betwixt and in equal opposition to both, that at the departure of the Romans, and *before* the Saxons came into the island, the Provincials were "a people so rude, that they had not, without the assistance of the Romans, art of masonry sufficient to raise a stone rampart for their own defence." How are these positions to be received? Shall we take the two extremes, and leave unnoticed the middle? Or shall we take the middle, which has so many facts appendant to it, and reject the others, which have none? Or shall we rather, with Mr. Hume, unite them all together and form them into one system? But this is impossible to be done. For how could *they* build country-seats, who were too ignorant to erect even a wall of stone? Or could they, notwithstanding this, do more? Could they even construct villages, when they were so uncivilized as not to know the common principles of masonry? And could they yet do infinitely more than all this? Could they rear a great number of both, even adorn their country with eight and twenty considerable cities, and even embellish these with "all the conveniences of life," temples, market-places, baths, and porticos, and yet be incapable of making a rampart of any other materials than turf?

It gives me pain to lay open such glaring inconsistencies as these, the natural effusion of unsettled principles and inattentive spirits. And it pains me the more, as Mr. Hume deserves so well from the historical world, and stands so respectable there for that first of all literary qualities, the power of thought. But there is a justice that every writer owes to himself, to the publick, and to truth. And Mr. Hume owes it to all, I think, to revise these early parts of his history immediately; by a more diligent attention to the old historians, to rectify the errours which now mislead his readers; by a more manly consideration of the course of the history, to remove the unmeaningness, the equal child of ignorance and fear, which sheds a sleepy insipidity over it; and, by a more rigorous examination of his own ideas, to reconcile the contradictions which perplex his narrative and entangle his reflections; that he, who has been ranked for years at the head of our national historians, may not seem to be placed there by the momentary wantonness of fashion; that the man, who in the regions of theology has shewn a bold activity of spirit and a wild originality of sentiment, should not meanly truckle to be the copyer of Mr. Carte in history; and that the writer, who in many parts of our annals has no superiour and in some no equal, should not be content to appear in others, appear even to the eye of friendship, too hasty to be accurate, too indolent to be authentick, and too unthinking to be even consistent.

24
JOHN OGILVIE

John Ogilvie, *Philosophical and critical observations on the nature, characters and various species of composition. By John Ogilvie, D.D. In two volumes.* London: printed for G. Robinson, 1774, 2 v.
Note to Volume 1, Section 4 (pp. 206–208); from 1774 edition.

Scottish clergyman John Ogilvie (1733–1814) was a minister for 55 years, and the author of several books on poetry, rhetoric, and theology. Ogilvie is best known in Hume scholarship for his *Inquiry into the Causes of Infidelity* (1783), which attacks various aspects of Hume's philosophy. His earlier *Philosophical and Critical Observations* (1774) is a work on rhetoric that discusses several methods of composition. In a section entitled "Of Penetration or Discernment, as it regards Composition," Ogilvie contrasts rational with imaginative approaches to composition, and, in a note to his discussion, he shows how Rapin and Hume use these techniques in their respective histories. According to Ogilvie, Rapin is rational, but "tedious and uninteresting." By contrast, Hume's imaginative approach paints an environmental context in which "the observations that are happily thrown into the narration without *breaking* it, form altogether an highly interesting exhibition."
The *Critical Review* commended Ogilvie's insight into human thinking:

Literary composition has employed the pens of the most eminent ancient and modern critics, but has never been treated more scientifically than in the elaborate production now before us. Not content with drawing his observations from examples, the author as ascended to the sources of intellectual sensation, and developed the influence of the several faculties of the mind, both separately and when combined, on the art which is the subject of his enquiry. [*Critical Review*, August 1774, Vol. 38, pp. 81–89, September, pp. 187–194]

Writing for the *Monthly Review*, John Langhorne was more neutral and suggested that the last portion of Ogilvie's work, which is less theoretical and abstract, will be "more useful and engaging" (October 1774, Vol. 51, pp. 249–254). William Baron, in the *Edinburgh Magazine and Review* criticizes Ogilvie's work for its poor organization and manner of expression:

His division and account of the faculties of the mind are whimsical and unsatisfactory. What he calls the faculty of discernment, in particular, and the use he makes of it, appear to us to be replete with absurdity.

The language in which he expresses himself is in many respects faulty. The sentences are generally too long and involved, void of harmony and variety; the arrangement is inverted and embarrassed, and loaded with a number of trivial circumstances, that obscure, but illustrate not the sense. He is now pompous and vulgar, now quaint and uncouth. [*Edinburgh Magazine and Review*, May 1774, Vol. 2, pp. 484–489]

In 1779, under a Dublin imprint, a reissue appeared with cancel title pages of the 1774 London edition of Ogilvie's *Philosophical and Critical Observations*. The work was not again republished. The following is from the 1774 London edition.

VOLUME 1.
SECTION IV.
Of Penetration, or Discernment, as it regards Composition.

...

The illustrious Roman orator and philosopher has wrote a treatise entitled, De Natura Deorum, which has reached the present times. The same subject is treated by Phurnutus, a Greek philosopher, who explains very succinctly, and at the same time with much perspicuity, the various parts of nature which the deities represented. Yet the first of these (though not the most shining of Cicero's writings) is universally known: the last is as much neglected. The reason is, that the Roman, who is formed in a great measure upon the Athenian philosopher formerly referred to, rangeth his diversified materials in such a manner as that these throw mutual light upon each other; and by going out of his way as it might seem, upon some occasions, to bring illustrations of his sentiments, he keeps attention always awake while a succession of pleasing ideas passeth before the imagination. The other, on the contrary, just dispatcheth his business in the fewest words, and without taking any compass to give a beautiful variety to his Composition, pursues one topic with the same uniform brevity, and after he hath finished a former.

What shall we say of these writers when thus compared together? – That the last mentioned treats his subject like a man of understanding, who comprehends and unfolds it with perspicuity. But the former are *discerning* judges of human nature, who keep in their eye the complicated qualities of which characters are formed; and in order to accomplish a purpose with one of these effectually, judge it proper to have recourse alternately to each.

{[Note:] It is the same in history as in philosophy. The man of judgment will relate facts with great perspicuity, and will accompany these with solid and edifying observations. But there is a method of instructing and fatiguing the mind at the same time; and where these two accompany each other, the sphere of the former must be very much contracted. This happens when there is an uniform recital of facts and observations drawn from these regularly carried on; the marks always succeeding the narration of events periodically, instead of being happily interwoven with it, so as to grow as it were out of the action, and to be pursued no farther than as it serves for illustration. Among modern historians who have fixed on the same general subject, Rapin and Hume are the historians of England. The first is a circumstantial and judicious writer, whose relation of facts is both distinct and particular; and whose observations on these are usually just and natural. In perusing his extensive work we find one uniform method invariably pursued. The transactions are first related at full length. The remarks on these are commonly placed by themselves likewise, so that the reader is never at a loss in the narration to know what will be the strain of a whole paragraph, unmixed with incidental sentiment or illustration, by casting his eye on the margin. This stiff method of procedure renders this valuable work tedious and uninteresting to readers who desire to be entertained as well as edified in reading history, and who neglect the *useful* when the *agreeable* is not united with it. The detail of events in Hume's History (which taken altogether is, in the author's opinion, one of the most complete performances of its kind) is much more concise. But he fixeth with great propriety upon circumstances that render us acquainted at once with the manners of the times and with the characters of the principal personages. These, in consequence of their own importance, and of the observations that are happily thrown into the narration without *breaking* it, form altogether an highly interesting exhibition. We are pleased with the historian's arrangement of such various materials, as well as with their selection, and consider the end of history as accomplished by the whole. The inference deducible here with regard to the *judgment* of one writer and the *discernment* of the other, is too obvious upon the principles laid down in this work to be particularly insisted on.}

25
JOHN CURRY

John Curry, *An historical and critical review of the civil wars in Ireland, from the reign of Queen Elizabeth, to the settlement under King William. Extracted from Parliamentary records, state acts, and other authentic materials. By J. C. M.D.* Dublin: printed and sold by J. Hoey, and T. T. Faulkner; G. Burnet; and J. Morris, 1775, [4], xxi, [3], 447, [7] p.
Selections from Introduction and 5.7; from 1775 edition.

John Curry (d. 1780) was an Irish Catholic physician, and author of several medical works on the subject of fevers and historical works on various Irish uprisings. Curry's first work, *A Brief Account... of the Irish Rebellion* (1747), draws from Protestant writers on the Irish massacre who suggest that Protestants themselves are to share in the blame for the tragedy. Curry continues this theme in *Historical Memoirs of the Irish Rebellion in the Year, 1641* (1758), a copy of which he mailed to Hume in 1764. The work was successful and went through five editions over the next 12 years. In 1771 Curry published *Observations on the Popery Laws*, which discusses the laws against Catholicism enacted by Queen Anne in 1704. In this work Curry cites "the profound historian Mr. Hume" regarding Catholic loyalty to the Monarchy. In 1775, Curry's *An Historical and Critical Review* appeared, a work that defends the role of Irish Catholics in Irish uprisings from 1569 to 1697. Discussions of Hume appear in the Introduction and Book 5. The Introduction was written by someone other than Curry, and the anonymous author in fact criticizes Curry for not having more strongly exposed the falsehoods of recent accounts of Irish struggles. He thus supplies some criticism himself, taking Hume to task for his misrepresentations. In Book 5 Curry criticizes Hume for relying on John Temple's gross distortion of the events. Curry believes that the Parliamentary documents included in his book supplies ample evidence for Hume to reject Temple's account.

The most important feature of Curry's comments on Hume is the inclusion of a footnote that contains portions of a letter from Hume to Curry – the original of which has not yet surfaced.[1] The letter fragment probably consti-

---

[1] If the original manuscript of Hume's letter exists, it may be among the possessions of Charles O'Conor, the executor of Curry's papers after his death. The letter is not included in *Letters of David Hume* or *New Letters of David Hume*, but has been transcribed from Curry in a recent journal article.

tutes the substance of Hume's letter. Curry's comments in the footnote indicate that Hume and Curry were not previously acquainted, and consequently the correspondence exchange would not likely have included personal information. The purpose of Hume's letter would have been to acknowledge the presentation copy of Curry's *Historical Memoirs*, and to respond to Curry's request for Hume to revise the relevant parts of his *History*. The first of these tasks, which would have been brief, is missing from Hume's letter. The second of these tasks is probably addressed in its entirety within the surviving letter. Given Hume's disclaimer that, "I am here at such a distance from my authorities, that I cannot produce all the arguments which determined me to give the account you complain of," little else could be said other than what Hume presents. What we lose by having only a truncated version of Hume's letter, we gain in terms of the background that Curry himself provides. Curry initiated the exchange, and his motives are clearly presented. The year "1764" cited by Curry is almost certainly accurate. First, this date corresponds with the dates during which Hume was in France (1763 to 1766), and Curry's account of Hume's purpose for being in France at this time is remarkably accurate. Second, Hume's correspondences are usually dated, and Curry clearly had Hume's letter in hand when penning the above footnote.

The significance of Hume's letter to Curry is that Hume did not feel obligated to re-evaluate Temple's testimony as Curry hoped. Since, Hume says, he was without access to his original sources, he relied on the integrity of his initial assessment: "I only remember I sought truth, and thought I found it." Hume's failure to change his account of the rebellion in subsequent editions of the *History* suggests that Curry's evidence against Temple's testimony carried little weight for Hume.

Ralph Griffiths favourably reviewed Curry's *Historical and Critical Review* in the *Monthly Review* and applauded Curry's attempts at impartiality:

> The Author of the elaborate work before us does not seem to have entered this field of controversy, armed with the weapons of religious bigotry and party prejudice. He appears to be a moderate, sensible, and philosophic inquirer after truth, though not destitute of zeal for that Church in behalf of which he has employed his researches and his pen: and he professes to have intended his work rather to 'conciliate than irritate;' to 'instruct, not to misrepresent.'

As to the Introduction Griffiths concludes that Hume is "perhaps not unjustly, censured." Griffiths quotes Curry's footnote from Book 5, which he prefaces with the following:

> Mr. Hume is not *now* alive, to render that justice to the Roman Catholics, which this Writer apprehends to be their due; but, we are informed, he has

left behind him a corrected copy of his History, in order to a new impression, with the Author's last improvements. When that edition shall appear, it will then be seen what effect was produced by a certain application to Mr. Hume; of which Dr. Curry has, in this Historical Review, given us the following anecdote... [*Monthly Review*, December 1776, Vol. 55, pp. 444–453]

Curry's *Historical and Critical Review* was published again in 1786, 1793, and 1810. The following is from the 1775 edition of that work.

INTRODUCTION

Had the learned Author of the following Review, proposed to himself no other end, than to detect the misrepresentations of contemporary writers, who derived an interest from the circulation of false history, his service to the public would not be deemed inconsiderable. His merit would be still greater, had he sat down professedly, to expose the mistakes of other less interested, but more dangerous writers, who have gained reputation from genius, and authority from rank, to give a currency to false facts, and to pronounced false judgments on the true. His merit in both these cases, is indeed clear; but it is secondary to a nobler object. ...

The Earl of Clarendon has left us an account of those times in the style rather of a pleader, than an historian. He was doubtless a nobleman of great abilities, but very unjust to the Irish nation. In representations anticipated by spiritual hatred and national prejudices, this man of strength, resigns all his vigour. No longer master of his subject, he yields himself up a willing captive, to such informations as were correspondent to his prior ideas of the people he undertakes to describe. He appears to have been incapable of receiving second impressions, and we can hardly on this account, charge him with delivering us a conscious untruth. History in such hands is neither better nor worse, than what the writer is enabled to make it, according to the degree of his partiality or aversion; and he must have little knowledge of men, who knows not, that this species of human infirmity, is but too often an ingredient in some of the best, as it always is in the worst characters, with whom the infirmity ends in vice. In the best, it resembles a cancerous excrescence on a beautiful face, and grows but too often out of our fairest principle, that of religion, from which it should, if possible, be rooted. Were religious indifferences useful in any instance, it would be in this before us, where the more a man is lukewarm in religious party-zeal, the nearer he approaches to the character of a true patriot and good citizen. But there is strength of mind superior to religious indifference itself, which gives all the qualifications necessary to constitute a good man, and judicious historian. This strength the Earl of Clarendon and other great men

(Protestants and Papists) wanted, and still want. As painters of former times, they may give a good likeness: as contemporaries they are intolerable; of all men the most likely to be deceived, and the more laborious to deceive. The mischief they circulate is in proportion to their abilities, and that rank in like, which render those abilities conspicuous.

It is, indeed, to be lamented, that Mr. Hume, one of the ablest writers of the present age, should as an historian suffer himself to be so far led astray by such contemporaries as we have hinted at, as to transfer all or most of the mischiefs of the year 1641 in Ireland, from the original authors, to the unfortunate Irish alone. Parties less aggrieved in Scotland were up before them, and drew the sword not only with impunity but with advantage. The Irish in Ulster who wanted to regain the lands they lost, followed the example. We do not justify the act in either kingdom. We only advance the alleviation of the Irish crime, that the majority of the nation have, in the two reigns of James and Charles, suffered a cruel bondage of thirty eight years with little intermission, and had now the most alarming prospect of extirpation before them. They did not mean to withdraw their allegiance from the King; even the weak leaders of the Northern rabble had no such intention. The latter began, and acted singly. Their outrages on their first setting out were kept within some bounds; most of the innocent Protestants in the neighbouring districts had time to escape into places of security, before many murders were committed. The Papists in the other provinces had no share in their guilt; they immediately published their detestation of it.

In general, they were steady to their duty as christians, and to their loyalty as subjects. They in their own defence took up arms, not against the King, but against the King's enemies, who announced their excision in public resolutions, and parliamentary votes. This is the truth of the fact. Mr. Hume passes it over as of no importance to the subject of his history.

He appears to have sat down with an intention to cure us of our unhappy-party prejudices, by pointing out their terrible consequences, in the last age, of our conduct as legislators, and our feelings as men. In general his observations are admirable, and stand in the place of excellent instructions, enforced by striking examples. His mistakes at the same time are hurtful, and a wound from such a hand must be painful. But happily it cannot be mortal, in the case before us, as abundant materials of true information are still preserved entire. The documents in the following Review will shew that Mr. Hume's representation of Irish affairs in 1641, is not true history, but fine and pathetic writing. Pity it is, to find such a man adopting the untruths of Sir John Temple, and spreading them on a new canvas heightened with all the colourings of his art. The piece has certainly cost him some labour; for horror and pity are wrought up here in high tragical strains. But the Irish certainly have not sat for the picture; and Mr. Hume in this part of his history must admit the justness of a charge, that he has given a wrong direction to the passions, he has taken so much pains to excite.

Mr. Hume is still alive to review and correct some mistakes in his history; and should he decline doing justice in the case before us (what must not be supposed) he, and not truth, will be affected.

...

BOOK V.

CHAP. VII.

The Humanity of the Chiefs of the Insurgents.

Mr. Hume, strangely misled by Temple's stupid legend, (for I will not suspect him of conscious misrepresentation,) asserts in a style better suited to romance than history, that, "an universal massacre of the English commenced with this insurrection;[2] that no age, no sex, no condition, was spared; that destruction was every where let loose, and met the hunted victims, at every turn; that all connections were dissolved, and the death was dealt by that hand, from which protection was implored, and expected." In short, "that, without provocation, without opposition,[3] the astonished English were massacred by their nearest neighbours, with whom they had long upheld a continued intercourse of kindness, and good offices." Not content with imputing these, and many other, if possible, greater barbarities, to the first insurgents, he confidently affirms, on the same exploded authority, "that the English Catholics of the pale, joining these old Irish, rivalled them in every act of cruelty, towards the English Protestants." Thus, the grossest, and most palpable fictions, which, when stupidly retailed by a noted and malicious libeller, have little or no chance to be believed by any, may yet be afterwards dressed out by a more artful writer, in such plausible colours, and with such semblance of truth, as will render them credible and affecting, even to some readers, of a moderate share of understanding. What a pity it is, that in all this historian's fine declamation on this tragical event, there is so very little of its true history to be found.

---

[2] Hist. of England, Dub. ed. vol. iv.

[3] This demonstrates a strange unacquaintedness in this writer, even with those historians, some of whose prejudices he has all along adopted in this part of his history. For to omit other instances, Borlace has given us a journal of Sir William Cole's services against the insurgents, wherein it is boastingly asserted, "that, from the 23d of October, 1641, to some time in 1642, the said Sir William killed with his regiment of 500 foot, and one troop of horse, 2417 swordsmen of the rebels; and starved and famished, of the vulgar sort, (whose goods were seized on by the regiment,) 7000. And that he rescued and relieved 5467 Scotch and English Protestants." Borlace adds, "after this rate the English in all parts fought." Hist. of the Irish Rebel. fol. 112. Colonel Gibson having taken the strong castle of Caric-main, belonging to the Walshes, near Dublin, in which several hundreds of the Irish had taken refuge, "put them all to the sword, sparing neither man, woman, nor child." Id. ib. fol. 97. Numbers of such instances of barbarous, and indiscriminate opposition and revenge, are to be met with in all the adverse writers on this subject.

{[Note:] In the year 1764, a copy of the historical memoirs of the Irish rebellion, wherein all these calumnies are clearly refuted by unquestionable authority, was sent to Mr. Hume, when Secretary of the embassy at Paris, under Lord Hertford, in hopes of inducing him to correct these flagrant, and injurious mistakes, in a subsequent edition of his history. But the expected effect has not since appeared. He, indeed, returned a polite but evasive answer, on that occasion, in which he says, "I am here at such a distance from my authorities, that I cannot produce all the arguments which determined me to give the account you complain of, with regard to the Irish massacre. I only remember I sought truth, and thought I found it. The insurrection might be excused, as having liberty for its object. The violence also, of the puritanical parliament, struck a just terror into all the Catholics. But the method of conducting the rebellion, if we must call it by that name, was certainly such (and you seem to own it) as deserved the highest blame, and was one of the most violent efforts of barbarism and bigotry united." The authorities sent to him in the memoirs above-mentioned, demonstrating his mistakes, are by both parties confessed to be undeniable. And indeed, it appears from the softer style of this letter, that since the writing of his history, he has abated somewhat of his declamatory virulence with respect to those insurgents, probably from the perusal of these authorities.}

In truth, the Irish engaged in this war, did not suffer more in their persons, by the swords of their enemies, while it was carrying on, than they have since done, in their characters, by the pens of some of those historians, who have either carelessly or maliciously commented upon it. The best, the noblest, and most loyal men in the kingdom, who, after having patiently endured numberless galling injuries and oppressions, were, at last, driven to the fatal necessity of taking arms in their defence, are confounded by these libellers, with the meanest of the Irish rabble, who followed them meerly for plunder. But I will now, from a motive of meer justice, produce a few signal instances out of many, of the humane and christian behaviour of some of the chiefs of these insurgents, towards such of those English and Protestants, as happened to fall under their power. And this I shall do, not from writers of their own party, or persuasion, but from such adverse historians, as have otherwise too hastily condemned all their constrained efforts of natural self-defence, as so many overt acts of treason, and rebellion.

...

26
ADAM SMITH

An inquiry into the nature and causes of the wealth of nations. London, W.
Strahan and T. Cadell, 1776, 2 v.
Selections from 5.i.g.; from 1784 edition.

Born in Kirkcaldy, Fife, Scotland, Adam Smith (1723–1790) attended
Glasgow college, where he was a student of Francis Hutcheson, and later
Balliol College, Oxford. Briefly delivering public lectures at Edinburgh
University, he was appointed professor of Logic at Glasgow in 1751, and a year
later was transferred to the chair of moral philosophy. Taking a lucrative job
as a tutor, he resigned this position in 1763, which was subsequently filled by
Thomas Reid. Smith's two principal works are his *Theory of Moral Sentiments*
(1759) and *Inquiry into the Nature and Causes of the Wealth of Nations*
(1776), both of which contain comments on Hume (see *Early Responses to
Hume's Moral Theory* for his critique of Hume's view of utility). Smith met
Hume around 1748 while in Edinburgh, and remained one of Hume's closest
friends until Hume's death in 1776. He is best known in Hume scholarship for
his letter to William Strahan concerning Hume's final days, which was
published along with Hume's "My Own Life". Smith shared many of Hume's
views, as is reflected in the following:

> [Smith] is a very unprejudiced and good man I see him every week at least
> once, and we are upon a very friendly footing together; he was an intimate
> friend of the late David Hume and has the same principles. [François Xavier
> Swediauer to Jeremey Bentham, September 14, 1784][1]

In Chapter 29 of the *History*, Hume argues in favour of state-controlled
religion. He recognizes that businesses will thrive in an environment of liberty,
insofar as they will increase their "skill and industry" in response to consumer
demands. However, he argues that granting free rein to religion will only
generate superstition and fanaticism, as the clergy sensationalize their message

---

[1] The Correspondence of Jeremy Bentham, Volume 3 (London: University of London,
The Athlone Press, 1971).

"to prevent their flock from straying in quest of new pastures." In 5.i.g., Smith opposes Hume's position. He argues that the zeal of the clergy will adversely affect religion only when there are just a handful of religious denominations. However, when there are hundreds or thousands of sects, many clergy will see that zeal is fruitless and instead learn "candour and moderation." Eventually, he thinks, these sects may evolve into a "pure and rational religion, free from every mixture of absurdity, imposture, or fanaticism." Although some clergy will retain their zeal, he believes that it will be harmless, especially if those sects subdivide into tinier units. Also, smaller sects tend to preserve common morality in an orderly fashion. Nevertheless, Smith feels that, with minimal intrusion, the state may guard against possible abuses of religion in two ways. First, the state may mandate "the study of science and philosophy" for people of middle rank, since "Science is the great antidote to the poison of enthusiasm and superstition." Second, the state may encourage artistic and cultural activities, which will divert people away from fanaticism. State religions, he argues, create special problems since they may act in direct opposition to the sovereign, and are of sufficient power even to instigate the overthrow of a monarch.

After the *Wealth of Nations* appeared, Hume wrote to Smith commending his work:

Euge! Belle! Dear Mr Smith: I am much pleas'd with your Performance; and the Perusal of it has taken me from a State of great Anxiety. It was a Work of so much Expectation, by yourself, by your Friends, and by the Public, that I trembled for its Appearance; but am now much relieved. Not but that the Reading of it necessarily requires so much Attention, and the Public is disposed to give so little, that I shall still doubt for some time of its being at first very popular: But it has Depth and Solidity and Acuteness, and is so much illustrated by curious Facts, that it must at last take the public Attention. It is probably much improved by your last Abode in London. If you were here at my Fireside, I shoud dispute some of your Principles. [Hume to Adam Smith, April 1, 1776]

The reviews of Smith's *Wealth of Nations* were unanimously favourable.[2] For example, in the *Monthly Review* William Enfield praises the content of Smith's work, although he is more reserved about its style:

The style and composition of this work, though suited to the subject, and except in a few instances sufficiently correct, is by no means its principal

---

[2]   *Critical Review*, 1776, Vol. 41 pp. 193–200, 258–264, 361–369, 425–433; *Edinburgh Magazine and Review*, 1776, Vol. 5, pp. 411–419; *London Review*, March 1776, Vol. 3, pp. 177–187, 271–277; *Monthly Review*, April 1776, Vol. 54, pp. 299–308, Vol. 55, July, pp. 15–25, August, pp. 81–92; *Annual Register*, 1776, Vol. 19, p. 341.

excellence. Its merit is of an higher order, and arises chiefly from the depth and accuracy with which the Author has investigated a subject of so complex and intricate a nature, from the truth of the principles which he has established, and from the importance and utility of the conclusions which he has enabled his readers to deduce. [*Monthly Review*, 1776, Vol. 54, pp. 299–308]

Smith revised his *Wealth of Nations* in a second edition of 1778 and a third edition of 1784.[3] The selection here follows the third edition, which contains no substantial changes from the first two.

ARTICLE III
Of the Expense of the Institutions for the Instruction of People of all Ages

The institutions for the instruction of people of all ages are chiefly those for religious instruction. This is a species of instruction of which the object is not so much to render the people good citizens in this world, as to prepare them for another and a better world in a life to come. The teachers of the doctrine which contains this instruction, in the same manner as other teachers, may either depend altogether for their subsistence upon the voluntary contributions of their hearers, or they may derive it from some other fund to which the law of their country may entitle them; such as a landed estate, a tythe or land tax, an established salary or stipend. Their exertion, their zeal and industry, are likely to be much greater in the former situation than in the latter. In this respect the teachers of new religions have always had a considerable advantage in attacking those ancient and established systems of which the clergy, reposing themselves upon their benefices, had neglected to keep up the fervour of faith and devotion in the great body of the people; and having given themselves up to indolence, were become altogether incapable of making any vigorous exertion in defence even of their own establishment. The clergy of an established and well-endowed religion frequently become men of learning and elegance, who possess all the virtues of gentlemen, or which can recommend them to the esteem of gentlemen: but they are apt gradually to lose the qualities, both good and bad, which gave them authority and influence with the inferior ranks of people, and which had perhaps been the original causes of the success and establishment of their religion. Such a clergy, when attacked by a set of popular and bold, though perhaps stupid and ignorant enthusiasts, feel

---

[3] For a discussion of the key editions of the *Wealth of Nations*, see William B. Todd's introduction in the Oxford University Press critical edition of the *Wealth of Nations* (1979), reprinted by Liberty Press (1981).

themselves as perfectly defenceless as the indolent, effeminate, and full-fed nations of the southern parts of Asia when they were invaded by the active, hardy, and hungry Tartars of the North. Such a clergy, upon such an emergency, have commonly no other resource than to call upon the civil magistrate to persecute, destroy, or drive out their adversaries, as disturbers of the public peace. It was thus that the Roman catholic clergy called upon the civil magistrate to persecute the protestants, and the church of england to persecute the Dissenters; and that in general every religious sect, when it has once enjoyed for a century or two the security of a legal establishment, has found itself incapable of making any vigorous defence against any new sect which chose to attack its doctrine or discipline. Upon such occasions the advantage in point of learning and good writing may sometimes be on the side of the established church. But the arts of popularity, all the arts of gaining proselytes, are constantly on the side of its adversaries. In England those arts have been long neglected by the well-endowed clergy of the established church, and are at present chiefly cultivated by the dissenters and by the methodists. The independent provisions, however, which in many places have been made for dissenting teachers, by means of voluntary subscriptions, of trust rights, and other evasions of the law, seem very much to have abated the zeal and activity of those teachers. They have many of them become very learned, ingenious, and respectable men; but they have in general ceased to be very popular preachers. The methodists, without half the learning of the dissenters, are much more in vogue.

   In the church of Rome, the industry and zeal of the inferior clergy is kept more alive by the powerful motive of self-interest than perhaps in any established protestant church. The parochial clergy derive, many of them, a very considerable part of their subsistence from the voluntary oblations of the people; a source of revenue which confession gives them many opportunities of improving. The mendicant orders derive their whole subsistence from such oblations. It is with them, as with the hussars and light infantry of some armies; no plunder, no pay. The parochial clergy are like those teachers whose reward depends partly upon their salary, and partly upon their fees or honoraries which they get from their pupils, and these must always depend more or less upon their industry and reputation. The mendicant orders are like those teachers whose subsistence depends altogether upon the industry. They are obliged, therefore, to use every art which can animate the devotion of the common people. The establishment of the two great mendicant orders of St. Dominick and St. Francis, it is observed by Machiavel, revived, in the thirteenth and fourteenth centuries, the languishing faith and devotion of the catholick church. In Roman catholick countries the spirit of devotion is supported altogether by the monks and by the poorer parochial clergy. The great dignitaries of the church, with all the accomplishments of gentlemen and men of the world, and sometimes with those of men of learning, are careful enough to maintain the necessary discipline over their inferiors, but seldom give themselves any trouble about the instruction of the people.

"Most of the arts and professions in a state," says by far the most illustrious philosopher and historian of the present age,

> "are of such a nature, that, while they promote the interests of the society, they are also useful or agreeable to some individuals; and in that case, the constant rule of the magistrate, except, perhaps on the first introduction of any art, is, to leave the profession to itself, and trust its encouragement to the individuals who reap the benefit of it. The artizans finding their profits to rise by the favour of their customers, increase, as much as possible, their skill and industry; and as matters are not disturbed by any injudicious tampering, the commodity is always sure to be at all times nearly proportioned to the demand.

> But there are also some callings, which, though useful and even necessary in a state, bring no advantage or pleasure to any individual, and the supreme power is obliged to alter its conduct with regard to the retainers of those professions. It must give them public encouragement in order to their subsistence, and it must provide against that negligence to which they will naturally be subject, either by annexing particular honours to the profession, by establishing a long subordination of ranks and a strict dependence, or by some other expedient. The persons employed in the finances, fleets, and magistracy, are instances of this order of men.

> It may naturally be thought, at first sight, that the ecclesiastics belong to the first class, and that their encouragement, as well as that of lawyers and physicians, may safely be entrusted to the liberality of individuals, who are attached to their doctrines, and who find benefit or consolation from their spiritual ministry and assistance. Their industry and vigilance will, no doubt, be whetted by such an additional motive; and their skill in the profession, as well as their address in governing the minds of the people, must receive daily increase, from their increasing practice, study, and attention.

> But if we consider the matter more closely, we shall find, that this interested diligence of the clergy is what every wise legislator will study to prevent; because, in every religion except the true, it is highly pernicious, and it has even a natural tendency to pervert the true, by infusing into it a strong mixture of superstition, folly, and delusion. Each ghostly practitioner, in order to render himself more precious and sacred in the eyes of his retainers, will inspire them with the most violent abhorrence of all other sects, and continually endeavour, by some novelty, to excite the languid devotion of his audience. No regard will be paid to truth, morals, or decency in the doctrines inculcated. Every tenet will be adopted that best suits the disorderly affections of the human frame. Customers will be drawn to each conventicle by new industry and address in practising on the passions and credulity of the

populace. And in the end, the civil magistrate will find, that he has dearly paid for his pretended frugality, in saving a fixed establishment for the priests; and that in reality the most decent and advantageous composition, which he can make with the spiritual guides, is to bribe their indolence, by assigning stated salaries to their profession, and rendering it superfluous for them to be farther active, than merely to prevent their flock from straying in quest of new pastures. And in this manner ecclesiastical establishments, though commonly they arose at first from religious views, prove in the end advantageous to the political interests of society."

But whatever may have been the good or bad effects of the independent provision of the clergy; it has, perhaps, been very seldom bestowed upon them from any view to those effects. Times of violent religious controversy have generally been times of equally violent political faction. Upon such occasions, each political party has either found it, or imagined it, for its interest, to league itself with some one or other of the contending religious sects. But this could be done only by adopting, or at least by favouring, the tenets of that particular sect. The sect which had the good fortune to be leagued with the conquering party, necessarily shared in the victory of its ally, by whose favour and protection it was soon enabled in some degree to silence and subdue all its adversaries. Those adversaries had generally leagued themselves with the enemies of the conquering party, and were therefore the enemies of that party. The clergy of this particular sect having thus become complete masters of the field, and their influence and authority with the great body of the people being in its highest vigour, they were powerful enough to overawe the chiefs and leaders of their own party, and to oblige the civil magistrate to respect their opinions and inclinations. Their first demand was generally, that he should silence and subdue all their adversaries: and their second, that he should bestow an independent provision on themselves. As they had generally contributed a good deal to the victory, it seemed not unreasonable that they should have some share in the spoil. They were weary, besides, of humouring the people, and of depending upon their caprice for a subsistence. In making this demand therefore they consulted their own ease and comfort, without troubling themselves about the effect which it might have in future times upon the influence and authority of their order. The civil magistrate, who could comply with this demand only by giving them something which he would have chosen much rather to take, or to keep to himself, was seldom very forward to grant it. Necessity, however, always forced him to submit at last, though frequently not till after many delays, evasions, and affected excuses.

But if politics had never called in the aid of religion, had the conquering party never adopted the tenets of one sect more than those of another, when it had gained the victory, it would probably have dealt equally and impartially with all the different sects, and have allowed every man to choose his own priest and his own religion as he thought proper. There would in this case, no doubt, have been a great multitude of religious sects. Almost every different congregation might probably have made a little sect by itself, or have entertained some peculiar tenets of its own. Each teacher would no doubt have felt himself under the necessity of making the utmost exertion, and of using every art both to preserve and to increase the number of his disciples. But as every other teacher would have felt himself under the same necessity, the success of no one teacher, or sect of teachers, could have been very great. The interested and active zeal of religious teachers can be dangerous and troublesome only where there is, either but one sect tolerated in the society, or where the whole of a large society is divided into two or three great sects; the teachers of each acting by concert, and under a regular discipline and subordination. But that zeal must be altogether innocent where the society is divided into two or three hundred, or perhaps into as many thousand small sects, of which no one could be considerable enough to disturb the public, tranquillity. The teachers of each sect, seeing themselves surrounded on all sides with more adversaries than friends, would be obliged to learn that candour and moderation which is so seldom to be found among the teachers of those great sects, whose tenets, being supported by the civil magistrate, are held in veneration by almost all the inhabitants of extensive kingdoms and empires, and who therefore see nothing round them but followers, disciples, and humble admirers. The teachers of each little sect, finding themselves almost alone, would be obliged to respect those of almost every other sect, and the concessions which they would mutually find it both convenient and agreeable to make to one another, might in time probably reduce the doctrine of the greater part of them to that pure and rational religion, free from every mixture of absurdity, imposture, or fanaticism, such as wise men have in all ages of the world wished to see established; but such as positive law has perhaps never yet established, and probably never will establish in any country: because, with regard to religion, positive law always has been, and probably always will be, more or less influenced by popular superstition and enthusiasm. This plan of ecclesiastical government, or more properly of no ecclesiastical government, was what the sect called Independents, a sect no doubt of very wild enthusiasts, proposed to establish in England towards the end of the civil war. If it had been established, though of a very unphilosophical origin, it would probably by this time have been productive of the most philosophical good temper and moderation with regard to every sort of religious principle. It has been established in Pennsylvania, where, though the Quakers happen to be the most numerous, the law in reality favours no one sect more than another, and it is there said to have been productive of this philosophical good temper and moderation.

But though this equality of treatment should not be productive of this good temper and moderation in all, or even in the greater part of the religious sects of a particular country; yet provided those sects were sufficiently numerous, and each of them consequently too small to disturb the public tranquillity, the excessive zeal of each for its particular tenets could not well be productive of any very harmful effects, but, on the contrary, of several good ones: and if the government was perfectly decided both to let them all alone, and to oblige them all to let alone one another, there is little danger that they would not of their own accord subdivide themselves fast enough so as soon to become sufficiently numerous.

In every civilised society, in every society where the distinction of ranks has once been completely established, there have been always two different schemes or systems of morality current at the same time; of which the one may be called the strict or austere; the other the liberal, or, if you will, the loose system. The former is generally admired and revered by the common people: The latter is commonly more esteemed and adopted by what are called people of fashion. The degree of disapprobation with which we ought to mark the vices of levity, the vices which are apt to arise from great prosperity, and from the excess of gaiety and good humour, seems to constitute the principal distinction between those two opposite schemes or systems. In the liberal or loose system, luxury, wanton and even disorderly mirth, the pursuit of pleasure to some degree of intemperance, the breach of chastity, at least in one of the two sexes, etc. provided they are not accompanied with gross indecency, and do not lead to falsehood or injustice, are generally treated with a good deal of indulgence, and are easily either excused or pardoned altogether. In the austere system, on the contrary, those excesses are regarded with the utmost abhorrence and detestation. The vices of levity are always ruinous to the common people, and a single week's thoughtlessness and dissipation is often sufficient to undo a poor workman for ever, and to drive him through despair upon committing the most enormous crimes. The wiser and better sort of the common people, therefore, have always the utmost abhorrence and detestation of such excesses, which their experience tells them are so immediately fatal to people of their condition. The disorder and extravagance of several years, on the contrary, will not always ruin a man of fashion, and people of that rank are very apt to consider the power of indulging in some degree of excess as one of the advantages of their fortune, and the liberty of doing so without censure or reproach, as one of the privileges which belong to their station. In people of their own station, therefore, they regard such excesses with but a small degree of disapprobation, and censure them either very slightly or not at all.

Almost all religious sects have begun among the common people, from whom they have generally drawn their earliest as well as their most numerous proselytes. The austere system of morality has, accordingly, been adopted by those sects almost constantly, or with very few exceptions; for there have been some. It was the system by which they could best recommend themselves to that order of people to whom they first proposed their plan of reformation upon what had been before established. Many of them, perhaps the greater part of them, have even endeavoured to gain credit by refining upon this austere system, and by carrying it to some degree of folly and extravagance; and this excessive rigour has frequently recommended them more than anything else to the respect and veneration of the common people.

A man of rank and fortune is by his station the distinguished member of a great society, who attend to every part of his conduct, and who thereby oblige him to attend to every part of it himself. His authority and consideration depend very much upon the respect which this society bears to him. He dare not do anything which would disgrace or discredit him in it, and he is obliged to a very strict observation of that species of morals, whether liberal or austere, which the general consent of this society prescribes to persons of his rank and fortune. A man of low condition, on the contrary, is far from being a distinguished member of any great society. While he remains in a country village his conduct may be attended to, and he may be obliged to attend to it himself. In this situation, and in this situation only, he may have what is called a character to lose. But as soon as he comes into a great city, he is sunk in obscurity and darkness. His conduct is observed and attended to by nobody, and he is therefore very likely to neglect it himself, and to abandon himself to every sort of low profligacy and vice. He never emerges so effectually from this obscurity, his conduct never excites so much the attention of any respectable society, as by his becoming the member of a small religious sect. He from that moment acquires a degree of consideration which he never had before. All his brother sectaries are, for the credit of the sect, interested to observe his conduct, and if he gives occasion to any scandal, if he deviates very much from those austere morals which they almost always require of one another, to punish him by what is always a very severe punishment, even where no civil effects attend it, expulsion or excommunication from the sect. In little religious sects, accordingly, the morals of the common people have been almost always remarkably regular and orderly; generally much more so than in the established church. The morals of those little sects, indeed, have frequently been rather disagreeably rigorous and unsocial.

There are two very easy and effectual remedies, however, by whose joint operation the state might, without violence, correct whatever was unsocial or disagreeably rigorous in the morals of all the little sects into which the country was divided.

The first of those remedies is the study of science and philosophy, which the state might render almost universal among all people of middling or more than middling rank and fortune; not by giving salaries to teachers in order to make them negligent and idle, but by instituting some sort of probation, even in the higher and more difficult sciences, to be undergone by every person before he was permitted to exercise any liberal profession, or before he could be received as a candidate for any honourable office of trust or profit. If the state imposed upon this order of men the necessity of learning, it would have no occasion to give itself any trouble about providing them with proper teachers. They would soon find better teachers for themselves than any whom the state could provide for them. Science is the great antidote to the poison of enthusiasm and superstition; and where all the superior ranks of people were secured from it, the inferior ranks could not be much exposed to it.

The second of those remedies is the frequency and gaiety of publick diversions. The state, by encouraging, that is by giving entire liberty to all those who for their own interest would attempt, without scandal or indecency, to amuse and divert the people by painting, poetry, musick, dancing; by all sorts of dramatic representations and exhibitions, would easily dissipate, in the greater part of them, that melancholy and gloomy humour which is almost always the nurse of popular superstition and enthusiasm. Publick diversions have always been the objects of dread and hatred, to all the fanatical promoters of those popular frenzies. The gaiety and good humour which those diversions inspire were altogether inconsistent with that temper of mind, which was fittest for their purpose, or which they could best work upon. Dramatic representations besides, frequently exposing their artifices to public ridicule, and sometimes even to public execration, were upon that account, more than all other diversions, the objects of their peculiar abhorrence.

In a country where the law favoured the teachers of no one religion more than those of another, it would not be necessary that any of them should have any particular or immediate dependency upon the sovereign or executive power; or that he should have any thing to do, either in appointing, or in dismissing them from their offices. In such a situation he would have no occasion to give himself any concern about them, further than to keep the peace among them, in the same manner as among the rest of his subjects; that is, to hinder them from persecuting, abusing, or oppressing one another. But it is quite otherwise in countries where there is an established or governing religion. The sovereign can in this case never be secure, unless he has the means of influencing in a considerable degree the greater part of the teachers of that religion.

The clergy of every established church constitute a great incorporation. They can act in concert, and pursue their interest upon one plan and with one spirit, as much as if they were under the direction of one man; and they are frequently too under such direction. Their interest as an incorporated body is never the same with that of the sovereign, and is sometimes directly opposite to it. Their great interest is to maintain their authority with the people; and this authority depends upon the supposed certainty and importance of the whole doctrine which they inculcate, and upon the supposed necessity of adopting every part of it with the most implicit faith, in order to avoid eternal misery. Should the sovereign have the imprudence to appear either to deride or doubt himself of the most trifling part of their doctrine, or from humanity attempt to protect those who did either the one or the other, the punctilious honour of a clergy who have no sort of dependency upon him, is immediately provoked to proscribe him as a profane person, and to employ all the terrors of religion in order to oblige the people to transfer their allegiance to some more orthodox and obedient prince. Should he oppose any of their pretensions or usurpations, the danger is equally great. The princes who have dared in this manner to rebel against the church, over and above this crime of rebellion, have generally been charged too with the additional crime of heresy, notwithstanding their solemn protestations of their faith and humble submission to every tenet which she thought proper to prescribe to them. But the authority of religion is superior to every other authority. The fears which it suggests conquer all other fears. When the authorized teachers of religion propagate through the great body of the people doctrines subversive of the authority of the sovereign, it is by violence only, or by the force of a standing army, that he can maintain his authority. Even a standing army cannot in this case give him any lasting security; because if the soldiers are not foreigners, which can seldom be the case, but drawn from the great body of the people, which must almost always be the case, they are likely to be soon corrupted by those very doctrines. The revolutions which the turbulence of the Greek clergy was continually occasioning at Constantinople, as long as the eastern empire subsisted; the convulsions which, during the course of several centuries, the turbulence of the Roman clergy was continually occasioning in every part of Europe, sufficiently demonstrate how precarious and insecure must always be the situation of the sovereign who has no proper means of influencing the clergy of the established and governing religion of his country. ...

27
GILBERT STUART

Gilbert Stuart, *A view of society in Europe, in its progress from rudeness to refinement: or, Inquiries concerning the history of law, government, and manners. By Gilbert Stuart, LL.D.* Edinburgh: printed for John Bell; and J. Murray, London, 1778, xx, 433, [3] p.
Selections from 2.1.1; from 1778 edition.

Son of an Edinburgh Latin professor, Gilbert Stuart (1742–1786) studied law at the University of Edinburgh. He made his career as an author, though, writing for review journals and authoring several historical works on the subjects of Scotland, European society, and the English constitution. Stuart's and Hume's professional lives overlapped by eight years. Their relation began amicably enough when the young Stuart mailed Hume a copy of his *Historical Dissertation concerning the Antiquity of the English Constitution* (1768), a work that earned him a doctor of laws degree the following year. Stuart's cover letter to Hume is as follows, only portions of which have appeared elsewhere:

Sir,
    Allow me to have the pleasure of presenting to you a copy of a small treatise concerning the English constitution which I have ventured to publish. If you are so kind as to receive it as a mark of high regard which your writings have made me conceive for you, I shall be very happy. The subject is well known to you, and the publick has profited very much from the learned and masterly reflections you have communicated concerning it. I have presumed to take a different road from that which you have followed, and if I have taken the liberty to differ from you in several particulars, it has been alwise with the greatest deference and respect. I have the honour to subscribe myself with the highest esteem,

Sir,
Your most obedient,
humble servant
Gilbert Stuart

Edin. College
2^d May 1768

Hume's general position on the subject was that individual freedom was not an integral part of the British constitution and "The commons came very late to be admitted to a share in the legislative power" (*History*, Appendix 2). Stuart opposes this contention in his *Historical Dissertation*, and raised this as a point of dispute with Hume in his subsequent publications. After sending his book to Hume, Stuart was eager to receive a response, as the following letter from Gilbert Elliot to Hume indicates:

> The young feudal author, Gilbert Stewart, is just now in my neighbourhood; and, his father tells me, impatient, to a great degree, for your letter. It seems he is much your admirer. However, I hope my criticisms, on some parts of his work, may keep him from carrying his admiration, on some points, too far. [Gilbert Elliot to Hume, July 11, 1768]

Hume responded to Elliot shortly after, addressing Stuart somewhat patronizingly:

> I send you my Letter enclosd to Mr Stewart, which I hope is calculated to encourage a young Man of Merit, without overstraining the Compliment. It were better, however, for him, and for every body, to pursue, in Preference to the idle Trade of Writing, some other lawful Occupation, such as Cheating like an Attorney, Quacking like a Physician, Canting & Hypocrising like a Parson &c &c &c. It is for very little Purpose to go out of the common Track. Does he expect to make Men wiser? A very pretty Expectation truly! [Hume to Gilbert Elliot of Minto, July 22, 1768]

In 1771, writing for the *Monthly Review*, Stuart boldly defended Hume against criticisms by Henry Griffet in his *Nouveaux éclaircissements* (for selections from Stuart's review see the entry on Griffet earlier in this collection). Stuart soon became an agitator of disputes and, in his capacity as editor of the *Edinburgh Magazine and Review*, he entangled Hume in a controversy (see the selection from Isaac Disraeli's *Calmaties of Authors* in *Early Responses to Hume's Life and Reputation*). Attacks on Hume made their way into Stuart's most important book, *A View of Society in Europe* (1778). He takes issue with Hume's account of feudal government as it appears in Appendix 2 of his *History* and concludes that "his history, from its beginning to its conclusion, is chiefly to be regarded as a plausible defence of prerogative." Stuart's *View of Society* was well-received by the major review journals. The *London Review* places Stuart among an impressive line-up of literary figures who have attempted to write on the Middle Ages:

> His [i.e., Montesquieu's] example was quickly followed by several writers of our times most conspicuous for genius and erudition, and a Kames, a Dalrymple, and a Hume have respectively attempted and illustrated with success many important topics in the history of the middle ages. But after all the investigations

of these authors much remained to be atchieved. They had circumscribed too much their enquiries, or having undertaken them with a view to the illustration of some favourite subject, had pursued them under the partial influence of a system. For these reasons, though they present us with many curious and instructive researches, which throw much light on the progress of improvements during the dark and barbarous ages, there was still wanting an inquirer who should traverse the field in its utmost extent; who, armed with patience, industry, and ability, and provided with leisure and enthusiasm for the subject, might embrace the investigation as a lover of truth, disengaged from partial views and unseduced by system. As such an inquirer, we will venture to pronounce the author of the performance before us. [*London Review*, March 1778, Vol. 7, pp. 194–201, April, pp. 254–258, May, pp. 329–339]

Writing for the *Monthly Review*, John Gillies applauds Stuart's research and the uniqueness of his interpretations:

... it adds peculiar merit to Dr. Stuart's performance, that on a subject of curiosity and importance sufficient to attract the universal regard of the learned and ingenious of the present age, he has brought forward many interesting facts hitherto neglected, opened a variety of views, and started many ideas, which lead to new and useful reflections. His observations concerning the state of society, and of government, in Europe, on the downfall of the Roman empire, as well as on the feudal system, and the Gothic manners, are essentially different from those of the most approved modern historians: and it must be acknowledged, that while he defends his opinions with uncommon acuteness, he supports them by authorities which shew that he has made the deepest researches into the history and antiquities of the middle ages.

However, Gillies faults Stuart on style:

With regard to the Author's style, we may, briefly, characterise it in the terms in which he speaks of the *knightly* manners that prevailed in the times of ancient chivalry. It has, in general, 'a majestic air' and 'ceremonious dignity;' but we must observe, that the stately *airs* and *dignities* are necessarily attended by a degree of stiffness, to which the lovers of elegant simplicity will ever prefer the more natural forms, and easier deportment, of those who move in less exalted spheres, and fill, with propriety, the middle walks of life, – which they love to frequent, and which are equally removed from the artificial splendours of a throne, and the untutored rusticity of a cottage. [*Monthly Review*, Vol. 58 March 1778, pp. 198–207]

Stuart's *View of Society* was also favourably reviewed by the *Critical Review* (1778, Vol. 45, p. 161 ff.). In "Hume and his Influence upon History" (1826), contained later in this collection, Francis Palgrave favourably mentions Stuart's critique of Hume.

The following year Stuart published his *Observations Concerning the Public Laws and the Constitutional History of Scotland* (1779), in which he once again locks horns with Hume on the nature of the English constitution. Specifically, Stuart contests Hume's view that the burgesses originally had no representation in English or Scottish national councils. Stuart's *View of Society* was published again in 1782, 1783, 1792, 1797, and 1813. The following is from the 1778 edition of that work. For more on Stuart, see the introductory comments to *Critical Observations* (1782) later in this collection.

BOOK II.

CHAPTER I.

SECTION I.

...

(4) The state, I know, of the people of old, as described by Dr Brady, and Mr Hume, by Dr Robertson, and a multitude of other authors, was uniformly most abject; and yet the power of the nobles is represented as most exorbitant. They dwell on what they term the aristocratical genius of the times, and seem to take a pleasure in painting the abjectness of the people.

It is remarkable, that these notions are contradictory and inconsistent. The nobles had immence influence; but, in what did this influence consist? Was it not in the numbers and the attachment of their vassals? These were their power; and, did they oppress them? The reverse is the truth. They treated them with the utmost lenity, and it was their interest to do so. The cordiality, accordingly, of the nobles and the vassals, was maintained during a long tract of time, of which the history as been repeatedly written, without the necessary attention to its nature and spirit. The decay, indeed, of this cordiality, was to create confusions and oppression; and, what confirms my remark, it was in this situation, that the power of the nobles was to be humbled.

The error I mention was first thrown out by a writer of ability, because it suited the theory he inculcates. It was adopted, for the same reason, by a writer of still greater talents; and nothing more is necessary to give currency to an absurdity. For, the authors who do not think for themselves, but who gain a fashionable and temporary reputation, by giving dress and trappings to other men's notions, will repeat it till it is believed.

(5) Mr Hume has the following very singular passage. 'None of the feudal governments in Europe had such institutions as the *county-courts*, which the great authority of the conqueror still retained from the Saxon customs. All the freeholders of the county, even the greatest barons, were obliged to attend the sherrifs in these courts, and to assist him in the administration of justice.' *Append*. II.

In every feudal kingdom, notwithstanding this strong affirmation, the *comes* was known, and the *comitatus*. The *comitatus*, or county, was the territory or estate of the *comes*; and the court he held, and in which he presided, was the *county-court*, to which the freeholders and feudators were called, and acted as assessors or judges. *Du Cange, and Spelman, voc. Comites.*

There might, indeed, be a *comes* who enjoyed not the property of the county, but only a part of it; and, in this case, he was constituted to exercise jurisdiction in it. The sheriff originally was a very subordinate officer. He was sometimes no more than the depute of the *comes.* Hence *vicecomes* was the term by which he was known. Sometimes he was only vested with the care of the king's interest in particular counties. And, in reality, he began only to figure when the jurisdiction of the nobles, in the decline of fiefs, had died away to a shadow.

It is said by Mr Hume, That the great authority of the conqueror retained the county-courts from the Saxon customs. He thus infers, that these courts were favourable to the royal authority. The fact, however, is exactly the reverse. The greater jurisdiction there is in the nobles and the people, the more limited is the prerogative of princes. The county-courts were eminent and formidable supports of the liberty of the subject. And, instead of giving them encouragement, it was the interest of the conqueror to employ his great authority in their suppression.

Mr Hume adds, in the spirit of a writer who had made a discovery, 'Perhaps this institution of the county-courts *in England*, has had greater effect on the government, than has yet been distinctly pointed out by historians, or traced by antiquaries.' *Ibid.*

I have remarked these and other weak places in the works of this illustrious man, that I might show the danger of implicit confidence even in the greatest names. The undue weight of what are called *great authorities*, gives a stab to the spirit of inquiry in all sciences.

(6) ... By a curious testimony, it is even obvious, that the word *sapientes* must have meant the *commons*. In the supplication *del county de Devonshire*, to Edward III. there are these expressions, '*que* luy please par l'avys des prelats, countees, barons, et *auters sages* in cest present parliament ordeiner,' &c. This supplication is printed in the 4. Inst. p. 232. In the reign of the third Edward, from the *auters sages* expressing the commons, it may surely be decisively inferred, that *sapientes* had the same meaning in older times.

In fact, the expressions which denote the Anglo-Saxon assemblies, allude to their nationality. 'Comune concilium, conventus omnium, concilium cleri et populi, omnium principum et omnium sapientum conventus,' &c. are appellations which mark forcibly the interference and assistance of the *commons*.[1]

---

[1]   Mr Hume has observed, indeed, that 'None of the expressions of the antient historians, though several hundred passages might be produced, can, *without the utmost violence*, be *tortured* to a meaning which will admit the *Commons* to be constituent members of the great council.' Append. II. It is painful to remark a want of candour so glaring in so great a man.

In the annals of Winchelcomb, an. 811. there is to be seen the term *procuratores*, as expressive of a branch of the wittenagemot. It also occurs in a charter of King Athelstane. And, that the persons denoted by it were the deputies of the people, seems past all doubt, when it is recollected, that, in the Spanish writers, this order of men is expressed by *procuradores de las cividades y villas*. Nay, in Polydore Virgil, we meet the expression *procuratores civium populique. p.* 478. *ap. Whitelocke, vol.* 1. *p.* 378.

To these notices I might add a multitude of authorities, respectable and positive. But I mean not now to enter fully into the dispute concerning the importance of the people. To give completeness to the spirit of my present volume, it is sufficient for me to assert the antiquity of the commons, in opposition to an opinion of their late rise, which a modern historian, of great reputation, has inculcated, with that hardiness which he displays in all his writings, but with little of that power of thought and of reasoning which does honour to his philosophical works.

Mr Hume, struck with the talents of Dr Brady, deceived by his ability, disposed to pay adulation to government, or willing to profit by a system, formed with art, and ready for adoption, has executed his history upon the tenets of this writer. Yet, of Dr Brady it ought to be remembered, that he was the slave of a faction, and that he meanly prostituted an excellent understanding, and admirable quickness, to vindicate tyranny, and to destroy the rights of his nation. With no less pertinacity, but with an air of greater candour, and with the marks of a more liberal mind, Mr Hume has employed himself to the same purposes; and his history, from its beginning to its conclusion, is chiefly to be regarded as a plausible defence of prerogative. As an elegant and a spirited composition, it merits every commendation. But no friend to humanity, and to the freedom of this kingdom, will consider his constitutional inquiries, with their effect on his narrative, and compare them with the antient and venerable monuments of our story, without feeling a lively surprise, and a patriot indignation.

28
JOSEPH TOWERS

Joseph Towers, *Observations on Mr. Hume's History of England. By Joseph Towers*. London: printed by H. Goldney, for G. Robinson, 1778, vii, [1], 151, [1] p.[1]
Complete book; from 1778 edition.

B orn in the London borough of Southwark, Joseph Towers (1737–1799) was son to a second-hand bookseller. He briefly worked as a printer, was later a dissenting clergyman, and throughout his adult life a prolific political pamphleteer. In 1766 he spent time at the British Museum, which allowed him to consult material for compiling the seven-volume *British Biography* (1766–1772) and his *Observations on Mr. Hume's History of England*, published 12 years later. Drawing on other histories as authorities, Towers attacks selected passages from all volumes of Hume's *History*. Although he principally targets the 1763 and 1773 editions, he also cites the 1754 and 1778 editions, the latter of which, Towers says in a note midway into the volume, "was not published till a considerable part of these observations was printed off." Ideologically, Towers's *Observations* is a Whiggish defence of constitutional rights and critique of Hume's view of royal prerogative. Aside from the brief Preface, Towers's *Observations* contains no section divisions or chapters. To assist in following the dominant themes of the text, I have created section titles and inserted them within brackets in appropriate places. Accordingly, the contents of the text are as follows:

Preface
1. Early Periods
2. House of Tudor

---

[1] Title page: OBSERVATIONS | ON | MR. HUME's | HISTORY OF ENGLAND. | By JOSEPH TOWERS. | Sunt duo genera hominum, qui ex antiquis monumentis Histo- | rias contexere, – Alii, quantum licet, veritatem expiscari | conantur, et diligenter omnia expendunt, ut verisimillimam | sequantur narrationem, cum non licet res exploratus proferre. | Alii vero de veritate non multum laborantes ea eligunt, quæ | maxime mirabilia videntur; quia facilius exornari possunt, | & grandiori orationi materiam suppenditant. | LE CLERC. | LONDON: | Printed by H. GOLDNEY, | For G. ROBINSON, PATER-NOSTER-ROW. | M DCCLXXVIII.

3. House of Stuart
4. Concluding Observations

In the opening paragraphs, Towers accuses Hume of intentionally and systematically distorting history in an attempt to be novel and gain fame. Regarding the early periods of English history, he argues that Hume was prejudicial against the indigenous inhabitants of England and wrongly presents Henry I's government as arbitrary. For Towers, Hume exaggerates the extent to which King John laid waste the Kingdom, and "we find him grossly palliating the conduct and administration of Edward II. [and] Richard II." Regarding the latter, Towers says, "It must, indeed, excite some surprize in the unprejudiced reader, to find, that our historian is so far from giving a just representation of the despotic administration of Richard, that he even makes it a matter of doubt, whether this prince had been guilty of any acts of oppression at all."

Turning to the House of Tudor, Towers writes, "his representation of it is, in some respects, much exaggerated; his design in which manifestly was, to make their conduct serve as an apology for the princes of the House of Stuart." To this end, Hume plays up the despotic and arbitrary nature of the Tudor governments. Contrary to Hume's view that the English constitution contained no regular plan of liberty prior to the House of Stuart, Towers holds that "the English government, from the earliest ages, has manifestly been characterised by a spirit of liberty." Like MacQueen and Maclaine, Towers finds fault with Hume's account of superstition and enthusiasm during the Reformation.

Regarding the House of Stuart, Towers charges that Hume grossly distorts the facts. He portrays respectable parliamentary leaders "in a ridiculous or unfavourable light." As to Strafford – Charles I's leading advisor who was ultimately executed by Parliament – Towers argues at length that his conduct "was so far from being either *innocent* or *laudable*, that it was in a very high degree criminal, and that he was a just object of national indignation, and of public prosecution." As to Hume's account of Charles I, Towers contends that it "may be considered rather as a specious and artful apology for that prince's conduct, than a just history." In his concluding observations he charges that Hume poorly represents scientists and literary figures, specifically Shakespeare, Bacon, Milton, and Boyle. He concludes that Hume's *History* "may be read with considerable advantage, if it be read with caution." But, as an educational tool, it "may be highly pernicious to the minds of youth," particularly in matters of "a free state" and religion.

Duly impressed with the *Observations*, the University of Edinburgh conferred on Towers the degree of Doctor of Laws. The *Observations* was prominently reviewed by the leading review journals. The author of the article for the *Critical Review* sides with Hume's view that in previous centuries the English constitution favoured the prerogative of the sovereign more than it did public freedom:

The author of these Observations is not the first that has accused Mr. Hume of partiality in the character of historian; yet, how far such a charge is well founded, may perhaps be matter of dispute. Though the civil broils which agitated this kingdom towards the middle of the last century, have long since been extinguished, so have not likewise the principles by which the opposite parties were actuated; and he who relates those contests with the greatest moderation, may frequently, on that very account, be exposed to particular censure.

One of the most material objections urged against Mr. Hume is, that he has represented the government of England, under the princes of the House of Tudor, as more despotic than it really was, with the view of extenuating the conduct of the subsequent sovereigns. In answer to this objection we should agree with Mr. Hume, that the English constitution was far from being rightly poised in those ages; and it seems to be unquestionable, from numerous facts, that the prerogatives of the crown were then frequently exerted in measures which seem inconsistent with a regard to public freedom, as the latter has since been ascertained. Nor is it indeed to be expected, that before the privileges of the people were fixed with greater precision, a degree of authority much superior to what is vested at present in the crown, should not, on many occasions, have been assumed by the executive power. If those arguments be admitted, the principal objections against Mr. Hume's representation of the English government before the time of the civil wars, will fall to the ground.

Although disagreeing ideologically with Towers, the reviewer nevertheless concludes by commending the work:

> These extracts are sufficient to give a favourable opinion of Mr. Towers's ingenuity and candor; and though himself, perhaps, may not be entirely void of modifications of the same qualities which he ascribes to the historian, his remarks, even where they seem not to be strictly just, are rendered extremely plausible, and may be read with advantage. [*Critical Review*, April 1778, Vol. 45, pp. 289–292]

Writing for the *Monthly Review*, Andrew Kippis (who was a member of the Constitutional Society along with Towers) gives a largely neutral account of Towers's work, noting only that it "contains no small degree of instruction and entertainment" (*Monthly Review*, July 1778, Vol. 59, pp. 19–25). The article for the *London Review* likewise offers a largely neutral summary of Towers's work, offering occasional comments in footnotes. In one note, the reviewer censures Hume for systematically misrepresenting the facts:

> It may not be improper to observe, that there is a wide difference between occasional and accidental errors, into which the most impartial historian may

sometimes fall, and a kind of systematic misrepresentation, which runs through the greatest part of a considerable work. This appears to be the case with Mr. Hume's history. [*London Review*, May 1778, Vol. 7, pp. 347–355]

In a second note, the reviewer sides with Hume's view that the generality of people are unqualified to examine the foundations of religion themselves: "But is not the latter assertion, at least *true*, Mr. Towers, if such an examination depends (as it is in these times become the fashion to represent it) on scholastic enquiry and philosophical investigation?"

Towers's *Observations* appeared a second time in 1796 in his three-volume *Tracts on Political and other Subjects, Published at Various Times* (London: T. Cadell). According to his "Biographical Memoir" (see below) only about half of his published works made their way into this collection. In their review of his *Tracts*, the *Critical Review* opens noting that Towers "has maintained the character not only of a zealous advocate for liberty, but of an honest uncorrupted man." Concerning his work on Hume, the reviewer believes that "Dr. Towers's observations are pertinent, and will be read with pleasure by such as admire the composition of Mr. Hume, but disapprove of some of his principles." The reviewer concludes by noting that Towers's various tracts "are distinguished by a clear and forcible, rather than a brilliant style; that the doctor's observations are rather direct and pointed, than moralising or sententious" (*Critical Review*, 1796, Vol. 18, pp. 306–311). The *Tracts* was also favourably reviewed in the *Analytical Review*, which comments that "we have no doubt, that the friends to the liberties of britons, and the rights of men, will be pleased to find these pieces collected, and reprinted in a form in which they may find a respectable place in their libraries" (*Analytical Review*, 1796, Vol. 24, pp. 206–207).

Towers's *Observations* was favourably mentioned by Francis Jeffrey in his 1824 review of Brodie's *History* and Francis Palgrave in "Hume and his Influence upon History" (1826), contained later in this collection. A "Biographical Memoir" and list of Towers's publications appear in James Lindsay's *Sermon occasioned by the death of the Rev. Joseph Towers* (London: Johnson, 1799). The following is from the 1778 edition.

OBSERVATIONS

ON

Mr. HUME's

HISTORY of ENGLAND.

By JOSEPH TOWERS.

Sunt duo genera hominum, qui ex antiquis monumentis Historias contexere;—Alii, quantum licet, veritatem expiscari conantur, et diligenter omnia expendunt, ut verisimillimam sequantur narrationem, cum non licet res exploratus proferre. Alii vero de veritate non multum laborantes ea eligunt, quæ maxime mirabilia videntur ; quia facilius exornari possunt, & grandiori orationi materiam suppeditant.

LE CLERC.

LONDON:

Printed by H. GOLDNEY,

For G. ROBINSON, PATER-NOSTER-ROW.

M DCC LXXVIII.

PREFACE.

The writer of the following Observations on the work of a late celebrated author, regrets that his death happened before their publication. He apprehends, however, that this circumstance is not of such a nature, as to preclude their being printed. The merit of Mr. Hume's history, as a fine composition, will make it long read, whatever may be its deficiencies in other respects; and it is, therefore, of some consequence, that a just idea should be formed of it. And as no man supposes, that there is any impropriety in criticising the works of Addison, or Pope, or Milton, there can be no just reason for objecting to a criticism on a work of Mr. Hume, though his death be of a more recent date. Whatever respect may be due to the memory of a departed genius, a much greater is due to the interests of truth; nor can the proper instruction be derived from an historical composition, unless we are acquainted with the views of the writer, and with the degree of credit that is due to his narrations.

OBSERVATIONS, &c.

Few of our modern historical performances have been more read, or more celebrated, than the HISTORY OF ENGLAND by Mr. DAVID HUME: and as an elegant composition, and the production of real and distinguished genius, it is unquestionably entitled to great applause. But though beauty of diction, harmony of periods, and acuteness and singularity of sentiment, may captivate the reader, yet there are other qualifications essentially necessary to the character of a good historian. Fidelity, accuracy, and impartiality, are also requisite: and in these, it is apprehended, Mr. Hume is frequently deficient; so that those who read his work, with a view to obtain just ideas of the most remarkable transactions and events which have happened in this country, will, if they rely solely on his authority, be led to form conceptions exceedingly erroneous respecting matters of very considerable importance.[2] It is, therefore, the design of the following Observations to evince, that those who wish to acquire an accurate knowledge of the real state of facts, and to think justly of the persons and transactions treated of in Mr. Hume's history, should read his work with some degree of caution and circumspection, without too implicit a reliance on his integrity as an historian, and that they should compare his relations with those of other authors.

The great object of Mr. Hume's ambition, as we are informed by himself, was literary fame. And in order to excite public attention, he seems to have thought

---

[2] It may not be improper to observe, that there is a wide difference between occasional and accidental errors, into which the most impartial historian may sometimes fall, and a kind of systematic misrepresentation, which runs through the greatest part of a considerable work. This appears to be the case with Mr. Hume's history.

it necessary to be singular. Accordingly, we find an affectation of singularity of sentiment, very predominant in his writings. But though opinions are not therefore true, because they are common; yet he who affects, on almost every occasion, to differ from the generality of mankind, will much more frequently be wrong than right. To oppose the sentiments of others, when they appear to be the result of prejudice or ignorance, is, in many cases, extremely laudable: but to contradict established opinions only for the sake of being singular, may justly be considered as a censurable affectation.

Mr. Hume appears to have been misled by his prejudices, as well as by affectation. And men who write under the influence of any particular biass, are apt to deceive others as well as themselves; unless their readers are aware of the prepossessions to which they are addicted, and the false views by which they are misled. And it sometimes happens, that men affecting great freedom of thought, and originality of sentiment, and who pretend to despise vulgar prejudices, are, at the same time, under the influence of inveterate prejudices of another kind, and as slavishly attached to a favourite hypothesis, as the meanest of the vulgar can be to those prepossessions which they have imbibed in their youth, and which their want of education, knowledge, and more enlarged views, has prevented them from shaking off.

No man can judge properly of the credit due to Mr. Hume's narrations, who does not compare his representations of facts, circumstances, and characters, with other historical writers. And this is a trouble which few readers are disposed to take: but those who do, will be convinced, that Mr. Hume is an historian by no means to be implicitly relied on. Some foreign writers have commended Mr. Hume's history in the most lavish terms. The reason is, they could judge of his eloquence as a writer, and of the beauty of his work as a literary composition; but their knowledge of our history was not sufficiently accurate and extensive, to enable them to judge of his partialities and prepossessions, and his deviations from historic truth.

I shall not attempt, in the following pages, to take a complete view of so large a work as Mr. Hume's History of England. But I shall point out sundry passages in that celebrated performance, which may tend to throw some light upon the character of the author as an historical writer, which may point out some of the prepossessions by which he was frequently misled, or, in consequence of which, he endeavoured to mislead his readers. And the writer of these observations flatters himself, that they may not wholly be without their use; because so far as it may reasonably be supposed, that men are influenced in their political conduct and sentiments by the reading of history, so far it may be of some importance to the public, what opinions are disseminated in a history of so much celebrity as that of Mr. Hume.

[1. EARLY PERIODS]

That Mr. Hume was very superficially acquainted with the earlier periods of the British History, has been shewn in a very able manner by the learned and ingenious Mr. Whitaker.[3] And it may also be observed, that in many passages of his history, Mr. Hume seems to take a particular pleasure in degrading the national character of the inhabitants of England: and, therefore, in the earlier part of his history, he passes very slightly over those circumstances and transactions which reflect honour on the natives of this country, or which make their courage and aversion to slavery; whilst he dwells in a very copious manner on those circumstances and transactions in which they appear to disadvantage. It may possibly be supposed by some, that this accusation against Mr. Hume, is only founded on his having guarded against the national prepossessions and prejudices of preceding English historians. But this is far from being the case: and those who will take the pains to compare Mr. Hume's work with the most authentic and impartial writers on the history of this country, will find that in many instances he has done great injustice to our ancestors. Whether he was led to this by his affectation of singularity, or by what other motive, I shall not take upon me to determine.

The spirited opposition made by the Britons to Julius Cæsar and the Romans, the heroism and noble behaviour of Caractacus, the bravery of Boadicia, and other striking events characteristic of the courage of the ancient Britons,[4] are very slightly passed over by this historian; whilst he dwells very minutely on the meanness of their applications to the Romans for assistance against the Picts and Scots, when the Romans had deserted this island, and when many of the Britons had quite lost that martial spirit by which they had formerly been distinguished, in consequence of the luxury and effeminacy which had been artfully introduced amongst them by the Romans.[5]

Mr. Hume was extremely desirous of representing the government of England as arbitrary, at least as much so as he could with any degree of plausi-

---

[3] [John Whitaker (1735–1808), *The History of Manchester* (1771–1775), selections from which are contained earlier in this collection.]

[4] It is observed by Mr. Whitaker, that 'it is one of the most singular events in the Roman annals, and reflects a peculiar honour upon the bravery of the Britons, that, in the long course of more than three centuries, the Romans could never make an entire conquest of the island. And this was the only country in the world, I think, in which Romans reduced the greatest part of the natives, and yet were for ever beat off by the small remainder of them. The conquest was attempted by some of the greatest generals that were produced in the armies of Rome, was prosecuted with the greatest vigour and conduct, and yet was never accomplished. All the efforts of the Romans, however successful at first, were finally baffled by the Britons. And they still lived independent in their mountains, and looked down with pity upon the rest of the brethren, stooping to the power, and adopting the manners of Italy." Hist. of Manchester, vol. ii, p. 211.

[5] Vid. Hume's History of England, vol. i, p. 12, 13, 14. edit. 8vo. 1763.

bility, in the periods preceding the accession of the House of Stuart: and this he was led to do by his desire of vindicating, or extenuating, the tyranny of that family, under the pretence, that they found the government despotic, or nearly so, on their accession to the throne of Great Britain. But notwithstanding all that he, or others, may have advanced upon this subject, there appears to have been a considerable degree of liberty in this country, from the earliest periods of which there are any notices in history. The inhabitants of Britain were anciently divided into distinct communities, governed by distinct kings. And it is observed, by that very able antiquarian, Mr. Whitaker, that

> "the monarchies of Britain acknowledged no indefeasible right of succession. And they were as little absolute and arbitrary in their nature. The Britons were not unacquainted, though history has never supposed them to be actually acquainted, with that properest restraint upon monarchical despotism, the rational, the manly, and the free institution of parliaments. No power but the royal could either make or abrogate a public law. And fixed upon this necessary principle hangs the central balance of every monarchy. But even the king could not make or abrogate one without the consent of the country. And grounded upon the basis of this maxim stands all the fair structure of popular liberty. The most antient constitutions of Wales have expressly recorded the exception. The terms of it carry sufficiently a reference to parliamentary concurrence. And we have a decisive argument for the existence of British parliaments, in the prefaces to the laws of Howel Dha, the most authentic registers of the legislative authority by which they were made. We there find six men summoned out of every commot or century in Wales, the most wise and powerful persons in the kingdom, in order to meet and assist the king in the great work of legislation. The parliament being assembled, by common council and consent, they examined the antient laws, reformed and cancelled some, added others, and digested both into a regular code. And this they presented to the king. The monarch approved of it, and gave it the ratifying sanction of his own authority. And both he and the senators concurred to imprecate the wrath of God, the parliament, and all the country, upon such of the people as should violate, and such of the kings as should abrogate, any of these constitutions; unless they were annulled in a council, equally national as that in which they had been recently made."[6]

And, indeed, Mr. Hume himself bears some testimony to the freedom of the antient Britons, before the invasion of the Romans, in the following passage: "The Britons," he says,

---

[6] History of Manchester, vol. i. p. 336, 337. 8vo. edit. 1773.

"were divided into many small nations, or tribes; and being a military people, whose sole property was their sword and their cattle, it was impossible, after they had acquired a relish of liberty, for their princes or chieftains to establish any despotic authority over them. Their governments, though monarchical, were free, as well as those of all the Celtic nations; and the common people seem even to have enjoyed more liberty amongst them, than among the nations of Gaul, from whom they were descended."[7]

Lord Lyttelton, speaking of the Welsh government, observes, that there was no tincture of despotism in it. "The nobles and clergy," his lordship says,

"were consulted in all matters of state: the people were free, and seem to have assisted in the making of laws, and other acts of great moment. They were oppressed by no taxes, nor by any toilsome work: and to this an antient author, who was himself of that nation, ascribes their magnanimity and courage in war. *For nothing* (says he) *so raises and excites the minds of men to brave actions, as the chearfulness of liberty: nothing, on the contrary, so dejects and dispirits them, as the oppression of servitude.*"[8]

And to these observations it may be added, that even after the Britons had been overcome by the Romans, it appears, that many of their antient privileges were continued to them, and that their internal government was regulated by their own laws and customs.[9]

Under the English Saxon kings, it appears, that the legislative power was in the great council, conjointly with the king; and it hath been shewn by Mr. Tyrrel, that "none of these Saxon kings could pass any laws, or make any considerable alterations in the state, without not only the advice, but consent of the great council."[10] And it is remarked by Nathaniel Bacon of the Saxons, that they were "a free people, governed by laws, and those made not after the manner of the Gauls (as Cæsar noteth) by the great men, but by the people; and therefore called a free people, because they are a law to themselves."[11] And it hath also been observed by an author just cited, and who was eminently skilled in the political history of this country, that if an exact inquiry be made into the government of William the Norman, commonly called William the Conqueror, "it will be found, that he had no more power of making laws,

---

[7] Hume's History of England, vol. i. p. 3.

[8] History of the Life of king Henry II. vol. ii. 38. edit. 4to. 1767.

[9] Vid. Whitaker's History of Manchester, vol. i. 334.

[10] Bibliotheca Politica, p. 222. Vid. also p. 226–313.

[11] Historical and Political Discourse of the Laws and Government of England, p. 9. 4th edition.

without the consent of his great council, than any of his predecessors,"[12] The case was similar under the other princes of the Norman line: and from the Norman invasion to the present time, a period of more than seven hundred years, though there have been various occasional exertions of regal tyranny, it is certain, that a despotic government was never regularly established in this country. And it hath been observed by Lord Clarendon, in his piece against Hobbes, that "those laws and customs which were before the conquest, are the same which this nation or kingdom have been ever since governed by to this day." It is likewise remarked, by a still superior authority in matters of this kind, Lord Coke, that "the grounds of our common laws at this day, are beyond the memory or register of any beginning, and the same which the Norman conqueror then found within the realm of England."

At the battle of Hastings, the great battle which opened the way for William the Norman to the throne of England, the English, under Harold, fought with great valour. The engagement lasted from morning till sun-set; and, even according to Mr. Hume's account, there fell near fifteen thousand Normans in this memorable engagement. It is probable, however, that William would not have succeeded in his enterprise, if it had not been for the death of Harold: but that event left William no formidable competitor. Edgar Atheling, the presumptive heir to the crown, was thought by the English themselves incapable of the duties of government. And it is well known, that William the Norman set up a different claim to the crown from that of conquest.[13] And though after his victory at Hastings, the English submitted to him, it was not merely as to a conqueror, who in consequence became possessed of despotic power, but as to a prince, whose authority was to be limited by the laws and customs of the kingdom. At his coronation, Aldred, archbishop of York, who performed the

---

[12] Bibliotheca Politica, p. 223.

[13] It is justly observed, in the learned Bishop Hurd's *Moral and Political Dialogues*, that "William's claim to the crown was not *conquest*, (though it enabled him to support his claim), but *testamentary succession*. A title very much in the taste of that time, and extremely reverenced by our Saxon ancestors.: – And "even waving this specious claim, he condescended to accept the crown as a free gift; and, by his coronation-oath, submitted himself to the same terms of administration, as his predecessors." He also "confirmed the Saxon laws, at least before he had been many years in possession of his new dignity." – "Is there any thing in all this that favours the notion of his erecting himself, by the sole virtue of his victory at Hastings, into an absolute lord of the conquered country? Is it not certain, that he bound himself, as far as oaths and declarations could bind him, to govern according to law; that he could neither touch the honours nor estates of his subjects, but by legal trial; and that even the many forfeitures in his reign are an evidence of his proceeding in that method?" Vol. ii. p. 121, 122. edit. 1765. It is also very properly observed, in the same excellent dialogue, "that, without connecting the system of liberty with that of prerogative, in our notion of the English government, the tenor of our history is perfectly unintelligible, and that no consistent account can be given of it, but on the supposition of a *legal limited constitution*." P. 126.

ceremony formally asked all the English present, whether they gave their consent to have the duke of Normandy crowned king, to which they assented; and William took an oath of the same kind with that which was formerly taken by the Anglo-Saxon kings. "From whence we may observe," says Tyrrell, "that this prince was so far from claiming as a conqueror, that he accepted the crown upon the same conditions, and took the like oath, which the Saxon kings, his predecessors, had done before,"[14] Indeed, Mr. Hume himself remarks, that, "in his whole administration, he (William I.) bore the resemblance of the lawful prince, not of the conqueror; and the English began to flatter themselves, that they had changed, not the form of their government, but only the succession of their sovereigns, a matter which gave them small concern."[15]

When William, in 1067, went over into Normandy, he took with him many of the most considerable nobility of England: and Mr. Hume says, that

"his English courtiers, willing to ingratiate themselves with their new sovereign, endeavoured to outshine each other in equipages and entertainments; and made a display of riches, which struck the foreigners with astonishment. William of Poictiers, a Norman historian, who was present, speaks with admiration of the beauty of their persons, the size and workmanship of their silver plate, the costliness of their embroideries, an art in which the English then excelled; and he expresses himself in such terms, as would much exalt our idea of the opulence and cultivation of the people."

But Mr. Hume adds in a note, that "as the historian chiefly insists on the silver plate, his panegyricks on the English magnificence shows only how incompetent a judge he was of the matter. Silver was then of ten times the value, and was more than twenty times more rare than at present; and consequently, of all species of luxury, plate must have been the rarest."[16] This seems an extraordinary remark, and by no means sufficient to impeach the judgment of the Norman historian. If the English made a great display of silver plate, and plate was at that time extremely scarce and valuable, nothing could be more natural, than that the historian, describing the magnificence of the English, should dwell particularly upon this circumstance.

William the Norman, soon after he was firmly settled on the throne, violated his coronation oath, and was guilty, especially in the latter part of his reign, of various acts of tyranny, inconsistent with the engagements into which he had entered. It should, however, be observed, that many of his English subjects soon

---

[14] Hist. of England, vol. ii. p. 10.

[15] Hist. of England, vol. i. p. 254. In the edition of 1773, this passage is in page 238 of the first volume.

[16] Hist. vol. i. p. 255, 256.

gave the strongest indications of their aversion to a despotic government; and their various insurrections, though not attended with success, prove that their minds were by no means fitted to the yoke of slavery.

It is observed by Lord Lyttelton, that

> "a distinction is to be made between the *government* of William the First, which was very tyrannical, and the *constitution* established under him in this kingdom, which was no absolute monarchy, but an ingraftment of the feudal tenures and other customs of Normandy upon the antient Saxon laws of Edward the Confessor. He more than once swore to maintain those laws, and in the fourth year of his reign confirmed them in parliament; yet not without great alterations, to which the whole legislature agreed, by a more compleat introduction of the strict feudal law, as it was practised in Normandy; which produced a different political system, and changed both power and property in many respects; though the first principles of that law, and general notions of it, had been in use among the English some ages before. But that the liberty of the subject was not destroyed by these alterations, as some writers have supposed, plainly appears by the very statutes that William enacted, in one of which we find an express declaration, '*That all the freemen in this kingdom should hold and enjoy their lands and possessions free from all unjust exaction, and from all tallage; so that nothing should be exacted or taken of them, but their free service, which they by right owed to the crown, and were bound to perform.*' It is farther said, '*That this was ordained and granted to them as an hereditary right for ever, by the common council of the kingdom.*'"[17]

These observations of the noble historian are unquestionably just; and yet we are told by Mr. Hume, that William the First "acted in every thing as *absolute master* over the natives, whose interests and affections he totally disregarded;" and that "it would be difficult to find, in *all history*, a revolution more destructive, or attended with a more *compleat subjection* of the ancient inhabitants."[18] These are very extraordinary assertions, and as ill-grounded as they are extraordinary; but such unwarrantable assertions are not uncommon in Mr. Hume's history.

Our historian also says, that William "had rendered himself *universal proprietor* of England;"[19] and he speaks of the English as having "tamely surrendered themselves, without resistance, to a tyrant and a conqueror."[20] But

[17] Hist. of the Life of King Henry the Second, vol. i. p. 41, 42. edit. 4to. 1767.
[18] Hume's Hist. vol. i. p. 302, 303.
[19] P. 295.
[20] P. 263.

this is certainly a very gross misrepresentation. The English had fought against the Normans, at the battle of Hastings, with great gallantry;[21] and if they submitted afterwards to William, it was because their prince Harold, in whom only they had any confidence, was killed, and because the Norman claimed a right to the crown by a supposed destination of king Edward the Confessor; and when they received William as their king, it was under the idea of a lawful prince, who was to govern according to the antient customs and usages of the kingdom. Mr. Hume also speaks of the natives of England as being "universally reduced to a state of meanness and poverty" in the reign of this prince; but that this was by no means the case, has been sufficiently shewn by Lord Lyttelton.[22]

Our accounts of the transactions of the great council of the nation, are very imperfect during the reigns of the first princes of the Norman line: but when we reflect how scanty an account is given of parliamentary proceedings even in much later reigns, in some of our general histories of England of very modern date, we can hardly wonder, that in the dark and monkish ages, when ignorance and barbarism had over-spread the face of Europe, our accounts of the proceedings of the great national assemblies should be exceedingly imperfect: and yet, in the darkest ages, we find that there were national assemblies in England, and that the power of the prince was limited, though not with the accuracy and precision that it ought to have been: but this could not justly be expected, in ages when the true principles of government and legislation were so little understood.

In a speech made by king Henry I. youngest son to William I. in a meeting "of the great men of the realm," which is preserved by Matthew Paris, is the following passage: "I, truly a king, meek, humble, and peaceable, will preserve and cherish you in your *antient* liberties, which I have formerly sworn to observe."[23] And a charter was also granted by this prince, for the securing and confirming to the people the possession of their antient liberties;[24] and Lord Lyttelton observes, that "in some respects, this charter of Henry the First was more advantageous to liberty than Magna Charta itself." The noble historian also remarks of this charter, from Sir Henry Spelman, that "it was the original of king John's Magna Charta, containing most of the articles of it, either particularly expressed, or in general, under the confirmation it gives to the laws of Edward the Confessor." – "So mistaken are they," says Lord Lyttelton,

---

[21] Mr. Tyrrell observes, that though the number of the killed at the battle of Hastings is not exactly ascertained; yet "it is acknowledged on all hands that there were so many on the Normans side, as well as the English, that nothing but the overruling providence of God, by the death of their king, could have given it (the victory) away from them to their enemies." Vol. i. p. 114.

[22] Hist. vol. i. p. 58.

[23] Parliamentary Hist. of England, vol. i, p. 10.

[24] Ibid. p. 20. Vid. also lord Lyttelton's Hist. of Henry the Second, vol. i. p. 98, 99.

"who have supposed that all the privilege granted in Magna Charta were *innovations*, extorted by the arms of rebels from king John! a notion which seems to have been first taken up, not so much out of ignorance, as from a base motive of adulation to some of our princes in latter times, who, endeavouring to grasp at absolute power, were desirous of any pretence to consider these laws, which stood in their way, as violent encroachments made by the barons on the antient rights of the crown: whereas they were, in reality, restitutions and sanctions of antient rights enjoyed by the nobility and people of England in former reigns; or limitations of powers which the king had illegally and arbitrarily stretched beyond their due bounds."[25]

Mr. Hume, speaking of this charter of Henry I. observes, that after the present turn was served, that prince *"never once thought*, during his reign, of observing *one single article* of it; and the whole fell so much into neglect and oblivion, that, in the following century, when the barons, who had heard an *obscure tradition* of it, desired to make it the model of the great charter, which they *exacted* from king John, they could only find one copy of it in the whole kingdom." Our historian appears here to have done great injustice to the administration of Henry I. whose government was far from being of that arbitrary nature which he hath represented it;[26] and as to his assertion respecting the obscurity into which this charter had fallen, it is founded on a passage in Matthew Paris, which lord Lyttelton hath shewn to be of very little weight;[27] in which opinion the noble writer is supported by the learned judge Blackstone.

In a meeting, which the writers of the parliamentary history of England term "a convention of the estates," held in 1136, by king Stephen, successor to Henry I. that prince signed a charter, in which he promised, that he would "well and truly keep all the good old laws and customs in all cases whatsoever."

In 1155, a parliament was assembled by king Henry II. for a remarkable purpose, of which no notice is taken by Mr. Hume, but of which the following account is given by lord Lyttelton.

"Henry called a parliament to meet him at Wallingford, soon after Easter, in the year eleven hundred and fifty-five, which settled the succession of the crown, after his decease, upon his eldest son William, who was then but three years old; and, in case of the death of William, (which happened soon afterwards) upon prince Henry, a second son, born to him at London in the month of March this year. Oaths of fealty were accordingly taken to both;

---

[25] Hist. of Henry II. vol. i, p. 99. 4to. edit.

[26] See this very clearly shewn by lord Lyttelton, Hist. vol. i. p. 100, 101, 158.

[27] Hist. vol. i, p. 487, 488.

and we may assuredly infer from this, as well as many other facts, that no right of birth, how indisputable soever, was thought, in those days, a sufficient title to convey the succession, without a parliamentary acknowledgment of it, followed and confirmed by feudal engagements. For if the crown had then descended of course to the eldest son of the king, it would not have been necessary to summon a parliament purely on this account."[28]

His lordship also observes, that "in another parliament held at London soon after this time, or rather in the same, adjourned to that city, he (Henry II.) granted to his people a charter of liberties, confirming that of his grandfather, king Henry the First."[29] And the same noble writer, speaking of the state of the English government at this time, says, that though it was not equal to the wisdom of the present constitution, yet "from the mixture of Saxon customs, which mitigated and tempered the Norman institutions, it was the best feudal government subsisting, at that time, in any part of the world."[30]

In the representation which Mr. Hume has given of the ravages committed by king John, and his foreign troops, after he had resolved to violate the great charter, which he had solemnly sworn to observe, these violences and depredations of the king and his foreign mercenaries seem to be much exaggerated, at least, as to their extent. John unquestionably acted like a perjured tyrant; and the barbarity and injustice which he exercised towards his subjects, in various parts of England, rendered him a just object of detestation. But there appears no sufficient reason for supposing, that he laid waste the kingdom to the extent that is represented by Mr. Hume.[31] And though the barons did not make so vigorous an opposition as might have been expected to the outrages of John, and though the opposition they did make was not conducted in the most judicious manner, it yet appears, that many of them immediately took up arms, and made some very spirited efforts against those, whom they considered as the supporters of the tyranny of the king.[32]

Mr. Hume's observations relative to the charter granted by king Henry III. at the beginning of his reign, and the other charters granted by the preceding princes, appear to be very just; though, perhaps, not quite consistent with his representations and remarks in other places. These famous charters, he says,

"were, during many generations, the darling of the whole English nation, and esteemed the most sacred rampart to national liberty and independence. As

---

[28] History of the life of king Henry the Second, vol. ii. p. 14.

[29] P. 15. The charter mentioned above, is inserted in the appendix to lord Lyttelton's history.

[30] P. 16.

[31] Hist. vol. ii. p. 96. edit. 1763.

[32] Vid. Tyrrell's Hist. of England, vol. ii. p. 787.

they secured the rights of all orders of men, they were regarded with a jealous eye by all, and became the basis, in a manner, of the English monarchy, and a kind of original contract, which both limited the authority of the king, and insured the conditional allegiance of his subjects. Though often violated, they were still claimed and recalled by the nobility and people; and as no precedents were supposed valid that infringed them, they rather acquired, than lost authority, from the frequent attempts made against them in several ages, by regal and arbitrary power."[33]

But notwithstanding these liberal remarks, Mr. Hume, in other passages of his work, mentions one of Henry the Third's charters, as being "copied from the former *concessions extorted* from John;"[34] he also speaks of the barons having "*imposed* on John and his successors limitations of the royal power;"[35] and says farther, that the licentious and powerful barons" had "*broke the reins of subjection* to their prince, and *obtained, by violence*, an enlargement of their liberties and independence."[36]

Those princes who have been dethroned, in consequence of the folly or iniquity of their government, seldom fail to meet with an advocate in Mr. Hume. Thus we find him grossly palliating the conduct and administration of Edward II. Richard II. and Charles I. Of Edward II. he says, that "it is not easy to imagine a man more innocent and inoffensive than this unhappy king; nor a prince less fitted for governing that fierce and turbulent people, subjected to his authority."[37] That Edward was a weak prince is very certain; and it appears also sufficiently manifest, that he was vicious as well as weak. If his incapacity was not a sufficient ground for the opposition of his subjects, the vices of his administration certainly were. At the very commencement of his reign, and before the interment of his father, he arbitrarily imprisoned Walter de Langton, bishop of Litchfield and Coventry, and seized his effects. And this appears to have been an act of personal revenge in the king, and is not very consistent with that inoffensive character which Mr. Hume attributes to him.[38]

Pierce Gaveston, his favourite, distinguished himself by the arrogance of his behaviour: he was also charged with abusing the king's ear by obtaining immod-

[33] Hist. vol. ii. p. 149, 150. In the edition of 1773, this passage stands in the 147th page of the second volume.

[34] P. 148.

[35] P. 179.

[36] P. 155.

[37] Hist. of England, vol. ii. p. 360. edit. 8vo. 1773.

[38] The above-mentioned prelate had complained to king Edward I of the improper attachment that his son, prince Edward, had to Pierce Gaveston, who gave him ill counsel, and led him into loose and debauched courses. And this young Edward shewed his resentment of, in the most arbitrary manner, when he ascended the throne.

erate grants for himself, with embezzling the treasure of the kingdom, and taking the best jewels of the crown to his own use; all which occasioned a sentence of perpetual banishment to be solemnly passed against him in parliament in 1308; and though the king himself agreed to this sentence, and publickly ratified it, yet Gaveston afterwards returned to England, where the king openly took him into favour, and transacted public affairs solely by his advice. The favourite also, after his return, treated the most considerable men in the kingdom with the greatest insolence; which so exasperated them, that we are informed, by some of our historians, the earls and barons "plainly told the king, that unless he would banish Pierce Gaveston, they would all rise against him as a perjured prince." But he was so far from being inclined to consent again to the banishment of his favourite, that he sent over to Gascoigny, to procure troops to defend Gaveston, by force, in his continuance in England.

Such was the folly of this prince, that "he acted all things by the sole influence of his favourite; whose indiscretion, as well as covetousness, was such, as to leave the king's coffers so bare of money, that he had not sometimes wherewithal to defray the usual expences of his family: and the queen herself was so straitened for her necessary allowance, that she was forced to write letters of complaint to her brother, the king of France."[39] And it was alledged by the lords, in their accusation against Gaveston, "that the laws and customs of the kingdom were not observed, nor the ordinances, lately made, regarded, but openly violated and broken at his pleasure."

After the death of Gaveston, the affairs of the kingdom were committed, by Edward, to his two other favourites, the Spensers, father and son, and their acts of violence and injustice ratified by him. The earl of Lancaster, though a prince of the blood, was put to death in an irregular and illegal manner. This nobleman, whilst he lived, was some check upon the king; but of his administration, after the death of Lancaster, the following representation is given: "After the return of the Despensers, and the death of the Earl of Lancaster, the king, looking upon himself as absolute lord and master over all his kingdom, grew much worse than ever he had been before; slighting the nobility, and giving himself up to avarice, by invading other men's properties, and to as great luxury in the spending of it, sparing none that had opposed him, but made it a pretence to enrich himself by the forfeiture of their estates."[40] And in the articles of mal-administration, brought against this king in parliament, it is said, that "whereas he was bound by his oath to do right to all, he would not do it for his own profit, and the covetousness of him and his evil counsellors who were with him; neither regarded the other points of the oath which he made at his coronation, as he was obliged. Also he abandoned his realm, and did as much as in him lay to destroy it, and his people; and, what is worse, by the cruelty and the defaults

[39] Tyrrell's General Hist. of England, vol. iii. p. 234.

[40] Tyrrell, vol iii, p. 293.

of his person, he is found incorrigible, and without hopes of amendment. All which things are so notorious, they cannot be gainsaid."

In Mr. Hume's representation of the transactions in the reign of king Richard the Second, he is also extremely partial to that prince. He admits, indeed, that he was "a weak prince, unfit for government;" but he takes abundant pains to palliate his misconduct and tyranny. And in the introduction to his account of the civil wars between the two houses of York and Lancaster, he says, "the English were now to pay the severe, though late penalty, of their *turbulence* under Richard II. and of their *levity* in violating, *without any necessity or just reason*, the lineal succession of their monarchs."[41] It is, however, certain, that the government of Richard II. was sufficiently oppressive to justify an opposition to it; and we cannot suppose, that any faithful or impartial historian, would have imputed the deposition of this prince either to the *turbulence* or *levity* of the English.

Early in this king's reign, by his own authority, and that of his privy council, he assumed a power of dispensing with the laws which had been solemnly agreed upon in parliament.[42] And when both houses joined in an accusation against his favourite, Michael de la Pole, earl of Suffolk, and desired that he might be removed from the chancellorship, he sent them word, that "he would not for them, or at their instance, remove the meanest scullionboy in his kitchen."[43] He also threatened the parliament afterwards, on their making a vigorous opposition to his proceedings, that he would call in his cousin, the king of France, and from him ask advice and aid; nay, even submit himself to him, rather than truckle to his own subjects.[44] And in the articles exhibited against Richard, at the time of his deposition, it was asserted, that, in the presence of many lords, as well as commoners, he had frequently said and affirmed, "that the life of every one of his subjects, and his lands, tenements, goods, and chattels, are his, the said king's, at his will and pleasure, without any forfeiture."[45]

Richard was also guilty of the most unjustifiable practices with respect to the parliament, and the election of its members.[46] And by tampering with the

---

[41] Hist. of England, vol. i. p. 180. edit. 1773.

[42] Vid. Parliamentary Hist. of England, vol. i. p. 393.

[43] Tyrrell's Hist. of England, vol. iii, p. 891.

[44] Tyrrell, p. 892, 893.

[45] Parliamentary History, vol. ii. p. 21.

[46] Tyrrell says, "The king, by certain indirect practices, and tampering with the sheriffs of several counties, whom he had now made for this purpose, caused them to return such knights of shires, without any due elections, as he had before named, and sent down to them; and this is worth our observation, because it is the first example of any king's making use of an arbitrary and illegal power in this kind." P. 964. And we are informed, in the *Parliamentary History*, that Richard's council of state commanded the sheriffs "to suffer none to be returned as knights or burgesses in parliament, but *such as the king and his council should nominate*." Vol. i. p. 432.

judges, he brought them to give the most shameful opinions, in support of his arbitrary proceedings. Among other opinions which were given by these judges, Tresilian, Belknappe, &c. were the following: That no matters ought to be brought on in parliament, but agreeable to the king's directions: "and if any act contrary to the king's pleasure made known therein, they are to be punished as traitors." That the lords and commons cannot, without the will of the king, impeach in parliament any of his judges or officers: "and if any one should do so, he is to be punished as a traitor."[47] But infamous as these opinions are, Mr. Hume informs us, that *there want not plausible reasons to justify these opinions of the judges.*[48] The parliament of that age, however, thought more justly, and these prostituted judges were afterwards convicted of high treason for advancing these opinions, nor were any *plausible reasons* then found sufficient for their exculpation.

Mr. Hume says, that Richard did not impose "any arbitrary taxes: even the parliament, in the articles of his deposition, though they complain of heavy taxes, affirm not that they were imposed illegally, or by arbitrary will."[49] But a very different account is given by Mr. Tyrell, and much more conformable to truth. He says,

"that the profits and revenues of the crown, nay, of the whole kingdom, was let to farm to certain favourites, who cruelly racked and oppressed the subjects. And, as an instance of this, great sums of money were, by new-found and unwonted means, every day rather extorted than borrowed from all sorts of people, whereof no advantage accrued to the kingdom, only the king's private pleasures were maintained at an extravagant rate, and unworthy favourites advanced. To which we may add, that the king was so exceeding liberal, or rather prodigal, that he was forced to borrow and extort money from many persons, to supply this vain, lavish humour; undoing many without cause, to enrich a few without desert. Over and above tenths and fifteenths, and other usual taxes, which were sometimes gathered twice in a year, other strange impositions were devised and put in practice; for he had often extorted great sums from the people, under the colour of benevolence, besides what was borrowed upon privy seals; so that no man of ability could escape those loans, though of these seldom any repayment was made."[50]

---

[47] Parliament. Hist. vol. i. p. 433, 434.

[48] Hist. vol. iii. p. 19. edit. 1773.

[49] Hist. vol. iii. p. 43.

[50] Hist. of Eng. vol. iii. p. 992.

Mr. Hume treats, in a very slight and cursory manner, the articles exhibited against Richard at the time of his deposition, as if the accusations brought against him in parliament were not very considerable. But in these articles he was charged with violating his coronation oath, with countenancing acts of the greatest violence, even robberies, rapes, and murders; and with imposing oaths on his subjects at his pleasure, *that he might the more freely execute and follow the humour of his foolish and unlawful will.*

One of the articles against Richard is, that "the said king, not willing to keep or protect the just laws and customs of his kingdom, but, according to his arbitrary will, to do whatsoever should occur to his desires, sometimes, and very often, when the laws of his kingdom have been expounded and declared to him by the judges and others of his council, and that they have desired that he would do justice according to those laws, hath expressly, and with an angry and haughty countenance, said, *That his laws were in his mouth;* and sometimes, *That they were in his breast;* and, *That he himself alone could make and change the laws of his kingdom:* and, being seduced with that opinion, did not suffer justice to be done to very many of his liege people; but, by threats and terrors, hath forced very many to cease from the prosecution of common justice."[51]

In the twenty-fifth articles against him, it is said, that "he was so variable and dissembling in his words and actions, and so contrary to himself, especially in writing to the pope, kings, and other lords out of the kingdom, as well as within it, and also to his other subjects, that no man living, knowing what he was, could confide in him; yea, he was reputed so unfaithful and inconstant, that he not only became a scandal to his own person, but also to the whole kingdom, and to all foreigners, when once they came to know him."

Richard attempted, in an arbitrary and unjust manner, to deprive Henry, duke of Hereford, of his succession to the honours and estates of his father, the duke of Lancaster; and ordered Henry Blewett to be banished for life, for no other crime than acting as the duke's agent, and endeavouring to obtain justice for him. He also seized the charter of the city of London, and gave such great offence to the citizens by his arbitrary treatment of the corporation, that this is supposed greatly to have facilitated his deposition.

To enumerate all the articles exhibited against Richard the Second, or to examine how far each of them can be supported by evidence, would exceed the intended limits of this publication. It will be sufficient for our purpose, if what has been already advanced relative to the government of this prince, proves its tyrannical nature, and that the account of his reign given by Mr. Hume is partial and fallacious.

---

[51] Parliamentary Hist. vol. ii. p. 18.

It must, indeed, excite some surprize in the unprejudiced reader, to find, that our historian is so far from giving a just representation of the despotic administration of Richard, that he even makes it a matter of doubt, whether this prince had been guilty of any acts of oppression at all. "Had he," says our author, "possessed the talents of gaining, and still more those of over-awing, his great barons, he might have escaped all the misfortunes of his reign, and been allowed to carry much further his oppressions over the people, *if he really was guilty of any*, without their daring to rebel, or even to murmur against him."[52]

[2. HOUSE OF TUDOR]

When Mr. Hume comes down to a lower period, to the history of the princes of the house of Tudor, he is not equally chargeable with extenuating their tyranny. On the contrary, his representation of it is, in some respects, much exaggerated; his design in which manifestly was, to make their conduct serve as an apology for the princes of the House of Stuart. It may be considered as a kind of favourite hypothesis with him, that the English government was little better than despotic at the accession of James the First; and, in order to support this, he has laboured to carry the ideas of his readers, respecting the arbitrary government of the Tudors, far beyond the truth. It cannot be denied, that there were many flagrant stretches of power under the princes of the House of Tudor. But it may be remarked, that several causes prevented the people from making, at this period, a more vigorous opposition to the encroachments of the crown. It is justly observed by Lord Lyttelton, that "there is no time of greater danger to liberty, than the first calm that succeeds to a long continuance of intestine commotions." This was precisely the case at the accession of the house of Tudor. The nation was wearied and exhausted by the long and destructive wars between the houses of York and Lancaster. The ancient nobility were in great part cut off in the course of these wars; and the people, dispirited and enfeebled by the calamities they had suffered, were inclined to bear considerable injuries with a degree of patience to which they had not been accustomed, rather than involve themselves again in the miseries of civil war.

Henry the Seventh, the first prince of the Tudor line, was a wary and a crafty prince, studious to enrich his coffers, and to extend his prerogative; and he artfully availed himself of every circumstance in his favour. Nathaniel Bacon says of him, that "casting his eye upon the government, and finding it of a *mixt temper*, wherein if royalty prevails not, popularity will; like a good soldier, whilst his strength is full, he sallies upon the people's liberties, in regard of their persons, with such cunning conveyance, as he taught the people to dance more often and better to the tune of prerogative and allegiance, than all his predecessors

---

[52] Hist. of Eng. vol. iii. p. 53.

had done. Nor did the people perceive it, till they were over their shoes; and then they clearly saw their condition."[53] However, it is mentioned by lord Bacon, as one of the reasons which induced Henry to hasten the calling his first parliament, that "he made this judgment, that it was fit for him to hasten to let his people see, that he meant to govern by law, howsoever he came in by the sword."

The son and successor of this prince, Henry the Eighth, who was arrogant, fearless, and impetuous, and who yet had many popular qualities, was not a prince under whose administration the nation could have any great probability of regaining any privileges which had been usurped from them; unless by the most animated exertions, and by drawing the sword against him. But they were not prepared for this, and therefore submitted to many violent acts of power, and to great extensions of the prerogative. It must not, however, be supposed, that the people of that age did, therefore, generally consider the prince, as possessed of a right to act in that manner by the antient constitution. They certainly did not consider him as having that right: and though the prerogatives of the prince, and the privileges of the people, were not exactly ascertained; yet the latter considered themselves as having as just a claim to their ancient and accustomed privileges, as the prince had to the prerogatives of his crown. Nor can occasional instances of tyrannical behaviour in the prince, be admitted to be any just proof of an established despotism.

Henry the Eighth was one of the most arbitrary princes who ever swayed the scepter of England; and yet in his reign it was solemnly declared, that the supreme authority was vested in the king, lords, and commons: which can give us no other idea than that of a limited monarchy. In the preamble to an act passed in the twenty-fifth year of the reign of this prince, is the following passage:

"It standeth, therefore, with natural equity and good reason, that in all and every such human laws made within this realm, or induced into this realm by the said sufferance, consents, and custom, your royal majesty, and your lords spiritual and temporal, and commons, representing the whole state of your realm, in this your high court of parliament, have full power and authority not only to dispense with those, and all other human laws of this your realm, as the quality of the persons and matter shall require: also the said laws, and every of them, to abrogate, annul, amplify, and diminish, as it shall seem to your majesty, and the nobles and commons of your realm, present in your parliament, meet and convenient for the wealth of your realm."

---

[53] Historical and political Discourse on the laws and government of England, part ii. p. 114.

However arbitrary, on some occasions, might be the behaviour of the king and his ministers, it is manifest, that the people thought they had rights and privileges by the antient constitution of the kingdom, which the king ought not to violate. It is also evident, that they considered themselves as having a right to judge of the propriety of granting subsidies to the king, and that their property was not to be taken from them without their own consent. And when cardinal Wolsey, in the height of his power, went to the house of commons, in order to reason with those who opposed granting the taxes required by the king, they refused to reason with him upon the subject.[54]

In 1525, when commissions were issued for levying taxes without parliamentary authority, lord Herbert says, "the people in general took it so ill, that it was like to have grown to a rebellion; alledging," among other reasons, "that these commissions were against the law." And though Henry, and his minister the cardinal, occasionally used very arbitrary language, yet this haughty monarch, on finding the opposition of the people, thought proper to lower his tone, and, "by letters sent through all the counties of England, declared, he would have nothing of them but by way of benevolence."[55]

This arrogant prince also, on other occasions, sometimes thought it necessary to cajole his subjects, and even to assume some appearance of humility, and to testify his gratitude for the supplies they afforded him. Thus, in a speech made by him in parliament, in 1545, in answer to an oration addressed to him by the speaker of the house of commons, Henry expressed himself in the following terms:

"I, taking upon me to answer your eloquent oration, Mr. Speaker, say, that where you, in the name of our well-beloved commons, have both praised and extolled me for the notable qualities that you have conceived to be in me, I most humbly thank you all, that you have put me in remembrance of my duty, which is to endeavour myself to obtain and get such excellent qualities, and necessary virtues, as a prince or governor should or ought to have; of which gifts I recognize myself both bare and barren: but of such small qualities as God hath endued me withal, I render to his goodness my most humble thanks, intending, with all my wit and diligence, to get and acquire to me such notable virtues and princely qualities, as you have alledged to be incorporated in my person. These thanks for your loving admonition and good council first remembered; I eftsoons thank you again; because that you, considering our great charge, not for our pleasure, but for your defence; not for our gain, but to our great cost which we have lately sustained, as well in defence against our and your enemies, as for the conquest of that fortress,

---

[54] Lord Herbert's Hist. of the Reign of Henry the Eighth, p. 146. edit. 1649.

[55] Herbert, p. 172.

which was to this realm most displeasant and noisome, and shall be (by God's grace,) hereafter to our nation most profitable and pleasant, have freely, of your own minds, granted to us a certain subsidy, here in an act specified, which verily we take in good part, regarding more your kindness than the profit thereof, as he that setteth more by your loving hearts, than by your substance."[56]

It is certain, that the power of the crown was exceedingly aggrandized, when the authority of the Roman pontiff was thrown off in England. His spiritual power being transferred to the king, and added to the other regal prerogatives, rendered the authority and influence of the prince much too great for the safety and happiness of the people. But it should be considered, that this accession of power to the crown arose from an extraordinary coincidence of circumstances, which the nation could not foresee, for which they were not prepared, and with the tendency and consequences of which they were not acquainted. They had severely felt the evil of papal usurpations and oppressions; they were therefore anxious to throw off the Roman yoke; and did not sufficiently consider, the danger to which they exposed themselves and their posterity, by transferring a similar authority to the king. Had they been sufficiently enlightened, they would have thrown off the authority of the Roman pontiff, without investing the crown with powers of a similar nature.

In his account of the reign of queen Elizabeth, whose disposition and conduct were sufficiently arbitrary, Mr. Hume says, that "the maxims of her reign were conformable to the principles of the times, and to the opinion which was generally entertained with regard to the constitution;"[57] and at the same time informs us, that the following was "the opinion which Elizabeth entertained of the duty and authority of parliaments." –

"They were not to canvass any matters of state: still less were they to meddle with the church. Questions of either kind were far above their reach, and were appropriated to the prince alone, or to those councils and ministers with whom he was pleased to intrust them. What then was the office of parliaments? They might give directions for the due *tanning of leather*, or *milling of cloth*; for the *preservation of pheasants and partridges*; for the reparation of bridges and highways; for the punishment of vagabonds or common beggars. Regulations concerning the police of the country came properly under their inspection; and the laws of this kind which they prescribed, had, if not a greater, yet a more durable authority, than those derived solely from the proclamations of the sovereign."[58] &c.

[56] Herbert, p. 534, 535.

[57] Hist. vol. v. p. 188 edit. 1763.

[58] Hist. *ubi supra*, p. 187.

But notwithstanding this extraordinary representation of Mr. Hume, it is certain, that even in that reign, much juster sentiments were entertained of the power and authority of English parliaments. Of this we have the fullest and most unquestionable evidence, in the writings of John Aylmer, Bishop of London in the reign of Queen Elizabeth, and of Sir Thomas Smith, secretary of state to that princess. In a piece written by Aylmer, and printed in 1559, is the following passage:

"The regiment of England is not a mere *Monarchy*, as some, for lack of consideration, think; nor a mere *Oligarchy*, nor *Democracy*; but a mixed rule of all these. Wherein each one of these have, or should have, like authority. The image whereof, and not the image, but the thing indeed, is to be seen in the parliament-house; wherein you shall find these three estates, the king or queen, which representeth the *Monarchy*; the noblemen, which be the *Aristocracy*; and the burgesses and knights, the *Democracy*. The very same had Lacedemonia, the noblest and best governed city that ever was. They had their king, their senate, and *hippagretes*, which were for the people. As in Lacedemonia, none of these could make or break laws, orders for war or peace, or do any thing without the other; the king nothing without the senate and commons, nor either of them, or both, without the king; albeit the senate and *ephori* had greater authority than the king had. In like manner, if the parliament use their privileges, the king can ordain nothing without them; if he do, it is his fault in usurping it, and their *folly* in permitting it. Wherefore, in my judgment, those that in king Henry's days would not grant him, that proclamations should have the force of a statute, were good fathers of the country, and worthy commendation in defending their liberty."[59]

Sir Thomas Smith, in his treatise of the "Common-wealth of England," also expresses himself thus concerning the power and business of parliaments:

"The parliament abrogateth old laws, and maketh new; giveth order for things past, and for things hereafter to be followed; changeth right and possessions of private men, legitimateth bastards, establisheth forms of religion, altereth weights and measures, giveth form of succession to the crown, defineth of doubtful right, whereof is no law already made; appointeth subsidies, tailles, taxes, and impositions; giveth most free pardons and absolutions, restoreth in blood and name; as the highest court, condemneth or absolveth them whom the prince will put to that trial. And, to be short, all that ever the people of Rome might do, either in *Centuriatis Comitiis*, or *Tribunitiis*, the same may be done by the parliament of England."[60]

These extracts are sufficient to prove the fallacy of Mr. Hume's representations,

---

[59] Vid. Strype's life of Bishop Aylmer, p. 26, 27, 28.

[60] Smith's Common-wealth of England, p. 77. edit. Lond. 1633. Vid. British Biography, vol. iii. p. 241, 242.

notwithstanding the high notions which Elizabeth herself entertained of the prerogative. But our author sometimes loves to make his readers stare; and therefore he has taken pains, in another part of his account of the reign of queen Elizabeth, to point out those particulars in which the government of England resembled that of Turkey.[61] In this Mr. Hume displayed the originality of his genius as an historic writer; for certainly no common author would have thought of comparing the constitution of the English government, which has been so long celebrated for its freedom, to one of the most despotic governments in the world.

Mr. Hume says, in his account of his own life, lately published, p. 23, that "It is ridiculous to consider the English constitution, before the period of the accession of the house of Stuart, as a *regular plan* of liberty." And it is very true, that the liberties of the people were not ascertained with the accuracy that they ought to have been, and that unjust stretches of power in the prince were too frequently submitted to: but notwithstanding this, the English government, from the earliest ages, has manifestly been characterised by a spirit of liberty; and the traces of a limited government are discernible, even in the darkest ages.

Mr. Hume, in his essays, quotes a passage from Sir Walter Raleigh, in which the king of England is spoken of under the title of an *absolute monarch*;[62] in order to shew, that men's ideas of the English government were then very different from what they are at present. But upon this it may be observed, that when the phrase *absolute king* was formerly sometimes applied to the king of England, it was evidently used in a different sense from that which we now affix to the words *absolute prince*. It was equivalent to the assertion, that the crown of England was imperial; by which nothing more was meant, than that the king of England was an independent prince, and not under the controul of any foreign power. In an act passed in the 24th year of the reign of Henry the Eighth, it is said, that "this realm of England is an empire, governed by one supreme head and king, and the crown or royal authority is also thereby declared imperial:" upon which it is justly observed by Mr. Tyrrell, who supports his opinion by the authority of Selden, "that this supremacy or freedom from all subjection, is not only challenged by our English sovereigns; but also by the kings of Denmark, Sweden, and Poland; the former of which yet was so far from being an absolute monarch, that before the reign of this king's father,[63] he might have been deposed for tyranny, or misgovernment, by the states of the kingdom, as the king of Poland may at this day. And, therefore, these titles may indeed prove a freedom from all foreign jurisdiction, but do not prove that the king is endued with an absolute sovereign power within the

---

[61] Hume's Hist. vol. v. p. 479.

[62] Political Discourses, second edition, Edinb. 1752, p. 257.

[63] The government of Denmark was rendered despotic in 1660, in the reign of Frederick the Third.

kingdom."[64] No just argument, therefore, in support of Mr. Hume's hypothesis, can be drawn from the passage cited by him from Sir Walter Raleigh, nor from another which he hath quoted from Winwood for the same purpose.

In his account of the origin of the reformation, Mr. Hume has given an injurious representation of the circumstances and motives which induced Martin Luther to promote that great event; and Dr. Maclaine, in his translation of Mosheim's Ecclesiastical History, has very properly animadverted on the insinuations against Luther, thrown out by Mr. Hume, and shewn them to be erroneous and ill-grounded.[65] But, indeed, his account of the reformation in general, and his characters of those by whom it was effected, are by no means fair and impartial, but, in many respects, justly deserving of great censure. In his first edition of the history of Great Britain, under the house of Stuart, printed at Edinburgh in 4to. in 1754, his account of the reformers was, however, more injurious than in the present editions of his work. In that edition is the following passage:

"The first reformers, who made such furious and successful attacks on the Romish superstition, and shook it to its lowest foundations, may safely be pronounced to have been *universally* inflamed with the highest enthusiasm. These two species of religion, the superstitious and fanatical, stand in diametrical opposition to each other; and a large portion of the latter must necessarily fall to his share, who is so courageous as to control authority, and so assuming as to obtrude his own innovations upon the world. Hence that rage of dispute which every where seized the new religionists; that disdain of ecclesiastical subjection; that contempt of ceremonies, and of all the exterior pomp and splendor of worship. And hence too that inflexible intrepidity, with which they braved dangers, torments, and even death itself; while *they preached the doctrine of peace*, and *carried the tumults of war*, through every part of Christendom."[66]

A few pages after this, in the same edition, Mr. Hume gives an account of the nature of the Roman Catholic religion; and this he was induced to do, he informs us, because "History addresses itself to a more distant posterity, than will ever be reached by any local or temporary theology;" and because "the characters of sects may be studied, when their controversies shall be *totally*

---

[64] Tyrrell's Bibliotheca Politica, or an enquiry into the antient constitution of the English government, p. 215.

[65] [Archibald Maclaine (1722–1804), in Mosheim's *An Ecclesiastical History* (1765), selections from which are contained earlier in this collection.]

[66] P. 7, 8. Besides the above passages, fifty lines more, immediately following, are omitted in the latter editions; but it is not thought necessary to recite them here.

forgotten." He seemed to suppose, that his history would survive, when the Romish religion was forgotten, or at least, when it should cease to be understood; and there is little reason to doubt, but that he entertained similar ideas respecting the Protestant religion. And, indeed, it was fortunate, that the memory of these two inconsiderable sects should be transmitted to posterity, through the channel of Mr. Hume's history. However, in his account of popery is the following passage:

"It has been observed, that upon the revival of letters, very generous and enlarged sentiments of religion prevailed throughout all Italy; and that, during the reign of Leo, the court of Rome itself, in imitation of their illustrious prince, had not been wanting in a just sense of freedom. But when the *enraged* and *fanatical reformers* took arms against the papal hierarchy, and threatened to rend from the church at once all her riches and authority; no wonder she was animated with equal zeal and ardour, in defence of such antient and invaluable possessions."[67]

This passage, and others in our author's work, were animadverted upon, with much good sense and spirit, in a small piece published at Edinburgh, in 8vo. in 1756, under the title of "Letters on Mr. Hume's History of Great Britain:" and both the passages which have been just cited, appear to have been omitted in the latter editions of this history. At least, they are wholly omitted in the editions which I have chiefly used; that is, the octavo editions of 1763 and 1773. And unfortunately for future ages, the whole of that curious paragraph, containing an account of popery, and which was addressed "to a more distant posterity than will ever be reached by any local or temporary theology," is entirely omitted. Though, if the uncastrated edition should happily be preserved in public libraries, posterity may yet be in some degree enlightened.

Mr. Hume speaks of it as one of the advantages the first reformers had over the Romish clergy, and which contributed towards the reformation, that the latter "were totally unacquainted with controversy, much more with every species of true literature; they were unable to defend themselves against men, armed with authorities, citations, and popular topics, and qualified to triumph in every altercation or debate."[68] But though we may readily admit, that a very large part of the Romish clergy were immersed in great ignorance, yet it is not

---

[67] P. 26 – As the above passages are omitted in the latter editions of Mr. Hume's history, the writer of these observations hath not particularly animadverted on, or examined, the strong charge brought against the reformers, of being *universally inflamed with the highest enthusiasm*. He was, however, of opinion, that these passages, and the omission of them, were not unworthy the notice of the public. Though it should be observed by the reader, that all the other passages in Mr. Hume's work, on which remarks are here made, are cited as they stand in the later editions.

[68] Hist. vol. iv. p. 42, edit. 8vo. 1763.

to be supposed, but that there were many among them capable of defending the papal see, and the doctrines of the Romish church, with sufficient ability for that age, if the cause in which they were engaged had been capable of being defended. But Mr. Hume was willing to attribute the success of the reformers to any cause, rather than to the force of truth, or rational investigation. He probably considered every species of religion, or, as he would rather term it, every species of superstition, as equally indefensible on the principles of reason.

Our historian also mentions "the invention of printing," and "the revival of learning," as among the causes of the progress of the reformation. And it is true, that both these causes did considerably contribute to facilitate that great event. But notwithstanding what he has insinuated to the contrary, neither of these causes would have operated in any great degree in favour of the reformation, if the Romish religion had not been of such a nature, that the extension of knowledge, and the increase of books, must tend to render its absurdity, and the injustice of its pretensions, more obvious and more generally known. As men became more enlightened, in consequence of the resurrection of letters, and of the facility with which books were multiplied by the important invention of the art of printing, it was highly natural, that a system of superstition should give way, which had derived its existence from the ignorance and credulity of mankind, and which was utterly incapable of standing the test of free enquiry and rational examination. But Mr. Hume gives it as his opinion, that reason did not bear "any considerable part in opening men's eyes with regard to the impostures of the Romish church:"[69] and in another place he says, that the reformation "owed not its success to reason and reflection." Indeed, our historian seems to have had but a very low idea of the efficacy of reason in religious controversy. For he says, that there is no instance, "where argument has been able to free the people from that enormous load of absurdity with which superstition has *every where* overwhelmed them."

John Lambert, who lived in the very age of which Mr. Hume was writing, and who was burnt for heresy in the reign of Henry the Eighth, appears to have had juster sentiments upon this subject. In his answer to the articles exhibited against him, speaking of the writings of Luther, he expresses himself thus: "He (Luther) coveteth above all things, as all his adversaries do well know, that all his writings, and the writings of all his adversaries, might be translated into all languages, to the intent that all people might see and know, what is said of every part, whereby men should *the better judge* what the *truth* is."[70] Lambert thought, and justly thought, that it was the truth and reason manifested in Luther's writings, which occasioned them to have so much effect upon the minds of men, and to become so formidable to the Romish church. Indeed,

---

[69] P. 40.

[70] Fox's Acts and Monuments, vol. ii. p. 398. edit. 1641.

Lambert, considering the age in which he lived, appears to have been well acquainted with the reasonableness and importance of free enquiry in matters of religion.

Mr. Hume speaks of the age of the reformation, as being generally *seized with a spirit of innovation*;[71] and *the novelty of the doctrines* of the reformation, he mentions as one of the circumstances which facilitated that great event. But it is certainly not very common for large bodies of men, to shew a great readiness in embracing opinions, either in theology, or any other subject, merely because they are new. And the fact seems rather to be, that men have always had a strong attachment to their antient opinions, and that it is with difficulty they are brought to reject them. Nor does it appear very philosophical to suppose, that in the age of the reformation, men were influenced by sentiments and propensities so exceedingly different from those by which they are ordinarily actuated. But Mr. Hume was willing to admit any supposition, however improbable, rather than acknowledge, that the reformation owed its success to the force of truth and reason.

Indeed, Mr. Hume, notwithstanding the liberties which he has himself taken in his writings, appears to have been no friend to the established Protestant principle, that all men have a right to examine for themselves the foundation of those religious opinions which are proposed to them, or to which their teachers endeavour to procure their assent. At least he asserts, that the generality of mankind are utterly unqualified for inquiries of this kind. "Nothing," says he, "forwarded more the first progress of the reformers than the offer, which they made, of submitting all religious doctrines to private judgment, and the summons given every one to examine the principles formerly imposed on him. Though the multitude were *totally unqualified* for this undertaking, they yet were highly pleased with it."[72]

He seems to have thought, that the Protestants have treated the fopperies of the Romish church with too much ridicule, though his own enumeration of some of them is sufficiently ludicrous. And he endeavours to persuade his readers, that these absurd superstitions were not so disgraceful to Popery as many have been apprehended. Speaking of the dissolution of the monasteries, he says,

"Protestant writers mention on this occasion, with great triumph, the sacred repositories of convents; the parings of St. Edmund's toes; some of the coals that roasted St. Laurence; the girdle of the virgin shewn in eleven several places; two or three heads of St. Ursula; the felt of St. Thomas of Lancaster, an infallible cure for the head-ach; part of St. Thomas of Canterbury's shirt,

[71] Hist. vol. iv. p. 141.

[72] P. 137.

much reverenced by big-bellied women; some reliques, an excellent preventative against rain; others, a remedy to weeds in corn. But," the historian adds, "such fooleries, as they are to be found in all ages and nations of the world, and even took place during the most refined periods of antiquity, form no PECULIAR nor VIOLENT reproach on the Catholic religion."[73]

Our historian's hypothesis respecting ecclesiastical establishments, is somewhat curious. He admits, that if the support of ecclesiastics were left to "the liberality of individuals, who are attached to their doctrines, and who find benefit or consolation from their spiritual ministry and assistance; their industry and vigilance" would "be whetted by such an additional motive; and their skill in the profession, as well as their address in governing the minds of the people, must receive daily increase from their increasing practice, study, and attention."[74] But this diligence of the clergy, which he stiles *interested*, Mr. Hume thought "every wise legislator would study to prevent." He considered the clergy as of so much utility to society, that the more indolent they were the better. "In reality," says he, "the most *decent* and *advantageous* composition which he can make with the spiritual guides, is to *bribe their indolence*, by affixing stated salaries to their profession, and rendering it *superfluous* for them to be *farther active*, than merely to preserve their flock from straying in quest of *new pastures*."[75] These observations are introductory to his account of the reformation, but they are of so general a nature, that they are equally applicable to the clergy of any other church, as to that of the church of Rome.

Mr. Hume seems generally unwilling to suppose, that any persons could suffer martyrdom from good motives; and, therefore, his accounts of persons under such circumstances, are often extremely destitute of candour and of equity. Thus in his narrative of the case of Lambert, who was burnt in the reign of Henry the Eighth, with circumstances of great barbarity, for denying the doctrine of the real presence in the sacrament, Mr. Hume says, that "Lambert possessed that courage which consists in obstinacy;" though he had no other reason for this assertion, than that Lambert would not publickly abjure his opinions, to save his life. And he also suggests, that the fortitude with which he underwent his public examination and sufferings, was the result of *vanity*; a suggestion as void of probability as of equity. He who can suppose, that vanity will support a man at the stake, must possess no ordinary portion of credulity. But Mr. Hume was willing to attribute the heroic firmness of Lambert to motives of any kind, however improbable, rather than to such as would have done honour to his integrity, and to the religion he professed. Our historian

[73] P. 194, 195.

[74] P. 33.

[75] P. 34.

seems to have been fond of propagating the notion, that persons suffering martyrdom for their opinions, might be more influenced by vain glory, than by motives of strict integrity, and a regard to the sacredness of truth. Thus speaking of Anne Askew, and three other persons who were burnt with her for heresy, in 1546, he says,

> "They were all tied to the stake; and in that dreadful situation, the chancellor sent to inform them, that their pardon was ready drawn and signed, and should instantly be given them, if they would merit it by a recantation. They only regarded this offer as a *new ornament* to the crown of martyrdom; and they saw with tranquility the executioner kindle the flames which consumed them. Wriothesely did not consider, that this *public* and *noted situation* interested their honour the more to maintain a steady perseverance."[76]

John Lambert, who hath been just mentioned, was a clergyman, and seems to have been a man of considerable learning and abilities, and was entitled, from any candid and equitable historian, to a much more honourable representation than is given of him by Mr. Hume. His real name was John Nicolson; but he told king Henry, that he had been compelled to change his name by the bishops.[77] He taught the Latin and Greek languages in London. He appears to have been a truly conscientious man; and the insinuations thrown out against him by Mr. Hume, of his being influenced by vanity, are wholly without foundation; and arose only from our historian's unwillingness to admit, that any man could suffer death for his religious opinions, and be wholly actuated by motives truly virtuous and commendable. But however lax may be the sentiments of some modern sceptics, respecting the sacred nature and importance of truth, I have no doubt, but that there have been many virtuous heathens, who would have suffered death, rather than have made an open and solemn profession of their belief in opinions, of the falsehood of which they were well persuaded.

Mr. Hume seems to have thought, that the situation of affairs may be such, as to justify persecution for religious opinions. Thus, speaking of the persecutions in Scotland in the reign of James the Fifth, and of those in Germany and France, under Charles the Fifth, and Francis the First, he says, 'the extremities to which all these princes were carried, proceeded *entirely* from the situation of affairs during that age, which rendered it impossible for them to act with greater temper or moderation, after they had embraced the resolution of supporting the antient establishments. So violent was *the propensity of the*

---

[76] P. 279.

[77] Vid. Fox's Acts and Monuments, vol. ii. p. 425. edit. 1641.

times towards innovation, that a toleration of the new preachers was equivalent to a formed design of changing the national religion.'[78]

The attempts made to enslave the French nation, and, in particular, to reduce the Protestants to submit to the will of their monarch, Mr. Hume seems to mention with much approbation. Speaking of the attempts of Richlieu for this purpose, and more immediately of the reduction of Rochelle, he says, 'This was the first *necessary step* towards the *prosperity* of France. Foreign enemies, as well as domestic factions, being deprived of this resource, that kingdom began now to shine forth in its full splendor. By a steady prosecution of wise plans, both of war and policy, it gradually gained an ascendant over the rival power of Spain; and every order of the state, and every sect, were reduced to pay submission to the lawful authority of the sovereign.'[79]

[3. HOUSE OF STUART]

Mr. Hume appears to have considered the reign of James I. as the æra of English national felicity, at least with respect to persons of fortune. 'Could human nature,' says he, 'ever reach happiness, the condition of the English gentry, under so mild and benign a prince, might merit that appellation.'[80] And now, for the first time, such it seems were the public advantages of the accession of the house of Stuart, the people became acquainted, that, as Englishmen, they possessed some privileges. 'In all European monarchies,' says our historian, 'the people have privileges, but whether dependant or independant on the will of the monarch, is a question, that, in most governments, *it is best to forbear.* Surely that question was not determined (in England) before the age of James I.'[81] So that, if we were to give credit to Mr. Hume, we must suppose, that the people of England did not know, before the reign of James the First, that they held any of their privileges by any other tenure, than the pleasure of the prince. But this is a groundless and indefensible notion. And as to enjoying privileges *dependant on the will of the monarch,* this may be done in the most despotic country upon earth. The inhabitants of Russia, of Turkey; of Morocco, may certainly enjoy privileges at the will and pleasure of their princes.

In order to extenuate the conduct of king James I. in the case of Sir Walter Raleigh, Mr. Hume seems to have been much inclined to blacken the character of that celebrated person.[82] And his principal authority for much of what he

---

[78] Hist. vol. iv. p. 250, edit. 1763.

[79] Hist. vol. vi. p. 203.

[80] Vol. vi. p. 112.

[81] In the edition of 1773, the above passage is in the 570th page of the sixth volume.

[82] Vid. Hist. vol. vi. p. 31, 34, 35, 36, 37. edit. 1763.

says upon this subject, is king James's "Declaration of the demeanour and carriage of Sir Walter Raleigh, knight, as well in his voyage, as in and sithence his return; and of the true motives and inducements which occasioned his majesty to proceed in doing justice upon him, as hath been done." But notwithstanding what our historian hath urged to make this royal publication[83] appear of "undoubted credit," it is certain, that an artful defence, published by the court, of an odious and unpopular measure, is not very implicitly to be relied on. Indeed, king James himself has, in some degree, borne testimony to the merit of Sir Walter Raleigh, though to his own dishonour: for soon after Sir Walter's execution, the king beginning to see that he should probably be deluded by the Spanish ministry, made one of his ministers write to his agent in Spain, to let that court know they would be looked upon as the most unworthy people in the world, if they did not now act with sincerity, since his majesty had given so many testimonies of his; and now of late,

"by causing Sir Walter Raleigh to be put to death, *chiefly for the giving them satisfaction*. Further, to let them see how, in many actions of late, his majesty had strained upon the affections of his people, and especially in this last concerning Sir Walter Raleigh, who died with a great deal of courage and constancy. Lastly, that he should let them know how able a man Sir Walter Raleigh was, to have done his majesty service. Yet, *to give them content*, he hath not spared him, when, by preserving him, *he might have given great satisfaction to his subjects*, and had at command, upon all occasions, as useful a man as served any prince in Christendom."[84]

---

[83] In the preamble to this Declaration it is said, "Although Kings be not bound to give account of their actions to any but God alone; yet such are his majesty's proceedings, as he hath always been willing to bring them before sun and moon, and carefully to satisfy all his good people with his intentions and courses, giving as well to future times, as to the present, true and undisguised declarations of them." Harleian Miscellany, vol. iii. p. 18. It appears, that Sir Walter Raleigh was apprehensive, that somewhat would be published after his death to traduce his memory: for when he was upon the scaffold, he particularly requested lord Arundel, "to desire the king, that no *scandalous writing* to defame him, might be published at his death."

Mr. Hume speaks of the king's Declaration rather ambiguously, and in a manner that might lead his readers to suppose, that this was subscribed by six privy-counsellors: but the fact is, it was not subscribed by any privy-counsellor. But reference is made in the Declaration to examinations taken in the presence of six privy-counsellors, which examinations were subscribed by them, and made use of in drawing up the Declaration. But the Declaration itself was not subscribed by any of them. Vid. the edition of this, in 4to. printed by Norton and Bill, in 1618.

[84] Life of Sir Walter Raleigh by Mr. Oldys, prefixed to his History of the World, edit. 1736. p. 232, and British Biography, vol. iv. p. 71.

In his account of the reign of Charles the First, Mr. Hume is desirous of leading his readers to consider the parsimony of the house of commons, at the commencement of this reign, as the source of the subsequent troubles. But this sentiment, which he hath laboured so much to establish, appears to be very ill grounded.[85] There is very little reason to believe, that Charles would have restrained his power within the proper limits, whatever liberality the commons might have displayed in granting him supplies. A desire of extending the prerogative ever appeared to be predominant in him. And it was surely rational in the house of commons, not to be too lavish in their grants of the public money, without endeavouring to obtain some redress of the national grievances. When they found the duke of Buckingham continued to be the royal favourite in this reign, as he had been in the preceding, they had abundant reason to conclude, that the public grievances would be continued, and probably increased, if proper measures were not adopted for their prevention. It was certainly a just ground for caution and jealousy in the house of commons, when they saw the most important offices of the nation, and the management of its affairs, still continue to be entrusted to a weak, incapable, and headstrong minister, to an arrogant and all-grasping

---

[85] It is observable, that lord Clarendon, though a known partizan of the court, seems to have had different ideas upon this subject, and to have been less partial in his representations in this respect than Mr. Hume. Speaking of the three first parliaments of Charles, he says, 'It is not to be denied, that there were, in all those parliaments, especially in that of the fourth year, several passages, and distempered speeches of particular persons, not fit for the dignity and honour of those places, and unsuitable to the reverence due to his majesty and his councils. But I do not know any formed act of either house, (for neither the remonstrance nor votes of the last day were such) that was not agreeable to the wisdom and justice of great courts, upon those extraordinary occasions. And whoever considers the acts of power and injustice of some of the ministers, in those intervals of parliament, will not be much scandalized at the warmth and vivacity of those meetings.'

'In the second parliament there was a motion, and intention declared of granting five subsidies, a proportion (how contemptible soever in respect of the pressures now every day imposed) scarce ever before heard of in parliament. And that meeting being, upon very unpopular and unplausible reasons, immediately dissolved, those five subsidies were exacted, throughout the whole kingdom, with the same rigour as if, in truth, an act had passed to that purpose. Divers gentlemen, of prime quality, in several counties in England, were, for refusing to pay the same, committed to prison, with great rigour, and extraordinary circumstances. And could it be imagined, that those men would meet again in a free convention of parliament, without a sharp and severe expostulation, and inquisition into their own right, and the power that had imposed upon that right? And yet all these provocations, and many other, almost of as large an extent, produced no other resentment than the petition of right (of no prejudice to the crown) which was likewise purchased at the price of five subsidies more, and, in a very short time after that supply granted, the parliament was likewise, with strange circumstances of passion on all sides, dissolved.' Hist. of the Rebellion, vol. i. p. 5. edit. 8vo. 1705.

favourite.[86] It is absurd to maintain, that because the parliament would not grant to Charles those supplies which he had, or supposed he had, occasion for, that therefore he was in any degree justified in the various arbitrary, unjust, and oppressive acts, of which he was afterwards guilty. The withholding supplies till justice was done to the subject, was the true constitutional check upon the crown: and it is doing extreme injustice to the great parliamentary leaders at the commencement of Charles's reign, to attribute the subsequent misfortunes of the nation to their conduct on this occasion.

Of the Petition of Right, Mr. Hume says, that "it may be affirmed, without any exaggeration, that the king's assent to it produced such a change in the government, as was almost equivalent to a revolution."[87] But this must surely appear a very extraordinary assertion, when it is considered, that the privileges and liberties claimed by this petition were unquestionably founded on the ancient laws of the kingdom. And it is a most absurd idea to suppose, that because the people had occasionally submitted to unjust stretches of the prerogative, that therefore they were under any obligation to acquiesce in the attempts made to establish a compleat despotism. It should also be observed, that lord Clarendon, notwithstanding his known partiality to Charles, acknowledges that the petition of right was *of no prejudice to the crown*. Though a great lawyer, who lived in the same age, a servant of Charles, and personally attached to him, he acknowledged, that the petition of right was of no injury to the crown: the very same act that Mr. Hume asserts to have "produced such a change in the government, as was almost equivalent to a revolution." Either, therefore, lord Clarendon had no ideas of the nature of the English government in his own time, or these notions of Mr. Hume are the mere reveries of a sportive imagination.

Our historian frequently takes pleasure in representing, in a ridiculous or unfavourable light, the most respectable of the parliamentary leaders. Thus he

---

[86] The following were the titles and offices of the duke of Buckingham: 'George, duke, marquis, and earl of Buckingham, earl of Coventry, viscount Villiers, baron of Whaddon, great admiral of the kingdoms of England and Ireland, and of the principality of Wales, and of the dominions and islands of the same, of the town of Calais, and of the marches of the same, and of Normandy, Gascoigne, and Guienne, general governor of the seas and ships of the said kingdom, lieutenant-general admiral, captain general and governor of his majesty's royal fleet and army lately set forth, master of the horse of our sovereign Lord the King, lord warden, chancellor, and admiral of the Cinque Ports, and of the members thereof, constable of Dover-castle, justice in eyre of the forests and chaces on this side the river Trent, constable of the castle of Windsor, gentleman of his majesty's bedchamber, one of his majesty's most honourable privy council in his realms both of England, Scotland, and Ireland, and knight of the most honourable order of the garter.' Rushworth's Historical Collections, vol. i. p. 303.

[87] Hist. vol. vi. p. 259, edit. 1773.

mentions the celebrated JOHN HAMPDEN as one of those, "who had resolved
for ever to abandon their native country, and fly to the other extremity of the
globe, where they might *enjoy lectures and discourses of any length or form
which pleased them.*"[88] Upon this it is sufficient to remark, that though
Hampden had probably much more religion, yet he appears to have been as
little of an enthusiast as David Hume himself.[89]

Our author, speaking of the year 1640, says, that "*noise and fury, cant and
hypocrisy,* formed the sole *rhetoric,* which, during this tumult of various prejudices and passions, could be attended to."[90] That many of the performances
of this period were violent and enthusiastical, may be readily admitted; but that
noise, fury, cant, and *hypocrisy,* constituted the *sole rhetoric* which the people
attended to at that time, is known not to be a truth, by every man who is
accurately acquainted with the publications and speeches of this period. The
terms in which Mr. Hume has expressed himself on this occasion, are the
language of a mere party writer, and not of an impartial historian.

He has also said of the house of commons, in 1642, "that they were resolved,
if possible, to excite the king to some violent passion; in hopes that he would
commit indiscretions, of which they might make advantage."[91] But this appears
to be a very unwarrantable method of writing history. It is imputing the most
unworthy motives to the great parliamentary leaders, without producing the
least evidence in support of what is advanced.

Extreme partiality is also manifested by Mr. Hume, in his representation of
the character, conduct, and trial, of the earl of Strafford. He says, "Such was
the capacity, genius, presence of mind, displayed by this magnanimous

---

[88] Vol. vi. p. 311. In another place he says, that the whole discourse and language of Pym,
Hampden, and Vane, were "full of the lowest and most vulgar hypocrisy." P. 325. edit.
1763.

[89] In the last edition of his history, that of 1778, which was not published till a considerable part of these observations was printed off, Mr. Hume has added the following
remark relative to his notion of Mr. Hampden's being tinctured with enthusiasm. He
says, that Hampden's "intended migration to America, where he could only propose
the advantage of enjoying puritanical prayers and sermons, will be allowed a proof
of the prevalence of this spirit (the enthusiastical) in him." Vol. vi. p. 587. But surely,
when measures were carrying on in this country to establish despotism both in church
and state, there can be no just reason for considering Hampden as an enthusiast, merely
because he had formed a design to go into America, in hopes of enjoying there the
blessings of civil and religious liberty. Or if this must be considered as enthusiasm, it
is of that kind which has animated some of the noblest of the human race, both in
ancient and in modern times. However contemptuously an ardent love of liberty may
be treated by a Hume, it was this which greatly contributed to ennoble much superior
characters, not only a HAMPDEN, but a LOCKE and a SYDNEY, a SELDEN and a
MILTON.

[90] P. 314.

[91] Vol. vi. p. 401. edit. 1763.

statesman, that, while argument and reason and law had any place, he obtained an undisputed victory. And he perished, at last, overwhelmed, and still unsubdued, by the *open violence* of his *fierce* and *unrelenting* antagonists."[92]

Our historian had before observed, that Strafford was "sensible of the load of popular prejudices under which he laboured."[93] That the people of England, Scotland, and Ireland, were extremely incensed against this nobleman, is very true; but there is no occasion to impute this to *prejudice* of any kind. It was the natural result of his conduct, which had been arbitrary, oppressive, and unconstitutional, and calculated to excite universal indignation.

But Mr. Hume says, that "though four months were employed by the managers in framing the accusation, and all Strafford's answers were extemporary; it appears from comparison not only that he was free from the crime of treason, of which there is not the least appearance, but that his conduct, making allowance for human infirmities, exposed to such severe scrutiny, was INNOCENT, and even LAUDABLE."[94]

Whether the conduct of Strafford was either *innocent* or *laudable*, may be best determined by a view of some of the facts that were proved against him upon his trial: and which may, perhaps, be sufficient to convince every unprejudiced reader, that his fate is not greatly to be deplored; unless by those who are of opinion, that men who act under the authority of kings, and, by their command, may be justified in the commission of the most atrocious crimes.

It was proved against him, that he had acted in a very arbitrary and illegal manner, as lord president of the court and council of the North.[95] As lord

---

[92] *Ibid.* p. 335.

[93] P. 304.

[94] P. 335, 336.

[95] Vid. the account of lord Strafford's trial in Rushworth's Historical Collections, vol iv. p. 140, 141, 142, 144.

The court and council of the North, (or, as it was often called, the court and council of York) was first erected, after some insurrections, by a patent from king Henry VIII, without any authority from parliament. Its power had been extended by degrees, but was never so great as it was after Wentworth was made president, king Charles having thought proper to invest him and the council with extraordinary discretionary powers. It was afterwards complained of by the people in the North, as an intolerable grievance; and Mr. Hyde, afterwards earl of Clarendon, was appointed, by the house of commons in 1641, to represent to the house of peers the pernicious consequences of this court. In his speech on this occasion, which is still extant, Mr. Hyde stiles this court "a great and crying grievance; which, though (says he) it be complained of in the present pressures but by the northern parts, yet, by the logic and consequences of it, it is the grievance of the whole kingdom." He also says, that it had "almost overwhelmed that country under the sea of arbitrary power, and involved the people in a labyrinth of distemper, oppression, and poverty." He likewise observes, that after Wentworth was made president, new clauses were added to the commission, which crowded in a mass of new, exorbitant, and intolerable power." He proceeds,

lieutenant of Ireland, he had also acted in a still more despotic manner, and treated persons of the best quality in Ireland with the utmost arrogance, insolence, and injustice. The earl of Corke deposed, that when he had commenced a suit at law in a case in which he apprehended himself to be aggrieved, the earl of Strafford, in the most arbitrary manner, forbad his prosecuting his suit, saying to him, "Call in your writs, or if you will not, I will clap you in the castle; for I tell you, I will not have my orders disputed by law, nor lawyers."[96] Lord Corke also farther deposed, that he being prosecuted in the Star-chamber, for having made a lease of a parsonage, contrary to an act of state made in king James's reign; and thereupon representing to lord Strafford, that it was merely an act of charity, and that he was not apprized of any such act of state, and intimating that he thought he could not legally be prosecuted for violating an obsolete act of state, lord Strafford answered, "I tell you, my lord, as great as you are, I will make you, and all the subjects of Ireland know, that any act of state made, or to be made, shall be as binding to you, and the subjects of Ireland, during my government, as an act of parliament."[97]

Sir Pierce Crosby deposed, that soon after Strafford came to Ireland, being at dinner in the deponent's house, with several others of the privy-council, he took occasion to say, that "if he, the earl of Strafford, lived, he would make an act of state to be of equal power with an act of parliament;" and added, that Ireland was a conquered nation, and the conqueror should give the law."

John Waldron deposed, that in a cause between the merchants of Galloway and others, concerning a church lease, at the council-table, Mr. Martin, who

---

"What hath the good northern people done, that they only must be disfranchised of all their privileges by Magna Charta, and the petition of right; for to what purpose serve these statutes, if they may be fined and imprisoned without law, according to the discretion of the commissioners? What have they done, that they, and they alone, of all the people of this happy island, must be disinherited of their birth-right, of their inheritance?" – "Truly, my lords, these vexed worn-out people of the North are not suitors to your lordships to regulate this court, or to reform the judges of it, but for extirpating these judges, and the utter abolishing this court." [Vid. this speech of Hyde at length, in Speeches and passages of the parliament of 1641, edit. 4to, 1641, p. 409, 416.] Mr. Guthrie observes, (Hist. Eng. vol. iii. p. 916.) that had Strafford "been guilty of no other demerit, he deserved to lose his head, for accepting what no king of England can give, and no free-born subject ought to execute; I mean a commission, that, in effect, set aside the laws of the land, and left no other visible tenure of justice, than the wills of men, always fallible, and often corrupted, influenced by sentiments of gratitude, fear, or expectancy towards the crown; resentments of hatred, envy, and malevolence against the subject." Vid. British Biography, vol. iv. p. 388, 389.

[96] Trial of Strafford, as published in Rushworth, p. 175. It should be observed, that the account of this memorable trial printed in Rushworth, is much more copious and accurate than that in the State Trials; in which the speeches of Pym, Maynard, Glyn, &c. are wretchedly mutilated; and many other important particulars wholly omitted.

[97] Rushworth, p. 176.

acted as council for the merchants, mentioning an act of parliament, which, he said, made for his client, Strafford said, "He would make him know, that an act of that board should be as good as a statute:" or to that purpose. Lord Killmallock, and John Kay, also deposed to the same effect.

Mr. Lotts deposed, that the commons having rejected some bills, particularly one which made it felony for a private person to have gunpowder, without a licence; and being sent for up to the house of lords, Strafford told them, that notwithstanding they had voted against it, yet he would make that, and some other bills they had voted against, acts of state, that should be as good."[98]

It was also proved, that, by Strafford's influence, lord Mountnorris was sentenced to be shot to death, for making use of an expression that the lord lieutenant disliked, and which, it was pretended, had a mutinous meaning; and, in his defence, Strafford spoke of this infamous sentence as "being only intended to discipline lord Mountnorris, and to teach him to govern his speech with more modesty."[99] It appears also, that lord Mountnorris was, for a considerable time, imprisoned, and deprived of an estate, though on other pretences.

Robert Kennedy deposed, that on the 30th of September, 1633, he was the king's remembrancer in Ireland, and that day the new mayor of Dublin was presented to lord Strafford; and the recorder made a speech on the occasion, reciting the many graces they had received from the kings of England, and among the rest, a charter that no soldier should be billetted on the city of Dublin. That the lord lieutenant answered several passages in the speech; and particularly said, "That they were a conquered nation, and the king might do with them as he pleased: and for their antiquated charters, they were binding no farther than he pleased." The earl of Corke also gave evidence to the same purpose.

Archbishop Usher being ill, his examination was read, in which that prelate declared, that discoursing with the earl of Strafford in Ireland, concerning some levies of money made upon the subject, Strafford said, that "he agreed with those in England, who thought that, in case of imminent necessity, the king might make use of his prerogative to levy what he needed." But added, that, "in his opinion, his majesty was first to try his parliament, and if they supplied him not, then he might make use of his prerogative as he pleased himself;" or words to that effect.

The earl of Bristol deposed, that discoursing with lord Strafford of the distractions of the times, after the breaking up of the last parliament, and the deponent proposing the summoning a new parliament as the best means to compose matters; lord Strafford did not dislike the proposal, but said it was

[98] Rushworth, p. 184.

[99] Rushworth, p. 200.

not adviseable at that time; for that the present dangers of the kingdom were so pressing, they could not "admit of so *slow* and *uncertain* a remedy as a parliament was." That the parliament had, in the great distress of the king and kingdom, refused to supply the king in the ordinary and usual way of subsidies: "and, therefore, the king must provide for the safety of his kingdom, by such ways he should think fit in his wisdom." And farther, "That the king was not to suffer himself to be mastered by the frowardness and undutifulness of his people."

Thomas Wiseman deposed, that the lord-mayor and aldermen of London being called before the council for not levying the ship-money, Strafford said, "They would never do their duties well, till they were put to fine and ransom;" and that he also said, "You will have no good of this man, (meaning the lord-mayor, as he supposed,) till he is laid by the heels."

Sir Henry Garraway, the lord-mayor, deposed, that having been obliged to attend the privy-council on account of the affair of ship-money, and having set forth the difficulties of levying ship-money before his majesty and council, it was ill taken; and lord Strafford said to the king, "Sir, you will never do good on this man till you have made him an example; he is too diffident: unless you commit him, you shall do no good upon him." That being also summoned with the aldermen before his majesty and the council, about a loan, and being desired to give in lists of those that were able to lend in their several wards, they refused; whereupon Strafford burst out into these words: "Sir, you will never do good to these citizens of London, till you have made examples of some of the aldermen: unless you hang some of them, you will do no good upon them."[100]

Strafford was also accused by the commons with having cited jurymen to appear in the Irish Star-chamber, where pains and penalties were inflicted on them for their verdicts. He admitted the charge, and contented himself with vindicating or extenuating what he had done.[101] It was likewise proved, in the course of the evidence against him, that in Ireland he had imprisoned and fined men by the authority of himself and the council only; that he had levied taxes on goods without any parliamentary authority; that he had arbitrarily caused the goods of persons to be seized, who had refused to obey his commands, though those commands were unwarrantable, and altogether unsupported by any law; and that he caused soldiers to be quartered on private persons, if they did not obey his orders.

Upon the whole, it is unquestionably certain, that the conduct of Strafford was so far from being either *innocent* or *laudable*, that it was in a very high degree criminal, and that he was a just object of national indignation, and of

---

[100] Vid. Rushworth, p. 584, 585.

[101] Rushworth, p. 125.

public prosecution. As lord president of the North, as lord lieutenant of Ireland, and as a privy-counsellor in England, he had laboured to trample on the rights of the people, and had been guilty of acts of great injustice and oppression. That he defended himself with great eloquence and address, and that he applied, with great art, to the passions of his auditors, is very true; but all this proves nothing as to his general innocence of the charges that were brought against him; and there is surely little reason for the assertion of Mr. Hume, that "though his death was loudly demanded as a satisfaction to justice, and an atonement for the many violations of the constitution; it may safely be affirmed, that the sentence, by which he fell, was an enormity greater than the worst of those which his implacable enemies prosecuted with so much cruel industry."[102]

Whether all the proceedings against Strafford, and his final sentence, were in every respect strictly legal, I shall not take upon me to determine. The law, perhaps, may not have made the same provision for bringing iniquitous ministers of state to justice, that it has for inferior criminals. But however this be, it is certain, that Strafford did not fall undeservedly; and that there is very little reason for those pathetic lamentations that are thrown out upon this subject by Mr. Hume. If Strafford had not been guilty of treason against the person of Charles, he had been guilty of treason against the rights of the people: and if this be a species of treason not yet to be found in our statute-books, it is high time that it should find a place there. Of all public crimes, attempts to subvert the rights of the people, and to overturn a free constitution, are the greatest, and ought to be the most severely punished. The idea that the personal security of the king is of more consequence, than the preservation of the rights and privileges of a whole nation, can arise only from the most contemptible servility.

Mr. Hume says, that "even a few weeks after Strafford's execution, this very parliament remitted to his children the more severe consequences of his sentence; as if conscious of the violence with which the prosecution had been conducted."[103] But no such consciousness can justly be considered as implied in this. Nothing more can fairly be inferred from it, than that the parliament had too much magnanimity and generosity, to desire that the children of Strafford should suffer for the crimes of their father.

Of the political maxims which Strafford recommended to Charles, and the advice which he gave him, some idea may be formed from such of his dispatches as have been published. In one of these, addressed to the king, concerning the calling a parliament in the kingdom of Ireland, after mentioning the obligations which an Irish parliament would be under to grant the king supplies, he says, "Should they not conform themselves to your gracious will, their unthank-

[102] Vol. vi. p. 354. edit. 1763.
[103] P. 335.

fulness to God, and the best of kings, becomes inexcusable before all the world, and the regal power more warrantably to be at after extended for redeeming and recovering your majesty's revenues thus lost, and justly to punish so great a forfeit as this must needs be judged to be in them."[104] In the same dispatch are also the following passages: "Conditions are not to be admitted with any subjects, less with this people, where your majesty's absolute sovereignty goes much higher than it is taken, *perhaps*, to do in England."[105]

It appears also from the same dispatch, that Strafford was sufficiently skilled, for that age, in the modelling and managing of parliaments. "I shall endeavour," says he, "the lower house may be so composed, as that neither the recusants, nor yet the protestants, shall appear considerably more one than the other, holding them, as much as may be, upon an equal balance; for they will prove thus easier to govern, than if either party were absolute." – "I will labour to make as many captains and officers burgesses, as possible I can, who, having immediate dependance upon the crown, may almost sway the business betwixt the two parties, which way they please." – "In the higher house, your majesty will have, I trust, the bishops wholly for you."[106]

In another of his letters, he recommends it to the king, to be ready to give reasonable *rewards* to the *judges* for occasional services; and afterwards adds, "I am most confident, were your majesty purposed but for a while to use the excellent wisdom God hath given you in the constant, right, and quick applying of *rewards* and *punishments*, it were a thing most easy for your servants, in a very few years, under your conduct and protection, so to settle all your affairs and dominions, as should render you, not only at *home*, but abroad also, the most *powerful* and considerable king in Christendom."[107]

It appears, from several of his letters, that he was very solicitous to promote the imposition of *ship-money* both in England and in Ireland; and in one of his dispatches he says, "It is plain, indeed, that the opinion delivered by the judges, declaring the *lawfulness* of the assignment for the shipping, is the *greatest service*[108] that profession hath done the *crown* in my time. But unless his majesty hath the *like power* declared to raise a *land army* upon the same exigent of state, the crown seems to me to stand but upon one leg *at home*, to be considerable but by halves to foreign princes abroad."[109] And Strafford was

---

[104] Earl of Strafford's letters and dispatches, published by Dr. Knowler, folio, 1739, vol. i. p. 183.

[105] *Ibid.* p. 184.

[106] Ibid. p. 187.

[107] Strafford's letters and dispatches, vol. ii. p. 41.

[108] This was probably one of that kind of services for which Strafford thought it would be proper to *reward the judges*: and it is certainly not reasonable to expect, that men should violate their consciences for nothing.

[109] Ibid. p. 61.

certainly in the right, that it would have been an improvement of Charles's regal power, if the judges, by proper douceurs and encouragements, could have been prevailed upon to invest him with an authority to raise money for both fleets and armies, without the concurrence of parliament.

In the same dispatch, he speaks of "vindicating the royalty at home from under the conditions and restraints of subjects;" and observes, that an army raised by the king's prerogative, would insensibly gain a precedent, and settle an authority and right in the crown to levies of that nature, which thread draws after it many huge and great advantages, more proper to be thought on at some other seasons than now." He adds, "By this time his majesty will find, how little I look upon my own *safety*, where his greatness and prosperity come in place."[110]

In one of his letters to Charles, Strafford speaks of himself as being "reported to all the world rather for a Basha of Buda, than the minister of a pious and Christian king."[111] In another he says,

> "Sir, my faith enforceth me, with all humility, to inform your majesty, that the liberty of such as mutiny the hierarchy, and would, I fear, in the next place, do as much for monarchy itself, increaseth very much: (a gradation which that wise and excellent king, your blessed father, had found, by experience, in the beginnings of his reign in Scotland) and worthy it will be of your majesty's wisdom and providence, that we have your direction how to carry ourselves. With longing we wait for it: and were it left to us, should not fail to give all such in this kingdom current and sound payment."[112]

And in another of his dispatches he says,

> "I understand that party (the Scotch) is much blown up with their expectations of help from their countrymen on this side, and sure such an assimilation of humours there is amongst them, as the conjecture is probable enough; yet, Sir, be you pleased to restore us but these five hundred men you borrow from this army, and I durst, with the peril of my life, be answerable to contain all here in quietness: but then I must have present and *full authority* to take every little inclination in the first appearance of it, *and to crush the serpent in the egg.*"[113]

---

[110] Ibid. p. 62.

[111] Vol. ii. p. 27.

[112] Ibid. p. 229.

[113] Ibid. p. 235.

It is evident, from the letters of Strafford, as well as from what was proved against him at his trial, that he was a most dangerous and arbitrary minister; that he violated himself every principle of law and of a free constitution; that he gave the most pernicious advice to the king; and that he well deserved the fate he met with.

Of archbishop Laud, Mr. Hume says, that "the maxims of his administration were the same which had *ever prevailed* in England."[114] Without particularly animadverting upon this, it may be sufficient to remark, that our historian's apology for this prelate, has in it much more of art and sophistry, than of sound argument and solidity. But even the unjust and barbarous sentences passed in the court of Star-chamber, though Mr. Hume does not formally defend them, yet he speaks of them in very gentle terms. "The severity of the Star-chamber," he says, "which was generally ascribed to Laud's passionate disposition, was, *perhaps*, in itself SOMEWHAT BLAMEABLE."

From the letters of Laud to Strafford, it appears, that the views and inclinations of the archbishop agreed extremely well with those of the lord-lieutenant: and that they were both equally disgusted with the restraints of law. In one of Laud's letters he says,

"I must desire your lordship not to expect more at my hands than I shall be able to perform, either in church or state; and this suit of mine hath a great deal of reason in it; for you write, that ordinary things are far beneath that which you cannot chuse but promise yourself of me in both respects. But, my lord, to speak freely, you may easily promise more in either kind, than I can perform: for, as for the *church*, it is so bound up in the forms of the common law, that it is not possible for me, or for any man, to do that good which he would, or is bound to do. For your lordship sees, no man clearer, that they which have gotten so much power in, and over the church, will not let go their hold; they have, indeed, fangs with a witness, whatsoever I was once said in passion to have. And for the *state*, indeed, my lord, I am for *thorough*, but I see that *both thick and thin* stays somebody, where I conceive it should not; and it is impossible for me to go *thorough* alone."[115]

In another letter to Strafford the archbishop says,

"I have received the copy of the sentence against Paterson, and am verily of your lordship's mind, that a little more quickness in the government would cure this itch of libelling, and something that is amiss besides, but you know what I have written, and truly I have done expecting of *thorough* on this side,

---

[114] Vol. vii. p. 41.

[115] Strafford's letters and dispatches, vol. i. p. 111.

and therefore shall betake myself to that which you say, and, I believe, is the next best; and yet I would not give over neither. As for Challenour, it was the weakest part that ever Mr. secretary Coke did, to leave him in the hands of a messenger, and not commit him to a very safe prison. But what can you think of *thorough*, where there shall be such slips in business of consequence? But what say you to it, that Prynee and his fellows should be suffered to talk what they pleased while they stood in the pillory, and with acclamations from the people, and have notes taken of what they spake, and these notes spread in written copies about the city, and that when they went out of town to their several imprisonments, there were thousands suffered to be upon the way to take their leave, and God knows what else."[116]

In another letter he says, "Your lordship apprehends right *the ill consequences of the liberty of these times*, both in speech and otherwise, and that Prynne is not the first that hath done mischief in this kind; nor do I think he will be the last; nor have I any great hope to see these things settle, nor other things as considerable as these, till reward and punishment[117] *have their full course*, and attend merit, not persons."[118]

Mr. Hume's account of the reign of king Charles I. may be considered rather as a specious and artful apology for that prince's conduct, than a just history. In some respects, it is more partial than the celebrated history of lord Clarendon, though that nobleman was an avowed partizan of Charles. But this seems to have been necessary, in order to enable Mr. Hume to support his favourite hypothesis. And with respect to lord Clarendon, it appears to have been a sentiment never entertained by him, that the government of England was little better than despotic[119] at the accession of the house of Stuart. This was a discovery for which we are indebted to the acuteness of more modern writers.

Charles's arbitrary administration of government for eleven years, without the intervention of one parliament, was certainly sufficient to exasperate the people, and a natural source of the civil war that followed. It is to his tyranny,

---

[116] Strafford's letters and dispatches, vol. ii. p. 99.

[117] From hence it appears, that the severity with which Prynne was treated, was not sufficient in the good archbishop's opinion. He was sentenced to have his book against plays, masquerades, &c. burnt by the hands of the common hangman, to be removed from the bar, and to be for ever rendered incapable of his profession, to stand twice in the pillory, to lose his ears, to pay a fine of 50000l. and to suffer perpetual imprisonment. But all this was not enough. He was *permitted to speak in the pillory*; and this gave the archbishop great uneasiness. This evil was, however, in some degree prevented, in the case of John Lilburne; for he was gagged in the pillory, by order of the court of Star-chamber; of which Laud was one of the principle members.

[118] Strafford's letters and dispatches, vol. ii. p. 131.

[119] Mr. Hume stiles the English government *a monarchy almost absolute*. Vol. vi. p. 312. edit. 1763.

and to his obstinacy, that the national calamities are justly to be attributed, notwithstanding all the specious glosses, and artful representations of Mr. Hume.

Our historian says of Charles, that had the limitations on prerogative been, in his time, quite fixed and certain, his integrity had made him regard, as sacred, the boundaries of the constitution." But this assertion will appear totally groundless, if we consider, that his administration of government, for a series of years, was little better than one continued violation of the Petition of right, which he had himself solemnly passed into a law. This is a demonstration, that however exactly the constitution might have been ascertained, the integrity of Charles would never have afforded a security to his subjects. If we could suppose him to have been totally ignorant of Magna Charta, and of every law made to restrain his predecessors from invading the rights of the people, or that he imagined those laws not binding upon him, we cannot suppose him ignorant of the petition of right, which he had bound himself to adhere to in the most explicit manner. And yet, for a series of years, he continued to trample on the right of his subjects in the most wanton manner, and in direct violation of this statute. To suppose, that this can be defended on any solid principles, or that such a conduct was consistent with integrity, is to suppose, that the most solemn engagements which can be entered into amongst men, are not binding on the parties; and that the humour of princes, or political expediency, may justify the greatest enormities. It is, indeed, not unworthy of observation, that in the very same page in which Mr. Hume speaks of the *virtuous and gentle temper of Charles*, he also gives it as his opinion, that it is not improbable, if he had been possessed of a sufficient military force, he would have enslaved his subjects.[120] So that such a conduct, according to Mr. Hume's ideas, would have been perfectly consistent with a *virtuous and gentle temper*.

Our historian, though he was certainly not fond of giving very favourable representations of the efficacy of piety, yet finds it productive of the best effects in the case of king Charles I. "While every thing around him," says he, "bore a hostile aspect; while friends, family, relations, whom he passionately loved, were placed at a distance, and unable to serve him; he reposed himself with confidence in the arms of that Being, who penetrates and sustains all nature, and whose severities, if received with piety and resignation, he regarded as the surest pledge of unexhausted favour."[121] It may, however, very reasonably be questioned, whether a prince, who had involved his subjects in all the horrors of civil war, merely to support his own unjust and tyrannical claims, could have any just grounds for confiding in the favour of the Almighty.

[120] Vid. Hist. vol. vi. p. 161.

[121] Vol. vi. p. 118.

In speaking of the extravagant notions and practices which prevailed in England after the execution of king Charles I. Mr. Hume says, that "it became a pretty *common doctrine* at that time, that it was unworthy of a Christian man to pay rent to his fellow-creatures; and landlords were obliged to use all the penalties of law against their tenants, whose conscience was scrupulous."[122] So extraordinary an assertion as this certainly deserved some evidence to support it, but with this we are not favoured; and, indeed, that such a doctrine should ever have become *pretty common,* is too incredible to be believed.

Our historian's representation of the propensity of the people of England, at this period, to form new systems of government and religion, is certainly much more ludicrous than just. "*Every man,*" he says, "had framed the model of a republic; and, however new it was or fantastical, he was eager in recommending it to his fellow-citizens, or even imposing it by force upon them. *Every man* had adjusted a system of religion, which, being derived from no traditional authority, *was peculiar to himself*; and being founded on supposed inspiration, not on any principles of human reason, had no means, besides cant and low rhetoric, by which it could recommend itself to others."[123] He also speaks of the more moderate republicans, as being "so intoxicated with their *saintly character,* that they supposed themselves possessed of peculiar privileges; and *all professions, oaths, laws,* and *engagements* had, (he says) in a great measure, lost their influence over them."[124] An author, who takes such liberties as these, may draw amusing pictures, but he surely cannot justly be considered as writing history.

Mr. Hume, in a great degree, attributes the civil war, and the calamities which attended it, to the irregularities of the English constitution of government; and to the prerogative of the king, and the privileges of the people, not being exactly ascertained. And yet, with much inconsistency, he speaks with approbation of Charles II. being restored, without any conditions, or new limitations. "Had the parliament," says he, "before restoring the king, insisted on any farther limitations than those which the constitution already imposed; besides the danger of reviving former quarrels among parties; it would seem that their caution had been *entirely superfluous.*"[125] What he urges in support of this opinion is, that, "by reason of its slender and precarious revenue, the crown in effect was *still* totally dependent." But as this had been the case before the civil war, and was not then sufficient to prevent regal tyranny, and the consequent national commotions, it was certainly not a suffi-

---

[122] Vol. vii. p. 173. edit. 1763. In the edition of 1778, this passage is in p. 528 of the same volume.

[123] Hist. vol. vii. p. 155. edit. 1778.

[124] P. 156.

[125] Vol. vii. p. 355, edit. 1778.

cient security to the people after the Restoration. When the nation had been so long struggling against tyranny, and the power was in their own hands, it was manifestly in the highest degree irrational, to invest the son of the late king with regal dignity, without stipulating proper conditions for the future security of the liberties of the people.

The conduct of Charles II. in the cases of Russel and Sydney, was too gross to be defended; and, therefore, Mr. Hume does not attempt this: but he endeavours to lessen our ideas of the criminality of those transactions, and to palliate, as much as possible, the behavior of the king. In the latter case, that of Algernon Sydney, after giving a sketch of his character and conduct, our historian says, "it may easily be conceived how obnoxious he was become to the court and ministry: what alone renders them inexcuseable, was the illegal method which they took of effecting their purpose against him."[126] And yet, after having thus admitted that illegal methods were adopted by the court to bring Sydney to the scaffold, he endeavours to throw the guilt of the transaction chiefly on the jury. "The evidence against him, it must be confessed, was not legal; and the jury who condemned him, were, for that reason, very blameable. But that after sentence passed by a court of judicature, the *king* should interpose and pardon a man, who, though otherwise possessed of great merit, was *undoubtedly guilty*,[127] who had ever been a most inflexible and inveterate enemy to the royal family, and who lately had even abused the king's clemency, might be an act of *heroic generosity*, but can never be regarded as a necessary and indispensible duty."[128]

Our historian says, that "Charles II. in 1672, may with reason be deemed the aggressor, nor is it possible to justify his conduct:"[129] and yet he immediately urges all he can in extenuation of it. And he was so desirous to apologize for the conduct of the Stuarts, that though it is certain that Charles II. had formed schemes to enslave his subjects, and engaged in intrigues with France of such a nature, that they must for ever render his memory infamous, and of which there is the most unquestionable evidence; yet our historian says, that all the enormities of his government, "if fairly and candidly examined, may be imputed, in a great measure, to the *indolence of his temper*; a fault, which, however unfortunate in a monarch, it is impossible for us to regard with great severity."[130]

---

[126] Vol. viii. p. 192.

[127] Sydney was *undoubtedly guilty* of a strong attachment to the liberties of his country, and an incurable aversion to every species of despotic government.

[128] P. 193.

[129] Vol. viii. p. 321, edit. 1778.

[130] Vol. viii. p. 206. edit. 8vo. 1763. Vol. vi. p. 371. edit. 4to. 1767.

Mr. Hume labours to place, in a very unfavourable light, the conduct of lord Churchill, afterwards duke of Marlborough, at the Revolution. "Lord Churchill," says he,

> "had been raised from the rank of a page, and had been invested with a high command in the army; had been created a peer, and had owed his whole fortune to the king's bounty: yet even this person could resolve, during the present extremity, to desert his unhappy master, who had ever reposed entire confidence in him. He carried with him the duke of Grafton, natural son to the late king, colonel Berkely, and some troops of dragoons. This conduct was a signal sacrifice to public virtue of *every duty in private life*, and required, *for ever after*, the most upright, the most disinterested, and most public spirited behaviour, to render it *justifiable.*"

Our historian afterwards adds:

> "But Churchill had prepared a still more mortal blow for his distrest benefactor. His lady and he had an entire ascendant over the family of prince George of Denmark; and the time now appeared *seasonable for over-whelming the unhappy king*, who was already staggering with the violent shocks, which he had received. Andover was the first stage of his majesty's retreat towards London, and there prince George, together with the young duke of Ormond, Sir George Huet, and some other persons of distinction, deserted him in the night-time, and retired to the prince's camp. No sooner had this news reached London, than the princess Anne, *pretending* fear of the king's displeasure, withdrew herself, in the company of the bishop of London and lady Churchill. She fled to Nottingham; where the earl of Dorset received her with great respect, and the gentry of the county quickly formed a troop for her protection." – "It is, indeed, singular, that a prince, whose chief blame consisted in *imprudences* and *misguided principles*, should be exposed, from *religious antipathy*, to such treatment as even Nero, Comitian, or the most enormous tyrants that have disgraced the records of history, never met with from their friends and family."[131]

At the very close of his history, and in the last edition of it, in the course of his reflections on the revolution, Mr. Hume still persists in apologizing for the conduct of James I. and Charles I. "The inconveniencies," he says, "suffered by the people under the two first reigns of the family of Stuart (for in the main they were fortunate) proceeded, in a great measure, from the *unavoidable situation of affairs*; and scarcely any thing could have prevented those events,

---

[131] Vol. viii. p. 286, 287, 288, edit. 1763.

but such vigour of genius in the sovereign, attended with such *good fortune*, as might have enabled him *entirely to overpower the liberties of the people.*"[132]

[4. CONCLUDING OBSERVATIONS]

Our author, in the course of his history, seems studious to lessen the reputation of some of the most celebrated English geniusses. He generally begins with bestowing some compliments upon them, and then contrives, with great dexterity, to throw out such insinuations against them, and so magnifies their defects, real or imaginary, as almost wholly to overturn what he has said in their favour: and the ideas which he endeavours to convey are such, as, if we adopt them, must greatly lessen our opinion of the merit of the eminent persons of whom he speaks. Thus, after several complimentary expressions of SPENSER, and stiling him "the finest English writer of his age," he says, "Yet does the perusal of his work become so tedious, that one never finishes it from the mere pleasure which it affords: It soon becomes a kind of task-reading; and it requires some *effort* and *resolution* to carry us on to the end of his long performance." – He "was employed in drawing the affectations, and conceits, and fopperies of chivalry, which appear ridiculous, as soon as they lose the recommendation of the mode. The tediousness of continued allegory,[133] and that too *seldom striking or ingenious*, has also contributed to render the *Fairy Queen* peculiarly tiresome."[134]

Of SHAKESPEARE, Mr. Hume says, that if he "be considered as a man born in a *rude age*, and educated in the lowest manner, *without any instruction*, either from the *world* or from *books*, he may be regarded as a prodigy." That is, Shakespeare may be regarded as a prodigy, if he be viewed in a light in which he never was, or could be viewed, by any human creature. It has been supposed, that Shakespeare was little versed in the antient languages; but that he had derived no instruction either from the world or from books, was never yet seriously supposed by any man. It may, indeed, be pretended, that Mr. Hume's meaning only was, that Shakespeare had not received the advantages of a liberal education, or had any opportunity of improving his sentiments by a converse with the higher classes of mankind. But if this be his meaning, he has

---

[132] Vol. viii. p. 320, edit. 1778.

[133] The writer of these observations does not mean to controvert the propriety of every sentiment advanced in the passages cited from Mr. Hume. Part of what the historian says may be just, though the other part be manifestly unjust; and, in making quotations, it is sometimes difficult to separate the one from the other. It will be sufficient for our purpose, if the passages cited prove, upon the whole, that Mr. Hume has *endeavoured*, without just reason, to *lesson the reputation of some of the most celebrated English geniusses.*

[134] Hist. vol. v. p. 492. edit. 1778. 8vo.

certainly not expressed it with much accuracy; and the evident design of his remarks is, to lessen the reputation of Shakespeare. "In his compositions," he says, "we regret, that many irregularities, and even absurdities, should so frequently disfigure the animated and passionate scenes intermixed with them; and at the same time we perhaps *admire the more those beauties, on account of their being surrounded with such deformities.* A striking peculiarity of sentiment, adapted to a singular character, he frequently hits, as it were by inspiration, but a reasonable propriety of thought he cannot, for any time, uphold." He also observes, that there may "remain a suspicion, that we over-rate, if possible, the greatness of his genius; in the same manner as bodies often appear more gigantic, *on account of their being disproportioned and mishappen.*"[135]

Of lord BACON, Mr. Hume says, that if we consider the variety of talents displayed by this man, as a public speaker, a man of business, a wit, a courtier, a companion, an author, a philosopher; he is justly the object of great admiration. If we consider him merely as an author and philosopher, the light in which we view him at present, though very estimable, he was yet inferior to his contemporary Galilæo, perhaps even to Kepler." There does not appear to be the least judgment or propriety in these parallels, which are calculated for no other purpose, but to lower our ideas of Bacon's merit: and yet, to those who think justly, they can have no such effect. We may admit the superiority of Galilæo and Kepler in astronomy, mechanics, and some particular branches of physical knowledge; and yet it will by no means follow, that either of them were equal to Bacon as philosophers, or as writers for the instruction of mankind, and the advancement of universal science. This is the light in which Bacon should be viewed, and it is the light in which he has always been viewed, by those who were the best acquainted with his writings, and the best judges of his merit.[136] But Mr. Hume farther observes, that "that *national spirit*, which prevails among the English, and which forms their great happiness, is the cause, why they bestow on all their eminent writers, and Bacon among the rest, such praises and acclamations as may often appear partial and excessive."[137] Unhappily for Mr. Hume's remark, lord Bacon is one of the worst instances that could have been produced, as an evidence of the national partiality of the English. For it appears evident, that foreigners, at least for a considerable time, had a much higher opinion of Bacon's merit, than his own countrymen;

---

[135] Hist. vol. vi. p. 191, 192. edit. 1778.

[136] We must have a very high opinion of the importance of lord Bacon's writings to the learned world, if we admit the truth of the assertion of Dr. Beattie, and it appears to be well founded, *viz.* that "science had made more progress since his time, and by his method, than for a thousand years before."
    Essays, edit. 4to. Edinb. 1777. p. 263.

[137] Vol. vi. p. 194, 195. edit. 1778.

so that Francis Osborne, who lived in the same age, observes of him, that he "was over-balanced by a greater weight of glory from strangers;" and the author of Bacon's article in the *Biographia Britannica* says, that "the memory of this admirable man, expanded more fragrantly abroad for many years, than here in his native country." And it is remarkable, that lord Bacon himself appears to have foreseen this. For in his will is the following passage: "For my name and memory, I leave it to men's charitable speeches, and to foreign nations, and the next ages." It is, therefore, manifest, that the attributing the high commendations that have been bestowed on Bacon to the national partiality of the English, is an imagination at once groundless and absurd.

Mr. Hume seems, in some respects, to have been more inclined to do justice to MILTON; and yet it is manifest, that he was sufficiently ready to urge whatever could plausibly be advanced, in diminution of the character of this great and illustrious poet. In his character of him, and of his writings, he says, that "in the Paradise Lost, his capital performance, there are very long passages, amounting to *near a third of the work*, almost wholly devoid of harmony and elegance, nay, of *all vigour of imagination*:" and that his prose writings are disagreeable, though *not altogether defective in genius.*" He also says, that he "was deeply engaged with fanatics, and even prostituted his pen in theological controversy, in factious disputes, and in justifying the most violent measure of the party."[138] But notwithstanding all that has been said upon this subject, there is no reason whatever to suppose, that Milton wrote, either in politics or theology, what was contrary to his own private judgment. It is, therefore, highly injurious to say of such a man, that *he prostituted his pen*. Milton was republican from principle; and he thought a tyrant ought to be put to death as much as any inferior malefactor; and on this ground he vindicated the execution of Charles the First. It may also humbly be presumed, that a man does not necessarily *prostitute his pen* by engaging in theological controversy, by giving his opinion on matters, supposed at least to be of importance among Christians, any more than Mr. Hume would imagine he did by writing in support of the glorious cause of infidelity and irreligion.

That Milton thought he had no reason to be ashamed of his political writings, nor had any ideas of his having *prostituted his pen*, is evident from his sonnet to Cyriac Skiner, on his blindness.

"Cyriac, this three years day, these eyes, tho' clear,
To outward view, of blemish or of spot,
Bereft of light their seeing have forgot,
nor to their idle orbs doth sight appear
Of sun, or moon, or star throughout the year,

[138] Vol. vii. p. 343, edit. 1778.

Or man, or woman. Yet I argue not
Against heaven's hand or will, nor bate a jot
Of heart or hope; but still bear up and steer
Right onward. What supports me, dost thou ask?
The conscience, friend, to have lost them overply'd
In Liberty's defence, my noble task,
Of which all Europe talks from side to side.
This thought might lead me thro' the world's vain mask
Content, tho' blind, had I no better guide."

It will be sufficient barely to recite the character which our historian has given of the celebrated ROBERT BOYLE, without making any remarks on it, to convince those who are acquainted with his merit and his writings, how little inclined Mr. Hume was to do him justice. "Boyle," he says,

"improved the pneumatic engine, invented by Otto Guericke, and was thereby enabled to make several new and curious experiments on the air, as well as on other bodies. His chymistry is much admired by those who are acquainted with that art: his hydrostatics contain a greater mixture of reasoning and invention with experiment, than any other of his works; but his reasoning is still remote from that blindness and temerity, which had led astray so many philosophers. Boyle was a great partizan of the mechanical philosophy; a theory, which, by discovering some of the secrets of nature, and allowing us to imagine the rest, is so agreeable to the natural vanity and curiosity of men."[139]

And, after having spoken in very high terms of NEWTON, he closes the whole with the following curious observation: that while that great man seemed to draw off the veil from some of the mysteries of nature, he shewed, at the same time, the imperfections of the mechanical philosophy; and thereby *restored her ultimate secrets to that obscurity*, in which they ever did and ever will remain."[140]

Notwithstanding the defects of Mr. Hume's History of England, it may be read with considerable advantage, if it be read with caution, with a due attention to the prevailing views, sentiments, and prepossessions of the writer, and if it be compared with other English historical authors. Independent of its merit as a composition, it may be admitted, that much real information, and many remarks equally just and acute, are to be found in Mr. Hume's history; but those who read his work, without such a previous acquaintance with

[139] Vol. viii. p. 333, 334. edit. 1778.
[140] P. 334.

other English historians, as will, in some degree, enable them to judge of the truth and impartiality of his representations, will often be led into the most erroneous conceptions. And it is certainly by no means a proper book to be put into the hands of British youth, in order to give them just ideas of the history and constitution of their own country; though this is an use to which it is sometimes applied. It requires a maturity of judgment, and a considerable degree of historic knowledge, to be able to read it without being misled by the political prejudices of the author, and by the art and dexterity which frequently attend his misrepresentations. There are sentiments in it which may be highly pernicious to the minds of youth, especially when considered in the light of subjects of a free state: and in many places the observations of this historian are calculated to infuse into his readers principles of scepticism, and to give them views very unfavourable, not only to superstition and enthusiasm, but to genuine and rational religion. For as our author had very unfavourable ideas of Christianity, he seldom let slip a plausible opportunity of throwing out insinuations against it, as well as against its teachers.

Though Mr. Hume's language is, in general, extremely elegant, yet there are in his work no inconsiderable number of unauthorized modes of expression, and grammatical inaccuracies; of which the ingenious Dr. Priestley, in his English grammar, hath afforded a very copious specimen.[141] It may also be observed, that, in the whole course of his history, Mr. Hume has hardly ever excelled in the description of a battle; almost all his descriptions of that kind being unanimated and uninteresting. He could describe a theological disputation with abundantly more energy and spirit than any warlike actions, though of the most brilliant kind. His descriptions of the battles of Cressy, Poictiers, or Agincourt, are much inferior, in point of spirit, to his account of king Henry the Eighth's disputation with John Lambert. And it may also be observed, that in the descriptions given by him of the most celebrated military actions of the English, he generally appears much inclined to lessen their splendor, and to speak disparagingly of the nation and their exploits.[142]

In his short narrative of his own life, Mr. Hume says, p. 23, "Though I had been taught by experience, that the Whig party were in possession of bestowing all places, both in the state and in literature, I was so little *inclined to yield* to their *senseless clamour*, that in above an hundred alterations, which farther study, reading, or reflection engaged me to make in the reigns of the two first Stuarts, I have made all of them invariably on the Tory side." But did this really

---

[141] [Joseph Priestley (1733–1804), *The Rudiments of English Grammar* (1768), selections from which are contained earlier in this collection.]

[142] Mr. Hume says, "the English never left their own country, but when they were conducted by a king of extraordinary genius, or found their enemy divided by intestine factions, or were supported by a powerful alliance on the continent." Hist. vol. iii. p. 98.

arise from conviction, or did the objections made by the Whigs to Mr. Hume's history, excite in him so much resentment, as to encrease his prejudices against them? That pure, unbiassed reason, should have dictated to him, to make all his alterations on one side only, or that there should have been no just cause for making a single alteration on the opposite side, is an improbability, that Mr. Hume would not easily have admitted in the case of any other writer.

He complains, that since the revolution, the influence of the Whigs "has proved destructive to the truth of history." And "no man," he says, "has yet arisen, who has *payed an entire regard to truth*, and has dared to expose her, without covering or disguise, to the eyes of the prejudiced public."[143] This defect, we are probably to understand, is now supplied by the publication of Mr. Hume's history. He likewise informs us, that in consequence of the influence of the Whigs, "compositions the most despicable, both for stile and matter, have been extolled, and propagated, and read; as if they had equalled the most celebrated remains of antiquity."[144] These *despicable compositions*, he informs us in a note, are those of RAPIN THOYRAS,[145] LOCKE, SYDNEY, HOADLY, &c.[146] Is it possible, that any friend to the interests of civil and religious liberty, and the common rights of mankind, or any man that has a just regard to characters of distinguished merit, can endure to hear such treatises as those of Locke and Sydney on government, not to mention the works of bishop Hoadly, spoken of as *compositions the most despicable both for style and matter*, without feeling the strongest indignation? Or can such a method of speaking of the productions of authors so truly respectable and illustrious, be vindicated by the most partial of our historian's friends?

There is a neatness, an elegance, and a perspicuity, in Mr. Hume's narrations, which cannot fail to captivate his readers. But those who read history from rational motives, must wish to be instructed, as well as entertained: and no elegance of composition can atone for gross misrepresentations of the real state of facts. Indeed, the greater the liberties may be which are taken by an historian, in disguising and ornamenting facts and characters, and the more what is called history approaches to romance, it may be the more pleasing, but it must be the less instructive. It may also be remarked, that an historian may be thought profound, when he points out, or seems to do so, the motives by which those were actuated of whom he writes; though it may often happen, that these

---

[143] Vol. viii. p. 322, edit 1778.

[144] P. 323.

[145] P. 323. It is observable, that, in his *Political Discourses*, Mr. Hume stiles Rapin *the most judicious of historians*. But it is surely somewhat singular, that the writings of the most judicious of historians, should be *despicable both for style and matter*. Vid. Hume's Political Discourses, p. 268. edit. Edinb. 1752.

[146] Hist. vol. viii. p. 323, edit. 1778. This note is not in the edition of 1763, nor probably in any but the last.

are nothing but the mere imaginations of the writer; and the motives which he suggests, may be totally different from those by which the parties were really influenced. There is reason to believe, that this is not unfrequently the case in Mr. Hume's history.

Though our historian, from his desire of placing the princes of the house of Stuart in a favourable point of view, frequently palliates the most exceptionable parts of their conduct; yet it is but justice to him to acknowledge, that there are sundry passages in his histor
y highly favourable to the general interests of liberty, and the common rights of mankind. But these are much more than counterbalanced, by a great number of passages and sentiments of so different a nature, that we have little reason to applaud our author for his consistency. And, upon the whole, it is apprehended, that the Observations which are offered to the public in these pages, must be sufficient to evince, that whatever commendation may be due to Mr. Hume as an ingenious, elegant, and polished writer, he is not entitled to equal praise as an exact, faithful, and impartial historian. Whatever may be the beauties of his stile, and however we may admire the eloquence with which his work is embellished, it is nevertheless certain, that we must have recourse to other sources of information, if we would obtain an accurate knowledge of the English history, if we would form just ideas of the most remarkable transactions and characters which occur in the annals of this country.

FINIS.

29
WILLIAM HAYLEY

William Hayley, *An essay on history; in three epistles to Edward Gibbon, Esq. with notes.* By William Hayley, Esq., London: printed for J. Dodsley, 1780, [4], 159, [1] p.
Selections from Epistle 2; from 1780 edition.

William Hayley (1745–1820) was the author of more than twenty poetical and other literary works, and was most noted for his biography of William Cowper (1803–1804). Exceptionally popular for some decades, his fame dissipated by the time of his death. His *Essay on History* – among his earlier works – is a commentary in verse on classical and modern historians. Well acquainted with literary figures of his day, he addressed the book to his friend Edward Gibbon. The selection below is from the close of Epistle Two (lines 368–493), which discusses recently deceased British historians. In this selection, Hayley attacks Hume for his sophistry, partiality and scepticism, and he contends that Hume's fame is dying. The *Critical Review* praised both the style and content of Hayley's *Essay*:

> This is a subject worthy of Mr. Hayley's muse, and he has treated it with that care and attention which it so highly deserves. The poem is written in a nervous, animated, and expressive style, adorned in many parts with glowing imagery and description. The observations are in general excellent, and the sentiments new and striking. [*Critical Review*, July 1780, Vol. 50, pp. 10–13]

Writing for the *Monthly Review*, Edmund Cartwright – who favourably reviewed Hayley's *Epistle to a Friend* earlier that year – speaks highly of this work as well:

> We are happy to find this new star in the poetical hemisphere, whose appearance we noted with so much pleasure, continues to shine, if possible, with increasing splendor. The province of literature affords hardly any subject of critical discussion that is of higher dignity and importance than that to which Mr. Haley has now directed his attention.

Cartwright is particularly impressed with Hayley's depiction of Hume and Clarendon:

> To point out, to Readers of taste, the masterly touches of the pencil and the strength of colouring that are observable in these, and indeed all his portraits, would be needless. The characters of Hume and Clarendon are of peculiar excellence. [*Monthly Review*, July 1780, Vol. 63, pp. 30–38]

Hayley's *Essay* was published again twice in 1781 and twice in 1782. The following is from the first edition of 1780.

EPISTLE TWO.

...

Hail to thee, Britain! hail! delightful land!
I spring with filial joy to reach thy strand:
And thou! blest nourisher of Souls, sublime
As e'er immortaliz'd their native clime,
Rich in Poetic treasures, yet excuse
The trivial offering of an humble Muse,
Who pants to add, with fears by love o'ercome,
Her mite of Glory to thy countless sum!
With vary'd colours, of the richest die,
Fame's brilliant banners o'er thy Offspring fly:
In native Vigour bold, by Freedom led,
No path of Honour have they fail'd to tread:
But while they wisely plan, and bravely dare,
Their own atchievements are their latest care.
Tho' CAMDEN, rich in Learning's various store,
Sought in Tradition's mine Truth's genuine ore,
The waste of Hist'ry lay in lifeless shade,
Tho' RAWLEIGH'S piercing eye that world survey'd.
Tho' mightier Names there cast a casual glance,
They seem'd to saunter round the field by chance,
Till CLARENDON arose, and in the hour
When civil Discord wak'd each mental Power,
With brave desire to reach this distant Goal,
Strain'd all the vigour of his manly soul.
Nor Truth, nor Freedom's injur'd Powers, allow
A wreath unspotted to his haughty brow:
Friendship's firm spirit still his fame exalts,
With sweet atonement for his lesser faults.

His Pomp of Phrase, his Period of a mile,
And all the maze of his bewilder'd Style,
Illum'd by Warmth of Heart, no more offend:
What cannot Taste forgive, in FALKLAND'S friend?
Nor flow his praises from this single source;
One province of his art displays his force:
His Portraits boast, with features strongly like,
The soft precision of the clear VANDYKE:
Tho', like the Painter, his faint talents yield,
And sink embarrass'd in the Epic field.
Yet shall his labours long adorn our Isle,
Like the proud glories of some Gothic pile:
They, tho' constructed by a Bigot's hand,
Nor nicely finish'd, nor correctly plan'd,
With solemn Majesty, and pious Gloom,
An awful influence o'er the mind assume;
And from the alien eyes of every Sect
Attract observance, and command respect.
    In following years, when thy great name, NASSAU!
Stampt the blest deed of Liberty and Law;
When clear, and guiltless of Oppression's rage,
There rose in Britain an Augustan age,
And cluster'd Wits, by emulation bright,
Diffus'd o'er ANNA'S reign their mental light;
That Constellation seem'd, tho' strong its flame,
To want the splendor of Historic fame:
Yet BURNET'S page may lasting glory hope,
Howe'er insulted by the spleen of POPE.
Tho' his rough Language haste and warmth denote,
With ardent Honesty of Soul he wrote;
Tho' critic censures on his work may shower,
Like Faith, his Freedom has a saving power.
    Nor shalt thou want, RAPIN! thy well-earn'd praise;
The sage POLYBIUS thou of modern days!
Thy sword, thy Pen, have both thy name endear'd;
This join'd our Arms, and that our Story clear'd:
Thy foreign hand discharg'd th' Historian's trust,
Unsway'd by Party, and to Freedom just.
To letter'd Fame we own thy fair pretence,
From patient Labour, and from candid Sense.
Yet Public Favour, ever hard to fix,
Flew from they page, as heavy and prolix.
For soon, emerging from the Sophists' school,

With Spirit eager, yet with Judgment cool,
With subtle skill to steal upon applause,
And give false vigour to the weaker cause;
To paint a specious scene with nicest art,
Retouch the whole, and varnish every part;
Graceful in Style, in Argument acute;
Master of every trick in keen Dispute!
With these strong powers to form a winning tale,
And hide Deceit in Moderations's veil,
High on the pinnacle of Fashion plac'd,
HUME shone the idol of Historic Taste.
Already, pierc'd by Freedom's searching rays,
The waxen fabric of his fame decays. –
Think not, keen Spirit! that these hands presume
To tear each leaf of laurel from thy tomb!
These hands! which, if a heart of human frame
Could stoop to harbour that ungenerous aim,
Would shield thy grave, and give, with guardian care,
Each type of Eloquence to flourish there!
But Public Love commands the painful task,
From the pretended Sage to strip the mask,
When his false tongue, averse to Freedom's cause,
Profanes the spirit of her antient laws.
As Asia's soothing opiate Drugs, by stealth,
Shake every slacken'd nerve, and sap the health;
Thy Writings thus, with noxious charms refin'd,
Seeming to soothe its ills, unnerve the Mind.
While the keen cunning of thy hand pretends
To strike alone at Party's abject ends,
Our hearts more free from Faction's Weeds we feel,
But they have lost the Flower of Patriot Zeal.
Wild as thy feeble Metaphysic page,
Thy Hist'ry rambles into Sceptic rage;
Whose giddy and fantastic dreams abuse
A HAMPDEN'S Virtue, and a SHAKESPEAR'S Muse.
   With purer Spirit, free from Party strife,
To soothe his evening hour of honour'd life,
See candid LYTTLETON at length unfold
The deeds of Liberty in days of old!
Fond of the theme, and narrative with age,
He winds the lengthen'd tale thro' many a page;
But there the beams of Patriot Virtue shine;
There Truth and Freedom sanctify the line,

And laurels, due to Civil Wisdom, shield
This noble Nestor of th' Historic field.
   The living Names, who there display their power,
And give its glory to the present hour,
I pass with mute regard; in fear to fail,
Weighing their worth in a suspected scale:
Thy right, Posterity! I sacred hold,
To fix the stamp on literary Gold;
Blest! if this lighter Ore, which I prepare
For thy supreme Assay, with anxious care,
Thy current sanction unimpeach'd enjoy,
As only tinctur'd with a slight alloy!

30
CRITICAL OBSERVATIONS

Critical observations concerning the Scottish historians Hume, Stuart and
Robertson: including an idea of the reign of Mary Queen of Scots, as a portion
of history. London: printed for T. Evans, 1782, [2], 53, [1] p.
Part 2, complete; from 1782 edition.

By 1780, Scotland boasted several prominent historians, most notably,
William Robertson, Tobias Smollett, Robert Henry, Gilbert Stuart, and
David Hume. A favourite pastime of critics was to compare the merits and
demerits of various historians, and in 1782 an anonymous pamphlet, *Critical
Observations*, appeared evaluating three of these figures: Stuart, Robertson,
and Hume. In this case, though, there was an apparent agenda behind the
comparison. In 1779 Stuart was unsuccessful in obtaining the professorship of
public law at the University of Edinburgh. He blamed Robertson for this
failure and subsequently hoped to undermine his reputation as an historian.
Although *Critical Observations* was probably not written by Stuart, it was
undoubtedly penned by one or more of his friends. The first of this two-part
work compares Stuart's and Robertson's respective views on the Mary Queen
of Scots controversy. Laying their narratives side by side, the pamphlet
highlights Robertson's attempt to place blame on the Queen, and Stuart's to
defend her. The author gives high marks to Stuart for originality, historical
narration, drawing characters, and style. Robertson is judged sorely deficient
in all of these areas. The second part of the pamphlet, presented below,
contrasts Robertson with Hume. The author argues that Robertson was
popular for the moment as a religiously conservative answer to Hume, but
Hume's value is long lasting. "The one is a philosopher, and a historian; the
other a sophist and a rhetorician."

The review of this pamphlet in *The European Magazine and London Review*
was mixed, agreeing with its content, but condemning its manner of expression.
As the second part of the pamphlet is rhetorically much harsher than the first,
the reviewer suggests that the work had two authors. The complete review is
as follows:

This pamphlet is interesting, and will probably excite curiosity and
attention. The observations are acute, and discover that the author is an

119

excellent judge of good writing. His remarks upon Mr. Hume and Dr. Stuart are very favourable, and even flattering. But this is by no means the case with what is said of Dr. Robertson. This historian is treated with the greatest severity. The strictures indeed, have generally a propriety as being founded in truth. But the manner in which they are expressed is harsh and cruel. It would be difficult to answer them. Yet the point that is given to them is offensive. In the first part of this pamphlet, Dr. Robertson is contrasted with Dr. Stuart. In the second part he is compared with Mr. Hume. In both he is censured and exposed. There are good sense and masterly observations in the first part. But it is far exceeded by the second part or section. This leads us to conceive that this publication is the work of two writers. But while we totally disapprove of the severity exercised by both of them, we are desirous to censure the author of the latter piece in a more particular manner. As his abilities appear to be very considerable, he ought to employ them better than in satire. To harrow up the soul of any individual is an unworthy occupation. To blast the fame of an author, who has obtained reputation with the public, and to hold out his weaknesses with acrimony, is wicked. The air of affectation which this writer communicates to his work is artful, and gives the keener poignancy to the satire. His performance is characteristical in a high degree; but men of wit and learning while they will acknowledge the happiness of the portrait, will exclaim against the maliciousness of the painter. [*European Magazine and London Review*, August 1782, Vol. 2, pp. 131–132]

Around the time of this review, the *European Magazine* published a series of anecdotes on Robertson and Stuart, and in their September issue they discuss the controversy that erupted upon the appearance of *Critical Observations*:

Upon its appearance in Scotland, a great and loud outcry was made against Dr. Stuart, on the pretended foundation of his being the real author of the comparison between his own work and that of Dr. Robertson. The pamphlet was indeed very decidedly in his favour. This, however, with impartial readers, was a reason why the offensive criticism ought not to have been imputed to him. But the partizans of a faction are sometimes more than blind; they are deceitful. [*European Magazine and London Review*, September 1782, Vol. 2, pp. 215–216]

The author continues noting that word of the controversy reached Stuart in London, which prompted him to deny in writing authorship of the pamphlet; his statement was then printed in Scottish newspapers. After presenting Stuart's statement, the author concludes, "The censure conveyed by Dr. Robertson and his friends, by the propagation of invented accusations, is too obvious to be insisted on – but we industriously abstain from every reprobation."

Writing for the *Monthly Review*, William Enfield presumes that the pamphlet was authored by a friend of Stuart's and accordingly condemns its efforts to elevate Stuart at the expense of Robertson. Enfield's complete review is as follows:

> The intended services of injudicious friends are often nothing better than real injuries. It is impossible that Dr. Stuart should not think so, with respect to his ill-judged attempt to establish his reputation upon the ruins of Dr. Robertson's. The encomiums which the unknown Writer has lavished upon Dr. Stuart are too extravagant to pass with the public for any thing more than the ebullitions of the most partial friendship: And the censures which he has heaped upon Dr. Robertson are so illiberal, that every one will, without hesitation, impute them to personal resentment and spleen.
>
> According to the decision of this profound Critic, whilst Dr. Stuart is all perfection, in originality of invention, in perspicuity of arrangement, and in simplicity, chasteness, strength, elegance, animation, and dignity of Style; Dr. Robertson has not a single theory, or a single thought, which is not borrowed: he has no pretensions to any kind of genius; his intellect is shallow and indolent, unenlightened by philosophy, and undisturbed by science; he has no powers of reasoning, no knowledge of the world, no extensive acquaintance with the dead or the living languages; no knowledge of the philosophy of grammar; he imposes upon the public wherever he affects originality: his narrative is only supported by daring and unscrupulous affirmations and insidious surmises, and, with shameless audacity, assassinates the truth: and lastly, his style is mechanically uniform, gaudy, unchaste, and poor, fit for no other purpose than to express the cant of the pulpit, and only adapted to amuse women and children. – The public, who are insulted by such an *unsupported* censure of their judgment in the approbation which they have bestowed upon Dr. R. will doubtless treat this *anonymous* defamation with the contempt which it deserves. [*Monthly Review*, November 1782, Vol. 67, pp. 390–391]

The following is from the 1782 and only edition of *Critical Observations*.

II.

A LITERARY PICTURE of *Dr.* ROBERTSON, *in a contrasted Opposition with the celebrated Mr.* HUME.

Qui dedit hoc hodie, cras, si volet, auferet: ut, si
Detulerit fasces indigno, detrahet idem.
Pone, meum est, inquit. Pono, tristisque recedo.
   HORAT.

There is a good fortune in letters as well as in life; and authors as well as men often rise to an eminence which does not belong to them. When the whole christian world, forgetting its charity, looked out for a rival to Hume, they found one in the very bosom of the church. Dr. Robertson gave his History of Scotland to the public. This incident was capricious; and he was indebted to it for the highest popularity. He addressed himself to the multitude at the most favourable moment; and his abilities were courtly and engaging. The flattery of panegyric was exhausted, and abused. It was said, that Mr. Hume had found not only a rival, but a superior. The philosophic Historian was forgot, for a time, in the respect that was paid to an orthodox and flowery Narrator. The palm of history was snatched in haste from his hand. Sagacity, research, and argument, submitted to garniture and dress; and ingenuity and genius gave way to gaudy paintings and pastimes for children.

But the reputation which is sudden, is often temporary and perishable; while that which advances by degrees under opposition, is almost always lasting and durable. When the 'Spirit of Laws' was first published in France, it attracted no notice. It was necessary that men of sense should meditate its merit, and pronounce their decision. In twenty years the genius of Montesquieu began to be understood, to be admired, and to be immortal. The author who is showy and shallow has a very different fate. He catches in the very hour of publication. His celebrity is at once at its height; and he smiles over the imposing parade of his easy and well-dressed labours. But his praise dies away in the mouths of the vulgar. While the sturdy oak rises slowly to its greatness and its honours, the transitory flower glitters in the sun, droops, and perishes. The dying Hume foretold his bursting fame. The living Roberson bewails his decaying reputation.

In the works of the one you perceive the most momentous weightiness of matter, the utmost depth of penetration, and the profoundest erudition. In those of the other, you are amused with pettiness and romance: you desiderate nerves, blood, and spirit. You give a willing admiration to Hume; you are disposed to be pleased with Robertson. The one forces you to collect all your powers and all your attention. The other tickles your fancy, and charms you to idleness. The strength of the former is commanding; the softness of the latter allures. Hume is grave, severe, and sublime; Robertson is smiling, popular, and plausible. The one is a philosopher, and a historian; the other a sophist and a rhetorician.

Robertson is rich in promises and magnificent in apparatus; but his writings disappointed all the fair hopes that are brought to their perusal. The powers of his understanding nowhere instruct us. His shallow and indolent intellect, unenlightened by philosophy, and undisturbed with science, cannot preserve itself from error, even when surveying the surface of objects. His industry, though painful, is not connected with knowledge; his elegance, though considerable, is disgraced by affection; and his arrangements, though laboured, are deficient in art, correctness, and consistency. His matter is hectic with weakness, and sickly with languor; and the purple and the ermine in which it is arrayed, cannot conceal its infirmity and nothingness.

In the absence of the talent of invention, and of any active power of reflection, Robertson discovers the unequivocal characteristics of the common composer. He has 'no words that breathe, no thoughts that burn.' He can get no assistance at home. He goes abroad to ransack every corner for the materials of his mimetic fabricks. Crouching in the trammels of authority, and seeming to contemn them, he adopts without a blush other men's sentiments and observations, often ignorant of their utility and value; but always strenuous to give them the embellishment of dress, and the unmeaningness of declamation. Not insensible himself to his want of originality, he even injudiciously exposes the defect by industriously attempting to conceal it. He affects to place facts in new lights; he affects to draw characters with new colours. But go to his historic predecessors, consult the vouchers to which he is too prudent to appeal; and you are somewhat scandalized to meet with his new lights, and his new colours. The trick, indeed, imposes upon the supineness of ignorance, and makes it stare, and gape, and wonder. But it is more than lost with the learned. They anticipate the artifice, and despise it. No blossoms of a new spring, no fruits of a new autumn, gladden their sight, or solace their palate.

To weigh with skill the degrees of probability and evidence, to dive into the views and the artifices of parties, to perceive the strength and the foibles of actors, to catch the truth while it floats in uncertainty, to keep an even and a steady course, undiverted and undeceived by the prejudices, the passions, and the caprices of preceding historians and his own, are atchievements far beyond his utmost reach. He is fond of system; but he cannot attain it. He is fond of philosophy; but he faints in the pursuit of its shadow. Causation and effect are his Scylla and Charybdis. When he reasons, all his cunning forsakes him: he posts and wanders from contradiction to absurdity. In his solicitude to offend no party, the eye of discernment discovers the habits of selfishness or the meanness of adulation. In the uniform propagation of high principles of monarchy, the most simple recognize the adorer of prerogative and the worshipper of a pension. In the habitual search after a fineness of motive to which to impute the conduct of statesmen, there are perceivable an affected knowledge of the world, and the decisive proofs of a monkish ignorance of its concerns.

But the more candid friends of this historian are ready enough to give up his matter. They allow that he has no pretensions of any kind to genius, and that his judgment is not that of a great master. It is his composition that they extol; and his taste is, doubtless, the happiest feature of his mind. Yet even here criticism, without being anxious or severe, may exert with success the province of correction. His tone is elevated, but it is uniform. One key is struck, and the ear is fatigued with eternal reverberations of the same sound. The note is musical and soft; but being incessantly repeated, it is the more disgusting upon account of its sweetness. Its merit acts against itself. A sameness of phraseology corresponds with this identity of cadence, and augments its sleepy insipidity. The former defect is to be traced to an untutored ear; the latter is the evident effect of a limited skill in the grammatical art, and of the want of erudition. For varied and artificial constructions, which constitute the harmony of composition, require a knowledge in the philosophy of grammar; and the endless multiplicity of vocables, which diversify the writings of the most finished composers, are the result of an extensive acquaintance with the dead and the living tongues. Now these advantages were never imputed to this author, even by the partiality of friendship, or the impudence of flattery. While the ability, however, of cultivated scholars turns away with disgust from the unvaried and monotonous structure of his periods and diction, this deficiency affects not the multitude. The great mass of the people are infinitely delighted both with his manner and his expression. His elegance is even the more alluring to them, for being imperfect and effeminate. They are melted with languor, and in raptures with his tinsel. Circumlocution, epithet, antithesis, and ostentation, engage completely their affections; and women and children still pursue the glittering butterfly. The jewels are very pretty, indeed, and have a dazzling lustre; but they are deceitful, and false. Like the tresses and the paint of the courtezan, they draw the youthful and unwary; and like them, too, they cover a body rotten at the core, tottering with fragility, and putid with disease.

These remarks are not made without thought, or at random; and it is not in their direct meaning only that they have their use. Convert them all into their opposites, turn to the other side of the medal, collect their antipodes; and you have a just and correct picture of the accomplished and unrivalled Hume. Robertson is a puny stream losing itself in its mud; Hume is the voice of history speaking to ages, and living in the eternity of time. Imposture and learning, genius and the want of it, cannot long be confounded. The operations of caprice and party are passing, and transient. Truth and justice ever vindicate their rights. The approbation of the select few is immortality. The applauses of the giddy many are flattering and ominous. The fame of Hume is ever to grow in its brightness. That of Robertson, like the flame expiring in the socket, hastens to its dissolution. His admirers among the clergy of Scotland, have waited long for his apotheosis, like the Jews for their Messiah. A more melancholy task now employs their humanity. They try to sooth the peevishness of their desponding idol, hold up to it the milk of adulation, and, vainly credulous, think to fit to its itching brows the reluctant and uncomplying laurel.

31
ABBE DE MABLY

Abbé de Mably, *De la maniere d'écrire l'histoire*, Paris: Chez Alexandre Jombert, jeune, 1783, [4], 342 p.
Selections from Dialogue 2; from *Two dialogues, concerning the manner of writing history. From the French of Abbé de Mably*. London: printed for G. Kearsley, 1783, [8], 298, [6] p.

Born in Grenoble, France, historian Gabriel Bonnot, Abbé de Mably (1709–1785) was a prolific writer in Greek, Roman and French history, and also European and American political thought. His *De la maniere d'écrire l'histoire* is a study of the principles and style required for writing history. In dialogue two, Eugenius, the principal character of the dialogue, argues that order is the most important feature of history writing. Hume, he believes, lacks that quality, particularly in his history of the Stuarts, which is little more than a sketch constructed out of memoirs. Hume has not understood the natural relationship between the various parts. The successful historian, Eugenius continues, must grasp a fundamental theme that unifies the whole, otherwise "He will cut up occurrences, fritter them into pieces, and, of course, never bring them forward in their just proportions." Further into the dialogue Eugenius criticizes the writing abilities of Hume, Gibbon, and Robertson in their respective histories. He charges that Hume did not know his nation and thus was "unable to mark out and ascertain the influence of the national character as blended with the events which he relates."

The *English Review*, founded in 1783 by Gilbert Stuart, gives a largely favourable review of the work, noting the somewhat extreme way that Mably both praises and criticises historical writers:

In explaining his opinions, the Abbé gives way to his sensibilities; and while he sometimes lavishes his praise with a prodigality that wounds justice, he at times also scatters his censure with some degree of levity. But in general we cannot but commend the freedom with which he has written. Upon Mr. Hume, Mr. Gibbon, and Dr. Robertson, he has uttered some strictures which deserve to be noticed. [*English Review*, August 1783, Vol. 2, pp. 124–130]

Regarding Mably's comments on Hume, the reviewer says "In this portrait there are sense and invective; but the latter perhaps is most prevalent." By contrast, he suggests that the criticisms of Robertson are justly formed. The reviewer concludes stating that the work "contains much profound criticism, and the marks of an extensive knowledge." Writing for the *Monthly Review*, William Enfield states more negatively that Mably "appears to us to have considered history too much in the light of a work of fancy and genius" (*Monthly Review*, January 1784, Vol. 70 pp. 32–38).

CONCERNING THE MANNER OF WRITING HISTORY.
THE SECOND DIALOGUE.

Particular Histories. Their requisite object. Observations on common Rules for all kinds of History.

EUGENIUS. ... But, this subject would draw us into endless investigations; and, therefore, Theodosius! let us relinquish it, and proceed to take notice of *order*, without an adherence to which no Historian can ever expect to enjoy even a tolerable share of literary reputation.

Order is, of all points whatsoever, the most necessary to the composition of a Work: nor need we produce a stronger proof of the justice of this assertion than that heap of books which, though filled with excellent things, affords not the least instruction, because they tire and disgust the generality of readers. *This* we have all experienced. A truth appears doubtful, unless it is prepared for by *that* truth which has preceded it; and a beauty displaced becomes a defect; but, *properly* arranged, grows more estimable.

> *Ordinis hæc virtus erit et Venus, aut ego fallor,*
> *Ut jam nunc dicat jam nunc debentia dici;*
> *Pluraque differat, et præsens in tempus omittat.*

If *that* of which you have just informed me explains to me, before-hand, *what* you are going to relate, the attention of my mind will not meet with any interruption, and I shall eagerly run through the perusal of a work which draws me on with pleasure from the first page to the last. But, I know not whether an Historian would not experience more difficulty than any other kind of Writer, amidst his endeavours to find out this *Order* concerning which we are now speaking. The Historian bends under the prodigious weight of his materials; and, if he cannot so arrange them as to form out of the whole one regular edifice, I shall lose myself in a labyrinth from whence no path is open to favor my escape. All this I have felt during the perusal of the History of the Stuarts by Mr. Hume. Instead of what was promised to me, I have found nothing except memoirs which might have served for the materials of his History; and how could I possibly regard with approbation a work which the Historian, whether from an ignorance of his art, or from indolence, or from a dullness of comprehension, has only *sketched*? All these facts, unripped from each other, elude my recollection; I have wasted my time, and cannot form a proper judgment concerning those events of which the narrative is placed before me.

In vain would you flatter yourself that you enjoy the power of establishing this luminous order throughout the pages of your History, if you have not separately meditated upon each of its respective parts. Draw them near to each other, in order that you may perceive wherein consists their most natural relation. Aided by your preliminary studies, endeavour so to place them that they may reciprocally throw light, the one upon the other. In a word, follow the precept of Horace. Make yourself master of your subject.

> ... *Cui lecta potenter erit res,*
> *Nec facundia deseret hunc, nec lucidus ordo.*

This *Order*, in a great measure, consists in the exposition relative to which I have so lately troubled you with my remarks. When the Historian has once acquired an extremely clear idea of all those points which he proposes to investigate, he will not find it difficult (I should imagine) to throw aside the mention of facts almost barren in their nature, or foreign to his purpose, and to bring his readers acquainted with the influence which the several events maintain, the one upon the other. Remark, let me intreat you, that there are in all States, in all enterprizes, and in all affairs, one or more principal points which decide upon the success of the whole, and which draw after them all particular accidents, like a torrent. In the government, or the administration of a Society, it is the knowledge of these decisive points which form the accomplished Statesman; nor must he promise himself success but in proportion to the steadiness and perseverance with which he strongly attaches himself to them, and keeps them always in his view. So is it with the Historian. On these objects should he fix both *his* attention and my own. Then, with the greatest facility, will he discover the most luminous order. Every point becomes clear and simple. The several facts will remain deeply engraven upon my memory, because I shall not, at any time, lose sight of that chain which, like the thread of Ariadne, will serve as a clue, to prevent my reason from wandering out of the right track. Such is the admirable art of Livy from the commencement of his History to the end; and (to remind you only of one example) recollect how, in his third Decad, when he is under the necessity of presenting to us, all at one time, a vast croud of objects, he rivets our regard and attention upon Hannibal, whose genius holds in the balance the fortune of the Romans, and even occasions it to totter. Whatsoever happens out of Italy relates only to this

General of the Carthaginians. Rome, by making diversions, is employed only in endeavors to diminish the forces of Hannibal, and to prevent Carthage from repairing those losses which are caused even by her victories.

When a state is either so happy, or so wise as to have acquired a *proper* knowledge of its own strength, to have learned the art of managing it to advantage, and of not venturing upon too many enterprizes at one time, the Historian will find himself more at ease; and, for the purpose of putting his relation into great order, he need only follow, with fidelity, the order of events. But, if *this* State, whether from an ignorance of its real interests, or from a kind of fatality, plunges, at once, into a variety of undertakings, without making the *proper* distinction between *that* which ought to have the principal lead and those which should be considered merely as simple accessaries, I should fear that the Historian would find himself entangled amidst equal perplexities and as little able to acquit himself with credit as the Republic the History of which he is composing. Whilst the persons in administration know not either what they do, or what they want to do, you will perceive that the Historian, not more enlightened than themselves, will string one event upon another, and fatigue and disgust the Reader by narratives which do not lead to any serviceable point whatever. Even the Author, tired out amidst his labors to arrange materials so meagre and so forbidding, will only throw before you a set of wretched pictures of which the first glance is too discouraging to make us wish to look a second time. Without a principal view before him, he will, at one moment, injudiciously relinquish the subject concerning which he treats; at another moment, he will resume it with equal impropriety; and, after all this, he will, a second time, discard it upon as frivolous and indefensible a ground. He will cut up occurrences, fritter them into pieces, and, of course, never bring them forward in their just proportions.

... [Hume] is indeed, learned; but, he wants taste. The descriptions in Hume run on more rapidly than in Rapin; yet, not knowing his nation, he is, of course, unable to mark out and ascertain the influence of the national character as blended with the events which he relates. His own reflections are common; and result too frequently from those false politics of which morality must disapprove. Having begun his narrative at the end, and without examining and unravelling the chain which connects together all the ages and all the occurrences of a nation, it is not astonishing that his History of the Stuarts should prove deficient in a multitude of desirable particulars. Afterwards, he carried his work up to the ancient Britons; and, here, we discover only an Historian whose reading is confined to Chronicles. Of the law of the Normans, he, certainly, was ignorant; and all his remarks concerning the polity of Fiefs are unintelligible; or, at least, I could not understand them.

32
DAVID DALRYMPLE, LORD HAILES

[David Dalrymple], *Miscellaneous remarks on "The enquiry into the evidence against Mary Queen of Scots."* London: printed for J. Robson; and G. Robinson, 1784, [2], 41, [1] p.
Sections 2 and 5, complete; from 1784 edition.

Born in Edinburgh, David Dalrymple (1726–1792) studied law at Utrecht, and subsequently became a prominent lawyer in Scotland. In 1766 he was appointed judge of the Court of Session, from which he obtained the title Lord Hailes. He was a prolific author of historical and legal works. Hume's letters reflect a somewhat checkered relationship with Dalrymple. The two interacted in a professional capacity beginning around 1752, when Hume was appointed keeper of the Advocates Library; Dalrymple was one of the library curators. Out of religious conviction, Dalrymple opposed Hume's appointment, but Hume nevertheless forgave the "very pretty fellow." Hume admired Dalrymple's literary abilities and in 1753 Hume solicited stylistic and substantive comments from him on the *Enquiry Concerning the Principles of Morals*; Dalrymple obliged, and Hume incorporated the suggestions into a revision of the work. Hume felt close enough to him that, in 1754, he requested use of a book that Dalrymple owned. Just one month later, though, Dalrymple and other curators removed three controversial books from the library that Hume had just ordered. Hume was offended by the rebuff and for almost half a year after considered resigning his position. Around this time, a club of Edinburgh's literary elite – the Select Society – was formed; Hume and Dalrymple were both members, which gave them another regular forum for interaction. In 1760 the two corresponded on the issue of the authenticity of James Macpherson's allegedly discovered fragments of Scottish Highland poetry. In 1772, Dalrymple attempted to move James Beattie from his teaching position at Marischal College, Aberdeen to the University of Edinburgh. Hume was the principal target of Beattie's *Essay on the Nature and Immutability of Truth* (1770), and Beattie's promotion to Edinburgh would have been a slap in the face to Hume and his Edinburgh supporters. The protests were strong enough to keep Beattie in Aberdeen. Hume died in 1776, and 11 years later Dalrymple published a Latin translation of Hume's brief autobiography, *The Life of David Hume*.

In 1784 Dalrymple entered the Mary Queen of Scots controversy with a short pamphlet titled *Miscellaneous Remarks on "The Enquiry into the Evidence against Mary Queen of Scots."* The work critiques the 1760 *Enquiry* of his friend – and fellow Select Society member – William Tytler. Dalrymple is sympathetic with Tytler's position in the dispute, but he nevertheless points out factual errors in Tytler's arguments. All parties in the controversy held that Mary's guilt or innocence hinged on the authenticity of her alleged letters to Bothwell (for background see the general introduction to this collection). Dalrymple too focuses on this point, and in Sections 2 and 5 he considers Hume's view on the subject. In Section 2, Dalrymple addresses the issue of whether the letters were either written in her hand, or signed by her, or both. The historical records are inconsistent on this point. Hume attributes the inconsistency to an error by a clerk, who mixed together one document that was only written by her with another that was only signed by her. Dalrymple, though, suggests that the documents were only written by her, but since the terms "written and subscribed" go together in common language, the clerk simply fell into this locution. Tytler attributes the confusion to an act of fraud on the part of Mary's enemies – a theory that Dalrymple finds implausible. In Section 5 he considers Hume's argument that there was an original – and subsequently lost – French version of the letters; for Hume, the surviving Scottish version of the letters contains French words, which suggests that they were originally written in French. In response, Tytler argued that the Scottish language at the time abounded with French words and Gallicisms; he gives several examples to support his contention. In defence of Hume, Dalrymple argues that the words cited by Tytler are not really of French origin.

The *Critical Review* commends Dalrymple's abilities, but does not feel that he resolved the controversy:

> ... the author appears to be actuated with the spirit of a scrupulous enquirer after truth. But his observations, however well founded, being for the most part drawn from verbal criticism, and the doubtful authority of contending idioms, are not sufficiently forcible towards deciding this celebrated controversy. [*Critical Review*, August 1784, Vol. 53, pp. 129–132]

Dalrymple's *Miscellaneous Remarks* was harshly criticised by John Whitaker in *Mary Queen of Scots Vindicated* (1787), selections from which appear later in this collection. The following is from the 1784 and only edition of the *Miscellaneous Remarks*.

SECTION II.

It is remarked by the author of the *Enquiry*, that the first appearance of the famous Letters is in an Act of Privy Council, 4th December, 1567; in which there is mention made of the Queen's "privie letters, written and *subscrivit* with her awin hand, and send by her to James Erle of Bothwell."

Here, there is said to be an *ugly jarring* between two public instruments, and it is conjectured, that, when the *crafty* politicians, Murray, Morton, and the others came to consider *deliberately* and with *cool reflection*, they thought that it might shock the credulity of many people to believe that the Queen could be so far deprived of common sense as to put her name to such letters, and, therefore, "they might very naturally, in the copies they produced before the Parliament, *withdraw the subscription*, and, in place of mentioning the letters to be *written and subscrivit* by the Queen, substitute the words, *halelie with her awin hand.*"[1]

Mr. Hume ascribes the difference to an inaccuracy of the Clerk of the Privy Council. "The letters, says he, were only *wrote* by her, the second contract with Bothwell was only *subscribed*, a proper description [distinction] was not made; and so they are said to be *wrote* and *subscribed*;" this is the sense of Mr. Hume's remark, as given by the author of the *Enquiry*.

The remark is not contemptible, however, much it may be despised by some men; for, as "letter of tack," and "letter of pension," are phrases used in Scotland, so, "letter of espousals" may be proper enough.

But another, and a more easy and obvious solution may be suggested.

He who writes a deed with his own hand does generally sign it, and it is hardly possible to figure a case of a *perfect* deed written by the parties own hand and not signed by him: hence, *written and subscribed* constantly go together in common language, just as *heirs and executors*. As every one, conversant in law business, must have seen *executors* joined to *heirs*, in consequence of what may be termed the customary affinity between them, although the maker of the deed meant not to speak of *executors*, so, in like manner, the Clerk of Privy Council might have added, *subscrivit* to *written*; it appears, that this inaccuracy was observed and immediately corrected.

This hypothesis seems more simple than that, adopted by the author of the *Enquiry*; it is not probable that crafty politicians, who had *deliberated* for weeks, and perhaps for months, on a most capital forgery, should have been so late in discovering the impropriety of making Queen Mary *sign* the letters, and then, in a sudden fit of *cool recollection*, should have discovered it.

Besides, "to *withdraw* a subscription" is no easy matter; it can only be effected by the means of some chemical preparation, or by the making a

[1] *Enquiry*, P. 13.

rasure, and to have attempted *this* on *eight* different letters would have been a work of infinite hazard and of doubtful success.

There is no reason to believe that *all* the members present at the Privy Council, 4th December, 1567, and in the Parliament, 15th December, 1567, were the obsequious tools of the Earl of Murray; if, in those assemblies, there was any one independent man, or any one favourer of the Queen and of justice, (the Earl of Errol for instance) this fraud, accomplished by the singular method of *withdrawing subscriptions* must have been detected.

The fraud, as it is called, was not discovered at the time; but, after an interval of two hundred years, there appears a dubious conjecture, importing that there *might* have been a fraud.

The innocence of Queen Mary ought to be maintained on more solid grounds.

SECTION V.

In opposition to Mr. Goodall's hypothesis, it has been said, "that the original French of the *first* letter, excepting the few words already quoted, is lost, that the Scottish copy, so often published, may have been a translation from that original, and that the French copy, still extant, may have been made, at second-hand, from the Scottish copy."

The author of the *Enquiry* will not even allow a rehearing on this argument.

He says, with some warmth, "since the Dissertator has been drove to deny that the French letters before us are true copies of the originals, *by all laws of proof and criticism*, it was his business to produce the originals."[2]

I trust, that *the rules of proof and criticism* are not so imperious, as to require a writing to be produced, whether it exist or not, and to preclude all exceptions against a supposed copy, if he, who excepts, be not in possession of the original.

The honour of Queen Mary is to be vindicated by moral evidence; it must not take shelter under the screen of municipal forms.

Bishop Lesley, although his intentions were good, hurt the cause of his Sovereign at the very commencement, by treating it too much in the style of a lawyer; he demanded proof *comparatione literarum*, and, at the same time, he insisted that such proof was, of all others, the weakest and most inconclusive; he said, that the letters were forged, and that they had nothing criminal in them.[3]

---

[2]   *Enquiry*, P. 85.

[3]   *Defence of the Honour of Queen Mary*, P. 15–20, ap. *Anderson* i.

The author of the *Enquiry* adds, "how is it possible to fix men who, *after having for two hundred years*, quoted and insisted on those letters as originals – have now recourse to other letters which they acknowledge to be lost."

If any man should, for *two hundred years*, persist in one hypothesis, and, at length, on being driven out of it, adopt another, we might well say, that it is hard to fix such a man.

But, "it is none of the least advantages which we now enjoy, that *bigotry and party-rage* have, at length, subsided," and in our times, he who writes on any subject, is *neither heir nor slave to another man's opinions.*

In this view of the case, it matters not what the adversaries, or the apologists of Queen Mary may have said in times past.

Ill would it have fared with the honour of that Princess, had another rule been established, for then her apologists might have found themselves tied down to say, as bishop Lesley did, "Albeit Darnley was her head in wedlock, yet was he otherwise but a member of her commonweale, subject to her, as to his principal and supreme governesse, and to her lawes, by the due and ordinary processe and course whereof he might justly have been convicted, condemned and executed, as wel for the murder committed upon David her secretarie, in whose body his dagger was found stabbed, as for the imprisoning of the Queene, and for the attempting to remove her from civil government, to intrude himself thereto, and for divers other the like pageants by him plaid."[4]

The truth is that, in *former times*, the apologists as well as the adversaries of Queen Mary were rather too warm, and applauded and reviled with little attention to evidence.

Mr Goodall first placed the controversy on its proper ground of argument and criticism, and on that ground, if it has not been decided already, must, it, in the end, be decided.

The hypothesis, mentioned in the beginning of this section, was first suggested by Mr. Goodall.[5] But the arguments, that he employed for confuting it, did not satisfy his antagonists, as we shall presently see.

Mr. Hume observes, that the Scottish copy of the first letter abounds in French words and Gallicisms; and, from that circumstance, he concludes, that it is merely a translation from a French original.

---

[4] *Defence of the Honour of Queen Mary*, P. 7. ap. *Anderson* i. This sentiment is more forcibly expressed in the marginal summary; "it is nothing like, that the Queene would have sought the destruction of Lord Darnley by these meanes, [by strangling or gun-powder] when *she might have openly put him to death by justice.*" I suppose that this quotation will be a sufficient answer to the query, whether Bishop Lesley ought to be termed, "a faithful and *discreet* servant of "Queen Mary," or, "a man heated with faction." See *Enquiry*, P. 157 *not.* *.

[5] *V. P.* 99.

To this observation the author of the *Enquiry* makes answer, "Any person, conversant with the language and writings in Queen Mary's time, will see, that from the long and continued intercourse and connexion between the Scottish and French nations at that time, the Scottish language abounded with Gallicisms and even French words; [he meant, with French words and *even* with Gallicisms] some of which, though now almost worn out in our writings, yet remain to this day in our language, especially among the vulgar."[6]

Notwithstanding the popular credit given to this assertion, there is some reason to believe that, as our ancient intercourse with France did not add much to our importance and prosperity, so it did not add twenty words and phrases to our language, such, at least, as ever became current in good company.

Our language, no doubt, has French words in it, and, perhaps, Gallicisms also, but they are, in general, derived from the Anglo-Norman, rather than from the French.

The examples, produced by the author of the *Enquiry*, do not greatly tend to prove the supposed prevalency of French words and gallicisms in the Scottish language.

His quotation from Secretary Cecil, who says, "And because it was *bruited*," seems not to the purpose, for Cecil was an Englishman, and *bruited* is not a French word. Besides, Throkmorton, also an Englishman, uses *bruite* for *rumour*.[7]

Neither is it of moment, that Melvil, who had passed much of his time in France, used *finest*, for "The most penetrating genius," thus forming, by analogy, a superlative from the French *fin*.

As to what the author says of *fin* and *finet* having the same sense, he might as well have said, that *smatterer* in the French language and an *adept* are synonymous.

Thus much having been premised, let us consider the remaining examples of French words and even of Gallicisms that the author of the *Enquiry* opposes to the Observation of Mr. Hume.

It is said, "Mr. Hume himself, and every Scotsman knows well what the vulgar mean, by giving a *bonne allé*, or parting cup."

Bonne allé, if it be a French phrase at all, means "a garden-walk, convenient and well-kept."

Giving ones foy, also means giving a parting cup.

But does *foi* mean "a parting-cup" in French, or "donner sa foi," to give a parting cup? – the "Dutch phrase, de *foy* geven," means, according to Skinner, who writes an English Etymological Dictionary, "coenam profectitiam dare, *i.e.*

---

[6] *Enquiry*, P. 109.

[7] *Hardwicke*, i. 139.

fidem amicitiæ, etiam par absentiam duraturæ, dare;" this is exactly our *foy*: and, as the phrase *is* Dutch, and is *not* French, it may be concluded that we got it from the Low-Countries, and not from France.

"To give a *bennison*, or blessing, is still a vulgar phrase."

Bennison, however, is not a French word, and, if corrupted from *Benediction*, it may, with more probability be derived from the English, than from the French. Littleton has "*Benison*, blessing, *Benedictio*."

"Old people still give the name of *montre* to a watch."

Old people, *who have been* in France, or who *affect* French words, may give the name of *montre* to a watch; the old fashioned word, within my memory, was "*orloge*," which may be from the Latin or German, as well as from the French.

There follows a criticism on *jardelow* or *gare de l'eau*, as the author expresses it, a word of which Scotsmen, unless superior to national reproaches, are not wont to treat. It means, "foul water or other noisome things thrown from a window." The vulgar amongst us have turned a French phrase, *gare l'eau*, into a single word, and have perverted both its sound and its signification; and this example is produced for proving that, in the days of Queen Mary, the Scottish language abounded in French words and even in Gallicisms.

By the like mode of reasoning we might prove, that, at this day, the French language abounds in Anglicisms, for the French call a large piece of veal, "un grand *rosbife* de veau."

"Moyen," also produced in illustration by the author of the *Enquiry*, is merely the word *mean*, spelt in a different way.

The two remaining examples are the adverb *meschantlie*, a word formed from the French *meschant*, and used by the queen herself; and *appuy* used by Secretary Lethington.

Some better evidence will be necessary before we can account for the numerous Gallicisms that occur in the Scottish copy.

That such Gallicisms do often occur in it, is hardly disputed, and the following examples, all taken from the *first* letter, will compleatly establish the proposition.

"Maid my *estait*," "faire un état," means in French, "to make up a list of the officers of one's household."

"He belevit to die for glaidness." – "Cuidoit mourir d'allegresse."

"Mak fault." – "faire faûte" – I suppose that no one will dispute the certainty of the Gallicism *here*. "He schews me *of* sa mony lytil flatteries" – in the Scottish language, this means, "he *gave me an account* of so mony lytil flatteries." Now this is plainly wide of the sense, and we must translate the words into French in order to discover their import: "m'a tant montrée *de* petites flateries."

"Before, flattering;" this is very remarkable. The French were wont to use the word *force* as an adjective; hence, "par force flaterie," means, "by *much* flattering."

33
JOHN PINKERTON

[John Pinkerton], *Letters of literature. By Robert Heron, Esq.* London: printed for G. G. J. and J. Robinson, 1785, [8], 515, [1] p.
Letter 42, complete; from 1785 edition.

Edinburgh native John Pinkerton (1758–1826) was an apprentice to a solicitor but at age 22 moved to London to pursue a career as a writer. Throughout his life he authored and edited many works on the subjects of history, geography, poetry, and Scottish culture. His *Letters of Literature* (1785) is an earlier composition which appeared under the pseudonym "Robert Heron" – the surname of Pinkerton's mother. The work is a collection of miscellaneous essays on topics such as Virgil, Shakespeare, Bacon, benevolence and genius; it gained attention because of its assault on classical Greek and Roman authors. Letter 42 discusses Hume and was sparked by a critique of Hume by Thomas Gray (1716–1771). Shortly after Gray's death, his friend William Mason published *The Poems of Mr. Gray* (1775), which also included Gray's memoirs. One of Gray's letters is exceptionally critical of Hume:

> ... I have always thought David Hume a pernicious writer, and believe he has done as much mischief here as he has in his own country. A turbid and shallow stream often appears to our apprehensions very deep. A professed sceptic can be guided by nothing but his present passions (if he has any) and interests; and to be masters of his philosophy we need not his books and advice, for every child is capable of the same thing, without any study at all. Is not that *naiveté* and good humour, which his admirers celebrate in him, owing to this, that he has continued all his days an infant, but one that unhappily has been taught to read and write? That childish nation, the French, have given him vogue and fashion, and we, as usual, have learned from them to admire him at second hand. [Gray to James Beattie, July 2, 1770, in *The Poems of Mr. Gray*, York: A. Ward, 1775, pp. 384–385]

In response, Pinkerton writes that Hume's "History of England, nay his Essays, display talents very far superior to any that Gray hath ever shewn." Nevertheless, he believes that Hume prostituted himself by making his entire *History* a defense of royal prerogative. Pinkerton believes that Hume was motivated by a desire to be rich: "The king is the surest fountain of wealth: and to flatter him is the path to preferment, and to opulence." Pinkerton contends that Scotland is "a whole century behind England in point of civil liberty," and Scottish writers such as Hume perpetuate this conservative stance, particularly as they seek approval from royalty and the upper class. He also criticizes Hume for attacking religion in a popular manner since "Religion is the only bond of society for the mob." Even though "it is impossible for man to know the truth," he argues that the true moralist should never undermine society's happiness, regardless of whether it "be founded on truth, or on delusion."

Reviews of Pinkerton's *Letters* were mixed. The *Critical Review* states that the letter on Hume is "the most able and animated one in the present volume" and "The remarks on Hume's History, and the tendency of his other works, are in general just." Writing for the *Monthly Review*, Samuel Badcock contends that "It seems to have been one leading object of this writer [i.e., Pinkerton] ... to excite attention by singularity."[1]

Two years after his *Letters*, Pinkerton briefly discussed Hume in his *Dissertation on the Origin and Progress of the Scythians or Goths* (1787):

> Mr. Hume, who knew nothing about Goths, nor the Gothic constitution, and who is so *shallow*, that far from reaching the *bottom*, he has not reached the bottom of the *surface*, but merely skimmed its top, observes in his own life, that it is ridiculous to look on the English constitution as a regular plan of liberty before the death of Charles the First. A profound remark truly, and most sagacious! Is it a regular plan now? Did regular plans of government ever exist, save in Utopia? Have not all governments, save despotism, been ever totally irregular? While a man has life, his pulse must ever be liable to irregularities; when he is dead, it is *regular enough*! [*Dissertation*, London: Nicol, 1787, p. 142]

Commenting on this passage, the *English Review* states, "It is to be feared that Mr. Pinkerton will never be able to imitate the *shallowness* of Mr. Hume till he acquires that regularity of pulse which is the consequence of death" (1787, Vol. 10 pp. 131–137). The following is from the 1785 and only edition of Pinkerton's *Letters*.

---

[1] *Critical Review*, December 1785, Vol. 60, pp. 405–413, January 1786, Vol. 61, pp. 18–26; *Monthly Review*, March 1786, Vol. 74, pp. 175–182. The work was also reviewed in the *European Magazine and London Review*, 1785, Vol. 8, pp. 106–110, 195–200, 290–293, 376–379.

LETTER XLII.

I grant you that Mr. Gray's censure of David Hume is the most exceptionable part of his Letters; but it is very vindicable, being written in confidence to a friend; and with no intention that the public should see it. His trite application of the remark, that muddy rivers seem deep, shews that it was written in an unlucky moment, when thought is absent; and perhaps in the fluster of evening wine: which last is indeed the only apology that can be made for the remainder of the stricture. No writer can be more clear and manly than Hume; I mean as to his sense; nay, what is wonderful, his style is always easily intelligible, tho full of solecisms and every species of barbarity: his gaiety is always that of an innocent and truly wise man. His History of England, nay his Essays, display talents very far superior to any that Gray hath ever shewn. Mr. Hume might have ruled a state: Gray's utmost views would only have ruled a college. Hume's reputation in France was only the echo of his fame in England. Mr. Gray shewed himself less than a child when he called Hume one. Such mad calumnies recoil upon their author's judgment, and crush it to nothing. Yet all this censure lights upon the Editor; for Gray would have called upon mountains to cover his shame, if he had seen his name publicly branded with throwing dirt from Billingsgate upon a contemporary lord of fame, because his envy saw that he was richer drest, and of far higher rank than himself.

The History of Mr. Hume is indeed very far from being laudable. It is a mere apology for prerogative from beginning to end:[2] and, tho the best apology which hath been offered, is yet very weak; which shews the cause must be desperate when even so great an advocate utterly fails in its defence. At the same time that his political principles led him to exalt the prerogative, his philosophic opinions forced him to depress the church: while every body knows that *no church, no king.* Hence his work is one chaos of heterogeneous axioms, and misrepresented events. His opinions even combated his natural sensibility; for I remember that, in narrating some of the most flagitious acts of cruelty of the blessed reign of Charles I. or II. he displays due sense of the atrocity of such calm deeds of tyranny, as make the frenzies of Nero or Domitian mere jests: but when he hath got thro them, and his opinion begins to resume cooler operation, he gravely begins his next paragraph thus: "These acts of severity (if they can be called such)."

What was the reason, do you think, that could induce a writer of such talents to prostitute them so basely? that could induce such a philosopher to suppose that millions of human beings were to hold their life and happiness at

---

[2] [Gilbert Stuart wrote similarly, "his history, from its beginning to its conclusion, is chiefly to be regarded as a plausible defence of prerogative" (*A View of Society in Europe*, 1778, included earlier in this collection).]

the nod of *one of them*: of a thing called a king; perhaps in corporeal and in mental powers less than the least of his subjects?

This is easily accounted for. Hume was poor, and wished to be rich. The king is the surest fountain of wealth: and to flatter him is the path to preferment, and to opulence. Hence public spirit is almost unknown in monarchies; for one man centers in himself the wealth and praise of his subjects. Hume tells us himself, Chap. LX. 1651. "Though the established government was but the mere shadow of a commonwealth, yet was it beginning by proper arts to encourage that public spirit, which no other species of civil polity is ever able fully to inspire." Hear him! Hear him! Then your History Mr. Hume wishes to extinguish PUBLIC SPIRIT, that is, to destroy the most laudable principle of society.

I know not how it is that the whole late Scotish writers of any eminence have been on the tyrannic side, if we except Dr. Stuart, a man of real abilities, but strangely misapplied in pulling down those of others.[3] Yet presbytery, the religion of that country, hath always been considered as necessarily connected with whig principles; and the common people of Scotland are almost universally whigs. The peers are however almost all tories; owing to the feudal spirit of tyranny and slavery not being wholly extinguished in that kingdom till 1747, when heretable jurisdictions were abolished. The court can only judge of Scotland by the nobility; the fathers of whom having been tyrants to slaves, the sons are willing to be slaves to tyrants; for such is the spirit of the feudal system: a later emancipation from which hath thrown Scotland a whole century behind England in point of civil liberty. Now the writers, in general, naturally adapt their principles to those of their superiors, and the court, *unto whom they look for their reward.*

Hence in our times Junius, Wilkes, Churchill, and other men of talents, have judged of that ancient and warlike kingdom very unjustly. A *Scot* is, with them, synonymous with a *tory*, a *slave*. Nothing can be more opposite to the spirit of the nation; however, it may apply to the noble *scum* on the *top*, or the *dregs* of mercenary writers at the *bottom*. But the nation is full of generous liquor, and hath nothing to do either with its *scum*, or its *dregs*; which are always worst, when the liquor is best. Indeed Churchill's work have passed thro more editions, and are more read, in Scotland, than here; which shews that the love of the country for liberty is superior even to the most inveterate national prejudices.

By a necessary chain, Scotish tories and Jacobites are now court favorites,

They taste the sweets of the Saturnian reign.
Epistle to Sir W. Chambers.

---

[3] [See, for example, Stuart's attack on Robert Henry, discussed in the introductory comments to the selection by Gilbert Stuart earlier in this collection.]

while the real nation, and its real interests, are neglected and despised. It is certainly fortunate that Scotland hath not been *free* above forty years, as to that circumstance we are indebted for its happy quiet, at a time when every province of the British empire evinces, in commotion, or in rebellion, the odious and most deplorable, but natural and unavoidable effects of those tory principles of government which have prevailed thro this pitiful and miserable reign, and have made it one blot in the British Annals.

It is no less wonderful than true, that, ever since the name of Whig hath been known, the nation hath been indebted for all its glorious events to men of that description; and for its miseries to the Tories. Indeed, my friend, if any one will shew me that a tory ministry ever did the least good to this country, or even did not do a great injury, I shall turn tory instantly: but if, from the reign of James I. to this hour, tory ministers have, by every measure, brought calamity and disgrace on their country, then must every Briton view such principles as the seeds of death in our constitution; and on those who profess them, and foster them in the chief magistrate, as deserving of the execration of every good man, and in fact of the highest punishment which the laws of society can ordain for those who mediate the utter perdition of the community.

A king of Great Britain who knows that, by the present constitution, he is only elective chief magistrate of the country, and will comply with the station (it is a glorious one!), hath it in his power to appropriate to himself all the fame rising from the public spirit of the greatest of modern nations. But if he wishes to extend his prerogative, that is, to extinguish that public spirit, he is a *suicide*, and the jury of posterity will bring it in *lunacy*. For he is the enemy of his own power, not to say of his own existence: the power of an English king being directly opposite to his prerogative; for his power is drawn only from the confidence of the nation, which his prerogative will infallibly destroy, if displayed, and not kept, as a sword in the scabbard, never to be drawn by a brave man but upon most urgent occasion. If he makes himself little, he will be great indeed! but if he bites the curb, which our fathers have put in his mouth, it is of steel, and he will only spoil his teeth. If he wishes to be an ox, he will feel himself only the frog in the fable.

You will know that I mean still less to defend the philosophic tenets of David Hume; tho he be a great and elegant writer of philosophy. But I detest the principles of any man who writes popularly against the religion of his country, let it be what it will, if it does not injure political freedom, the first of human blessings. I say popularly, because if treated in an high and abstract, or in a poetical style, as Lucretius hath done, it will not injure the vulgar faith, but only afford speculation to the learned. Religion is the only bond of society for the mob; and they ought not even to suspect that their superiors despise it; as they will, in that case, from their ignorance of moral theory, imagine that their superiors have no laws, and consequently that they ought to have none. Philosophy will never do for the vulgar. They must be bound in the chains of prejudice, and so led thro the road of life; and not trusted to themselves after proper information.

Besides, my friend, the consolations of human life are by no means too numerous. Religion is one of the chief of these consolations to thousands of people; and among these to many possest of qualities superior to genius, knowledge, or philosophy; qualities that constitute the GOOD, the first order of society. Shall I, with rash and sacrilegious hand, burst open the temple of their happiness, and steal away the palladium of their peace? Forbid it Humanity! Forbid it even Philosophy! The philosophy that is not benevolent is false and destructive. It is impossible for man to know the truth: but it is of no importance whether his felicity be founded on truth, or on delusion.

34
JOHN MILLAR

John Millar, *An historical view of the English government: from the settlement of the Saxons in Britain to the accession of the House of Stewart*, London: Printed for A. Strahan, and T. Cadell, and J. Murray, 1787, vii, [9], 565, [19] p.
Selections from 2.11; from 1803 edition.

B orn in Shotts, Lanarkshire, John Millar (1735–1801) was educated in law at Glasgow, during which time he attended lectures on the history of civil society by Adam Smith – whom Millar referred to as the "Newton" of the subject. He was subsequently a tutor for the son of Henry Home, Lord Kames; during this time he met Hume. In 1761 he was made professor of law at the University of Glasgow. A regular speaker at Glasgow's Literary Society, he defended Hume's philosophical theories against Reid's critique. Around 1775, Hume's nephew, David (later Baron Hume) was Millar's student and boarded with Millar. Hume encouraged the arrangement and paid his nephew's expenses. Hume and Millar corresponded during this time, although none of their letters has yet surfaced (Hume's manuscripts contain one letter from Millar, but this appears to be written to the nephew). However, a letter from Hume to his nephew at this time indicates the great respect that Hume had towards Millar, and also how the two differed politically – Millar advocating a free republic and Hume advocating a strong monarchy:

[Republicanism] is only fitted for a small State: And any Attempt towards it can in our [Country], produce only Anarchy, which is the immediate Forerunner of Despotism. [Will he] tell us, what is that form of a Republic which we must aspire to? Or [will the Revol]ution be afterward decided by the Sword? [One] great Advantage of a Commonwealth over our mixt Monarchy is, that it [woud consid]erably abridge our Liberty, which is growing to such an Extreme, as to be incom[patible wi]th all Government. Such Fools are they, who perpetually cry out Liberty: [and think to] augment it, by shaking off the Monarchy. [Hume to his nephew David Hume, December 8, 1775; the original manuscript is torn, and bracketed words are Greig's conjectures.]

142

Millar's views were exceptionally liberal for his time. He opposed various forms of oppression, such as slavery and the subjugation of women, and he defended the American and French revolutions. Paralleling Adam Smith's views, he argued that key social institutions ultimately progress over time. Strongly Whiggish in his political sentiments, he nevertheless strived for impartiality in his writings. He published two major works, both of which mention Hume. His *Origin of the Distinction of Ranks* (1771) traces the distinction between social classes, defending the individual liberty of the lower classes. He briefly argues here that Hume's "Of the Populousness of Ancient Nations" quite arbitrarily estimates the number of ancient Athenian slaves at 40,000. His *Historical view of the English Government* (1787) makes the case that England was traditionally a limited rather than an absolute monarchy. Here he opposes Hume on a variety of issues. In 1.7 he addresses the issue of the makeup of the Saxon Witenagemot. The Tory side of the issue – as held by Brady and Hume – is that the commons were excluded from the Witenagemot. The Whig side – as held by Tyrrel, Lyttleton and Stuart – is that they were included. Millar argues for the middle ground. In 2.6.3 he notes that the relaxation of the feudal system strengthened the House of Commons. Hume contended that this took place as an act of Parliament in the reign of Henry IV; Millar argues that it was prior to that time. In 2.11, he criticizes Hume's depiction of Elizabeth's reign – from Chapter 38 of his *History* – as exceptionally despotic. Although ideologically opposed to Hume, throughout his work, Millar footnotes Hume as an authority.

The *Critical Review* favourably appraised Millar's *Historical View*, noting that his "observations are every where supported by reason and probability."[1] Writing for the *Monthly Review*, Samuel Rose applauds the work for its "diligence of investigation" and "acuteness and soundness of argument." Rose criticizes Hume for not paying enough attention to the early periods of English history, and recommends Millar's work for addressing this deficiency:

> Mr. Hume, whose name, as an historian, will ever be mentioned with a considerable degree of respect, has not paid that minute attention to the *earlier* that he has to the *later* periods of our history. He probably considered them as immaterial, and apprehended that a diligent investigation of them would be no more amusing to the writer, than entertaining to the reader. In this instance, however, though supported by the respectable authority of Sir William Temple, and many others, we may venture to affirm that he was mistaken; he should have remembered, that in the Saxon period, a period he

---

[1] *Critical Review*, May 1787, Vol. 63, pp. 369–377, July, Vol. 64, pp. 49–57. The work was also favourably received by the *English Review*, 1787, Vol. 10, pp. 11–223.

has passed over in too cursory a manner, those foundations were laid which were adapted to the superstructure that future hands were to erect, and which succeeding ages have concurred in admiring. Such a period, with such circumstances attending it, could never be unfruitful; there must be in it many pleasing and agreeable views to diversify the attention, and many prolific spots to gratify the taste of the reader.

A good account of the Saxon times has long been much wanted, though that want is in a partial degree supplied by the labours of the animated and acute Mr. Whitaker, in his History of Manchester; but his plan is necessarily of too circumscribed a nature to give all that information which curiosity would require. The present volume comes seasonably to our assistance, and promises us much rational entertainment, by a view of those times, which, hitherto, have not attracted a sufficient degree of attention. [*Monthly Review*, Vol. 77. August 1787, pp. 106–116]

In 1803 a four-volume posthumous edition of the work appeared, which contains a previously unpublished narrative of the house of Stuart, based on Millar's surviving manuscripts. The new discussion presents a less sympathetic account of the House of Stuart than Hume's; throughout that narrative, Miller footnotes Hume's *History*, but does not discuss it in any detail. This edition was reviewed in the *Edinburgh Review* by Francis Jeffrey. Jeffrey attended Glasgow while Millar was there, although Jeffrey's politically conservative father prohibited him from attending lectures by the famous Whig professor. Jeffrey opens noting that, stylistically, the work lacks the flair of Millar's actual spoken words:

The reputation of Professor Millar, we are inclined to think, stands somewhat higher with his pupils, and those who had the benefit of his acquaintance, than it is likely to do with those who may merely peruse his publications. ...

The style of conversation, indeed, in which most of his lectures were delivered, is not very easily adapted to the purposes of publication. The great merit, and the great charm of this style consists in its varying and judicious adaptation to the taste and situation of the hearers, and in the facility and animation with which every thing is communicated and explained. ...

But though, for these, and for other reasons, the written style of Mr Millar be certainly inferior in force and effect to his conversation, the character of his genius is very clearly imprinted upon both: and though it must go down to posterity with some disadvantage from his contempt or unskilfulness in the art of composition, his writings will long continue, we have no doubt, to command the respect and admiration of his readers.

Jeffrey contrasts Hume's and Millar's respective views of the English constitution, finding faults and merits with both; he agrees with Millar that England
historically had a limited monarchy, but disagrees with his liberal interpretation
of the English Parliament:

> The greater part of his treatise upon this subject [of the house of Stuart] may
> be considered as a formal answer to Mr Hume's history, or a specific antidote
> to the poison which he imagines it to contain. Though the differences that
> prevail upon this subject will probably never be composed with the consti-
> tution of this country exists, it is not a little remarkable, that all parties are
> now agreed upon the principle by which they should be determined, and that
> the dispute relates only to the degree or extent of its application. Mr Hume
> admits, that Charles the First attempted many arbitrary things, and was guilty
> of great errors and imprudence; and only apologizes for him on the ground
> of his hereditary prejudices, the necessity of his situation, and the distrust
> which was naturally inspired by the increasing boldness and exaction of his
> Parliament. Mr Millar, on the other hand, without absolutely rejecting these
> apologies, acknowledges that the Parliament ultimately carried their
> precaution and their vengeance a little too far; that their patriotism was
> tainted with fanaticism; that their republicanism was not seconded by the
> voice of the nation; and that it paved the way for the usurpation of military
> despotism of the protector.
>
> There is undoubtedly a great deal of truth, and a great deal of partiality
> in the statements of both writers: neither of them suppresses or falsifies
> facts; but they both give them that disposition and arrangement that is
> calculated to favour their party. Mr Hume certainly magnifies the tyranny
> and arbitrary conduct of Elizabeth, when he compares it to that of a
> Turkish sultan, in order to extenuate the unpopular measures of her
> successors; and Mr Millar certainly does not make a very satisfactory
> answer to this representation, when he proves the constitution of England
> to be a limited monarchy, from the writings of Fortescue in the days of
> Henry II. Upon this general point, however, we are satisfied that Mr Millar
> is in the right, and that the government of England was always considered
> as distinct from the absolute monarchies that existed over the greater part
> of the Continent.
>
> On the other hand, though Mr Hume has certainly aggravated the absur-
> dities of the puritanical leaders of the age, and omitted no opportunity to
> hold up the fanaticism of the Parliament itself to derision, it can scarcely be
> doubted that Mr Millar has ascribed to them a far more unmixed and liberal
> spirit of patriotism, than they really appear to have possessed. ... [*Edinburgh
> Review*, October 1803, Vol. 3, p. 154–181]

Millar's *Historical View* is favourably mentioned by Francis Jeffrey in his 1824 review of Brodie's *History*, contained later in this collection. Millar's work was also published in 1790. The following is from the 1803 edition.

BOOK I.
CHAP. VII.
Of the Wittenagemote.

...

In consequence of the disputes between the king and the people, that took place in England after the accession of the house of Stewart, there arose two political parties; the followers of which have maintained very opposite opinions concerning the constituent members of the Anglo-Saxon Wittenagemote. The supporters of the prerogative, in order to shew that the primitive government of England was an absolute monarchy, and that the privileges enjoyed by the people have all flowed from the voluntary grants and concessions of the sovereign, were led to assert that the original members of the Wittenagemote were persons under the king's immediate influence and direction; from which it was concluded, that, so far from being intended to controul the exercise of his power, the council was called of his own free choice, for the purpose merely of giving advice, and might of consequence be laid aside at pleasure. Hence it was contended, that beside the bishops and abbots, and the aldermen, both of which were supposed to be in the nomination of the crown, the other members of the Wittenagemote, who received the appellation of *wites* or *wise men*, were the lawyers or judges of the kingdom, who sat in the privy council, and were likewise in the appointment of the sovereign.[2]

Those writers, on the contrary, who defended the rights of the people, appear, from their eagerness in combating this opinion, to have been betrayed into the opposite extreme. In their endeavours to prove the independent authority of the ancient national council, they were induced to believe, that, from the beginning, it had been modelled upon the same plan as at present; and that it was originally composed of the nobility, the knights of shires, and the representatives of boroughs.[3]

It requires no great sagacity or attention, at this day, to discover that both of these opinions are equally without foundation. They may be regarded as the delusions of prepossession and prejudice, propagated by political zeal, and

---

[2] Hume's Hist. of England, Appendix to Anglo-Saxon period.

[3] Sir Robert Atkyns' Power, Jurisdiction, and Privileges of Parliament, – Petyt, Rights of the Commons asserted. – Jani Anglorum facies nova. – Argumentum Antinormanicum. – Tyrrel's Bibliotheca Politica. – Lyttleton's Hist.

nourished with a fondness and credulity of party attachment. Nothing can be more improbable, or even ridiculous, than to suppose that the lawyers or judges of England were, immediately after the settlement of the Anglo-Saxons, a body of men so considerable as to compose the principal part of the Wittenagemote, and, from a title peculiar to themselves, to fix the general denomination of that great assembly. In a very rude age, the business of pleading causes is never the object of a separate profession; and the deciding of law-suits does not form a characteristical distinction in the chiefs or leading men, who are occasionally employed in that manner. We may as well suppose that, in the period of English history now under consideration, the Anglo-Saxon *wites*, or *wise men*, were the physicians, the surgeons, and apothecaries, or the mathematicians, the chymists, and astronomers of the country, as that they were the retainers of the law. We have surely no reason to believe that the latter were, by their employment, more distinguished from the rest of the community than the former.

Besides, if the *wites* are understood to be judges and lawyers, it will follow, that the ancient national assembly was often composed of that class of men exclusive of all others; for, in ancient records, it is frequently said, that laws were made, or public business was transacted, in a council of *all the wites* of the kingdom. But it is universally admitted, that the bishops and abbots, as well as the aldermen or governors of shires, were members of the Wittenagemote; from which it is a natural inference, that these two sets of people were comprehended under the general appellation of *wites*.

This may easily be explained. The term *wite* signifies, primarily, a man of valour, or military prowess: and hence a man of high rank, a nobleman.[4] It has been used, in a secondary sense, to denote a *wise man*, from the usual connection, especially in a rude age, between military skill and experience or knowledge: in the same manner as *an old man*, or *grey-headed man*, is, according to the idiom of many languages, employed to signify a ruler or governor. As far as any conclusion, therefore, can be drawn from the appellation of Wittenagemote, or council of wites, it is likely that this national assembly comprehended neither judges nor lawyers, considered in that capacity, but that it was composed of all the leading men, or proprietors of landed estates; in which number the dignified clergy, and the governors of shires, if not particularly distinguished, were always understood to be included.[5]

The other opinion is not more consistent with the state of the country, and the condition of its inhabitants. It supposes that in England, soon after the

---

[4] Somner's Sax. Dict. v. *Wita*.

[5] By a law of king Ina, it is enacted, that if any person fought in the house of an alderman, *or of any illustrious wite*, he should pay a fine of sixty shillings. See Wilkin's Anglo-Saxonica, Leges Inæ, c. 6.

settlement of the Anglo-Saxons, the lower ranks of men were so independent of their superiors, as to form a separate branch of the community, invested with extensive political privileges. This opinion supposes, in particular, that the mercantile part of the inhabitants were become a distinct order of the people, and had risen to such opulence and authority as entitled them to claim a share in the conduct of national measures. There is not, however, the least shadow of probability in this supposition. Whatever improvements in trade and manufactures had been made in Britain, while it remained under the provincial government of Rome, these were almost entirely destroyed, by the convulsions which attended the Saxon conquest, and the subjection of a great part of the island to the dominion of a barbarous people. The arts which remained in the country after this great revolution, were reduced to such as procure the mere necessaries, or a few of the more simple conveniencies of life; and these arts were hardly the objects of a separate profession, but were practised occasionally by the inferior and servile part of the inhabitants. How is it possible to conceive, in such a state of manufacturers, that the trading interest would be enabled to assume the privilege of sending representatives to the great council of the nation? Even in those European states, whose advancement in arts was much earlier than that of the Anglo-Saxons, the formation of the trading towns into corporations was long posterior to the period we are now examining; yet this event must have preceded their acting in a political capacity, and, consequently, their being represented in the national assembly. ...

It has been imagined by some authors, that the privilege of sitting in the Wittenagemote was originally confined to such as possessed forty hides of land; a property of great extent, which few individuals, it is natural to suppose, could have an opportunity of acquiring; whence it seems to be inferred, that a small part only of the landed gentry were admitted into the councils of the sovereign.[6] This opinion is founded upon a passage in the register of Ely, which mentions a distinction in point of rank, enjoyed by such of the nobles as possessed estates amounting to forty hides of land. But this passage refers to the state of the kingdom in the reign of Edward the confessor, when property had been subjected to the most important revolutions, and government had widely deviated from its original institution. No inference can thence be drawn, concerning the primitive constitution of the national council; which must have arisen from the state of the inhabitants at the time when it was framed. How far the authority above mentioned is sufficient to justify that conclusion, with respect to the later periods of the Anglo-Saxon government, will fall to be afterwards examined. It is therefore highly probable that the Wittenagemote of the Anglo-Saxons was originally so constituted, as to admit a great portion of the

---

[6]   Dugdale's preface to his Baronage. Hume's Hist. of England, appendix to Anglo-Saxon period.

people into a share of its deliberations; and it merits attention, that even such of the inhabitants as were excluded from this assembly, were either the slaves, or the tenants and vassals of those who sat in it. The former were thus placed under the protection of the latter. Men of inferior rank, though not formally represented in the national council, enjoyed, therefore, a degree of security from the influence of their master or superior, who had an interest to defend them from every injustice but his own, and whose jealousy was ever watchful to guard them from any oppression of the sovereign. ...

BOOK II.

CHAP. VI.
History of the Parliament in the same Period.

SECTION III.
Concerning the Manner of electing the national Representatives, and the Forms of Procedure in Parliament.

...

By this relaxation of the feudal system, the foundation of the house of commons was enlarged; and its establishment was rendered more extensively useful. The knights of the shires became properly the representatives, not of one class, but of the whole gentry of every rank and description. All the independent property in the kingdom was, according to this constitution, represented in parliament: the lords appeared in behalf of their own possessions; the inferior landed interest fell under the care of the country members; and the burgesses were entrusted with the protection of that wealth which was employed in trade.

Such, in all probability, were the circumstances, from which the rear-vassals obtained a share in the election of county-members; but at what time this change was produced is very uncertain. Mr. Hume has concluded, that it took place in consequence of an act of parliament in the reign of Henry the fourth. But when we examine that statute, it does not appear to have introduced any such regulation: on the contrary, it supposes that proprietors of land, not holding directly of the crown, had been formerly entitled to vote for the country-members; and makes a general provision for securing that freedom of their election, as well as for preventing undue returns by the sheriff.[7]

---

[7] 7 Henry IV. c. 15. See a farther provision to the same purpose, 11 Henry IV. c. 1.

CHAP. XI.

Of Edward the Sixth – Mary – and Elizabeth. – General Review of the Government. – Conclusion of the Period from the Norman Conquest to the Accession of the House of Stewart.

...

The great historian of England, to whom the reader is indebted for the complete union of history with philosophy, appears very strongly impressed with a notion of the despotical government in the reign of Elizabeth, and of the arbitrary and tyrannical conduct displayed by that princess.

1. He observes, that

"she suspended the laws, so far as to order a great part of the service, the litany, the Lord's prayer, the creed, and the gospels, to be read in English. And, having first published injunctions, that all the churches should conform themselves to the practice of her own chapel, she forbade the hoste to be any more elevated in her presence; an innovation, which, however frivolous it may appear, implied the most material consequences."

But we must not forget, that, in this case, the dispensing power was exercised under great limitations, and in very singular circumstances. Upon the accession of Elizabeth, the Protestants, who now formed the greatest part of her subjects, exasperated by the late persecution, and in full confidence of protection, began to make violent changes; to revive the service authorized by Edward the sixth, to pull down images, and to affront the priests of the Roman catholic persuasion. The queen had called a parliament to settle the national religion; but, in order to stop the progress of these disorders, an immediate interposition of the crown was necessary. It was even pretended by some, that the parliaments, in the late reign, had not been legally held, and that of consequence the laws of Edward the sixth, relating to the government of the church, were still in force.[8] But, whatever regard might be due to this, a temporary indulgence to the protestants, with respect to the external forms of religious worship, was highly expedient for quieting their minds, and for preventing the commission of greater enormities. This indulgence was followed by a proclamation prohibiting all innovations, until the matters in dispute should be finally determined by parliament; and, considering the circumstances of the case, ought to be regarded rather as a measure calculated for the present security of the established religion and its professors, than as a violent exertion of the prerogative, in opposition to the laws of the land.

[8]   Burnet.

2. But this author, not contented with ascribing to the crown a power of suspending the laws, has gone so far as to assert, that it was entitled, at pleasure, to introduce new statutes. "In reality," says he, "the crown possessed the full legislative power, by means of proclamations, which might affect any matter, even of the greatest importance, and which the star-chamber took care to see more rigorously executed than the laws themselves."[9]

In answer to this, it will perhaps be thought sufficient to observe, that anciently the crown possessed no legislative power; that royal proclamations were first declared to have the force of laws, in the latter part of the reign of Henry the eighth; that even then, this force was given them under great restrictions, and in singular cases; and that in the beginning of the subsequent reign, it was entirely abolished by the same authority from which it had proceeded.

In the star-chamber, therefore, supported this power in the reign of Elizabeth, it must have been in direct violation of the constitution; and it is not likely, that stretches of this kind would often be attempted. But let us consider what were the proclamations issued in this reign, which the star-chamber had an opportunity to enforce. In virtue of the papal supremacy, with which she was invested, Elizabeth prohibited *prophecyings* or particular assemblies instituted for fanatical purposes, and not authorized by the church.[10] Having the regulation of trade and manufactures, she also prohibited the culture of *woad*, a plant used for the purpose of dying. And, as a director of ceremonies, prescribing rules for the dress of those who appeared at court, or in public places, she gave orders that the length of the swords, and the height of the ruffs then in fashion, should be diminished. These are the important instances adduced in order to prove that Elizabeth superseded the authority of acts of parliament, and assumed the legislative power in her own person.

3. The same historian appears to conceive, that, among other branches of prerogative exercised by Elizabeth, was that of imposing taxes. "There was," he remarks, "a species of *ship-money* imposed at the time of the Spanish invasion: the several ports were required to equip a certain number of vessels at their own charge; and such was the alacrity of the people for the public defence, that some of the ports, particularly London, sent double the number demanded of them."[11] And in a subsequent period of the English history,

---

[9]   Hist. of Engl. vol. V. Appendix 3.

[10] In the fifth of Elizabeth there was passed an act, conformable to a preceding one in the reign of Edward the sixth, against *fond and fantastical prophecies concerning the queen and divers honourable persons*, which, it seems, had a tendency to stir up sedition. From the name, it is not unlikely that the assemblies, alluded to in the proclamation above-mentioned, were supposed guilty of the like practices, and that Elizabeth was merely following out the intention of an act of parliament.

[11] Vol. V. Appendix 3.

having mentioned a requisition made by Charles the first, that the maritime towns, *together with the adjacent counties*, should arm a certain number of vessels, he adds; "This is the first appearance, in Charles's reign, of ship-money; a taxation which had once been imposed by Elizabeth, but which afterwards, when carried some steps farther by Charles, occasioned such violent discontents."[12]

Ship-money was originally a contribution by the maritime towns, for the support of the fleet, corresponding, in some measure, to the scutages which were paid by the military people, in room of personal service in the field. When it came, therefore, to be a regular assessment, exacted by public authority, it fell of course under the regulation of parliament; and, like other taxes, being gradually pushed beyond its original boundaries, was extended to the counties in the neighbourhood of the sea, and at length to the most inland parts of the kingdom. To oppose an invasion which threatened the immediate destruction of her empire, Elizabeth had recourse to the customary assistance of the sea-port towns; and, so far from using compulsion to procure it, was freely supplied with a much greater force than she required. How can this measure be considered as analogous to the conduct of Charles the first, in levying that *ship-money*, which gave rise to such violent complaints? The contribution obtained by Elizabeth was altogether voluntary: that which was levied by Charles was keenly disputed by the people, and enforced by the whole power of the crown. The supply granted by Elizabeth was furnished by the maritime towns only; who, by their employment and situation, were connected with the equipment of vessels: that which was extorted by Charles, had been converted into a regular tax; and was imposed upon the nation at large. The ship-money of Elizabeth was procured in a single case, and one of such extraordinary necessity, as would have excused a deviation from the common rules of government. But the ship-money of Charles was not palliated by any pretence of necessity: it was introduced, and, notwithstanding the clamours of the people, continued for a considerable period, with the avowed intention of enabling the king to rule without a parliament.

4. But the chief ground of this opinion, concerning the tyrannical behaviour of Elizabeth, and the despotical nature of her government, appears to be her interference in the debates of parliament; her imprisonment of members for presuming to urge the prosecution of bills, after she had put a negative upon them; and the tameness with which parliament submitted to those exertions of prerogative.

It must be confessed, that if, in the present age, a British monarch should act in the same manner, and should meet with the same acquiescence from parliament, we might reasonably conclude that our freedom was entirely destroyed. But the

[12] Vol. VI.

submission of that assembly, at a period when the order, in which the king's negative should be interposed, was not invariably determined, does not argue the same corruption; and therefore will not warrant the same conclusion. Whatever might be the view entertained by some members of parliament in that age, the greater part of them were probably not aware of the consequences with which those exertions of the crown might be attended; and as, with reason, they placed great confidence in the queen's intentions, their jealousy was not roused by a measure which did not seem to violate any fixed rule of the government.

Neither have we any good reason to infer, that, because this point had hitherto been left undetermined, the constitution was of no value or efficacy to maintain the rights of the people. It was, no doubt, a great defect in the political system, that the king might put a stop to any bill depending in parliament, and prevent any farther debate with relation to it. But even this power of the sovereign was far from rendering the government despotical. By means of it, he might the more effectually defend his own prerogative, but it could not enable him to encroach upon the liberty of the subject. The parliament, without whose authority no innovation could be made, was the less capable of introducing any new regulation; but not the less qualified to maintain the government as it stood. The power of taxation, at the same time, threw a prodigious weight into the scale of parliamentary influence. By the increasing expence of government, a consequence of the improvement of arts, and the advancement of luxury, the old revenues of the crown became daily more inadequate to the demands of the sovereign; which laid him under the necessity of making frequent applications to parliament for extraordinary supplies. This, as it reduced him to a dependence upon that assembly, enabled it to take advantage of his necessities, and to extort from him such concessions as experience had shown to be requisite for securing the rights and privileges of the people.

5. According to Mr Hume,

"the government of England, during that age, however different in other particulars, bore, in this respect, some resemblance to that of Turkey at present: the sovereign possessed every power, except that of imposing taxes: and in both countries this limitation, unsupported by other privileges, appears rather prejudicial to the people. In Turkey, it obliges the Sultan to permit the extortion of the bashaws and governors of provinces, from whom he afterwards squeezes presents, or takes forfeitures. In England, it engaged the queen to erect monopolies, and grant patents for exclusive trade: and invention so pernicious, that had she gone on, during a tract of years, at her own rate, England, the seat of riches, and arts, and commerce, would have contained, at present, as little industry as Morocco, or the coast of Barbary."[13]

---

[13] History of England, vol. V. Appendix 3.

But surely, in England, the sovereign was not possessed of every power, except that of imposing taxes. The power of legislation was vested in the king, lords, and commons. The judicial power was not, in ordinary cases, exercised by the crown, but was distributed among various courts of justice; and though, in these, the judges, from the manner of their appointment, might be supposed to favour the prerogative, yet the modes of their procedure, and the general rules of law, were in most cases too invariably determined, to permit very gross partiality. The institution of *juries*, besides, which had long been completely established in England, was calculated to counterbalance this natural bias of judges, and to secure the rights of the people. Is it possible that, in such a government, the power of the monarch can be seriously compared to that which prevails in Turkey?

The sovereign, indeed, was entitled to erect monopolies, and to grant exclusive privileges; which, in that period, were thought necessary for the encouragement of trade and manufactures. That these grants were often bestowed for the purpose merely of deriving a pecuniary advantage to the crown, it is impossible to deny. But who can believe that the perquisites, arising from this branch of the prerogative, or from such of the feudal incidents as were still of an arbitrary nature, were ever likely to defray the extraordinary expences of the crown, and to supersede the necessity of soliciting taxes from parliament?

The star-chamber, and the court of high commission, were doubtless arbitrary and oppressive tribunals; and were in a great measure under the direction of the sovereign. But their interposition, though justly the subject of complaint, was limited to singular and peculiar cases; and, had it been pushed so far as to give great interruption to the known and established course of justice, it would have occasioned such odium and clamour, as no prince of common understanding would be willing to incur.

To be satisfied, upon the whole, that the English constitution, at this period, contained the essential principles of liberty, we need only attend to its operation, when the question was brought to a trial, in the reigns of the two succeeding princes. At the commencement of the disputes between the house of commons and the two first princes of the Stewart family, the government stood precisely upon the same foundation as in the time of Elizabeth. Neither the powers of parliament had been encreased, nor those of the sovereign diminished. Yet, in the course of that struggle, it soon became evident, that parliament, without going beyond its undisputed privileges, was possessed of sufficient authority, not only to resist the encroachments of prerogative, but even to explain and define its extent, and to establish a more compleat and regular system of liberty. It was merely by withholding supplies, that the parliament was able to introduce these important and salutary regulations. Is the power of taxation, therefore, to be considered as prejudicial to the people? Ought it not rather to be regarded as the foundation of all their privileges, and the great mean of establishing that happy mixture of monarchy and democracy which we at present enjoy?

35
JOHN WHITAKER

John Whitaker, *Mary Queen of Scots vindicated. By John Whitaker,* ... London: printed for J. Murray, 1787, 3 v.
Selections from Preface, 1.5.4, 1.6.3, 1.7.7, 2.6.7; from 1790 edition.

John Whitaker (1735–1808) was the author of *The History of Manchester* (1771–1775), selections from which are contained earlier in this collection. In *Mary Queen of Scots Vindicated*, Whitaker defends Mary's innocence by attacking the authenticity of the eight letters, twelve sonnets, and two marriage-contracts attributed to Mary. Throughout the work he criticizes Hume and other historians who hold them to be authentic. In the Preface, he sketches the history of the controversy from the 16th century to his own day. He notes there that Hume's response to Tytler reflected a "ferocity of spirit" and "a real imbecility of exertion." Like Tytler, Whitaker believes that the letters ascribed to Mary are forgeries, and one indication of this is the inconsistent statements about whether they were both written and signed by her. In 1.5.4 he criticizes Hume's and Dalrymple's attempts to rectify the inconsistency. In 1.6.3 he considers the fact that Lord Huntly – a defender of Mary – was an alleged witness to one of the signed contracts; according to Hume, if the document was a forgery, Huntly or Mary would have immediately spoken out about this fact, which they did not do. In response, Whitaker argues that Huntly or Mary did not have access to the documents and thus did not know that his name was down as a witness to the document. In 1.7 he responds to Hume's attack on Goodall, that "So far as I know, no man ever denied" the present French copy to be only a translation from the Scottish. Whitaker replies, "But did any man ever *assert* it, *before* Mr. Goddall?" In 2.6.4 he considers Hume's argument in favour of a French original based on the presence of French words and idioms in the Scottish version. Whitaker replies that, when comparing the Scottish phrases with the alleged French idioms, we find more dissimilarities than similarities among the words.

Whitaker's work was favourably reviewed by James Anderson in the *Monthly Review,* who notes that "Mr. Whitaker follows nearly the same path that Goodall had marked out, and Tytler had smoothed before him; but with an acuteness of penetration."[1] The article on Whitaker in the *Critical Review* was largely negative, suggesting that the work did not add much to the discussion:

> We have, in this article, chiefly given a specimen of our author's manner, with some remarks on the management of the controversy; and we have selected rather those parts which are subservient to this design, than those in which he has materially elucidated the question. The latter are, indeed, found with much difficulty. He has amplified hints, and has extended the sentences of others to whole pages.

However, the reviewer sides with Whitaker against Hume:

> The real letters had no signature, and we cannot avoid joining Mr. Whitaker in his suspicion, that though they could forge the hand of Mary, they could not imitate her seal. Of course unsealed letters, on such subjects, could not properly have a signature; and such letters must be consequently obscure and illusive. We are aware of Mr. Hume's answer to this point; and though we allow his arguments to have great weight, and that they are not sufficiently considered by Mr. Whitaker, yet, in this instance, from the language of the report it is impossible to apply the subscription to the contract. [*Critical Review*, February 1788, Vol. 65, pp. 81–87]

Whitaker's *Mary Queen of Scots Vindicated* appeared again in 1788, 1789, and 1790. The following is from the 1790 edition. Bracketed comments in the text are those of Whitaker.

PREFACE.

The eight letters, twelve sonnets, and two marriage-contracts; which either in their subscriptions, in their composition, or in both, have been attributed to the pen of the unfortunate Mary; and on which, principally, is founded all the slander that has been raised against her; have been as singular in their fortune, as they are in their nature. Suspected for forgeries by numbers, at the time of their original appearance; and condemned equally by numbers, for certain

---

[1] *Monthly Review*, December 1787, Vol. 77 pp. 472–478, January 1788, Vol. 78, pp. 1–15. Whitaker's *Mary Queen of Scots Vindicated* was also reviewed in the *English Review*, 1787, Vol. 10, pp. 100–111, and *European Magazine and London Review*, 1787, Vol. 12 pp. 373–378, 457–460.

forgeries; they gained by degrees upon the good opinion of the publick, till they nearly came at last into the full possession of it. In this kind of pre-eminence, they continued to our own days. They carried a commanding boldness, in their air and manner. And nothing imposes more readily upon the easy faith of the world, than the bold testimony of a confident witness.

The most important of these papers, however, the letters, had been very strongly encountered at first by a *Defence of Mary's honour*; which was published by her worthy adherent, Lesley, bishop of Ross; and which was at once lively, convincing, and pointed. But this was instantly suppressed, by the violence of Queen Elizabeth. No vindication of Mary was suffered to appear. Many were published on the continent; yet none of them durst venture upon English ground. And, at the same time, the *Detection of Mary's Doings* by Buchanan; that daring effort of fabricated calumny, in which the principal of the two contracts, all the sonnets, and all the letters were originally published; received every recommendation, that could be lent it by authority. It was presented in form to Elizabeth herself. It was circulated with industry by her ministers. In that period of our government, such artifices of tyranny would carry a peculiar efficacy with them. They could not fail of success. The reputation of Mary was assaulted on every side, in vigourous and artful appeals to the publick. She was debarred from all counter-appeals, in her own defence. From the malicious partiality of mankind to slander, the energy of a vindication is no ways equal to the force of an accusation. What then must be the force of the one, when the other is not permitted to accompany it; when this is suppressed, and that is supported, by all the exertions of authority in the government, and by all the habits of obedience in the people? The consequence was very natural. The sonnets, contracts, and letters were received as authentick testimonies of Mary's guilt. The opinion of the publick became fixed upon the point. And a slander, that has once got possession of the general faith, is the most difficult of all prejudices to be removed.

But in 1754 a wonderful revolution began to take place, in the history of these established evidences. Mr. Goodall, keeper of the Advocates' library at Edinborough, stepped forward with a courage, that seemed to border upon rashness; in order to prove them mere forgeries, and to disabuse the deceived publick. He was a man very conversant with records. He was, therefore, in the habit of referring assertions to authorities. He was also actuated perhaps by a spirit of party, as a party had been then formed in the nation concerning the point. Something more vigourous than the abstracted love of truth, is generally requisite to every arduous undertaking. But, whatever were his motives, his enterprize was honourable, and his execution powerful. He entered into an examination of the papers, with considerable spirit. He went through it, with considerable address. He even proved the letters to be forgeries, in so clear a manner; that one is astonished, it had never been done before. *This* shews, indeed, the little attention which had been paid to the subject; in care to substantiate, or in zeal to destroy, the fundamental credit of the whole. And *that* forms one of those grand discoveries, which must necessarily be very rare in the history of any nation, and therefore reflect a peculiar honour, upon the individual who makes them.

Yet such was the factious credulity then prevailing generally in the island, that this work, one of the most original and convincing which ever were published, made its way very slowly among us. Even some of our first-rate writers, presumed to set themselves against it. Dr. Robertson, a disciple of the old school, wrote a formal dissertation in opposition to it. Even Mr. Hume, who in *history* had learned to think more liberally than the Doctor, still professed and defended his adherence to the ancient errour, in some incidental notes to his History of England. And the nation stood suspended between the authority of great names, and the prejudices of "the million," upon one side; and a new name, new arguments, and demonstration, on the other. Then Mr. Tytler arose. He generally took the same ground, which Mr. Goodall had taken before him. He generally made use of his weapons. He brightened up some. He strengthened others. With both and with his own, he drove an enemy out of the field. Dr. Robertson quitted it directly. Mr. Hume rallied, after a long interval of eleven or twelve years. He rallied with a seeming ferocity of spirit, and with a real imbecillity of exertion. He, who never replied to an adversary before, now replied to Mr. Tytler in a note to a new edition of his history. He laid himself out there, in reproaches against Mr. Tytler, and in vindications of himself. But he touched upon the cause of Mary, in a single point only. And his efforts of proving in all, were slight in their aim, and feeble in their operation. Mr. Tytler, however, very properly advanced upon him again, in a postscript to a new edition of his own work; and Mr. Hume retired finally with Dr. Robertson. Mr. Tytler deservedly gained great honour, by the contest. His work is candid, argumentative, acute, and ingenious. Only, his success seems to have injured his master's reputation. The glory was in no small measure Mr. Goodall's own. Yet such is the capriciousness of fame conferred by men, that the laurels are still shading the brow of Mr. Tytler, while the original proprietor is almost forgotten. It is a justice due to the memories of illustrious masters, not to let their names be lost in the succeeding splendour of their scholars, when a large share of that splendour is derived from the masters themselves.

In this state of the controversy, the nation continued for many years. The new truths were gradually gaining ground. None opposed them. Numbers embraced them. And at last, in the natural progress of conviction, Dr. Stuart appeared about four years ago; with a regular history of Mary's reign, modelled upon the authority of records, and therefore vindicating the character of the Queen. He even challenged Dr. Robertson, as the preceding historian of her reign, to leave the retreat which he had kept so long, to come forward from his covert at last, and either justify or retract his slanders against her. This was fair and manly. But the Doctor was too prudent to accept the challenge. He had gained his first honours in historical composition, from that very history. These indeed had withered on his head. But he might lose them entirely, in attempting to freshen them. The notion was no longer in that high state of faction, in which it stood when he published first. And to retract what he had said, could not be expected from that measure of generosity, which ordinarily falls to the share of man.

It was the perusal of Dr. Stuart's spirited and judicious History, in the second edition of it; that put me upon examining the evidences, on which the whole is founded. I had formerly read the controversy, just as thousands must necessarily have read it, with a transient attention to the cited records, and with a full conviction on the side of Mary. But I now resolve to go deeper. The result was, that I quickly saw some particulars concerning the letters, sonnets, and contracts, as I thought; which had not yet been opened with sufficient clearness, had not yet been pressed with sufficient vigour, or had been totally overlooked hitherto. These would serve, I saw, to vindicate more fully the character of a Queen, to whom the nation owes so much in reparation, for two centuries of unremitted obloquy. And these have been so successively continued from point to point since, that they have at last, I find, embraced the whole history and evidence of the writings, within their ample circle.

Yet, in justice to my own candour, I ought to acknowledge; that, in doing this, I have found myself compelled at times to avoid the ground, which the preceding champions for Mary have generally occupied. From a prudential regard for myself, I have been careful not to take any that was untenable. From a more dignified respect for facts, I have been upon my guard against that generosity of compassion, for a highly injured woman; which is so apt to steal over the spirits, and to impose upon the judgment, of an honest man. And, while I profess myself a warm friend to Mary, I wish to be considered as a much warmer one, to the truth of history in writing, and to the exercise of integrity in life.

VOLUME 1
CHAPTER 5.
§ IV.

...

In the act of council the letters are described, as "written AND SUBSCRIVIT with hir awen hand;" and in the act of parliament, as "WRITTIN HALELIE with hir awin hand." Whence arises this difference? it is apparently a very extraordinary one. It strikes strongly upon the mind. And it is authenticated in the clearest manner. The letters, no doubt, were *exhibited* before the council. Even Murray could not have had the effrontery, to ask and to procure a *charge* of *murder* against Mary, upon the testimony of writings *not seen*. The council therefore saw them. yet they represented them, "as written *and subscribed* with her own hand." They were certainly seen by the parliament too. I know, indeed, that the friends of Mary to this day contend they were not. But I am constrained by the force of truth, to separate from them in this, as well as in some other points. Murray could still less than before have had the effrontery, to ask and procure a *sentence* of *murder* against Mary, upon the authority of writing that dared not to show their faces. And Murray and Mary's nobles concur to say expressly, that they were seen. On the Duke of Norfolk's privately proposing to Murray at York, not to produce his letters to the commissioners; "my reply to that was," says Murray himself, "how the matter had passed in parliament, and THE LETTERS SEEN TO MANY, so that the abstracting of the same could not then secure her to any purpose."[2] Murray's word indeed will not be readily admitted upon a dubious point, by either the friends of Mary or myself, without the concurrences of some other testimony. I hasten therefore to such a testimony. What pretended to be "hir Majestie's writing," the very nobles of Mary's party say, was "PRODUCIT IN PARLIAMENT."[3] Yet the parliament described the letters, from an equal view of them with the council itself, in a manner essentially different; as NOT "written *and subscribed* by her own hand," but only as "written" by it, and as written "wholly" by it. Here we have vision against vision, and record against record. Which of them shall we take? We know not which to take. We are floating betwixt two opposite tides. One drives us, to suppose the letters only *written* by the Queen. The other compels us, to believe them both *written and subscribed* by her. And which shall carry us away by its impulse, at last?

The former must, says Mr. Hume. The whole difficulty, according to his solution of it, results from "the inaccuracy or blunder of the clerk." and "the mistake is easily accounted for: the letters were only wrote by her, the second contract with Bothwell was only subscribed; a proper accurate distinction was not made, and they were all said to be wrote and subscribed."[4] Nor is "a proper accurate distinction" *yet* made. The *second* contract, indeed, pretended only to be subscribed. But the *first* pretended, equally with the letters at one time, to be both written and subscribed.[5] Having cleared up this little confusion, let us attend to the argument itself. And let us observe, in order to give a full energy to it, that the rebels on the 10th of December, 1568, when they declared at Westminster, "good honest men, full surely!" how they came by the evidences against Mary; spoke of them, "as written OR subscrivit be hir hand."[6] But then

---

[2] Robertrson, ii. 397.

[3] Goodall, ii. 360 – 361.

[4] Hist. v. 148.

[5] Appendix, No. v. and xi.

[6] Goodall, ii., 92.

they speak of "divers missive letteris, sonnettis, obligatiounis or contractis for marriage, betwix the Quene – and Erle Bothwille."[7] And the acts of council and of parliament, as Mr. Tytler has very justly replied,[8] speak only of "her privie letters." These alone are said by the parliament, to have been written wholly by her own hand. These alone are said by the council, to have been both written and subscribed by it. These alone *could* be mentioned or meant at all, by either. THEY ALONE WERE PRODUCED TO EITHER. The *contracts*, either first or second, were *not* produced. The *sonnets* were equally *not* produced. They could neither of them, therefore, be within the purview of the council. They could neither of them be, in the contemplation of the parliament. And Mr. Hume's clerk, instead of being set down for a blunderer by his ingenious employer, must have been a much more ingenious man than himself; as he was professed of the peculiar faculty, a superior kind of second-sight in memory perhaps, of alluding to papers which he had never seen, of combining the stores of sight with the treasures of revelation in his mind, yet marking with some distinctness the real boundaries of both, and so referring half of his description to the one and half to the other.

So contemptible does Mr. Hume's solution appear, when we bring it to the slightest test of trial! Yet a writer has recently stepped forth, in opposition to Mr. Tytler; and pronounced it "not" a "contemptible" solution. This writer has given himself to the world, in "Miscellaneous Remarks" on Mr. Tytler's work.[9] He is plainly an enemy to Mary, a disciple of Dr. Robertson's or Mr. Hume's. Most probably he is a pupil to the former.[10] But, whatever he is, he is evidently *very young*. He should have staid longer at the feet of his political Gamaliel, before he had ventured to become a teacher himself. He should have "staid at Jericho, till his beard was grown." And if a young man chose to be artful; if his youthful integrity would permit him to assume a disguise, he should have taken care to wrap it closely about him. He affects the air of one of Mary's friends. Yet he writes with the venom of her enemies. He has not much indeed, because he has little strength. But he shows as much, as his strength will permit him to show. And to apply the witty remark of a *Cavalier*, "young Sir Harry Vane, if he lives, will come to be old Sir Harry." He informs

[7]   Goodall, ii. 92.

[8]   P. 9. Edit. 1st, which is the edition that I invariably use, except when I say to the contrary. [William Tytler (1711–1792), *An Historical and Critical Enquiry* (1760), selections from which are contained earlier in this collection.]

[9]   Printed for Robson and Robinson, London, 1784. [David Dalrymple (1726–1792), *Miscellaneous Remarks* (1784), selections from which are contained earlier in this collection.]

[10]   Dr. Robertson accordingly, in 1. 137, edit. xi. appeals to his work, as containing "several ingenious remarks."

us in his first page, that "the intercourse between Mary and the Earl of Bothwell was ill-fated, and in its consequences disastrous; *but with respect to her, it was innocent.*" Yet, even after such an assertion, he plainly is endeavouring to make the epistolary part of that intercourse, appear to be genuine, and therefore guilty indeed; by answering the objections, that have been made to its genuineness. And this he does, under the disingenuous pretence of clearing the cause of Mary's vindication, from some arguments that injure it. Such has been the influence of the late writings in favour of Mary, upon the mind of the publick; that even an enemy is now obliged to put on the uniform of her friends, to place himself in the ranks with them, and to pretend a zeal for their cause.

He accordingly takes part with Mr. Hume, concerning this extraordinary variation in the records. He is even gallant enough, to come and assist him at the very moment of his defeat. And he has the generosity, to wish to cover the retreat which he had not power to stop. But his gallantry is greater than his prudence, and his generosity is superiour to his force. He has induced me by his interference, to follow the stunning blow which Mr. Tytler had given Mr. Hume, to pursue the enemy which he had obliged to retire, and to improve the success (I trust) into a complete discomfiture. And having done this, I turn upon the auxiliary himself. Mr. Hume's solution, he says, is "not contemptible, however much it may be despised by some men: for as *letter of tack* and *letter of pension* are phrases used in Scotland, so *letter of espousal* may be proper enough."[11] This gentleman appears from many circumstances, to be a Scotchman. Indeed the subject of Mary's innocence or of Mary's guilt, has been almost entirely confined to the Scotch. and I know not whether I am not the first Englishman, that has written a large treatise professedly on the point. Yet, though a Scot, he is not much conversant with the idioms of the Scottish language. Had he been, he might have given a greater force to his argument, than he has done. I will do it for him, before I attack it. This will be acting with the honourableness of an old knight-errant. I acted with a little of this spirit, to Mr. Hume before. And I ought not to be less generous to his kind assistant. He wants it as much as he, though he came as an assistant to him.

The Scotch formerly denoted; and do denote still, I suppose; *all* sorts of writings, by the appellation of LETTERS. We do so in some measure ourselves, in the use of the word *letters* for literature. Hence come our authour's "letter of tack," and "letter of pension." Hence also a contract for marriage, may very analogously be denominated a "letter of espousal." And, what is decisive upon the topick, even *the very contract* mentioned by Mr. Hume, is expressly styled *a letter* by an author *of the very time.* That authour is MURRAY himself.

[11] P. 7.

In ennumerating the written evidences which he produced against Mary, he mentions "the contractis or obligatiounis for marriage, – and all *utheris* LETTERIS."[12] The Earl of Morton, also, speaks of them afterwards in the very same style exactly, as "contractis or obligatiounis for marriage, – and utheris LETTERIS."[13] But then they both distinguish very carefully, what common-sense requires every language to distinguish, betwixt epistolary and other writings. Murray mentions "all *missive letteris*, contractis or obligatiounis for marriage, sonettis or luif-ballettis, and all utheris letteris." Morton specifies "the *missive letteris*, contractis or obligatiounis for marriage, sonettis or luif-ballettis, and utheris letteris." The acts of council and parliament also, observing the same distinctiveness of language, speak of "her *privie* letters." These are evidently the same, with the "missive letters" of Morton and Murray. They are even said expressly by both the parliament and the council, to have been actually missive; being described by both, as "divers hir previe lettres, *writtin and subscrivit*" or "*writtin halelie*," "with *hir awin hand*, and SENT by hir to James sumtyme Erll of Bothwell." And, as I have already noticed, *these* were the *only* letters or writings, that were produced before the council, or presented to the parliament.

So easily is the auxiliary defeated, as well as the principal! But the former afterwards comes forward, from his subordinate situation as an auxiliary; and assumes the tone and stalk of a principal himself. He thinks Mr. Hume's argument not a bad one. But he has *a better of his own*. "Another," he says, "and a more easy and obvious, solution may be suggested." It is this. "He who writes a deed with his own hand," he says,

> "does generally sign it; and it is hardly possible to figure a case of a perfect deed, written by the party's own hand, and not signed by him: hence *written and subscribed* constantly go together in common language, just as *heirs and executors*. As every one, conversant in law-business, must have seen *executors* joined to *heirs*, in consequence of what may be termed the customary affinity between them, although the maker of the deed meant not to speak of executors; so, in like manner, the clerk of privy council might have added *subscrivit* to *written*. It appears that this inaccuracy was observed, and immediately corrected."[14]

Such is the "more easy and obvious solution" suggested by this gentleman! But whether it is *more* obvious and easy than Mr. Hume's may soon be settled. It

[12] Appendix, No. iv.

[13] Appendix, No. iv.

[14] P. 7.

is neither easy nor obvious at all. The very confusedness of it, shows this suffi-ciently. And nothing but the natural partiality, which the mind always bears to its own conceptions; or the equally natural unfixedness of a frivolous mind; could have induced him to mention it. It has two advantages, however, over Mr. Hume's. It does not militate against the positive fact mentioned before. And, what perhaps is equally useful, it has so little pointedness in it, that it is not easy to meet its force.

The confusion of ideas, that prevailed in the authour's understanding when he conceived the argument, appears very evident in his management of it. Even as he states it himself, it amounts only to this, that so it might be. Yet, in the very next words, he assumes this argument of mere possibility, for an absolute evidence of reality. "The Clerk of privy council," he says, "MIGHT have added *subscrivit* to *written*." And yet, as we are instantly told, "IT APPEARS" that he did add it; that "this inaccuracy" was actually committed by him, actually "OBSERVED," and "IMMEDIATELY CORRECTED."

Such is the whole of the argument, as stated by himself! Let us now examine the parts of it, as they stand before us. "He who writes a deed with his own hand, does generally sign it." This is surely a very strange position. Who writes a *deed* with his own hand? Not one in ten thousand. And if this gentleman be in the law, as from his allusion I take him to be, he hopes for the sake of the profession, I presume, that not one in ten thousand will ever do it; unless indeed he is one of those peculiarly malignant lawyers, who would be glad of confusion for the sake of advantage, would sacrifice the world to their gains, and are ready, in their rage for profit, to cry out with "the enraged Northumberland,"

Let heaven kiss earth! now let not nature's hand
Keep the wild flood confin'd! Let order die!

But when any one does write a deed with his own hand, it seems, he *generally* signs it. He *always* signs it, if it be a deed. If he draws it up as a deed, he will equally as a deed sign it. But what connection has all this, with the letters before the council and parliament? It has this. "Hence *written and subscribed* constantly go together in common language, just as *heirs and executors*." The technical union of heirs and executors is very natural, because these are legally two grand and parallel links, in the chain of transmitted property. But is there any such union, or any such reason for an union, between the subscribing and the writing of a paper, whether a law deed or not? Do deeds generally, or even ever, make use of the combination "written and subscribed," as they do of "heirs and executors?" Certainly not. The subscriber is almost always a different man, from the writer. And, even when he is not, none but an affected simpleton would think, if ever *one* thought, of recording upon his deed, that he *wrote* as well as subscribed it.

But even if all this was true; if the terms "written and subscribed" were as common associates in the language of the law, as "heirs and executors" are; what then? Would every or would any lawyer, from his frequent recurrence of the phrase, always superadd "subscribed" to "written," whenever he had occasion to mention the letters? Would he particularly, in mentioning any writing that was *not* subscribed, from the force of a merely mechanical bias, and in direct opposition to his own view of it, mention it as equally subscribed and written? The supposition is sufficiently refuted, by the statement. The very question precludes all answer. But, even if he would, was the clerk of the council a lawyer, and the clerk of the parliament none; and were the acts, either of the parliament or of the council, usually drawn up in the law-language, practised within this gentleman's *forum justitiæ?* It does not appear, that either was. Nor were the acts of the council, any more than those of the parliament, ever said by the clerks to be written and subscribed by the members. They were both *subscribed* by them. Both these were particularly so.[15] But they were neither of them *written.* And this very act of council does not purport, to be either written or subscribed by them.[16]

I have pursued this ridiculous argument at a greater expence of time and words, than it had a right to claim at my hands; in order to show it ridiculous, in every principle and particle of it. It may thus serve as an useful specimen of the wretched reasoning, in which the adversaries of Mary are now compelled to take refuge. ...

CHAPTER 6.
§ III.

...

As to the smaller and un-dated contract, this is still more plainly a forgery of the rebels. It is expressly averred above the commissioners at York, to have been "of the Quene's own hand," and by Murray himself to have been "*written* be the said Quenis awin hand;*" while the other is asserted to have been "*signed* with the Quene's hand, and also with Bothwell's," but "*written* – with the Earl of Huntley's own hand." We have here, therefore, a peculiar evidence of forgery. This little contract, from some extraordinary but unknown circumstances in its history, is *the only one of all these attributed writings, that was not published in the Detection of Buchanan,* being first printed by Mr. Goodall in 1754; what is more surprising, is *the only one of all these attributed writings,*

---

[15] Appendix, No. i. and ii.

[16] Ibid. ibid.

that *was left at London in the original* by the rebels; and, what is more surprising than either, is *the only one of all these attributed writings, that remains in the original at present.* It remains in the Cotton library, *Caligula, C. 1. fol.* 202. From that original Mr. Goodall published it. AND THAT IS APPAR-ENTLY NOT WRITTEN BY THE QUEEN'S HAND. This is a full proof of the general forgery. It is a proof addressed to the very senses. The *subscription* of it is in a different hand, from the *contract* itself. It is also different from Mary's hand. The letters of it, in general, carry no great resemblance to the writing of Mary. The first letter, in particular, is entirely different. In all the genuine subscriptions of her name, the first letter is constantly of the same length with the rest; while, in the bastard subscription before us, it is *twice* as long as they. And, what crowns the whole, the contract itself, which is asserted by Murray, and asserted by the commissioners, to have been written with the Queen's own hand; is actually written in one totally different, in the formal hand of a lawyer, and in a kind of chancery hand. So palpably gross is the forgery here![17]

Yet let me add another remark. When this contract was shown at York, it was certainly *written* in the *same* hand, in which it was *subscribed.* This is plain from the account of it, given equally by the commissioners and by Murray. But when it was exhibited to Cecil, and lodged among his papers now in the Cotton library, it was very different. Cecil's contract is written in one hand, and subscribed in another. So far Cecil's contract *pretends* not to be written in the Queen's hand, though the contract of the commissioners and the contract of Murray does. *That* pretends only to be *subscribed* by Mary, when *this* pretends to be *written* by her. They are therefore not the same. The contract shown at York, and reported by Murray, has been suppressed. Another has been formed upon another plan, and yet given to Cecil as the same. This demonstrates the forgery again, in the fullest manner. And, to mark still more the confusedness of guilt in Murray, he exhibited a contract all written in the Queen's hand at York, changed it afterwards into a contract only subscribed by her, presented the latter to Cecil, and still says he presented the former to him.

But was not the assumption of Lord Huntly's name, as a witness to one of these counterfeits, and even as the very writer of it; a most extraordinary circumstance, *if* the whole was forged? The whole was certainly forged. The actual appearance of the real contract, and the late production of the mimick one; the appearance also of another contract, as all written by Mary's hand,

[17] See iii. 4. 2, and Goodall, i. 126. So also says Ruddiman in his notes upon Buchanan's Hist. xix. 462. "Quem autem hic contractum," he tells us, "a Reginæ manu scriptum asseverat Buchananus, *aliâ manu* ex *diversâ literarum formâ et modulo* exaratum contendit David Crafordius, *qui eum cum aliis genuinis Reginæ scriptis composuit.* Vide *acta publica ac literas* ab ipso collectas in Biblioth. Jurid. Confer etiam appendicem ad Anglicam Detectionis et Actionis in Mariam interpretationem, Pag. 1."

and its re-appearance, as only subscribed by her; concur decisively to prove it a forgery. The use of Huntly's name, therefore, *was* a most extraordinary circumstance. He was then alive. He was then warm against the rebels. He was full of loyalty and spirit. And would not such a man as this, exult in exposing the impudence of falsehood in the rebels, and glory in blasting their reputation by proclaiming their forgery? He certainly would. Yet he did not. In the beginning of the year 1569, appeared what is called "the protestatioun of the Erlis of Huntly and Argyll, touching the murthour of the King of Scottis." In this, Argyle and Huntly are seen producing some very violent presumptions against Murray and Lethington, of their guiltiness in the murder; and making this very pointed conclusion from the whole, against them: "We judge in our consciences, the haldis for certane and treuth, that the sadis Erle of Murray and Secretarie Lethingtoun wer auctoris, inventaris, devyseris, counsallouris, and causeris of the said murthour, in quhat manner or be quhatsumever perfounis the samin was execute."[18] And "was not this also the time," says Mr. Hume, "for Huntly to deny his writing [and witnessing] Mary's contract with Bothwell, if that paper had been a forgery?"[19] It certainly was the properest of all times. Only we should be certain also, that he actually DREW UP the protestation; and that, when he did it, he actually KNEW of the writing and testimony, thus attributed to him by the rebels. These two circumstances must be ascertained, before we can expect him to deny. Mr. Hume indeed has taken it for granted that Huntly knew, – because he himself knows. On the same principle, many a spectator in the playhouse is astonished, that the persons moving before him do not act very differently from what they do, by availing themselves of all that insight into characters and incidents, which he himself enjoys. And in fact the Earl of Huntly, *when* he drew up the protestation, was as little apprized of the contract affirmed by the rebels to be written and witnessed by him, as he was of the power of gravitation, or the motion of the fixed stars. He *did not draw up the protestation at all.* It was composed by Lord Boyd and the Bishop of Ross, of whom the former had just come to Mary; was immediately sent by her to the Earls Huntly and Argyle, for their seals and subscriptions; and was intercepted on the way, remitted to Cecil, and so lodged among Cecil's papers, in the state in which it now appears, un-sealed, un-subscribed, and un-dated in month, day, or place.[20]

"Ze sall ressave," says Mary in covering dispatch to Huntly of the 5th of January 1569, "one letter be this beirar, to be subscryvit be zou, and our

[18] Goodall, ii. 320.

[19] Hist. v. 151.

[20] Goodall, ii. 321. It is but fair to acknowledge, that Dr. Robertson in Diss. 7 – 9 first taught me to see this fact, in opposition to the friends of Mary.

cousigne the Erle of Aryle." It "is maid be my Lord Boyd's adwyse," she adds, "conform to the declaratioun ze maid to our traist [trusty] counsallour the Bishop of Ross, he knawing zour deliberation and will thairin-till." It was therefore drawn up by Lord Boyd, from the minutes of conversation, which the earls had reported formally to the bishop; and in consequence of an agreement then made betwixt him and them, that they would authenticate the particulars, and assert their inference from them, whenever it was thought expedient for the honour of Mary. But, as she subjoins,

"we refer to zour discretiounis to eik and pair the said letter, as ze sall think best, and extend it in sic form, as ze sall think maist necessare: praying zou to send us the samin agane, subscrivit and seillit, the soonest ze may; to the effect it may be producit, togidder with the rest of the accusatiounis, quhilk we intend to give in aganis [against] our tratouris."[21]

Mary sent it, for their seals and subscriptions; authorized them to lengthen or shorten it previously, as they thought requisite; and desired to have it returned, with all expedition: that she might produce it with some other proofs, to the commissioners at Westminster; in order to substantiate the charge, which she had brought against Murray and his associates, of being, as they plainly were, the very authours of the murder, that they had the audacity to charge upon her. Murray, accordingly, expected the protestation to be shown in London against him, after he was gone for Scotland. He was within five days of his departure, when the paper came into Cecil's hands. He sat down on the 19th of January, 1569, to reply to it before it was published. "Because," he says,

"the custume of my adversaris is, and has bene, rather to calumpniate and backbite me in my absence, than befoir my face; and that it may happen thame, quhen I am departit furth of this realme, sclanderouslie and untrewlie to report untreuthis of me, and namelie towards sum spechis haldin in my hearing at Craigmillar, in the moneth of November, 1566,"

---

[21] Goodall, ii. 315 and 316. The protestation, and the covering letter, are both in the same hand-writing; which is different from Mary's (Diss.9), and is, no doubt, that of Lord Boyd. Only, the letter is *subscribed* by Mary (Diss. 9.). And Dr. Robertson assigns this reason for the letter being only subscribed, and not written also, by Mary; that "she seldom chose to write in the English language" (Diss. 9). The fact is as untrue, as the reason is ridiculous. She appears frequently writing letters in English (Haynes, 376, &c.). She actually appears writing in *English*, to her embassadour in *France* itself (Keith, pref. vii – viii); and to her agents, Englefield, Morgan, and Page, in *France* and *Spain* (Murdin, 469, 514, 515, 519, 531, and 532. And the true reason for her only signing the covering dispatch, was obviously this; that it and the protestation had been written ready for her by Lord Boyd, and that she had nothing more to do, than to sign the one and to send off both.

about three months before the murder; for this reason he replies to the protestation. He replies to it, as if already sanctioned by the earls. And Cecil, with whom the reply was left, indorses it in form, as "an answer of the Erle of Murray, to a wryting of the Erle of Huntly and Argyle."[22]

But in this answer does he, with Mr. Hume, ask Lord Huntly, why he did not deny his writing and witnessing the contract? Let us see. The accusation from the earls, naturally comes first. Yet he plainly replies to this, with all the movements of a detected villain,

With all the forc'd pace of a shuffling nag.

He is bold in denying – *what is not asserted*, concerning subscriptions and bands. But to the conversation asserted, he answers in the most evasive manner. "In cais ony man will say and affirm," he says, "that ever I was present quhen ony purposis wer haldin at Craigmillar in my audience;" NOT, as he would have answered if he had been innocent, *such or of such a nature as are stated in the protestation*; but "tending to ony unlauchful or dishonorabill end;" then he denies it. He goes off from the *reality* of the fact asserted against him, and is ready to discuss with the earls the *quality* and *tendency* of it. He does not dare to deny the conversation stated, either in the matter or in the manner. He indeed acknowledges it in effect. And it certainly carries, as Mary thought it would carry, a very damnatory aspect against him. But it carries a ten times more damnatory one, from the authority which he has stamped upon it, by the evasiveness and the frivolousness of his reply. And thus that infamous addition of injury to the imprisonment of Mary, which shows Elizabeth, not merely to have confined her person, but to have also *intercepted her letters*; and that infamous addition of evidence for the conspiracy between Elizabeth and Murray, which proves Elizabeth, not only to have precluded all possibility of Mary's defending herself against Murray's accusations of murder, but to have equally precluded her from *fixing the murder upon Murray,* by intercepting *her formal dispatches for that purpose*; all has now turned out eventually, to the

---

[22] It is remarkable, that the conversation alluded to by Huntly and Argyle, is stated by them to have been held "in zeir of God 1566 zeiris, *in the moneth of December or thairby*" (Goodall, ii. 317). Yet Murray himself states it to have happened, "in the moneth of November, 1566" (Goodall, ii. 321). He knew the conversation so exactly, we see, that he could instantly and at once ascertain the *period* of it, and *better* than those peers themselves. This single circumstance serves of itself, to mark the general truth of Huntly's and Argyle's suggestion, and the general guilt of Murray in it. So a cunning Friar in Shakespeare, one well read in human nature, tries and tests the innocence of the accused lady; by putting a question to her, instantly upon her recovery from that fainting-fit, into which the accusation had thrown her.

Lady, WHAT man is he you are accused of, he asks; when no man had been specified, and when only her guilt, if she had been guilty, could have suggested the name to her.

ampler vindication of Mary's innocence, and to the fuller attestation of Murray's and Elizabeth's guilt.

Murray, however, gives us another reply to the charges in protestation. This *must* be satisfactory. *He had confessed the whole truth*, he says, *to Elizabeth*; a proper confessor for such a confessionary! "I have alreddie declarit to the Quene's Majestie," he tells us, "the effect of the haill purposis spokin in my audience at the samin tyme, sincerely and trewlie, as I will answer to Almychtie God; unconceiling ony part to my remembrance, as hir Hienes, I traist, will report."[23] The publick is put off with an elusory answer; that however, to the confusion of Murray, tells all which he wants to hide. But Elizabeth is indulged with a full account. The publick was not likely to *shrive* him so gently, as she would. She was selected for this good work, on the same principle that the Jesuits were lately selected by all the popish sovereigns in Europe, from the happy laxity of her sentiments and morals. He could be explicit in his auricular disclosures to her. And she was very ready, no doubt, to administer ghostly comfort to him, and to give him a plenary absolution. Father Gerard and Kitty Cadiere at Thoulon in 1731, easily settled the ritual of their confessions and absolutions together.

This is the whole of his answer. He therefore does not take up Mr. Hume's objection, and express his wonder at Huntly's silence concerning the contract. He knew indeed, though Mr. Hume did not; that Huntly had no other concern in the protestation, than, in concert with the Earl of Argyle, to furnish those particulars of a very remarkable conversation, which constitute the body of it. These must have been furnished to the bishop of Ross, when he was last in Scotland; when he was appointed a commissioner there, by the Lords of Mary's party on Sept. 12, 1568;[24] and, consequently, when the contracts had not hitherto made their appearance at all.

Yet still Mr. Hume's question recurs, and is only to be applied to a different person. And "was not this the time," let *me* ask in his name, "for Mary's commissioners, the bishop and Lord Boyd, to make Huntly deny his writing [and witnessing] her contract with Bothwell, if that paper had been a forgery?" It certainly was. But still why does not Murray ask the question himself, in his reply before? For this plain reason, because he was aware that Mary and her commissioners knew as little of the contract, the witnessing, or the writing, as Huntly himself. Neither she nor they, at the time, *knew of any thing except the letters*. This is very remarkable. It ought to be particularly noticed, as a circumstance singularly striking, even amidst all the singularities of this strangely conducted accusation. The commissioners of Mary, who from their residence

[23] Goodall, ii. 321 – 322.

[24] Goodall, ii. 351 – 353.

in London, as well as their employment there, were the regular channels of intelligence to her; but who could not convey what they had never received; were not only precluded from all inspection of the original writings adduced against her, were not only debarred from all copies of them, but did not even hear, either by publick report or by secret communication, of these writings being any thing more than the letters. ...

CHAPTER 7.

§ VII.

The French letters, then, were only a translation from the Scotch. This had been much disputed formerly. Mr. Goodall was the first who suspected it. And the suspicion appears at present, to have done high honour to his sagacity. It is now carried into certainty. It is now founded upon the basis of FACTS. But he saw it only from a view of the letters themselves, by the light which they bore in their own bosom. Yet this is managed so well, that he illustrated his position very strongly by it. He gave indeed such convincing proofs of the point, that no man of candour in the business of thinking, no man of honour in the intellectual commerce of life, could possibly deny the force of them.[25] Yet Mr. Hume and Dr. Robertson did. For the dignity of literature, and, what is infinitely more in value, for the majesty of virtue itself, I am sorry I am compelled to say it. They denied it in reality, when they were obliged to acknowledge it in appearance. They owned the French copy which we have at present, to be undoubtedly a translation from the Scotch. But then they begged leave to suppose, and even presumed to maintain; that *the present copy was not the same, as was exhibited at Westminster.* "We have not," says Mr. Hume, "the originals of the letters, "which were in French; we have only a Scots and Latin translation from the original, and a French translation professedly done from the Latin."[26] "We may observe," says Dr. Robertson, "that all this authour's," Mr. Goodall's, "premises may be granted, and yet his conclusion will not follow; *unless* he likewise prove that the French letters, as we now have them, are a true copy of those, which were produced by Murray and his party, in the Scottish parliament, and at York and Westminster –. Our authour might have saved himself the labour of so many criticisms, to prove that the present French copy of the letters is a translation from Latin. The French editor himself acknowledges it, and, so far as I know, no person ever denied it."[27] This is surely the last and desperate effort of a baffled credulity. Having no longer any footing upon earth, they endeavour to fix themselves in the clouds. And they

---

[25] Goodall, i. 81 – 98.

[26] Hist. v. 147.

[27] Diss. 30 – 31.

are ready to raise supposition upon supposition, and to pile assertion upon the head of assertion, "imponere Pelio Ossam;" in order to ascend thither. But let us pursue them into this, their last, retreat. And we shall soon bring them back to earth again.[28]

It is very observable, that Dr. Robertson does not positively assert the existence, of such an imaginary original. He only *insinuates* it. And he calls upon Mr. Goodall to disprove it. This is the very *policy* of literature, the joint device of prudence and of fear. But what is Mr. Goodall called upon to prove, in order to disprove that? He is to show, that "the French letters, as we now have them, are a true copy of those that were produced by Murray and his party, in the Scottish parliament, and at York and Westminster." This indeed would be a labour for Hercules. This would be a task for Jupiter himself. It would be to prove, what I have historically disproved. It would be to prove, in contradiction to FACTS themselves. And I have already shown it would be this, by showing the copy presented to the parliament, and produced at York, NOT to be French at all. So little had Dr. Robertson attended to the HISTORY of the letters!

But both he and Mr. Hume expressly acknowledge the *present* French, to be a translation from the Scotch, and, what is much more, a translation through the medium of the Latin. Mr. Hume assumes it, as a certain principle. Dr. Robertson adds, that he never knew any person to deny it. Yet who taught this principle to them both? MR. GOODALL. Who proved the certainty of it to them both? MR. GOODALL. From the publication of the French letters, to the very day of Mr. Goodall's writing concerning them; the published French had been taken by all, to be the very original of the whole. Mr. Goodall demonstrated this universal belief,to be false in itself. Conviction flashed upon all the thinking and ingenuous part of the nation. But there were some MOLES in criticism, it seems; who had been long in the habit of throwing up dirt against Mary; to whom the light was peculiarly painful; who therefore took refuge from it again in darkness, and there began to throw up their dirt again. The divine and the sceptick united together, to treat the intelligence which they acquired from Mr. Goodall's reasoning, just as sceptics are very apt to treat the knowledge, which the derive from scripture; to admit what they cannot deny, to appropriate all without any acknowledgment, and then to turn their borrowed science against the very lender of it. Mr. Hume and the Doctor secretly renounced all their former errours, under the impression of Mr. Goodall's arguments. And they then pretended, that these errours had never existed in

---

[28] Mr. Hume and Dr. Robertson have not even the *intellectual* merit, of *inventing* this poor subterfuge. It was first suggested by Mr. Goodall himself. He foresaw and exposed it. And yet these two fellow-labourers in the cause were so much distressed, that they condescended to take up this objection from him. See Goodall, i. 99 – 102

their or any other heads, at all. Mr. Hume silently pretends it, and Dr. Robertson openly. With an affectation of liveliness to colour over a want of candour, the latter lets his spirits ferment; till at last they break out in the very extreme of disingenuousness. "So far as I know," he cries at the end, "no man ever denied" the present French copy, to be only a translation from the Scotch. But did any man ever *assert* it, *before* Mr. Goodall? The doctrine of gravitation, "so far as I know," was never denied by any man. But was it ever affirmed *before* Sir Isaac Newton? And would it not reflect dishonour upon the spirit of a philosopher at present, a disciple (we will suppose) of Mr. Hutchinson's; if feeling too powerfully the weight of Sir Isaac's arguments, for the credit of his understanding, to deny assent to his conclusions; he should yet take shelter from conviction in littleness, should catch at some pretended hints of gravitation in an ancient authour, and then exclaim with an *acted* admiration at the proofs in the real discoverer, that "he might have saved himself the labour of so many criticisms," and that, "so far as he knew, no person had ever "denied" the doctrine?

But *is* the French copy that we have at present, say, or mean to say, these confessors and martyrs for political prejudice; the very same, with the copy produced by Murray at Westminster? And *is* the Scotch copy that we have at present, *I* add, the very same that was exhibited by him at York? The one may be questioned, as well as the other. Some anti-confessor or anti-martyr to the same sort of prejudice, may determine the question as affirmatively on the one side, as they have done it on the other. And how shall we, who are not for being confessors or martyrs to either, be able to determine betwixt them? One answer will be effectual to both. We have some remains, as Dr. Robertson himself allows, of the *French* copy that was exhibited by Murray. We have also some remains, as every one must allow, of the *Scotch* copy exhibited by him. "In the Scottish translation of the Detection," says the Doctor, "two or three sentences of the original French, were prefixed to each letter; which breaking off with an &c. the Scottish translation of the whole followed."[29] And I have already given some passages out of the original Scotch, which the commissioners at York have afforded me. But are these passages, and these sentences, *greatly* different from those in the present copies? No! Are they different in any *one important word*? No! They are nearly to a word the same *Scotch*. They are actually the same to a word in *French*. This Dr. Robertson himself admits. And where therefore, in the name of common-sense, can a possibility of doubt be lodged? No where within the regions of *commonsense*. But in the refinement of understanding, which is only the result of disingenuousness; and which is a kind of intellectual juggle, that an uncandid mind exercises upon itself; there will still be scope for evasion. These passages, so exactly the same in the

---

[29] Diss. 31.

Doctor's pretended original, and the present copy, of the French, *may* have been, he will be bold to suppose; and actually *were*, he will be more bold to assert; taken from that original into the present copy, and so came to be exactly the same in both. "The French editor," the Doctor tells us, "laid hold of these sentences and tacked his own translation to them."[30] And the extracts from the Scotch may be also asserted, by an antagonist of equal bravery, if such a one can be met with; to have been equally borrowed by the present copy, from the letters of the commissioners at York, and for that reason to be so entirely conformable in both. When the human mind once puts itself under the dominion of chicane, it is constantly punished by its own folly. Its vigour is debilitated by its fraudulence. The strength of the lion, sinks away into the wily weakness of the fox. And, in the just retributions of Providence, the dishonesty is repaid by ridiculousness.

This will appear still more strongly, if we consider the conduct of these brother-champions for credulity, in another view. They are eminent patterns of that very credulity, which they want to enforce upon us. They want to fix our faith upon an imaginary copy of the French letters, which once (they say) existed upon earth, but is now *in nubibus*; or rather is mounted to the moon,

As all things lost on earth are treasured there.

There it is secure from all the calamities of life. No critick eye can follow it thither, and expose its pretensions to originality. It there may rest with all its infirmities about it, safe from the GOODALLS of every age. And every one must applaud the wisdom of these gentlemen, in the sudden *translation* of the original to such a state of repose; just at a time, when the voice of war was beginning to disturb it in its old possessions, and to threaten even its very existence. But alas! all human wisdom is greatly tempered with folly. In this act of prudent attention to one point of the charge against Mary, they forgot another. In their zeal to lodge the French original in some unknown sphere, they deprived themselves of any original at all. The present Scotch is merely a version. The present French is also a version. And the present Latin is equally one, with both. The Scotch is also asserted by Messieurs Robertson and Hume, to be very faulty. The Latin is allowed by them, to be still more so. And the great faultiness of the French, is their principal argument for its spuriousness. All may be exceedingly vitiated. Each certainly differs from the other. This argues all to have been strangely corrupted, as we have no original for the trial of any. The French, particularly, we know to talk egregious nonsense at times. It changes Mary's *letter of adultery* into her BIBLE; that edition of it anticipated

---

[30] Diss. 34.

(I suppose), in which the commandment ran, "thou *shalt* commit adultery." It confounds her letter again, with her *first day's journey*; and so makes her to promise, with a happy Hibernism, to *finish this* her *first day's journey* the NEXT DAY. It even mistakes *irkit* for *nakit*; strips the delicate Queen in the month of January, and at the hour of midnight; and keeps her in this situation "*toute* nuë," without even the cover of a smock upon her, writing a long letter to her lover. How can we rely then, upon the testimony of such a blundering witness as this? And, what is more, as the Scotch can depose to what it knows at second hand only, so the Latin and the French can attest only at third and at fourth hand. The original French transmitted its intelligence, to the Scotch; the Scotch imparted it to the Latin; and the Latin communicated it to the bastard French. To such hearsay, such vitiated, and such contradictory evidences, are we now reduced; by dispatching the original away from earth. And, with such a preposterous policy, have these two advocates for the letters been labouring to defend their genuineness; that they have almost annihilated their credibility.

...

VOLUME 2
LETTER 6.
§ VII.

Here let us examine an argument, which has been strongly urged in favour of a French original to the letters. Mr. Hume, I think, was the first, who insisted upon the Gallicisms in the Scotch copy, and alledged them as a proof of its being a translation from the French.[31] Mr. Tytler replied to him. And the Miscellaneous Remarker has rejoined to Mr. Tytler. It is pleasing enough to a philosophical surveyor of the human mind, to see it contending with such weak weapons on either side, when history would have furnished it with weapons of force and power. Such have been actually produced, I trust, in the course of the present work. Nor can any Gallicisms in the Scotch, have the weight of a feather at present, against the full measure of historical evidence before. Yet it may be useful to notice the argument, in order to answer it as an objection; as one that is really light in itself, but has been made respectable by the contest about it.

The objection, as advanced by Mr. Hume, consisted of various IDIOMS, and of one WORD, that were Gallick. To the idioms we need not say much. They are such unsubstantial evidences, that there is hardly any grasping of them. They run thus: "make fault, faire des fautes;" "make it seem that I believe, faire semblant de le croire," which is literally, to make a semblance of believing it, and therefore different from the Scotch: "make brek, faire breche;" "have

---

[31] v. 147.

you not desire to laugh, n' avez vous pas envie de rire," which is plainly no idiom, and has no similarity at all; "the place will hald unto the death, la place tiendray jusqu'a la mort," where the point of similarity lies only in *the* and *la*, the former of which was then used in this connection, though it seldom is now, and the latter is sometimes not used at present; "he may not come forth of the house this long time, il ne peut pas sortir du logis de long temps," which is no idiom, and has no more similarity than what a translation necessarily gives; "to make me advertisement, faire m'avertir," which is different from the Scotch, and signifies only, to *make advertise me*; "put order to it, mettre ordre a cela," which is different again, and as different as to *put* and to *send*; discharge your heart, decharger votre cœur," and "mak gud watch, faites bon gard," in both which the similarity is in one word, and the dissimilarity in two and three. And at the close we may ask, If such arguments as these can prove any thing, what will be too difficult to be proved? Yet the Miscellaneous Remarker[32] has even heightened the folly, by adducing these additional Gallicisms out of one of the letters, though these are as much Anglicisms, as almost any modes of speech in our language; "the disdaine that I can not be in outward effect yours," "my only wealth," "fall not part furth of my bosom," "to quhilk I pretend," and "for evil nor gude fall nevir mak me go from it." And I cannot but observe upon both, that, if we were to listen to such empiricks in language as these, we should be like the honest Alderman with his *prose*, and stare to find we had been talking FRENCH all our lives.

The languages of France and England, were originally the same. They were so, in the days of our British ancestors. They were so still, in the time of our Saxon fathers. And *Frenchmen were brought hither by Augustine and his fellow-missionaries, to be their interpreters to the English*. The fact is little known. But it ought to be called out into general notice. It is recorded by Bede himself:[33] "acceperunt autem, præcipiente beato Papâ Gregorio, DE GENTE FRANCORUM INTERPRETES." This being the case, the two languages may well retain a variety of similar idioms to the present day. They must still be *substantially* the same. They apparently are so. The same words, and the same combinations of words, are perpetually recurring in both. And we may as well argue in general, from any coincidences of this nature, *that the French are derived from the English*; as that the English are borrowed from the French. Yet, from the natural variations of time in two separate kingdoms, there are many idioms and words peculiar to each at present. Some of the French were common once to our own language, though they are retained only in the other now; and some are still common. Thus, "to *discharge* your heart" was used at the period of

---

[32] P. 33.

[33] Hist. i. 25. Smith.

the letters, and is still used among us, as it is among the French; though it is almost superseded in familiar life among us, by the expression to *open* your heart." Thus also, "to *make* good watch," was used then for "to *keep* good watch;" though the French still adhere to their old expression, "*faire* de bon guard." The French and we also once said, "*faire* un faut," *or* "*to* make a fault," as the Scotch letters say; but we now say, "to *do* a fault," while the French preserve their ancient term. And "to make a breach" is as good English, as "pour faire breche" is French.

Having thus dispatched the idioms, I turn to the words. Mr. Hume mentions only one; "this is my first JOURNEY, c'est ma premiere JOURNE'E." He thought *journey* in this sense, to be purely French. Though a Scotchman; though so thoroughly a Scotchman, that even to the last he could not clear his tongue, from his native provinciality of pronunciation; yet he had never heard the word, it seems, among his cotemporaries of the town or country about him. In itself, and in its derivatives, it forms a very important set of words in the English language. In all the English extremities of the island, it signifies just as it does in the letters, a day's work. And, as Mr. Tytler has justly observed,[34] *journey-man* and *journey-work* are common to all parts of it.

This single instance furnishes us with a striking proof, of the hasty superficialness and the wanton decisiveness, with which Mr. Hume pretended to disprove the originality of the Scotch letters. In the violence of his assault upon it, he forgot his native tongue. His zeal operated, with all the forces of a fever upon his brain. He did, as Rousseau said he did afterwards in his hearing. *he talked nothing but French in his sleep.* The whole English language was lost to him, during the continuance of the paroxysm. And the loudest conversation of the street or the farm, could not awaken him from his delirium.

But the English language, *at the period of the letters,* appears to have been particularly furnished with words, that either in their nature, or in their orthography, were purely French. Indeed the foppery of adopting such terms, seems to have been fully as prevalent among the grave statesmen then; as it is among our writing and conversing coxcombs at present. And some of these actually make their appearance, in the letters.

...

[34] P. 87.

36
WILLIAM BELSHAM

[William Belsham], *Essays, philosophical, historical, and literary*. London: printed for C. Dilly, 1789–1791, 2 v.
Selections from Essay 3; from 1799 edition (Essay 18 in that edition).

Born in North Bedfordshire and son of a dissenting minister, William Belsham (1752–1827) made his living as a writer, principally on historical and political subjects. His brother was Unitarian minister Thomas Belsham. His two volume *Essays, Philosophical, Historical, and Literary* appeared anonymously in 1789 and 1791, although he put his name to the revised edition of 1799. The work is a collection of 35 essays on a variety of philosophical, theological, and political subjects. Several of the essays criticize Hume (for selections from his essays on Hume's moral theory, see *Early Responses to Hume's Moral Philosophy*). His essay on Queen Elizabeth, excerpted here, defends the Queen against Hume's portrayal of her government as "odious and tyrannical" – a view which Belsham believes overturns two centuries of high regard for the monarch. According to Hume, praise for her is inconsistent with the contempt usually shown toward James I and Charles, since her reign was no less tyrannical than that of the two Stuart kings. Belsham counters Hume by noting two key points of distinction between Elizabeth and her successors. First, Elizabeth's actions had "the stamp and sanction of national approbation," and, second, she acted within the bounds of a limited monarchy, rather than an absolute one.

All reviews of Belsham's work were generally favourable, but many noted some limitation. The *Analytical Review* comments that there is an "inequality in the merit of the different performances, and still more ... [an] apparent discrepancy in some of the opinions which they exhibit." They nevertheless call it an "excellent treatise." The *European Magazine and London Review* concludes that Belsham should "confine his studies to the metaphysics, to which his genius seems best adapted." According to the *English Review*, a minor fault of Belsham's work is that its "temper [is] somewhat too sanguine." The *Monthly Review* comments that the essays "discover more extent and variety, than depth, of thinking." In contrast to these responses, the *Critical Review* uniformly praised both volumes of the work. In their review of the 1791 volume, they noted that their positive assessment of Belsham stood in contrast with reviews in other journals: "On referring to our account [of Volume 1 of

Belsham's *Essays*], we can scarcely reconcile it with the accusation we have more than once heard, that Mr. Belsham's Essays ... have not been treated by the periodical critics with sufficient respect."

Responses to Belsham's essay on Queen Elizabeth were mixed. The *Critical Review* calls this essay "an able apology for the despotic daughter of Henry." The *English Review* writes, "we cannot but applaud our author's boldness, in taking what seems at present the unpopular side of the argument; and though we are ready to admit he has allowed the Queen a few failings, yet had he admitted a few more, in our opinion, he would not have exceeded the truth." The *European Magazine and London Review* says more critically that "Our essayist, to vindicate his favourite fully, compares her measures with those of her successors, the Stuarts; but the absurdity of this must strike the meanest capacity: for if she was blest with more spirit and cunning, yet the history of her reign sufficiently proves, that she wished to be as arbitrary as the worst of the Stuarts."[1]

A four-volume edition of Belsham's *Essays* was published in Dublin in 1790–1791. The following is from the revised 1799 and final edition of that work.

BOOK II.

ESSAY XVIII.

ON THE REIGN AND CHARACTER OF QUEEN ELIZABETH

During a reign of almost half a century, and for a period of a century and half succeeding her death, Queen ELIZABETH was the object of universal reverence and admiration: and to this very day her name, to the bulk of the people, carries with it a sort of magic in the sound. They consider her reign as a kind of golden age, as the halcyon days of perpetual prosperity and felicity. But several persons, eminent for the depth of their historical researches, have recently discovered that the maxims of her government were odious and tyrannical; that her authority was

---

[1] *Analytical Review*, 1789, Vol. 6, pp. 169–175, August 1791, Vol. 11, pp. 18–26; *Critical Review*, December 1789, Vol. 68, pp. 459–469. December 1791, Vol. 3, pp. 361–392; *English Review*, November 1789, Vol. 14, pp. 365–377; *European Magazine and London Review*, November 1789, Vol. 16, p. 336, January 1792, Vol. 21, pp. 25–28, March, pp. 201–203, April, 281–283; Vol. 22, July, pp. 33–35; *Monthly Review*, [Gilbert Stuart] May 1790, Vol. 2, pp. 1–7, [William Enfield] April 1792, Vol. 7, pp. 428–435.

despotic, and that the political constitution of this country, in her days, bore a remarkable resemblance to that of Turkey at present. This and much more has Mr. Hume, in particular, asserted in a very high and peremptory tone; and as a necessary consequence of these assertions, he has taken much pains to exculpate the two first princes of the House of Stuart, from the accusations brought against them, of introducing arbitrary and unconstitutional principles of government into their administration. According to the representation of the eloquent historian, those monarchs have been treated, both during their lives and since their deaths, with the highest ingratitude and injustice. And if this representation is just, England must pass for the most whimsical and capricious of all nations: for without any reasonable or assignable cause, Queen Elizabeth has ever been, and still is, the object of the highest admiration and applause; whilst the unfortunate James and Charles are regarded, the one with contempt the other with detestation. But this account cannot give entire satisfaction to those who believe human nature to be constituted on certain fixed and immutable principles, and who are consequently inclined to believe that opposite effects cannot well proceed from similar causes in similar circumstances.

Certainly Mr. Hume has no reason to expect that we should entertain a very high idea of that philosophy which cannot account for moral phænomena upon moral principles, or which satisfies itself with a vague or general solution, without attempting to trace the connection between the supposed causes and their respective effects. This remarkable opposition of sentiment, it were far more reasonable to account for and justify by a general review of the leading features of her political character and administration, contrasted with those of her successors of the house of Stuart.

During the civil contests which so long prevailed between the rival Houses of York and Lancaster, the regal authority, irregular as the exertions of it sometimes appear, was subjected to a variety of important and salutary restraints. As the one or the other party prevailed, popular laws were enacted in order to acquire and preserve the good-will of the nation, which the opposite faction, when in power, could not venture to repeal. And in the reign of Edward IV. Lord Fortescue was able to demonstrate, in striking colours, the superiority of the English constitution and government, compared with those of the surrounding nations;[2] which indeed was sufficiently manifest from the

---

[2] Non potest Rex Angliæ ad libitum suum leges mutare regni sui. Principatu namque nedum regali sed et politico ipse suo populo dominatur. Si regali tantum ipse præ-esset eis, leges regni sui mutare ille posset; tallagia quoque et cætera onera eis imponere ipsis inconsultis; quale dominium denotant leges civiles cum dicant, "Quod principi placuit legis habet vigorem." Sed longè aliter potest Rex politicè imperans genti suæ, quia nec leges ipse sine subditorum assensu mutare poterit, nec subjectum populum retinentem onerare impositionibus peregrinis; quare populus ejus liberè fruetur bonis suis; legibus quas cupit regulatus nec per Regem aut quemvis alium depilatur.

FORTESCUE DE LEG. ANG.

reign of the English Justinian Edward I. In the short period that Richard III. held the sceptre, many excellent regulations were made: And when the battle of Bosworth placed the crown on the head of Henry VII. he endeavored, at least in his early years, to recommend himself to the favor of the nation, who were in general much attached to the House of York, by similar means. Though it must be confessed that upon the whole, and before the conclusion of his reign, the royal authority was greatly augmented. By his artful policy, the jurisdiction of the arbitrary court of Star-Chamber was much enlarged, and the power of the aristocracy in a great measure broken: and towards the latter end of the reign of his successor, by a remarkable concurrence of causes the royal prerogative had established itself to appearance above all control. But, in proportion as those adventitious circumstances which had occasioned this extraordinary exaltation disappeared, new limits were set to the power of the Crown. And during the minority of Edward VI. the constitution was in its most essential points restored. In the succeeding reign, notwithstanding the violence of religious persecution, the parliament gave signal proofs of its attention to the security and preservation of the civil privileges of the nation: and Queen Elizabeth at her accession found herself in possession of a crown, invested indeed with ample and splendid, and in some measure indefinite powers; but these powers were to be exercised over subjects possessing privileges of the most important nature: some of them of high antiquity, of the value of which they were perfectly sensible, and which nothing short of the most outrageous violence could deprive them of. It may even be affirmed, that the condition of the lower classes of people was at that time in many respects preferable to what it now is. ...

... But not to dwell in generals, there is no difficulty in specifying several particulars, in which the political character and conduct of Elizabeth differ very essentially from her immediate successors.

And, 1st, Nothing can be more evident, throughout the whole course of her reign, than her constant and anxious solicitude, that all her political transactions should have the stamp and sanction of national approbation. Her great popularity is sometimes represented as the effect of artifice. She was possessed, it is said, of the arts of insinuation; she knew how to cajole, how to soothe, and to flatter. But can any one believe, that, in the course of more than forty years, these arts should not have been detected? If, at that time, a full persuasion of her sincerity prevailed, it is certainly harsh and unjustifiable at the distance of 200 years, to stigmatize her laudable endeavours to please with the appellations of deceit and simulation. ...

But if we pass on to the reign of this monarch [i.e., King James VI of Scotland] to his son, the unfortunate Charles, what a contrast! In what single instance do we find the interests of the people consulted, or their wishes gratified? Not in the countenance and encouragement given by the court to the Catholic religion, at a time when the principles and practices of the Puritans became every day more prevalent. Not in sacrificing the gallant Raleigh to appease the anger and resentment of Spain – Not in the desertion of his own children, the King and queen of bohemia, under their accumulated distresses – Not in the mean and servile court he paid to the House of Austria, in his attempts to procure the restoration of the Palatinate, and to accomplish that great object of his ambition, the marriage of his son with the infanta. Neither can it be said that his son and successor, Charles, discovered any greater condescension, for the opinions or prejudices of his subjects, in espousing a Catholic Princess, and granting, in consequence of this alliance, additional privileges and immunities to the professors of that religion – or by involving the nation in two dangerous and successless wars, to gratify the preposterous vanity and resentment of a worthless favorite – By levying taxes, in a time of profound peace, by virtue of the regal authority – By a professed intention of governing without parliaments – By violent attempts to suppress Puritanism in England; or, by still more violent attempts to introduce the most odious innovations of a religious nature in Scotland. But no farther enlargement is necessary on this point. It is too plain to be denied, that the public measures of Elizabeth were, in general, agreeable to the sense of the nation; and that she wished and endeavored they should be so; and it is as plain, that in the succeeding reigns public opinion was wholly disregarded, and that almost all the measures of government were the result of pride, obstinacy and folly.

2dly, The contrast between that great Princess and her successors appears equally striking, if we consider their respective characters in what may be termed a legal point of view; or as sovereigns possessed of a limited authority. Though it must be confessed that the deportment of Queen Elizabeth, notwithstanding her general affability, was upon some occasions sufficiently imperious, it does not appear that she ever had an idea of advancing such exorbitant principles and pretensions as James I. perpetually insisted upon in his reasonings and speculations upon government; and which Charles, fatally for himself, attempted to reduce to practice. Mr. Hume asserts that the only business of parliament in this reign was to grant subsidies. "They pretended, indeed," says he, "to the right of enacting laws." Pretended! and did they not exercise this right? If Mr. Hume had taken the trouble to consult the statute book, he would have known that very important and salutary laws were enacted in this reign; though the absurdity of multiplying useless, complex, and oppressive legislative regulations and restraints was wisely and happily avoided. Lord Chief Justice Fortescue entertained, certainly, much more lofty ideas respecting the authority of this assembly, when he refused "in any wise to determine the extent of the privileges of the high court of parliament. For," says he, "so high and mighty is it in its nature, that it may make that which it pleases to be law; and that which is law, it may make no law; and the determination and knowledge of the privilege of parliament belongs to parliament only." It was a famous apothegm of the Lord Treasurer Burleigh, that England could be

ruined only by a parliament; and Sir Edward Coke says, "the power and jurisdiction of parliament is so transcending and absolute that it cannot be confined
either for causes or persons wthin any bounds. *Si antiquitatem spectes,* he adds,
*est vetustissima; si dignitatem est honoratissima, si juridictionem est
capacissma.*" The parliament, indeed, did not assume a power of controlling
the crown in "matters of state," as they were called, or, in other words, of
directing the transactions of the sovereign with foreign powers. And the
Queen's conduct, in this respect, gave such entire satisfaction to the public, that
they were under little or no temptation to interfere; but they usually confined
themselves to the less splendid but more useful employment of superintending
the domestic concerns of the nation. And it is observable, that to this day
parliament possesses no authority, properly speaking, respecting foreign affairs;
though the extensive powers vested in that body, and the utter inability of the
crown to support itself without assistance, give it the highest degree of influence
whenever it judges interference necessary. On the other hand, the influence of
the crown over the legislative assemblies is, in modern times, by the most
unconstitutional and unexpected means, so enormously increased that the
control of parliament over the crown is become the mere echo of a sound.

Mr. Hume is pleased to assert that England had less reason to boast of her
liberties in the reign of Elizabeth than the generality of foreign nations at
present. But let us for a moment suppose that the authority of the general
assembly of estates in France were restored; that all traces of vassalage were
abolished; that trials by jury were introduced; that in the regular courts of
judicature nothing were regarded as law but what had been virtually assented
to, or expressly enacted by the representatives of the people; that individuals
of every rank in public stations were divested of all discretionary powers, and
obliged to conform their conduct to the standard of the laws; that the formidable standing army of that kingdom were annihilated, and taxes levied only
by the authority of the estates of the realm;[3] would any man in his senses take
upon him to say, notwithstanding that the authority which remained to the
crown might be in a great degree indefinite; notwithstanding the existence of
irregular courts which might be empowered to take cognizance of extraordinary
cases; notwithstanding that the sovereign might sometimes use very lofty and
imperious language to the legislative body; and even dare occasionally to
violate their established rights and privileges; would any man venture to say
that liberty had not made very great advances in that kingdom; could it be

---

[3]   In the short space of time which has elapsed since the above was written, all this, and
much more than this, incredible as it must then have appeared, has been actually
accomplished in France; which has exhibited to an astonished world the unprecedented
example of a great and enlightened nation, by one daring and glorious effort, shaking
off the chains and fetters of despotism, though rivetted by the prescription of ages, "as
dew-drops from a lion's mane."

denied that they were in fact possessed of a constitution, on the basis of which a regular and permanent system of liberty might easily be founded? If, indeed, the government of a country in such circumstances was conducted with address and ability; if the public interests were upon the whole understood and pursued; if the extraordinary and irregular exertions of prerogative were such as the necessity of the state seemed to justify; if a due regard was paid to public opinion, and a just reverence maintained for the authority of the laws in the common and ordinary course of proceedings; the general satisfaction and popularity attending such a government must naturally preclude any vigorous attempts to improve the constitution, or establish the principles of liberty on a more secure or extensive foundation. These speculative ideas nearly correspond with the real state of things in the times of Elizabeth. But if the sceptre should, in similar circumstances, devolve to weak or obstinate princes who held public opinion in contempt; who pursued measures in compatible with the public interests; who had the imprudence upon every occasion to advance speculative principles utterly subversive of civil or political freedom; who insisted that the privileges of the subjects were derived merely from the grace and favor of the sovereign, and the power of the sovereign from GOD alone; and especially if these despotic principles were reduced to practice; if they were converted into fundamental maxims of government; if there were evident marks of a regular and concerted plan for the extinction of popular privileges, and for reducing the nation to the most abject state of submission to the will of the monarch; if no other reason than "Such is our pleasure" were assigned for the most irregular and violent exertions of power; a nation must be destitute of every spark of public virtue and public spirit, and even deaf to the dictates of common sense, who did not, in consequence of such alarming inroads upon the constitution, take occasion to scrutinize with more accuracy into the nature and foundation of human authority; who did not make use of the advantages they possessed to circumscribe within narrower limits, and to ascertain by more exact boundaries those powers and that prerogative which had excited such just and general apprehension. This representation is perfectly applicable to the state of affairs in the reigns of James and Charles.

Mr. Hume expresses his surprize that so different a fate should attend the memories of Henry VIII. and Charles I. but there is, in fact, nothing very extraordinary or singular in the case: Henry VIII. was, undoubtedly, a tyrant, but he was at the same time possessed of qualities which will always command a certain degree of respect; and it must be considered, that though a variety of causes then concurred to disturb the balance of the constitution, and to throw a prodigious weight of power into the scale of the crown, yet the parliament was usually made, even in that reign, the instrument of regal tyranny; by which means he not only gave dignity and efficacy to the measures, but escaped a great share of the popular odium which would otherwise have attended him. Let it be considered, too, that Henry never went the lengths in the delicate and dangerous business of taxation which Charles ventured to do: not to mention that, in the long period of a century, very essential alterations in a political system may reasonably be supposed to take place. And it is as preposterous to attempt to justify or palliate the arbitrary conduct of Charles I. by appealing to precedents drawn from the reign of Henry VIII. as it would be to vindicate any illegal or unconstitutional practices of the present reign by an appeal to the direful precedents of the latter days of Charles II. In the beginning of the seventeenth century the maxims of the reign of Henry VIII. were become obsolete. Men were accustomed to another mode of government. Their minds were occupied by the recollection of the glorious and prosperous times of Elizabeth, when uninterrupted affection and harmony subsisted between the sovereign and the people: and if the prerogative was occasionally exerted in an irregular and arbitrary manner, those very exertions were seen or were thought at least to be necessary, and no apprehensions were entertained that they were the result of a fixed and preconcerted plan to enslave the nation. Charles I. was a tyrant as well as Henry VIII. but he attempted to part at a period far more unfavorable to the success of his designs. Mr. Hume pretends that the circumstances in which he was placed were in the highest degree critical; and plausibly apologizes for him by saying, that his capacity was not equal to situations of such extreme delicacy. But his situation at the commencement of his reign was not to be compared, in point of difficulty, with that of Elizabeth. In the progress of it, indeed, it must be confessed that he frequently involved himself by his own imprudence, or rather infatuation, in circumstances of such extreme difficulty, that had he even possessed the capacity of Elizabeth, he could not have extricated himself with honor. But it surely required nothing more than a common share of common sense, to see that the temper of the times would not endure even those stretches of prerogative which were thought necessary, or excusable at least in the days of Elizabeth; much less any wonton or novel exertions of power; and least of all, would it bear an open and almost avowed design, to reduce the nation to a state of such abject and unreserved submission, that if it had succeeded, Mr. Hume might indeed have had reason sufficient for his assertion, respecting the resemblance of the English government to that of Turkey.

It must, without doubt, greatly surprise those who conceive of Queen Elizabeth, as a Princess possessed of despotic authority, which is the idea Mr. Hume labours to inculcate, to be made acquainted with many circumstances of her conduct and management during the course of her reign. In the very commencement of it, the odious and sanguinary instruments of her sister's cruelties escaped with impunity, because they had acted under the sanction of the law. So mild were the maxims of the government at this period, that the detestable and inhumane Bonner himself could venture to appear in public, and even at court, with perfect security. The queen, indeed, it is remarked, averted her eyes, no doubt with horror, from the man of blood; but no other mark of disgrace or resentment followed. Bishop Burnet informs us, that Cecil and the other counsellors of Elizabeth, were unanimously of opinion, "that no steps should be taken by the Queen's highness to restore the Protestant religion, till a Parliament could be summoned." And we accordingly find, that nothing of consequence was done in that important business without the sanction of legislative authority. In the ensuing Parliaments of the affair of the succession, which had been slightly touched on by the preceding one, was resumed with great warmth, and the Queen was reduced to a very disagreeable dilemma. The right of blood clearly rested in the House of Stuart; but the will of Henry VIII. the validity of which, though founded on an act of Parliament, was nevertheless the subject of much dispute, was express in favor of the House of Suffolk. An authoritative and ultimate decision in favor of either, must be attended with obvious inconveniences to the reigning sovereign.

...

37
FRANCIS GARDEN

Francis Garden, *Miscellanies in Prose and Verse*, Edinburgh: [Printed by J. Robertson], 1791, [3]-7, 240 p.
Selections; from *The New-York Magazine, or Literary Repository*, New Series, 1797, Vol. 2, pp. 295–299.

Francis Garden (1721–1793) was a Judge on the Scottish Court of Session, from which he received his title Lord Gardenstone in 1764. A popular anecdote relates that a favourite pig followed him around. The pig even slept with Garden until it grew too large for the bed and thereafter stayed on the floor, covered with Garden's clothes. In the 1760s, Hume and Garden were on opposing sides of the Douglas Cause. The issue involved a dispute between two possible heirs to the estate of Archibald, Duke of Douglas, who died childless in 1761. One contender was the Duke of Hamilton, a young blood-relative, whose guardians were Baron Mure and Andrew Stuart, Hume's close friends. The other contender was Archibald James Edward Steuart, a nephew who, as alleged by Hamilton's guardians, was adopted in France and thus not a true blood-relative. Garden and James Burnet – later Lord Monboddo – were, respectively, senior and junior council for Steuart on this issue. Hume strongly supported his two friends on the Hamilton side and, in a letter to Mure, comments on Garden and Burnet: "Can any thing be more scandalous and more extraordinary than Frank Garden's Behaviour? Can any thing be more scandalous & more ordinary than Burnet's?" (Hume to Baron Mure of Caldwell, June 22, 1764).

Garden's *Miscellanies in Prose and Verse*, published near the end of his life, contains a brief discussion of Hume's *History*. He criticizes Hume's assessment of Rapin's *History* as "the most despicable, both for style and matter." Although applauding Hume's own style, Garden nevertheless faults him on several issues, including his limited historical research and Tory ideology. He questions why Hume would defend Laud since Hume himself would likely have been executed in those days for his infidel writings. In conclusion, Garden says of Hume's *History* that, "As an epitome of English History, it is too large; but as a complete history, it is by far too short." Garden's *Miscellanies* was published a second time in 1792. The section on

Hume was reprinted in the *New-York Magazine, or Literary Repository* in 1797, from which the following is taken.[1]

Critical Remarks on some of the most eminent Historians of England

Though we are now in the close of the eighteenth century, the history of this island has never been studied with proper attention. That portion of it, in particular, which precedes the reformation, seems, at present, buried in profound neglect. For this misfortune, sufficient reasons may be assigned; and hundred and fifty years were wasted in theological frenzy, or in defeating the tyranny of the house of Stuart, and a modern compiler of general history is strongly tempted to rush with precipitation over the remoter periods, and to reserve his abilities and research for those later scenes, in which a reader of the present day is more heartily interested. – On some of these modern authors, a few candid observations may repay a perusal.

The name of RAPIN is now almost forgotten; and Mr. Hume, in the end of his English History, has branded him as an author "the most despicable both in style and matter." The censure is invidious, and unjust: His work contains an immense multitude of interesting circumstances, wholly omitted by the Scottish author. From his personal situation, a classical composition was not to be expected. He wrote a more complete General History of England than had ever appeared in this country; and whatever be his faults, it would be ungenerous to deny his uncommon merit.

SALMON made an essay on the same subject. Though short, it contains much information, which is not to be found in more voluminous historians of England. His own reflexions are brief, lively, and sensible. It is usual to represent Richard III, as deformed and decrepid; yet these very authors inform us, that he unhorsed and killed with his own hand the standard-bearer of Henry VII. who was reputed to be the strongest knight in the rebel army. The inconsistency of these two stories is pointed out by Salmon. He has left behind him no work of very superior value, yet he must have been an author of superior abilities; for, without becoming tiresome, he has written more than most of us have read.

The same remarks apply with equal justice to Dr. SMOLLET. The immense bulk of his writings proves that he composed with greater facility than ordinary men are able to converse. By his own account, in the expedition of Humphrey Clinker, it appears that he very often wrote merely for wages; and on such occasions, nothing above mediocrity can with reason be demanded. The contin-

---

[1] I thank Mark Spencer for bringing this item to my attention and providing me with the following transcription of it.

uation of his English History, from 1748 to 1764, is a mere catchpenny chaos, without even a spark of merit. There is great reason to believe that he, or rather his journeymen, copied at random from somebody else, most of the quotations and references arranged with so much parade on the margin of his text.

GUTHRIE has left behind him more than one ponderous fabric on British history. He had sense, learning, candour, and industry. He had an original manner, and wished to think for himself: But to elegance, he was an entire stranger, and to that happy choice of circumstances which forms an instructive historian; he was often familiar without perspicuity, and prolix without completeness. No writer is at present less popular. A geographical grammar has been printed under his name; but it is generally understood, that he had no share in its composition.

In point of style, Mr. HUME may be studied as a perfect model. Pure, nervous, eloquent, he is simple without weakness, and sublime without effort. In the art of telling an humorous story, he can never be excelled; and when he chose to exert himself, he was even a considerable master of the pathetic: But it was his misfortune to despise accuracy of research, and fidelity of citation: He was a bitter Tory; and while detection flashed in his face, he commonly adhered to whatever he had once written. His account of the house of Stuart is not the statement of an historian, but the memorial of a pleader in a Court of Justice. He sometimes asserts a positive untruth, contradicted by the very author whom he pretends himself to be quoting; but more commonly gains his purpose, by suppressing the whole evidence on the opposite side of the question. His conduct in the controversy with Mr. Tytler, can hardly be defended:[2] And his injurious treatment of Queen Mary of Scotland is not more disgusting than his farcical panegyrics on the virtues of her posterity. When we examine Mrs. Macaulay's performance on the same period, we meet with a profusion of interesting intelligence, of which the mere reader of Hume has not the most distant conception. The Scottish historian gives but short and partial excerpts from the writers of the times. His female antagonist, on the other hand, gives large extracts from the original writers; and though to a superficial eye, her work assumes an air less pleasing and classical, what is lost in elegance is fully repaid in authenticity. He is a zealous advocate for the ceremonies of the Church of England. He censures those brave and able men who resisted and defeated her usurpations; and to whom we are, at this day, indebted for our liberties. He attempts to prove, that Episcopacy is preferable to Presbyterianism, and that Laud may be vindicated for persecuting the dissenters. Had Mr. Hume been serious in his opinion, he might have deserved an answer. But on turning over to his Essays, we are surprised by the most stupendous and

---

[2] [William Tytler (1711–1792), *An Historical and Critical Enquiry* (1760), selections from which appear earlier in this collection.]

unblushing contradiction. One chief end of his metaphysical writings is to extinguish every sentiment of religion. The same Court, therefore, which sent Bastwick and Prynne to the pillory, would, with far less injustice, have sent our historian himself to *a more decided situation*. What are we to think of a professed infidel defending the barbarous insolence of the priesthood?

Mr. Hume has expressed much indignation at that memorable act of justice, the execution of Charles I. His two elder sons ought to have shared the same fate. Their annals are distinguished by endless usurpations, plots, rebellions, and massacres; by two foreign wars, and a revolution. We cannot but observe with the honest Dutchman, that their predecessor "was quite another man." Had Cromwell survived but for ten years longer, we should have heard no more about the posterity of "The Holy Martyr."

James I. butchered Sir Walter Raleigh, without the form of a trial. Mr. Hume tells us, that this measure "was esteemed an instance of the utmost cruelty and injustice;" and his vindication of James is one of the most elaborate passages in his whole work. The best of his arguments appears to be, "that no jury would have found Raleigh guilty!"

At the sentence of Lord Bacon, Mr. Hume adds, that James "conferred on him a large pension of eighteen hundred pounds a year, and employed every expedient to alleviate the weight of his age and misfortunes." This pension would have been equivalent to six or eight thousand pounds sterling at the present day: And as his Majesty had nothing of his own, it must have been transferred from the pockets of his subjects. The transaction at best could have but resembled an apprentice interfering with his master's till; a comparison which applies to most other examples of royal munificence. But the fact is, that Bacon, from the time of his sentence, lived as he died, in beggary. On this point, the reader may consult Mrs. Macaulay and her authorities.

Mr. Hume has canted much about the death of Strafford, and claims the merit of having shed some "generous tears" on that subject. All that he says, put together, is not worth a single expression of honest Pym. When Strafford, then a leader of Opposition, for the sake of a place at Court, deserted the public cause; "you have left us," said Pym, "but we shall not leave you while your head is on your shoulders;" and he kept his word.

No part of our historian's performance has been more controverted than that relative to Queen Mary. Perhaps the next age may consider her conduct in a light equally different from her present accusers and her apologists. I would meet the former on their own ground, and frankly reply, that the brutal insolence of Darnly to his wife, his sovereign, his benefactress, deserved ten deaths; and that Mary, if connected with the conspirators, was at worst but an executioner of justice. If she wanted to depose and destroy Elizabeth, still the ruin of her country, the massacre of her friends, the loss of her kingdom, her liberty, and her child, justified her revenge. Let us, for example, suppose that Mr. Hume had been confined in one of the dungeons of the Holy Office at

Lisbon, and that he had obtained a chance of escaping. *Query*, Would he have refused freedom, for fear of injuring the inquisitor who arrested him? Surely he could not have scrupled at knocking out the brains of the whole fraternity? Many modern historians, and among others, Mr. Hume, have fallen into the practice of quaint wiredrawn portraits. The virtues and literary genius of James I. for instance, are expanded by our author into a quarto page, which can be regarded but as waste paper. As a man of taste, Mr. Hume is often extremely singular. He affirms that Shakespeare "was totally ignorant of *all* theatrical art and conduct; that it is in vain we look either for continued purity, or simplicity of diction; and that he cannot for *any* time uphold *a reasonable propriety of thought.*" There is much more to the same purpose.

Mr. Hume, in common with most of our historians, has omitted to give an account of his materials. A judicious reader, when he sees them perpetually referred to, will ask who is Froissart, and who is Rhymer? Till the accession of the house of Tudor, his narrative is abrupt. For example; the reign of Edward III. extended to almost half a century, and is one of the most busy and memorable in ancient or modern annals. It is compressed by Mr. Hume within an hundred octavo pages, while the reign of Elizabeth alone fills one of his largest volumes. His warmest admirers must allow, that he betrays a wide disproportion of parts in the execution of his plan: But in truth, it was by far too extensive to be completed by any single pen. It was necessary to write a book of a saleable size. As an epitome of English History, it is too large; but as a complete history, it is by far too short. We often see whole folios printed on the antiquities of a single town, or a single country parish. Why then should we think it tiresome to read twenty or thirty volumes on the national history of our ancestors? Mr. Hume, like many men of eminence, has performed too little, by attempting to perform too much; yet his writings afford universal and lasting pleasure. The distinctness of his manner, and the acuteness or plausibility of his general observations, cast a veil over the errors and deficiencies of his narrative.

38
THE CRITICAL REVIEW

Review of *The History of England, Abridged from Hume* (1795), in *The Critical Review*, January 1795, Vol. 13, pp. 76–79. Complete review.

Although Hume's *History* was written for a general audience – as opposed to an audience of specialists – it was nevertheless too long and detailed for student use. Several one-volume histories of England were available, many abridged from Smollett's *History*. In 1793, the first single-volume abridgment of Hume's *History* appeared, edited by George Buist. Two years later, a two-volume abridgment appeared, anonymously edited by historian and clergyman Charles John Ann Hereford (b. 1757). In addition to abridgments, continuations of Hume's *History* were also called for. The most notable continuation was derived from Smollett's *History*. This was both incorporated into Hume's volumes and issued as a separate series of volumes under the title *The History of England from the Revolution to the Death of George the Second, Designed as a Continuation of Mr. Hume's History*. One such continuation appeared in 1795. The preface to this work states "A considerable part of the volume ... was written by a very eminent historian lately deceased. The continuation, from the middle of the reign of George II, is added by a person conversant in modern history" (p. iii). This and the 1795 abridgment of Hume's *History* were reviewed in both the *Critical Review* and the *Monthly Review*. The article below, though critical of Hume, is complimentary of both of these books.

An Abridgment of Hume's History of England. By the Author of the Abridgement of Gibbon's Roman History. 2 Vols. 8vo. 14s. Boards. Kearsleys. 1795.

The History of England, from the Revolution to the Commencement of the present Administration. Written in Continuation of Mr. Hume's History. 8vo. 7s. Boards. Kearsleys. 1795.

In our Review of Dr. Coote's History we are conscious that we hazarded in some degree our popularity, by frankly giving our sentiments on the history of

Hume. From that opinion we feel no inclination to retract; and we are satisfied that, sooner or later, the judgment of the public will bear us out. As long, however, as Mr. Hume's continues a popular history, we can recommend the present as a good and useful abridgement.

Of the Continuation, as it has more claim to originality than a professed abridgement can have, it may be expected that we should treat more at large. We confess, indeed, that we have been much gratified by the perusal of it. Though the author adheres with tolerable fidelity to his profession, of intro-ducing 'no disquisitions on the principles of government,' yet it is written with more liberality, we might say with more honesty, than Hume, or than Goldsmith, and the other smaller histories of England, which are almost literally copied from Smollett, who was a decided Tory. One circumstance, however, we cannot but regret respecting this Continuation, viz. that it is rather too concise. We are conscious that some plausible arguments may be urged in favour of this circumstance. In a history of recent events, it may be said, that the more prominent facts are all that can be wanted, to refresh the memory, and recall the attention of the reader; that the causes and motives of events are not known for a series of years after their occurrence, and, conse-quently, to investigate these circumstantially, would be little better than a loss of time. – In a history designed, in part at least, if not principally, for the use of young persons, it may be added, that as little unnecessary matter as possible should be introduced to distract their attention; and the minute discussion of minute circumstances would frequently appear to them trifling, or dull at the best. Notwithstanding, however, these and other arguments, which might possibly be alleged by the author, we cannot forego our opinion, that, as the history is not exclusively meant for young persons, he might in some instances have extended his narrative to advantage, especially since the judicious obser-vations and reflexions on political subjects, which frequently occur, will naturally extend the circulation of the book to readers of mature years, and of well-informed understandings. We must, however, do the author the justice to say, that the volume presents us with a very judicious compendium of the History of England, during the period of which he treats. All the great public events, we must add, are distinctly related, and as an instance, we can truly say that the volume contains the clearest and most candid history of the late American war which we have hitherto met with.

The following are our author's reflections on the advantages resulting from the Revolution:

'The revolution of 1688 is justly regarded by Britons as the most brilliant transaction in their history. The important ends which it accomplished, compared with the moderate and equitable measure by which it was atchieved, most properly render it the object of our veneration. By the Revolution, and the Bill of Rights, which was the immediate consequence of that event, the existence of a virtual compact between the king and people was confirmed beyond the possibility of a question; as well as the right of the latter to dismiss even the highest officer of the state, when he should be found to abuse the trust reposed in him. The Revolution prevented many and great evils; it conferred some substantial benefits; and it sanctioned, by a solemn act of the legislature, all the legal privileges of the subject, in such a manner, as, we trust, will render it for ever impossible to establish in these kingdoms an arbitrary system of government. To those who may be led to imagine, that this glorious reform in our government did not go far enough in securing the political liberties of the nation, and in abridging the royal prerogatives, many sound arguments might be adduced; but it will be suffi-cient for the present to request their attention to the state of the external dominions of Great Britain, and of Ireland in particular, and even to the state of parties in this kingdom, at the momentous period which we have to record.'

The character of Sir Robert Walpole does honour to the candour and humanity of the author.

'A general and frantic joy overspread the nation on the dismission of sir Robert Walpole; but while the errors of his administration have been freely exposed, equal justice demands that his merits should not be concealed or caste into shade. With all his blemishes, it will not be easy to find a minister from the period of the revolution that deserved on the whole better of his country. That he was notoriously corrupt, and professedly governed by a venal influence, has already been sufficiently exposed; but which of the agents of this government has ever depended upon the integrity of his principles and the wisdom of his measure for parliamentary support? This circumstance it is true does not afford an apology for the shameless practice of corruption and venality; a practice which is not only destructive to the principles of the constitution, but ruinous to the morals of the nation. But while this charge is admitted in its amplest extent, it must be added on the other hand, that no minister ever understood the true political interests of Britain, better than sir Robert Walpole. He loved, and cultivated peace, which is the only system that can be salutary for a commercial people. He saw the gross absurdity of this island, interfering in the debates or dissentions, of the continent; and, saw that the subsidizing of the petty despots of Germany, was the great gulph that swallowed up the treasures of England. He saw nothing to be gained by war, but an increase of taxes, and that no accessions could compensate for the burthens, and the miseries, which it brought upon the people.

To this wise and pacific system, sir Robert Walpole may be considered as having fallen a martyr; for it must be confessed, that it was neither his corruption of the parliament, nor his patronage of the excise, that effectually excited the public indignation against him. The people of England have a natural infatuation which induces them to love war. While the genius of the nation is really not military; their distance from the scene of action, enables them to be entertained at home with the details of bloodshed; and they absurdly affect the most unqualified claims to the epithet humane, while they feast with avidity on the calamities of their fellow creatures, and rejoice that thousands have been slaughtered "for the honour of England." Thus no pacific minister has ever been popular, and the most trifling cause of dispute has always been sufficient to raise a party in favour of war, and consequently adverse to the statesman who studies the real interest and welfare of the country.'

The work concludes with a few prejudicious strictures on the coalition, and the succeeding administration formed under Mr. Pitt, which we shall extract.

'The burst of public indignation which produced the downfall of the coalition ministry, has been mistakenly attributed to the India bill presented by Mr. Fox. It was really the effects of that resentment, which all mankind involuntarily feel against a dereliction of sentiment and principle. It was the mean and dishonourable coalition of the Portland party, with those men whose measures they had reprobated, and whose characters they had stigmatized, that fortified the king in the opinion of the people, and enabled him on this occasion to exercise the royal prerogative with effect. The transactions of Mr. Pitt's administration, are too recent to be recorded with propriety in this history, and the violence of party would, perhaps, be an effectual impediment to the discovery of the truth. To future historians we must therefore consign the task, and can only express a wish, that, agreeably to his own predictions so confidently asserted, the public finances (the sinews of the nation) may, at the termination of his ministry, be found in an improved state; and the population, wealth, and commerce of the island, increased and flourishing.'

From these specimens the reader will perceive that the style of this volume is perspicuous, correct, and animated. We think the publisher has acted judiciously in selling the Continuation separate from the Abridgment, as it will afford an opportunity to those who may be already in possession of Rapin's, Coote's, or other histories of England, to furnish themselves at an easy expence, with a lively and pleasant Continuation of the History from the Revolution to the present time.

39
WILLIAM ENFIELD,
THE MONTHLY REVIEW

[William Enfield], review of *The History of England, Abridged from Hume* (1795), in *The Monthly Review*, January 1796, Vol. 19, pp. 73–74. Complete review.

Born in Sudbury, Suffolk, William Enfield (1741–1797) was a teacher at the dissenting academy at Warrington and the author of several theological and philosophical books. He was also a regular contributor to the *Monthly Review* in the areas of religion and philosophy; quotations from his reviews of Smith's *Wealth of Nations* (1776), the anonymous *Critical Observations* (1782), and de Mably's *De la maniere d'écrire l'histoire* (1783) are contained earlier in this collection. In this review, Enfield praises the 1795 abridgment of Hume as the best brief history of England available. However, comparing the abridgment with Hume's original, he points out some unwarranted liberties that the editor had taken. He also notes that, of necessity, the editor removed Hume's own reflections and explanations of the "measures and causes of events."

ART. XVIII. *The History of England, abridged from Hume.* By the Author of the Abridgment of Mr. Gibbon's Roman History.[1] 2 Vols. 8vo. pp. 600 in each. 14s. Boards. Kearsleys. 1795.

The history of England is so interesting to every Englishman, and the important train of facts of which it is composed must be represented so faintly in the most judicious abridgment, that no one, who has an opportunity of perusing it in detail, should content himself with the imperfect information which he can obtain from two octavo volumes. Nevertheless, since many persons either have not sufficient leisure or sufficient industry to undertake the reading of voluminous works, and who yet may wish not to be wholly ignorant of the history of their native country, it is desirable that, for the use of such persons,

---

[1] See Rev. January 1791, p. 82.

abridgments should be provided, somewhat more attractive than a mere dry chronicle of occurrences. We are acquainted with no method in which this can be better done, than by copying select parts of some approved historian, in which the more important facts are detailed at some considerable length, and in the words of the original author. Our readers will perceive, from these remarks, that the design of the present volumes has *so far* our approbation; and, after having compared, with some attention, the abstract with the original, we do not scruple to give it as our opinion that the abridgment is made with a considerable share of judgment. Though some of the most valuable parts of the original work, – those in which the historian explains at large the grounds of measures and causes of events, and gives the result of his own reflections, – are omitted; this was unavoidable in a work, the great object of which was to comprize within a narrow compass a narrative of the great events of the English history during a period of 1700 years.

Towards the beginning of the abridgement, we find the present writer attempting alterations in the language of his author, which certainly are not improvements on the original: but we were glad to observe, as we proceeded, that the abridger, either growing tired of the labour of correcting the style of Hume, or discovering that the attempt was unnecessary, commonly contents himself with only such deviations from the original text, as were necessary to present the reader with an unbroken narrative. In some places, we have remarked that the sense of the author is very imperfectly given; for example, in the abstract of the state of learning at the close of the reign of James I.; and in a few instances, the abridger has offered an opinion different from that of Mr. Hume, without apprizing the reader; for instance, in his account of the celebrated philosopher Hobbes, at the close of the history of the common-wealth; a freedom which an abbreviator cannot take without doing manifest injustice to his author.

Notwithstanding these and other occasional defects, we readily allow to the editor the general merit of having executed his task faithfully, and of having furnished those to whom abridgments are desireable, with a better *Brief History of England* than had before appeared – within the same compass.

40
WILLIAM ENFIELD,
THE MONTHLY REVIEW

[William Enfield], Review of *The History of England, from the Revolution to the Commencement of the present Administration* (1795), in *The Monthly Review*, January 1796, Vol. 19, pp. 74–76.
Complete review.

William Enfield (1741–1797) was the author of the previous item in this collection. As with that review, his article here praises Hume's *History*. Unlike the reviewer for the *Critical Review*, Enfield does not think that the 1795 continuation is up to Hume's standards, and he hints that a better one will be published shortly.

ART. XIX. *The History of England*, from the Revolution to the Commencement of the present Administration. Written in Continuation of Mr. Hume's History. 8vo. pp. 250. 7s. Boards. Kearsleys. 1795.

To abridge Hume's History of England is a much easier task than to write a continuation of it. A work which should merit that title must closely follow this justly celebrated historian, in the exercise of sound judgment, in the selection and arrangement of facts, in sagacity in tracing back events to their sources, in solidity and depth of reflection, and in a copious command of the energies and graces of style. In all these respects, it must be fairly owned, the writers of this volume retire at an almost immeasureable distance behind their leader. This we shall not scruple to declare, notwithstanding the assurance given to the reader in an advertisement prefixed to this history, that a considerable part of the volume was written by a very eminent historian lately deceased; and that, from the middle of the reign of George II. the work is continued by a person conversant in modern history. Had the editor been contented to offer the work to the public under the modest title of Annals of England, from the revolution to the termination of the American war, we should have reported the publication to our readers as a compilation which might be useful to those who wished to inform themselves of the general train of events during that period, without taking the trouble of examining the original documents, or perusing more minute details. In this view, we readily recommend it as a proper supplement to the set of historical abridgments with which the publisher had lately provided the world: but we think it of importance that it should be generally understood, that the Continuation of Hume's History of England is, notwithstanding this publication, a *desideratum* in British literature. Expectations, however, have been raised, from different quarters, that this defect will hereafter be supplied.

As a brief specimen of the style and spirit of this volume, we shall copy the general remarks which conclude the reign of George I.

'The political conduct of George the First has been viewed through the medium of party as coloured by the prejudices of the eye through which it was surveyed; but whatever might be the virtues, vices, or errors of his political conduct, he was liked and even loved by individuals who had the honour of a familiar conversation with him, and was generally regarded by those who do not examine closely or critically into the nature of virtue and vice, or the motives and principles of human conduct, as a man who had an honest heart, and whose faults in his government, if there are faults to be found, were entirely owing to the suggestions of a venal ministry, who, having neither sufficient virtue, nor sufficient understanding, to govern parties by the confidence which these great qualities give, their power and influence were solely grounded on corruption.

This narration has furnished many proofs of the liberal, nay, the profuse manner with which every parliament gave away the money of the people. – George the First was almost always in war, or entangled in expensive alliances. Bremen and Verden were bought, with the sweat of the brow of the English subject: and though the nation was fifty millions in debt, the wretched people, who were regarded in no other light but as the means to raise money for the use of their betters, were almost every year saddled with the burthen of near seven millions; and the heavy taxes which produced this sum were carried through the two houses without any considerable opposition, except in the first parliament of this king's reign. Yet such were the prejudices of a prince, who it has been said governed his German dominions in so absolute a manner, that the miserable slaves of the principality were obliged to pay a tax to the government for every joint of meat they laid down to the fire; such were the prejudices of this German elector, that Lord Chesterfield informs us, that George the First was exceedingly hurt, even with the weak opposition he met with in parliament, on account of subsidies; and could not help complaining to his most intimate friends, that he was come over to England to be a begging king; that is, that he could not command without asking, and issue out mandates to raise arbitrary taxes by the royal authority singly.'

From the preceding passage, it may be inferred that this history is drawn up on whig principles, and this will be found to be the general political character of the work; though the writer professedly avoids all disquisition on the principles of government, because he conceives 'that such enquiries would be not only superfluous, but even impertinent, as we have one *certain criterion of political wisdom and virtue*, namely, the established doctrines of the British constitution.' – Friends and admirers as we are of the constitution with which we are blessed through the sagacity and the firmness of our ancestors, we are no advocates for such hyperbole of language, as that which pronounces any effort of human power to be the *certain criterion of political wisdom and virtue.*

41
ROBERT BISSET

Robert Bisset, *The life of Edmund Burke. Comprehending an impartial account of his literary and political efforts, and a sketch of the conduct and character of his most eminent associates, coadjutors, and opponents. By Robert Bisset,* ... London: printed and published by George Cawthorn; and sold also by Messrs. Richardson; J. Hatchard, and J. Wright, 1798, xvi, 592 p. Selections; from 1800 edition.

Historian Robert Bisset (1759–1805) was the author of the six-volume *History of the Reign of George III* (1804) and is perhaps best known for writing the first substantial biography of Irish-born philosopher and statesman Edmund Burke (1729–1797). At several places in the biography Bisset discusses Burke's connections with Hume, two of which involve their respective views of the Irish massacre. In the first of these Bisset notes that Burke denied the Irish massacre, and, when pressed by Hume on the evidence, Burke irrationally argued that the testimonies of the Irish proved nothing. In the second, Bisset relates a conversation on the subject between Hume and Burke, and Bisset himself defends Hume's view of the subject. Bisset provides us with the most detailed account of Hume's and Burke's relationship. In Hume's letters we learn further that he admired Burke's *Sublime and Beautiful* (1757), gave Burke a copy of Adam Smith's *Theory of Moral Sentiments* (1759), and showed sympathy for Burke regarding a poorly received speech he made in Parliament in 1767. From Burke's writings, we know that Burke either authored or at least endorsed the flattering assessment of Hume's *History* in the 1761 review of that work in the *Annual Register* (included earlier in these volumes), and Burke writes approvingly of Hume's *History* in *Thoughts on French Affairs* (1791). Nevertheless, Bisset's depiction of Burke's growing dislike for Hume is confirmed by James Boswell, who reports that Burke spoke with Hume only because the liberal state of society required it.[1]

Reviews of Bisset's *Life* were favourable, but with some reservations. The *Analytical Review* writes "The subject before us, indeed, furnishes ample

---

[1] *Private Papers of James Boswell* (1928–1934), Vol. 11, p. 268, as mentioned by Mossner, *Life of David Hume*, p. 394.

materials, and if we be inclined occasionally to doubt, as to the *impartiality* of which he boasts, we must, at the same time, make every allowance for his industry." Writing for the *Monthly Review,* Thomas Wallace concludes that Bisset fails "to prove the consistency of Edmund Burke," and that Bisset should "appear *less* learned" in his composition. The *Critical Review* similarly stated "Of the writer's style we may observe, that it sometimes exhibits an unpleasing pomp and affectation."[2] Bisset's biography was published again in 1800 and 1809. The following is from the 1800 edition.

...

The genius, wisdom, and learning of Burke did not prevent him from entertaining some opinions totally unfounded. Through life he had certain prepossessions, to which he was warmly attached, and respecting which, though in most of his conversations he was mild and unassuming, he could brook no contradiction. He most strenuously denied the Irish Massacre: he said it was all a fiction. Being at one time intimately acquainted with Hume, he used to battle this point with him with great zeal: when pressed hard by the strong testimony and powerful arguments adduced by Hume, he used to say that the testimony proved nothing; and to quote an absurd story, to which, he affirmed, thousands of Irish most confidently bore witness, "that the ghosts of numbers of those that had been killed, and thrown into the Shannon, often made their appearance on the banks of the river, to the great disturbance of the neighbourhood." This mode of reasoning, that one believed portion of history was false, because a story obviously false had been believed, was certainly very unworthy of Burke, and very unlikely to convince Hume; although he himself, when it favours his own prejudices, reasons in the same manner. I am assured that Hume alludes to Burke in the following note to the fifth volume of the *History of England:* "There are three events in our history which may be regarded as touchstones of party men. An English whig, who asserts the reality of the popish plot; an Irish catholic, who denies the massacre in 1641; and a Scotch Jacobite, who maintains the innocence of queen Mary; must be considered as men beyond the reach of argument, and must be left to their own prejudices."

So great is the inequality often to be found in men of the highest genius, that Burke could not bear to have this favourite notion attacked. There were three subjects on which he could not speak without being transported into a rage, as violent as Johnson, if whigs were praised, the Americans defended, or

---

2   *Analytical Review,* July 1798, Vol. 28, pp. 9–16; *Monthly Review,* August 1798, Vol. 26, pp. 361–378, September, Vol. 27, pp. 23–38; *Critical Review,* 1799, Vol. 25, pp. 291–298.

episcopacy censured: – Burke's were, through life, the Irish Massacre; during the latter part of it, the conduct of Hastings, and the French revolution. He never forgave Hume; and I am informed that, even so late as the last Christmas he saw, in conversation with a counsellor of the first talents, he inveighed most bitterly against the historian for having alluded to him in his note.

...

Mr. Burke about this time received a visit from a very eminent literary gentleman, who has been so kind as to communicate to me various particulars of the conversation which took place, and the deportment of his host. Part of the communications is interspersed in different parts of the volumes; the remainder I shall insert here.

The visitant went prepossessed with the very highest idea of merit which he could analyse, comprehend, and appreciate. The first address of the host [i.e., Burke] was extremely striking, and suggested to the guest the idea of chivalrous hospitality. His powers of conversation were wonderful: in extent and minuteness of detail, as well as the most profound and expanded philosophy; in playfulness, in humour, wit, serious imagery, beautiful, grand, and diversified. An instance of his correctness in point of fact, he exhibited in a statement of the poor's rates of fifty parishes in Buckinghamshire, during the time he had been at Beaconsfield; he also gave the history and progress of the farming, the improvements, rents, and taxes. The conversation having turned upon literary subjects, the guest had an opportunity of hearing him talk of David Hume. The reader will remember, that Mr. Hume, in a note on his account of Mary, mentions three sets of persons that are not to be argued with, but left to their own prejudices: a Scotch Jacobite, who believes in the innocence of Mary; an Irish Catholic, who denies the truth of the Irish massacre; and an English Whig, who believes in Titus Oates's plot. Mr. Burke considered himself though no Catholic, as referred to on the subject of the massacre. Mr. Hume and he had met at Garrick's, and the massacre was one of the subjects discussed. Mr. Burke endeavoured to prove that the received accounts were in a great degree unfounded, or at least very much exaggerated, and quoted affidavits deposited in Trinity College, Dublin. He described various absurd stories that had been propagated and believed by many concerning the Irish; among others, that the ghosts of the murdered Protestants frequented the banks of the Shannon almost from its source to the sea. Mr. Hume maintained the justness of the account, which makes a part of his history. It must be owned that the evidence is much stronger in favour of Mr. Hume's position than Mr. Burke's. In the first place, independent of testimony, it is perfectly consonant to the ferocious and bloodthirsty character so often exhibited by the Irish in their most enormous atrocities. Let us consider their conduct: when driven on by furious bigotry, they supported the contemptible priest-ridden James against the wise and glorious deliverer of Europe. Let us view their conduct in the late rebellion: the cruelties imputed to them in the former part of the 17th century are not greater than those which they are known to have perpetrated towards its close, and in our own days; they proceeded, at the instance of their priests, like wild beasts, purposely infuriated by their keepers, and let loose. So much for internal evidence in the character of the Irish. But the authorities received by Hume are those of annalists and historians near the time; Rushforth, Temple, Nalson, and Whitlocke. It is certain, however, that Mr. Burke did not regard Hume's memory with great affection, however highly he must have admired his talents.[3] Perhaps the religious sentiments of Hume might have been one cause of Mr. Burke's disapprobation, as no one was more strongly impressed with the necessity of religion to the well-being of society.[4]

---

[3]   Some paltry antiquarian, I forget the man's name, has lately been nibbling at our illustrious historian, and raking into some old Saxon books with a view to prove that he is erroneous in the names of one or two monks. The Spectator has a very fine paper on a fly which, viewing St. Paul's Cathedral, from its diminutive optics, might, he conceived, discover some roughness in the surface of a particular part, though so totally unable to comprehend the beauty and grandeur of the whole building.

[4]   It does not appear that Mr. Hume, notwithstanding his penetration, at his first acquaintance with Burke, discovered his extraordinary talents, as in a letter to Mr. Adam Smith, he speaks of him as 'a Mr. Burke, an Irish gentleman, who has written a very pretty book on the Sublime and Beautiful.' The reader will remember a case somewhat parallel, not in the writer, but in the subject, when Whitlocke speaks of *one Milton.*

42
JEREMY BENTHAM

Jeremy Bentham, *A plea for the Constitution shewing the enormities committed to the oppression of British subjects, innocent as well as guilty; in breach of magna charta, the petition of right, the habeas corpus act, and the bill of rights.* London: Mawman, Poultry, 1803, ix, 68 p.
Selections from Section 14.4; from *The Works of Jeremy Bentham*, edited by John Bowring (London: 1838–1843), Vol. 4.

Born in London, son of an attorney, Jeremy Bentham (1748–1832) is among the most noted moral and political philosophers of the late eighteenth and early nineteenth centuries. He studied law, but never practised it, and instead devoted much of his life to writing on issues of legal reform. Throughout his writings, Bentham took regular notice of Hume, and was particularly influenced by his moral theory (see *Early Responses to Hume's Moral Theory and Essays*). In *A Plea for the Constitution*, Bentham discusses the ill effects of British leaders violating various parts of the British constitution. In a lengthy note he draws on Hume's *History* and argues that Hume himself was acutely aware of the adverse consequences of this in the time of Charles I. Bentham warns that the constitution will lose its protective force if continually trampled upon.

IV. *Transgressions in breach of the several Transportation Acts, by which that Punishment has been appointed for limited lengths of time.*

[Note:] Without a thought of any application to existing circumstances, I happened but now to open the reign of Charles I., in *Hume*. If prejudices of any kind be deemed imputable to that prince of historians, they will hardly be of that cast, which would dispose a man to exaggerate the mischief resulting from a transgression of the limits prescribed by the constitution to the power of the crown. Whether to that dispassionate, acute, and comprehensive mind, the wounds given to the constitution on the ground of penal colony would have presented themselves as matters of indifference – as incidents in which the body of the people have no concern – is a question, the answer to which may be read, I should suppose, without much difficulty, in the following passages: –

Vol. VI., 8vo, p. 316, anno 1637. Speaking of ship-money, "What security," says the arguments which he exhibits as conclusive, "what security against the further extension of this claim? ... Wherever any difficulty shall occur, the administration, instead of endeavouring to elude or overcome it by gentle and prudent measures, will instantly represent it as a reason for infringing all ancient laws and institutions: and if such maxims and such practises prevail, what has become of national liberty? What authority is left to the *great charter*, to the *statutes*, and to that very *petition of right*, which in the present reign had been so solemnly enacted by the concurrence of the whole legislature?" So far Hume. The breach of those two constitutional safeguards constituted in those days, according to the historian, the superlative of tyranny. The *Habeas Corpus act* and the *Bill of Rights* have since been added. To triumph over those more ancient laws, the violation of which cost Charles the first his crown and life, was not enough: the violation of the Habeas Corpus act, and the bill of Rights – a course of systematic violation persevered in for fourteen years – has accordingly been added to the triumphs of ministers in these our times.

Along with those two fundamental laws, other "statutes" are mentioned by the historian in general terms: and, as an aggravation of the tyranny, the *then* present reign is noted as the period that gave birth to the *Petition of Right*, one of those two fundamental laws. Statutes of inferior account, in crowds, contribute to swell the triumph obtained over law (with grief I say it) in the *now* present reign: and among them the several *transportation acts*, to which, in numbers too great for reference, this same reign has been giving birth.

Ib. p. 314, anno 1637. – "It was urged," ... continues the historian, "that the plea of necessity was in vain introduced into a trial at law; since it was of the nature of necessity to abolish all law...." p. 315. "And as to the pretension that the king is sole judge of the necessity, what is this but to subject all the privileges of the nation to his arbitrary will and pleasure? To expect that the public will be convinced by such reasoning, must aggravate the general indignation, by adding, to violence against men's persons, and their property, so cruel a mockery of their understanding."

Ib. p. 421, anno 1641. – "In those days," observes the historian, "the parliament thought" – and according to him – "justly thought that the king was too eminent a magistrate to be trusted with discretionary power, which he might so easily turn to the destruction of liberty. And in the event it has hitherto been found, that, though some sensible inconveniences arise from the maxim of adhering strictly to law, yet the advantages overbalance them, and should render the English grateful to the memory of their ancestors, who, after repeated contests, at last established that noble, though dangerous, principle." Established it? So *they* thought (it seems) in *their* times: so Hume thought (it seems) in *his* time. In these *our* times, does that valuable principle *remain* established? or, after having been overthrown and trampled upon for these fourteen years, is it now finally to be abandoned, and to remain lifeless and extinct for ever?

In one point, indeed, at least according to the view given of it by this historian, the parallel would be found to fail. "The imposition of ship-money, independent of the consequences," (viz. the anti-constitutional consequences above spoken of) "was a great and evident advantage to the public," viz. "by the judicious use which the king made of the money levied by that expedient.

Ib. p. 319, anno 1637. – So far as to the unconstitutional impost of *that* day. As to the anti-constitutional system of the present times, what degree of "judiciousness" there was, either in the design of it or in the *"use"* made of it, may be seen in the Letters to Lord Pelham, by any man when conscience will permit him to look the subject in the face.

Ib. p. 360, anno 1640. – "The lawyers had declared, that *martial law* would not be exercised, except in the presence of the enemy; and because it had been found necessary to execute a mutineer, the generals thought it advisable, for their own safety, to apply for a pardon from the crown." – So much greater was the respect paid to the constitution by the king's servants – Strafford of the number – in those days, than in these. See above.

Ib. p. 319, anno 1587 – The cause of the unfortunate pertinacity on the part of the misguided king, and the deceitful ground on which it rested, are thus delineated. "Though it was justly apprehended, that such precedents, if patiently submitted to, would end ... in the establishment of arbitrary authority; Charles dreaded no opposition from the people, who are not commonly much affected with consequences, and require some striking motive to engage them in a resistance to established government."

Such at that time had been the *reliance*, but now follows the *result*.

Ib. p. 317, anno 1637. – "Hampden, however," observes the historian, "obtained by the trial the end for which he had so generously sacrificed his safety and his quiet: the *people* were roused from their lethargy, and became sensible of the danger to which their liberties were exposed. Then national questions were canvassed in every company; and the more they were examined, the more evidently did it appear to many, that liberty was totally subverted ... slavish principles, they said, concur with illegal practices; ... and the privileges of the nation, transmitted through so many ages, secured by so many laws, and purchased by the blood of so many heroes and patriots, now lie prostrate at the feet of the monarch. What though public peace and national industry increased the commerce and opulence of the kingdom? This advantage was temporary, and due alone, not to any encouragement given by the crown, but to the spirit of the English, the remains of their ancient freedom. What though the personal character of the king, amidst all his misguided counsels, might merit indulgence, or even praise? He was but one man; and the privileges of the people, the inheritance of millions, were too valuable to be sacrificed to his prejudices and mistakes."

Ib. p. 375, anno 1640. – The jealousy of the people was roused; "and, agreeably to the spirit of free governments, no less indignation was excited by the view of a violated constitution, than by the ravages of the most enormous tyranny." Such was the language – such the spirit – of the people of that day: such their language and their spirit, when both as yet were temperate, and had not burst forth into the wild explosions that ensued. In the case of New South Wales, *both* provocations – the *"violated constitution,"* and the *"enormous tyranny"* – go hand in hand: the tyranny, the end; the violation of the constitution, the means. What will now be the spirit of a British parliament? what will now be the spirit of the British people? It remains to be seen in what degree, if in any, the people of this day retain the virtues of their ancestors.

They must be degenerate indeed, if they are to be lulled into any such persuasion, as that the constitution will be capable of retaining for their benefit its protecting force, after it has been made apparent, that, with ultimate impunity, it may thus be trampled upon in the most vital parts of it, for such a course of years.

43
HANNAH MORE

Hannah More, *Hints towards forming the character of a young princess: in two volumes.* London: Printed for T. Cadell and W. Davies, 1805, 2 v.
Selections from Chapter 10; from *The works of Hannah More*, Philadelphia: Edward Earle, 1818, vol. 7.

Hannah More (1745–1833) was born in Stapleton, Gloucestershire, England. When a young girl she knew Hume's friend John Peach, a linen draper from Bristol, and from that acquaintance conveyed an anecdote about Hume's stay in that city (see *Early Responses to Hume's Life and Reputation*). Around 30, she became close friends of David Garrick, Samuel Johnson, and, as a noted poet and playwright herself, she was included in London's famed literary circles. Her religious convictions intensified with age and, no longer attending theatrical productions, many of her writings focused on religious themes. In her 1805 *Hints towards Forming the Character of a Young Princess* she criticizes the political and religious bias in Hume's otherwise elegant *History*. She calls it "a serpent under a bed of roses," and warns young readers to be cautious about being swayed by Hume's subtle insinuations against religion.

CHAP. X.
REFLECTIONS ON HISTORY – ANCIENT HISTORIANS.

...

MR. HUME

Hume is incomparably the most informing, as well as the most elegant, of all the writers of English history. His narrative is full, well arranged, and beautifully perspicuous. Yet, he is an author who must be read with extreme caution on a political, but especially on a religious account. Though, on occasions where he may be trusted, because his peculiar principles do not interfere, his political reflections are usually just, sometimes profound. His account of the origin of the Gothic government is full of interest and information. He marks, with exact precision, the progress and decay of the feudal manners, when law and order began to prevail, and our constitution assumed something like a shape. His finely painted characters of Alfred and Elizabeth should be engraved on the heart of every sovereign. His political prejudices do not strikingly appear, till the establishment of the house of Stuart, nor his religious antipathies till about the distant dawn of the reformation under Henry V. From that period to its full establishment, he is perhaps more dangerous, because less ostensibly daring than some other infidel historians. It is a serpent under a bed of roses. He does not (in his *history* at least) so much ridicule religion himself, as invite others to ridicule it. There is in his manner a sedateness which imposes; in his scepticism, a sly gravity, which puts the reader more off his guard than the vehemence of censure, or the levity of wit; for we are always less disposed to suspect a man who is too wise to appear angry. That same wisdom makes him too correct to *invent* calumnies, but it does not preserve him from doing what is scarcely less disingenuous. He implicitly adopts the injurious relations of those annalists who were most hostile to the reformed faith; though he must have known their accounts to be aggravated and discoloured, if not absolutely invented. He thus makes others responsible for the worst things he asserts, and spreads the mischief, without avowing the malignity. When he speaks from himself, the sneer is so cool, the irony so sober, the contempt so discreet, the moderation so insidious, the difference between Popish bigotry, and Protestant firmness, between the fury of the persecutor and the resolution of the martyr, so little marked; the distinctions between intolerant phrenzy and heroic zeal so melted into each other, and though he contrives to make the reader feel some indignation at the tyrant, he never leads him to feel any reverence for the sufferer; he ascribes such a slender superiority to one religious system above another, that the young reader who does not come to the perusal with his principles formed, will be in danger of thinking that the reformation was really not worth contending for.

But, in nothing is the skill of this accomplished sophist more apparent than in the artful way in which he piques his readers into a conformity with his own views concerning religion. Human pride, he knew, naturally likes to range itself on the side of ability. He, therefore, skillfully works on this passion, by treating with a sort of contemptuous superiority, as weak and credulous men, all whom he represents as being under the religious delusion; and by uniformly insinuating that talents and piety belong to opposite parties.

To the shameful practice of confounding fanaticism with real religion, he adds the disingenuous habit of accounting for the best actions of the best men, by referring them to some low motive; and affects to confound the designs of the religious and the corrupt, so artfully, that no radical difference appears to subsist between them.

It is injurious to a young mind to read the history of the reformation by any author, how accurate soever he may be in his facts, who does not see a divine power accompanying this great work; by any author who ascribes to the power, or rather to the perverseness of nature, and the obstinacy of innovation, what was in reality an effect of providential direction; by any who discerns nothing but human resources, or stubborn perseverance, where a Christian distinguishes, though with a considerable alloy of human imperfection, the operation of the spirit of God.

Hume has a fascinating manner at the close of the life of a hero, a prince, or a statesman, of drawing up his character so elaborately as to attract and fix the whole attention of the reader; and he does it in such a way, that while he engages the mind he unsuspectedly misleads it. He makes a general statement of the vices and virtues, the good and bad actions of the person whom he paints, leaving the reader to form his own conclusions, by casting up the balance of the vices and virtues, of the good and bad actions thus enumerated: while he never once leads the reader to determine on the character by the only sure criterion, the *ruling principle*, which seemed to govern it. – This is the too prevailing method of historians; they make morals completely independent of religion, by thus weighing qualities, and letting the preponderance of the scale decide on virtue, as it were by grains and scruples: thus furnishing a standard of virtue subversive of that which Christianity establishes. This method, instead of marking the moral distinctions, blends and confounds them, by establishing character on an accidental difference, often depending on circumstance and occasion, instead of applying to it one eternal rule and motive of action.[1]

But, there is another evil into which writers far more unexceptionable than Mr. Hume often fall, that of rarely leading the mind to look beyond second causes and human agents. It is mortifying to refer them to the example of a pagan. Livy thought it no disgrace to proclaim, repeatedly, the insufficiency of man to accomplish great objects without divine assistance. *He* was not ashamed to refer events to the direction and control of providence; and when he speaks of notorious criminals, he is not contented with describing them as transgressing against the state, but represents them as also offending against the gods.

Yet, it is proper again to notice the defects of ancient authors in their views of providential interference; a defect arising from their never clearly including a future state in their account. They seem to have conceived themselves as fairly *entitled* by their good conduct to the divine favour, which favour they usually

---

[1] If these remarks may be thought too severe by some readers for that degree of scepticism which appears in Mr. Hume's *history*, may I not be allowed to observe that he has shown his principles so fully, in some of his other works, that we are entitled, on the ground of these works, to read with suspicion every thing he says which borders on religion? – A circumstance apt to be forgotten by many who read *only* his history.

limited to present prosperity. Whereas all notions of divine justice must of necessity be widely erroneous, in which a future retribution is not unambiguously and constantly included.

44
MONTHLY REPOSITORY

"On Mr. Hume's Political Inconsistencies as an Historian," in *Monthly Repository*, 1821, Vol. 16, pp. 472–473.
Compete article.

T he *Monthly Repository and Review of Theology and General Literature* was a Unitarian periodical founded in 1806 by Robert Aspland and published in London. By the beginning of the 19th century, Hume had been criticized for making inconsistent statements in his *History* and for his Tory ideology. The author of this brief article – who identifies himself only with the initial "N." – attacks Hume for making inconsistent statements about the role of individual liberty in English history. In some places, according to the author, Hume seems to recognize a strong liberty tradition, but in others denies this.

On Mr. Hume's Political Inconsistencies as an Historian

"Though our historian, from his desire of placing the princes of the House of Stuart in a favourable point of view, frequently palliates the most exceptionable parts of their conduct; yet it is but justice to him to acknowledge, that there are sundry passages in his history highly favourable to the general interests of liberty, and the common rights of mankind."

TOWERS.

A few of these passages, contrasted with others of a different character, I shall lay before the readers of the *Monthly Repository*, who will hence perceive that Mr. Hume's most objectionable statements are refuted by himself, and that "we have little reason to applaud our author for his consistency."
Speaking of Charles I., he says, "the king had, in some instances, stretched his prerogative beyond its just bounds; and, aided by the church, had well nigh put an end to all the liberties and privileges of the nation."[1] This, assuredly, is no exaggerated statement; within a few pages, however, the same historian

---

[1]   History, &c. VII. (1793), 220; and see VI. 228, 229, 231.

remarks, "All Europe stood astonished to see a nation, so turbulent and unruly, who, for some doubtful encroachments on their privileges, had dethroned and murdered an excellent prince, descended from a long line of monarchs, now at last subdued and reduced to slavery."[2]

Mr. Hume, in his narrative of the trial of Algernon Sidney, observes, "In ransacking the prisoner's closet, some discourses on government were found; in which he had maintained principles, favourable indeed to liberty, but such as the best and most dutiful subjects in all ages have been known to embrace; the original contract, the source of power from a consent of the people, the lawfulness of resisting tyrants, the preference of liberty to the government of a single person."[3] To this representation, who that deserves the name of an Englishman can object? It is the representation, nevertheless, of an historian, who stigmatizes certain writings of "Rapin Thoyras, Locke, *Sidney*, Hoadly," &c. as "Compositions the most despicable both for style and *matter*"![4]

Of Charles II. this writer acknowledges that he was "negligent of the interests of the nation, careless of its glory, averse to its religion, jealous of its liberty, lavish of its treasure." – The admission is less astonishing than the manner in which Mr. Hume attempts to qualify it: for he adds, "Yet may all these enormities, if fairly and candidly examined, be imputed, in a great measure, to the indolence of his temper; a fault which, however unfortunate in a monarch, it is impossible for us to regard with great severity." In a paragraph, which almost instantly follows, the historian intimates, that Charles II. had an "appetite for power:" and he confesses that this monarch's "attachment to France, after all the pains which we have taken, by inquiry and conjecture, to fathom it, contains still something mysterious and inexplicable."[5] Whatever *mystery* existed on the subject, has been completely solved.[6]

Concerning James II. Mr. Hume asks, "What was wanting to make him an excellent sovereign? A due regard and affection to the religion and constitution of his country. The sincerity of this prince (a virtue on which he highly valued himself) has been much questioned in those reiterated promises which he had made of preserving the liberties and religion of the nation. It must be confessed, that his reign was almost one continued invasion of both."[7] Truth and justice required this acknowledgment, which comes, notwithstanding, with an

---

[2]   Ibid. VII. 225.

[3]   History, &c. VIII. 197.

[4]   Ibid. VIII. 323.

[5]   Ibid. VIII. 212. Nor is Mr. Hume consistent with himself in his views of O. Cromwell's character. VII. 286, 290.

[6]   See Hume, VIII. 32, 41; the Appendix to Fox's Hist. of James II.; and the Life of William Lord Russell (4to.) p. 63.

[7]   History, &c. VIII. 306.

extremely ill grace from the man who, in the account of his own life, tells us that "it is ridiculous to consider the English constitution before" the Revolution "as a regular plan of liberty."[8]

In the *ridicule* which, according to Mr. Hume, such an opinion merits, my readers will perhaps be content to share, together with individuals who have diligently studied the history of the English constitution. Let me refer, in particular, to Bishop Hurd's excellent dialogue on the subject: and I more gladly make this reference, because justice has not always done to the Prelate's consistency as a political writer.[9]

What shall we finally pronounce of Mr. Hume in this character? Dr. Johnson said of him, that "he was a Tory by chance."[10]

N.
July 19, 1821

---

[8] Ibid. I. p. xi.

[9] The question is well considered, and satisfactorily determined, in Mon. Repos. III. 460–462, and in *Extracts from the Diary of a Lover of Literature*, (1816,) p. 71. It were to be wished, however, that the animated *Postscript* in the original edition of the *dialogues* (1759) had been retained in the subsequent impressions.

[10] Boswell's Life of Johnson, (ed. 3,) IV. 202.

45
GEORGE BRODIE

George Brodie, *A history of the British Empire, from the accession of Charles I. to the Restoration; with an introduction, tracing the progress of society, and of the constitution, from the feudal times to the opening of the history; and including a particular examination of Mr. Hume's statements relative to the character of the English government*. Edinburgh, Printed for Bell & Bradfute, 1822, 4 v.
Preface, selections from Chapter 2; from 1866 edition.

Born in East Lothian, Scotland, George Brodie (1786?–1867) was an attorney and is remembered for his principal work, *A History of the British Empire*, first published in 1822 and retitled *A Constitutional History of the British Empire* in the revised second edition of 1866, published a year before his death. An ardent Whig, Brodie attacks Tory accounts of recent British political history. Approximately one quarter of the work contains criticisms of Hume, which often appear in lengthy footnotes. In general, Brodie opposes Hume's claims for the existence of a royal prerogative throughout English history. The most sustained attack on Hume appears in Chapter 2 of the introductory volume, which examines Hume's accusation in Appendix 3 that Elizabeth's reign was arbitrary to the point of bearing "some resemblance to that of Turkey at present." Hume specifically argued that Elizabeth relied heavily on institutions that were antithetical to liberty, such as the Star-Chamber, martial law, imprisonment, torture, and forced loans. Examining these accusations one at a time, Brodie presents evidence to the contrary. Throughout this Chapter, Brodie is direct, but not rhetorically harsh towards Hume. His footnotes in later portions of the work, though, are more heated, as the following sample indicates:

"Mr. Hume's account of Cromwell is, like almost every character he draws, and transaction he relates, utterly erroneous" (Vol. 3, Ch. 2, p. 115)
"Hume's note at the end of vol. vii. upon the death of Laud, is as uncandid as it is possible to conceive." (Vol. 3, Ch. 2, p. 177)
"That any writer who had the slightest respect for his own character, not merely as an historian but as a man, should have written thus is truly astonishing." (Vol. 3, Ch. 3, p. 209)

"After all this, the candour of Hume, I doubt, cannot longer be defended, any more than that of the monarch whose cause he undertook. But, possibly, the reader may conceive that he has afforded to Charles a defence of an unexpected nature. For if an historian can be vindicated for sitting down coolly to misrepresent facts, through so many volumes, in defence of that misguided prince, we cannot condemn the infatuated individual himself." (Vol. 3, Ch. 3, p. 217)

"As Hume's own marks are still in the copy of Herbert's *Mem.* [i.e., Thomas Herbert, *Memoirs of ... Charles I*] belonging to the Faculty of Advocates, and now on my table, it has been well observed that he could have no excuse for following such a writer as Clement Walker, who is contradicted by every other." (Vol. 3, Ch. 4, p. 335)

"I have already said a good deal about the religion of the age. Hume's account is always extravagant; but I am astonished that even he should have written note G to vol. vii. The story of the six soldiers, taken from Clement Walker, is, considering the authority, worthy of no consideration. The remainder of the note is unsupported altogether." (Vol. 3, Ch. 5, p. 367)

Brodie's *History* was reviewed by Francis Jeffrey in the *Edinburgh Review* and John Stuart Mill in the *Quarterly Review*; selections from both of these appear later in this collection. Both reviews were somewhat mixed, criticising his style but commending his decisive refutation of Hume. Jeffrey closes his review as follows:

> In concluding, we have to thank Mr. Brodie for a great deal of information and sound doctrine – but we cannot part with him without a word of advice. His book has been too hastily published – and must, in fact, be entirely new cast in another edition. It contains a great deal of needless repetition – and, in spite of this, the facts and views that bear upon the same topics are frequently scattered in very distant passages, and divided between text and notes in a very unskilful and perplexing manner. ...
> When he is at the work of revisal, it might not be amiss if he were to revise some of his opinions. He is too bitter and too indiscriminate a disputant, – believes every thing against the royalists, and will find no fault in their opponents.... [*Edinburgh Review*, March 1824, Vol. 40, pp. 92–146]

Mill concludes his review as follows:

> From what we have said, it will readily be understood, that his [i.e., Brodie's] principal merits are diligence, accuracy, and perseverance. He displays, too, considerable skill in evolving the facts from a number of scattered, and seemingly unconnected, articles of circumstantial evidence. In the higher qualities of an historian, in acquaintance with the great principles of

legislative philosophy, and in that comprehensiveness of intellect, which traces up effects to their causes, and teaches the reader to take in by a *coup d'œil* the mutual connexion of all the great events of the age, Mr. Brodie has not evinced any extraordinary degree of excellence. His style, though not strikingly deficient, has no peculiar merit. He has produced, nevertheless, one of the most important historical works of which modern English literature has to boast.... [*Westminster Review*, October 1824, Vol. 2, pp. 346–402]

William Smyth, in his *Lectures on Modern History* (excerpted later in this collection), writes of Brodie's work that "it appears to me for ever to have damaged, and most materially damaged, the character of Mr. Hume as an accurate historian."

The following is from the 1866 and final edition of Brodie's *History*. Most of Chapter 2 of the introductory volume appears here. I have excluded a 20–page discussion of Edward Coke that appears at the outset, and, in the interest of space, also excluded Brodie's frequent and often lengthy footnotes.

PREFACE
TO
THE NEW EDITION.

It is now many years since I published my History of the British Empire, and often since then I have been urged to produce a new edition; but other avocations so occupied me that I was obliged to delay it for a season, though I never renounced the idea.

During that time – induced by the remarks of some whose sentiments on various subjects differed from my own – I have subjected my work to the most searching scrutiny, and carefully perused my authorities. I have endeavoured as far as possible to correct my errors, making alterations and additions wherever by so doing I considered I could throw more light on any subject. What is the value of History but to present truth? Dr. Robertson the great Historian used to say, that he considered himself on oath in every statement he made; this was a just view, and such as no one who undertakes history should lose sight of.

This work was formerly entitled 'A History of the British Empire;' but in the present edition I have adopted a title which explains more definitely the scope of my book.

PREFACE
TO
THE FIRST EDITION.

From the celebrity of Mr. Hume's Work, it may be thought to have been equally presumptuous and hopeless to enter the field which he is supposed to have so fully preoccupied. The portion of British History, however, embraced by the following volumes is so important – the picture there presented so different from the one drawn by that elegant writer, that, if it shall be found to be sufficiently supported by authority, I flatter myself that I shall be absolved from the charge of either presumption or rashness.

For the task of an historian, Mr. Hume was in many respects most eminently qualified; but, having embarked in his undertaking with a predisposition unfavourable to a calm inquiry after truth, and being impatient of that unwearied research which, never satisfied while any source of information remains unexplored, or probability not duly weighed, with unremitting industry sifts and collates authorities, he allowed his narrative to be directed by his predilections, and overlooked the materials from which it ought to have been constructed. Many documents of essential consequence have, since his time, enriched the public stock; but it may appear, from the following pages, that he either did not avail himself or make the proper use of those open to his inspection. From the short period, indeed, devoted by him to that portion of British History, I conceive it to have been morally impossible for him to have become master of the necessary materials.

The work which I now submit to the public has occupied my leisure hours for many years; and though, to my regret, I perceive that in some respects, particularly in certain expressions which had escaped me, it might still be improved, I trust that it will be found deficient neither in research nor accuracy. Not contented with merely glancing through or dipping into the numerous publications referred to, I have, by a collation of the various parts, endeavoured to ascertain the truth. The manuscripts relative to my subject – whether in the Advocates' Library at Edinburgh, the British Museum, the Archbishop of Canterbury's Library at Lambeth, (and here I must acknowledge my obligations to Mr. Todd for his kind attention,) or the Bodleian Library – I have carefully examined. From a manuscript copy of Baillie's Letters shown to me by my valuable friend, Dr. M'CRIE, I have, to illustrate my text, extracted some passages which the Editors have omitted to publish.

As it is impossible to understand events without a thorough knowledge of all the circumstances out of which they emerged, and as Mr. Hume's view of the government, and of public opinion – on which is founded his defence of the unfortunate Charles I. and his minister Strafford – appears to me altogether erroneous, I have devoted a whole volume to introduction. From the variety and importance of the matter which it contains, I believe that, as it was not the least difficult part of my undertaking, that volume will be regarded as not the least valuable. On religion – a subject on which the celebrated historian alluded to seems to me no less unhappy than in his ideas of the government – I have been particularly copious. Endeavouring to keep steadily in view the principles of toleration, I have yet made it my study to present such a faithful picture of the sentiments of the times as may enable the reader to form a just estimate of transactions which flowed from a more contracted policy. In recording civil events, it has ever been my object to abstain from all unnecessary indulgence in abstract speculations, and to appreciate men and things, in relation to the state of the government, of society, and of public opinion, as the only standard by which they ought to be tried.

CHAPTER II.

CONTAINING A PARTICULAR ACCOUNT OF THE VARIOUS INSTITUTIONS AND USAGES UNDER THE TUDORS AND THEIR PREDECESSORS, WHICH EITHER WERE PREJUDICIAL TO FREEDOM, OR ARE SUPPOSED TO HAVE BEEN SO; TOGETHER WITH AN EXAMINATION OF MR. HUME'S STATEMENTS IN HIS THIRD APPENDIX, UPON WHICH HE CONCLUDES THAT THE ENGLISH GOVERNMENT UNDER ELIZABETH 'BORE SOME RESEMBLANCE TO THAT OF TURKEY.'

The various institutions and usages under the Tudors and their predecessors, which were, at a subsequent period, abolished or discontinued, have been so little understood, or so generally misconceived, that, without presenting a particular account of them, and examining the statements of Mr. Hume – which are remarkably plausible, and have made a deep impression on the public mind – we should in vain attempt to convey a correct idea of the views of parties during the stormy period we have selected as the subject of our work; and the discussion of such topics here will save us from the necessity of interrupting the narrative with explanations.

Court of Star-Chamber. The Court of Star-Chamber, as holding a Conspicuous rank amongst arbitrary institutions, demands our earliest attention.

Anterior to the time of the Tudors, there does not occur, either in any publication or record, so much as the mention of any court called the Court of Star-Chamber: and the advocates for its antiquity are obliged to admit that the few instances referred to by them, in Proof of its antiquity, passed under the council, as it was then called, or, as we should now denominate it, the privy council. ...

Mr. Hume gives an account of this court in the following words: –

'One of the most ancient and most established instruments of power was the Court of Star-Chamber, which possessed an unlimited discretionary authority of fining, imprisoning, and inflicting corporal punishment, and whose jurisdiction extended to all sorts of offences, contempts, and disorders, that lay not within the reach of the common law. The members of this court consisted of the privy council and the judges – men who, all of them, enjoyed their offices during pleasure; and when the prince himself was present, he was sole judge, and all the others interposed only with their advice. There needed but this one court in any government to put an end to all regular, legal, and exact plans of liberty; for who durst set himself in opposition to the Crown and ministry, or aspire to the character of being a patron of freedom, while exposed to so arbitrary a jurisdiction? I much question whether any of the absolute monarchies in Europe contain at present so illegal and despotic a tribunal.'

The erroneousness of this view, in regard to the antiquity and power of the court, must be sufficiently clear from what we have already said upon the subject; but we may remark, in respect to its constitution – first, that it is not correct to say that the judges of the land, who were entitled to sit there, held their offices during pleasure, as it was reserved for Charles I., in whose vindication the learned historian so eagerly makes the statements, to alter the patents of the judges from *quamdiu se bene gesserint* (during good behaviour), to *durante bene placito* (during pleasure). We shall have occasion to give instances of integrity in Elizabeth's judges in opposition to the court, which cast a deeper stain upon the reign of Charles I.; secondly, that there never occurred an instance of any king arrogating a right to exercise the judicial function in this court, till James I., with the pedantic pretensions peculiar to him, embraced an opportunity to exhibit there his Solomon-like powers; and even he never attempted it a second time. In the next place, it is extraordinary indeed to find this learned author assuming it as an incontrovertible point, that such a court necessarily put an end to all regular legal and exact plans of liberty, when, within a few years of the period he is now treating of, the plans of liberty adopted by parliament proved fatal to the prince. The true answer to his question – 'Who durst set himself in opposition to the Crown and ministry, or aspire to the character of being a patron of freedom, while exposed to so arbitrary a jurisdiction?' – is, Elliot, Hampden, and the rest who did it. When this part of Mr. Hume's work is compared with that where he represents Charles I. as in so miserable a plight, from the encroachments of parliament on his prerogative, one would be apt to conclude that the powers of the Court of Star-Chamber had either ceased or been abridged, whereas they were vastly extended, and the court had entirely lost the very decency and appearance of justice which had characterised it under the Tudors. 'The slavish speech of whispering,' says even Hudson, 'was not heard to come from the noble spirit of those times, in that honourable presence, and not familiarly introduced there, till a great man of the common law, and otherwise a worthy justice, forgot his place of session, and brought it in this place too much in use.' 'The slavish punishment of whipping,' says another writer, 'was not heard to come from the noble spirits in those times sitting in that honourable presence.' (This is not exactly correct, but nearly so).

'When once this court began to swell big, and was delighted with blood, which sprung out of the ears and shoulders of the punished, and nothing would satisfy the revenge of some clergymen but crept ears, slit noses, branded faces, whipt backs, gag'd mouths, and withal to be thrown into dungeons, and some to be banished, not only from their native country to remote islands, but, by order of that court, to be separated from wife and children, who were by their order not permitted to come near the prisons where their husbands lay in misery; then began the English nation to lay to heart the slavish condition they were like to come to if this court continued its greatness.'

But it is not easy to conceive what Mr. Hume meant by questioning whether any of the absolute European monarchies in his time contained so despotic a tribunal. Had he never heard of the Inquisition? Was he a stranger to the existence of the Bastile, and to the very issuing of *lettres de cachet* to immure within its dungeons, without a hope either of trial or reprieve, all who were obnoxious, not only to the executive, but even to the mistresses and minions of the court? Nay, had he never heard that those *lettres de cachet* were notoriously sold by the minions or mistresses of the court, in order that the purchasers might gratify revenge, or accomplish some sinister object by oppression? The very best French institution was worse than the Court of Star-Chamber; for the aeneral excellency of the English institutions operated as a check upon this, where all proceedings were public, while in France the judgment-seats were sold, and every tribunal held out, by its example, an encouragement to an arbitrary course in all the rest.

Court of High Commission. The next subject that demands attention is the Court of High Commission, which was founded upon a clause of the Act that restored the supremacy to the Crown, in the 1st of Elizabeth. The words are these:

'The queen and her successors shall have power, by their letters patents under the great seal, to assign, name, and authorise, when and as often as they shall think meet and convenient, and for as long time as they shall please, persons, being natural-born subjects, to exercise, use, occupy, and execute, under her and them, all manner of jurisdiction, privileges, and pre-eminences, in anywise touching or concerning any spiritual or ecclesiastical jurisdiction within the realms of England and Ireland, and to visit, reform, redress, order, correct, and amend all such errors, heresies, schisms, abuses, contempts, offences, and enormities whatsoever, *which, by any manner, spiritual or ecclesiastical power, authority, or jurisdiction, can or may lawfully be reformed, ordered, redressed, corrected, restrained, or amended:* Provided that they have no power to determine anything to be heresy but what has been adjudged to be so by the authority of the canonical scripture, or by the first four general councils, or any of them; or by any other general council, wherein the same was declared heresy by the express and plain words of canonical scripture; or such as shall hereafter be declared to be heresy by the high court of parliament, with the assent of the clergy in convocation.'

This statute confers no power whatever to fine, imprison, or inflict corporal punishment; and when the court transgressed its limits, the remedy was always in the power of the injured, by applying to the ordinary courts for a prohibition. The real object was to correct the heresies of the clergy by suspension and deprivation; and surely, if there be a national establishment, all that enjoy functions under it ought to conform to its rules. Were it otherwise, the office might be converted to a very different purpose. And here it may be remarked, that the numerous suspensions and deprivations in this reign (their number, by the way, may be fairly doubted) afford no ground for charging the government with tyranny, since the doctrine and conduct of the ecclesiastics were irreconcilable to the establishment under which they accepted of livings. At this day the same consequences would follow. Various commissions were issued by this princess; and in 1584 she granted one to forty-four individuals, by which she empowers them to enquire into all misdemeanors, not only by the oath of twelve men, and by witnesses, *but by all other means and ways they can devise.* Mr. Hume, following Mr. Neal, says that this included the rack, torture, inquisition, imprisonment; but, besides that the rack never was attempted, the other clauses distinctly show that it never was contemplated. The very next clause distinctly appoints them to punish all who obstinately absent themselves from church, &c., by censure, or any other *lawful* ways and means, and to levy the penalties according to the forms prescribed by the Act of Uniformity. The third clause authorises them to visit and reform heresies, &c., which may *lawfully be reformed or restrained by censures ecclesiastical, deprivation, or otherwise, according to the power and authority limited and appointed by the laws, ordinances, and statutes of the realm.* The fifth clause empowers them to punish 'incest, adulteries, and all grievous offences punishable by the ecclesiastical laws, according to the tenour of the laws in that behalf, and according to your wisdom, consciences, and discretions; commanding you, or any three of you, to devise all such *lawful* ways and means for the searching out the premises, as by you shall be thought necessary.' Having cleared up this point, we may observe, that the commission was extremely arbitrary in authorising the oath *ex officio*, by which the accused was bound to answer interrogatories against himself, and in empowering the commissioners to fine and imprison. Of its illegality the queen and commissioners were so fully aware, that, as we learn from Sir Edward Coke, the commission was not, as it ought to have been, enrolled in chancery, lest it should have been questioned. Besides, though fines were *imposed*, not one was *levied* in Elizabeth's time by any judicial process out of the exchequer; 'nor any subject, in his body, lands, or goods, charged therewith.'

Many arbitrary acts were committed by the commissioners; but though Mr. Neal is pleased in one place to say that the privilege of prohibition from Westminster Hall was seldom allowed by the commissioners, there does not appear, even from his own writings, to have been an instance of the prohibition having been refused. Indeed, when it came to that, the ordinary courts were bound to support their own jurisdiction, and the judges in that reign afforded many proofs of their readiness to assert the laws. The great cause of so many submitting to injustice and oppression from this court seems to have been their unwillingness to forfeit all hope of ecclesiastical preferment; for they never scrupled to accept of livings under an establishment, which yet they would not allow to be a church. The commissioners used to send pursuivants to ransack houses; but, when an individual defended his rights by killing the officer who attempted to enter his house by virtue of a warrant from the commissioners, the ordinary judges declared that he was not liable to prosecution, and dismissed him from the bar. It was in the time of Charles I. that this court lost all decency, and was no longer under the control of the laws, as the judges, who were governed by Laud, and changed at the pleasure of the king, did not longer vindicate their own jurisdiction.

'The queen,' observes Mr. Hume, 'in a letter to the Archbishop of Canterbury, said expressly, that she was resolved that no man should be suffered to decline, either on the left or on the right hand, *from the direct line limited by authority and by her laws and injunctions.*' But the learned author has not attended to the express words of the letter, which he quotes erroneously and has thus committed a mistake of no small consequence to a thorough knowledge of Elizabeth's government. The letter, which is dated in August 1571, runs thus: – 'Wher we required you, as the metropolitan of our realme, and as the principall person in our commission for causees ecclesiasticall, to have good regard that such uniform ordre in the divyne service and rules of the chirch might be duly kept, *as in the lawes in that behalf is provyded,* and by our injunctions also declared and explaned' (the injunctions were issued in the 1st of her reign by virtue of the Act of Uniformity):

'and that you shuld call unto you for your assistance certen of our bishopps to reform the abuses and disorders of sondry persons, sekyng to make alteration therin. We understandyng that, with the help of the reverend Fathers in God, the Bishops of Wyncester and Ely, and some others, you have well entred into some convenient reformation of thyngs disordred, and that now the said Bishop of Ely is, by our commandment, repayred into his diocess, whereby you shall want his assistance, we myndyng to have a perfect reformation of all abusees attempted to deforme the unyformyty prescribed by owr lawes and injunctions, *and that none shall be suffred to declyne ether on the left or on the right hand from the direct lyne lymitted by authority Of our sayd lawes and injunctions, do earnestly, by our authority royall, will and chardg you, by* all means *lefull, to procede herein as you have begon;'* &c.

Taken as a whole, this letter cannot be considered indicative of an arbitrary character in the government. The queen does not pretend to act by her own authority, but by that which had been committed to her by the legislature; and, however the policy of enforcing uniformity may be arraigned (we shall not repeat what we have said on that point in the preceding chapter), Elizabeth cannot be accused, in this instance, of exceeding the limits prescribed by parliament.

Martial Law. 'But martial law,' says Mr. Hume, 'went beyond even these two' (the Courts of Star-Chamber and High Commission), 'in a prompt, and arbitrary, and violent method of decision. Whenever there was any insurrection or public disorder, the Crown employed martial law, and it was during that time exercised, not only over the soldiers, but over the whole people: anyone might be punished as a rebel, or an alder or abettor of rebellion, whom the provost-marshal, or lieutenant of a county, or their deputies, pleased to suspect.' In opposition to so bold and sweeping an assertion, we shall set the following authorities. Sir Thomas Smith, who held the office of secretary of state under Edward VI., and afterwards under Elizabeth, writes thus upon martial law:

'In warre time, and in the field, the prince hath also absolute power, so that his word is a law; he may put to death, or to other bodily punishment, whome hee shall thinke so to deserue, without processe of lawe or forme of judgment. *This hath beene sometime used within the realme before any open warre in suddaine insurrections and rebellions, but that not allowed of wise and grave men, who, in that their judgement, had consideration of the consequence and example, as much as of the present necessity, especially when, by anie meanes, the punishment might have been done by order of lawe.* This absolute power is called martiall law, and euer was, and necessarily must be, used in all camps and hosts of men, where the time nor place doe suffer the tarriance of pleading and processe be it neuer so short, and the important necessitie requireth speedie execution, that with more awe, the souldier might be kept in more straight obedience, without which neuer captain can doe any thing vaileable in the warres.'

'If a lieutenant, or other that hath commission of Marshall authority,' says Sir Edward Coke, 'in time of peace, hang or otherwise execute any man by colour of Marshall law, *this is murder,* for this is against magna charta, cap. 29, and is done with such power and strength as the party cannot defend himself; and here the law implieth malice' *(vide* Pasch. xiv. c. 3, in Scacario, the Abbot of Ramsey's case). Thom. Countee de Lancaster being taken in an open insurrection, was by a judgment of marshall law put to death, in anno 14 Ed. IV. This was adjudged to be unlawful, '*eò quòd non fuit arrainiatus, seu ad responsionem positus tempore pacis, eò quòd cancellaria, et aliæ curiæ regis fuerunt tunc apertæ, in quibus lex fiebat unicuique, prout fieri consuevit, quòd contra cartam de libertatibus cum dictum Thomas fuit unus parium et magnatum regni non imprisonetur, &c. Nec dictus rex super eum ibit, nec super eum mittet, nisi per legale judicium parium suorum, &c., tamen tempore pacis absque arraniamento, seu responsione, seu legali, judicio parium suorum, &c., adjudicatus est morti.*'

In the preceding chapter, a view has been taken of the state of society, and it has been shown that the higher and even the middling classes, instead of deprecating certain commissions of martial law, eagerly desired them, the aristocracy conceiving that they had no cause to dread those commissions when the execution was left to themselves, who arrayed the military. The insurgents could only be put down by force; and I have not met with evidence of any executions by martial law of those taken with arms in their hands, while the legal authorities held that the commission was so far from warranting a recourse to martial law, except in the case of actual necessity, that the act would have been murder in the agents. Proclamations, containing threats of punishment against law, were frequently made; but they were only used *in terrorem*, without the slightest intention of being carried into effect; and we may conclude that, as it was perfectly understood, the commission of martial law would not justify any illegal act, so the object was the same as in the case of proclamations – to inspire terror. The mere commissions, therefore, and Mr. Hume refers only to them, prove nothing.

Mr. Hume proceeds thus: 'Lord Bacon says that the trial at common law granted to the Earl of Essex and his fellow-conspirators was a favour, for that the case would have borne and required the severity of martial law.' The authority of Bacon's name demands attention, though the great philosopher was ever ready to prostitute his talents and his pen to any state purpose which promised to advance his own fortune; but what says he of the very production from which Mr. Hume draws his statement? – that it was written at the express desire of the queen, and repeatedly perused and altered both by her and her council. 'Myself,' says he, 'indeed, gave only words and form of style in pursuing their directions.' In order to understand the meaning of this state paper (for it was nothing else), entitled 'The Declaration of the Practices and Treasons of Robert Earl of Essex,' it is proper to remark that Essex was a great favourite with the people, who (after that nobleman had paid the mulct of his offences, apparently the offspring rather of a disordered mind than of any purpose to overturn the government, and yet such as no government could overlook) were so enraged at his fate, that it was deemed necessary to quiet them by this state paper. But, though it be said in the outset that the case would have borne and required the severity of martial law, that point is barely touched, not dwelt on, and the production must be considered an homage to public opinion to which the monarch would not have descended, had she not felt the influence of the popular voice. Surely, however, a state paper published with a view to compose the public mind, and to impress the idea of her majesty's clemency as well as of the greatness of the insurrection, cannot be regarded as a proof either of the powers really exercised or arrogated by the sovereign; nor ought the historian to have quoted Bacon as his authority, without mentioning that he had virtually disclaimed the publication. Elizabeth's conduct in regard to the unfortunate Essex, on a former occasion, sufficiently bespeaks her respect for the laws and her solicitude for popularity. She had resolved to bring that nobleman to trial, but was dissuaded by Bacon, who told her that, as the earl was well spoken, and possessed 'the eloquence of accident – the pity and benevolence of his hearers' – it would not be for her honour to bring his case into public question.

'We have seen instances,' continues Mr. Hume, 'of its' (martial law) 'being employed by Queen Mary in defence of orthodoxy.' Now, in the first place, Mary's reign, as we have already observed, ought never to be cited in illustration of the ancient government of England. In the second place, though it be true that a proclamation was issued against books of heresy, treason, and sedition, wherein it is declared that whosoever had any of these books, and did not presently burn them without reading them or showing them to any other person, should be esteemed rebels, and without any further delay be executed by martial law, yet it does not appear ever to have been acted upon, or even to have been followed by any commission of martial law. Besides that, as we have already seen, upon the highest authority, proclamations with illegal penalties were often issued without any view to their being carried into effect; the proclamation, unaccompanied with such a commission, was innocuous, since no person was authorised to act upon it.

The proclamation was issued on the 6th of June 1558, only a few months before her death, as she died on the 17th of November following; and we may remark, in passing, that it is strange Mr. Hume has stated the fact under the head of 'Transactions' in the year 1555. Bad as Mary's government was, it never arrived at the stage of despotism ascribed to it by this historian; and as it became worse towards the close of her reign, so the people indicated by many circumstances that they could not have endured it much longer.

'There remains a letter,' proceeds Mr. Hume, 'of Queen Elizabeth's to the Earl of Sussex, after the suppression of the northern rebellion, in which she sharply reproves him because she had not heard of his having executed any criminals by martial law; though it is probable that near eight hundred persons suffered one way or another on account of that slight insurrection.' Now, besides that there appears to be a great mistake in regard to the number that suffered, it may be remarked, with all deference to this accomplished writer, that the very fact of criminals not having been executed by martial law in this case, is a striking proof of the general feelings and understanding of the age; for the northern rebellion was not by any means a slight insurrection, even according to Mr. Hume's account of it in the proper place. Some of the chief nobility were concerned in the conspiracy; foreign powers encouraged and assisted it; and it was only prevented from being most formidable by a discovery of their designs having obliged the rebels to take the field too soon. As it was, however, the insurgents, regularly trained and headed by the Earls of Northumberland and Westmoreland, were four thousand foot and sixteen hundred horse strong – a considerable army for the time; and, independent of an expected supply of troops and arms from the Duke of Alva, governor of the Low Countries, they confidently anticipated a junction with all the Catholics in England – an event no less dreaded by the Protestant party than hoped for by their enemies. Indeed, the activity of government prevented another rising in Suffolk. The leaders issued proclamations in a regular form, and everything bore the appearance of a terrible convulsion. Dismay prevailed amongst Protestants, who had so lately escaped from the cruel tyranny of Mary; and, if we may draw an inference from their general complaints of her Majesty's ill-judged clemency to Catholics, they burned with a fury towards the insurgents at least equal to her own. A fact must always be taken alone with all its circumstances; and whoever weighs all these matters, will cease to regard this as indicating that arbitrary character in the government which has been ascribed to it.

But the kings of England,' continues Mr. Hume, 'did not always limit the exercise of this law to times of civil war and disorder. In 1552, when there was no rebellion or insurrection, King Edward granted a commission of martial law, and empowered the commissioners to execute it, as should be thought by their discretions most necessary.' In order to understand the object and cause of this commission, the reader must recall to his remembrance the state of the country at the time. The lower classes, reduced, by the chance in manners as well as by the Reformation, to beggary, and detesting the nobility and gentry as the authors of their misery, were almost in a continual state of insurrection during Edward's reign; and, as the aristocracy were threatened by the insur-

gents, so they ardently desired sanguinary measures against that unhappy class
– a desire in which most who profited by the new system appear to have
concurred. On the other hand, the prince, or rather protector, was so far from
acting out of any arbitrary spirit, that he pitied the poor, and endeavoured to
alleviate their misery by executing the laws for preserving the old state of
things. The protector's lenity, by the hostility it excited against him amongst
the higher classes, proved the main cause of his ruin – a symptom of weakness
rather than of exorbitant power in the executive. But, after his removal, the fury
of the aristocracy against the tumultuous being no longer restrained, that
commission, which Mr. Hume has referred to, was procured from the Throne;
and, as the very class who solicited were allowed to execute it, they had no
apprehensions of their own rights being affected by such a grant. It is inconceivable, however, upon what principle the learned historian should have said
that there was no insurrection at that time, for Strype, his own authority,
besides, in various parts of his work, describing the country as subject to the
most dreadful commotions during this reign, thus expresses himself in the
very passage on which the historian founds his statement: – 'Popular disturbances and tumults seemed now to be very frequent; and the common people,
uneasy under the present juncture, which occasioned, surely, that severe
commission which was given out this month of March to John, Earl of Bedford
– &c., to put in execution all such martial laws as should be thought necessary
to be executed, and instructions were also given in nine distinct articles.' The
commission may be pronounced cruel and impolitic; but it argued anything
rather than power in the prince; and there is no evidence of its having been
acted upon.

'Queen Elizabeth, too,' says Mr. Hume,

'was not sparing in the use of this (martial) law. In 1573, one Peter Burchet,
a Puritan, being persuaded that it was meritorious to kill such as opposed
the truth of the gospel, ran into the street, and wounded Hawkins, the
famous sea-captain, whom he took for Hatton, the queen's favourite. The
queen was so incensed, that she ordered him to be punished instantly by
martial law; but, upon the remonstrance of some prudent counsellors, who
told her that this law was *usually* confined to turbulent times, she recalled
her order, and delivered over Burchet to the common law.'

Of the two authorities referred to by Mr. Hume (Strype and Camden), Strype's
account of the matter is the most particular; and, in illustrating a case of such
importance to the constitutional history of England, we shall make no apology
for giving his words: – 'This wicked principle of murthering for God's sake, the
queen apprehended so much danger in as that of her own life, as well as that
of others of chief rank about her, and so enraged her, that at first she
commanded this murtherer to be immediately executed by martial law; and a

commission for that purpose was drawn up. And this she resolved to do, as her sister Queen Mary had done, in that severe reign, towards Wyat' – it must have been towards one of Wyat's followers, if towards any, for he was himself regularly tried –

'especially having heard it by report of the Earl of Leicester, and he from the admiral. Yet not with any their approbation of such rigorous doings. So the queen in her great closet, at service therein, gave order to Mr. Secretary to bring to her the commission for execution of this man by martial law, to be signed by her after dinner. But the Earl of Sussex, Lord Chamberlain, and the Lord Admiral were much against it; and the Lord Treasurer was not then at court, whose only advice was then wanted, to prevent it. The earl, therefore, even while he was at dinner, wrote to him, it being the 28th of October, "first praying God to put it into the queen's heart to do the best, and then acquainting him with the particulars: as that the Lord Admiral was greatly grieved with the speech that he should devise it, when as he was directly against it; that, indeed, he had told my lord of Leicester of the execution done in London, in the rebellion of Wyat, but he never told it to the queen; that the Earl of Arundel was also very vehement against it in speech to him (the Lord Chamberlain). He added, that the queen asked for the Lord Treasurer, and seemed to look for his being at court, because it was holy-day." At length, by the counsel, as it seems, of the Lord Treasurer, the queen set aside that purpose of hers of Burchet's speedy execution after that manner.'

Of Wyat's adherents, fifty are said to have been executed in London, and twenty-two elsewhere; but these appear to have been regularly arraigned and condemned. Wyat was taken on the 7th of February, and the execution took place on the 14th; and had it been otherwise, the matter must have been too notorious to have been unknown either to Elizabeth, who was confined on suspicion of having been engaged in the conspiracy, or to anyone else, and would have been particularly mentioned by historians. There must have been only one execution, therefore, by martial law, not executions; indeed, it is execution which is mentioned. If any such execution really occurred, the probability is that it was one of Bret's soldiers, who, having been sent against the insurgents, went over with their leader to the opposite party. Whoever he was, he was a man of no note, as all such were regularly condemned. If any case could have justified a resort to martial law upon the captives, it was Wyat's, for the insurrection was at one time most formidable. He expected, and the other party apprehended, that the Londoners would join him; and, had he not been too irresolute and feeble-minded for such an enterprise, it might have been attended with a different result.

Camden's account of Elizabeth's intention towards Burchet is this: – 'The queen was so extraordinarily incensed at Burchet's assassinating Hawkins, who was in great favour, that she commanded that the man should be presently executed by martial or camp law, till she was informed by some prudent persons that martial or camp law was not to be used but in camps, and in turbulent times; but that at home, and in times of peace, the proceedings must be carried on in the way of a judiciary process.'

It is unnecessary to observe, in regard to that case, that it is so far from supporting the statement of Mr. Hume, that it does exactly the reverse. Had martial law been common, could it ever have happened that one solitary instance, and that doubtful too, which is said to have occurred in the hour of a great rebellion carried into the very capital, afforded the only pretext for the queen's intended proceeding? When is it, too, that courtiers so strenuously oppose an arbitrary purpose in the sovereign? Only when it is inconsistent with the general spirit of the government.

'But,' proceeds Mr. Hume, 'she' (the queen) 'continued not always so reserved in exerting this authority. There remains a proclamation of hers, in which she orders martial law to be used against all such as import bulls, or even forbidden books and pamphlets, from abroad; and prohibits the questioning of the lieutenants, or their deputies, for their arbitrary punishment of such offenders, *any law or statute to the contrary notwithstanding*.' It has already been said, upon the highest authority, that proclamations were frequently issued, containing a threat of penalties which were not meant to be carried into effect, but were published merely for the purpose of creating a wholesome terror amongst certain classes. Yet, though the proclamation alluded to by the historian was not acted upon, the reader may perhaps be of opinion that, if the fact were as stated by him, the government must have been very arbitrary, and therefore it will be necessary to investigate the matter.

In entering upon this point, we must repeat that a case must always, with a view to understand it, be considered along with all its adjuncts, and never was this more necessary than on the present occasion. Besides the open rebellion in the north, by the Catholic party, during this reign, the Papists were ever engaged in plots and conspiracies against the queen's life and the established government. To encourage these designs, the pope issued a bull, in the early part of the reign, absolving the subject from his allegiance, and instigating him, under the pain of damnation, to dethrone Elizabeth, and proclaim a Catholic prince. The bull, after having been privately circulated, and having occasioned the northern rebellion, was affixed by John Felton to the Bishop of London's gates, and set up at Pont St. Etienne, in Paris, on the same day: the sensation created by it may be imagined from the language of Bishop Jewel, who, in a sermon, characterised it 'as a practice to work much in quietness, sedition, and treason against our blessed government: for it deposed the queen's majesty (whom God long preserve) from her royal seat, and tore the crown from her head; it discharged all her subjects from their true obedience; it armed one side of them against the other; it emboldened them to burn, to spoil, to rob, to kill, to cut one another's throats.' Parliament, justly alarmed by this and other practices of the Romish party, passed acts, making the importation of bulls from Rome, which had been previously punishable with the pains of premunire, high treason; and likewise declaring it to be treasonable to compass, or imagine to depose the queen, or intend her bodily harm, or advisedly to deny her title, or to affirm that she was a heretic, schismatic, illegitimate, &c., or to incite foreigners to invade the kingdom, &c., or to deny the power of parliament to regulate the succession. These statutes were evaded, and therefore it was after-wards made treason to practise, to withdraw the subjects from their obedience to their prince and the established religion, or to be reconciled to the church of Rome. Even this, however, did not frighten Catholics into submission, who, esteeming it a glory to destroy an heretical princess, no sooner failed in one conspiracy than they engaged in another. Of the public feeling, some idea may be formed from the voluntary association into which the peers and commons of parliament, not in their character of legislators, but of noblemen and gentlemen, entered in the year 1584 or 1585, binding themselves by oath to revenge the queen's murder, should the malice of her enemies prove successful. The Babington conspiracy followed, and in 1588, the *annus mirabilis,* as it is called, the Spanish armada threatened general destruction. The invaders expected that the English Catholics would flock to the standard of the Duke of Parma the instant be landed, and, though a few of that body proclaimed their determination to resist the invasion, the Protestants apprehended the event of which their enemies were so confident. While general consternation prevailed, as it was scarcely believed that the kingdom possessed resources to meet so mighty an armament, and the fear of internal commotion increased the alarm; while every preparation testified the greatness of the emergency, and Elizabeth displayed a heroism which must render her memory respectable to the latest ages, the pope issued a bull, declaring her accursed, and deprived her of her crown, and committing the invasion and conquest of the realm to the Catholic king, with power to execute his purpose by sea and land, and to take the crown to himself, or to limit it to such a potentate as should be agreed on by his holiness and him. This bull was followed by a great many copies of an English book, the production of Cardinal Allen, which was printed at Antwerp, and sent into the kingdom even while the armada was daily looked for (and another by the same author was ready for publication), denouncing Elizabeth as a usurper, heretic, and schismatic, as illegitimate, &c., equally unworthy of rule and of life; charging all to join the Duke of Parma, and proclaiming it to be lawful to lay violent hands on the queen. Other works of a similar tendency were published at the same time. At so awful a crisis, when the existence of everything dear to Englishmen was at stake, the importation of bulls from Rome, or of forbidden books, acts of high treason in themselves, assumed the blackest dye, and may fairly be pronounced, in familiar yet expressive language, a beating up for recruits to rebellion, for the purpose of forming a junction with an invading and inveterate enemy. But there was no time left to assemble parliament, that new measures against treason of so audacious a nature might be devised in the usual course; and on such an occasion the executive was justified in adopting, for the common safety, an extraordinary and illegal remedy for the evil. The plea of necessity ought ever to be received with caution; but where it does exist, it is, of course, paramount to all law. It is to the credit of Elizabeth's government, however, that this proclamation, which Mr. Hume has adduced as a proof of the despotism of the times, was merely used *in terrorem*, according to a practice, as has already been seen, sometimes resorted to; and that it was not followed by any commission even verbally authorising the carrying of it into effect. It is worthy of remark, that after the danger was past, parliament, while it gave to the queen the tribute of applause which her conduct had so fairly earned, testified its watchfulness over the public liberty by petitioning for leave to bring in a bill of indemnity for all illegal imprisonments in the season of alarm.

Thus the case which Mr. Hume has represented as the abstract of tyranny, appears, upon examination, in a very different light indeed: and had that eminent writer attended to the date of the proclamation, he could not have fallen into such a mistake; for, in relating the affairs of that memorable period, he says that Elizabeth, 'while she roused the animosity of the nation against popery, treated the partisans of that sect with moderation, and gave not way to an undistinguishing fury against them.' 'She rejected all violent counsels, by which she was urged to seek pretences for dispatching the leaders of that party: she would not even confine any considerable number of them.'

'We have another act of hers' (Elizabeth's), continues the historian, 'still more extraordinary. The streets of London were much infested with idle vagabonds and riotous persons. The lord mayor had endeavoured to repress the disorder; the Star-Chamber had exerted its authority, and inflicted punishment on the rioters; but the queen, finding these remedies ineffectual, revived martial law, and gave Sir Thomas Wilford a commission of provost-martial, granting him authority, and commanding him, upon Signification given by the justices of peace in London or the neighbouring counties, of such offenders worthy to be speedily executed by martial law, to attack and take the same persons, and in the presence of the said justices, according to the justice of martial law, to execute them upon the gallows or gibbet openly, or near to such place where the said rebellious and incorrigible offenders shall be found to have committed the said great offences.' 'I suppose,' observes Mr. Hume, 'it would be difficult to produce an instance of such an act of authority nearer than Muscovy.' The only authority quoted by this writer is the commission itself; but, surely, an insulated state paper is not calculated to afford sufficient information upon so important a subject, since it is impossible to estimate a measure correctly without a thorough knowledge of all the circumstances out of which it emerged, and with which it was accompanied; particularly as proclamations and commissions were sometimes issued *in terrorem*, though it would have been murder in the commissioners to have acted upon them. The state of society, as we have described it in the preceding chapter, was, throughout England, wretched; and London at this time was greatly infested with vagrants, some of them discarded soldiers, others assuming that and various fictitious characters, who, colleaguing with the apprentices, then a powerful as well as a numerous body, excited alarming insurrections. Some years before, the vigilance of the city government had frustrated one great attempt by the apprentices against the foreigners, who were generally hated as engrossing the trade which the people conceived to be their own by birthright. This failure did not curb the licentiousness of that body, who had now acquired such an increase of strength by their junction with the vagrants; and as milder remedies were resorted to in vain, the city magistracy, who about this period evinced a high spirit in support of their privileges, themselves applied to the Throne, through their mayor, for martial law, as the only means of repressing the disorders – a clear proof that they apprehended no danger from such a precedent. Elizabeth, at their request, granted the commission to Wilford; but he, apparently satisfied that it could not warrant the exercise of the illegal power it verbally conferred, patrolled the streets with a band of armed followers, and, having secured five of the ringleaders, carried them before the justices for examination only. The justices committed them for trial; and the offenders, having been regularly arraigned and convicted at Guildhall of high treason, suffered the punishment of their crimes. Most assuredly the learned historian might have discovered an instance of a proceeding much more arbitrary than this, without travelling to a great distance, much less to Muscovy; and he must have been ignorant indeed of the temper of the French government, to which he was so much attached, not to know that such disorders in that country would have immediately provoked the most sanguinary measures.

Offices of High Constable and Earl Marshal. 'The patent of high constable,' says Mr. Hume, 'granted to Earl Rivers, by Edward IV. proves the nature of the office. The powers are unlimited, perpetual, and remain in force during peace as well as during war and rebellion. The parliament in Edward IV.'s reign acknowledged the jurisdiction of the constable and marshal's court to be part of the law of the land.' The accomplished writer has not, in other respects, given a true picture of that age; but in this instance he has outraged the case to a most extravagant degree. The office of high constable was hereditary, and ceased with Edward Duke of Buckingham, beheaded on a charge of treason in the 12th of Henry VIII.; and as the earl marshal was, by some, supposed to have been the constable's deputy, it was questioned whether one could be legally constituted to that office after the other ceased. Earls marshal were, however, subsequently created, and the office was at times put into commission. But the judicial powers of the office extended only to the authority belonging to a Court of Chivalry, and were not permitted to interfere with the administration of justice in anything which regarded the common law.

The steward and marshal of the household had early attempted to extend their very limited jurisdiction, which related to contracts and trespasses within the verge of the court, and repeated statutes repressed the usurpation; but the high constable and marshal had, probably owing to the jealousy which the monarch must have entertained of an hereditary office like the constable's, exercised their powers with moderation till the time of Richard II., when the Commons complained of a late encroachment from that quarter upon the common law; and by the 8th of that king, c. 2, these great officers were ordained to confine themselves within the ancient limits of their offices. This, however, did not repress the evil, and, therefore, by the 13th of the same king, c. 5, it was provided, 'at the grievous complaint of the Commons, that the court of constable and marshal hath encroached, and daily doth encroach contracts, covenants, trespasses, debts, and detinues, and many other actions pleadable at the common law, in great prejudice of the king and of his courts, and to the great grievance and oppression of the people;' that this court should not interfere with anything determinable by the common law; and declared that its duty related exclusively 'to contracts touching deeds of arms and of war out of the realm, and also of things that touch war within the realm, which could not be determined and discussed by the common law,' &c. The law was never altered upon this subject, and it was not till the time of Edward IV. that the people had again reason to complain of the high constable, in consequence of the monstrous patent granted by that prince, in the 7th of his reign, to his father-in-law, Earl Rivers. But whoever calls to mind the state of public affairs at that period, convulsed as the country was with intestine dissension, and enjoying only a respite from a ferocious civil war, will never consider such a patent, when the country was necessarily under a sort of military government, as affording any evidence of the constitutional principles of England, in contradiction to the united force of all other authorities. Sir Edward Coke pronounces it 'a most irregular precedent,' and says that, 'therefore, by no means the same, or the like, is to be drawn into example.' But it is inconceivable how Mr. Hume should have adduced this as a proof of the tyranny of Elizabeth's time, when the office of high constable had so long ceased. Had he consulted any authority whatever – for all authorities agree upon this point – he must at once have been satisfied of the error into which he had fallen. The nature of the constable's and marshal's jurisdiction is thus described by Lambard, whom we quote because we have already seen how far he goes in support of the prerogative, and he dedicated his work to Sir Robert Cecil, then secretary of state: – 'The Court of the Constable or Marshal of England determineth contracts touching deeds of arms out of the realm, and handleth things concerning war within the realm, as combats, blazons, armoury, &c., but it may not deal with battle in appeals, nor, generally, with any other thing that may be tried by the laws of the land.' Crompton, Camden, Cotton, Coke, and others agree with Lambard. As to the Act of Edward VI., which, according to Mr. Hume, acknowledged the constable's and marshal's jurisdiction to be part of the law of the land, it does not appear how such an enactment could affect the present question, unless it had abrogated the statutes of Richard II., which, according to the highest authorities, Coke, Hale, &c., never were annulled; and surely the learned author must have committed some strange mistake in quoting the 7th Edward VI. c. 20, for there is no such chapter, and I have not been able to discover any statute during that reign applicable to the court of constable and Marshall It was during the was erected, which made such grievous encroach-ments upon the privileges of the people that Lord Clarendon pronounces it 'a monstrous, usurped jurisdiction;' and, indeed it was he, then Mr. Hyde, who moved for its abolition, declaring it 'a court newly erected, without colour or shadow of law, which took upon itself to fine and imprison the king's subjects, and to give great damages for matters which the law gave no damages for.'

Imprisonment by Warrant of a Secretary of State, or of the Privy Council.
'There was,' continues Mr. Hume,

'a grievous punishment very generally inflicted in that age without any other authority than the warrant of a secretary of state, or of the privy council, and that was imprisonment in any jail, and during any time that the ministers should think proper. In suspicious times, all the jails were full of prisoners of state, and these unhappy victims of public jealousy were sometimes thrown into dungeons, and loaded with irons, and treated in the most cruel manner, without their being able to obtain any remedy from law. This practice was an indirect way of employing the rack.'

It is very unfortunate that the learned author has not thought proper to adduce some instances of this atrocious proceeding, and of justice having been denied by courts of law; for the English, regarding imprisonment as torture and civil death, were ever jealous of their personal liberty, and had provided many statutes beside *Magna Charta* to secure themselves from that evil. To such a degree did they carry their apprehensions of any encroachment of prerogative against their personal rights in this respect, that after the defeat of the Spanish armada, the Commons, as we have already mentioned, petitioned for leave to bring in a bill of indemnity for the illegal imprisonment of some Catholics on that momentous occasion; and during Elizabeth's time, as well as during that of her predecessors, the judges liberated individuals who had been imprisoned by the express command of the sovereign and council. In the 34th of Elizabeth, certain great men, having been offended at the liberation of some prisoners, procured a command to the judges not to proceed; but that venerable body continued to discharge their duty by setting the prisoners at liberty in the face of this order: and having been desired to specify in 'what cases a person sent to custody by her majesty or her council, some one or two of them, is to be detained in prison, and not to be delivered by her majesty's court or judges,' they gave it as their opinion (which they delivered in writing to the chancellor and treasurer),

> 'that if any person be committed by her majesty's command, from her person, or by order from the council board, or if any one or two of her council commit one for high treason, such persons so in the cases before committed may not be delivered without due trial by the law, and judgment of acquittal had. Nevertheless, the judges may award the queen's writ to bring the bodies of such persons before them, and *if, upon return thereof, the causes of the commitment be certified to the judges as it ought to be,* then the judges in the cases before ought not to deliver him, but to remand the prisoner to the place from whence he came, which cannot conveniently be done unless notice of the cause in generality or else specially be given to the keeper or gaoler that shall have the custody of such a prisoner.'

Thus the power of the queen and her council to imprison at will was denied, for the cause must be certified, as well as be one which it is the object of government to bring to a trial. The opinion is ill expressed, but it would appear that the words 'high treason,' as the cause of commitment, applied to all the cases of custody as well as to the last; and it will be observed that the question put to the judges was not whether the queen and her council could imprison at pleasure, but in what cases the commitment was good; and that they asserted their right to grant a *habeas corpus*, that the cause might be ascertained. The construction put upon the opinion appears to be fully warranted, not only by the case to which it referred, as well as an after case in that reign, but by the use which was made of it in the year 1627; for Coke and Selden quoted it as decisive against the right to commit without assigning the cause, then claimed by the Crown, and the lawyers on the other side did not oppose what was said, while they could not adduce a single precedent in support of the principle for which they had contended.

Had such a power been exercised by Elizabeth, it would have been such a flagrant violation of law as could not be too soon repressed; and submission to it could only have been attributed to the extraordinary situation in which she was placed.

The Uses of Torture. 'But,' says Mr. Hume, 'the rack itself, though not admitted in the ordinary administration of justice, was frequently used, upon any suspicion, by authority of a warrant from a secretary of state.' Torture has at all times been abhorrent to the feelings of Englishmen, and unknown to the laws of that country. Sir John Fortescue, who, as we formerly observed, sat long as chief justice under Henry VI., and was afterwards nominated chancellor, founds his panegyric on the English laws partly upon their being uncontaminated with this horrid practice – a practice which, he justly remarked, ought not to be accounted law, but rather the highway to the devil, but which was yet common in France and other countries where the civil code obtained.' Sir Thomas Smith, who held the office of secretary of state both under Edward VI. and Elizabeth, and who wrote his work with much the same view as Fortescue – to contrast the free government of his native country with that of surrounding states – likewise expresses abhorrence at such a practice, and congratulates England on its being free from it. Harrison, a popular writer of Elizabeth's time, takes the same view. Sir Edward Coke expresses his abhorrence of torture in the strongest terms, declaring that there is no law to warrant it. 'And,' says he, 'the poet, in describing the iniquity of Rhadamanthus, that cruel judge of hell, saith –

Castigatque, auditque dolos, subigitque fateri.

First, he punished before he heard; and when he had heard his denial, he compelled the party accused, by torture, to confess it.' He then shows that this is not only against the law of God, but against magna charta; and proceeds thus: – 'Accordingly, all the said ancient authors are against any pain or torment to be put or inflicted upon the prisoner before attainder, nor after attainder, but according to the judgment; and there is no one opinion in our books or judicial records (that we have seen and remember) for the maintenance of tortures, torments,' &c. 'The trial by rack,' says Blackstone,

'is utterly unknown to the law of England; though once, when the Dukes of Exeter and Suffolk, and other ministers of Henry VI., had laid a design to introduce the civil law into this kingdom as the rule of government, for a beginning thereof they erected a rack for torture, which was called, in derision, the Duke of Exeter's daughter, and still remains in the Tower of London, where it was occasionally used as an engine of state, not of law, more than once in the reign of Queen Elizabeth.'

Nothing can justify a resort to anything so horrid; but the conspiracies of Papists were endless, as well as of the most alarming kind – and men under the influence of fear are generally cruel, while the party who support administration are too apt not to condemn an illegal act which strikes at enemies of whom they live in constant alarm. During Elizabeth's reign, some Catholics, believed to be engaged in the deepest treason, were put to the rack to extort confession; but the circumstance raised such a clamour against the government that, in 1583, Burghley himself wrote and published a vindication of it, in which he states that the Popish party had exaggerated the matter beyond all bounds; that very few had been racked, and these very gently; and that 'none of them had bene put to the racke or torture, no not for the matters of treson, or partnership of treson, or such like, but where it was first known and evidently probable by former detections, confessions, and otherwise, that the party so racked was guylty, and did knowe, and coulde deliver trueth of the things wherewith he was charged; so as it was first assured that no innocent was at any time tormented, and the racke was never used to wring out confessions at adventure upon uncertainties, in which doing it might be possible that an innocent in that case might have bene racked.'

The excuse is a sorry one, but it proves the real feelings of the age; and, though the period of publication was a critical juncture, Elizabeth herself ordered the practice to be forborn. It was again employed after the Revolution, in the time of William III., to extort confession from a state delinquent; yet who will say that it was not at that time as repugnant to the feelings of Englishmen as to their laws?

'Even the council in the marches of Wales was empowered, by their very commission, to make use of torture whenever they thought proper.' Now, with regard to this, it is only necessary to remark, that this commission was issued by Queen Mary, a princess whose reign ought not to be quoted; that, at all events, Wales did not fully enjoy the administration of the English laws, as by 34 Henry VIII. cap. 26, the president and council were empowered to execute justice according to their discretion; and that, such was the state of society in that principality, even in the time of Hudson, who wrote either towards the close of James's reign or in that of Charles, that there was no possibility of obtaining a regular conviction there of any man of a certain rank.

'There cannot be,' continues the historian,

'a stronger proof how lightly the rack was employed than the following story, told by Lord Bacon. We shall give it in his own words: – "The queen was mightily incensed against Hayward on account of a book dedicated to Lord Essex, being a story of the first year of Henry IV., thinking it a seditious prelude to put into the people's heads boldness and faction. She said she had an opinion that there was treason in it, and asked me if I could not find any places in it that might be drawn within the case of treason. Whereunto I answered, For treason, sure, I found none; but for felony, very many. And when her majesty hastily asked me wherein? I told her the author had committed very apparent theft; for he had taken most of the sentences of Cornelius Tacitus, and translated them into English, and put them into his text. And another time, when the queen could not be persuaded that it was his writing whose name was to it, but that it had some more mischievous author, and said, with great indignation, that she would have him racked to produce his author, 'replied, Nay, madam, he is a doctor; never rack his person, but rack his style. Let him have pen, ink, and paper, and help of books, and be enjoined to continue the story where it breaketh off, and I will undertake, by collating the styles, to judge whether he were the author or not." Thus, had it not been for Bacon's humanity, or rather his wit, this author, a man of letters, had been put to the rack for a most innocent performance. His real offence was dedicating a book to that munificent patron of the learned, the Earl of Essex, at a time when that nobleman lay under her majesty's displeasure.'

Essex, once the great favourite of Elizabeth, had fallen into disgrace, and from his popularity had become an object of jealousy. At this juncture, Doctor (afterwards Sir John) Hayward published his 'History of the Early Part of the Reign of Henry IV.,' in which he treats almost exclusively of the misconduct and disposition of Richard II., uttering, on so delicate a point, sentiments bold enough to startle princes, and dedicated the work to Essex, whom he addressed in these words – '*Magnus siquidem es, et presenti judicio et futuri temporis expectatione.*' No wonder that Elizabeth was offended; and, though Mr. Hume has ascribed her resentment solely to the dedication, all contemporary authorities attribute it to the sentiments as well as to the dedication, which was particularly offensive, from the ambitious designs imputed to Essex, and from another work, questioning her title, having been dedicated to the same nobleman. It must be admitted, however, that there is a wide difference between the use and the execution of a violent threat, pronounced in a moment of irritation, and therefore much weight cannot be given to her threat of putting Hayward to the rack. Indeed, it appears that she did not soon drop her resentment; and therefore we cannot admit that her rage was diverted by Bacon's wit.

Mr. Hume further remarks, that 'the queen's menace of trying and punishing Hayward for treason could easily have been executed, let his work have been ever so innocent. While so many terrors hung over the people, no jury durst have acquitted the man, when the court was resolved to have him condemned.' He then makes an observation about witnesses not being confronted with the prisoner; declares that scarcely an instance occurred during all these reigns of the sovereign or the ministers having been disappointed in the issue of a prosecution, and proceeds thus: – 'Timid juries, and judges who held their offices during pleasure, never failed to second all the views of the Crown; and as the practice was anciently common of fining, imprisoning, or otherwise punishing the jurors, merely at the discretion of the court, for finding a verdict contrary to the direction of these dependent judges, it is obvious that juries were then no manner of security to the liberty of the subject.' In this there is some truth mixed up with much gratuitous assumption. In the first place, the queen made no menace of trying Hayward for treason, though she evinced great anxiety to have the case brought within the compass of treason – a fact which of itself goes far to negative all the historian's unqualified account of the state of the government, particularly about the judges, who, by the way, did not, as we have already observed, hold their places during pleasure, but during good behaviour. The juries, too, though occasionally summoned into the Star-Chamber for their verdicts, were not reduced to such a deplorable condition as the historian imagined. But, in the next place, we may observe that, in Elizabeth's time, the judges displayed an integrity which forms a strong contrast with the conduct of the sworn guardians of the law during the two succeeding reigns. Elizabeth's judges put a check upon the proceedings of the High Commission, and, in spite of the interest used to have the individual condemned who killed the pursuivant that attempted to enter his house by virtue of a warrant from the commissioners, they dismissed him from the bar, as having only vindicated the rights of an Englishman. They asserted the privileges of the people in regard to illegal imprisonments; and they declined to sanction, by their opinion, an imposition laid upon merchandise without an Act of Parliament. The following circumstance, too, is in point: – One Bloss had affirmed that King Edward was alive, and that Elizabeth was not only married to the Earl of Leicester, but had borne four children to that nobleman. ministers were eager to chastise him; but having found that there was no statute which authorised his punishment, they instantly set him at liberty.

Impressments. 'The power of pressing both for sea and land service,' continues the historian, 'and obliging any person to accept any office, however mean or unfit for him, was another prerogative totally incompatible with freedom.' Osborne gives the following account of Elizabeth's method of employing this prerogative: – 'In case she found any likely to interrupt her occasions, she did seasonably prevent him by a chargeable employment abroad, or putting him upon some service at home least grateful to the people; contrary to a false maxim since practised with far worse success by such princes as thought it better husbandry to buy off enemies than reward friends.' 'The practice,' says Mr. Hume, 'with which Osborne reproaches the two immediate successors of Elizabeth, proceeded partly from the extreme difficulty of their situation, partly from the greater lenity of their dispositions.' Legally, no one could be sent out of the kingdom against his will; and though every man was obliged, for the public defence, by law, to provide himself with arms according to his quality, he was not, except in a case of invasion, bound to go beyond his own shire. Everything is, however, liable to abuse, people of influence in the state being too apt to overlook oppression which does not touch themselves; and labourers and artificers were pressed for sea as well as land service, and sent out of the kingdom; but no instance, so far as I know, is adduced of individuals of high rank having been impressed under the Tudors, except the famous one of Alderman Read, in the time of Henry VIII., for refusing a benevolence – an act generally condemned as tyrannical. Had such cases occurred, however, under Elizabeth – as the persons must have been men of note to interrupt her occasions – they would doubtless have been handed down to us. With regard to the assertion of Osborne, unvouched by contemporary or any authority, it is little to be regarded. A writer of the present age, of no great ability, like Osborne, who should make a general assertion of what had happened fifty or a hundred years back, would not be entitled to much credit; and, luckily, the accuracy of this author, in regard to Elizabeth's reign, can be brought to the test. In some sentences immediately preceding the passage quoted by Mr. Hume, Osborne says that Elizabeth called parliaments often, and that 'it was not the guise of those times to dissolve them in discontent, but to adjourne them in love.' 'And,' says he, 'it is no less remarkable that, in so long a reign, she was never forced, as I have heard, to make use of her negative power, but had still such a party in the House of Lords as were able to save her from that trouble.' Now, it may be observed that this alleged good correspondence with her parliaments is not altogether consentaneous to the idea of her having sent upon expensive employments abroad leading men from whom she dreaded opposition; but the statement is incorrect, for on one occasion she sharply rebuked the Commons on dissolving them. And with regard to her never having been forced to make use of her negative power, it is only necessary to state that, in the 39th of her reign, she refused no less than forty-eight several bills which had passed both houses. But it is indeed extraordinary to find both Osborne and Hume giving so different a character to the government of Elizabeth's two next successors (Osborne's may partly be ascribed to the general indignation excited by the favour shown to Wentworth, afterwards Earl of Strafford, for becoming a creature of the court), since it could not be unknown to them that, in the year 1621, some of the most distinguished members of the Commons were sent abroad by James on the most frivolous pretences, because they discharged their duty in parliament; that, in the year 1623, a citizen of London was by the same monarch ordered to carry a despatch to Ireland, because he refused to comply with a demand of a benevolence, a species of imposition never attempted by Elizabeth; and that Charles I. carried his tyranny in this respect to the most odious height.

The historian has justly observed, that men of inferior rank often abused the power of pressing, as officers frequently exacted money for freeing persons from the service. But, however great the grievance was – and it undoubtedly was an enormous one – it may fairly be questioned whether it ought not rather to be ascribed to the state of society than to the uncontrolled power of the Crown. The only instance given by Mr. Hume proves the readiness of the queen to afford redress to the sufferers the instant the fact reached her ears.

Forced Loans. Forced loans and benevolences are, by Mr. Hume, numbered amongst the arbitrary engines of government possessed by Elizabeth, though that princess never attempted the latter illegal mode of raising money. Forced loans were as directly against the principles of the constitution as any tax without the assent of the legislature. But the evil could not be so easily repressed; since, while the request of a prince, especially in disorderly times, is too apt to degenerate into a demand, the illegality of the measure was sheltered under that pretext; and people in general were not likely to dispute the request to lend small sums for a short time, though they lost the interest upon the ground then current and established by law, that it was unjust to take anything for the use of barren money. The lender, however, could not recover his money by any legal process, and a dishonourable prince might defraud him. Accordingly, this formed one of the charges against Richard II., and parliament *generously* liberated Henry VIII. from repayment of his loans, which, however, might be borrowed at interest. Elizabeth frequently borrowed large sums of money at the enormous rate of 14 per cent.; and as, while she borrowed at such a charge, she appears to have applied only twice (Mr. Hume says *often*) to her subjects, on the most momentous occasions too, and for a short period, for loans in an irregular way, we may safely conclude that, had it been carried farther, the temper of the kingdom could not have submitted to the grievance. The first occasion on which Elizabeth resorted to this mode of raising money was upon the northern rebellion; and it will be perceived from the warrant, a copy of which is to be found in Haynes' Collection, that it is in the form of a request, and that the lenders are assured of repayment within twelve months. The measure was justified on the principle of necessity, as treasure 'now, without parliament, cannot be had but by way of lone,' and it was said that 'the prince is not here the borrower, but God and our naturall cuntry.' The influence of the Crown in the country was at this time very great, in consequence of the number that had obtained a share of the church lands; and the request does not appear to have encountered opposition there amongst the higher ranks, while, says Mr. Bertie, in a letter to Secretary Cecil, 'the perverse in this' (the lower) 'rancke shall be, by shame, constreyned to contribute with their goods.' At the year's end the queen was not, owing to the great expense incurred, in a condition to repay the money, and therefore she thus instructed the collectors

'to use all good meanes, ether by your letters, or by your conference with the partyes that have so lent to us any monny, as for the reasons above sayd, and at our request they will be content to forbeare the demand of their monny from the daye the same is or shall be due, for the space of seven monthes; at which tyme, or before, you may assure to them an undoubted payement, for so we have fully determyned by advise of our counsell to perform the same.'

She concludes by saying that, 'as the lenders had given her cause to think well of them by their readiness to lend, she hoped they would give her reason to increase her good opinion by forbearing their demand according to her request.'

This was the identical loan which gave occasion to the historian for the following statement: – 'There remains a proposal made by Lord Burleigh for levying a general loan on the people, equivalent to a subsidy; a scheme which would have laid the burthen more equally, but which was, in different words, a taxation imposed without consent of parliament.' Now, there is no further proposal in the case than an order for letters of privy seal. Yet the author referred to compares this, *'which he says was proposed without any visible necessity,'* to the imposition of a sixth part of men's goods, attempted by Henry VIII., which, enormous in itself, was not even to be repaid, and to the after exactions of Charles I., who was, says the historian, 'enraged by ill usage from his parliament.' But what sets this in a different light is, that, though the queen succeeded in the counties, where there was less public spirit and greater court influence, she failed in the metropolis; for the citizens refused to lend, and she borrowed 16,000*l.* at the rate of 6 per cent. for six months, or 12 per cent. per annum, granting at the same time a discharge from the statute of usury. At the end of the six months she was unable to refund the money, and prolonged the term of payment for other six months, with 6 per cent. more, besides brokage. It is curious, too, that Mr. Hume elsewhere states the fact of her having borrowed from the city, through the influence of Sir Thomas Gresham, and yet he totally overlooked the date of the loan, as well as the refutation which it carried with it of his own statement; since, if Elizabeth could have borrowed without interest, she would not have paid for the loan at so enormous a rate. The other loan raised by Elizabeth was immediately after the defeat of the Spanish armada, when vigorous preparations were still deemed requisite against any after attempt: then it was that the mayor of London officiously imprisoned some citizens for refusing to lend. But the season was fit for an illegal proceeding. From the extraordinary Charges to which the government had been put, and the treasure still requisite, necessity seemed to justify such a loan; while the victorious triumph over the Spaniards threw into the shade the irregularity of the means employed to compass the object.

Benevolences. 'The demand of benevolences,' says Mr. Hume, 'was another invention of that age for taxing the people. This practice was so little conceived to be irregular, that the Commons in 1585 offered the queen a benevolence, which she very generously refused, as having, at that time, no occasion for money.' By the fundamental principle of the constitution, confirmed by magna charta, &c., money could not at any time be exacted from the people without an Act of the legislature; but Edward IV., taking advantage of the particular state of affairs, two years after the battle of Tewkesbury, and just on the eve of a war with France, when the kingdom had been rent with civil dissension, and his power, upon the reduction of his adversaries, was great, instead of summoning a parliament from which he might ask a benevolence (from time immemorial every legislative grant has passed under that name), directly applied to the people, pretending that he demanded nothing of right, but appealed to their generosity. The people, however, considered his request as approaching to a demand, and resented it so deeply that the device was urged by the Duke of Buckingbam, in his discourse to the citizens at Guildhall, as a proof of the oppression practised by Edward, and as a reason for not permitting respect for that prince's memory to prevent their setting aside the succession of his children. Richard III. himself, with both houses of parliament, by stat. i. c. 2, of that prince, stigmatised it not only as illegal, but as an act of the grossest injustice and oppression. Henry VII., whose situation in regard to the influence of the Crown has been already described, had, in 1492, resolved upon something of the kind, leviable at a certain rate, but the people resisted it till parliament lent its authority to the particular tax proposed. In 1505 he repeated the measure successfully without the interposition of the legislature. His son and successor, instigated, as it is alleged, by Cardinal Wolsey, attempted to levy money without an Act of Parliament; but violent symptoms of rebellion obliged him to recall the warrants and disavow the measure, when he declared that he meant only to appeal to their goodwill, not to ask anything of right. In the year 1546, when the Reformation had so greatly extended the influence of the Crown, Henry a second time resorted to this unlawful way of raising money; but, though he sent Alderman Read to Scotland, and practised severities against others for refusing, it is extraordinary – and the fact has escaped historians – that he was obliged to apply to parliament for its authority to levy the sums proposed. As a statute was passed at his request, the demand ceased to be irregular. Nothing of the kind was ever afterwards attempted by the house of Tudor. Thus, anterior to the dynasty of the Stuarts, there had been only five attempts at benevolence, of which two obtained the authority of parliament, and consequently became legal taxes.

As on this subject of real importance to the political history of the country, Mr. Hume has successfully led public opinion, the reader will deem a strict scrutiny of that celebrated writer's statements no trespass upon his patience. In treating of the benevolence levied by Edward IV., he says – 'But, as the king deemed these sums unequal to the undertaking, he attempted to levy money by way of benevolence, a kind of exaction which, except during the reigns of Henry III. and Richard II., *had not been much practised in former times,* and which, though the consent of the parties was pretended to be gained, could not be deemed entirely voluntary.' In the apparent support of this statement, there is an array of references, whence the natural conclusion is, either that the whole of it was warranted by them, or that he had alluded to the practice of former times, from having himself adduced instances of it in the preceding parts of his history. The conclusion is, in both respects, erroneous. All the writers, with the exception of Fabian – and his language likewise implies it – pronounce, in the most direct and explicit terms, the benevolence by Edward IV. a new device. No instance is in the 'History of Richard II.' insinuated by the author himself against that king; and, though in his 'History of Henry III.,' it is said that 'Henry demanded benevolences, or pretended voluntary contributions, from the nobility and prelates,' the assertion derives little support from the only authority to which he refers, or from any other. Henry's long reign was full of civil dissension, and marked with many violations of public rights which he was obliged to acknowledge, and solemnly to swear never to repeat. He was guilty of extortion, not only from the Jews, who appear to have been thought lawful prey, but from the citizens of London, whose pardon afterwards he was forced to beg with tears in his eyes. It is even alleged, that some of his household were freebooters, and that he shared in the spoil. Having reduced himself to great straits, and disposed of his very plate and jewels, he summoned a parliament; but that assembly, far from relieving his wants, assailed him, as usual, with the most bitter reproaches. Disappointed in his hopes of procuring money from them collectively, he endeavoured to obtain it by applying to them individually, promising each a return of favour, pleading his debts, and even feigning that he meant to make war with France. But his request was received with every mark of contempt and scorn. Turning from the barons, he applied to the ecclesiastics, to whom he used the miserable whine of a mendicant, declaring that it would be greater charity to assist him than the wretch who begs from door to door. 'Asserens majorem eleemosynam fore sibi juvamen conferee pecuniare quam alicui ostiatim mendicanti.' But, with the exception of two abbots, he was not more successful with that body. In this part of Mr. Hume's work, as elsewhere, we encounter bold assertion. He roundly states that this and other practices were uniformly continued by Henry's successors.

In another place, he argues that the legislative enactment which empowered Henry VII. to levy *one* benevolence, indirectly established the general principle in favour of the Crown. But with equal justice may it be said that a statute which imposes one tax for the public exigencies, implies a power in the sovereign to assess the people at discretion. The statute of Richard III. was not abrogated by that in favour of Henry VII., and the existence of the latter fully imports the understanding of both king and people, that money could not be, in this way, any more than by an ordinary subsidy, legally raised without the intervention of parliament. Mr. Hume's view has, however, the merit of originality. Wolsey contended that Henry VIII. was not bound by the statute of Richard III., because it was passed under a usurpation; yet, though a pretext for injustice was eagerly hunted after, the ingenuity of Henry's adviser never started such a plea. Nor were the Stuart family more successful.

'The Commons' (*his own authority calls it the parliament*), 'in 1585,' says Mr. Hume, 'offered Elizabeth a benevolence, which proves that it was little conceived to be irregular.' Now, as the grand, the only objection to what in *common speech* is termed a benevolence, arises from its being a real extortion under the pretext of a voluntary gift (for, were the practice to prevail, individuals would be exposed naked to the influence and indignation of the

Crown), it is utterly impossible to conceive upon what ground a legislative grant, pregnant with no injustice to any particular class of the community, could, under one name, be more repugnant to the theory or spirit of the constitution than under another. Against such a species of benevolence the law of Richard III. neither was, nor could be, directed; for parliament ever continues to be invested with the same power, and its acts must, therefore, be equipollent. But had this author bestowed a little more investigation on the subject, he would have discovered that the word 'benevolence' had, in parliamentary and common language, totally different meanings – importing in the first, an ordinary legislative supply to the Throne; and in the other, a species of extortion at the mere will of the prince. So deeply rooted is the first meaning, that, from time immemorial, the assent of the sovereign to a money bill has been thus expressed in Norman French: 'Le roy, or la roigne, remercie ses loyaulx subjects, accepte lour benevolence, et aussi le veult.' – 'The king, or queen, thanks his or her loyal subjects, and wills it to be so.' Let us now take the passage founded on by Mr. Hume, which is part of a speech by Sir Robert Cecil, in the year 1592 or '93, and we shall probably perceive small cause to infer that there had been any irregular offer of money. A very large supply, according to the opinion of those times, had been moved for; and many contended that it would form a precedent for future grants prejudicial to the nation. Sir R. Cecil, then secretary of state, in order to remove this apprehension, observed that, 'In her Majesty's time, it was not to be feared that this precedent would ever do them harm, for her Majesty would never accept anything that was given unwillingly. Nay, in the *parliament* the 27th of her reign, she refused a benevolence offered her, because she had no need of it, and would not charge her people.' Now, on a strict examination of the journals for the year 1585, nothing of this kind appears; and the only occasion on which she declined an offer of money was in the 9th of her reign, when she remitted the third payment of a subsidy *tendered by bill in ordinary form*, alleging that she had no need of money at that time, and that it was better in her subjects' pockets than her own, though her real motive was to evade a condition of marriage on her part, which the gift imported. To this, then, must we presume that Sir Robert referred; and we do it with the greater confidence, because we are informed by the editor of the 'Journals' that the speech founded on by Mr. Hume was extracted, not from the original Journals of the house, but from an anonymous Journal (taken by some member), which he had in his possession, and it is easy to conceive that an error of a date may have crept into it. But perhaps the word 'benevolence' may still startle the reader, since there may reasonably be supposed a difference betwixt a formal and unvaried response of the sovereign, and the common language of the two houses of parliament. To remove this impression we may observe, that upon a strict investigation of D'Ewes' Journals from beginning to end, we have discovered that the word 'benevolence,' employed to denote a regular legislative grant, occurs not seldomer than twenty times. Nay, in reference to that very subsidy which Cecil was strenuously endeavouring to obtain, and to which his speech related – the word 'benevolence' is used four times, once by the secretary himself. Nor should the double meaning of the word be matter of wonder; for subsidy had also two significations, denoting in one sense a general grant of money in whatever shape; in another, a specific assessment: so that sometimes one subsidy was given, with tenths and fifteenths; at others, two, three, four, and so on. A supply was likewise called a free gift, a free grant, a contribution.

Having cleared up this subject, and displayed upon what a sandy foundation the historian builds, it will be proper to mention, that the two houses of parliament did, in the year 1586, depart from the regular course, by contributing amongst themselves a certain sum for the purpose of assisting her majesty in her wars in the Low Countries. Their object was to aid the sovereign without burthening the inferior classes, who groaned under the load of taxation; and who shall dare to censure this manly act, because they unanimously performed it without the formality of a bill, entertaining no groundless cold-hearted fears of danger from the precedent? Has there ever been, or is there now, any principle, either in the theory or spirit of the constitution, to blast such generosity? And, instead of indulging in absurd deductions against those times, ought we not to lament that the precedent of that assembly has been lost upon their successors? But, lest it should be imagined that Cecil alluded to this contribution, it may be again observed that her majesty thankfully received it. The clergy, in convocation, also granted one, which was not confirmed by Act of Parliament. The resolution of the Commons, in the 4th of Charles I., affords additional proof in support of our statement: – 'That it is the ancient indubitable right of every freeman, that he hath a full and absolute property in his goods and estate; that no tax, tallage, loan, *benevolence,* or other like charge, ought to be commanded or levied by the king or any of his ministers *without common assent by Act of Parliament.*'

The Power to Impose Customs, &c. 'Queen Mary, also,' says Mr. Hume, 'by an order of council, increased the customs in some branches, and her sister imitated the example.' Magna Charta, which merely confirmed the common law, expressly provides against everything of the kind; and so firmly was the principle established, that there does not occur an instance of any imposition on merchandise having passed without being complained of in parliament as a grievance, and being redressed; nor even of any attempt to impose, from the time of Edward III. till the 4th of Queen Mary – a period of nearly two hundred years. The military achievements of Edward III. gave him great influence in such an age, and he availed himself of his popularity to impose new duties on commerce; but parliament never permitted anything of the kind to pass unnoticed, and he, far from pretending to the power of imposing, adopted the readiest way to recover his popularity, by recalling the measure, applying in the regular form for subsidies, and thankfully accepting of them as gifts – thereby directly disclaiming the idea of exacting anything as a right. Queen Mary, who revived a practice which had been so often reprobated and repressed, and so long unattempted, did not arrogate the right of imposing, but evaded the law, which she did not venture avowedly to break. The custom of wools had, in consequence of the improvement in the English manufactures, greatly decayed, as, instead of the raw produce, much woollen cloth had been exported; and the same quantity of wool which, in its raw state, would, owing to later duties, have paid 40s., was, when wrought up, chargeable with 4s. 8d. only. The regulation was calculated to promote English manufactures; but Mary (whose government should never be cited as illustrative of the ancient constitutional principles), alleging that the wool was liable for the duty in whatever shape it was exported, and being then engaged in a war with France, and much in want of money, laid an additional assessment upon the cloth, which, however, did not nearly equalise the duties. She died the next year, and a loud clamour against the imposition was raised by the merchants in the 1st of Elizabeth. That princess assembled the judges to deliberate upon the measure and give their opinion upon its legality; but, though her successors readily obtained both judicial and extra-judicial sanctions to their extortions, it was to the credit of Elizabeth that her judges would not prostitute their office by an opinion in her favour; while all the great lawyers, including Plowden, openly condemned the tax as altogether unconstitutional; nay, Plowden composed an argument against it. She herself did not pretend to any right to alter the customs, but rested her plea entirely on the equity of the thing, arguing that, though it did not fall within the words, it did within the spirit of the laws in regard to wool, and therefore ranked it under the old customs to disguise its illegal origin. With this, possibly, the merchants were satisfied, and parliament, with the nation at large, then occupied with the most important affairs that can engross the attention of any state, and perceiving no disposition to extend the precedent into a right, permitted the illegality of the measure to fall into oblivion. Even in Philip and Mary's reign the right to impose was directly questioned, and the judges decided against the Crown. The town of Southampton obtained an exclusive grant by letters patent to import Malmsey wines, and all others were prohibited under the pain of treble customs – a mere device to raise the duties. But when the matter was tried in the Exchequer, upon an information by the attorney – general against certain merchants, 'two points were,' says Sir Edward Coke, 'resolved by all the judges: 1, That the grant made in restraint of landing of the said wines was a restraint of the liberty of the subject against the laws and statutes of the realm; 2, That the assessment of treble Custom was merely void, and against law: as it appeareth by the report of the Lord Dyer, under his hand, which I have in my custody.' There occurred in that reign, however, another instance of evasion of the law. On the breaking out of the war with France, she prohibited intercourse with that country – a measure that might have been proper in itself, had she not evinced that it proceeded from an improper motive, and then allowed it to those who procured a license to trade at a certain rate of duty on the articles imported. Elizabeth pursued the same course in regard to sweet wines on the war with Spain. The injustice of both queens is sufficiently manifest from these instances; but, independently of the judgment against Mary, and the legal opinions in the next reign, the very subterfuges to which they resorted afford the best evidence of the feelings and understanding of the age on that subject.

Embargoes on Merchandise. 'Embargoes on merchandise,' says Mr. Hume, 'were another engine of royal power by which the English princes were able to extort money from the people. We have seen instances in the reign of Mary. Elizabeth, before her coronation, issued an order to the custom-house, prohibiting the sale of all crimson silks which should be imported till the court were first supplied. She expected, no doubt, a good pennyworth from the merchants while they lay under this restraint.' As the learned historian had alluded to the embargo in the time of Queen Mary, under the head of customs imposed by her, he ought not to have repeated it, as if it had been another engine to extort money; and with regard to the instance in the reign of Elizabeth, it is necessary to do little more than quote the words of the authority to which this elegant writer refers: 'That the coronation,' says Mr. Strype, the only authority referred to, 'might be done with the greater magnificence, the customers of London were appointed to stay all crimson-coloured silk as should arrive within their ports until the queen should first have her choice towards the furniture of her coronation; and to give warning to the lords of the council if any such should arrive there; *but, nevertheless, to keep the matter secret.*' This argues a lamentable meanness in Elizabeth, but does not support the historian's statement. She does not pretend to stop the goods by her prerogative – for, in that case, secrecy would have been impracticable: she evidently trusted to the ingenuity of the customers to invent excuses for detaining the goods, and affords the clearest proof of the illegality and novelty of the measure by sending the injunction 'to keep the matter secret.' Upon the subject of embargoes in general, we shall only observe that the law does not appear to have undergone any material change. There had been no fewer than thirty Acts about opening and shutting the ports. The power entrusted to the sovereign on this head is conceived to be requisite, in order to prevent a greater evil; but it was always held as law, that no dispensation or license contrary to the embargo could be granted for money by the prince. Sir Edward Coke, amongst others, is explicit on this point; and Sir Matthew Hale, who has told us that proclamations with various penalties which neither could be nor were intended to be enforced, were occasionally issued, observes, that

'if it were admitted that in these particular cases of arms, ammunition, victuals, and money such proclamations might be made, and thereby the offenders might be subject to fine and imprisonment, yet it could not be extended to other things, neither ought or might this inhibition be an engine to gain money by licenses; for, if the proclamation had any strength, it was because of the inconvenience of the exportation of those things. If it were not a public inconveniency, it could not be inhibited barely by proclamation; and if it were a public inconveniency, it might not be licensed for private profit. If it might, the strength of the proclamation would consequently cease.'

Power assumed by the Sovereign over Foreign Trade, and over the Persons of Individuals in Preventing them from Travelling without a License. 'The sovereign even assumed a supreme and uncontrouled authority over all foreign trade; and neither allowed any person to enter or depart the kingdom, nor any commodity to be imported or exported, without his consent.' The slightest examination might have satisfied Mr. Hume that his statement was altogether erroneous and unfounded, and that the law in regard to embargoes, and to opening and shutting the ports, differed then very little from what it was in his own time. As to the right of individuals to enter or quit the kingdom, the utmost liberty was allowed at common law, unless the prince laid a positive prohibition; but by the 4th chapter of the 'Constitutions' of Clarendon, ecclesiastics were restrained from going abroad, because, from their attachment to the Romish see, they promoted its usurpation over the liberties of England. And by the time of Edward I. peers were also restrained, because they were the regular counsellors of the Crown; knights, because they were bound to defend the kingdom from invasion; archers and artificers, because they carried the arts out of the kingdom. But by 5th Rich. II. c. 2, matters were so far reversed that great men and notable merchants only were permitted to pass beyond the seas at pleasure. By the 25th of Henry VIII., it was provided that 'no person resident within any of the king's dominions should depart out of any of those dominions, to any visitation, congregation, or assembly for religion.' This was revived for a -limited period by the 1st Eliz. c. 1. The powers granted to the Crown may be imprudent, or impolitic; but where the legislature thinks it necessary to make a provision against any supposed evil, it is, surely, not logical to rank this under the head of prerogative. The prince is bound to execute the laws, though these may not always be consonant to strict principles of policy or general liberty. When the supposed necessity for the act ceases, or more enlarged notions are entertained, an alteration is made upon the law. This accordingly happened on the point we are now discussing, the law of Richard II. prohibiting the people from going abroad having been repealed; but the prerogative was not abridged, nor yet is it, since the prince has always possessed the power of restraining, under severe penalties, any individual from leaving the kingdom, by the writ *Ne exeat regnum.* The principle of the law is, that certain individuals might, on great occasions, injure the state by carrying information abroad; and it is thought better to lodge in the king a power that may be abused to the oppression of an individual, than expose the nation to the hazard of ruin. This branch of the prerogative, however, has long been unexercised; and, even in Elizabeth's time, restraint was rarely used. 'No man could travel,' says Mr. Hume, 'without the consent of the prince. Sir William Evers underwent a severe prosecution because he had presumed to pay a private visit to the King of Scots.' The true answer to this account of the prerogative is the view which we have given of the law. But this case of Evers, when investigated, shows that the government of Elizabeth, in the exercise of powers committed to her by the legislature, was not characterised by rigidness. It happened about the close of that queen's reign, when she had the mortification to discover that her courtiers turned their eyes towards the rising sun. Evers went to Scotland for the purpose of intrigue, and he was detected: yet, while he might legally have been punished for leaving the kingdom without a license, he suffered imprisonment for merely having solemnly denied that he had been at the Scottish court. Whether his confinement was long continued does not appear.

The Species of Ship Money said to have been Imposed by Elizabeth at the Time of the Spanish Invasion. 'There was,' says Mr. Hume, 'a species of ship money imposed at the time of the Spanish invasion. The several ports were required to equip a certain number of vessels at their own charge, and, such was the alacrity of the people for the public defence, that some of them, particularly London, sent double the number demanded of them.' In other words, the seaports, animated, like the rest of the nation, with zeal for the public defence at such a crisis, volunteered ships and men. It does not appear that any compulsive means were attempted, and it cannot be denied that, if ever a case could justify an illegal mode of calling out the resources of the country, it was the one in question, when an invasion, which threatened every thing valuable in existence, was daily apprehended. At such a crisis, such as do not show alacrity in the public defence may be considered concealed enemies. And at that period, as it was ships and men, not money, that were required, so all classes volunteered their services. Surely, therefore, it would be a poor return for that noble spirit which baffled the attempt of the enemy, and preserved for their posterity so many blessings, to cast obloquy upon conduct that ought to endear their memory to us, as if they had sanctioned an illegal tax; or to liken a measure which, though imperiously called for, was yet voluntary, to a proceeding by the prince that arose from a determination to overturn every constitutional principle of government, by raising money without the intervention of the legislature. In 1601, the city of London, on an apprehension of a fresh attempt by the Spaniards, again raised men for the public defence, and fitted out a certain number of galleys – conduct for which they received the royal thanks. It may be imagined that, possibly, the city might not, on the last occasion, have been so forward had it not been for their secret conviction of the overwhelming influence of the Crown; but as they maintained at least the appearance of volunteering, while they, with the rest of the kingdom, knew that any compulsory demand of the kind was unconstitutional, it must be admitted that they reserved their right to resist anything of the kind, whenever they perceived that they could do it with effect. The grand constitutional limits to the prerogative, at least, still remained unaltered in the estimation of all men.

New-Year's Gifts. 'New-year's gifts were expected at that time,' says the historian, 'from the nobility, and from the more considerable gentry.' In support of this statement, he quotes from Strype an account of new-year's gifts to Henry VIII. in the year 1532. But had that very document been examined, it must have satisfied him of his mistake. The value of the whole gifts amounted to 792*l.* 10*s.* 10*d.*, and the number of the granters was thirty-eight, of whom twenty-four were ecclesiastics. Had such gifts been expected from all the nobility, we should have found all their names in the list; yet it contains the names of fourteen laymen only, and of these just seven were peers. The fact is, that new-year's gifts were then in fashion, and that those who depended upon the court, or desired its patronage, embraced that method of testifying respect for their master; while, if they did not always obtain similar presents in return – which, however, appears to have been the case – they expected something, in another way, infinitely more valuable. Accordingly, of the seven commoners whose names as donors appear in this list, one was master of the rolls, and another was 'Hasilwood of the receipt.' But what sets this matter completely at rest, and evinces how readily the historian caught hold of every insulated circumstance which seemed to afford a basis for his theoretical view of the ancient English government, is an original document in the British Museum, being a long roll of vellum signed by Elizabeth in three different places, which contains an exact account not only of all new-year's gifts to the queen, but of those by her, in the eighteenth year of her reign. Those to whom gifts were made were ladies of quality, maids of honour and other ladies, statesmen, noblemen, bishops, and gentlemen, including those of the bedchamber. The presents were in plate, almost all gilt, and the weight of the whole was 5,109½ oz. On the other side of the roll is a list of gifts to the queen, and these are by the identical individuals to whom she had made them. The gifts to the sovereign were in money, and the whole amount was 1,032*l.* 16*s.* 8*d.*, which, I presume, would be about the value of the plate. In short, this mighty affair, from which, amongst other things, Mr. Hume infers that 'the inventions were endless which arbitrary power might employ for extorting money,' turns out to have been a mere reciprocity of politeness and kindness between the monarch and the principal subjects who had access at court; and the latter just appear to have given, on those occasions, the price of what they received, while those mutual favours were calculated to secure for their benefits of a far higher kind.

Power of Dispensing with the Laws. 'The legislative power of parliament,' says Mr. Hume, 'was a mere fallacy, while the sovereign was universally understood to possess a dispensing power, by which all the laws could be invalidated and rendered of no effect. The exercise of this power was also an indirect method practised for erecting monopolies. Where the statutes laid any branch of manufacture under restrictions, the sovereign, by exempting one person from the laws, gave him in effect the monopoly of that commodity. There was no grievance at that time more universally complained of than the frequent dispensing of the penal laws.' We shall first speak of dispensations from the penal laws, which, according to the historian, were so much complained of. One of the powers annexed to the Crown has always been that of pardoning criminals and remitting penalties, while the sovereign is not legally obliged to prosecute in any particular instance. Hence sprang the exercise of another power, which, though illegal, was analogous to the undoubted privileges of the monarch – that of granting dispensations to individuals from the penalties of certain statutes that were supposed to press particularly hard upon them (and, from the number about apparel, for instance, 'some of them fighting with and cuffing one another,' as well as those about uniformity, &c. in religion, such must frequently have been the fact), that they might not be vexed by informers. But one departure from law seldom fails to introduce another. In bad times, those of Henry VII. during the ministry of Empson and Dudley, and of Mary particularly, power to grant dispensations and compound for forfeitures was procured from the Crown by certain persons who, by that authority, oppressed the people. This last, however, was always held to be grossly illegal; and Sir Edward Coke lays it down, that 'all grants of the benefit of any penal law, or of power to dispense with the law, or to compound for the forfeiture, are contrary to the ancient fundamental laws of the realm.' He informs us also, that 'it was one of the articles wherefore the Spencers, in the reign of King Edward II., were sentenced, that they procured the king to make many dispensations.' The understanding of people in Elizabeth's time, and the general practice of government, may be estimated from the following passage in Smith's 'Commonwealth:' –

'The prince useth to dispense with lawes made, whereas equine requireth a moderation to be had, and with paines of transgressing of lawes, where the paine of the lawe is applied only to the prince. But where the forfaite, as in popular actions it chaunceth many times, is part to the prince, the other part to the declarator, detector, or informer, there the prince doth dispense with his part only. Where the criminal action is intended by inquisition (that manner is called with us at the prince's suite), the prince giueth absolution or pardon, yet, with a clause, *modo stet rectus in curia,* that is to say, that no man object against the offender. Whereby, notwithstanding that he hath the prince's pardon, if the person offended will take upon him the accusation (which in our language is called the appeale) in cases where it lieth, the prince's pardon doth not serue the offender.'

With regard to dispensations which laid any particular branch of commerce or manufactures under a restriction, they could not be too much reprehended, and parliament itself had early exerted its powers to prevent so great a grievance. 'In the 50th of Edward III.,' says Coke, 'Richard Lions, a merchant of London, and the Lord Latimer, were severely sentenced in parliament for procuring licenses and dispensations to transport wools.' On the subject of monopolies in general, we shall only observe in passing that they were carried in Elizabeth's time to a monstrous height, and that they were clearly illegal; but that Mr. Hume has not been fortunate in an instance adduced by him to exemplify the effect of dispensations from a law that laid any particular manufacture under restriction. A statute, passed in 1576, prohibited goldsmiths from selling articles under the fineness of twenty-two carats. An individual, however, had, long anterior to the Act, manufactured certain articles of a lower standard; and, as the statute threatened him with ruin, the queen granted him a dispensation for the sale of the particular articles which he had prepared before the passing of the Act, and which are specially described in a schedule annexed to the patent. This was illegal; but not such as could excite any considerable discontent.

Proclamations. 'But, in reality,' says Mr. Hume,

'the Crown possessed the full legislative power by means of proclamations, which might affect any matter even of the greatest importance, and which the Star-Chamber took care to see more rigorously executed than even the laws themselves. The motives for these proclamations were sometimes frivolous and even ridiculous. Queen Elizabeth had taken offence at the smell of woad, and she issued an Act prohibiting any from cultivating that useful plant. She was also pleased to take offence at the long swords and high ruffs then in fashion. She sent about her officers to break every man's sword, and clip every man's ruff – which was beyond a certain dimension. This practice resembles the method employed by the great Czar Peter to make his subjects change their garb.'

This is a very extraordinary statement. The legislature had conferred a certain power upon the Throne in the time of Henry VIII. to issue proclamations, which, to a limited extent, were to have the effect of laws; but the power was withdrawn in the next reign, by the authority that conferred it, and no one ever ascribed to the prerogative, of itself, any right to alter the laws of the land. With regard to the instances referred to by Mr. Hume, they do not warrant his statement. Elizabeth, deeming the smell of woad a nuisance, because she could not herself endure it, interdicted the cultivation of the plant; but parliament complained of the proclamation, and it was instantly recalled. As for the others, they may be supposed too ridiculous to require any remarks, since people might not choose to impugn the illegal exercise of the royal power on such trivial occasions, and yet upon examination the matter will appear in a very different light. It was the practice of that age for people not only to go about with remarkably long swords, and to wear them in a threatening manner, but to carry a species of pocket-pistols called daggs, and to wear besides privy coats or doublets of defence. Thus arrayed, they disturbed the public peace, quarrelling with, and making frays upon, the unarmed. The quiet part of the community complained, and the queen issued proclamations prohibiting the use of privy coats, &c., as well as daggs and similar weapons, which, she well observes, 'in time of peace were only meet for thieves, robbers, and murderers.' She enjoined, at the same time, that the swords should be reduced to a more moderate length, not exceeding a yard and half a quarter – a size supposed to be less formidable to the peaceful – and that they should not be worn in the '*hectoring*' way then in fashion. It must immediately occur to the reader that, had no statute devolved upon the executive the right of correcting such an evil, it belonged to the queen as conservator of the public peace; but parliament had not been so inattentive to the general safety, for it had provided laws against going armed, by which penalties, such as forfeiture of the arms, fine, and imprisonment were imposed upon the guilty. Elizabeth, therefore, proceeded upon powers vested in the Throne by the legislature, and which subsist at this day. The proclamations were founded on statutes which were specially quoted, and were perfectly legal as well as expedient. Sir Edward Coke observes, that such writs might be devised for the better execution of the statutes; and then says emphatically, in speaking of this subject, 'Note, proclamations are of great force when they are grounded upon the laws of the realm.' Nor was it she who sent about officers to measure the swords, but the mayor of London, who, in carrying the proclamations into effect, sent select citizens to the several gates to ascertain whether they were obeyed. Far from censuring this proceeding, we ought to mark it with approbation. – the case of the ruffs is more questionable in law, and luckily also in point of fact. It was the mistake of those times for the legislature to interfere with matters that ought to be left to the regulation of individuals, and many statutes had, from time to time, been devised against excess of apparel, which, it was imagined, tended to impoverish the nation, and draw after it a train of evils. During Elizabeth's reign, parliament did not allow this subject to escape its notice, but passed three laws against that supposed mischief, while several bills were rejected. In conformity with the laws, the queen issued proclamations, in which she threatened to exact the penalties; but as none of the statutes entitled her to meddle with the ruffs, so there appears to be only one authority for the story about them, and that a questionable one – Howes, the continuator of Stow. According to that writer, the ruffs began to be worn exceedingly high, and foreigners ridiculed the fashion as barbarous. To prevent this imputation, as well as the offence to the eye, the queen sent about grave citizens to measure that article of dress, and curb the licentious use of it. If Howes be correct, the acquiescence of the people may easily be accounted for, without even supposing that they connived at such a usurpation Upon their privileges. When the royal proclamation had been issued, the common council applied to the Throne for a mitigation of the laws; and, as this was granted, it is possible that Elizabeth might, at their request, consent to relax the rigour of the statutes, on condition of their restraining the offensive size of ruffs; and that those who were obnoxious to punishment by statute-law for excess of apparel (such only would be likely to wear uncommon ruffs), would be satisfied to suffer in that respect, when they found themselves relieved from the legal penalties in another. But, indeed, this is a point scarcely worth investigation, as it would not be any great proof of slavishness in the people that they were above contesting a trifle of this kind with a beloved monarch, whom they, with the rest of Europe, considered the bulwark of the Protestant cause; and unless it be supposed that the historian could have produced something more important to justify his general statement, few will be inclined to adopt his view of the government in that age.

Stopping the Course of Justice by Particular Warrants. Stopping the course of justice by particular warrants is reckoned by Mr. Hume amongst the abuses of those times, and one of the strongest proofs of arbitrary power: he says also, that parliament, in the 13th of the queen, praised her for not imitating this practice, which was usual amongst her predecessors; but he has scarcely done justice to his authority. In those days, the speaker of the Commons, when presented to the sovereign for his or her approbation, used to make a fulsome oration upon the excellency of the present ruler: high compliments passed on both sides, and abuses of former times were brought forward to form a contrast with the felicity of the present. In the course of his harangue, the speaker, on the occasion alluded to in the 13th of Elizabeth, 'said something in commendation of her majesty, who had given free course to her laws, not sending or requiring the stay of justice as heretofore *sometimes* hath been by her progenitors used. Neither hath she pardoned any, without the advice of such before whom the offenders have been arraigned, and the cause heard.' The historian says that 'the queen, in refraining from the practice, was very laudable, But she was by no means constant in this reserve. There remain in the public records some warrants of hers for exempting particular persons from all lawsuits and prosecutions; and these warrants, she says, she grants from her royal prerogative, which she will not allow to be disputed.'

This abominable practice early attracted the attention of the legislature, and is expressly provided against, not only by magna charta, but by other statutes. Nor were the laws on this head considered a dead letter, as courts of justice had repeatedly adjudged the warrants to be void. Mr. Hume has referred merely to the warrants themselves, which neither show the circumstances out of which they emerged, nor the consequences with which they were attended; and he holds that because the queen in common form declares that she will not allow her command to be disputed, these warrants could not be impugned; but had he consulted Coke's 'Institutes' upon this point, he would have discovered that, not only in early reigns, but in those of Henry VII. and Henry VIII. and even of Elizabeth herself, these warrants had been resolved by the judges to be against law, and the sheriffs had been amerced for not executing the writs. Nay, it is very singular that one of the three warrants referred to by Mr. Hume is also specially referred to by Sir Edward Coke, as having been adjudged void.

Monopolies. The great grievance of Elizabeth's reign was monopolies. When an individual, by applying talent, time, and industry to any particular object, has made a discovery, there seems to be no way so well calculated to remunerate him, without injury to the community, as to grant him the exclusive right to the benefit of the invention for a certain term of years. This principle was early understood; but Elizabeth, availing herself of it, granted exclusive patents for ordinary manufactures, either as gifts to her courtiers, or as a mean of procuring money for the Crown; and the whole nation sensibly felt the effects of such a system, which was not only against the fundamental laws of the realm, but had been often adjudged to be so, even in parliament, as well as in the ordinary courts of justice. In the course of Elizabeth's time, the evil swelled to that magnitude that the people at large bitterly – cried out against it; and though parliament adopted language on the occasion little consonant to the public spirit of that assembly in the former parts of the same reign, the ministers of the Crown, with the queen herself, perceived it to be full time to yield to the public voice. Sir R. Cecil, when he announced to the Commons her majesty's purpose to recal the patents, complained that 'parliament matters were ordinarily talked of in the streets.' 'I have heard myself,' says he, 'being in my coach, these words spoken aloud – "God prosper those that further the overthrow of monopolies. God send the prerogative touch not our liberty." The time was never more apt to make ill interpretation of good meanings. I think these persons would be glad that all sovereignty were converted into popularity.' Mr. Hume has justly remarked that, had the system of monopolies been continued, England would have contained at present as little industry as Morocco or the coast of Barbary; but he ought to have seen, at the same time, that since such a spirit was abroad, it would have required a band of Janizaries to have supported the Throne in such an unconstitutional proceeding. Elizabeth herself politicly pretended to have been misled, and expressed the utmost indignation against the patentees, vowing vengeance upon them for their crimes, and solemnly protesting, with an appeal to heaven, that she never had granted one patent which she did not believe to be conducive to the public good. Some of the patents were then remitted to the courts of law, by which they were condemned and made void as illegal.

Wardship. Wardship, as one of the feudal incidents, it is unnecessary to describe, because every reader of intelligence is acquainted with it. It has been generally regarded as a sad grievance of former times; but in my opinion the point may admit of a doubt. They who suffered under it possessed advantages of the highest kind over the rest of the community; and this was just one of the conditions upon which they held so eminent a station, while it possibly was a mean of preventing the aristocracy from acquiring the most pernicious influence in society, by accumulations during the infancy of heirs. As society improved, wardship was properly abolished, because the other ranks had acquired such a standing in the community that they could form a counterpoise to the aristocracy. In short, it was just a species of tax upon property; and we may observe, that the wards of the Crown had better treatment than those of subjects. The right of giving the ward in marriage was one of the conditions of the holding; but the resistance of the ward was only attended with a definite pecuniary forfeiture.

Restraint upon the Marriage of the Nobility. 'None of the nobility,' says Mr. Hume, 'could marry without permission from the sovereign. The queen detained the Earl of Southampton long in prison, because he privately married the Earl of Essex's cousin.' With the exception of wardship, which applied to other immediate vassals of the Crown as well as the nobility, I know of no law that permitted the sovereign to interfere in those matters. But, with the Tudor family, the nobility, who began to decline in influence in the community, became attached by many ties to the court, and it was usual with them to consult the monarch in the grand affair of their marriage. This sprang from a feeling of interest, a desire of patronage , not from any notion of right in the Crown to interpose in such affairs, and the non-observance of this practice appears to have provoked the royal displeasure, which, I presume, showed itself in banishing or debarring the parties from court. Camden informs us that Elizabeth resented the conduct of Southampton, in privately marrying without consulting her, and took deep offence at Essex for appointing him master of the horse contrary to her orders; but the authority for the statement about the imprisonment is the following passage in a letter by Essex: – 'Was it treason in my Lord of Southampton to marry my poor kinswoman, that neither long imprisonment, *nor any punishment besides, that hath been usual in like cases, can satisfy or appease?*' What that punishment, besides imprisonment, was, except the loss of royal favour and banishment from court, I cannot comprehend. But we may observe, that it does not appear that Southampton was ever prosecuted in any court of justice, even the Star-Chamber; so that his case affords no proof of a right in the Crown to meddle with such matters. His imprisonment, However, admits of an easy solution.

The openings for talent and enterprise in that age were so extremely limited, that young men of the first families entered into the service even of subjects, while they who had the prospect of the royal countenance eagerly crowded to court. The treatment which servants were then exposed to, however, is revolting to our ideas. The sons of distinguished families could submit to personal chastisement; nor was this a matter which could be remedied by law, because submission was voluntary. Those servants might easily have cast off their bondage, but they must have dismissed with it all hope of promotion; while what was common, and deemed a necessary ordeal through which enterprise passed to an eminent sphere in the state, reflected no disgrace upon the individual. Courtiers were also under a rigid discipline, and confinement in the Tower was a species of punishment to which they were exposed. Sir Walter Raleigh was imprisoned three months for debauching a maid of honour, the daughter of Sir N. Throckmorton, whom he afterwards married. I presume that Southampton suffered as a courtier, and that he quietly submitted from the Hope of regaining her majesty's favour, and with it, honours, place, and other rewards, to which he eagerly aspired.

Purveyance. Purveyance was reckoned one of the grievances of that age; and it will be proper to give some account of it. Originally, the king's household was provided with necessaries from the royal demesnes; and the deficiency was supplied by a constant market kept at the court-gate. As this was discontinued, purveyance began. At first, however, nothing could be lawfully taken without the owner's consent, the purveyors being merely caterers employed by the court. But, acting under the royal authority, they at times abused their office, by not sufficiently consulting the will of the sellers. The legislature was not inattentive to the evil, while it sufficiently regarded the comforts of the sovereign, who, in his progress through the kingdom, in ages when, from bad roads, &c., there were so many impediments in the way of quickly transporting provisions, must have often had the greatest difficulty in procuring the necessaries of life, and there had been no fewer than forty-eight statutes passed on the subject. By the early statutes, the sale to the purveyors was voluntary; but, by later ones, those officers, provided they had a commission under the great seal, were entitled to take certain articles for the household, at prices which should be fixed by the constables, or other discreet men in the neighbourhood, who were first duly sworn to do justice to both parties. In spite of all the forty-eight statutes, purveyance was abused by the officers, whom Elizabeth herself, in indignation, called harpies; and she expressed an intention of substituting for the practice some other arrangement.

Persecuting Statutes. The historian remarks that 'it is no wonder the queen, in her administration, should pay so little regard to liberty, while parliament itself, in enacting laws, was entirely negligent of it.' He then condemns the persecuting statutes which were passed against Papists and Puritans, as extremely contrary to the genius of freedom; and observes, that 'their conferring an unlimited supremacy on the queen, or, what is worse, acknowledging her inherent right to it, was another proof of their voluntary servitude.' In the preceding chapter we have had occasion to speak of the supremacy, and it will be perceived from it that Mr. Hume has not taken a correct view of the matter. It is true that Elizabeth affected to have derived from it a discretionary power of regulating religious matters; but she confined her government within the pale of the laws. Sir Edward Coke proves that the supremacy was always vested in the Crown of England; but his grand object was to vindicate the independence of that country on any foreign power. After quoting some old statutes, &c., he says that it was settled 'by three other Acts of Parliament' – viz., by the statute 25th Henry VIII. c. 21, 'Wherein by authority of parliament it is enacted and declared (directing their declaration to the king) that this your grace's realm, recognising no superior under God but only your grace, hath been, and is, free from subjection to any man's laws, but only to such as have been devised, made, and ordained within this realm for the wealth of the same, or to such other as, by sufferance of your grace and your progenitors,

'the people of this your realm have taken at their free liberty by their own consent to be used amongst them, and have bound themselves by long use and custom to the observance of the same; not as to the observance of the laws of any foreign prince, potentate, or prelate, but as to the customed and ancient laws of this realm, originally established as laws of the same; by said sufferance, consents, and customs, and none otherwise. And by the statutes 25th Henry VIII. c. 21, 1 Elizabeth, c. 1, and 1 Jac. c. 1, the Crown of this kingdom is affirmed to be an imperial crown.'

Having cleared up this point, it may be observed, that Mr. Hume, in speaking of the persecuting statutes against Papists and Puritans, seems to have forgotten the question which he was endeavouring to settle – the power of the Crown in regard to the parliament; for his account of what the parliament did, unless he had shown – which he does not pretend to do – that, in this instance, they were obliged implicitly to obey the dictates of the sovereign, merely proves that the legislature, in imposing its principles by cruelty on the people, was not actuated by wisdom or policy. The same laws might – nay, most probably would – have been passed under the purest republic; and the Presbyterian party, had they prevailed, would have devised still more severe statutes against every sect that differed from them, while they reduced the power of the Crown to a nonentity.

But because they abused their power, could it thence be inferred that they did not possess it?

Mr. Hume properly pronounces the law of the 23rd of her reign, 'making seditious words capital, as also a very tyrannical statute;' and it was no less impolitic, for, independently of all other objections, it may be remarked that severity ever defeats its object. But the question is, whether the statute sprang from such an overwhelming influence in the Crown over both houses of parliament as really deprived them of the legislative power, or from erroneous views of policy in them, or even from personal attachment to the sovereign. That statute made seditious rumours and words, *verbally uttered*, punishable, on the first conviction, with the loss of ears, six months' imprisonment, and a fine of £200; and on the second conviction it was made felony without benefit of clergy. Writing and publishing seditious words, &c., were likewise felony without benefit of clergy. But, besides that the offence was to be tried within a year of its being committed, and proved by two witnesses confronted with the prisoner, the Act was to expire with the life of the queen. It may be observed, that the very fact of Elizabeth's being obliged to apply to parliament for protection against personal wrongs, together with the cautious limitations of the statute, disproves Mr. Hume's idea of the unlimited extent of her prerogative.

Cases of Udal and Penry. He has most justly condemned as tyrannical the use which was made of this statute in the cases of Udal and Penry. The whole proceedings against the first were irregular; but, as he had attacked the bishops very bitterly, denied the Church of England to be a church, and held that she was destitute of a lawful ministry, sacraments &c., the clergy eagerly drove on the prosecution. Udal, however, was not executed, every means being in vain taken to prevail upon him to recant, and he died in prison. Udal had refrained from any personal attack upon the sovereign, and the charge against him was constructive – that he had abused the ecclesiastical government, and consequently her majesty as its head. But the case of Penry was very different. Not content with the most scurrilous abuse of the bishops, whom he denominated a troop of bloody atheistical soul – murderers and sacrilegious church robbers, and as such desired to strip them of all their livings, fully intending to reserve their revenues for his own party – not satisfied with telling the people that they ought not to wait for authority to establish a proper ecclesiastical government, but to proceed in spite of prohibitions -- he published that her majesty envied her subjects a saving knowledge of the true God; that she was yet unbaptised, while her people remained in infidelity, and stood generally condemned to hell; that an honest man could not possibly live under her government in any vocation whatever; and that she might as well make a new religion as new laws for religion. That this language fell under the statute cannot be questioned; but when a warrant was issued for his apprehension, be fled to Scotland, where he remained for three years. Fired with additional zeal in that country, he at last returned to England with a petition to her majesty, which he intended to have delivered in person. In it he declares that

> 'he had cause to complain, nay, the Lord and His church had cause to complain, of her government; that her subjects were sold to be bond-slaves, not only unto their affections, to do what they would, so that they kept themselves within the compass of established laws, but also to be servants to the Man of Sin (the Pope) and his ordinances; that she ought to rank herself amongst those who opposed the Gospel; that the practice of her government showed, if she could have ruled without the Gospel, it never would have been established, and that it flourished more under her sister's reign than hers.'

While he thus rails, he at the same time shows in plain terms that he desired her concurrence to root out every sect but his own. This also was assuredly seditious within the statute, and was calculated to disturb the state; but then it had not been published, and of course was as yet no libel. For his former writings he could not be arraigned, as the time limited by the statute was expired, and therefore he was unjustly charged with this, which had been in his custody as yet unpublished. It is said that the queen regretted his death; but the fury of the prelates exceeded her own.

'It was also,' says Mr. Hume, 'imputed to Penry by the lord keeper Puckering, that, in some of his papers, "he had not only acknowledged her majesty's power to *establish* laws, ecclesiastical and civil, but had avoided the *usual* terms of *making, enacting,* decreeing, and ordaining laws, which imply," says he, "a most absolute authority."' Hence the author infers that the queen's power was acknowledged to be absolute; but in this, as in other instances, be only affords a proof of the danger of many conclusions regarding the laws and opinions of any age or country, and particular expressions from isolated passages. In strict constitutional language, the sovereign is the fountain of all law, and, as it must be known to everyone, all statutes bear, *in germio,* to have been made by him, with the advice and consent of the lords spiritual and temporal and the commons in parliament assembled. When, therefore, in the next reign, the king pedantically claimed absolute power, he was answered that his notion was correct, but that this absolute power could only be exercised by means of his great council the parliament. In Elizabeth's time, no one ever pretended that laws could be made by the sovereign without the intervention of the legislature; and the very usual terms of making, enacting, &c., ought to have set Mr. Hume right, while it is somewhat inexplicable how the whole passage referred to should not have had that effect. That portion of the puritanical party to which Penry was attached denied the power of the legislature to make laws about religion, while they confidently asserted that they derived from heaven a legislative authority, which the civil government was bound to ratify. When it was argued against them that their ecclesiastical government was incompatible with the civil, they plainly avowed that, if such were the fact, the civil government, as the result of human policy, ought to be made conformable to the ecclesiastical, which was divine – not the ecclesiastical to the civil. Their ideas about deposing princes, too, were equally bold. In short, as we have shown in the preceding chapter, from the notes of this very lord-keeper Puckering, their notions would have necessarily led to the subversion of the state, while they who exclaimed against the tyranny of forcing consciences declared it, at the same instant, to be the duty of the magistrate to root out every sect which dared to impugn their decrees. It was under this impression that Puckering drew up his observations in Penry's case; and his real words, which Mr. Hume has neither quoted correctly nor fully, leave no doubt on the point. He endeavours to prove, from many grounds, that Penry is not, as he pretends, a loyal subject, but a seditious disturber of her majesty's peaceable government; and, in the sixth place, he says this appears 'by so many of his protestations, wherein he acknowledgeth her majesty's power only to establish laws ecclesiastical and civil, shunning the usual terms of making, enacting, decreeing, ordaining laws, which import a most absolute authority; *as though her majesty had no such power, but only a prerogative to establish and ratify such laws as are made to her hand by the omnipotent presbytery, as he and others of his crew have both taught and written.*' The language of Puckering is certainly not commendable, for he might have alluded to the parliament; but, while it was soothing to the royal ear, for which this courtier prepared it, it was not unconstitutional, and could not be misunderstood. The queen acted with, not against, the legislature.

Burghley's Proposal to erect a new Court for the Correction of all Abuses, &c. What we have just said, partly explains the language of Burghley, when, in a speech to the council, he proposed that the queen 'should,' to use Mr. Hume's words, 'erect a court for the correction of all abuses, and should confer on the commissioners a general inquisitorial power over the whole kingdom;' 'To proceed therein indeed,' says Burghley, 'as well by direction and ordinary course of your laws, as also by virtue of your majesty's supreme regiment and absolute power from whence law proceeded.' 'This proposal,' says Mr. Hume, 'needs not, I think, any comment. A form of government must be very arbitrary indeed, where a wise and good minister could make such a proposal to the sovereign.' The minister who proposes to overturn the laws of his country by an arbitrary act of the chief magistrate, can neither be accounted good nor wise; and, had such an attempt ever been made, Burghley might himself have fallen a sacrifice to his guilty rashness, or would, doubtless, on the first change in administration, have suffered the fate of Empson and Dudley, to whose actions he alluded. But, though the whole speech be in the grossest style of adulation, I do not conceive that it will be difficult to rescue his memory from this imputation, and to prove that he never intended that the sovereign should act without the interposition of the legislature. Our inquiry, too, will throw light upon that statesman's plan, which would otherwise be scarcely intelligible. The scheme was first developed by the lord-keeper Bacon in his address, in her majesty's name, to both houses, at the dissolution of parliament, in the 13th of her reign. After adverting to the state of the country, and showing that inquests were overborne, the guilty acquitted, the innocent condemned, and the laws, which were good of themselves, made 'instruments of all injuries and mischiefs,' by the very individuals who were selected by the prince to enforce justice throughout the kingdom, he intimates that there should, with authority, be a triennial visitation of all temporal officers and ministers by commissioners nominated by the queen, upon the principle of the visitation of the church, who should be authorised 'to try out and examine by all good ways and means, the offences of all such as have not seen to the due execution of the laws, and according to the offences so found and certified, to be sharply punished without omission or redemption.' The scheme, which the lord-keeper had thus intimated at the dissolution of that parliament, he proposed, in the queen's name, at the opening of the next, but he introduced the topic by telling them that 'he left it to their judgments.' Had Elizabeth's influence been really so great in parliament as has been imagined, she could have had little difficulty in carrying a measure which she appears to have so much desired; but it struck too forcibly against the power of the aristocracy to be listened to, and it never was heard of again till about the year 1594, when Burghley gratified his mistress by the speech referred to. It cannot be imagined, however, that he could advise her to attempt a measure without parliament, which she could not accomplish with it; and therefore we must presume that her absolute power was to be exerted through her grand council. Elizabeth was so pleased with the speech, that she desired a copy of it; but the scheme seems never to have been thought of more.

Sentiments of the Age regarding the English Constitution. We have now examined the grounds upon which Mr. Hume conceived that the English government bore some resemblance to that of Turkey, as well as given an account of the particular institutions and usages of that period; and it remains to make a few remarks upon his assertion, that the established principles of the times attributed to the prince such an unlimited and indefeasible power, as was supposed to be the origin of all law, and could not be circumscribed by any. In support of this statement he refers to the homilies, which, he observes, inculcate absolute obedience; and thence he concludes that people complained with small reason in the next age, 'because some court chaplains were permitted to preach such doctrines; but there is,' continues the historian, 'a great difference between these sermons and discourses published by authority, avowed by the prince and council, and promulgated to the whole nation.' Indeed, we must admit that there was a decided difference in the cases. The homilies against disobedience and rebellion were prepared in consequence of, and immediately after, the northern rebellion, when the fears of the best patriots alarmed them with the idea of an overturn of the state by a religious faction, and when, therefore, they desired the assistance of religion to support the whole frame of the civil government, which zeal of a different kind would have torn to pieces. The queen was not then attempting to subjugate the nation by acting without the concurrence of parliament, but openly avowed herself its head. In the next age, the court chaplains preached up damnation to those who pretended to resist the prince in assuming to himself the whole powers of the legislature, after he had quarrelled with his parliaments; nor were they barely permitted to preach thus, but keenly encouraged in that pious undertaking. We have already shown that, instead of that tameness of spirit which the historian has attributed to the age, there was a very numerous party, whose doctrine savoured deeply of republicanism, and that their writers maintained very bold sentiments about deposing princes.

The learned author has said that the English were not aware of enjoying any political advantages beyond their continental neighbours, and has remarked that he has met with no writers that speak of the English government as anything else than an absolute monarchy. But surely his research has been limited, or his inattention great, for proofs of this are to be found in most writers of the age. Fortescue's work, 'De Laudibus legum Angliæ,' was printed in Henry VIII.'s reign, and was then referred to by lawyers, nay, was even quoted from the bench in Mary's reign. In 1567, an edition in Latin and English was published, and dedicated by the translator to one of the judges of the Queen's Bench; and in 1599, the translation was published alone, with the following title – 'A Learned Commentary of the Politic Laws of England, wherein, by most pithy reasons and demonstrations, they are plainly proved to excel, as well the civil laws of the empire, as also all other laws of the world; with a large Discourse of the difference between the two Governments of Kingdoms, whereof the one is only regal, and the other consisteth of regal and politic administration conjoined.' Did no other document remain, which, fortunately, is not the fact, this of itself would refute Mr. Hume's notion. We have already referred to Smith's 'Commonwealth,' and to Hayward's 'History,' and we shall not return to them. Many passages might be quoted from various works published in Elizabeth's time, but we shall content ourselves with the following: Aylmer, afterwards Bishop of London, in the tract which he published anonymously in answer to Knox's 'First Blast of the Trumpet against the Monstrous Regiment of Women,' defends female government in England expressly on the principle of the superiority of the English government, where the laws governed the magistrate, not the magistrate the laws. 'Well,' says he, 'a woman may not reigne in England: better in England then any where, as it shall wel appere to him that without affection will consider the kinde of regiment: whyle I conferre ours with other as it is in itselfe, and not maymed by usurpacion, I can fynde none either so good or so indifferent. The regiment of England is not a mere monarchie, as some for lacke of consideracion thinke, nor a mere oligarchie, nor democratie, but a rule mixte of all those, wherein ech one of these have or shoulde haue like authoritie. Thimage whereof, and not the image, but the thinge in dede, is to be sene in the parliament hous, wherein you shal find these 3 estats. The king or quene, which representeth the monarche; the noble men, which be the aristocratie; and the burgesses and knights, the democratic. The verye same had Lacedemonia, the noblest and best city gouerned that euer was; thei had their kings, their senate, and Hippagretes, which wer for the people. As in Lacedemonia none of these could make or breake lawes, order for warre or peac, or do any thing without thother, the king nothinge without the senate and commons, nor either of them or both withoute the king (albeit the senate and the ephori had greater authoritie then the kinge had). In like maner, if the parliament use their priuleges, the king can ordein nothing without them. If he do, it is his fault in usurping it, and their follye in permitting it.' 'But to what purpose is all this? To declare, that it is not in England so daungerous a matter to have a woman ruler as men take it to be.' 'If, on thother part, the regiment were such, as all hanged uppon the kinge's or quene's wil, and not upon the lawes wrytten; if she might decre, and make lawes alone, without her senate; if she iudged offences accordange to her wisdome, and not by limitation of statutes and laws; if she might dispose alone of war and peace; if, to be short, she wer a mere monark, and not a mixte ruler, you might, peraduenture, make me to feare the matter the more, and the les to defend the cause. But the state being as it is or ought to be (if men wer wurth theyr eares), I can see no cause of feare.'

He afterwards presents a picture of the wretchedness of the French, and compares their condition, and that of other states, with the situation of England. Thus much for Aylmer. Cartwright, in defending his system of church government, which he, of course, calls divine, says,

'The churche is gouerned with that kind of gouernment whiche the philosophers, that wryte of the best commonwealths, affirme to be the best. For in respecte of Christe the head, it is monarchie, and in respect of the aunciens and pastours that gouern in common, and with lyke authoritie amongst themselves, it is an aristccratie, or the rule of the best men; and, in respecte that the people are not secluded, but have their interest in churche matters, it is a democratie or a popular estate. An image whereof appeareth in the pollicie of thys realme; for in respecte of the Queen her maiestie, it is a monarchie, so in respecte of the most honourable counsel, it is an aristocratie; and having regard to the parliament, which is assembled of all estates, it is a democratie.'

Harrison, who published in 1577, gives this account of the parliament: –

'This house hath the most high and *absolute* power of the realme; for thereby kings and mightie princes haue from time to time beene deposed from their thrones; lawes either enacted or abrogated; offendors of all sorts punished; and corrupted religion either disannulled or reformed. To be short, whatsoeauer the people of Rome did in their *centuriatis* or *tributintiss comitiis*, the same is and may be doone by authoritie of our parlement house, which is the head and bodie of all the realme, and the place wherein euerie particular person is intended to be present, if not by himselfe, yet by his aduocate or attornie. For this cause also any thing ther enacted is not to be misliked, but obeied of all men without contradiction or grudge.'

No language can be stronger than this; but as Mr. Hume has brought together every circumstance which could convey a contemptible idea of parliament, we shall make a few observations on that point, and produce some instances to prove the general spirit that pervaded that assembly.

Conduct of Parliament, with the Ideas Entertained by that Assembly of their Powers and Privileges. In the previous chapter we have traced the causes of the influence which the Crown then enjoyed in the state: it remains to say, that Elizabeth, having had certain powers in regard to religion devolved upon her, objected to the introduction of bills which tended to abridge her authority; and, in the course of her reign, even sent members to the Tower who disobeyed her injunctions on this head, as well as some who insisted upon her marriage, and her naming a successor, &c. That the proceeding was unconstitutional, no one doubted; and, in the 13th of her reign, when she first attempted an encroachment upon the privileges of the Commons, by ordering a member to abstain from attendance in his place till he received further orders, the circumstance created such a flame in the Lower House, that she instantly restored the member; but her popularity and influence enabled her to repeat the measure, and even to send the members to the Tower. Not choosing, at such a moment, to contest the matter with the Crown, he submitted to the hardship.

In the year 1566, Mr. Onslow, then speaker of the Commons, *in his address to the Throne* at the conclusion of the session, pronounces a panegyric upon the common law. 'For,' says he, 'by our common law, although there be for the prince provided many princely prerogatives and royalties, yet it is not such as the prince can take money or other things, or do as he will at his own pleasure, without order; but quietly to suffer his subjects to enjoy their own, without wrongful oppression, *wherein other princes, by their liberty, do take as pleaseth them.*' 'He tells her, that, as a good prince, she was not given to tyranny contrary to the laws, had not attempted to make laws contrary to order, but had orderly called this parliament, who perceived certain wants, and thereunto had put their helping hand,' &c. Onslow was, at the very time, though prolocutor of the Commons, the queen's solicitor; and his speech was so far from giving offence, that, while the Commons were reprehended for having trenched upon the prerogative, by questioning her right to grant patents for monopolies, &c., it was pronounced wise and eloquent. To smooth down and justify the reprimand, the lord-keeper, in her majesty's name, tells the parliament that 'she meant not to hurt any of their liberties.' At the opening of the next parliament, in the 13th of that reign, both houses were informed from the Throne that the first reason for calling them 'was to establish or dissolve laws as best should serve for the governance of the realm;' and that, 'because in all councils and conferences, first and chiefly, there should be sought the advancement of God's honour and glory, as the sure and infallible foundation whereupon the policy of every good public weal is to be erected and built, &c., therefore they were to consider whether the ecclesiastical laws concerning the discipline of the church be sufficient or no, and, if any want should be found, to supply the same.' Now, it will not be forgotten that it is chiefly on religious matters that Elizabeth's government has been censured: it has even been alleged that a divine right on that head was arrogated by the Crown. The lord-keeper, who delivered the royal address, reminded the parliament in no less liberal terms of their duty, in reforming, abrogating, or altering the temporal laws. It was even treason by an Act of that queen to deny that parliament had power to determine the succession, or other matters regarding the Crown. 'It were horrible to say,' observed Mr. Mounson, in that very session, 'that the parliament had not authority to determine of the Crown, for then would ensue, not only the annihilating of the statute 35 Henry VIII., but that the statute made in the 1st year of her majesty's reign, of recognition, should also be void.' 'For the authority of parliament,' said Serjeant Manwood, on the same subject, 'it could not, in reasonable construction, be otherwise; for who should deny that authority, denied the queen to be queen, and the realm to be a realm.' It was during this session that Mr. Strickland, for having intro- duced and pressed a bill about religion, which was said to be injurious to the prerogative, was summoned before the council, and commanded to attend their further pleasure, and in the meantime not to return to the house; but, as has just been said, this infringement of their privileges was taken up with so high a spirit, that though the ministers affected to defend the restraint, the member was restored on the following day. Mr. Yelverton, in arguing for the liberty of the house, and representing the danger of the precedent, if they did not vindicate their privileges, said that 'all matters not treason, or too much to the derogation of the imperial Crown, were tolerable there, where all things came to be considered of, and where there was such fulness of power, as even the right of the Crown was to be determined, and by warrant whereof we had so resolved. That to say the parliament had no power to determine of the Crown, was high treason. He remembered how that men are not there for themselves, but for their countries. He showed it was fit for princes to have their prerogatives, but yet the same to be straitened within reasonable limits. The prince, he showed, could not herself make laws, neither ought she, by the same reason, break laws.'

He concluded with defending Strickland's bill. Now, though one member argues that the house ought to petition the Throne as the only way to obtain redress, not one courtier rose to object to these general principles. Peter Wentworth, in the 18th of that reign, was committed to the Tower by the house for undutiful expressions towards the queen; but though he defended what he had said, instead of showing regret for it, her Majesty interposed in his favour, and restored him to his place. Now, it is remarkable that the general positions which be laid down, as that the prince must be under the law, for the law makes him king, &c., never were impugned even by the council.

We have Perhaps said enough, but as the learned historian has repeatedly stated that the English did not suppose that they enjoyed superior privileges to their neighbours, we shall further observe – 1st, that if the people enjoyed privileges, as it is evident they did, it would not lessen our opinion of their enjoyments, that they were unacquainted with the situation of the continental states, and that it would be incumbent on Mr. Hume to prove that France enjoyed anything of the kind. 2ndly, that the wretched condition of France, governed and taxed at the will of the prince, and oppressed by foreign military, seems to have been a fact with which most men were acquainted, and that proofs of it not only occur in books, but in the journals of parliament. Sir Humphrey Gilbert, in support of the prerogative to grant patents, advised the house, in language similar to what was adopted in a future reign, to abstain from such topics, lest

'her majesty might look to her own power, and thereby finding her validity to suppress the strength of the challenged liberty, and to challenge and use her power any way, to do as did Lewis of France, who, as he termed it, delivered the crown there out of wardship, which the said French king did upon like occasion. *He also said that other kings had absolute power, as Denmark and Portugal,* where, as the Crown became more free, so are all the subjects thereby the rather made slaves.'

This speech was disliked, but no notice was taken of it at the time. At the next meeting of parliament, however, on a question about the residence of burgesses within the boroughs they represented, a member, after stating to the house that it belonged to them 'to consider of all, and, as occasion may serve, to alter, constitute, or reform all things as cause should be,' alludes to Gilbert's speech in the following terms:

> 'We know that such as have spent their whole time in service, or have seen only the manner of government of other nations, and can tell you how the Crown of France is delivered out of wardship, or otherwise tell a tale of the King of Castile and Portugal, how they, in making laws, do use their own discretion, the King of Denmark useth the advice of his nobles only, and nothing of the commons: or can point you out the monstrous garments of the common people in some parts of Germany, or the mangled commonwealth of the allies, or shadows of the great cities, which now are to be seen in Italy; surely all those men, except they know also our own homes, are not to be trusted to conclude for our home affairs.'

Wentworth, on a future day, declared Gilbert's speech to be an injury to the house, and reprobated that individual in the coarsest terms for his disposition to flatter and fawn upon the prince, comparing him to the chameleon, which can change itself into all colours save white; 'even so,' said he, 'this reporter can change himself into all fashions save honesty.' No evidence can be more direct or complete than this.

We have now travelled over a vast variety of ground, and it must be apparent that, though there were some institutions, as the Star-Chamber, &c., not consonant to the genius of a free government, and occasional proceedings of a dangerous kind, the grand constitutional principles were clearly defined as well as recognised by the monarch in the general course of administration.

46
FRANCIS JEFFREY

[Francis Jeffrey], Review of Brodie's *History of the British Empire* (1822), in *Edinburgh Review*, March 1824, Vol. 40, pp. 92–146. Selections.

The *Edinburgh Review* was founded in 1802 by Francis Jeffrey, Henry Brougham, and Sydney Smith. The journal's first editor was Jeffrey (1773–1850), a struggling lawyer at the time who, with his two friends, sought an outlet for their liberal views. The journal developed into a strong advocate of the Whig party, and when that party came to office in 1830 Jeffrey was appointed Lord Advocate. Jeffrey authored the 1803 review of Millar's *Historical View*, quotations from which appear earlier in this volume. In 1822 George Brodie published his *History of the British Empire* – a boldly Whig attack on Hume's Tory views of royal prerogative (selections from Brodie's work are contained earlier in this collection). Jeffrey reviewed this work and, not surprisingly, was very favourable towards Brodie. The first half of his article, presented below, is an analysis of Hume's *History*. The greatest merits of Brodie's work, Jeffrey believes, "would be to counteract the many bad effects" of Hume's *History*. Jeffrey contends that practical Toryism is motivated by the desire to obtain undeserved distinctions; however, he holds open the possibility of a more speculative Toryism, which is principally defended in Hume's *History*. It is this feature of Hume's work, he believes, that makes it so dangerous. He thinks highly of Hume's character and abilities, and speculates that Hume was led to Toryism since advocates of liberty were commonly associated with Protestant fanaticism – a religious attitude that Hume disdained. For Jeffrey, there are two kinds of history writing: one that merely chronicles events, and another that furnishes "a satisfactory *theory* of their connexion and mutual dependency." Hume has done the latter, but, in the process, was directed by prejudice. Hume also violated the rules of good history writing by inventing motives and dialogue for the principal actors, rather than conveying an authentic account of events.

  Contrasting Hume's Tory interpretation of English history with Brodie's Whig view, Jeffrey takes a middle ground. He agrees with Brodie that the English Government was "greatly more free than those of the Continental kingdoms," but concedes to Hume that "the checks upon royal power were in its early periods brought very irregularly into action." Jeffrey concludes his discussion of Hume by faulting the dramatic inconsistencies in the *History*, and also the way that Hume links patriotism with Protestant fanaticism. Regarding the inconsistencies, he thinks that Hume began modestly enough by trying to explain the unique circumstances that led the Stuart monarchs to arbitrary rule. But, "intoxicated with his success," he shifted from "excuses to justification." As to the alleged Protestant fanaticism of the patriots, Jeffrey argues that at the time zeal was justified since Catholicism was the cause of despotism, wars, and persecutions. The second half of Jeffrey's article – not included here – excerpts from and summarizes Brodie's attacks on Hume as they appear in the introductory volume of his work.

ART. V. *A History of the British Empire, from the Accession of Charles I. to the Restoration; with an Introduction, tracing the progress of Society, and of the Constitution, from the feudal Times to the opening of the History; and including a particular Examination of Mr Hume's Statements relative to the Character of the English Government.* By GEORGE BRODIE, Esq. Advocate. 4 vols. 8vo. Edinburgh, Bell & Bradfute. London, Longman & Co. 1822.

This is the work of a resolute, learned, and industrious Whig; and forms, we think, the most valuable contribution to the constitutional history of our country that has appeared since the commencement of our labours. It is not particularly well written; nor digested, in all places, in the most lucid order; and, on some of the nicer questions of prudence or principle, the author is not perhaps entitled to the praise of uniform moderation or absolute impartiality. Yet the work is by no means passionate or declamatory; but grave, conscientious, and argumentative; – while nothing can be more exemplary than the zeal and diligence with which the author has addressed himself to the task he has undertaken – nor any thing better than the general spirit of his performance. He proceeds on the principles of taking no fact on the credit of any recent historian without the strictest examination of his authorities, and admitting no questionable opinion, without the freest and most fearless discussion of the grounds on which it rests. In this way he has traced up almost all the leading statements of the history to their original sources; and thus not only secured for his own narrative the best and most authentic evidence that could in any way be obtained, but made innumerable corrections on the accounts of less scrupulous writers, and detected an incredible multitude of errors and misrepresentations in the most material and least suspected parts of their productions.

    The author upon whom he has chiefly exercised this wholesome but severe discipline, it will readily be supposed, is Hume – to whose history of the same period the work before us may indeed be regarded as a professed answer or antidote – and who is here convicted of so many inaccuracies and partial statements, that we really think his credit among historians, for correctness of assertion, will soon be nearly as low as it has long been with theologians for orthodoxy of belief. It is this, indeed, we do not scruple to confess, that gives the work its chief value in our eyes – for, though an exact and trust-worthy history of the memorable period it embraces, must have been at all times of great interest and importance, we cannot help feeling that the greatest good it can do at present would be to counteract the many bad effects which the unlucky, though in many respects well merited, popularity of Mr Hume's work has had on the public mind. The true source of *practical* Toryism, or, in other words, of personal servility to the Government, is no doubt self-interest, or a strong desire for unearned emoluments and undeserved distinctions – but the great support of *speculative* servility and *sincere* Tory opinions – to which we are liberal enough to allow an actual existence, has of late years been found chiefly in Hume's history: – and we have really very little doubt that both the prejudices which infect the few genuine Tories of the present day, and the apologies by which the crowds who care nothing either for prejudice or principle, are enabled to make a plausible defence for their conduct, may be justly ascribed to the impression which the artful colouring and delusive reasonings of that book have made on public opinion – an impression which the excellence of the writing, the acuteness of the observations, and the apparent fairness of the deductions, have all tended powerfully to confirm. We are aware that to many practical politicians it may appear fantastic and even ridiculous to ascribe such effects to a book – and especially to a book in four quarto volumes, published near seventy years ago: But when it is considered how universally, and at how early an age, it has been read, especially during the latter half of that period – how pleasant it is to read, and how easy to understand and remember – how much clearer, in short, and concise and comprehensive it is than any other history of equal extent – how reasonable and sagacious are the greatest part of the observations it contains – and how plausible the most erroneous of its conclusions, – nay even how *just*, upon the premises of facts which it assumes, while so very few of its readers can be supposed to have either leisure or inclination to inquire into the truth of these assumptions, – our readers will cease perhaps to wonder at the influence we have ventured to ascribe to it, and acknowledge that principles which fall in with so many of the baser parts of our nature, may be promoted almost as much by artful apologies as by present and actual temptation. But, However this may be, the errors of the most popular of our historians, as to the true origin and character of English liberty, are certainly of importance enough to give interest to any work which pretends to expose or correct them – and in the account we are now to give of Mr Brodie, we shall regard him accordingly chiefly as the censor of Mr Hume.

Let us begin, however, by doing justice to that admirable writer and most excellent man. He was, in his own person, of the most independent character; and utterly incapable of the mercenary subserviency for which his doctrines have furnished so many with an apology: and indeed, when he first published, these doctrines were not the best passports to promotion. He was also, we believe, on the whole, a sincere inquirer after truth, and thought his opinions substantially just; – though he could scarcely fail to be aware that he had not sought very curiously for facts and arguments that might make against them, and had given them the advantage not only of an artful and attractive statement, but of some exaggeration and some suppression of the evidence. In what circumstances his Tory partialities originated, it would perhaps be idle now to inquire. He had early in life conceived an antipathy to the Calvinistic divines, and his temperament led him at all times to regard, with disgust and derision, that religious enthusiasm or bigotry with which the spirit of English freedom was, in his opinion, inseparably associated. His intellect was also, perhaps, too active and original to submit, with sufficient patience, to the preparatory toils and long suspended judgment of an historian; and led him to form premature conclusions and precipitate theories, which it then became the pride of his ingenuity to justify. His personal character, too, which, though eminently kind and cheerful, was remarkably averse from all sorts of enthusiasm or strong emotion, and even somewhat indolent and timid, naturally disposed him rather to submit quietly to established authority than to question or withstand it; while the vanity of giving to the world a new view of the history and progress of the English Constitution, held out an almost irresistible temptation to exaggerate and overstate all those points on which he wished to prove that the common opinions had been erroneous.

The least of these considerations, we fear, would be sufficient to account for all the partiality and infidelity with which we think this eminent writer chargeable. Impartiality, or even tolerable fairness of statement, is a far rarer and more difficult virtue than is commonly imagined. We see every day, that the existence of the slightest controversy, an inclination towards the most paltry theory, makes the most honest and candid individuals incapable of seeing what is before them, or describing truly what they see. In the account of a chemical experiment, an anatomical operation, or a geological survey, no man acquainted with the history of these sciences, peaceful and tranquilizing as they appear, will place much reliance on the statement of the most honourable and conscientious persons, if they are known advocates of a theory, or parties to a dispute, the merits of which may be affected by the result; and every body, at any rate, takes it for granted, that the facts would be differently represented by an observer of opposite inclinations. In questions of religion and politics, however, these disturbing forces must obviously act with still greater power, – and in the history of our own country, and especially in that mode of writing history of which Mr Hume is the great example, their influence may fairly be calculated to be it its *maximum*. For his sake, as well as for that of the subject, we must be indulged, on this last point, with a few words of explanation.

History may plainly be composed on two separate plans. According to the first and most simple, it should contain little more than a clear statement of facts, arranged in a lucid order, and interspersed perhaps with a few moral reflections on the most striking occurrences – giving *all* the accounts of the matter where good authorities differ, and only rejecting such as are manifestly absurd and incredible, – but being in substance and reality nothing more or other than *a narrative*, and pretending to no higher qualities than fidelity and perspicuity. The other plan is far more comprehensive and ambitious – professing not only to make *a selection* of the facts most worthy to be recorded, by abridging some and dwelling at length on others, but also to pass an authoritative judgment on the wisdom or folly, the merit or demerit, of all the acts and actors with which it is conversant – to trace memorable events back to their causes, and forward to their consequences – to furnish, in short, not only a true account of the facts as they occurred, but a satisfactory *theory* of their connexion and mutual dependency, and thus to teach far more of their true character and value than was probably known to those who produced them. Now, it is quite true, that this last sort of history requires far greater talents, and is, when suitably executed, not only infinitely more interesting, but greatly more instructive than the simple story of the chroniclers. In the latter ages of the world indeed, when records have accumulated, and affairs become complicated, some such concentrated and digested views of its past experience become almost indispensable; as few ordinary readers could be expected to labour through a mass of indigested annals – and still fewer to separate and connect what was valuable and important, or to deduce from them those great lessons of policy or morality, of which they are the most authentic teachers. In the course of time, therefore, more philosophical, discriminating, and concise histories naturally take the place of the diffuse compilations of their predecessors: and, for the great proportion of readers, Sismondi extinguishes Muratori and his followers in Italy, and Hume puts out Hollinshed and Speed and Eachard in England.

But however superior in dignity and attraction this way of writing history may appear, it is obvious that it is attended with infinitely greater hazards, both to the writer and the reader; and affords scope and temptation to all kinds of erroneous impressions. When the business of the historian is no longer merely to make his readers acquainted with the facts he has ascertained, as they really occurred in past time, but also to furnish him with the opinions and moral impressions to which they should give rise, it is plain that he has it in his power, in most cases, to give any colour his own prejudices and passions may suggest, to every delicate or important transaction he records; and thus to dictate to posterity, with almost absolute authority, the sentiments they should entertain of their ancestors. Even if his partialities are not strong enough to suborn his integrity, they will generally be sufficient not merely to direct or misguide his eloquence, but substantially to distort his representations of truth. He will not only lend all the colours of his style to enhance the merits, and palliate the crimes of his favourites, and to aggravate those of their opponents, but he will slur and abridge in his narrative the facts which it gives him pain to record, while he expatiates with graphic and circumstantial accuracy on those which seem to lend a triumph to his peculiar opinions. He will, perhaps unconsciously, be careless and negligent in investigating the details which tend to discredit the theories to which he is partial, and collect with malicious industry all the scattered intimations which seem to support them. In this way he will often give what are truly exceptions to the general rule, as illustrations of its actual tendency; or represent the whole scanty facts which the most anxious research could discover in favour of his conclusions, as instances taken carelessly and at random from an immense multitude of still stronger examples. Above all, when he comes to describe and estimate the views and motives by which, at any critical period, the different parties in the State were actuated, he will not only bring prominently forward the prejudices or follies by which the wisdom or virtue of one side were alloyed, while all these debasing elements are kept out of sight in his representation of the other – but will lend to his favourites all the finer views and plausible apologies which his own ingenuity and the improved sagacity of his age can suggest for persons in their situation, without the least evidence of their having been actually entertained by those to whom they are ascribed; while their adversaries are left without addition or assistance to any crude and improvident exposition of their reasons which they may have happened to put on record.[1]

---

[1]   Mr Hume's summaries of the conflicting views of different parties at particular eras, have been deservedly admired for the singular clearness, brevity, and plausibility with which they are composed: – But, in reality they belong rather to *conjectural* than to authentic History; and any one who looks into contemporary documents will be surprised to find how very small a portion of what is there imputed to the actors of the time had actually occurred to them, and how little of what they truly maintained is there recorded in their behalf. The object of the author being chiefly to give his readers a clear idea of the scenes he described, he seems to have thought that the conduct of the actors would be best understood by ascribing to them the views and motives, which, upon reflection, appeared to himself most natural in their situation. In this way, he has often made all parties appear more reasonable than they truly were; and given probability and consistency to events, which, as they actually occurred, were not a little inconceivable. But in so doing, he has undoubtedly violated the truth of history – and exposed himself to the influence of the most delusive partialities. Such a hypothetical *integration* of the opinions likely to prevail in any particular circumstances, seems at all times to have been a favourite exercise of his ingenuity. Very early in life, for example, he composed four Essays, to which he gave the names of the Epicurean, the Stoic, the Platonist, and the Sceptic – and prefixed to them the following very characteristic notice. 'The intention of these Essays is not so much to explain accurately the sentiments of the antient sects of philosophy, as to deliver the sentiments of the *sects which naturally form themselves in the world,* and entertain different ideas of human life and of happiness. I have given each of them the name of the philosophical sect to which it bears the greatest affinity.' These very words, we think, might be applied, with very little variation to most of the summaries of which we have been speaking. They, too, are mere conjectural views of the different sentiments that may be supposed naturally to arise in the world at particular periods; and they are given under the name of the historical party to which they bear the greatest affinity.

Such are a few of the obvious temptations to partiality, and even to abuse, in the composition of that more exalted and ambitious sort of history which an advanced period of civilization requires; and, as Mr Hume's work must be allowed to have combined, in an eminent degree, many of the excellencies and attractions of that species of writing, so it is not to be wondered at, though very much to be lamented, that it has also afforded a most conspicuous example of its dangers and defects. For, not to leave the matter on the ambiguous footing of insinuation, we mean distinctly to assert, that there is not one of the forms of partiality to which we have just been referring, of which he does not afford habitually the strongest examples. It is, if possible, still more unfortunate, however, that while the temptations to give false impressions are thus seductive and abundant, the task of correction and exposition should be so peculiarly difficult and ungrateful. A clear flowing and elegant narrative, interspersed with lively sarcasms, brilliant explanations, and artful remarks, is easily followed, readily remembered, and willingly believed – while the business of pointing out exaggerations, detecting inaccuracies, and supplying omissions, has always a heavy and cumbrous effect, and not only carries with it an air of petty cavilling and unreasonable austerity, but, in truth, can rarely be made intelligible to those who have not the precise tenor of the faithless story in their recollection, without so much resumption and repetition as deservedly to incur the reproach of tediousness and inelegance. When a work, therefore, like Mr Hume's, has once got possession of the public, it is wonderful to observe with what slowness and difficulty the proofs of its inaccuracy are received; and when the natural partiality with which we cling to early impressions, and recur to clear and elegant delineations, is reinforced by the seductions of self-interest and the applauses of a prevailing party, it may easily be conceived how unprosperous his task is likely to be who brings forward detached and laborious truths, to destroy the symmetry we had admired, and discredit the pretexts under which we were willing to yield to temptation. The cause of Truth and Liberty, however, is sure to triumph in the end; and their advocates may console themselves with the reflection, that they are always making more progress than they appear to do. The misrepresentations of Hume are every day more known and admitted; and the unostentatious labours of his correctors have already shaken the very foundations of his authority with all intelligent readers. Professor Millar has done much to counteract the effect of his errors as to the earlier Part of our history, and Mr Laing still more as to that portion of it which relates to the administration of the Stuarts in Scotland. Bishop Hurd, in the first edition of his 'Dialogues on the English Constitution' for the latter are pitifully altered – has made a strong appeal against the partial statements and unconstitutional prejudices of this author. Dr Birch, in a very exact and elaborate treatise, has completely discredited his account of Galmorgan's transactions in Ireland – and Dr Towers, in a valuable tract published by him in 1778, has brought together many new proofs of his extraordinary misrepresentations.[2] A great deal, however, was left to Mr Brodie; and as he has done his work with great vigour and perseverance, the result, we have no doubt, though not perhaps immediately conspicuous, will be strong and decisive. The truths here brought so forcibly into view will sink imperceptibly but deeply into the minds of the public; and – though their triumph will not probably be complete till some eloquent and philosophical writer shall arise, to recast the whole rude materials that have been collected, and supersede *all* our present histories by one more exact, comprehensive and emphatic – there can be no doubt that account is now taken of the value of these materials, and a proportionate deduction made from the credit against which they are placed.

It may now fairly be said, we think, to be the main scope and object of Mr Hume's history to show, that the English government, before the accession of the Stuarts, was an arbitrary and absolute monarchy; and that, though the Barons, in rude feudal times, asserted a barbarous and rebellious sort of independence, the body of the people had as little notion of liberty as in Turkey; or any of the Asiatic despotisms – that at this era the people encroached on the settled prerogative of the sovereign, and not the sovereign on the liberties of the people – that this new and audacious questioning of authority rose neither from any sense of actual oppression, nor any speculative ideas of fitness and justice, but from the fermentation of religious zeal and bigotry, by which the whole proceedings of the pretended patriots were actuated, and their notions debased – that the sovereigns, and especially the unfortunate Charles, made, though with natural reluctance, all reasonable concessions, and having, with perfect good faith, divested themselves of the power to do mischief, were trampled upon by the usurping Commons, and overwhelmed, with all the known principles of order and authority, under the ruins of the monarchy and old constitution of the country, – from which they were at last revived, with the universal assent of the nation, at the Restoration, though alarm cast down, with less violence, by the same great agent of religious antipathy, at the Revolution.

Now, Mr Brodie holds the very reverse of this to be the true state of the fact. The English government, he maintains, was founded on principles of liberty from the time of the Saxons; and, though assimilated to the feudal kingdoms of the Continent at the period of the Conquest, was fortunately enabled, by its insular situation, to escape the subjugation which the establishment of standing

---

[2] [John Millar (1735–1801), *An Historical view of the English Government* (1787); Richard Hurd (1720–1808), *Moral and Political Dialogues* (1759); Thomas Birch (1705–1766), *An Inquiry into the Share, which King Charles I. had in the Transactions of the Earl of Glamorgan* (1756); Joseph Towers, *Observations on Mr. Hume's History of England* (1778); selections from these works are contained earlier in this collection.]

armies soon after imposed on its neighbours. He proves accordingly, by the citation of numerous authorities, that the government of England was always spoken of, both by native and foreign authors, as clearly distinguished from those of the continent by its greater freedom, and the higher rights of its people; and shows, that both these objects were provided for by various anxious statutes, long before the accession of the house of Tudor. The wars of York and Lancaster, by breaking the power of the grater Barons, had the double effect of strengthening the Crown by their suppression, and leading the formation of Burghs and free associations among the lower people, whose vocation of private war was now in a great measure destroyed – and who were therefore driven both on the pursuits of industry and the independent assertion of the rights, by this revolution in the state of society. The Commons, therefore, grew into consideration precisely as the Barons declined; and succeeded naturally to the benefit of those limitations on the royal power, which the latter had established chiefly with a view to themselves.

The suppression of religious houses under Henry VIII. operated substantially in the same manner; and though the temper of that prince, and the wealth he had thus acquired, enabled him to venture on stretches of power unknown to his predecessors, there are the plainest indications both of a spirit of resistance in the Parliament, and of an independent supremacy in the law, that marks the true character of the Government as a limited, and not an absolute monarchy. The reign of Mary was that of a bigotted and vindictive faction – and that of Elizabeth, as to the true character of which Mr Hume has indulged in the greatest exaggerations, was that of a Sovereign deservedly popular for her wise administration, and naturally looked upon with peculiar veneration and indulgence, as the great stay of the Protestant cause in Christendom. These advantages armed her with more power than belonged, in ordinary circumstances, to the crown she inherited – while the alarms excited by the machinations of Mary of Scotland and her adherents, and by the threatened invasion from Spain, tempted and almost justified her in occasionally using it in a way which, in other times, would have been more impatiently endured. Mr Brodie however maintains, and we think upon conclusive evidence, that, in spite of some arbitrary proceedings, the reign of Elizabeth was, on the whole, the reign of a constitutional sovereign; and afforded no warrant, in its general tenor, for those broad and systematic assumptions by which the succeeding monarchs endeavoured to establish for themselves an arbitrary and truly unlimited power. He alleges, therefore, and sets himself deliberately to prove, that the Stuarts originated and first proclaimed those tyrannical pretensions by which the whole spirit of the constitution was innovated and debased, and acted, or attempted to act, systematically and habitually upon maxims of government that had never been asserted before – turning occasional acts of power, on which their predecessors had ventured on great emergencies, into the habitual rule of their conduct – and not only claiming prerogatives beyond the warrant of any former precedent, but denying rights to their people, and privileges to their Parliaments, that had never been questioned in any preceding reign. He conceives, therefore, that the Commons were perfectly justified in insisting on the redress of those grievances, and the recognition of those rights, as conditions precedent to their granting any supplies; and that the consequent discontinuance of Parliaments and levying of money without their sanction, were as much without apology from the circumstances, as they were in themselves against all law and precedent. He farther maintains, and we think on strong grounds, that the conduct of Charles was throughout so faithless and insincere as entirely to justify the distrust which the Parliament showed of him, and to render necessary those extraordinary restrictions on which they ultimately insisted, and by the rejection of which the appeal to arms became unavoidable. The blame of the war, therefore, he lays wholly on the king; and contends that it was, in fact, a war waged by him on his people for the purpose of reestablishing his tyranny – and not a rebellion of subjects resolved, at all events, to cast off the trammels of monarchy. He justifies the Parliament accordingly, not only in all their belligerent measures, but in their proceedings against the king; and, looking favourably on the Commonwealth, reprobates the inconsiderate servility of the Restoration, and this poor vindictiveness with which it was followed up.

For our own parts, we are inclined to mediate between these opposite representations. Though we think Mr Brodie quite right in considering the English Government as greatly more free than those of the Continental kingdoms, we cannot but admit to Mr Hume, both that the checks upon royal power were in its early periods brought very irregularly into action, and that the influence of the Commons House of Parliament was very small, and the interests of the great body it represented very subordinate, in the original scheme of the constitution; and though we think it quite correct to assert, that when, from the increase of wealth and industry, they acquired more consideration, they proceeded legitimately in building upon those foundations of independence which the feudal Barons had laid for themselves, it is difficult to deny that this assertion of rights in the Third Estate was substantially a novelty in the government, and directed in many respects to new ends and objects; – although it should never be forgotten, that from the earliest periods, the protection of personal liberty, and the exclusive power of imposing taxations, had been jealously asserted by the Parliament for the benefit of all classes of the population. These, too, constitute undoubtedly the great securities and indications of political freedom; and though the civil expenses of the sovereign were in a great measure defrayed by his hereditary property, and the charges of war greatly diminished by the feudal services he could require, it is certain that these checks did at all times operate as an effectual limitation of his power, though greatly strengthened by the changes that took place on the general pacification of society. The Barons imposed their restrictions rather with their arms than their purses – and controlled the sovereign, not so much by withholding money, as by refusing to furnish men, – or plainly intimating that they would employ them if necessary to compel the concessions they required. When this untractable feudal army was dissolved, and with it the habitual threat and dangers of rebellion, the necessity of obtaining pecuniary supplies became of course more urgent and imperative, and the right of withholding them infinitely more valuable, and more likely to be used.

In like manner, we think it must be admitted to Mr Hume, that the pretensions of the Commons were at this time brought forward with more confidence and precision, and advanced with more systematic steadiness, than at any former period – and that we now find the idea of public liberty for the first time embodied in clear definitions, and asserted upon broad argumentative principles. But if this could at any time have been regarded as an usurpation or encroachment, and was not plainly to be referred to the greater intelligence of the age, it ought at all events to be remarked, that there is room for a similar observation, and to a much greater extent, as to the principles of arbitrary power; and that the advocates of servility undeniably took the lead and set the example in this mutual provocation to the assertion of extreme opinions. It was the reign of James chiefly, and in a particular manner in the acknowledged writings of that monarch himself, that the first solemn and precise claim of absolute authority was made in behalf of an English sovereign, and a naked and elaborate exposition attempted of the duty of passive obedience on the part of his subjects. That these doctrines should have called forth contradictions and denials, and led the way to the angry assertion of opposite opinions, was of course unavoidable; and if extravagant notions were ultimately maintained, upon either side, in the course of a controversy that could not well be altogether impartial or dispassionate, the chief blame should certainly rest on those who first gave the challenge, and courted that appeal to theory and first principles, which is often as hazardous in politics as it is beneficial in the abstract sciences. The truth is, however, that to a certain extent this had become unavoidable – not only because the age had become more speculative and intelligent, but because the increasing numbers and wealth in the body of the nation, together with the decay of the great nobility and the dilapidation of the royal demesnes, had deranged the old balance of the constitution; and brought on a crisis which could not possibly be managed without a thorough examination of those *reasons* upon which the pretensions of the conflicting parties were rested. But though the controversy itself was perhaps unavoidable, it is impossible to forget that the excesses by which it was so fatally embittered, all originated with that party by whom it had been first provoked. The cruel imprisonments, fines, pilloryings, brandings and cuttings of ears, by which the authors of offensive writings were punished in this season of contention, not only began with the government, but were never retorted to any thing like the same extent, even after their exasperated adversaries had succeeded to the possession of power.

The question of practical aggression is substantially resolved by that of the aggression of principal and pretensions – since the one was merely carrying into effect what the other authorized or commanded. Nor is it less idle to take a distinction between aggression by actual force, or menace of force, and aggression by the exercise of prerogative, or of legislative authority. If the last was justifiable, so of course was the former; and one was an obvious and unavoidable consequence of persisting in the other. If the Parliament was guilty of rebellion when they voted an army to support their pretensions, they were no less guilty when they set forth those pretensions in their votes and resolutions – and if the blame of the war is to be laid on the king, it must be, not for raising his standard at Nottingham, but for insisting on those powers for the recovery of which it was lifted. The true beginning of the contest was when the king dissolved his first parliament for refusing to grant a supply till they obtained a redress of grievances; and war, we have always been of opinion, was substantially proclaimed, when he announced, on calling his second, that if they were not more liberal than their predecessors, he would have recourse to other counsels, raise a revenue by his own authority, and govern for the future without their assistance. When these threats were afterwards carried into execution, when members were ordered into arrest for their speeches in parliament – when parliament itself was again dissolved, money extorted by forced loans, monopolies and ship money, and commissions issued to fine and imprison those who resisted these exactions; we hold it to be quite plain that the constitution was violently invaded on the part of the sovereign, and that force might have been justifiably employed to restore it.

It seems impossible, therefore, to deny that the first aggression, in every sense of the word, was on the part of the crown – and, indeed, Mr Hume has himself distinctly admitted, that up to the period of which we have been speaking, the Commons had nothing which they were not clearly entitled to do by the law and constitution of the country, while the king had proceeded on the precedent of a few irregular acts of authority, in the face of the most clear and express enactments. He rests his allegations, therefore, of the reasonableness of the king's conduct and the aggression of the Commons, on the concessions which he *subsequently* made, and the extravagant nature of the demands that were notwithstanding pressed upon him. The liberties of the people, he says, were sufficiently secured by the Petition of Right and the bill for triennial parliaments; and when the Commons afterwards insisted on his giving up to Parliament, though for a limited time, the appointment of military officers and Privy councillors; this, he maintains, was such an unprovoked invasion of the very principle of monarchical government as made all further concession impossible, and threw upon those who made it the whole blame of the hostilities to which it inevitably led. Nothing, however, we conceive, can be more glaringly partial and even absurd than such a determination. The historian should have remembered that he had himself recorded, that when the king dissolved his second parliament, 'it was not improbable that if he had possessed any Military force on which he could rely, he would *at once have taken off the mask*, and governed without any regard to parliamentary privileges: But *his army was new levied, ill paid, and nowise superior to the militia*, who were in a great measure under the influence of the county gentlemen.' For these reasons, and these alone, the sovereign is represented as continuing to wear the mask – and postponing the war which, it is thus admitted, he was disposed to wage for the maintenance or recovery of his prerogatives. He did, to be sure, afterwards pass the petition of right, but confessedly with the greatest possible reluctance, and it is equally certain that he violated it in almost every article within a few years after its enactment. He restored monopolies, increased the tonnage and poundage – extorted loans, arrested members for their speeches in Parliament – and studiously and anxiously appointed to the lieutenancy of counties, and to other military commands, only such men as were implicitly devoted to his cause. The discontents in Scotland and Ireland had enabled him to increase and improve his forces – and left him, after their pacification, in possession of a very formidable army. It was in this situation and those dispositions, and when, as the eloquent historian observes, 'he had begun to speak in a firmer tone, and to retort the accusations of the Commons,' that the proposition for vesting in Parliament the substantial controul of the militia was brought forward, which is here represented by Mr Hume as an unprovoked attack on the monarchy, and a far more inexcusable breach of the constitution, than all that had been charged on the Sovereign. It was a strong, certainly, and extraordinary measure. But the disorders of the time were not to be met by common remedies – and, so far from having been the immediate cause of the war, we are fully persuaded, both that the concession might have saved all the horrors of that unnatural contest, and that the assumption of this power by Parliament rather retarded than accelerated the actual commencement of hostilities. The king was evidently preparing for war – and, being completely deserted in both Houses, had indeed no other means of contention – and, after his retreat to York, was obviously employed in extending his military resources – nor do we believe that any intelligent reader of his history can now doubt that, if he had been allowed to settle the militia on his own plan, he would in a very short time have employed it against the Parliament – and thus not only precipitated, but rendered still more sanguinary and protracted, a struggle that could, after all, have but one result.

We differ from Mr Brodie as to many of the measures of the Parliament during the war – as to the necessity of the king's death – and the merits of the Commonwealth and the Long Parliament. But we differ still more from Mr Hume as to most of these matters – and especially as to the triumph and satisfaction with which he speaks of that unqualified and unconditional Restoration by which all the fruits of this costly experiment were thrown away, and the necessity of a new contest created. We have altogether as little sympathy with his continual leaning to the side of the royalists, after the contention was begun – his plain wishes for their success, and almost ludicrous uneasiness at being obliged to record their defeats. Whatever difference of opinion there might be as to the merits of the controversy before it went to the arbitriment of force, we really do not understand how any candid man can doubt that, after it had come to that extremity, the liberties and the peace of the country could only be secured by the success of the Parliament. Even after that success, by which the rights of the people were necessarily established – the principal and foundation of the monarchy might still have been saved by large and timely concessions: – shorn indeed of its splendour, and deprived for a time of some of its most salutary powers, but still sound at the root, and capable of blossoming forth anew when the season of tempest was over. By the success of the royalists, on the other hand, liberty was disheartened for ages – if not extinguished for ever – for even Mr Hume himself could not believe that, if Charles had been triumphant in the field, he would ever again have allowed a free parliament to assemble, or left himself unprovided with a devoted army to control and put down all popular resistance: And time, which must have allayed the republican fervour, would only have added strength to the system of oppression: For authority has such a tendency to grow and expand itself, that the most limited monarchy requires constant watching and exertion, to prevent it from becoming tyrannical; while the excesses of liberty speedily correct themselves, and are in no danger of becoming perpetual.

We should now proceed to the details of Mr Brodie's arguments and corrections. But, before leaving Mr Hume to his castigation, we must be allowed to make one observation upon that eloquent writer's *inconsistencies*, and another on his rage for ascribing all the measures of the patriots to *religious bigotry* and insane enthusiasm.

The first, we think, is really curious. The History of Mr Hume is the most acute work of one of the most acute men that ever existed. It is carefully, and even artfully composed, and was several times revised and corrected with the greatest pains and diligence – and yet we will venture to say, that it contains more irreconcilable opinions, and indeed more contradictory representations and sentiments, than are to be found in any historical work in existence. That its general tendency and spirit is what we have already attempted to describe, cannot, we suppose, be denied – but the author seems not to have had courage to keep up systematically to the same point – and has made so many remarks and admissions directly at variance with his favourite doctrines, as to have furnished, almost out of his own mouth, conclusive proof of their unsoundness. The key to all this inconsistency and wavering is to be found, we think, partly in a reluctant deference to the liberal maxims established at the Revolution, which could not, in his day, be decently or even safely impugned; and partly in some uncertainty or change of purpose which seems to have come over him in the course of the composition. At the time this history was written, the

Whigs, it should be remembered, were still the predominant party in the State – and it was not allowable directly to question any of their principles, which had been solemnly sanctioned at the settlement of 1688. Nor did the author, we imagine, design at first indirectly to discredit or contest them. His original design, we are persuaded, was by no means so bold or lofty – and aimed at no more than an *apology* for the erroneous and *unjustifiable* conduct of the Stuarts. Admitting that their pretensions were utterly unjust, and that the principles of liberty had been happily established in despite of them, he seems to have thought that sufficient allowance had not been made for the difficulties of their situation – the prejudices incident to their state – the novelty of the circumstances in which they were placed – and the provocations they succes- sively received; and that, without at all depreciating the benefits that had been derived from their expulsion, an explanation might be given of their conduct and that of their adherents, both more favourable to them, and more consistent with the truth of history and the ordinary principles of human nature, than had hitherto been offered. The design we think was fair, and certainly neither unreasonable nor ungenerous – and a great, and perhaps the best part of the work, is dedicated with sufficient correctness to its execution. As he went on, however, the author seems to have been intoxicated with his success; and without entirely renouncing the style of an apologist, to have assumed the feeling and adopted the character of a defender and eulogist – proceeding from excuses to justification – mixing up recrimination with defence, and presuming at last to question, by plain implication, the value of that liberty, and the merit of that patriotism, for which he was every now and then professing in set terms the most profound veneration. Thus his whole history of the Stuarts is composed on a double and discordant tone. Mild, but very distinct censures of the king are interchanged with pathetic exaggerations of the harshness with which he was treated – splendid encomiums on the genius and virtues of the patriots, are followed up by the most contemptuous representa- tions of their virulence, fanaticism, and vulgarity – acknowledgments of the strict legality of their proceedings are balanced by broad assertions of their invasions of the constitution – and tributes to the inestimable value of parlia- mentary privilege and popular rights, neutralized by remarks on the superior despatch and authority which belongs to an executive and irresponsible magis- trate.

It would be idle to think of exhibiting in this place, any part of the proofs which every page almost affords of these assertions. To make their meaning clear, however, we shall mention one or two instances which have happened to catch our eyes in turning over the volume before us. Thus, after saying of the leaders of opposition in Charles's first parliament, that 'these generous Patriots, animated with a warm regard to liberty, saw with regret an unbounded power exercised by the crown, and resolved to seize the opportunity which the king's necessities afforded them, of reducing the prerogative within reasonable compass;' and adding 'that to grant or refuse supplies was the undoubted privilege of the Commons;' he chuses to represent their refusal to grant more than two subsidies till they had been heard on the national griev-ances, as 'a cruel mockery of the sovereign, and a proceeding unprecedented in an English Parliament;' and shortly after, stigmitizes the very persons of whom he had spoken in terms we have now cited, as ambitious fanatics, who advocated 'furious measures,' and 'under colour of redressing grievances, which, during this short reign, could not have been very numerous, proposed to control every part of the government which displeased them.

Of Hampden, he says, in an elaborate character, in itself neither very generous nor very consistent, 'Then was displayed the might ambition of Hampden, taught disguise, not moderation, by former restraint; supported by courage, conducted by prudence, embellished by modesty; but whether founded in a love of power or zeal for liberty, is still, from his untimely end, left doubtful and uncertain.' Now, if ambition means any thing, and especially a mighty, disguised and immoderate ambition, it *must* mean, we should think, a love of power; – but, while such an ambition is assumed as the undoubted basis and denominator of the character, it is admitted to be uncertain whether a love of power had any thing to do with it! But the eloquent writer does not startle even at greater inconsistencies than this, when the object is to lower the character of an anti-royalist. This illustrious person had at one time resolved, it seems, along with Pym and Cromwell, 'to abandon his native country and fly to the other extremity of the globe,' – and then, he who could be actuated only by mighty ambition – founded either in a love of power or a zeal for liberty, is eagerly degraded into a crazy fanatic, who had no other object but 'to enjoy lectures and discourses of any length or form that might please him!'

In the same reckless spirit of flagrant inconsistency, or rather perhaps we should say, of alternate candour and partiality, he first represents the people of England at the commencement of the war in these glowing colours. 'Never was there a people less corrupted by vice, and more actuated by principle, than the English at this period. Never were there individuals who possessed more capacity, more courage, more disinterested zeal. To determine his conduct in the approaching contest, every man hearkened with avidity to *the reasons* proposed on both sides.' But, both before and after, while we meet with perpetual and unvarying praise of the gallantry and generous loyalty of those who adhered to the king, we find nothing but invectives and sarcasms upon the furious bigotry, the base hypocrisy, and low arts of popularity by which their opponents are said to have been actuated. In like manner, he first says of Laud, that though not exactly a Papist, 'the genius of his religion was the same with that of the Romish, and that not only the puritans believed the church of England to be relapsing fast into that superstition, but the court of Rome itself entertained hopes of regaining its authority in this island, and twice offered him privately a Cardinal's hat,' which he declined with great civility;

and then, when he comes to the account of his trial, does not scruple to say, that 'the *groundless* charge of popery, *though belied by his whole conduct*, was continually urged against him.' In the same spirit, when he comes to the agitating scene of the king's trial and condemnation, he first represents it in these words as a proceeding of the most awful grandeur and sublimity. 'The pomp and dignity, the ceremony of this transaction, corresponded to the greatest conception that is suggested in the annals of human kind! The delegates of a great people sitting in judgment on their supreme magistrate, and trying him for his misgovernment and breach of trust!' This, it must be confessed, is, at least, lofty and liberal enough; and would satisfy, we should imagine, the ambition of a professed regicide. But by and by, all this theatrical pomp is conjured away, and this magnificent temple of Justice converted into a den of paltry and contemptible assassins. Instead of his judges being really the delegates of a great nation, we find even the Parliament by whom they were appointed dwindled into 'a diminutive assembly, no longer deserving that honourable name,' and disavowed by the body of the nation; while they themselves are called 'hypocritical parricides, who, by sanctified pretences, had long disguised their treasons,' and now consummated 'the height of all iniquity and fanatical extravagance.'

It is needless, however, to multiply instances of what is so conspicuous in every part of the work; and we shall conclude this slight and passing notice of those glaring inconsistencies, which have hitherto been too little insisted on, by merely observing, that while he repeatedly, and with much emphasis, maintains that 'the king's assent to the petition of right produced such a change in the government, as was almost equivalent to a revolution,' he has himself cited it at length, as if to show, that *it is in every one clause a mere re-enactment of former statutes* of the greatest notoriety and undisputed authority! – while he seems to have forgotten that Clarendon has himself been compelled to admit, that 'it was of no prejudice to the Crown' – so rash and open to refutation are some of the most confident and fundamental of his assertions!

With regard again to *fanaticism*, even the few extracts we have now casually made may show with what exaggerated eagerness he refers to this as the moving spring of all great transactions he records. It is the perpetual theme indeed of his derision and invective – of contemptuous ridicule and bitter abuse. An insane horror of Popery – a ludicrous antipathy to certain vestments and ceremonials of worship, are everywhere represented by him as the true causes of that pretended zeal for liberty which was the source of so many disorders; and all the resources of his pen are employed to darken and degrade the characters of the parliamentary leaders by the imputation of these vulgar and unphilosophical propensities. Now, though it may sound very liberal and reasonable at the present day to speak of Popery and Protestantism as mere varied forms of the same holy faith, and to smile at the intolerant zeal with which the external symbols of each were mutually rejected, it was otherwise, and *reasonably otherwise,* in the times to which Mr Hume would transfer these sentiments; and it is in truth as illiberal as it is absurd to judge the statesmen of that day by the feeling of ours. This very insignificant distinction of Papist and Protestant had, in point of fact, covered Europe with blood and crime for upwards of a century. This *now* innoxious Popery was *then* not only inseparably connected with the principles of political despotism, but had been the cause of the most sanguinary wars, the most inhumane persecutions – the most atrocious massacres. It had produced the eye of St Bartholomew and the massacres in the Netherlands and Switzerland – the wars of the League, of Flanders, and of Holland. In England itself, and so lately as Queen Mary's time, it had lighted up the fires of Smithfield – in Elizabeth's it had produced various rebellions and alarms, and fitted out the Spanish Armada; and in James's it had occasioned the gunpowder treason, and various other plots and disorders. It was in those circumstances, with a war of extermination waging against the Huguenots in France – with a bigotted princess of that family married to the uxorious King of England – with the Primate more than half a Catholic – with a resident nuncio from the Pope, – and under a Prince who, after reluctantly enacting laws against the Papists, raised an unconstitutional revenue by dispensing with their execution – who chose many of his chief counsellors from men of that persuasion – and towards the end of his reign actually treated secretly with the court of Rome and other bigotted Catholic powers for supplies of men and arms to beat down by force the Protestant fanaticism and Protestant liberties of his people – it is with reference to these times, and to these recent and pending transactions that Mr Hume thinks fit to hold up as altogether ludicrous and contemptible those 'eternal complaints against Popery,' and that 'suspicion of a Popish faction about the person of the king,' to which he perpetually directs the attention of his readers as the mainspring of all the discontent and seditions he commemorates. Religious zeal formed, no doubt, one of the great agents in the important events of that age – and in the acrimonious controversies to which it gave rise, a spirit of intolerance was unquestionably generated, and importance attached to matters, that in a more tranquil state of men's minds would have been considered as insignificant: But nothing, we conceive, can be more uncandid and absurd than to represent the nation as on this account incapable of any other impulse, and actuated by a mere delirium of fanaticism, which superseded the use of reason in those under its influence. The truth is, that in spite of the existence of a good deal of bigotry – and a good deal of cant and hypocrisy, there never was an era in the history of the world where the leaders of a popular body were so little the dupes of their own passions or those of their followers – where the spirit of reformation was so uniformly tempered by respect to precedent and authority, or where sober judgment and patient research were so largely blended with national zeal and individual genius and courage.

The most interesting part, perhaps, of Mr Brodie's book, is the volume which contains his Introduction; which is dedicated to an examination of Mr

Hume's Theory of the English Constitution, as it existed before the accession of the Stuarts; and in a particular manner of the doctrines contained in his three memorable Appendixes to the reigns of Elizabeth, James, and Charles, in which he attempts to show, that up to that period the government was substantially arbitrary, and 'bore indeed a considerable resemblance to that of Turkey.' These extraordinary chapters are here subjected to a very minute dissection; and the statements and authorities they contain sifted and canvassed with such effectual severity, as entirely to change the character of the picture they present; and, as we think, totally discredit the theory of the author. It is impossible for us, of course, to give more than a slight abstract of some of the points of correction – and these we must select, fully as much with a view to their admitting of abridgment, as of their absolute importance.

...

47
JOHN STUART MILL

[John Stuart Mill], review of George Brodie's *History of the British Empire* (1822) in *Westminster Review*, October 1824, Vol. 2, pp. 346–402. Selections.

The *Westminster Review* was founded by Jeremy Bentham and James Mill in 1824 as a vehicle for expressing the political views of the philosophical radicals – a utilitarian political group advocating economic and political liberalism. An early contributor to the journal was the young John Stuart Mill (1806–1873), who later became one of the foremost British philosophers of the nineteenth century and, along with Bentham, a chief advocate of utilitarianism. Mill's review of Brodie is principally an attack on the literary "romance" that Hume presents in his account of the Stuart monarchs. In the interest of space, only the opening pages are presented here, which contain his general critique of Hume. The remainder of the article compares Hume's and Brodie's narratives of Charles I; Mill almost always disagrees with Hume, and frequently disagrees with Brodie. Invoking utilitarian reasoning, Mill argues that Hume's caricature of Charles I is especially immoral since it places the selfish pleasure of a single individual (i.e., Hume) against the pleasure of society as a whole – a pleasure involving society's right to know the truth. For Mill, Hume is a master rhetorician who wilfully and systematically suppressed truth: "The direct lies are not a few; the insinuated are innumerable." Hume, argues Mill, did not necessarily invent his lies, but merely perpetuated them from his unscrupulous Royalist sources, namely, Clarendon, Carte, Walker, and Perinchief. This, Mill believes, is just as bad as if he did invent them.

Art. V. *A History of the British Empire, from the Accession of Charles I., to the Restoration; with an introduction, tracing the Progress of Society, and the Constitution, from the Feudal Times, to the Opening of the History; and including a particular Examination of Mr. Hume's Statements, relative to the Character of the English Government.* By George Brodie, Esq., Advocate. In Four Volumes, 8vo. Edinburgh. Bell & Bradfute. London. Longman & Co. 1822.

Mr. Brodie has rendered no mean service to his country by these volumes. We allude, not so much to the merits of his work as a history, though these are considerable, as to the unexampled exposure which he has furnished of the demerits of former writers, and particularly of Hume. In no portion of our history has mis-representation more extensively prevailed, because in no portion of it have the motives, which lead to misrepresentation, been more strong.

Hume possessed powers of a very high order; but regard for truth formed no part of his character. He reasoned with surprising acuteness; but the object of his reasonings was, not to attain truth, but to shew that it is unattainable. His mind, too, was completely enslaved by a taste for literature; not those kinds of literature which teach mankind to know the causes of their happiness and misery, that they may seek the one and avoid the other; but that literature which without regard for truth or utility, seeks only to excite emotion. With the earlier part of his work, we at present have no concern. The latter part has no title to be considered as history. Called a history, it is really a romance; and bears nearly the same degree of resemblance to any thing which really happened, as Old Mortality, or Ivanhoe, while it is far more calculated to mislead. As every romance must have a hero, in his romance of the Stuarts, the hero is Charles the first: and in making a pathetic story about Charles the first, the thing he gave himself least concern about was, whether it was true.

Romance is always dangerous, but when romance assumes the garb of history, it is doubly pernicious. To say nothing of its other evils, on which this is no place to expatiate, it infallibly allies itself with the sinister interests of the few. When events come to be looked at, not as they affect the great interests of mankind, but as they bear upon the pleasures and pains of an individual; a habit is engendered of considering the pleasures and pains of an individual as of more importance than the great interests of mankind. That this is one of the most pernicious of all habits, is proved by merely telling what it is; that it is one which the prevailing system of education carefully fosters, is too true; that it is a habit into which the mind has of itself too strong a tendency to fall, is matter of universal experience. The pleasures and pains most interesting to an ill-cultivated mind, are those of the one and of the few; of the men in exalted stations, whose lot is most conspicuous, whose felicity, to the ignorant, appears something almost divine, and whose misfortunes, from their previous elevation, most powerfully affect the imagination. The sufferings of the many, though multiplied almost beyond calculation from their indefinite extent, are thought nothing of: they seem born to suffer; their fall is from a less height; their miseries lie hidden, and do not meet the eye. Who is there that would not admit, that it is better one should suffer than a million? Yet among those who can feel and cannot reason, nothing is so rare as to sympathize with the million. The one, with them, is every thing, the million, nothing; merely because the one is higher in rank, and perhaps suffers rather more, than any one assignable individual among the million. They would rather that a thousand individuals should suffer one degree each, than that one individual should suffer two degrees.

This propensity is so thoroughly incompatible with the pursuit of the only true end of morality, the greatest happiness of the greatest number, that genuine and enlarged morality cannot exist till it be destroyed; and to this object, he who writes to benefit his species will bend his most strenuous efforts: but he who writes for effect, without caring whether good or evil is the consequence, must address himself to the prevalent feeling, and to this, one of the strongest of prevalent feelings. He must select a hero; if possible a monarch, or a warrior; and to excite a strong interest in this hero, every thing must be sacrificed. If he be an historian, he will probably have to relate, among the actions of his hero, some by which the many are made to suffer; these it is necessary for him to justify or excuse. He may have to relate attempts on the part of the many, to guard themselves against those actions of his hero by which they are made to suffer; these attempts he must represent as extremely wicked, and the many as villains for engaging in such attempts. In short, whenever the interests of mankind, and of his hero, are at variance, he must endeavor to make the reader take part with his hero against mankind.

Such was the object of Hume; and the object to which he deliberately sacrificed truth, honesty, and candour. When, in order to attain the most mischievous of ends, a man does not scruple to employ the most mischievous of means, it makes very little difference in the degree of his immorality, whether he be himself the dupe of his own artifices or not. To that extent, Hume may very possibly have been sincere. He may, perhaps, have been weak enough to believe, that the pleasures and pains of one individual are of unspeakable importance, those of the many of no importance at all. But though it be possible to defend Charles 1st, and be an honest man, it is not possible to be an honest man, and defend him as Hume has done.

A skilful advocate will never tell a lie, when suppressing the truth will answer his purpose; and if a lie must be told, he will rather, if he can, lie by insinuation than by direct assertion. In all the arts of a rhetorician, Hume was a master: and it would be a vain attempt to describe the systematic suppression of truth which is exemplified in this portion of his history; and which, within the sphere of our reading, we have scarcely, if ever, seen matched. Particular instances of this species of mendacity, Mr. Brodie has brought to light in abundance; of the degree in which it pervades the whole, he has not given, nor would it be possible to give, an adequate conception, unless by printing Mr. Brodie's narrative and Hume's in opposite columns. Many of the most material facts, facts upon which the most important of the subsequent transactions hinged, and which even the party writers of the day never attempted to deny, Hume totally omits to mention; others, which are so notorious that they cannot safely be passed over in silence, he either affects to disbelieve, or mentioning no evidence, indirectly gives it to be understood that there was none. The direct lies are not a few; the lies insinuated are innumerable. We do not mean that he originated any lies; for all those which he could possibly need were ready made to his hand. But if it be criminal to be the original inventor of a lie, the crime is scarcely less of him who knowingly repeats it.

The authorities from which the history of those times is to be collected are various. There are royalist writers, and republican writers; and there are original documents, letters, and others, from which the facts may be gathered, free from that colouring which is put upon them in the apologetical writings of either party. There are, in particular, a variety of letters, written, some of them by Charles himself, others by Strafford, and other eminent persons in the royal party, where they unfold to one another designs which were carefully concealed from the public, and which, when imputed to them by their opponents, they repelled as the vilest of calumnies. Almost the whole of these documents Hume passes over, as if they did not exist: because they prove his hero, not only to have been an adept in dissimulation and perfidy, but to have been in the constant habit of making asseverations, and corroborating them by the most solemn appeals to Heaven, which asseverations, when he uttered them, he perfectly well knew to be totally false. And as this fact, if known, would have spoiled him for a hero, Hume makes a point, not only of concealing, but of constantly and unblushingly denying it.

Exclusively of these documents, the authorities which remain are the publications of the two parties at the time, and those of their partisans afterwards. If compelled to draw his whole information from these questionable sources, a fair historian would at least take nothing upon trust from either party; would compare their statements with one another, reject the exaggerations of both sides, and while he would repose tolerable confidence in their admissions against their own cause, would attach little weight to their assertions, when tending to asperse an adversary, or vindicate themselves. As for Hume, had he never looked into any but the royalist publications, the spirit in which he has written his history might have been pardoned, as the effect of blind credulity and partiality. But the names of Whitelocke, Ludlow, Rushworth, May, appear so often at the bottom of the page, as to leave no doubt that, with regard to many of the events which he relates, he knew the truth, and wilfully concealed it. The republican writers are believed – when they bear testimony in favour of the royalists; while the royalists are never disbelieved, except when ,by any chance, they make admissions against themselves.

If we consider who these royalists were, we shall be able to form some estimate of the credibility of a history, nearly the whole of which is copied from them.

The first, and, on the whole, the most respectable, is Clarendon; whom, though he was himself an actor in the scenes which he describes, and was not the more likely to be impartial, that he was a renegade, it has been usual to regard as a man of unimpeachable veracity, for no other reason that we can discover, but because Hume says so; for it surely is no proof that a man will tell truth, because, like every man of sense and prudence, he is sparing of foul language. The question, however, concerning the veracity of Clarendon, may not be considered as settled; see Brodie, vol. iii. pp. 110, 263, 265, 306, 316, 334, 336, 389, 552, *et passim*, for various instances of his dishonesty and bad faith. It is too much to require that we should believe what Hume says of Clarendon rather than what Clarendon says of himself. A writer who makes a boast of the dexterity with which he fabricated speeches, and published them in the names of some of the parliamentary leaders, was not likely to be over scrupulous, when he sat down to write an express vindication of himself and of his party.

If such be the character of the most candid of the royalist writers, it may be judged what credit is due to the more furious partisans. Even Clarendon, indeed, is too honest for Hume; for he occasionally lets out facts which it suits Hume to conceal. His other authorities were less scrupulous. The chief of these are Carte, Clement Walker, and Perinchief; particularly the former, whom he seems almost to have taken as his text book, but whom he rarely ventures to quote; and he frequently commits the dishonesty of referring to Whtelocke or Rushworth for a story, of which the important features are to be found only in Carte. It is chiefly towards the latter end of the story that Perinchief and Walker come into play. Of these three, it is difficult to say which is least deserving of credit. Carte was a vulgar fanatic on the side of royalty, who believed every thing in favour of Charles, and nothing against him; and it is some presumption in favour of his sincerity, that, by the documents published in his Appendix, he furnished, in a great measure, the materials of his own refutation. Of Walker we shall say more hereafter. Of Perinchief we need say nothing, because we are quite sure that no man who has ever read a page of his work, will pay the least regard to any thing that he asserts.

The arts by which Hume has succeeded in obtaining belief for a period so much exceeding the ordinary duration of party lies, are various, and well worthy of examination.

In the first place, he avoids the appearance of violence, and yields some points, in order to make a show of moderation; knowing well that a writer, if he acknowledges only a tenth part of what is true, obtains a reputation for candour which frequently causes people to overlook the mis-statement of the other nine-tenths. Such points, therefore, as are wholly untenable, he gives up with a good grace. He allows some merit to the popular leaders, and acknowledges that they had some reason to complain. Yet, though the people may sometimes have been in the right, he will not allow that Charles can ever have been in the wrong; and if he allows that the people can have been right, it is only to a trifling extent. To extenuate the abuses of the government, there is no sort of concealment which he does not practise: for those which cannot be concealed, while, by an ordinary artifice, he represents them as solitary instances, and exceptions to the general rule, he industriously supplies every palliation which the most refined ingenuity can devise. In the first place, however bad the government might be, it was milder under Charles than under his predecessors; as if that were true; or any thing to the purpose of it were. In the next place, we are told, in at least twenty places, that he was driven to these abuses by an appearance of necessity; when Charles himself never pretended to be moved by necessity, but asserted that he had a right to do all that he did. The religious grievances are expressly declared to be of no consequence; as if it were of no consequence when a king attempts to force his own religion down the throats of the people; as if this were not of itself one of the most tyrannical of all acts of power; and as if a king who would do this, would not do any thing. If it be fanaticism to resist the introduction of a superstitious observance, how much greater is the fanaticism of upholding that observance, by cutting off men's ears and imprisoning them for life? Or, if Charles was himself conscious of the frivolity of the ceremonies which he imposed, what more charitable supposition remains, than that he supported Laud's religion, that Laud might support his power?

Another of the artifices of Hume consists in attempting to prepossess the reader for or against a particular person, while he is still in ignorance of those actions of that person, from which, and not from the assertions of his partisans, or of his enemies, his character ought to be inferred. Thus, every opportunity is taken of holding up king Charles as a person distinguished by every moral excellence: many of his actions indicate the reverse; but as the character has the advantage of coming first, it is hoped that the reader will credit the character rather than the actions. The parliamentary leaders, on the other hand, he represents as hypocrites or fanatics, and (when he dares) as uneducated, coarse, and brutal in their manners and in their character. All this, as Mr. Brodie has shown, is untrue; but it answers the purpose; and the reasoning amounts to this: Vane, Ireton, and Harrison were fanatics, therefore king Charles's government was good: a specimen of argumentation which, if not strictly logical, is, at any rate, extremely convenient, since it is hard if a partisan, however weak his cause, cannot contrive to pick a hole either in the intellectual or moral character of some one or more of his opponents.

We might fill a whole article with an analysis of the artifices of Hume; but a few specimens are necessary, to convince the reader that we have not brought charges which it is not in our power to prove; imperfect as the conception is which can be given by specimens, of a work of which almost every sentence contains in it more or less of misrepresentation. And as it is also incumbent on us to give some idea of what Mr. Brodie has done to throw light upon that portion of history, it seems to us that these two objects may best be united by such a concise sketch of the events of the period as is compatible with the narrow limits of an article; and to this, after requesting the indulgence of the reader to the very general view which it is in our power to afford, we shall proceed. ...

48
JOHN ALLEN

[John Allen], review of John Lingard's *A history of England*, in *Edinburgh Review*, April 1825, Vol. 42, pp. 3–7.
Selections.

Edinburgh native John Allen (1771–1843) was a student of James Gregory at the University of Edinburgh, receiving his medical degree in 1792. He moved to London and became a prominent member of the Whig intelligentsia around Brougham and Macaulay. Beginning in 1811 he was appointed supervisory roles at Dulwich College, during which time he authored several books on legal and political issues concerning British government, most notably his *Inquiry into the Rise and Growth of the Royal Prerogative* (1830). Allen is known in Hume scholarship for *Illustrations of Mr. Hume's Essay Concerning Liberty and Necessity* (1795), his first work, in which he defends Hume against the attack by his professor James Gregory (included in *Early Responses to Hume's Metaphysical and Epistemological Writings*). A contributor to the *Edinburgh Review*, in 1825 his article on the second edition of John Lingard's *History of England* appeared.

In this review, Allen praises Lingard's writing style and scholarship, but feels that it lacks the "profound knowledge of human nature" that we find in Hume's *History*. Hume, he believes, also excels in tragic description. He notes that "Hume has been accused of a childish partiality for Kings," which Allen attributes to the fact that Hume was averse to violence, and, in contests between government and the people, the latter "are sudden and violent." Nevertheless, he feels that "no historian had a stronger sense than Mr Hume of the benefits of civil liberty." An exception to this, though, is Hume's defence of the Stuart monarchs, which, Allen believes, reflects Hume's youthful but lingering bias towards Jacobite views. Insofar as Hume is the leading representative of philosophical historians, Allen notes that Lingard harshly denounced that approach, calling it the philosophy of romance. According to Allen, Lingard misunderstood the nature of the philosophy of history: it is not concerned with divining the secret motives of actors, but with tracing the general causes of social conditions "in spite of the individuals who appear to conduct them."

Allen's review is favourably mentioned in Francis Palgrave's "Hume and his Influence upon History" (1826), contained later in this collection.

ART. I. *A History of England, from the first Invasion of the Romans.* By JOHN LINGARD, D.D. Second edition. 8vo. London, 1823.

...

But it must not be inferred from these remarks, that Dr Lingard has confined himself to a mere recital of events, without comment or observation, or that he is an indifferent spectator of the progress of society and manners. Availing himself of the information accumulated in the two last centuries, and profiting by the labours and researches of his predecessors, he has on the contrary inter-woven in his narrative many valuable episodes, on the character, customs, and institutions of our forefathers, and on the important alterations successively effected in their laws and constitution, in their judicatories, ecclesiastical and civil, and in their administration military and financial. On all these subjects we find much minute and curious information in his history; but we shall look in it in vain for those general and comprehensive views, that sagacity and judgment, those masterly lessons of political wisdom, that profound knowledge of human nature, that calm philosophy, and dispassionate balancing of opinions, which delight and instruct us in the pages of Hume.

It was a practice of that great historian, on grave and important questions, where the justice or expediency of the course to be taken was doubtful or disputed, to bring forward the arguments that might be used on both sides; and to give a more historic form to these discussions, it was not uncommon for him to state them as having been actually proposed and urged at the time, by the contending parties. Dr Lingard appears to disapprove of this practice, and calls it fiction. We are sure that no fraud was intended by it on the part of Mr Hume, and doubt whether he has ever had readers simple enough to believe, that controversial discussions inserted in his history took place in the form and manner there related. Like the speeches in Livy, we have always regarded them as political disquisitions, applicable to all times and places; and believing it to be the object of history to store the mind with knowledge, and not merely to load the memory with events, we have studied them, we confess, with attention, and, we flatter ourselves, with profit. Mr Hume, to be sure, did not extract them from the monkish chronicles, where Dr Lingard has probably sought for them in vain, but drew them from the recesses of his own mind: And, so just and true are his reflections, and yet so natural and obvious do they appear, when presented to us in his admirable sketches, that though no authority may be found for them in contemporary annals, we cannot help believing, that they contain the sentiments and views, not only of the statesmen and parties to whom he ascribes them, but of politicians and nations, at all times and on all occasions when similar questions have arisen, since men were first united in society, and governed by their reason and reflection.

In pathetic and dramatic narration, Dr Lingard must not be compared to Mr Hume; and in moral feeling he is not less inferior. To be oppressed with calamity, was at all times sufficient to excite the sympathy of Mr Hume. To rouse his indignation, it was enough to place before his eyes a scene of cruelty, hypocrisy, or injustice. Dr Lingard has little talent for pathetic description. His humanity is apt to slumber where none but laymen suffer; and his indignation against oppression is seldom warm, unless when churchmen are wronged.

Both historians have their defects. Mr Hume has been accused of a childish partiality for Kings. Dr Lingard worships a more jealous idol – the Church.

Paradoxical as the assertions may seem, it has always appeared to us that Mr Hume was in reality an admirer of popular government in preference to monarchy. But, though in his speculative tenets as republican, it cannot be denied that the general tenor of his History of England is unfavourable to the popular party in our Constitution. From temper, disposition and character, he was averse to violence and turbulence; and therefore, in civil contests, he was always inclined to side with the party that seemed to him to be acting on the defensive. But such, to appearance, is in general the relative situation of a government when contending with its subjects. The encroachments of power are commonly slow and imperceptible; its invasions of popular rights are made without tumult or confusion, disguised by pretences of public good, and often effective for the time in repressing disorder and maintaining tranquillity. The efforts of the people, on the other hand, are sudden and violent, provoked by resentment and oppression, and leading directly to civil war. Mr Hume had, besides, adopted from Brady strained and exaggerated notions of the ancient prerogatives of the Crown; and, seduced by the specious theory of that learned and acute, but disingenuous inquirer, he was led, on many occasions, to mistake the efforts of the people to recover their rights, for invasions of the legitimate authority of the Crown. He did not perceive that the contested prerogatives were usurpations; and forgot that, though sometimes acquiesced in from convenience, and at other times submitted to from necessity, they had been always disputed, and had been frequently resisted with success.

But, though too much disposed, in his History of England, to take part with the Crown against the people, no historian had a stronger sense than Mr Hume of the benefits of civil liberty; no one has pleaded with more success, or defended with steadiness, the cause of humanity and toleration; and, on great occasions, no one has expressed a deeper interest in the struggles for liberty and limited government. It is impossible to read the beautiful and animating passage, where he describes the opening of the Great Parliament, and pourtrays, with such force and truth, the great men there assembled, destined to revive the ancient spirit of their country, without participating in his admiration of their genius, and his applause of their designs. It is true, that dislike of the fanaticism, which at once inspired and clouded their virtues, and commiseration for the victims, justly, though irregularly sacrificed to their resentment, made him afterwards judge harshly, if not unfairly, of their characters, and withdraw from their exertions the sympathy he lavishes on their opponents. But, even in his aberrations from the cause of liberty, we never find him an apostate from its principles. He never deigns to varnish or embellish, with his eloquence, the *speculative* dogmas of slavery. He uniformly treats with scorn and indignation the palliations for cruelty and injustice, whether urged by laymen or churchmen, by kings or demagogues.

We are far from intending, by these remarks on Mr Hume's general character as an historian, to vindicate or palliate his history of the Stuarts. We are thoroughly sensible of its deficiencies in what constitute the chief merit of an historian, fidelity and regard to truth. Various reasons may be given, though no satisfactory excuse can be offered, for his partiality to an unhappy race, whose faults and errors were redeemed by fewer great or good qualities than have fallen to the lot of any family that has ever worn the Crown of England. He had received from education a strong tincture of Jacobitism, which was then fashionable in Scotland among all who felt, or affected, a regard for the honour and ancient independence of their country; and, though his manly understanding rejected with disdain the principles of the Jacobites, his early bias in their favour led him, in his pity for the misfortunes of the Stuarts, to extenuate their guilt. He had encountered opposition too, and narrowly escaped prosecution from the sour and intolerant bigotry of the Calvinistic Clergy, that indisposed him to a party of which they had been the champions and supporters. When he began to write, there was an appearance of gallantry in maintaining a cause, which had been abandoned for half a century by the worshippers of Fortune; for the same turn of character that makes men Tories at present, made them at that time Whigs.

But, setting aside his errors from prejudice and education, his great defect as a friend of liberty and popular government seems to have been a morbid horror of whatever tended to disturb for a time the peace and order of society. Disgusted with the cruelty and ferocity of civil contests, provoked by the hypocrisy of some, indignant at the ambition of others, alarmed at the fury and madness of all, his reflections tend to damp our ardour for exertion, and, without inculcating the principles, lead to the practice of passive obedience. The pupils formed in his school are apt, in their dread of temporary confusion, to overlook or undervalue the permanent evils of slavery; and, in their desire to secure the repose of one generation, to sacrifice the happiness of many. They are no friends to despotic rule, and value, as they ought, the blessings of liberty; but they are better qualified to enjoy its benefits with temper and moderation, when conferred by others, than to earn or maintain it by their own exertions.

Dr Lingard also, we are sorry to say, has no generous sympathy in the cause of freedom. He appears to take little interest in the struggles for liberty that form the brightest part of our annals. He relates, with lifeless coldness, the establishment of Magna Charta, seems unconscious of the importance of the contests between Henry III. and his people, and commemorates the termination of the struggle in the time of Edward I. with freezing indifference. In short, it is only when the honour or the interests of the Church are affected, that his passions are warmed; and even churchmen appear to suffer in his estimation, when they contribute to the civil liberties, or devote themselves to the temporal interests of mankind. One cold sentence of approbation suffices for Winchelsea and Langton: Pages are devoted to the vindication of Dunstan and of Becket.

Dr Lingard, we need scarcely say, is a decided partisan of the Church of Rome. That he should be devoted to her doctrines, was to be expected from the faith he holds, and the profession he has embraced. But he is not only a believer in the creed, and advocate for the discipline of his church; he is the defender of all her saints and confessors, the eulogist of all who have laboured or suffered in her cause, the decrier of all who have resisted her usurpations. From the days of Austin to the dawn of the Reformation, his thermometer for personal merit is of spiritual manufacture. In his own church, he prefers the regular to the secular clergy, and seems to regard the monastic profession as the perfection of Christian virtue. On some occasions he has objected to the claims of temporal authority, and to other usurpations of the Popes; but he is ever faithful to the church. In no instance that we recollect has he renounced any one of her immunities, or abandoned any one of her pretensions. In his account of the celebrated controversy with Becket, he has amused his readers with an historical disquisition on the antiquity of the exemption claimed by the clergy from secular jurisdiction, expressed his doubts of the extent to which that privilege gave impunity to crimes, dropped some hints of the superiority of the ecclesiastical over the lay tribunals, but never unequivocally expressed his disapprobation of the claim itself.

Dr Lingard pronounces his anathema against the philosophy of history, which he is pleased to term the philosophy of romance. He compares the philosophic historian to the novelist, 'whose privilege,' he tells us, it is 'to be always acquainted with the secret motives of those whose conduct and character he delineates.' (Preface). More is not wanted to show, that he entirely misconceives the nature and purpose of what has been called the philosophy of history. The philosophic historian troubles himself little with the characters of individuals, or with the motives that influence their actions. His object is to trace the general causes in the state and condition of society that determine events, independent, and often in spite of the individuals who appear to conduct them. He neglects the fly, to study the wheel on which it revolves. The fault to which he is most prone, is indifference about individuals. He neither interests himself nor his readers in their fate or fortunes. Instead of a dramatic story, his work becomes a dry dissertation. Content with enlarging our views, and enlightening our understanding, he aspires not to warm our passions, or excite our feelings. The mistake of Dr Lingard, if it is not a sacrifice to the vulgar cant of the day, must have arisen from his aversion to Hume, who is justly placed by common consent at the head of our philosophic historians. But Dr Lingard should understand, that Mr Hume is not more distinguished for his philosophy, than for his sagacity and judgment, his feeling and pathos. In diligence and critical research he must yield the palm to Dr Lingard; but in no other point of view are they to be put for one moment in comparison.

Dr Lingard next proceeds gravely to tell us, 'that the writer of history can know no more than his authorities have disclosed, or the facts themselves necessarily suggest.' If, by *necessarily* in this passage, Dr Lingard means that which follows by inevitable consequence, he has himself departed from his own rule.

...

49
FRANCIS PALGRAVE

[Francis Palgrave], "Anglo-Saxon History," in *Quarterly Review*, London, June 1826, Vol. 34, 248–298.
Selections.

The *Quarterly Review* was founded in 1809 by London publisher John Murray as a Tory answer to the Whig ideology of the *Edinburgh Review*. An active contributor to both journals was London native Francis Palgrave (1788–1861). Born to Jewish parents and originally having the surname "Cohen", in 1823 he converted to Christianity and changed his name to "Palgrave" – a family name on his mother's side. He worked in the legal profession, authored numerous works on history and law, and was knighted in 1832. Palgrave critiques Hume in two *Quarterly Review* articles: "Anglo-Saxon History," excerpted here, and almost 20 years later in his 1844 "Hume and his Influence upon History," included later in this collection. The earlier article appears as a book review of the 1825 edition of Hume's *History*, with the running head titled "Anglo-Saxon History." Only the opening few pages are on Hume, though, and the remainder of this lengthy essay discusses ancient sources of English history, with no further reference to Hume. In the opening pages Palgrave condemns Hume's uncritical reliance on secondary sources: "Hume has not even observed the obvious rule of avoiding to adduce secondary evidence when an original witness can be obtained." He notes that Hume indeed footnotes "a cabbalistic array of names, and syllables," but most of these are secondary glosses, rather than primary sources.

"Anglo Saxon History" is reprinted in *Palgrave's Collected Historical Works* (Cambridge, 1922, Vol. 9, pp. 375–428). In the introduction to that volume, editor H.E. Malden states that Palgrave's assault on Hume seems unnecessary now, but was certainly valid in Palgrave's day:

The slaughtering of the historical authority of Hume may appear unnecessary. No one now thinks that he is an authority. In Sir Francis Palgrave's own day, his own labours were rapidly establishing a different standard of historical evidence from that of Hume. It is a perfectly fair indictment that the philosophic stickler for good evidence with regard to miracles was content to accept the weakest evidence for non-miraculous events in history, and about views and motives of eminent men of the past, if such evidence happened to coincide with his own unphilosophic assumption of what events and motives were likely to have been. But the anti-religious or immoral influence of Hume upon the rising generation was not perhaps so very dangerous as Sir Francis feared. When Hume was distilled through the mouths of Mrs Markham and her terrible children, he might be very trivial, and was of course very incorrect, but he was not deeply corrupting. ... He was a great historian to an age which was content that Goldsmith should write school histories, because "he wrote like an angel," and should write a Natural History, when he just knew a horse from a cow.

Malden reiterates his point specifically regarding Palgrave's article on "Anglo-Saxon History":

The article upon "Anglo-Saxon History" has a new edition of Hume as its supposed *raison d'être*, but is mainly a consideration of the authorities for our earlier history. We again meet with what is to us a superfluous slaying of the slain, the pseudo-Ingulph is exposed as an evident fabrication. That this is so is a matter of course to us, but he had imposed upon everyone for a long time, and nearly up to the date of the article, 1826. [Introduction, p. xxix-xxx]

The following is from the original article in the *Quarterly Review*.

ANGLO-SAXON HISTORY.

ART. XI. – *The History of England, from the Invasion of Julius Caesar to the Revolution of 1688.* By David Hume, Esq. New Edition. London. 1825.

Whatever opinions may be entertained respecting the faith which ought to be placed in a modern narrative of ancient history, there is, generally speaking, hardly any doubt concerning the truth of the materials from whence the composition is derived. Perhaps the inferences of the writer may be denied, or his arguments may be deemed fallacious, but the sources of his work are admitted, without contest, as authentic testimonies. We are sufficiently careful to guard against the errors of the *author*, particularly when the subject is such as to offer a probability of his being either deceived himself, or inclined to deceive his readers, a misled follower or a fallacious guide. Should any suspicions arise, we contest his qualifications, we examine his principles, we ask for his creed. And if we are disposed to try the history by the severest test, we compare it with the 'original authorities,' and we examine whether the facts which rest upon ancient evidence are fairly and faithfully recited or rendered.

If the author's text and the 'authorities' which he quotes are found to agree, we are satisfied. After this investigation has been performed our inquiries end. The vigilance awakened by the modern historian is rarely excited by the ancient chronicler. Upon our ancestors we willingly bestow the faith which we withdraw from our contemporaries, and consider all as 'very sooth' which has the venerable sanction of grave antiquity.

Our disinclination to examine into the positive veracity and comparative value of the ancient sources of ancient history may be easily explained. The individuals who flourished in the many, long, remote centuries, which we denote by the comprehensive term of the 'middle ages,' are so essentially distinguished by language, manner and mind, from the individuals of the living age, that they seem to form but one class when contrasted with our contemporaries. All minor distinctions amongst them are lost in the general conformity. The Nun of Sion prays beside the Benedictine Monk of Lindidarne. Mailed crusaders unite with the ranks of the gallant chivalry of the Tilt Yard. Plantagenets and Tudors meet in the same presence-chamber. The interval by which they are separated from us appears to place all their forms at the same distance. All are equally uncouth and strange. Enveloped alike in mist and gloom, we are impressed with a vague idea of remoteness, and we do not sufficiently measure the gradations in which they recede.

Hume, in the first chapters of his history, affords a curious exemplification of the deceptions thus produced by the aerial perspective of the mind. It might be anticipated that the author of the Essay on Miracles would have prefaced his historical inquiries by carefully scrutinizing the value of his authorities. In endeavouring to establish his facts by an appeal to historical testimony, we might have expected some recollection of his own rules. We have been taught by him to attend to the character of the witnesses, to balance every circumstance which can occasion doubt, and to mark every cause of suspicion. Such, however, is far from being his mode of proceeding, when he had occasion to practise his own maxims. Hume has not even observed the obvious rule of avoiding to adduce secondary evidence when an original witness can be obtained. At the foot of his pages we have, certainly, a cabalistic array of names, and syllables, and figures; but this host of quotations can only betray the reader into the belief that the history has resulted from a careful comparison of testimonies. A more minute examination of the authorities will dispel our reliance on the judgment of the historian. Without any selection, any attempt at discrimination, we find the Saxon Chronicle and Florence of Worcester, William of Malmesbury, Ralph Higden, and Matthew of Westminster, all considered as the vouchers for the events of the reign of the Confessor, and, apparently, with equal confidence and satisfaction. Yet, how different are the grounds upon which they are to be trusted! – The Saxon Chronicle may be considered, in this portion, as coeval with the events which it relates. – Morence of Worcester, in the corresponding sections of his Latin Chronicle, is merely a translator of the Saxon Chronicle; and his version, though of great importance in affording an assistance to the right interpretation of the Anglo-Saxon text, is without any weight if quoted as cumulative testimony. – William of Malmesbury, removed but by one generation from the Anglo-Saxon age, was enabled to consult authorities which cannot be traced in any other ancient historian. – Ralph Higden flourished towards the close of the reign of Edward III., and his Chronicle, a new edition of a compilation formed by Roger of Chester, who wrote a few years before, consists entirely of excerpts from original writers, all of which are extant, connected by his own remarks and annotations. – Matthew of Westminster is a phantom who never existed. – If such an un-critical use of ancient authorities was made by Hume, a reasoner gifted with singular acuteness and sagacity, and trained and exercised in the very school of scepticism, we may well account for the impression usually received respecting those passages of history which are as familiar to us as household words. The authorities being all admitted to be valid, it follows as a necessary consequence that the facts remain unchallenged. Adventures inseparably associated to well-known names; deeds which have been recounted to us from our earliest childhood; monarchs whose grim imaginary portraitures have been presented to us so often that we recognise them as easily as the countenances of our own parents, form the popular materials and characters of popular history. Seldom do they offer themselves in such a guise as to excite any degree of hesitation. The utmost extent of our incredulity is to disbelieve that Saint Dunstan really pulled the devil by the nose. From the Trojan war to the battle of Bosworth field, the scenes of 'ancient history' rise up successively with undiminished vividness and unimpeached credibility.

If, however, we pause, and reflect upon the nature of the sources of history, our confidence must in some measure forsake us. Every nation has passed through an heroic age, during which no evidence, in the strict sense of the term, can be preserved of historical facts. Truth maintains a perpetual conflict with fiction. The causes which stamp such an era with its distinguishing character destroy the fidelity of its records. During the various stages of incipient civilization, the might of some one individual, preeminent either for physical or moral power, is the main-spring of the fortunes of society. When the skill and prowess of one chieftain enable him to decide the battle, his achievements obtain a much more minute and favoured narrative than the fate of the nation whom he leads to victory. Recollections are attached to the glory of the warrior, not to the annals of the commonwealth. Giants overshadow the subject world, and beneath the colossal forms of legislators and leaders we lose all sense of the importance which belongs to the herd of human-kind.

...

50
THOMAS JEFFERSON
AND GEORGE TUCKER

Thomas Jefferson and George Tucker, "Jeffersoniana: Hume's Political Principles," *Virginia Literary Museum*, No. 1, June 17, 1829, pp. 13–15. Complete.

Thomas Jefferson (1743–1826) – third president of the United States – founded the University of Virginia in 1818, and appointed former Congressman George Tucker (1775–1861) professor of moral philosophy in 1825. Tucker and a fellow professor, Robley Dunglison, founded the *Virginia Literary Museum* in 1829 as a scholarly outlet for the University faculty. The journal folded a year later for the failure of the faculty to meet publishing deadlines, and the burden this placed on Tucker and Dunglison to write most of the articles. Beginning around 1807, Jefferson's private letters display his negative attitude towards Hume's *History* and its Tory ideology. This is also reflected in Jefferson's commonplace book, which, in one section, contains a list of passages from Hume's *History* that were particularly disregarding of individual liberty. Tucker gained access to Jefferson's commonplace book and, in the first issue of the *Virginia Literary Museum*, he transcribes these passages from Hume. He notes further that Hume's political views have indeed sparked opposition in both Britain and the United States, and Jefferson "entertained doubts of letting Hume's *History* hold a place in the University library." Contrary to Jefferson, though, Tucker argues that British concerns about Hume's *History* do not affect Americans, and youth may read his work "without any danger of being contaminated by his principles of government." The article was published anonymously, subscribed with the initial "V", which was an abbreviation that Tucker used for several articles that he personally authored. Comments in square brackets are those of the original article; those in curly brackets are mine.

JEFFERSONIANA

{Tucker:} The kindness of Thomas Jefferson Randolph, Esq. – the grandson of the Patriot and Philosopher, whose actions occupy so large a space in the history of his country's glory, — will enable us to lay before our readers, under this head, several extracts from the Common-Place Books of that illustrious individual, which are not destined to meet the public eye in any other form. They will be additional evidences of the indefatigable industry, in the prosecution of knowledge, which so preeminently distinguished him through the whole course of his long and useful life.

No. 1. – HUME'S POLITICAL PRINCIPLES

{Jefferson:} 'The following are specimens of Hume's political principles.

"I shall only ask, whether it be not sufficiently clear, from all these transactions [to wit, temp. Elizabeth," that in the two succeeding reigns [to wit of James and Charles,] it was the people who encroached upon the sovereign: not the sovereign who attempted, as is represented, to usurp upon the people." Note AA. to chap. 42. "The grievances, under which the English laboured [to wit, whipping, pillorying, cropping, imprisoning, fining, &c.] when considered in themselves, without regard to the constitution, scarcely deserved the names, nor were they either burthensome on the people's properties, or any wise shocking to the natural humanity of mankind." c. 53.

"Had the preceding administration of the King [Charles,] which we are apt to call arbitrary, proceeded from ambition, and an unjust desire of encroaching on the antient liberties of the people, there would have been less reason for giving him any trust, or leaving in his hands a considerable share of that power which he had so much abused; but if his conduct was, in a great measure, derived from necessity, and from a natural desire of defending that prerogative which was transmitted to him from his ancestors, and which his parliaments were visibly encroaching on, there is no reason why he may not be esteemed a very virtuous prince and entirely worthy of trust from his people." Note CC. c. 56.

"That the letter of the law, as much as the most flaming court sermon, inculcates passive obedience, is apparent: and though the spirit of a limited government seems to require, in extraordinary cases, some mitigation of so rigorous a doctrine, it must be confessed, that the preceding genius of the English Constitution had rendered a mistake in this particular very natural and excusable." c. 57. ch. I. "It is seldom, that the people gain any thing by revolutions in government," c. 59. "The Commons established a principle, which is noble in itself and seems specious, but is belied by all history and experience, *that the people are the origin of all just power*," c. 59. "Government is instituted in order to restrain the fury and the injustice of the people; and being always founded on opinion, not on force, it is dangerous to weaken, by these speculations, the reverence which the multitude owe to authority, and to instruct them before hand that the case can ever happen, when they may be freed from their duty of allegiance: or, should it be found impossible to restrain the license of human disquisitions, it must be acknowledged that the doctrine of obedience ought alone to be *inculcated*, and that the exceptions, which are rare, ought seldom or never to be mentioned in popular reasonings and discourses." c. 59. "Amidst the passions and prejudices of that period, that he [Cromwell] should prefer the parliamentary to the legal cause, will not appear extraordinary, since, even at present, some men of sense and knowledge are disposed to think that the question with regard to the justice of the quarrel, may be regarded as doubtful and uncertain." c. 61. *sub fine.* In a debate, in the House of Commons, March 23, 1824, Sir James Mc'Intosh quotes Burke as having said in some speech "I believe we shall all come to think, at last, with Mr. Hume, that an absolute monarchy is not so bad a thing as we supposed." – *Globe*, March 24, 1824.'

{Tucker:} In offering the preceding extracts, which Mr. Jefferson has grouped together for the sake of making the author's political tenets more flagrant and odious, we cannot forbear to add some passing remarks.

The principles here exhibited by Hume, taken in connexion with his unquestioned partiality for the house of Stuart, have excited vehement opposition to his history of that ill fated race among the friends of civil liberty, in this country as well as England, notwithstanding the admiration they could not but feel for the beauties of his style and his just and profound views of men and things. Nay, these very charms of his diction and philosophy served but to heighten the hostility to his history, from the influence they would naturally exert in recommending acts of tyranny and arbitrary principles of government to his readers, who are thus made to swallow poison and to believe it as wholesome as it is palatable. They have therefore long wished to see a well written history of this important era in English annals, which would counteract Hume's political principles, by refuting his constitutional doctrines, and proving him mistaken in his facts. It was by this feeling that Mr. Fox was induced to undertake that history which he never lived to finish – that Godwin and Sir James Mc'Intosh have also, as we are told, been long engaged in similar undertakings – and that Brodie, in the work he has lately published, has laboured so diligently to shew the want of authenticity in Hume's statements.

Mr. Jefferson, who was so sensitive to every thing that seemed to have the least bearing on the cause of human freedom, partook largely of the same feeling. He even once entertained doubts of letting Hume's History hold a place in the University library; and he never failed, when an occasion presented itself, to warn his youthful acquaintance of its dangerous heresies, and to recommend, as its antidote, that work of Brodie, by whom he used to say Hume had been '*pulverized.*'

This opposition to Hume has acquired force in England from a circumstance which has no application with us. In that country, precedent has great weight in determining the principles of an ancient and unwritten constitution as well as in the administration of justice. Both the Whigs and Tories therefore, endeavour to support their several views of the English Constitution, by past examples; and history acquires with them an additional interest from its bearing on the political struggles of the day. A natural consequence of this interest is that it often influences men in the interpretation of such historical facts as are doubtful or obscure, and even in their estimation of the historians themselves.

But the cause is otherwise in this country, where the fundamental principles of government are not founded on precedent and usage, but on the interests of the people, as indicated by their will; and where it is held that every generation has the right, as well as the power, to make its own laws, whether primordial or municipal. We may, therefore, and ought to take the same cool and dispassionate views of these disputes about the ancient Constitution of England, as of those between the Patrician and Plebian orders of the Roman Republic; and we may admit the weight of argument to be on either side, without conceding any thing unfavourable to popular rights.

Besides, we are not only exempt from the bias arising from the supposed force of precedent, but our political principles are inculcated in so many thousand ways – they have been taught us from our earliest infancy – and we are so accustomed to see them in daily and beneficent operation, that, with most of our citizens, Hume's political tenets, however speciously recommended, must be altogether innoxious; and although we do not wonder that Mr. Jefferson should have continued to feel apprehensions that were well founded in his early life, in the same way as a fond mother who has been alarmed for the safety of her infant offspring, is ever afterwards alive to the dread of the same danger, yet we must think that his fears are unfounded, and that our youth may safely read Hume's History, and profit by his profound sagacity, n tracing events from their first causes to their remote effects; his accurate discriminations between semblance and truth; his thorough penetration into the motives of human conduct, and the inimitable ease and beauty of his style, without any danger of being contaminated by his principles of government, which, with the safeguards that have been mentioned, they would hold to be detestable, if they did not perceive them to be absurd.

V.

51
HENRY HALLAM

[Henry Hallam], review of John Lingard's *A history of England*, in *Edinburgh Review*, March 1831, Vol. 53, pp. 1–43. Selections.

An attorney by training, Henry Hallam (1777–1859) authored three major works in European and British history: *A View of the State of Europe during the Middle Ages* (1818), *The Constitutional History of England* (1827), and *The Introduction to the Literature of Europe* (1837–1839). His views of English political history were Whiggish and thus opposed to Hume's. He opens his review of Lingard's *History* by comparing the merits of other recent histories of England. He says of Hume's *History* that it is "not only the greatest monument of historical literature in our language, but in many respects equal perhaps to any which either ancient or modern Italy has produced." However, he charges that there are strong parallels between Hume's and Thomas Carte's respective histories, particularly regarding the earlier periods of English history. Thomas Birch's *Inquiry* (1756), John Whitaker's *History of Manchester* (1771–1775), and John Stuart Mill's review of Brodie (1825) had also noted Hume's heavy reliance on Carte. These earlier critics faulted Hume specifically for relying on Carte as his principal source of information, rather than consulting more ancient authorities. Hallam takes the issue a step further, though, and argues that Hume's sentence structure very often parallels what we find in Carte. To illustrate his contention he presents paragraphs from Hume and Carte that compellingly show the parallels. He believes, though, that a charge of plagiarism would be absurd, and, instead, feels that it is to Hume's credit that he kept "a valuable model before his eyes in composition."

ART. I. – *A History of England, from the Invasion by the Romans*. By John Lingard, D.D. Eight vols. 4to. London: 1819–1830.

... Carte is certainly no concise writer. On a loose calculation, we find that, down to the reign of James I., his letter-press is to that of Rapin about as three to two; to that of Hume as nine to four; and to that of Dr Lingard, less than two to one. This prolixity, and the inconvenience of the folio size, which

313

excludes so many books of ancient repute from the tables of a more indolent generation, have rendered Carte's History, comparatively even with Rapin, an obscure book. As far, however, as the reign of James I. inclusive, he is incomparably superior to Rapin, in copiousness of materials and accuracy of statement. Instead of confining himself, like his predecessor, to the more common printed authorities, he sought access to original papers, both in Paris and London; and perhaps fell sometimes into the not unusual fault of relying too much on rare and unpublished documents when they disagreed with popular history. It is hardly necessary to observe, that Carte is to be read with great caution on all subjects of constitutional privileges.

The last volume of Carte had not issued from the press, when an eminent writer, conspicuous already for a diversified and brilliant, though sometimes too eccentric, career over the fields of literature and philosophy, undertook a labour not apparently very congenial to the habits of his mind, as they had hitherto been displayed, in a History of the House of Stuart. Hume published the first volume of this in 1754, and the second in 1756. The History of the House of Tudor followed at equal length in 1759; and two more volumes in 1761, by a curiously retrograde process, completed the usual course from Julius Cæsar to the Revolution. Eulogy is superfluous on a work which is not only the greatest monument of historical literature in our language, but in many respects equal perhaps to any which either ancient or modern Italy has produced. Many have excelled, and others will hereafter excel Hume in their knowledge of the spirit of antiquity, in their exactness and circumstantiality of narration, and, what is more important, in their rigorous adherence to the laws of moral and historical truth, in the estimate of political transactions and characters. But we can hardly hope to see his rival in reflections usually just, and often profound, without the involution of mystical pedantry, in the harmonious subordination of illustrative digressions to the main stream of history, or, still less perhaps, in a style equally fitted for narration and for dissertation, – easy without being feeble, simple without dryness, and, if not always free from a little affectation in idiom, never losing its elegance in redundant ornament, or learned abstraction.

It has been often asserted that Hume has made great use of Carte's History, especially in his first two volumes; and he has even been called his copyist.[1] We have had the curiosity to compare a few passages at random, and the result is, to a great extent, in confirmation of this fact. We mean only, that Hume appears to have written with Carte always open before him, and to have followed him, generally speaking, not only in the arrangement of events, but

---

[1] [John Whitaker (1735–1808), in *The History of Manchester* (1771–1773) writes "In all the earlier parts of our history Mr. Hume is merely the copier of Mr. Carte" (see selections from Whitaker included earlier in this collection).]

in the structure of his exposition of them; giving, however, the colour of his own thoughts and style to the whole narration, and continually, as we believe, both verifying the statements of his predecessor, and adding what he thought requisite to his own by a reference to the original sources. As this is a matter of some literary curiosity, we will insert two very short extracts in order to exhibit this parallelism.

'Henry was hunting in the New Forest, when he heard the news of his brother William's death; and resolving to make a push for the throne, went immediately to the Castle of Winchester, to demand the keys of the royal treasury, which the guards made some difficulty in delivering. They were in the custody of William de Breteuil, (the eldest son of William Fits-Osborn, formerly Earl of Hereford,) who was likewise in another quarter of the forest; when, being surprised with an account of the king's death, he made all possible haste home to take care of his charge; and, arriving in the middle of the dispute, told the young prince that neither the treasure nor the sceptre of England belonged to him, but to his elder brother Robert, to whom he and others of the chief nobility had already done homage. High words arose, and blows were likely to follow, when Robert, Count of Meulant, with a great number of the late king's attendants, coming in, took the part of the prince present, and forced William to leave him master of the treasure, with which they hoped, perhaps, to be rewarded for their service.' – *Carte*, vol. i. p. 480.

'Prince Henry was hunting with Rufus in the New Forest, when intelligence of that prince's death was brought him; and, being sensible of the advantage attending the conjuncture, he immediately galloped to Winchester, in order to secure the royal treasure, which he knew to be a necessary implement for facilitating his designs upon the crown. He had scarcely reached the place when William de Breteuil, keeper of the treasure, arrived, and opposed himself to Henry's pretensions. This nobleman, who had been engaged in the same party of hunting, had no sooner heard of his master's death, than he hastened to take care of his charge; and he told the prince, that this treasure, as well as the crown, belonged to his elder brother, who was now his sovereign; and that he himself, for his part, was determined, in spite of all other pretensions, to maintain his allegiance to him. But Henry, drawing his sword, threatened him with instant death if he dared to disobey him; and as others of the late king's retinue, who came every moment to Winchester, joined the prince's party, Breteuil was obliged to withdraw his opposition, and to acquiesce in this violence.' – *Hume*, vol. i., p. 222. 4to. 1762.

It will be understood by the reader that we produce these passages as an example, not as sufficient proof, of Hume's use of Carte. A single incident cannot, of course, display this so conclusively as a series of events expanded into several paragraphs, which we have not room to insert. But we believe that any one will satisfy himself of what we have said by a comparison of the two volumes in different parts. If it should be conceived that historians, relating the same events from several authorities, will naturally adopt an identical arrangement, even in the structure of their sentences, the contrary will be shown by trying the experiment upon Rapin or Lingard. It will appear, if a fair number of instances be tried, that the diversities in the order and tone of impressions made on the mind of an historian who compares and meditates upon his materials, will prevent two wholly independent writers, as soon as they leave the track of mere translation, from presenting similar narrations to the reader's eye. In these observations we have not the slightest intention of bringing the absurd charge of plagiarism against our philosophical historian. On the contrary, we think that having ascertained, as he undoubtedly did, the judiciousness and veracity of Carte, he acted much more fairly by his readers in keeping a valuable model before his eyes in composition, than if he had endeavoured to weave a new web of a texture which he would, perhaps, himself have felt to be inferior. It had not been the occupation of his life to investigate the early annals of England; and those who can only devote a limited time to any historical study, know well the importance of a standard work to marshal and methodize their enquiries.

The unpretending and elegant, though necessarily superficial, abridgment of Goldsmith, hardly deserves notice in this place; much less an epitome of that abridgment, entitled 'History of England, in Letters from a Nobleman to his Son,' which the booksellers' catalogues ridiculously attributed to Lord Lyttleton. Nor has Smollett in the slightest degree better pretensions than Goldsmith to authority as an historian, while he is utterly deficient in the qualities of style which belong to the latter. His continuation of Hume, nevertheless, having been generally bound up in the same series by those Mezentiuses, the booksellers, who yoke the dead to the living, and the high-bred courser to their own battered hackney, has obtained, not a reputation, but a sale which it little deserves. The history of the same period, which we hope to obtain from the pen of Sir James Mackintosh, will send Smollett to the cheesmongers. Not more than a few years had elapsed since the publication of Hume's last volumes, when Dr Henry announced a History of Britain upon a new plan. Each volume, of which he promised twelve, as to be divided into seven chapters, for the civil and the military, the ecclesiastical, the legal and constitutional, the literary history, that of arts, of commerce, and of manners, for the several periods which the entire work was to comprehend. It seems that he had contemplated its continuance to his own time; but death intercepted his progress in the sixth volume, at the death of Henry VIII. The success of Henry's history for many years after its appearance, cannot be ascribed to any grace of his style, which is homely, though not absolutely bad, nor to any depth of research, for he is superficial, perhaps inevitably so, in every portion of his multifarious narrations, but to the increasing avidity for information upon arts and learning, and upon the domestic life of our ancestors, which his peculiar scheme of composition led him to display on a far greater scale than had been usual with the historian of public events. The scheme itself merits no great praise; even as an arrangement to facilitate reference, it does not supersede the necessity of an index, though he has given none; and the reader, who undertakes the perusal of the whole, is distracted by continually passing from one subject to another of a totally different nature. The important accessions to our knowledge on the subjects of many chapters in Dr Henry's history since its publication, have diminished its usefulness; though they cannot, of course, take away from his just praise of having made much accessible which was then beyond the reach of an ordinary reader.

...

52
WILLIAM SMYTH

William Smyth, *Lectures on modern history: from the irruption of the northern nations to the close of the American Revolution*. London: William Pickering; J. and J.J. Deighton, 1840, 2 v.
Selections from Lectures 5, 10, 14 and 18; from 1840 edition.

Whig historian William Smyth (1765–1849) was born in Liverpool, the son of a banker. Educated at Cambridge, in 1807 he was appointed regius professor of modern history at Cambridge, a position which he held for 42 years until his death. His two principal lecture subjects were modern history and the French revolution. In 1817 he published a pamphlet for his students titled *List of Books Recommended and Referred to in the Lectures in Modern History*. Revised over the decades, Smyth's course material finally appeared in his *Lectures on Modern History* (1840) and *Lectures on the French Revolution* (1840). Smyth mentions Hume throughout his *Lectures on Modern History*; four sustained discussions are excerpted here. In Lecture 5, on England, he contends that the principal defining issue in English history is prerogative versus privilege, and writers on history invariably construe their narratives according to one or the other of these ideologies. Hume is an example of a defender of prerogative. This, Smyth believes, should be duly noted since "Hume is the historian, whose views and opinions insensibly become our own." Although Hume could be challenged on all points of his interpretation, to do so would be very tedious, and no one but a few scholars would read such a critique. To this end, though, Smyth selects and dissects two passages from Hume. The first, from Chapter 16, discusses the arbitrary levying of taxes by Edward III. Sentence by sentence, Smyth argues that Hume inaccurately represents his authorities. The second, from Chapter 17, discusses the bishop of Carlisle's speech in defence of Richard II. Smyth argues that Hume fabricates his account of the speech, which illustrates more generally how Hume attributes "to the personages of history the sentiments of his own philosophic mind." But it is not the job of the historian, Smyth believes, to offer "modern views and sentiments of his own."

In Lecture 10, on the Reformation, Smyth notes Hume's bias against religion, but nevertheless recommends Hume's discussion: "The most religious man may be taught lesson by some of the comments of this powerful writer." In Lecture

14 he largely agrees with Hume's view of the arbitrary nature of the constitution under Elizabeth, but objects that at least occasionally she gave way to the wishes of the commons. In Lecture 18 he criticizes Hume's distorted picture of Charles II, and he laments the poor use Hume made of two important manuscripts, which he accessed in France.

Smyth's *Lectures* is favourably mentioned in Francis Palgrave's "Hume and his Influence upon History" (1826), contained later in this collection. His work was revised and published several times in Britain and America in the 1840s and 50s; an abridged version appeared a century later in 1955. The following is from the 1840 first edition of the *Lectures*.

LECTURE V.
ENGLAND.

... [H]istorians and philosophers are affected by different feelings, and give different representations of the same periods; and every student must refer to authorities and judge for himself.

Turn, for instance, to the history of Hume. We are scarcely entered upon the work and referred to the notes, before we see the symptoms of some contrariety of opinion between the historian and other writers with respect to the original nature of our constitution. If we have recourse to the authors whom he quotes or alludes to, the shades of controversy soon thicken around us, and we perceive that the same dispute exists among our own writers that will be found among the historians and antiquarians of the French nation; between those who insist upon the popular, and those who contend for the aristocratic and monarchical nature of the original constitutions and governments of Europe.

Controversies of this kind have arisen not only from the curious and disputable nature of these topics, but from a difference of sentiment, which has always existed among the writers and reasoners that have lived under the mixed governments of Europe: secretly or avowedly they have always fallen into two divisions – those who think the interests of the community are best served by favouring the monarchical part of a constitution, and those who think the same end best attained by inclining to its popular privileges. The result has been, that writers of the first description have been eager to show that the prerogatives of the monarch were from the earliest times predominant; and that those of the last description have been equally earnest to prove that all power, not only in theory but in fact, was first derived from the people.

Such discussions may be thought by many little more than the natural, though unimportant, occupation of speculative writers and antiquarians; for the real question (it will be said) must always be, by what form of government the happiness of the community is best secured, – not, what was in fact the form that happened to exist among our ancestors a thousand years ago; their mistakes or misfortunes can be no rule or obligation to us; we may emulate or avoid their example, but cannot be bound by their authority.

All this must be admitted, yet it must be remembered that the affairs of men are not disposed of by the rules of logic or the abstract truths of reasoning; these may remain the same, and may always exhibit to the monarch and to the people, to the courtier and the patriot, those principles and maxims, which are best fitted to promote the happiness of the community. Neither the one nor the other are, however, likely to see such truths very clearly, or to examine them very accurately. It is by a certain loose and coarse mixture of right and wrong in the reasoning, and of selfishness and generosity in the intention, that the *practical* politics of mankind are carried on according to the varying circumstances of the case: not only, therefore, are the reasonings of philosophy produced, but arguments are urged, drawn from precedent and ancient usage, which thus appear to moderate, as it were, between the contending parties, and to be unaffected by the heats and prejudices of the moment. It seems, for example, more reasonable to insist upon privileges which have been *before* enjoyed, more reasonable to maintain prerogatives which were *originally* exercised. Topics of this nature, which can in no respect be slighted by any sound philosopher, much the contrary, are perfectly adapted to the loose, sweeping, and often irrational decisions of the generality of mankind; and, therefore, the discussions of antiquarians and philosophic historians, with respect to the original state of prerogative and privilege, can never be without their interest and importance. In the practical politics of mankind, usage, prescription, custom, are every thing, or nearly so; but, in this country, such discussions are fitted to excite a more than ordinary degree of interest. The language of the statesmen and patriots, to whom we are so much indebted for our constitution, has always been, that they claimed their undoubted rights and privileges, their ancient franchises, the laws and liberties of the land, and their immemorial customs. One monarch has been obliged to capitulate with his subjects, and acknowledge their immunities and franchises formally by charter; one has perished on a scaffold; another been exiled from the throne. Revolutions and a civil war have marked the influence of opposite opinions with respect to the popular nature of our constitution. These dreadful and perilous scenes could not fail to transmit this original division of sentiment to us their posterity. The distinction between those who incline to the popular part of the constitution and those who incline to the monarchical, exists to this hour, and can only cease with the constitution itself.

The great leading idea which should be formed of our constitutional history is, that there has always been a constant struggle between prerogative and privilege.

Open, for instance, a volume of Hume, in any reign after the House of Commons had obtained an existence – any extract may serve as a specimen of the whole – it will instantly be seen that the points at issue between the crown and the subject were *always* nearly the same (precisely the same in principle), from the earliest struggles of the barons down to the Revolution in 1688.

Take, for example, a paragraph in his reign of Edward III., page 490, 8vo.: –

"They mistake, indeed, very much," says he, "the genius of this reign (of Edward III.), who imagine that it was not extremely arbitrary. All the high prerogatives of the crown were to the full exerted in it; but what gave some consolation, and promised in time some relief to the people, they were always complained of by the Commons: such as the dispensing power, the extension of the forests, erecting monopolies, exacting loans, stopping justice by particular warrants, the renewal of the commission of trailbaton, pressing men and ships into the public service, levying arbitrary and exorbitant fines, extending the authority Of the privy council or star-chamber to the decision of private causes, enlarging the power of the mareschal's and other arbitrary courts, imprisoning members for freedom of speech in parliament, obliging people without any rule to send recruits of men-at-arms, archers, and hoblers to the army."

Now, if the references of Mr. Hume are consulted, it will be found, as he asserts, that traces of such arbitrary exercises of power appear on our records.

But, says Mr. Hume, they were always complained of by the Commons.

On consulting the references, this, too, will be found to be the case.

And here, then, we have before us a picture of the whole subject, – a continued struggle between prerogative and privilege, and of the same nature in the reign of Edward III. as afterwards in the reigns of Charles I., and even of James II.

Grievances like these continually occurred from the irregular nature of government and society in such barbarous times; but the natural feelings of mankind, operating upon the example transmitted by more ancient times, continually revived the spirit of resistance. This virtuous spirit found in the House of Commons a regular and legal organ through which the rights of the community could be asserted; and this is the struggle and this the merit of our ancestors – this the inherited duty (if necessary) of ourselves.

Now, such being the real picture of our constitutional history, the student is in the next place to be reminded of what we have already stated to him, and must, in the course of these lectures for ever repeat, the natural divisions, not only of mankind, but of philosophers, on political subjects; and the manner in which they separate into two classes: those, for instance, who are anxious first and principally for the prerogative of the crown; and those, on the other hand, who are zealous first and principally for the privileges of the people.

It may be very true, that could the selfishness and the irrationality of men allow them to weigh and consider the reasonings of each other, the real interests of both crown and people would be found to consist in their mutual support, and are always in truth the same; but the rude warfare of human passions admits not of such salutary adjustments, and as mutual offences are in practice constantly given and received, men who naturally kindle at the sight of what they conceive to be insolence and usurpation on the one side, or on the other to be cruelty and wrong, are not only inflamed, when they live at the time, and are witnesses of the scene, but they are unable to give an accurate representation even of the transactions of the past; they cannot consider them, with proper calmness, even when they observe them, in a subsequent period, at a secure distance of time and place; so true is this, that not one thoroughly impartial historian of our annals can be mentioned; and it is necessary to warn my hearers that they are to adopt no train of reasoning, nor even the narrative of any important proceeding, without a due examination of different writers, and a careful consideration of their particular prejudices.

Take, as specimens, the reruns of Edward II. and Richard II.; let them be considered first in Hume and afterwards in Rapin, the reader will be impressed with the difference between the representation of the one historian and the other. Let him then turn to the account given of these reigns by Millar, the difference will be still more striking; the reign of Richard III. for instance is represented by Millar as perfectly analogous to that of James II.; a king, neglecting the interests and violating the rights of his subjects, and justly deposed. In Hume, on the contrary, we see only the picture of a prince unfitted to contend with a turbulent people, and a factious aristocracy, and perishing by a cruel death, rather from weakness of understanding than from any malignity of disposition.

The discordant observations of these two distinguished philosophers, when viewing the same actors and events at the distance of four centuries, sufficiently exemplify that division of sentiment, which has been described as existing more or less among all political reasoners on similar occasions. Throughout all our history it may be observed, that all violence and resistance is imputed by Hume to faction and barbarism, by Millar and most other writers to a laudable spirit of freedom and independence.

These are the observations that I have to address to those students who are disposed to search diligently into the records of our history.

But I must now turn again to the general reader, who may not have the same ardour of inquiry or patience of study. Rapin and Hume are our two great historians.

But it is Hume who is read by every one. Hume is the historian, whose views and opinions insensibly become our own. He is respected and admired by the most enlightened reader; he is the guide and philosopher of the ordinary reader, to whose mind, on all the topics connected with our history, he entirely gives the tone and the law.

The two great histories which we read, as I must again observe, are those of Rapin and Hume: their political sentiments are different; but Hume is the author who, from his conciseness, the charms of his style, and the weight of his philosophical observations, is always preferred, and is far more universally and thoroughly read.

It is impossible, indeed, that the confidence of a reader should not be won by the general air of calmness and good sense, which, independent of other merits, distinguishes the beautiful narrative of Hume. If he should turn to his authorities (speaking first on the favourable side of the question), he will then, and then only, be able to perceive the entire merit of this admirable writer; the dexterity and sagacity with which he has often made out his recital, the ease and grace with which it is presented to the reader, and the valuable and penetrating remarks by which it is enriched.

But to speak next on the unfavourable side, by turning to the same authorities, we shall then only perceive the entire demerit of his work. It is understood, indeed, by every reader, it has been proclaimed by many writers, that Hume always inclines to the side of prerogative; that in his account of the Stuarts his history is little better than an apology; his pages are therefore read, in this part of his work at least, with something of distrust, and his representations are not considered as decisive. But what reader turns to consult his references or examine his original authorities? What effect does this distrust after all produce? Practically none. In defiance of it, is not the general influence of his work, on the general reader, just such as the author would himself have wished; as strong and as permanent as if every statement and opinion in his history had deserved our perfect assent and approbation?

I must confess that this appears to me so entirely the fact, judging from all that I have experienced in myself, and observed in others, that I do not conceive a lecturer in history could render (could offer at least) a more important service to an English auditory than by following Mr. Hume, step by step, through the whole of his account; and shewing what were his fair, and what his unfair inferences; what his just representations, and what his improper colourings; what his mistakes, and above all, what his omissions; in short, what were the dangers, and what the advantages, that must attend the perusal of so popular and able a performance.

But such lectures, I apprehend, could not be listened to, Were they even formed into a treatise, they would only be in part perused by the general reader; nor would they be properly and thoroughly considered, by any but the most patient inquirers.

I would wish, however, to make some effort of this kind, however slight and imperfect. A sort of specimen perhaps may be offered, a general notion may I hope be given; and as investigations of this nature are very repulsive and fatiguing, I shall fix only upon some one paragraph, the first that occurs, and examine it in all its important parts; and contenting myself with this example leave my hearers to draw their own reflections, and pursue such inquiries to any further extent, which they may hereafter judge expedient.

I have already quoted a paragraph from the reign of Edward Ill., to shew that the nature of the contest between prerogative and privilege always turned upon the same points through the whole of our history. It may be also remembered that I have always represented the right of taxation as the most important question of all: now the paragraph that immediately follows in Mr. Hume, is this:

"But there was no act of arbitrary power more frequently repeated in this reign than that of imposing taxes without consent of parliament. Though that assembly granted the king greater supplies than had ever been obtained by any of his predecessors, his great undertakings, and the necessity of his affairs, obliged him to levy still more; and after his splendid success in France had added weight to his authority, these arbitrary impositions became almost annual and perpetual. Cotton's Abridgment of the Records affords numerous instances of this kind, in the first year of his reign, in the thirteenth year, in the fourteenth, in the twentieth, in the twenty-first, in the twenty-second, in the twenty-fifth, in the thirty-eighth, in the fiftieth, and in the fifty-first.

The king openly avowed and maintained this power of levying taxes at pleasure. At one time he replied to the remonstrance made by the Commons against it, that the impositions had been exacted from great necessity, and had been assented to by the prelates, earls, barons, and some of the Commons; at another, that he would advise with his council. When the parliament desired that a law might be enacted for the punishment of such as levied these arbitrary impositions, he refused compliance. In the subsequent year, they desired that the king might renounce this pretended prerogative; but his answer was, that he would levy no taxes without necessity, for the defence of the realm, and where he reasonably might use that authority. This incident passed a few days before his death, and these were, in a manner, his last words to his people. It would seem that the famous charter or statute of Edward I., 'de tallagio non concedendo,' though never repealed, was supposed to have already lost by age all its authority. These facts can only shew the practice of the times; for as to the *right,* the continued remonstrances of the Commons may seem to prove that it rather lay on their side; at least, those remonstrances served to prevent the arbitrary practice of the court from becoming an established part of the constitution."

Now, here we have certainly very important statements. Let my hearer observe them.

"But there was no act of arbitrary power more frequently repeated in this reign, than that of imposing taxes *without* consent of parliament." – "These arbitrary impositions became almost annual and perpetual." – "The king openly avowed and maintained this power of levying taxes at pleasure." – Such are Mr. Hume's expressions to represent the facts.

"These facts," he continues, "only shew the practice of the times, for as to the right, the continual remonstrances of the Commons may *seem* to prove that it *rather* lay on their side." – Such is the general air of his reasoning upon these facts.

Now, it cannot be supposed that a writer like Mr. Hume will be palpably and entirely unfair either in his facts or his reasonings, yet he may be sufficiently so, to give his reader an impression on the whole not so favourable to the constitutional rights of the subject, as the case admits.

The authority quoted is Cotton's Abridgment of the Records; and on consulting the references of Mr. Hume, they will be seen to prove, as he asserts, that money was raised by the king, without the authority of parliament. This must be considered as proved by the occasional complaints of the Commons, which in the references constantly appear; but the still more important consideration is this, – what were the *answers* of the king to these complaints of the Commons? Mr. Hume's assertion is, that "the king openly avowed and maintained this power of levying taxes at pleasure. At one time," says Hume, "he replied to the remonstrance made by the Commons, "that the impositions had been exacted from great *necessity* and had been *assented* to by the prelates, earls, and barons, and some of the commons." Now, even this answer, thus given by Mr. Hume, does not justify him in the assertion, that the king openly avowed and maintained the power of levying taxes at pleasure – quite the contrary; for the king alleged not his right but the necessity of the case, and the *assent* of the lords and part of the Commons. Upon looking, however, at Mr. Hume's reference in Cotton, page 53, the real answer appears to have been as follows: – "If any such imposition be made, the same was made upon great necessity, and with the assent of the prelates, counts, barons, and other great men, and some of the Commons then present, notwithstanding the king wills not, that such undue impositions be drawn into consequence."

These last words, "notwithstanding, &c. &c." are totally omitted by Mr. Hume in his representation of the king's answer; but they are evidently very material and entirely opposed to Mr. Hume's affirmation, that the king openly avowed and maintained this power of levying taxes at sure, in so much so, that they are the very words which are always used, when a particular exception is made to a general rule, and it is thought necessary to assert and acknowledge the general rule, and leave it as, it stood before. The king's answer in every part of it, particularly in this last omitted part, implies that the right of levying money could not be regularly exercised without the parliament.

Again. At another time, says Mr. Hume, the king replied, "that he would advise with his council;" but the real answer in the reference in Cotton, page 57, is this, – "that the subsidy (of which they seem to have complained) was *granted for a time yet enduring,*" within which time the king will advise with his council, what shall be best to be done therein for the good of the people.

The first part of this answer (that the subsidy *was granted* for a term *yet enduring*), which acknowledges the right of the Commons, is again totally omitted by Mr. Hume, and his representation is that the king answered, "that he would advise with his council." Again. "When the parliament," says Mr. Hume, "desired that a law might be enacted for the punishment of such as levied these arbitrary impositions, the king refused compliance."

Upon consulting the reference, the petition of the Commons runs thus. They petition, "that such as shall of their own authority lay new impositions without assent of parliament, may lose life, member, and other forfeitures." In the House of Commons this was surely a most violent and objectionable mode of asserting their right of taxation, and well deserving the resistance of the king.

The answer of the king was, "Let the common law heretofore used, run."

Now this is not so much to refuse compliance, as to give a proper answer.

On the whole, we have here neither the exact petition nor the exact answer that would have been supposed from the account given by Mr. Hume: the words of the Commons would have been supposed, from Hume's expressions, more reasonable, and those of the king more authoritative and arbitrary, than they really were; that is, an improper representation is given of both the one and the other.

"In the subsequent year," says Mr. Hume, "they desired that the king might renounce this pretended prerogative." The reference which is printed in the margin of Hume, in some editions, 132, should be 152, and is more exactly represented by Mr. Hume than any of the rest. For the part of the parliament roll referred to, we are indebted to the diligence not of Cotton, but of his editor, the famous Prynne.

The petition from the Commons was for a *general* surrender of the right totally and formally.

But the king, whose end was now approaching, having nothing further to hope or fear from his people, and not inclined by his own act formally to abandon for his successor a power which he had sometimes found it so convenient to exercise, returned for answer, as might have been expected, – "That with respect to laying any charge upon the people without common assent, that the king is not at all willing to do it without great necessity and for the defence of the realm, and where he may do it with reason."

In those other instances which are produced by Mr. Hume, to prove the practice of arbitrary impositions, instances where Mr. Hume quotes no answer, there is either no answer from the king on record, or one that is soothing and apologetical, or one that is favourable to the right of the House of Commons. Indeed, the king's very silence must be considered as favourable to their right.

In one of the first instances of complaint referred to by Hume, the answer was – "For as much as these charges were ordained (alluding to charges ordained by the Privy Council without the Commons) for safe conduct of merchandises into the realm and forth to foreign parts, upon which conduct the king hath spent much, which before Michaelmas cannot well be levied, it seemeth that the levying of it, for so small a time to come, should not be grievous."

This is apologetical. Again, some merchants had farmed the customs and subsidies, and raised the rate above that mentioned by parliament; the Commons complained; the answer was – "Let the merchants be called into parliament and answer." In another instance of complaint *not* mentioned by Mr. Hume, the answer was the same as one already cited – "That the imposition was made upon great necessity, with the assent of the courts, &c. and some of the Commons, and that the king wills not, that such imposition be unduly drawn in consequence."

The student, after having weighed these answers, is then to reflect upon the great ability, attractive qualities, military talents, and brilliant victories of this renowned monarch, of Edward III; and he must then consider, whether no stronger conclusion can be drawn from the whole than what Mr. Hume leaves with his readers, which is this: that "as to the right of taxation, the continued remonstrances of the Commons may *seem* to prove that it rather lay on their side."

The Paragraph that has been thus taken from Mr. Hume was not selected as one in which he was either faulty or otherwise in his representations, but as one that exhibited , in the smallest compass, the nature of the constitution at that time, and ever after, till 1688, and as one that involved more especially the question of the right of taxation. It was literally the first that I tried.

On examination, however, it turns out that we do not arrive it the conclusions which Mr. Hume has drawn for us: far from it; and we are thus taught to be more than ever suspicious of the historian's particular prejudices. And on the whole, this instance will show you that you must not take it for granted that Mr. Hume accurately represents even the very authorities he quotes: so irresistible in these cases is the influence of the sentiments of the mind over the operations of the understanding.

I stop to observe, that as a lecturer on history, I can only point out to you fields of inquiry and trains of reasoning, and it must be left for you to do the rest.

Thus I have just now drawn your attention to one great line of objection to Mr. Hume's history, his inaccurate representation of the very authorities he quotes. You must yourselves pursue the subject.

But I will now mention another: the colouring which he gives to his materials, and this more particularly in a manner of his own. He ascribes to the personages of history, as they pass before him, the views and opinions of later ages; those sentiments and reasonings, for instance, which his own enlightened and powerful mind was enabled to form, not those, which either really were or could be formed by men thinking and acting many centuries before.

But this is to mislead the reader, and in fact to draw him aside from all the proper instruction of history, much of which lies in the comparison of one age with another.

I will refer to an instance, taken from the times we are now considering, as a general specimen of what I conceive to be one of the most common and serious faults that can be objected to in the attractive pages of his history.

In his account of the unfortunate close of the reign of Richard II., Mr. Hume observes, that one man alone, the Bishop of Carlisle, had the courage, amid the general disloyalty and violence, to appear in defence of his unhappy master, and to plead his cause against all the power of the prevailing party.

He then gives a representation of the speech; but if we turn to Sir J. Heyward's history (the authority which Hume himself quotes) we may there see the speech fully given; and it will be found not without its beauties, but certainly very inferior to the representation of it, which is exhibited in Hume. The philosophic observations which are interwoven and added by Mr. Hume, serve to give a great force and finish to the expostulations of the bishop in favour of the fallen monarch; but the more important consideration is, that they serve also to throw over the proceedings of the barons an air of greater violence and criminality, than properly belong to them; for their conduct rises up in still stronger contrast, if such views of the English constitution and of the principles of government could indeed have been taken and urged in such an assembly by a contemporary statesman, a man of like passions and like information with themselves.

I will venture to take up your time by considering more minutely the instance before us. Observe, first, the beautiful reasonings of Hume: it would be not a little marvellous if they had been produced by the Bishop of Carlisle in the time of Richard II. "He represented," says Hume, "to the parliament, that all the abuses of government which could justly be imputed to Richard, far from amounting to tyranny, were merely the result of error and youth, or misguided counsel:" this, though in different words, the bishop did say. "And that this admitted," continues Mr. Hume, "of a remedy more easy and salutary than a total subversion of the constitution:" this, which is of a more philosophic cast, the bishop did *not* say. Now mark what immediately follows in Hume; not any such observation, as was very likely to be offered by the bishop to the barons, or even to have occurred to the mind of Sir J. Heyward himself, two centuries afterwards, but the very observation which contains the whole of the philosophy of Mr. Hume while writing the History of England; the great principle by means of which he defends all the arbitrary proceedings of our monarchs, and by which he reconciles his unwary readers to the admission of sentiments and opinions unfavourable to the best interests and assured rights of the popular part of our constitution. "The bishop represented to the Lords," continues Mr. Hume, "that even if these abuses of government had been much more violent and dangerous than they really were, they had chiefly proceeded from former examples of resistance, which, making the prince sensible of his *precarious* situation, had obliged him to establish his throne by irregular and arbitrary expedients:" the bishop said nothing of the sort. And now observe the next remark that follows in Hume; how worthy of the generalizing mind of the philosopher of the eighteenth century – how little likely to have been addressed by a warm hearted ecclesiastic to the disorderly barons of the fourteenth. "That laws could never secure the subject which did not give security to the sovereign; and if the maxim of inviolable loyalty, which formed the basis of the English government, were once rejected, the privileges belonging to the several orders of the state, instead of being fortified by that licentiousness, would thereby lose the surest foundation of their force and stability."

All this is very true and worthy of a great reasoner like Mr. Hume, when applying the powers of his mind to the subject of government; and all this may be cheerfully assented to by the warmest partisan of popular privileges: and the more so, because it is at length understood, that the king can act only by his ministers; and that though the king must be secure, that his mind may be at rest on the subject of his prerogative, and that the security also of his people may be thus undisturbed, still that his ministers need not; that they are responsible at least, though the sovereign be not; that in short there is some one responsible, and that the community is not left at the mercy of fortune, and without any reasonable means of watching over its own interests.

No such interpretation however of this great principle of government is added by Mr. Hume; and neither the principle, so stated, nor the interpretation, are to be found in Sir J. Heyward; and it was not in this philosophic manner that the bishop reasoned according to the representation of Sir J. Heyward; his arguments were founded merely upon the obvious doctrines of passive obedience and the divine right of kings. "I will not speak," said the bishop, (according to Sir J. Heyward) "what may be done in a popular state or a consular. In these and such like governments, the prince hath not legal rights; but if the sovereign majesty be in the prince, as it was in the three first empires, and in the kingdoms of Judea and Israel, and is now in the kingdoms of England, France, Spain, Scotland, Muscovy, Turkey, Tartaria, Persia, Ethiopia, and almost all the kingdoms of Asia and Africke – (very like the philosophic reasonings of Hume, all this! England! Ethiopia! and Africke!) – although for his vices he be unprofitable to the subjects, yea hurtful, yea intolerable, yet can they lawfully neither harme his person nor hazard his power, whether by judgment or else by force; for neither one nor all magistrates have any authority over the prince from whom all authority is derived, and whose only presence doeth silence and suspend all inferiour jurisdiction and power. As for force, what subject can attempt, or assist, or counsel, or conceal violence against his prince and not incur the high and heinous crime of treason?"

The bishop then goes on to quote the instance of Nebuchadnezzar, of Baltazar, of Saul, and there insists that not Only our actions but our speeches also and our very thoughts are strictly charged with duty and obedience unto princes, whether they be good princes or evil; that the law of God ordaineth that he which doeth presumptuously against the ruler of the people, shall dye; that we are not to touch the Lord's anointed, nor rail upon the judges, neither speak evil against the ruler of the people; that the apostles do demand further that even our thoughts and soules bee obedient to higher powers; and least any one should imagine that they meant of good princes only, they speak generally of all; and further to take away all doubt, they may (make) expresse mention of the evil princes, &c. &c.

The bishop then goes on to illustrate his doctrine by the consideration of the domestic relation of parent and child. "The son must not lift up his hand," says he, "against the father, though for all excesse of villanies, odious and execrable both to God and man; but our country is dearer unto us than our parents, and the prince is Pater Patriæ the father of our country, and therefore, &c. &c. not to be violated. Doth he (the prince) command or demand our persons or our purses, we must not shun for the one nor shrink for the other – for, as Nehemiah saith, continues the bishop, kings have dominion over the bodies and over the cattle of their subjects at their pleasure. Yea, the church hath declared it to bee an heresie to hold that a prince may be slain or deposed by his subjects for any disorder or fault either in life or else in government." Such is the reasoning of the bishop, as given by Sir J. Heyward. And his philosophy, when it appears, is the following: "There will be faultes so long as there are men; and as we endure with patience a barren year, if it happen, and unseasonable weather, and such other defects of nature, so must wee tollerate the imperfections of rulers and quietlye expecte eyttier reformation or else a change."

This is the first specimen of it, and the only remaining philosophic position that I can observe, is the following:

"Oh! how shall the worlde be pestered with tyrantes, if subjects may rebell upon every pretence of tyranny!" The instances that followed to illustrate this remark are not well chosen by the bishop. "If they levy a subsidy or any other taxation, it shall be claymed oppression," &c. &c.

And now what will my hearer suppose, if I tell him that I believe the speech thus given by Sir J. Heyward to the good bishop is wholly a composition of Sir J. himself; and that though the general statement of passive obedience may have been expressed by the bishop, no such words were uttered as he describes. Walsingham takes no notice of the bishop's speech. Another historian, Hall, but about the time of Sir J. Heyward, says that the bishop did rise up in his place and speak; and the doctrines of passive obedience are put into his mouth by Hall. The same is done in the play of Richard II. by Shakspeare, and these doctrines were probably the topics that he chiefly insisted upon; but the only fact that can now be ascertained, is, that he was thrown into prison for words spoken in parliament in opposition to the usurpation of Henry; and on this has been founded the very elaborate speech of Sir J. Heyward, and the very improbable arguments ascribed to him by Hume. Now all this is not to write history either in Mr. Hume or in Sir J. Heyward.

And this instance will be sufficient to shew you, as before, the particular description of fault, which may be objected to Mr. Hume, that of colouring the materials before him, and attributing to the personages of history the sentiments of his own philosophic mind: and this second description of fault is to be added to the former, which I have mentioned, that of not accurately representing the very passages he quotes.

In the next page of his history indeed, when Mr. Hume comes to comment upon the title of Henry IV. to the crown, he attributes a speech to the king, and properly, for he can extract from the rolls of parliament the very words which the king made use of. This Mr. Hume does, and this is to write history.

The words extracted are certainly very remarkable, and very descriptive of the scene and the age; but it is relics of this kind, that an historian should produce and make the subject of the philosophic meditation of his reader, not offer him modern views and sentiments of his own.

A few barbarous words or any distinct fact, that can be shewn to be authentic, are worth volumes of reasonings and conjectures to a thinking mind; or rather it is, on such relics and facts that the student must in the first place alone depend when he collects materials for his instruction, and he must never lose sight of them, when he comes afterwards to build up his political reasonings and conclusions.

It is upon this account, and it is to impress this lesson upon your recollection, that I have gone into this detail, and perhaps, not a little exercised your patience. It is for this reason and for another, to shew you the importance of the political principles of men; a point which I must for ever enforce in the course of these lectures. First observe the general remarks of Hume. – "Though some topics," says Mr. Hume, while introducing the passages I have just quoted from him, "though some topics employed by that virtuous prelate the bishop of Carlisle, may seem to favour too much the doctrine of passive obedience, &c. &c. the intrepidity as well as disinterestedness of his behaviour proves," says Mr. Hume, "that whatever his speculative principles were, his heart was elevated far above the meanness and abject submission of a slave." Undoubtedly it does: this observation of Mr. Hume is very just, and therefore it is more incumbent upon me, as your lecturer, to impress upon your minds the importance of your political principles, that you may endeavour to be wise, as well as virtuous. It is but too plain from the historian's own account, that men of the most noble feelings and honourable character, (such as the bishop is here supposed by Mr. Hume to have been) may on public occasions act upon principles and enforce political doctrines, which can have no tendency but to make their fellow creatures base and servile, (whatever they may be themselves) by injuring and destroying the only source of all elevated character in a people, the free principles of the constitution of their government. It is of little consequence that men may not have, themselves, the feelings of slaves, if they propagate doctrines that will practically and in the result make a nation of slaves around them.

But to return to Hume. Gilbert Stuart, a very able though somewhat impetuous inquirer into the earlier parts of our history, has pronounced his opinion upon the work of Mr. Hume in the following words, "From its beginning to its conclusion, it is chiefly to be regarded as a plausible defence of prerogative. As an elegant and a spirited composition, it merits every commendation. But no friend to humanity, and to the freedom of this kingdom, will consider his constitutional inquiries, with their effect on his narrative, and compare them with the ancient and venerable monuments of our story, without feeling a lively surprise, and a patriot indignation."[1]

This opinion, however severe, is not very different from that which is in general entertained by others, who from previous study are competent to decide; and this, while the literary merits of the history are universally acknowledged. The student will therefore read, with more than ordinary care, what he is told is so fitted at once to charm his taste and to mislead his understanding.

Since I drew up this lecture, a work has been published by Mr. Brodie, of Edinburgh; it is not well written in point of style, and the author must be considered as a writer on the popular side, but he is a man of research and independence of mind. It is a work of weight and learning, and it appears to me for ever to have damaged, and most materially damaged, the character of Mr. Hume as an accurate historian. It justifies the opinion I have just alluded to, as pronounced by Gilbert Stuart, and maintained by others competent to decide.

I must observe, before I conclude, that it is the general effect of the narrative of this able historian that is of so much importance. Particular passages might be drawn from his work of every description, favourable as well as unfavourable to the privileges of the subject. But the sentiment conveyed by such particular passages, taken singly, do in fact stand opposed to the general impression that results from the whole.

Were a popular writer to seek for observations favourable to the cause of the liberties of England, he would often find them no where better expressed; but their being found in the history of Hume is a circumstance quite analogous to what constantly obtains, in every literary performance, where the author has (on whatever account) a general purpose to accomplish, which the nature of his subject does not in strict reason allow. Truth is then continually mixed up with misrepresentation, and the whole mass of the reasoning, which in its final

---

[1] [Gilbert Stuart, *A View of Society in Europe* (1778), selections of which are contained earlier in this collection.]

impression is materially wrong, is so interspersed with observations, which are in themselves perfectly right, that the reader is at no time sufficiently on his guard, and is at last betrayed into conclusions totally unwarrantable and at variance with his best feelings and soundest opinions.

Observe the writings of Rochefoucault or Mandeville; you will there see what I am describing, as indeed you may in every work, where the author is deceived himself or is deceiving others.

One word more and I conclude, one word as an estimate of the whole subject between Mr. Hume and his opponents.

In the first place, we may agree with Mr. Hume, that the whole of our history during the period from Edward I. to Henry VIII. was a scene of irregularity and of great occasional violence; that the laws could neither be always maintained, nor could the principles of legislation be ever said to be well understood; we must admit, therefore, that it is not fair to imagine, as Mr. Hume complains we do, that all the princes, who were unfortunate in their government, were necessarily tyrannical in their conduct, and that resistance to the monarch always proceeded from some attempt on his part to invade the privileges of the subject. This we must admit.

But, in the second place, it must be observed that the struggle between the subject and the crown was constantly kept up in the times of the most able, as well as of the weakest monarchs; that they, who resisted the prerogative, never did it, without producing those maxims and without asserting those principles of freedom, which are necessary to all rational government, which are by no means fitted in themselves to produce anarchy, and by no means inconsistent with all those salutary prerogatives of the crown, which are requisite to the regular protection of the subject.

In the third place, that if these maxims and principles had not been from time to time asserted, and sometimes with success, that the result must have been, that our constitution would have degenerated, like that of France and of every other European state, into a system of monarchical power, unlimited and unrestrained by the interference of any legislative assemblies.

And that therefore, in the last place, Mr. Hume tells the story of England without giving sufficient praise to those patriots who preserved and transmitted those general habits of thinking on political subjects which have always distinguished this country, and to which alone every Englishman owes, at this day, all that makes his life a blessing and his existence honourable.

LECTURE X.
REFORMATION.

...

Turning to the account, which now remains in Mr. Hume's work after his last corrections and omissions (for those who wrote against him wrote against passages which you will now not find), I have the following observations to submit to your reflection.

The cause of the reformers, in their first struggle with the church of Rome, which I distinguish from their subsequent contests with each other, was the cause of truth, of religion, and of all the best interests of society. Now, the proper and just and natural influence of so sacred a cause on the Human mind is not duly observed or properly respected by Mr. Hume, and the student must not suffer himself to be insensibly led into so striking an injustice to such virtuous men, and into so thoughtless an indifference to such sacred principles. It would not be fair to try Mr. Hume by a single sentence which may have been inconsiderately written, but the reader may proceed through all the causes of the progress of the Reformation which are mentioned in this part of his history, and he will see those that are secondary and those that are not creditable to the reformers chiefly and indeed alone insisted upon. It is not that causes are mentioned that did not operate, but that the natural and just efficacy and influence of truth and religious inquiry, when opposed to the gross doctrines and abuses of the papacy, are overlooked. The fault here is considerably analogous to the fault committed by Mr. Gibbon in his fifteenth and sixteenth chapters, with respect to the propagation of Christianity. He produces and dwells upon every cause but the main and the right one; that on which the rest depended.

Again, – Objections that belong to some of the reformers are transferred to all, and made characteristic of the whole cause.

In all questions, civil as well as religious, there is no species of injustice against which the student should be so much on his guard as this. None is so common; good and wise men are continually made to answer for the bad principles and bad conduct of others, with whom they indeed agree, but agree only as to certain points. It is often the ungenerous artifice of their opponents, and always the custom of the vulgar, to confound these distinctions, however real.

Again, – Improper motives are sometimes imputed to the reformers. Our nature is made up, as it is well known, of various ingredients; our best principles readily associating with, and often assisted by motives not the most dignified. But it is not philosophical, neither is it a part friendly to mankind, to rob our virtues of their due share in those actions which they so *contribute* to produce, if they do not entirely produce. A species of injustice like this, is one of the chief fallacies in the works of Rochefoucault, Mandeville, and the licentious moralists.

Again, – The people are represented by Mr. Hume as passive with respect to religion, and as ready to receive any form or description of it. But the student is not from thence to conclude, as too many have done, that this is an argument against *all* religion. True religion as well as false religion may be taken upon authority. The original question of the truth or falsehood of a religion remains the same.

An argument indeed may be hence adduced for the freedom of religious inquiry, that the people may see that others inquire, though they cannot; but this is the proper conclusion, not an indiscriminate conclusion against all religion whatever.

Lastly, there is through the whole of Mr. Hume's recital a certain air of carelessness with respect to religion, and a readiness to represent all warmth on the subject, even in these very peculiar times, as fanaticism. Mr. Hume's opinions in religion are well known, and all this might have been expected. You will therefore take into your account these particular opinions. Assuredly Mr. Hume, as an historian, should not have taken his own view of the question of religion for granted, and should not have confounded the warmth of men, when opposed to the abuses of religion, with their fury when encountering each other; when contending not for the opening of the Bible, but for some speculative point in divinity, or when persecuting each other on account of some vestment or ceremony, in itself of no importance.

When these cautions have been premised, I am not aware that you can be otherwise than materially instructed by the penetrating remarks of this historian on the effects of the religious principle during these singular times. No man should turn entirely away from the criticisms even of his enemy. The most religious man may be taught lesson by some of the comments of this powerful writer; and the more blind tenets of the Papists on the one hand, and the more fantastic whims of the Puritans on the other, whenever they appear, may surely be surrendered to his mercy.

Along with Hume, I would recommend Burnet's History of the Reformation; no cautions need be suggested before the perusal of the laborious work of this impartial and liberal churchman, an ornament to his order, and who deserved the name of Christian. ...

Robertson must be compared with Hume; some differences may be observed in their accounts. Hume certainly intended to make the reformers of Scotland odious and ridiculous. ...

LECTURE XIV.
ELIZABETH.

...

I hasten to the reign of Elizabeth. "In order to understand," says Mr. Hume, "the ancient constitution of England, there is not a period which deserves more to be studied than the reign of Elizabeth." And it happens, that there can be no period of our history which may be more thoroughly studied. Camden has written her life. There are very valuable collections of letters and papers; you may trace them in the references of Hume and Rapin, and many curious and amusing, and sometimes important particulars, have been lately drawn from these sources, and presented to the ordinary reader in a very agreeable and sensible manner by Miss Aikin, in her Memoirs of the Reign of Queen

Elizabeth. It is, however, the constitutional part of this history that I can myself alone allude to.

Hume, after making the remark I have alluded to, proceeds to state the very arbitrary nature of the constitution, as exhibited in the conduct and maxims of that queen, and of the ministers at that time. On the whole, he makes out a strong case to show the existence of such tribunals, such principles, and such practices, as seem in themselves totally inconsistent with all civil freedom, however qualified the idea which we should affix to the term.

But this reign, it must on the other hand be remembered, exhibits not only (as Hume endeavours to prove) the strength and extent of the royal prerogative, but also unveils and shows, though at a distance, all those more popular principles which equally belonged to the constitution of England, and all those reasonings and maxims, and even parties and descriptions of patriotism, which grew up afterwards into such visible strength and form, during the reigns of her successors, James and Charles.

For instance, and to illustrate both views of the constitution – the arbitrary and the popular nature of it.

Whatever concerned the royal prerogative, was considered by Elizabeth as forbidden ground, and she included within this description, in a religious age, every thing that related to the management of religion, to her particular courts, and to the succession to the crown; she insisted in her own words, "that no bills touching matters of state, or reformation in concerns ecclesiastical, should be exhibited." – Cobbett, p. 889.

This will give you some idea of Hume's view of the reign, and of the arbitrary nature of it; and certainly it is quite disgusting to observe the slavish submission of some of the greatest men that our country has produced, to the authority and caprices of this female sovereign; the manner in which they became her knights, rather than her statesmen, and the sort of scuffle which the court exhibited, between men of the first capacities and highest qualities, for mere patronage and power, rather than for any worthier objects connected with the civil and religious liberties of their country and of mankind. But on the other hand, and in opposition to the views of Hume, it must be remarked, that from the nature of Elizabeth's pretensions and claims, such as I have just alluded to, it certainly did happen, that the members of the commons did often offend her by their words, and were sometimes brought into direct collision with her supposed authority, by the measures they proposed; that a real struggle ensued, and that Elizabeth, with becoming wisdom, generally gave way.

...

LECTURE XVIII.
CHARLES II.

...

After Burnet we may turn to Hume, and read him in conjunction with the debates in the houses. Nothing can be more attractive, nothing can more strongly exemplify the charms and the merits of his seductive pages, than his Life of Charles II. Ready, however, as every reader will naturally be to give his confidence to so masterly a writer, he cannot but perceive that the character of Charles II., as given by the historian, reflects not to his mind the true image of the original; but resembles rather one of those portraits which we so often see presented to us by the skill of a superior artist, where every grace and beauty, that can consist with the likeness, is transferred to the canvass, while every the most inherent deformity or defect is withdrawn or disguised.

It had not escaped the most ordinary politicians in the times of Charles, that there must have been some secret alliance between the king and Louis. It was indeed known as a fact to some of the popular leaders; proofs of the corruption of Charles were at last produced, even in the House of Commons, and became the apparent cause of Danby's impeachment. All the political writers of this period evidently suppose, that not only the House of Commons was bribed by the king, but the court itself by France. In the fourth page of the eighth volume of Hume, there is a remarkable passage, in which he says, that, on the whole, we are obliged to acknowledge (though there remains no direct evidence of it), that a formal plan was laid for changing the religion and subverting the constitution of England, and that the king and the ministry (the cabal) were in reality conspirators against the people.

But after his sagacity and good sense had dragged him into this conclusion, be made inquiries in France during his residence there, and saw with his own eyes that direct evidence which he had not supposed in evidence. This evidence was found in some MS. volumes kept in the Scotch college at Paris, and which Mr. Hume was permitted to peruse. These MS. volumes were neither more nor less than a journal written by James II. in his own hand, of his own life, during the most critical period of our history.

From such a treasure as this, it is a matter to be lamented, and indeed deserving of extreme surprise, that such an historian as Hume did no more than produce a single extract. This extract was important, but it might surely have been conceived, that such MSS. would have opened a boundless field of observation to one who was so capable of remarking on human character and political events. But on some account or other, not explained (and which I think cannot be explained favourably to Hume), he contented himself with adding to his history a single note, and nothing more.

There is yet again in Mr. Hume's History a second note on this reign of Charles (page 206), which deserves our attention; this second note is drawn from another source, not from the papers or Life of James II. but the papers of Barillon, who was the French ambassador at the time.

Charles, towards the close of his reign, dismissed his parliament (says Mr. Hume in his text), and determined to govern by prerogative alone; whether any money (he continues) was now remitted to England, we do not certainly know, but we may fairly presume that the king's necessities were in some degree relieved by France. And then follows a note, the note I now allude to, in which be gives an extract from one of the letters of Barillon, containing an account of a regular agreement verbally entered into, between Charles and Louis, where good services are promised by the one and money by the other, for the purpose, it is said, of putting his Britannic majesty out of the reach of all constraint, from his parliament, which could interfere with his new engagements with Louis.

This curious treaty was communicated to Mr. Hume while in France, and by him to the public; but Mr. Hume gives no account of any farther attempt to become acquainted with these dispatches for the French ambassador, which it was however evident would unveil, wherever they could be inspected, the most curious scenes of intrigue and corruption. Hume himself thought them important, as appears by one of his letters to Robertson. ...

53
ROBERT CHAMBERS

Robert Chambers, "David Hume," in *Cyclopædia of English literature; a history, critical and biographical, of British authors, from the earliest to the present times.* Edinburgh, W. and R. Chambers, 1844, 2 v. Selections; from 1867 Philadelphia edition, Vol. 2, pp. 169–170.

Scottish biographer and publisher Robert Chambers (1802–1871) was born in Peebles and at the age of sixteen began work as a bookseller. He soon authored several works in Scottish culture and history. He is most remembered for the editorial and supervisory work he and his brother William did on *Chambers's Edinburgh Journal*, established in 1832, and the ten volume *Chambers's Encyclopædia* (1859). Fifteen years before the *Encyclopædia*, Chambers compiled the *Cyclopædia of English Literature*, a two-volume collection of biographies and short selections of British writers. Most of the articles were written by Robert Carruthers (1799–1878), who also substantially revised the work in later editions. The article on Hume in the *Cyclopædia* is largely negative, and reflects the growing sentiment among 19th century historians that Hume was a biased and inaccurate historian, and should not be taken as an authority. The article highlights limitations of Hume's *History*, such as his reliance on secondary sources, his contempt for struggles for personal liberty, and the hundreds of factual errors contained throughout the work. Nevertheless, the article praises the engaging style and philosophical insight of the work. The *Cyclopædia* was reprinted dozens of times in Britain and America during the 19th century. The following is from the 1867 edition, which reflects revisions by Robert Carruthers (1799–1878).

HISTORIANS.
DAVID HUME.

Relying on the valuable collections of Carte; animated by a strong love of literary fame, which he avowed to be his ruling passion; desirous also of combating the popular prejudices in favour of Elizabeth and against the Stuarts; and master of a style singularly fascinating, simple, and graceful, the celebrated DAVID HUME left his philosophical studies to embark in historical composition. ...

The *History* of Hume is not a work of high authority, but it is one of the most easy, elegant, and interesting narratives in the language. He was constantly subjecting it to revision in point of style, but was content to take his author- ities at second-hand. The striking parts of his subject are related with a picturesque and dramatic force; and his dissertations on the state of parties and the tendency of particular events, are remarkable for the philosophical tone in which they are conceived and written. He was too indolent to be exact; too indifferent to sympathise heartily with any political party; too sceptical on matters of religion to appreciate justly the full force of religious principles in directing the course of public events. An enemy to all turbulence and enthu- siasm, he naturally leaned to the side of settled government, even when it was united to arbitrary power; and though he could 'shed a generous tear for the fate of Charles I. and the Earl of Strafford,' the struggles of his poor countrymen for conscience' sake against the tyranny of the Stuarts, excited with him no other feelings than those of ridicule or contempt. He could even forget the merits and exaggerate the faults of the accomplished and chivalrous Raleigh, to shelter the sordid injustice of a weak and contemptible sovereign. No hatred of oppression burns through his pages. The careless epicurean repose of the philosopher was not disturbed by any visions of liberty, or any ardent aspirations for the improvement of mankind. Yet Hume was not a slavish worshipper of power. In his personal character, he was liberal and independent: 'he had early in life,' says Sir James Mackintosh, 'conceived an antipathy to the Calvinistic divines, and his temperament led him at all times to regard with disgust and derision that religious enthusiasm or bigotry with which the spirit of English freedom was, in his opinion, inseparably associated: his intellect was also perhaps too active and original to submit with sufficient patience to the preparatory toils and long-suspended judgment of a historian, and led him to form premature conclusions and precipitate theories, which it then became the pride of his ingenuity to justify.' A love of paradox undoubtedly led to his formation of a theory that the English government was purely despotic and absolute before the accession of the Stuarts. A love of effect, no less than his constitutional indolence, may have betrayed the historian into inconsistencies, and prompted some of his exaggeration and high colouring relative to the unfortunate Charles I., his trial and execution. Thus, in one page we are informed that 'the height of all iniquity and fanatical extravagance yet remained – the public trial and execution of the sovereign.' Three pages further on, the historian remarks: 'The pomp, the dignity, the ceremony of this trans- action, corresponded to the greatest conception that is suggested in the annals of humankind; the delegates of a great people sitting in judgment upon their supreme magistrate, and trying him for his misgovernment and breach of trust.' With similar inconsistency, he in one part admits, and in another denies, that Charles was insincere in dealing with his opponents. To illustrate his theory of the sudden elevation of Cromwell into importance, the historian states about the meeting of parliament in 1640, the name of Oliver is not to be found oftener than twice upon any committee, whereas the journals of the House of Commons shew that before the time specified, Cromwell was in forty-five committees, and twelve special messages to the Lords. Careless as to facts of this kind – hundreds of which errors have been pointed out – we must look at the general character of Hume's *History*; at its clear and admirable narrative; the philosophic composure and dignity of its style; the sagacity with which the views of conflicting sects and parties are estimated and developed; the large admissions which the author makes to his opponents; and the high importance he everywhere assigns to the cultivation of letters, and the interests of learning and literature. Judged by this elevated standard, the work of Hume must ever be regarded as an honour to British literature. It differs as widely from the previous annals and compilations as a finished portrait by Reynolds differs from the rude draughts of a country artist. The latter may be the more faithful external likeness, but is wanting in all that gives grace and sentiment, sweetness or loftiness, to the general composition.

54
FRANCIS PALGRAVE

[Francis Palgrave], "Hume and his influence upon history," in *Quarterly Review*, March 1844, Vol. 73, pp. 536–592. Complete article.

Francis Palgrave (1788–1861) was the author of the 1826 *Quarterly Review* article, "Anglo-Saxon History," excerpted earlier in this collection. His 1844 article on Hume appears as a book review of the 1842 edition of Par Augustin Thierry's *Histoire*, with the running head titled "Hume and his Influence upon History." Only the short opening paragraph mentions Thierry. The lengthy essay contains only three section divisions near its close. To assist in following the dominant themes of the text, I have created additional section titles and inserted them within brackets in appropriate places. Accordingly, the contents and organization of the essay is as follows:

1. A Dialogue on Hume's value as a Historian
2. Assessment of British Historians Prior to Hume
3. Hume's Method of Writing the History
4. Hume's Anachronisms and Inaccuracies
5. Hume's Bias against Religion
6. Hume's Falsified account of Charles I
   a. Hume's Narrative
   b. Hume's Authorities
   c. Religious and Moral Character of Charles I as Deduced from Hume

The essay opens with a Dialogue discussing whether Hume's *History* is useful at all. One character argues that it may be valuable if an editor annotates Hume's mistakes; the other character argues that it is unsalvageable. In the second part, Palgrave discusses the limitations of historians prior to Hume, who wrote general histories of England, namely, Brady, Tyrrell, Eachard, Guthrie, Rapin, Salmon, and Carte. Of the seven, he feels that Carte was unquestionably the best scholar, but none had narrative flair. In part three he attempts to expose the unsoundness of Hume's method in writing the *History*. He argues that Hume tried his hand at philosophical essays, but none were "very brilliant." But, as a writer of history, he finally found the right instrument for

his talent. Palgrave surveys the important events leading up to Hume's composition of the *History*, offering interesting anecdotes and insights into Hume's
motivations. He argues that Hume drew heavily on Carte, Tyrell, and Brady,
and neglected important primary sources. As such, "Hume's history is made
out of the cast of a cast, in which all the sharpness of the original has been lost."

In Part 4, Palgrave argues that Hume was unable to look beyond his
eighteenth-century vantage. His anachronisms and inaccuracies are "specks on
the rind, which betray the unsoundness of the fruit, rotten to the core." In Part
5 he argues that, in spite of his intellectual abilities, he perverted his *History*
into a panegyric of infidelity – "Infidelity for the million," Palgrave believes,
is the real title of Hume's history. His perversion of religious truth, though, is
"crafty," and he is as much a "fraudulent opponent of revelation" as a fraudulent partisan of prerogative. And even a small acquaintance with medieval
divinity would show Hume's "amazing misrepresentations." As an illustration
of Hume's craftiness, Palgrave contends that Hume felt public pressure to
speak highly of Alfred, but did so by leaving out most of the religious compo-
nents of Alfred's life and actions.

In Part 6, Palgrave compares quotations from Hume with those of his
authorities, showing specifically how Hume ignored most of the religious
aspects of Charles I's character. Palgrave then creates a fictitious student essay,
suggesting what young readers might deduce from Hume about Charles's
religious and moral character. Such readers would conclude that, in his dying
days, Charles was free from any religious convictions, and even parted with his
children for the last time "without a prayer." Even Charles's dying words were
not religious, but instead aimed to "support the royal prerogative." This is
especially troubling for Palgrave since several educational histories are based
on Hume's religion-neutral account.

Palgrave's "Hume and his Influence upon History" was reprinted in
Palgrave's Collected Historical Works (Cambridge, 1922, Vol. 9, pp. 535–592).
In the introduction to that volume, editor H.E. Malden makes the following
comments regarding this essay:

> The Essay upon Hume's History concludes with an exposition of the
> systematic way in which he suppressed evidence of religious feeling in
> historical characters. But the main purpose of most of it is the exposure of
> his want of system in selecting his authorities. [Introduction, Vol. 9, pp. xxx]

The following is from the original article in the *Quarterly Review.*

ART. VII. – *Histoire de la Conquête de l' Angleterre par les Normands.* Par
Augustin Thierry, de l'Institut Royal de France. Quatrième édition. Bruxelles.
1842.

Thierry, largely and approvingly quoted by Sir James Mackintosh, and praised by many English reviewers, has, without absolutely superseding any of our " standard " authorities, become, through the medium of translations and cheap editions, a popular book. So much attention has been excited by the novelty of his very doubtful views, which we trust to have ere long an opportunity of discussing, that it has tended to revive the scheme, often suggested but never yet adopted, of publishing an *annotated Hume.*

[1. A DIALOGUE ON HUME'S VALUE AS A HISTORIAN.]

[Alciphron:] "Hume, after all" – it was urged by an able advocate of the plan, whom, according to the fashion of the days of Berkeley and Hervey, we will designate as *Alciphron* – "Hume, after all, retains his literary ascendancy. People will turn to him naturally as the educational book, the unchallenged source of authority. New histories, such as Thierry, may enjoy a flash of reputation, but they will not be considered as the sober, regular book, the outfit of the new book-case in the newly-furnished breakfast-room, newly occupied by the newly-married expectants of a numerous family. As Professor Smyth says, in his Lectures, *It is Hume who is read by every one. Hume is the historian whose views and opinions insensibly become our own. He is respected and admired by the most enlightened reader: he is the guide and philosopher of the ordinary reader, to whose mind, on all the topics connected with our history, he entirely gives the tone and law.*[1] Were, however, the merit of Hume's history less than it is, the stamp given by the name of a standard work will always sustain its value as a literary or commercial speculation. Hume may be truly characterized as History for the Million. In our active age, the prevailing desire is to acquire the largest show of information with the smallest expense of thought. Just as you buy a tool-chest or a medicine-chest, because it contains all the hammers and chisels, or tinctures and powders which you want, all ready chosen for you without any trouble of your own – even so do people purchase the standard work for their handsome, select libraries, because they expect, and rightly, that it will fill up the gap on their shelves and the void in their heads, without any further pains."

[Euphranor:] "Your comparison, however apposite" – was the reply of *Euphranor* – "cannot be carried entirely through. He who purchases the tool-chest endeavours to ascertain the temper of the tools; he assures himself that the shear-steel is Holtzapfel's and not Sheffield ware. It is not the mere 'town made' which will satisfy him. In the medicine-chest, you take pains enough to ensure that the contents of phials and boxes shall be the right thing, – no willowbark instead of Battley's cinchona, – genuine unadulterated senna. Still

---

[1]   [William Smyth (1765–1849), *Lectures on Modern History* (1840), selections from which are contained earlier in this collection.]

more anxiously would you keep away from the shop, however gay and attractive, if you knew that the pharmaeopolist had been tried and convicted for selling oxahe acid in the place of Epsom salts, or arsenic for magnesia.' But with respect to the 'standard work,' or the whole legion of educational works, equally 'standards' in their degree, is the same salutary caution employed? Rarely does the teacher, who places the book before the pupil, take the trouble to consider the character of the mind whence the work emanates, or the tendency of the doctrines which it may boldly display or coyly conceal. How often does the careful mother, who anxiously guards her children against opening any but 'Sunday books' on the Lord's-day, resume on the Monday her regular course of readings-lessons on history, lessons on botany, lessons on geology, taken from productions in which, either in express terms or by inference, Holy Scripture is either so excluded as to destroy all trust in its reality, or represented as a fable!"

[Alciphron:] "Surely not so," – said *Alciphron*: – "name them."

[Euphranor:] "Nay" – quoth *Euphranor* – "it is mamma's business, not mine; let her set her wits to work, and examine the first dozen of the rubbish which she shoots upon the school-room table."

[Alciphron:] "We are wandering from our question," – resumed *Alciphron*; – "do not suppose that I contend for the absolute perfection of Hume's history. In many respects, it may not satisfy the awakened curiosity of the public mind. Copious sources of information, unexplored in Hume's day, have been made known since his time by the diligence of our modern antiquaries. Sounder criticism is employed in judging the medieval period: more truly do we appreciate the poetical character of the middle ages, the splendours of chivalry, the charm of romance, the beauty of the structures, the merit of the artists who, sixty years since, were equally contemned by the man of letters and the virtuoso. Above all, we begin to understand how extensive is the inquiry involved in the annals of mankind; for the enlarged researches of our own times, make us now far more sensible of the exact extent of our ignorance. There is as much graphic archæology and curious quaintness, in any one number of Charles Knight's London or *Old England,* or my friend Felix Summerly's Guide Books, as, under Pitt's administration, would have set up an Antiquarian Society – president, council, director, and all the members to boot. But our abundance will facilitate the editorial task. Hume's short-comings may be completely remedied by the note, the excursus, the appendix, and the essay. All those who possess the information and talent needed for correcting Hume's errors or making good his deficiencies, will have a far better chance of profit or fame by annexing their information to his pages, than through any independent production of their own. Embark in the vessel which has so long braved the storms of criticism: the good ship Hume will always make a prosperous voyage, and find a market for her wares in ports which to every other flag will be closed. *It is in vain* – as observed by a shrewd critic of our own day – *that we shall look elsewhere for those general and comprehensive views, that sagacity and judgment, those masterly lessons of political wisdom, that profound knowledge of human nature, that calm philosophy and dispassionate balancing of opinion, which delight and instruct us in the pages of Hume. Hume is justly placed, by common consent, at the head of our philosophic historians: he is not more distinguished for his philosophy than for his sagacity and judgment, his feeling and pathos.*[2] – Hume may be deficient in diligence and research, but, as I have before said, how easily can any defects arising from imperfect information, be supplied by those, who, with less genius and philosophy, have more opportunity of collecting materials, more assiduity, more knowledge! And if there be any tendencies at variance with received opinions, surely a calm and temperate correction of his errors, will sufficiently enable the reader to maintain a due impartiality."

[Euphranor:] "You are quoting, O *Alciphron*" – was the reply of *Euphranor* – "the words of the late John Allen, who, as an acute, diligent and critical investigator of history, is entitled to great respect; but the task of correction would not be so easy as you suppose. Fully do I acknowledge the cleverness displayed in Hume's history, though I should not characterize his qualities exactly in the same terms. Allen's language is even more tinged by affection than that of the lover; for in the very same article he says: – '*We are thoroughly sensible of its deficiencies in what constitute the chief merit of an historian, fidelity and regard to truth.*' – Professor Smyth goes a deal further. He warns us to be '*ever suspicious*' of the author's '*particular prejudices.*' He virtually accuses his favourite writer of a perpetual falsification of his subject, '*by ascribing to the personages of history, as they pass before him, the Views and opinions of later ages: those sentiments and reasonings which his own enlightened and powerful mind was able to form, not those which either really were or could be formed by men thinking or acting many centuries before.*' And he sums up the literary character of the '*beautiful narrative*' by telling us that '*in Hume's history truth is continually mixed up with misrepresentation, and the whole mass of the reasoning, which in its final impression is materially wrong, is so interspersed with observations which are in themselves perfectly right, that the reader is at no time sufficiently on his guard, and is at last betrayed into conclusions totally unwarrantable, and at variance with his best feelings and soundest opinions.*'[3]

---

[2]   [John Allen, review of John Lingard's *A History of England*, in *Edinburgh Review*, April 1825, Vol. 42; selections from this review are included earlier in this collection.]

[3]   The passages quoted by Alciphron and Euphranor will be found in the Edinburgh Review, vol. 42, p. 5, etc.; and in Smyth's Lectures vol. i, Lecture V., which we request our readers to peruse attentively, comparing it with this article. [In Palgrave's original article, the volume number of Allen's *Edinburgh Review* essay appears as "83".]

"How can an editor deal with such a writer – an historian who neither knows the truth, nor cares to know it, and whose wilful perversions must provoke a continual, though ineffectual, refutation? – The perpetual commentary must become a perpetual running fire against the text. Let it be further recollected that the *'particular prejudices'* of Hume may chance to run counter to an editor's best interests and feelings. If you, *Alciphron*, held a good estate in the county of Berks, by your father's will, would you like to attempt the correction of a topographer who had such a *'particular prejudice'* against testamentary devices as to represent them to be grounded, in every case, upon fraud? How could any Englishman bear to edit a general history of England, composed by Monsieur De Nigrement the Frenchman, who, entertaining the most *'particular prejudices'* against the British sea-service, always advocates his own opinion by so artfully mixing up truth with misrepresentation, as to make all our naval men appear odious or ridiculous; and to induce us to believe that our naval service is equally mischievous and contemptible; our wooden walls, not the defences of the realm, but useless sources of extravagant expense; our sailors, ruffians, serving merely for plunder; the *'whole scope'* of all our Admiralty orders directed to the same wicked object; our commanders, knaves or fools, traitors or cowards; who represents Howe as a ninny, and Collingwood as a brute; and who, in narrating the last days of Nelson, fraudulently omits his 'England expects every man to do his duty;' lest, by quoting these emphatic words, he should preserve a memorial of the ardent and sincere patriotism of the dying hero?

"An editor appears to me to be nearly in your position when you introduce a stranger to your friend. In this case, you wish – if consistent with truth – to become the entire voucher for the character of the party: if you cannot go to that full extent, then, in connexion with the introduction, you feel yourself obliged to put your friend sufficiently upon the *qui vive* to protect himself in his intercourse. As the world goes, you may often be compelled, even for your friend's benefit, to place him in close quarters with an individual whose connexion or acquaintance cannot be pursued or cultivated without caution. – 'Chipchase is an honest workman, but very cross. – John Bean takes good care of his horses, though he is not a teetotaller. – Sir Richard enjoys capital credit upon Change, but he is apt to be tricky.' In all such cases the merit or talent, such as it may be, is accepted as a compensation for the defect. So far as concerns the particular purposes required, the balance is on the right side. But you would find it rather awkward, had you to state

'Lorenzo is a delightful companion, full of wit, talent and information; he has only one fault, his whole heart and soul is given up to gallantry: he never loses sight of his purpose. He has written a most clever essay upon *"the natural history of chastity"* – to prove, not only the bad influence exercised by the *"popular notions of chastity"* upon morality, but that, in point of fact, chastity never exists; and that she who is apparently the most virtuous differs only from the most profligate by "cant and grimace." Lorenzo is most actively consistent – he tries to seduce every woman he can get at. When you have him in your house he will endeavour on all occasions to put his doctrines into practice, whether he meets your smart lady's maid in the park or your staid governess on the stairs, plays an accompaniment to your spinster cousin, assists your wife at the dinner-table, reads a sermon to your budding daughter, or escorts your well matured sister to the opera.' –

Would it not probably occur to you that your friend would consider it rather inexpedient to begin by shaking hands with a scoundrel, whom he would soon be compelled to get rid of by kicking him out of doors?"

———

[2. ASSESSMENT OF BRITISH HISTORIANS PRIOR TO HUME.]

Hume's merits must be examined with reference to the era in which he flourished. Previously to Hume, it can hardly be said that England possessed historical literature in the aesthetic sense of the term. Adopting the Gibbonian phrase, it was our reproach that no British altars had been raised to the muse of History. All who, since Hume, have earned any commanding reputation, are more or less his disciples; and all our juvenile and educational histories, and conversations, and outlines, are, in the main, composed out of Hume's material – occasionally minced up with a few pious reflections, or even with texts, in order to correct the taint of the food thus dished up for the rising generation. Even Turner strongly partakes of his flavour.

Before Hume, we had many valuable and laborious early writers, such as Hall and Grafton, Speed and honest Stow, who chronicled events with diligence, giving that instruction which facts, faithfully though unskilfully narrated, afforded to the multitude, when the comparative sterility of the press rendered reading scarcer and reflection more abundant. 'Baker's Chronicle, in the hall window, the one book conned over by the fine old English gentleman, taught him to think for himself. May be his chaplain helped him a little. The modern English gentleman thinks as he is taught by his newspaper. Besides such Gothic chroniclers, for we name Baker only as the exemplar, there were other writers who had made a nearer approach to the science of history, by treating the subject with reference to the principles of government, or the doctrines of party. They aspired to the more ambitious rank of instructors; yet we had not any works which, viewed as literary compositions, were distinguished either by style or sentiment. Many might be consulted for information, none had striven for literary eminence.

Omitting the writers confined to particular eras or reigns, there were six who, as precursors of Hume, had, with more extended views than mere annalists, planned or executed the task of compiling a general history of England.

First appears Brady. The functions of this learned man exhibited an odd combination of pluralities: a doctor of medicine by profession, an antiquary by fancy, he united in his person the offices of Regius Professor in his faculty at Cambridge, Master of Caius College at Cambridge, and Keeper of the Records in the Tower; being, moreover, one of the household physicians of James II., and as such one of the attesting witnesses of the birth of his unfortunate son. Brady was also much connected with Sydenham. Strange to say, he pursued his literary studies, and preserved his reputation for professional skill. In our days, the 'three black graces' respectively impose three degrees of literary exclusiveness upon their respective professors. Mother Church is most indulgent towards her children; provided they 'perform' one service on Sunday, she nods and allows them to expatiate as they may. Themis shows more jealousy: when she is courted by the student, she smiles and says,

'Young man, recollect I must have you all to myself. It is not for the like of you to suppose that you are to be indulged like the suitors of whom I have been sure – a Brougham or a Jeffrey, a Talfourd or a Merivale. No, – when you have wedded me, you must give up all flirtations with the Muses. If you forget yourself, you shall not touch a shilling of my property, and I dare say I shall end by suing for a divorce from such an unfaithful partner.'

Esculapius is the harshest of all: if his son prints his footsteps upon ground forbidden to medical intellect, he at once cuts off the extravagant heir with an empty pill-box.

In Brady's time, far more toleration was allowed. He grew rich, received fees, and flourished, albeit he was a distinguished antiquary and historian. The first, or introductory volume of Brady's History, containing a summary of the origin and progress of the constitution, with a valuable Glossary, was published in 1684; the second in 1685; the third, which ends with the reign of Richard II., in 1700. Brady was sincere in his belief that the people had no political rights, excepting what they had begged, bought, or stolen from the king. Considered as an historical investigator of constitutional law, rather than as a narrator of facts, Brady has much merit, though he draws erroneous conclusions from authentic evidence. He assumes that, whenever any grant in favour of the people proceeded from the Crown, their right originated out of the grant; whereas, in fact, it more frequently happens that such a grant is only a confirmation of a previously existing right, or the recognition of a prevailing principle in the constitution, subsisting by custom and usage, but which now required to be defined, because government sought to violate the understanding, or refuse the concessions which might render the struggle unnecessary: popular rights previously held in solution, but precipitated by excess of royal prerogative or party pertinacity.

'Our late great parliamentary revolution' said *Alciphron*, hearing this observation, 'is a case in point: it was the refusal of the franchise to Manchester which solidified parliamentary reform-a few drops more of *Eldonine*, and we should have had the People's Charter.' But this is a vexed question, which Euphranor advises us for the present to decline, and we must therefore return again to our historians.

Partial, however, as Brady may have been, he was an honest writer; rigidly accurate in his quotations, and, having appended numerous original documents to his text, he affords us the means of refuting his own mistakes, and is still in many points a useful guide.

Brady was the champion of Toryism and hereditary right; Tyrrell took up the gauntlet on the side of the Whigs and the Revolution, by producing, in 1698, 'The General History of England, both Ecclesiastical and Civil, from the earliest accounts of time to the Reign of his present Majesty William III., taken from most ancient Records, MSS., and printed Historians, with Memorials of the most eminent Persons in Church and State, as also the foundation of the most noted Monasteries and both Universities.' Four successive volumes followed; the last appeared in 1704, when, like Brady, he was silenced in his controversy by death, and the same era, the conclusion of the reign of Richard II., ends his 'Complete History.'

As a necessary consequence of Tyrrell's antagonism to Brady, he runs fast and far away from the truth in the opposite direction. If not absolutely the founder, yet he gave a great help to the respectable, but somewhat prosy school, who systematise Anglo-Saxon liberty; believe that King Alfred instituted trial by jury; portray King John as signing Magna Charta with a long goose-quill; and, always confounding the means with the end, consider political freedom as identical with national happiness. His 'History' is a Whig pamphlet in five volumes folio. Puzzle-pated, and yet sincere, Tyrrell waded diligently through the best authorities; he neglected no source of information. We believe that he has hardly omitted any one fact of importance: and yet you read through his history without being able to recollect one of the events which he has narrated with drowsy fidelity. Like all writers of his class, he is a telescope with dulled glasses; he brings the object nearer to you, but so dim and confused that you have no distinct image at all.

With better fortune than his predecessors, Lawrence Eachard was enabled to fulfil his plan of 'giving to the Englishman his own country's story.' He undertook his useful and important work, for such it certainly is, under the clear conviction that he was called to the task by a sense of duty as a divine. England wanted a church *and* state history, a history which might teach Englishmen to respect their national constitution as well as their national religion, without egging one on against the other: he therefore wrote as a professed teacher, influenced by doctrines which it was his calling openly to propagate and confirm. Eachard's principle, however he may have carried it through, was the right one. A soldier would deem it an insult if you supposed he forgot his commission when he appears in plain clothes. Equally should a clergyman make all around him constantly know and remember his order, although his surplice may be put off. The first volume, which extends to the end of James I., is the least important. He did not neglect original authorities, but, according to the prevailing fashion, he considered the 'monastic writers' as 'being highly disagreeable to the taste and genius of our refined age.' In the second and third volumes, which carry on the history to the 'late happy Revolution,' Eachard becomes a writer of intrinsic worth. He exercised a satisfactory diligence in collecting all the printed authorities, not merely such as are historical in the strict sense of the term, but of that miscellaneous illustrative class, pamphlets, lampoons, trials, and the like, neglected by his contemporaries, but of which he fully knew the value. Eachard was also assisted by manuscript and oral information, so that in the latter portion of the work he becomes an original authority. It is a grave, magisterial, sober, sensible book, in Oxford binding. His narration is deficient in talent or liveliness; but want of elegance and spirit is compensated by the business-like clearness of his style, and the excellent arrangement of his matter. His work, in spite of the attacks of scurrilous Oldmixon, and the criticism of the miserable free-thinker, Conyers Middleton, acquired considerable credit, and may be read with advantage by those who value plain historical information, full and solid: but they must not look for any solution of difficult problems, or any nice elucidations of character.

In the capacity of the patriarch of book-makers, the earliest professional author known to have been paid by the sheet, Guthrie, whose ponderous Geographical Grammar still lingers in its fourteenth edition, deserves a memorial. Let subscriptions be raised at every trade-dinner for the erection of the statue in papier mâché, in the dark court opposite Stationers' Hall, in the centre of the little grubby, scrubby, shabby green. As an historian, few words will suffice for poor Guthrie. He was a Tory by principle and an author by necessity. Steadily did he fill page after page, under the stimulus of political feeling and the pressure of domestic penury. Such was the patient complacency of his customers, that Guthrie's history, being intended to be popular, fills two enormous folios, a stone-weight of literature. Guthrie's work is decently and comprehensively executed; but he has omitted references to proofs and authorities, so that his compilation, far too unwieldy for any ordinary reader in our degenerate days, is nearly useless to historical enquirers.

The history of reputations ill deserved, would form a large and interesting chapter in the annals of literature. When it shall be investigated by some future D'Israeli, a prominent station must be found therein for Rapin. Laborious and yet superficial, pompous and shallow, his foreign birth, education, and *habitat*, all unfitted him for the task. We must recollect, however, in judging him, that he wrote for foreigners; that is to say, for the continental public, and not for ourselves. Rapin tells us so with a candour which excuses the author, though it does not neutralize the errors which he has propagated. Rapin had some appreciation of the higher qualities of an historian – but his model of composition was Mezeray; his sentiments those of Bayle. He judged all matters, religious or political, in the spirit of a French refugee: feelings fully natural and excusable in one who had escaped the persecutions sanctioned by the name of Louis le Grand. Yet our toleration for his opinions must not induce us to conceal that Rapin, in his worthless farrago, is consistently an enemy to monarchy. Whenever the subject gives him an opportunity, he never fails to speak out: his sober republicanism is wholly different from the radicalism of the present day, and yet it is not without its influence in the same cause. Rapin's history ends with Charles I. The remaining portions of the French text (of his avowed English continuators we do not speak) are all written by different hands. Salmon says that the history was worked up by a club or society of Dutch Calvinists, French Huguenots (Durand, the minister of the Savoy, being one), English Presbyterians, and Scotch Cameronians. There may have been something of design, but there was more of bookmaking. Amsterdam was then the Manchester of this manufacture; and Rapin dying before he had completed his work, Abraham Rogissart, the bookseller, had it 'got up' from his papers, in order not to lose the benefit of a publication from which much profit was derived.

To counteract Rapin, Thomas Salmon, whom we have just quoted, produced his History of England, comprehending, as we are informed by his elaborate title-page, printed with a wonderful variety of type – upper-case, lower-case, roman, italic, red letter and black letter – 'Remarks on Rapin, Burnet and other Republican writers, vindicating the just Right of the Established Church, and the Prerogatives of the Crown against the wild schemes of Enthusiasts and Levellers, no less active and diligent in promoting the subversion of this beautiful frame of government, than their artful predecessors in hypocrisy, who converted the Monarchy into a Commonwealth and the Church into a Chaos of impious Sects.' Salmon did not come from a bad stock: he was brother of the well-known historian of Essex. His fortunes, however, had been oddly chequered: he had served in the wars in Flanders (we suspect as a private), had been much at sea, twice to the Indies, and had kept two coffeehouses in a small way, first at Oxford and then in London. Whilst following the last-mentioned avocation, he compiled the 'Modern Universal History,' in which the English history is included, and several other useful works. His English history is fairly executed, and has occasionally those touches of liveliness which knowledge of the world imparts even to inferior talent. As a critic, Salmon has given many useful corrections of the 'republican writers,' not only in his history, but in his 'Examination' of Burnet's Life and Times.

Brady and Tyrrell, but more particularly the former, well understood research. An historical antiquary now arose, in the person of Thomas Carte, who far surpassed any of his predecessors. Carte was an indefatigable investigator of unpublished documents, particularly of state-papers, but he was somewhat deficient in the gift of knowing when to undervalue the result of his own researches. Alas! it is a common error of antiquaries to reckon the worth of the prey by the difficulty of the chase, and to consider that the mere accident of the information existing in manuscript – and above all in a manuscript *penes me* – must of necessity ensure the value of the article. He has overlooked important authorities, amongst others, strange to say, some of the publications of Tom Hearne; a great wonder, because Tom Carte ought to have turned to him by pure instinct as an *unsworn* brother. Adhering to the unfortunate house of Stuart, and having become cognizant of some plot for their restoration, Carte attained the uncomfortable honour of having his name placarded on the walls, in a proclamation which offered one thousand pounds for his apprehension; but he was able to escape to France, where he continued many years. The Benedictine school was flourishing there, and he had good opportunity of profiting by their labours. These excellent men were busily employed in editing the various sources of mediaeval history; and their example, as well as the general tone of their erudition, so different from the Parisian coteries in which Hume afterwards flourished, gave Carte a deeper insight into the mode of conducting historical inquiry, than he could have obtained in England. Patronised by Dr. Mead, Carte had previously published his noble edition of Thuanus, which, after his recall to England, was followed by the 'History of the Duke of Ormond.' In the latter work he necessarily examined the character of Charles I. This production opened the way for a task of greater magnitude. Feeling, in common with others, the need of opposing a more effectual antidote to the erroneous views of Rapin, than the well-meant, though not profound, attempts of Salmon, he planned his 'Society for encouraging the writing of a History of England,' with the avowed view of being supported by such encouragement. Carte fully knew his ground, and the difficulties he should have to encounter, and he went to work as a man determined to overcome them.

A great number of 'noblemen and gentlemen signed an instrument, obliging themselves to contribute, the former their twenty, the latter their ten guineas a year, towards the charges of the work and materials.' The documents which our author circulated amongst his subscribers, before he began to publish the History, entitled 'A Collection of the several Papers published by Mr. Carte in relation to his History of England,' show how thoroughly he had considered the subject in all its bearings. A full knowledge of the contents of our own archives, many of which were then of difficult access, a thorough acquaintance with the continental collections, a due and critical appreciation of the value of the ancient sources of information, all testify to his qualifications for the task. He received munificent support. Oxford University and five of the principal colleges appeared as subscribers. Prudent Cambridge wholly kept aloof; but the reserve of Alma Mater was more than compensated by the solid patronage of the Corporation of London and of the opulent city companies. The first volume of the 'General History of England, by Thomas Carte, *an Englishman*,' was worthy of the ample assistance the author had obtained. His quaint denomination must be explained. Carte, though in holy orders, dared not write himself *clerk*, and would not write himself *gentleman*; he was a member of a secret and proscribed hierarchy; therefore he probably thought, that, since he could not add any designation of station, he would claim no other description save that which he derived from his country. Carte exercised great control over his principles: his Jacobitism can only be detected in his fairness towards monarchy, nor is the allegiance due to the House of Hanover ever endangered by the historian's affection to the Stuart cause. Without doubt, he was rather desirous not to put the Treasury again to the trouble of offering a thousand pounds for lodging him in any of his Majesty's gaols. Throughout the whole of the work, which Carte continued till the year 1642, there is only one passage in which his Jacobitism crops out, betraying the sentiments of the party to which he belonged. Never was the love of the White Rose more innocently, some folks would say more absurdly, displayed.

Speaking of the right of anointing, practised, according to ancient usage, at the coronation, he refutes the injudicious arguments of those who rest the jurisdiction of the Crown in ecclesiastical matters upon this ceremony, contending that such power is incident to royalty, and inherently vested in all sovereigns. Had he stopped there, and then taken the oaths, all would have been excellent. Even a Whig minister might have 'thought of him,' as the phrase is; or his friends might have told him so. But, unluckily, he was tempted on a little bit further; and he proceeds to confute another opinion, that the gift of healing the scrofulous humour, called the king's evil, by the royal touch, a belief which has furnished an entertaining chapter in Mr. Pettigrew's very curious history of 'Medical Superstitions,' was to be attributed to the virtue imparted by the same ceremony; 'for,' says he, 'I myself have seen a very remarkable instance of such a cure, which could not possibly be ascribed to royal unction.' The individual supposed to have received this miraculous healing, was a certain Christopher Lovel, a native of Wells, who, having resided at Bristol as a labourer, was sorely afflicted with the disease. During many years, as Carte tells us, had he tried all the remedies which the art of medicine could administer, without receiving benefit. An old sailor, his uncle, about to sail to Cork, received Lovel on board his vessel: another voyage brought him to St. Malo in the Isle of Rhé. Hence Lovel crossed the country to Paris; ultimately he reached Avignon. 'At this last place,' says Carte, 'he was touched by the eldest lineal descendant of a race of kings;' and, upon returning to his birthplace, he appeared, as people thought, entirely cured. Upon hearing this story, the first impression is, that Christopher Lovel was benefited by change of air and scene, diet and exercise, in the course of his long peregrinations by land and by sea; and any wise man, even though not a doctor, would assuredly, before he committed himself, have said, 'Let us wait awhile, and see whether the disease be entirely removed.' Accordingly, at no long period afterwards, the disease did in fact reappear. Whilst the unfortunate Jacobite thus lost his cause by failing in the ordeal which he had waged, he suffered all the odium of gaining a victory. Carte's enemies, and they were many in his own craft, took up the matter no less fiercely than as if the patient had been really and thoroughly healed, thereby giving the most undisputable proof of the legitimacy of the Pretender. Had Christopher Lovel been produced, as fresh as a rose and as sound as an apple, at the bar of the House of Lords – for the purpose of giving evidence to set aside the Act of Settlement, a louder hurly-burly could not have been raised. Pamphlets abounded. Silvanus Urban, usually open to all parties and influenced by none, lost all fellow-feeling. Mysterious paragraphs appeared, in which significant letters interchanged with more significant dashes – 'N–j–r, P–t–r,' excited all the horror of loyalty against the luckless T–s C–e. London citizens took fright. Pursuant to a vote of Common Council, Mr. Chamberlain, by order of Mr. Town, withdrew their subscription. Many other of Carte's supporters followed their example from a real horror of Jacobitism; more, lest they should incur suspicion of favouring the Stuart cause – thus saving at once their reputation and their money. Still Carte's spirit was unsubdued: he continued to labour at his work. The remaining volumes appeared in due succession; and, had not death arrested his pen, he would, without doubt, have completed the book to the Revolution. As before mentioned, it ends with 1642. Carte's transcripts form a very valuable and extensive collection, and are now deposited in the Bodleian, where they constitute a memorial of conscientious honesty; for though Carte did not live to complete his plans, still he fully performed his duty towards those who supported him. He brought together all the materials for the edifice, which he was bound to raise.

[3. HUME'S METHOD OF WRITING THE HISTORY.]

Such were the precursors, who, with unequal qualities and success, had prepared the way for Hume. Being in 1752 appointed librarian of the Faculty of Advocates, an office from which he received little or no emolument, but which gave him the command of the largest library in Scotland, he then, as he tells us, formed the plan of writing the 'History of England;' 'but, frightened with the notion of continuing a narrative through a period of 1700 years, I commenced with the accession of the House of Stuart, an epoch when I thought the misrepresentations of faction began chiefly to take place.' Two years elapsed before the appearance of the first volume of the 'History,' containing the period from the accession of James I. to the Revolution. The second followed in 1756. The history of the House of Tudor was next published in

1759; and the more early part, beginning, according to custom, with the Druids and Julius Caesar, was given to the public in 1761. This retrograde process is not ill adapted for the purpose of giving an effective and persuasive unity: it better enables the writer to single out such results as may agree with the causes which he chooses to assign. Keen novel-readers often begin with the catastrophe, in order to judge of the conduct of the tale. A writer of history may follow an analogous plan in order to ensure a striking development. Hume's 'History' thus falls into three sections, and there are diversities of execution in each. Unquestionably, the portion in which Hume shows most grasp of mind is the Stuart history, yet one spirit pervades the whole.

Previously to the appearance of the history, the Librarian, petted and favoured as he may have been by private friendship, had not manifested any ability reasonably leading to the supposition, that he would ever be numbered among the great men of the age. Had it not been for the notoriety attached to his 'philosophical' principles, no impartial observer would have anticipated that David was likely to attract the notice of posterity, amidst the crowd of gentlemen who write with ease. He had tried a profusion of little essays, little treatises, little didactic dialogues upon metaphysics, philosophy, political economy, arts and sciences, trade, commerce, and polygamy,[4] politics and constitutional policy, and historical antiquities – none very brilliant. Until he became a narrator, he never discovered the means of exerting his influential powers. Hume was destined to become a magnificent performer; but he began professing upon the wrong instruments: they had not sufficient compass – they wanted power and depth of tone; he kept hitting and hammering arias and fantasias upon the harpsichord, instead of expatiating in all the mazes of a grand concerto upon the violoncello. When he did change for the right instrument, he made it speak: and he took his proper place in the orchestra; but of that hereafter.

Hume's first offering to the literary world, as we are told in 'My own Life,' was 'a Treatise *of* Human Nature, being an Attempt to introduce the Experimental Method of Reasoning, into moral subjects'; not a very intelligible title, even when, by substituting *on* for *of,* we render it somewhat more conformable to the vulgar idiom of our language. 'Never,' adds he, 'was any literary attempt more unfortunate than my Treatise: it fell dead born from the press, without reaching such distinction as even to excite a murmur among the zealots.' And he proceeds to represent how cheerfully he sustained the disappointment, and then recovered from the blow. In this autobiographical confession, which contains two facts, the failure of the work and Hume's own

---

[4] [In *Palgrave's Collected Historical Works* (1922), the previous four words appear as "trade and commerce, polygamy," indicating a likely typographical error in the original *Quarterly Review* publication.]

conduct, there are two misrepresentations: the baby was not still-born – it was quite alive, and cried lustily, so as to excite the ogres, that is to say, the reviewers, to strangle it: an operation effectually performed, in the Journal entitled 'The Works of the Learned.' In the next place, Hume, instead of submitting with stoical indifference to the loss of said baby, raged like a lioness deprived of her cubs. Rushing into the shop of Jacob Robinson, the publisher of the Review, he out with his sword and demanded satisfaction. Jacob took refuge within his proper stronghold, and entrenched himself behind the counter, and thus escaped being pinked after the most approved fashion. Both parties acted very naturally – the stoical philosopher in being furious at the criticism, and the bookseller in declining to become a martyr for his editor; but 'My own Life' is wholly silent about the matter. 'My own Life,' indeed, belongs to a class of compositions rarely commanding much confidence: say, one in a hundred. Autos usually takes a good care not to tell any tales, which, in his own conceit, would lower his repute with Heteros – not one in a thousand. In all such compositions there is a great root of self-deception. We are far more proud of confessing our secret sin, than of recalling the recollection of our open follies. But the Philosophical Historian is superlatively egotistical and self-adulatory; he rolls and swelters in vanity.

All his miscellaneous productions, excepting only his 'Natural History of Religion,' and some slight Essays upon 'the passions,' 'tragedy,' and 'taste,' appeared before the publication of the first Stuart volume. Hume's general information, his apparent mildness and good temper, his gentleman-like flow of language when he was not provoked, his conversational powers, and the general tendency of his moral and philosophical essays, gained him much notoriety and favour in the literary circles and coteries at Edinburgh. Deism was spreading, with exceeding rapidity, amongst the more intellectual classes of the northern capital. Philosophy became almost indispensable for preserving literary caste. Free-thinking, however, was then a quasi-aristocratical luxury. It had not yet descended to the Lord Provost and the Town-Council; and when Hume became a candidate for the chair of Moral Philosophy, the 'zealots' having been bold enough to assert that he was an apostle of infidelity, he lost his election.

Such contests are usually poor tests of sound principle: however, on this occasion, the opposition was honest and sincere. It was instigated by the more orthodox and uncompromising members of the Kirk, who really adhered in heart and life to Christianity as taught by Calvin and John Knox; and Hume hated them thenceforward with his whole soul. But the 'enthusiasts' constituted a minority-both a moral and a numerical minority; all the ministry who professed liberal opinions, valued and sought Hume's friendship. Stigmatized as the propagandist of unbelief, he was consoled, supported, protected by the cordial friendship of the most distinguished members of the Scottish estab-lishment, – Blair, Wallace, Drysdale, Wishart, Jardine, Home, Robertson, and

Carlyle. This reverend patronage, not any ability or cleverness of the writer, gave activity to Hume's venom. It removed the reproach previously attached to infidelity. It at once took off the interdict. Those who are the warmest adherents to Hume's irreligion have never dared to risk their own literary reputation by praising the talent of Hume, as evinced in the most offensive of his publications, such as the 'Natural History of Religion,' which includes the 'Bad Influence of Popular Religions on Morality,' the 'Essay on Miracles,' and the 'Inquiry concerning the Human Understanding;' and when Magee (On Atonement and *Sacrifice*, vol. ii. p. 276) spoke of them as 'standing memorials of a *heart as wicked, and a head as weak, as ever pretended to the character of philosopher and moralist*,' it is the harshness of the language, not the injustice of the sentiment, which can in any degree dispose us against the criticism. Deficient in any sustained argument, prolix and inconclusive, his hold upon your attention principally arises from the effort which you are constantly compelled to make, in order to follow the reasoning, which vanishes as soon as it begins to assume a definite form. If you are an antagonist, he wearies you, not by his blows, but by continually slipping out of your grasp. Such works would absolutely have destroyed Hume's reputation as a philosophical reasoner, had he not been an unbeliever – had not opposition to faith been usually in those days considered as a *primâ facie* proof of a strong and vigorous mind.

The 'Inquiry concerning the Principles of Morals' may stand high in the scale of mediocrity. What have we in this pragmatic dissertation? A favourable approbation of qualities commonly favoured; a dislike of vices commonly odious; commonplace observations brought forth with placid solemnity; obvious truths, intermixed with as obvious fallacies. Cold approbation is the utmost Hume bestows. He has no objection to the more amiable of the natural good qualities of mankind, if they trouble him not in his easy way. Without seeking to encourage any vice which might diminish the safety of society, he is apathetic even in the cause of pagan virtue.

The best of Hume's miscellaneous productions are his political and constitutional essays: they are clear and sensible, and they have all the force resulting from a shrewd and tranquil intellect. He recommends himself by his *disinvoltura* and worldly good sense, and a due appreciation of the popular fallacies by which the multitude are deluded. These pieces have the value of slight sketches by a good artist, free and expressive, but they need finish and carrying out into compositions. The most elaborate of them is the 'Essay upon the Populousness of Ancient Nations.' Its reasonings received an elaborate reply from Wallace; and Gibbon, in his valuable 'Adversaria,' has pointed out some striking inaccuracies. It is now chiefly remarkable, as having elicited from Hume, an important and instructive description of his peculiar tactics. In a second edition, he added the following curious note: –

'An ingenious author has honoured this discourse with an answer full of politeness, erudition, and good sense. So learned a refutation would have made the author suspect that his reasonings were entirely overthrown, *had he not used the precaution from the beginning to keep himself on the sceptical side; and, having taken this advantage of the ground*, he was enabled, though with much inferior force, to preserve himself from a total defeat. That reverend gentleman will always find, where his antagonist is so entrenched, that it will be very difficult to force him. Varro, in such a situation, could defend himself against Hannibal, Pharnaces against Cæsar.'

But becoming afterwards aware, that this was an unguarded disclosure of the trick which gave most success to his sophistry, he omitted it, when, for a third time, he republished the essay in an octavo form.

In the large library, which, as he tells us, suggested his work, Hume wanted, like his predecessors, important materials then concealed in manuscript, but now familiar to every historical inquirer. Domesday, the groundwork of Anglo-Saxon and Anglo-Norman territorial organization, was enshrined in the Chapter House at Westminster, protected strictly under lock and key: rarely could the edifice be entered; if the antiquary sought to consult the treasure, thirteen shillings and fourpence of lawful money must be paid for each inspection of the volume; guarded so jealously that the finger was never allowed to wander beyond the margin, lest the characters should sustain injury from the contact with unexchequered hands. He had to labour under many other similar disadvantages, removed by more recent editorial diligence.

Such deficiencies, though they may diminish the completeness of history, are not detrimental to the literary character of the historian. Ordinary and vulgated sources will usually give all that is needed for a broad outline, which may be rendered sufficiently effective, as a test of the author's talent, with few minor details. 'Here are some new and unpublished materials for the History of the Siege of Rhodes, M. l'Abbé.' The reply of M. l'Abbé Vertot – as we have it in the facetious, anecdotic chapter of the French school-grammars of the last age – was, 'Mon siège est fait.' In the case of Vertot, the answer has become a standing joke against his memory, but the point of the sarcasm is given by his general untrustworthiness. Had M. l'Abbé been faithful to the extent of his knowledge, no candid fellow-labourer would be inclined to blame him, for being content to work well upon a limited stock. In discussing Hume's claims to be adopted as 'the guide and philosopher,' who, 'on all topics connected with our history entirely gives the law'; it is therefore important to ascertain whether he employed due diligence, in studying the materials which were accessible to him, and in availing himself of the ample library, which, as he informs us, stimulated him to his enterprise. Gibbon thought not: he describes Hume's History as 'elegant, but *superficial*:' apparently a slight epithet of blame, but which, employed by Gibbon, obtains great intensity. Congenial, unhappily, as their opinions might be in some respects, no two literary characters could be more distinct. Hume's historical Muse is dressed à la Pompadour: she is so painted that you never see her true complexion, you never get deeper than the rouge and the fard. Hume, in his best moods, only fluttered about the truth; never sought to know it. Gibbon sought to know the truth; but for the purpose of wickedly and perfidiously perverting it. Yet how admirable was the talent exerted by Gibbon, in hostility to the Power by whom the gift was bestowed – his nice sense of the due subordination of the different branches, into which he divided his studies; the good sense which taught him to intersperse them amidst each other, so varied as to relieve the mind, and yet so continuous as not to distract attention – to slacken the bow, but never leave it unstrung! His constant vigilance to improve every opportunity – recovering his Greek, to the sound of the fife and the tattoo, when on duty at Devizes; placing Homer in parallel with the verse of Pope and the geography of Strabo; comparing the returned numbers of the establishment of the Berkshire militia, with its actual rank and file, 560 nominal and 273 effective, and hence drawing his inferences respecting the real magnitude of the armies commemorated in history.

Hume, at least in the papers which have been published, abstains from affording us any similar information. 'My own Life' is silent concerning my own studies during the progress of the history; nor have we any means 'of visiting the fattest of epicurean hogs in his stye,' – this is Gibbon's kind phrase, explained by the ingenious index-maker as a 'jocose allusion to Mr. Hume's indolence.' The only glimpse we gain is through a story told by a late venerable Scottish crony. Some one having hinted that David had neglected an authority he ought to have consulted, the old gentleman replied, – 'Why, mon, David read a vast deal before he set about a piece of his book; but his usual seat was the sofa, and he often wrote with his legs up; and it would have been unco fashious to have moved across the room when any little doubt occurred.'

In the absence of more precise information, we must endeavour to ascertain, by internal evidence, the books which Hume had by his side, when, compiling the earlier portions of his history, he worked in this somewhat American guise. It has been ably shown by the most competent judge amongst our contemporaries *(Ed. Rev.* vol. liii. p. 15),[5] that, from Carte, Hume borrowed not only the arrangement of events but the structure of his expressions, giving, however, the colour of his own thought and style to the narration, and occasionally verifying Carte's statement by referring to his quotations. Hume made nearly as much use of Tyrrell, balancing the

---

[5] [Henry Hallam, review of John Lingard's *A history of England*, in *Edinburgh Review*, 1831, Vol. 53, selections from which are included earlier in this collection.]

narratives of the two historians, wisely availing himself of the hints given by Whig and Tory. Brady was his principal help for constitutional information. Original sources were occasionally consulted by him, though very uncritically and sparingly; some of considerable importance are wholly passed by: for example, the anonymous life of Richard II. published by Hearne. The reason is obvious; Carte unaccountably neglected it, therefore Hume was ignorant of the book's existence. Hume may have turned over the leaves of the chroniclers, but he never rendered them the object of study, and never distinguished between primary and secondary authorities. Of Church history, he knew absolutely nothing. Slight references to the imperfect English Concilia by Spelman, testify his ignorance or neglect of the more complete edition which we owe to Wilkins; a book which, a quarter of a century ago, was estimated as waste paper, but which now is worth more pounds than it was then worth shillings. Hume was entirely unacquainted with any of the ample collections, in which the transactions of the Church are recorded. A few passages, relating to Ecclesiastical law and history, are borrowed from the pungent satires of Fra Paolo Sarpi: his facts for the Crusades, from Maimbourg or Vertot; his notices of continental history, generally, from the *Essai sur les Mœurs* by Voltaire, and some other of the then fashionable works of French infidel literature. In the Stuart portions, Hume worked more freely and independently, from original writers; though Eachard, and also Bishop Kennet's compilation, useful for the documents and textual extracts it contains, were serviceable in saving the walk across the room.

Possibly many elucidations of Hume's literary character might be derived from the large collection of his correspondence, now deposited in the Library of the Edinburgh Royal Society. An editor would, however, find difficulty in dealing with the papers, so as to afford sufficient instruction, and, at the same time, avoid public offence. Selections from correspondence are worth little, unless they are sufficiently ample to exhibit a continuous view of the mind and pursuits of the man, and the mutual interchange of thought. Those who have examined the Hume papers – which we know only by report – speak highly of their interest, but add, that they furnish painful disclosures concerning the opinions then prevailing amongst the clergy of the northern metropolis; distinguished ministers of the Gospel encouraging the scoffs of their familiar friend, the author of the 'Essay upon Miracles,' and echoing the blasphemies of their associate, the author of the 'Essay upon Suicide.' Can we doubt but that Hume, who possessed within him the natural germ of many virtues, was exceedingly strengthened in his infidelity, by the inconsistency of those whom he terms 'religionists' leading him to the conclusion that

'their conviction is in all ages more affected than real, and scarcely ever approaches in any degree to that solid belief and persuasion, which governs us in the common affairs of life? The usual course of men's conduct belies their words, and shows that their assent in these matters is some unaccountable operation of the mind between disbelief and conviction, but approaching nearer to the former than the latter.'[6] –

Thus generalizing from his knowledge of the private sentiments of these betrayers of their Lord, these preachers of the Gospel, honouring the reviler of their Saviour, whose talents and worldly respectability added to their evil influence, he became firmly convinced that 'priests of all religion are the same,' seeking merely the gratification of their own sordid and selfish passions and propensities.

[4. HUME'S ANACHRONISMS AND INACCURACIES.]

The 'careless inimitable beauties of Hume,' as they are styled by Gibbon, that is to say, his solecisms, his Scotticisms, his Gallicisms, his violation of the rules of English grammar, and still more of English idiom, were criticised with some severity by Dr. Priestley, in his 'English Grammar,' the rarest of his productions.[7] 'The mere language of an historian,' as Dr. Arnold observes, 'will furnish us with something of a key to his mind – will tell us, or at least give us cause to presume, in what his main strength lies, and in what he is deficient.'

Hume's language shows us that his main strength lies in his art of rhetorical persuasion – in his striving always to lead the hearer to form inferences beyond his words – in his being able to throw out his written discourse with the ease of conversation, avoiding its triviality – and in a thorough appreciation of the respect which an author gains, who can neither be depreciated for vulgarity nor ridiculed for bombast. On the other hand, Hume's language equally discloses his deficiency in historical knowledge, evinced by his inability to relate his history in appropriate diction: he wants the happy medium between that paraphrase which obliterates the character of the original, and the untrue fidelity, which even still more would disguise its real features. Whoever writes the history of remote times, is virtually a translator; and a strict and literal translation fully meets the meaning of the German term. It is an *übersetzung*, an oversetting. Translation, it has been well observed, is 'a problem, how, two languages being given, the nearest approximation may be made in the second, to the expression of ideas already conveyed through the medium of the first.' Perhaps the worst solution is the conceit of rendering sound for sound, in which the sound usually ceases to be an echo of the sense. Speak, in translating from Norsk or Anglo-Saxon, of the *stink* of a rose, that is to say, the rose's *smell* – the *dream* of a fiddle instead of its *tone* – the green *beam* for the growing tree

---

[6]   [Hume, "The Natural History of Religion," Section 12.]

[7]   [Joseph Priestley (1733–1804), *The Rudiments of English Grammar* (1768), selections from which are contained earlier in this collection.]

– the *smear-monger* for the *butter-merchant*; – represent a mother as lamenting that her *knave's lungs are addled*, instead of her *boy* being ill of *consumption*; – describe the preacher holding forth from his pulpit as the *beadle spelling* from the *steeple*; – or, recurring to the original *sense*, when *sound* fails you, praise the excellent taste of his majesty of Bavaria in erecting the marble *slaughter-house* to the honour of Germania's worthies – such Teutonisms would not add to the clearness of our ideas. Very insidious, in all cases, are the deceptions suggested by titles of dignity, designations connected with state or office, of which the signification changes so rapidly from age to age, whilst the symbol remains the same. *Dominus*, or lord, conveys in the originals no peculiar notion of pre-eminence. It is sufficiently humble in the familiar compound of *landlord*; but speak of the *lord of the land*, and what a vision it raises of feudal dignity! In words which according to the laws of language, you must employ, the great difficulty consists in guarding against ambiguities, arising from the change of meaning. Parliament is not a senate occupied in making speeches and passing laws, but the king, enthroned at the head of his great court of remedial justice; a bishop's palace, nothing regal, but a *place*, a mansion; throne, unconnected with royalty, and only the official seat of the prelate. The historian should consider himself as an interpreter, standing between two nations, and he cannot well execute his task, unless he has lived with both. He must be familiarised, not merely with their language, but with their habits, and customs, and thoughts. He must be able to reduce all the conventional phrases of society into truth, to know when the speech which makes the roof resound means nothing – and be equally able to find the expressive meaning of silence. A very useful introduction to the study of patristical latinity – a main source, together with the Vulgate, of the mediæval idioms – will be found in Mr Woodham's Tertullian. It is unnecessary to remark that the baser latinity of the mediæval writers differs widely from that of classical authors; but the discrepancy lies far deeper than the adoption of barbarous words, whose signification can be disclosed by a glossary, or the solecisms which can be corrected by grammatical rules. Their rough refectory – and kitchen – Latin, came natural to them; they thought in it; hence, though employing uncouth and ungraceful language, they expressed themselves, when needed, with terseness and power. It also exhibits strong idiomatical peculiarities, not merely of individuals, but of æras. Anglo-Norman latinity differs much from the later Plantagenet latinity. Compare, for example, a few sentences of Ordericus Vitalls, or William of Malmesbury, with the pseudo-Ingulphus, forged, as we have shown, subsequently to the reign of Edward II.,[8] or Knighton. Hume, compiling chiefly from dull and vapid translations and compilations, and quite unable to catch a

---

[8] Sources of English History, 'Quart. Rev.,' vol. XXXIV. p. 296; in which article we have spoken fully of Hume's uncritical use of the ancient sources.

distinct perception of the originals, never approaches to the *truth* of historical diction, though he fully attains its rhetorical beauty.

Helped onwards by such guides as Carte and Tyrrell, it was impossible that so acute a writer as Hume could commit any palpable blunder in the main facts of his history; but he absolutely teems with all the errors which can be committed by talent, when endeavouring to disguise ignorance by putting on the airs of knowledge. Hume's history is made out of the cast of a cast, in which all the sharpness of the original has been lost. He gives great effect to the dull and rounded forms, by touching up the figures with his chisel, and recutting them so as to suit his conception; but this process, cleverly as it may be executed, only denaturalizes them the more.

We are amused at the absurdity of the Romancers of the middle ages, who portray Alexander in full armour, and Nectanebus hearing mass in the temple of Termagaunt. These anachronisms, the proofs of a total misconception of the Grecian age, are not a whit greater than when Hume speaks of 'Anglo Saxon gentlemen.' The notion of a gentleman is a complex idea, entirely belonging to our own times – it implies courtesy of manners, education, a qualification of property not defined by pounds, shillings, and pence, but which places him above poverty, though not necessarily in opulence; and belongs to a state of society which never could have existed in the Anglo-Saxon age – nor could the term ever have been employed by any writer who had the Saxon Chronicle before him.

The Gallicism *Tiberiade* reveals Hume travelling to Tiberias in the Holy Land, under the guidance of the Abbé, and not of William of Tyre.

Edwin, in Hume's History, retires 'to his *estates* in the North, with the view of commencing an insurrection' – just as a Cumberland squire might have done in the '45. Possibly Hume may have found in Rapin, that Edwin fled to his *éstats*. Unless Hume's readers obtain information elsewhere, it will be difficult for them to understand that Edwin retreated to his great earldom, his great feudal earldom, as it would be called, which he possessed with quasi-regal power.

Another example is somewhat more complicated. What confidence would be placed in a writer, who, expatiating upon the policy of our own times, were to say that landed property may be recovered, by *filing a bill* in the Court of Common Pleas, or bringing *an ejectment* in the Court of Chancery? True, this is a misapplication of mere technical terms, but the technicality involves essentials: a writer thus blundering, would at once exhibit himself as woefully incompetent to discuss the merits or demerits of our jurisprudence. Hume, in stating that Henry II. 'admitted either of the parties to challenge a trial by *an assize or jury* of twelve freeholders,' as if the terms were synonymous, displays exactly the same species of ignorance. The assize was an array of recognitors of twelve knights, elected by four other knights, under a special ordinance of Henry II.; the jury was summoned by the sheriff, by assent of the parties. The difference between the assize and the jurata constitutes one of the most instructive portions of the learning of our ancient law.

Hume is fierce against the middle ages for their ignorance of geography. – 'The imperfect communication amongst the kingdoms, and their ignorance of each other's situations, made it impracticable for them to combine in one project or effort.' – Hume was no less ignorant of the political geography of those times, without which it is quite as impracticable for an historian to combine his facts for the instruction of his readers. He creates a kingdom of *Naples* in the twelfth century, when the continental dominions of the *King of Sicily* consisted of the duchy of Apulia and the principality of Capua. He speaks of Italy and Germany in relation to the disputes between pope and emperor. Now his Italy is merely Lombardy. Germany, as we now see it coloured on the map, did not then exist. The countries which he means are the territories of the empire, bounded by the Rhone on the one side, and the wilds of the Lithuanians, and Prussians and Sclavonians, on the east.

Whilst Hume discusses, describes, condemns the manners and customs and ignorance of the middle ages, he, with dogmatic confidence, betrays in every allusion, that he never can remove himself out of the eighteenth century. Unreal ideas of the past are constantly united to a more real sense of the present; his descriptions remind one of a showman's booth in a fair – a scene with daubed temples and dingy groves, and, around and behind, the shops and lamp-posts of the market-place. Thus, speaking of the Anglo-Saxon free pledge, 'No man,' he says, 'could change his habitation without a warrant or certificate from the borsholder of the tithing to which he formerly belonged.' Farmer Ethelwolf puts on his great coat, and, going to the shop of Mr Grimbald, a tithing-man and tobacconist, walks up to the counter, and tells him that he is about to move next Michaelmas, and requests his certificate, which Grimbald duly delivers, and receives a shilling for his pains. This is the train of ideas which Hume's description of the proceeding suggests.

Suppose that an historian, describing the reign of George I., were to observe, 'There were not many bills of exchange in circulation in those days, and losses for want of such securities – a sure mark of a rude state of commerce – were *very frequent; for the art of copperplate engraving was so little known* that you could hardly ever buy blank bills of exchange in the stationers' shops.' – Even such is the reasoning of Hume in the following passage: – 'And it appears from Glanville, the famous justiciary of Henry II., that, in his time, when any man died intestate, an accident *which must have been very frequent when the art of writing was so little known*, the king, or the lord of the fief, pretended to seize all the moveables, and to exclude every heir, even the children of the deceased – a sure mark of a tyrannical and arbitrary government.'

Hume evidently supposed that writing was essential for declaring testamentary intentions. But, according to the jurisprudence of the middle ages, it was not essential; nuncupative testaments, or bequests made by word of mouth, might be equally effectual. Writing was no more needed, in the first instance, for the purpose of preventing a man in the reign of Henry II. from dying intestate, than copper-plate engraving was in the reign of George I. for the purpose of giving a legal bill of exchange. Practically, the greater proportion of wills in the middle ages were unwritten deathbed declarations, made in the presence of witnesses – who subsequently appeared before a competent authority; and to this circumstance we may trace some of the most marked characteristics of mediæval testamentary dispositions, as distinguished from our own.

When Hume personifies the papal authority in the twelfth century by 'the triple crown,' and represents the pontiff, at the same era, as launching his thunders from the 'Vatican,' he shows that he deserves the same confidence in his knowledge of the papal history, as if, writing the history of France, he were to embody the valour of France during the crusades under the symbol of the tricolor, or describe St. Louis as issuing his ordinances from the Tuileries. The second crown did not appear on the tiara till after Boniface VIII. (1294–1303), whilst the third was only added in the fourteenth century by Boniface IX. (1389–1404); and the Vatican never became the official residence of the popes, until the widowhood of Rome ceased, by the return of the pontiffs from Avignon.

In every touch we detect the inaccuracy of the picture. Hume tells us that, in the twelfth century, parish registers were *not regularly* kept. Not *regularly* kept! Parish registers were never kept in any part of the world until the sixteenth century. The only mode by which the Piovano of San' Giovanni, the baptistery of Florence, took an account of the infants whom he baptized (and all the infants of the city were brought thither), was by putting beans into a bag – a white bean for a girl, and a black bean for a boy – and then casting them up at the end of the year.

During the Anglo-Saxon period, Hume informs us that 'deeds relating to civil transactions, bargains and sales, manumissions of slaves, and the like, were inserted in the blank leaves of the *parish Bible*,' kept, it is to be presumed, in the vestry, printed by his Majesty's printer, and bound in rough calf. We shall soon have to speak of the Bible during the Anglo-Saxon period. If Hume had consulted history with any attention, he would have said that such instruments were occasionally recorded in the blank leaves of a Missal, or the Gospel, or the Psalter, or some other portion of the Scripture, treasured in a great monastery; but the examples are rare, and do not require the prominence which he has bestowed upon them.

Hume's inaccuracies go at once to the competency of the historian – the flaws in the metal, which show that the piece will not stand fire – specks on the rind, which betray the unsoundness of the fruit, rotten to the core.

Our philosopher was free from one sin – the pride which apes humility. His autobiography lies like an epitaph. He discounted his own legacy of posthumous praise, and exonerated his executors from the liability of payment.

He extols his own sobriety and his own industry in the strongest terms. – Had he these qualifications? If exerted, they would have enabled him, like Carte, to emulate the exactness of the French Benedictines; and his negligence discredits him the more.

Hume the librarian, labouring, like Guthrie, to earn an honest penny by writing for the booksellers at so much a sheet, might have been useful, or at least innocuous.

Hume the metaphysician possessed the rare gift of being able to compare probabilities, and, at the same time, to suspend his judgment. Hence the ability with which he has treated the character of Mary, a question upon which either side may be taken with equal scepticism or equal credulity. If he had been gifted with a truth-seeking mind, this talent would have conducted him to the best principles of historical investigation. He would have disciplined us in the least cultivated branch of historical science, the logic of history.

Hume the politician, as we can fully judge from his slight but able constitutional essays, might have conveyed wise practical lessons through the medium of our national history. Calm and unimaginative, great names had no influence over him: there was no object to which he bowed; he entered the temple of Fame, refusing to worship any popular idol. Head or stamp would not induce him to receive base metal as precious coin. He who had the courage to designate the works of Locke, and Sidney, and Hoadley, as 'compositions the most despicable both for style and matter,' was truly able to count the cost of exposing himself to the hostility of literary prejudice and party feeling. No one had shown more clearly than Hume the utter fallacy of the original-compact doctrines: he could admit the lovely vision of a government framed upon philosophical theory, and yet refute the Utopian absurdity of reducing it into practice. Hume was not one of those who repudiate Oxford, and graduate at Laputa. Do we seek a demonstration of the inoperativeness of popular election, as the means of collecting popular opinion – where can more able arguments be found than in Hume?

Hume the travelled scholar, inspired by the ambition of literary fame, the ruling passion, as he tells us, of his life, had it fully in his power to have composed a history, in which an even flow of style, polished though not forcible, a courteous and gentlemanlike dignity, a happy disposition of incidents, and the delicate taste which, preventing his attaining the sublime, always guarded him against the ridiculous, would have furnished a narrative in which instruction pleasantly conveyed might have compensated for the absence of original inquiry. Hume is a great master in historical discourse. He is a *consummate Rhetor*. As a composition, considered without reference to truth or principle, his Stuart apology is unrivalled.

[5. HUME'S BIAS AGAINST RELIGION.]

But all his powers – they were great, and might have been noble – are rendered useless by the *consummate Rhetor's* continued perversion of *history* into a panegyric of infidelity. His metaphysical writings have always been more known than read – so dull, that even the zest of doing a wrong thing can hardly now persuade a reader to grapple with their drowsy inanity. Even the warmth and talents of his opponents could never criticism them into popularity. At last he discovered his peculiar talent. It was this acquisition of self-knowledge, and not the opportunities of his office, which induced him, like Voltaire, to adopt history as the more effective vehicle of his opinions; and he fully succeeded. 'INFIDELITY FOR THE MILLION' is the heading for Hume's history, than which only one other – and is it needful to name Gibbon? – has exerted a more baneful influence upon English literature, and through English literature upon the civilized world. Antipathy to faith had become engrafted upon his moral constitution. Like Gibbon, he was possessed with malignant hatred against all goodness and holiness. 'Never lose an opportunity,' was the advice given by a kindred spirit, 'of placing gunpowder, grain by grain, under the gigantic edifice of superstition, until the mine shall be charged with a sufficient quantity to blow up the whole.' Hume did not dare to fire the train. He would have dreaded the smoke and noise of an explosion. Adopting the coarse but forcible expression, suggested by a crime unknown in the 'dark ages,' and generated in the full blaze of civilization, he always tried to *burke* religion. Temper, as well as prudence, had from the first beginning rendered him sober. Personal considerations had due influence: he courted not the honours of martyrdom. Opinion imposed some check, law more. In England there was a boundary which could not be quite safely passed. Some examples had occurred sufficient to warn him. Like Asgill, or Toland, or Woolston, or Peter Annet, he might be seduced beyond the bounds of conventional impunity granted to free-thinking, and find himself in the presentment of the grand jury, with a prospect of Newgate and the pillory in the background: far enough off, yet disagreeable objects, looming in the horizon. At Edinburgh, an ecclesiastical prosecution brushed by him. 'An overture' was made in the General Assembly, for appointing a committee to call the philosopher before the synod, as the author of books 'containing the most rude and open attacks upon the Gospel; and principles evidently subversive even of natural religion and the foundations of morality, if not establishing direct atheism.'

A further examination of this very remarkable transaction would exceed our limits: the endeavour thus made by the orthodox members of the Kirk, to testify against the progress of infidelity, was frustrated not by dint of reasoning, but by the indefatigable exertions of his clerical friends. We have seen what high and influential names were numbered amongst them. The strongest argument which these ministers of the Gospel employed *on behalf* of their client, was, 'that Mr. Hume was really no Christian, had not so much as the profession of it, and therefore was to be considered as one who is *without*, and not a subject of, Christian discipline.' Thus did the most eminent, in the world's opinion, of the teachers of Christianity in Scotland plead Hume's declared infidelity, as the reason for espousing his cause, and protecting him from ecclesiastical censure. Pending the proceedings, the more faithful of the clergy did their duty, by endeavouring to warn their people against him. His chief opponent was Anderson, 'the literary champion of the fanatics,' who dealt with Hume by '*constantly appealing to the Bible, the usual resource of the priest in every difficulty.*' We take the words of his biographer, as the best exponent of the antagonist feelings by which Hume was supported or opposed.

Yet Hume did not escape entirely without damage. Infidelity stood between him and the much-coveted professorial chair. By the rebound of the attack made in the General Assembly, he was compelled to resign his librarianship. Though little hurt, he was somewhat scared; and whilst it increased his grim antipathy to the faithful Calvinistic clergy, the 'fanatics' and 'enthusiasts,' he was the more wary in avoiding any very tangible opportunity of falling into their power – a power fast diminishing, but yet sufficiently formidable to disturb the Sybarite on his rose-leaves. Caution, therefore, was always needed: a restraint to which he submitted the more willingly, since he conceived that his own quiet plan of operation would be quite as sure, in the long run, as the more brilliant and sounding measures adopted by the other active members of the philosophical circle, the 'sensible, knowing, and polite company – with which Paris abounds more than any other city in the world.' He comforted himself in his dying hours with the hope of the ultimate advent of unbelief triumphant. 'Have a little patience, good Charon: I have been endeavouring to open the eyes of the public; if I live a few years longer, I may have the satisfaction of seeing the downfall of some of the prevailing systems of superstition.'

To this one object, the destruction of 'religious fictions and chimeras,' all Hume's endeavours were directed. It was the one end and intent of the History, which gives to the whole the epic unity, whence its seductive merit is in great measure derived. Hume's mode of dealing with religion shows the cowardice of his heart: he dreaded lest conviction should come upon him against his will. He was constantly trying to stupefy his own conscience, lest the pain of perceiving any reality in things unseen should come on. The first object of Hume is to nullify religion. All the workings of Providence in worldly affairs are denied: or blurred, when he cannot deny them. All active operation of holiness, all sincerity, is excluded. He constantly labours to suppress any *belief in belief*, as an efficient cause of action: he will rather infer any other influential motive. Silence, argumentation, equivocation, absolute falsity, are all employed with equal dexterity, and in sovereign contempt of all the laws by which the conscience of an historian should be ruled. But if he cannot blot out religion entirely, he lowers, degrades, deforms it; yet he prefers to affect contempt, rather than express absolute aversion; he treats faith rather as a meanness, which the enlightened philosopher is ashamed to notice, than as an enemy who needs to be actively expelled. Ever and anon, however, his hatred becomes apparent; and he forgets even the conventional decencies of language in the bitterness of his heart. When his so-called history is not an inferential argument against religion, it is an invective. Could the powers of Belial be described more forcibly, than in the following remarkable passage?[9] –

'*Hume, ... without positively asserting much more than he can prove, gives prominence to all the circumstances which support his case. He glides lightly over those which are unfavourable to it. His own witnesses are applauded and encouraged; the statements which seem to throw discredit on them are controverted; the contradictions into which they fall are explained away; a clear and connected abstract of their evidence is given. Everything that is offered on the other side is scrutinized with the utmost severity; every suspicious circumstance is a ground for comment and invective; what cannot be denied is extenuated or passed by without notice. Concessions even are sometimes made; but this insidious candour only increases the effect of this vast mass of sophistry.*' –

And in every shape, Hume is the Belial advocate of infidelity.

When reading Hume's History, we must carefully keep in view the meaning of the terms which he employs; his technical language must be translated by turning to his own dictionary – Religion is with Hume either *Superstition* or *Fanaticism*. He so applies and counter-changes these opprobrious terms as to include every possible form of Christianity. In the Churches of Rome and England, superstition predominates; in the Calvinistic Churches, which he detested most, fanaticism; though all are equally assailed. When he bombards St. Peter's, his shells glance off upon St. Paul's. His spear pierces through Archbishop Anselm, and pins Archbishop Howley to the wall. The filth with which he bespatters the Lateran Council, defiles the General Assembly. But, alas! each religious body, viewing only the damage done to its opponents, has been insensible of the hurt which its own cause receives from the bitter enemy of their common Head. Too successful has been the policy adopted by him, of 'opposing one species of superstition to another,' and thus profiting by the dissensions which he helps to raise.

---

[9]   From Mr. Macaulay's article upon 'History,' Edinburgh Review, No. xlvii. p. 359. We have no hesitation in affixing Mr. Macaulay's name to this admirable and in most respects incontrovertible essay. Since he has not reprinted it in his collection, we trust he will reproduce it in an enlarged form, perhaps reconsidering his judgment of the Greek historians. [In Palgrave's original article, the volume number of Macaulay's essay appears as "xciv".]

All who oppose Hume's *political* principles – Towers, Stuart, Brodie, Fox, Laing, Allen, Smyth, Macaulay[10] – reproach him with unfairness and insincerity – correct his misrepresentations, brand his crafty perversion of truth. The most lenient, and yet in some respects the most severe, of his critics, Professor Smyth, warns us to be '*ever suspicious*' of the historian's *particular prejudices*. Every accusation they prefer against him, by reason of his fraudulent partisanship of prerogative, applies with far greater force against him as a fraudulent opponent of revelation.

Hume's estimate of the merit or demerit belonging to any institution – or any individual – is exactly in proportion to the absence of so deleterious an influence as Christianity. Hume is always on his guard; no holiness, no beauty, no purity, no utility, can by any chance betray or seduce him to find an excuse for the sin of religion.

Professor Smyth, warning his readers against the continued fraud and falsity of the 'guide and philosopher,' and expatiating upon the sagacity and skill displayed by Hume in perverting the authorities whom he employs, proceeds, –

'But what reader turns to consult his references, or examine his original authorities? What effect does this distrust after all produce? Practically, none. In defiance of it, is not the general influence of his work on the general reader just such as the author would have wished; as strong and permanent as if every statement and opinion in his History had deserved our perfect assent and approbation?

I must confess that this appears to me so entirely the fact, judging from all that I have experienced in myself and observed in others, that I do not conceive *a lecturer in history could render (could offer, at least) a more important service to an English auditory than by following Mr. Hume, step by step, through the whole of his account; and showing what were his fair, and what his unfair inferences*; what his just representations, and what his improper colourings; what his mistakes, and, above all, what his omissions: in short, what were the dangers, and what the advantages, that must attend the perusal of so popular and able a performance.' – *Lectures on Modern History*, vol. i. pp. 127, 128.

Some few observations and examples will exemplify how truly the Professor's censures are deserved: but we must be content to await an explanation of the

[10] [Gilbert Stuart (1742–1786), *A View of Society in Europe* (1778); Joseph Towers (1737–1799), *Observations on Mr. Hume's History of England* (1778); George Brodie (1786?–1867), *History of the British Empire* (1822); John Allen, Review of Lingard's *History* in *Edinburgh Review* (1825); William Smyth (1765–1849), *Lectures on Modern History* (1840); selections from these works are contained earlier in this collection.]

principles which justify the public teacher of youth in bestowing the most affectionate and warmest praise upon such a propagator of falsity. Would it not
have been desirable that an instructor of the rising generation should pass some
censure upon these violations of natural morality, some regret for talents thus
misapplied?

Hume's sagacity taught him in most cases to avoid absolute falsehoods.
You can rarely apprehend him in flagrant delict. Hume's misrepresentations are
usually couched in those vague broad general charges which he propounds as
certain, without bringing forward any proof. Now, it is very difficult to refute
charges so propounded, because their contradiction must always be a negative
pregnant, involving counter assertions, which throw the whole burden of
proof upon those who wish to dispel the error. To revert to Euphranor's illustration, if a French writer were to state that the *whole scope* of our Admiralty
orders since the reign of Queen Elizabeth 'is directed to the purpose of plunder,'
there would be no incontrovertible refutation, excepting by producing the
whole series of documents. So it is in Hume: his calumnies are couched in those
stereotyped phrases, which, through him, and, we may also add, through
Robertson, are now adopted as first principles of historical information and
knowledge – 'ignorance and absurdity;' 'days of ignorance;' 'disputes of the
most ridiculous kind, and entirely worthy of those ignorant and barbarous
ages;' – assertions that the clergy 'subsisted only by absurdities and nonsense;'
– that 'nonsense passed for demonstration;' – that 'bounty to the Church
atoned for every violence against society;' that 'the people, abandoned to the
worst crimes and superstitions, knew of no other expiation than the observances imposed upon them by their spiritual pastors.' To demonstrate the
prejudice, the unfairness, the wicked untruths of such accusations, the first step
in the process must necessarily be to know what they mean. 'Ignorance' may
be ignorance of evil – absurdities may be the highest truths. According to
Hume, belief in a special Providence is a gross absurdity. It is painful to us to
be compelled to notice impiety in a conversational tone, but the nature of our
subject compels us to do so. In the next place, the general influence of Hume's
general propositions can only be counteracted by a faithful development of the
practice and doctrine, life and conversation, of the ages and persons so
recklessly defamed. The task, we rejoice to say, has been nobly begun by Mr.
Maitland, in his Essays upon the Dark Ages, which have appeared in their
present form, since this article was first sent to the printer. Terse, witty,
powerful in reasoning, pious in spirit, and profoundly learned, Mr. Maitland
has, by a well-chosen selection of topics, enabled every reader to judge of the
gross misrepresentations which have been promulgated by those popular
writers, who, in Professor Smyth's words, have hitherto given the tone and the
law to the public mind. We trust that such a work as Mr. Maitland's will not
be confined to the instruction of readers. Let us hope that it will produce
students: encouraging those who, deriving knowledge from original sources by

patient assiduity, thence acquire self-reliance and independence of judgment, so much needed in this over-active age, when so many endeavour to be up and doing, and so few sit down and think. For this purpose there must be a diligent study of medieval divinity.

Considered merely as affording the means of historical information, this pursuit will become indispensable, when, with more philosophy than has hitherto been exerted, we endeavour to penetrate into the moral organization of medieval society. Are we interested by the structure of the abbey or the cathedral? – Is it not at least as important to become acquainted with the doctrines which were taught by those who ministered at the altar? Our present love of antiquity may lead to unsound conclusions. Many are tempted to a blind and indiscriminate worship of past times, not only shutting their eyes against unfavourable facts, however clearly proved – but ascribing to the middle ages gifts of impeccability and perfect holiness, which revelation teaches us to be incompatible with human nature; others, constituting a more numerous class, are caught by the vulgar bait of antiquarianism. Our attention is in danger of being engrossed by the archæology of the curiosity shops. Unless this tendency be corrected, we shall be overwhelmed with literary dealers in the *rococo* of history – Archaeology, if pursued merely with reference to art or decoration, to manners and customs, to incident and romance, is little more. Without doubt, in a subordinate relation, all such inquiries are useful, but they are only secondary and subordinate: it is the bane of sound instruction to consider them in themselves as objects of knowledge. History so treated, substitutes the illuminated miniature of a manuscript, with its bright colours and false perspective, for a real view of the state of society. How has the study of classical antiquity been rendered beneficial to the intellect? It is because the history and philosophy and literature of Greece and Rome have been rendered ethical; because they have been pursued for the purpose of distinguishing between the transitory forms which they assume, and the principles of permanent application and utility which they include. To the Christian teachers of the middle ages, we deny the honour and worship which we lavish upon the wise among the heathen. In place of seeking the highest utility, we play with the eccentricities and peculiarities which amuse us from their novelty or singularity, which minister to intellectual frivolity, which gratify the ear or the eye – the baubles supplying the subject of a melodrama or the drawing for an album, the arrangement of a tableau, the poetry of an annual, or the frippery of a fancy-ball.

Very important are these doctrinal works in explaining how the comparative paucity of copies of the Holy Scriptures influenced, and, paradoxical as it may appear, promoted, their study during the middle ages. Until about the twelfth century, the productions of the inspired writers were not commonly found otherwise than in separate manuscripts, as is the case in the East at the present day. 'So scarce are the copies,' is the remark of a recent traveller, 'that I have not found but a single Nestorian, and that was the patriarch, who possessed an entire Bible; even that was in half-a-dozen volumes. One man has the Gospels, another the Epistles, and so on.'[11] It was, therefore, only with much trouble and expense that a complete set of the detached pieces of Holy Writ could be formed. The donor of the Book of Kings or the Book of Chronicles is recorded as a benefactor in the annals of the monastery. Few libraries before the Hildebrandian era – the great era of revival – possessed Law and Prophets, and historical and poetical books, and Gospels, and Acts, and Epistles, and Apocalypse, transcribed uniformly in the one volume which we call the Bible – a term unknown till about the thirteenth century, such a volume being previously designated as the *Bibliotheca,* or the *Pandects.* The scarcity of a complete textual copy of the entire Scriptures – the deep feeling of their inestimable value – the exertions bestowed by monks and clergy for their diffusion – all appear from a remarkable anecdote in the life of St. Ceolfrid (ob. 716). This holy man, the abbot of Wearmouth and Jarrow, caused three *Pandects* to be copied. Two were placed in his monastery, in order that the whole body of Scriptures might be conveniently ready and at hand for consultation or perusal in any particular chapter; the third he himself conveyed to Rome, and presented to St. Peter's: thus proving equally the value of the volume and the diligence of the Anglo-Saxon Church – Northumbria, so lately a pagan realm, aiding by her industry and learning the capital of the Christian world.

New generations arose; time advanced; the patient industry of the inmates of the Scriptorium multiplied the copies of Holy Writ, until the wider diffusion of Scripture was permitted by a process – art, it cannot be called-so easy, so familiar, so long known, that the concealment of the printing-press from mankind until these our latter ages is one of the most remarkable instances, revealing to us the constant control exercised over human intellect by the Power from Whom it flows. In the meanwhile, and until printing was thus called into operation, the whole course of religious instruction consisted in a constant endeavour to imbue the learned clergy, and the unlettered laity, with the knowledge of the Word of God. Hence, for the clergy, the formation of the Concordance, binding, as it were, the Holy Scripture into one whole, and rendering the inspired writers their own commentators; and it was in the 'darkness' of the thirteenth century, that, by Hugo de Sancto Caro, this great and laborious work was performed. Hence, for the laity, the common use of pictures. Objectionable as such a mode of instruction may become, it was then beneficially employed, as the means of realising an historical knowledge of Holy Writ. How few amongst us identify, in our own minds, the personality of the individuals, and the actual occurrence of the events, mentioned or recorded in sacred history! How rarely do we strengthen ourselves in the conviction that

---

[11] Grant on the Nestorians, p. 67.

the Deluge is as real an event as the fire of London! Historical belief and doctrinal belief are inseparably combined; take either away, the other fails. Reject the historical event, and you destroy the sacrament which it typifies. Even the mystery or stage-play, in which the events of Scripture were dramatized, was beneficial. In certain states of society, there is scarcely any sense of the ridiculous. The rude dramas which amuse the half-scoffing antiquary, conveyed sound instruction to the wondering multitude. The more the volumes of the Holy Scriptures were scarce, the more was Scripture knowledge valued. Scriptural knowledge acquired activity from its concentration. The narrowness of the stream added to the force of the current; what was lost in breadth was gained in intensity. Scripture was forced upon the reader, upon the hearer, upon the monk in his cell, upon the crowd assembled round the cross. Consult the medieval sermons and homilies: what are they but continuous lectures upon the Holy Scriptures? The Song of Songs alone furnishes *eighty-six* sermons to St. Bernard, of singular excellence. Their treatises of divinity, properly so called (for the scholastic dialectics belong to a different class), overflow with Scriptural knowledge; and generally may be designated as Scripture extracts connected by ample glosses and expositions. Above all, was the Bible brought home to the people by the constant appeal to Holy Writ – in discourse or in argument, in theory or in practice, for support or example – connecting it with all the affairs of human life. The Scriptures entered as an element of all learning, of all literature, of jurisprudence, and of all knowledge. Theology was honoured as the queen of science. The opening speeches to Parliament were scriptural discourses; and this circumstance has been alluded to with ridicule, by the very writers who most strongly condemn the middle ages for their neglect and concealment of Holy Writ. Every theory, every investigation, was based and founded upon Scripture; for, in the memorable words of the venerable Primate of our Church, mankind truly and practically acknowledged the all-important duty of 'approaching the oracles of Divine truth with that humble docility, and that prostration of the understanding and the will, which are indispensable to Christian instruction.'[12] Can we say that the far greater diffusion of Scriptural knowledge in our times produces that vital result? Do we, like them, obey the whole tenor of the volume, which teaches us the duty of bringing intellect into continual subjection to revelation? Considered merely as a book, none was perused with greater delight – no poem had so great a hold upon the imagination. The Bible, in all its variety, was presented to them, not as a huge bundle of texts, but as one wonderful epic, beginning before time – ending in eternity.

---

[12] Charge delivered to the Clergy of London, at the Primary Visitation, 1814, by William, Lord Bishop of London.

It would require years – years well employed – to investigate the literature of medieval divinity. Even the most moderate tincture is sufficient to correct the amazing misrepresentations which have been propagated respecting the religious morality of the middle ages; and, with respect to Hume's wholesale falsities, take the following passage: –

'However little versed in the Scriptures, they [the ecclesiastics] had been able to discover that, under the Jewish law, a tenth of all the produce of land was conferred on the priesthood; and forgetting, what they themselves taught, that the moral part only of that law was obligatory on Christians, they insisted that this donation conveyed a perpetual property, inherent, by divine right, in those who officiated at the altar. *During some centuries, the whole scope of sermons and homilies was directed to this purpose; and one would have imagined, from the general tenor of these discourses, that all the practical parts of Christianity were comprised in the exact and faithful payments of tithes to the clergy.*'

Such are the accusations preferred by the philosopher, who, denying the miracles of the Gospel, confessed that he had never read through the New Testament. Of the knowledge possessed by the clergy, whom the sneering enemy of revelation represents as 'little versed in Scripture,' we have already spoken. With respect to the accusation which charges *the entire body of Christian teachers* with the foul and deliberate perversion of the whole scope of their teaching, for the purpose of ministering to their own sordid avarice, it is not merely an untruth, but an untruth destitute even of a pretence by which it could be suggested. In no one of the sermons or homilies of Bede, Ælfric, Gregory, Anselm, Bernard, Gerson, or Thomas à Kempis (names amongst the most important of the ministers of the Gospel during the middle ages), or in the treatise of Alan de Lisle, destined for the instruction of the extempore preacher, is there a single passage by which the payment of ecclesiastical alms or tithes is recommended, enforced, or enjoined. Nor do we believe that, if the whole body of medieval divinity, printed or manuscript, were ransacked, any evidence could be found by which the calumny could be in the slightest degree sustained. The Historian would not have dared to broach the falsity, had he not been able to rely upon an ignorance amongst his readers, to which his own impudence could be the only parallel.

As history unfolds, and each successive personage is put upon his trial before Hume, he very carefully examines into character. Can it be shown that king or statesman has reviled the Word of God, oppressed the priesthood, robbed the church – then the Judge charges the jury to take the evidence of good character into consideration. If, on the contrary, witnesses come forward, showing that the culprit has been guilty of Christianity – then, in passing sentence, this previous conviction calls for aggravation of punishment. We have thus, in all

Hume's delineations of character – delineations far more frequently displaying the common-place contrasts of a theme, than the skill of a philosophical inquirer – a constant source of falsification. 'Rufus,' says Hume, 'was a violent and tyrannical prince, a perfidious, encroaching, and dangerous neighbour, an unkind and ungenerous relation, and was equally prodigal and rapacious in the management of his treasury. If he possessed abilities, he lay so much under the government of impetuous passions, that he made little use of them in his administration.' Yet Hume lets him off with many a good word. His open profaneness is excused, as the result of 'sharp wit;' and, with great kindness and consideration, he warns us, that we must be 'cautious of admitting every thing related by the monkish historians to the disadvantage of this prince;' he, Hume, having already admitted and enlarged upon every fact related by the monkish historians, which shows his profligate and reckless tyranny.

Because Henry I. persecuted Archbishop Anselm, he receives Hume's high praise for his 'prudence and moderation of temper;' the proofs of these good qualities being, *e.g.*, his cutting off the noses of his grandchildren, the offspring of his illegitimate daughter Juliana, and plucking out the eyes of Lucas de la Barre.

Whenever it is possible, by misrepresentation, or by concealment, or by sophistry, to calumniate any individual exercising religious functions, or to depreciate any one in whose character religion forms an element, or to carp at any action grounded upon religion, Hume never fails to improve the opportunity. We have thus a perpetual source of falsification in the biographies of the leading personages. Ecclesiastics were compelled, from their situation, to take a prominent part in the business of the world; they were statesmen, politicians; now the leaders of opposition, now the prime ministers of the sovereign. Whether it was expedient that the members of the hierarchy should be called upon thus to mix in secular affairs, whether it were a privilege or a burden, or a temptation, are questions which we shall not discuss. But this constant unfairness ruins the mere historical narrative.

Take, for example, Lanfranc. 'Lafranc was a Milanese monk.' Lanfranc was *not* a Milanese monk; he was born in an independent and hostile state, the city of Pavia. Hume, turning to Guthrie's Grammar, and finding that Pavia was included in the Duchy of Milan, supposed that it was equally so in the eleventh century. Moreover, though Lafranc was a monk, he did not become so till long after he had crossed the Alps, when he professed in the rising monastery of Bec Hellouin: afterwards he became abbot of Caen, whence he was translated to Canterbury.

'This prelate was rigid in defending the prerogatives of his station; and, after a long process before the Pope, he obliged Thomas, a Norman monk, who had been appointed to the see of York, to acknowledge the primacy of the Archbishop of Canterbury. Where ambition can be so happy as to cover his enterprises, even to the person himself, under the appearance of principle, it is the most incurable and inflexible of human passions,' etc. –

True enough, but the maxim, ingeniously hitched in between the account of Lanfranc's contest and a falsified statement of his zeal for the papacy, does not apply to either. Whether Canterbury or York should possess the primacy was a mixed question of legal right and constitutional privilege. The primacy had been long disputed, upon grounds as strictly technical as those which give an individual a right to an estate. York acted with considerable pertinacity. Some of the earlier evidences were ambiguous. Adverse possession might, in some cases, be surmised; the suit was to be decided, therefore, by the construction of legal instruments and by evidence. Archbishop Lanfranc brought his suit against Archbishop Thomas, in the same manner as two peers might have contested the possession of a barony in Parliament. Moreover, the claim was one which Lanfranc could not surrender. Had he yielded, he would have sacrificed the rights of his successors, the liberties of the English people. As primate, he was the first member of the Great Council of the realm. Through the Archbishop, upon each coronation, the compact was concluded between the sovereign and the subject. Furthermore, Lafranc's success established the principle, that whatever rights had legally subsisted before the Conquest, were to be preserved and maintained, unaffected by the accession of the new dynasty. Lafranc, maintaining the rights of his see, protected all his successors – all his order. It is they who, at the present time, are still reaping the benefit: it was their battles which Lanfranc fought. The decision given in Lanfranc's case governed all similar cases; and, followed by the resistance of his successor Anselm to the spoliations and oppressions of Rufus and Beauclerck, protected the rights of every diocese and diocesan, every dean and deanery, every parish priest and parish throughout the kingdom. Every churchman in England holds his preferment as the heir of Lanfranc and of Anselm.

Hume accuses Lanfranc of 'zeal in promoting the interests of the papacy, by which he himself augmented his own authority.' But the fact is, that Lanfranc in no manner augmented his authority through the papacy; and his conduct contributed greatly to keep the Church of England in that state of isolation from the other portions of the Western Church, which so remarkably characterizes the Conqueror's reign. William, who had been willing enough to support his claims by the sanction of Alexander II., presented a firm front to Hildebrand. 'No pope shall be acknowledged in England without my assent,' was the declaration of the Conqueror. Lanfranc, the 'Milanese monk,' acted so completely in conformity to this declaration, as to lead to the supposition that he obeyed a course which he himself had advised. The 'process' before the pope went off without effect. The contest between him and the archbishop of York was decided as if it were entirely a civil question, by the king and the Great Council or Parliament – and not by papal authority, as Hume leads his readers to suppose. When Guibert of Ravenna was appointed to the papacy by the emperor, Lanfranc maintained an armed neutrality. He refused to acknowledge Clement III., and did *not* send his adhesion to Gregory VII. Had Lanfranc's successors adopted the same course, England would have been lost to Rome. Yet all these important facts are concealed by Hume, in order to establish a charge of 'zeal for the papacy.' Hume's notice of Lafranc's learning is confined to a silly sneer; 'he wrote a defence of the real presence against Berengarius; and in those ages of stupidity and ignorance he was greatly applauded for that performance.' Lanfranc's treatise possesses singular dialectic acuteness and dexterity. Without being in the least convinced by his arguments, we may fully admire his skill. Lafranc contended for doctrines which he conceived he was bound to support; he appealed to public opinion, and by argument gained the victory.

But Lanfranc's fame had been long since established; it did not depend upon his polemic discussions. Lafranc led the intellectual movement of his age; Lanfranc was acknowledged to be the great teacher of Latin Christendom. Hume remarks, that 'knowledge and liberal education were somewhat more common in the southern countries.' But the seat of liberal education was more truly in the North. From the remotest parts, not only of Latin or Western Europe, but even of Greece, students of all classes and ages resorted to Bec Hellouin, as to another Athens. Removed from his university, for such his humble monastery had become, to Caen, and thence exalted to the primacy of England, his pastoral duties compelled a new application of his literary labours. He entered a less ambitious, but not less useful career. Lanfranc now employed himself upon his edition of the Holy Scriptures. The texts of the biblical books had been miserably corrupted, by the ignorance of the later Anglo-Saxon transcribers, one of the many results of the calamitous invasion of the Danes, which no exertion had been able wholly to remove. Much of this correction was effected by Lanfranc's own application and learning: manuscripts, with his autograph corrections, existed in France previous to the Revolution; others may perhaps lurk in our libraries. But he also provided, as far as he could, for futurity – by training up many disciples for the same important task. Of Lanfranc's character and influence as prime minister, Hume says absolutely nothing. Lanfranc's letters or despatches, to which the historian never makes a single reference, display his vigilance and his charity. Whilst defending the power of his sovereign, he became a father to the English. He rejoiced to adopt the name of Englishman. Rufus was educated by Lanfranc. One of the most remarkable proofs of the archbishop's intellectual power, and of the good use to which he turned that power, was that, so long as he lived, the wickedness and tyranny of his pupil were utterly restrained. Hence Lafranc's death was lamented as the greatest calamity which England could sustain. Of all these characteristics, not a word is to be found in Hume. Concerning all these practical effects of good sense, and learning, and talent, and piety, exhibited in the most distinguished character of the early Anglo-Norman era, the historian of England is entirely silent.

Bentham amused himself, and his readers also, by proposing that criminals should be exhibited to public contempt, with masks emblematical of the bad passions which seduced them to crime. Hume, as a writer, has anticipated the utilitarian jurist. He has two sets of such masks, in which he usually exposes his churchmen to scorn and contempt: the wolf-mask, and the fox-mask.

Gregory the Great is shown up as wolf: the unwearied and successful labours of this pontiff for the conversion of the English, arise simply from raving, craving ambition. Augustine, the apostle of the English, wears the fox-mask: his mission is a consistent and successful course of hypocrisy. Whenever religion can be laid to the charge of any individual, conclude him, says Hume, to be either knave or fool: consider it as an incontrovertible principle, 'that a general presumption lies against either the understanding or the morals, of *any one who is dignified with the title of Saint* in those ignorant ages.'

When victimizing Pope Gregory, or Augustine, or Lafranc, Hume knew he was on the safe side, and that his readers would go with him; but what, if, by a strange contingency, some individual thoroughly besotted and perverted by faith, should happen to be a popular favourite? Now it does so happen that Hume, by the pressure from without, feels himself under the awkward and imperative obligation of joining in the homage universally rendered to an individual, holding a proud and eminent station in English history, but of whom it must be most truly said that 'superstition' was the ruling passion. The materials for the biography of this bigot are peculiarly ample. Not merely do the contemporary historians abound with minute details of his life and actions, but we possess also his own declarations of his sentiments, for he happens to have been an author, as well as a patron of literature. Moreover, as a royal author, he speaks in the public documents dictated by his own heart and mind. From these materials, so unusually trustworthy and abundant, and which form the sources of this sovereign's history, we can collect that he 'received every word uttered by the clergy as the most sacred oracles,' and 'admitted all their pretensions to superior sanctity.' 'Stupidly debased,' he was 'wholly given up to an abject and illiberal devotion.' In every trial, every emergency, this 'weak and superstitious prince trusted to supernatural assistance:' 'his whole mind was sunk into the lowest submission and abasement, and devoted to the monkish virtues of mortification, penance, and humility.' If there was any individual in whom, more than another, all the miserable absurdity of superstition is thus exemplified, it is in this prince. Yet, in spite of all this ignorance and folly, it was needful that Hume, if he wished to preserve the favour of his readers, should represent him – and it is *Alfred* of whom we are speaking – as 'the model of that perfect character, which, under the denomination of a *sage or wise man*, philosophers have been fond of delineating, rather as a fiction of their imagination than in hopes of ever seeing it really existing;' and as 'the wisest and best prince that had ever adorned the annals of any nation.'

What, therefore, was to be done in this dilemma? how was Alfred to be rendered such a sage, such a wise man, as the philosopher could applaud? The process was quite easy. In Hume's very elaborate life of Alfred, which occupies one-fourth of the *History of England* up to that period, he has *concealed every passage, every fact, every incident, every transaction, displaying that active belief in Christianity, which governed the whole tenor and course of*

Alfred's life. The sedulous care which Hume has bestowed, in obscuring and deleting the memorials of Alfred's Christianity, may be judged of by the three following specimens: –

'He usually divided his time into three portions: one was employed in sleep and the refection of his body by diet and exercise; another, in the dispatch of business; a third, in study and devotion ... and by such a regular distribution of his time, though he often laboured under great bodily infirmities, this martial hero, who fought in person fifty-six battles by sea and land, was able, during a life of no extraordinary length, to acquire more knowledge, and even to compose more books, than most studious men, though blessed with the greatest labour and application, have, in more fortunate ages, made the object of their uninterrupted industry.'

Without containing anything which is absolutely false, the above passages contain nothing which is true. Alfred's mind and exertions, according to the impression produced by Hume, were all but wholly engrossed by his temporal concerns: the regular distribution of his time was solely intended to enable him to combine the character of an active warrior and a vigilant sovereign with that of a literary student. Whereas the whole end and intent of Alfred's course of life, of which *one half* was given to God, was to combine the active duties of a sovereign with the strict devotion of the recluse; to keep his heart out of the world, in which he was compelled, by God's appointment, to converse – to bear the crown as his cross; so that the performance of his duties towards God might not be rendered a temptation for shrinking from those labours and responsibilities which God had imposed.

'Alfred set apart a *seventh* portion of his own revenue for maintaining a number of workmen, whom he constantly employed in rebuilding the *ruined cities, castles, palaces, and monasteries.* Even the elegancies of life were brought to him from the Mediterranean and the Indies; and his subjects, by seeing those productions of the peaceful arts, were taught to respect the virtues of justice and industry, from which alone they could arise.'

Who, in this narrative, could discover that Alfred set apart *one-half* of his entire revenue for pious purposes, in order that, so far as his station admitted, he might fulfil the obligation of poverty?[13]

---

[13] Stinted as we are for space, we cannot, as we should wish, bring before the reader the passages from the original writers, which would show how entirely all trustworthiness must be denied to Hume. In the following extracts, relating to the employment of Alfred's revenues, besides suppressing the application of one-half to religious purposes, he has falsified the portion relating to the *expenditure upon the workmen.* Asser says nothing whatever of monasteries in his account of the appropriation of *the building-third* of the

'Sensible that the people at all times, especially when their understandings are obstructed by ignorance and bad education, are not much susceptible of speculative instruction, Alfred endeavoured to convey his morality by apologues, parables, stories, apophthegms, couched in poetry: and besides propagating amongst his subjects former compositions of that kind which he found in the Saxon tongue, he exercised his genius in inventing works of like

secular portion of Alfred's revenue (being *one-sixth* of the whole revenue, and not *one-seventh*). This sixth was employed upon secular buildings, probably fortresses or bridges, or other public works; but as Hume might apprehend that some of his readers would recollect Alfred did found *two* monasteries of great celebrity, and repair many others, he has artfully introduced them as an incidental item in the general estimates of the expenditure.

'His ita deffinitis, solito suo more, intra semetipsum cogitabat, quid ad huc addere potuisset, quod plus placeret ad piam meditationem; non inaniter incepta, utiliter inventa, utilius servata est: nam jamdudum in lege scriptum audierat, Dominum decimam sibi multipliciter redditurum promisisse; atque fideliter servasse, decimamque sibi multi-pliciter redditurum fuisse. Hoc exemplo instigatus, et antecessorum morem volens transcendere, *dimidiam servitii sui partem*, diurni scilicet, et nocturni temporis; nec non etiam *dimidiam partem omnium* divitiarum, quæ annualiter ad eum cum justitia moder-anter acquisitæ pervenire consueverant, Deo devote et fideliter toto cordis affectu pius, meditator se daturum spopondit; quod et quantum potest humana discretio discernere et servare, subtiliter ac sapienter adimplere studuit. Sed ut solito suo more cautus evitaret, quod in alio divinæ Scripturæ loco cautum est; si recte offeras, recte autem non dividas, peccas: quod Deo libenter devoverat quo modo recte dividere posset, cogitavit: et, ut dixit Salomon, Cor regis in manu Domini, id est, consilium; consilio divinitus invento omnium unius cujusque anni censuum successum bifarie, primitus ministros suos dividere æqua li lance imperavit.'

A very interesting account of the application of the first third of the half amongst his soldiery and household being given, the coeval historian proceeds: –

'Talibus itaque primam de tribus prædictis partibus partem, unicuique tamen secundum propriam dignitatem, et etiam secundum proprium ministerium largiebatur: secundam autem *operatoribus*, quos ex multis gentibus collectos et comparatos propemodum innumerabiles habebat, in omni terreno *ædificio edoctos*; tertiam autem ejusdem partem advenis ex omni gente ad eum advenientibus, longe propeque positis, et pecuniam ab illo exigentibus, etiam et non exigentibus, unicuique secundum propriam dignitatem mirabili dispnsatione laudabiliter, et (sicut scriptum est, Hilarem datorem diligit Deus) hilariter impendebat.

'*Secundam vero partem omnium divitiarum suarum, quæ annualiter ad eum ex omni censu preveniebant, et in fisco reputabantur* (sicut jam paulo ante commemoravimus) *plena voluntate Deo devovit*, et in quatuor partibus etiam curiose suos ministros illam dividere imperavit; ea conditione, ut prima pars illius divisionis pauperibus uniuscujusque gentis, qui ad eum veniebant, discretissime erogaretur: memorabat etiam in hoc, quantum humana discretio custodire poterat, illus sancti Papæ Gregorii observandam esse sententiam, qua discertam mentionem dividendæ eleemosynanæ ita dicens agebat; Nec parvum cui multum: nec multum cui parvum: nec nihil cui aliquid, nec aliquid cui nihil. Secundam autem duobus monasteriis, quæ ipse fieri imperaverat, et servientibus in his Deo (de quibus paulo ante latius disseruimus); teriam scholæ (*Oxford University?*) quam ex multis suæ propriæ gentis nobilibus studiossissime congregaverat; quartam circum finitimis in omni Saxonia et Mercia monasteriis, et etiam quibusdam annis per vices in Britannia et Cornumbia, Gallia, Armorica, Northymbria, et aliquando etiam in Hybernia, ecclesiis et servis Dei inhabitantibus, secundum possibilitatem suam aut ante distribuit, aut sequenti tempore erogare proposuit, vita sibi et prosperitate salva.' – *Asser, 64–67.*

nature, as well as in translating from the Greek the elegant fables of Æsop. He also gave Saxon translations of Orosius and Bede's histories; and of Boethius concerning the Consolations of Philosophy.'

In this enumeration of the works produced by Alfred, or under his direction, Hume, extracting from Spelman's Life, in which the catalogue is complete, quietly *leaves out all* such as are contaminated by Christianity. All Alfred's translations of the Pastoral of St. Gregory – the Dialogues of the same pope – the Soliloquies of St. Augustine – the Psalms – several other portions of the Bible – and his 'Hand-Book' – (selections from the Scriptures, with commentaries and reflections), constantly borne about him – and to which he added at every interval of leisure, even in the midst of his secular employments. The whole object of Alfred's instruction was intended for the diffusion, not of literature in its modern sense, but of such portions of human knowledge as might be rendered subservient to Faith. Hume, by repainting Alfred's portrait in coarse and gaudy colours, has thus daubed out all the characteristics of Alfred's individuality – his religious foundations, his devotional charity – his labours for the diffusion of the Scriptures – his constant seeking comfort and support from divine truth – his bodily penances and mortifications – and, above all, that, as king and legislator, Alfred entirely based his laws upon the Bible, declaring to his people that immutable truth which *no* other king or legislator has been sufficiently enlightened to proclaim, that if they obeyed the precepts of Almighty God, no other law would be required. Read Alfred's character as it is presented by Hume to the reader, particularly to the youthful reader, and the 'sovereign, the warrior, the politician, and the patron of literature' becomes the counterpart of Frederick of Prussia, whose epithet of 'the Great' is the very curse of the kingdom over which he ruled.

[6. HUME'S FALSIFIED ACCOUNT OF CHARLES I.]

Yet one proof more must be given of Hume's falsification of history, resulting from his inveterate hostility against religion. Relating not to the 'dark ages,' but to a period near and familiar, it will best enable the readers of Hume to comprehend and abhor the deceptions practised upon them by their philosopher and guide. As the moral fraud – for to call it a literary fraud would be far too lenient a designation – which he has perpetrated in his narrative of the death of Charles I., possesses singular interest, and has been wholly unnoticed and undetected, we shall lay the evidence before our readers as fully as the limits of this publication will admit, in order that they may judge for themselves.

Hume *quotes*, as his groundwork, Herbert's 'Memoirs,' which he consulted carefully; the copy he used being in the Advocates' Library, and containing his pencil-marks; and Walker's 'History of Independency.' – But he does not quote Lloyd's 'History,' Whitelocke's 'Memorials,' and Warwick's 'Memoirs,' from whence he derived the most important passages relating to the king's interview with his children and his conduct upon the scaffold, including his dying speech; and we cannot think that this suppression of references is the result of accident. We give the *whole* of Hume's narrative in continuity; and request our readers will take the trouble to read it attentively, and then to read the authorities, to which *we* have made references in Hume's text, with equal attention. From the latter we have extracted all the most important passages.

[a.] HUME'S NARRATIVE.

(I.) – 'Three days were allowed the king between his sentence and his execution. This interval he passed with great tranquillity, chiefly in reading and devotion.'

(II.) – 'All his family that remained in England were allowed access to him. It consisted only of the Princess Elizabeth and the Duke of Gloucester; for the Duke of York had made his escape. Gloucester was little more than an infant: the princess, notwithstanding her tender years, showed an advanced judgment; and the calamities of her family had made a deep impression upon her. After many pious consolations and advices, the king gave her in charge to tell the queen, that, during the whole course of his life, he had never once, even in thought, failed in his fidelity towards her; and that his conjugal tenderness and his life should have an equal duration.'

(III. IV.) – 'To the young duke, too, he could not forbear giving some advice, in order to season his mind with early principles of loyalty and obedience towards his brother, who was so soon to be his sovereign. Holding him on his knee, he said, "Now they will cut off thy father's head." At these words the child looked very stedfastly upon him. "Mark, child! what I say: they will cut off my head! and perhaps make thee a king: but mark what I say, thou must not be a king, as long as thy brothers Charles and James are alive. They will cut off thy brothers' heads when they can catch them! and thy head too they will cut off at last! therefore, I charge thee, do not be made a king by them!" The duke, sighing, replied, "I will be torn in pieces first!" So determined an answer from one of such tender years, filled the king's eyes with tears of joy and admiration.'

(V. VI.) – 'Every night, during this interval, the king slept sound as usual; though the noise of workmen, employed in framing the scaffold, and other preparations for his execution, continually resounded in his ears. The morning of the fatal day (30th Jan.) he rose early; and calling Herbert, one of his attendants, he bade him employ more than usual care in dressing him, and preparing him for so great and joyful a solemnity. Bishop Juxon, a man endowed with the same mild and steady virtues by which the king himself was so much distinguished, assisted him in his devotions, and paid the last melancholy duties to his friend and sovereign.'

(VII. VIII.) – 'The street before Whitehall was the place destined for the execution: for it was intended, by choosing that very place, in sight of his own palace, to display more evidently the triumph of popular justice over royal majesty. When the king came upon the scaffold, he found it so surrounded with soldiers that he could not expect to be heard by any of the people: he addressed, therefore, his discourse to the few persons who were about him; particularly Colonel Tomlinson, to whose care he had lately been committed, and upon whom, as upon many others, his amiable deportment had wrought an entire conversion. He justified his own innocence in the late fatal wars, and observed that he had not taken arms till after the Parliament had enlisted forces; nor had he any other object in his warlike operations than to preserve that authority entire, which his predecessors had transmitted to him. He threw not, however, the blame upon the Parliament; but was more inclined to think that ill instruments had interposed, and raised in them fears and jealousies with regard to his intentions. Though innocent towards his people, he acknowledged the equity of his execution in the eyes of his Maker; and observed, that an unjust sentence, which he had suffered to take effect, was now punished by an unjust sentence upon himself. He forgave all his enemies, even the chief instruments of his death; but exhorted them and the whole nation to return to the ways of peace, by paying obedience to their lawful sovereign, his son and successor. When he was preparing himself for the block, Bishop Juxon called to him, "There is, Sir, but one stage more, which, though turbulent and troublesome, is yet a very short one. Consider, it will soon carry you a great way; it will carry you from earth to heaven: and there you shall find, to your great joy, the prize to which you hasten, a crown of glory." – "I go," replied the king, "from a corruptible to an incorruptible crown, where no disturbance can have place." At one blow was his head severed from his body. A man in a vizor performed the office of executioner: another, in a like disguise, held up to the spectators the head streaming with blood, and cried aloud, *This is the head of a traitor!*'

[b.] HUME'S AUTHORITIES.

(I.) 'The king, at the rising of the Court, was with a guard of halberdiers returned to White-hall in a close chair, through King-street, both sides whereof had a guard of foot-soldiers, who were silent as his Majesty pass'd. But shop-stalls and windows were full of people, many of which shed tears, and some of them with audible voices pray'd for the king, who through the privy-garden was carried to his bed-chamber; whence, after two hours space, *he was removed to St. James's*....'

'The king now bidding farewell to the world, *his whole business was a serious preparation for death*, which opens the door unto eternity; in order thereunto, he laid aside all other thoughts, *and spent the remainder of his time in prayer and other pious exercises of devotion*, and in conference with that meek and learned Bishop Dr. Juxon, who, under God, was a great support to him in that his afflicted condition; and resolving to sequester himself so, as he might have no disturbance to his mind, nor interruption to his meditations, he order'd Mr. Herbert to excuse it to any that might have the desire to visit him....'

'At this time also came to S. James's Mr. Calamy, Mr. Vines, Mr. Carryl, Mr. Dell, and some other London-Ministers, who presented their duty to the king, with their humble desires to pray with him, and perform other offices of service, if his Majesty pleas'd to accept of 'em. The king return'd them thanks for their love to his soul, hoping that they, and all other his good subjects, would, in *their addressed to* 'God, be mindful of him. But in regard he *had made choice of Dr. Juxon* (whom for many years he had known to be *a pious and learned divine, and able to administer ghostly comfort to his soul,* suitable to his present condition) he would have none other. These Ministers were no sooner gone, but Mr. John Goodwyn (Minister in Coleman-street) came likewise upon the same account, to tender his service, which the king also thank'd him for, and dismiss'd him with the like friendly answer....'

'That evening, Mr. Seamour (a gentleman then attending the Prince of Wales in his bed-chamber) by Colonel Hacker's permission, came to his Majesty's bed-chamber door, desiring to speak with the King from the Prince of Wales; being admitted, he presented his Majesty with a letter from his Highness the Prince of Wales, bearing date from the Hague the 23rd day of January -48 (Old Stile). Mr. Seamour, at his entrance, fell into a passion, having formerly seen his Majesty in a glorious state, and now in a dolorous; and having kiss'd the king's hand, clasp'd about his legs, lamentably mourning. Hacker came in with the gentleman and was abash'd. But so soon as his Majesty had read his son's sorrowing letter, and heard what his servant had to say, and imparted to him what his Majesty thought fit in return, the Prince's servant took his leave, and was no sooner gone *but the king went to his devotion, Dr. Juxon praying with him, and reading some select chapters out of sacred Scripture.*' – Herbert, p. 117.

(II.) 'Morning being come, the Bishop was early with the king, and *after prayers* his Majesty broke the seals open, and shew'd them what was contain'd in it; there were diamonds and jewels, most part broken Georges and Garters. You see (said he) all the wealth now in my power to give my two children. Next day Princess Elizabeth, and the Duke of Gloucester, her brother, came to take their sad farewel of the king their father, and to ask his blessing. This was the 29th of Jan. The princess being the elder, was the most sensible of her royal father's condition, as appear'd by her sorrowful look and excessive weeping; and her little brother seeing his sister weep, he took the like impression, though, by reason of his tender age, he could not have the like apprehension. The king rais'd them both from off their knees; he kiss'd them, *gave them his blessing,* and setting them on his knees, admonished them concerning their duty and loyal observance to the queen their mother, the prince that was his successor, love to the Duke of York, and his other relations. The king then gave them all his jewels, save the George he wore, which was cut in an onyx with great curiosity, and set about with 21 fair diamonds, and the reverse set with the like number; and again kissing his children, had such pretty and pertinent answers from them both, as drew tears of joy and love from his eyes; and then *praying God Almighty to bless 'em*, he turned about, expressing a tender and fatherly affection. Most sorrowful was this parting, the young princess shedding tears and crying lamentably, so as mov'd others to pity, that formerly were hardhearted; and at opening the bed-chamber door, the king return'd hastily from the window, and kiss'd 'em *and blessed 'em;* so parted.

'This demonstration of a pious affection exceedingly comforted the king in this his affliction; so that in a grateful return *he went immediately to prayer,* the good bishop and Mr. Herbert being only present.' *Herbert,* p. 125.

(III.) 'His (the king's) last words being taken in writing, and communicated to the world by the Lady Elizabeth his daughter, a lady of most eminent endowments, who though born to the supreamest fortune, yet lived in continual tears, and died confined at Carisbrook (whither her father was cheated) in the Isle of Wight – are to this effect:' –

'A True Relation of the King's Speech to the Lady Elizabeth and the Duke of Gloucester, the Day before his Death.

'His children being come to meet him, he first gave his blessing to the Lady Elizabeth, and had her remember to tell her brother James, whenever she should see him, that it was his father's last desire that he should no more look upon Charles as his eldest brother only, but be obedient unto him as his sovereign, and that they should love one another and forgive their father's enemies. Then said the king to her, "Sweet-heart, you'l forget this." "No," said she, "I shall never forget it, whilst I live;" and pouring forth abundance of tears, promised him to write down the particulars. Then the king, taking the Duke of Gloucester upon his knee, said "Sweet-heart, now they will cut off thy father's head;" upon which words the child looking very stedfastly at him, 'Mark, child, what I say; they will cut off my head, and perhaps make thee a king; but mark what I say, you must not be a king, so long as your brothers do live, for they will cut off your brothers' heads, when they can catch them, and cut off thy head too at last, and therefore I charge you do not be made a king by them." At which the child sighing, said, "I will be torn in pieces first;" which falling so unexpectedly from one so young, it made the king rejoyce exceedingly.'

'Another Relation from the Lady Elizabeth's own Hand.

"What the king said to me, Jan. 29th, 1648, being the last time I had the happiness to see him: He told me, he was glad I was come; and although he had not time to say much, yet somewhat he had to say to me, which he had not to another, or leave in writing, because he feared their cruelty was such as that they would not have permitted him to write to me. He wished me not to grieve and torment myself for him, for that it would be a glorious death that he should dye, it being for the laws and liberties of this land *and for maintaining the true Protestant Religion. He bid me read 'Bishop Andrews' Sermons,' 'Hooker's Ecclesiastical Polity,' and 'Bishop Laud's Book against Fisher,' which would ground me against Popery.* He told me he had forgiven all his enemies, and hoped God would forgive them also, and commanded us and all the rest of my brothers and sisters to forgive them. He bid me tell my mother that his thoughts never strayed from her, and that his love should be the same to the last. Withal he commanded me and my brother to be obedient to her, and bid me send his blessing to the rest of my brothers and sisters, with commendation to all his friends. So after he had given me his blessing I took my leave.

"Further, he commanded us all to forgive those people, but never to trust them, for they had been most false to him and to those that gave them power, and he feared also to their own souls; and desired me not to grieve for him, for he should dye a Martyr, and that he doubted not but the Lord would settle his throne upon his son, and that we should be all happier than we could have expected to have been, if he had lived; with many other things, which at present I cannot remember.

"(Signed) Elizabeth."

– *Lloyd's Life of Charles I., 215.*'

(IV.) '*That day the Bishop of London, after prayers, preached before the king: his text was the second chapter of the Romans, and sixteenth verse;* the words are, "At that day when God shall judge the secrets of men by Jesus Christ," etc., inferring from thence, that although God's judgments be for some deferred, he will nevertheless proceed to a strict examination of what is both said and done by every man; yea, the most hidden thoughts and imaginations of men will most certainly be made to appear at the day of judgment, when the Lord Jesus Christ shall be upon his high tribunal; all designs, tho' conceal'd in this life, shall then be plainly discovered; he then proceeded to the present sad occasion, and *after that, administered the Sacrament.* That day the king *eat and drank very sparingly, most part of the day being spent in prayer and meditation*; it was some hours after night, e'er Dr. Juxon took leave of the King, *who willed him to be early with him the next morning.*

'After the Bishop was gone to his lodging, *the king continu'd reading and praying more than two hours after.* The king commanded Mr. Herbert to lie by his bed-side upon a pallat, where he took small rest, that being the last night his gracious sovereign and master enjoy'd; but nevertheless the king for four hours, or thereabouts, slept soundly, and awaking about two hours afore day, he opened his curtain to call Mr. Herbert; there being a great cake of wax set in a silver bason, that then, as at all other times, burned all night; so that he perceiv'd him somewhat disturb'd in sleep; but calling him, had him rise; "For," said his Majesty, "I will get up, having a great work to do this day;" however, he would know why he was so troubled in his sleep? He reply'd, "May it please your Majesty, I was dreaming." "I would know your dream," said the king; which being told, his Majesty said, "It was remarkable. Herbert, this is my second marriage day; I would be as trim to-day as may be; for before night *I hope to be espoused to my blessed Jesus.*" He then appointed what cloathes he would wear; "Let me have a shirt on more than ordinary," said the king, "by reason the season is so sharp as probably may make me shake, which some observers will imagine proceeds from fear. I would have no such imputation. I fear not Death! Death is not terrible to me. I bless my God I am prepar'd."

'These, or words to this effect, his Majesty spoke to Mr. Herbert, as he was making ready. Soon after came Dr. Juxon, Bishop of London, precisely at the time his Majesty the *night before had appointed him.* Mr. Herbert then falling upon his knees, humbly beg'd his Majesty's pardon, if he had at any time been negligent in his duty, whilst he had the honour to serve him. The king thereupon gave him his hand to kiss, having the day before been graciously pleased, under his royal hand, to give him a certificate expressing that the said Mr. Herbert was not impos'd upon him, but by his Majesty made choice of to attend him in his bed-chamber, and had serv'd him with faithfulness and loyal affection. At the same time his Majesty also deliver'd him *his bible, in the margin whereof he had with his own hand writ many annotations and quotations,* and charged him to give it the Prince as soon as he returned; repeating what he had enjoyned the Princess Elizabeth, his daughter, that he would be dutiful and indulgent to the queen his mother (to whom his Majesty writ two days before by Mr. Seymour), affectionate to his brothers and sisters, who also were to be observant and dutiful to him their sovereign; and for as much as from his heart he had forgiven his enemies, and in perfect charity with all men would leave the world, he had advised the prince his son to exceed in mercy, not in rigour; *and, as to episcopacy, it was still his opinion, that it is of Apostolique institution, and in this kingdom exercised from the primitive times, and therein, as in all other his affairs, pray'd God to vouchsafe him, both in reference to Church and State, a pious and a discerning spirit; and that it was his last and earnest request, that he would frequently read the Bible, which in all the time of his affliction had been his best instructor and delight;* and to meditate upon what he read; as also such other books as might improve his knowledge....'

'He likewise commanded Mr. Herbert to give to the Princess Elizabeth *"Doctor Andrews' Sermons," "Archbishop Laud against Fisher the Jesuit,"* which book (the king said) would ground her against Popery, and *"Mr. Hooker's Ecclesiastical Polity."* To the Duke of Gloucester, *"King James's Works,"* and *"Dr. Hammond's Practical Catechism."*' – Herbert, p. 126.

(V.) 'His Majesty then bade him withdraw; *for he was about an hour in private with the Bishop; and being call'd in, the Bishop went to prayer; and reading also the 27th Chapter of the Gospel of St. Matthew, which relateth the Passion of our Blessed Saviour. The king, after the service was done, ask'd the Bishop "If he had made choice of that Chapter, being so applicable to his present condition?" The Bishop reply'd, "May it please your Gracious Majesty, it is the proper Lesson for the Day, as appears by the Kalendar;"* which the king was much affected with, so aptly serving as a seasonable preparation for his death that day.'

'*So as his Majesty, abandoning all thoughts of earthly concerns, continu'd in prayer and meditation, and concluded with a chearful submission to the will and Pleasure of the Almighty, saying, "He was ready to resign himself into the hands of Christ Jesus, being, with 'the Kingly Prophet, shut up in the hands of his enemies; as is expressed in the 31st Psalm, and the 8th verse."'* – Herbert, p. 132.

(VI.) 'The Chapter of the day fell out to be that of the Passion of our Saviour, wherein it was mentioned that they led him away for envy and crucified their king, which he thought had been the Bishop's choosing; but when he found it was the Canon *of the* Rubric, he put off his hat, and said to the Bishop, "God's will be done."' – *Warwick's Memoirs*, p. 385.

(VII.) '*Upon the king's right hand went the Bishop*, and Colonel Tomlinson on his left, with whom his Majesty had some discourse by the way; Mr. Herbert was next the king; after him the Guards. In this manner went the king *through the Park*; and coming to the stair, the king passed along the galleries unto his bed-chamber, *where, after a little repose, the Bishop went to prayer;* which being done, his Majesty bid Mr. Herbert bring him some bread and wine, which being brought, the king broke the manchet, and eat a mouthful of it, and drank a small glassful of claret-wine *and then was some time in private with the Bishop*, expecting when Hacker would the third and last time give warning. Mean time his Majesty told Mr. Herbert which satin nightcap he would use, which being provided, and the king at private prayer, Mr. Herbert address'd himself to the Bishop, and told him, "The king had ordered him to have a white satin night-cap ready, but he was not able to endure the sight of that 'violence they upon the scaffold would offer the king." The good Bishop bid him then give him the cap, and wait at the end of the Banqueting-House, near the scaffold, to take care of the king's body; "for," said he, "that, and his interment, will be our last office."' – *Herbert*, p. 134.

(VIII.) '"I think it is my duty, *to God first* and to my country, for to clear myself both as an honest man and a good king, and a *good Christian*. I call *God to witness*, to whom I must shortly I render an account, that I never did intend to encroach upon their privileges. As to the guilt of those enormous crimes which are laid against me, *I hope in God that God* will clear me of it. God forbid that I should be so ill a Christian as not to *say that God's judgments are upon me*. For to show you that I am a *good Christian*, I hope there is a good man," pointing to Dr. Juxon, "that will bear me witness that I have forgiven all the world, and even those who have been the chief causes of my death: who they are *God knows*, I do not desire to know; I pray *God forgive them*. I *pray God with Saint Stephen*, that this be not laid to their charge. Sirs, to put you in the right way, believe it you will never do right, *nor God will never prosper you, until you give him his due*. You must give God *his due by regulating rightly his Church according to his Scripture*. A national synod, freely called, freely debating amongst themselves, must do this. I declare before you *all that I die a Christian according to the profession of the Church of England as I found it left me by my fathers.*"' – *Whitelocke's Memorials*, p. 375.

Has the reader performed our injunction? Has *he compared Hume with the original authorities*; and will not the comparison convince him, that Hume's narrative, tranquil, clear, and pathetic – unquestionably possessing a very high degree of rhetorical merit – persuasive without the show of argument, solemn without affectation, dignified without grandiloquence, the more impressive from its apparent simplicity – combines every species of untruth: the *suppressio veri*, the *suggestio falsi*, and the fallacy, more efficient, because less susceptible of detection, than either – the artificial light thrown on peculiar incidents, for the purpose of disguising others by comparative shade?

But now we must venture to impose a *second* injunction. In order to test the effect which this wonderful piece of sophistry is intended to produce, read Hume again, *compare Hume with Hume*, and throw yourself into the mind of a student required by the examination paper, to '*Give the religious and moral character of Charles I. as exemplified in his death; and state the reasons of your opinion as deduced from the work of Hume.*' Then pause, and decide whether the following answer does not contain the opinions which Hume has taught you to deduce and to form.

[c.] RELIGIOUS AND MORAL CHARACTER OF CHARLES I.
AS DEDUCED FROM HUME.

'That the virtue of Charles I. was in some degree tinctured by superstition, cannot be denied; but whilst the elegant historian, whom we deservedly consider as the soundest champion of monarchy, most candidly admits this tendency as the chief defect of the king's character, it is equally evident that the blemish existed only in the smallest degree, so as to be an evanescent quantity, scarcely to be discerned. Possibly nothing more than the doubt, the uncertainty, the suspense of judgment, naturally resulting from our most accurate scrutiny into religion.

'Consider the manner in which Charles passed the three awful days allowed to him between his sentence and his execution. Lay your hand upon your heart, and, after giving the most serious consideration to the natural history of religion, as exemplified in the whole history of the human race, declare whether you can think that the king's conviction approached in any degree to that solid belief and persuasion, which governed him in the common affairs of life. He now avowed by his acts the doubts he entertained; and fully showed, that, whatever assent his outward demeanour may at any previous time have given to the doctrines of superstition, it was an unaccountable operation of the mind between disbelief and conviction, but approaching much nearer to the former than to the latter. Charles, in the awful hour of death, never betrayed any weakness which a philosopher would despise.

'When dissolution is brought on by the ordinary course of malady or the decay of nature, the- last symptoms which the intellect discovers are disorder, weakness, insensibility, and stupidity, the forerunners of the annihilation of the soul; and it is then always most susceptible of religious fictions and chimeras. The griefs and afflictions which Charles had sustained, the horror of a public execution, might have troubled his mind even more than pain or sickness; yet – instead of making any of the preparations suggested by popular credulity, whether nursed by superstition or inflamed by fanaticism, as the means of appeasing an unknown and vindictive being – the main, and, as it should seem, almost the only object which occupied his thoughts, was securing the succession of the throne to his son, by the prerogative right of primogeniture. On the morning of his execution, during his most pathetic interview with his infant children, his mind was wholly engrossed by that object. Young as these infants were, he would, had religious conviction predominated over doubt, have endeavoured, at such a solemn moment, to impress on their tender hearts some notions of the faith which has been ascribed to him. No such effort was made by him. Equally removed from superstition and fanaticism, he may have endeavoured to comfort them by the usual commonplaces; but he received them without a blessing, and dismissed them for ever without a prayer.

'Indeed, there are no incidents in the life of the King that more strongly mark the noble independence of his mind, than the minuter circumstances attending this, the most affecting passage in his history. One of his own chaplains, Hammond, had been remarkable for his diligence in catechising youth, that is to say, instructing them in the nonsense which passed for religion. – Did Charles deem it right to enable his infant boy, the Duke of Gloucester, to obtain any perplexing knowledge of such absurdities? No! Charles wholly discarded it. – The Princess Elizabeth was a child endowed with judgment beyond her years, and capable of appreciating any advice which he might have bestowed, and of understanding the doctrinal works advocating the theological extravagances then so much in vogue. But when any man of sense takes up a volume of divinity, what are the questions which he asks? – Does it contain any abstract reasoning concerning quantity or number? No. Does it contain any experimental reasoning concerning matter of fact and existence? No. Commit it then to the flames, for it contains nothing but sophistry and illusion. So thought Charles, now that intellect asserted her full empire. Of these writers, many were familiarly known to Charles, both through their works and his personal connexion with the men; and he had quoted them with sufficient point, when he could employ their arguments against his political enemies. But what was his conduct now? – Did he attempt to strengthen the religious obedience of his child by recommending to her the sophistries of Hooker? No. – Did he teach her to seek consolation in the superstitions of Andrews? No. – With philosophical contempt he rejected them all.

'Indeed many men of sense might think that Charles carried his indifference almost too far, considering the need of conciliating the predominant opinions of the vulgar. The mere suspicion of being inclined to the Popish superstition had been most calamitous to him; and he was now consigning his children to the care of a mother zealously affected to that superstition, and yet without bestowing the slightest caution against the errors which she might instil into their minds. But it will be answered, Was it to be expected that Charles, with his dying breath, would adopt any course which might diminish the affection of his children towards the wife whom he so tenderly loved, or encourage them to depreciate the parent whom he taught them to respect and honour? Certainly not; but, had he been sincere in his religious convictions – and let it be recollected, that the great lesson to be derived from the contemplation of the death of Charles I. is the absence of any practical influence possessed by religious tenets – he might have afforded the most efficient caution to his children, without expressing the slightest want of confidence in their mother, or even mentioning her name. Amongst the works of Laud is his celebrated reply to Fisher, which all zealots must consider as the most cogent refutation of Popery ever produced; for whilst the crafty archbishop annihilates his antagonist, he never uses any argument which could be employed against the superstition of the Church of England by the fanatics; yet Charles, anxious, no doubt, that his children should be preserved, as far as possible, from the contagion of all religious opinions, never even alluded to a book which might have influenced their conscience in favour of any positive belief.

'On the scaffold, his dying words contained a most earnest exhortation to his subjects to pay obedience to his son as their lawful king. Whilst he thus employed the last moments of his existence in labouring to support the royal prerogative, by the sympathy which his fate excited amongst his bitterest enemies, he purposely, deliberately, and advisedly abstained from any expression or exhortation displaying any attachment or feeling of duty towards the Church, for which he had contended so earnestly, when its interests were connected with the rights of the crown.

'The total want of any allusion to the late established religion is most remarkable. The more we investigate the character of Charles as delineated by Hume, the more shall we be confirmed in the opinion that his superstition had now entirely passed away; at least not a trace of it can be found in Hume's accurate narrative. The only incident which might tend to show that Charles had the slightest recollection of the Church of England, any veneration for its priestcraft, is the circumstance that Bishop Juxon assisted him in some species of devotion when on the scaffold. Yet, as far as we can discover from the conduct of Charles, he justly regarded priests as the invention of a timorous and abject superstition. Rejecting the foundation of a priesthood, the absurd super-structure of an apostolic succession would of course fall to the ground. We have no reason to suppose that Bishop Juxon was chosen by the king, or that Charles would not equally have accepted of what were then termed spiritual consolations from the fanatical ministers, or indeed that he required any religious consolation at all. It was only in the capacity of a friend that the bishop paid the last melancholy duties to his sovereign. In every respect the conduct of Charles, in repudiating all adherence to the superstitions of the Church of England, was calm and solid. The period of dissimulation had passed by. Whatever ridicule may, by a philosophical mind, be thrown upon pious ceremonies, they are unquestionably advantageous to the rude multitude; and upon that ground, no doubt, Charles I. had so strenuously contended for the share of popish ceremonies which the Church of England, as is well known, had retained. They were now wholly and entirely cast off. Charles discarded all the mummery of a liturgy, all the solemn farces of lessons and gospels, rubrics and set forms of prayer; and, freeing himself from all superstitious influ-ences, he disdained to partake of the Communion which, according to the rites of the Church of England, he was enjoined to have sought in his dying hour.

'No philosophical mind can doubt the origin of the works which superstition and fanaticism equally receive as the production of those who have been tempted to appear as prophets or ambassadors from Heaven; books presented to us by a barbarous and ignorant people, written in an age when they were still more barbarous, and resembling those fabulous accounts which every nation gives of its origin. Charles fully appreciated the insufficiency of such testimony. We have the strongest proofs that he never entered into the delusion, from the marked circumstance, that, during the three days which, as before mentioned, were allowed him between his sentence and his execution, an interval which he passed in great tranquillity, the Scriptures, as they are called, were never in his hands; nor did he, according to the practice of all religionists, whether guided by superstition or fanaticism, seek any comfort in his affliction from a book so contrary to human reason. Charles neither saw the Bible, nor heard the Bible, nor read the Bible, nor touched the Bible, nor expressed any belief in the Bible, nor recommended the Bible to his children or his friends. Do we need any stronger proof that Charles was a philosopher in the fullest sense of the term? His devotions, as we must style them according to the conventional language of society, appear to be nothing more than that reverence which every philosopher renders to the hypothesis by which he endeavours to account for the unalterable and immutable order of the universe. His allusions to passing from a corruptible to an incorruptible crown, where no disturbance can take place, if they mean anything beyond a species of rhetorical play upon words, only imply that he contemplated the eternal rest of annihilation. For they were wholly detached from any other expressions implying any belief in a future state. Charles may have admitted its possibility, but nothing more. And how could it be otherwise? Even at this day, the Christian religion cannot be believed by any reasonable person without a miracle; and whoever is moved by faith to assent to it, is conscious of a continued miracle in his own person, which subverts all the principles of his understanding, and gives him a determination to believe what is most contrary to custom and experience. This miracle was not worked in Charles; and he died without making the slightest, the most remote, the most transient profession of Christianity.'

—

Such, then, are the inferences intended to be deduced by Hume, who, in his most dishonest statement, has, as will be seen by comparison with his sources, purposely omitted every historical memorial or record testifying either the king's allegiance to the Church, or his unshaken faith as a Christian. Charles truly suffered death for the belief that Christianity, according to the profession of the Church of England, was the fundamental law of the state, unchangeable by any political or constitutional power, being an obligation contracted with the Almighty, from which he could not be absolved by any human authority. Let it further be remarked, that, whilst Hume falsifies the narrative by expunging all the particulars teaching the reader to profit by the religious sentiments of the monarch, he endeavours to excite a factitious sympathy, by the false and theatrical representation of the king's hearing the noise of the scaffold, which authentic accounts entirely disprove.[14] And, for the same purpose of effect, whilst Hume gives to the interview with the children more prominence of detail than its *relative importance* requires, he suppresses that portion of the king's advice which most *peculiarly discloses the mind of the dying father*, namely, the recommendation made by Charles of *Hammond, Hooker, Andrews*, and *Laud*, as the expositors of the doctrines of that Protestant Church of England, for which *he and Laud* equally died as martyrs.

Detrimental as Hume may be, when speaking his own sentiments in his own book, the evil which he effects in person is small when compared to the diffusion of his irreligion, by those who are frequently unconscious of the mischief which they perpetrate; – we mean the writers who have been guided by him in what is at this day the most important branch of our literature – the

[14] This has been done so effectually by Mr. Brodie, and by Mr. Laing, that it is unnecessary to go into further particulars.

numerous compilers of educational works; and in order that our readers may pursue the inquiry for themselves, we wish them to consult three of the most popular histories of this class, Keightley, Gleig and Markham; and selecting the death of Charles I., judge for themselves whether this event – of all others in our annals, the most interesting to the imagination – has been presented by those writers to the rising generation in such a tone or spirit as to inculcate any dutiful affection towards the Church, or aid the parent in bringing up the child in the nurture and admonition of the Lord.

These three writers may in some measure elucidate the manner in which Hume's influence has operated upon his successors, according to their individual characters and opportunities. Mr. Keightley, a man of considerable diligence and energy, has been taught by Hume's scepticism to *boast* that he 'belongs to no sect or party in religion or politics;' hence he gives only 'a moderate preference to the Church of England, without taking upon him to assert that it absolutely is the best;' and the same indifference has caused him, in his Outlines of history, to obtrude upon youth some of the most offensive doctrines which German neology can afford. In the death of Charles, all he finds edifying is that *Hugh Peters* prayed for him!

Mr. Gleig is an amiable and most pleasing writer; when he works freely upon his own ground, speaks his own sentiments, and embodies his own observations, he produces narratives of rare and unaffected vigour and elegance;[15] but when he is tempted to put on the sleeves and apron of a bookmaker, his genius deserts him. He is above such work, and goes about it accordingly. The circumstances under which he produced his 'Family History' as a mere bespoken task, to be put on the list of a Society, rendered it, we can suppose, needful that he should take what he found most ready at hand. He perhaps went a step beyond Hume; but the only word of instruction which he can insert in the narrative of the death of the royal martyr, is the dry historical fact, that Charles avowed himself a member of the Protestant Church of England. There is nothing positively wrong in Mr. Gleig's work – but, out of sight, out of mind; Christian knowledge is as diligently weeded out from this 'Family History' as Hume himself could desire.

Yet perhaps the strongest case of the treacherous seductions of Hume is to be found in Mrs. Markham's history. We do not in the least doubt, from a close examination of the work, that when the author began it for the use of her own children, she resorted at once to the historian whom she had been taught to consider as her philosopher and guide. From her father, the inventor of the power-loom, she may have heard the name of Adam Smith mentioned with the highest honour; and Adam Smith, in the letter prefixed to the history, has told

---

[15] We are pleased to notice 'The Light Dragoon' of the present season, as entirely worthy of the pen that wrote 'The Subaltern' and the 'Narrative of the American Campaign in 1814.'

her – as he tells *our* children, if we place Hume in their hands – that Hume's character approached as nearly to the idea of a perfectly wise and virtuous man as perhaps the nature of human frailty will permit; and therefore there is hardly any portion of the work in which the professors of religion are mentioned, into which the sentiments of Hume are not infused. These passages are fortunately not numerous; and we do most earnestly hope that, if a production, in many respects so useful, and which has obtained so much currency, should come to another edition, they may be *all* modified or expunged.

Hume has been, and is still, valued by many, as a defender of monarchical principles; but his support kills the root of loyalty. By advocating the duty of obedience to the sovereign, simply with reference to human relations, he deprives allegiance of the only sure foundation upon which it can rest.

Perhaps the speculative atheism of Hume – for it is a violation of the warning not to call evil good, if, when required to pass judgment, we designate his principles by any other name – may render his history, in some respects, more pernicious, if that be possible, than the ribald aggressive infidelity of Gibbon. Arsenic may warn us by the pain which the poison occasions, but narcotics steal life away. Hume constantly tempts us to deny the existence of the Supreme Being, before whom he trembles. He raises his foul and pestilential mists, seeking to exclude from the universe the beams of the Sun of Righteousness, whom he hates and defies. The main object and end of history is the setting forth God's glory, so as to show that national happiness arises from doing His appointed work, and that national punishments are the results of national sins; yet let it not be supposed that, in order to render history beneficial, it must of necessity be expressly written upon religious principles, still less that facts should be coarsely and presumptuously wrested, for the purpose of justifying the ways of God to man. If there be one thing worse than a pious fraud, it is a pious fallacy. Any narrative of the affairs of the world, when not corrupted by the Lying Spirit of unbelief, sufficiently declares the superintending power of the Almighty. Fire and hail, snows and vapours, wind and storm, all the inanimate objects of nature, are seen fulfilling His word: and the simple statement of the vicissitudes and fortunes of the kings and nations of the earth will always declare the terrors of His judgments, and the mercies of His love. But the Deistical philosopher – the foolish and impotent rebel against the Almighty – strives to annul the evidence given by the light of nature. He would deprive mankind of all the hope, and trust, and joy, which can sustain us in our pilgrimage, seducing us to be his companion in the downward path, conducting to the portals of the shadow of death –

> 'Per me si va nella città dolente,
> Per me si va nell eterno dolore,
> Per me si va tra la perduta gente –
> ... Lasciate ogni speranza, voi ch' entrate'

55
MISCELLANEOUS COMMENTS
ON HUME'S HISTORY

During the 18th and 19th centuries, hundreds if not thousands of references to Hume's *History* appeared in various publications. Many of these were passing quotations in which the authors relied on Hume as an authority. Presented here are some brief critical discussions of the *History*, which are noteworthy because of the authors' importance or their intrinsic merit. Selections are presented chronologically.

THOMAS COMBER

Though [Hume's *History* is] more decried than ever book was, and certainly with faults, I cannot help liking much. It is called Jacobite, but in my opinion is only not *George-abite*; where others abuse the Stuarts, he laughs at them; I am sure he does not spare their ministers. [Comber, Thomas (d. 1778), *Vindication of the great revolution in England*, London, J. Robinson, 1758, p. 131.]

HORACE WALPOLE

Mr. Hume has published his History of the House of Tudor. I have not advanced far in it, but it appears an inaccurate and careless, as it certainly has been a very hasty, performance. (Walpole to Henry Zouch, March 15, 1759.)

All the histories of England, Hume's, as you observe, and Smollett's more avowedly, are calculated to whiten the house of Stuart. (Walpole to Henry Zouch, May 14, 1759)

Can I think that we want writers of history while Mr. Hume and Mr. Robertson are living? It is a truth, and not a compliment, that I never heard objections made to Mr. Hume's History without endeavouring to convince the persons who found fault with it, of its great merit and beauty; and for what I saw of Mr. Robertson's work, it is one of the purest styles, and of the greatest impartiality, that I ever read. (Walpole to David Dalrymple, July 11, 1759.)

Mr. Hume shall publish a few remarks he has made on my book: they are very far from substantial; yet still better than any other trash that has been written against it, nothing of which deserves an answer. (Walpole to Cole, April 16, 1768.)

You have placed that defence on sound and *new* grounds; and, though very briefly, have very learnedly stated and distinguished the landmarks of our constitution, and the encroachments made on it, by justly referring the principles of liberty to the Saxon system, and by imputing the corruptions of it to the Norman. This was a great deal too deep for that superficial mountebank, Hume, to go; for a mountebank he was. He mounted a *fretaeu* in the garb of a philosophic empiric, but dispensed no drugs but what he was authorized to vend by a royal patent, and which were full of Turkish opium. He had studied nothing relative to the English constitution before Queen Elizabeth, and had selected her most arbitrary acts to countenance those of the Stuarts: and even hers he misrepresented; for her worst deeds were levelled against the nobility, those of the Stuarts against the people. Hers, consequently, were rather an obligation to the people; for the most heinous part of despotism is, that it produces a thousand despots instead of one. Muley Moloch cannot lop off many heads with his own hand; at least he takes those in his way, those of his courtiers; but his bashaws and viceroys spread destruction every where. The flimsy, ignorant, blundering manner in which Hume executed the reigns preceding Henry VII, is a proof how little he had examined the history of our constitution. (Walpole to Pownall, October 27, 1783.)

Both assure me that you will not take ill the liberty I have used in expressing my doubts on your plan for amending our language, or for any I may use in dissenting from a few other sentiments in your work; as I shall in what I think your too low opinion of some of the French writers, of your preferring Lady Mary Wortley to Madame de Sévigné, and of your esteeming Mr. Hume a man of a deeper and more solid understanding than Mr. Gray. In the two last articles it is impossible to think more differently than we do. In Lady Mary's Letters, which I never could read but once, I discovered no merit of any sort; yet I have seen others by her (unpublished) that have a good deal of wit; and for Mr. Hume give me leave to say that I think your opinion, "that he might have ruled a state," ought to be qualified a little; as in the very next page you say, his History is "a mere apology for prerogative," and a very weak one. If he could have ruled a state, one must presume, at best, that he would have been an able tyrant; and yet I should suspect that a man, who, sitting coolly in his chamber, could forge but a weak apology for the prerogative, would not have exercised it very wisely. I knew personally and well both Mr. Hume and Mr. Gray, and thought there was no degree of comparison between their understandings; and, in fact, Mr. Hume's writings were so superior to his conversation, that I frequently said he understood nothing till he had written upon it. What you say, Sir, of the discord in his history from his love of prerogative and hatred of churchmen, flatters me much; as I have taken notice of that very unnatural discord in a piece I printed some years ago, but did not publish, and which I will show to you when I have the pleasure of seeing you here. (Walpole to John Pinkerton, June 22, 1785.) [Horace Walpole (1717–1797), *Letters of Horace Walpole*, Philadelphia: Lea And Blanchard, 1842, 4 v.]

CLAUDE FRANCOIS XAVIER MILLOT

Mr. Hume unites perspicuity and precision, solidity and elegance; he copies nature in his paintings, without the appearance of art; he usually seizes the most interesting point of view, and there places his objects, which seem to arrange themselves; sparing us the barren and gazette like sameness of military operations; without passing over in silence the memorable exploits of heroes, he principally sets before our eyes the manners, the laws, the passions, the follies of mankind, the changeful caprices of fortune, the regular connection of causes with effects. No author was ever more superior to the prejudices which darken historical truth. If, as a protestant, he sometimes affronts the sanctity of our tenets, yet he does not disguise the madness or the wickedness of his own sect; if, as a subject of Great Britain, he is attached to the principles of his own country, he attempts not to palliate the excesses which the fanaticism of liberty has produced there; he is not unjust to other nations; he as little flatters popular prejudices as the interests of the court; always impartial between the violent factions which divide the kingdom, he seems to be the organ of the judgement of posterity, and his countrymen would applaud him, as well as less prejudiced foreigners, if parties would unite in favour of a writer who has the singular merit of favouring none. In short, philosophy and policy have dictated the history of Mr. Hume, one of the best adapted ever written, under proper restrictions, to form the sage, the statesman, and the citizen. [Claude Francois Xavier Millot (1726–1785), *Élémens de l'histoire d'Angleterre*, 1769; tr. *Elements of the history of England*, London: J. Johnson, 1771, 2 v.]

JOSEPH PRIESTLEY

Mr. Hume, whose evidence may well be allowed in this case [regarding Puritan revolutionaries such as Hampden and Pym], has given a very different account of those heroes. He also acknowledges, that whatever civil liberty we now enjoy in Great Britain, is owing to our ancestors, the Puritans; and I trust that every wise and virtuous ministry, who have the liberties and natural rights of their fellow-citizens at heart, will always have reason to depend upon the Dissenters; And that only a wicked, tyrannical, and profligate administration, who are intent upon making a tool of the king, and thereby grasping all the power of the state to themselves, will ever entertain any jealousy of them. A wise, just, and moderate prince will value such subjects; though a prince of a different character may rather choose to be without them. [Joseph Priestley

(1733–1804), *Remarks on some paragraphs in the fourth volume of Dr. Blackstone's Commentaries*, 1769, Section 2]

Mr. Hume, though a friend to the *Stuarts*, somewhere acknowledges that this country is chiefly indebted to the principles and spirit of the *Puritans* for its civil liberties. [Joseph Priestley (1733–1804), *Familiar Letters*, Birmingham: printed by J. Thompson, 1790.]

ANONYMOUS

I have the charity to believe that Herodotus and Tacitus were both honest men, and wrote with the best intentions; yet this enlightened age has produced a historian, who is indeed much read and admired, I mean Mr Hume, but whose history of England must be considered by every impartial man as a work unfriendly to the cause of religion. The most judicious arrangement, together with all the elegance of composition, can never justify those licentious principles which this ingenious writer was well known to have adopted, and which he endeavours to inculcate in all his writings; – a work which has a tendency to promote the cause of infidelity, and which, in many places, breathes the most violent prejudices and party-spirit which could actuate a narrow and bigotted mind, will certainly be condemned by an impartial posterity. As a friend to the cause of truth and religion, I am not afraid to express my sentiments in this public manner concerning "The History of England;" and I hope the reader will excuse me for a digression which was thought too material to be omitted. ["Academicus," "Observations on Antient and Modern History," in *Weekly Magazine, or Edinburgh Amusement*, November 13, 1777, Vol. 38, pp. 146–148.]

WILLIAM BURGH

Whatever occurs in the antient writers of history, of a speculative nature, we find to be an inference from a fact stated, without any seeming view to the deduction, but to the unadulterated representation of which the historian appears to have religiously attended. Whatever occurs in the modern writers of history of a narrative nature, we find to be an inference from a system previously assumed, without any seeming view to the truths of the fact recorded, but to the establishment of which the historian appears, *through every species of misrepresentation*, to have zealously directed his force. The late Mr. *Hume*, for instance, converted the history of this nation into a defence of the Stuarts' principles of government: to this end he has adduced facts only as arguments, has warped the train of events from the real course of succession, and, in order to render them subservient to his predetermined conclusion, has bestowed on each that false colouring which may give it, in some degree, the appearance of a case in point. A similar plan has been since pursued; and as the subversion of freedom was the evident purpose of Mr. Hume in writing *the History of England*, so, I fear, we may with too much justice affirm the subversion of Christianity to be the object of Mr. Gibbon in writing *the History of the Decline and Fall of the Roman Empire*. As a narrative founded on the authority of antient writers must have defeated his end, it is curious to observe the subtlety and variety of those artifices with which this gentleman has endeavoured to work away their credit, and thus to obtain a favourable reception for his own *substituted conjectures* , as a superior ground of history. [William Burgh (1741-1808), *An Inquiry into the Belief of the Christians of the First Three Centuries*, York: printed by A. Ward, 1778, p. 70.]

EDWARD GIBBON

As the ancient world was not distracted by the fierce conflicts of hostile sects, the free and eloquent writers of Greece and Rome had few opportunities of indulging their passions, or of exercising their impartiality in the relation of religious events. Since the origin of Theological Factions, some Historians, Ammianus Marcellinus, Fra-Paolo, Thuanus, Hume, and perhaps a few others, have deserved the singular praise of holding the balance with a steady and equal hand. Independent and unconnected, they contemplated with the same indifference, the opinions and interests of the contending parties; or, if they were seriously attached to a particular system, they were armed with a firm and moderate temper, which enabled them to suppress their affections, and to sacrifice their resentments. [Edward Gibbon (1737–1794), *Vindication of some passages*, London, Strahan, 1779, Ch. 8.]

The perfect composition, the nervous language, the well-turned periods of Dr. Robertson inflamed me to the ambitious hope that I might one day tread in his footsteps: the calm philosophy, the careless inimitable beauties of his friend and rival often forced me to close the volume, with a mixed sensation of delight and despair. [Edward Gibbon (1737–1794), *Memoirs*, in *Miscellaneous works of Edward Gibbon*, London: Strahan, 1796, 2 v.]

You tell me of a long list of Dukes Lairds and Chieftains of Renown to whom you are recommended; were I with you I should prefer one David to them all. When you are at Edinburgh I hope you will not fail to visit the Stye of that fattest of Epicurus's Hogs, and inform yourself whether there remains no hope of it's recovering the use of it's right paw. There is another animal of great, though not perhaps of equal and certainly not of similar merit; one Robertson; has he almost created the new World? [Edward Gibbon (1737–1794), *Miscellaneous works of Edward Gibbon*, London: Strahan, 1796, 2 v.]

JEREMY BENTHAM

Hume has fallen into a mistake on this subject, in supposing that in the reign of Henry II. moveables [i.e., moveable property] were the prey, not of the spiritual power but the temporal. "It appears," says he, vol. 1. anno 1100, "from Glanville, the famous justiciary of Henry II., that in his time, where any man died intestate, an accident which must have been frequent when the art of writing was so little known, the king, or the lord of the fief, pretended to seize all the moveables, and to exclude every heir, even the children of the deceased, – a sure mark of a tyrannical and arbitrary government." So far Hume, referring to Glanville, I. vi. c. 16. But what Hume understands of inter-states in general, Glanville confines to bastards. [Jeremy Bentham (1748–1832), *Supply without burden; or escheat vice taxation*, London: J. Debrett, 1795, Sect. 10.]

JANE AUSTIN

"Historians, you think," said Miss Tilney, "are not happy in their flights of fancy. They display imagination without raising interest. I am fond of history – and am very well contented to take the false with the true. In the principal facts they have sources of intelligence in former histories and records, which may be as much depended on, I conclude, as anything that does not actually pass under one's own observation; and as for the little embellishments you speak of, they are embellishments, and I like them as such. If a speech be well drawn up, I read it with pleasure, by whomsoever it may be made – and probably with much greater, if the production of Mr. Hume or Mr. Robertson, than if the genuine words of Caractacus, Agricola, or Alfred the Great." [Jane Austin (1775–1817), *Northanger Abbey*, London: John Murray, 1818, 4 v.]

ANNE BOTTA

12th [January, 1838]. The last volume of Smollett's continuation of Hume I finished last night. Thank heaven, it is read through! Though his history is good as a reference, and it may be a duty to read it, it is hardly a pleasure. He could not easily be more uninteresting. [Anne Charlotte Lynch Botta (1815–1891), *Memoirs of Anne C.L. Botta*, New York, J. Selwin Tait, 1894, p. 359]

GEORGE L. CRAIK

We would scarcely attempt to defend the prejudices and the minor inaccuracies of Hume: but, it seems to us, that sufficient account is not made of the wonderful quickness and sagacity of that great writer, and most admirable of narrators, whose intuitive perception generally made up for his indolence in examining records and original authorities. [George L. Craik (1798–1866), *The pictorial history of England: being a history of the people*, London, 1840, 4 Vol.]

HERMAN MERIVALE

But all the ability of Hume has scarcely rescued him from the comparative neglect which change of style has occasioned. We doubt whether he has so many readers now as formerly. [Herman Merivale (1806–1874), review of Craik's *Pictorial History*, in *Edinburgh Review*, Vol. 74, January 1842, pp. 430-473]

ANONYMOUS

If, however, we judge from the incredibly small circulation which his work at first obtained, we must be led to the conclusion that Hume was somewhat too early, at least in England, with a historical work, manifesting such bold scepticism, such keen criticism, and the art of using facts for the purpose of building up a particular system. To account for this limited circulation, it is more than probable, that the principles of the new philosophy which the work promulgated, had not yet much descended below the literary aristocratic coteries in England, of whom Hume, no less than his brother philosophers, Voltaire and Montesquieu, may be regarded as the leader and the organ. [Review of Schlosser's *History*, in *Eclectic Magazine*, January 1847, pp. 38–46.]